McGRAW-HILL DICTIONARY OF ART

McGRAW-HILL

● McGRAW-HILL BOOK COMPANY   NEW YORK

DICTIONARY OF ART

Edited by
BERNARD S. MYERS
Consulting Editor, *Encyclopedia of World Art*
Editor, *Encyclopedia of Painting*
Formerly New York University, Rutgers University,
University of Texas, The City University of New York

Assistant Editor
SHIRLEY D. MYERS

Assistant Editor, *Encyclopedia of Painting*

Volume 2   CEZANNE – GRECO-ROMAN STYLE

TORONTO   LONDON   SYDNEY   JOHANNESBURG

McGRAW-HILL STAFF

Executive Editor: David I. Eggenberger
Director of Design and Production: Gerard G. Mayer
Associate Editor: Beatrice Carson
Editing Managers: Tobia L. Worth; Margaret Lamb
Research Editor: Donald Goddard
Proof Editor: Gordon L. Gidley
Administrative Editor: M. Barat Kerr Sparks
Bibliographers: Sally Evans; Donald Goddard; Marian Williams
Editorial Assistant: Ethel M. Jacobson
Copy Editors and Proofreaders: Monica Bayley; Olive Collen; Beatrice Eckes
Art and Design: David Ross-Robertson; Edward Fox; Ann Bonardi

ART AND DESIGN STAFF

Picture Editor: Giorgio Marcolungo

Art Director: Fiorenzo Giorgi

Assistants: Massimo Bucchi
Raffaele Curiel
Isabella Piombo
Adolfo Segattini
Maurizio Turazzi

Line Drawings Prepared by: 5 Lines Studio - Rome
Design Italiana - Milan

C

CEZANNE, PAUL. French painter (b. Aix-en-Provence, 1839; d. there, 1906). He attended the Collège Bourbon at Aix (1852–58), where he befriended Emile Zola. From 1859 to 1861 Cézanne studied law at Aix, but at the same time, and with greater enthusiasm, took art lessons at the Académie de Dessin. At Zola's prompting, he left for Paris in 1861, to join his friend there and to become a painter. Teacherless, he worked at the free Académie Suisse, where he met Camille Pissarro. Between 1861 and 1866 Cézanne gradually hardened in his determination to continue his training in Paris, despite his failure to be admitted to the Ecole des Beaux-Arts and the handicap of a passionate, stubborn perfectionism, forever frustrated by technical clumsiness. Zola's encouragement was of crucial importance at this time. Little remains of Cézanne's earliest work.

By 1866 he had achieved an individual style, somewhat influenced by Courbet and Manet, marked by striking darkness of tone and rough vigor of handling. The colors, applied in thick smears with the palette knife, sculpt the forms in harsh contrasts of light and shadow. Energy and awkwardness, crudity and originality are curiously mingled in such works as the *Self-portrait* (ca. 1865) and *The Artist's Father Reading* (1866), both in the Lecomte Collection, Paris, and *Uncle Dominic* (ca. 1866) in the Museum of Modern Art, New York.

About 1867 Cézanne's manner began to lose some of its earlier, excessive heaviness. The tones become lighter, the pigment thinner and smoother. Though the emphasis is still on vigorous light-dark contrasts, the colors, particularly the blues, now play a more important role. Cézanne experimented with large figure compositions of a portraitlike character, such as *Overture to Tannhäuser* (ca. 1867; Moscow, National Museum of Fine Arts), and with dramatic subjects of erotic flavor, conceived in a neobaroque style reminiscent of Delacroix. *The Abduction* (1867; J. M. Keynes Collection) and *The Rape* (ca. 1870; Paris, E. Roche Collection) are examples of the latter type.

Paul Cézanne, *Paul, the Artist's Son*. National Gallery, Washington, D.C.

Throughout this period he remained in obscurity. He exhibited at the Salon des Refusés in 1863 without being noticed; he submitted work to the official Salons from 1864 to 1869 and was regularly rejected. Through his conversations with Zola, he influenced the latter's art criticism; Zola dedicated his pamphlet *Mon salon* (1866) to him. Occasionally, Cézanne visited the Café Guerbois, the haunt of Manet, Degas, Bazille, and Pissarro, but remained an outsider to this circle of future impressionists. In 1870–71, at Aix and L'Estaque, near Marseilles, he concentrated on landscape painting.

In 1872–74 Cézanne came strongly under the influence of the impressionists, particularly of Pissarro, with whom he worked at Pontoise and Auvers. In 1874 he participated in the first group show of the impressionists. A radical change then occurred in his development. He abandoned his earlier lavish use of black and of somber colors in favor of the primary colors, used at high intensity and in light tonalities, and applied in smaller, more supple strokes than had been his custom. On Pissarro's advice, he sought to build form with color, rather than with strong tonal contrasts. Like the impressionists, he now turned more particularly to open-air landscape painting, without abandoning still life or figure composition altogether (*House of the Hanged Man*, ca. 1873, Paris, Louvre; *Hermitage at Pontoise*, ca. 1875, Moscow, National Museum of Fine Arts; *Landscape near Auvers*, ca. 1874, Chicago, Art Institute; *Apple Still Life*, ca. 1876, and *Man with Vest*, ca. 1876, both Merion, Pa., Barnes Foundation). A significant difference between Cézanne's landscapes of that time and those of the impressionists proper is, nevertheless, evident. Less concerned than Monet or Pissarro with the scintillation of light or the haze of atmosphere, he stressed the tangible substance of objects and gave a more definite compositional structure to his paintings.

During these years he found supporters in the person of Choquet, an early collector of his work, and of Père Tanguy, his first dealer. Still regularly rejected by the official Salons, he exhibited once again with the impressionists in 1877. His association with Pissarro, Monet, and

Guillaumin continued, although Cézanne gradually emancipated himself from impressionism to develop his own, thoroughly independent style. After 1881 he spent more and more time in the provincial isolation of Aix, deeply absorbed in the search for a way of painting that would combine the luminosity of impressionism with the grand stability and harmony of classical art.

During the 1880s and 1890s he achieved his fullest mastery. Never satisfied by his results, embroiled in a constant, despairing struggle for the complete "realization" of his visual experience, he painted landscapes, still lifes, and figure compositions that rank among the highest achievements of 19th-century painting (*Chestnuts at Jas de Bouffan*, ca. 1885, Minneapolis Institute of Fine Arts; *Mont Ste-Victoire*, ca. 1887, Washington, D.C., Phillips Collection; *L'Estaque*, ca. 1888, Chicago, Art Institute). The architectonic clarity of form and coloristic radiance that distinguish the best of the later landscapes are to be found equally in the still lifes, the portraits, and the series of *Card Players* (ca. 1890–92; New York, Metropolitan Museum of Art; Barnes Foundation; Louvre; London, Courtauld Institute). Of special importance are the various compositions of *Bathers* (Barnes Foundation; Philadelphia, Museum of Art; Moscow, National Museum of Fine Arts; and others), which are recapitulations of the classical theme of nude figures in a landscape and are exceptional among his later works in that they are based on invention rather than on the observation of visual reality. Most of the compositions date from between 1890 and 1906.

Cézanne's paintings then began to be sought after. In 1895 Vollard organized the first one-man show. The same year two of Cézanne's paintings entered the Luxembourg (Caillebotte bequest); the Berlin National Gallery bought two others in 1897. From 1900 on he frequently exhibited in Paris, Brussels, Berlin, and Vienna. Young artists (Emile Bernard, Maurice Denis, and K. X. Roussel) formed an admiring coterie around him and recorded his pronouncements on art. In 1907, the year after his death, a retrospective exhibition of his work had an instant and profound effect on Matisse, Picasso, Braque, and other leading artists of the younger generation; the revolutionary impact of Cézanne's work on 20th-century art was beginning to be felt.

Cézanne's contribution to modern art was nothing less than a new concept of realism and pictorial form. In contrast to the lyrical naturalism of the romantics and the materialism of Courbet, he conceived of realism as being a matter of reconstruction rather than imitation. Painting for him was the "realization" of impressions received from nature, the translation into artistic equivalents (colors and shapes) of the unpaintable facts of space and corporeality. Instead of aiming for illusion, he strove for representational truth, for a recasting of observed nature into the quite different reality of pictorial form. This called for close observation on the one hand and, on the other, for a logical discipline of organization and transformation that excluded fantasy or improvisation.

Like the impressionists, Cézanne needed the experience of nature; unlike them, he did not try to record momentary visual sensations, fleeting effects of light and atmosphere.

Instead, he studied the permanent structures and relationships of objects. Convinced that forms are not established by lines (which do not exist in nature) but by gradations or contrasts of color and tone, he laboriously constructed his later paintings of interlocking color surfaces, stroking on the pigments in thin, almost transparent washes. Full realization for him meant the establishment of a continuous color relief that models the forms and at the same time defines their position in space.

BIBLIOGRAPHY. A. Vollard, *Paul Cézanne*, Paris, 1914, New York, 1923; E. Bernard, *Souvenirs sur Paul Cézanne*, Paris, 1920; L. Venturi, *Cézanne: Son art, son oeuvre*, 2 vols., Paris, 1936; R. Fry, *Cézanne*, London, 1927; J. Rewald, *The Ordeal of Paul Cézanne*, London, 1950.

LORENZ EITNER

CHABOT, HENDRIK. Dutch painter, sculptor, and graphic artist (1894–1949). Born in Sprang, he studied in Rotterdam and Vienna. Chabot was primarily an expressionist figure painter of strongly composed, emotionally colored, and distorted forms.

CHADWICK, LYNN. English designer and sculptor (1914–   ). He was born in London and was trained as an architect. Early influences, from González toward metal sculpture and from Calder toward sculpture in motion, resulted in a series of mobiles from 1947 on, for example, *The Fish Eater* (1950–51; London, Collection of the Arts Council of Great Britain). His next works were of thin sheets, singly or combined with armatures or other materials, as in *The Inner Eye* (1952; New York, Museum of Modern Art), where a lump of glass is suspended in a vaguely human framework of iron and wire. Chadwick's recent sculptures, such as *Moon of Alabama* (1957; artist's collection), are enclosed forms of welded iron.

BIBLIOGRAPHY. C. Giedion-Welcker, *Contemporary Sculpture*, rev. ed., New York, 1961.

CHAGALL, MARC. Russian painter (1887–   ). Born in Vitebsk, Russia, Chagall has lived mainly in Paris since 1910. His style, while reflective of cubist, surrealist, and expressionist affinities, is distinctly personal. His contribution to early modern painting and printmaking has been of the first order.

Chagall studied briefly with a local artist in Vitebsk and, in 1908, studied at the academy in St. Petersburg. In 1910 he went to Paris, where he met the poets Max Jacob, Blaise Cendrars, and André Salmon and the painters Modigliani, Delaunay, La Fresnaye, and other cubists and independents.

The complexities of Chagall's aesthetic are apt to be obscured somewhat by the whimsical, fantastic subject matter. It does not detract from Chagall's uniqueness of expression, however, to attribute to cubism an early and formative influence upon this gifted Russian. His *Half Past Three* (*The Poet*, 1911; Philadelphia Museum of Art) is a testimonial to cubist structure, although Chagall has refuted the programmatic orthodoxy of the French manner and substituted a sensitive adaptation of his own; moreover, his color is altogether original. The impact of cubist structure and spatial handling continues in his *I and My Vil-*

Marc Chagall, *The Feast of Tabernacles*, 1928. Gouache on paper. J. B. Belmont Collection, Binningen, Germany.

lage (1911) and *Over Vitebsk* (1916; both New York, Museum of Modern Art). Thereafter his style becomes increasingly unique and the cubist aspects operate less evidently.

Apollinaire introduced Chagall to Herwarth Walden, the German publisher and dealer, in Berlin in 1914. This resulted in Chagall's first one-man show in the same year. He returned to Russia to marry, and after the revolution of 1917 he was appointed commissar of fine arts for Vitebsk and founded an art school there. He designed murals for the Moscow Jewish Theater in 1922 and then left for Paris by way of Berlin, where he remained long enough to make engravings as illustrations for a book.

The poet Cendrars was responsible for Chagall's meeting the dealer Ambroise Vollard. A commission for engraved illustrations for Gogol's *Dead Souls* followed (these were not published until 1949, although Chagall had completed them long before).

Chagall's first retrospective exhibition was given at the Galerie Barbazange-Hodebert, Paris, in 1924. His style became increasingly romantic and devoted to fantastic narratives during the middle 1920s. *The Jewish Wedding* (1926; New York, Museum of Modern Art), a gouache-and-chalk composition, discloses another tendency of Chagall's expression: his persistent, refreshing summoning of folk memories of his Russian origin. His first New York show dates from 1926. In 1927 he undertook the illustration of La Fontaine's *Fables*, completing the 100 plates in 1930. In 1931 he traveled to Palestine and Syria to study themes for Biblical engravings, another Vollard commission. *The Arabian Nights, Daphnis and Chloë,* and Boccaccio were also illustrated as a result. Chagall's own book, *Ma vie,* was published in 1931.

Chagall by now had become internationally famous, and a large retrospective in 1933 at the Basel Art Museum increased his prestige. He was disquieted, however, by political developments in Europe during the early 1930s, and the increasingly severe persecutions and threat of war led him to paint religious works of a darkly exciting kind. His apprehensions were aggravated by a visit to Poland in 1935.

First prize in the 1939 Carnegie International, Pittsburgh, was given to Chagall, and in 1941 he settled in the United States at the invitation of New York's Museum of Modern Art. At first rejuvenated by the new environment, he was to be deeply saddened by the death of his wife in 1944. Before returning to Paris in 1946, he completed the sets for Stravinsky's *Firebird* and other theatrical designs.

Chagall had retrospective shows in 1947 in Paris, Amsterdam, and London, and was represented at the 1948 Venice Biennale. In 1949 he worked in Vence, especially with ceramics. In that year he also painted an important canvas, *The Red Sun*, an allegory invoking memories of his late wife and rich with strikingly colored imagery referring once again to the Russian folk fantasy, which is so much an aspect of his art.

The 1950s brought additional honors to Chagall, not the least of which was the commission from the architect Joseph Neufeld and the Women's Zionist Organization of America to design twelve stained-glass windows for the synagogue of the Hadassah-Hebrew University Medical Center near Jerusalem. These windows were exhibited in Paris and New York before being installed in Israel in 1962. In 1967 and 1968 a triptych of tapestries designed by Chagall was woven at the Gobelins factory. The triptych, representing *The Creation*, *The Exodus*, and *Entry into Jerusalem*, was ordered by André Malraux, French Minister of Cultural Affairs, for presentation to the Israeli parliament. *See also* NICE: CHAGALL MEMORIAL.

BIBLIOGRAPHY. W. George, *Marc Chagall*, Paris, 1928; M. Chagall, *Ma vie*, 1st ed., Paris, 1931; new ed., Paris, 1957; J. J. Sweeney, *Marc Chagall*, New York, 1946; U. Apollonio, *Marc Chagall*, Venice, 1951; A. Werner, "Chagall's Jerusalem Windows," *Art Journal*, XXI : 4, 1962.

JOHN C. GALLOWAY

CHAH-SINDEH (Shah-Zinda): MOSQUE OF QASIM IBN-ABBAS. Tomb mosque in Samarqand, now in the Uzbek S.S.R. It was built in 1334. Characteristic of Muslim art of the period, it has a domed prayer hall, on each side of which is a vaulted chapel, one of which contains the tomb. Arches and canopies, with glazed tiles carved in relief, adorn the mosque.

BIBLIOGRAPHY. A. Pope, ed., *A Survey of Persian Art*, vol. 2, New York, 1939.

CH'AI. Chinese ceramic ware that is recorded in literary sources as an imperial ware of the 10th century. Supposedly extremely thin and light blue in coloration, it has not been positively identified among existing examples of Chinese porcelains.

CHA-IRE. Small container, about 2 to 3 inches high, of glazed pottery or stoneware, used to hold the powdered green tea of the Japanese tea ceremony. This type is made of red, brown, or grayish ware, with lids of ivory. The shapes vary widely, but the decoration is of extreme simplicity, consisting of a mottled brown glaze sometimes ornamented by a patch of glaze in another color. When not in use, they are stored in silk brocade bags. Some of the most important examples of *cha-ire* date from the Kamakura and Muromachi periods.

BIBLIOGRAPHY. E. Hannover, *Pottery and Porcelain*, vol. 2: *The Far East*, London, 1925.

CHAISE-DIEU, LA. French town, situated in the Department of the Haute Loire. It is the site of a Benedictine abbey, rebuilt between 1344 and 1378, with a great for-

tified donjon added between 1378 and 1420. The canopied tomb of Pope Clement VI was erected in the church before his death in 1352. Between 1440 and 1450 three long fresco panels depicting the *danse macabre* were painted on the church walls. The paintings are an interesting example of a theme widely popular in France at the time.

BIBLIOGRAPHY. J. Evans, *Art in Mediaeval France, 987–1498*, London, 1948.

CHAITYA (Caitya) HALL. An Indian Buddhist temple resembling in form and function the Roman basilica and Early Christian church but having, in place of an altar, a votive stūpa (also called a chaitya). The fully developed chaitya hall consists of a central nave, an apsidal end, and pillared side aisles that continue around the apse to provide a circumambulatory passage (*pradaksiṇā*) around the sacred stūpa. A barrel vault rises over the nave, and another vault half its size covers each side aisle. The basic façade consists of an entrance (usually facing the stūpa) above which is a lofty opening, or chaitya window, shaped like a horseshoe with an ogee point.

The earliest chaitya halls are known through ruined foundations of freestanding constructions possibly from the period of Aśoka the Great (r. ca. 273–236 B.C.), for example, at Sāñchī, Sārnāth, and Sonari. But, with few exceptions (one being Chezārla), most extant chaityas are cave temples carved from solid rock, particularly in the mountainous areas of western India (for example, the caves of Bhājā, Kondāne, Pitalkhorā, Ajaṇṭā, Bedsā, Nāsik, Kārle, and Ellorā). These chaitya halls represent one of two types of Buddhist cave architecture, the other being the adjoining living quarters for monks (vihāras). Chaitya halls date from the 3d century B.C. to about the 7th century A.D., but the greatest periods of production were from the 1st century B.C. to the 2d century A.D. and again in the 5th and 6th centuries. While the scale and degree of ornamentation vary considerably, some of the rock-hewn sanctuaries achieved the grandeur of a Gothic cathedral.

The chaitya hall, whether rock-cut or freestanding, copies wooden prototypes, none of which remain. But imitation and even incorporation of wood forms and techniques extended to the degree of affixing, as if for support, a framework of curved wooden ribs to a barrel-vaulted roof cut into the living rock (for example, Kārle). Decorative elements from woodwork and wickerwork were also adapted by the stone carver. Stone columns in the earliest chaitya caves (for example, Kondāne and Bhājā, ca. 100 B.C.) have a slight inward slope, evidently imitating a feature that wood examples required to counteract the pull of bentwood arches over the entrance doorways. Later, the device of a tie rod to hold the wood arch together, as seen in illustrations of buildings in bas-reliefs, was used about the beginning of the Christian era at Sāñchī and in later chaitya halls, such as Kārle. *See* AJANTA; BEDSA; BHAJA; CHEZARLA; ELLORA; KARLE; KONDANE; NASIK; PITALKHORA; SANCHI; SARNATH.

BIBLIOGRAPHY. R. C. Majumdar, ed., *The History and Culture of the Indian People*, vols. 2 and 3, Bombay, 1951 and 195?; P. Brown, *Indian Architecture*, 4th ed., 2 vols., Bombay, 1959; B. Rowland, *The Art and Architecture of India*, 2d ed., Baltimore, 1959.

J. LEROY DAVIDSON

CHAKRA, *see* CAKRA.

Chaitya hall. The main votive stūpa, or shrine, of Cave XIX, Ajaṇṭā, ca. A.D. 550.

Chaldean art. Ornamental detail of the reconstructed Ishtar Gate, from Babylon. Former State Museums, Berlin.

CHALCOGRAPHY, *see* CALCOGRAPHY.

CHALCOLITHIC EPOCH. Final phase of the Neolithic period, in the second half of the 4th millennium B.C., when metal was discovered and used simultaneously with stone. The name is derived from the Greek *chalkos* (copper) and *lithos* (stone). The discovery of metal brought a radical change in man's living conditions, and during this period the first cultures began to develop in the Middle East. Until then, raw materials for tools and weapons were stone, clay, wood, and bone.

Asia Minor, Urartu, Elam, and Cyprus all produced copper, and metal came into general use because it was easy to use and durable. Weapons, tools, and other objects manufactured of metal followed the old patterns. The flat axe of pure copper was a reproduction of the polished stone axe, but changes and innovations were later introduced. Triangular daggers appeared, as did swords, spearheads, arrowheads, battle axes, and sickles. Practically everywhere in Asia excavations have brought to light axes with metal sockets for the handles, metal chisels, drills, tools for engraving, and sickles, which previously had been made of flint and had had handles of wood or occasionally of the jawbones of animals.

In the Chalcolithic period, when agriculture expanded and the standard of living improved, works of art began to be produced in abundance. Painted pottery of excellent quality appeared, giving evidence of the cultural progress of the times. Shell was used, and an even more precious substance, ivory, was continually in demand from very early times. Used occasionally in the Paleolithic period, ivory came into general use in the Chalcolithic period. With great herds of elephants in an extensive area of the ancient world (Syria, Mesopotamia, and the Indus Valley), ivory could be obtained in abundance. Earlier shell carvers had developed the technique of carving.

Painted pottery of excellent quality was produced in abundance over a vast area of Asia, giving evidence of a superior culture as exemplified in the works of Tell Halaf, al-'Ubaid, Uruk, and other centers.

In the early 3d millennium B.C. copper began to be mixed with small quantities of lead, zinc, and especially tin, and this process produced bronze, which was harder, stronger, and easier to work with than pure copper. Bronze was the first metal alloy to come into general use and marked the beginning of the Bronze Age, during which metal weapons increased in number and variety. Not only weapons and tools but also vases and various vessels and containers, figurines, statues, and even jewelry were made of bronze. About 1200 B.C. the Bronze Age was superseded by the Iron Age.

BIBLIOGRAPHY. A. Parrot, *The Arts of Assyria*, New York, 1961; L. Woolley, *The Art of the Middle East*, New York, 1961.

LUCILLE VASSARDAKI

CHALDEAN ART. The Chaldean, or neo-Babylonian, kingdom was established in 612 B.C. and retained its independence until 539 B.C., when Babylon was invaded by Cyrus the Persian. The reliefs show Babylonian or Kassite rather than Assyrian influence: the boundary stone of Mardukapaliddina, which records the gift of land to a vassal, recalls the soft, rounded forms of the Stele of Hammurabi. Seal designs betray a gentle elegance far removed from the Assyrian's angularized fierceness. Unlike the Assyrians, who always showed the shoulders frontally, the neo-Babylonians rendered a true profile.

Great palaces featuring the architectural use of baked brick were built at Babylon and at Ur. Nebuchadnezzar's palace at Babylon (900 by 600 ft.) was composed of a maze of small units. An architectural innovation of the period was a mud-brick wall in short sections set at an angle to the frontage, giving the wall the effect of a toothed saw. This fashion was adopted for private houses. The throne room of the palace was not flanked, as in Assyria, by awe-inspiring demonic guardians. Rather, there was a resplendent façade of glazed bricks showing an architectural pattern with flower designs against a blue background. *See* BABYLON.

The Ishtar Gate of Babylon was erected on the Processional Way beyond the inner town. A double gate, it was decorated with glazed bricks depicting, in relief, bulls and lions with yellow bodies and blue hair. (At Khorsabad, panels of polychrome glazed brick had been used, but there the figures were flat.) On the walls of the Processional Way, against a blue background studded with rosettes, there appeared in glazed tile sixty life-size lions. *See* ISHTAR GATE, BABYLON.

South of the palace stood Marduk's ziggurat, of which only the ground plan and the three steps leading up to it survive. The palace was situated roughly in the middle of the northern town wall, between the Euphrates on the west and the main north-south avenue.

In the late neo-Babylonian period, during the reign of Nabonidus (555–539 B.C.), a new style of ziggurat appeared. The best preserved of these, at Ur, featured seven stages instead of the previous three. Herodotus relates that each stage was given a different and, beginning with the bottom, a progressively brighter color, and that there was a shrine at the top of blue-glazed brick. *See* UR.

BIBLIOGRAPHY. O. E. Ravn, *Herodotus' Description of Babylon*, Copenhagen, 1942; A. Parrot, *Ziggurats et tour de Babel*, Paris, 1949; H. Frankfort, *The Art and Architecture of the Ancient Orient*, Baltimore, 1954.

CHALGRIN, JEAN-FRANCOIS-THERESE. French architect (1739–1811). He worked in Paris. Established under the *ancien regime*, his major work was the influential Church of St-Philippe-du-Roule. He is better known, however, as the designer of the Arc de Triomphe de l'Etoile, which was completed after his death. Associated in proportions and monumentality with François Blondel's Porte St-Denis, the arch is considered his masterpiece. Chalgrin followed Boullée's and Servandoni's lectures, was associated with Soufflot, and was attracted by the strict archaeological classicism of more advanced architects; his work falls in the transitional period between the French baroque tradition, the abstraction of the romantic classicists, and the pompous grandeur of the Napoleonic era. *See* ARC DE TRIOMPHE DE L'ETOILE, PARIS; SAINT-PHILIPPE-DU-ROULE, PARIS.

BIBLIOGRAPHY. L. Hautecoeur, *Histoire de l'architecture classique en France*, vol. 4, Paris, 1952.

CHALICE. Liturgical vessel containing wine used in the celebration of the Mass, or Eucharist. It consists of a foot, a shaft with a nodus, and a cup (Latin, *cuppa*). In the early Middle Ages and in the Romanesque period, the parts were basically spherical; Gothic vessels were elaborated into trefoil and hexafoil shapes.

CHALK DRAWING. Natural chalk, which is found in several colors and forms, has been used as a drawing material since the earliest times. In its natural form it occurs in black, white, and a limited range of reds. These three, therefore, are the traditional colors for chalk drawing, though they have been artificially produced since the 16th century. Colored chalks other than the traditional three are more correctly called pastels.

Earlier, a combination of black and red chalk was used on white papers to achieve a variety of luminous and textural effects. Red chalk, or "sanguine," was favored for figure studies in the 16th, 17th, and 18th centuries, and was particularly popular in Italy after 1500. Perhaps the most famous early chalk drawing is a study for the *Head of Emperor Sigismund* (Paris, Louvre) by Pisanello. Leonardo, who often used it with the pen, and colorists such as Andrea del Sarto and Correggio were especially fond of red chalk. Black-and-white chalk drawings, called *aux deux crayons*, were made in the 16th and 17th centuries; by the 18th century, an elaborately systematized procedure, called *aux trois crayons* (red, white, and black), was in use by rococo artists. Watteau was by far the greatest exponent of the *trois crayons*.

BIBLIOGRAPHY. B. Degenhart, *Europäische Handzeichnungen*, Berlin, 1943; C. de Tolnay, *History and Techniques of Old Master Drawings*, New York, 1943.

JULIA M. EHRESMANN

CHALONS, SIMON DE (Simon de Mailly or Malhy). French painter (b. Châlons-sur-Marne; d. Avignon, 1561/62). Little is known of his life, except that he was active in Avignon from about 1535 until his death; he consistently signed and dated his paintings. The strong influence of the 1530s Antwerp school in his work indicates that Mailly was apprenticed in Flanders. Italian influence is also present. Many of his paintings have remained in Avignon, for example, *The Adoration of the Shepherds* (1548; Calvet Museum).

BIBLIOGRAPHY. A. Blunt, *Art and Architecture in France, 1500-1700*, Baltimore, 1954.

CHALONS-SUR-MARNE: NOTRE-DAME-EN-VAUX. French cathedral, begun after a fire in 1230. The main portal, in the classic style, dates from 1628-34, as do the west front and the first two bays of the nave. As in many eastern Romanesque churches, the choir is flanked by two towers, the north dating from the 12th century and the south, from the early 13th. The nave and transepts date mostly from the second half of the 13th century. The triforium has blind arcades in the choir but handsome glazing along the nave. There is some fine 12th-century glass (especially the window of the Passion) and an excellent 13th-century north rose window. In the south aisle is a series of 16th-century windows of considerable distinction.

BIBLIOGRAPHY. M. Aubert and S. Goubet, *Gothic Cathedrals of France and their Treasures*, London, New York, 1959.

CHAM (Amedee de Noe). French graphic artist (b. Paris, 1819; d. there, 1879). Cham was one of the foremost caricaturists of the Second Empire. He achieved considerable

Chalk drawing. Jean Antoine Watteau, *Masked Men*. Louvre, Paris.

fame for his political cartoons, particularly the sketches of French and Algerian life that appeared in *Charivari*.

CHAMBERLAIN, JOHN. American sculptor (1927–   ). Born in Indiana, he studied at the Art Students League in New York (1951–52) and began working in metals. He taught at Black Mountain College in North Carolina (1955–56) and has had one-man exhibitions in Chicago and New York, where he now lives. Most of his works are constructions using metal sheets from automobiles, crumpled and jammed together in dynamic relationships and, in recent years, brightly painted with industrial paints.

CHAMBERS, SIR WILLIAM. English architect (b. Sweden, 1723; d. London, 1796). He early traveled to China, was a pupil of J. F. Blondel in Paris, and began to practice in London in 1755. He was favored by the royal family, designing at Kew from 1757 and eventually becoming the first Comptroller and Surveyor General of the Works.

His *Treatise on Civil Architecture* (1759), a standard work, reflects Chambers's impeccable taste in the use of the orders. His excursions into the Chinese style, in both literature and building, were more of a *jeu d'esprit*, and he hated the Gothic mode. His practice was extensive. Somerset House (1776–86) is his best-known official work; and the Casino at Marino, Dublin (1761), perhaps the most perfect.

CHAMBIGES, MARTIN DE. Parisian architect (d. 1532). Fully Flamboyant in style, his work includes the transept façades of Sens Cathedral (1490–1512), the south transept façade of Beauvais (begun in 1500), and Senlis (after 1504). He was sometimes assisted by his son Pierre. *See* SENS: SAINT-ETIENNE.

BIBLIOGRAPHY. V. Leblond, *La Cathédrale de Beauvais*, 2d ed., Paris, 1956.

CHAMBORD, CHATEAU OF. Royal château in the Loire Valley, originally planned as a hunting lodge by King Francis I of France. Construction was begun in 1519. The vast building encompasses more than 350 rooms. Its nucleus is the square, three-storied donjon, bounded at its four corners by tremendous, circular towers. This structure (220 ft. sq.) serves as the *corps-de-logis*, or main residence. Two wings extend from the donjon, doubling the width of the north façade. The wings also terminate in corner towers and act as a boundary wall for the château. Conical roofs, surmounted by cupolas, cover the towers. This expansive north façade has a royal grandeur unequaled in other surviving domestic buildings from the early part of the 16th century.

The south side of the château has low, wall-like buildings that begin at taller pavilions on the east and west sides. These low structures, with terracelike flat roofs, enclose a large courtyard from which the donjon rises as a huge mass of white limestone. Originally the château was bordered on all four sides by a moat, but this feature, always more decorative than defensive, has been supplanted by walks and lawns on all but the north side.

The walls of the *corps-de-logis*, with their sturdy masonry and comparatively simple ornament of paired stringcourses between stories, are in the French Gothic tradition of heavily fortified domestic buildings. Flat, vertical pilasters at regular intervals between the stringcourses, and rising from basement to roof, help to create an interesting surface pattern. The massive towers have a double window at each floor; the topmost are high, decorated dormers capped by impressive gables. Single windows also appear alongside the paired ones, and a few random light apertures pierce each of the towers. The windows of the middle spans, however, are both large and ornamental and serve as a reminder that Chambord was conceived by its designer, who may have been Domenico da Cortona, as a gracious and well-organized Italianate villa.

A model for the château existed until the 17th century, when it was sketched by Félibien. His drawings show that the general proportions and the four-partite arrangement of the model were retained during construction. Much of the work was done during the reign of Francis; the main residence was roofed in 1537 and the east wing in 1539. The west wing was roofed in 1550 during the reign of Henry II. He and later monarchs were probably responsible for the elaborations that rise from the rooftop of the main building. The basically flat roof became a foundation for a fantastic array of steeply pitched roofs, dormer windows, richly trimmed gables, and tall chimneys, decorated with insertions of black slate. These features are Flamboyant Gothic in spirit, but they utilize a wealth of Renaissance classical motifs. The roof edge has deep consoles, a shell-work frieze, and a heavy, Italianate balustrade.

Château of Chambord, begun 1519, north façade.

A unique cupola rises over the central point of the roof, supporting a series of radiating piers that, in turn, carry a delicately balanced lantern tower. The tower crowns an ingenious interior staircase, probably the most noteworthy single feature of Chambord. The staircase consists of two spiral stair runs, both rising within a single confined space, and so arranged that they interlock within it. Richly carved coffers cover the ceilings above the stairs as well as the ceilings of the four hallways on each floor. These halls, spanned by elliptical arched ceilings, divide each story of the *corps-de-logis* into four separate *appartements*, with the central staircase at their intersection.

BIBLIOGRAPHY. H. Guerlin, *Le Château de Chambord*, Paris, 1912; F. Gebelin, *Les Châteaux de la Loire*, Paris, 1927; A. Blunt, *Art and Architecture in France, 1500–1700*, Baltimore, 1954; C. Terrasse, *Les Châteaux de la Loire*, Paris, 1956.   EMMA N. PAPERT

CHAMFER. Surface formed when the arris, or sharp edge at the intersection of two surfaces, is cut off diagonally. Chamfers are often used to prevent sharp corners from chipping. In heavy mill-wood construction, chamfering reduces the hazard of fire's attacking exposed corners.

Chamfer. A beveled edge at the intersection of two surfaces.

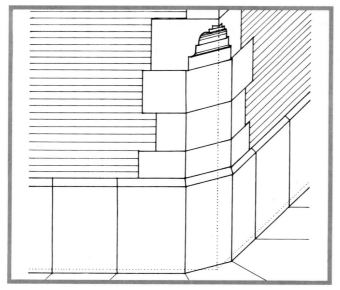

CHAMPAGNE SCHOOL. Important 16th-century school of sculpture and stained glass, centered in Troyes. The school's first major works of sculpture are in the Church of La Madeleine at Troyes: the choir screen (1508–17) by Jean Gailde, and the renowned statue of St. Martha, by an unknown master of the so-called "atelier de la Ste-Marthe." They show a departure from the Gothic Flamboyant style, and the easy charm characteristic of the school.

The arrival of Domenico del Barbiere from Fontainebleau about 1537 marked a new phase in the evolution of Champenois sculpture toward mannerism, as can be seen in the now dismembered choir screen from St-Etienne at Troyes, Domenico's major work. Another important sculptor of the Champagne school is Ligier Richier, whose chief work, composed of thirteen statues, is the *Holy Sepulchre* in the Church of St-Etienne at Saint-Mihiel. See BARBIERE, DOMENICO RICOVERI DEL; RICHIER FAMILY.

The most important examples of stained glass of the school of Champagne are in the Cathedral of Troyes (upper windows of nave, finished by 1498–1501), in the Cathedral of Châlons-sur-Marne (window of St. Stephen, 1498), and in the Cathedral of Sens (rose window of south transept arm, commissioned in 1500).

BIBLIOGRAPHY. R. Koechlin and J. J. Marquet de Vasselot, *La Sculpture à Troyes et dans la Champagne méridionale au seizième siècle*, Paris, 1900; P. Biver, *L'Ecole troyenne de la peinture sur verre*, Paris, 1935– ; *Congrès archéologique de France, 1955*, Orléans, 1957.
                    JOHN B. CAMERON

CHAMPAIGNE, JEAN-BAPTISTE DE. French religious and portrait painter (b. Brussels, 1631; d. Paris, 1681). He was the nephew and pupil of Philippe de Champaigne. He became an academician in 1663 and professor at the Royal Academy in 1673. He was anti-Le Brun, a partisan of "drawing" as opposed to "color," and an exponent of austere Jansenist realism and a predicator of that faith.

BIBLIOGRAPHY. A. Fontaine, *Académiciens d'autrefois...*, Paris, 1914.

CHAMPAIGNE, PHILIPPE DE. French portraitist, landscape and religious painter, and decorator (b. Brussels, 1602; d. Paris, 1674). Though reputedly denied apprenticeship under Rubens, he was the pupil of Jacques Fouquières and perhaps of Theodore van Loon and Gaspard de Crayer, whose Bolognese strain his early works reflect.

In 1621 Champaigne moved to Paris, where, at lodgings in the Collège de Laon, he knew Poussin. He worked briefly under G. Lallemand and in the Luxembourg Gallery, where Rubens's *Life of Marie de' Medici* was being installed, under Nicolas Duchesne. He succeeded Duchesne as First Painter and married Duchesne's daughter Charlotte in 1628. Until 1635 he worked for Marie de Médicis (a series for the Carmelite convent on the rue St. Jacques) and for Louis XIII (*La Rochelle Victory Portrait*, Paris, Louvre, in a style recalling Frans Pourbus). From 1636 to 1642 he worked mainly for Cardinal Richelieu, doing decorative works at the Palais Royal, in the dome of the Sorbonne chapel, and at Bois-Le-Vicomte, Rueil, and Richelieu; he also did portraits (Paris, Louvre, and London, National Gallery) suggesting Van Dyck, though more sculpturesque, for Anne of Austria (Val-de-Grâce), for the Canon of Notre-Dame (*Life of the Virgin* tapestry series, 1636; Strasbourg, Museum of Fine Arts; drawings in the Louvre), and for Louis XIII (Vincennes and the Tuileries).

In 1643 Hardouin de Péréfixe introduced Champaigne to Jansenism, an anti-Jesuit, reformative sect established at Port-Royal. This heroically purist order greatly influenced his work. The Italian, or Rubenist baroque, tendencies of his earlier works (*Adoration of the Magi*, Le Mans, Museum of Fine Arts; *Adoration of the Shepherds*, London, Wallace Collection) gave place to a classical formalism that was (from the early 1630s) concurrent with, but independent of, Poussin's similar development in Rome, and more devoutly expressive. Champaigne's religious subjects became more stiff and cold (*Martyrdom of St. Protasius*, 1655, Louvre; *St. Gervasius*, 1655, Lyons, Museum of Fine Arts). The restrained bust portraits of ascetic friends at Port-Royal (the Arnaulds, Saint-Cyran) and of civic and clerical leaders impose awareness not only of his gravely humane perception of the intellectually great of the period but also of his adaptation into lucid French terms of the Flemish veristic tradition of physiognomical naturalism, translated by Robert Nanteuil and Gerard Edelinck into engraving.

Champaigne was among the original twelve academicians in 1648 and delivered lectures after 1655 professing his partisanship of "drawing" as opposed to Venetian "color," which he eschewed for strong, clear local tones. After his daughter Suzanne, a nun at Port-Royal, was miraculously cured of paralysis, he painted a votive portrait of her and Mère Agnès Arnauld (1662; Louvre). This portrait, painted twelve years before his death, synthesized his lifelong tendencies of abstraction and realism and epitomized his sincere faith. Though Champaigne was of Flemish origin and never studied in Italy, he completely assimilated the form and content of evolving French 17th-century thought, suppressing the mannerism of the early century and stabilizing the incipient Italian baroque domination of the later half.

BIBLIOGRAPHY. A. Félibien, *Entretiens . . .*, vol. 4, Amsterdam, 1706; A. Gazier, *Philippe et Jean-Baptiste de Champaigne*, Paris, 1893; A. Mabille de Poncheville, *P. de Champaigne*, Paris, 1938; Orangerie des Tuileries, *Philippe de Champaigne* (exhibition catalog by B. Dorival), Paris, 1952; A. Blunt, *Art and Architecture in France, 1500–1700*, Baltimore, 1954.

GEORGE V. GALLENKAMP

CHAMPLEVE ENAMEL. Enameling technique in which the design, hollowed out of the background metal, is filled with colored vitreous pastes; the whole is fired and subsequently polished, leaving an enameled design flush with the metal background. Champlevé enameling contrasts with cloisonné technique, in which the enamel is raised above the surface. It reached a high degree of refinement in the Maas region in the 12th and 13th centuries, as seen in the work of Nicolas de Verdun.

BIBLIOGRAPHY. H. Maryon, *Metalwork and Enameling*, New York, 1955.

CHAMPMOL, CHARTREUSE DE, DIJON, *see* DIJON.

CH'AN BUDDHISM, *see* ZEN.

CHANCE CONFIGURATION. Deliberate use of accidental elements in a work of art. Chance was given a central role in the creative activities of the Dadaists. Arp was the first to cut out shapes blindly and to arrange them "according to the laws of chance." Duchamp dropped pieces of thread randomly on canvas and then traced them where they lay, one example of a widespread practice. Since then chance configuration has been an important

Philippe de Champaigne, *La Rochelle Victory Portrait*, with Louis XIII of France. Louvre, Paris.

Champlevé enamel. Nicolas de Verdun, scene representing the crossing of the Red Sea, detail of the altar of the Abbey Church of Klosterneuburg.

element in modern art—in the surrealists' use of found objects and in the abstract expressionists' dependence on random strokes and accident.

CHANCEL. Section separated by a screen from the body of the church. This word is derived from the Latin *cancelli,* meaning "crossbars." Occupied by the clergy and the choir, the chancel contains the altar or Communion table.

CHANDELIER. Fixture with multiple light sources suspended from the ceiling. Early medieval chandeliers were constructed chiefly of architectural elements, such as towers and doors, and were mostly variations of the wheel format. The 11th-century chandelier in Hildesheim Cathedral is an example. In the Gothic period, the chandelier received its characteristic multiple branching arms arranged in tiers of diminishing size. Some chandeliers have figural decoration.

CHANDHU-DARO, *see* INDUS VALLEY CIVILIZATION.

CHANDIGARH. New capital city of the Punjab, in northwest India at the foot of the Himalayas. Begun in 1950, it was conceived as a planned ensemble of modern architecture. The designs are the work of several planners and architects, the chief among whom was Le Corbusier. The capital itself is a monumental whole, a vast grid upon which the government buildings are placed. Major structures include the Secretariat and the Palace of Justice; a large number of housing units have also been erected. The Palace of Justice, built of roughly surfaced concrete and completed in 1956, is most striking with its brightly colored network of rectangles below a series of magnificent sheltering vaults.

BIBLIOGRAPHY. Le Corbusier, *Oeuvre complète 1952–1957,* Zurich, 1957.

CH'ANG-AN (Sian; Hsi-an). Ancient Chinese administrative center, located by the Wei River in Shensi Province. Ch'ang-an was first established as a capital during the Han dynasty, but nothing significant remains of the ancient city. During the Sui reunification of China in 589 a new capital was built on the south side of Ch'ang-an and further extensions were made to the west. The T'ang emperors took Ch'ang-an as their capital also, enlarging and modifying the city started by the Sui. Under the T'angs, Ch'ang-an became an internationally famous cosmopolitan center, the heart of Chinese civilization and one of the greatest single metropolises of the world. Anti-Buddhist persecutions in the 9th century destroyed all the temples, however, and the city was repeatedly sacked from the 8th through the 10th century. After the fall of the Northern Sung (1126–27) the city lost forever its prestige as a cultural center.

Ch'ang-an under the T'angs was a model of city planning. Without the restriction of having to cope with previous foundations, the planners could start afresh and use the experience gained in the layout of such older cities as Lo-yang. The cities were laid out according to a grid system, contained by an outer wall. At each of the east, west, and south walls was a major gate; the Imperial Palace was located in the northern section of the city. Market districts were situated in both the western and the eastern sections and a broad central avenue divided the city on a north-south axis, leading from the south gate to the northern imperial section. The simplicity and clarity of the plan provided the inspiration for the Japanese in designing their capital city of Nara in 710. Among the surviving early monuments of Ch'ang-an is the famous White Goose Pagoda, built in 652 and rebuilt from 701 to 705. *See* PAGODA.

BIBLIOGRAPHY. K. Adachi, *Chōan shiseki no kenkyū (A Study of the Historic Remains at Ch'ang-an),* 2 vols., Tokyo, 1933; W. Willets, *Chinese Art,* vol. 2, Harmondsworth, 1958.

MARTIE W. YOUNG

CHANG HSUAN. Chinese painter (fl. early 8th cent.). He was renowned principally for his meticulously detailed paintings of court ladies and children. Chang Hsüan's precise dates are not recorded, and no original work from his hand has survived. Chinese historians, however, have traditionally considered him and his younger contemporary Chou Fang to be the two leading exponents of the courtly figure-painting style in the T'ang dynasty. *See* CHOU FANG.

BIBLIOGRAPHY. O. Sirén, *Chinese Painting, Leading Masters and Principles,* vol. 1, London, 1956.

CH'ANG-KANG, *see* CHO SOK.

CHANG LU. Chinese landscape painter (fl. late 15th–early 16th cent.). He was born in Ta-liang (K'ai-feng); his *tzu* was T'ien-chih and his *hao* P'ing-shan. His style of painting most often resembles that of Tai Chin, the ack-

Ch'ang-an. White Goose Pagoda, rebuilt 701–705.

nowledged leader of the Che school; thus Chang Lu is usually placed in the Che school of painters. His loosely painted landscapes featuring broad washes of ink are best seen in Japanese collections. *See* CHE SCHOOL; TAI CHIN.

BIBLIOGRAPHY. O. Sirén, *Chinese Painters, Leading Masters and Principles*, vol. 4, London, 1958.

CHANG SENG-YU. Chinese painter (fl. Liang dynasty, 502–557). Chang Seng-yu executed numerous wall paintings for the Buddhist temples around Nanking as well as secular portraits for the Liang emperors. None of his original paintings has survived, and later copies such as the well-known "Constellation" scroll (Abe Collection, Osaka Municipal Art Museum) barely suggest his style. Literary sources contain great praise given him by both his contemporaries and his later critics, chiefly for the startlingly realistic effects he achieved through the use of a method of relief shading.

BIBLIOGRAPHY. Abe Kōjirō, ed., *Sōraikan kinshō*, vol. 4, Osaka, 1939.

CH'ANG-SHA. Chinese city, located in Hunan Province. One of the most important cities in the central interior, Ch'ang-sha was the center of the Ch'u kingdom during the late Chou dynasty. Before World War II, numerous relics datable to the period from 600 to 200 B.C. were discovered in the marshes outside the city, among them the spectacular pair of cranes and serpent now in the Cleveland Museum of Art. In 1949 another major find, a painted silk fragment that may be the earliest example of its kind, was made in the southeastern suburbs of the present city. Systematic excavations at Ch'ang-sha since 1951, principally to the north of the city and in the southeastern suburbs, have revealed hundreds of tombs that can be dated with certainty to the late Chou period. The great quantity of lacquer excavated establishes the importance of the ancient city as a leading center for painting under the Ch'u rulers, whose control had extended over a major part of the modern provinces of Hunan and Anhui in the late Chou dynasty.

BIBLIOGRAPHY. "Ch'ang-sha Ch'u-mu (The Ch'u Tombs of Ch'ang-sha)," *K'ao-ku hsüeh-pao*, no. 1, 1959.

CH'ANG SHENG-FO, *see* AMITAYUS.

CHANG SHU-CH'I. Chinese painter (1899–1957). Chang Shu-ch'i studied at the Shanghai Academy and in the 1930s taught art at the National Central University in Nanking. He went to the United States in 1942 and spent a good part of his later career there. A traditional painter, Chang Shu-ch'i had a period of great popularity in the United States, and his works are widely distributed in American collections.

CHANG TA-CH'IEN. Chinese painter (1899–   ). Chang Ta-ch'ien is a native of Nei-chiang in Szechwan Province. His given name was Yüan, but he is best known by the name Ta-ch'ien, bestowed upon him as a novice in a Buddhist temple in Sun-chiang in 1919. He visited the famous cave temples of Tun-huang in 1941 and stayed two and one-half years, making more than 200 color copies of the frescoes there. His full-scale copies were the first major attempts by any Chinese artist to duplicate the inaccessible works from the great site. The paintings were widely ex-

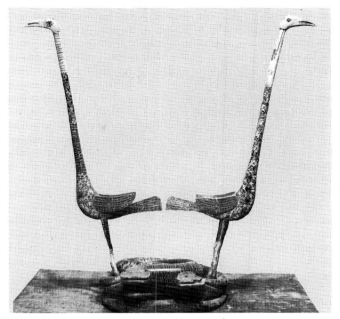

Ch'ang-sha. Pair of cranes with serpent. Lacquered wood. Cleveland Museum of Art.

hibited in such places as New Delhi, Tokyo, and Paris. In 1949 Chang Ta-ch'ien left China permanently and lived in various countries, finally settling in South America.

Chang Ta-ch'ien has been considered China's last great traditional painter. He ranges over a full spectrum of past Chinese styles, showing a dazzling command of history. Like Ch'i Pai-shih, the only other 20th-century Chinese painter who has had similar prolific skills, Chang has been a great admirer of the 17th-century Chinese individualists and eccentrics. Among the best of his works are the large-scale ink studies of flowering plants executed late in his career. He has exhibited widely and is represented in the Metropolitan Museum and the Museum of Modern Art in New York and the Museum of Fine Arts in Boston. His own collection of ancient masterpieces is famous among scholars of Chinese painting. *See* CH'I PAI-SHIH.

BIBLIOGRAPHY. Hirschl & Adler Galleries, Inc., New York, *Exhibition [of the Works of] Chang Daichien*, New York, 1963.

MARTIE W. YOUNG

CHANG YEN-YUAN. Chinese critic and collector (fl. mid-9th cent.). His background and personal life are not known in any detail. Although he was active as both a collector and an amateur practitioner of painting and calligraphy, his lasting contribution was made as a writer. He is the author of the *Li-tai ming-hua chi* (Records of Famous Painters of All Dynasties) that was completed in 847. The first four chapters give general observations by the author on a variety of topics such as the six principles of Hsieh Ho, the origins of painting, problems of connoisseurship, and the history of painting. The last six chapters contain biographical notes on painters from the earliest times to the year 841. Taken as a whole, the *Li-tai ming-hua chi* is an invaluable store of information on T'ang and pre-T'ang painting. Although he is not the earliest critic or historian of painting in China, Chang Yen-yüan is a basic source of biographical material on early painters and knowledge concerning late T'ang aesthetic attitudes.

BIBLIOGRAPHY. W. R. B. Acker, ed., *Some T'ang and pre-T'ang Texts on Chinese Painting*, Leyden, 1954; O. Sirén, *The Chinese on the Art of Painting* (Sinica leidensia, vol. 8), Peking, 1936.

CHANNEL. Groove, as in a column, such as one of the Corinthian order. *See also* FLUTE.

CHA-NO-YU. Tea ceremony originated in China by Ch'an (Zen) monks as an inducement to contemplation of the refined and eternal aspects of life. It was introduced by this Buddhist sect into Japanese circles around the Ashikaga shogun Yoshimasa (1435–90). The ceremony became a cult under the tea master Sen-no Rikyu (1520–91) and influenced pottery, architecture, and painting toward a studied simplicity, according to the Zen perception of beauty in the humblest object.

CHANTILLY: CHATEAU. Medieval fortress in a small town of the Ile-de-France. The château was rebuilt at the behest of Anne de Montmorency, constable of France, in the 16th century. The Condé family made further alterations in the 17th and 18th centuries. After a disastrous sacking in the French Revolution the château was finally rebuilt between 1876 and 1882. In 1876 the Duc d'Aumale gave the château, its collections, and its grounds to the Institute of France. It is now the Condé Museum.

See CHANTILLY: CONDE MUSEUM.

BIBLIOGRAPHY. G. Macon, *Chantilly et le Musée Condé*, Paris, 1910; E. de Ganay, *Chantilly au XVIIIe siècle*, Paris, 1925.

CHANTILLY: CONDE MUSEUM. French collection. The 19th-century Grand Château, containing the splendid collection of pictures assembled by the Duc d'Aumale, was given to the Institute of France in 1876. In accordance with the duke's wish, the presentation of the furnishings and works of art has remained unchanged. In addition to the French and Flemish primitives in the Condé Museum, there are canvases by Clouet, Memling, Poussin, Watteau, Ingres, and Delacroix. The choice collection of drawings is highlighted by 100 examples from the hand of Poussin. Among the 150 manuscripts are three of the greatest masterpieces of Western illumination, the Psalter of Queen Ingeborg of Denmark, the Très riches heures du Duc de Berry by the Limbourg Brothers, and the Book of Hours of Etienne Chevalier by Jean Fouquet.

BIBLIOGRAPHY. J. Meurgey, *Les Principaux manuscrits à peintures du Musée Condé à Chantilly*, Paris, 1930.

CHANTILLY PORCELAIN. French soft-paste porcelain. The Chantilly factory was founded in 1725 by Cignaire Cirou under the protection of Louis-Henri de Bourbon, Prince de Condé. Until Cirou's death in 1751, Chantilly was distinguished by its use of a tin glaze that produced a milky white opaqueness uncommon to soft-paste porcelain. After 1751, the usual lead glaze was used. Oriental motifs, particularly those from Kakiemon and Imari porcelains, inspired many Chantilly designs, some of which were adapted from existing Meissen patterns. The Chantilly factory continued in operation until the turn of the 19th

century; during its later years, its mark was changed from a red to a blue hunting horn.

BIBLIOGRAPHY. H. Frantz, *French Pottery and Porcelain*, London, 1906; W. Honey, *European Ceramic Art*, 2 vols., London, 1949–52.

CHANTRY, SIR FRANCIS. English sculptor (1781–1841). He was one of the most prolific early 19th-century sculptors. His works number in the hundreds, and many are of studio quality. Chantry could, however, depict great feeling (*Lady Stanhope*, 1823; Kent, Chevening) and nobility (*Marianne Johnes*, 1811; Haford).

CHANTRY. Endowment, or a chapel or altar so endowed, for the chanting of Masses and the offering of prayers. Chantries were generally small chapels within a church, or extending from it, that contained the tombs of the founders who endowed them. In medieval England, chantry chapels were most numerous in abbeys and cathedrals, where burial privileges commonly accompanied a benefaction.

CHAO CH'ANG. Chinese painter of flowers and fruits (fl. 1000–20). Born near Cheng-tu, he gained considerable honor and prestige at the imperial court in the early years of the Sung dynasty, chiefly for his delicate use of colors in the depiction of various species of flowers. In early Chinese histories of painting Chao Ch'ang is usually grouped with Hsü Hsi and Huang Ch'üan to form the triumvirate of masters who initiated the bird-and-flower category of painting. *See* HUANG CH'UAN; HSU HSI.

BIBLIOGRAPHY. O. Sirén, *Chinese Painting, Leading Masters and Principles*, vol. 1, London, 1956.

CHAO LING-JAN (Chao Ta-nien). Chinese painter of landscapes (fl. late 11th cent.). He was a direct descendant of the first Sung-dynasty emperor, T'ai-tsu (r. 960–76). His landscapes were described by contemporaries as being very soft and almost effeminate in their visual effect. The number of surviving paintings attributed to Chao Ling-jan seems to agree with such descriptions, for most show a characteristic misty, low-lying marshland or river's edge bathed in a late-autumnal glow.

BIBLIOGRAPHY. O. Sirén, *Chinese Painting, Leading Masters and Principles*, vol. 2, London, 1956.

CHAO MENG-FU (Chao Tzu-ang). Chinese painter (d. 1322). Born in Hu-chou (Wu-hsing), Chekiang Province, Chao Meng-fu was known also by his *tzu* Tzu-ang, his *hao* Sung Hsüeh, and his posthumous title Wen-min. He received his education under the Southern Sung dynasty at the capital of Hang-chou and pursued an official government career until the dynasty fell in 1279. He later joined the court of Kublai Khan and, from 1286 on, served the Mongol conquerors in various high administrative posts and as a court painter. Chao Meng-fu gained a great measure of fame in his own time as a calligrapher, painter, and scholar. Later critics have occasionally discounted his contribution to Chinese art because, although a descendant of the Sung imperial family, he collaborated with the Mongols.

In calligraphy Chao Meng-fu was highly regarded for his skill in all the accepted styles of script, and in painting

Chao Meng-fu, *Horses Crossing a Stream*. Freer Gallery, Washington, D.C. A work long attributed to this artist.

he had a similar diverse repertoire in subject matter. But to the Western audience Chao Meng-fu was first known as a great painter of horses, a category of subject matter that appealed naturally to the horse-conscious Mongols. A number of paintings in American and European collections have had long-standing attributions to Chao Meng-fu (for example, *Horses Crossing a Stream*, Freer Gallery, Washington, D.C.; *Two Horses*, formerly Stoclet Collection, Brussels), but few if indeed any can be unconditionally accepted as authentic. Another category of subjects that suffers from overly optimistic attributions to the Yüan master is that of bamboo paintings. Several fine specimens in the National Palace Museum Collection, Sun Yat-sen Museum, near Taipei, do reveal the sure and gifted hand of Chao Meng-fu in the handling of various textures of ink to define forms.

The most reliably attributed works of Chao are probably in the category of landscape painting, notably the fine hand scroll in the National Palace Museum collection entitled *Autumn Colors of the Ch'iao and Hua Mountains*. With its low sweeping horizon line the scroll gives a more normalized view of a panoramic landscape than the monumental and idealized products of the 11th century. The two mountains of the title appear as strange humps of blue on the horizon. The reference is both to the past and to the present, to the blue-and-green T'ang-dynasty style and to the new emerging realism of the Yüan period. The overpowering grandeur of the earlier landscapes has been replaced by an interest in ink tones and carefully contrasted brushstrokes defining trees, rocks, weeds. The archaistic reference appears not only in the use of the special color of blue but in the deliberately awkward scale employed for houses and other objects in the landscape. The painting is a clear visual statement of Chao Meng-fu's own writing, in which he contends that his "rough and simple" style comes close to the ancient masters. A conservative traditionalist, Chao married his calligraphic interest to landscape depictions, and such works as *Autumn Colors* reveal his genius far better than the many horse paintings traditionally ascribed to his brush.

See also BLUE-AND-GREEN STYLE.

BIBLIOGRAPHY. L. Binyon, "A Landscape by Chao Mêng-fu in the British Museum," *T'oung Pao*, ser. 2, VI, 1906; S. Shimada and Y. Yonezawa, *Painting of the Sung and Yüan Dynasties*, Tokyo, 1952; O. Sirén, *Chinese Painting, Leading Masters and Principles*, vol. 4, London, 1958.

MARTIE W. YOUNG

CHAO PO-CHU. Chinese painter (fl. mid-12th cent.). He was active in the court of Emperor Kao-tsung (r. 1127–62) at the beginning of the Southern Sung dynasty. Chao Po-chü, known also by his *tzu* Ch'ien-li, was a direct descendant of the first Sung emperor and had served in the academy of Emperor Hui-tsung. After Hui-tsung's fall he moved south to the newly established capital at Hang-chou along with a few other members of the academy. In this new location he continued to paint landscapes, illustrative narratives, and portraits in a meticulous and refined style that Chinese critics traditionally refer to as the "blue-and-green" manner. To this highly coloristic style of painting, credited to the inventive genius of the T'ang-dynasty master Li Ssu-hsün, Chao Po-chü added gold outlines to heighten the effect of visual richness and to create a jewellike surface. A fine example of this coloristic style is the long hand scroll in the Museum of Fine Arts, Boston, which illustrates the army of the first Han-dynasty emperor making its victorious entry into the city of Kuan-chung. The scroll bears the seal and signature of Chao Po-chü.

See also BLUE-AND-GREEN STYLE; HUI-TSUNG; LI SSU-HSUN.

BIBLIOGRAPHY. K. Tomita, "Entry of the First Emperor of the Han Dynasty into Kuan-chung: A Chinese Scroll-Painting by Chao Po-chü . . .," *Boston, Museum of Fine Arts, Bulletin*, XXX, October, 1932.

MARTIE W. YOUNG

CHAO TA-NIEN, *see* CHAO LING-JAN.

CHAO TSO. Chinese landscape painter (fl. first quarter of 17th cent.). Chao Tso was active in the city of Sung-chiang, Kiangsu. He was a close friend of Tung Ch'i-ch'ang, and his manner of painting with muted tonal washes and strong brushwork was modeled after Tung to some extent. Chinese historians sometimes refer to Chao Tso as the founder of the "Su-sung" school of painting. Chao Tso is also the author of a short treatise on painting entitled *Hua-yu-lu*. See TUNG CH'I-CH'ANG.

BIBLIOGRAPHY. O. Sirén, *Chinese Painting, Leading Masters and Principles*, vol. 5, London, 1958.

CHAO TZU-ANG, see CHAO MENG-FU.

CHAO YUNG. Chinese painter (b. 1279). A native of Hu-chou (Wu-hsing) in Chekiang Province, he was the son of the illustrious Chao Meng-fu. Chao Yung served in the court of Kublai Khan and, like his father, had a successful government career. His paintings follow his father's in both variety of subjects and general style, although Chao Yung was never considered so gifted or so influential as his famous father. See CHAO MENG-FU.

BIBLIOGRAPHY. O. Sirén, *Chinese Painting, Leading Masters and Principles*, vol. 4, London, 1958.

CHAPEL. Place of worship, usually in honor of a particular saint. It is a room or recess containing an altar and is dedicated separately from, for example, the church in which it may be located. Chapels may be private places of worship, as found in palaces, or oratories in which Masses are sung for the dead, as found in mausoleums.

CHAPEL, LADY. Chapel dedicated to the Virgin Mary, an outgrowth in medieval architecture of the increasing veneration of the Virgin. The Lady chapel was generally situated at the east end of the church, behind the altar and on an axis with the nave: it was the most important of the cluster of chapels forming the *chevet*. In England it was often a church within a church, as in the Cathedrals of York, Winchester, and Salisbury.

CHAPEL, RADIATING. Chapel usually situated at the east end of a medieval church, forming part of a semicircular cluster behind the sanctuary. The French Gothic Cathedrals of Reims, Amiens, Chartres, and Beauvais have chapels radiating from the sanctuary and opening from an ambulatory.

CHAPELLE EXPIATOIRE, PARIS, see PERCIER AND FONTAINE.

CHAPIN, JAMES ORMSBEE. American painter (1887–). He was born in West Orange, N.J., and studied at the Antwerp Academy and in New York City. Chapin paints portraits, landscapes, figures, and genre subjects in a style related to American Scene realism, but, since the 1940s, with a looser handling.

CHAPMAN, DAVE. American industrial designer (1909–). Chapman was born in Gilman, Ill. After studies at the Armour Institute of Technology in Chicago, he started with the Century of Progress in Chicago (1932–33) and moved on to product design at Montgomery Ward (1933–35). He established his own firm in Chicago (1935) and became head of Design Research, Inc. (1955).

CHAPTER HOUSE. Place where abbot, prior, and other members of a monastery or cathedral chapter may meet to transact their affairs. Chapter houses were often reached from cloisters, as at Westminster. French medieval chapter houses were usually double-aisled, vaulted, and rectangular; those in England (often separate structures) were more often polygonal in plan, their vaults springing from a central pillar, as at Lincoln, Wells, and Salisbury Cathedrals.

CHAPU, HENRI MICHEL ANTOINE. French sculptor (b. Mée, 1833; d. Paris, 1891). He studied at the Ecole des Beaux-Arts in Paris with Pradier and Duret and spent five years in Rome. While conforming in some respects to the academic classicism of his time, Chapu used a degree of naturalism to offset the coldness of the antique. This pleasing combination can be seen in the rhythmically lovely female figure *Youth* paying homage to the bust of Henri Regnault on Regnault's tomb (1872; Paris, Ecole des Beaux-Arts). Chapu's other emphasis, on naturalism, is visible in his figure *Jeanne d'Arc* (ca. 1870; Paris, formerly Luxembourg).

BIBLIOGRAPHY. O. Fidière, *Chapu: Sa vie et son oeuvre*, Paris, 1894.

CHARCOAL DRAWING. Charcoal is obtained by roasting thin sticks or vines of a close-grained wood, such as linden, box, or willow, in a closed vessel. Depending on the wood, charcoal varies from soft to hard. A charcoal line applied directly is a deep mat black, while one that is rubbed is less bright, even gray. Charcoal is usually used on a soft grainy paper and is almost always fixed with a thin spirit varnish such as shellac.

Until the late 19th century, when it was widely used as an autonomous medium, charcoal drawing was mainly associated with preparatory sketches, cartoons, and layouts. The nature of the line, which can vary from very dark and precise to very soft and smudgy, makes it ideal for blocking out a composition in its roughest aspects. The extreme impermanence of unfixed charcoal made it somewhat impractical as a highly developed drawing medium.

The first independent charcoal drawing is Dürer's *Portrait of Willibald Pirckheimer* (1503; Berlin, former State Museums, Print Cabinet). Michelangelo and Raphael both used charcoal for studies and layouts, the latter for a cartoon preparatory to *School of Athens*, in which the charcoal line is supplemented with black and white chalk. The Venetians used charcoal, especially in the late 16th century, for portraits and portrait studies. Titian, Tintoretto, and Veronese all found charcoal well suited to their temperaments and often used it in conjunction with white lead.

BIBLIOGRAPHY. B. Degenhart, *Europäische Handzeichnungen*, Berlin, 1943; J. Watrous, *The Craft of Old-Master Drawings*, Madison, Wisc., 1957.

JULIA M. EHRESMANN

CHARDIGNY, BARTHELEMY FRANCOIS. French sculptor (b. Rouen, 1757, d. Paris, 1813). He was awarded the Prix de Rome in 1782 and lived in Rome until 1786. Chardigny worked for various cities and churches in Provence, sometimes producing imaginative sculpture in a classicizing style.

CHARDIN, JEAN-BAPTISTE-SIMEON. French painter (1699–1779). He was born in Paris and inherited high standards of craftsmanship from his father, Jean Chardin, a master cabinetmaker. He was apprenticed about 1713 to P. J. Cazes, a mediocre history painter and a disciple of Le Brun. Cazes's shop, though devoid of living models, offered Chardin early exposure to academic principles. He did subsequent work under Noël-Nicolas Coypel, whose

Jean-Baptiste-Siméon Chardin, *Boy Playing with Cards*. Uffizi, Florence.

emphasis on the correct placing and lighting of a gun or dog for an official portrait afforded Chardin his first chance to paint directly from nature, encouraging habits of cautious visual analysis. This gave him an early opportunity to handle paint boldly and intimately without the necessity of making preparatory drawings. Chardin rarely drew, except to record a passing notion.

Enrolled in the Academy of St. Luke, he did not compete for the Prix de Rome. He never traveled farther than Fontainebleau, where, under Jean-Baptiste Van Loo, he assisted in the restoration of the 16th-century decorative works in the palace galleries. Local renown in his Saint-Germain quarter came about 1726, however, when a signboard he painted for a surgeon was hung: it depicted the aftermath of a duel and in its teeming genre spontaneity evoked Guardi and especially Watteau's *Enseigne de Gersaint*. Professional recognition was immediate at a showing, among recognized artists' works, of twelve of his own, including *The Ray* and *The Buffet* (both Paris, Louvre), at the Exposition de la Jeunesse in 1728. In that year he also won membership in the Royal Academy. His advancement in that body was marked by appointment as councilor (1743), treasurer (1755–74), royal pensioner (from 1752), and *tapissier* (from 1755), responsible for hanging works of exhibitors at the Royal Salons. Finally, Chardin was the beneficiary of quarters in the Louvre from 1757 until his death.

The critics, including Diderot, who had been exuberantly enthusiastic about his art before 1750, began to express reservations after that time. They misjudged his working with consecrated intensity upon a limited number of themes as weakening of inventiveness caused by newly acquired domestic comfort and royal favor, and compared him unfavorably with the industrious but more decorative Jean-Baptiste Oudry, his arch and unique rival. Only briefly in 1765 and 1766, when he executed two series of overdoor paintings (*Attributes of the Arts and Sciences* for the Château de Choisy and *Civil and Military Music* for Bellevue; some are in the Louvre, others have disappeared) for the Marquis de Marigny, director of fine arts, was there an upsurge of critical enthusiasm. Diderot subsequently remarked, however, "Chardin's art is dying." Thereafter Chardin was neglected in favor of his more facile pupils and imitators: in genre, Lépicié, E. Aubry, F. Duparc, and Jeaurat; in still life, Mme. Valloyer-Coster and Roland de LaPorte.

Chardin was individualistic and a laborious perfectionist, and he shyly avoided observation as he worked. He was therefore ill-suited to communicate to others, for example, to Fragonard, who was briefly his pupil. He could not convey the secrets of his personal poetry by teaching the highly technical elements of his craft. His celebrated speech, entitled "Indulgence" (*Oeuvres de Diderot: Le Salon, 1765*), amply indicates his goodwill toward students, and his encouragement of Jacques-Louis David confirms it. He was entirely disinterested in profits and modestly undercharged for his master works, which were, paradoxically, prized internationally by Catherine of Russia, Frederick the Great, Louis XV, the Prince of Liechtenstein, the Count of Tessin, and others, and were assiduously copied by engravers (genre only, by Cochin, LeBas, Lépicié, Fillouel, and Surugue).

Though Chardin was sensitive to critical neglect, his preoccupations with aesthetics were paramount, permitting him to pursue his own criteria in the exploration of visual reality until convinced he had something important to say. Such a statement constitutes the conclusive and unexpected triumph of his career, his turning, during the last eight years of his life, from genre and still life in oils to pastel portraiture. Not only were his powerfully sensitive portraits of himself and his wife (Louvre) acclaimed at the Salon of 1775, but his own high tradition was consummated in a medium and a domain that had been considered exclusively those of Maurice-Quentin de La Tour.

Chardin's earliest works reflect an independent predilection for the Netherlandish still-life masters (J. Fyt, Metsys, and A. Cuijp) whose cabinet pieces were enjoying a vogue. Though Chardin monumentalized them more in the French manner of Desportes and of Oudry, late baroque drama is still implied by the contrasts of living and dead animals, the glitter and opacity of vessels, and the moist repellence of marine life with elaborate dessert pieces, asymmetrically arranged in recessional curves. In the early 1730s, perhaps goaded by his friend Aved, he attempted the representation of the human figure, experimenting first with monkeys (*The Monkey Painter* and *The Antiquarian*, both Louvre). He developed slowly into genre, suggesting the manner of Jean-François de Troy (*Lady Sealing a Letter*, Berlin, former State Museums) and portraiture (*Aved*, known as *The Prompter*, Louvre).

He found his stride with sixteen works exhibited at the 1734 Exposition de la Jeunesse and eight at the 1737 Salon. Mostly scenes of bourgeois life, they represent industrious mothers and grave children, simply but fastidiously dressed, in quiet interiors furnished with sober elegance. In an age of opulence these provoked a nostalgia for a simpler way of life and resuscitated a synthesized memory of Vermeer, A. Bosse, and the Le Nains.

His portraiture in oil, in which he always felt deficient, is focused around 1746. Though the paintings represent specific individuals, they usually remain unqualified under genre titles. From 1751 to 1771 he concentrated mainly on still lifes, composed of modest wooden, copper, glass, and earthenware utensils, ripening fruits, and the ingredients for meals. They were flawlessly rendered in creamy impasto and pearly, glowing tones, eliciting the perfect and eternal qualities proper to each object. These motifs are so judiciously selected and discreetly composed through his science of balance of varied shapes, silhouettes, and textures, through contours softened by diffused light, subtle reflections, and highlights, that essential monumentality becomes secondary to the impact of gratification in the contemplation of our "daily bread," sanctified without sentimentality in paint. Chardin's works breathe a spiritual solitude that results from fusing classical norms of beauty with a naturalism based upon the undisturbed observation of routine life.

Stable, independent, never sacrificing his art or peace of mind to wealth or prestige, Chardin is fundamentally an artist's artist. Though the explicit content of his art has, like Rembrandt's, universal appeal, he felt himself primarily accountable for the formal means. His poetry is, therefore, the by-product of sincere dedication to his own evolving aesthetic standards. Like earlier masters, he is con-

Enguerrand Charenton, *The Coronation of the Virgin*. Hospice, Villeneuve-les-Avignon.

cerned with abstract problems of perspective and foreshortening, and with problems of the total visual effect. Like modern painters, while challenging the tensions between surface and space and the color patch, he is ulteriorly preoccupied with the minimum means to an expressive end. Though his methods understandably frustrated contemporary imitators and occasioned a long period of neglect, fundamental questions about optics, structure, and expression raised in the mid-19th century have automatically generated more understanding and a reassessment of his methods and content. Through Chardin, still-life painting has been raised from the least distinguished of all the genres to one of the most flexible and utilitarian in the development of modern painting.

BIBLIOGRAPHY. G. Wildenstein, "Le Caractère de Chardin et sa vie," *Gazette des Beaux-Arts*, 6th series, X, 1933; G. Wildenstein, *Chardin, biographie et catalogue critiques...*, Paris, 1933; E. L. de Goncourt and J. A. de Goncourt, *French XVIII Century Painters*, New York, 1948; J. Seznec and J. Adhémar, *Diderot Salons*, vol. 1, Oxford, Eng., 1957.

GEORGE V. GALLENKAMP

CHARENTON (Quarton), ENGUERRAND. French painter (b. Diocese of Laon, Picardy, ca. 1420; d. Avignon, ca. 1470). He is known from documents to have been in Provence at least from 1444 until 1466. Charenton's surviving work shows him as schooled in the Franco-Flemish tradition, with its Gothic play of lines. This he blended in a unique way, with elements reminiscent of Sienese 14th-century paintings in Avignon and with the strong contrasts and three-dimensional quality with which the southern light endowed Provençal painting, to create altarpieces that are major monuments of the period.

Contracts preserved in Avignon connect Charenton with the two paintings on which his reputation rests. In 1452 he was commissioned to paint a *Virgin of Mercy* with posthumous portraits of Jean Cadart and his wife and with St. John the Baptist and St. John the Evangelist (Chantilly, Condé Museum). The towering Virgin and saints and the smaller praying figures project in sculptural volumes against a flat gold ground. Charenton was associated in this commission with the painter Pierre Villate; it appears that Villate painted only the missing predella called for in the contract, for there is no evidence of a second hand that might be involved in the execution of the existing Chantilly panel.

The contract of 1453 in which the priest Jean de Montagnac commissioned Charenton to paint *The Coronation of the Virgin* (Villeneuve-les-Avignon, Hospice) reveals to what degree the details of the composition were dictated by the donor and how much was contributed by the painter. The altarpiece presents the whole of the Christian cosmos in a way that brings to mind the sculptured tympanum of a northern French cathedral. The dominant figures are those of the stylized hieratic Virgin and the Holy Trinity, "with no difference at all between Father and Son," as stipulated in the contract. Surrounding them in Paradise are the blessed, depicted in rich variety on a much-reduced scale. Beneath is shown the earth in the form of a naturalistic landscape of impressive depth and assurance. The landscape faithfully portrays areas of Avignon and its environs, expertly abstracted and organized, as are details of the city scenes representing Rome and Jerusalem. The holy cities are separated by a Crucifixion. Below, in the position of lintel or predella, is a lively scene of Purgatory and Hell.

Recently Charenton has been credited with the famous *Avignon Pietà* (Paris, Louvre), painted before 1457, which shares with the two paintings described above such characteristics as organization in large arabesques, idealized physiognomies with large skulls, sculptural quality, and masterly simplification of many of the forms, as well as certain details.

BIBLIOGRAPHY. L. H. Labande, *Les Primitifs français: Peintres et peintres-verriers de la Provence occidentale*, 2 vols., Marseilles, 1932; C. Sterling, *Le Couronnement de la Vierge, par Enguerrand Quarton*, Paris, 1939; G. Ring, *A Century of French Painting, 1400–1500*, London, 1949; M. Laclotte, *L'Ecole d'Avignon: La Peinture en Provence aux XIVe et XVe siècles*, Paris, 1960.

MADLYN KAHR

CHARIOTEER OF DELPHI. Greek bronze statue, excavated in the Delphic sanctuary of Apollo in 1896, and now in the museum at Delphi. It was part of a quadriga group that stood on the terrace of the Temple of Apollo. Fragments of the chariot, the horses, and a groom have also been found. According to an inscription on its stone base blocks, the group was set up by Polyzalos, the younger brother of Gelon, tyrant of Syracuse, to commemorate a victory in the Pythian games. The inscription and the style of the statue itself indicate a date in the 470s, perhaps the Pythian games of 474 B.C. The charioteer is a masterpiece of austere, Doric simplicity and may be said to be the sculptural equivalent of the poetry of Pindar.

BIBLIOGRAPHY. F. Chamoux, *L'Aurige*, Paris, 1955.

CHARITES, see GRACES, THE.

CHARLEMAGNE. The rebirth of late-antique form in the art of the Carolingian Renaissance is directly attributable to the emperor Charlemagne (ca. 742–814). In rivalry with Byzantium, he strove to make the Holy Roman Empire the true heir to Constantine's empire. He personally directed the building activity at Aachen and, by importing Early Christian and Byzantine manuscripts that were used as models in the many scriptoria he patronized, played an important role in the development of manuscript illumination. *See* AACHEN. *See also* CAROLINGIAN ART AND ARCHITECTURE.

CHARLES I, PORTRAIT OF. Oil painting by Van Dyck, in the Louvre, Paris. *See* DYCK, ANTHONY VAN.

CHARLES IV, EQUESTRIAN MONUMENT OF, MEXICO CITY, *see* TOLSA, MANUEL.

CHARLES V, PALACE OF, GRANADA, *see* ALHAMBRA, GRANADA.

CHARLES V AT MUHLBERG. Oil painting by Titian, in the Prado, Madrid. *See* TITIAN.

CHARLES BORROMEO, ST., *see* BORROMEO, CHARLES, ST.

CHARLES THE BALD, PSALTER OF. Carolingian illuminated manuscript, in the National Library, Paris. *See* CAROLINGIAN ART AND ARCHITECTURE; CORBIE SCHOOL; SAINT-DENIS STYLE.

CHARLESTON, S.C.: CITY HALL. Formerly the Bank of the United States, the City Hall was begun in 1800. It has been suggested that Gabriel Manigault was the architect. The use of curved lines, marble trim, and circular basement windows and the general effect of delicacy seem characteristic of his work.

BIBLIOGRAPHY. B. Ravenel, *Architects of Charleston*, 2d ed., Charleston, S.C., 1964.

CHARLESTON, S.C.: ST. MICHAEL'S CHURCH. Begun in 1752, St. Michael's is one of the largest and most sophisticated American Georgian churches. The spire, with its position above the giant portico (the first giant portico on a Colonial church), places the design close to James Gibbs's St. Martin-in-the-Fields, London (1721–26). The architect is unknown, but Peter Harrison of Newport, R.I., has been suggested.

BIBLIOGRAPHY. H. S. Morrison, *Early American Architecture*, New York, 1952.

CHARLET, NICOLAS-TOUSSAINT. French painter and lithographer (b. Paris, 1792; d. there, 1845). In 1817 Charlet entered the studio of Gros, where he became familiar with the Napoleonic subjects that occupied him throughout his career.

His first series of lithographs, which was entitled *Suite de costumes militaires* and *La Vieille armée française* (1820), appeared while he was still associated with Gros. During the 1830s his works contributed to the "Légende Napoléonienne" and soon brought him considerable fame. Charlet continued to produce series of lithographs with subjects drawn from the military exploits of Napoleon; the greatest were the illustrations for Napoleon's diary of St. Helena, *Le Mémorial de Sainte-Hélène*. He executed a few oil paintings (*Episode de la retraite de Russie*; Lyons, Museum of Fine Arts), which he used for his debut in the

Jean Charlot, detail of mural in the School of Journalism, University of Georgia, Athens, Ga.

Salon of 1836. Charlet's works are particularly important as a source of the cultural history of France between 1820 and 1840.

BIBLIOGRAPHY. J. F. L. de La Combe, *Charlet*, Paris, 1856; A. Dayot, *Charlet et son oeuvre*, Paris, 1893.

CHARLIER, GUILLAUME. Belgian sculptor (1854–1924). Born in Ixelles, Charlier studied under Geefs and De Groot in Brussels and under Cuvelier and Carolus-Duran in Paris. Later he worked in the studio of Van der Stappen and traveled to Italy on a Prix de Rome. His early portraits and classical works are unexceptional. More characteristic are the later works that depict fishermen and other working people with sentimental and anecdotal realism.

CHARLIEU, ABBEY CHURCH OF. SS. Peter and Paul, a French Benedictine church, was founded in the 9th century and rebuilt in the grand manner of Cluny in the late 11th and the early 12th century. Little remains except the unusually fine two-storied narthex with its profusion of late Burgundian Romanesque sculpture. The tympanum and border decorations are especially noteworthy.

BIBLIOGRAPHY. J. Evans, *The Romanesque Architecture of the Order of Cluny*, Cambridge, Eng., 1938.

CHARLOT, JEAN. Mexican painter (1898–   ). Born in Paris of French-Mexican ancestry, Charlot studied at the Ecole des Beaux-Arts. He reached Mexico in 1921 and became a pioneer of the mural movement. Late in 1922 he completed his first Mexican mural, *Fall of Tenochtitlán*, for Mexico City's new Preparatory School. After helping Diego Rivera decorate the auditorium of this school, Char-

lot collaborated with him and others in frescoing the two courts of the Ministry of Education (1923). Dismissed from this venture, Charlot turned temporarily to easel painting. In 1928–29 he served the Carnegie expedition at Chichén Itzá, Yucatán, where contact with the ancient Maya intensified his admiration for primitive art.

In 1929, as a result of artistic exposure to the United States, Charlot became instructor of mural painting for the Art Students League of New York. Next he taught at such institutions as Smith College, Black Mountain College, and the universities of Georgia and Iowa. Charlot has been a director of the College Art Association and a recipient of a Guggenheim Fellowship. Leading museums in Latin America, Europe, and the United States possess his works. Since 1951 Charlot has been professor of art at the University of Hawaii.

His chief production in the United States comprises three murals in Athens, Ga., for the Fine Arts and School of Journalism buildings (1941–42 and 1943–44, respectively) at the University of Georgia and for the McDonough Post Office (1941–42). In 1955 Charlot frescoed Psalm 22 for the Church of Christ the Good Shepherd, Lincoln Park, Mich. He executed murals for the Waikiki Beach branch of the Bishop National Bank as well as for the Hawaiian Village Hotel in 1956. He has also won fame as a pioneer of color lithography.

Charlot has investigated aesthetic and technical problems of the most varied nature, making rich contributions to the study of pre-Columbian, colonial, folk, and graphic art. Representative publications are *The Temple of the Warriors* (Washington, D.C., 1929), *Art from the Mayans to Disney* (New York, 1939), and *Mexican Art and the Academy of San Carlos, 1785–1915* (Austin, 1962).

As an artist, Charlot has achieved a sophisticated blend of primitive and modern elements. He refines and simplifies forms into basic cubes and cylinders evocative of either Léger and Picasso or Toltec and Aztec sculpture. Typically, saw-cut Indian masks and streamlined shapes are combined in formal unions within interlocking, tightly organized designs. Charlot, however, is more than a formalist; he has striven also to discover appropriate aesthetic solutions to problems of modern religious art.

BIBLIOGRAPHY. V. Stewart, *45 Contemporary Mexican Artists*, Stanford, Calif., 1951; A. Reed, *The Mexican Muralists*, New York, 1960; J. Charlot, *Mexican Mural Renaissance, 1920–25*, New Haven, Conn., 1963.

JAMES B. LYNCH, JR.

CHARNEL HOUSE. In the Romanesque and Gothic periods, a place similar to a mortuary chapel where dead bodies were deposited. Charnel houses were small round or polygonal buildings usually erected near the church; sometimes the church crypt served the same function. A special chantry chapel was often built above the charnel house.

CHARON. The shabby, bearded old man who was thought by the ancient Greeks to ferry the souls of the dead across the river Styx to the various regions in Hades. Since his charge for this service was one to three obols, mourners placed a coin in the mouth of the deceased. Charon is shown wearing a workman's chiton and hat as he pushes his pole into the river current.

CHARTERHOUSE, *see* ABBEY.

CHARTRES CATHEDRAL. Great French Gothic cathedral. Immediately after a fire destroyed its 11th-century façade in 1134, work began anew, first on the north bell tower and then on the south tower. About 1150 a new façade was brought forward flush with the west side of the towers and was then superbly embellished with the sculptures of the Royal Portal as well as with incomparable windows. In 1194, however, another disastrous fire reduced the timber-roofed cathedral to rubble. Again work resumed immediately, and the nave was completed by 1220. Between then and 1264, when the Cathedral was dedicated, the transepts, transept porches, choir, ambulatory, and radiating chapels were finished. In the 14th century the chapter house with the Chapel of St-Piat above was added. Another major addition was the graceful north spire built (1507–13) by Jean Texier, known as Jean de Beauce. He also added the ambulatory screen (1520–29) decorated with scenes from the story of the Virgin and Christ.

In many ways Chartres stands midway between the late Romanesque Abbaye-aux-Hommes and the High Gothic of such buildings as Amiens. The façade shows this transitional character in a greater verticality, resulting from the prominent angle towers and the doubled-up buttresses. Its massive form echoes the Romanesque style, but the portals and window openings have been enlarged. The portals are still recessed, however, in comparison with those of Amiens and other High Gothic structures, where they protrude.

Historically, Chartres may perhaps be considered the first High Gothic building, and it may be supposed that it was planned to utilize the flying buttress system, with all that this implies. In some ways, particularly in the elevation of its interior with its three-story divisions accenting the large clerestory windows (comparable in height with that of the nave arcade), the Chartres system set the standard for the Gothic architecture of Europe.

The façade is perhaps less impressive than those of later buildings, such as Reims and Amiens, which represent the next step in the evolution of Gothic architecture, but the sculptures are incomparable in richness and variety. The Royal Portal is one of the greatest achievements of Romanesque art; its harmonious calm and monumental style already suggest the grandeur of the 13th century. The jamb figures, with their downward-pointing feet, their magnificently modeled draperies, and their restraint and with elongation and observance of the rigid rules of frontality, preserve a perfect relationship with the architectural whole. There is rich variation in the colonnette bases on which these Old Testament patriarchs and prophets rest. In turn, they hold above their heads scenes of the New Testament, even as the Old Testament supports the New. The capitals of columns and colonnette figures tell the story of Christ.

The tympanum to the right, with the Virgin and Child enthroned above the two panels, deals with the Nativity and the Presentation. On the voussoirs are the liberal arts and women bearing the trivium and quadrivium, assisted by the sages of antiquity. On the left door we see the Ascension in the tympanum, while the voussoirs show the occupations of the months. The central door tympanum represents Christ set against the *mandorla*, surrounded by the symbols of the Evangelists. The Apostles are represent-

Chartres Cathedral. The façade is transitional between the late Romanesque and the High Gothic styles.

ed on the lintel and the old men of the apocalypse on the archivolts.

The north transept sculptures deal primarily with the Triumph of the Virgin. The central tympanum represents the Death, Assumption, and Coronation of the Virgin, and on the splayed jambs are superb figures of prophets and saints. The left door shows the Annunciation, the Visitation, and the Nativity, and the right shows scenes from the Old Testament. Decorative statuettes representing the active life and the contemplative life, the creation of the world, and the occupations of the months fill the surrounding spaces.

On the south porch, the central theme on the tympanum is the Last Judgment. The central *trumeau* supports a marvelously human "Teaching" Christ, surrounded on the jambs by the Apostles. The *Door of the Martyrs* to the left, with especially fine figures of SS. Theodore, Maurice, and George, represents the chivalrous ideal of the time of St. Louis. The latter figures date from 1230–40. The right door deals primarily with the stories of SS. Martin and Nicholas, and the jamb figures (1220–30) portray with great vigor and comprehension the Princes of the Church and saints. The whole complex of figures represents an aggregate of 12th- and 13th-century sculptured ideals.

All the sculpture, like the windows, displays an iconographical organization that stems from the sensitive lofty realms of Scholastic thought that emanated from the school of Chartres. This school, since the time of Bishop Fulbert (11th cent.) had stressed the highest aspects of humanism, particularly through the influence of Bernard de Chartres, Thierry, and John of Salisbury (bishop 1176–80).

Chartres is the richest of all French cathedrals in the glories of its stained-glass windows. The oldest are the three windows of the west front and *Notre Dame de la Belle Verrière* in the south choir aisle (all 12th cent.). Their age is evident from the tracery, the wide borders with floral decorations, the rather Byzantine elongation of the figures, and especially the richness of the blues. The blue used is a special flax blue, unknown to the 13th century, a glorious color that has not faded with the passing centuries. Of the west front windows, the left represents the Passion, the Crucifixion, and the Redemption. The center window shows scenes from the childhood and later life of Christ, arranged in alternating circular and square medallions set against blue and red backgrounds, in turn confined by the leads and pearl-colored borders. The right window shows the tree of Jesse. *Notre Dame de la Belle Verrière*, the most venerated of all, was saved from the fire of 1194 and reerected within the framework of a 13th-century stained-glass window.

Since vast spaces were offered by the new style of architecture after the fire of 1194, Chartres soon became one of the great centers of glass painting. Within a few years 173 windows were produced, representing more than 2,000 square yards of surface. Many windows were donated by the faithful, as is proved by coats-of-arms, and were dedicated to favorite saints. This is especially true of the clerestory windows executed between 1200 and 1250.

The windows of the apse and the rose window of the north transept were donated by the bakers and consecrated to the Virgin. The arcaded clerestory underneath represents David, Melchizedek, St. Anne, Solomon, and Aaron (1230–35). The southern rose window glorifies Christ (1221), and below it are the figures of the Evangelists mounted on the shoulders of the prophets. This symbolizes a mystical idea, a favorite of Bernard de Chartres, that the men of his time were dwarfs, seated on the shoulders of giants (the ancients) that they might see more and farther. The two rose windows span 43 feet 9 inches.

Beneath the choir is the Carolingian burial vault of St. Leobinus, and under the aisles of the choir and nave is the crypt of Bishop Fulbert's cathedral, which extends as far back as the towers of the entrance. There are interesting fragments of Romanesque frescoes. In the north gallery is the well of the *Saints Forts* and *The Virgin in Majesty with the Christ Child*. The much-venerated 12th-century *Virgin of Chartres* was burned in the French Revolution, but was replaced by a copy in 1857.

Fragments of the superb 13th-century rood screen are in a chapel off the south aisle. These are some of the finest examples of Gothic sculpture, notably the *Angels Appearing to the Shepherds*, the *Awakening of the Magi*, and the exquisitely sensitive and human scene of the *Nativity*. The last shows the Virgin pushing aside the swaddling clothes of her first-born, the better to admire Him; her face is already stamped with sadness as she mystically perceives the Cross of Calvary in the distance.

BIBLIOGRAPHY. H. Adams, *Mont Saint Michel and Chartres*, Washington, D.C., 1904; M. Aubert and S. Goubet, *Gothic Cathedrals of France and their Treasures*, London and New York, 1959.
ALDEN F. MEGREW

CHARTREUSE, LA GRANDE, *see* GRANDE CHARTREUSE, LA.

CHASE, WILLIAM MERRITT. American painter and teacher (b. Nineveh, Ind., 1849; d. New York City, 1916). He studied in Indianapolis and at the National Academy of Design in New York and worked briefly in St. Louis, painting flowers and still lifes. In 1872 he went to Munich, where he studied with Wagner and Piloty at the Royal Academy. His five-years stay in Munich was successful; besides working and exhibiting independently, he was offered an instructorship at the academy. In 1877 Chase visited Venice with his fellow Munich students Duveneck and Twachtman. While there he received an invitation to teach at the Art Students League in New York; he accepted and taught there until 1896, when he established his own school in New York.

William Merritt Chase, *Portrait of a Lady in Black*. Metropolitan Museum of Art, New York.

Chase's early paintings, done in the dark tonality of his training, were mostly figures and portraits, such as the exotic subject *The Turkish Page* (1876; Cincinnati Art Museum). A concern for portraits and figures continued in his middle years with such works as *Lady in Black*, known also as *Mrs. Leslie Cotton* (1888; New York, Metropolitan Museum), and the fine *Lady in a White Shawl* (ca. 1893; Philadelphia, Pennsylvania Academy of Fine Arts). After his Munich studies, Chase's style was influenced by the broad, rich painting of Hals and Velázquez and, in his own time, Manet and Whistler. Impressionism, with the exception of his late Long Island landscapes, only moved him to heighten his palette.

In his long and influential career, Chase taught the method that made him so popular: a flashing and virtuoso brushstroke that rendered the surface appearance of the objects within the visual field. This fluent aspect of his style can best be seen in the bric-a-brac-laden pictures of his studio, such as *Tenth Street Studio* (ca. 1890; Pittsburgh, Carnegie Institute) with its profusion of glitter and highlights, or in his greatly skilled later still lifes, mostly including fish, for example, *An English Cod* (1904; Washington, D.C., Corcoran Gallery). Although primarily a realist and opposed to most forms of modernism, he did, for a while, produce handsomely decorative pictures under the influence of Japanese prints.

In 1892 Chase established a home and summer school at Shinnecock, Long Island. From this time date such Long Island landscapes as *Near the Beach, Shinnecock* (ca. 1895; Toledo Museum of Art). Chase was elected president of the Society of American Artists in 1879 and a national academician in 1890.

BIBLIOGRAPHY. K. M. Roof, *The Life and Art of William Merritt Chase*, New York, 1917; Art Association of Indianapolis, *Chase Centennial Exhibition*, Indianapolis, 1949.

JEROME VIOLA

CH'A SHIH-PIAO. Chinese landscape painter (1615–98). Ch'a Shih-piao is known also by his *tzu* Erh-chan and *hao* Mei-ho (or Mei-ho San-jen). A native of Hai-yang in Anhui Province, he is counted among the "Four Masters of Anhui." Born of a wealthy family that possessed an extensive collection of old masters, Ch'a Shih-piao had the opportunity to study closely the works of famous painters; this familiarity with paintings of the past partly explains the diversity of styles to be found among his own works. But it was primarily for the somber and melancholy landscapes done in the manner of the Yüan painter Ni Tsan that Ch'a Shih-piao was best known among his contemporaries. *See* NI TSAN. *See also* ANHUI SCHOOL, FOUR MASTERS OF.

BIBLIOGRAPHY. O. Sirén, *Chinese Painting, Leading Masters and Principles*, vol. 5, London, 1958.

CHASHITSU. Japanese term for a room or a detached structure constructed for the performance of the tea ceremony. The tradition of building a small, independent structure for the tea ceremony, usually with a room 4½ *tatami* (mats) in size, goes back to the late Muromachi period. The size and style of *chashitsu* changed in the Momoyama period under the guidance of the great tea master Sen-no Rikyū (1522–91). Tearooms of two or three mats were built, in rough and unfinished materials, thereby

Chashitsu. The *tokonoma* (alcove) of the Tai-an of the Myōki-an, Kyoto.

creating an impression of a rustic country hut or farmhouse. A usual *chashitsu* includes a sunken hearth for heating water and a *tokonoma* (alcove) for displaying a painting or calligraphy scroll and a flower arrangement. A small window and entrance create a barrier against the outside world. Many examples of *chashitsu* have undergone extensive repairs, but a few preserve their original forms. The Tai-an of the Myōki-an and the Shōnan-tei of the Saihōji, both in Kyoto, date from the Momoyama period. The Jo-an of the Mitsui residence in Kanagawa prefecture was originally built in the Kenninji in Kyoto sometime between 1615 and 1624. The Mittan of the Ryūkō-in in the Daitokuji in Kyoto and the Tōshin-tei in the Minase Shrine in Osaka are good examples from the early Edo period.

BIBLIOGRAPHY. H. Kitao, *Cha-no-yu Houses in Detailed Illustrations*, Tokyo, 1953; R. T. Paine and A. Soper, *The Art and Architecture of Japan*, Baltimore, 1955; W. Blaser, *Japanese Temples and Tea-Houses*, New York, 1956; J. B. Kirby, *From Castle to Teahouse: Japanese Architecture of the Momoyama Period*, Rutland, Vt., 1962.

CHASING. General term in metalwork applied to any method of ornamenting the surface by embossing or engraving to produce a raised pattern. Chasing is accomplished with a variety of steel tools.

BIBLIOGRAPHY. E. F. Kronquist, *Art Metalwork*, New York, 1942.

CHASSERIAU, THEODORE. French painter (b. 1819, Samaná, Hispaniola; d. Paris, 1856). In 1822 the young Creole was taken to Paris by his father. In 1830–31 he

Théodore Chassériau, *Two Sisters*. Louvre, Paris.

entered Ingres's studio and remained there until 1834, when Ingres went to Italy. Delacroix's influence appeared in Chassériau's Bedouin subjects, done in 1836 in Marseille, and in his *Susanna and the Elders* (1839; Paris, Louvre). In *Two Sisters* (Alice and Adèle Chassériau, 1843; Louvre) he attempted a synthesis of Ingres and Delacroix styles, using bright colors within linear contours. A freer manner prevailed in *St. Mary of the Egyptians* for the Church of St-Merri in Paris; other decorations in this city are those for St-Roch (1854), for St-Philippe-du-Roule (1855), and for the old Cour des Comptes (1844–48; fragments *Peace, War, and Commerce* now in the Louvre).

In 1844 his series of engravings on Othello appeared; other Shakespearean subjects followed in oils: *Romeo and Juliet* in 1845 and *Othello* and *Desdemona* in 1850 (both in the Louvre). In 1846 Chassériau went to Algeria, where he painted melancholy native scenes; for one of these, *The Bath in the Seraglio* (1849; Louvre), his beloved Alice Ozy posed. He produced a number of excellent portraits in oils, of himself and Ernest Chassériau in 1835, his mother and sister Adèle the next year, and Lacordaire in 1841 (all in the Louvre); and in pencil, of Principessa di Belgioioso (Paris, Petit Palais), Marie Cantacuzène (later Mme Puvis de Chavannes) in 1855, and others.

Chassériau transmitted a svelte romantic version of the Ingres and Delacroix traditions to Gustave Moreau, who in 1865 dedicated to him the *Painter and Death*; to Puvis de Chavannes, who admired his mural compositions; and to Redon. Most of his work was collected by his nephew Baron Arthur Chassériau and donated to the Louvre. A few fine examples are outside France, for example, those at the Fogg Art Museum, Cambridge, Mass.

BIBLIOGRAPHY. V. Chevillard, *Un Peintre romantic, Théodore Chassériau*, Paris, 1893.

NORMAN SCHLENOFF

CHASSIS. A wooden frame either fitted or prepared to be fitted with material reaching from one edge to the other. In painting, it is the stretcher for a canvas; in sculpture, the revolving modeling stand on which an armature is placed. The term is also used in the French theater to mean either a coulisse or, figuratively, the personnel of a theater.

CHASUBLE. Garment of Roman Catholic and Greek Orthodox priests worn over the alb during Mass. It is sleeveless, made of two pieces of cloth joined at the shoulders, and worn front and back over the body. Chasubles are decorated with a cross on the back and frequently bear other Christian symbols on the front.

CHATEAU. Castle or fortress in feudal France; also a seigneur's mansion or a large country residence. The château in medieval France was usually erected on a height above a river to command a valley. With thick walls and small windows it was built to withstand attack. The 14th-century Château de Pierrefonds, standing on a rocky height with its entrance guarded by a drawbridge over a moat, had massive round towers, battlemented parapets, and outer walls 20 feet thick. The 16th-century Château de Chambord with its semifortified character shows a later development. *See also* KEEP.

CHATEAU, *see* name of château or location.

CHATEAUNEUF-SUR-CHARENTE: SAINT-PIERRE. French church of the second quarter of the 12th century, with a 15th-century reconstruction of the east end. The barrel-vaulted nave and aisles contain Romanesque capitals richly decorated with foliage, animals, and figures of all sorts. The fine west façade, gabled with triple arcades on two levels divided by a row of corbels, is reminiscent of façades in Saintonge. The façade sculpture includes four Apostles, one of the best examples of an equestrian "Constantine"—a symbol of the triumphant Church—and a portal with Virtues and Vices on the voussoirs.

BIBLIOGRAPHY. J. George, *Charente*, Paris, 1933.

CHATELET, CLAUDE-LOUIS. French painter (b. Paris, 1753; guillotined, 1797). He collaborated with H. Robert, his teacher, and with Fragonard on the illustrations for Saint-Non's *Voyages pittoresques de Naples et de Sicile* (1781–86). His pen and water-color drawings are vaporously delicate landscape and architectural views in the Louis XVI style.

CHATRA. Sanskrit term meaning "umbrella." The *chatra* is the topmost finial on a stūpa.

CHATRI. In Indian architecture, a Hindu funerary shrine, a chapel built over a tomb, or a rest house for pilgrims.

Chelsea porcelain. Candelabrum with cherub. Metropolitan Museum of Art, New York.

CHATSWORTH. William Talman's most important house, executed between 1687 and 1696 for the Earl of Devonshire in Derbyshire, England. The exterior, with its giant Ionic order, and the rich interiors were models of grandeur for the English private palace. The west front was by Thomas Archer, the stables and bridge by James Paine.

BIBLIOGRAPHY. J. Summerson, *Architecture in Britain, 1530–1830*, 3d ed., Baltimore, 1958.

CHATTUSA, see BOGHAZKEUY.

CHAUDET, ANTOINE DENIS. French sculptor (b. Paris, 1763; d. there, 1810). He studied in Rome, where he was influenced by Canova. Later Napoleon I made him a court sculptor. He executed numerous portraits of the Emperor and made the colossal statue of him that was placed on top of the column at the Place Vendôme. The statue was removed in 1814, but was replaced in 1862–63 by another sculpture of Napoleon, the work of Augustin Dumont (1801–84). Typical Chaudet works are *Paul and Virginia*, *Amour*, and *Oedipus and Phoebus*, all in the Louvre. Chaudet's art is characterized by excessive sentimentality, pompousness, and self-conscious gracefulness.

BIBLIOGRAPHY. F. Novotny, *Painting and Sculpture in Europe, 1780–1880*, Baltimore, 1960.

CHAUMES, NICHOLAS DE. French architect (fl. ca. 1310–40). The royal architect in Paris, he directed the works at the Cathedral of Sens from 1319 to 1339.

CHAUVIGNY. Small town in the Department of the Vienne, in the Poitou region of France. Chauvigny is noted for the sculpture on its two 12th-century Romanesque churches. The sculpted capitals, stylistically *retardataire*, are painted in a colorful and decorative manner.

BIBLIOGRAPHY. P. Deschamps, *French Sculpture of the Romanesque Period, Eleventh and Twelfth Centuries*, Florence, 1930.

CHAVEZ MORADO, JOSE. Mexican painter (1909–   ). Chávez Morado was born in Silao, Guanajuato. During the thirties he concentrated on prints and drawings, and in 1933 he was appointed chief of the graphic arts department of the Ministry of Education. From 1938 to 1941, he was a guiding light of the Workshop for Popular Graphic Art. Also in the 1930s he designed sets and costumes for the state.

Since the late 1930s Chávez Morado has distinguished himself as a muralist. He has turned increasingly to the Indian past for subject matter and technique. His gigantic mural of 1954 for the Ministry of Communications and Public Works, Mexico City, is a mosaic composed of colored stone, tile, glass and terra cotta, while his wall decorations for the Medical Center (1958), Mexico City, feature stone reliefs.

BIBLIOGRAPHY. A. Reed, *The Mexican Muralists*, New York, 1960.

CHAVIN ART. The Chavín culture flourished in Peru from 1200 B.C. to A.D. 200. It takes its name from Chavín de Huántar in the northern Peruvian highlands. It was most important from about 1200 to 400 B.C., and there is evidence that its influence extended into later periods. The extensive stone masonry and sculpture indicate that it was a major ceremonial center. The art products usually have a stylized feline form that was an underlying theme in other cultural artifacts over a wide area of Peru. Chavín art was therefore the first to have a Pan-Peruvian style. The delicately incised Stele Raimondi in the Anthropological Museum in Lima is the best example of Chavín sculpture. Ceramic remains from Cupisnique are of a Chavín type and the carved slabs of Cerro Sechín in northern Peru are also mentioned in association with Chavín.

See also AMERICAS, ANCIENT, ART OF (PERU AND BOLIVIA: FORMATIVE PERIOD).

BIBLIOGRAPHY. P. Kelemen, *Medieval American Art*, New York, 1943; W. C. Bennett, *Ancient Arts of the Andes*, New York, 1954; J. A. Mason, *The Ancient Civilizations of Peru*, Harmondsworth, Middlesex, 1957.

CHEERE, SIR HENRY. English sculptor (1703–81). He was remarkably versatile, with a love for combining contrasting marbles in a rococo setting. He is better known for his beautiful monuments; that of the Earl of Kildare in Christ Church Cathedral, Dublin, is typical.

CHEESMAN, THOMAS. English engraver (b. 1760; d. London, probably 1834/35). A close follower of Francesco Bartolozzi, Cheesman made highly prized colored engravings in a stipple technique, as well as engravings after paintings by Romney, Hogarth, Lawrence, and others.

CHEF D'ECOLE. In the fine arts, the declared or undeclared head, founder, or leader of a school, group, or movement. Usually he has a profound influence on the artists who follow him. Jacques-Louis David is an outstanding example in French 18th–19th-century painting.

CHELLEAN (Abbevillian) EPOCH. Earliest cultural stage of the lower paleolithic age, dating from the first interglacial period. The term derives from stone artifacts discovered at Chelles, France, on a river terrace of the Marne Valley. The epoch is characterized by irregularly flaked hand axes and simple flake tools. Evidence found in Europe, North Africa, and Asia indicates that man was a primitive hunter and food gatherer at this time and lived in temporary, open encampments.

CHELLES, ABBEY OF. Located eleven miles from Paris, Chelles was the site of an important medieval abbey founded in the 6th century by St. Clothilde; it was re-established in the mid-7th century by St. Bathilde, wife of King Clovis II. The choir of the former abbey church, rebuilt in the 13th century, survives in part. Chelles was the birthplace of the 13th-century architect Jean de Chelles.

BIBLIOGRAPHY. L. Cottineau, *Répertoire topo-bibliographique des abbayes et prieurés*, 2 vols., Mâcon, 1935–37.

CHELSEA PORCELAIN. Product of England's foremost porcelain factory of the 18th century. Started before 1745, the factory operated until 1784, when its models were transferred to Derby. The earliest examples, inspired by silver forms, include naturalistic designs such as the milk jug in the form of two reclining goats and the crayfish saltshaker. After 1750, first Meissen and later Sèvres influence can be detected. The sculptor Roubillac is thought to have been responsible for some of Chelsea's more outstanding figures. Etuis, small bottles, and boxes compose the category of "Chelsea toys," which show inventiveness and quality. Examples are at the Metropolitan Museum of Art, New York, and the Victoria and Albert Museum, London.

BIBLIOGRAPHY. W. B. Honey, *Old English Porcelain*, London, 1948.

CHENAVARD, PAUL. French painter (b. Lyons, 1808; d. there, 1895). He lived in Italy from 1827 to 1829. Derivative in composition and lifeless in style, he was primarily a painter of ideas. His never-completed Pantheon decoration was a vast mystical interpretation of the history of man.

BIBLIOGRAPHY. J. C. Sloane, "Paul Chenavard," *Art Bulletin*, XXXIII, December, 1951.

CH'EN CHI-JU. Chinese scholar, critic, poet, and amateur painter (1558–1639). His birthplace was Hua-t'ing in Kan-

su Province, and he is known under a variety of names, among them his *hao* Mei-kung. He is among the leading theoreticians of the late Ming dynasty and helped to formulate the *wen-jen-hua* (literati-painting) ideas that dominated 17th-century aesthetics. *See* WEN-JEN-HUA.

BIBLIOGRAPHY. A. W. Hummel, ed., *Eminent Chinese of the Ch'ing Period, 1644–1912*, vol. 1, Washington, D.C., 1944.

CH'ENG-TEH, *see* JEHOL.

CH'EN HSIEN. Chinese painter of Buddhist subjects (fl. mid-17th cent.). Nothing is known of him in standard Chinese sources, his chief works being located in various Japanese collections. He was an adherent of the Huang-po sect of Buddhism and seems to have been particularly inspired by the subject of Kuan-yin.

BIBLIOGRAPHY. Tajima Shiichi, ed., *Tōyō bijitsu taikan*, vol. 10, 1908–18.

CH'EN HUNG-SHOU. Chinese painter of figures and landscapes (1599–1652). A native of Chekiang Province, he spent most of his mature years in Peking and Nanking during the confused period of the Manchu conquest, and the degree to which the change in governments affected Ch'en Hung-shou personally is not clearly understood. His highly charged eccentric paintings, with their free distortions and archaic overtones, combined with an almost naïve air, seem to reflect the troubled age in which he lived.

BIBLIOGRAPHY. Tseng Yu-ho, "A Report on Ch'en Hung-shou," *Archives of the Chinese Art Society of America*, XIII, 1959.

CH'EN JUNG. Chinese painter (fl. mid-13th cent.). His *tzu* was Kung-ch'u and his *hao* So-weng. A native of Ch'ang-lo in Fukien Province, he held a minor government post and gained a modicum of distinction for his poetry and general scholarship. His exceptional paintings of dragons brought him a reputation for works of his particular subject. His somewhat eccentric personality and style of painting, combined with a number of extant paintings attributed to his brush, make him the outstanding

Ch'en Jung, *Nine Dragons Scroll* (part 2), mid-13th century. Museum of Fine Arts, Boston.

Château of Chenonceaux. Built in the 16th-century on the Cher River.

painter of all Chinese history in this special category of subject matter.

His technique of painting was quite striking, for according to contemporary literary accounts Ch'en Jung first blocked out rough areas of tonal contrasts by impressing a cloth dipped in ink onto the surface and then completed the painting with a brush to define his dragons, clouds, water, and rocks. He also splattered ink over his painting by snapping the end of his brush, adding to the rich texture of the surface. The final effect was the marvelous evocation of the special, mysterious world of the dragons, where forms emerge and disappear in whirls of dense ink representing clouds, water, or vapor. Excellent examples of Ch'en Jung's dragon paintings can be found in the Museum of Fine Arts, Boston, and the William Rockhill Nelson Gallery of Art, Kansas City.

BIBLIOGRAPHY. Tseng Hsien-chi, "A Study of the Nine Dragons Scroll," *Archives of the Chinese Art Society of America*, XI, 1957.
MARTIE W. YOUNG

CHENONCEAUX, CHATEAU OF. French residential château built in 1515 by the wealthy bourgeois Thomas Bohier and his wife, Catherine Briçonnet. Chenonceaux was built on the site of a mill that had stood in the waters of the Cher River, a tributary of the Loire. The property had included a fortified castle of the mid-15th century, a single, round tower of which was left standing. The tower was then decorated, possibly by Italian workmen, with a mixture of Flamboyant Gothic and classical relief ornament and used as a gatehouse. The remaining area was utilized as a terraced forecourt from which the château could be reached by a drawbridge. The passage of river water

through the foundation was made possible by an arched corridor transversing it from west to east.

The square château, of white limestone, features four small and purely decorative turreted towers at its corners. Its interior has large rooms, with somewhat top-heavy mantelpieces, on either side of a wide hall running the full length of the building from the entrance portal. The north and west façades demonstrate great regularity of design. Large mullioned windows, framed by Italianate pilasters, appear in the two main stories. Stringcourses between stories create horizontal accents, as do a heavy classical frieze and cornice just below the roofline. These details demonstrate the deep impression made by Italian Renaissance forms as a result of the repeated French invasions of Italy.

Both Gothic and Renaissance building methods are employed in the interior. The entrance hall is covered by ribbed, Gothic vaulting, but the main staircase presents a straight ascent that doubles back on itself in the second flight rather than spiraling in the Gothic manner. The small chapel projecting out of the east façade has Gothic windows and buttressing. Under Henry II, the estate was given to the King's favorite, Diane de Poitiers. She ordered construction of the bridge to the south bank, and it was carried out according to the plan of Philibert de l'Orme, from 1555 to 1559. The bridge consists basically of a roadway carried on five arches, each reinforced by piers jutting into the river. An Italian *parterre* and gardens were installed along the northeast bank.

After the death of the King, Diane was forced to give Chenonceaux to the widowed queen, Catherine de Médicis, in exchange for the château of Chaumont. Catherine planned widespread additions, but only a few were carried out. One new wing was constructed to accommodate the many fêtes and banquets held during the reigns of Catherine's sons. This is the long gallery built above the bridge in 1560, now attributed to Jean Bullant. A fairly simple building with a pitched roof, the two-storied wing lends a picturesque and original appearance to the château and doubles its size.

BIBLIOGRAPHY. C. Terrasse, *Le Château de Chenonceaux*, Paris, 1928; R. Dutton, *The Châteaux of France*, London, 1957.
EMMA N. PAPERT

CH'EN SHUN (Ch'en Tao-fu). Chinese painter (1483–1544). Ch'en Shun was active in the Wu school in the Su-chou district. He had a high reputation among contemporary connoisseurs for his flower-and-bird paintings, but his reinterpretation of the Mi Fu landscape style is perhaps his most distinctive contribution in terms of Chinese painting history. *See* MI FU.

BIBLIOGRAPHY. O. Sirén, *Chinese Painting, Leading Masters and Principles*, vol. 4, London, 1958.

CHEOPS, PYRAMID OF (Great Pyramid). Largest of the three pyramids at Giza. "Khufu-belongs-to-the-horizon" was built by Cheops (Khufu) as a monumental tomb symbolizing his own solar destiny. It is impressive by reason of size (about 750 ft. square and 480 ft. high) as well as by the accuracy of its orientation and by its masonry. Its inner apartments reveal three stages of construction; the final one consists of a great corbeled gallery (over 50 ft. high) ascending to the burial chamber situated beyond a lobby having three granite portcullisses. Five superimposed ceilings and a gable form an overcautious provision against the weight above this chamber. Known as one of the wonders of the ancient world, its construction out of local stone was described by Herodotus (II, 124) with many interesting details. *See also* EGYPT.

BIBLIOGRAPHY. S. Hassan, *The Great Pyramid of Khufu and Its Mortuary Chapel*, Cairo, 1960.

CHEPHREN, PYRAMID OF. "Great-is-Kha'fre'," built by Chephren (Kha'fre') southwest of the pyramid of Cheops, is slightly smaller in size (about 700 ft. square and 470 ft. high, with a 52°20′ inclination) and of poorer workmanship. The pyramid of Chephren retains part of its limestone casing near the top and two courses of unpolished granite at the bottom. The inner apartments are simple, consisting of a granite-lined passage that descends from the north face and continues horizontally at ground level until it reaches the burial chamber. This chamber is located slightly northeast of an imaginary vertical line drawn from the apex and is roofed with gabled and painted limestone blocks. This latter apartment was connected to the underground chamber of an earlier, abandoned project located farther to the north. *See also* EGYPT.

BIBLIOGRAPHY. W. F. Petrie, *The Pyramids and Temples of Gizeh*, London, 1883; I. E. S. Edwards, *The Pyramids of Egypt*, Harmondsworth, Middlesex, 1947.

CHEPSTOW: CASTLE AND WALLS. One of the earliest and best-constructed Norman keeps. It was built about 1070 on a narrow ridge sloping up from the Wye River on the English-Welsh border. Its finely designed great hall was later divided into two rooms by an open arcade. Thirteenth-century strategy required the addition of curtain walls, towers, and gatehouses to protect its two baileys. Stately residential buildings, added along the north cliff, are now in ruins.

BIBLIOGRAPHY. H. Braun, *The English Castle*, London, 1936; S. Toy, *The Castles of Great Britain*, 3d ed., London, 1963.

CHERET, JULES. French lithographer, poster artist, and printer (b. Paris, 1836; d. Nice, 1931). The son of printer, he was apprenticed at fourteen to a lithographic letterer, from whom he learned commercial design. Inhibited by working within small areas, he went to London in 1859; there he learned to produce larger compositions and in effect created a new style in poster art. He returned to Paris in 1866, successfully installing himself on the Rue de la Tour des Dames and Rue Brunel. In 1881 he turned over his printing establishment to Monsieur Chaix but kept the direction of his own atelier on the Rue Brunel. After 1890 he joined with Chaix under the name Ateliers Chéret, on the Rue Bergère.

BIBLIOGRAPHY. J. Laran and J. Adhémar, *Inventaire du fonds français, après 1800*, vol. 5, Paris, 1949.

CHERMAYEFF, SERGE. American architect, designer, and educator (1900–   ). He was born in the Caucasus, Russia, and educated at Harrow School, Cambridge, England. From 1933 he practiced architecture with Eric Mendelsohn in England, where they collaborated on the De La Warr Pavilion at Bexhill (1934–35). Chermayeff, who has taught and practiced architecture in the United States since 1940, is a professor of architecture at Yale University.

Pyramid of Cheops. The largest of the three pyramids at Giza, near Cairo.

CHERSIPHRON. Greek architect from Ephesus, who with his son Metagenes, undertook the construction of the first great peripteral temple of Artemis at Ephesus about 560 B.C. They afterward wrote a book, perhaps the earliest architectural treatise, describing architectural features and engineering problems (such as the raising and placement of the huge architrave) involved in building the temple.

BIBLIOGRAPHY. W. B. Dinsmoor, *The Architecture of Ancient Greece*, 3d ed., London, 1950.

CHERUBIM. Type of angel, frequently found in representations of the Madonna and Child, which has four wings covered with eyes. Together with seraphim and thrones, the cherubim form the first hierarchy of angels. According to Dionysius the Areopagite, cherubim symbolize Divine Wisdom; hence they are shown holding books.

CHE SCHOOL. School of Chinese painting. Its name is derived from the region of Chekiang Province, the "Che" being the first of the two characters employed in the name of the province. The acknowledged leader of the school, at least by later Chinese critics, was Tai Chin, who was active in the first half of the 15th century. *See* TAI CHIN.

The region of Chekiang was of great importance during the Southern Sung period (1127–1279) since the city of Hang-chou had served as the capital. The style of the Southern Sung Academy painters thus lingered throughout the Yüan dynasty and into the early decades of the Ming. Many painters from Chekiang became influential in the Ming Academy at Peking, and the Che school is often equated with the academy style for this reason. The notion of a school of painting bearing the appellation "Che," therefore, must be qualified in the light of Ming academicism in general. *See* HANG-CHOU.

The relationship between painters in Peking and those in Chekiang is not always clear, but art historians normally regard the Ming restoration of the Ma-Hsia style as typical of both the academy style and the Che school. Classification of painters under the Che-school label is sometimes tenuous: Chu Tuan, Wu Wei, Chang Lu, and Chou Wen-ching are some of the painters loosely grouped under that heading. The last great painter of the school is considered to be Lan Ying, who carried the school into the 17th century. *See* CHANG LU; CHOU WEN-CHING; CHU TUAN; LAN YING; MA-HSIA SCHOOL; WU WEI.

BIBLIOGRAPHY. L. C. S. Sickman and A. C. Soper, *The Art and Architecture of China*, Baltimore, 1956; Y. Yonezawa, *Painting in the Ming Dynasty*, Tokyo, 1956.
MARTIE W. YOUNG

CHESTER. English town in Cheshire, in the Midlands. Chester was the Roman Deva, and the impressive amphitheater is the largest Roman building surviving in Britain. The medieval town walls with their many gates and the Cathedral (formerly the abbey; begun in 1093) are built in the characteristic local red sandstone.

BIBLIOGRAPHY. C. E. Jarman, *Chester*, London, 1953.

CHEVALIER, ETIENNE, BOOK OF HOURS OF AND DIPTYCH OF (Melun Diptych), *see* FOUQUET, JEAN.

CHEVALIER, GUILLAUME SULPICE, *see* GAVARNI.

CHEVET. End of a church containing the sanctuary, particularly the east end. Its circular or polygonal apse contains radiating chapels. The *chevet* developed with the need for chapels to display sacred relics and is associated in its early form particularly with monastic churches. The great pilgrim church of St. Martin of Tours, France (997–1015), is said to be one of the first with a *chevet* of radiating chapels linked to a processional ambulatory. *See* CHAPEL, RADIATING.

CHEVET EN ECHELON, *see* APSE ECHELON.

CHEVRIER, JEAN. French manuscript illuminator (fl. ca. 1300–50). Chevrier was a member of the workshop of Jean Pucelle, and his name appears on folios 268 and 300 of the Belleville Breviary (before 1343). It is probable that he was responsible for some of the borders and terminal figures in this and possibly other works by the master.

CHEVRON. Zigzag ornament of repeated V's frequently found in Norman architecture. Examples are in Waltham Abbey, North Hinksey, and Bredgar.

CHEYENNE INDIANS, *see* NORTH AMERICAN INDIAN ART (PLAINS).

CHEZARLA. Site in Krishna District, Andhra Pradesh, India. Chezārla is known for the Kapoteśvara temple, which is one of the few examples of a Buddhist freestanding chaitya hall in its original condition. The temple, built in the 5th century A.D., has since been converted to Hindu usage and dedicated to the god Siva. A rectangular hall (*maṇḍapa*) has been added to make the structure appropri-

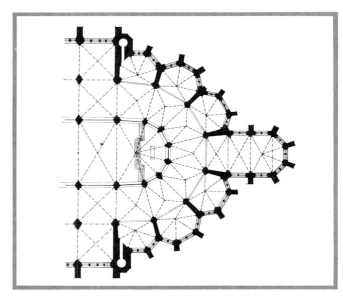

Chevet. Plan of the apse with radiating chapels of Amiens Cathedral.

Chevron. Zigzag ornament found in Norman architecture.

ate to Hindu worship. Near the temple are a small rectangular cella and several small monolithic votive shrines, each decorated with a single chaitya arch. A similar temple exists at Ter in Sholāpur District, Maharashtra.

BIBLIOGRAPHY. P. Brown, *Indian Architecture*, 4th ed., vol. 1: *Buddhist and Hindu Periods*, Bombay, 1959; B. Rowland, *The Art and Architecture of India*, 2d ed., Baltimore, 1959.

CHIA. Class of ancient Chinese bronze ritual vessels that includes a number of variant shapes. Used as wine containers, the *chia* have three (sometimes four) legs, a wide flaring mouth, two bottle-shaped horns, and a handle perpendicular to the horns. The vessels occur throughout the Shang and early Chou periods and have some resemblance to the *chüeh*. *See* CHUEH.

CHIANG TS'AN. Chinese painter (fl. first half of 12th cent.). Chiang Ts'an was born in Wu-hsing, Chekiang Province; his *tzu* was Kuan-tao. He gained some fame for his landscapes in the manner of Tung Yüan and for his water-buffalo paintings. Summoned to the court of Kao-tsung (r. 1127–62), he died the evening before he was scheduled to be presented.

BIBLIOGRAPHY. O. Sirén, *Chinese Painting, Leading Masters and Principles*, vol. 2, London, 1956.

CH'IAO-TA-MA, see GAUTAMA.

CHIAO-T'AN.
Chinese term meaning "altar of heaven," used in Chinese ceramic history to refer to the area where commercial kilns produced imperial ceramic wares during the Southern Sung period (after 1127) and later. The kiln site was discovered in the early 1930s, but in some earlier publications the site was called the "Suburban Altar" kiln to mark the products of the Southern Sung–dynasty kilns located in the suburbs of the capital at Hang-chou. *See also* KUAN WARE.

CHIARAVALLE, ABBEY OF.
Large Romanesque Cistercian church near Milan, Italy, begun after a foundation in 1136 and consecrated in 1196. The domed rib vaults of the red-brick nave may date from about 1160; the heavy octagonal crossing spire is later, after 1196.

BIBLIOGRAPHY. K. J. Conant, *Carolingian and Romanesque Architecture, 800–1200*, Baltimore, 1959.

CHIAROSCURO.
Descriptive term, from the Italian, applied to the opposition of light and shade in painting and graphics, and by extension in all art forms. A painter's chiaroscuro (French, *clair-obscur*) technique is his method of treating shadows. Rembrandt's was masterly handling.

CHIARUTTINI (Chiarottini), FRANCESCO.
Italian painter (1748–96). Born in Cividale, Chiaruttini first studied in Venice with Fontebasso. He executed numerous frescoes and scenographic paintings, such as those in the Palazzo Brusadola in Cividale, which are full of decorative detail and fantastic imagery. He approaches in the picturesque style of his perspective paintings the art of both Bigari and Pannini, whom he met on a trip to Rome in 1788. His art reveals both an intelligent use of perspective and chiaroscuro and a rich imagination for fanciful ornament.

BIBLIOGRAPHY. C. Donzelli, *I pittori veneti del Settecento*, Florence, 1957.

CHIA-YEH-PO, see KASYAPA.

CHICAGO.
City, county seat of Cook County in northeastern Illinois, on the southeastern shore of Lake Michigan in the central United States. It is one of the largest commercial and industrial centers and is of major consequence in the history of contemporary architecture.

Its cultural facilities include the Illinois Institute of Technology, founded in 1940 as a result of a merger of Armour Institute and Lewis Institute, and the Art Institute, which contains a major collection of modern French painting as well as the Burnham Library, a center of material on the development of architecture in this country. Important for the history of modern design in this country, Chicago was the location of the New Bauhaus in the 1930s after the closing of the Bauhaus in Dessau, Germany. *See* CHICAGO: MUSEUMS.

The city is particularly noteworthy as the focus of 20th-century architectural development. The balloon frame, which revolutionized vernacular architecture, was invented in Chicago during the 1830s. This technique was made possible by the development of inexpensive nails and the steam saw mill for cutting standardized wooden members—two by fours, two by sixes, and so forth. It was initiated because of the increasing demand for rapid, simple construction methods that could be handled by unskilled labor. Thus it replaced the older system of handhewn logs, laboriously joined, with a peculiarly semimodern system of prefabricated members that could be assembled by relatively unskilled craftsmen.

On a practical level, the balloon frame expedited settlement of the West; on an aesthetic plane, it led to the Stick style and Shingle style in domestic American architecture, forerunners of much contemporary work.

The skyscraper, one of America's first contributions to the mainstream of Western culture, was spawned and developed in this architecturally fertile city. With the phenomenal growth of commerce in Chicago after the Civil War, land became disproportionately expensive with respect to building cost. The skyscraper was initiated as a means of commercially exploiting the space above land. The Chicago fire of 1871, which destroyed large areas of the city, gave impetus to the demand for new building. Rapid vertical development was made possible by the low cost of steel, the safe and efficient elevator, and the invention of the steel frame—all these developments took place in the 1860s and 1870s. A complicating factor, however, was the soil of this prairie region, which is loose, gravelly, and sandy, deposited in a flat lake plain. This condition was overcome by imaginative foundation design that pioneered engineering techniques in both masonry and reinforced concrete.

The architects and engineers who attacked the skyscraper problem—the Chicago school—included such masters as Daniel Burnham, John W. Root, William Le Baron Jenny, and the firm of Dankmar Adler and Louis H. Sullivan. Produced in Chicago during this era were such world-famous buildings as the Auditorium (Adler and Sullivan, 1887–89); the Monadnock Building (Burnham and Root, 1891), the last masonry skyscraper; the Reliance Building (Burnham and Root, 1890); and the Carson, Pirie, Scott Store (Sullivan, 1899–1904). Chicago was also the nursery of Frank Lloyd Wright during this period, when he built scores of homes in and around the city.

Important also for the history of city planning, Chicago was the location of the Columbian Exposition of 1893, a vast assemblage of bone-white Imperial façades. For the first time since Charles L'Enfant's dream (by then a nightmare) of a grandiose scheme for Washington, D.C., and Thomas Jefferson's magnificent University of Virginia, the United States produced a group of buildings that approached the dignity and order of much-admired European cities such as Paris. The Exposition's format, established by Burnham, Richard Morris Hunt, Charles F. McKim, and Frederick L. Olmsted, stimulated national interest for several decades in revitalizing American cities—the City Beautiful movement.

In 1922, the *Chicago Tribune* conducted a world-wide competition for its new headquarters, attracting distinguished designs by Walter Gropius and Eliel Saarinen, who won second prize. The executed building (1923–25), by Hood and Howells, is a compact shaft encrusted with Gothic veneer. *See* CHICAGO TRIBUNE BUILDING.

Chicago is again a major center of architectural activity, stemming in part from the influx of European artists during the 1930s, particularly Mies van der Rohe and Moholy-Nagy. Mies's design for the Illinois Institute of Technology (1945–61), his Lake Shore Drive Apartments (1952), and B. Goldberg's Marina City (1962) are among the seminal works to come out of the recent period in Chicago. Among others are the Chicago Civic Center by C. F. Murphy Associates and Skidmore, Owings and Merrill (1963–65), with its monumental plaza sculpture by Picasso; their Chicago Circle Campus of the University of Illinois (1965–68); and the 100-story John Hancock Mutual Life Insurance Co. Building (1967–68) by Skidmore, Owings and Merrill.

See also MARSHALL FIELD WAREHOUSE.

BIBLIOGRAPHY. T. E. Tallmadge, *Architecture in Old Chicago*, Chicago, 1941; V. J. Scully, *The Shingle Style: Architectural Theory and Design from Richardson to the Origins of Wright*, New Haven, Conn., 1955; J. D. Randall, *A Guide to Significant Chicago Architecture of 1872 to 1922*, Glencoe, Ill., 1958; C. W. Condit, *American Building Art: The Nineteenth Century*, New York, 1960; C. W. Condit, *The Chicago School of Architecture*, Chicago, 1964; M. L. Peisch, *The Chicago School of Architecture*, New York, 1965.

THEODORE M. BROWN

CHICAGO: MUSEUMS. Important public art collections in Chicago, Ill., are located in the museums listed below.

Art Institute of Chicago. Founded in 1879, when it merged with the Academy of Fine Arts, the Art Institute continues to operate one of the largest and most prestigious schools of art in the United States. Its museum collections derive primarily from the donations of private collectors in the Chicago area. The Palmer and Bartlett bequests, in particular, enabled the museum to assemble a collection of French 19th-century painting of first rank. The building was constructed in a Renaissance style to the plans of Shepley, Rutan, and Coolidge in 1892, and additions have been made many times since.

The survey of paintings from before the 19th century is somewhat limited, although there are interesting and important works. Of paintings dating from the 13th to the 16th century, special attention might be called to Meliore Toscano's *Madonna and Child Enthroned*, Giovanni di Paolo's six panels depicting scenes from the *Life of St. John the Baptist*, Gentile Bellini's *Two Orientals*, Tintoretto's *Tarquin and Lucretia*, Martorell's *St. George and the Dragon*, El Greco's *Assumption* and *St. Martin and the Beggar*, diptychs by Memling and Van der Weyden showing the Madonna and a donor, Gerard David's *Lamentation*, Lucas van Leyden's *Adoration of the Magi*, portraits by Mor, and Cranach's *Crucifixion* and *Adam and Eve*.

Notable in the baroque and rococo group are works by Guercino, Reni, and Strozzi, Tiepolo's series on *Rinaldo and Armida*, Velázquez's *The Servant*, Zurbarán's *Crucifixion*, Goya's series on *The Capture of the Bandit Maragato*, Poussin's *St. John on Patmos*, a Claude landscape, Chardin's *White Tablecloth*, Rembrandt's *Girl at the Half-Open Door*, Ruisdael's *Ruins of Egmond*, and works by Van Dyck and Rubens.

All major French 19th-century painters are represented, many by important works. The prize is Seurat's master-

Chicago Tribune Building, Chicago, 1922.

piece, *Sunday Afternoon on the Island of La Grande Jatte.* Best-known works of other artists include Delacroix's *Lion Hunt*; Géricault's *After Death*; Corot's *Interrupted Reading*; Courbet's *Mère Grégoire*; Manet's *Races at Longchamp* and *Bullfight*; Degas's *Uncle and Niece*, *Café Singer*, and *The Millinery Shop*; Fantin-Latour's *Portrait of Manet* and *Corner of a Table*; Monet's *Beach at Saint-Adresse*, *Gare St-Lazare*, *Artist's Garden at Argenteuil*, *Etretat*, three versions of *Haystack*, and scenes of London and Venice; Renoir's *On the Terrace* and *Two Little Circus Girls*; Cézanne's *Gulf of Marseilles*, *The Bathers*, *Portrait of Mme Cézanne*, and several still lifes; Redon's *Woman among the Flowers*; Gauguin's *Human Misery* and *Day of the Gods*; Van Gogh's *Self-Portrait* and *Bedroom at Arles*; Toulouse-Lautrec's *At the Moulin Rouge* and *The Ringmaster*; and Henri Rousseau's *The Waterfall*. English paintings of note from this period are Constable's *Stoke by Nayland*, Turner's *Dutch Fishing Boats* and *Valley of Aosta*, and Rossetti's *Beata Beatrix*.

The less extensive 20th-century collection has some important early Kandinskys; several paintings by Matisse, Klee, and Léger; such works as Picasso's *Old Guitarist*, *Portrait of D. H. Kahnweiler*, and *Mother and Child*; Gris's *Portrait of Picasso*; Modigliani's *Jacques Lipchitz and His Wife*; Picabia's *Edtaonisl*; Rouault's *Three Judges*; and Chagall's *Praying Jew*. Highlighting the American collection is a room devoted to landscapes by Inness, several works each by Cassatt, Copley, A. B. Davies, Dove, Hartley, Hassam, and Whistler, and such outstanding individual works as Glackens's *Chez Mouquin*, Homer's *Herring Net*, Sheeler's *The Artist Looks at Nature*, and Wood's *American Gothic*.

The museum also has fine collections of drawings and prints, medieval art, English ceramics, and Oriental art. Japanese woodcuts are particularly well represented.

BIBLIOGRAPHY. *Paintings in the Art Institute of Chicago*, Chicago, 1961.

DONALD GODDARD

Oriental Institute of the University of Chicago. The institute supports a museum at the university as well fieldwork in Egypt and the Near East. The collection includes objects of art of the ancient Near East. There is an important group of Chinese ceramics of the 3d to the 5th century, together with Chinese bronzes and sculpture. The Japanese paintings, sculpture, and graphic arts collection is outstanding; the development of woodblock printing is illustrated in the graphic arts section. Korean ceramics are also represented, and there are examples of Indian and Cambodian sculpture.

CHICAGO DAILY NEWS BUILDING, CHICAGO, *see* HOLABIRD AND ROOT.

CHICAGO TRIBUNE BUILDING, CHICAGO. In 1922, the *Chicago Tribune* announced an international competition to secure for Chicago the most beautiful office building in the world. Two hundred sixty-three designs were received from twenty-three countries in styles ranging from Egyptoid to modernistic, reflecting a broad cross-section of opinion on the nature and form of the tall building. John Mead Howells and Raymond M. Hood of New York submitted the winning design. Second prize went to Eliel Saarinen of Finland, and third prize to Holabird and Roche of Chicago. The winning entry was an intricately detailed Gothic extravaganza capped by a fanciful tower based on the Butter Tower of Rouen Cathedral.

Howells, who had previously designed Gothic skyscrapers, probably suggested the basic form and style, and Hood then worked out the details. Relatively unknown before 1922, Hood was catapulted to fame even before the building was completed. His major contribution to the design was the harmonious bridging of the shaft to its crown. This was accomplished by projecting the vertical members of the façades upward in the form of bogus buttressing. Though a handsome tower-type building, it did not particularly advance the design of skyscrapers; its major contribution was a unified composition.

Even more than in Cass Gilbert's Woolworth Tower (1911–13), where the vertical members at least indicate the steel skeleton underneath, the Tribune Building expressed a contradiction of the times. In it, a traditional style was applied to a contemporary architectural form. Reflecting as it did the traditional tripartite divisions of base, shaft, and crown, the building terminated an epoch in skyscraper design, rather than beginning one, and its influence was limited.

The famous architect Louis Sullivan denounced the result and praised Saarinen's entry for the manner in which the Finn had grasped the problem of designing a lofty, steel-framed structure. This design, in its feeling for geometrical form, handling of setbacks, and its abrupt skyward termination, influenced many architects in subsequent years, including Hood. Because of the relative opacity and density of its walls, however, Saarinen's design was not as advanced as the one submitted by the Germans Walter Gropius and Adolph Meyer. Apparently ignored by jury and architects alike, their entry had the openness and flexibility that were characteristic of the earlier Chicago school skyscrapers and the subsequent tall building designs of the 1930s and after.

MATTHEW E. BAIGELL

CHICHEN ITZA. Chichén Itzá was a Mayan ceremonial center near two cenotes, or openings to subterranean rivers, of the Yucatán Peninsula in Mexico. A large part of an earlier site was rebuilt in the 12th century of the Christian era under the dominance of Toltec peoples. It includes

Chichén Itzá. Pyramid of Kukulcán (El Castillo), with an earlier temple in its base.

Chichester. The Cathedral, established 1091.

the largest pre-Columbian ball court, the imposing pyramid of Kukulcán (El Castillo), which has an earlier temple in its base, the Temple of Warriors and the Temple of Jaguars with relief sculptures as in Toltec Tula, and a circular astronomical observatory called El Caracol (The Snail). The remains have been extensively studied and restored by the Carnegie Institution of Washington. Mural paintings are found in the Temple of Warriors and the Temple of Jaguars. Other religious buildings include the Temple of the Three Lintels, the Red House, the Iglesia, and the Nunnery.

See also AMERICAS, ANCIENT, ART OF (MAYA); TOLTEC ART.

BIBLIOGRAPHY. P. Kelemen, *Medieval American Art*, New York, 1943; S. G. Morley, *The Ancient Maya*, rev. by G. W. Brainerd, 3d ed., Stanford, Calif., 1963; I. Marquina, *Arquitectura prehispánica*, 2d ed., Mexico, 1964.

CHICHESTER. City in Sussex, England. Originally a Roman town, it still follows the line of the ancient wall and principal Roman streets. There is a 13th-century guildhall; and near the Bishop's Palace a 13th-century chapel containing the *Chichester Roundel*, a painting depicting the Virgin and Child. The Market Cross at the center of town, erected in 1500, is an octagonal stone building with flying buttresses. The medieval city was almost entirely rebuilt during the 18th century. The Grammar School was designed by Sir Christopher Wren.

The Cathedral was established in 1091. Its old Norman clerestory was rebuilt in early English Gothic style, and work continued on the building until the 15th century. Dating from the 15th century is the only English example

of a separate bell tower. The 19th-century spire by Sir Gilbert Scott replaced a fallen 14th-century spire.

BIBLIOGRAPHY. W. Page and L. F. Salzman, eds., *The Victoria History of the County of Sussex*, 6 vols., London, 1905-53.

CHIEN-CHEN, *see* GANJIN IN TOSHODAIJI, NARA.

CH'IEN-FO-TUNG, *see* TUN-HUANG.

CH'IEN HSUAN. Chinese painter (ca. 1235–after 1300). Born near Wu-hsing in Chekiang Province, he was known also by his *tzu* Shun-chü and his *hao* Yü-t'an. His pupil Chao Meng-fu and six other friends joined Ch'ien Hsüan to form the group called the "Eight Talents of Wu-hsing." This circle was disbanded in 1286, when Chao Meng-fu and several others left to serve the Mongol conquerors, while Ch'ien Hsüan chose to retire to private life. *See* CHAO MENG-FU.

The painting style of Ch'ien Hsüan has been studied closely, but the lack of sufficient extant examples from his hand makes a simple summary difficult. He was a complex painter, skilled in a number of categories of painting: birds and flowers, figures, and landscapes. Of the landscape category no unquestioned example seems to have survived, although literary sources indicate that he did some in the blue-and-green manner associated with the T'ang dynasty as reinterpreted by Chao Po-chü. The tendency toward a kind of archaism or revival of earlier masters (especially the literati painters) is also evident in his figure paintings, in which the fine-line style of Li Kung-lin was employed by Ch'ien Hsüan in conjunction with rather bright colors. The paintings in the bird-and-flower category are the most numerous in terms of attributions, and among the paintings must be cited the evocative *Early Autumn* in the Detroit Institute of Arts (bearing the signature and seal of Ch'ien Hsüan) and the well-known *Squirrel on a Peach Branch* in the National Palace Museum Collection, Sun Yat-sen Museum, in Formosa. The diversity of styles in these nature studies attributed to the late Sung master (particularly evident in the many Ch'ien Hsüans in Japanese collections) is too great to permit generalizations; at present we can only note the strong flavor of naturalism and the high refinement of execution reminiscent of early Sung academic traditions in the works of this category by Ch'ien Hsüan. *See* BLUE-AND-GREEN STYLE; CHAO PO-CHU; LI KUNG-LIN.

BIBLIOGRAPHY. R. Edwards, "Ch'ien Hsüan and 'Early Autumn'," *Archives of the Chinese Art Society of America*, VII, 1953; J. Cahill, "Ch'ien Hsüan and His Figure Paintings," *Archives of the Chinese Art Society of America*, XII, 1958; W. Fong, "The Problem of Ch'ien Hsüan," *The Art Bulletin*, XLII, Sept., 1960.

MARTIE W. YOUNG

CH'IEN KU. Chinese painter (1508–after 1574). His *tzu* was Shu-pao and his *hao* Ch'ing-shih. A native of Su-chou, he is usually classified with the Wu-school painters and spent some of his adult years in studying the classics at the home of Wen Cheng-ming. Many of his paintings were executed on fans, a popular format in the 16th century in the Su-chou area. *See* WEN CHENG-MING.

BIBLIOGRAPHY. O. Sirén, *Chinese Painting, Leading Masters and Principles*, vol. 4, London, 1958.

CH'IEN TSAI. Chinese painter of orchids and bamboos (1708–93). Ch'ien Tsai was a native of Hai-yen, Chekiang Province. A popular painter during the Ch'ien-lung period

Ch'ien Hsüan, *Early Autumn*, bearing the artist's signature and seal. Detroit Institute of Arts.

(1736–96), he gained his reputation principally for his beautifully executed brush paintings of small facets of nature. He is not well known in Western collections, but Japanese collectors have sought his work eagerly for years.

CHIEN WARE, *see* TEMMOKU.

CHIERICATI PALACE, VICENZA. Originally a private residence and now the Civic Museum of Vicenza, Italy. It was begun in 1551 after the completion of Andrea Palladio's designs in 1550. The spatial recession of the side wings, the coupled columns of the façade, and the contrasts of light suggest a baroque approach. However, such mannerist features as the tall second-story windows, with elongated Michelangelesque figures above the pediments, reveal Palladio's mastery of contemporary forces in his own majestic, rhythmically controlled form of 16th-century classicism. The Tuscan order is used on the first story of the façade, and the Ionic on the second. The monumental portico, biapsidal salon, garden vestibule, and flanking rooms divide the first floor. Designed to turn away from Vicenza and face, with large loggias, the then open country, it is one of Palladio's most elegant residences—half villa and half palace.

BIBLIOGRAPHY. G. Chierici, *Il palazzo italiano dal secolo XI al secolo XIX*, Milan, 1957.

CHIGI. Japanese term for the scissors-shaped finials placed over the gables of Shinto shrines. *Chigi* are also found on the *haniwa* house models from the Tomb period (ca. 3d–6th cent.). They were originally functional devices to hold down the ridge pole, but later they became merely decorative, as on the Ise Shrine.

BIBLIOGRAPHY. R. T. Paine and A. Soper, *The Art and Architecture of Japan*, Baltimore, 1955.

CHIHIL SUTUN PALACE, ISFAHAN. Safavid palace in the royal gardens to the west of the Maidan-i-Shah in Isfahan. It was constructed by Shah Abbas about 1620. Behind a lofty open porch with twenty wood columns were private rooms and a very large hall, decorated with mural paintings, for royal receptions. *See* MAIDAN-I-SHAH, ISFAHAN.

BIBLIOGRAPHY. A. U. Pope, ed., *A Survey of Persian Art*, vol. 2, New York, 1939.

CHIKUDEN (Tanomura Chikuden). Japanese painter (1777–1835). Born into a family of physicians, he later served a feudal lord as a Confucian scholar and political adviser. After retiring from service, he led the life of a poet and painter. He studied painting briefly with Bunchō Tani. Tender lyricism is created in his ink paintings by soft brushwork and lightly applied colors. *See* BUNCHO (TANI BUNCHO).

BIBLIOGRAPHY. J. E. H. C. Covell, *Japanese Landscape Painting*, New York, 1962.

CHIL, MANUEL, *see* CASPICARA.

CHILANDARI, MONASTERY OF, *see* MOUNT ATHOS.

CHILCAT INDIANS, *see* CHILKAT INDIANS.

CHILDREN'S ART. From the art of children can be learned, on the one hand, something of the characteristics of different stages of development and, on the other, something of the motivations and expressive uses of the art of adults. Free fantasy and uninhibited spontaneity generally prevail in the art of children up to the age of about seven, starting usually with nonrepresentational experiments that lead to schematic figurative pictures. Gratification is felt in the very act of painting. This freedom, and the self-satisfaction that ordinarily accompanies it, is usually lost sometime after that age, as attempts at naturalistic representation, the wish to communicate, and submission to exterior standards intrude on the creative process.

The very young child, starting with a scribble, gradually develops the muscular control needed to make at will the marks that will serve as schematic symbols. Random marks suggest images, which may be clarified by deliberate modifications (a method not unlike that recommended by Leonardo and used by such artists as Klee and Dubuffet). Such images become formulas that are used repeatedly, sometimes in complex combinations, along with newly invented formulas that are added as the interests of the child require them. What he feels as significant in his experience is what he is interested in communicating through his pictures. To the age of about ten, he may be satisfied to repeat a single theme monotonously for long periods. Usually, by age ten the child has become concerned with logical relations of scale. He begins to conceive ground and sky as areas rather than as simple lines, learns to indicate depth by overlapping forms, and attempts to depict the functional relations of parts.

Developmental social changes between the ages of nine and twelve frequently lead to a decline in the self-confidence of the earlier years and with it the loss of the freedom of expression through art. At this time, too, the child may find it difficult to invent the more complex symbols

Chimu art. Stirrup-spout vessel. Archaeological Museum, Cuzco, Peru.

needed to express what he wishes to communicate. At this point, "calendar art" and cartoons, easy to imitate and to have peers understand, attract some children to such a degree that they never supplant them as criteria of artistic value. Those who fear they lack the ability to copy such stereotypes may renounce any further attempt at graphic expression. If they can avoid this trap, they may find new impetus in the challenge of working from observation and in concern for the mastery of representational skills. Only later are they likely to go beyond the aims of literal representation to other and more varied aesthetic goals.

BIBLIOGRAPHY. J. Piaget, *Play, Dreams, and Imitation in Childhood*, New York, 1951; V. Lowenfeld, *Creative and Mental Growth*, rev. ed., New York, 1952; M. Lindstrom, *Children's Art*, Berkeley, 1957.

MADLYN KAHR

CHILKAT (Chilcat) INDIANS. A subtribe of the Tlingit in southeastern Alaska, the Chilkat are known for their textile arts, especially the woven blankets that are actually used as shoulder capes or dance aprons. The blankets are made of mountain-goat wool combined with cedarbark. The traditional weave is a close diagonal pattern. Although women do the weaving itself, men paint the complex designs in advance on boards. These designs are carefully executed. Life-forms of Northwest Coast sculpture—split-form interpretations of animals, birds, and killer-whales—dominate the designs. The wearing of such blankets among the Chilkat Indians denotes tribal status and identification. Yellow, white, black, green, and blue are the traditional colors.

See also NORTH AMERICAN INDIAN ART (NORTHWEST COAST); TLINGIT INDIANS.

BIBLIOGRAPHY. G. T. Emmons, *The Chilkat Blanket* (Memoirs of the American Museum of Natural History, vol. 3), New York, 1907; R. B. Inverarity, *Art of the Northwest Coast Indians*, Berkeley, Calif., 1950; F. Dockstader, *Indian Art in America*, Greenwich, Conn., 1961.

CHILLIDA, EDUARDO. Spanish sculptor (1924–   ). Chillida was born in Saint-Sebastian. He studied architecture at the University of Madrid (1943–47) but turned to sculpturing in 1947. In Paris (1948–51) he began to work in iron, which he uses primarily in an abstract manner. One of his many prizes was an award at the 1964 Pittsburgh International Exhibition.

BIBLIOGRAPHY. New York, Museum of Modern Art, *New Spanish Painting and Sculpture*, New York, 1960.

CHIMAERA. Legendary fire-breathing monster of ancient Lycia, with a lion's head, a goat's body, and a serpent's tail. Her depredations were ended by the deadly arrows of the hero Bellerophon, aided by the flying horse Pegasus. The Chimaera, depicted in various media, appears also on coins of the Greek cities Corinth and Sicyon.

CHIMENTI, JACOPO (Jacopo da Empoli). Italian painter (b. Florence, ca. 1554; d. there, 1640). Except for a visit to Genoa, he remained in Tuscany (Florence, Empoli, Pisa, Livorno), closely tied to the local traditions. The *Immaculate Conception* in S. Remigio, Florence (1591), is one of his finest works. During his late years, he produced some attractive still lifes.

BIBLIOGRAPHY. S. de Vries, "Jacopo Chimenti da Empoli," *Rivista d'arte*, series 2, V, 1933.

CHIMNEYPIECE. Projecting hood of a medieval fireplace. Originally meant to divert smoke, the chimneypiece became a decorative framework often carried to the ceiling. It subsequently evolved into a mantel or shelf.

CHIMU ART. The Chimu culture was a powerful urban development with a capital, Chan-Chan, near the present Trujillo, Peru. Their peak was from about 1300 to 1438. Extensive irrigation projects near their walled, grid-plan, adobe cities in northern Peru enabled them to control the coastal areas and the Andean streams. Many remaining wall surfaces have painted relief designs of anthropomorphic and geometric origin. The Chimu, a partial reemergence of the Mochica, were excellent craftsmen in gold and silver. They produced blackware ceramics, often with relief decoration and in stirrup-spout, effigy, and aryballoid forms. For a period they rivaled and threatened the expanding Incas. *See* INCA ART; MOCHICA ART.

See also AMERICAS, ANCIENT, ART OF (PERU AND BOLIVIA).

BIBLIOGRAPHY. P. Kelemen, *Medieval American Art*, New York, 1943; W. C. Bennett, *Ancient Arts of the Andes*, New York, 1954; W. C. Bennett and J. B. Bird, *Andean Culture History*, 2d and rev. ed. (American Museum of Natural History, Handbook Series, no. 15), New York, 1960.

CHINA. Although other civilizations have had earlier beginnings than the Chinese, none has presented as continuous and unbroken a record as this dominant culture of east Asia, and none has had as long a history of artistic achievements. The actual physical boundaries of the country we call China today have altered considerably through the centuries, but when we speak of China we generally mean the region south of the Great Wall, framed by the Gobi Desert and steppes to the north, the Tibetan plateau to the west and southwest, and the plain of the Red River to the south. *See* GREAT WALL OF CHINA.

This vast area has been variously subdivided, the designation "eighteen provinces" (*shih-pa-sheng*) eventually being established in the Manchu (Ch'ing) period (1644–1912) and accepted until the early 20th century. The regional districts or provinces can be conveniently grouped around three great river systems: in the north, the famous Yellow River (Huang-ho); in the central area, the great Yangtze; and in the south, the West River (Hsi-chiang). The basic ingredients of a definable civilization or distinct culture were first assembled in the Yellow River Valley, the area referred to accurately as the "cradle of Chinese civilization," and the China we know today can be traced directly back to the neolithic inhabitants who first settled in the fertile valley. These early settlements led a precarious existence, constantly buffeted by aggressive nomadic tribes to the north and west, and the idea of *chung-kuo*, or "central states" (later mistranslated to become the "Middle Kingdom" in Western references), was eventually formulated. One of the small states, the Ch'in, managed to unify the area north of the Yangtze under one ruling house for a brief period of time beginning in 221 B.C., and it is from the name of this dynasty that the word "China" is ultimately traced.

Our recognition and knowledge of Chinese achievements in the visual arts have come slowly and at times quite haphazardly. Chinese writings on art have always existed in abundance, and habits of collecting and connoisseurship were established by the Chinese remarkably early. But the physical remoteness of China, major differences in language, and uncertainties concerning Chinese methods of scholarship have made much of the great record inaccessible to Western scholars until recent times. The Romans knew the Chinese through their trade in silk, over the famous Silk Route of central Asia, but referred to China only as the "land of Seres." Marco Polo's account of "Cathay" under the Mongols of the 14th century was mostly ignored or derided. The far-flung T'ang-dynasty empire of China, surely the most developed and most powerful civilization in the world during the 7th and 8th centuries, was largely unknown to medieval Europe at a time when Japan, southeast Asia, India, and the Middle East were paying tribute to Chinese emperors in Ch'ang-an. *See* CH'ANG-AN.

When the Portuguese took the Strait of Malacca in 1511, the fabulous porcelains of China began to reach the Western world. The history of the trade between Europe and China in ceramics, ivories, jades, and other portable art forms has been well documented, the Portuguese and Dutch being active in the 17th century and England assuming a major role in the 18th century. American participation in the lucrative China trade came later in the 18th century, but much of what returned from China to the shores of the New World may not qualify as great art; indeed, much of the porcelain was made by the Chinese for the express purpose of export. A fondness for the luxurious, the romantic, and the exotic underlies 19th-century taste, as seen in such excellent collections of China-trade items as that of the Peabody Museum in Salem, Mass. Occasionally some native examples of Chinese art found their way into the stream of trade; but, more important, the way was open and curiosity aroused, signaling the serious exploration of China that was to come in the 20th century. *See* CHINA: CERAMICS.

The intellectual probing of Chinese aesthetics and attitudes toward art was a sporadic affair. The Jesuit missions, established and well received in the 17th century, especially during the K'ang-hsi period (1662–1722), introduced Western ideas of painting, along with medicine, science, and mathematics, to the court at Peking. But the initial direct confrontation of East and West in art had neither immediate nor lasting effects on either party. Matteo Ricci, perhaps the greatest mind among the Jesuits, was an enthusiastic admirer of Chinese porcelains but had little to say that was complimentary about landscape painting, the highest and most distinctive art practiced by the Chinese at the time. Skill and craftsmanship, so clearly demonstrated in the smaller utilitarian arts of China, remained the qualities most admired by Westerners. Of Chinese painting, sculpture, and architecture, the Europeans had little understanding until almost the end of the 19th century.

A new chapter in our knowledge of Chinese art was initiated in the late 19th century by men somewhat prepared to cope with the vast Chinese literature on art and by the beginnings of archaeological exploration of the mainland. On the American side a handful of men—Bigelow, Fenollosa, and Morse, among others—developed a keen interest in Asian art, and with their help the Museum of Fine Arts in Boston soon acquired the finest representative collection of Chinese art anywhere in the Western world. Other American museums began following the path marked out by the Boston museum, and in the first half of the 20th century the Chinese collections of the Freer Gallery in Washington, D.C., the Metropolitan Museum in New York, the Philadelphia Museum of Art, the Art Institute of Chicago, and the William Rockhill Nelson Gallery of Art in Kansas City, to name only a few of the prominent ones, expanded quickly and began reflecting the wider achievements of the Chinese in areas besides those of export ceramics. Some of the earlier attitudes about the charming exoticism of the Orient underwent significant alterations, but only to be replaced by other myths that either extolled constantly the spiritual superiority of Chinese art or emphasized the mystic "oneness" of man and nature. The gradual awakening of American scholars and museum curators to the wider range of Asian art and subsequent changes in taste and attitude need not be labored. The results of American concerns throughout this century are clearly evident in the remarkable quantity and quality of Chinese art in the United States.

Another major landmark in the study of Chinese art was established with the beginning of archaeological excavations conducted by trained personnel in the 1920s and 1930s. J. G. Andersson's explorations in the north of China did much to help identify early neolithic settlements, and the excavation of the great city An-yang by the Academia Sinica and the Freer Gallery gave substance to the literary evidence for China's long and rich past. Since World War II further archaeological excavations have added immensely to the slowly accumulated body of knowledge concerning a great artistic civilization, and, although the assessment of new materials is far from complete, a picture of Chinese art has emerged with some clarity and balance to offset the earlier romanticizing. More recently, the art of painting in China has come under intensive reevaluation, again led by American scholars, and some of the subtleties and strengths of this branch of Chinese art are becoming apparent at last. *See* AN-YANG.

Although the details are often blurred or lacking, a general outline of the development of Chinese art over the span of more than 3,000 years seems to have now at least a recognizable form. The earliest major aesthetic expression of the Chinese is admirably recorded in the art of ceremonial bronzes and weapons, and the missing links between the Bronze Age and the neolithic civilizations are gradually being established. Not only are the bronzes themselves invaluable records of the first great phase of Chinese culture, extending from the Shang rulers in the 2d millennium B.C. through the earlier Han dynasty (to about the time of Christ), but they document the gradual shift from an almost total preoccupation with symbolic imagery to a delight in luxurious surface forms and effects.

The time span represented by the Han dynasty, from 206 B.C. to A.D. 221, appears now to be an age of great experimentation and exuberance in the arts. Some sculpture of monumental scale was attempted, partly stimulated no doubt by the wider contacts the Chinese were experiencing with other major civilizations to the west. The art of painting found a receptive audience, and lacquer products appeared in increasing numbers. And the message of Confucianism and Taoism, the two major philosophies of early China, was propagated in a variety of ways during the Han dynasty by the Chinese artist. With the introduction of Buddhism by the end of the Han period, sculpture became a major mode of expression as the demand for religious images became the main stimulus for art in China. Painting also entered the service of the Buddhist church in the centuries after the Han, and the first recorded painters are often connected with developments in the new religion. Buddhism brought a new fervor to the arts, and to this remarkable gospel, with its incessant demand for icons, the Chinese artist responded with the greatest period of sculptural activity. For nearly six centuries the concern for the spiritual representation of the Buddha and attendant deities dominated the mind and hand of the Chinese artist. *See* BUDDHIST TERMS, CORRELATION OF. *See also* CHINA: ARCHITECTURE, PAINTING, SCULPTURE.

If it is possible to single out a first peak of achievement in Chinese art, it would have to be the 7th and 8th centuries, the period of the T'ang dynasty. Like the earlier empire of the Han, the T'ang was a time of great enlightenment and expansive exuberance in all branches of art but one marked by an underlying classicism and rational restraint. Pottery achieves its first period of real distinction both in terms of technical innovations in glazing and firing and in the vigor of shape and decoration. Secular figure painting expressed another facet of a rich and dynamic age that found poetry emerging as a great literary form. And Buddhist sculpture achieved a level of naturalism and plasticity never again to be equaled on Chinese soil.

The decline of Buddhism and the collapse of the T'ang in the 9th century signaled another burst of creative energy that was to find its most characteristic expression in landscape painting. At the apex of this next major phase of Chinese art stands the Sung dynasty, the period lauded so often by earlier writers on Chinese art (including the Japanese) as the supreme age of painting in China. However much this may be true, such adulation has obscured many of the crucial questions concerning the nature of vision being explored by the Chinese artist in this critical

period of the 9th through the 12th century. The question of why landscape dominated the painter's vision at the expense of figure painting, still life, history, or other subjects is only partially answered by resorting to the mystique of man and nature or of Zen and enlightenment. Beneath the dazzling surface of marvelous paintings, questions about realism or abstraction, technical skill or intellectual virtue, and traditional values or contemporary interpretations were involved even if not always clearly articulated. There is no denying, however, that the Sung was indeed a great period of art, in ceramics as well as in painting, and although time has taken a severe toll, what remains from this era is enough to testify to the glory of a refined, aesthetically oriented age.

The history of Chinese art from the 14th century to the modern period is enormously complex and less understood than the preceding millennium. The number of surviving works of art is so much greater, creating a paradoxical embarrassment of riches that defies simple or immediate categorization. Earlier books on Chinese art often solved the question by dismissing entirely most of post-Sung art or by drastically compressing the Yüan, Ming, and Ch'ing periods and seeing the artist of these dynasties as bound by tradition and devoted to the copying of older styles. The sheer diversity of output and the multiplication of names of painters, shapes and types of ceramic wares, and regional schools of art do place severe strains on our present capabilities for handling the material in an intelligible fashion. Perhaps only the grossest kinds of generalizations can be attempted now about the experiences through which the Chinese artist of the last 600 years has passed. Certainly the weakening of a central academy, or court sponsorship, and the resulting freedom for experimentation appear as a major factor in the 14th and 15th centuries. The literati viewpoint, stressing the pursuit of learning and intellectual activities while deemphasizing technical virtuosity in the art of painting, was one avenue that was fully explored, and this view was to dominate painting in the 16th and 17th centuries. Tendencies toward mannerism or pure decoration are detectable in other art forms, and technical innovations moved porcelains into the front rank of Chinese efforts in the utilitarian arts. *See also* GLASS.

The rejection of realism and the denial of the past partially explain the emergence of the 17th-century radical expressionist painters usually labeled the "unorthodox masters" in China. How much affectation, both in personal behavior and in unconventional painting, is detectable in the wild painters of later China is a question that was, or perhaps still is, applicable to modern art in the West. Indeed, many of the trials and tribulations of Chinese artists of the later periods appear now as a longer paraphrase in time of the problems with which the Western artist grappled in a much shorter span in our modern age. The art of the later centuries in China should be seen as a complex tapestry, made up of many interwoven strands held together by the common bond of a rich tradition that was always the core to which every Chinese artist returned, no matter how much he wished to reject what had gone on before him. A recognition of the parallel nature of the problems facing the Chinese artist and those of the modern painter and sculptor will go a long way toward erasing

China, architecture. Courtyard and first building of the T'ai-ho Men (Gate of Supreme Harmony), Summer Palace, Peking.

the last remnants of previous attitudes that made Chinese art something always mysterious, inscrutable, and inaccessible to all but the chosen few.

BIBLIOGRAPHY. P. Pelliot, "L'Origine du nom de 'Chine,' " *T'oung Pao*, XIII, 1912; G. Creel, *The Birth of China*, London, 1936; G. D. Guest and A. G. Wenley, *Annotated Outlines of the History of Chinese Art*, Washington, D.C., 1946; H. G. Creel, *Chinese Thought, from Confucius to Mao Tsê-tung*, Chicago, 1953; S. H. Hansford, *A Glossary of Chinese Art and Archaeology*, London, 1954; L. Sickman and A. Soper, *The Art and Architecture of China*, Baltimore, 1956; L. C. Goodrich, *A Short History of the Chinese People*, 3d ed., New York, 1959; S. E. Lee, *A History of Far Eastern Art*, New York, 1964; M. Medley, *A Handbook of Chinese Art*, London, 1964; W. Willets, *Foundations of Chinese Art*, New York, 1965.

MARTIE W. YOUNG

CHINA: ARCHITECTURE. The 3,000 years of architecture in China are matched only by Egyptian architecture in longevity and slowness of change. Such changes as occur are largely variations on a few themes.

GENERAL CHARACTERISTICS

Materials. The chief building material of China is wood. The reason is not the unavailability of stone but the love of flexibility and the lack of desire for great height or monumentality. Stone, brick, and stucco are used to a limited degree.

Buildings were usually erected on platforms of tamped earth as strong as concrete. Remains of these foundations are found as far back as Shang, the first historical dynasty. Few traces of early wooden buildings remain. The types and construction methods, however, were imported by Japan, and several well-preserved examples of Chinese styles can be studied there.

Plan: Buildings and cities. The basic unit of a building or a city is a walled square or oblong along a north-south axis. This unit may have developed from the earth altar, a square, or from *ching-t'ien*, the well-field system. Land was divided into a unit of nine squares, eight families farming one square each. The ninth, and central, square was farmed communally and the produce paid to the landlord.

Within the walled city are units consisting of administrative or religious structures and domiciles with courtyards. The units are on a north-south axis with the most important building facing the south. The north is considered the source of evil.

The chief building has little visible dominance, nor is there a great difference between secular and religious architecture. There is no philosophy of architectural monuments. Buildings differ in size and luxury, not in basic design. In general, luxury was not conspicuous, for extravagance in architecture was considered one of the signs of misgovernment and was severely criticized.

Architectural elements. The basic structure is a hall, usually on a raised platform. It is divided into units of floor space or bays (*chien*). The areas east and west of the larger central area, called *hsiang*, can become wings with their own roofs and internal pillars.

Across the front or on the two sides of the center is a porchlike space (*t'ang*) for social ceremonies. There may be another appendage, a two-story porch or balcony (*hsien*) with a separate roof.

Sometimes within the courtyard there is a *t'ai*; originally a lookout tower, it later became a raised platform, roofed or not. There may also be a wood-framed tower of two or more stories (*lou*), the prototype of a pagoda (*t'a*).

The pagoda is typically a building of several stories made by repetition of the basic story and its roof. Each stage diminishes in size, and the structure is capped by a tall spire and disks. The pagoda is usually placed as an isolated tower in a temple courtyard in front of the hall that contains the altar and the images. Buildings are assembled around courtyards and are balanced to right and left. The main hall is centered at the rear. The courtyards are along the north-south axis and in Buddhist temples are often enclosed by galleries. They usually have two side gates as well as the main front gate. This gate is actually an entrance building with side chambers. The large doorway is flanked by paired elements (*ch'üeh*), which sometimes become lookout towers. Behind the main gate is the screen wall, a short freestanding wall across the axis to bar direct entrance. Its original purpose was to stop evil spirits, who travel principally in a straight line. (For the iconography of the pagoda, *see* INDIA.)

Roofs are generally tiled, and the buildings may or may not have a ceiling beneath the structural beams. Such a ceiling may be flat, coffered, or in the form of a cupola.

One of the most distinctive features of Chinese and Japanese architecture is the manner in which the heavy roof is supported, the weight being distributed by an elaborate system of projecting arms and impost blocks. The main elements of this construction are the *hua*, an arm projecting from the column head; the *kua-tzu*, a longitudinal bracket on the end of the outer arm of the column head; the *man*, a bracket placed above the *hua* and *kua-tzu* for height; the *ang*, a slanting transverse arm helping to brace the weight of the eaves; and the *ling*, a longitudinal bracket on the *ang*.

The arch was known as early as the Han period, but it was used sparingly and usually only for utilitarian purposes, as in vaulted grave chambers. It may be either the corbeled arch or the true arch. The arch is frequently used in the doorways of Buddhist pagodas, showing the influence of Indian models.

HISTORICAL PERIODS

The historical development of Chinese architecture may be traced from the 2d millennium B.C. through the various dynastic periods.

Shang (before ca. 1027 B.C.). Excavations at An-yang, the capital of the Shang dynasty, have revealed traces of pillared halls, one 90 feet long, on tamped-earth platforms, as well as the foundations of the city walls fortified with towers. Several square tombs have also been discovered, the chief one being 40 feet deep with a ramp on the south and steps on the other sides. *See* AN-YANG.

Chou (ca. 1027–256 B.C.). Traces of Chou walls, platforms, and roof tiles have been excavated, and many references to Chou architecture can be found in the classic Chinese texts. The testimony concerning the *ming-t'ang* is contradictory. Apparently it was a royal hall containing a series of apartments used in sequence according to the seasons of the year.

Ch'in (221–207 B.C.). The beginnings of a national architecture appear within this short period of one generation. Shih-huang-t'i, the first national emperor, built in the capital a series of pleasure palaces, which copied those of the feudal lords he had conquered. The regional differences in these buildings were later fused into an imperial style. The palaces of the Emperor were huge and far more splendid than those of his predecessors.

Han (206 B.C.–A.D. 221). This was a period of much government architecture. Ch'ang-an, the first capital, was a walled square but had no central axis. Lo-yang, capital of the Later (or Eastern) Han, was more regular. Both cities had very large buildings; the audience hall of the Ch'ang-lo Palace is said to have been 497 by 120 Han feet. The *lou* tower was first seen in this period. All important buildings were ornamented with sculpture and painting. The most pretentious structure must have been the *ming-t'ang* of Wang Mang, which combined a round superstructure with a square base and embodied a cosmological symbolism. *See* CH'ANG-AN; LO-YANG.

The small stone grave chapel of Hsia-t'ang-shan with engraved wall decorations is the only building remaining from this period. Our knowledge comes largely from texts and from the great mass of pottery models found in tombs. *See* HSIA-T'ANG-SHAN.

Six Dynasties (221–589). Domestic and government buildings of this period repeat the Han style. The major portion of the great amount of construction is due to the rapid growth of Buddhism. Lo-yang had 42 temples in the early 4th century and 500 by the 6th century; 30,000 were scattered over north China between 530 and 570.

The Buddhist temple compound followed the tradition of walls, gatehouses, galleries, and monumental halls and was dominated by the pagoda (*t'a*), partly derived from the Han *lou* tower. Another probable origin was the famous tower built by Kanishka near Peshawar in present-day Pakistan, which had thirteen stories surmounted by an iron mast carrying thirteen gold disks. The Chinese type can be seen in the rock-cut pagodas of the Yün-kang and Lung-men caves and in examples at the Hōryūji, Hōkiji, and Hōrinji monasteries in Japan. *See* HORYUJI; LUNG-MEN; YUN-KANG.

The earliest masonry survivor from the 6th century is the Sung-yüeh-ssu on Mt. Sung in Honan (*ssu* is a generic term for monastery). It is a twelve-sided brick structure with a high plain plinth and a first story with corner columns. A series of corbeled eaves diminishing in size makes up the rest of the building, which is surmounted by a mast and disks. The sculptured details of arched recesses, miniature arches, and pagodas in relief are purely Indian. A simple one-story version in stone is seen in the pagoda Ssu-men-t'a of Shen-t'ung-ssu in Shantung, dated 544.

Sui (589–618). China was reunited in this dynasty, and the volume and scale of building increased greatly. A new rank was accorded engineer-architects, and there were several men of marked talent. Yang Su laid out a new city of Lo-yang and was also a noted naval architect. Yü-wen Kai was a hydraulic engineer and the designer of an ingenious rotating pavilion for the Empress and an intricate version of the *ming-t'ang*. Ho T'iao was a military engineer and constructed the mausoleum of the Dowager Empress. Yen Pi, painter and architect, restored the Great Wall, built a pleasure palace, and constructed a canal. *See* GREAT WALL OF CHINA.

The first Sui emperor contributed to the expansion of Buddhist building by distributing a set of relics to the provinces. Each relic required a new pagoda to house it.

T'ang (618–906). This is one of the great periods of Chinese history and one of the richest in all expressions of art. It had both the wealth and the talent to fulfill the demands of an active and creative age for a very considerable length of time. The capital of Ch'ang-an, laid out by the Sui and inherited and developed by the T'ang, was a walled city, symmetrical in plan, with an inner imperial enclosure on a north-south axis that housed all the government offices.

One of the 7th-century rulers, the usurper empress Wu Hou, like Queen Hatshepsut of Egypt, impressed her image on the country by the fantastic feats of her architects. One item was an openwork *lou* of stone 100 feet high, a kind of a Chinese Eiffel Tower. A more important construction was an extraordinary *ming-t'ang*, 294 feet high, built in 688 at Lo-yang. According to descriptions, its lower story had four faces in the colors of the four seasons. The middle story symbolized the twelve branches of the time cycle and was crowned by a cupola supported by nine dragons. The top story, also with a cupola, signified the twenty-four solar periods and was crowned by a 10-foot iron phoenix. Through the middle of the whole structure was a great wooden shaft, probably symbolic of the axis joining earth and heaven.

The emperor Ming-huang, like a Sui predecessor who had built a rotating pavilion, prized ingenious luxuries. He had a small pavilion cooled by artificial rain pouring on the roof and a heated pool large enough to hold boats and miniature islands. But the persistent strain of Confucian austerity was also present in this period. The mountain palace of the emperor T'ai-tsung was roofed with thatch. A decree of 827 limited the number and types of architectural ornament used by government officials and assigned a maximum size for halls and gatehouses according to their ranks.

The buildings of the Buddhist temple compounds were made of wood, and almost nothing has survived. The pagodas, however, were generally made of masonry or stone, and several examples remain. The general T'ang type has a square base with a corbeled cornice and a pyramidal superstructure topped by a spire. One such example, dated 712, is at Lai-shui-hsien in Hopei. A common and more elaborate version has the superstructure divided into stories, usually seven, each with eaves. The pagoda of Yün-chü-ssu near Peking is an example of this type.

One of the most famous remains at Ch'ang-an is the White Goose Pagoda (Ta-yen-t'a), 190 feet high, at Tz'u-en-ssu, the monastery of the pilgrim Hsüan-tsang. It was built in 652 and renovated from 701 to 705. This structure has seven stepped-back stories. The walls are divided by flat pilasters, and the combination of beams, intercolumnar struts, and capitals is derived from carpentry techniques. A closer imitation of wood construction is seen in the tomb pagoda of Hsüan-tsang south of Hsi-an-fu, which has simulated octagonal pillars with brackets above the capitals. The pagoda was erected in 699 but may have been restored much later.

An octagonal plan, a T'ang innovation, survives in the tomb pagoda of Ching-ts'ang, a noted Buddhist teacher, in the compound of Hui-shan-ssu on Mt. Sung. With its simulated doors and windows the pagoda has both wooden and masonry features. The superstructure has an octagonal lotus-petal cornice, above which it develops into a round form as a base for the spire. Similar pagodas can often be seen in the Tun-huang paintings. Another type is found at the Wu-t'ai-shan temple of Fo-kuang-ssu. This is single-storied and domed like the stūpas in the Ajanṭā caves.

One T'ang wooden building has survived: the main hall of Fo-kuang-ssu on Wu-t'ai-shan, built about 850. It is one-storied, measures seven bays by four (about 113 by 65 ft.), and has a hipped roof. The interior is spacious, with a large platform altar facing south; the back is closed. Five bays on the front are doors; each end wall has a set of windows, vertically barred. The eaves are held by massive bracketing complexes.

Sung (960–1279). The period between the T'ang and Sung, that of the Five Dynasties, is too short for any noticeable change. Political and economic circumstances and a more conservative spirit made the Sung itself less experimental and extravagant than the T'ang. Architectural refinements and elaborations took the place of vigor and power. Architects liked to play with color and proportions; to use glazed roof and floor tiles; to add porches, wings, and galleries to achieve picturesque massing; and to enrich interiors with decoration, which often included elaborate miniature buildings set into ceilings and walls. They liked towers and the graceful lightness of curved roofs, a style they perfected in this period. An architectural manual of these construction techniques, the *Ying-tsao fa shih*, composed about 1100, has been handed down in copies to the present day. *See* Ying-tsao fa shih.

After the Kin (Chin) Tatar invasion, the court fled to Hang-chou in the south. The architecture was probably a modest copy of the previous styles, but we know little about it except for the type that influenced the 13th- and 14th-century Zen buildings in Japan.

The Northern Sung capital was built at Pien-ching (modern K'ai-feng) on a T'ang site. The necessary enlargements made it irregular at first, and the desired symmetry was reached just before the Tatars burned it in 1126. *See* K'AI-FENG.

About sixty pagodas have survived from the Five Dynasties and Sung periods. Most of these are of the 11th century; by the 13th century Buddhism was waning in power, and the sect that was popular, the Ch'an (Zen), did not favor pagodas. Most of the existing pagodas are of the now standard type: constructed of brick and hexagonal or octagonal in form. An example that has the characteristic Sung elaboration is the thirteen-story T'ieh-t'a at K'ai-feng, built about 1044. This pagoda has two tiers of closely set corbel blocks, curved eaves with roof tiles, corner columns and column top beams imitating wood, fake balconies above the first story, and a colorful tile casing. Iron was occasionally used for small-sized pagodas in this period. Of the few remaining, the one at Ching-chou in Hopei Province is in the best condition.

The monastery Lung-hsing-ssu at Cheng-ting remains sufficiently intact to give some impression of its original state. A ruined pavilion housing a large Kuan-yin is at the end of the axis. It is seven bays by five and has stucco reliefs on the end and rear walls. The rear courtyard has a two-storied library on the west and a similar Maitreya pavilion on the east. An ordination platform of later date is in front of these structures; beyond it is a monumental hall, the Mo-ni-tien, probably of mid-10th-century date. Farther on are the ruins of another Sung hall, an earthen terrace, and the traces of bell and drum towers. *See* Lung-hsing-ssu, Cheng-ting.

The historically important Mo-ni-tien has certain unique features as well as an early development of standard forms. It has an unusual narrow entrance vestibule projecting from each of the four sides. Each vestibule has a low hip-and-gable roof, the entrance a pedimentlike gable. The two-aisled central hall is square and may reflect the original building, known from records to have been built in 586. The scale of the bracketing is massive, and the column head has a T section, an early example of the Sung standard type.

The south seems to be the major source of the Sung style, and the most influential architect of the period is from that region. It was Yü Hao of Hang-chou, master architect and author of a now-lost builders' manual, who among other innovations is credited with bringing the curved-roof style to the north. Only one documented wooden building of Southern Sung remains in fair condition. This is the main hall, San-ch'ing-tien, of the Taoist monastery Yüan-miao-kuan in Su-chou. It is a large building, 150 by 84 feet, nine bays by six.

Japan imported Ch'an (Zen) Buddhism from the Hangchou region, and these buildings of Southern Sung can actually be better studied through their modified Japanese copies, called Kara-yō, or "Chinese style." A good discussion of the type, with specific examples, has been made by A. C. Soper in *The Evolution of Buddhist Architecture* (1942).

Liao, Kin (Chin), Yüan (1279–1368): Barbarian rule. In the early 10th century the Khitan Tatars from Mongolia took the Liaotung Peninsula. By the 11th century they had forced the Sung government south of the Yellow River. In 1114 the Jurchen, a Tungusic people, formed an alliance with the Chinese, destroyed the Liao, and established the Kin (Chin) dynasty. This was overcome in 1234 by the Mongols, who as the Yüan dynasty ruled China until 1368.

For more than 400 years China, or a large part of it, was dominated by barbarian warriors and hunters. Although they had few creative interests, they were impressed by the Chinese achievements and were ambitious to continue and reproduce the culture for themselves.

Architecture, like all other arts, followed the Sung type with the exception of a brick pagoda type created by Liao Tantric Buddhism. The plan of this pagoda type is octagonal, the base is high and grooved with narrow sculptured bands, and the shaft is decorated with large Buddhist figures against a plain surface. The shaft is surmounted by a crown of closely set roofs, usually thirteen, diminishing in size and surmounted by a spire. The lower eaves have an imitation wooden bracketing of the most complicated and forceful type, which produces strong light and dark accents. The result is one of impressive richness with three dramatically differentiated divisions quite unlike the simpler clarity of the Sung type. The best examples are found only in the north. Among those in good condition are that of Pei-chen at Chin-hsien, Manchuria, of mid-11th-century date, and the White Pagoda of Pai-t'a-ssu at Ch'ing-chou, Jehol, of the 11th–12th century.

The Yüan pagodas of the Sung type have no new interest. The Tibetan chorten, a bottle-shaped stūpa, was imported by the court, which favored the Lamaist form of Buddhism. A huge chorten built in the time of Kublai Khan still exists in Peking.

The two oldest Liao wooden buildings (984) are a gatehouse and a pavilion in the Tu-lo-ssu compound at Chihsien in Hopei. The gatehouse is a simple structure, 55 by 29 feet, with a hipped roof and a ridge acroterium. The pavilion is 67 by 47 feet and has three floor levels; the upper two levels are inner balconies with latticework railings surrounding a huge clay statue of Kuan-yin. Twenty-four types of bracketing are used in this building to fit every structural condition.

Marco Polo writes of the stupendous and luxurious court of the Mongols, but no buildings survive to give us an idea of the grandeur. The Ming catalog, the *Chou-keng lu*, suggests that Sung usage was followed, probably with emphasis on rich color, dramatic massing, and diversity.

Ming and Ch'ing (1368–1912). Although many monumental buildings were erected in this period, architecture underwent a slowly progressive decadence. The Sung style became a traditional formula and was generally interpreted without sensitivity or fresh imagination.

The Chih-hua-ssu, a temple in Peking completed in 1444, is typical. It has the traditional layout of a narrow oblong with a succession of courtyards. The first court is balanced on east and west by bell and drum towers; a gatehouse leads to the second court, which also has balancing side buildings, the western one a Lamaist-style library. At the back of this court is a Buddhist hall on axis. The third court contains the chief building, the Ju-lai-tien. All the buildings are small; even the main hall is only 60 by 40 feet. Neither the structural planning nor the carpentry details of the Ju-lai-tien are of first-class craftsmanship. The pillars are poorly spaced, and the bracketing is crowded and not entirely functional, the load being carried mainly by poorly designed big beams. The arch used in the three doorways of the upper story is a novelty. The interior is richly decorated with eye-catching details and once had an ornately carved and impressive cupola (now in Kansas City, William Rockhill Nelson Gallery of Art).

BIBLIOGRAPHY. E. Boerschmann, *Die Baukunst und religiöse Kultur der Chinesen*, vol. 3: *Pagoden*, Berlin, Leipzig, 1931; O. Sirén, *The Walls and Gates of Peking*, London, 1924; E. Boerschmann, *Chinesische Architektur*, Berlin, 1925; O. Sirén, *The Imperial Palaces of Peking*, 3 vols., Paris, 1926; O. Sirén, *Histoire des arts anciens de la Chine*, vol. 4: *L'Architecture*, Paris, Brussels, 1930; J. Prip-Møller, *Chinese Buddhist Monasteries*, Copenhagen, London, 1937; L. Sickman and A. Soper, *The Art and Architecture of China*, Baltimore, 1956.

ELIZABETH LYONS

CHINA: BRONZES. Bronze ritual vessels and other metal objects furnish the master key to the early civilizations of China, from the 2d millennium B.C. to the period of the great Han empire in the 2d century A.D. For several thousand years bronze casting was a major art form, and

China, bronzes. Ritual vessel from the Chou dynasty (ca. 1027–256 B.C.).

even after the time of the Han it enjoyed continued popularity as a medium for the artist in the form of Buddhist icons, mirrors, and other implements. But when we speak of Chinese bronzes the reference is inevitably to the bronzes of the early dynasties, from the Shang and Chou periods principally. The bronzes from these two great ages in Chinese history are numerous, are fairly well preserved, and are the principal documents of the aesthetic achievements of the early Chinese peoples.

Although the history of bronzes in China is very complex in terms of its relative chronology, the broad lines of development seem fairly well defined. The pioneering works of such scholars as Li Chi, Bernard Karlgren, and W. P. Yetts, to mention only a few, have reconstructed a part of that vast history. Some hard questions undeniably remain, among them the fascinating problem of the origins of this great bronze art, which seems to appear fully mature on Chinese soil in the 2d millennium B.C. Both internal and external factors appear to be involved: contacts with the West through such areas as Siberia on the one hand and rapid development of the necessary vocabulary of forms and designs that seem to draw directly upon native Chinese inspiration on the other. Closely related to the matter of origins is the question of the precise technical means by which the bronzes were cast. Fragments of molds that have been discovered in excavated sites indicate that the piece-mold process was the principal means employed for the majority of bronzes, but the earlier theories of the lost-wax (*cire-perdue*) process cannot be entirely discounted. Nor do we know the exact makeup of the piece molds and the procedures followed by the caster to achieve such almost perfect examples. Yet if our knowledge of the bronze art of China is admittedly incomplete, there is considerable promise of major progress in this area of study in the excavations now being conducted in mainland China by trained archaeologists. The extensive publications of these excavations have already begun to alter the conception of the first major visual expression of the Chinese.

Shang dynasty. The date of the advent of the Shangs is not certain, and various dates have been used. For the study of the first flush of bronze art, however, there is a more or less fixed point in time: the capital of the Shangs at An-yang in Honan Province, at which excavations began in 1928 and continued sporadically to 1937. This great city was the last capital of the Shang sovereigns, covering some 300 years, from roughly 1350 to about 1027 B.C. The more recent discovery of an earlier Shang capital near the modern village of Cheng-chou in Honan provides evidence for the striking technical advances of the An-yang casters, for the more primitive stage of Cheng-chou is quite marked by contrast and points to the long formulative period necessary for the development of this technically sophisticated art form. The sequence of Cheng-chou and the overlap with An-yang are not certain by any means, nor is the date for the establishment of Cheng-chou known. But clearly, for a period of time before the move to An-yang, the art of bronze casting was under way, so that by about 1350 the art was well established and the mature Shang style was in florescence. *See* AN-YANG.

Generally speaking, Shang bronzes not only are supreme examples of skillful casting but are visually complex and compelling in terms of surface design. The decoration may cover the entire vessel or only a part, and it is usually composed of a background motif consisting of geometric spirals called by the Chinese *lei-wen*, or thunder pattern. Against this tightly controlled, incised background there is in raised relief a combination of various stylized animal designs, of which the *t'ao-t'ieh*, or "ogre mask," is most striking. The mask appears in various shapes but is always seen frontally, as though some animal head had been split down the center and spread out over the surface. The form is not completely naturalistic, the lower jaw being missing in all forms of the mask, and in the Shang pieces there are various degrees of stylization in the handling of this motif, but its ubiquitous appearance in the Shang makes it a prominent feature in the decorative vocabulary. Along with the *t'ao-t'ieh* mask there are other hybrid creatures of semimythical and seminaturalistic form: the *k'uei* (one-legged) dragon, varieties of snakes, and birds. These motifs (actually few in number) are combined with such ingenuity and imagination that the inventory of animal forms at first seems much too large to encompass, a great tribute to the highly developed sense of design of the Shang artist. *See* K'UEI DRAGON; T'AO-T'IEH.

Where the Shang designer acquired this extensive vocabulary of designs has not been satisfactorily explained. Li Chi has suggested an earlier origin in painting on wood, and other scholars have advanced different types of earlier materials now lost. The meanings attached to such elements as the *t'ao-t'ieh* mask and the *k'uei* dragon are also shrouded in speculation, some of it quite intriguing and within the realm of possibility. But whatever else one can say about the specific purpose of an animal on a given bronze, the general zoomorphic fantasies on these bronzes are not mere decoration. Much of the belief of the Shangs and their way of looking at the world is contained on the surface of the vessels that were cast as a part of their ritual program.

The shapes of the bronze vessels are even more varied than the animals that appear on their exteriors. About forty types of Shang vessels have been classified, although some are minor variations on a major type. The Chinese have employed identifying names for the various shapes, some of the names being traced to inscriptions of the Shang or Chou and others being those given to the vessels in the Sung dynasty during the great antiquarian revival of interest in ancient bronzes.

Of the many shapes mention should be made of the very common *ting*, a three- or four-legged vessel used for cooking or heating food in the ritual ceremony. This particular form of vessel is often cited for comparison with the prehistoric pottery form called the *li* tripod, a functional cooking vessel composed of a round body and three hollow bulbous legs. Certainly prototypes such as the *li* tripod do account for some of the shapes found in the bronzes, and the indebtedness of the Shang artist to earlier neolithic cultures, particularly the pottery of Lung-shan, cannot be denied. Many of the bronze shapes, however, have no immediate antecedents in the prehistoric past. Among these should be included the types of vessels in the form of animals, *tsun* and *kuang*. The term *tsun* is often applied to vessels that are not easily classified; the *kuang* refers to a wine container shaped like a modern gravy

boat with a lid in the form of an animal's head and back. The type of Shang vessel termed *huo* is probably the most interesting variation on the theme of animal-shaped containers. The Freer Gallery, Washington, D.C., possesses a *huo* with a human-faced lid and the body of a snake with wings, a marvelously evocative piece that typifies so much of the Shang attitude toward the physical and spiritual world. *See* KUANG; TING; TSUN.

Chou dynasty. When the vigorous rulers of Chou, a small state to the west, overthrew the great Shangs and occupied An-yang about 1027 B.C., there was no abrupt change in the art of bronze making. Karlgren has isolated some elements that form a transitional Shang-Chou phase, but the differences in style between An-yang vessels and those that can be assigned to the early Chou rulers are not visually compelling. Some shapes were discontinued, and a few minor variations occurred, but essentially the early Chou peoples continued the great tradition of bronze casting inaugurated by the house of Shang, at least for a period of time.

About 900 B.C., after the Chou state had solidified itself for a number of generations, a very marked change in bronze style occurred, perhaps the first really radical departure from the long, slow evolution of the bronze art form. This stylistic break has been referred to as the "second phase" by Yetts and is termed "middle Chou" by others. The exact date for the inception of the new style is not definite, but it seems to have been in evidence by about 900 B.C. and to have continued for some 300 years. The changes are marked enough so that we may infer a total kind of deliberate reorientation toward the bronze craft, responding to a new demand and resulting in a new system of aesthetics to replace the older zoomorphic vocabulary of Shang and early Chou times.

The number of existing bronzes of the middle Chou period is not numerous compared with those of Shang and early Chou, and controlled excavations datable to this period are lacking. But the available evidence shows the characteristics of the second-phase style clearly. The bronzes from Hsin-cheng, Honan Province, and from the site of Chia-hsien in the same area are definitely expressions of a radically new outlook: the decoration is subdued by comparison with the richness of the earlier vessels, and the shapes are more rugged and squat close to the ground, emphasizing the horizontal rather than the vertical. The horizontality of some of the vessels is enhanced by parallel grooving or ribs, and a heavy, almost ponderous quality seems to be the effect sought after by bronze designers in the middle Chou period. The zoomorphic flights of imagination and the lively exuberance of the Shang style have given way to an aesthetic that concentrates on the symbolic and visual nature of pure power: vigorous, monumentally conceived forms with a singular directness of decoration. Grim austerity seems to be the prevailing standard. *See* KUEI.

The new attitude toward animal forms is nowhere better demonstrated than in the pair of bronze tigers in the collection of the Freer Gallery. Compared with the typical animal-shaped vessels of Shang or early Chou, with their "loaded" surface designs of wings, snakes, dragons, and t'ao-t'ieh masks, the Freer tigers appear as sterling examples of greater visual unity. The sides of the tigers no longer have any reference to stylized animal forms, the decorations now functioning as another element within the total scheme. The massive and bulky effect of these animals stems from a consistency of approach and handling, and an awareness of the expressive potential of shape is clearly indicated in these impressive pieces of middle Chou bronze art. This sense of a greater cohesiveness of visual effect is revealed in other examples of animal sculpture in bronze from the same period, for example, in the crouching buffalo of the Pillsbury Collection, Minneapolis.

The austerity that keynotes the middle Chou style was superseded by another major reorientation of the art of bronze design about 600 B.C. (again the dates are very rough approximations). This last major change in bronze casting seems to be the direct opposite of the stringent middle Chou style, and the period is referred to by a series of confusing terms: the "third-phase" style used by Yetts, Eastern Chou, late Chou, Warring States, or Huai River style after the name of an important region. The time span extends from about 600 B.C. to the beginning of the Han dynasty in 206 B.C. This period is a rich one in many ways: it was a time of sweeping philosophical inquiry as well as material achievement, of great literary records, and of dazzling metalwork. *See* HUAI STYLE.

The archaeological evidence of the late Chou is fairly extensive compared with the middle Chou period. Finds datable to the late Chou come from sites such as Chin-ts'un in Honan, Shou-chou in Anhui, Ch'ang-sha in Hunan, and Li-yü in Shansi. The geographical distribution is wider than in the previous periods, but the record is far from complete. It is apparent that the ancient state of Ch'u in the south of China, represented by the rich finds of Ch'ang-sha, was one of the dominant if not most important centers for late Chou culture. But if there were local or regional variations in bronze making in the late Chou, as evidence seems to indicate, there is nonetheless an overall unity to all bronzes of this period. Their visual effect can be summed up by one word: sumptuous. The use of inlays of precious metals, for example, gained great importance in the late Chou. Silver, gold, and semiprecious stones incrust the surface and enhance the pictorial splendor of the design. The vocabulary of motifs ranges back to the Shang and early Chou zoomorphic patterns but is handled now with a new polish and elegance. Naturalistic animal forms appear, sometimes as almost independent sculptures attached to the bronzes. Patterns become intricately interwoven around the surface, and a dazzling brocadelike effect is achieved at times. The shapes of the vessels tend to swell, as though to afford the largest possible surface for the complexity of rich pictorial elements that move or twist across the field of vision. The masculine vigor of middle Chou bronzes has been clearly replaced by an almost feminine delicacy. The change is less sudden and probably less conscious than had been the case with the shift from Shang to middle Chou, but the style of these later bronzes speaks clearly for a new age and society. *See* CH'ANG-SHA.

The great outward expansion of the Chinese in late Chou times in terms of new techniques and knowledge is also evidenced by the greater variety of material available. Mirrors and bells, for example, were cast in large number, as were belt hooks and other items of personal adornment.

At least a part of this increase in both design vocabulary and types of objects was caused by influences stemming from contact with the so-called animal art of the steppes region. The many fine bronzes of the *hu* type, with their scenes of hunting and combat, stem directly from the influence of nomadic art on the Chinese of late Chou times. And the whole lively character of these hunting bronzes matches perfectly the exuberant nature of late Chou art in general. The political agitation and ferment of this period seem to have produced a remarkable conscious aestheticism that is quite distant from the magic-oriented world of the Shang artist. *See* HU. *See also* TOU.

Han dynasty and later periods. With the new religious and political outlook that accompanied the Han empire bronze casting lost its preeminence as a major form of art. A general decline in technical quality and less interest in the possibilities of shapes are clearly evident by even a superficial examination of existing Han bronze vessels. The large and functional shapes tend to echo those of the potter, indicating the shift from the ritual or ceremonial to the practical in use. Inlays occasionally continue from the late Chou into Han times, with a modification of ornamentation reflecting the linear stylization of other Han arts, but normally the Han vessel is not decorated except for ribs or grooves. In other types than the vessels, however, there is a continued reflection of late Chou flamboyance: the mirrors are particularly notable for their complexity of cosmic symbolism, and cylindrical caskets or toilet boxes decorated with animals of the four directions capture the quality of Han life, elegant and civilized.

After the Han dynasty the ceremonial bronze vessel completely disappeared, to be revived only as an antiquarian's pastime at a much later date. The medium of bronze was limited to the service of religious sculpture or to occasional personal ornaments. The mirrors continue into the T'ang period as a happy exception to the general decline of bronze art. The many mirrors datable from early Han through to the T'ang period remain essentially the only vestige of what had been the great art of bronze casting.

See also CHINA: SCULPTURE.

BIBLIOGRAPHY. S. Umehara, ed., *Nihon shūcho Shina kodō seikwa* (Selected Ancient Chinese Bronzes in Japanese Collections), 6 vols., Osaka, 1934–64; S. Umehara and S. Hamada, *Senoku seishô* (The Sumitomo Collection of Old Bronzes), rev. ed., Kyoto, 1934; B. Karlgren, "Yin and Chou in Chinese Bronzes," *Bulletin of the Museum of Far Eastern Antiquities*, VIII, 1936; B. Karlgren, "New Studies on Chinese Bronzes," *Bulletin of the Museum of Far Eastern Antiquities*, IX, 1937; W. P. Yetts, *The Cull Chinese Bronzes*, London, 1939; B. Karlgren, "Huai and Han," *Bulletin of the Museum of Far Eastern Antiquities*, XIII, 1941; Freer Gallery of Art, *A Descriptive and Illustrative Catalogue of Chinese Bronzes*, Washington, D.C., 1946; B. Karlgren, *A Catalogue of the Chinese Bronzes in the Alfred F. Pillsbury Collection*, Minneapolis, 1952; M. Loehr, "The Bronze Styles of the Anyang Period," *Archives of the Chinese Art Society of America*, VII, 1953; *Hsiao-t'un* (The Yin-Shang Site at Anyang, Honan), vol. 3: *Artifacts*, Taipei, 1956; M. Loehr, *Chinese Bronze Age Weapons*, Ann Arbor, Mich., 1956; Li Chi, *The Beginnings of Chinese Civilization*, Seattle, 1957; W. Willets, *Chinese Art*, vol. 1, Harmondsworth, 1958; T. K. Cheng, *Archaeology in China*, vol. 2: *Shang China*, Cambridge, 1960; vol. 3: *Chou China*, Cambridge, 1960–63; N. Barnard, *Bronze Casting and Bronze Alloys in Ancient China*, Tokyo, 1961; W. Watson, *Ancient Chinese Bronzes*, London, 1962.

MARTIE W. YOUNG

CHINA: CALLIGRAPHY.

In premodern China calligraphy and painting had always been considered sister arts, inti-

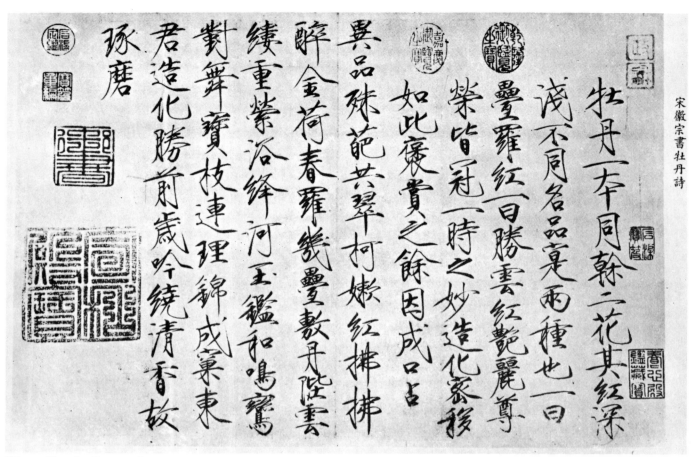

China, calligraphy. Poetry written by the hand of the emperor Hui-tsung, Sung dynasty.

mately linked together because of the employment of identical methods and materials. The work of a famous painter could be prized as much for the inscription in his hand accompanying the work as for the aesthetic qualities of the pictorial representation, and the collecting of specimens of calligraphy was pursued with as great a vigor as the search for examples of painting. In general, however, calligraphy has had a much longer history and a wider base of appeal than painting, for its utilitarian aspects meant that it was more commonly encountered in all its forms than its sister art. Calligraphy was one type of art that could be practiced by many and was held in high esteem as a symbol of learning and as an aesthetic delight. Painting, by contrast, was considered a skill belonging to the artisan until almost the 5th century A.D.

The differences between Chinese and Western calligraphy are considerable. In the Western world the basis for admiration of writing can rest on the qualities of touch and style in a manner analogous to the situation in China. But the alphabet script is limited in its appearance, and, since words are formed of linear combinations of basically few elements, there is little visual interest as such in the structure of a particular word. In Chinese writing, on the other hand, each character constitutes an entity, designed to fit visually into the confines of a square, conceived as a total independent unit. Each separate character in the vocabulary of Chinese thus becomes an individual problem of

design, although the various strokes occur in similar combinations among groups of characters. The pattern of strokes must, of course, have intellectual meaning, but the basic visual appeal is of a magnitude hardly approached in Western calligraphy.

Calligraphy as an art in China extends back in time to the latter half of the 2d millennium B.C. and can be traced through inscriptions on bones, shells, and bronzes. The Chinese script, based originally on pictographs, developed into a highly organized system of writing in which brush and ink were employed and some principle of design observed. The early script is broadly categorized under the term *chüan-shu*, sometimes referred to as archaic or seal script. There are variations in the style of the archaic form of early characters, but in general the script may be described as very linear, with lines of even thickness and great clarity. The pictographic nature of the script is detectable at times, but by the 1st millennium B.C. new characters that reveal the process of stylization and abstraction had come into being. The archaic form of script is still used in modern times on seals (something in the manner of the Western monogram) and occasionally is practiced for calligraphic purposes.

In the 2d century B.C. a simplified and speedier style of rendering characters called the *li-shu* (clerical script) was developed, and it is from this script that the modern Chinese characters directly evolve. In the *li-shu* the strokes making up the character vary in width and end with broad flourishes or rough, jagged ends. In other words, the nature of the brush handling becomes quite visible. The *li-shu* became the accepted script in the Han dynasty (206 B.C.–A.D. 221) and remained preeminent to the 4th century.

From the *li-shu* emerge three basic variations. The first of these is called *k'ai-shu*, or "regular" (official) script, featuring sharp corners and clear lines of varying thickness. *K'ai-shu* can be considered a stylized offshoot of *li-shu*, more graceful and formal in appearance. Eventually *k'ai-shu* provided the model for printed characters. By the 5th century A.D., *k'ai-shu* had completely supplanted *li-shu*, and classic examples of the *k'ai* style can be found in Buddhist inscriptions of this period. Connected with the rise of *k'ai-shu* is the most celebrated of all Chinese calligraphers, Wang Hsi-chih (321–379), who reputedly had a great deal to do with an important modification of the *k'ai-shu* script. This modification resulted in the style called *hsing-shu*, or running script, a cursive style in which the angular nature of *k'ai-shu* is replaced by a fluid movement of the brush, strokes blending together to produce a powerful rhythmic effect. The inception of this cursive style is not historically certain and the borderline between *k'ai* and *hsing* is not always clear, but by the 7th century both had been firmly established as the norms.

The final variant of the clerical script is commonly called *ts'ao-shu*, or "grass writing." This is a very abbreviated and at times virtually illegible style of executing characters. Complicated characters can be reduced to a single scrawling movement of the brush, and the ends of strokes can have great variations. Subtle modulations of strokes are of utmost importance in this style. The distinct flavor of *ts'ao-shu* comes through its highly charged expressive effects, its personal and private connotations giving a more random quality to this script than that of the others. It is not all clear when the *ts'ao-shu* method came into being, but its origin is undoubtedly related to developments in *hsing*; indeed, all three of the major variations of *li-shu* can be seen as closely related, showing shifts of degree from the clerical script rather than differences in kind.

The great names in calligraphy are numerous in Chinese history. The periods of greatest florescence of calligraphy as an art are considered to be the T'ang dynasty (618–906) and the Sung period (960–1279). In the T'ang the names of Ou-yang Hsün (557–641) and Ch'u Sui-liang (596–658) stand out for their general excellence in all forms of script. The emperor Ming-huang was himself an excellent calligrapher, and imperial patronage of calligraphy as an art resulted in the numbers of major masters in this area of visual expression. In the Sung dynasty the high esteem in which this art was held led to the collecting and preservation of ancient specimens of calligraphy, as well as continued minor refinements. The emperor Hui-tsung, for example, developed a refined style of *k'ai-shu* that clearly echoes the precise and exquisite touch found in his paintings. The relationship between painting and calligraphy became quite close in the Sung period, and masters such as Su Shih and Mi Fu evolved the literati theory of painting partly through the recognition of the close interrelationship of the two arts. Both of these men were as well known (perhaps better known) for their calligraphy as for

their paintings. *See* HUI-TSUNG; MI FU; SU SHIH. *See also* WEN-JEN-HUA.

With the emergence of the literati theory and its eventual dominance, painting and calligraphy became more and more the proper pursuits of the scholar class. The later history of Chinese art is liberally sprinkled with names of great painter-calligraphers: Chao Meng-fu in the Yüan dynasty, Wen Cheng-ming and Tung Ch'i-ch'ang in the Ming period, and Chin Nung in the Ch'ing dynasty, to mention only a few. On another level, the many handbooks of calligraphy published in the later centuries provided a broad base, allowing students to follow an ancient style or to make even more individual and personal changes. The art remained a constantly vital one up to perhaps the introduction of the modern fountain pen into China. *See* CHAO MENG-FU; CHIN NUNG; TUNG CH'I-CH'ANG; WEN CHENG-MING.

BIBLIOGRAPHY. L. Driscoll and K. Toda, *Chinese Calligraphy*, Chicago, 1935; Lin Yutang, "The Aesthetics of Chinese Calligraphy," *T'ien Hsia Monthly*, I, December, 1935; Chiang Yee, *Chinese Calligraphy*, London, 1938; L. Sickman, ed., *Chinese Calligraphy and Painting in the Collection of John M. Crawford, Jr.*, New York, 1962.

MARTIE W. YOUNG

CHINA: CERAMICS. The ceramic wares of China that so charmed and delighted European audiences from the 17th century on were the products of a rich and stable tradition in this branch of art, going back some 4,000 years to the earliest settlements in the great Yellow River Valley. The conditions for fine pottery have existed almost since the dawn of China's history: settled living conditions and easy access to all types of clays. As a result China has enjoyed a preeminent position in the technical excellence and aesthetic standards of her pottery for the greater part of recorded history. By the 8th century A.D. China's reputation in this field extended well beyond her national borders. Chinese ceramics of this period have been found from Egypt east to Japan, including great areas of the South Pacific, as testimony to the great esteem given to the high-fired vitrified wares synonymous with the term "china" even today.

A high technical level of pottery making already existed in the dim past of neolithic China. The spectacular finds of the Yang-shao culture in northern China made by the Swedish archaeologist J. G. Andersson in 1921 moved the dates of the earliest Chinese pottery back to the period from 3000 to 2200 B.C. This decorated red pottery discovered by Andersson employed geometric designs of great variety and quality. The Yang-shao culture went through several apparent stages, seemingly having been widespread over northern China. It was succeeded by the Lung-shan culture, the name of which is taken from the type site in Shantung Province. The pottery from this period, also referred to as the "black-pottery" culture, was undecorated, thinly potted, and hard-baked, with a remarkably fine lustrous surface. This culture was widespread along the northern coastal areas of China and dates from about 2500 B.C. to the beginnings of the Shang dynasty. The advent of Shang culture is not definitely fixed in time, but there is little doubt that as the Chinese emerged into this first historical dynasty their pottery had reached a refined stage and preliminary experiments with feldspathic glazes as well as some high firing of wares with kaolin had begun.

For the following period of Chou rule (ca. 1027–256 B.C.) developments in pottery art are not as yet clearly defined, most of what is known resembling closely Shang wares. In the later Chou period (5th cent.–256 B.C.) the general exuberance of decoration found on lacquer products and inlaid bronze vessels also appears in pottery, which is painted with broad designs, either geometric or of figures, in strong colors. From about the 2d century B.C. to the T'ang dynasty (618) lead glazing was developed, perhaps being derived from the Middle East. Also, a high-fired stoneware was produced in the ancient Yüeh district of Chekiang Province. The green-glazed stoneware from this area resembles in shape the bronze vessels of the period, and the restricted vocabulary of design also is closely related to the metal art. The Yüeh kilns continued to be active through the T'ang dynasty, but by the 7th century other types of pottery had been developed in competition, and the full florescence of pottery as an art was under way. *See* YUEH WARE.

Much of the visual evidence for the "golden age" of T'ang comes to us today in the form of pottery remains, for not much of the painting and virtually none of the architecture of this great period are left. Buddhist sculpture gives us examples of the spiritual achievements of the artists of the age; pottery tells us something of their secular concerns and preoccupations. A great deal of the T'ang ceramic industry was devoted to producing tomb figures of every type. The best-known glaze of the T'ang period was the famous *san-tsai*, or "three-color," ware, in which amber, green, blue, and yellow appear over a white slip. The glazes are allowed to intermix and run freely, sometimes over an incised design on the clay. In addition to the funerary figures, the T'ang potters produced a variety of wares for utilitarian uses; the shapes are powerful and virile, sometimes being influenced by the extensive contact with foreign sources in this period. Some of the ewers, in particular, seem to have derived directly from Middle Eastern metal shapes, and impressed rosettes and other exotic Western designs appear frequently on pottery bodies. The production of high-fired stoneware in the T'ang dynasty reached considerable proportions, supplying the outside world with works of great technical skill. *See also* T'ANG FIGURINES.

The development of true porcelain in all probability occurred in the T'ang period. The porcelain ware known as Hsing (after the name of the district in Hopei Province) is recorded in literature of the 9th century. Fine hard white porcelains were exported to Samarra and might be identified with early products of the famous porcelain kilns at Ting-chou in Hopei Province, a site that flourished in the following period. *See* PORCELAIN.

The pottery of the Sung dynasty (960–1279) has often been referred to by Chinese and Westerners as the great classic pieces. By this time the production of translucent porcelains had reached great technical refinement, and both shaping and glazing take on tremendous sophistication. A variety of distinct wares emerges in the Sung, some two dozen types having been identified by Chinese in their standard sourcebooks, the *T'ao-shu* and *T'ao-lu*.

Of the many types of wares associated with the Sung the styles known as Ting, Lung-ch'üan, and Chün have gained common acceptance. All three are the names of

China, ceramics. Female figure, T'ang dynasty. Victoria and Albert Museum, London.

famous pottery districts connected with a special kind of ware. *See* CHUN WARE; LUNG-CH'UAN WARE; TING WARE.

Other names attached to Sung ceramics, however, may refer to the quality of a glaze; for example, the well-known celadon glaze refers to the olive green produced by iron oxides and was probably produced over many areas of northern China and Korea (hence the term northern celadon). The type of ware called Chien by the Chinese refers to the location in northern Fukien Province that first specialized in tea bowls (the ware is called Temmoku by the Japanese), but the characteristic black–dark-brown glaze connected with these tea bowls was also found in northern kilns in Hopei and Honan. Even more mystifying are the ceramics described as *ch'ing-pai* or *ying-ch'ing*, a recent term coined to match the color of glaze and translated as "blue white" or "shadow blue." Where these particular wares were produced in China is not certain, although there seems little tendency to question their Sung date. *See* CELADON, NORTHERN; TEMMOKU; YING-CH'ING.

Although there is still considerable confusion over the precise classification and terminology of Sung ceramics, the general stylistic characteristics of pottery from this great age are fairly distinct. The glazes are monochromatic (that is, the coloristic effects are achieved through the single glaze alone) and are usually quite subdued. Shapes are kept simple and dignified yet have a rich variety and compelling beauty. The clarity and precision of much of Sung pottery seems to echo on a lower level the great developments in the nobler arts of painting and calligraphy.

The history of post-Sung ceramics mainly centers on the new techniques of underglazing and overpainting with enamels. The greatest single triumph of technique was that of underglazing with cobalt blue, begun in the Yüan dynasty about the early 14th century. In the Ming period (1368–1644) an imperial factory was established at the site of Ching-te-chen in Kiangsi, and this remained one of the great centers of ceramic industry to the 19th century. The underglazed blue-and-white wares were the basic product of this flourishing kiln site. Various modifications were made in this basic technique throughout the long relatively peaceful Ming period, and it is common to speak of various imperial reigns in tracing and classifying the many subtle changes made in wares of these later centuries. Porcelain completely supplanted earthenware and stoneware (both had been produced throughout the Sung), and the ceramic industry reached such gigantic proportions that much of the individual quality of Sung pieces was lost in the standardization and mass-production process. However, fine wares were produced, many of them to find their ultimate destination in the imperial collection. *See* BLUE-AND-WHITE; CHING-TE-CHEN.

Of the great variety of later Chinese ceramics brief mention can be made of only a few principal types: blue-and-white, marked with a wealth of painted motifs ranging from human figures to geometric floral decorations, dominated; but along with it came polychrome pieces of equal technical refinement. The reign of Ch'eng-hua (1465–87) saw several innovations in the polychrome enamels, sometimes in combination with underglazed blue-and-white. Large ceramic items also began to appear in the Ming: garden seats and huge, imposing vases. At the same time small exquisite cups and bowls were produced, testifying to the range of activity and complete assurance of the Ming potter. *See* TOU-TS'AI; UNDERGLAZE RED.

In the Ch'ing dynasty (1644–1912) the finest pieces were still made for the Imperial Palace, but blue-and-white continued to be produced in great quantities for export, as it had been throughout the Ming. Enameled wares became increasingly popular, however, and finally replaced blue-and-white in favor. The two great reigns associated with Ch'ing ceramics are those of K'ang-hsi (1662–1722) and Ch'ien-lung (1736–96). During the reign of K'ang-hsi the type of enameled porcelain called *famille verte* in the West was turned out in great numbers. At the same time that these highly decorated enameled works were being developed, monochromatic wares continued, depending now on refinements of clear colors, oxblood and apple green among others. *See* FAMILLE-GROUP PORCELAINS; K'ANG-HSI WARE. *See also* CLAIR DE LUNE; CRACKLE AND CRACKLEWARE; EGGSHELL PORCELAIN; SWATOW WARE.

BIBLIOGRAPHY. B. Rackham, "The Earliest Arrival of pre-Ming Wares in the West," *Transactions of the Oriental Ceramic Society*, III, 1923–24; L. Bachhofer, "Characteristics of T'ang and Sung Pottery," *The Burlington Magazine*, XV, 1934; B. Leach, *A Potter's Book*, London, 1940; W. B. Honey, *The Ceramic Art of China and Other Countries of the Far East*, London, 1945; G. Sayer, *Ching-tê-chên T'ao lu*, London, 1949; S. Jenyns, *Later Chinese Porcelain*, London, 1951; *Sekai Toji Zenshu* (Ceramic Art of the World), vols. X–XII, Tokyo, 1951–56; B. Gray, *Early Chinese Pottery and Porcelain*, London, 1953; H. Garner, *Oriental Blue and White*, London, 1954; G. Gompertz, "Some Notes on Yüeh Ware," *Oriental Art*, II, 1956; J. Pope, *Chinese Porcelain from the Ardebil Shrine*, Washington, D.C., 1956; W. Willetts, *Chinese Art*, vol. 2, Harmondsworth, 1958.

MARTIE W. YOUNG

CHINA: INK. In both painting and calligraphy the quality of the ink used is of primary importance, and from the earliest times the Chinese have expended great care in making their inks. The Chinese word *mo* refers to black carbon mixed with glue, a mixture that was in use as early as the 3d century B.C. The carbon for early inks was drawn from a variety of natural sources, including petroleum derivatives. In later periods wood soot was the most common source for lampblack, pine soot traditionally being accorded the place of highest esteem since it yielded an exceptionally rich lustrous ink. However, artists of the later periods had individual preferences, some using oil as the base for lampblack since it gave a lacquerlike quality to the ink. In many instances artists made their own inks to suit their particular needs.

Whatever the source for black, the ratio of glue to carbon was usually maintained at 2 to 1, the whole mixture being formed into sticks or cakes that were often elaborately ornamented and were minor works of art in themselves. The art of ink-cake manufacture reached its zenith in the Ming dynasty (1368–1644), when elaborate illustrated catalogs were published by manufacturers. Chinese collectors have long cherished old ink sticks, and in the Ming period it was possible for an artist to obtain prized Sung-dynasty ink.

The ink stick was ground on an abrasive surface of bronze, stone, or pottery and was mixed with water to the desired consistency. The ink slabs were also minor works of art, and from ancient times collectors have highly valued them as well as antique specimens of actual ink.

BIBLIOGRAPHY. C. C. Wang, "Notes on Chinese Ink," *Metropolitan Museum Studies*, III, December, 1930; R. H. van Gulik, *Chinese Pictorial Art as Viewed by a Connoisseur*, Rome, 1958.

MARTIE W. YOUNG

CHINA: JADE. Jade has been cherished and worked in China from the prehistoric age to the present; in fact, the continual and persistent preoccupation with this material is a marked feature of Chinese cultural history. The usage and purpose of jade have changed through the centuries from utilitarian neolithic tools to ritual emblems and to objects of personal adornment, but jade has always retained the status of an uniquely precious stone invested with symbolic and mystical properties. The modern Chinese language still contains a reflection of that attitude: a "jade girl" is a lovely one; a "jade heart" is pure; a talented, brave, and handsome young man is a "tree of jade."

The Chinese term for jade is *yü*, which actually refers to any very hard and finely grained stone that will take a high polish, such as agate, quartz, and serpentine. In the West only two minerals, nephrite and jadeite, are considered jade, but neither of these is found in China proper. Nephrite, the mineral worked since the prehistoric age, came from the rivers and mountains of eastern Turkestan and Siberia. The Yüeh-chih (Yuechi) tribe seems to have been the intermediary that brought it to China in the form of river pebbles and boulders or of blocks crudely mined from mountain veins. Jadeite, not used in China until the 18th century, was imported from Burma through Yünnan. Both materials are found in an almost infinite range of colors, with black, white, grays, browns, and greens predominating. Jadeite is often more vivid and glassy in appearance, but the only reliable way to differentiate between the two minerals is by X-ray diffraction.

In the Neolithic period jade was the material par excellence for implements used in grinding or for sharp-edged tools and weapons. It was, however, never an ordinary material, and excavated specimens are not numerous. No doubt this rarity, combined with its qualities of color, lustrous surface, translucence, and sonority, helped create the ritual and metaphysical significance that it soon acquired.

The early Chinese considered jade to be of supernatural origin and to contain the essence of life, virtue, and eternity. Confucius says it is endowed with the virtues of charity, integrity, wisdom, and justice; that it is a white rainbow, a thing of heaven; that it is also of earth because it emanates from mountains and streams; and that it is of the way of virtue because everyone honors it.

From the earliest historical period, the Shang, certain insignia were made of jade. These emblems, forbidden to be sold on the general market, were used by the rulers to communicate with the heavenly powers and were conferred on feudal princes as a symbol of rank and authority. The names of the ceremonial jade emblems and notes on their usage are given in the early classic texts, but unfortunately the descriptions of the objects were made later by commentators in the Han period after the rites themselves had changed or disappeared.

The emblems used in the Shang and Chou periods and somewhat less extensively in the Han are the *kuei*, an oblong flat blade or scepter; the *ts'ung*, a tube squared on the outside with the inner cylinder projecting slightly from the top and bottom; the *chang*, which is a half *kuei*; the *pi*, a flat disk with a center opening; the *huang*, a half *pi*; and the *hu*, described as being in the design of a tiger. Also of a ritualistic nature are the jade weapons: axes, daggers, knives, and spearheads, either in miniature form or so thin and finely worked that their purpose is obviously symbolic, not functional.

The ceremonial jade most frequently mentioned in the texts is the *kuei*, the insignia of the ruler, perhaps the symbol of his right to rule. Feudal princes in recognition of his mandate may offer a *kuei* to the emperor and a *chang* to the empress. The emperor uses the *kuei* to render homage to the east and in certain sacrificial ceremonies. When an envoy is sworn in for an official mission, he is given a *kuei* and must present himself at the foreign court or outpost with this jade tablet, evidently serving as his credentials, in his hand.

The *pi* is a jade disk with a perforation half the width of the rim. It is generally referred to as a symbol of heaven but has other ceremonial uses and is a principal token of enfeoffment. In the Chou wars between feudal states a vanquished prince had to surrender this emblem to the victor. One form of the *pi* disk with three or four evenly spaced serrated areas around the rim is thought to be an astronomical instrument, since the stars of the constellation Ursa Major can be neatly aligned along the toothed notches of the disk.

Other jade rings, the *yüan*, with a perforation double the width of the rim, and the *huan*, with perforation and rim of equal width, were used in some sacrificial ceremonies connected with the fertility of the soil but were chiefly prized tokens and gifts awarded for loyalty and service.

The *huang*, rarely mentioned, is said to have been used in worship of the north. The *ts'ung* is a symbol of earth, of the male principle, and of fertility. There is some evidence that it may also have had an astronomical use as a sighting tube in connection with the notched jade disk.

Burial jades. The Taoist philosophers taught that jade, when swallowed under certain physical and ritual conditions, could prevent the decay of the body and even produce immortality. If this result was not easily evident to the population, the number of jades excavated from graves would suggest that at least many persons supported the theory that by blocking all the passages of the body with pieces of jade the corpse could be preserved from disintegration. Tubes, plugs, and eye covers were made expressly for this purpose.

The mouth amulet is the most common burial jade and goes back to Shang, perhaps, and certainly to pre-Taoist early Chou. The usual form is that of a cicada, which because of its seemingly mysterious appearance from the earth after a long subterranean existence became the symbol of resurrection.

One item of unknown use that frequently appears in Han graves is a pair of stylized and blocky pigs. They are considered to have been held in the hands, placed under the armpits, or used as shroud weights, but there is no actual archaeological evidence to provide support for any of these theories.

Complete sets of burial jades are rare and are not found before Han. Very often such jades are calcified or stained by contact with the corpse.

The great ceremonial jade emblems were not made for funeral use, but from Shang times on they were frequently buried with the corpse of a nobleman. The texts cite the

China, jade. Openwork perforated disk, with intertwined dragons, Six Dynasties. British Museum, London.

position in which each object should be placed in relation to the body, but excavations have not revealed much concordance.

Pendants and amulets. The texts frequently mention girdle ornaments of jade. These small objects were suspended from the belt of a courtier, and when he moved they chimed together with clear bell-like notes to remind him of the way of virtue. Other pendants hung from the ceremonial headgear, were sewn to the bonnet as a sign of rank, were worn as amulets, or were used as coiffure ornaments.

Unlike the great emblems that were conferred officially and used only for purposes of state or court appearances, the small jades were less sacred and might be types of medals, gifts between friends, or good-luck tokens. One must remember that even in objects that might be classed as personal ornaments a mystical significance was inherent in the mineral itself.

The usual form of these pendants and amulets is either miniature weapons, knives, axes, or daggers (probably rank or fealty symbols) or stylized animals, birds, or fishes. Much of the iconography of the latter type has been explained by Florence Waterbury. The tiger, for example, one of the earliest symbols, is a protective animal for an agricultural people because it kills rabbits, boars, and other pests that could destroy the crops. Birds, the only creatures that can soar into the sky, are the messengers to the spirits, the link between heaven and earth. Fish are

a symbol of fertility and abundant harvest. Fish (*yü*) may also have been a pun for jade (*yü*), as were deer and prosperity (*lu*) and bat and happiness (*fu*). Composite or fantastic animals such as the *kuei*, a one-footed, feline creature, or the well-known dragon are often found, and there are occasional representations of human figures or anthropomorphic deities. Other early objects of jade include handles, sword furnishings, finials and appliqués, cups and cup stands, belt buckles, and items of jewelry.

Post-Han jade. During the period of widespread Buddhism after Han, the sacred and ceremonial role of jade was greatly diminished, although it never entirely lost its hallowed significance and certainly none of its aesthetic appeal. Jades made in the Wei, Sui, and early T'ang periods are mainly bowls, cups, jewelry, ornaments, animal figurines, and decorative pieces. Strong animal forms, famous for their freedom of movement, were also produced in the T'ang period.

Scholarly interest in the archaic age reappeared in the Sung dynasty, and with it came archaistic imitations or re-creations in jade of Shang and Chou bronzes or interpretations of the ritual emblems based on the imaginative Han descriptions. Original work of great charm and vigor can also be found, particularly in objects for the scholar's desk: deeply carved brush holders, waterpots, and small sculptures. The sculptures, used as paperweights or to hold down the end of an unrolled scroll, were also meant to inspire the scholar by the feel of their lustrous surface or their symbolism.

From this period through the 19th century artisans worked the beautiful and intractable material into *objets d'art* of nearly incredible virtuosity: eggshell-thin bowls, intricate scepters, jewelry, complicated incense burners, jars, and ornaments. These were costly gifts, cherished possessions, and great prizes for the collectors of both East and West in the 18th, 19th, and 20th centuries.

See also JADE.

BIBLIOGRAPHY. P. Pelliot, *Jades archaïques de Chine, appartenant à M. C. T. Loo*, Paris, Brussels, 1925; A. Salmony, *Carved Jade of Ancient China*, Berkeley, 1938; Huang Chün, *Ku Yü T'u Lu*, 4 vols., Peiping, 1939; S. H. Hansford, *Chinese Jade Carving*, London, 1950; S. Jenyns, *Chinese Archaic Jades in the British Museum*, London, 1951; A. Salmony, *Archaic Chinese Jades from the Edward and Louise B. Sonnenschein Collection*, Chicago, 1952.

ELIZABETH LYONS

CHINA: LACQUER. The sap of the lacquer tree (*Rhus vernicifera*) has been used extensively by the Chinese since earliest times. Among the ancient literary reference to lacquer is the Book of Songs (*Shih-ching*), compiled between 800 and 600 B.C., in which lacquer is mentioned in connection with the decoration of musical instruments. The *Chou-li*, a compilation of rituals dating from the later Chou dynasty, records the use of lacquer in the decoration of a variety of implements, and the excavations at Ch'angsha, Chin-ts'un, and elsewhere confirm the wide usage of lacquer as a method of both decorating and preserving wood, leather, and other materials in the pre-Han period. *See* CH'ANG-SHA.

The lacquer tree (*ch'i-shu*) is native to China's southern and central provinces and is today also found in Korea and Japan. The trees are tapped in summer to obtain the white resinlike sap, which turns to gray and then black when exposed to air. After the sap has been boiled and strained to reduce moisture and remove impurities, the juice is ready for use and is applied with a brush or a spatula. A wide range of colors is obtained by the addition of coloring agents to lacquer in the fluid state, crimson (from cinnabar) and deep black (from iron oxide) being the most common colors in early Chinese lacquer.

The unique properties of lacquer made it an ideal substance for a variety of purposes. Lacquer is almost impervious to water and was found by the Chinese to be excellent for coating almost any surface. Excavations in Lolang, Korea, revealed tombs that had been under water for centuries, yet the lacquered objects contained in the chambers dating to the Han dynasty were in an almost perfect state of preservation. In the fluid state lacquer could be brushed on almost any material and was widely used to coat war gear as a utilitarian device to protect against rot as well as to give a dazzling decorative surface to basketwork or wood. When dried and hardened, lacquer could be carved or engraved with considerable precision, and it also could be inlaid with precious stones or ivory to create particularly stunning surface effects.

The history of lacquer art in China is still not very well known, and many gaps in the chronology remain to be filled. The extensive finds at Ch'ang-sha, Chin-ts'un, Hui-hsien, and Ku-wei-ts'un provide an adequate testimonial to the state of the art in the late Chou dynasty and suggest that painting in lacquer was the forerunner of later Chinese pictorial art. That the lacquer industry had become widespread in the Han period is indicated clearly by the finds in Lolang, where a Chinese colony existed about the 1st centuries B.C. and A.D. The use of lacquer on common household items points to the development of state factories in China for its manufacture, and the famous painted lacquer basket with portraits of the paragons of filial piety found in Lolang remains one of the most important single examples of Han painting. *See also* CHINA: PAINTING (HISTORICAL DEVELOPMENT: PRE-T'ANG PAINTING).

For the period of some four centuries between the end of the Han and the beginning of the T'ang dynasty, knowledge of lacquer usage in China is nonexistent save for several fleeting remarks contained in literary sources. Lacquers from the T'ang period (7th and 8th cent.), however, have been preserved in the Shōsōin in Japan. A number of very important pieces in this splendid collection, which had been deposited in the precincts of the Tōdaiji in Nara by the widow of the emperor Shōmu after his death in 756, show the high state of the lacquer industry during the golden period of Chinese civilization. It is still a matter of dispute as to whether the many lacquered bronze mirrors and the famous painted and inlaid musical instruments called the *biwa* are actually the work of Chinese workmen in Japan or imported products from Korea. But the skill and level of work in these objects reflect certainly the kinds of lacquer being produced in China during the 7th and 8th centuries.

According to literary sources, carved red lacquer began to appear in some quantity during the Sung dynasty (960–1279), although precise identification of any actual Sung lacquers that correspond to descriptions in Chinese and Japanese sources of the period is still to be made. A few lacquers datable to the Sung period have been found at Chü-lu-hsien in Hopei Province, a site that was destroyed

China, lacquer. Chair lacquered in dark brown and gold, 17th century. Ontario Royal Museum, Toronto, Canada.

by flood in 1108. Most of the lacquers from this site, however, are plain red or black without carving and without the extensive inlay mentioned in literary records. For the subsequent Yüan period (1279–1368) the names of two lacquer artists are recorded as active in the 14th century, indicating that lacquer was prized by collectors and had emerged as a true art form. Few examples of the Sung and Yüan periods have survived.

The majority of existing Chinese lacquers belong to the Ming and Ch'ing dynasties, and a number of inscribed and dated pieces give us a general notion of the development of the art in these centuries. Of the many lacquer techniques practiced throughout the two periods, carved lacquer in particular seems to have been valued. The lacquer was applied thickly and often in different-colored layers so that when it was carved a multicolored line appeared throughout the design. Early-15th-century lacquer, considered by some the finest ever produced in China, had a multitude of floral, animal, and landscape patterns to draw upon. The carving of intricate designs on round or scalloped boxes with close-fitting lids was developed to exceptional heights during the early Ming period and apparently was practiced extensively in many parts of China. Further refinements in methods of carving lacquer were made in the later Ming period, and it is possible to classify carved red lacquer on the basis of the colors employed in the layers and the types of incisions used. Painted and inlay lacquers were made in almost great quantities during the Ming and Ch'ing, but the more fragile nature of these types of lacquer have made for generally poorer preservation than in the case of the huskier multilayered carved lacquers.

The first major exportation of carved Chinese lacquer occurred during the reign of K'ang-hsi (1662–1722), and at that time lacquered screens, which are found in Europe and America in some quantity, became popular. The production of Coromandel lacquer also began at about this time. In the Ch'ing period lacquer was produced in great quantities, but it was not always of high quality. The emperor Ch'ien-lung (r. 1736–96) was particularly fond of ornately worked lacquer, as witnessed by his famous red throne (London, Victoria and Albert). *See* COROMANDEL LACQUER.

BIBLIOGRAPHY. O. Mänchen-Helfen, "Materialien zur Geschichte des chinesischen Lacks," *Ostasiatische Zeitschrift*, XXIII, 1937; R. S. Jenyns, "Chinese Lacquer," *Transactions of the Oriental Ceramic Society*, XVII, 1939–40; F. Löw-Beer, "Chinese Lacquer of the Early 15th Century," *Bulletin of the Museum of Far Eastern Antiquities*, XXII, 1950; F. Löw-Beer, "Chinese Lacquer of the Middle and Late Ming Period," *Bulletin of the Museum of Far Eastern Antiquities*, XXIV, 1952; W. Watson, "Chinese Lacquered Winecups," *British Museum Quarterly*, XXI, 1957; W. Willets, *Chinese Art*, vol. 1, Harmondsworth, 1958; H. Garner, *Ming Lacquer*, London, 1960; K. Herberts, *Oriental Lacquer: Art and Technique*, London, 1962.

MARTIE W. YOUNG

CHINA: PAINTING.

Although other arts of China have been appreciated in the Western world for more than three centuries, Chinese painting has only recently gained comparable recognition. In the opening decades of the 20th century Western students of Chinese art were greatly influenced by the taste of cultivated Japanese scholars, who favored small paintings of birds and flowers, the ink plays of the Ch'an (Zen) Buddhist school, and the romantic Southern Sung landscapes. Only in very recent years has a more catholic view begun to prevail, particularly among scholars and collectors in the United States. (For the correlation of Chinese, Indian, and Japanese Buddhist terminology, *see* BUDDHIST TERMS, CORRELATION OF.)

Another discouraging factor in early studies was the problem of authenticating originals and distinguishing them from later copies and outright forgeries. From the earliest times the Chinese have considered copies—sometimes freely paraphrasing but often closely following the original—not only a proper means for training students but also a legitimate way of perpetuating the style of an ancient master. Even a painter famous in his own right could execute a copy of another master, which would be valued as highly as the original. The fake or imitation done for deception did, however, exist in China as elsewhere. Because of the Japanese influence, Sung-dynasty works (960–1279) were favored in the West, and the number of copies or dubious originals from this period is far greater than that from later centuries. *See* CHINA: PAINTING (COPIES).

The seals and inscriptions that frequently appear on Chinese paintings can be a positive aid to understanding. The inscriptions may represent the opinions of another Chinese, a contemporary of the artist or a later connoisseur. The red seals on a painting might be those of the painter or an early owner and thus furnish a valuable clue to its history. With improved analytical methods and with better research tools such as encyclopedic references for identification of signatures or seals, the study of Chinese painting has made significant progress.

FORMAT, MATERIAL, AND TECHNIQUES

The actual forms of Chinese painting are basically only four: the hand scroll, the hanging scroll, the wall painting, and the album leaf. Only the last two have any relation to Occidental painting forms, and the common easel painting of the Western world was unknown in China.

The hand scroll (widely known by the Japanese term *makimono*) is the earliest in time after the wall painting. The scroll consists of a long horizontal piece of silk or paper that is kept rolled for storage. It is unrolled section by section, moving from right to left, and each section that has been viewed is then rerolled on the right. The paintings were never designed to be seen in their entirety but rather section by section, the painting thus having a definite existence in time and offering the painter exciting possibilities for dramatic compositions.

The hanging scroll (Japanese, *kakemono*), also painted on either silk or paper, was meant for a wall, hung so that the entire composition could be seen at once. Like the hand scroll, however, it was never intended for permanent display but was rerolled and stored. In both cases the painting is backed for strength and is bordered by brocade or other material that is pliable yet strong.

Wall paintings in China are not true frescoes, that is, done while the surface was still partially wet. Wall paintings were executed by the Chinese artist for palaces, temples, and tombs, usually with ink and mineral colors on a thin slip or ground of white clay.

The album leaf has no real parallel in the West. Medieval manuscript illuminations and the familiar artist's sketchbook are comparable only in that they use a book (hence, album) format. Some of the album paintings still extant from earlier periods suggest by their shape that they were originally fans, later mounted into an album for preservation. The scale of the album is a limiting factor not present in the other forms, and the format is most often employed when an intimate kind of scene dictates the small scale.

The surfaces for most Chinese painting consist of silk or paper. Silk was used as early as the 3d century B.C. as a surface for writing and painting and has continued as a popular ground up to the present. There are slight variations in the texture, weight, and weave in the silks used in different periods, but not enough is yet known about this to enable dating on the basis of silk alone. The silk is sized or primed by several means; the most common method beginning in the 10th century was to brush on a mixture of alum and glue and then to rub or to beat the surface until it was suitable for receiving the ink. The relatively high cost in terms of time and energy to prepare silk may have caused the early development of paper as a cheaper substitute. There is evidence that papermaking was practiced by the Chinese during the Han dynasty (206 B.C.–A.D. 221). Paper was made from a range of materials, depending on the locale, hemp and bamboo being quite common. The paper was sized or unsized depending on the effect desired. *See* CHINA: PAPER, SILK.

Colors in Chinese painting resemble Western water colors in consistency and stem from both mineral and vegetable sources. The pigment is suspended in a mixture of fine glue and water. With the exception of paintings in the "boneless method," colors always appear in conjunction with black ink. Ink is manufactured in the form of a solid compressed tablet, formed of pine or oil soot that has been mixed with glue. When ready for use, it is ground on a flat stone and mixed with varied amounts of water, consistency depending on the particular tone desired. *See* BONELESS METHOD; CHINA: INK.

Ink and color or ink alone must be transferred to the painting surface by means of a brush, which resembles in general appearance the water-color brush used in the West. However, Chinese brushes come in a wide variety of shapes and sizes, and any one brush can produce a remarkable range of strokes, wet to dry, fine to blunt. The flexibility that is inherent in the nature of the Chinese brush combined with ink that can be controlled for tonal range results in paintings with the dynamic calligraphic qualities that constitute the unique contribution of the Asian artist. The techniques developed by the Chinese artist are always related directly to the two factors of ink and brush, and the method of painting is the most direct of any in the world. The paper or silk is laid flat on a table, the brush held above vertically. The moment when the loaded brush touches the clean prepared surface for the first time is the moment of truth for the Chinese artist, for once the brush drops (termed by the Chinese *lo-pi*) the painter has made his commitment. There is no opportunity for correction, for preliminary underdrawing that can later be removed. Strength and directness of brushwork, therefore, determine success, and the endless preoccupation with line and all its varied possibilities is intense. Understandably, then, the exploitation of linear effects is more important than other elements such as composition (which can be copied) or accuracy of depiction, and no understanding of Chinese painting is possible without a careful consideration of linear qualities. *See also* TS'UN.

HISTORICAL DEVELOPMENT

In this account the T'ang dynasty is used as an arbitrary dividing line. The T'ang period can be considered the first golden age of painting, the culmination of efforts by the Chinese to develop a branch of art that had its inception almost a millennium earlier.

Pre-T'ang painting. Painting was certainly practiced on some scale in the late Chou dynasty (5th–3d cent. B.C.), as some fragmentary evidence clearly testifies. Brushes have been found at sites near Ch'ang-sha in Hunan Province; and in 1949 a fragment of actual painting on silk was excavated in this region, one of the apparent early centers of painting activity in China. More indirect evidence of the state of the painting art comes from such sources as the bronze ceremonial vessels inscribed with hunting scenes, the numerous ornately decorated lacquer objects from the Ch'ang-sha region, and a few rare painted bronze mirrors such as the example in the Fogg Art Museum, Cambridge, Mass. The pair of shells with painted hunting scenes in the Cleveland Museum of Art preserve some of the vividness of handling that characterizes so much of late Chou art. From such widely varied sources as these it is apparent that late Chou painting was sprightly and energetic in tone. *See* CH'ANG-SHA.

Painting from the Han dynasty (206 B.C.–A.D. 221) also survives only in fragmentary manner, and a great deal must be inferred. Actual examples consist principally of funerary art such as the famous basket with paragons of filial piety painted on the lid and sides excavated some years ago in Lolang, Korea. More recently discoveries have been made in mainland China of tomb paintings dating from the Han

dynasty, the most notable being the tombs at Wang-tu in Hopei Province, where the remarkably well-preserved wall murals depict portraits of governmental officials. Earlier Japanese excavations in Manchuria, near Liao-yang, also revealed mural paintings of some quality in a tomb; these were devoted to the subjects of life, death, and the supernatural. The highly stylized yet fluid figures of animals in the tomb are very closely related in both subject matter and style to other Han dynasty paintings on mirrors and lacquer objects and the engraved or bas-relief tomb tiles from scattered sites within China proper. The best known of these engravings are the stone slabs that make up the offering shrine of Wu Liang, near Chia-hsiang in Shantung Province. The engravings were probably copied from now-lost cycles of wall paintings. The composition and designs of these slabs testify to the skill and imagination of the Han-dynasty artist in the organization of complex subject matter. Other tiles of impressed design from sites in Szechwan furnish further evidence for claiming that the artistic outlook of the Han painter was one of sheer exuberance, his style a consistent one in which the dynamic and moving silhouette prevailed. *See* LIAO-YANG TOMB; WU LIANG TOMBS.

Although the numerous tomb tiles may give us a fairly complete picture of the compositional devices employed by the Han painter, they tell us nothing of his brushwork. Only a few examples of actual brushwork remain from this period, and the most revealing of these are the painted tiles in the Ross Collection of the Museum of Fine Arts, Boston. The very fluid shorthand style used in these tiles speaks for a highly developed sense of painting and the clear beginnings of a calligraphic technique by the end of the Han.

The period of the Six Dynasties (221–589) was one of intellectual and social upheaval; Buddhism was introduced during this time, with profound consequences for the art of painting. Although more paintings are extant from the Six Dynasties period than from the two preceding periods, visual evidence is still far from adequate for a complete understanding. Examples indicate that in the Six Dynasties painting had moved out of its early infancy and, although not yet of age, was reaching a stage of adolescence at least. One of the unmistakable signs of the new growth is the emergence of literature that is directly concerned with painting. The most notable of these early literary sources is the *Ku-hua p'in-lu* of Hsieh Ho, a treatise written at the end of the 5th century in which the author sets forth his famous "six principles" of painting. *See* HSIEH HO; SIX PRINCIPLES OF CHINESE PAINTING.

Related to the development of literature on painting was the lifting of the cloak of anonymity that had enveloped earlier painters. Names that can be attached to a particular style of painting begin to appear, and the artistic personality comes alive. The dominant genius in the period was Ku K'ai-chih, a court painter active in the late 4th century in Nanking. Several copies after Ku K'ai-chih have survived, the most famous being the *Admonitions of the Instructress to the Court Ladies* scroll in the British Museum, London. The painting is certainly a copy of very early date and may be an accurate reflection of Ku's style. The handling of the figures in the scroll contrasts strongly with the Ross tiles just noted. The tendency toward the expressive thickening-thinning line of the late Han seems to have been completely arrested by Ku K'ai-chih, replaced in the *Admonitions* scroll by a firm controlled line of a delicate but even thickness. The graceful and wispy figures delineated by Ku K'ai-chih continue a century later in an exceptionally fine engraving after a painting on a sarcophagus (ca. 525) in the William Rockhill Nelson Gallery of Art, Kansas City, but here the figures are set into a landscape rather than existing against the indeterminate space of blank silk as in the *Admonitions* scroll. About 525 another famous figure painter, Chang Seng-yu, was working in the court at Nanking. He gained considerable attention for his use of a method of chiaroscuro whereby he darkened edges of his contours with bands of ink or color to approximate a relief effect, a method that was also used in Central Asia and India. *See* CHANG SENG-YU; KU K'AI-CHIH.

The link to foreign systems of painting suggested by Chang Seng-yu is further supported at the site of Tun-huang in Kansu Province. The wall paintings decorating the Buddhist shrines at this site are exceptional documents for the study of Six Dynasties painting, and the stylistic changes among the caves show the gradual assimilation and modification not only of the Buddhist religion but also of the style of painting as well. The foreign religion of Buddhism supplied the initial subject matter, and the Central Asian artist greatly influenced the style in the beginning, but both style and subject matter were soon adapted by the Chinese to conform to their own aesthetic-philosophical outlook. *See* TUN-HUANG.

T'ang dynasty (618–906). Chinese civilization reached one of its greatest peaks in the age of T'ang, and the temper of the period is reflected succinctly in painting as well as in the other arts. The literature on painting increases, highlighted by the appearance of what could be termed the first major history of painting, Chang Yen-yüan's *Li-tai ming-hua chi* (847). From these pages a glorious picture of Chinese painting emerges, and giant personalities step onstage to challenge the course of history. The greatest of these masters was Wu Tao-tzu, active in the early 8th century, of whom Chang Yen-yüan speaks in terms so reverent they approach religious awe. Nothing remains of this artist now save some engraved stones that copy several of his figure paintings, but so dominant was his personality that we feel his presence constantly and tend to look for his influence in much of T'ang painting. A slightly earlier but also famous painter, Yen Li-pen, is represented by a well-known scroll in the Museum of Fine Arts, Boston, depicting thirteen emperors. The style retains some aspects of Chang Seng-yu, the scale is still hieratic, and the poses of the figures are stiff and formal, but the faces of the emperors are clearly differentiated. Like that of Ku K'ai-chih, the drawing of Yen Li-pen is firm, the line controlled and of even thickness, but the figures are heavier in their proportions and are no longer ethereal as in the Six Dynasties. The contrast here with the more expressively charged and energetic line of Wu Tao-tzu (as described in the literary sources) is quite notable, enough so that two distinct manners of treating the human figure seem to have characterized T'ang painting. *See* CHANG YEN-YUAN; WU TAO-TZU; YEN LI-PEN.

The polarization of style that is suggested in a comparison between Yen Li-pen and Wu Tao-tzu in figure painting emerges quite clearly in landscape painting. Knowledge again must still depend on scanty evidence, but enough remains so that the main developments seem clear. It is obvious that by the T'ang period landscape painting had undergone some fundamental changes since the time of Ku K'ai-chih, and landscape was no longer treated as a mere adjunct to figure painting. According to Chang Yen-yüan, the great Wu Tao-tzu was also a leading exponent of "pure" landscape painting, but no faint suggestion of his style is left. Rather it is the poet-painter Wang Wei who gives us a more positive point of departure, for he is usually credited with the beginnings of the monochromatic ink landscapes and the *p'o-mo* ("broken-ink") technique. From existing copies after Wang Wei it is clear that this technique depended strongly on a calligraphic linear style combined with a controlled shading for depicting structural masses. About the same time a quite dissimilar manner of treating landscapes developed with the appearance of the blue-and-green style associated with the names of Li Ssu-hsün and his son Li Chao-tao. Their paintings stress meticulous fine lines and bright colors in which blues and greens predominate. This rich polychrome approach differs from earlier coloristic efforts in the total consistency of handling to achieve the effect of a dreamlike wonderland of lushness. The painting that comes closest to catching the flavor of the style ascribed to the Li family is the unsigned work in the Sun Yat-sen Museum in Formosa, which depicts travelers on horseback passing through a mountain gorge, sometimes entitled *Ming-huang's Journey to Shu.* The overwhelming pageantry of this work is indeed a far cry from the poetically conceived landscapes of Wang Wei and his school. *See* BLUE-AND-GREEN STYLE; LI SSU-HSUN; P'O-MO; WANG WEI.

The increasing complexities of Chinese painting can be graphically demonstrated in the development of specialists in various categories of subject matter during the T'ang period. Han Kan, for example, distinguished himself as a painter of horses and was employed in the court of Ming-huang to portray the magnificent imperial steeds. Another court painter, Chou Fang, excelled in the representation of females drawn from the life of the nobility. The tradition for this particular specialization had already been established a generation earlier by Chang Hsüan. The popularity of such specialists in the T'ang is expressive of the age: luxury loving to an extent, always cosmopolitan and urbane. *See* CHANG HSUAN; CHOU FANG; HAN KAN.

Although secular life appears in the paintings of the period, religious painting was not neglected. From all accounts Buddhist paintings were executed in great numbers to decorate the interiors of temples and large meeting halls. All of these have been destroyed, most of them during the violent Buddhist persecutions in 842–845. Tun-huang did survive and remains a principal source of information concerning religious painting of the T'ang. More than half of the wall paintings from this site are T'ang in date, testifying to the flourishing life along the great desert highway to India and the West. The style of Tun-huang painting can be classified as international, being related closely to both India and the Far East. In this connection, supplementary evidence for the development of the international style of both secular and religious art is furnished by the wall frescoes in the temple of Hōryūji, Nara, Japan (now destroyed) and examples of various types of painted objects preserved in the storehouse called the Shōsōin, also in Nara. The paintings here, although in Japan, are closely related to styles current in 8th-century China.

Tenth century. After the fall of the T'ang empire China entered another period of disunity called the Five Dynasties (906–960). This brief period is especially critical for the development of landscape painting. A real sense of turbulence underlies most of the 10th century, yet this period produced some extraordinarily gifted painters and a wide range of output. The elevation of landscape painting to the highest rank in the hierarchy of subject matter was only one of the many developments in the century. Ch'an (Japanese, Zen) Buddhism had its first real repercussions in the Five Dynasties, as witness the unconventional paintings of Kuan-hsiu early in the century and the very spontaneous ink handling of Shih K'o a few decades later. The paintings of these two masters express one side of Ch'an in painting: emphasizing the grotesque, intentionally shocking, they seem to be a direct mocking of the labored, carefully composed icon paintings of traditional Buddhism. A comparison of their works with the British Museum's 10th-century exquisitely painted banner from Tun-huang, *Kuan-yin as Guide of Souls*, states the position of the new emerging Ch'an style emphatically. *See* KUAN-HSIU; SHIH K'O.

The break with T'ang traditions was not so clean-cut as a cursory examination of a few Ch'an paintings might indicate. The artistic climate of the Southern T'ang court at Nanking under Li Yü (937–975) echoed the former glories of the T'ang at its height. The courtly ladies of Chou Fang found another champion in Chou Wen-chü. His charming women, slightly slimmer perhaps than the hefty beauties of Chou Fang, capture something of the atmosphere of forced charm and gentility that dominated a court basking in the long twilight of the T'ang. Other painters at the several southern courts of China chose to develop another new category of subject matter, that of birds and flowers. Among the great 10th-century masters who started to explore the visual possibilities of the smaller realms of nature were Huang Ch'üan, who painted for the court at Szechwan, and Hsü Hsi, who was active in Nanking. Their paintings exploited the notion of seasonal change and the transience of all living things in nature, reflecting perhaps something of the climate of impending doom that must have hung so heavily over these effete courts in the south. *See* CHOU WEN-CHÜ; HSU HSI; HUANG CH'UAN.

The painters of figures, birds and flowers, and Ch'an subjects all made a distinct impression on the 10th century, and their importance for the development of later painting is undeniable. But the lasting influence of the 10th-century masters was most keenly felt in landscape painting. A remarkable triumvirate of painters worked in the northern part of China during this century, producing highly original and significant landscapes, which drew high praise from later painters. In terms of actual remaining examples, however, these men remain mostly shadows today. Ching Hao, the oldest of the group, was active in the first part of the century. The works now attributed to him hardly do justice to his name, but his thoughts on landscape painting are

preserved in a short, beautiful essay called *Pi-fa-chi* (Notes on Brush Method), the first serious discussion of a Chinese painter's attitude toward nature. His younger contemporary and pupil Kuan T'ung is even more of a mystery, and only one painting left today seems to echo dimly his style. An impressive mountain landscape in the Sun Yat-sen Museum has had a long-standing attribution to Kuan T'ung. The towering mountain façade that dominates this painting is bold and startling, as is the compressed flat foreground, and the dramatic contrast between the high rear and low forward planes produces the effect of monumental grandeur that was to become a cliché in some later landscape paintings. The third and youngest member of the landscape group, Li Ch'eng, represents still another stylistic facet of the Five Dynasties. His landscapes were concerned with atmospheric mood, wintry and barren in tone for the most part. He excelled in flat, level views and in depicting the branches of gnarled pine trees with a special kind of stroke said to resemble the claws of a crab. Such enrichments of stroke vocabulary are contributions of many painters in this active period. *See* CHING HAO; KUAN T'UNG; LI CH'ENG.

On the basis of existing evidence it is clear that the northern painters of the 10th century viewed the world in entirely different terms from those of earlier landscapists such as Li Ssu-hsün of the T'ang dynasty. The highly coloristic panoramas of the Li family tradition have been replaced by a greater clarity and simplification stemming from an intense interest in working a few select motifs: a mountain peak, a valley floor, a waterfall, a few species of trees. In the south of China, however, a different manner was developing, under the guiding genius of Tung Yüan, who painted in the Nanking region. The stark, monumental grandeur of Ching Hao and his followers found no equivalent here, but rather it was the well-weathered, grass-covered rolling hills of the southern landscape that were depicted by Tung Yüan and continued by his follower Chü-jan until his departure for the north. But Tung Yüan's technique was just as radical a departure from T'ang traditions, and his very "rough ink" strokes and forms blurred by low-hanging mist elicited considerable praise later for the sheer boldness of handling. *See* CHU-JAN; TUNG YUAN.

Sung dynasty (960–1279). Dynastic divisions are somewhat arbitrary in a discussion of artists of both the Five Dynasties and the early Sung period. The first great phase of landscape painting occupied most of the 10th and 11th centuries, and there is a continuity that has little to do with the transfer of political power. Li Ch'eng, Tung Yüan, and Chü-jan, for example, are often classified as Sung painters. In general, the early Sung painters in the north continued directly the monumental vision of nature created by the earlier painters; so the distinction is not clear or vital. Hsü Tao-ning, a follower of Li Ch'eng, takes us into the Sung by definitely echoing his master's brooding landscape style. The masterful hand scroll by Hsü Tao-ning in the William Rockhill Nelson Gallery of Art, entitled *Fishing in the Mountain Stream*, is a refinement of the Li Ch'eng mode, a marvelous and compelling evocation of the fantastic creations of nature. The consummate master of the heroic vision, however, was Fan K'uan, who in the early decades of the 11th century carried on the powerful and dramatic works of Ching Hao and Kuan T'ung. *The Travelers among Mountains and Streams* by Fan K'uan

China, painting. Ma Yüan, *Solitary Fisherman on the River*, first half of the 13th century. Paint and ink on silk. National Museum, Tokyo.

in the Sun Yat-sen Museum is conceived on a gigantic scale, with its bare mountain cliff rising like a great tower over dark and somber woods, the contrast of the tiny human figures wending their journey in the lower portion adding to the sense of grandeur and magnificence. Fan K'uan was regarded, rightly so we suspect on the basis of this painting, as being the greatest painter of his age by his contemporaries. *See* FAN K'UAN; HSU TAO-NING. *See also* CH'ING-LING.

In the second half of the 11th century there was considerable modification of the simplicity and clarity that are the hallmark of the monumental style. In the hands of Kuo Hsi, the greatest painter among the second wave and considered by some the climactic figure of Northern Sung landscape painting, nature was interpreted in terms equally as broad in scope as in the 10th century, but now the mountain forms are molded into restless moving masses, swallowed by mist, stabbed by flickering light. Trees and temples are reduced to accents within the total configuration of nature, and the view becomes truly macrocosmic. The stately undulating rhythms of Hsü Tao-ning are charged by Kuo Hsi with new perception and a sense of dynamic energy. A comparison of Hsü s *Fishing* scroll mentioned above with Kuo Hsi's *Early Spring* of 1072 in the Sun Yat-sen Museum reveals the change in outlook clearly. There is less of an involvement on the part of Kuo Hsi with the mystery and awesomeness of nature, more of realism tempered by a rather romantic attitude toward the world in general. *See* KUO HSI.

The concern with verisimilitude in the rendering of the visual world is borne out in the writings of Kuo Hsi as well as indicated by his extant paintings. His *Shan-shui hsün* (Remarks on Landscapes), a collection of notes edited by his son, states this concern vividly. The question of realism in painting is insisted upon even more vigorously by the emperor Hui-tsung, who upon his accession to the throne in 1101 issued an edict exhorting painters to truthfulness of form and color. A painter of great talent himself, Hui-tsung led the way for his academy, not by struggling with the immense world of mountains but by immortalizing the small world of birds and flowers, painting them with exquisite precision and a nearly flawless meticulousness of touch. For the next quarter of a century the academy of Hui-tsung produced painters who followed the edict rather closely. Among landscape painters in the academy a decided sense of calmness appears, as exemplified in the low, marshy, tranquil river views of Chao Ling-jan. *See* Chao Ling-jan; Hui-tsung.

About 1100 another group of painters appeared whose concerns were of an entirely different order from those of the academy. Gathered around the great poet and calligrapher Su Shih were a number of painters who were not intent on pursuing the literal recording of the visual world but on capturing the more elusive qualities of mind and spirit. Painters such as Mi Fu, Li Kung-lin, and Wang Shen, among others, executed paintings diametrically opposed to those of the academy. This group denied Hui-tsung's contention that representational value determined artistic quality. They boldly claimed that painting need not depend on skillful handling to achieve true likeness; rather, the inner feelings of the artist and the pure act of creation itself were what mattered. Developed in large part from the close connections between painting and calligraphy, this line of reasoning led to the formulation of the "literati" theories of painting (Chinese, *wen-jen-hua*, meaning "scholar-gentleman painting"). What was important in this view was the power of painting to reveal some facet of the intellectual qualities of the artist. This concept was to have wide ramifications in the later periods. *See* China: Calligraphy; Li Kung-lin; Mi Fu; Su Shih; Wen-jen-hua.

A distinctly different phase of Sung painting begins with the capitulation of Hui-tsung at the capital of K'ai-feng in 1126. Northern China was occupied by the Jurchens; a new capital was set up in the south at Hang-chou. The period of the Southern Sung lasted until the final conquest of all China by the Mongols in 1279. Painting in this period came under the total dominance of the Imperial Academy. The first director of the newly established academy at Hang-chou was an older painter, Li T'ang, who had been active in the former academy at K'ai-feng. The landscapes inaugurated by Li T'ang featured a broad handling and emphasized one type of brushstroke as a unifying device. The "broad ax" stroke (*ts'un*), as it was called, used the side of the brush laid horizontally to produce the effect of a sharply split rock or boulder, and the stroke was immediately adopted into the vocabulary of Southern Sung painters. But changes within the first years of the new academy were not always immediate or profound. A number of painters followed Li T'ang "across the river" to the new court and simply perpetuated the styles they had developed under Hui-tsung. Li An-chung continued painting birds and flowers, Mao I worked on quiet themes of domestic animals, Li Ti imitated Li T'ang in the painting of water buffaloes, and Chao Po-chü turned his attention to re-creating the great events of history in a tight blue-

and-green style. *See* Chao Po-chu; Li An-chung; Li T'ang; Li Ti; Mao I; Ts'un.

It remained for the second generation of Southern Sung artists to produce spectacularly different results, and again the new developments came first in landscapes. The leaders were Ma Yüan and Hsia Kuei, both having joined the academy late in the 12th century. The style they developed was totally different from that of the monumental manner of the 11th century. Their works are characterized by faultless execution, simplicity and gracefulness in placement of forms, and a widespread use of an asymmetrical composition with the corresponding exploitation of empty spaces. Thus came the suggestive "void" that has so often intrigued the Western viewer on first glance. The broad ax stroke of Li T'ang was highly favored by the Ma-Hsia school since it was appropriately suggestive in itself: literal texturing of rocks had no place in their scheme, so the slashes of ink that characterize the ax stroke were used to evoke rather than describe the concrete world. The compositions are correspondingly more intimate, and the fact that the album leaf became one of the more favored forms for the landscape painter is no mere accident. The world of soaring mountain peaks with its concentration on the overwhelming sense of nature has been scaled down to manageable size and veiled in allusions. The tiny and insignificant 10th-century travelers of Fan K'uan, dwarfed as they were by the sheer majesty of the towering cliffs, have been replaced in the Southern Sung by the philosopher-sage sitting in contemplation by a modest-sized boulder or rock. Yet for the Southern Sung audience this intimate and fragmentary glimpse of the world was enough, and in this way the southern artist continued the great dialogue with nature that had typified Chinese painting since the Five Dynasties. *See* Hsia Kuei; Ma-Hsia School; Ma Yuan.

So pervasive was the influence of the academy during the Southern Sung period that little is known about painting outside the court, with the single exception of the Ch'an school of Buddhist painting. The Ch'an temples around Hang-chou produced some truly remarkable painters in the early 13th century. The best known were Liang K'ai, who started his career as an academician but later took up residence in a Ch'an monastery, and Mu-ch'i, a monk who turned to painting. It is misleading to speak of a "Ch'an style" of painting in referring to these men since there is little uniformity to their works. Much of their pictorial language, the basic vocabulary of brushstrokes with which they worked, was drawn from the same sources used by all Southern Sung painters, and in this respect the "unconventional" works of the Ch'an painters are merely the logical and inevitable extension of the methods employed by the Ma-Hsia school. The ink splashes of Ying Yü-chien can be seen as pushing the art of pure suggestion to its furthest limits, where an entire mountain range, village and all, is reduced to a misty blur of ink from which forms appear and disappear. The very real and solid world of the 10th-century masters has been so dissolved that the empty void of Ma Yüan now becomes virtually the entire subject of the Ch'an landscapes. Mu-ch'i, considered the greatest of all the Ch'an painters, did not indulge in the spontaneous ink splash idea to such an extreme but preferred dealing with conventional subject matter cast into new relationships. His famous *Six Persimmons* in the Daitokuji, Kyoto, is not the product necessarily of the "inspired moment" but rather a controlled and studied exercise in formal relationships, suggestive and evocative in the same manner as a Southern Sung academician's landscape but without any of the overtones of nostalgia or romanticism. The art of total expressive suggestion reaches its fruition under the Ch'an masters, never to be equaled in the same way again on Chinese soil. *See* LIANG K'AI; MU-CH'I; YING YU-CHIEN.

Yuan dynasty (1279–1368). The Mongol conquest presented the painters of the academy (and other intellectuals as well) with a serious decision: whether to heed the call to join the court under the khans or retire to private life. One of the greatest of China's painters, Chao Meng-fu, chose eventually to join the new government and take a position, while his famous teacher Ch'ien Hsüan refused and thus remained loyal or "virtuous." But regardless of their political decisions the painters of the first generation of the Yüan period attempted in general to discard the Southern Sung style in theory. Thus a new interest in pre-Sung painting arose, and an archaistic revival of sorts took place. Ch'ien Hsüan looked back to the fine-line style of Li Kung-lin (who had in turn based his style on earlier T'ang models). Chao Meng-fu also evinced more than mere curiosity in the ancient masters with his interpretation of the blue-and-green manner in landscape. Both painters rejected the immediate past, turning to older styles to express this rejection. *See* CHAO MENG-FU; CH'IEN HSUAN.

The aversion to the Southern Sung overtly romantic landscape style is even more marked in the works of the second generation of Yüan painters. Wu Chen took up the life of a recluse in this unsettled age and painted landscapes that seem at times deliberately awkward, as his *Old Fisherman* in the Sun Yat-sen Museum reveals. The mood here is still poetic, but it is poetry of an entirely different order from the skillful presentations of the Ma-Hsia school. The world that Wu Chen depicted was no longer to be seen in such simple and deceptively alluring terms. Even more extreme in the portrayal of bleakness and grimness are the landscapes of Ni Tsan, one of the outstanding and most imitated of all Yüan masters. His influence on later painters was enormous, in part because of the very consistent and unique pictorial devices he used to describe his environment. His sparse style, in which both ink and brushstrokes are kept to the barest minimum, resulted in refined, pristine landscapes totally forbidding and barren of all human warmth. Both Ni Tsan and Wu Chen often accompanied their paintings with poems, which are rich in allusions to the past, and this combination of painting and poetry is fundamental for later centuries of *wen-jen* painting. In the concentration on individual moods, the intellectual position of Ni Tsan and Wu Chen was close indeed to the earlier theories of the literati painters. But other artists of the Yüan exploited the art of painting for other aims. Wang Meng, for example, concentrated on achieving dense effects of surface, and his turbulent, impenetrable landscapes reveal an orientation entirely different from that of Ni Tsan. Huang Kung-wang was also interested in the pictorial surface, but the exuberance of Wang Meng is under better control. Huang Kung-wang gives us a few combinations of elements repeated and manipulated as in a Cézanne, and his paintings such as the *Dwelling in the Fu-ch'un Mountains* in the Sun Yat-sen Museum are examples of studied relationships of lines and planes but are still tied to the visual world in a very real and direct way. *See* HUANG KUNG-WANG; NI TSAN; WANG MENG; WU CHEN.

What is apparent in an examination of Yüan painting is the wide diversity of styles in this short period. The great masters of the Yüan, and there are many, produced distinctly different pictorial effects, and each worked according to his particular temperament, unbound by academic rules. The diversity and individuality are tied together only in the common rejection of the Southern Sung and the search for new expressive possibilities in painting.

Ming dynasty (1368–1644). The very loose bonds that hold the Yüan painters together as a group completely disappear in the following centuries that make up the two long epochs of Ming and Ch'ing rule. The diversification of styles already so apparent in the Yüan accelerates to the point where it becomes implausible to speak of a "Ming style" or "Ch'ing style" as such in painting. There are as many styles in these later centuries as there are great creative painters or centers of activity, and major masters now number in the scores. We can speak now only of individual painters and local schools, not of a unified national style.

A number of painters make the transition from the Yüan to the Ming in painless fashion. Wang Fu and his pupil Hsia Ch'ang, for example, kept part of the literati tradition alive in the face of a new burgeoning Imperial Academy. Among the academicians the names of Lü Chi and his teacher Pien Wen-chin have gained some stature. But the major movement that separates out rather clearly in the early part of the Ming was the group of painters later labeled as of the "Che" school. Tai Chin, considered the founder of the school (which took its name from the region of Chekiang), was an academy painter at first, but his temperament was better suited to the bohemian existence he eventually chose to lead. It was after he had left the academy that many of his best works, devoted to scenes of life on the river, were done. Others who followed his trail in the Che school were content to revive the Ma-Hsia tradition, sometimes with remarkable skill and deftness recapturing the quality and flavor of the Southern Sung. *See* CHE SCHOOL; HSIA CH'ANG; LU CHI; TAI CHIN; WANG FU.

A countermovement to the revival of the Ma-Hsia lyricism can be found in the works of the Wu-school masters (taking their name from the region of Wu-hsing, which includes modern Su-chou). The principles that motivated the Yüan literati painters found a new champion in Shen Chou, a poet-painter of extraordinary refinement of spirit and purity of soul. His paintings are cast in the deceptively casual mold of the true intellectual who shuns all pretense at mere skill, and an element of the awkward is kept in his works. Wen Cheng-ming, his acknowledged disciple and perhaps the true leader of the Wu school, remains for us one of the most talented personalities in Chinese painting: cultivated, sensitive, and a scholar of all the arts, he shows in his paintings shifts of style that are revealing. Behind the façade of self-control he presented to his contemporaries one suspects a sense of turbulence that is strikingly akin to the modern 20th-century temper. *See* SHEN CHOU; WEN CHENG-MING.

Not all painters in the Ming period can be attached so easily to a label of either school or academy. The 16th century in particular was a time of many prodigious talents who defy easy classification. T'ang Yin and Ch'iu Ying, for example, are considered members of the Wu school because they lived in the region. But the styles they pursued seem contrary at times to the basic literati tradition that motivated the majority of Wu-school painters. Ch'iu Ying, especially, demonstrates a skilled mastery of styles and subject matter bordering on the encyclopedic. Both Ch'iu Ying and T'ang Yin, furthermore, were professional painters in that they lived by their art, and both remained essentially uncommitted to any particular theory or school. They were exceptional painters who existed by talent alone among the galaxy of great artists in the area of Su-chou. *See* CH'IU YING; T'ANG YIN.

Toward the end of the Ming period another clear shift of attitudes seems to have taken place. A group of theoreticians centered in the Sung-chiang region around the genius of Tung Ch'i-ch'ang represents the final triumph of the literati tradition. Under Tung and others working in related locations in the 17th century, history and painting become inseparably intertwined. The paintings of Tung Ch'i-ch'ang and his pupils may appear at first glance to be highly formalized works, totally lacking in the comfortably easy identification one makes with paintings in the Southern Sung style. But Tung Ch'i-ch'ang's many studies after old masters of what he termed the "southern school" are almost art-historical studies in a modern sense: they deal with the fundamental qualities of style that distinguish the individual masters of the past. And this was no mere antiquarian's interest on the part of Tung and his followers but rather a seriously conceived and systematically executed total reevaluation of the history and philosophy of painting. *See* NORTHERN AND SOUTHERN SCHOOLS OF CHINESE PAINTING; TUNG CH'I-CH'ANG.

Ch'ing dynasty (1644–1912). Tung Ch'i-ch'ang's intellectual position dominated not only his own age but the following generation of early Ch'ing painters as well. His startling theories became the accepted standard by the time of the "Four Wangs." With these early Ch'ing masters eclecticism is not only accepted, it is adulated. Wang Hui, perhaps the most facile of the four, literally raided the ancient past for his sources. Meanwhile, the academic tradition continued at the court of Peking, producing mostly painters of average ability but occasionally revealing a brilliant master such as Kao Ch'i-p'ei. *See* KAO CH'I-P'EI; WANG HUI. *See also* WANG CHIEN; WANG SHI-MIN; WANG YUAN-CH'I.

In other areas of China painting flourished along entirely different lines, and the centuries of Ch'ing rule witnessed a proliferation of schools: the "Yang-chou eccentrics," the "Four Masters of Anhui," and the "Eight Masters of Nanking." These movements were widely divergent from each other, and even within a given school there was no absolute stylistic consistency. The monk-painter Hung-jen, for example, interpreted Ni Tsan in a novel way and effected fragile, delicately thin landscapes of a unique character. Ch'a Shih-piao, also an Anhui painter, chose to emphasize

the cold, sober side of Ni Tsan with a far more fluid brush than his "colleague" Hung-jen. Among the masters at Nanking a similar diversity of style is evident. Kung Hsien, one of the major figures in this school, painted somber and gloomy landscapes laden with heavy skies. Fan Ch'i, another member, worked in a finer and more meticulous manner to produce exquisitely airy landscapes, entirely opposed to those of Kung Hsien. The tie that binds these men into various schools is a loose one, and it is quite apparent that in these later centuries painters were less and less restricted in the stylistic sense. *See* ANHUI SCHOOL, FOUR MASTERS OF; CH'A SHIH-PIAO; FAN CH'I; HUNG-JEN; KUNG HSIEN; YANG-CHOU, EIGHT ECCENTRICS OF.

The sense of heightened individualism is nowhere better exemplified than in the works of those painters who are usually referred to as the "Great Individualists." The departure from the orthodoxy of the Four Wangs is radical among these painters, and each sought his own particular way to depart. The paintings of Chu Ta are remarkable and highly personal statements, not merely in style but in subject matter as well. His curiously humanized birds and large-eyed animals, painted with a bold brush, are seen in a distinctly bizarre manner, speaking an utterly private message. His landscapes are impulsive, spontaneous creations, as chaotic in their total visual effect as was the mind of the artist. Chu Ta was an impassioned spokesman for individualism in the Ch'ing period. But the supreme master of these gifted individualists was Tao-chi, a Buddhist monk whose opposition to the orthodox tradition is summed up beautifully in his famous statement, "The method of no method is the perfect method." Thus, by professing no allegiance to the past masters, Tao-chi turned to himself to discover a whole new world within. His paintings are not necessarily essays into the subconscious, however, and at times there are a note of humor and nuances of brush control that betray the game he seems to be playing with the ancient masters. *See* CHU TA; TAO-CHI.

What is striking about Chu Ta and Tao-chi, and indeed about other painters of these later centuries who were not necessarily labeled as eccentrics, is the very complexity of their works. These new men do not lend themselves to simplification and universal statements. It is perhaps just this complexity that has made these painters so inaccessible to the Western observer in the past, but in much of their efforts there are striking parallels in Western art.

BIBLIOGRAPHY. B. March, *Some Technical Terms of Chinese Painting*, Baltimore, 1935; K. Harada, *Shina Meigwa Hokan: The Pageant of Chinese Painting*, Tokyo, 1936; Kuo Hsi, *An Essay on Landscape Painting*, London, 1936; S. E. Lee, *Chinese Landscape Painting*, Cleveland, 1954; A. Priest, *Aspects of Chinese Painting*, New York, 1954; L. Sickman and A. Soper, *The Art and Architecture of China*, Baltimore, 1956; O. Sirén, *Chinese Painting, Leading Masters and Principles*, 7 vols., New York, 1956–58; Y. Yonezawa, *Painting in the Ming Dynasty*, Tokyo, 1956; N. Wu, "The Toleration of Eccentrics," *Art News*, LVI, May, 1957; J. F. Cahill, "Ch'ien Hsüan and His Figure Paintings," *Archives of the Chinese Art Society of America*, XII, 1958; R. H. van Gulik, *Chinese Pictorial Art*, Rome, 1958; P. Swann, *Chinese Painting*, London, Paris, 1958; M. Sullivan, *Chinese Art in the 20th Century*, London, 1959; Wang Shih-chien, ed., *Three Hundred Masterpieces of Chinese Painting in the Palace Museum*, 6 vols., Taichung, 1959; J. F. Cahill, *Chinese Painting*, Geneva, 1960; W. Watson, *Archaeology in China*, London, 1960; F. van Briessen, *The Way of the Brush*, Rutland, Vt., 1962; R. Edwards, *The Field of Stones*, Washington, 1962; M. Sullivan, *The Birth of Landscape Painting in China*, Berkeley, Calif., 1962.

MARTIE W. YOUNG

CHINA: PAINTING (Copies). No moral sanction existed in China against copying older masters, as the sixth principle of Hsieh Ho indicates. The Chinese painter frequently, but not always, labeled his copies by one of several terms when he signed the painting. Thus the three terms *mo-fang*, *lin*, and *fang* are often encountered on copies, for example, in the format of X (the painter), *lin* Y (the old master), or some variant of this. *See* SIX PRINCIPLES OF CHINESE PAINTING.

The three terms mentioned indicate degrees of copying, but their exact meaning may not be precisely the same for each artist or in different periods. In general, *mo-fang* (sometimes *mu-fang* or *mu*) means an extremely faithful copy after an old painting, occasionally made by tracing, and is used primarily to preserve the composition of a master. *Fang* refers to a freer interpretation of an antique painting and is usually translated in Western sources as "in the style of" or "in the manner of." *Lin* is perhaps the most frequently encountered term in signatures and appears to mean a more liberal, "freehand" copy of the painting in which the style of the master may be kept with some alterations of handling or composition; it is sometimes translated by the term "after." But the distinction between *lin* and *fang* would seem delicate under the best of circumstances, and the terms might have been used interchangeably, given different shades of meaning at different times. Copies of the *lin* or *fang* class presumably could be executed for purposes of training, as study pieces, but they could also be a form of honor bestowed upon old masters by another master.

What is fundamental to the understanding of Chinese painting is to realize the role of such various copies in preserving so much of the fragile history of painting in China and to distinguish the spirit motivating such works from the less high-minded (but just as frequently encountered) efforts of the forger and faker.

MARTIE W. YOUNG

CHINA: PAPER. As a support for writing and eventually painting, paper was used in China more than 1,000 years before it was known in Europe. It was in use certainly by Han times (2d cent. A.D.), and there is a tradition that a certain Ts'ai Lun invented the material in A.D. 105 as a cheap substitute for expensive silk. The date may be somewhat arbitrary, but other literary sources mention the use of paper at about this time. Some of the papers recovered by Stein in Tun-huang can be dated to at least the early 4th century, if not earlier, and the exceptionally high quality of the Tun-huang samples clearly speaks for a long period of development of papermaking as an art. *See* TUN-HUANG.

Papers of the earliest periods were almost pure rag in content; Ts'ai Lun's papers, for example, were made from linen waste and rag materials. Most of the Tun-huang papers, however, were made from raw fibers rather than waste materials. The pulp for paper varied from region to region, depending on the nature of the supply; hemp, bamboo, mulberry, and rice stalks all have served as sources for fibers. By the time of the Sung dynasty (960–1279) papermaking had achieved some status as an art, with numerous "brand" names known to connoisseurs. By the latter part of the T'ang dynasty (9th cent.) painting on paper had come into general use, perhaps as a natural

China, sculpture. Buddha head, from Yün-kang, Northern Wei dynasty. National Museum, Tokyo.

consequence of developments in the ink monochrome techniques.

Both sized and unsized papers have been used in Chinese painting and calligraphy. The unsized paper, being more absorbent, lends itself to exuberant effects of the brush, but it was more common to employ a sized paper. Sizing was accomplished by adding a hardening agent to the pulp in the liquid stage, a mixture of glue and alum being most widely used. The durability of well-sized papers is attested to by the Tun-huang finds, and at the same time a surprising range of effects can be achieved by the use of sized papers.

BIBLIOGRAPHY. R. H. Clapperton, *Paper: An Historical Account of Its Making by Hand from the Earliest Times to the Present Day*, Oxford, 1934; T. F. Carter, *The Invention of Printing in China and Its Spread Westward*, 2d rev. ed., New York, 1955.

MARTIE W. YOUNG

CHINA: SCULPTURE. The art of sculpture in China is basically religious in inspiration, and the finest examples of Chinese sculpture essentially stem from attempts to embody in concrete form the intangible qualities of great deities, be they Confucian, Taoist, or Buddhist. There is little secular sculpture per se in China. Indeed, the history of Chinese sculpture is closely related to the history of Buddhism, that religion of both infinite compassion and infinite demands for icons. It is no accident that the acknowledged great periods of Chinese sculpture coincide with the florescence of Buddhism on Chinese soil. And since Buddhism was an imported religion, the art of sculpture reflects more clearly than any of the other arts the direct influence of foreign styles. (For the correlation of Chinese, Indian, and Japanese Buddhist terminology, *see* BUDDHIST TERMS, CORRELATION OF.)

GENERAL CHARACTERISTICS

Unlike the arts of painting and calligraphy, sculpture was never accorded a high place in the scheme of things by the Chinese connoisseur. The sculptor remains fundamentally anonymous, tied to the tradition of the craft guilds, submitting his services to the demands of a higher metaphysical order; and his success was not measured in terms of personal glory or identification. It is not surprising, therefore, that taken as a whole Chinese sculpture lacks the impact of some of the other arts where personal style is a major factor.

For the most part Chinese sculpture remains linear and frontal in its orientation, with little of the complexity of plastic form and moving mass that typifies the greatest examples of Indian religious art. Lacking also is the feeling for the inherent quality of materials—the grain of a piece of wood, the granular texture of a block of stone—those tactile sensations that are so pleasurable to the modern observer. But even if Chinese sculpture does not charm the eye in precisely the same manner as do the more sophisticated arts of painting and calligraphy, there are many fine qualities that cannot easily be denied in the Chinese handling of plastic form. Among the great masterpieces of Chinese sculptural art are some of the most brilliantly executed works of any in the world: distinctive and imaginative evocations of spiritual deities, majestic testimonials to the force of religion at certain times in particular places. And among the thousands of lesser votive pieces are many that possess a freshness of concept and a vigor of handling that make them high points in true folk art, meaningful in their historical context yet compelling today.

HISTORICAL DEVELOPMENT

Until the introduction of Buddhism China had little in the way of a consistent sculptural tradition, aside from the magnificent bronze ceremonial implements. *See* CHINA: BRONZES.

Pre-Buddhist sculpture. The Neolithic age is not yet well documented in terms of sculpture, although excavations have yielded a few scattered examples of figure sculpture in clay datable to neolithic cultures. The earliest examples of stone sculpture come from the so-called royal tombs of the Shang-dynasty capital at An-yang. The marble and limestone configurations of animals, both mythical and natural, and the images representing kneeling or seated human beings are all the more remarkable when contrasted with the primitive quality of neolithic attempts to handle plastic form in clay. The incised decorations on the surfaces of these stone pieces are drawn from the vocabulary of the bronze caster, but their massive and powerful character springs from an awareness of both the limitations and the potentials of stone carving. They possess a monumental quality that belies their relatively small size. *See* AN-YANG.

Closely related to the marble carving from An-yang are some small bronzes that must be classified as sculpture. The well-known rhinoceros in the Brundage Collection, San Francisco, for example, is a beautifully modeled sculptural masterpiece although it functioned as a vessel. The surface of this bronze is entirely undecorated, the interest

being centered on the animal itself. It stands as a remarkable example of naturalistic observation in which the ponderous quality of the beast seems perfectly captured, and it testifies to another side of the zoomorphic interest of the Shang peoples.

The sensitivity to three-dimensional forms exemplified in the Shang pieces of marble or bronze disappeared almost as mysteriously as it appeared, for no monumental sculpture of any equal quality appears for more than 1,000 years after the Shang dynasty in China. No trace of stone sculpture has as yet been identified with the immediate successors of the Shang rulers, although the casting of bronze vessels and other metal implements continued without interruption. Why the promising beginnings of marble carving were discontinued under the house of Chou remains an unanswered question. Our knowledge of the art of sculpture during the Chou dynasty rests primarily on the evidence of bronzes: the fine pair of tigers in the Freer Gallery, Washington, D.C., dating from the middle Chou (ca. 900 B.C.); the lively wrestling figures in the Spencer-Churchill Collection, Gloucestershire; and the Mongolian servant in the Museum of Fine Arts, Boston, of later Chou date.

The practice of burying objects in tombs as a substitute for human sacrifices was apparently established during the Chou period. These tomb objects, or *ming-ch'i*, of the Chou dynasty are not of outstanding quality. The controversial Hui-hsien figures are quite lively and indicate a sense of spontaneity and freedom, but they appear rather dubious in date. The best of Chou sculpture comes from the later Warring States period (480–221 B.C.), when sculptors working in the state of Ch'u in central China produced some remarkable wood sculptures for burial purposes. These attenuated, almost totemic, wooden human figures of strongly stylized design have been excavated in large numbers from Ch'ang-sha. Closely related to these Ch'ang-sha pieces are the monster masks of animals with long protruding tongues and deer antlers from the site of Chang-t'ai-kuan in Honan. The lively and expressive qualities of such examples of Ch'u-state sculptures supply us with a pocket of creativity in an otherwise rather undistinguished sculptural period. *See* CH'ANG-SHA.

What could be termed the first major effort at monumental stone sculpture after the period of An-yang is also related to a tomb: the monument at the tomb of General Ho Ch'ü-ping (d. 117 B.C.) at Hsin-p'ing in Shensi Province. Standing outside the tomb is a large carved boulder representing a horse trampling the prostrate form of a human warrior between his legs. Iconographically the reference would seem to be to the conquest of the barbarian tribes by the famous Han general, but the combat motif also echoes the earlier Shang-dynasty concern with animals and men. The horse is barely disengaged from the gigantic boulder, and the whole seems to be less three-dimensional sculpture than two reliefs pressed together. Despite the crudity of the carving there is still something powerful and impressive in the concept. The other carved boulders at this tomb are no more than barely incised reliefs, conforming to the shape of the rock; again the combat motif dominates the stones scattered about the tomb. *See* HO CH'Ü-PING, TOMB OF, HSIN-P'ING.

The stone monuments from the Later Han Dynasty (25–221) are more numerous, consisting principally of tomb pieces from Szechwan and Shantung provinces. The mythical tigerlike creatures with wings and horns, sometimes called chimaeras, are sturdy, bulky works that reveal the blocklike character of the stone from which they were hewn. They too appear to be less plastic in concept than like freestanding reliefs, but the quality of execution is more polished than the performance at Ho Ch'ü-ping's tomb. The relief type of sculpture is also to be seen on the various pillars that marked the so-called spirit road that led to the burial mounds. The best of these are the Pillars of Shen in Szechwan, notable for the beautiful low reliefs on the shafts that depict the creatures of the four directions. The upper portions of the pillars, by contrast, are carved in very high relief in imitation of tiled roofs. The atlantean-type figures on each of the four corners of the pillars seem almost to function as visual supports for the architectural mass of the roof. They are solidly conceived full-bodied forms, quite at variance with the usual linearization that is typical of Han art in general. The numerous impressed tomb tiles from the same areas of Szechwan and Shantung, on the other hand, appear to capture the real spirit of the Han age: dynamic, moving silhouettes that dance across the surface. These bas-reliefs of Han date are less sculptural than painterly in concept, and many of the conventions used relate more immediately to the art of painting. *See* SHEN, PILLARS OF.

The clay figurines from Han tombs are abundant: men and animals, models of boats, houses, rice fields. The exuberance of this outpouring matches the lively character of the bas-reliefs that formed the inner walls of the chambers, and, when viewed in conjunction with the reliefs, the tomb figures give us an accurate and surprisingly real view of Han life and culture. Compared with the works in stone, the funerary sculpture may strike the observer as being more childlike and naïve, totally lacking in the sense of monumentality that accompanies the efforts in resistant materials like granite or limestone, but the directness and vigor of their execution place them in the mainstream of Han art.

Six Dynasties period. By the time that Buddhism reached China and created the demand for images of the great savior there was a more than ample store of experience behind the Chinese sculptor's immediate response. The iconography and style of the Buddha images may have depended on India for basic inspiration, but the earliest images of the Buddha in China are clearly modified by Chinese aesthetics. No wholesale direct imitation of Indian models seems to have taken place with the onslaught of the new religion. But there is certainly little doubt that the vital Buddhist art of India exerted considerable influence on the Chinese sculptor, changing his concepts of three-dimensional art and providing a fresh new impetus for the creation of the human figure.

Buddhism had reached China in the later years of the Han dynasty, but it was not until the 4th century that Buddhist images occurred in any number. The Six Dynasties period (221–589) has been labeled the "archaic" phase of Chinese Buddhist sculpture, a somewhat misleading term used to describe the whole of the Six Dynasties style in sculpture. The earliest-known dated image in this initial phase of Buddhist art is the small bronze seated Buddha in the Brundage Collection (338). The end of this first

stylistic wave may be exemplified by the exceptionally beautiful bronze Śākyamuni and Prabhūtaratna in the Guimet Museum, Paris (518). The Brundage bronze is a simple, direct evocation of the majestic Buddha, frontal in concept, crude in its attempt to overpower, rigid in the handling of drapery, depending on the rule of symmetry in its presentation. An echo of the Gandhāra style is still evident in this 4th-century work. The Guimet bronze provides a strong and striking contrast in both iconography and style, revealing the distance traversed by the Chinese sculptor in the 180 years that separate the two works. The subject matter deals with the dialogue between the Buddha of the present, Śākyamuni, and the Buddha of the distant past, Prabhūtaratna, typifying the complexity of the involved Mahāyāna doctrine in the 6th century. The style is correspondingly sophisticated: slender, ethereal figures with their bodily substance suppressed, they evoke the sense of the nonphysical, spiritual realm so appropriate to this great event. The drapery cascades over the throne, ending in the sharp-edged points so characteristic of the mature Six Dynasties style. While the frontality and conventionalized nature of drapery folds seen in the 338 Buddha are maintained to some degree in the later bronze, the fluid and graceful execution reveals the complete mastery of the Chinese sculptor. *See* GANDHARA; MAHAYANA.

In the north of China, on the terminal fringes of the great caravan routes over the Central Asian desert, cave temples were being hollowed out during the period spanned by the two bronzes. Under the patronage of the Tatar tribes known as the T'o-pa, Buddhism became an official doctrine, and the demand for images was immense. Taking the Chinese name "Wei" for their dynastic title, these tribes exploited the new faith as a means of extending their control over the northern regions of China (hence the term "Northern Wei" used sometimes synonymously with the Six Dynasties sculptural style). The first major undertaking was the cave complex at the site of Yün-kang, begun in 460 and continuing to 494. Burrowing into the sandstone cliffs, the sculptors literally hacked out gigantic images in the deep recess of the caves. The earlier caves, such as Cave 20, show a mixture of stylistic elements, Central Asian basically but with traces of Gandhāran and Chinese influence as well. This hybrid style relates to the 338 bronze: the execution is stiff, frontal, and hieratic in concept, with a strong linear treatment in drapery folds. The gradual modification of the hybrid formula can be traced throughout the span of Yün-kang, and the slimmer models of Cave 5 show this process rather clearly. But it was not until the shift of the Wei capital south to Lo-yang in 494 that the new style emerged with great vigor. *See* LO-YANG; YUN-KANG.

At the site of Lung-men, a few miles south of the new capital, the Wei sculptors found a fine-grained limestone suitable for the close carving. The cave temples at this site were continued into the T'ang dynasty (618–906), but the finest caves are usually considered to be the earlier 6th-century examples. The Pin-yang cave was probably contemporary with the Guimet Museum bronze mentioned above, and there are many similarities in the handling of the sculptures occupying the niches: the same slender, elongated quality is captured in limestone as in the bronze, and the hybrid style has been replaced by the Chinese interest in the flickering silhouette and rhythmical linear patterns that are so characteristic of earlier Han art. *See* LUNG-MEN.

The mature Six Dynasties style was relatively short-lived, lasting until the breakup of the Wei dynasty in 535. The latter half of the 6th century is sometimes referred to as a "transitional period," indicating a shift in style once again from the "archaic" linear handling to the full-bodied T'ang style that begins in the 7th century. The term "transitional" may not be an accurate description of the stylistic change, however, for it implies a natural internal sculptural development toward more three-dimensional forms. The cause for the shift in aesthetics appears to be more closely related to another wave of influence from India, notably in the fully developed Gupta style.

The two dynastic houses known as Northern Ch'i and Northern Chou, the immediate successors to the Wei rulers, and the short period of Sui reunification of China (589–618) produced a series of homogeneous sculptural pieces featuring a columnar type of Buddha image. The Bodhisattvas produced during this period have an opulence of jewelry that distinguishes them from the stately dignity of the Buddha, but both types of image stress the idea of the deities' physical presence. The ethereal grace of the Six Dynasties style is replaced by more worldly figures in such temple complexes as those of Hsiang-t'ang-shan in Honan (Northern Ch'i), the Mai-chi-shan series in Kansu, and the Yün-men-shan caves in Shantung of Sui-dynasty date. Some excellent examples of this columnar style of sculpture exist in the collection of the University of Pennsylvania Museum, Philadelphia, and one of the finest Buddhist masterpieces of any period is the Sui-dynasty bronze group *Amitābha and Attendants*, dated 593, in the Museum of Fine Arts, Boston. *See* HSIANG-T'ANG-SHAN.

T'ang dynasty. The full glory of T'ang-dynasty sculpture develops directly out of such antecedents as the Boston *Amitābha* altarpiece. All the elements suggested in the Sui pieces, the sense of emerging plastic form, the carefully controlled relationship maintained between linear decoration and solid mass, and the awareness of surface finish, are continued in the period of T'ang rule. Carried another step forward, the drapery of the T'ang figures becomes even more closely integrated with the body beneath, and a voluptuousness of form takes over in the 7th and 8th centuries. The Gupta style becomes completely absorbed, and a new naturalism permeates the flesh and bones of the T'ang Buddha image. The high point of the T'ang Buddhist sculptural style can be seen in the caves of T'ien-lung-shan, begun under the tutelage of the Northern Ch'i rulers. In such caves as number 20 from this site the easy postures of the seated Bodhisattvas seem typical of the worldly, self-assured quality of so much T'ang sculpture. The figures appear almost as though they had been carved in the full round and moved into the cave rather than having been wrested out of the mountain rock, as they were. Along with the self-assured nature of stone sculpture during the 7th and 8th centuries comes an almost self-satisfied earthiness of attitude that marks the beginning of the end in the later examples from T'ien-lung-shan. *See* T'IEN-LUNG-SHAN.

Little remains of T'ang sculpture outside the major caves, and even these have been largely despoiled over the years.

Virtually nothing remains of wood, lacquer, or the other media of the sculptor. One happy exception is the art of funerary sculpture: under the T'angs tomb art reaches its greatest peak, as the hundreds of examples in Western collections testify. Most of these pieces exist because of the enterprise of earlier generations of grave robbers, but controlled excavations of T'ang tombs in recent years indicate that an extensive inventory of figures accompanied the T'ang official to his grave. The wealth of material supplied by these funerary figurines presents us with a lucid picture of courtly life and interests: polo players, musical groups, animals of every description, mythical guardians, court officials and ladies, foreigners in native dress, evoking the rich and cosmopolitan character of the T'ang period. Much of this mass-produced tomb furnishing relates to the ceramic industry rather than to the art of sculpture, and the summary treatment of so many of the pieces does not make a comparison with Buddhist sculpture of the 7th and 8th centuries particularly valid. However, among the numerous glazed and unglazed earthenware figures are many of striking and handsome design. The tomb horses are world-famous, reflecting the same naturalism of form that is observable in the major Buddhist monuments of the period. Taken as a whole, the art produced for the tombs helps to broaden our view of T'ang achievements, providing a balance to the religiously inspired yet curiously worldly art of Buddhist sculpture. *See* KAO-TSUNG, TOMB OF. *See also* T'ANG FIGURINES.

Sculpture in the later periods. The decline of Buddhism after the violent and destructive persecutions of 842–845 brings to a close the greatest chapters of Buddhist sculpture in China. The history of sculptural art after the T'ang is uneven and not particularly notable, although isolated fine examples do exist along with the continuation of some local schools. The imposing image of Udayana type in the Seryōji temple, Kyoto, bearing a date of 984, was supposedly made in China and taken to Japan by the priest Chōnen. But it is an obvious archaistic work, an attempt to recapture something of the spirit of early Buddhist sculpture, and is not significant of any stylistic innovations after the T'ang period. Some fine examples of stone sculpture dating from the northern dynasties, particularly that of the Liao in the 10th and 11th centuries, have occupied the attention of art historians. The Khitan and Jurchen tribes that swarmed into the north of China after the fall of the T'ang brought a revival of interest in Buddhism to the same area dominated earlier by the Wei rulers in the Six Dynasties period. An archaistic revival of sorts took place as one aspect of the interest in Buddhist sculpture, and the site of Yün-kang received renewed attention for a very brief period. Along with the archaistic interest there developed a distinctly different style of Buddhist sculpture, rooted in T'ang traditions but in no way to be seen as a simple degeneration. The clay images at the "Lower" Hua-yen-ssu in Ta-t'ung, Shansi Province, for example, still evoke the majesty of the mature T'ang style but add a strong note of serenity and calm. *See* HUA-YEN-SSU, TA-T'UNG.

In the southwestern province of Szechwan the T'ang tradition continued, but almost as a provincial appendix. Many stone sculptures have been found in this region, some of them bearing dates and providing a relatively

China, sculpture. Bronze Buddha, early T'ang Dynasty. Metropolitan Museum of Art, New York.

clear picture of developments in the plastic arts from the 9th through the 12th century. The changes are gradual here, as we witness a long twilight period in which the powerful naturalism of T'ang forms undergoes slow modification toward an anecdotal type of realism. The great 12th-century sculptural complex at Ta-tsu, which has been extensively published, may be seen perhaps as the culmination of this tendency.

The most commanding images produced after the T'ang are probably the many wooden statues, well represented in American and European collections, of Kuan-yin (Sanskrit, Avalokiteśvara), the Goddess of Mercy. Most of these come from Shansi Province and date from the Sung and Yüan dynasties (11th–14th cent.). Only a few of them bear inscriptions, and the dating is not always precise. The tradition of these rather portly, sometimes sensuous figures may well have continued into the Ming period. Taken as a whole, however, the wooden images of the favored Bodhisattva of later Buddhism in China are remarkably homogeneous in style. The figures are nonmystical in concept, appealing to the visual senses, highly polychromed, sumptuously clothed, stately in bearing. The robes and ornaments swirl about restlessly; the carving is deep for maximum contrast of light and dark. The whole effect seems oriented toward the pictorial, and at times the sculptor appears to be painting in three dimensions. The seated Kuan-yin (*potala* Kuan-yin) images are exceptional in this respect. The figure is placed on a rocky ledge or installed in a rocklike grotto symbolizing Kuan-yin's abode in the South Seas, one arm draped over a knee that has been casually drawn up. The pose has been labeled that of "royal ease,"

a rather fitting description in many ways for all these wooden images. The relaxed quality of the figures typifies the attitude of the later carvers: serenity and tranquillity have become the supreme ideal.

By the end of the 14th century these wooden figures of Kuan-yin appear as almost meaningless clichés, repulsively overweight and clumsily executed for the most part. They signal the end, in a general way, of great sculpture in China. Sculpture produced during the Ming and Ch'ing dynasties does exist in quantity, some dedicated still to Buddhism, some Taoist-inspired, and there are some portraits of a memorial nature and images of popular folk heroes. A few of these later examples of sculpture are of high quality, but the general level of plastic art in the later periods is hardly commensurate with the quality of works produced on a national scale during the Six Dynasties and T'ang. Whatever inclination the Chinese sculptors had toward the handling of forms seems to have found a more suitable outlet in the smaller-scaled objects of jade and ivory.

BIBLIOGRAPHY. E. Chavannes, *Ars Asiatica*, vol. 2: *Six monuments de la sculpture chinoise*, Brussels, 1914; O. Sirén, *Chinese Sculpture from the Fifth to the Fourteenth Centuries*, 4 vols., London, 1925; D. Tokiwa and T. Sekino, *Shina Bukkyo Shiseki (Buddhist Monuments in China)*, 6 vols., Tokyo, 1926–38; O. Sirén, "Studien zur chinesischen Plastik der post-T'angzeit," *Ostasiatische Zeitschrift*, XIV, 1927; O. Sirén, *History of Early Chinese Art*, vol. 3: *Sculpture*, London, 1930; B. Rowland, "Notes on the Dated Statues of Northern Wei Dynasty and the Beginnings of Buddhist Sculpture in China," *Art Bulletin*, XIX, 1937; L. Bachhofer, "Two Chinese Wooden Statues," *The Burlington Magazine*, LXXIII, October, 1938; O. Sirén, "Chinese Marble Sculpture of the Transition Period," *Bulletin of the Museum of Far Eastern Antiquities*, XII, 1940; S. Mizuno and T. Nagahiro, *Ryūmon Sekketsu no Kenkyū: A Study of the Buddhist Cave Temples at Lung-Mên, Honan*, Tokyo, 1941; O. Sirén, "Chinese Sculpture of the Sung, Liao, and Chin Dynasties," *Bulletin of the Museum of Far Eastern Antiquities*, XIV, 1942; A. Priest, *Chinese Sculpture in the Metropolitan Museum of Art*, New York, 1944; H. Münsterberg, "Buddhist Bronzes of the Six Dynasties Period," *Artibus Asiae*, IX, 1946; S. Mizuno, *Chinese Stone Sculpture*, Tokyo, 1950; S. Mizuno and T. Nagahiro, *Unkō Sekkutsu: Yün-Kang, The Buddhist Cave Temples of the Fifth Century A.D. in North China*, 16 vols., Kyoto, 1951–56; R. Rudolph and Wen Yu, *Han Tomb Art of West China*, Berkeley, Calif., 1951; J. L. Davidson, *The Lotus Sūtra in Chinese Art*, New Haven, 1954; L. Sickman and A. Soper, *The Art and Architecture of China*, Baltimore, 1956; W. Willets, *Chinese Art*, vol. 1, Harmondsworth, 1958.

MARTIE W. YOUNG

CHINA: SILK. Silk must rank among the foremost of China's many contributions to the material culture of the world. A knowledge of sericulture existed in China in Shang times (2d millennium B.C.), well before it was practiced in the Western world. The Chinese silk that reached the Greco-Roman world was regarded as a precious commodity, and the inhabitants of the lands producing the fine materials were referred to as Seres. The connection between the Seres and the Chinese, however, was not made until the Jesuits began their explorations of the Far East. By then Chinese silk had a long history and had become a major industry.

As a surface for painting and writing, silk was used by the Chinese as early as the 3d century B.C. The earliest paintings now known are on fragments of silk recovered from Ch'ang-sha in Hunan, and there are reasons to believe that silk may have been used earlier as a support for painting, as it certainly was for writing. Even after the invention of paper silk remained a very popular ground, particularly for paintings that employed a good deal of color since heavy pigments adhered better to the textured surface of woven silk than to paper. Chinese literary sources record a variety of silks used throughout Chinese painting history: T'ang silk, called *seng chüan*, was described as coarse in weave, while a kind of Sung silk referred to as *yüan chüan* was highly prized by academic painters for its very fine and densely woven surface. But it is extremely difficult to correlate existing specimens of silk with the excellent and detailed descriptions given in ancient literary sources. Also, it was common practice in the Ming period to use old silks, just as fakers today use ancient materials to make their objects appear antique. *See* CH'ANG-SHA; CHINA: PAINTING.

The original color of silk, a pale golden tone, is rarely visible on old Chinese paintings since silk tends to darken when exposed to light for long periods of time. Despite its fragile appearance silk is remarkably durable, and when properly primed and sized it offers a fine surface for accepting ink and colors. The priming of silks was sometimes attended to personally by the artist since it was a matter of great importance. The standard method of priming, at least after the 10th century, was to employ glue mixed with alum.

BIBLIOGRAPHY. A. Priest and P. Simmons, *Chinese Textiles*, New York, 1931, 1935; V. Sylwan, "Silk from the Yin Dynasty," *Bulletin of the Museum of Far Eastern Antiquities*, IX, 1937; W. Willets, *Chinese Art*, 2 vols., Harmondsworth, 1958.

MARTIE W. YOUNG

CHINA (Porcelain). Term applied originally to the Chinese hard-paste porcelain exported to eager buyers in Europe and America. Commencing with the last decades of the 17th century, great quantities were purchased for serving tea, coffee, and chocolate; soon complete dinner sets became popular. German, Austrian, and French makers of both hard- and soft-paste porcelain eventually captured some of this luxury trade; with the development of English bone china, less expensive dinner wares became generally available. *See* CHINA: CERAMICS; PORCELAIN.

See also BERLIN PORCELAIN; BOW PORCELAIN; BRISTOL PORCELAIN; BUEN RETIRO PORCELAIN; CAPODIMONTE PORCELAIN; CHELSEA PORCELAIN; COPENHAGEN PORCELAIN; DERBY PORCELAIN; DOCCIA PORCELAIN; FRANKENTHAL PORCELAIN; FULDA PORCELAIN; FURSTENBERG PORCELAIN; HOCHST PORCELAIN; LUDWIGSBURG PORCELAIN; NYMPHENBURG PORCELAIN; ROSENTHAL PORCELAIN; SAINT-CLOUD PORCELAIN; VINCENNES-SEVRES PORCELAIN; VIENNA PORCELAIN.

BIBLIOGRAPHY. H. D. Eberlein and R. W. Ramsdell, *The Practical Book of Chinaware*, rev. ed., Philadelphia, 1948.

CHINA CLAY, *see* PORCELAIN.

CHINARD, JOSEPH. French sculptor (b. Lyons, 1756; d. there, 1813). He studied with B. Blaise and in Rome. Chinard is best known for his portrait busts of women, in which his sensitivity to individual features outweighs the classical accessories.

CH'IN ART, *see* CHINA: ARCHITECTURE (HISTORICAL PERIODS: CH'IN).

CHINA STONE, *see* PORCELAIN.

CHINESE CHIPPENDALE, *see* CHIPPENDALE, THOMAS.

CHINESE IMPERIAL TREASURES, *see* FORMOSA (TAIWAN): SUN YAT-SEN MUSEUM.

CH'ING ART, *see* CHINA: ARCHITECTURE, CALLIGRAPHY, CERAMICS, JADE, LACQUER, PAINTING, SCULPTURE.

CHING HAO. Chinese landscape painter (fl. first half of 10th cent.). Ching Hao's life spanned the period of turmoil that marked the end of the T'ang dynasty and the age of disunity that followed. He was born in Honan Province but fled to the mountains of T'ai-hang, where, in a manner suggestive of the later Thoreau at Walden, he supported himself by tilling the soil. None of his paintings seems to have survived (although a number of questionable works exist), but he is still a major figure in the development of landscape painting because of his writings. The *Pi-fa-chi* (Notes on Brush Method), sometimes known under its subtitle *Hua shan-shui lu* (Essay on Landscape Painting), records a conversation between an elderly sage and a young painter in which emerges a new attitude toward nature and art. The essay also contains a major reevaluation of the "six principles" expounded earlier by Hsieh Ho.

BIBLIOGRAPHY. S. Sakanishi, *The Spirit of the Brush*, London, 1939.

CH'ING-LING. Chinese tomb site in Inner Mongolia. Here are located three tombs that belong to the emperors of the Liao dynasty (907–1125). In the mountainous region near the border of Mongolia and Manchuria the Liao emperors had hunted deer at their leisure, and they gave orders that their tombs be built in this area. The sixth emperor, Shen-tsung, located his tomb on the Mien-shan mountain, and his son and grandson also chose to be buried at this site, now known as Ch'ing-ling.

The wall paintings which decorate the mausoleum of Shen-tsung can be dated to 1031 and for this reason are important documents in the history of landscape painting. On the four walls of the central chamber there are landscapes of the four seasons executed in a decorative coloristic style reminiscent of the preceding T'ang dynasty. The heavy polychrome and the archaic space conventions seen in these wall paintings would seem to make them rather provincial works, but the charm and liveliness of these Liao works reflect something of the growing interest in depicting the natural world in China of the 11th century.

BIBLIOGRAPHY. J. Tamura and Y. Kobayashi, *Tombs and Mural Paintings of Ch'ing-ling, Liao Imperial Mausoleums of the Eleventh Century A.D. in Eastern Mongolia*, 2 vols., Kyoto, 1953.

MARTIE W. YOUNG

CH'ING-LU, *see* BLUE-AND-GREEN STYLE.

CH'ING-PAI, *see* YING-CH'ING.

CHING-TE-CHEN. Famous ceramic center near Fou-liang in Kiangsi Province, China. It was active perhaps as early as the Han dynasty (206 B.C.–A.D. 221). Located where there were excellent deposits of clay, the kilns at this site eventually supplied the great imperial wares of the Ming and Ch'ing dynasties, and from the 14th century on the enormous output of the pottery factories included blue-

and-white wares and the elusive *ying-ch'ing* type of porcelains. *See* BLUE-AND-WHITE; YING-CH'ING.

BIBLIOGRAPHY. A. Brankston, "An Excursion to Ching-te-chen and Chi-an-fu in Kiangsi," *Transactions of the Oriental Ceramic Society,* XVI, 1938–39.

CHIN NUNG. Chinese painter and calligrapher (1687–after 1764). Chin Nung was born in Hang-chou but spent most of his life in the Yang-chou area. He belongs to the circle of "eccentric" painters known as the "Eight Strange Masters of Yang-chou" and is considered the most prominent member of this group. His biographers record that he did not begin painting until after he had reached the age of fifty, and there seems to be a cultivated amateurish quality about his small-scale paintings of landscapes, plum blossoms, and the like. In his very late years Chin Nung turned to Buddhism and led the life of a monk-recluse. *See* YANG-CHOU, EIGHT ECCENTRICS OF.

BIBLIOGRAPHY. O. Sirén, *Chinese Painters, Leading Masters and Principles,* vol. 5, New York, 1958.

CHINOISERIE. An 18th-century style of furniture and decorative art deriving its principal motifs from Chinese decoration and art. Chinoiserie arose out of the rococo style in France. Jean Henri Riesener created furniture in this style for the French court in the last decades of the 18th century. *See* RIESENER, JEAN HENRI.

BIBLIOGRAPHY. M. Jourdain and R. S. Jenyns, *Chinese Export Art in the 18th Century,* New York, 1950.

CHIOS, *see* NEA MONI, CHURCH OF, CHIOS.

CHIOS, SCHOOL OF, *see* GREECE.

CHIOZZOTTO, IL, *see* MARINETTI, ANTONIO; SCHIAVONI, MICHELE.

CH'I PAI-SHIH. Chinese painter (1863–1957). His name was Ch'i Huang, and his *tzu* was Pin-sheng, but he was best known by his *hao* Pai-shih. A native of Hsiang-t'an, Hunan Province, he is generally recognized as the leading modern Chinese painter. Largely a self-taught artist and scholar, he began working as a carpenter for his uncle. At the age of fifteen he took up wood carving and

Thomas Chippendale, desk ornamented with neoclassic motifs. Art Gallery and Temple Newsom House, Leeds.

became acquainted with the *Mustard-seed-garden Painting Manual.* He took pride in his peasant beginnings and often signed his paintings *K'e-mu lao-jen* ("The Old Woodcutter"). Late in his twenties he took up poetry, calligraphy, and writing. In his early forties he traveled throughout China, sketching and painting. He finally settled in Peking at the age of sixty and for more than thirty years he dominated the artistic circles of the great capital. In 1953, at the age of ninety, he became president of the Peking Institute of Chinese Painting. *See* MUSTARD-SEED-GARDEN PAINTING MANUAL.

Ch'i Pai-shih's painting style is highly individualistic. He is most famous for his powerful sketches, in black and white or in color, of crabs, insects, and birds and flowers, but he also executed numbers of figure studies and landscapes. Always boldly conceived and stunningly executed, his paintings link him historically to the Chinese eccentrics and individualists of the 17th century, especially Shiht'ao (Tao-chi) and Chu Ta. Ch'i Pai-shih's paintings, however, are narrower in range and have a more humane and gentle quality. He was also a prolific painter whose total *oeuvre* appears as variations on a singular theme: a limited but well-explored world of small creatures and human beings possessing an underlying spirit of gaiety and spontaneity. *See* CHU TA; TAO-CHI.

BIBLIOGRAPHY. G. Pommeranz-Liedtke, *Tschi, Pai-schi,* Dresden, 1958; Li Chin-hsi and Ch'i Liang-i, eds., *Ch'i Pai-shih tso p'in hsuan chi,* Peking, 1959; *Ch'i Pai-shih tso p'in chi,* 3 vols., Peking, 1963.
MARTIE W. YOUNG

CHIPPENDALE, THOMAS. English cabinetmaker and designer (b. Worcester, 1709/18; d. London, 1779). He was the son of a Worcester cabinetmaker who was also named Thomas, and by 1730 both were established in London in a business that was continued by Thomas Chippendale III. The three Chippendales produced fine furniture for about a century and are probably best known for their chairs and chests of drawers on legs and for the design book published by the second Thomas. Entitled *The Gentleman and Cabinet Maker's Director,* it appeared in 1754, 1759, and 1762. It is actually a compilation of designs by several English artists, the epitome of the English version of the rococo style in ". . . the French, Gothick and Chinese taste." Generally in natural woods, especially mahogany, the designs were of tremendous influence in England, on the Continent, and in the English colonies, although they appeared just as the reaction to the rococo style, neoclassicism, was first introduced.

The *Director* reflected strong French influence, and the designs were in many cases easier for an engraver than a cabinetmaker to execute. Suggestions for heavy carving (backs) and elaborate curves (legs and arms) dominate. By Gothic was meant the pointed arch-and-trefoil pattern used primarily on chair backs. The Chinese taste referred to designs that had pierced patterns of fretwork applied on flat areas, straight legs (instead of the more typically Chippendale curving cabriole leg with its claw-foot termination), and obvious elements of chinoiserie such as pagoda forms on chair backs. Essentially the Chippendale style consists of designs related to those of the *Director,* an elaborately carved, flamboyantly rococo style in fashion from about 1740 to 1770. There is no documented furniture in the French taste by Thomas Chippendale. Of the furniture known to have been made at his shop, the best-documented work is that made under the supervision of the neoclassic architect Robert Adam for Harewood House in Yorkshire. Possibly another group would be for the Chinese bedroom at Claydon House in Buckinghamshire, where Chippendale is known to have supplied some of the decorative work.

Little is known of the Chippendales, although the list of subscribers to the book, which reveals a most substantial clientele, and the fact that Thomas II and Thomas III were members of the Royal Society of the Arts, suggest successful craftsmen who had achieved the status of gentlemen.

BIBLIOGRAPHY. O. Brackett, *Thomas Chippendale: A Study of His Life, Work, and Influence*, London, 1924.
MARVIN D. SCHWARTZ

CHI-RHO MONOGRAM. Sacred monogram of Christ, formed from the first two letters of the Greek word for Christ. In use since the 4th century, it is one of the earliest Christian symbols. The Chi-Rho emblem appears on numerous works of art, notably on early Christian sarcophagi. (See illustration.)

CHIRICO, GIORGIO DE. Italian painter (1888–). He was born of Italian parents in Volos, Greece, and studied at a technical school in Athens. In 1905 he went to Italy and painted after Botticelli, Uccello, and other Quattrocento masters. De Chirico studied in 1909 with Hackl at the Munich Academy of Fine Arts and was influenced by the styles of Böcklin and Klinger. He lived in Florence in 1910 and began his unique, compelling series of landscapes with figures or antique statuary and the architecture of Italian city squares. One of the earliest of these haunting, shadow-ridden canvases is the 1910 *Enigma of an Autumn Night*. The same melancholy and evocative green tonality continues in 1911 works such as the *Enigma of the Hour* (Milan, private collection), the 1913 *Soothsayer's Recompense* (Philadelphia Museum of Art), and the 1914 *The Melancholy and Mystery of a Street* (private collection). It is remarkable that De Chirico, who was fully aware of the dynamic futurist movement in Italy, with its derision of Italy's antiquarian glories, and was similarly abreast of cubist activities in Paris, remained singularly free from influence of either aesthetic. He was, in fact, almost the only major European painter of the 1910s to avoid those sources, and this despite his knowing Picasso, the poets Paul Guillaume and Max Jacob and other cubist affiliates, and certain of the futurists.

No little of De Chirico's pervasive unearthly effect results from his bringing together elements which are illogically related in time—a modern clock and a locomotive in a medieval architectural setting which also contains a late classical statue, for example. Such arrangements are made more enigmatic by the plunging lines of perspective and the shadows that cut across them from inconsistent angles. The nostalgic atmosphere—or curiously vacuum-like space—of the 1910–14 "city square" canvases is rarely matched in its intensity by any of the surrealist efforts of the 1920s and later which were strongly influenced by De Chirico's style.

In 1915 De Chirico shifted his themes to include mannequin figures and a bizarre span of still-life objects—biscuits and toys, for example. De Chirico's dreamlike imagery and much of the quality of his earlier technique persisted during the years 1915–25, his so-called Metaphysical Period. Thereafter the uniqueness of his style waned, and soon after 1930 he strangely converted to an academic and uninspired program. A quasibaroque flair has marked most of the portraits he began painting in 1933. He disclaimed his fine early works. *See* PITTURA METAFISICA.

De Chirico remains one of the most original artists of his time on the strength of his 1911–14 canvases; and the surrealists, with whom he exhibited in 1925 without fully committing himself to the movement, owe much to his visionary temperament.

BIBLIOGRAPHY. C. Carrà, *Pittura metafisica*, Florence, 1919; G. de Chirico, "Sull'arte metafisica," *Valori Plastici*, IV, V, 1919; J. T. Soby and A. H. Barr, Jr., *Twentieth-Century Italian Art*, New York, 1949; J. T. Soby, *Giorgio de Chirico*, New York, 1955.
JOHN C. GALLOWAY

CHITEI (Hata Chitei). Japanese court painter (fl. 11th cent.). He decorated the walls of the Picture Hall of the Hōryūji in 1069, illustrating scenes from the life of Prince Shōtoku, the ardent supporter of Buddhism in the 6th century. In the same year Chitei also added colors to a seated statue of the prince in the Hōryūji carved by the sculptor Enkai.

CHITON. Principal garment of the ancient Greeks, similar to the Roman tunic. It consisted of an oblong piece of cloth wrapped around the body, open on one side, and often belted at the waist; two corners were fastened together by a clasp on one shoulder. There were two styles: the Doric (short) and the Ionic (long).

BIBLIOGRAPHY. A. Baker, *Classification of the Chitons Worn by Greek Women as Shown in Works of Art*, Philadelphia, 1923.

CHITRA (Citra). Hindu representative art (sculpture, relief, painting). *Chitra* also means "picture" or "pictorial."

Chi-Rho monogram. Emblem found on many early Christian art works.

Giorgio de Chirico, *The Mysterious Swimmer*. Rosina Jaffe Collection, Turin.

CH'IU YING. Chinese painter (fl. Su-chou region, 1530–55). Ch'iu Ying was known by his *tzu* Shih-fu and occasionally by his *hao* Shi-chou. He is considered by Chinese critics to be one of the "Four Great Masters" of the Ming dynasty, but little is known of his life, principally because he held no government position and was not himself a poet, scholar, or writer. He is recorded as being a pupil of Chou Ch'en, and at one time he had his own studio; the greater part of his mature years, however, was apparently spent in residence with various Su-chou collectors, among them the famous Hsiang Yüan-pien, and at least part of his time was spent in copying early masterpieces in these collections. His general skill and dexterity in the art of painting won him high praise from some members of the Wu school, and colophons by Wen Chia, P'eng Nien, and other literati of the elite can be found on many of his paintings. *See* CHOU CH'EN; HSIANG YUAN-PIEN.

The true contribution of Ch'iu Ying to the history of painting has been obscured by the many works in the blue-and-green manner usually attributed to him; many of these attributions are at best very poor imitations of the coloristic style associated with Ch'iu Ying's name. There seems little doubt that Ch'iu did execute a number of paintings in the *kung-pi*, or meticulous, style that forms a part of the blue-and-green tradition, and among such works is the fine scroll of the *Lute Song* in the William Rockhill Nelson Gallery of Art, Kansas City. But a study of literary sources and existing works of this master indicate that such tightly controlled, coloristic works form but a small fraction of his output, and his diversity of styles was considerable, ranging from the free, bold monochromatic ink paintings to the carefully executed polychromatic works. The *Musicians under Banana Trees* in the National Palace Museum Collection, Sun Yat-sen Museum, near Taipei, serves as an effective contrast in style to the Kansas City painting, while the *Fisherman Listening to the Flute* in the Crawford Collection, New York, shows the balanced, rational style of Ch'iu Ying, which derived ultimately from the Sung master Li T'ang. *See* BLUE-AND-GREEN STYLE; LI T'ANG.

BIBLIOGRAPHY. Y. Yonezawa, *Painting in the Ming Dynasty*, Tokyo, 1956; L. Sickman, ed., *Chinese Calligraphy and Painting in the Collection of John M. Crawford*, New York, 1962.

MARTIE W. YOUNG

CHI-WARA, *see* AFRICA, PRIMITIVE ART OF (WEST AFRICA: MALI).

CH'I-YUN, *see* SIX PRINCIPLES OF CHINESE PAINTING.

CHLAMYS. Light overwrap, similar to a soldier's mantle, worn by the ancient Greeks. It consisted of an oblong piece of woolen cloth thrown over the left shoulder and fastened on the right by a clasp or simply by tying. It corresponds to the Roman paludamentum.

BIBLIOGRAPHY. L. M. Wilson, *The Clothing of the Ancient Romans*, Baltimore, 1938.

CHLUDOFF PSALTER. Byzantine illuminated manuscript, in the Historical Museum, Moscow.

CHO DENSU, *see* MINCHO.

CHODOWIECKI, DANIEL NICHOLAS. German painter and engraver (b. Danzig, 1726; d. Berlin, 1801). As a boy, under the direction of an aunt who was a miniaturist and an enamel painter, he copied etchings of Callot and prints of the Dutch and Flemish masters. Later he obtained engravings after Watteau and Lancret and made small-size reductions. Early in his career he also decorated boxes and painted enamels. In 1743 he moved to Berlin, where he was influenced for a time by the realism of Christian Bernhard Rode, a Polish artist who had settled there. Chodowiecki himself stayed mainly in Berlin until his death, though he revisited Danzig in 1775 and made journeys to Dresden, Hamburg, Leipzig, and other northern German cities, where he accumulated a number of studies that he used in paintings and book illustrations.

Though his figure types are close to those of his French contemporaries Watteau, Lancret, and Pater, thematically Chodowiecki's art reflects the rise of the *bourgeoisie*. His many sketches of lower-middle-class Berlin life have an unaffected air about them; rarely do they contain the formal poses and gaudy trappings favored by the upper classes. In Chodowiecki's melodrama and theatricality, Hogarth and especially Greuze were his models, as can be seen in the moving *Callas Taking Leave of His Family* (1767; Berlin, Charlottenburg Castle).

Among other works, Chodowiecki illustrated Voss's *Luise*, Goethe's *Werther* and *Hermann und Dorothea*, Schiller's *Die Räuber* and *Kabale und Liebe*, Lessing's *Minna von Barnhelm*, Goldsmith's *Vicar of Wakefield*, and Sterne's *Sentimental Journey*. He was most prolific; Engelmann's catalog of 1906 lists the titles of 2,075 distinct designs. Chodowiecki may be said to have introduced a new era of book illustration in Germany.

Daniel Nicholas Chodowiecki, *Lotte Offering the Pistol to Werther's Servant,* illustration for Goethe's *Werther.*

In the collection of Dr. and Mrs. Franz Blumenthal in Ann Arbor, Mich., are six pen-and-pencil illustrations to Shakespeare's *Hamlet*, done at the play's first performance in Berlin in 1778. For his book illustrations Chodowiecki made literally thousands of sketches, some of which show admirable freshness and skill in composition. The backgrounds are simple, the surroundings plain.

BIBLIOGRAPHY. W. Engelmann, *Nachträge und Berichtigungen zu Daniel Chodowieckis sämtliche Kupferstiche*, 2d ed., Leipzig, 1906.
ABRAHAM A. DAVIDSON

CHOFFARD, PIERRE PHILIPPE. French ornament engraver (1730–1809). He lived in Paris and was apprenticed to Dheulland, a cartographic engraver, and to the ornament engraver P. E. Babel, from whom he learned to make cartouches and the other small vignettes that characterize his work. In 1804 Choffard published *Notice historique sur l'art de la gravure en France*.

BIBLIOGRAPHY. V. Salomons, *Choffard*, London, 1912.

CHOGA-ZAMBIL (Dur Untashi; Tchoga-Zanbil). Elamite site in the province of Khuzistan in Iran, 30 miles from Susa, with remains of an Elamite city founded in the 13th century B.C. and destroyed by Assurbanipal about 640 B.C. A votive ax found in the Temple of Kiririsha, now in the Louvre in Paris, has a bronze blade inscribed with the name of Untash-Gal, an Elamite king of the 13th century B.C., who built the city's ziggurat. The haft of the ax is adorned with a boar of electrum. Trilingual inscriptions, old Persian, Elamite, and Babylonian, have also been found here, and glass objects give evidence that the glass industry was highly developed. A Temple of Inshushinak, built inside the seven-story ziggurat about 1250 B.C., had a wooden door adorned with hundreds of long rods in white glass paste, decorated with entwined ribbons of black glass paste.

BIBLIOGRAPHY. R. Ghirshman, *The Arts of Ancient Iran: From Its Origins to the Time of Alexander the Great*, New York, 1964.

CHOIR. Part of a church used for singers, usually between the nave and the sanctuary in medieval cathedrals. The choir was generally set off by a choir screen, often of wood, wrought iron, or bronze. Medieval choir stalls were sometimes enclosed and at times surmounted by canopies. *See also* CANCELLI; CHANCEL.

CHOIR STALL. Row of seats on either side of the choir occupied by the clergy while they attended common service. Choir stalls appear to have evolved from the bishop's throne. They first appeared in characteristic form in the 13th century and usually consisted of lower and upper rows of seats behind which rose the dorsal. Most choir stalls are membered by architectural elements such as arcades and baldachins, and many have elaborately carved figural decoration such as those in St. Paul's Cathedral, London.

CHOJIRO. Japanese potter (1515–92) of Kyoto who developed Raku ware. He originally made roof tiles but after 1572 made tea ceremony utensils. Chōjirō was a favorite of both Oda Nobunaga and Toyotomi Hideyoshi. *See* RAKU WARE.

BIBLIOGRAPHY. R. A. Miller, *Japanese Ceramics*, Rutland, Vt., 1960; M. Feddersen, *Japanese Decorative Art*, London, 1962.

CHOKI (Eishosai Choki). Japanese Ukiyo-e printmaker (fl. late 18th cent.). Prints of great delicacy and beauty were produced by Eishōsai Chōki between 1789 and 1795. His portraits of idealized women are like those of Harunobu in their quiet color combination and delicate lines, which evoke a sense of purity and lyricism.

BIBLIOGRAPHY. L. V. Ledoux, *Japanese Prints, Sharaku to Toyokuni, in the Collection of Louis V. Ledoux*, Princeton, 1950.

CHOKUAN (Soga Chokuan). Japanese painter (fl. late 16th–early 17th cent.). He produced many flower and bird paintings in brilliant colors, showing realistic details of animal life. These works are closely related to a group of flower and bird screen paintings attributed to Sesshū. Chokuan's ink paintings show a stiffness in brushwork and the speedy execution typical of the period. *See* SESSHU TOYO.

BIBLIOGRAPHY. R. T. Paine and A. Soper, *The Art and Architecture of Japan*, Baltimore, 1955.

CHOLULA. One of the holy cities of pre-Hispanic Mexico, located in the State of Puebla, traditionally associated with the worship of Quetzalcoatl. The great pyramid, about 44 acres in area and the largest structure of ancient America, consisted of four superimposed temple platforms, the earliest of which is stylistically related to preclassic Teotihua-

Choir. The part of a church set aside for the singers.

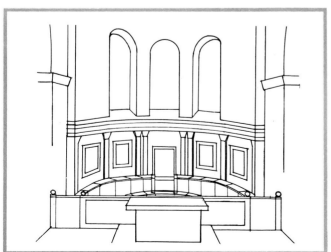

Cholula, Mexico. Domed roof of the mosquelike Royal Chapel.

cán. The first Spaniards mentioned the great number of temples at Cholula, and tourists are still assured that there are 365 churches, "one for every day of the year." Although the number is an exaggeration, the city is rich in colonial structures, some built on the ruins of Indian temples. The mosquelike Royal Chapel (16th cent.) and the "fortress" church of S. Gabriel (1549–52) are of especial interest. At nearby Acatepec and Tonantzintla are two outstanding 18th-century polychrome tile churches.

BIBLIOGRAPHY. D. Angulo Iñiguez, *Historia del arte hispano-americano*, 3 vols., Barcelona, 1945-56; F. de la Maza, *La ciudad de Cholula y sus iglesias*, Mexico City, 1959.

CHONG SON (Kyom-jae; Ran-gok). Korean painter (1676–1759). He was a master landscapist of the Yi period, known for his firm yet delicate brushstrokes. Instead of copying the famous paintings of China, he painted many scenic spots in Korea in an unusually realistic style, providing models for the later Korean landscapists. Among his better-known masterpieces are *The Diamond Mountains* and *Mount In-wang*, both in the collection of Mr. Jai-hyang Sohn, and *The Rock Gate at Tongchon*, in the collection of Mr. Hyung-pil Chun.

BIBLIOGRAPHY. R. T. Paine, ed., *Masterpieces of Korean Art*, Boston, 1957.

CHORA, CHURCH OF THE, ISTANBUL, *see* KAHRIE-DJAMI, ISTANBUL.

CHORAGIC MONUMENT. Shrine celebrating a victory in a music festival in Greek antiquity. Erected by a successful choragus, or chorus leader, or by one who endowed one of the dramatic choruses, the choragic monument usually displayed the prize tripod won in competition. The Choragic Monument of Lysicrates on the Street of the Tripods in Athens originally featured a bronze tripod set 34 feet above the ground on an ornamented roof. The Street of the Tripods contained several such shrines. *See* LYSICRATES, CHORAGIC MONUMENT OF, ATHENS.

CHORIN, CONVENT CHURCH OF. German Cistercian convent church dedicated in 1334. It is the most important example of early Gothic brick architecture in northern Germany. Today it is partly in ruins. The plan of the church is that of a three-aisled basilica with a crossing, a short choir, and a 7:12 termination.

BIBLIOGRAPHY. J. A. Schmoll gen. Eisenwerth, *Das Kloster Chorin*, Berlin, 1961.

CHORNY, DANIEL (Daniil Tschorny). Russian painter (fl. early 15th cent.). A monk and a friend of Andrei Rublev, Chorny assisted the great painter on the frescoes and icons for the Cathedral of the Dormition, Vladimir (1408–09) and for the Church of the Trinity in the Trinity–Saint Sergius Monastery near Moscow (1425–27; destroyed). *See* RUBLEV, ANDREI.

CHORTEN. Tibetan term for a chaitya or stūpa.

CHOSHUN (Miyagawa Choshun). Japanese painter (1683–1753). Chōshun first studied the style of the Tosa school. He quickly rose to fame through his brilliant portrayals of beautiful women in lavish colors, as well as of scenes of the gay quarters and theaters. Although Chōshun influenced later Ukiyo-e printmakers, he himself never made prints. *See* TOSA SCHOOL; UKIYO-E.

BIBLIOGRAPHY. T. Akiyama, *Japanese Painting* [Geneva] 1961.

CHO SOK (Ch'ang-kang). Korean painter (b. 1595). He excelled in flower and bird paintings. Some of the famous extant examples of his works are *Pair of Birds* and *Plum Tree* (both Seoul, National Museum) and *Birds on a Tree* and *Crows on an Old Tree* (both Seoul, Toksu Palace Museum). These paintings show his masterful strokes and subtle composition.

BIBLIOGRAPHY. E. McCune, *The Arts of Korea*, Rutland, Vt., 1962.

CHOSROES, PALACE OF (Taq-i-Kisra), CTESIPHON. Brick palace at Ctesiphon, on the Tigris River in Iraq. Ctesiphon was the principal city of the Sassanian dynasty (226–642). The palace is commonly dated in the reign of Chosroes I (531–579), but it may date from the 4th century. Its chief surviving portion is a vast banqueting room, open in front like the tents of tribal sheiks, and buttressed on either side by huge walls that screen private apartments. The banqueting room is roofed by an elliptical barrel vault (known as the Arch of Chosroes), 24 feet thick at the base, 120 feet from floor to crown of vault, and spanning a width of 83 feet. The huge flanking wall façades (almost completely destroyed) were 112½ feet high and showed Roman influence in their tiers of engaged columns and blind arcades.

BIBLIOGRAPHY. M. Dieulafoy, *L'Art antique de la Perse*, 2 vols., Paris, 1884; B. Fletcher, *A History of Architecture on the Comparative Method*, 17th ed., New York, 1961.

CHOU ART, *see* CHINA: ARCHITECTURE, BRONZES, CALLIGRAPHY, CERAMICS, JADE, LACQUER, PAINTING, SCULPTURE.

CHOU CH'EN. Chinese painter (fl. 1500–35). He is frequently cited by his *hao* Tung-ts'un. Since he was a professional painter, not much is known about his life, except that he was born in Su-chou and is often recorded as the teacher of both Ch'iu Ying and T'ang Yin. The relationship between Chou Ch'en and T'ang Yin was apparently a particularly involved one, and there is some evidence to suggest that T'ang may have on occasion signed his more famous name to the works of Chou. The style of painting employed by Chou Ch'en seems to be heavily dependent on that of Li T'ang, and Chou Ch'en's historical importance lies in his revival of the Li T'ang mode in the early 16th century. *See* CH'IU YING; LI T'ANG; T'ANG YIN.

BIBLIOGRAPHY. O. Sirén, *Chinese Painting, Leading Masters and Principles*, vol. 4, New York, 1958.

CHOU CHI-CH'ANG. Chinese painter (fl. late 12th cent.). He was active in the region of Ning-p'o, Chekiang Province. Nothing is recorded of this painter in Chinese sources, and he is known only for the series of 100 paintings depicting the 500 lohans, which he executed along with Lin T'ing-kuei (also unrecorded). Ten of the paintings from this series are in the Museum of Fine Arts, Boston, two in the Freer Gallery, Washington, D.C., and the bulk of the remainder in the Daitokuji, Kyoto. *See* LIN T'ING-KUEI.

BIBLIOGRAPHY. Wen Fong, "The Lohans and a Bridge to Heaven," *Freer Gallery of Art, Occasional Papers*, III, 1958.

CHOU FANG. Chinese court painter (fl. late 8th cent.). Chou Fang, who was active under the T'ang emperor Te-tsung (r. 780–805), is considered traditionally the successor to Chang Hsüan in figure painting. Chou Fang first gained a reputation for his paintings of Buddhist and Taoist subjects, but his lasting fame is based on his depictions of court ladies. Some echo of his style can be found in copies after him in the William Rockhill Nelson Gallery of Art, Kansas City, and the Freer Gallery, Washington, D.C. His portly women with their pensive air and the monumental quality of their poses make them effective and striking examples of the international style of figure painting that existed in the 8th century. *See* Chang Hsuan.

BIBLIOGRAPHY. O. Sirén, *Chinese Painting, Leading Masters and Principles*, vol. 1, New York, 1956.

CHOU WEN-CHING. Chinese painter (fl. mid-15th cent.). His *hao* was San-shan. A native of P'u-t'ien in Fukien Province, he joined the Ming court as a fortuneteller but eventually gained some recognition for his abilities as a painter. He is considered to be the foremost follower of Tai Chin in the Che school, and there are a number of older attributions to this master in American collections. *See* Che School; Tai Chin.

CHOU WEN-CHU. Chinese court painter (fl. early 10th cent.). He was in the employ of Li Hou-chou at the Southern T'ang court in Nanking. His refined court ladies were cast in the mold of Chou Fang, and Chou Wên-chü's principal claim to historical importance probably lies in the fact that he maintained the great T'ang figure-style traditions for a few more years during the twilight of the southern court. *See* Chou Fang.

BIBLIOGRAPHY. Y. Yashiro, "Again on the Sung Copy of the Scroll 'Ladies of the Court' by Chou Wên-chü," *Bijutsu Kenkyu*, IV, 1952.

CHRETIEN, FELIX. French history and portrait painter? (b. Auxerre, ca. 1500; d. there, 1570/75). Félix Chrétien was in the employ of François II Dinteville, and he followed his patron to Italy in 1538. Back in France by 1542, he was made canon of Auxerre Cathedral. In 1566 he wrote the biography of his patron. Three paintings are attributed to him: a *Ste-Eugénie Triptych* (1535; church of Varzy), *The Dinteville Brothers* (1537; New York, Metropolitan Museum), and *The Stoning of St. Stephen* (1550; Auxerre Cathedral). Since no document ever referred to Chrétien as a painter, there is no real proof that he was the author of these pictures or even a painter. The portrait heads betray the influence of Holbein, but more distinctive are the general cold and bright coloring and the sculptural monumentality of the figures.

BIBLIOGRAPHY. J. Thuillier, "L'Enigme de Félix Chrestien," *Art de France*, I, 1961.

CHRISM. Consecrated oil used in various rites of the Roman Catholic church, such as baptism and ordination. Mixed with balm, it is prepared on Holy Thursday and is kept in a special metal vessel, the chrismatory.

CHRIST AT THE COLUMN, *see* Flagellation, The.

CHRIST CHURCH, BOSTON, *see* Old North Church, Boston.

CHRIST CHURCH, PHILADELPHIA. Erected for the most part between 1727 and 1744; its design is traditionally ascribed to John Kearsley. The interior is said to be the first successful reproduction of the full English Palladian ordinance in the colonies. Its lavish decorations, particularly the urns crowning the balustrade, give the exterior a baroque flavor reminiscent of James Gibbs's style.

BIBLIOGRAPHY. G. B. Tatum, *Penn's Great Town: 250 Years of Philadelphia Architecture*, Philadelphia, 1961.

CHRIST CHURCH COLLEGE, *see* Oxford.

CHRIST DESTROYING HIS CROSS. Fresco painting by Orozco, in the Dartmouth College Library, Hanover, N.H. *See* Orozco, Jose Clemente.

CHRIST HEALING THE SICK (Hundred Guilders Print). Etching by Rembrandt. *See* Rembrandt Harmensz. van Rijn.

CHRISTIAN, JOHANN JOSEPH. German sculptor (b. Riedlingen, 1706; d. there, 1777). The principal works of Christian, who probably studied with the Flemish sculptor Quellinus, are the great complexes of sculpture done in collaboration with the Swabian architect Johann Michael Fischer at the churches of Zweifalten (1744–56) and Ottobeuren (1757–66). The statues of saints, the great altars, and the choir-stall reliefs show classical restraint in the profuse rococo scheme of decoration. Although agitated draperies, dynamic poses, ecstatic expressions, and slender, ethereal proportions are prevalent, the human forms have a certain monumentality and dignity that increase in the later works. Christian also worked in churches at Uhingen, Emmingen ab Egg, Bregenz, Feldhausen, and Buchau.

BIBLIOGRAPHY. R. Huber, *Joseph Christian, der Bildhauer des schwäbischen Rokoko*, Tübingen, 1960.

CHRISTINA OF BOLSENA, ST. Virgin martyr of Tyro, a town now submerged in Lake Bolsena (3d cent.). After being baptized, she refused to sacrifice to idols and broke silver and gold images of the gods of her father, prefect Urban. He had her tortured on a wheel and thrown into Lake Bolsena with a millstone around her neck, but she clung to the millstone, which floated. A later prefect had her bound to a stake and shot with arrows. Her attributes are a millstone, arrows, and a wheel. Her feast is July 24. *See also* Saints in Art.

CHRIST IN MAJESTY (Majestas Domini). The representation of Christ enthroned within a mandorla-shaped glory surrounded by the four evangelical symbols derived from the Apocalypse. It first appears in Early Christian art, for example, the mosaic in the 6th-century Church of S. Vitale, Ravenna. It becomes common in Western art after Carolingian times. Christ in Majesty is particularly important during the Romanesque and Gothic periods as a tympanum subject in church and cathedral doorways.

CHRISTOPHER OF LYCIA, ST. Gigantic Christian Hercules who carried people across a dangerous stream for Christ because he was the greatest power in the universe. Christopher (from the Greek "one who bore Christ") was originally called Reprobus. One night a child appeared wanting to cross; He was Christ, and His increasing weight, that of the world, was almost overwhelming. Christopher was supposedly martyred in Asia Minor in the 3d century. His attributes include the Christ Child on his shoulder and a staff, which sprouted miraculously. His feast is July 25. *See also* SAINTS IN ART.

CHRISTUS, PETRUS. Flemish painter (ca. 1410–1472/73). Listed as a citizen of Bruges from 1444, he was one of the generation of Flemish painters who carried on the innovations of the Master of Flémalle and Jan van Eyck. Although Christus was not of the major rank of Rogier van der Weyden (ten years his senior), his work represents most strongly the continuity of the Eyckian tradition.

Most evidence indicates that he was trained in the workshop of Jan van Eyck, and the relationship of Christus to Van Eyck is one of the major problems concerning Petrus's *oeuvre.* Generally, Christus continued the Eyckian approach to space and volume, albeit in a much less complex manner. The Christus-Van Eyck problem is especially apparent in such panels as the *St. Jerome in His Study*, in the Detroit Institute of Fine Arts, and the *Virgin, St. Barbara, and Donor* ("Rothschild Madonna"), in the Frick Collection, New York. The former is thought to have been a work by Van Eyck, finished in his workshop by Christus; the latter, although started by Van Eyck, was completely reworked by Christus. The *St. Jerome* bears the date 1442, while the "Rothschild Madonna" is known to have been completed before September, 1443.

The distinctive Flemish style of Christus becomes evident in such works as the small *Pietà* in the Louvre, Paris, and a much larger, expanded version of this subject in the Brussels Museum. Both works, as well as the *Money Changers* in the Lehman Collection, New York, show Christus's mature style—a heavy, somewhat placid simplification of the formal innovations and visual richness of Van Eyck.

Despite his indebtedness to Van Eyck, Christus is not to be regarded as a totally derivative, uninspired painter. In such works as his *Portrait of Lord Grymestone* (London, National Gallery) and *Portrait of a Carthusian* (New York, Metropolitan Museum), both of which are dated 1446, he shows himself capable of masterful, sometimes incisive painting, with an intense interest in the definition of space.

His early mastery of receding space is shown in the *Madonna and Child in a Gothic Room* (Kansas City, Mo., William Rockhill Nelson Gallery of Art). In this panel one room opens into another that in turn opens onto a street. Light streams in from windows and doors, revealing a convincing spatially organized interior. It is in this aspect of his work that Christus's historical significance lies. By simplifying Eyckian forms without adopting the linear, surface quality of Rogier, Christus "opened up" space to the spectator, presenting his figures as solid masses within this newly broadened stage.

BIBLIOGRAPHY. M. J. Friedländer, *Die altniederländische Malerei,* vol. 1, Berlin, 1924.

STANLEY FERBER

Petrus Christus, *The Wife of the Donor.* Panel. National Gallery, Washington, D.C.

CHROME. Bright, silvery metal noted for its permanency. It is used in the form of a protective plate and unifying coating for iron and steel objects, particularly for objects that are constantly exposed to weather. Oxides and similar compounds of chrome are used as pigments for chrome orange and chrome yellow paints.

CHROMO-LITHOGRAPHY. The practice, especially in the 19th century, of making color lithographs from as many as fifteen separate stones in order to imitate painting. The term "chromo-lithography" still has certain derisive connotations in contrast to the term "color lithography," which implies original work.

CHROMOLUMINARISM, see NEOIMPRESSIONISM.

CHRYSELEPHANTINE. Colossal statues whose wooden cores were covered with plates of ivory (for nude areas such as face, hands, and feet) and sheets of gold (for drapery). They were made for temple worship by famous sculptors in Greece during the 5th and early 4th centuries B.C., at enormous expense to state treasuries. Outstanding examples were the *Athena Parthenos* and the *Olympian Zeus* by Pheidias, the *Hera of Argos* by Polycleitus, and the *Asklepios of Epidaurus* by Thrasymedes.

BIBLIOGRAPHY. G. M. A. Richter, *The Sculpture and Sculptors of the Greeks*, rev. ed., New Haven, 1957.

CHRYSOGRAPHY. Obsolete term for the application of gold or silver letters to parchment, as in medieval illuminated manuscripts. Usually the letters were formed with gold and silver inks rather than by the application of gold leaf. Chrysography can be extended to include all forms of painting in gold.

CHUEH. Chinese term applied to a group of ancient ritual bronze vessels. Used as a wine dispenser, the *chüeh* has three blade-shaped legs, a body that is generally elliptical in section, an elongated spout with a flat extended lip opposite, two upright capped columns, and a handle. Most surviving examples of the type date from the Shang period (before 1027 B.C.) and appear to represent an experimental stage in the development of bronze shapes. There are a number of variants in this very interesting group of early bronzes.

CH'U-FU. City in Shantung Province, China. Ch'ü-fu is notable for the complex of Ming and Ch'ing structures that make up the Confucian Temple. The foundations of the main temple supposedly date back to A.D. 153, but alterations have been continuous throughout history. The present complex numbers more than 100 buildings, ranging in date from the 15th to the 19th century. The entire precinct measures ½ mile in length and 500 feet in width; it is enclosed by the usual wall.

BIBLIOGRAPHY. A. Boyd, *Chinese Architecture and Town Planning*, Chicago, 1962.

CHU-JAN. Chinese painter (fl. 2d half of 10th cent.). He is usually classified as a pupil of Tung Yüan. Nothing is known of the details concerning Chü-jan's personal life except that he was a Buddhist priest who resided in a temple in Nanking, the capital of the Southern T'ang dynasty. He gained his initial recognition as a painter in this city; when Li Yü, last of the Southern T'ang rulers, went to K'ai-feng in 975 to present his submission to the Sung emperor, Chü-jan was included in the official retinue. He remained at the Sung capital and entered a monastery. Chü-jan was apparently well received as a painter by the Sung court since the *Hsüan-ho hua-p'u* lists more than 100 paintings by the master in the imperial collection. He was particularly praised for the misty atmospheric effects that he achieved in his paintings. *See* HSUAN-HO HUA-P'U; TUNG YUAN.

Chü-jan's painting style undoubtedly reflects aspects of Tung Yüan's paintings methods: rough brushstrokes combined with a sense of spaciousness and soft landscape forms typical of the southern regions of China. His existing paintings reveal a remarkably consistent view, which combines some of Tung Yüan's qualities with the more monumental compositions associated with the northern landscape painters of the 10th century. Chü-jan's towering mountain forms are built up with many smaller rounded hills that are topped by wet dense dots of ink to convey the effect of natural vegetation. His foreground elements are carefully detailed and effectively employ the device of contrasts for rhythmic accents. Among the best known of the paintings attributed to Chü-jan is the *Seeking the Tao in Autumn Mountains* in the Sun Yat-sen Museum in Formosa. There are two monumental landscapes in Western collections, one in the Cleveland Museum of Art and the other in the British Museum, London.

BIBLIOGRAPHY. *Chinese Art Treasures*, Geneva, 1961; M. Sullivan, "A Masterpiece of Chinese Painting: Chü-jan's 'Mou-lin tieh-chang t'u,'" *Apollo*, LXXVII, July, 1962.

MARTIE W. YOUNG

CHULTUN. Irregularly shaped subterranean chamber with a well-like opening roofed by a slab, found in ancient Mayan construction. It is assumed to have been used as either a tomb or a reservoir.

CHU-LU-HSIEN. Former city in Hopei Province, China. Chü-lu-hsien was flooded in A.D. 1108, when the Yellow River changed its course. Excavations at this site have revealed a porcelaneous white ware of thick body and relatively robust design quite different from the Ting ware, which is so characteristic of imperial white wares of the Sung dynasty. *See* TING WARE.

CHUMASH INDIANS. Tribe of the Hokan linguistic group who lived in the vicinity of Santa Barbara, Calif. Like the neighboring Gabrielinos, the Chumash produced an impressive prehistoric stone art. Typical subjects were killer whales and swordfish. They also made canoe models, which were carved in steatite and sometimes inlaid with shell.

The Chumashan style is one of simplified, sophisticated naturalism. Although the dating of Chumashan sculpture remains conjectural, it is certain that the style had developed considerably before the time of Spanish missionizing in the early 16th century. By the 19th century the Chumash had all but disappeared; their art had died out even earlier.

See also NORTH AMERICAN INDIAN ART (CALIFORNIA).

BIBLIOGRAPHY. G. G. Heye, *Certain Artifacts from San Miguel Island, California*, New York, 1921; E. K. Burnett, *Inlaid Stone and Bone Artifacts from Southern California*, New York, 1944.

CHUNG. Chinese term applied to ancient ritual bronzes used as bells in ceremonies. There are a number of subtypes in this broad category. The *chung* is oval in section and varies considerably in size, a very large example measuring about 3 feet in height. The bells were struck, no clapper having been involved. The outside of the *chung* is usually ornamented with thirty-six bosses or nipples set in series of threes. Such bells occur in the middle and late Chou periods (ca. 900 B.C.–206 B.C.).

CHUNG K'UEI, THE DEMON QUELLER. Chinese legendary figure. According to popular legend, Chung K'uei first appeared in a dream of the T'ang emperor Ming-huang

Chün ware. Six-lobed flower pot, Sung dynasty (920–1280). Fogg Art Museum, Cambridge, Mass.

as a huge bearded man in rags. He subdued a demon who had entered the palace, and he identified himself to the grateful Emperor as a scholar who had committed suicide when prevented from attaining first place on a public examination. The emperor dubbed him official demon quell-

er, and his exploits provided Chinese artists with abundant material for demoniacal scenes, such as Kung K'ai's masterly scroll, *Chung K'uei, the Demon Queller, on his Travels* (1260–80; Washington, D.C., Freer Gallery). Chung K'uei's counterpart in Japanese lore is Shōki.

BIBLIOGRAPHY. L. Sickman and A. Soper, *The Art and Architecture of China*, Baltimore, 1956; F. M. Jonas, *Netsuké*, Rutland, Vt., 1960.

CHUNG-TU, *see* PEKING.

CHUN WARE. Imperial ceramic ware produced in China from the Sung dynasty into the Ming period. The name is taken from Chün-chou, a district in Honan Province where the kilns were located in the Sung period. The site was established as early as the 10th century, and later other kiln sites produced similar wares, which go under the general designation of Chün. The most characteristic features of the ware are a thick lavender glaze flushed with crimson and purple (often in large blotches) and a rather heavy form. The pieces include massive flowerpots and bulb bowls as well as dishes and smaller cups. A fine collection of Chün ware can be found in the Fogg Art Museum, Cambridge, Mass.

CHURCH, FREDERICK EDWIN. American landscape painter (b. Hartford, Conn., 1826; d. New York City,

Frederick E. Church, *Scene in the Catskill Mountains*, 1852. Walker Art Center, Minneapolis.

1900). He studied drawing with Benjamin A. Coe and painting with Alexander H. Emmons. Later he was a pupil of Thomas Cole and headed the second generation of Hudson River school landscape painters.

Church visited and painted in the Andes, Jamaica, Europe, the Near East, and Labrador. The *Catskill Mountains* (1852) illustrates his profound understanding of nature. He diligently painted panoramas with broad horizons, pure colors, and meticulous details. Luminous skies and sweeping aerial perspectives give his romantic natural scenes a spiritual quality.

BIBLIOGRAPHY. C. E. Sears, *Highlights Among the Hudson River Artists*, Boston, 1947.

CHURCH AND SYNAGOGUE.

Subject in medieval art personified by two young women known as *Ecclesia exaltetur* and *Synagoga deponitur*. Derived from a French theme dating from 10th-century ivories, they represented the Christian and Jewish religions and were shown together as an allegory on the fulfillment of the Old Law by the New. The Church was shown erect, crowned, and holding a chalice and banner. The Synagogue appeared as dejected, blindfolded, and holding a broken stave. The finest examples of the figures in Gothic sculpture are those used as jamb figures in the 13th-century Cathedral of Bamberg, as well as those at Reims.

BIBLIOGRAPHY. C. R. Morey, *Mediaeval Art*, New York, 1942.

CHURCH OF THE VIRGIN, *see* ST. PARASKEVI CHURCH, SALONIKA.

CHURINGA (Tsuringa) STONES.

Type of sacred object made by the Australian aborigines. Carved with ritual symbols, they are used in religious rites together with songs and chants. They are also made of wood.

BIBLIOGRAPHY. C. Barrett and R. H. Croll, *Art of the Australian Aboriginal*, Melbourne, 1943.

CHURRIGUERA, JOSE BENITO DE.

Spanish architect, painter, and sculptor (b. Salamanca, 1665; d. Madrid, 1723/25). José was the head of an architectural family dynasty during the last years of the 17th and the first quarter of the 18th century. This family consisted of three brothers and four sons, all of whom were active at the same time and several of whom worked together on certain projects. There has thus been much difficulty in distinguishing between them, resulting in frequent misattributions.

In the early 1690s José and his brother Joaquin (1674–1725) came to Madrid from Barcelona to continue the family trade of making large retables for altars, usually on the basis of someone else's designs. In 1689 José won a competition for a catafalque for the tomb of Queen Maria Luisa of Savoy, the first wife of Charles II. Although the catafalque may have been based on, and showed no improvement over, Bernardo de Pineda's 1671 monument to St. Ferdinand in the Cathedral at Seville, winning the competition opened José's career. The following year he was appointed court painter to Philip V but he was later dismissed after disagreements with Philip's favorite artist, the German Teodore Ardemans. Between 1693 and 1696

José moved back to Salamanca, where he was subsequently appointed *maestro mayor* of that city's Cathedral; within fifty years he and his family and their pupils had turned the city into a Churrigueresque show place.

The style this term denotes is characterized by the most frenzied exuberance of detail, representing the Spanish baroque fantasy at its fullest. However, the term has been, and frequently still is, used as a synonym for bad taste. Although the term is normally associated with the work of José himself, as head of the family, it is clear that in all his work he showed more restraint than did his brothers. Moreover, he never permitted sculptured stucco decoration to hide completely the architectonic structure of the work. The retable in S. Esteban, Salamanca (1693), is a good example of his work. Indeed, José is the least Churrigueresque artist of the whole family, and by no means should the general excesses of the style be attributed to him. His work has the admirable blend of the Gothic and the baroque spirit found in the work of Guarini in Italy.

BIBLIOGRAPHY. B. Bevan, *History of Spanish Architecture*, London, 1939; G. Kubler and M. Soria, *Art and Architecture in Spain and Portugal and Their American Dominions, 1500–1800*, Baltimore, 1959; J. Lees-Milne, *Baroque in Spain and Portugal and Its Antecedents*, London, 1960. CARL F. BARNES

CHU TA (Pa-ta shan-jen).

Chinese painter (1625–ca. 1700). He was a distant descendant of the Ming imperial house

José Benito de Churriguera, high altar and retable of S. Esteban, Salamanca, 1693.

and became a Buddhist monk about 1648, a few years after the fall of the Ming dynasty.

Few painters in Chinese history have been as enshrouded in colorful legends as Chu Ta, and few painters have presented more complexities of personality. Pa-ta literally means "Great Eight" and has sometimes been taken to refer to the four major and minor quadrants, in all of which there was supposedly none greater than Chu Ta himself. Chinese writers do not agree on his life chronology, but there seems little doubt that Chu Ta either effectively feigned or was actually touched by insanity and was also apparently a liberal drinker. The various accounts of his drunkenness and madness have a parallel with the life and career of Hsü Wei, and there is more than a passing similarity in their painting styles. *See* HSU WEI.

His bizarre personality aside, there is no question that Chu Ta ranks as one of the most brilliant of the individualistic monk painters in the 17th century. The side of his style that is best known to the Western audience centers on the depiction of birds, fishes, and animals, usually in the small-scaled album format. The paintings are extremely abbreviated statements, done with a brush that appears at first glance to be careless and somewhat spontaneous: scratchy and dry in places, overloaded and blurred in others, his brushstrokes take on expressive qualities that are tinged by the sense of personal aberration and mystery surrounding this quite uncommon painter. His subject matter also reflects the bizarre world in which he lived, his birds seen as insecure creatures, hunched on a single wavering flower stem. His animals are often misshapen, touched by a kind of whimsical humor at times, by a ponderous moroseness at others, but always with recognizable human qualities. Whatever his message in these homogeneous presentations, it was a private one, unfathomable for the rational mind. The landscapes of Chu Ta, however, speak in the more traditional manner in terms of subject matter at least, although the quality of the bizarre is also present.

His landscape studies seem related to those of Tung Ch'i-ch'ang, possessing a rather similar cold, formal air. But the obvious twists and turns of the brush that are evident in his landscapes, no matter how rational the construction and interwoven the surface may be, dynamically state the process of painting and give his landscapes a sense of true organic growth. *See* TUNG CH'I-CH'ANG.

BIBLIOGRAPHY. H. Franke, "Zur Biographie des Pa-ta shan-jen," *Asiatica, Festschrift Friedrich Weller*, Leipzig, 1954; Hsieh Chih-lu, *Chu Ta* (Chung-kuo hua-chia ts'ung-shu, vol. 18), Shanghai, 1958; O. Sirén, *Chinese Painting, Leading Masters and Principles*, vol. 4, New York, 1958.   MARTIE W. YOUNG

CHU TE-JUN. Chinese landscape painter (1294–1365). He was born in Sui-yang, Honan Province, during the Yüan dynasty and spent the better part of his life in Su-chou, the area that eventually became of major importance in the Ming dynasty. Chu Te-jun was well known to his contemporaries and played an influential role in the cultural life of the times. He was a gifted intellectual whose paintings were decidedly in the conservative vein, following Kuo Hsi, Li Ssu-hsün, and other "ancient masters." Time has not been too kind to Chu Te-jun, for his extant paintings are very few and hardly justify the reputation he had during his lifetime. *See* KUO HSI; LI SSU-HSUN.

BIBLIOGRAPHY. O. Sirén, *Chinese Painters, Leading Masters and Principles*, vol. 4, New York, 1958.

CHU TUAN. Chinese court painter (fl. first part of 16th cent.). He was known also by his *tzu* K'o-ch'eng. A native of Hai-yen in Chekiang Province, Chu Tuan gained a reputation for his landscape paintings, although he is included among the followers of Lü Chi, the famous Ming bird painter. His landscapes reveal a restrained but gifted painter, one who is well aware of the previous Yüan-dynasty experiments in this genre. Among the best-known Chu Tuans in American collections is the excellent and often-reproduced landscape in the Museum of Fine Arts, Boston, showing a scholar seated in a boat by a riverbank. *See* LU CHI.

BIBLIOGRAPHY. L. Sickman and A. Soper, *The Art and Architecture of China*, Baltimore, 1956.

C.I.A.M. (Congres Internationaux d'Architecture Moderne). International organization of Europe's leading modern architects, first assembled at the Château de la Sarraz, Switzerland, in June, 1928. It aimed to consolidate the gains of the 1920s; to further explore problems of environmental design; and to propagate the objectives of the new architecture. Among its early organizers were Siegfried Giedion, Le Corbusier, Ernst May, Victor Bourgeois, Walter Gropius, and others, who subsequently took little part in its proceedings. The organization eventually split and was disbanded in 1959. *See* GROPIUS, WALTER; LE CORBUSIER.

CIBBER (Cibert), CAIUS GABRIEL. English sculptor (b. Denmark, 1630; d. England, 1700). By 1693 he had established a great reputation, working in architectural settings, such as the *Chatsworth Altarpiece* (1687–90). His tomb to

Lodovico Cardi da Cigoli, *St. Peter Walking on Ashes*. Pitti, Florence.

Thomas Sackville (1677) at Withyham is a portrayal at once moving and among the great English monuments of the 17th century. His best-known works are *Melancholy* and *Raving Madness*, both in London.

CIBORIUM, *see* BALDACHINO.

CIFRONDI, ANTONIO. Italian painter (1657–1730). He was a student of the Bolognese figure painter Marcantonio Franceschini. Cifrondi became popular for his representations of scenes from bourgeois life. In the framework of this genre Cifrondi's work reveals the closest relationship with the series of etchings *Arti di Bologna* by Annibale Carracci. Like those earlier popular works, Cifrondi's paintings emphasize the narrative quality of homely scenes with frequent grotesque or bawdy inclusions.

BIBLIOGRAPHY. R. Wittkower, *Art and Architecture in Italy, 1600–1750,* Baltimore, 1958.

CIGNANI, CARLO. Italian painter (b. Bologna, 1628; d. Forlì, 1719). He studied with G. B. Cairo and then with Albani (ca. 1646–50) in Bologna, working in his native city except for trips to Leghorn (1655–58), Rome (1662–65), and Parma (1678–81), and transferring to Forlì in 1686, where he remained for the rest of his life. Cignani's exploration of the theme of pagan figures in a landscape (*Rape of Europa*, ca. 1678–81; Parma, Palazzo del Giardino) and "quiet" illusionism (*Assumption of the Virgin*, ca. 1686–1706; Forlì, Cathedral) is done in a style that combines a sense of sweetness, based on smooth curvilinear forms, with a latent baroque rendering of movement. Cig-

G. B. Cima, *The Madonna with the Orange Tree.* Academy, Venice.

nani thus forms a link between earlier Carraccesque and later 18th-century Italian artists.

BIBLIOGRAPHY. S. Vitelli Buscaroli, *Carlo Cignani, 1628–1719,* Bologna, 1953; *Maestri della pittura del Seicento emiliano* (catalog), ed. F. Arcangeli et al., 2d ed., Bologna, 1959.

CIGOLI, LODOVICO CARDI DA. Italian painter and architect (b. Castelvecchio di Cigoli, 1559; d. Rome, 1613). He studied with Allori and Buontalenti in Florence, working there and in Rome for the rest of his life. His early style depends on Florentine mannerism (*Noli me tangere,* ca. 1585; Florence, S. Miniato al Monte), but his horizons soon widen to include Correggio and the Venetians (*Martyrdom of St. Stephen,* 1597; Florence, Pitti Palace). These elements, in conjunction with the mysticism, fervent emotion, and immediacy that pervade such paintings as the *Stigmatization of St. Francis* (Pitti Palace), make Cigoli one of the founders of baroque painting.

BIBLIOGRAPHY. San Miniato, Accademia degli Euteleti, *Mostra del Cigoli e del suo ambiente* (catalog), ed. Mario Bucci et al., 1959.

CIMA, GIOVANNI BATTISTA (Cima da Conegliano). Venetian painter (ca. 1460–1517/18). He was born in Conegliano. His life was an uneventful series of commissions in Venice and nearby. He is best known for many half-length Madonnas, which have made him seem a secondary Giovanni Bellini. He uses the same compositions as Bellini in a more old-fashioned style and sometimes retraces his own early compositions in later works.

Cima's development is in lighting and modeling; his forte is forms suspended in light, not drama or feeling. His background is in the Vivarini group, parallel to Montagna's. His earliest certain work, the *Madonna with SS. John and Jerome* (Vicenza Museum), has a unique design with the Madonna in front of an arbor and the saints in front of a wall. This requires two lightings and thus gives a naturalistic force to the traditional divisions of altarpieces.

After the more standard Conegliano Cathedral altarpiece (1493), Cima concentrates on the architectonic forms of the figures. In *The Baptism* (1494; Venice, S. Giovanni in Bragora) and the *Madonna with the Orange Tree* (Venice, Academy) they are geometrically articulate, softened by delicate light, in a world romantically rich in incident. In interiors, similar geometric figures relate to cubic furniture or rooms (*Annunciation,* 1495; Leningrad, Hermitage). Smooth purity grows in the *Dragan Altarpiece* (1496–99; Venice, Academy) and in the one at Miglionico (1499).

After 1500 a change suggests the influence of Giovanni Bellini's late style, Leonardo's visit, and Giorgione. Forms soften, though they remain isolated, as they do not in the more advanced artists. At first they have elaborate folds and ornaments (*Constantine and Helena,* Venice, S. Giovanni in Bragora). Small mythological paintings are also Giorgionesque (Parma, National Gallery, and Philadelphia Museum of Art). Soon he simplifies in the new texture (*Incredulity of St. Thomas,* 1504; London, National Gallery) and is again geometric (*Peter Martyr,* 1506; Milan, Brera), developing dynamic diagonals. The last works are gentle and unemphatic, with diffuse light (*Montini Altarpiece,* 1507, Parma, National Gallery; *St. Peter Enthroned,* 1516, Milan, Brera).

BIBLIOGRAPHY. L. Coletti, *Cima da Conegliano,* Venice, 1960.
CREIGHTON GILBERT

CIMABUE (Cenni di Pepi or Pepe). Italian painter of the Florentine school (ca. 1240–after 1302). According to Dante, Cimabue was the most eminent painter in Italy before the advent of Giotto, who eventually surpassed him in fame. Cimabue is first mentioned, as a witness, in a document of 1271 concerning a nunnery of the Order of St. Damian in Rome that was to be put under the protection of Cardinal Ottoboni Fieschi. Cimabue is not recorded again until 1301, when he is mentioned as a master workman on the apse mosaic in the Cathedral of Pisa. A Pisan document of 1302 names him as the author of the still extant *St. John* there. Two other documents of 1301 state that Cimabue was commissioned to paint a *Virgin in Majesty* and a *Crucifix* for the hospital church of S. Chiara in Pisa. The last notice concerning him is a Florentine document of 1302 in which he is listed as a member of the society of the Piovuti.

In the course of time many works, both in fresco and tempera, have been attributed to Cimabue; modern scholarship, however, accepts as authentic only a small number. The majority of these are in the Church of S. Francesco at Assisi, where the vault of the choir and the walls of the transept and the apse in the Upper Church (dedicated in 1253) were decorated, beginning between 1277 and 1280, by Cimabue and his assistants. In the four quadrants of the choir vault Cimabue painted the *Four Evangelists*, depicting each as a seated scribe in front of a city, an iconographic type found on the title pages of Byzantine evangelistaries.

The walls of the left transept are painted with scenes from the Apocalypse (*St. John on Patmos*, *The Fall of Babylon*, *The Apocalyptic Christ with Angels*, *The Four Winds*, *The Infant Christ on the Throne*) and the *Crucifixion*. The chemical change that has blackened all these frescoes, obliterating their colors and exaggerating their linearity wherever the forms have not been partially effaced, has affected the *Crucifixion* with particular harshness. It is a composition of great size, covering the entire east wall and dominated in the center by a colossal figure of Christ. In grandeur and intensity of conception it is one of the greatest works in the history of Italian painting.

The upper part of the left transept contains figures and busts of angels, executed by assistants to Cimabue's designs, and the remains of *St. Michael Battling Demons* by Cimabue, which is thematically related to the Apocalypse cycle below it. The frescoes in the apse depict the *Apocryphal Legends of the Virgin*, beginning with four (*The Annunciation to Joachim*, *The Suitors Before the High Priest*, *The Nativity of the Virgin*, and *The Marriage of the Virgin*) in the two topmost recesses and continuing in the lower zone with four scenes from the *Death and Glory of the Virgin* (*The Last Hour of the Virgin*, *The Dormition*, *The Ascension*, and *Christ and the Virgin Enthroned*).

The right transept is devoted to the Apostles. The figures of the twelve Apostles set in the arcades have been ruined, but something, though no more than the minimal indications of form common to all the frescoes, has remained of the *Scenes from the Lives of SS. Peter and Paul* in the lower part of the wall (*St. Peter Healing the Lame Man*,

St. Peter Healing the Sick, *The Fall of Simon Magnus*, *The Crucifixion of St. Peter*, and *The Beheading of St. Paul*). The last two of these were executed by an assistant after Cimabue's designs. The east wall of the right transept is occupied by another *Crucifixion*, a collaborative work of Cimabue and his shop, equally large but not as impressive as the one flanking it on the left transept.

Although other parts of the fresco decoration in the Upper Church have also been assigned to Cimabue, the foregoing are his undisputed and, in the opinion of most scholars, his only works there. The choice and arrangement of subjects are dependent on St. Bonaventure's formulation of Franciscan religiosity, especially as it is recounted in his *Life of St. Francis*. One fresco in the Lower Church of S. Francesco at Assisi, a heavily repainted *Madonna and Child Enthroned with Angels and St. Francis*, may be attributed to Cimabue.

Only two works in tempera show the unassisted hand of Cimabue: the grandiose *Madonna and Child Enthroned with Angels and Prophets* from the Florentine Church of S. Trinita (Florence, Uffizi) and the *Crucifix* in S. Domenico at Arezzo. Another *Crucifix* (Florence, Museum of Sta Croce) is only in part by the master, and the *Madonna and Child Enthroned with Angels* from S. Francesco in Pisa (Paris, Louvre) appears to have been executed entirely by his shop. Even further removed from Cimabue's individual style, though generally associated with his shop, is the *Madonna and Child Enthroned with Angels* in the Church of the Servi in Bologna. Cimabue's importance in his time may in part be gauged by the number of painters who worked under his direct influence. With few exceptions, however, their identity has remained unknown. Their works are usually designated as by the school of Cimabue, such as the triptych with *Christ Between St. Peter and St. James Major* in the National Gallery of Art in Washington, D.C.

Although Cimabue's art is related to and partly comes out of the Byzantine style, he replaced its conventional compositions and shapes with the formulations of his own more vital, monumental, and structurally articulated manner, based to a much larger extent on the observation of real things. His particular signature exists in a partly angular, partly curved geometry that conveys concentrated and dynamic energy. Though nothing is known of his training, it may be said that he developed to its ultimate possibilities the monumental style of his slightly older contemporary Coppo di Marcovaldo. There is no evidence for the assumption that Cimabue was the teacher of Giotto. On the contrary, his art marks the culmination of one, Giotto's the beginning of another, phase in Italian painting.

BIBLIOGRAPHY. J. Strzygowski, *Cimabue und Rom*, Vienna, 1888; G. Vasari, *Le vite...*, ed. K. Frey, vol. 1, Munich, 1911; E. Benkard, *Das literarische Portraet des Giovanni Cimabue*, Munich, 1917; O. Sirén, *Toskanische Maler des XIII. Jahrhunderts*, Berlin, 1922; A. Nicholson, *Cimabue*, Princeton, 1932; E. Battisti, *Cimabue*, Milan, 1963; J. White, *Art and Architecture in Italy, 1250–1400*, Baltimore, 1966.

HELLMUT WOHL

CIMA DA CONEGLIANO, *see* CIMA, GIOVANNI BATTISTA.

CIMBORIO. Spanish term for a lantern or raised structure above a roof admitting light to the interior. Such an ar-

Cimabue, *Crucifix*, detail. S. Domenico, Arezzo.

Cimborio. Raised structure admitting light to the interior.

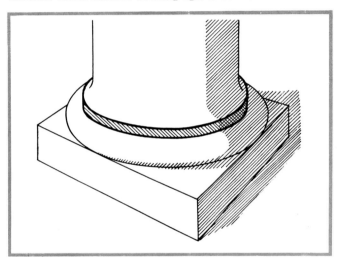

Cincture. Molding encircling a column base.

Jacopo di Cione, *The Coronation of the Virgin*. Academy, Florence.

rangement may be seen in S. Juan de los Reyes, Toledo, and the Old Cathedral, Salamanca.

CINCINNATI, OHIO: CINCINNATI ART MUSEUM. Opened in 1886. The museum contains painting, sculpture, and antiquities, including some rare Nabataean sculptures from Jordan and Israel and a masterpiece of Chinese painting, *The Four Sages of Shang-shan*, by Ma Yüan. The collection of European art contains distinguished works of all periods and schools, including Botticelli's *Judith with the Head of Holofernes*, Titian's *Philip II of Spain*, El Greco's *Crucifixion with View of Toledo*, and Zurbarán's *Legend of the Bell*. Perhaps the rarest painting is the Mantegna *Esther and Mordecai*, which is one of six works by Mantegna in the United States.

The museum sponsors a Color Lithography International and has amassed an extensive print collection. There is also a fine collection of decorative arts.

BIBLIOGRAPHY. E. Spaeth, *American Art Museums and Galleries*, New York, 1960.

CINCTURE. Annular fillet at the top or bottom of a classical shaft. Generally it is the upper member of the base.

CINERARIUM. Place to receive the ashes of the dead; in ancient Roman tombs the place for sepulchral urns.

CINQUECENTO. Italian for "500"; an abbreviation for the 16th century. In art, Cinquecento refers specifically to the Italian styles of the High and Late Renaissance and generally to the whole of the 16th century.

CINQUEFOIL. In tracery, having five foils (French *cinques feuilles*, "five leaves") or openings, terminating in cusps outlining the openings.

CINTRA, PALACE OF. Palace of Portuguese kings since its reconquest from the Moors in 1147. The building, around a nucleus that may be Islamic, has accreted an asymmetrical pile of Gothic, Mudejar, Manueline, and

Renaissance additions, dominated by the twin conical turrets of the kitchens. Tiled walls and floors, and painted, carved, and gilded ceilings of all periods abound.

BIBLIOGRAPHY. J. Pessanha, *Sintra*, Pôrto, 1932.

CIONE, ANDREA DI, *see* ORCAGNA, ANDREA.

CIONE, JACOPO DI. Italian painter of the Florentine school (fl. 1365–98). Jacopo was the brother of Nardo di Cione and of Andrea di Cione (called Orcagna) and may have been trained in the latter's shop. Jacopo's individual style is not easy to define. It has little in common with that of Orcagna but shows, rather, the influence of Maso di Banco and later of Nardo di Cione and Niccolò di Pietro Gerini. Jacopo is documented in 1368 as completing an altarpiece of *St. Matthew with Scenes from His Life* (Florence, Uffizi) that had been commissioned from Orcagna the year before. Originally set up in Or San Michele, it is a reversion common at its time to a type of altarpiece prevalent in the 13th century, with the standing figure of the saint in the center and the smaller scenes flanking him in vertical strips at either side.

In 1373 Jacopo completed a large altarpiece of the *Coronation of the Virgin* (Florence, Academy), ordered in 1372 by the Florentine Mint. A work of the same subject and in a similar style, but slightly smaller, is in the National Gallery, London. At least two other painters are known to have participated in the execution of these two works; their identity is not certain, but one of them may have been Niccolò di Pietro Gerini. Jacopo received payments in 1378, 1380, and 1382 for works in Florence that have not survived. A polyptych of 1383 (*Madonna and Child with Angels and Saints* and *The Adoration of the Magi and Six Saints* in the predella) is also in Florence (Academy). In 1382 he worked on the coloring of statues for the Opera del Duomo (the commission in charge of all construction and decoration in connection with the Cathedral of Florence).

Many panel paintings are attributed to Jacopo, among them a *Madonna of Humility with Angels* (New York, Lehman Collection), a *Madonna and Child with a Kneeling Donor* (Fiesole, Bandini Museum), and a portable altar with the *Madonna and Child with Saints*, the *Annunciation*, the *Nativity*, and the *Crucifixion* (Gloucester, Highnam Court).

BIBLIOGRAPHY. O. Sirén, "Pictures in America by Bernardo Daddi, Taddeo Gaddi, Andrea Orcagna and his Brothers," *Art in America*, II, 1914; B. Berenson, "Quadri senza casa," *Dedalo*, II, 1930–31; R. Offner, "Mostra del tesoro di Firenze sacra," *The Burlington Magazine*, LXIII, 1933; H. Gronau, "The San Pier Maggiore Altarpiece: A Reconstruction," *The Burlington Magazine*, LXXXVI, 1945.

HELLMUT WOHL

CIONE, NARDO DI. Italian painter of the Florentine school (fl. ca. 1343; d. ca. 1356). Nardo was the brother of Jacopo di Cione and of Andrea di Cione (called Orcagna). Our knowledge of Nardo's art is based on Ghiberti's attribution to him of the frescoes in the Strozzi Chapel in S. Maria Novella, Florence. Nardo joined the Florentine painters' guild about 1343. Nothing is known of his training; he was influenced by Maso di Banco and Orcagna. His frescoes in S. Maria Novella represent, on opposite walls of the chapel, *Paradise* and *Inferno*, and between them the *Last Judgment*. In the *Paradise* Christ and the

Virgin are seated in the upper part of a tall throne aedicule, surrounded by two-dimensionally superimposed rows of saints and the blessed. In the *Inferno* the elaborately compartmented structure, resembling a cross section, follows Dante's organization of hell in the *Divine Comedy*. In their overriding concern for enumeration these frescoes show the influence of popular Dominican sermons of the time.

Nardo also painted frescoes in the Chiostrino dei Morti of S. Maria Novella depicting the *Legend of the Virgin* and figures of various saints. Fragments of a fresco cycle of the *Passion of Christ* in the Giochi and Bastari Chapel in the Badia of Florence, the most extensively preserved of which is *Christ Carrying the Cross*, may also be attributed to him. Nardo's tempera works are greatly prized. They combine Florentine monumentality and severity with suaveness and subtlety of expression and refinement of color, qualities more often associated with Sienese than with Florentine painting.

Though Nardo painted many large altarpieces his most valued pictures are small, portable altars, such as the triptych in the National Gallery of Art in Washington, D.C. Among the larger works are a *Madonna and Child* (New York, New-York Historical Society), an altarpiece with *Three Saints* (London, National Gallery), two panels of *Saints* (Munich, Old Pinacothek), *St. Peter* and *St. John the Baptist* (New Haven, Conn., Yale University Art Gallery) and a polyptych (Prague, National Gallery). Next to Orcagna, Nardo was the most important and distinguished painter in Florence during his lifetime. His influ-

Nardo di Cione, *Madonna and Child with SS. Peter and John the Evangelist.* National Gallery of Art, Washington, D.C.

ence was significant in Florentine painting of the later 14th century, particularly in the circle of Giovanni del Biondo.

BIBLIOGRAPHY. R. van Marle, *The Development of the Italian Schools of Painting*, vol. 3, The Hague, 1924; R. Offner, "Nardo di Cione and His Triptych in the Goldman Collection," *Art in America*, XII, 1924; F. Antal, *Florentine Painting and Its Social Background*, London, 1947; M. Meiss, *Painting in Florence and Siena after the Black Death*, Princeton, 1951; R. Offner, *A Critical and Historical Corpus of Florentine Painting*, section 4, vol. 2, New York, 1960.

HELLMUT WOHL

CIPRIANI, GIOVANNI BATTISTA. Italian etcher and painter (b. Florence, 1726; d. London, 1785). His etchings are highly finished with the engraving tool and display the stylistic panoply of the hack reproductive engraver. He made prints after his own compositions and those of his teacher, A. D. Gabbini, as well as Van Dyck, Guido Reni, and others. There were many more prints made after Cipriani (by Bartolozzi and others) than by him.

CIRCIGNANI, ANTONIO (Pomarancio). Italian painter (b. Pomarance, 1570; d. Rome, ca. 1630). A student of his father, Nicolò Circignani, and of Cristoforo Roncalli, both of whom were also called Pomarancio, Antonio developed a pious and simplified mannerist style in his frescoes for Roman churches and palaces, which in some respects has an affinity with Spanish baroque painting.

CIRCIGNANI, NICOLO, *see* POMARANCIO.

CIRCUS. Long U-shaped structure used chiefly for chariot races and horse racing in Roman antiquity. The word means "circle" or "ring" in Latin. Circuses were divided longitudinally by a barrier called a spina. At the sides and rounded turn of the circus were tiered seats for spectators. The plan of the Roman circus resembles that of the Greek hippodrome, with *carceres*, or stalls for horses. The Circus Maximus and the Circus of Maxentius, both in Rome, are representative examples.

Circus Maximus, Rome. First and greatest of all Roman circuses.

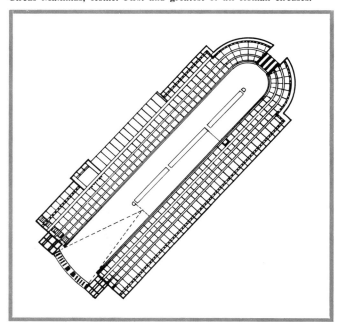

CIRCUS MAXIMUS, ROME. Ancient Roman circus situated in the valley between the Palatine and Aventine hills. The first and greatest of all Roman circuses, it was 1,968 feet long and 492 feet wide. The site was first chosen for a circus by the Tarquins. The early *carceres* (stalls at the starting places for the races) were built of wood; they were replaced by stone forms in the 2d century B.C. The circus was repeatedly destroyed by fire and was restored several times. It was rebuilt by Julius Caesar, who probably constructed the first stone foundations upon which the two upper tiers of wooden seats rested. The wooden structure of the circus burned down in 31 B.C.; it was restored by Augustus, who erected the imperial box on the side of the Palatine. He also placed in the center of the spina (central ridge) an obelisk from Heliopolis (today in the Piazza del Popolo).

The circus reached its greatest magnificence in the time of Emperor Trajan. The main structure was then of solid masonry covered with white marble. The exterior was three stories high, with arches and engaged Doric columns. The *cavea* (interior) was divided into three zones of seats, separated by corridors, and resembled in plan the *cavea* of the Colosseum. The west end consisted of several stories with towers that gave the appearance of a fortified wall. At the east end stood a gateway formed by the Arch of Vespasian and Titus, erected by the Senate in A.D. 81. A water channel called the Euripus encircled the arena. Placed there at an early date, it protected the spectators from attack by the wild beasts. The circus was used for gladiatorial combats and fights with wild animals. The last games are recorded to have taken place in A.D. 549. At that time the destruction of the Circus Maximus began.

The seating capacity of the circus has given rise to dispute. It is probable that it could accommodate about 200,000 spectators. Several altars of numerous divinities were placed within the circus on the spina or in the *cavea*.

BIBLIOGRAPHY. S. B. Platner, *The Topography and Monuments of Ancient Rome*, 2d rev. ed., Boston, 1911; D. M. Robathan, *The Monuments of Ancient Rome*, Rome, 1950.

EVANTHIA SAPORITI

CIRE-PERDUE, *see* CAST AND CASTING.

CIRQUE FERNANDO, AU. Oil painting by Toulouse-Lautrec, in the Art Institute of Chicago. *See* TOULOUSE-LAUTREC, HENRI DE.

CIST. Type of pre-Christian burial common to the Celtic peoples of the British Isles and France. It consisted of a crude stone chest arranged in the earth or hewn out of rock and covered by stone slabs. By extension, a cist is any sepulchral stone chest. It is known also as "cistvaen," from the Welsh word meaning "chest."

CISTA. Box or chest, usually of metal (also called cist). In antiquity cistae were used to contain toilet articles and sacred utensils pertaining to the mysteries of Demeter and Bacchus (bronze cistae from Praeneste, including the famous Ficorini cista in the National Etruscan Museum of the Villa Giulia in Rome). In Christian times cistae served as reliquaries and as protective coverings for parchment rolls.

CISTERCIAN ARCHITECTURE, *see* Cîteaux; Clairvaux, Abbey of; Fontenay, Abbey Church of; Fossanova, Monastery of; Fountains Abbey; Heiligenkreuz; Poblet, Abbey of.

CITADEL. That portion of a town, often placed on a commanding height, which was strongly fortified in order to dominate the local populace and to serve as a refuge for them in case of enemy attack. Originating during the Bronze Age, a time of urban growth, these walled enclosures also provided sites for important temples and for royal residences. The Acropolis of Athens and the Capitoline of Rome are outstanding examples.

CITEAUX. Site, about 15 miles south of Dijon, France, of the foundation of the Cistercian order. Founded by Robert de Molesmes in 1098, Cîteaux and the order grew and spread rapidly, especially under the impetus of the dynamic personality of St. Bernard of Clairvaux (ca. 1090–1153). By the year 1200 more than 700 monasteries were under the rule of Cîteaux and the Cistercian order.

The order, influenced by St. Bernard, followed a rigidly prescribed existence, one that did not allow for the flourishing of the arts common to the other monastic orders of the period. The austerity of the Cistercians is indicated by some of their rules: in 1124 sculptural decoration in churches was proscribed, as was manuscript illumination; in 1157 stone towers on churches were prohibited; and in 1182 stained glass was proscribed. The austerity of St. Bernard, in direct contrast to his art-loving contemporary Abbot Suger of St-Denis, perhaps accounts for the simplicity and conservatism of Cistercian architecture.

At Cîteaux, the founder's church, a small wooden building, was replaced in 1106 by a larger stone church, tunnel-vaulted and without transepts. Chapels forming a dwarf transept were soon added, but the whole retained a simple quality. Even when the large new church at Cîteaux (1125–93) was completed, it retained a good deal of Cistercian simplicity and directness. This was due in large part to the unmistakable quality of Cistercian masonry: fine, sharply cut, evenly mortared ashlar.

The general aspect of Cistercian architecture is that of contemporaneous Burgundy. In terms of specific appearance, this meant adherence to Cluniac-Burgundian "proto-Gothic" vaulting systems, general Romanesque stylistic qualities, and monastery planning derived and modified from the ideal plan of St. Gall. When the Cistercian churches adopted the Gothic mode (flying buttresses, pointed rib vaulting, the *chevet* complex), as in the no longer extant church at Clairvaux (1133–74), they still retained the pristine character of the order's austere foundations. *See* Clairvaux, Abbey of.

Typical of extant Cistercian monastic building is that at Fontenay (1139–47), the best-preserved, oldest Cistercian monastic complex in existence. The layout of Fontenay clearly indicates the emphasis on self-sufficiency and the desire for isolation. *See* Fontenay, Abbey Church of.

BIBLIOGRAPHY. M. Aubert, *L'Architecture cistercienne en France*, 2 vols., 2d ed., Paris, 1947; *Saint Bernard et l'art des Cisterciens* (exhibition catalog), Dijon, 1953.　　　　STANLEY FERBER

CITHARA. Greek musical instrument, consisting of seven or eight strings stretched from volute-like wooden supports

Cîteaux. Engraving of the Cistercian monastery complex, built mainly in the 12th century.

over a sounding box (usually a tortoise shell). In art, it is a characteristic attribute of Apollo and the Muses. An excellent example is shown on an amphora by the Berlin Painter from the Hearst Collection in the Metropolitan Museum of Art, New York.

BIBLIOGRAPHY. G. M. A. Richter, *Attic Red-Figured Vases: A Survey*, New Haven, 1958.

CITRA, *see* Chitra.

CITY PLANNING, *see* Town Planning.

CIUFFAGNI, BERNARDO DI PIERO. Italian sculptor (b. Florence, 1381; d. there, 1457). Trained in the Gothic tradition, he aspired to, but failed to attain, the expressive realism of Donatello. Ciuffagni worked chiefly for the Opera del Duomo and under this patronage carved in 1410–15 for the façade of the Cathedral the well-known statue of St. Matthew which is now in the Cathedral Museum.

CIVERCHIO, VINCENZO. Italian painter of Lombardy (fl. 1491–1539). Civerchio worked in his native Crema, in Brescia, and in small towns. Signed altarpieces are in Brescia, Crema, Budapest, Lecco, Lovere, and Palazzolo. He was an eclectic, echoing Leonardo, Foppa, Bramantino, and Butinone.

BIBLIOGRAPHY. A. Morassi, *Brescia*, Rome, 1939.

CIVIDALE DEL FRIULI, CHURCH OF, *see* Santa Maria in Valle, Tempietto of.

Matteo di Giovanni Civitali, *Altar of St. Regulus*. Cathedral, Lucca.

CIVITALI, MATTEO DI GIOVANNI. Tuscan stone sculptor (b. Lucca, 1436; d. there, 1501). He was active also in Carrara, Pisa, and Genoa. Civitali may have stayed in Florence during the 1460s, to judge from stylistic similarities to the Rossellino atelier and Desiderio da Settignano. Civitali's works include the tomb of the papal secretary Piero da Noceto (1472; Lucca, Cathedral), the 1481 Volto Santo Chapel in the nave of Lucca Cathedral for his patron Domenico Bertini, and the 1485 *Altar of St. Regulus* (Lucca, Cathedral), perhaps his greatest work. Civitali's style is primitive but approaches the High Renaissance.

BIBLIOGRAPHY. A. Venturi, *Storia dell'arte italiana*, vol. 6, Milan, 1908.

CIVITALI, NICOLO. Italian sculptor and architect (b. Lucca, 1482; d. after 1560). A pupil of his father, Matteo, Nicolò built the palace of the Bernardini at Lucca, of the Santini at Gattaiola, and of the Sinibaldi at Massa Pisana. As a sculptor, he is known only to have worked at Pietrasanta.

CLAESSEN (Claesz.), ALART (Allaert). Dutch painter of portraits and possibly also graphic artist (fl. Amsterdam, 1520–55). Nothing is known of his training and very little of his activity. Karel van Mander, the Dutch painter and artists' biographer, states that Claessen was a portrait painter and one of the best artists of his time. Van Mander noted that numerous portraits by Claessen were to be seen in Amsterdam (1604). He also tells us that Pieter Aertsen was his pupil. Claessen is sometimes identified with an engraver of the same name whose dated works fall between 1520 and 1555; however, Van Mander makes no mention of this aspect of Claessen's activity. A *Civic Guard Portrait with Eighteen Figures* (dated 1534 but not signed; Amsterdam, Rijksmuseum) is usually attributed to Claessen.

BIBLIOGRAPHY. A. Riegl, *Das holländische Gruppenporträt*, 2 vols., Vienna, 1931; A. B. de Vries, *Het Noord-Nederlandsch Portret in de tweede helft van de 16e Eeuw*, Amsterdam, 1934.

CLAESSENS (Claeissins; Claes), PIETER II. Flemish history and portrait painter (b. Bruges, ca. 1550; d. there, 1623). Master of the Bruges guild in 1570 and dean in 1587, 1600, and 1606, Claessens was the official town painter from 1581 to 1621. In 1584 he worked on the entry of Alessandro Farnese, duke of Parma, into Bruges. He painted topographical views of cities and portraits of Philip II and Charles V. Claessens' *retardataire* religious paintings and portraits, clinging to the tradition of Memling and Gerard David, are stiffly and naïvely painted.

BIBLIOGRAPHY. W. H. J. Weale, "A Family of Flemish Painters," *Burlington Magazine*, XIX, 1911.

CLAESZ., ALART (Allaert), *see* CLAESSEN, ALART.

CLAESZ., ANTHONY I. Dutch still-life painter (1592–1635/36). Little is known of the activity of this flower and fruit painter. His work, of which only a few paintings are known, is similar to that of such early still-life painters as Ambrosius Bosschaert and Balthasar van der Ast. His son Anthony II Claesz. was also a painter.

BIBLIOGRAPHY. I. Bergström, *Dutch Still-Life Painting in the Seventeenth Century*, New York, 1956.

CLAESZ., ANTHONY II. Dutch still-life and flower painter (1616–before 1652). A native of Amsterdam, he appears to have traveled considerably and was in England. In spite of his slightly archaic style he was one of the best Dutch flower painters of the first half of the 17th century. He was the son of Anthony I Claesz.

BIBLIOGRAPHY. I. Bergström, *Dutch Still-Life Painting in the Seventeenth Century*, New York, 1956.

CLAESZ., PIETER. Dutch painter of still lifes (b. Burgsteinfurt, 1597/98; d. Haarlem, 1660 or 1661?). He was born in Westphalia, seemingly of Dutch parents. In Haarlem in 1617 he was described as a painter. He may have been a pupil of Floris van Dijck, one of the early Haarlem still-life painters. Claesz.'s early work is related to that of Willem Claesz. Heda. Claesz.'s earliest certain work is a *Still Life* (West Monkton, Eng., E. C. Francis Collection) signed with his monogram and the date 1621. He is one of the foremost exponents of the Dutch monochromatic banquet still life.

Claesz. was influenced by the brushwork of his Haarlem contemporary Frans Hals, and the Hals influence is already discernible in Claesz.'s 1624 *Still Life* (Amsterdam, Rijksmuseum). In the 1630s Claesz.'s compositions became somewhat more refined and simplified (*Still Life*, monogram and dated 1636; Rotterdam, Boymans–Van Beuningen Museum). His works are extremely important for the development of Dutch still-life painting in the 17th century.

BIBLIOGRAPHY. A. P. A. Vorenkamp, *Bijdrage tot de geschiedenis van het Hollandsch stilleven in de zeventiende Eeuw*, Leyden, 1934; I. Bergström, *Dutch Still-Life Painting in the Seventeenth Century*, New York, 1956.

CLAEU, JACQUES, *see* GRIEF, JACQUES.

CLAIR DE LUNE. Term coined by Jacquemart in the 19th century to describe a group of 18th-century Chinese ceramic wares with a predominant lavender-gray or blue-gray tone in the glaze. The closest Chinese designation of the ware would be *yüeh-pai*, or "moon white," but the Chinese term covers a wider variety of wares than the French description.

CLAIR-OBSCUR, *see* CHIAROSCURO.

CLAIRVAUX, ABBEY OF. Former French abbey about 55 miles north of Dijon. It was founded in 1115 by St. Bernard, who became its first abbot and did much to aid the growth of the Cistercian order and to direct the order toward austerity and rigidity of rule. The present buildings date mostly from the 18th century; only a storehouse remains from the 12th century. The abbey church was originally square, with stone walls divided into nave and aisles by wooden posts supporting a wooden roof, and was rigorously unadorned. It was rebuilt in a much larger form between 1133 and 1174, with a Gothic ribbed high vault, a clerestory, flying buttresses, and a polygonal apse and ambulatory surrounded by angular radiating chapels. One of the major Cistercian churches in Burgundy, it was destroyed in the French Revolution.

BIBLIOGRAPHY. M. Aubert, *L'Architecture cistercienne en France*, 2 vols., Paris, 1943.

CLAPBOARD. Board, wedge-shaped in section, used as siding in buildings. The term is assumed to have derived from the German *Klappholz*, meaning "barrel stave." Colonial clapboards, so placed that each board overlapped another, were about 5 inches wide, distinguishing them from "weatherboards," about 6 to 8 inches wide, which were used during the 17th century in the southeastern counties of England.

CLAPEROS, ANTONIO, THE ELDER. Spanish sculptor (fl. ca. 1440–60). He worked in the Barcelona and Gerona Cathedrals, at times with his sons, Juan and Antonio Claperos the Younger. From what can be surmised, he treated figures and draperies with some naturalistic freedom, breaking with the rigid Gothic style.

CLARE OF ASSISI, ST. Founder of the Poor Clares and a patron of Assisi (1194–1253). She left home at eighteen,

Pieter Claesz., *Still Life*. Boymans–Van Beuningen Museum, Rotterdam.

Abbey of Clairvaux. Engraving of the former Cistercian abbey.

gave her possessions to the poor, and took vows administered by St. Francis. Joined by her sister and mother, she founded a community in the convent of St. Damian. They lived by the Franciscan rule, emphasizing poverty. St. Clare is portrayed wearing a Franciscan habit with a triple-knotted cord. Her attributes are a monstrance (with which she routed the Saracens), a lily, and a crucifix with olive branch. Her feast is August 12. *See also* SAINTS IN ART.

CLARK, LYGIA. Brazilian abstract painter and sculptor (1920–   ). Born in Belo Horizonte, Lygia Clark studied first with Burle Marx, then in Paris. In 1952 she had her first one-man show and won three prizes, including the Abstract Art Prize in Petrópolis. Cofounder of Brazil's neoconcrete group, she does relieflike painting and metal sculpture.

BIBLIOGRAPHY. F. Gullar, *Lygia Clark*, Rio de Janeiro, 1958.

CLARK (Sterling and Francine) ART INSTITUTE, WILLIAMSTOWN, MASS., *see* WILLIAMSTOWN, MASS.: STERLING AND FRANCINE CLARK ART INSTITUTE.

CLASSICAL ART. Specifically, a term applied to the culture of the ancient Greek and Roman world; but also a general stylistic term applied to any art that strives after the clear, rational balance characteristic of ancient art. The neoclassic style of the early 19th century and certain phases of the Italian Renaissance style, for example, are classical in the general sense of the term.

BIBLIOGRAPHY. B. Rowland, *The Classical Tradition in Western Art*, Cambridge, Mass., 1963.

CLASSICISM, *see* NEOCLASSICAL ART (NEOCLASSICISM).

CLASSICISM, ROMANTIC. A mode of designing rather than a specific style, it is predominantly French in origin, springing from the projects of such architects as Boullée and Ledoux, and consists of stripping architecture to an essential geometric form, often with symbolic associations. It is considered the antithesis of the contemporary picturesque architecture of the last decades of the 18th century and the first decades of the 19th. *See* BOULLEE, ETIENNE-LOUIS; LEDOUX, CLAUDE-NICHOLAS.

BIBLIOGRAPHY. H. R. Hitchcock, *Architecture, Nineteenth and Twentieth Centuries*, Baltimore, 1958.

CLAUDE, *see* LORRAINE, CLAUDE.

CLAUDE LORRAINE GLASS. Small, convex mirror of colored or black glass whose curvature reduces a landscape viewed in it to a compact and less detailed scene. The device, which appeared in the 16th century, has been erroneously connected with the landscapes of Claude Lorraine on the theory that their pervasive "golden" tone might have been obtained in this way. The dark mirror was especially useful to engravers who derived from it a reverse image required by reverse needle engraving.

BIBLIOGRAPHY. "Claude Lorraine Glass," *Apollo*, April, 1956 (s.v. "Letters and Answers to Correspondents").

CLAUSEN, GEORGE. English painter (b. London, 1852; d. there, 1944). He studied in London. In his landscapes

Clausen used a sort of hardened impressionism, at first influenced by Bastien-Lepage, later by Millet's rural sentiment.

BIBLIOGRAPHY. Contemporary British Artists, *George Clausen*, London, 1923.

CLAVE, ANTONI. French painter (1913–   ). Born in Barcelona, Clavé studied at the Barcelona School of Fine Arts. He lives in Paris. Clavé's work underwent a long evolution to reach a very personal style of predominant blacks, reds, and whites, as in *Nature morte aux pastèques* (1936; Paris, Fuentes Collection). He has designed theater décor and has illustrated several books, among them Mérimée's *Lettres d'Espagne*, Rabelais' *Gargantua*, and Pushkin's *The Queen of Spades*. In all his work there is a characteristically Catalonian excitement and vivacity. Clavé was awarded the Prix de la Gravure (1954), the prize of the São Paulo Bienal (1957), the Hallmark Prize, and the UNESCO Prix de la Gravure. His work is on exhibition at the National Museum of Modern Art, Paris. In October–November, 1958, a large Clavé exhibition was held at Arthur Tooth & Sons, London.

BIBLIOGRAPHY. J. Cassou, *Antoni Clavé: Catalogue, Clavé Exhibition*, London, 1958; J. Cassou, *Antoni Clavé*, Barcelona, 1960; R. Nacenta, *Ecole de Paris...*, Neuchâtel, 1960.

CLAVE, PELEGRIN. Mexican painter (1810–80). A Catalan by birth, Clavé was appointed director of the Mexican Academy of San Carlos in 1845. Biased toward French neoclassicism and German romanticism, he became artistic dictator of Mexico. Opposed by "nationalist" elements, Clavé was eventually supplanted under Juárez.

BIBLIOGRAPHY. J. Charlot, *Mexican Art and the Academy of San Carlos 1785-1915*, Austin, Tex., 1962.

CLEARSTORY, *see* CLERESTORY.

CLEEF (Cleve), JAN VAN. Flemish religious and historical painter (b. Venlo, 1646; d. Ghent, 1716). He studied in Brussels with Louis Cousin and Gaspard de Crayer and became a master in the Ghent guild in 1668. Van Cleef chiefly produced religious works for churches, and he also carried out some tapestry cartoons (begun by De Crayer) for Louis XIV of France. His painting style followed a static form of baroque.

BIBLIOGRAPHY. R. H. Wilenski, *Flemish Painters, 1430-1830*, 2 vols., New York, 1960.

CLEEF, JOOS VAN, *see* CLEVE, JOOS VAN.

CLEITIUS (Klitias) AND ERGOTIMOS. Attic vase painter and potter, respectively (fl. ca. 570 B.C.). Although they combined talents on several works, their most famous creation is the François Vase in Florence (Archaeological Museum), a large volute crater that is a masterpiece of early archaic ceramic art. In fact, on the basis of it, Cleitius must be considered the first great narrative painter in European art.

The decoration of the vase is arranged in a series of horizontal bands, filled with some formal patterns but mostly with elaborate mythological scenes in which a multitude of small figures, identified by inscription, are depicted. The dramatic power and humor, as well as the

Antoni Clavé, *King and Queen*. Museum of Modern Art, Paris. Characteristically Catalonian excitement and vivacity mark this artist's work.

magnificent draftsmanship of these scenes, marked a culminating point in early archaic painting and reflected the rich legacy of iconographic types that Cleitius and his contemporaries made available to later generations.

BIBLIOGRAPHY. J. D. Beazley, *The Development of Attic Black-Figure*, Berkeley, Calif., 1951.

CLEMENT, ST. Pope (92–101) and martyr. After being converted by St. Peter, he was banished by Trajan to Crimea, where he was condemned to work in a quarry. To slake his companions' thirst he caused water to flow from a rock. The anchor, symbol of his faith, was the source of a legend that he drowned in the Black Sea with an anchor tied to his neck and angels built him an undersea tomb. Two epistles were ascribed to him; one, the earliest existing sermon, is now attributed to other sources. His attributes are the papal tiara, a cross with triple bars, and an anchor. His feast is November 23. *See also* SAINTS IN ART.

CLEMENTE, IL, *see* SPANI.

CLEMENTI, *see* SPANI.

CLEMENTI, MARIA GIOVANNA BATTISTA (La Clementina). Italian portrait and miniature painter (b. Turin, 1690; d. there, 1761). She is reputed to have been a pupil of Marten Mijtens. Her sitters included such notables as Charles Emmanuel III and Cardinal Ferreri. Few of her works are extant.

CLENNELL, LUKE. English painter (1781–1840). Born in Northumberland, he began his studies under Bewick, the engraver, in 1797 and showed a precocious talent. Clennell also developed as an oil painter, and the success of his *Charge at Waterloo* secured him the commission to paint the festivities in London to celebrate the victory. The commission ran into insuperable difficulties, and he did not fulfill the assignment.

CLEOPHRADES PAINTER. Attic vase painter (fl. ca. 500–480 B.C.). His numerous extant works show several stylistic phases. He was one of the first artists to make experiments in the technique of shading. In his best work, such as an amphora in Munich showing Dionysos, satyrs, and maenads, he brilliantly combines outer action with a sense of inner life.

BIBLIOGRAPHY. J. D. Beazley, *Der Kleophrades-Maler* (Bilder griechischer Vasen..., vol. 6), Berlin, 1933.

CLEPSYDRA. Water clock (Greek *klepsydra*, "a stealing of water") that measures time by the regulated flow of water through a small opening, as in the Tower of the Winds in Athens. *See* TOWER OF THE WINDS, ATHENS.

CLERCK, HENDRIK DE. Flemish painter (b. Brussels, 1565/70; d. there, 1629). He was a pupil of Martin de Vos, and continued to produce elaborate religious works in his teacher's mannerist style. De Clerck painted small mythological compositions, and also did figures for the landscapes of Denis van Alsloot, Hendrik van Balen, Jan

Breughel I, Jacques d'Arthois, Josse de Momper, and others.

BIBLIOGRAPHY. W. Bernt, *Die niederländischen Maler des 17. Jahrhunderts...*, vol. 1, Munich, 1948.

CLERESTORY (Clearstory). Portion of a structure that rises above the roofs of adjacent parts and whose walls are pierced to admit light. The clerestory was used in the hypostyle hall of the Egyptian Temple of Amun in Karnak. Widely used in Roman basilicas and thermae, clerestories became the common means of lighting early Christian and later churches.

CLERISSEAU, CHARLES-LOUIS. French painter and architect (1722–1820). He studied architecture in Paris, and then went to Rome as a royal pensioner in 1749. He accompanied Robert Adam to Split, Yugoslavia, in 1757 to study the Roman remains there. Clérisseau is mentioned as a collaborator in Adam's publication on the ruins (1764). From 1773 Clérisseau lived in Paris, where he was a leader in the new enthusiasm for classical antiquity. This was expressed in his paintings of ancient ruins and in his architecture. His principal work is the Hôtel du Gouvernement (1776; now Courthouse) in Metz, which derives more from Italian mannerism than classical antiquity.

BIBLIOGRAPHY. J. Lejeaux, "Charles-Louis Clérisseau...," *La Revue de l'Art*, LIII, LIV, 1928.

CLERMONT-FERRAND: NOTRE-DAME-DU-PORT, *see* NOTRE-DAME-DU-PORT, CLERMONT-FERRAND.

CLESINGER, JEAN BAPTISTE. French sculptor (b. Besançon, 1814; d. Paris, 1883). He studied with his father, Georges Philippe. Jean Baptiste Clésinger's academically treated figures and personifications achieved a mixed reputation in Paris. In 1857 he settled in Rome but continued to exhibit each year at the Salon with some success.

BIBLIOGRAPHY. A. Estignard, *Clésinger: Sa vie, ses oeuvres*, Paris, 1900.

CLEVE, CORNEILLE VAN, *see* CORNEILLE VAN CLEVE.

CLEVE, CORNELIS VAN (Sotto Cleve), *see* CLEVE, JOOS VAN.

CLEVE, JAN VAN, *see* CLEEF, JAN VAN.

CLEVE (Cleef), JOOS VAN. Flemish painter (b. ca. 1485; d. Antwerp, 1540). Joos has most frequently been identified with the Master of the Death of the Virgin. Records of Joos are all related to Antwerp, where he became a master in 1511. He is listed in the Antwerp guild regularly and frequently until 1535, and appears to have established an active and successful workshop there.

It is believed that Joos was in Paris to paint a portrait of Francis I. That Joos should be called upon to portray the French king is consistent with his reputation as a portraitist, especially of royalty. A portrait of Francis I by Joos is in the Philadelphia Museum of Art, and there is a fine copy at Hampton Court. There are portraits by him of the emperor Maximilian I, dated 1510, and of Francis's second wife, Eleanor, in the Museum of Art History, Vienna.

The early date of the Maximilian portrait raises the question of Joos's pre-Antwerp training. Two wings by him of Adam and Eve (1507; Paris, Louvre) are stylistically close to the work of Jan Joest, and it is possible that Joos trained with that master, who worked at Kalkar. With these panels Joos's development can be traced from 1507 to the portrait of Maximilian (1510) and the listing in the Antwerp guild (1511). In 1515 Joos did a small triptych with the *Death of the Virgin* (Cologne, Wallraf-Richartz Museum), and shortly after he painted a larger version of the same subject (Munich, Old Pinacothek). The next dated works are a *Portrait of a Woman* (1520; Florence, Uffizi) and an altarpiece with the *Lamentation over Christ* (1524; Frankfurt am Main, Städel Art Institute). Undated, but slightly later, is the *Adoration of the Kings* (Dresden, State Art Collection, Picture Gallery).

Difficult to date are various copies and works after Rogier, Gerard David, Van Eyck, Dürer, and Leonardo. The influence of Leonardo is evident in the *Lamentation over Christ Altarpiece* (Louvre), which has a *Last Supper* on the predella that is very close to Leonardo's. Although Leonardo died in 1519, his presence at the French court must have left many mementos. Joos's familiarity with Leonardo's work speaks for his presence in Paris, and would date the portrait of Francis I at roughly the same time as the Paris *Lamentation*, that is, in the 1530s.

Stylistically, Joos was conservative and rarely changed his manner. He did adapt to prevailing taste, as in his early work under the influence of Quentin Metsys and his later Leonardesque works. Generally, Joos's works are pleasant and placid, graceful and lacking in profundity. They show a consistently high level of craftsmanship, in the tradition of Flemish painting.

Joos's son Cornelis (Sotto Cleve, 1520–67) was a history painter, but no work can be attributed to him with certainty.

BIBLIOGRAPHY. L. Baldass, *Joos van Cleve*, Vienna, 1925; M. J. Friedländer, *Die altniederländische Malerei*, vol. 9, Berlin, 1931.

STANLEY FERBER

Clerestory. A means of admitting light.

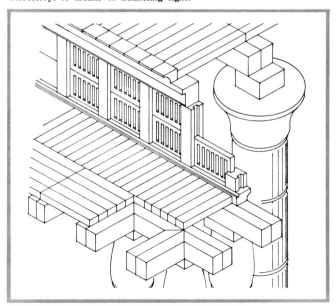

Joos van Cleve, *Joris W. Vezeler*. National Gallery, Washington, D.C. (Andrew Mellon Fund, 1962).

CLEVELAND, OHIO: CLEVELAND MUSEUM OF ART.
Situated in Wade Park, the museum is housed in a classical edifice by Hubbell and Benes (1916).

The collections survey the history of world art, starting with ancient Egypt and Mesopotamia. Among the Greek and Roman works are a kouros torso of the 6th century B.C., a kylix by Douris, a head of Alexander the Great, several Roman portraits, and a 3d-century sarcophagus.

Perhaps the most striking exhibition is the one devoted to Early Christian, Byzantine, Romanesque, and Gothic sculpture, textiles, ivories, jewelry, and miniatures. The prize of this collection is the group of nine objects from the Guelph Treasure of the early 11th century, including the Gertrudis Altar and crosses. Furniture, pottery, and minor arts from the 16th through the 18th century also abound.

The select group of European sculptures includes a German *Christ and St. John* of about 1280; 15th-century works by Claus de Werve, Antoine Le Moiturier, Luca della Robbia, and Amadeo; 16th-century works by Leinberger, Stoss, the Master of Rabenden, and Il Sansovino; and modern works by Rodin, Degas, Renoir, Lipchitz, Barlach, Brancusi, Marcks, and others.

The painting collection ranges from the 15th through the 20th century. Outstanding Italian paintings are Andrea del Sarto's *Sacrifice of Abraham*, Tintoretto's *Baptism of Christ*, and works by Lippo Memmi, Giovanni di Paolo, Carlo Crivelli, Cima, Lotto, Titian, Savoldo, Veronese, Strozzi, Magnasco, and Tiepolo. Prominent in the Flemish

and Dutch group are works by Memling, Geertgen tot Sint Jans, Bouts, Rubens, Van Dyck, Hobbema, Cuijp, Rembrandt, Hals, Ter Borch, and Teniers.

El Greco's *Crucifixion* and *Holy Family* and works by Huguet and Goya highlight the Spanish group. German painting is represented by the Master of Heiligenkreuz's *Death of the Virgin* and works by Altdorfer, Baldung-Grien, and Holbein. Turner, with *The Burning of the Houses of Parliament* and *Fluelen*, heads the list of English painters, which also includes Hilliard, Lely, Reynolds, Gainsborough, Raeburn, and Girtin. Some of the French painters represented are Poussin, Georges de La Tour, Watteau, Boucher, Fragonard, David, Delacroix, Corot, Manet, Renoir, Monet, Degas, Gauguin, Cézanne, Toulouse-Lautrec, and Rousseau.

Picasso's *Cycle of Life* is outstanding in the 20th-century collection, as are works by Bonnard, Matisse, Rouault, Soutine, and Mondrian. In the comprehensive survey of American painting Hicks's *Peaceable Kingdom* and Ryder's *Death on a Pale Horse* should be mentioned.

The museum also has one of the best collections of Oriental art in the United States, including Islamic, Indian, Japanese, and Chinese sculpture, paintings, and crafts. Particularly fine is the Chinese collection, which ranges from the Neolithic period through every phase of Chinese history.

BIBLIOGRAPHY. The Cleveland Museum of Art, *Handbook*, Cleveland, 1966.   DONALD GODDARD

CLEVENGER, SHOBAL VAIL.
American sculptor (b. Middletown, Conn., 1812; d. at sea, 1843). He worked in Cincinnati as a stonecutter, studied anatomy at Ohio Medical College, and studied sculpture briefly in Italy. A classically conceived bust of Henry Clay (1842; New York, Metropolitan Museum) is representative of the work of this short-lived sculptor.

BIBLIOGRAPHY. A. T. Gardner, *Yankee Stonecutters*, New York, 1945.

CLEVES, GOSPELS OF.
Carolingian illuminated manuscript, in the National Library, Berlin.

CLICHE-VERRE.
A process invented about the middle of the 19th century employing handmade negatives, the sun, and photosensitive paper to produce a so-called print. A sheet of glass is coated with a light-proof ground, and the design is scratched through the ground to create the negative. It is then printed in the same way as any other photograph.

Clipeus. Sarcophagus medallion with portrait of the deceased.

CLIPEUS. Large circular shield used by the Greeks and Romans. Also a term for a medallion, displaying a portrait of the deceased, on a sarcophagus. (See illustration.)

CLOACA MAXIMA, ROME. Subterranean sewer, which, according to tradition, was constructed by Tarquinius Superbus (6th cent. B.C.) to drain the Roman Forum. Originally the Cloaca Maxima was a natural watercourse flowing from the Argiletum through the Forum to the Tiber; later it was canalized, and after 200 B.C. it was arched over.

BIBLIOGRAPHY. S. B. Platner, *The Topography and Monuments of Ancient Rome*, Boston, 1904; E. Nash, *Pictorial Dictionary of Ancient Rome*, vol. 1, London, 1961.

CLODION (Claude Michel). French sculptor (b. Nancy, 1738; d. Paris, 1814). When he was seventeen years old, he went to Paris to study with his uncle, Lambert Sigisbert Adam. After his uncle's death, Clodion worked with Jean-Baptiste Pigalle. Clodion was quickly recognized for his work and in 1759 won the grand prize at the Académie Royale. He went to Rome in 1762, and while there he attracted the attention of Catherine II of Russia, who wanted him to come to Moscow. However, he returned to Paris in 1771 and thereafter remained there, except for a period of six years in Nancy (1792–98). Clodion produced numerous allegorical and decorative rococo sculptures; *Dying Cleopatra* and the *Nymph and Satyr* (New York, Metropolitan Museum) are typical.

BIBLIOGRAPHY. A. Jacquot, *Les Michel et Clodion*, Paris, 1897.

CLOISONNE. Type of enameling technique in which the design is constructed of wires soldered to the background

Clodion, *Nymph and Satyr*. Marble. Metropolitan Museum of Art, New York.

plate. The cells, or cloisons, formed between the wires are then filled with colored vitreous pastes and the whole is fired, fusing the pastes into colored glass. The glass is then polished off flush with the wires. Particularly well developed in Byzantine art, cloisonné reached its high point in Western art during the 10th and 11th centuries. The Pala d'Oro in S. Marco, Venice, is an outstanding example.

BIBLIOGRAPHY. K. F. Bates, *Enameling: Principles and Practice*, Cleveland, 1951.

CLOISONNISME. French term describing a late-19th-century method of painting in a compartmented fashion reminiscent of medieval stained glass. The technique was applied by some synthetist painters, but the term is often inaccurately used as a synonym for synthetism. *See* SYNTHETISM.

CLOISTER. Covered passage, often colonnaded, around an open space or garth; also a monastery or convent. Cloisters usually connected several elements of the medieval monastery, such as the chapter house and refectory.

CLOISTERS, THE, NEW YORK, *see* NEW YORK: MUSEUMS (THE CLOISTERS).

CLOMP, ALBERT JANSZ., *see* KLOMP, ALBERT JANSZ.

CLONMACNOISE. Ancient Irish religious center. The Cathedral has a late Romanesque doorway, a unique vaulted chancel, and a 15th-century north door. The Nun's Church of about 1166 contains fine Romanesque decoration, and St. Finghin's Church of the same period has a remarkable round tower belfry. *See also* CLONMACNOISE CROSS.

BIBLIOGRAPHY. H. G. Leask, *Irish Churches and Monastic Buildings*, vol. 1, Dundalk, 1955–60.

CLONMACNOISE CROSS. Hiberno-Saxon sculpture of A.D. 914, at the former monastery of Clonmacnoise, Ireland.

CLOONEAMERY (Cloone), CHURCH OF. Church in County Kilkenny, Ireland, one of a group of so-called "antae" churches, in which the side walls project beyond the face of the gables. The church, which may date from the 10th century, has a simple linteled doorway with a cross above.

BIBLIOGRAPHY. H. G. Leask, *Irish Churches and Monastic Buildings*, vol. 1, Dundalk, 1955–60.

CLOSE. Enclosure or court; also the precinct of a cathedral, monastery, or abbey. Thus, English medieval cathedrals, often part of a monastic group and containing cloisters, refectory, chapter house, and so on, are said to be set in a close rather than among houses in towns, as French Gothic examples were.

CLOTH HALL. Building used by cloth merchants in medieval times. A particularly fine example was the Halle des Drapiers of the cloth guild in Ypres, Belgium.

CLOTH HALL, YPRES. The Gothic Halle des Drapiers (ca. 1260–1380), in Ypres, Belgium, was part of the three-hall complex begun under Count Baldwin IX about 1200. Ypres was the most important center of cloth manufacture

Cloisonné. *The Crucifixion*, detail of an Evangelistary cover. Treasury of S. Marco, Venice. An example of 10th-century Byzantine art.

in Flanders in the middle of the 13th century, and this great Gothic guildhall was the most imposing commercial edifice of its period in northern Europe. Its façade (430 feet long) was the longest in the country, and its severe massiveness was unmatched for its impressive dignity by the later, more ornate town halls of such Flemish commercial centers as Brussels, Bruges, and Louvain. Restoration was begun in 1908, but the Cloth Hall at Ypres was all but completely destroyed by German artillery fire in World War I.

CLOUDBAND. Ubiquitous decorative and symbolic motif in Chinese art, representing the heavens. Sometimes the cloudband is considered the dwelling place and substance of the dragon. It was used variously schematized or free, alone or combined with dragons, animals, birds, flowers, and so on, from the time of the Warring States (480–221 B.C.) on.

CLOUET, FRANCOIS. French painter (b. Tours, before 1510; d. Paris, 1572). He carried on the tradition of his father, Jean Clouet, whom he succeeded in 1541 as court painter. In the *Portrait of Elizabeth of Austria, Queen of France* (Paris, Louvre), attributed to François, he was especially successful in maintaining delicacy and tact of rendition and delight in decorative pattern without loss of individualization of the sitter. More typical are the dry and conventional *Portrait of Charles IX* (Vienna, Museum of Art History) and the *Portrait of Henry II* (Florence, Uffizi), which exemplify standard royal portraiture of the period. Attributed to the master or to his workshop are several equestrian portraits of Francis I (Louvre; Uffizi).

Clouet's signed portrait of the botanist Pierre Quthe (Louvre), dated 1562, is clearly of Florentine mannerist inspiration. Another of the rare works of the artist authenticated by an inscription, his *Diane de Poitiers* (ca. 1571; Washington, D.C., National Gallery), presents a theme,

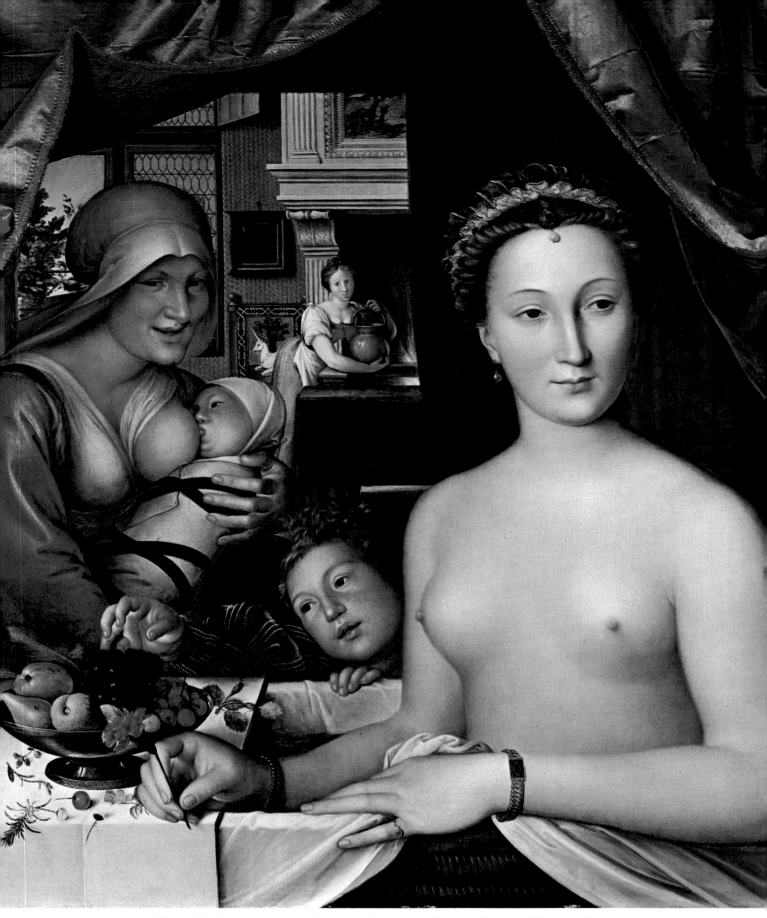

François Clouet, *Diane de Poitiers*, ca. 1571. Panel. National Gallery, Washington, D.C. (Samuel H. Kress Collection, 1961).

also with Italian references, that was fashionable among painters of the Fontainebleau school.

BIBLIOGRAPHY. E. Moreau-Nélaton, *Les Clouet et leurs émules*, Paris, 1924; P. du Colombier, *L'Art renaissance en France*, rev. ed., Paris, 1950.

MADLYN KAHR

CLOUET, JEAN (Janet). French portraitist (d. 1540). He is known to have worked at the French court from 1516. A series of crayon portrait drawings, mostly in the Condé Museum at Chantilly, have traditionally been attributed to him, and certain paintings associated with these drawings are presumed to be his work. Among these is a *Portrait of Guillaume Budé* (New York, Metropolitan Museum) and the *Man with a Petrarch* (London, Windsor Castle). Clouet is thought to have been born in Brussels, and his style is marked by the Flemish taste for particularization. His Italianate rendering of form, however, shows his understanding of the High Renaissance.

Portrait drawings of "Clouet type," usually in black or black-and-red crayon, became very popular with contemporary collectors and were turned out in great numbers. To the modern eye the best of them have the appeal of freshness and spontaneity that is generally lacking in the painted portraits for which they presumably served as preparatory drawings. *See also* CLOUET, FRANCOIS; CLOUET DE NAVARRE.

BIBLIOGRAPHY. E. Moreau-Nélaton, *Les Clouet et leurs émules*, Paris, 1924; A. Blunt, *Art and Architecture in France, 1500–1700*, Baltimore, 1954.

MADLYN KAHR

CLOUET DE NAVARRE. French painter (fl. 16th cent.). Hardly anything is known about this artist aside from a mention by Marguerite d'Angoulême, queen of Navarre, in a letter supposedly written by her in 1529. In it we find a reference to "the brother of Janet, who is the painter of the King." Janet is apparently Jean Clouet, court painter of Francis I. We do not know what commissions the brother executed for the Queen in Navarre or elsewhere. The Louvre ascribes to him the *Portrait of Baron de la Mothe-Saint-Heraye*.

BIBLIOGRAPHY. L. Dimier, *French Painting in the Sixteenth Century*, London, 1904.

CLOVIO, GIULIO (Jure Clovicic). Croatian-Italian painter and miniaturist (b. Grizane, Croatia, 1488; d. Rome, 1578). He went to Rome in 1516, and was especially influenced by Michelangelo. Clovio later learned the art of illuminating from Girolamo dei Libri. Clovio worked for Louis II of Hungary in 1524–25, then for Cardinal Marino Grimani, and finally, from 1537 until his death, for Cardinal Alessandro Farnese. No initiator, Clovio skillfully translated the monumental mannerist style of his time into minutely figured, colorful miniatures and illuminations. His masterpiece is the Farnese Book of Hours (1537–46; New York, Pierpont Morgan Library).

BIBLIOGRAPHY. J. W. Bradley, *The Life and Works of Giulio Clovio, Miniaturist . . .*, London, 1891; New York, Pierpont Morgan Library, *Italian Manuscripts in the Pierpont Morgan Library . . .*, comp. M. Harrsen and G. K. Boyce, New York, 1953.

CLUNY. Town in southern Burgundy, France, roughly halfway between Lyons and Dijon. It achieved fame because of the monastic order founded there. In Roman times

Jean Clouet, *Guillaume Budé*. Metropolitan Museum of Art, New York.

Giulio Clovio, Farnese Book of Hours. Morgan Library, New York.

it was a station called Cluniacum; later, under the Franks, it was the site of a large Gallo-Roman villa. During Carolingian times the area passed to the domains of Charlemagne's family, and finally, it came into the possession of William I, duke of Aquitaine. The duke, who was called "the Pious," gave the lands of Cluny to a group of Benedictine monks. The foundation charter of the new monastery was drawn up in 909 in Bourges, the ecclesiastical center of Aquitaine. This remarkable document accounts for the phenomenal growth of the house of Cluny. It granted Cluny complete independence, secular and ecclesiastical, and allowed it to develop, under proper leadership, into an almost independent state. As such, it was the first of the great independent orders (for example, the Cistercians, Carthusians, and Augustinians) that flourished in the later Middle Ages.

Berno was the first abbot of Cluny, from 909 to 927, a period that corresponds to the beginning and completion of the first abbey of Cluny, the so-called Cluny I (no longer extant). Berno brought several other monasteries under the nominal leadership of Cluny, and he left a legacy of about six affiliated abbeys. His successor, Odo (927–42), set about making Cluny the center of a monastic reform movement that was to strengthen its spiritual leadership and attract other Benedictine abbeys to its fold, among them Montecassino and Subiaco. Under subsequent abbots Cluny continued to grow.

The greatest force in Cluniac expansion was the abbot St. Hugh (1049–1109), who realized the power and potentialities of Cluny as a reform movement and monastic center. It was under Hugh that Cluny reached its apex, the control of almost 1,500 houses, at least 200 of which were of major significance. The power and wealth of Cluny led to a gradual decline in its high standards and achievements, so that under the last of its great abbots, Peter the Venerable (1122–56), Cluny itself was reformed. But before this occurred Cluny had succeeded in leaving an indelible mark on the monastic life and church building of western Europe.

Over Cluny's long history a distinct type of church building is distinguishable. Although some scholars have attempted to see Cluny as almost independent of and apart from general Romanesque developments, the Cluny type and derived church fall within the general framework of the Romanesque architectural style, contributing to it as well as drawing from it. The interesting aspect of the Cluny-related church is its demonstration of the transmission of architectural motifs along the route of monastic affiliations, which transcended geographic boundaries.

In this line of relationships the prototypical church seems to have been one, no longer extant, known as Cluny II (ca. 950–1000). It was a three-aisled cruciform building of basilica plan. It had three east apses (in a modified apse echelon) and, at the west end, an atrium and a galilee (a large groin-vaulted narthex, supporting a chapel on the gallery level—perhaps a survival of the Carolingian westwork). A tunnel-vaulted nave was combined with groin-vaulted aisles to give the entire building an appearance of substantial solidity. There were also low western flanking towers. This type of church was adopted, with minor local variations, by affiliated monasteries as far distant as Germany (SS. Peter and Paul, Hirsau) and Spain (S. Juan de

Cluny. Remains of the abbey church, showing south transept.

la Peña). Other churches, geographically closer to Cluny, with the same characteristics are the first church in Charlieu and that in Chapaize (after 1050). Some of the related churches had apse ambulatories and radiating chapels in place of the apse echelon. *See* CHARLIEU, ABBEY CHURCH OF; HIRSAU: SS. PETER AND PAUL. *See also* BERNAY, ABBEY CHURCH OF.

A more developed type began to appear after 1040. Still much like Cluny II, churches of this type were more ambitious, with wide transepts flanked by towers and frequently with fully developed apse echelons or an ambulatory with radiating chapels. There was the initial use of carving as a decorative element in capitals, around portals, and in decorative arcading. This might be the beginning of the famous Burgundian school of Romanesque sculpture, but the question is clouded by the parallel rise of the pilgrimage school of sculpture and the close interrelationship of the pilgrimage route and Cluny. Examples of this second development of the Cluny II type are in Payerne (1040–1100), in the second church in Charlieu (1030–94), and in La Charité-sur-Loire (1060–1107). *See* LA CHARITE-SUR-LOIRE; PAYERNE, PRIORY CHURCH OF.

The height of Cluniac architectural and sculptural achievement was reached under Abbot Hugh. Cluny III was started between about 1085 and 1088. It was immense (ca. 614 ft. long) and had two east transepts, five aisles, and a full ambulatory with radiating chapels. The barrel-vaulted nave was flanked by groin-vaulted aisles. A groin-vaulted forechurch with two western towers was added in the 12th century. Sculpture and frescoes enriched the surfaces of the buildings. *See* MONTECASSINO, ABBEY OF.

By 1100 tracer elements of Cluny architecture had diffused throughout Burgundy and France and in parts of Germany, Spain, Italy, and Switzerland. However, strong developments had occurred elsewhere (Normandy, Lombardy), so that the truly international admixture of regional Romanesque developments had diminished the impact of Cluny architecture on that of western Europe as a whole.

BIBLIOGRAPHY. J. Evans, *Monastic Life at Cluny, 910–1157*, London, 1931; J. Evans, *Cluniac Art of the Romanesque Period*, Cambridge, Eng., 1950; K. J. Conant, "Mediaeval Academy Excavations at Cluny, VIII," *Speculum*, XXIX, 1954; "Mediaeval Academy Excavations at Cluny, IX," *Speculum*, XXXVIII, 1963.
STANLEY FERBER

CLUNY, HOTEL DE. Originally the Paris town house of Jacques d'Amboise, abbot of the Burgundian abbey of Cluny. Built between 1485 and 1510, this Gothic stone building is composed of three wings surrounding a courtyard. Although the Flamboyant dormers remain from the 15th century, much of the ornament is the result of 19th-century restoration. A small entrance tower, which encloses a circular staircase, lends charm and dignity to the courtyard of what is now the Cluny Museum. *See* PARIS: MUSEUMS (CLUNY MUSEUM).

BIBLIOGRAPHY. Paris, Musée des Thermes et de l'Hôtel de Cluny, *Musée de Cluny*, introd. and notes P. Verlet and F. Salet, Paris, 1951.

CLUNY MUSEUM, PARIS, *see* PARIS: MUSEUMS (CLUNY MUSEUM).

CLUTTON, HENRY. English architect (1819–93). The significant event in the Gothic revival was his winning with William Burges the 1855 International Competition for Lille Cathedral. Clutton's works include many churches, schools, and houses. With Burges and George Edmund Street he helped to consolidate the ecclesiological attitude toward the Gothic.

BIBLIOGRAPHY. H. R. Hitchcock, *Architecture, Nineteenth and Twentieth Centuries*, Baltimore, 1958.

CNIDUS, DEMETER OF, *see* DEMETER OF CNIDUS.

CNIDUS, VENUS OF, *see* PRAXITELES.

CNOSSUS (Knossos). Site of a Minoan palace situated a few miles southeast of modern Heraklion, Crete. The extensive excavations of this palace, begun by Sir Arthur Evans in 1900 and still in process today, first brought to light the forgotten civilization of Bronze Age Crete.

Greek mythology preserved the memory of King Minos of Cnossus and of a complicated maze-like structure called the Labyrinth in which Minos offered victims to a monster called the Minotaur. Evans's excavations showed that Cnossus had indeed once been the site of a great sea power and that the palace did have a complicated maze-like plan. He proved, as Schliemann had done at Troy, that the Greek myths were based on historical fact. Evans

coined the term "Minoan" for early Cretan civilization and also devised a chronological scheme of three periods (Early, Middle, and Late Minoan, with appropriate subdivisions in each period), which still is used by most archaeologists in the field although some of its details are now controversial.

Evans's excavations revealed that Cnossus had a lengthy neolithic occupation, which ended about 2800 B.C. The Early Minoan period (ca. 2800–2000 B.C.), the first period of the Bronze Age, may have been initiated by a new wave of settlers from southwest Asia Minor. The palace of Cnossus first took shape at the beginning of the Middle Minoan period (ca. 2000–1580 B.C.) and was destroyed at the end of Middle Minoan II (1700 B.C.), probably by an earthquake. Most of the present remains belong to the second palace, which was begun immediately after the destruction of the earlier one and was in turn destroyed, according to its excavators, about 1400 B.C. (end of Late Minoan I). The nucleus of both palaces was the large rectangular courtyard, with its long axis running north-south.

The earlier palace was composed of a number of independent but closely related buildings, referred to as "insulae." The plan of these is largely obscured by the later palace, in which the insulae were unified into a labyrinthine series of rooms and corridors running all around the central courtyard. The chambers to the west consisted of storage magazines and rooms devoted to religious and state functions, such as the throne room and lustral chamber; those on the east were probably the domestic quarters of the Cnossian rulers and their retinue. The bright frescoes of the palace and its elaborate water supply and drainage system all point to an urbane, refined level of culture. The palace had two, perhaps in places three, stories. Its superstructure was probably built of wood and clay bricks, covered in places with stucco, and resting on foundations of stone. A grand staircase at the southern end of the west

Cnossus. Reconstructed courtyard of the palace.

Charles Nicolas Cochin the Younger, *The Laughing Man and the Fish.* Drawing. Ecole des Beaux-Arts, Paris.

block and a corridor flanked by bastions leading from the northern edge of the central court formed the main entrances of the palace. Northwest of the palace was a stepped "theatral area" and a paved processional highway. Surrounding the major palace are several smaller structures, the most important being a "Royal Villa" and a "Little Palace."

There is at present a controversy about whether the final destruction of Cnossus took place about 1400 B.C. (the view of Evans and his followers) or about 1200–1150 B.C. (the view of L. R. Palmer). The "Linear B" tablets from the palace indicate that its last occupants, presumably Mycenaean invaders, spoke Greek.

See also CRETE (PALACES: CNOSSUS); EVANS, SIR ARTHUR; MINOTAUR.

BIBLIOGRAPHY. A. J. Evans, *The Palace of Minos*, 4 vols. in 6 and index, London, 1921–36; J. D. S. Pendlebury, *The Archaeology of Crete*, London, 1939; R. W. Hutchinson, *Prehistoric Crete*, Baltimore, 1962; L. R. Palmer and J. Boardman, *On the Knossos Tablets*, Oxford, 1963; L. R. Palmer, *Mycenaeans and Minoans*, 2d ed., New York, 1965.

JEROME J. POLLITT

COADE, ELEANOR. English manufacturer of artificial stone (d. 1796). In partnership with John Sealy, she commercialized the artificial stone supposedly invented by her father or husband, employing the best sculptors and architects to make designs. The firm's most ambitious work in Coadestone was the tympanum in the west pediment of Greenwich Palace (1810–13).

COATES, WELLS W. British architect (b. Japan, 1895; d. Canada, 1958). After an eclectic education he went to London in 1929 and immediately stood apart from the traditionalists with his designs for shops and showrooms, which are essentially fundamental in their design and owe not a little to the Far East. His pioneer design was the Hampstead Lawn Road apartments (1934), almost "Brutalist" in its directness of style. He was a founder-member of several avant-garde groups such as the Architectural

Research Group and Unit One (1933). His later work included apartments, studios at Broadcasting House, and the National Film Theater of 1951. He spent his last years in Canada, where he engaged in town-planning projects.

BIBLIOGRAPHY. J. Richards, "Wells Coates, 1893–1958," *The Architectural Review*, CXXIV, 1958.

COATLICUE. Aztec sculpture, in the National Museum of Anthropology, Mexico City. *See* AMERICAS, ANCIENT, ART OF (MEXICO).

COBRA. Group of artists and critics formed in Paris in 1948. The name derives from the cities of the three countries from which the artists originated: Copenhagen (Co), Brussels (Br), and Amsterdam (A). Among the founding members were Jorn, Appel, and Corneille; later Atlan, Alechinsky, Dubuffet, and Pedersen joined. Like the abstract expressionists in the United States, the CoBrA artists were interested in the direct expression of creative energy, in art as a piece of reality. The human figure, although wildly distorted by violent brushstrokes and color in most of the work of the group, remains the central image. The artists of CoBrA worked together on murals, were given exhibitions in Amsterdam, Liège, and Paris, and published a magazine. The group disbanded in 1951 but had a great impact on the subsequent art of northern Europe. *See* ALECHINSKY, PIERRE; APPEL, KAREL; CORNEILLE; DUBUFFET, JEAN; JORN, ASGER.

COBURG: VESTE COBURG ART COLLECTIONS. German collections, founded between 1840 and 1850. The works are housed in the medieval fortress, renovated in the 19th century; part of the original citadel, the so-called Blue Tower, is still preserved. Graphic arts form the major part of the collection. German drawings range from the 15th to the 19th century, from the so-called *Sachsenchronik*, with its approximately 1,300 colored drawings of the school of Cranach, to later drawings by Chodowiecki, Goethe, and Richter. There are also about 300,000 woodcuts, copper engravings, and mezzotints, including the almost complete graphic work of Dürer and about 220 examples of Rembrandt's graphic work. Compared with these treasures, painting forms a minor part of the collection; there are, however, ten works by Lucas Cranach. About 100 sculptures, especially from Franconia and Thuringia, and all kinds of applied arts—textiles, metalwork, ceramics, and glass—are also on view.

BIBLIOGRAPHY. H. Jedding, *Keysers Führer durch Museen und Sammlungen*, Heidelberg, Munich, 1961.

COCA, CASTLE OF. Brick castle at Coca, in the province of Segovia, Spain. It was built in Mudejar style by Alonso de Fonseca (1418–73), archbishop of Seville. Recently restored, it retains remnants of decorative wall painting combining Gothic and Islamic motifs. No domestic apartments survive, and the walls now shelter an agricultural college.

BIBLIOGRAPHY. D. E. Tormo, "...Castillo de Coca," *Boletín de la Real Academia de Bellas Artes de San Fernando*, XXII, 1928.

COCHIN, CHARLES NICOLAS, THE ELDER. French engraver (b. Paris, 1688; d. there, 1754). The son of a painter, he married an artist, Magdeleine Horthemels; their son, C. N. Cochin the Younger, became one of the most famous French 18th-century engravers. Although the father's name is often eclipsed by that of the son, Cochin the Elder was one of the best engravers of his day. He worked carefully from an etched outline, which he then completed with the burin. He made large engravings after Watteau, Lancret, Chardin, and other contemporaries. However, it was from his son's drawings that he produced his most famous and ambitious plates, *Décoration du bal paré* and *Décoration du bal masqué*.

BIBLIOGRAPHY. S. Rocheblave, *Les Cochin*, Paris, 1893.

COCHIN, CHARLES NICOLAS, THE YOUNGER.

French painter, engraver, and draftsman (b. Paris, 1715; d. there, 1790). Cochin early learned the art of engraving from his father, but it was as a draftsman and portraitist that he excelled. His work for the court brought him to the attention of the Marquis de Marigny, brother of Mme de Pompadour. He accompanied the Marquis on a trip to Italy, and was his art adviser for the remainder of his life. In 1751 he became an academician, and in 1752 Keeper of the King's Drawings. Besides his many designs expressing French taste of the 18th century, he is especially noteworthy for his ability to depict large groups of people and for an important series of small portraits.

BIBLIOGRAPHY. S. Rocheblave, *Charles-Nicolas Cochin*, Paris, 1927.

COCK (Kock), HIERONYMUS.

Flemish painter, graphic artist, and publisher of prints (ca. 1510–70). Born in Antwerp, he was a publisher of prints after Raphael, Giulio Romano, Brueghel, and others, and in this capacity he contributed significantly to Netherlandish art. Through these prints the Romanizing motifs—views of ruins, grotesques, and Raphaelesque compositions—became available and made a strong impression on his contemporaries.

COCK (Wellens), JAN (de).

Flemish painter of religious scenes with ample landscape backgrounds (fl. early 16th cent.). The first known document that refers to him is his inscription in the register of the Antwerp Guild of St. Luke in 1503 as Jan van Leyden. According to G. Isarlo, the indication of Leyden as the presumptive place of origin might explain the relationship of his style to that of Cornelis Engebrechtsz. The inscription of a first pupil dates from 1506, and here the artist uses the name Jan Cock. In 1507 or 1508 there is a payment for menial work done for the Church of Notre-Dame in Antwerp. He died before the end of 1529, for his wife was mentioned as a widow that year in certain account books. His only documented work is *Landscape with St. Christopher* (Oberaudorf, Upper Bavaria, Baroness Elisabeth von Bissing Collection). All others are attributions.

BIBLIOGRAPHY. L. van Puyvelde, *La Peinture flamande au siècle de Bosch et Breughel*, Paris, 1962.

COCK, MATHYS WELLENS DE.

Flemish landscape painter (b. Antwerp, ca. 1509; d. there, 1548). Cock was a master in Antwerp by 1540. He traveled to Italy and according to Van Mander was the teacher of Jacob Grimmer. No certain work by Cock remains, but many landscapes grouping mountains, rivers, castles, and villages are attributed to him.

BIBLIOGRAPHY. R. H. Wilenski, *Flemish Painters, 1430-1830*, 2 vols., New York, 1960.

COCKERELL, CHARLES ROBERT.

English architect (1788–1863). Having completed his architectural training in his father's office, Cockerell embarked on the grand tour to Greece, Asia Minor, Sicily, and Italy, where he studied and measured ancient buildings. Shortly after his return to England in 1817, he succeeded his father as surveyor of St. Paul's, thus beginning his illustrious architectural career.

He was architect to the Bank of England, Royal Academy professor of architecture, and the first Royal Gold Medalist and professional president of the Royal Institute of British Architects. His artistic sensibility, together with a new vocabulary based on native English baroque and his Greek studies, revitalized late Georgian architecture. The Ashmolean Museum, Oxford (1841–45) and the Sun Fire Office, London (1841–42) are his best-known works.

COCKSON, THOMAS.

English engraver (fl. London, ca. 1591–1636). Cockson's known output is relatively small but is varied nonetheless. It includes a title page (1591) copied from a 1584 edition of J. Harrington's translation of Ariosto's *Orlando Furioso*; a map of Cadiz (1596), satirical allegories, and four equestrian portraits of English nobility. The portraits are his best-known works. Details of his life remain obscure.

BIBLIOGRAPHY. S. Colvin, *Early Engraving and Engravers in England, 1545-1695...*, London, 1905.

COCTEAU, JEAN.

French poet, playwright, essayist, film director, and illustrator (1892–1963). Cocteau was born in Maisons-Lafitte and received most of his formal training at the Lycée Condorcet. His family was cultivated and encouraged the young Cocteau to write and draw. They took him regularly to the Comédie-Française, and through them he met such notables as Rostand, Proust, and Anna de Noailles. Cocteau began to write and paint. He knew the work of the Fauves and cubists and had met Diaghilev and seen the Ballets Russes. Feeling a need for isolation in order to write, he closed himself off and turned out his first novel, *Le Potomak*, in 1913. He gained early fame and became a public figure with the success of a ballet, *Parade*, in 1917, which had sets by Picasso and music by Satie. In 1919 he published a critical work and a volume of poems.

Cocteau was interested in various movements, such as Dada and surrealism, but he never was officially a member of any group. He refused to conform to a group, no matter how nonconformist the group itself might appear. In 1920 he produced his ballet *Le Boeuf sur le Toit*, with music by Milhaud and, the following year, *Les Mariés de la Tour Eiffel*, with music by "Les Six." It was Cocteau who introduced their work to the public. In 1922 he published a volume of poems, *Vocabulaire*, and, the next year, *Plain-Chant*, in which he mourned the death of his friend, the young novelist Raymond Radiguet. His grief led him to experiment with opium, and he wrote about his experiences in *Opium*. In 1923 he wrote an essay on Picasso.

Cocteau gained a world public with his play *Orphée* in 1927. He later made a film based on it, which received the Grand Prix du Film d'Avant-garde in 1950. His first film was *Le Sang d'un Poète*, released in 1932. Cocteau sought to make the film a poem, a *poème cinématographi-*

que, as he wanted his ballets to be "choreographic poetry" and his critical writings to be "critical poetry." In 1950 he made a successful film of his 1929 novel, *Les Enfants terribles*.

He wrote his best known-play, *La Machine infernale*, in 1934. In 1938 he wrote *Les Parents terribles*, which scandalized the first audiences with its theme of incest, but which later, in 1945, was hailed as a triumph. Cocteau made a film of it three years later. In 1951 he wrote the play *Bacchus*. His play *La Voix humaine* was made into an opera, with music by Poulenc. In 1955 Cocteau was elected to the French Academy. In 1957 his surrealist art was used to express mystical concepts in his fresco decorations for the Chapel of St-Pierre, Villefranche-sur-Mer.

His drawings are most often illustrations for his own literary works. They emphasize the figure. He favors an unmodulated line and avoids chiaroscuro. The drawings recall the neoclassical period of Picasso, but lack Picasso's eloquence.

BIBLIOGRAPHY. M. Crosland, *Jean Cocteau*, New York, 1955; J. Cocteau, *Journals*, New York, 1956.

ROBERT REIFF

CODDE, PIETER JACOBSZ. Dutch painter of genre and portraits (b. Amsterdam, 1599; d. there, 1678). Little is known of Codde's early training. He was married in Amsterdam in 1623 and seems to have spent most of his life there. Codde seems to have had some direct contact with Haarlem, and in 1637 he completed Frans Hals's *Company of Captain Reynier Reael and Lieutenant Cornelis Michielsz. Blaeuw* (Amsterdam, Rijksmuseum). It is accepted that Codde worked on the right side of the Hals composition.

Codde is generally seen as a follower of Frans Hals. His style is also related to masters such as Antonie Palamedes Stevens and Willem Duijster; the latter seemingly was Codde's pupil. Codde's work in the 1630s, such as *The Ball* (signed and dated 1636; The Hague, Mauritshuis Art Gallery), represents his best stylistic period. He was also a poet.

BIBLIOGRAPHY. C. M. Dozy, "Pieter Codde, de Schilder en de Dichter," *Oud-Holland*, II, 1884; A. Bredius, "Iets over Pieter Codde en Willem Duyster," *Oud-Holland*, VI, 1888.

CODESIDO, JULIA. Peruvian painter (1892–   ). Julia Codesido studied in her native city of Lima and traveled in Mexico (1935). She has had important exhibitions in Lima (1929, 1931, 1939), New York (1936), San Francisco (1937), and Paris (1939). In Paris her work is owned by the Jeu de Paume Museum. She is a leading member of the Indigenist school, which stresses native themes, and her style employs large color masses in simplified designs.

BIBLIOGRAPHY. G. L. M. Morley, *An Introduction to Contemporary Peruvian Painting*, San Francisco, 1942.

CODEX. Manuscript bound in leaves or pages, as distinct from one that is rolled in scroll form (rotulus). The codex appears to have been known in antiquity, but it achieved the height of its popularity in Europe in the handwritten, illuminated manuscripts of the Middle Ages. In pre-Columbian America both the Mayas and the Mixtecs used the codex to record religious and historical events. Figbark paper or deerhide was given alternate folds like a screen. An example is the Mixtec genealogical record, the Codex Zouche-Nuttall (London, British Museum).

BIBLIOGRAPHY. E. A. Lowe, ed., *Codices latini antiquiores*, 6 vols., Oxford, 1934-53.

CODEX AMIATINUS. Hiberno-Saxon illuminated manuscript, in the Laurentian Library, Florence. *See* MANUSCRIPT WRITING; NORTHUMBRIAN ART.

CODEX AUREUS. Gospel book lettered in gold or silver ink on leaves of purple-dyed vellum. Luxurious manuscripts of this type were made for royal personages of the Carolingian and Ottonian courts from about the 8th to the 11th century. Among the most famous are the Codex Aureus of Canterbury (Stockholm, Royal Library), the Codex Aureus of St. Emmeram (or Charles the Bald; Munich, Bavarian State Library), and the Codex Aureus Epternacensis (or Golden Gospels of Echternach; Nürnberg, Germanic National Museum). *See* CAROLINGIAN ART AND ARCHITECTURE; OTTONIAN ART.

BIBLIOGRAPHY. A. Grabar and C. Nordenfalk, *Early Medieval Painting from the Fourth to the Eleventh Century*, New York, 1957.

CODEX AUREUS EPTERNACENSIS (Golden Gospels of Echternach). Illuminated Ottonian manuscript, in the Germanic National Museum, Nürnberg, Germany. *See* ECHTERNACH SCHOOL.

CODEX AUREUS OF ST. EMMERAM (Codex Aureus of Charles the Bald). Carolingian manuscript, in the Bavarian State Library, Munich. *See* CAROLINGIAN ART AND ARCHITECTURE; SAINT-DENIS STYLE.

CODEX CALIXTINUS. Mid-12th-century pilgrim's guide to the roads leading to Santiago de Compostela, Spain. The Codex, in the Santiago de Compostela Cathedral, contains information about routes, accommodations, and shrines along the way, as well as a detailed description of the Cathedral itself.

CODEX EGBERTI. Ottonian illuminated manuscript, in the Municipal Library, Trier.

CODEX PURPUREUS OF MUNICH. Early Christian illuminated manuscript (ca. 6th cent.) in the Staatsbibliothek, Munich. *See* EARLY CHRISTIAN ART AND ARCHITECTURE.

CODUCCI, MAURO DI MARTINO. Italian architect of the Venetian school (ca. 1440–1504). Coducci was the major exponent of Renaissance architecture in Venice during the 15th century. His chief works are the Church of S. Michele on the island of San Michele (1469–79) and the Church of S. Zaccaria in Venice (1483–90), where he developed the round-gabled façade that became characteristic of the architecture of Venice and the Veneto in the late 15th and the early 16th century. *See* SAN ZACCARIA, VENICE.

BIBLIOGRAPHY. P. Paoletti, *L'architettura e la scultura del Rinascimento a Venezia*, 2 vols., Venice, 1893.

COECKE (Koeck) VAN AELST, PIETER (Master of the Holy Feasts; Pseudo Lambert Lombard). Flemish history painter (b. Alost, 1502; d. Brussels, 1550). He was a

Pieter Coecke van Aelst, *St. Luke Painting the Virgin*. Museum, Nîmes.

student of Bernard van Orley and a master in the Antwerp guild in 1527. Pieter Coecke went to Rome and later, in 1529, was the teacher of Willem Key and Pieter Brueghel, the Elder. Coecke went to Constantinople in 1533 to work on tapestry cartoons; by 1534 he was back in Antwerp, where, in 1537, he was dean of the guild. He published a translation of Serlio's *Vitruvius* in 1545. In 1550 he settled in Brussels. No signed paintings of Coecke are known; his *Last Supper* (1531), now lost, was engraved by Goltzius (1585). Designs for tapestries include a *History of Joshua, The Seven Capital Sins*, and a *History of David*; drawings exist for most of these. Coecke designed the triumphal arches for the entry of Philip II and Charles V into Antwerp in 1549 and may be the author of the engravings of the *Procession* published in 1550. In 1553 his wife published *Les Moeurs et fachons de faire des Turcz* ... with his engravings. The triptych of the *Descent from the Cross* (Lisbon, National Museum) is now attributed to him. Coecke's style is closely related to that of Van Orley, though more mannered and lively.

BIBLIOGRAPHY. A. Corbet, *Pieter Coecke van Aelst*, Antwerp, 1950; L. van Puyvelde, *La Peinture flamande au siècle de Bosch et Breughel*, Paris, 1962; G. Marlier, *La Renaissance flamande: Pierre Coeck d'Alost*, Brussels, 1966.

PENELOPE D. MAYO

COELLO, CLAUDIO. Spanish painter (1642–93). He studied under Juan Carreño de Miranda and Francisco Rizi de Guevara. Endowed with talent as a draftsman, composer, and colorist in painting, Coello seems to have gone over the heads of his teachers to learn with a selective and independent eye from works by Raphael, Titian, Correggio, Rubens, Pietro da Cortona, and even Tintoretto. The re-

sult in his grandiloquent conceptions is distillation and transformation to a singular independence of expression. One after another of his religious compositions demonstrate an easy virtuosity.

The robust corporeality and rhythmic dynamism of *The Annunciation* (1663; Madrid, S. Plácido), although not unrelated to similar qualities in Rubens, are absolutely native to Coello's purpose of making tangible the supernaturalness of the event. *The Holy Family with Angels and Saints* (Madrid, Prado) has the enchantment of mood and spirited composition of a Correggio, but these are responsive to Coello's baroque intention of dissolving the barrier between the actual and the illusion.

The Adoration of the Holy Eucharist (1685–90; El Escorial) has been called the swan song of Spain's baroque Golden Age and of the Madrid school. It is imbued with profound religious reverence and, at the same time, is firmly mundane in its forthright compilation of portraits. Architectural grandeur is achieved with majestic proportions and geometric clarity in a manner reminiscent of Raphael. The tunnel space and the lively allegorical figures cavorting buoyantly are reminiscent of Tintoretto. Yet, as in all Coello's works, the ensemble is undeniably original.

His works stand apart also from those of his Spanish predecessors and contemporaries. The Spanish convention of expressing spirituality by revealing states of soul in strongly individualized personalities was abandoned by Coello for an Italianate reliance on the dramatic spectacle, within which individuals are subordinated to and absorbed by a charged emotional climate. Such religious scenes of

Claudio Coello, *The Adoration of the Holy Eucharist*. Sacristy, El Escorial, near Madrid.

House of Jacques Coeur, Bourges, built between 1443 and 1451 for a banker of Charles VII.

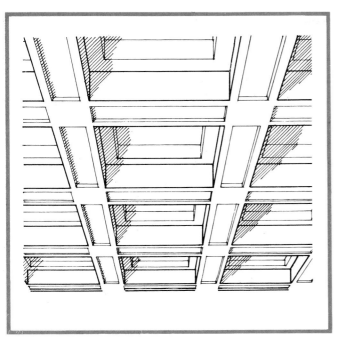

Coffer. Example of a coffered ceiling.

magnificent theater are Coello's forte, but he did occasionally achieve insightful portraits, an example being *Father Gabanillas* (Prado).

BIBLIOGRAPHY. F. Jiménez-Placer, *Historia del arte español*, 2 vols., Barcelona, 1955; J. A. Gaya Nuño, *Claudio Coello*, Madrid, 1957.

EILEEN A. LORD

COEMETERIA. Burial chambers in ancient Rome. Their subterranean vaults contained columbaria for ashes of the dead and loculi for interred bodies. Later *coemeteria* were called catacombs, from the district of Catacumbae near Rome. *See* CATACOMB.

COENACULUM. Supper room in the ancient Roman house. The custom of eating the *cena* (*coena*) in an upper room has led to the association of the term with upper rooms or suites. The coenaculum is also a banqueting hall.

COENE, JACQUES. Flemish painter, miniaturist, and architectural draftsman (fl. early 15th cent.). Coming from Bruges, Coene settled in Paris in 1398. There has been an attempt to identify him as the Boucicaut Master. Before 1402, with Jacquemart de Hesdin, he worked on some Hours for the Duc de Berry. *See* BOUCICAUT MASTER.

COEUR, JACQUES, HOUSE OF, BOURGES. Mansion in central France, built between 1443 and 1451 for a banker and councillor of Charles VII. With its picturesque irregularity of composition it represents one of the finest extant examples of Gothic secular architecture. In the chapel can be seen bas-reliefs and frescoes of the period. At present the house serves as a museum for sculpture of the Middle Ages and the Renaissance, notably statuary from the tomb of Jean, duc de Berry. *See* MASTER OF JACQUES COEUR.

COFFEE, WILLIAM JOHN. English-American sculptor (b. ca. 1774; d. New York State, ca. 1846). After study-ing in London and exhibiting at the Royal Academy, he went to the United States in 1816. Coffee lived in New York City, Newark, N.J., and Albany, N.Y. His portrait busts included those of his relatives and of Thomas Jefferson. He was also a painter.

BIBLIOGRAPHY. A. W. Rutledge, "William John Coffee as a Portrait Sculptor," *Gazette des Beaux-Arts*, XXVIII, 1945.

COFFER. Recessed panel in ceilings, domes, or vaults. An example of the coffered ceiling in ancient Greek architecture is found in the Temple of Epicurus in Bassae. Coffers were extensively used in Roman structures, as in the dome of the Pantheon, Rome, and in most classically influenced architecture.

COIGNET, GILLIS, *see* CONGNET, GILLIS.

COIL TECHNIQUE. A means of building up pottery from hand-rolled ropes of clay, which are connected to form a continuous coil. The coils are arranged concentrically until the vessel reaches its full height. At times the coiling process is done within a basket, which serves as a guide for shape and curve. Upon completion, the inner wall of the vessel is smoothed with water and flat implements. The outer wall can be smoothed or it can be allowed to retain its corrugated appearance.

BIBLIOGRAPHY. B. H. Leach, *A Potter's Book*, 4th ed., New York, 1949; H. H. Sanders, *The Practical Pottery Book*, London, 1955.

COIMBRA. University city in central Portugal. The Old Cathedral was begun in 1162 in the Romanesque style and altered in the early 16th century. The university boasts a

Coimbra. J. F. Ludovice, interior of the baroque university library, 1717–23.

Greek and Roman coinage. Left: Silver coin of Syracuse with head of the goddess Arethusa. Museum of Fine Arts, Boston. Right: Roman coin with bust of Marcus Junius Brutus, 42 B.C. Formerly collection of La Banque Leu, Zurich.

remarkable baroque library (1717–23), designed by J. F. Ludovice. The former archiepiscopal palace contains the Machado de Castro Museum, displaying paintings, tapestries, sculpture, and minor arts. *See* COIMBRA: OLD CATHEDRAL.

BIBLIOGRAPHY. Lisbon, Academia nacional de belas artes, *Inventário artístico de Portugal*, vol. 2: V. Correia and N. Gonçalves, *Cidade de Coimbra*, Lisbon, 1947.

COIMBRA: OLD CATHEDRAL (Se Velha).
Portuguese church, begun in 1162. It had two architects, Robert and Bernardo. Under the all-pervading influence of Santiago de Compostela, the plan has three aisles, a transept with a projecting bay at each end, and three east apses. The entire church is vaulted, but it derives its distinctive character from Moorish influences.

The façade is a sheer massive unit with one deep-set central arched portal. A high-relief corbel table separates the portal from an equally deep arched window above it. The entire façade is capped by Moorish crenelations and corner turrets, giving the Sé Velha a fortresslike appearance. Sixteenth-century additions by Jean de Rouen furnish interesting examples of early Renaissance architecture in Portugal.

The Flamboyant retable of the high altar was carved by the Flemings Olivier de Gand and Jean d'Ypres (early 16th cent.). There are many notable medieval tombs in the Cathedral.

BIBLIOGRAPHY. K. J. Conant, *Carolingian and Romanesque Architecture, 800–1200*, Baltimore, 1959.

COINAGE, GREEK AND ROMAN.
Sometime in the 7th century B.C. the Ionian Greeks were using coins, a practice that probably arose as a result of mercantile contacts with cultures farther to the east. Ingots of metal had been used for exchange in Egypt and Mesopotamia, but the new practice of coinage featured small pieces of metal stamped with some sort of guarantee as to their purity and weight.

The three most important early Greek centers of coinage were Aegina, Chalcis on Euboea, and Corinth, but coinage became much more general in the 6th century. The first great development of Athenian coinage occurred in the latter half of the 6th century under the tyrant Peisistratus.

Greek coins were almost exclusively silver or electrum until the 5th century B.C., but gold and bronze types were used later. Each city-state stamped on its own design and minted according to its preferred system of denominations. The principal standards for silver coinage were those of Aegina and Euboea, but many less important ones existed. In time, designs on coins became increasingly "artistic," reflecting the monumental art styles of their period and place of execution, a phenomenon of great importance to art historians. Very high-quality coinage was produced in Sicily, especially by Syracuse during the classical period, and it is generally true that there is a high correlation between the power and vigor of a city and the quality of its coinage. In the Hellenistic era coinage reflects the new world order by including rulers' images, usually on the obverse of coins bearing the conventional city emblems, but this was a characteristic of the Asiatic kingdoms rather than of Greece itself. As the Hellenistic world was absorbed by Rome, Roman coinage succeeded local types. Greek coinage may be considered to have ended with the establishment of the principate in 27 B.C.

The earliest Roman currencies were reckoned in terms of livestock and rough bronze bars (aes), evidence of primitive economic conditions. True coinage probably appeared no earlier than the 3d century B.C. The first silver coins, the so-called Romano didrachmas, were struck in 269 B.C., probably influenced by Alexandrian contacts. Thereafter silver and light "token" bronze coins were used primarily in the cities; heavy bronze, in the countryside. Gold coins were first struck in the late 3d century

B.C. Representations on Roman coinage were strongly influenced by Greek models from the outset. Thus, Roman coins are our only solid source of information about the appearance of some famous works of Greek art. During the republic the Senate maintained mints in Rome and in important Italian and provincial cities. With the advent of the principate the Emperor took over the minting of gold and silver coinage but left bronze coinage under the nominal control of the Senate. An important aspect of imperial coinage was its use as a herald of current events and hence as a propaganda medium.

BIBLIOGRAPHY. C. T. Seltman, *Greek Coins*, 2d ed., London, 1955; H. Mattingly, *Roman Coins from the Earliest Times to the Fall of the Western Empire*, 2d ed., London, 1960.

EVANTHIA SAPORITI

COLA DELL'AMATRICE (Nicola di Filotesio). Italian painter and architect (b. Amatrice, ca. 1480; d. soon after 1547). He was active in Umbria and in the Marches, mostly at Ascoli Piceno. His paintings reflect the influence of many masters, ranging from Carlo Crivelli (in the early works) to Michelangelo (in the later ones). Typical is a Raphaelesque *Way to Calvary* (Ascoli Piceno, Municipal Picture Gallery), one of several panels in different styles, all part of a huge altarpiece painted between 1516 and 1533. Equally characteristic are two of his most important constructions, both probably designed in 1525 but differing in style: the façade of S. Bernardino at Aquila is rather classic; that of the Ascoli Piceno Cathedral is almost baroque. A genius *manqué*, Cola produced work that is usually grand in intention, unsuccessful in effect.

BIBLIOGRAPHY. G. Fabiani, *Cola dell'Amatrice secondo i documenti ascolani*, Ascoli Piceno, 1952.

COLCHESTER, CASTLE OF. Largest of all Norman English keeps, built in Essex about 1080. Its plan and chapel are almost identical with those of the White Tower in the Tower of London, although it was completed only to the second story. The great hall is so enormous that an arcaded wall was built to support the roof. The building's interior walls have lacing courses of Roman brick over their rubble core; the exterior walls are dressed with freestone to a height of one story. Square turrets and pilaster buttresses provide added wall strength. Colchester is also the location of St. Botolph's priory church, dating from the 12th century. *See also* TOWER OF LONDON.

BIBLIOGRAPHY. H. Braun, *The English Castle*, London, 1936; S. Toy, *The Castles of Great Britain*, 3d ed., London, 1963.

COLDSTREAM, WILLIAM. English painter (1908–   ). Coldstream was born in Belford, Northumberland, and studied at the Slade School. He was a member of the London

Cola dell'Amatrice, the façade of S. Bernardino at Aquila, probably designed in 1525 by the painter-architect.

Thomas Cole, *Expulsion from the Garden of Eden*. Museum of Fine Arts, Boston (M. and M. Karolik Collection).

Group in 1933. With Victor Pasmore and Claude Rogers, he founded the Euston Road School in 1937 and taught there until 1939. Despite some experimentation with abstraction, Coldstream has continued his early style of a mild impressionism, influenced by Sickert, in landscapes, figures, and portraits of simple and restrained representation, for example, *Mrs. S. G. H. Burger* (1936–37; London, Tate).

BIBLIOGRAPHY. J. Rothenstein, *British Art since 1900*, New York, 1962.

COLE, THOMAS. American painter (b. Bolton-le-Moors, Lancashire, 1801; d. Catskill, N.Y., 1848). The chief painter of the Hudson River school was born in England. As a boy of fourteen, he worked as an apprentice to a designer of calico prints at Chorley, Nottinghamshire. A year later he was an engraver's assistant in Liverpool. He arrived in Philadelphia with his family in 1818 and there produced a series of illustrations for Bunyan's *Holy War*. The following year he and his family moved to Steubenville, Ohio, where he taught drawing and painting at his sister's school. He took up portrait painting under the influence of an itinerant artist but failed to support himself in this way. Between 1823 and 1825 he studied painting formally at the Pennsylvania Academy of Fine Arts in Philadelphia. At the end of this time the sale of three landscapes did

much to encourage him and ushered in a period of financial stability. In 1826 he was active in the group that founded the National Academy of Design.

Cole spent the years between 1829 and 1831 traveling in England and on the Continent. He admired the paintings of Claude and Turner and was greatly moved by the sight of the ancient ruins at Rome and Volterra. Upon his return to America, he found that his name was famous. From 1836 he made his permanent home in Catskill, N.Y., a region which was a lasting inspiration to him. A series of commissions for large works and whole ensembles of paintings kept him active throughout the 1830s and into the 1840s.

As a boy in England, Cole had read and dreamed of the grandeur of the American landscape which he later found embodied in the Hudson River Valley. Landscape painting was the love of his life, and wherever figures appear in his work they are dominated by their surroundings. *Expulsion from the Garden of Eden* (1828; Boston, Museum of Fine Arts) illustrates his use of chiaroscuro and calligraphic technique to underscore the drama of the scene, while *In the Catskills* (1837; New York, Metropolitan Museum of Art) is one of his masterpieces of visual lyricism. *The Titan's Goblet* (1833; New York, Metropolitan Museum) represents the peak of Cole's realization of romantic fantasies and anticipates certain devices of the surrealists. In *Dream of Arcadia* (1838; St. Louis, City Art Museum) he summoned up an imaginative reconstruction of an idyllic classical landscape. *The Voyage of Life* (1841; Utica, Munson-Williams-Proctor Institute), an ensemble of huge works that characterizes the four ages of man in landscapes, is the crowning achievement of his career and a major monument in the history of American painting.

BIBLIOGRAPHY. E. I. Seaver (intro.), *Thomas Cole, 1801–1848: One Hundred Years Later*, Hartford, Conn., 1949; V. Barker, *American Painting*, New York, 1950; E. P. Richardson, *Painting in America*, New York, 1956; L. L. Noble, *The Life and Works of Thomas Cole*, Cambridge, Mass., 1964.

FRANKLIN R. DIDLAKE

COLEMAN, GLENN O. American painter and graphic artist (b. Springfield, Ohio, 1887; d. Long Beach, N.Y., 1932). Coleman first studied painting at the Industrial Art School in Indianapolis and worked as a newspaper illustrator. He went to New York in 1905, studied with William Merritt Chase, Robert Henri, and Everett Shinn, and, only partly under their influence, was drawn to realistic subjects of urban genre. His own economic difficulties, his interest in socialism, and his concern for the lives of the poor also led him in the same direction. Many of his earlier drawings were published in *The Masses*. More than the other painters of the Ashcan group, however, Coleman depended on the picturesque qualities and atmosphere of his scenes, combined with a sentimental emphasis on local elements. Even in his most realistic work the figures are often seemingly less interesting than the charmingly ramshackle streets in which they move, as in *The Mews* (1926; Washington, D.C., Phillips Collection), or the street corners and elevated station of *Downtown Street* (1926; New York, Whitney Museum).

By the 1920s Coleman's paintings and the nostalgic lithographs he made from his early drawings were obviously anachronistic, harking back to an aesthetic of painting that was no longer viable under the impact of the artistic movements of the early 20th century. In his later work Coleman tentatively and personally absorbed these new movements. Massive buildings and skyscrapers were more solidly composed and increasingly stressed as the figures of city dwellers became less and less important. The new impersonality can be seen in *The Mirror* (1927; Whitney Museum), where the outside world of bridge and buildings is seen only in its reflection in an interior.

Despite the more formal order of his late work, Coleman retained a warm love for the changing experience of city life. Such a painting as *Bus View* (ca. 1930; formerly Glenn O. Coleman Estate) is a kaleidoscopic bringing together (with perhaps a hint of futurism) of alley, train tracks, skyscrapers, and other elements of the urban environment that could be seen from the window of a moving bus.

BIBLIOGRAPHY. C. A. Glassgold, *Glenn O. Coleman*, New York, 1932.

JEROME VIOLA

COLESHILL HOUSE. English house designed by the amateur architect Sir Roger Pratt from about 1650. It was a startling innovation, departing from the current Jonesian canon. The themes were varied and eclectic and were influential on later British architecture, especially as reflected in Pratt's Clarendon House, which burned in 1952.

BIBLIOGRAPHY. J. Summerson, *Architecture in Britain, 1530–1830*, 3d ed., Baltimore, 1958.

COLIJER (Colyer; Collier), EDWAERT. Dutch still-life and portrait painter (d. Leyden or Haarlem? in or before 1702). Born in Breda, Colijer entered the Guild of St. Luke at Leyden in 1673. He was also active in Haarlem and perhaps in London. He painted still-life representations of musical instruments and books with *vanitas* symbolism.

BIBLIOGRAPHY. I. Bergström, *Dutch Still-Life Painting in the Seventeenth Century*, New York, 1956.

COLIN, ALEXANDRE. Flemish sculptor (b. Mechlin, 1527/29; d. Innsbruck, 1612). Colin's specialty was the execution of fountains, mostly in the service of the emperor Maximilian, and he acquired great technical proficiency in working after painted models. His most important tomb sculpture was the grave of the banker Hans Fugger (1584–87; Innsbruck, Ulrichskirche). Colin worked in a brilliant Flemish style that was heavily Italianized.

COLIN, PAUL EMILE. French graphic artist (1877–ca. 1947). Born in Lunéville, Colin was a medical doctor. He gradually left his profession to become an illustrator, first in woodcut and then in etching. He is known for his romantic landscapes and woodcut illustrations for Jules Renard's *Les Philippe* and an edition of Zola's *Germinal* (1912).

BIBLIOGRAPHY. G. Geffroy, "La Gravure sur bois au XXe siècle: Paul-Emile Colin," *L'Art et les Artistes*, XI, April, 1910.

COLISEUM, ROME, see COLOSSEUM, ROME.

COLLAGE. Picture composed largely of such materials as paper, cloth, wood veneer, newspaper, and textured and colored papers held together by glue. The term is sometimes used interchangeably with *papiers collés* (from the French *coller*, "to stick, paste, or glue"). *Papiers collés* implies that only paper is employed, while a collage, the term suggests, may be made of a larger range of materials. Braque is thought to be the first artist to have made a collage, about 1911. Picasso soon followed. He used oil cloth, simulating chair caning in one of his first collages (artist's collection). A novel means of picture making then, the collage has since been accepted and is no longer unusual. *See also* PAPIERS COLLES.

BIBLIOGRAPHY. H. Janis and R. Blesh, *Collage: Personalities, Concepts, Techniques*, Philadelphia, 1962.

Glenn O. Coleman, *Downtown Street*. **Whitney Museum of American Art, New York.**

COLLANTES, FRANCISCO. Spanish painter (1599–1656). A pupil of Vicente Carducho, Collantes worked in Madrid, his native city. The influence of Ribera can be directly documented by a signed copy (London, Reder Collection) that Collantes made of a *St. Peter*. His more independently conceived landscapes, usually vehicles for Old Testament subjects, provide the basis for his reputation. He had a penchant for fantastic scenes filled with heroic architectural ruins, such as *The Vision of Ezekiel* (Madrid, Prado). A delight in total catastrophe is again given play in the awesomely inventive *Burning of Troy* (Granada University).

Such thematic choices were part of the baroque desire to recapture medieval man's intimate sense of the imminence of doomsday. Collantes's art, operatic in its use of a clamorously contrasted foreground chiaroscuro, is made palatable by its heroic character and by the ameliorating counterpoint of a greater, distant landscape, poetically luminous as though in a state of divine grace.

His romanticism was given expression also in more gracious themes such as the *Burning Bush* (ca. 1640–50; Paris, Louvre) and *Hagar and the Angel* (ca. 1640–50; Providence, Rhode Island School of Design, Museum of Art). Collantes edits the Biblical text in the manner of a playwright alert for dramatic effectiveness. Thus his artistic talent always served his classical sense of theater.

BIBLIOGRAPHY. J. Gudiol i Ricart, *Spanish Painting*, Toledo, Ohio, 1941; G. Kubler and M. Soria, *Art and Architecture in Spain and Portugal and Their American Dominions, 1500–1800*, Baltimore, 1959.

EILEEN A. LORD

COLLCUTT, THOMAS EDWARD. English architect (1840–1924). He was trained in the office of G. E. Street and practiced a Renaissance style. Collcutt's finest work—and the best-known one—is the Imperial Institute, London (1887–93), with one of the most strikingly elegant towers of the century.

COLLECTOR'S MARK. A monogram, personal stamp, or device impressed on the back of a print by the connoisseur-owner. The practice of print collecting dates back to the 16th century. Certain eminent collectors placed their marks only on prints of the highest quality.

Collector's mark. Stamp of the collector Leopoldo de' Medici (1617–75).

COLLEONI, IL. Bronze equestrian statue by Verrocchio, in the Campo SS. Giovanni e Paolo, Venice. *See* VERROCCHIO, ANDREA DEL.

COLLEONI CHAPEL, BERGAMO. Built in 1470, the chapel, which adjoins the Church of S. Maria Maggiore in Bergamo, Italy, was richly decorated by Giovanni Antonio Amadeo in Renaissance style. It contains the tomb of Bartolommeo Colleoni (d. 1473), general of the Venetian Republic, with reliefs from the life of Christ; a gilded equestrian statue of Colleoni by Sixtus Siry of Nürnberg (1501); and a monument to Colleoni's daughter Medea (d. 1470) by Amadeo.

BIBLIOGRAPHY. J. Pope-Hennessy, *Italian Renaissance Sculpture*, London, 1958.

COLLIER, EDWAERT, see COLIJER, EDWAERT.

COLLIER, THOMAS. English landscape water-colorist (1840–91). Born in Glossop, Derbyshire, Collier studied at the Manchester College of Art, but was largely self-taught. He began to exhibit in London in the 1860s and became a member of the Royal Institute of Painters in Water Colours in 1872. The airiness and atmosphere of his style won him distinction at the Exposition Universelle in Paris in 1878, and he was awarded the Legion of Honor.

COLLOT, MARIE-ANNE. French sculptor (b. Paris, 1748; d. Nancy, 1821). She entered Falconet's atelier at sixteen, specializing in portraiture, and was his most brilliant female pupil. In 1766 she accompanied Falconet to Russia and executed the head for his colossal equestrian statue of Peter the Great. In 1767 she became a member of the Royal Academy of Arts of St. Petersburg, and in 1777 she married Falconet's son. Her portrait style is vigorous and realistic, in contrast to such 18th-century female artists as Mme Vigée-Lebrun.

BIBLIOGRAPHY. C. Cournault, "Etienne-Maurice Falconet et Marie-Anne Collot," *Gazette des Beaux-Arts*, series 2, II, 1869; L. Réau, "Une femme-sculpteur française au XVIIIe siècle: Marie-Anne Collot (1748–1821)," *Bulletin de la Société de l'Histoire de l'Art Français*, November, 1924.

COLLOTYPE. Photographic process for the black-and-white reproduction of printed illustrations. An extremely high quality of tonal differentiation is achieved by printing from specially developed gelatin-covered plates, which are first exposed to a negative made from the original. Collotype can also be adapted for color reproduction.

BIBLIOGRAPHY. T. A. Wilson, *The Practice of Collotype*, Boston, 1935.

COLLYER, JOSEPH. English engraver and book illustrator (b. London, 1748; d. there, 1827). The son of the book publisher Joseph Collyer, he studied with Anthony Walker and probably also with Anthony's brother William Walker. Through his book illustration Collyer was able to attract the attention of English society. He eventually made portraits both from life and from paintings by other masters (*Portrait of the Prince of Wales*, 1792, after Russell).

BIBLIOGRAPHY. A. M. Hind, *A History of Engraving and Etching...*, 3d ed., rev., London, 1923 (repr. New York, 1963).

COLMAR: UNTERLINDEN MUSEUM. French collection. Among the Alsatian primitives exhibited in this former Dominican monastery, the *Isenheim Altar* of Matthias

Cologne. Cathedral, begun in 1248.

Grünewald is outstanding and culminates the expressionist tendencies emerging in the late Gothic period.

BIBLIOGRAPHY. C. Champion, *Le Musée d'Unterlinden à Colmar*, Paris, 1924.

COLOBIUM. Type of sleeveless tunic worn by women in ancient times. It is also an alternative designation for the priestly dalmatic.

COLOGNE (Koln). Cultural and commercial center on the middle Rhine River, in western Germany. The Roman city of Colonia Agrippina owes its origin to a military camp established at the site under Augustus. In A.D. 50 Cologne was made a colony and subsequently became the capital of the province of Germania Inferior. Industrial arts and crafts, especially glassmaking, flourished in Roman Cologne, and examples are in the Roman-German Museum.

Christians established an episcopal see here in the 4th century, and several churches show a continual history of worship from that time until the present. Cologne thus ranks as one of the main centers of continuity between ancient and medieval civilization in northwestern Europe. The Ottonian period (late 10th–early 11th cent.) marked the beginning of a golden age of the arts. Cologne developed a distinctive school of miniature painting characterized by subtle color harmonies. Gold- and silverwork emerged somewhat later, stimulated by influences from the Meuse Valley. The central medieval period (950–1250) saw the building of a number of important churches, culminating in the famous Gothic Cathedral. The later Middle Ages, when the city greatly prospered through its trade with England, were less important artistically. The interdiction

of this commercial link in the Reformation caused a decline, which was not reversed until the 19th century. Heavily damaged by bombing in World War II, Cologne has subsequently been the scene of interesting experiments in town planning. *See also* COLOGNE SCHOOL; RHENISH SCHOOL.

Remains of the Praetorium (palace of the military governor) and a tower of the city walls date from the Roman period. The original core of the Church of St. Gereon, which is built on an oval plan, dates to the second half of the 4th century. The ambitious Cathedral, begun in 1248 after French models, replaced an earlier Carolingian basilica; it remained unfinished until the 19th century. The Ottonian Church of SS. Aposteln was built in the early 11th century. St. Pantaleon retains an imposing westwork. St. Maria im Kapitol (10th cent.) has a trefoil plan that was much imitated in the Rhineland; its wooden doors are a noteworthy specimen of Ottonian relief sculpture. In the Gothic style are the Minoritenkirche, St. Andreas, and St. Ursula. The ruined Gurzenich Palace and the porch of the City Hall represent secular architecture of the late Gothic and Renaissance period respectively. *See* COLOGNE: CATHEDRAL; ST. GEREON; SANKT MARIA IM KAPITOL.

Noteworthy buildings erected after World War II include the Opera House by Wilhelm Riphahn, the Wallraf-Richartz Museum by Rudolf Schwartz (who was also responsible for the overall redevelopment plan), and several suburban churches by Dominikus Böhm. *See* COLOGNE: MUSEUMS.

Among the many churches in the center of the city rebuilt after the bombings of World War II are Sankt Maria im Kapitol and the Basilica of the Holy Apostles.

BIBLIOGRAPHY. P. Clemen, *Die Kunstdenkmäler der Rheinprovinz*, vols. 6, 7, Düsseldorf, 1911–30; H. Vogts, *Köln im Spiegel seiner Kunst*, Cologne, 1950; W. Meyer-Barkhausen, *Das grosse Jahrhundert Kölnischer Kirchenbaukunst, 1150–1250*, Cologne, 1952; H. Schnitzler, *Rheinische Schatzkammer*, 2 vols., Düsseldorf, 1957–59.

WAYNE DYNES

COLOGNE: CATHEDRAL. German Cathedral begun in 1248. Its choir was dedicated in 1332. Although the Cathedral was modeled after the Cathedral of Amiens in ground plan, form, and even proportions, it is no mere copy. Amiens has three aisles, but Cologne has five; yet no relationships can be traced between Cologne and five-aisled French cathedrals such as those at Bourges and Paris. Individual forms also deviate from the Amiens prototype.

The west front uses the twin-tower scheme of the French cathedrals, but here the towers are constructed of the open, lacy stonework that is characteristic of German Gothic architecture. It was not until 1841, during the archaeological phase of the Gothic revival, that the original plans were found and the building was finally completed. *See also* DREIKONIGENSCHREIN, COLOGNE CATHEDRAL.

BIBLIOGRAPHY. N. Pevsner, *An Outline of European Architecture*, 7th ed., Harmondsworth, 1963.

COLOGNE: MUSEUMS. Important public art collections in Cologne, Germany, are located in the museums listed below.

Archiepiscopal Diocesan Museum (Erzbischofliches Diozesanmuseum). Founded in 1858. It is dedicated to the art and applied arts of the church, with works especially from the Lower Rhine and Cologne proper. Two paintings by Stephan Lochner, the *Virgin with the Violet* and the *Nativity*, deserve special mention.

Michel Colombe, *St. George*. Relief from the chapel of the château at Gaillon. Louvre, Paris.

Schnuetgen Museum. Founded in 1906. Mainly a collection of medieval ecclesiastical art from the Lower Rhine region, the area around the Maas River, and Westphalia, the museum is appropriately housed in the former Collegiate Church of St. Cecilia, dating from about 1160. Among the Romanesque and Gothic sculptures a baptismal font from the Maas region (ca. 1200), the *Siegburg Madonna* (ca. 1150), figures of apostles and saints, and *Christ on the Donkey* (ca. 1500) are noteworthy. The museum also contains works in ivory from as far back as the 9th century, many liturgical objects, a fine collection of textiles ranging from Coptic pieces of the 6th century to a southern German wall covering of about 1500, manuscripts, and fine pieces of stained glass.

Wallraf-Richartz Museum. Collection founded in 1824 and now housed in a building of 1953–57. It consists mainly of European paintings from the Middle Ages to the present. The main accent is on German painting, beginning with Cologne altarpieces from the early 14th to the 16th century and German altarpieces mostly of the 15th and 16th centuries. There are works by Altdorfer, Hans Baldung-Grien, Lucas Cranach, and Dürer, and, perhaps the best-known work in this museum, Stephan Lochner's *Madonna in a Rose Bower*. Among other periods in German art, romanticism and 20th-century expressionism are especially well represented. Second in number among the other European schools is the collection of works by Dutch and Flemish painters (Hals, Rembrandt, Ruisdael, Rubens, Van Dyck, and others). Works of the French school (from Claude Lorraine through Braque) and the Italian school (mainly 18th-cent. masters), graphic arts of nearly all European schools (from the 15th cent. to the present), and sculptures of the 19th and 20th centuries are included.

LOTTE PULVERMACHER-EGERS

COLOGNE SCHOOL. The painting around the region of Cologne, Germany, in the last half of the 14th and the first half of the 15th century. It culminated in the work of Stephan Lochner and is marked by a mood of dreamy tenderness. Even when the scenes of Calvary are depicted, the horror is minimized. The polyptychs of Cologne, sumptuous with their gold backgrounds, are peopled with elegant figures described with a precise calligraphy.

Most painters of the school are known anonymously, such as the Master of the Legend of St. Ursula and the Master of the St. Bartholomew Altarpiece (so called from the altar in Munich, Bavarian State Picture Galleries). The first substantial figure is the Veronica Master, who has been identified with a Master Wilhelm or a Herman Wynrich, first mentioned in Cologne in 1387. The colors of his small devotional pictures are glowing and enamel-like.

Lochner, who came from southern Germany, moved to Cologne about 1430. He perpetuated the idyllic grace of the early Cologne painters, but fashioned heavier figures and deepened the picture space by replacing the gold background with a landscape. After Lochner, Cologne imitated the meticulous realism of the art of the Netherlands. The innocence and delicacy peculiar to the Cologne school disappeared. In the opening years of the 16th century, artists from the Netherlands, coming to Cologne to execute commissions, founded schools of their own. *See* LOCHNER, STEPHAN; MASTER OF THE ST. BARTHOLOMEW ALTARPIECE; MASTER OF THE LEGEND OF ST. URSULA; VERONICA MASTER.

BIBLIOGRAPHY. H. Dickinson, *German Masters of Art*, New York, 1914; F. J. Mather, Jr., *Western European Painting of the Renaissance*, New York, 1948.

ABRAHAM A. DAVIDSON

COLOMBE, JEAN. French miniaturist (fl. after 1467; d. Bourges, 1529). He was probably a brother of the sculptor Michel Colombe. Jean's name is first encountered in Bourges in 1467. He worked for Charlotte of Savoy and, later, for Charles I, duke of Savoy. He was one of the first northern artists to work in the Renaissance style, and his borders and architectural details are classical. Evidence of his great contemporary reputation are the commissions he received to complete two earlier manuscripts that were well known, one the *Très riches heures* of the Duc de Berry, and the other the *Apocalypse*. In each case the additions are in his own style.

BIBLIOGRAPHY. H. M. R. Martin, *Les Miniaturistes français*, Paris, 1906.

COLOMBE, MICHEL. French sculptor (ca. 1431–ca. 1512). His name appears first in connection with a tomb for Francis II, duke of Brittany (1499–1507; Nantes Cathedral). Colombe, Girolamo da Fiesole, and Jean Perréal seem to have worked jointly on this memorial, with Colombe producing the sculpture. This monument shows characteristics of Italian late Gothic tombs with certain Burgundian features. The four Virtues at the corners are Burgundian, and the altar tomb with reclining effigies (*gisants*) is Italian. Stylistically the figures and *gisants* are of native origin. A second sculpture definitely attributed to Colombe is a relief, *St. George* (1508–09; Paris, Louvre), from the chapel of the château at Gaillon. Colombe was important as an early 16th-century sculptor because he was able to combine native traditions with Italian Renaissance models.

BIBLIOGRAPHY. A. Blunt, *Art and Architecture in France, 1500–1700*, Baltimore, 1954; P. Pradel, *Michel Colombe: Le Dernier imagier gothique*, Paris, 1953.

COLONIA. Originally a term applied to the colonies established first by the Greeks and then by the Romans in various areas of the Mediterranean removed from the motherland. Later the term was expanded to apply to the culture of these areas. Important Greek colonies, such as Sicily, developed cultures that were in many ways different from and, at times, superior to those of the Greek mainland.

COLONIAL AMERICAN FURNITURE, *see* FURNITURE.

COLONIAL ART: LATIN AMERICA. The Spanish conquerors of Mexico, Central America, and South America in the early 16th century encountered a group of highly developed American Indian cultures that had evolved independently of the European tradition. The Spaniards tried to destroy the evidences of those earlier civilizations. The extent to which the firmly rooted native traditions resisted Spanish pressures ultimately determined the character of the new entity that resulted. It is the fusion of European Christian and American preconquest elements that constitutes the culture of Latin America and gives it a special flavor.

From the 16th through the 18th century all Latin America was a colonial territory ruled by viceroys of Spain, except for Brazil, which was owned by Portugal. The Spanish conquest brought a tremendous influx of Catholic monastic clergy: Franciscans, Dominicans, Augustinians, Mercedarians, and, somewhat later, Jesuits and Carmelites. In order to convert the great mass of Indians, monasteries were built to carry on missionary activities. These were rather modest buildings in the earliest days, but in a relatively short time ecclesiastical structures of considerable consequence were to be seen. By the early 17th century there were about 70,000 churches and 500 monastic establishments of various religious orders in the Spanish colonies. At that time it was observed, for example, that church properties in Lima, Peru, occupied more of the city than did all the rest.

Although the Catholic Church functioned universally in the colonial territories, there is no such thing as a common Latin-American style. The chief centers of colonial administration were usually set up in the destroyed capital cities of the earlier Indian nations, and churches in many cases were built on the actual ruins of earlier temples. The most important colonial cultural centers, therefore, were in those areas that had previous and separate civilizations, such as the Aztecs and Mayas in Mexico and Guatemala and the Incas in the highlands of Peru, Ecuador, and Bolivia. Thus the baroque style of Mexico, for instance, differs from that of Peru; furthermore, a metropolitan style of church or monastery in Cuzco can be distinguished from a nonmetropolitan one in some small Peruvian town.

Colonial art is, of course, deeply indebted to Spain in that its patterns were set by Spanish priests and objects of art and artists were imported from there. Nevertheless, Latin-American art of the colonial period remains essentially distinct from its Spanish parent. Some critics even consider that the colonial baroque of the 17th–18th century is superior to the Spanish baroque. The new-fledged composite culture, conditioned by the strength and persistence of indigenous cultural patterns, began to emerge in Latin-American works as early as the 16th century.

The fusion of Spanish and Indian talents produced new and, in some ways, more interesting artistic types. The Spaniards had destroyed all the Aztec and Maya temples and almost completely obliterated the great Inca Temple of the Sun in Cuzco, but native workmanship was permitted and even encouraged in the building of churches. It was felt that the use of indigenous techniques and motifs would be a means of spreading the faith. Certainly the priests in charge of erecting such a church as S. Lorenzo in Potosí in the Bolivian highlands were aware that there the Christian symbols were mingled with Inca signs for the sun and moon and that angels were replaced by sirens playing the *charango*, a native instrument made from an armadillo shell.

This free and even non-Christian decorative treatment was paralleled by certain innovations in the architecture itself. The special conditions of mass baptism, in the conversion of whole populations of Indians, brought forth such Mexican forms as the immense atrium, or open forecourt, with a shrine at each of the four corners, and the open chapel. On the other hand, fortress churches were built in far greater number in Latin America during the 16th century than in Europe during the Middle Ages. Practically all the earliest Mexican churches were of this character, not as a concession to the Indian's taste but rather as a defense against him.

MEXICO

Mexican art of the colonial period developed in several stages: the early colonial style, the Plateresque style, the Herreran style, Mexican baroque, and the Churrigueresque style.

Early colonial style. The most typical Mexican building of the early 16th century, the fortress church, is exemplified in Actopan, Acolmán, Huejotzingo, and Yecapixtla. These structures date from the time of the conquest (1519–20) to about the middle of the 16th century, when the tribes in the center of the country were overcome. The buildings show many traces of medieval style, which in the mother country was still being utilized at that late date. Gothic forms may frequently be seen in the ribbed and pointed vaulting of the interior of these Mexican churches, for instance, in Huejotzingo and Acolmán. It is also noteworthy that specific characteristics of the late Moorish, or Mudejar, style of Spain were often transmitted in the decorative work, not only on the ceilings of the fortress churches but also in the residences of the conquistadors. *See* Acolman, Monastery Church of; Huejotzingo, Monastery Church of.

Since there was enormous need for building and decorating talent, schools were established by the monks to teach the Indians various techniques. Thus there are early and somewhat naïve attempts to cover the church walls with paintings, as in Acolmán, where, in the absence of fresco prototypes, the natives copied woodcut illustrations from pious books. Many of the so-called frescoes are, therefore, in black and white and in a very precise linear style, in some cases actually reproducing in paint the cross-hatching of the original woodcut. Native ideas appear also in the carvings, both in subject matter and in the flattened and nonsculptural, almost Oriental, manner of carving. This early, flattened carving may well be compared with the technique of precolonial friezes in Chichén Itzá and other sites in the Yucatán Peninsula.

Plateresque style. A second stage of colonial development corresponded to the Renaissance in Spain. It arose from a period of relative calm in the New World, from the middle of the 16th through the first quarter of the 17th century, when the conqueror was able to turn from fighting to agriculture and mining. In architecture this period gave rise to the Plateresque style, a name derived from the fineness and richness of its ornamental work, comparable to products of the silversmith (*platero*). The open chapel of the monastery of Tlalmanalco shows a combination of Renaissance ornamental detail and Indian craftsmanship (that is, friezelike flattening) that yields the Mexican version of the Plateresque style. The great staircase of the monastery of Actopan shows the increasing influence of the Renaissance in Mexico.

Sculpture of the 16th century had been under the influence of the Andalusian, or southern Spanish, school. By the end of that century there appeared Renaissance retables covering the entire end of the church. In their elaborate combination of paintings, reliefs, and freestanding figures, they contrast strongly with the simplicity of the buildings. As in the mother country, these Plateresque altarpieces were decorated with saints carved in wood, sometimes covered with gold leaf and generally polychromed, as in the altarpiece of Huejotzingo.

The minor arts followed the Moorish tradition of Spain. Wealthy Spaniards imported many decorative objects from the home country, and native craftsmen with their centuries-old mastery of fine work in gold produced numerous pieces in that medium. In addition, fine furniture, wrought iron, and embroidery were plentiful. An interesting evidence of the persistence of Indian craft traditions may be found in the reappearance of the famous precolonial feather mosaics, now containing religious narratives and representations of saints.

As the 17th century moved forward, social stability and wealth grew and imposing mansions were built. More ecclesiastics arrived from Spain, and cathedrals were constructed, in addition to the monasteries. The Renaissance period in architecture was later matched in painting by the mid-17th-century arrival of professional painters from Europe, men in the Italo-Flemish tradition. Their influence, however, soon gave way to a more distinctly Spanish viewpoint, that of Zurbarán, Murillo, and others. Many monasteries at this later date continued to be built in Renaissance style, but the simplicity of the earlier medieval buildings was gone. Luxury and elaboration of decoration became increasingly evident in the church furniture of the time.

The first generation of Italo-Flemish painters in Mexico produced followers, and the painters from Spain added the emotive trend that had been popularized by Spanish emulators of the Caravaggio style. Prosperity meant a great expansion of artistic activity, as the greater number of paintings clearly indicates. Instead of frescoes, the walls of religious buildings were covered by huge oil paintings done by such artists as Baltásar de Echave Ibía. *See* Echave Ibia, Baltasar de.

Herreran style. The Plateresque style in architecture was followed by a brief period in the Herreran manner, a reserved and even dry mode best exemplified in Spain by that coldest of buildings, El Escorial, built by Herrera for the tomb of Philip II. Too severe for Mexico, it was a short-lived fashion there; but it produced some interesting examples, such as the Cathedral of Puebla (1649–64) with its controlled exterior, on which, however, some baroque elements already emerge. *See* Puebla Cathedral.

Mexican baroque. Although the earlier architectural forms never disappeared entirely, the whole conception of building veered in the latter part of the 17th century toward an art filled with dynamism and movement. As in European baroque, the surfaces were deeply cut; light and shade contributed to a restless emotive movement throughout these richly surfaced and deep structures. Greater wealth, particularly gold, and cheap labor were available to the colonists, and the religious and other buildings took on a sumptuous elaboration never seen before. By the end of the 17th century Mexican baroque became an identifiable style and an outstanding feature of the Mexican scene, to such an extent that whole cities sometimes appear to be baroque in character. *See* Baroque Art.

The churches in this style constitute a fairly uniform type throughout Latin America: they are spacious structures, cruciform in plan, with a dome over the crossing and often with towers dominating the façade. Deep shadowy carvings on the façade impart an intense emotional quality to the building. In the interior, rich decorations in the form of retables and other church furniture lend an air of splendor to the worship conducted there. The palaces of the baroque style also take on some of these features. The Cathedral of Oaxaca with its highly carved façade, its niches filled with statues, and its irregularity of surface and line has this distinctive effect, the American variant of European baroque.

Both Puebla and Oaxaca as cities convey a marked flavor of the past. Puebla is characterized by its almost completely colonial quality, imparted particularly by the tile-covered domes of its churches. Oaxaca is an example of a city that, in spite of its manifestly Christian stamp, is close in many ways to its Indian ancestry. The tilework so plentiful in Puebla (and on the dome, towers, and roof of the Cathedral of Oaxaca) is part of the Moorish heritage of Talavera ware brought over by the Spaniards and grafted onto techniques already known to the Indians. The tile-covered domes have become distinguishing features of Mexican churches, and tilework also serves secular purposes on fountains, wall facings, and town squares. Sculpture and the decorative arts (including both ecclesiastical and secular furniture) shared the generally more emotive character of the time—rich, splendid, and dramatically effective.

Churrigueresque style. As the art of Mexico assumed its own character, a change occurred in the direction of a more complex version of the baroque, known as the Churrigueresque style. Whereas the favorite baroque supporting element had been the spiral column, the Churrigueresque style used a kind of pier in the shape of an inverted obelisk covered with heavy ornaments. More important, while baroque buildings such as the Cathedral of Oaxaca had preserved the basic traditional values in plan and in spatial qualities, the new Churrigueresque structures tended toward designs in which movement and rhythm rather than structural discipline were stressed. The buildings and their retables approached the fantastic, expressing an almost dreamlike splendor. The 18th-century monastery of Tepotzotlán is one of the most luxurious and colorful examples of this ultrabaroque style. It points up, too, the limitless supply of gold and the use of the traditionally skillful and decoratively inclined Indian sculptors. Another instance is the Sanctuary of Our Lady of Ocotlán, near Tlaxcala (ca. 1745). *See* Ocotlan, Sanctuary Church of; Tepotzotlan. *See also* Churriguera, Jose Benito de.

This last flowering of colonial genius gave way, toward the end of the 18th century, to neoclassic influences coming again from Spain. Both architecture and sculpture display the evidence of that increasingly powerful strain. An architectural example is the Church of the Carmen (1804) in Celaya, Guanajuato, designed by Francisco Eduardo Tresguerras. In sculpture the trend is exemplified by the works of the Spaniard Manuel Tolsa, such as the equestrian monument of Charles IV (1803) in Mexico City. Tolsa, who was also an architect, was director of the Academy of S. Carlos in Mexico City. The entire hemisphere, north and south, was affected by the neoclassical development. *See* Tolsa, Manuel; Tresguerras, Francisco Eduardo.

In sculpture, the Churrigueresque period marked a serious decline. The fantastically elaborate and gilded retables with their polychromed and otherwise decorated figures were in themselves pictorial in viewpoint rather than sculpturesque. In some ways they seemed even to fulfill the illusionistic needs of the art of painting, with their naturalistic treatment of skin, of actual draperies, and of other adjuncts. Such elaborate carving left no flat surfaces on which paintings could be done or to which they could be attached.

On the other hand, the great demand for paintings throughout the increasingly wealthy colonies brought a serious drop in quality. Pictures were turned out wholesale, and the outward forms of the art of Murillo became pat and empty formulas. With the exception of the work of such portrait painters as Miguel Cabrera—for example, his portrait (1750) of Sor Juana Inés de la Cruz, the great religious poetess—and an occasional still-life painter such as Antonio Pérez de Aguilar, the bulk of the painting produced in the second half of the 18th century, mostly religious art, is of very dubious quality. *See* Cabrera, Miguel.

HIGHLANDS OF SOUTH AMERICA

While the fusion of Spanish and native genius may be traced in many Mexican examples, the Indian resistance to Spanish concepts seemed stronger in the South American highlands, and proportionately more native elements remained in the South American arts. On the shores of Lake Titicaca, the sacred lake of the Incas, such old cities as Zepita, Puno, and Pomata have churches that are almost un-Spanish in character, so heavy is the proportion of Indian details. In Potosí, Bolivia, as mentioned earlier, the Church of S. Lorenzo shows a façade (1728–44) replete with Indian motifs. This influence is felt, though less strongly, as far north as Quito, Ecuador. In Peru, the viceregal capital of Lima, a new city, remains almost completely Spanish; but Cuzco, built on the ruins of the earlier Inca civilization, reveals strong traces of that background in the materials that were used and in the generally cyclopean wall structure.

The two great centers of Hispanic-American arts, after Mexico, are Quito and Cuzco. Here, on the remains of destroyed Inca capitals, the conquerors built a pair of Christian cities. But Cuzco's resistance to the penetration of Spanish ideas was stronger because this area had been the heart of the great and powerful Inca empire and also because it was far removed from the Spanish administrative capital at Lima.

The architecture and art of Lima may be considered to duplicate that of Spain, for the most part. Spanish ships brought articles of luxury, particularly ecclesiastical furniture, paintings, and sculpture, as well as architects and sculptors. This literal transplantation of Spanish art and artists made for a minimum of Indian influence in Lima. What is found here, therefore, is a multitude of Moorish

Colonial art, Latin America. São Francisco, Ouro Preto, Brazil.

architectural elements, Mudejar woodwork patterns, tile-work of the Seville type, and furniture from the same source. A good instance of the kind of building produced is the Palacio de Torre Tagle (1730–35). *See* LIMA: CATHEDRAL OF LA ASUNCION; LIMA: SAN FRANCISCO.

Cuzco. In Cuzco the atmosphere changes. The conquerors, building on the ruins of Inca temples, in some cases preserved the earlier masonry for Christian purposes. However little of the original walls and foundations were employed, there was a strong tradition of stone building that gave a special direction to the church architecture of Peru and the Andean highlands in general. In this region emerged one of the most original styles of Spanish America.

The Cathedral of Cuzco, like most of the buildings there, postdates the destructive earthquake of 1650. Its simple outlines, squat towers, and heavy masonry illustrate very directly the Inca heritage; a relatively baroque doorway inserted into the whole ameliorates the severity of the façade. The Cathedral was built on the ruins of the temple of the Inca god Wiraqocha; the evenly cut brown-colored stones of that temple were reused in its construction. Less ornate than its Mexican contemporaries, it possesses a simplicity and a directness that remove it from the Herreran category. Compared with the elegance of the Herreran style, the Cathedral of Cuzco has an elemental strength, an almost primitive power. Walls like these suggest the massive masonry of the Inca citadel of Sacsahuaman in Cuzco or the awesome majesty of Machu Picchu. Within the building, heavy cruciform piers help support a system of Gothic brick vaulting. The curious wood ornamentation brings to mind the fact that as many as fifty Indians helped to build the façade. Indian influence can also be seen in the Church of S. Sebastián in Cuzco and that of La Compañía in the city of Arequipa. On these examples the Indian imprint is twofold: in the introduction of plant and animal forms and in the typical flattening of the carved ornament,

which suggests that of the Incas (and of the Moors). *See* CUZCO CATHEDRAL.

Cuzco retained its early importance throughout the colonial period. Its main square, the Plaza de Armas, is one of the largest in Latin America and has four churches. In addition to architecture, Cuzco also produced a great variety of church furniture, painting, and metalwork, as well as sculptures to be used for retables and crucifixes. *See also* BITTI, BERNARDO.

In Bolivia there was again a strong Indian carryover. The stonecutters responsible for the chief churches and civil buildings of La Paz and Potosí combined the tendencies of the great Tiahuanaco tradition and that of El Escorial, near Madrid. The austerity of the Cuzco style is felt here even more forcefully, probably because the Tiahuanaco tradition itself was inclined that way. The churches of S. Francisco in La Paz and of S. Lorenzo in Potosí offer a certain simplicity of general form that at first glance is obscured by the rich, flatly carved Indian type of ornament covering the façades (especially the portals). Definite and carefully balanced horizontal and vertical lines determine the movement of the façades, rather than the complex in-and-out movement of the more typically baroque monuments of Mexico. This is an altogether new version of the baroque style.

Quito. The other important center, Quito, is more Spanish and has many colonial buildings, principally churches and monasteries, such as the Franciscan Church of S. Francisco and the Jesuit Church of La Compañía (the Company of Jesus). *See* QUITO SCHOOL.

One of the most elaborate complexes in Spanish America, S. Francisco takes in an area of four city blocks and has four cloisters with altars and paintings. It was finished in the mid-17th century and has since been one of the showplaces of South America. The façade is long and low, with a slightly Renaissance portal accented by paired baroque columns and rusticated bands of stone that suggest 17th-century European baroque. This central section is capped by two towers and stretches away to left and right in long horizontal wings. The low, massive quality reminds us of other Andean churches, for example, the Cathedral of Cuzco. The exterior is in strong contrast to the rich interior, which has Mudejar work on the ceiling, gilded wood carving in the lower part of the nave, and a high altar that covers the entire apse and even flows round the corners into adjacent areas, contributing to one of the most impressive and luxurious effects in Latin America.

The Jesuit Church of La Compañía is more homogeneous in form and is, in various ways, more genuinely baroque. In plan and façade La Compañía suggests a combination of two famous Roman Jesuit churches: Il Gesù, the mother church of the order, and S. Ignazio, which was in the process of building while La Compañía was going up during the mid-17th century. But there is a clear difference between the academic baroque of Italy and the lively, varied, almost tumultuous baroque of Latin America. The gold in the interior of La Compañía, unlike the pure gold found in some other buildings, is tempered by red and white paint in the carved ornamentation and by the red background of the gilded strapwork. *See also* JESUIT STYLE.

Colonial art, Latin America. Church of Penha, Bahia, Brazil. Example of the Brazilian variety of Portuguese baroque.

BRAZIL

Settled by the Portuguese, Brazil does not manifest the same succession of styles that characterizes the Spanish-dominated centers. In this region, which shows practically no artistic or literary development during the 16th century, the Indians were not comparable in cultural achievement with those of the Spanish viceroyalties, especially Peru and Mexico. Trained craftsmen and traditions of building did not exist in the Brazilian area, and even good stone had to be imported from Portugal.

Moreover, Portuguese colonies in the Americas were not exploited so vigorously, and the religious orders were not involved there until late in the 16th century. With few exceptions, it was not until the end of the 17th century that significant buildings appeared with any degree of frequency in Brazil. The first of these were in the severe late Herreran style to be seen in the coarsened examples of Recife (Espirito Santo and Madre de Deus) and in Santos and Rio de Janeiro.

Salvador (or Bahia), capital of the colony until 1763, presents a cross section of the various artistic trends. One

of its earliest structures, the church of the Third Order of St. Francis (1703), illustrates the Brazilian variety of Portuguese baroque with its typical wrought-iron balconies and the rhythmical use of consoles and volutes, the decorative elements being so separated as to give a static rather than a flowing effect.

Another distinct style in Brazil is the so-called coastal baroque embodied in the Church of São Pedro dos Clérigos in Recife, the Venice of that part of the world. Its chief characteristics are tall, narrow façades, elaborate French windows (where Spanish-American baroque would show niches), an emphasized central doorway; a high pediment separated from the squarish towers, and whitewashed wall surfaces.

Unique in the architecture of the Americas is the type of church associated with the province of Minas Gerais, where gold and diamonds were mined. Here many handsome, even elegant, churches were built, in a style that has been classified as rococo rather than baroque, that is, light, airy, and graceful rather than florid, emotive, and heavy. A local quartz was used for its structural as well as its artistic value, and the availability of large quantities of fine hardwood for beams tended to exclude the arched vaults typical of the other schools of colonial architecture.

These mining-district churches, many of the finest occurring in the area of Ouro Preto, show a simple rectangular plan, a pair of formally round or square towers integrated into the shape of the façade rather than separate, a single doorway equipped with an elaborately carved cornice, handsomely shaped rococo windows directly over the cornice as well as above it at the sides, and window balconies. São Francisco in Ouro Preto is a fine example of the style; it exhibits all these features as well as a charming contrast in color and texture between the light (gray) hue of the main body of the building and the orange soapstone used for the engaged columns, bases, and cornices.

São Francisco and other churches in Ouro Preto are associated with the name of the architect-sculptor Antônio Francisco Lisboa, known as "the Little Cripple" (O Aleijadinho). It would seem that the carving around the portal of São Francisco and in the disk above it is by Aleijadinho, whose personality appears to have dominated the art of this section of Brazil in the 18th century. In this mode of expression, with its decoratively contrasting façade elements and colors, its gay motifs of garlands and scrolls, its graceful window carvings, and its eloquent sculpture, Brazil produced a style that can be matched only in part by that of Portugal. *See* ALEIJADINHO.

BIBLIOGRAPHY. New York, Museum of Modern Art, *Twenty Centuries of Mexican Art*, New York, 1940; M. S. Noel, *El Arte en la América española*, Buenos Aires, 1942; D. Angulo Iñiguez, *Historia del arte hispanoamericano*, 3 vols., Barcelona, 1945-56; M. Toussaint, *Arte mudéjar en América*, Mexico, 1946; P. Kelemen, *Baroque and Rococo in Latin America*, New York, 1951; Sociedad de Arquitectos Mexicanos, *4,000 años de arquitectura mexicana*, Mexico City, 1956.
BERNARD S. MYERS

COLONIAL ART: UNITED STATES. American art of the 17th and 18th centuries. Early in the 17th century the English colonist adapted for his use the Indian wigwam of the oblong plan by adding to it fireplaces, crude chimneys, and doors hung by wooden hinges to hewn door frames. By 1639, however, the frame house came into use in New England (Fairbanks House, Dedham, Mass.). It featured steep gabled (and sometimes gambreled) roofs, which usually made for a picturesque exterior; an overhanging second story; a single chimney for a large fireplace that served both for heating and cooking and spanned half the length of a wall; and few and small irregularly spaced windows with leaded casements. The house grew by lean-tos as the need arose, but did not rise beyond two stories in height. Decoration was meager: the Parson Capen House (Topsfield, Mass., 1683) had brackets attached to the corners of the overhang of the second story. It was one of the more affluent homes of the time, with the two downstairs rooms vertically sheathed and an oak lintel placed over the fireplace. The interiors of many of these frame houses were enlivened by damask linen and turkey-work chairs. *See* CAPEN HOUSE. *See also* FURNITURE.

Changes marking the Georgian style of the 18th century were the doubling of rooms to make deeper, four-square plans; the flattening of roofs; and the raising of the stories. The gable was gradually abandoned, and a level cornice was continued all around the structure. It was not unusual to have a great entrance hall freed from stairs (Mt. Pleasant, Philadelphia, 1752). About 1740 the Georgian was further enriched with elaborate doorways and Palladian windows. Also appearing were tall pilasters rising the height of the structure, porticoes sometimes placed one upon the other, ornate mantels and overmantels, carved staircases, and ornamented ceilings. Rooms were often completely paneled. Walnut and mahogany replaced the oak characteristic of 17th-century furniture, and the Chippendale and Sheraton styles became fashionable.

In ecclesiastical architecture churches that were built away from the large centers are rather plain on the exterior: St. James at Goose Creek, S.C., has as external ornament only quoins and a pedimented doorway. But at St. Michael's (Charleston, S.C., 1752) a great steeple rises behind a pedimented colonnade. English models came to be used as prototypes: Christ Church in Boston, designed in 1723 by William Price, is based on Wren's St. Andrew's in London. Designs in English architectural books came into vogue and were sometimes copied literally: parts of Peter Harrison's Touro Synagogue (1762) in Newport, R.I., are taken from Inigo Jones, Gibbs, Kent, and Langley. *See* CHARLESTON, S.C.: ST. MICHAEL'S CHURCH; OLD NORTH CHURCH, BOSTON.

Throughout the 17th century and even until the eve of the American Revolution, portraiture with but a few exceptions (Gustavus Hesselius's *Bacchus and Ariadne*, ca. 1725, Detroit Institute of Arts; John Greenwood's *Sea Captains Carousing at Surinam*, 1757–58, St. Louis, City Art Museum) was the only subject matter for painting. Newly arrived, the American colonist had not the proper perspective to create a school of history painting; busy wresting his living from the soil, he had not the detachment from nature to create a school of landscape painting; and the Puritans, controlling large portions of the seaboard, forbade the depiction of the nude that was necessary for mythological painting. *See* GREENWOOD, JOHN; HESSELIUS, GUSTAVUS.

The names of the early limners are for the most part unknown. Unable or, because of the heritage of English Tudor painting, unwilling to render objects as three-dimensional totalities existing in space, they painted in a hard, but often powerful, linear fashion. An outstanding example is the *Mrs. Freake and Baby* (1674; Worcester Art Museum), in which grays, blacks, dull reds, and greenish yellows have been brought together exquisitely and in which the baby, stiff as a doll, is held carefully, but not with overt sentimental affection. About 1720 the painters for the patroon families of New York produced brightly colored, full-length figures standing before a trimmed-down landscape over which floats a tranquil sky (*John van Cortlandt*, Brooklyn, N.Y., Brooklyn Museum). *See* FREAKE MASTER; LIMNING.

One of the first American painters of whom we possess definite knowledge is John Smibert, who became the leading portraitist in Boston before Copley and influenced many later artists. Robert Feke was a decorative painter of graceful figures and sensitively blended colors. Other portrait painters of the period were Joseph Blackburn and Joseph Badger. America's most brilliant colonial painter was John

Colonial art, United States. *Mrs. Freake and Baby*, 1674. Worcester (Mass.) Art Museum. An outstanding example of a portrait executed by a limner.

Singleton Copley, who combined the crystalline clarity of the limners with a three-dimensional solidity and a textural realism. *See* BADGER, JOSEPH; BLACKBURN, JOSEPH; COPLEY, JOHN SINGLETON; FEKE, ROBERT; SMIBERT, JOHN.

Though no sculptor of great repute appeared during America's colonial period, sculpture of a high quality occurred frequently in weather vanes, tombstones, and wooden figures for the prows of ships. In Boston, in the decades preceding the Revolution, Henry Christian Geyer specialized in tombs and frontispieces for fireplaces.

BIBLIOGRAPHY. F. W. Bayley, *Five Colonial Artists of New England*, Boston, 1929; A. Burroughs, *Limners and Likenesses: Three Centuries of American Painting*, Cambridge, Mass., 1936; O. Hagen, *The Birth of the American Tradition in Art*, New York, 1940; J. T. Flexner, *First Flowers of Our Wilderness*, Boston, 1947; C. Bridenbaugh, *Peter Harrison, First American Architect*, Chapel Hill, N.C., 1949; H. S. Morrison, *Early American Architecture*, New York, 1952.

ABRAHAM A. DAVIDSON

COLONNADE. Series of columns, arranged in regular intervals, as in Bernini's colonnade for St. Peter's Square, Rome. A colonnade in front of a building is called a portico, as in the Roman temple known as the Maison Carrée, Nîmes. One surrounding an open court or a building is called a peristyle, as in the Parthenon, Athens. *See* PERISTYLE; PORTICO.

COLONNADE OF ST. PETER'S, ROME, *see* BERNINI, GIAN LORENZO.

COLONNETTE. Small column, usually one of a cluster, as in Gothic columns, or in balustrades and parapets.

COLOR, BROKEN. A color that is varied or "broken up" by the addition of other colors. Optically, most colors are broken simply by their proximity to other colors, as can be seen in impressionist paintings.

COLOR, COMPLEMENTARY. Color produced by the mixture of two of the three primary colors (red, yellow, and blue), which is the complement of the third color. For example, green, the complement of red, is formed by the admixture of yellow and blue. The three complementary colors, when mixed together, theoretically produce white. Impressionist painting employed complementary colors in shadows cast by objects painted in primary colors. *See* CONTRAST, COLOR.

BIBLIOGRAPHY. M. Bernstein, *Color in Art and Daily Life*, New York, 1928.

COLOR, FUGITIVE. Color that, because of the impermanent nature of its pigment or the instability of its base, has a tendency to fade. This tendency is increased with the presence of dampness and, in some cases, extreme heat.

COLOR, LOCAL. Theoretically, the inherent color of an object when it is unaffected by the reflected light from another object. In practice, it is the color of an object in natural light.

COLOR, PRIMARY. One of the three colors—red, yellow, or blue—that by admixture with one or both of the other two can theoretically produce any other color. Secondary colors, such as orange, are obtained by a mixture of two primary colors.

COLOR, PURE. In general, color that is unmixed; therefore, a pure color is one that corresponds to the color divisions of the spectrum.

COLOR, RECEDING. Color that produces a type of perspective effect involving the phenomenon that when certain colors, such as blue and yellow, are placed on the same plane, one appears to recede and the other to advance. Aerial perspective, which creates the illusion of depth, is accomplished by varying the intensity of colors.

BIBLIOGRAPHY. W. Schöne, *Uber das Licht in der Malerei*, Berlin, 1954.

COLOR, REFLECTED. When an object stands in close proximity to a background of a different color, the color of the object is changed by the reflected light from the background. This phenomenon is called reflected color.

COLOR, SECONDARY. Color, such as green, produced by the mixture of two of the primary colors.

COLOR, SYMBOLIC. Chiefly, color that is associated with a certain personage in Christian art and is used to symbolize that personage. The Virgin Mary is clad in a blue mantle and red dress; Christ and St. John the Evangelist, in red and blue; Peter, in white and blue; Jews and Judas, in yellow. Symbolic colors are used in priests' vestments to signify various feasts. Modern painters such as Van Gogh and Gauguin also speak of symbolic colors employing the term in a personal sense.

COLOR ORCHESTRATION, *see* ORPHISM.

COLOR PERSPECTIVE, *see* PERSPECTIVE (AERIAL).

COLOR REPRODUCTION. Any printed reproduction of a work of art that also attempts to reproduce the color of the original. Until the late 19th century various graphic processes were developed for or adapted to color prints; for example, aquatint was adapted to color in 1768. In the late 19th century chromo-lithography was invented. Today various photomechanical processes, such as halftone, litho-offset, and collotype, are the primary means of color reproduction. *See* AQUATINT; CHROMO-LITHOGRAPHY; COLLOTYPE; HALF TONE; OFFSET.

BIBLIOGRAPHY. L. C. Martin, *Colour and Methods of Colour Reproduction*, London, 1923.

COLOSSAL ORDER. Term sometimes applied to columns or pilasters extending several stories, especially in 16th- and 17th-century architecture. It is typified by Palladio's Valmarana Palace, Vicenza, whose base, pilasters, and entablature unify in one order a building several stories high.

COLOSSEUM (Coliseum), ROME. Largest amphitheater and one of the most imposing buildings in the world, situated southeast of the Roman Forum. Known in antiquity as the Amphitheatrum Flavium, the Colosseum was built on the site of an artificial lake that had belonged to Nero's Golden House. Erected by Vespasian (r. A.D. 59–79), the Colosseum was dedicated by Titus in A.D. 80. It was used for gladiatorial combats throughout the Roman period. The building underwent several restorations, mainly under Alexander Severus from 222 to 224 and under the emperor Decius in 250. It was not used after 404. From the Middle Ages on it was used as a travertine quarry, and several Roman palaces were built of material taken from it. The building underwent major restorations in the 19th century under Canina, which somewhat obscured its original plan.

The Colosseum is elliptical in plan and measures 617 by 512 feet; its total height is 157 feet. The exterior is divided into four stories. The three lower floors are pierced by arches divided by three-quarter-engaged superposed columns of the Tuscan, Ionic, and Corinthian order respectively. All three orders carry an unbroken entablature all around the building. The three lower arcades belong to the original structure. The fourth story, of later date, is pierced by small rectangular windows and is decorated with Corinthian pilasters. Above the windows is a row of

Colosseum, Rome. Detail of two stories of the façade, with arches divided by Doric, Ionic, and Corinthian engaged columns.

consoles with sockets that served to carry the masts of the velarium (the awning that shaded the auditorium and extended over the entire space of the *cavea*). Access to the *cavea* was given through eighty entrances, two of which were reserved for the emperor.

The *cavea* consisted of three parts: (1) the podium; (2) the *cavea* proper, which was divided by a passage into two zones (the *maenianum primum* and the *maenianum secundum*) of marble seats reaching to the beginning of the third floor (the higher zones of seats, the *maenianum summum*, were of wood); and (3) eighty walls that radiated from the arena and supported the two main ranges of seats. Access to the seats was given by staircases built between the radiating walls and by passages between the zones of seats. The amphitheater had a seating capacity of 45,000. Its arena measured 287 by 180 feet and was surrounded by a wall 15 feet high. Under the arena were subterranean passages and chambers. The entire exterior of the structure and the principal corridors were built of travertine clamped with iron set in lead. Concrete was used for all the vaulting except that of the outer arches. Ambulatories between the outer wall and a second interior wall with corresponding arches encircled the building. The ceiling of the ambulatories had groined cross vaulting.

BIBLIOGRAPHY. G. T. Rivoira, *Roman Architecture*, Oxford, 1925; W. J. Anderson, R. P. Spiers, and T. Ashby, *The Architecture of Greece and Rome*, vol. 2: *The Architecture of Ancient Rome*, London, 1927; D. S. Robertson, *A Handbook of Greek and Roman Architecture*, 2d ed., Cambridge, Eng., 1945.   EVANTHIA SAPORITI

COLOSSUS. Term applied to any very large statue but especially to the bronze statue of Helios, the sun-god, which towered about 105 feet over the harbor of Rhodes. This work, one of the Seven Wonders of the World, was erected about 280 B.C. by Chares of Lindos, a pupil of

Lysippus, and was destroyed by an earthquake in 224 B.C.

BIBLIOGRAPHY. G. M. A. Richter, *The Sculpture and Sculptors of the Greeks*, rev. ed., New Haven, 1957.

COLQUHOUN, ROBERT. English painter (1914–62). He was born in Kilmarnock, Ayrshire, and studied in Scotland, Italy, France, Holland, and Belgium. Colquhoun's early paintings were influenced by vorticism, and some of the hard-edge linearity is still evident in his mature style, which, however, is closer to expressionism. He applies some of the analytic deformations of early cubism to settings and to groups of figures, usually women, social outcasts, or animals, with vaguely disquieting results. The feeling produced is often of a brooding anxiety, as in *Weaving Army Cloth* (1945; London, Imperial War Museum).

BIBLIOGRAPHY. Buffalo, Albright Art Gallery, *British Contemporary Painters*, Buffalo, 1946.

COLUMBARIUM. Recess containing ashes of the dead, deriving its name (from the Latin *columba*, "dove") from its resemblance to dovecotes. Columbaria in ancient Rome were storage places for cinerary urns bearing names of the deceased. Cut in the rock of *coemeteria*, or subterranean vaults, columbaria are a distinguishing feature of Roman catacombs.

COLUMBIA RIVER STYLE. Stylistic complex of American Indian prehistoric and early historic stone sculpture discovered in the Columbia River Valley of Oregon and Washington. These works, strongly represented in the Portland, Ore., Art Museum, are carved in animal, human, and geometric form. They probably date from the beginning of the Christian era. In addition to three-dimensional figurines, there are mortars, pestles, and other functional objects of sculptural quality. The technique was one of combined pounding, pecking, and carving with stone tools.

Columbia River sculptures were collected for prestigious reasons and may have served a ceremonial purpose as well. Several distinctive substyles exist, but the main style is one of conventionalized imagery, massive and complete even when surfaces are left rough. This art is important for its priority in the Northwest and for its blunt, powerful aesthetic.

See also FRASER RIVER STYLE; NORTH AMERICAN INDIAN ART (NORTHWEST COAST); NORTHWEST AMERICA, ART OF.

BIBLIOGRAPHY. P. S. Wingert, *Prehistoric Stone Sculpture of the Pacific Northwest*, Portland, Ore., 1952.

COLUMN. Supporting member of a building, acting in compression under an axial load. It may be a freestanding vertical post with capital, shaft, and base, as in classical architecture. When partly attached to a wall, it is called an engaged column. *See* COLUMN, ENGAGED. *See also* COLUMN, SPIRAL; COLUMNS, ANNULATED.

COLUMN, ENGAGED. Column partly attached to a wall or pier, as in the Temple of Zeus Olympeios in Akragas, where columns are attached to the front, sides, and rear of the cella wall, giving the appearance of a peristyle and accordingly being called pseudoperipteral. *See* PSEUDOPERIPTERAL.

COLUMN, PROTO-DORIC. Incorrect designation for the faceted pillar found in Egyptian architecture. It was formerly thought to be the ancestor of the Greek Doric column, but no significant connection between the two is now theorized to have existed.

COLUMN, ROSTRAL. Column commemorating a naval victory. Its name (*columna rostrata*) is derived from *rostrum*, or prow of a ship. It consists of a vertical shaft from which project the prows of captured ships. The rostral column of C. Duilius in the Roman Forum celebrating the victory over the Carthaginians in 260 B.C. is an early example.

COLUMN, SPIRAL. Reinforced-concrete column, usually round, whose main reinforcement consists in a vertical spiral of steel enclosing longitudinal or vertical bars.

COLUMN, TRIUMPHAL. Any column erected separately, that is, outside an architectural ensemble, as a monument to a victory. A triumphal column may or may not have crowning sculpture. A popular form of monument in ancient Rome was one on which campaigns of the emperor were set out in documentary narrative reliefs winding up the column, for example, the Column of Trajan (106–113). *See* TRAJAN, COLUMN OF, ROME. *See also* COLUMN, ROSTRAL.

COLUMNAR SARCOPHAGUS. Somewhat obsolete term for the tumba grave, which consisted essentially of a rectangular sarcophagus, with or without an effigy of the deceased on the lid, raised above the ground by columns, usually one at each corner. Sometimes, as was common in the late Middle Ages, the spaces between the supporting columns were filled with relief plaques. Earlier, the custom was to mount the columns on top of lion or griffin figures.

COLUMN OF TRAJAN, ROME, *see* TRAJAN, COLUMN OF, ROME.

COLUMNS, ANNULATED. Columns clustered together by rings or bands, as in English medieval architecture.

COLVILLE, ALEX. Canadian painter (1920–). He served as an official Canadian war artist, and since 1946 he has taught at Mount Allison University, in Sackville, New Brunswick, where he now lives. The author of some murals, he is known chiefly for his magic realist tempera paintings.

BIBLIOGRAPHY. Ottawa, National Gallery of Canada, *Catalogue of Paintings and Sculpture*, ed. R. H. Hubbard, vol. 3: *Canadian School*, Ottawa, 1960.

COLYER, EDWAERT, *see* COLIJER, EDWAERT.

COLYNS DE NOLE FAMILY, *see* NOLE, COLYNS DE, FAMILY.

COMFORT, CHARLES FRASER. Canadian painter (1900–). Born in Scotland, he immigrated to Canada in 1912 and has lived mainly in Toronto. He studied in Winnipeg and under Robert Henri. An official war artist

(1943–46), he has directed the National Gallery of Canada in Ottawa since 1960. He paints murals, water-color portraits, and landscapes in oil.

BIBLIOGRAPHY. Ottawa, National Gallery of Canada, *Catalogue of Paintings and Sculpture*, ed. R. H. Hubbard, vol. 3: *Canadian School*, Ottawa, 1960.

COMNENIAN ART. Byzantine art of the Comnenian dynasty (1081–1185), in which the advances of the Macedonian dynasty were continued. Comnenian art, marked by a lessened dependence on the antique, moves slowly toward a stiff, somewhat lifeless formalism. The religious intentions of the works themselves become the sole end. This, however, should not be seen as a condemnation of Byzantine art of the period, for it was this stiffened, highly stylized form that became the model for Byzantine provincial art in the Balkans and Russia for centuries.

The Comnenians, more successful in architecture, built the impressive palace of Blachernae. They were also responsible for the construction or reconstruction of the Church of the Chora (Kahrie-Djami) and the Church of the Pantocrator, both in Istanbul, for the mosaics in the Church of the Nativity, Bethlehem (ca. 1169), and for the frescoes and mosaics in southern Italy, Cappadocia, and Russia. *See* BETHLEHEM; KAHRIE-DJAMI, ISTANBUL.

COMO, GUIDO DA (Guido Bigarelli da Arogno). Italian sculptor from Pisa (fl. 13th cent.). With his half-brother Lanfranco and other assistants, he was active during the mid-13th century in Tuscany. His sculptures for the Cathedral of S. Martino, Lucca (ca. 1240), show the Lombard influence of the Campionesi. Guido has been credited with making the octagonal marble font in the Baptistery, Pisa (1246–48), and the monumental Archangel Michael in the façade of the Church of S. Giuseppe, Pistoia (1250). His style is characterized by a solid projection of simple sculptural volumes in which the squat figures stand out sharply against smooth backgrounds.

BIBLIOGRAPHY. W. G. Waters, *Italian Sculptors*, 2d ed., London, 1926; M. Salmi, *Scultura romanica in Toscana*, Florence, 1928.

COMOX INDIANS, *see* SALISH INDIANS.

COMPANIA, LA, JESUIT CHURCH OF, QUITO, *see* COLONIAL ART: LATIN AMERICA (HIGHLANDS OF SOUTH AMERICA).

COMPIEGNE, CHATEAU OF. French royal residence in the Department of the Oise. Although the importance of Compiègne as a royal residence goes back to Merovingian times, the present château was built in the 18th century by J.-A. Gabriel and Le Dreux de la Châtre. Alterations were carried out under Napoleon I and Napoleon III. The château houses the Museum of the Palace of Compiègne (furniture and minor arts) and the National Carriage and Travel Museum (vehicles of the 18th–20th cent.). The château and its park are situated in the midst of a large forest.

BIBLIOGRAPHY. J. Babelon, *Compiègne, Pierrefonds*, Paris, 1949; M. Terrier, *Le Château de Compiègne* [Paris?], 1950.

COMPLEMENTARY COLOR, *see* COLOR, COMPLEMENTARY.

Guido da Como, *St. Martin and the Beggar*, façade sculpture, Cathedral of S. Martino, Lucca.

COMPLUVIUM. Opening in the roof of the atrium of the Roman house. The roof sloped toward the compluvium to discharge its rainwater into an impluvium, or cistern, in the floor of the open court.

COMPOSITE ANIMALS, *see* ANIMALS, MYTHOLOGICAL COMPOSITE.

Compluvium. Opening in roof of the Roman atrium.

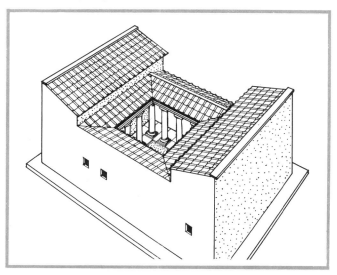

COMPOSITE ORDER. Architectural assembly with a distinguishing capital, its upper part Ionic with volutes, its lower part Corinthian and ringed with acanthus leaves. Ionic volutes superimposed on a Corinthian bell are found in late Greek work, although the Composite capital is more usually associated with Roman architecture.

COMPOSTELA, *see* SANTIAGO DE COMPOSTELA.

COMPOUND DOME, *see* DOME.

COMPTE, PEDRO. Spanish architect (d. 1506). His chief work is the silk exchange (Lonja) at Valencia (1482–98), which was modeled on the Lonja built by Guillem Sagrera at Palma de Mallorca earlier in the century. The Lonja at Valencia is rectangular in plan and has an interior of three naves of equal height divided by twisted columns supporting rib vaults.

BIBLIOGRAPHY. *Ars Hispaniae*, vol. 7: L. Torres Balbás, *Arquitectura gótica*, Madrid, 1952.

COMUNALE PALACE, PERUGIA. Italian Gothic palace, constructed between 1293 and 1297. The original architects were Giacomo di Servadio and Giovannello di Benvenuto. The palace was enlarged in 1443. Originally called the Palazzo dei Priori, it is a massive stone structure of several stories, capped with a crenelated parapet characteristic of this type of secular Gothic building.

COMUNALE PALACE, PISTOIA. Italian palace begun in 1295 on a site that had been occupied by houses belonging to exiled families. It was successively added to, resulting in an irregular ground plan. In 1348 the architect and goldsmith Michele di ser Memmo from Siena became master builder in charge of the work. The palace is a three-story building with an open arcade to the street and a narrow interior courtyard.

CONCA, SEBASTIANO. Italian painter (b. Gaeta, 1679; d. Naples, 1764). He worked as a portraitist in his early

Composite order. Capital combining Ionic and Corinthian elements.

years, after studying with Solimena, the Neapolitan fresco painter. Later Conca executed numerous works for Roman churches, including frescoes in S. Clemente and S. Giovanni in Laterano for Pope Clement XI and the ceiling fresco *The Crowning of St. Cecilia* (1725) in S. Cecilia. He was employed by the elector of Cologne and the kings of Spain, Portugal, Sardinia, and Poland. On his return to Naples in 1751 Conca created a number of works for churches there, including the fresco *Solomon and the Queen of Sheba* in S. Chiara. Working in the grand manner of late baroque painting, Conca emphasizes balanced compositions in the familiar celestial and architectural settings, modifying the turbulence, contrasts, and theatricality of earlier painting. His compositions are unified by a broad but flaccid linear movement.

CONCERT CHAMPETRE. Oil painting by Giorgione, in the Louvre Museum, Paris. *See* GIORGIONE.

CONCORD, TEMPLE OF, *see* AKRAGAS.

CONCORDE, PLACE DE LA, PARIS. Focal point of Paris, France, designed in 1755 by Gabriel to provide a setting for a statue of Louis XV. In 1792 the statue was demolished, and in 1793 the guillotine was erected there for the execution of Louis XVI and many others. The square was named "Concorde" during the Directory in an attempt to expunge its violent past.

It took from 1833 to 1836 to set in place at the center of the square the 75-foot-tall obelisk from Luxor, gift to France from the Egyptian viceroy Muhammad Ali. Two fountains were built, and eight statues representing cities of France were erected on the plinths built by Gabriel. Flanking the splendid view up the Champs-Elysées to the Arc de Triomphe are Coustou's *Horses of Marly*; the view in the opposite direction, toward the Place du Carrousel and the Louvre, is framed by the *Winged Horses* of Coysevox. The perpendicular axis offers equally famous views, toward the Church of the Madeleine in one direction and the Bourbon Palace in the other.

BIBLIOGRAPHY. M. Florisoone, *La Peinture française: Le Dix-huitième siècle*, Paris, 1948.

CONCRETE. Artificial stone made by cementing sand and aggregate, such as crushed rock and natural gravel. When hardened, concrete is strong in compression but weak in tension. The ancient Romans used a mixture of volcanic ash and hydrated lime, today known as slag or pozzuolana (puzzolan) cement, applying it to the construction of foundations, domes, and vaults. Their concrete walls often served as a structural binder for facing materials such as brick, marble, and stone, a practice later adopted by the Byzantines.

The first true hydraulic cement, one hardening under water, was developed about 1756 in England by Smeaton. The first natural cement was made in England at the end of the 18th century by calcining and grinding an argillaceous limestone, and in 1824 portland cement, so called because of its resemblance to stone quarried on the Isle of Portland, was patented in England.

Plain concrete is distinguished from reinforced concrete, which is combined with steel to compensate for the inherent tensile weakness of concrete. Precast concrete is prefabricated instead of being poured into forms on the site. Concrete plank is a precast concrete formed in planks, usually for floor and roof construction. Prestressed concrete is a concrete that is subjected to initial compressive stresses with the use of high-tensile steel. *See* CONCRETE, PRESTRESSED; CONCRETE, REINFORCED.   MILTON F. KIRCHMAN

CONCRETE, PRESTRESSED. Concrete subjected to compressive stresses before loads are applied so as to strengthen it and prevent it from cracking. Prestressing concrete is comparable to tightening steel bands around barrel staves to prevent them from opening when the barrel is filled with a liquid.

Pretensioning, or prestretching, indicates that the steel is stretched before the concrete has hardened. Generally the steel is stretched by devices such as hydraulic jacks and concrete is poured around it, the stresses from the stretched steel being transferred to the concrete on hardening by anchorages at the ends of the steel and by bond between steel and concrete. Posttensioning, or poststretching, is done by stretching steel after the concrete has hardened. Prestressing makes possible thin sections and large spans and has suggested new architectural forms.

CONCRETE, REINFORCED (Ferroconcrete; Concrete Steel). Concrete in which metal, usually steel, is embedded so that the two act together in resisting stresses. On hardening, the concrete mix adheres to the steel, the tensile strength of which compensates for the intrinsic tensile weakness of concrete. The concrete protects the steel from corrosion and fire, contributing to the widespread use of reinforced concrete in modern building. Reinforcement generally consists of round or square bars called plain bars; deformed bars have slight projections intended to help engage the concrete and prevent slippage under stress. Wire mesh is a steel fabric commonly used to reinforce slabs.

Because of its architectural plasticity and structural strength, reinforced concrete is being used extensively in the construction of shells, warped surfaces such as hyperbolic paraboloids, and domes. Prestressed concrete is a comparatively recent development in reinforced concrete. *See* CONCRETE, PRESTRESSED; CONSTRUCTION, SHELL; HYPERBOLIC PARABOLOID.   MILTON F. KIRCHMAN

CONCRETE ART. Term coined by Theo van Doesburg as an alternate to abstract art; he published a journal called *Concrete Art*. Today the term is seldom used.

CONCRETE STEEL, *see* CONCRETE, REINFORCED.

CONDE, JOHN. English engraver (fl. end of 18th cent.). Condé is known for his engravings in the dotted manner, and especially for full-length portraits of women, many of which are after Richard Cosway. Among them are portraits of Mrs. Bouverie and Mrs. Tickell and a small oval portrait of Madame du Barry.

BIBLIOGRAPHY. G. C. Williamson, "Jean and Pierre Condé," *The Connoisseur*, XXXIII, August, 1912.

CONDE MUSEUM, CHANTILLY, *see* CHANTILLY: CONDE MUSEUM.

CONDER, CHARLES. English painter and lithographer (b. London, 1868; d. there, 1909). He was in Australia with a surveying crew from 1885 to 1890 and also did newspaper drawings. He went to Paris in 1890. Although he exhibited with an Australian impressionist group, his work there was mostly tightly painted. In Paris, however, he began to paint in a thin and delicate manner, which gradually became richer. Conder is best known for his designs for fans, beginning in 1893, of festive and imaginary scenes with graceful ornament. Related in subject and style to his fans are his rapidly painted water colors on carefully chosen silk supports, for example, *L'Oiseau bleu* (1895; Melbourne, National Gallery of Victoria).

BIBLIOGRAPHY. F. Gibson, *Charles Conder*, London, 1914; J. Rothenstein, *The Life and Death of Conder*, London, 1938.

CONFESSIO, *see* CRYPT.

CONFESSIONAL. Place in a church where the priest sits to hear confession. In England the confessional was once called the shriving seat: the penitent knelt openly before the seated confessor, a custom still extant in the Greek Church. Confessional boxes, adopted in the Western Church in the 16th century, are generally placed against the wall or in a recess of the church.

CONFUCIUS, TEMPLE OF, PEKING (Ta Ch'eng Miao). Shrine dedicated to the greatest Chinese philosopher, located near the northeast corner of the Imperial City in Peking. Although there was a Confucian temple on the site as early as the 13th century, the present layout appears to belong to the Ming dynasty (1368–1644), and the shrine has been refurbished several times since then. A gracious courtyard containing six yellow-tiled pavilions leads to the Hall of the Great Perfection. The austere interior of the hall gains its effect through the careful proportions of the design. The Hall of Classics (Kuo-tzu-chien), which stands immediately west of the Confucian temple, has a fine gateway and gardens.

BIBLIOGRAPHY. J. Bredon, *Peking*, 2d ed., Shanghai, 1922.

CONGNET (Coignet; Quinetus), GILLIS. Flemish portrait and history painter (b. Antwerp, ca. 1538; d. Hamburg, 1599). A student of Lambrecht Wenslyns in 1554 and of Antoine van Palermo, Congnet was a master in Antwerp in 1561. He traveled to Naples and Sicily, painted frescoes with Stello in Terni, and became a member of the Florence Academy in 1568. Back in Antwerp by 1570, he became dean of the guild in 1585. The next year he left for Amsterdam, where he was made a burgher in 1589, and later settled in Hamburg. Very few certain works by Congnet are known. He is best in portraits, and these, Flemish in form, are painted in a quick style imitating Titian's.

BIBLIOGRAPHY. L. van Puyvelde, *La Peinture flamande au siècle de Bosch et Breughel*, Paris, 1962.

CONGO. Insofar as the sculptural traditions of Negro Africa are concerned, it remains necessary despite any recent modifications of political boundaries to define the Congo as that region combining the southeastern Cameroons, French Equatorial Africa to the south, Gabon, the Ogowe River, the Lower Congo, Belgian and Central Congo, and northern and certain central parts of Angola.

Congo. Bateki wooden figure.

Among the tribes or tribal groups distinguished for their art, the traditions of which are many centuries old throughout the Congo, are the Balumbo, Fang, Bakota, Bakwele, Ambete, Babembe, Bakongo, and Bayombe of the northeastern and Lower Congo regions; the Bushongo (Bakuba), Bateke, Bayaka, Bapende, Baluba, Bena-Lulua, and Basonge of the western and Central Congo; and the Manyema and Balega (Warega) of the east. The style of the southern Congo is best studied in Badjokwe (Batshioko) sculptures. The Mangbetu (Makere) and Azande are located more or less apart from the main complex, far to the east and north near the Wele River. The Congo has produced some of the most spectacular art known to Negro Africa.

See also AFRICA, PRIMITIVE ART OF (CENTRAL AFRICA).

BIBLIOGRAPHY. E. Torday, *Les Bushongo*, Brussels, 1910; F. M. Olbrechts, *Plastiek van Kongo*, Antwerp, 1946.   JOHN C. GALLOWAY

CONGRES INTERNATIONAUX D'ARCHITECTURE MODERNE, *see* C.I.A.M.

CONINXLOO, CORNELIS VAN. Flemish history painter (fl. 1525–58). *The Parents of the Virgin* (Brussels, Fine Arts Museum), signed and dated 1526, shows Cornelis to be a *retardataire* painter, a weak imitator of Jan Gossaert.

BIBLIOGRAPHY. L. van Puyvelde, *La Peinture flamande au siècle de Bosch et Breughel*, Paris, 1962.

CONINXLOO, GILLIS VAN. Flemish painter of landscapes (b. Antwerp, 1544; d. Amsterdam, 1607). He was,

successively, the pupil of Pieter Coecke van Aelst, Lenaert Cros, and Gillis Mostaert. Coninxloo became a master in 1570, and went first to Frankenthal, Germany, where he was active from 1585 to 1595, and then to Amsterdam. The artist is best known as the "poet of the forest," head of a significant school of landscape painters among whom we count Jan Breughel I and Roelant-Jacobsz. Savery, and the great innovator in the manner of treating foliage. Whereas the Flemings had formerly featured panoramic landscapes, Coninxloo leads the spectator into the center of the forest, which he represents as if the trees and their branches were imbued with enchanted life. His influence reaches far into the 17th century. *Wooded Landscapes* (1598 and 1604; Vaduz, Liechtenstein Collection) are representative.

BIBLIOGRAPHY. Y. Thiéry, *Le Paysage flamand au XVIIe siècle*, Brussels, 1953.

CONJEEVERAM, *see* KANCHIPURAM.

CONQUES: ABBEY CHURCH OF SAINTE-FOY. French pilgrimage church situated in a rugged mountain valley. It stands in the center of a village that has lost none of its medieval flavor. The church seems almost certainly to have been completed by 1130. The style of the famous *Last Judgment* tympanum of the west door suggests attachment to the school of Auvergne, with the scenes of *Heaven* and *Hell* in the bottom register depicted under sloping roofs. A superb and very complete *Christ in Majesty* fills the second and third registers. The capitals of the nave are also frequently reminiscent of Auvergne. The treasure is handsomely housed in a rebuilt section of the cloister and contains reliquaries and the gold and jeweled statue of Ste-Foy, all of the 10th century.

BIBLIOGRAPHY. P. Deschamps, *French Sculpture of the Romanesque Period*..., Florence, 1930; M. Aubert, *L'Eglise de Conques*, Paris, 1939; K. J. Conant, *Carolingian and Romanesque Architecture, 800–1200*, Baltimore, 1959.

CONSAGRA, PIETRO. Italian sculptor (1920–   ). Born in Trapani, Sicily, Consagra studied at the Academy of Fine Arts in Palermo and traveled to Paris in 1946. In

Gillis van Coninxloo, *Landscape with Judgment of Midas*, detail. Picture Gallery, Dresden.

1947 he established, with a group of painters, the first postwar movement of nonfigural art in Italy. Consagra now lives in Rome. He works chiefly in bronze and burned wood in a free abstract style.

BIBLIOGRAPHY. U. Apollonio, *Pietro Consagra*, Rome, 1956; M. Seuphor, *The Sculpture of This Century*, New York, 1960.

CONSERVATION. Works of art suffer changes and damage of many kinds. Effects of weathering, climatic changes, improper care, decay, willful or accidental destruction, and, more recently, the effects of industrial acids that form in the air—all threaten the original condition and state of a work of art. Preventing these destructive changes is the province of conservation; correcting the deterioration is the province of restoration. Both aspects of preserving works of art are usually spoken of as conservation and are intimately combined in practice.

Despite its young history as a science, conservation is an ancient practice. And since the beginning, the restorer has been faced with two choices: to restore the object as if it were new or to make basic repairs and restore it as a reasonable facsimile. The decision is a matter of taste, and that in turn is usually the reflection of the age in which the restoration is done. In general, the facsimile approach is fairly recent and reflects a historically sophisticated approach to conservation. Restorers of the past have, by and large, measured the success of their conservation by the extent to which the object appears new.

The Romans practiced conservation, as mentioned in their literature, in an effort to continue classical Greek culture. They scaled wall paintings from Greek walls and brought the pieces to Rome, and they copied Greek wall paintings in mosaic. The mosaic *The Battle of Issus* (Naples, National Archaeological Museum), depicting the struggle between Darius the Persian and Alexander, is an example of the latter practice.

The Middle Ages held an ahistorical position on conservation, taking what they considered valuable from older works of art and reworking them into a "modern" object. Therefore, certain restored objects show a mixture of styles and materials. Even during the Renaissance the restorers of damaged works, especially of antique sculpture, worked in such a way that some pieces are almost unrecognizable as Greek, Roman, or Renaissance. The "new" creation was valued far more than the fragment. This attitude is underscored by the fact that eminent artists such as Donatello, Michelangelo, and Cellini were called in as restorers. Their restorations could hardly be anything but original treatments, and yet the Renaissance believed it was practicing in the manner of the ancients by setting the best artists to work on these restorations. By the end of the 16th century isolated restorations of every kind were being made, most of them eclectic in material and style.

Restoration on a large scale first occurred in Italy in the 17th century. Among the notable efforts were the *Aldobrandini Marriage* frescoes (Rome, Vatican Museums), dating from the 1st century B.C. and unearthed in Rome in 1606. The fake seems to have come into being at this time as well, which reveals a growing sophistication about the venerability of works of art. By the 18th century the value of the fragment itself was recognized. Certain types,

Conques, Abbey Church of Ste-Foy.

busts and torsos particularly, were highly prized and studied. In addition, techniques for transferring paintings to more permanent backings were developed, and an effective permanent protective varnish was discovered.

The romantics in the 19th century brought historical criteria to bear on conservation; although many 19th-century restorations now seem highly biased, the attempts were honest. Restorers and conservationists were sought by museums and private collectors, and the first institutes for the preservation of architectural monuments were established. The wars of the 20th century have given great impetus to the conservation movement, and highly technical and scientific methods are now part of restoration and conservation. In general, the leadership has passed from the Italians to the Germans, British, and Americans.

In addition to the many and constantly improved techniques of restoration, there are a number of standard aids used to treat damaged and threatened works of art. A wall painting threatened by dampness may be sprayed with calcium casein. If extensive damage has occurred, the paint and plaster may be stripped and transferred to a drier spot, often a museum. Warping or split wood panels may be treated by cradling (parquetry), in which strips of wood are glued on the back of the panel in the direction of the grain and cross strips are inserted through slits in the strips in grid fashion. This prevents further damage but allows the panel its slight natural expansions and contractions. When worms threaten a panel, it may be sprayed with fumes of prussic acid, and in the case of severe worm

John Constable, *The Hay Wain.* **National Gallery, London. One of the best known of the artist's large exhibition canvases.**

damage the wood may be scraped from the back down to the paint ground and replaced entirely. Bubbling and flaking can be halted by inserting glue under the loose layers of paint, but this is an extremely delicate operation.

Paintings on damaged or deteriorating canvas can be restored by gluing a new layer of canvas to the back of the old and even, in extreme cases, by a careful transfer of the paint to another backing. The most advanced conservationists disapprove of retouching, or "inpainting," as it is called, except in extreme circumstances, such as when the design is unintelligible and the paint has peeled to the ground. Then inpainting is done only with egg tempera, which neither darkens with age nor becomes more transparent. The restorer who must retouch often uses X radiation or ultraviolet light to duplicate the original build-up of layers. As a general rule, he does not attempt to make his restorations imperceptible.

Weathering of wood sculpture is curtailed by impregnating the work with solutions of resin or beeswax, and worms are destroyed with fumes of prussic acid. Stone sculpture is cautiously restored with cement or plaster. Bronze and other metal sculptures are cleaned with acids, but never to the bare metal.

BIBLIOGRAPHY. F. G. H. Lucanus, *Die Praxis des Restaurators,* Halberstadt, 1929; M. C. Bradley, *The Treatment of Pictures,* Cambridge, Mass., 1950; *Studies in Conservation* (October, 1952–); H. J. Plenderleith, *The Conservation of Antiquities and Works of Art,* London, 1957; International Institute for Conservation of Historical and Artistic Works, G. Thomson, ed., *Recent Advances in Conservation,* London, 1963.

JULIA M. EHRESMANN

CONSERVATORI PALACE, ROME. The right lateral building of the complex designed (1537) by Michelangelo for the Capitoline hill. It is identical in plan with the Capitoline Museum Palace facing it across the square. The lower portico is spanned by stone beams, and a colossal order of Corinthian pilasters runs the height of the two-story façade. Both palaces were executed under the direction of Giacomo della Porta. *See* ROME: MUSEUMS (CAPITOLINE MUSEUMS).

BIBLIOGRAPHY. J. Ackerman, *The Architecture of Michelangelo,* 2 vols., London, 1961.

CONSOLE. Bracket, usually carved, supporting a cornice, window head, bust, or decorative element. It most commonly has an S-shaped profile and approximately parallel sides. When carrying the upper part of a cornice, consoles are sometimes called modillions.

CONSTABLE, JOHN. English painter (b. East Bergholt, Suffolk, 1776; d. London, 1837). He entered the Royal Academy of Arts in 1799 while in his early twenties. Still very much an amateur artist, he had had only casual training and gave no indication of great promise. He spent much time in copying, particularly the works of Claude Lorraine, whom he greatly admired, as well as those of Ruisdael, Gainsborough, and Richard Wilson. He did not, however, wish to follow directly in any established tradition.

Constable's art evolved quietly during the next decade. He spent most of each year working in London, but escaped to his beloved Suffolk during the summers. Recognition was slow in coming. He began exhibiting regularly at the Royal Academy, but, although several of the academicians (including the president, Benjamin West) commended his work, he was not elected an associate until 1819. To earn money he accepted a number of portrait commissions. Although he attained considerable success in this area, and his portraits commanded increasing respect, he fortunately withstood the temptation to make this work his principal occupation.

Constable's steady development brought his art to maturity about 1820. His earlier achievements had been most notable in the now greatly prized small oil sketches. But by 1820 he had mastered the large exhibition picture. In 1819 he exhibited *The White Horse* (New York, Frick Collection). There followed a whole series of "6-foot" canvases, which remain, in spite of vicissitudes of taste, the foundation of Constable's artistic reputation. The best known of these are *Stratford Mill* (1820; Major R. N. Macdonald-Buchanan Collection); *The Hay Wain* (1821; London, National Gallery); *View on the Stour near Dedham* (1822; San Marino, Calif., Huntington Art Gallery); and *The Lock* (1824) and *The Leaping Horse* (1825), both in the Royal Academy.

In 1824 recognition came from abroad. Three of Constable's paintings, including *The Hay Wain* and *View on the Stour*, were shown at the Paris Salon and were awarded a gold medal by Charles X. Constable's work was much admired by the French painters, primarily because of his fresh color and bold handling of pigment. His philosophy of landscape painting (in terms of the motifs he selected and what he chose to do with them) was less immediately appealing, although it did find echoes in the work of the Barbizon painters.

The comparatively happy and successful decade of the 1820s came to an abrupt end with the death of the painter's wife in 1828, a loss from which he never fully recovered. He became increasingly morose and depressed, even after his long-delayed election to full academician in 1829. There were also professional difficulties. An elaborate project for having some of his works engraved was a complete failure financially. The prints were not well received; they were condemned for their "blackness and coarseness," which had resulted simply from an attempt to convey a sense of the texture and tone of the paintings.

During the early 1830s Constable's uncertain health and the duties he accepted in supervising the life class of the Royal Academy and lecturing on landscape interfered somewhat with his own painting, and he was generally less productive than during the previous decade. His most important exhibition paintings during the 1830s were *Opening of Waterloo Bridge* (1832), which he had been working on in fits and starts for the previous twelve years, *The Valley Farm* (1835), and *The Cenotaph* (1836).

Constable's only serious competitor in the field of British landscape is his great contemporary, J. M. W. Turner. Constable's devotion to the quiet English countryside and his limiting himself for the most part to a half-dozen areas that he knew with great intimacy are in contrast with Turner's search for arresting themes. Constable has a less involved relation to the earlier traditions of landscape painting, but his art is more subtle in its intimate understanding of a particular motif and in its changing moods as reflected in transitory effects of weather.

Modern taste finds Constable's small oil sketches and drawings particularly congenial. The directness, spontaneity, and freedom of handling in these little pictures anticipate attitudes not frequently encountered before the latter part of the 19th century. To render the living, moving quality of nature in these visual impressions, Constable used broken touches of color. The spontaneity of his emotional reactions affected such romantic painters as Delacroix. The sparkles of light and color and the deliberately rough texture of Constable's canvases had an important influence on impressionist painters later in the century.

BIBLIOGRAPHY. C. R. Leslie, *Memoirs of the Life of John Constable, R. A.*, London, 1843, rev. ed. A. Shirley, London, 1937; P. Leslie, ed., *Letters of John Constable to C. R. Leslie*, London, 1931; S. J. Key, *John Constable, His Life and Work*, London, 1948; R. B. Beckett, *John Constable and the Fishers*, London, 1952; G. Reynolds, *Catalogue of the Constable Collection*, London, 1960.

ROBERT R. WARK

CONSTANTINE I. First Christian emperor (280–337); a great patron of both civic and church edifices (Arch of Constantine and Basilica of Constantine, Rome; Church of the Holy Sepulchre, Jerusalem). He is often represented in art, particularly in the scenes of his conversion (Piero della Francesca) and the battle at the Milvian Bridge (Raphael and Romano, Sala di Costantino, Vatican). *See* CONSTANTINE, ARCH OF, ROME; MAXENTIUS (CONSTANTINE), BASILICA OF, ROME. *See also* CONSTANTINOPLE.

BIBLIOGRAPHY. J. Burckhardt, *The Age of Constantine the Great*, New York, 1949.

CONSTANTINE, ARCH OF, ROME. Roman triumphal arch erected in honor of the emperor Constantine I to commemorate his victory over Maxentius at the Milvian

Arch of Constantine, Rome. The city's largest and best-preserved triumphal arch, completed A.D. 315.

Bridge in A.D. 312. This arch, completed in 315, is the largest and best preserved in Rome. It consists of three archways flanked by detached Corinthian columns carrying an entablature and raised on pedestals. The attic above the arches has a dedicatory inscription. The arch is richly decorated with reliefs taken from earlier monuments: Hadrianic medallions with hunting scenes on the side arches, Aurelian panels on the attic, and fragments of a Trajanic frieze on the sides of the central passageway. The narrow frieze as well as the remainder of the sculptural decoration is contemporary with the arch and exhibits the characteristic decadence of that period.

BIBLIOGRAPHY. W. J. Anderson, R. P. Spiers, and T. Ashby, *The Architecture of Greece and Rome*, vol. 2: *The Architecture of Ancient Rome*, London, 1927; H. P. L'Orange and A. von Gerkan, *Der spätantike Bildschmuck des Konstantinsbogens*, Berlin, 1939; B. Berenson, *The Arch of Constantine*, New York, 1954.

CONSTANTINE, BASILICA OF, ROME, see MAXENTIUS, BASILICA OF, ROME.

CONSTANTINOPLE (Istanbul). Great city located in European Turkey on the site of the ancient Greek colony of Byzantium. Constantinople was its Christian Roman name. The city was for 1,100 years the capital of the Eastern Roman or Byzantine Empire, having been dedicated in A.D. 330 by the emperor Constantine I and conquered by the Ottoman Turks in 1453. Situated on the Bosporus strait that separates Europe from Asia, Constantinople had a most rich and creative artistic history. This evolved from its mixed Greek, Roman, and Christian heritage and from the talent and pride of major but usually anonymous Constantinopolitan artists.

The city was magnificently sited on a roughly triangular peninsula and protected by all but impregnable fortifications. It was provided by Constantine with the institutions and building forms of ancient Rome and with an orderly administration of a typically Roman kind. This overlay of Roman forms and institutions did not, however, stifle the essentially Greek and Christian culture of the city; thus the buildings, mosaics, frescoes, ivories, coins, silks, and icons produced in Constantinople were not derived solely from pagan imperial art. Rather, the art of Constantinople effected a combination of certain pre-Christian late-antique principles with a renascent Hellenism. The result, always presented in a powerful Christian iconography, was a distinct style. As the city grew older and the neighbors of its empire became in varying degrees the recipients of its culture, Constantinopolitan, or Byzantine, art spread centrifugally and greatly influenced Slavic, Muslim, and western Christian art. Throughout its history the city was the center and focus of Byzantine art. *See also* BYZANTINE ART AND ARCHITECTURE.

First period (330–518). The great building programs of later periods destroyed or obscured most of the architecture of this period. The enormous triple walls of the landward side of the peninsula and the shell of the late-5th-century basilica of St. John of Studion remain. The figural arts are represented in Istanbul by such monuments as the base of the Obelisk of Theodosius I, which displays the late Roman court in an iconic frontality, and a geometrized head of the emperor Arcadius. A fine cameo of Constantius II and his wife is in the Louvre, Paris, and there is

some magnificent silver from the period in the Hermitage, Leningrad, and the Prado, Madrid. There are a number of consular and imperial ivories of great importance in the various European museums. In general these works are frontal, planar, somewhat abstracted, and of a sumptuous quality. During this period the number and importance of studios and workshops in Constantinople developed rapidly. *See* OBELISK OF THEODOSIUS I; ST. JOHN OF STUDION. *See also* SACRED PALACE, ISTANBUL.

Second period (518–565). This is the period of the ascendancy of Justinian, who, like Augustus and Hadrian, encouraged architects and artists to proclaim in tangible forms his Christian and imperial objectives. His scores of buildings are described by the historian Procopius; of them two still stand, SS. Sergius and Bacchus and Hagia Sophia, or Holy Wisdom. The latter, with its flowing geometry and rich interior colors, fully characterizes the style of the period. The Emperor himself appears in the great mosaics of S. Vitale in Ravenna, upon a cast, in the Louvre, of a lost medallion, and almost certainly in the Louvre's Barberini ivory. Dome-vaulted cisterns were built in the city, the Imperial Palace was in part reconstructed and decorated with mosaics of the Emperor's victories, and a bronze equestrian statue of Justinian was erected upon a tall column beside Hagia Sophia. In Justinian's age the basic principles of the Byzantine style were firmly established, and Constantinople became the central city of the Christian arts in the early Middle Ages. *See* HAGIA SOPHIA; SS. SERGIUS AND BACCHUS. *See also* HAGIA IRENE.

Third period (565–843). There is a paucity of monuments from this dark era because of fierce wars, first with Persia and then with Islam, and because of an intense struggle that developed between the government and those who espoused image worship (from 726 to 843 icons were officially prohibited, except for a short time). The resources of Byzantine society could not, during this period, be much devoted to the arts. But Justinian's successor, Justin II, built within the Imperial Palace a golden dining hall, the Chrysotriklinos, which is known from texts to have been a domed octagon somewhat similar to S. Vitale in Ravenna.

Fourth period (843–1204). This is the second great age of Constantinopolitan art. In architecture it was characterized by the development within the palace and in subsequent city examples of the five-domed church sheathed inside with hierarchically disposed mosaics (Our Lady of the Pharos; the Nea Ecclesia, or New Church). This type of church was a more or less standard model from which much Orthodox architecture later developed. Hagia Sophia received magnificent new mosaics, and the products of the Constantinople studios were widely exported. Manuscript painting in the city reached its apogee in such works as the Joshua Roll (Rome, Vatican Library) and the Paris Psalter (Paris, National Library), both of the 10th century. *See* NEA. *See also* ST. SAVIOR PANTEPOPTES.

Final period (1261–1453). After a half century of occupation and degradation by the adventurers of the Fourth Crusade, the relatively impoverished city again produced artists of magnificent talent. The Deësis Mosaic in Hagia Sophia combines an oncoming humanism with the inspiring formality of the past. Exquisite ivories and manuscript paintings continued to be made. The achievements of this period and, indeed, of Byzantine art in general can be measured by the quality of the mosaics and, especially, of the frescoes of the Church of the Chora. They have recently been uncovered and cleaned and must rank among the great masterpieces of medieval art. They display the genealogy and lives of Christ and the Virgin in mosaic and themes of Resurrection and Judgment in fresco, utilizing powerful combinations of reality and ethereality. *See* KAHRIE-DJAMI (CHURCH OF THE CHORA).

The artistic dynamic of Constantinople in part stemmed from the classical traditions of the city and the passionately Christian beliefs of its people and sovereigns. Also, the city was a nexus of ancient Near Eastern, Hellenic, and Roman influences. From these elements came first a style of fusion and then one of great creativity. The prestige of the city helped to ensure the continuity and influence of its art, which continue to this day. *See also* OTTOMAN ARCHITECTURE.

Istanbul (since 1930). In addition to the buildings mentioned, the modern city contains a large museum with important works dating from the Christian period. Many portable products of the artists of Constantinople may be seen in the museums of Europe. In the United States the chief collections are in the Dumbarton Oaks Research Library and Collection, Washington, D.C., the Walters Art Gallery, Baltimore, and the Metropolitan Museum, New York.

See also APOSTLES, CHURCH OF THE HOLY; ISTANBUL: ARCHAEOLOGICAL MUSEUM; ST. MARY PAMMAKARISTOS; ST. THEOTOKOS PAMMAKARISTOS.

BIBLIOGRAPHY. H. B. Dening, tr., *Procopius* (Loeb Classical Library, vol. 7), London, 1940; G. Downey, *Constantinople in the Age of Justinian*, Norman, Okla., 1960; J. Beckwith, *The Art of Constantinople*, New York, 1961; W. L. MacDonald, *Early Christian and Byzantine Architecture*, New York, 1962.

WILLIAM L. MACDONALD

CONSTRUCTION, IRON. The extensive use of iron in building was one of the effects of the Industrial Revolution and played a central role in the early development of modern architecture. The earliest significant structure of iron, a single arch bridge over the Severn River (1779), was erected by Abraham Darby, whose family first produced iron on a large scale in the early 18th century. Its use became popular but subsidiary in such structures as the roof of the Théâtre Français in Paris (1786), where methods of timber construction were employed, and John Nash's Brighton Pavilion (1818–21), where slim iron columns support the central dome framework. Boulton and Watt were the first to use both iron beams and columns, at the Salford Cotton Mill in Manchester (1801), establishing the prototype for the factory building. *See* NASH, JOHN.

Distinctive structural methods slowly emerged, devised mostly by engineers. Through the use of wrought-iron wire cables, suspension bridges were constructed by Seguin in France and Telford in England in the first quarter of the 19th century, and later by Roebling in the United States. Wrought-iron frameworks were used in conjunction with glass throughout the century to cover the immense spaces of exhibition halls, greenhouses, and arcades. *See* ROEBLING, JOHN AUGUSTUS; TELFORD, THOMAS.

More important for architecture, perhaps, was the advancement of the iron skeletal frame by Fairbairn in England and Bogardus in the United States during the middle years of the 19th century. Bogardus developed prefabri-

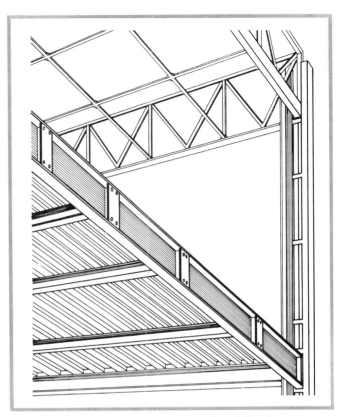

Iron construction. Building method that prefigured the skyscraper.

cated structures, using iron on the exterior as well as the interior. This framework and the extensive use of glass prefigured the form of the skyscraper, the conceptions of Leroy S. Buffington of Minneapolis and others. The earliest one built was the Home Life Insurance Building in Chicago (1883–85) by William Jenney. After this, however, steel became the predominant material in the construction of skyscrapers by the Chicago school. *See* BOGARDUS, JAMES; BUFFINGTON, LEROY S.; JENNEY, WILLIAM LE BARON.

In traditional architecture iron was first prominently and inventively used by Labrouste in his Bibliothèque Ste-Geneviève (1843–50) and Bibliothèque Nationale (1860s), both in Paris, and by Smirke in the dome for the British Museum in London (1823–47). The apotheosis of the uses and methods of iron construction occurred with the erection of the Eiffel Tower for the Paris Exhibition of 1889, just prior to the triumph of steel. *See* LABROUSTE, HENRI; SMIRKE, ROBERT. *See also* CONSTRUCTION, STEEL.

BIBLIOGRAPHY. S. Giedion, *Space, Time and Architecture*, 4th ed., Cambridge, Mass., 1962.

DONALD GODDARD

CONSTRUCTION, SHELL. Type of construction in reinforced concrete that is essentially a thin plate, curved or folded to add strength. A barrel shell has a cylindrical form. Barrel shells may be subdivided by transverse ribs or membranes to form multiple barrels. When the transverse distance, or chord width, is short in comparison with the span between ribs, the shell is called a long barrel. A short barrel has a large chord width in proportion to the span between ribs. A shell may be corrugated or folded, in such basic shapes as a V, W, or Z; it may have a doubly curved shape, such as the dome, or be composed of warped surfaces, such as the hyperbolic paraboloid, hyperboloids of revolution, conoids, cylindroids, and helicoids, as in spiral ramps. Shells spanning 300 feet have been constructed, and new forms in architecture have been derived. *See* HYPERBOLIC PARABOLOID.

CONSTRUCTION, SKELETON. Type of construction in which loads are transmitted to foundations by means of a structural frame of beams and columns, the enclosing walls being supported at each floor. Skeleton structures are commonly of steel or concrete or a combination of both. Reinforced-concrete skeletons generally have monolithic concrete floors with or without girders, as in flat-plate construction. In steel skeleton construction the building frame is of steel, often supporting slabs of reinforced concrete. Floor systems in steel frames may also consist of concrete plank or of light steel joists supporting a metal deck topped with a layer of concrete. In some types of modern reinforced-concrete skeletons, the walls as monolithic screens perforated by window openings are used in bearing.

Skeleton construction developed with the skyscraper and the use of steel. Steel as a structural material had been used extensively during the early 19th century. In 1792–93 the calico mill in Derby, England, employed an interior framework of iron columns and beams to support floors. Such construction soon became standard for warehouses and factories, the system being improved by embedding iron columns in exterior walls to carry the ends of iron floor beams, thereby minimizing the load-bearing function of walls. Cast-iron fronts were adopted as early as 1830 in Pottsville, Pa., and in 1847, in New York, James Bogardus attached cast-iron plates of an iron façade to an iron frame. Post offices and customhouses of the 1850s sponsored by the Treasury Department made extensive use of a structural system in which brick floor arches were supported by wrought-iron floor beams framing into cast-iron columns. The Crystal Palace in London (1851) had a structural-steel frame, although it was not a multistory building in the sense of a skyscraper. *See* BOGARDUS, JAMES; CONSTRUCTION, STEEL.

The idea of the skeleton frame has been attributed to Leroy S. Buffington in the United States, although various aspects of skeleton construction had been used by others before him. Buffington's Boston Block in Minneapolis (1880) made use of cast-iron columns independent of walls; his 8-story West Hotel, completed in 1883, employed spandrels to carry walls. In 1888 Buffington applied for a patent on skeleton construction, but his ideas have since been described as unscientific, and their priority was challenged by the claims of Fryer in 1869 and Hardy in 1875. Buffington himself did not completely incorporate his ideas in his buildings, although in 1881–82 he did conceive a 28-story and a 100-story building using skeleton construction. In 1883–85 William Le Baron Jenney used skeleton construction in the Home Life Insurance Building in Chicago, although its party walls of masonry on the north and east sides disqualify it as a pure example. The first complete skeleton frame has been attributed variously to Holabird and Root (1888) and to Jenney and Mundie (1889) in

Chicago. *See* BUFFINGTON, LEROY S.; HOLABIRD AND ROOT; JENNEY, WILLIAM LE BARON.

MILTON F. KIRCHMAN

CONSTRUCTION, STEEL. Type of construction in which the building frame is of steel, although the term "iron" is sometimes used as well, particularly for older buildings. Steel, although known in antiquity, was first adopted extensively as a structural component during the latter part of the 18th century.

Cast iron was used in the first metal bridge, completed in 1779 in Coalbrookdale, Wales. Thomas Paine in 1787 proposed the construction of an arched 400-foot iron bridge spanning the Schuylkill River at Philadelphia. The Paris Halle au Blé (1811) had a cast-iron dome inspired by the Pantheon in Rome. Robert Mills used iron structural elements in his Record Office in Charleston, S.C., in 1822–23. Iron sheds were used in the construction of the Madeleine Market in Paris in 1829; the Bibliothèque Ste-Geneviève, Paris (1843–50), employed iron columns and iron trusses. The Crystal Palace, London (1851), was a glass and

Shell construction (top); skeleton construction (bottom).

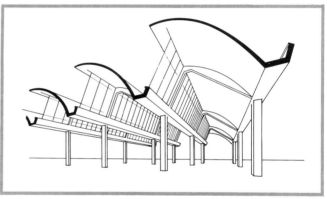

iron cage. Thomas Walter's dome for the Capitol in Washington, D.C. (1860–65), was largely of cast iron. *See* BIBLIOTHEQUE SAINTE-GENEVIEVE; CAPITOL, THE, WASHINGTON, D.C.

Wrought-iron structural members were imported and used in the United States in 1855, the firm of Jones and Laughlin manufacturing its own beams in 1889. Iron found its way into the construction of multistory buildings and into cast-iron fronts. By the late 1880s the true steel skeleton was developed, enabling the raising of buildings to greater heights. High-strength steels, welding, and advances in structural analysis have since yielded new forms such as the steel rigid frame.

The strength and flexibility of steel have made possible a greater openness and an increased use of glass in the great skyscrapers of the 20th century, such as Mies van der Rohe's Seagram Building in New York City. A great variety of new methods of steel construction, in addition to the rigid frame, have also been developed. These include the use of steel in reinforced concrete, various forms of cantilever construction, cables from which roofs are suspended, and space forms (for example, Buckminster Fuller's geodesic domes).
See CONSTRUCTION, SKELETON; SKYSCRAPER.

MILTON F. KIRCHMAN

CONSTRUCTIVISM. Movement and style of art that originated in Russia with the constructions, especially reliefs carried out in modern industrial materials, of Vladimir Tatlin, El Lissitzky, and Alexander Rodchenko beginning in 1913. In that year Tatlin created the first assembled works in abstract forms (Picasso and other cubists had begun high reliefs of the collage technique, and Boccioni in 1912 advocated the utilization of untraditional substances such as hair, glass, and cardboard). Tatlin exhibited them in 1915 as free, geometric constructions in space. While Tatlin and his colleagues were conversant with cubism through slightly earlier exhibitions in Moscow, the combination of essentially geometric abstraction and industrial materials assembled into abstract form was original and was immediately to influence Naum Gabo and his brother Antoine Pevsner, who, although they joined the constructivist movement in 1917 and issued a renowned manifesto in 1920 setting forth the principles of the style, were not in fact the pioneers of the association. Other artists who with Gabo and Pevsner helped to win acceptance of constructivism outside Russia were the Hungarian László Moholy-Nagy and, although his style belongs also to other phases of geometric abstraction, Josef Albers. *See* ALBERS, JOSEF; GABO, NAUM; LISSITZKY, LAZAR; MOHOLY-NAGY, LASZLO; PEVSNER, ANTOINE; RODCHENKO, ALEXANDER; TATLIN, VLADIMIR EVGRAFOVICH.

The excitement enjoyed by Tatlin and his followers over the constructivist innovations was short-lived insofar as it related to official encouragement in postrevolutionary Russia. Because this aesthetically radical abstract art was not readily comprehended by the people, who also failed to understand the earlier nonfigural paintings of Kandinsky, the constructivists were out of favor by about 1920, and several of them settled in Germany. Tatlin and Rodchenko remained in Russia, and, although the precise facts are

Constructivism. Antoine Pevsner, *Torso.* Formerly Katherine S. Dreier Collection.

presently obscure, it appears that they did not achieve significant further success with constructivism. Gabo and Pevsner, both strongly original artists, stayed in Berlin after 1922. Pevsner proceeded to Paris in 1923, and Gabo, after an active period in Germany, including the development of a motorized abstract sculpture, joined him there in 1932. *See* TATLINISM.

The constructivist aesthetic was amplified in the 1920s at the renowned Bauhaus at Weimar (later removed to Dessau). Moholy-Nagy, inspired by Lissitzky, who was in Germany during part of this period, brought together the major principles of constructivism and de Stijl, creating both paintings and architecture. As professor at the Bauhaus under the direction of Walter Gropius and later as founder of the New Bauhaus in Chicago, Moholy-Nagy helped to spread constructivism in the United States, where it has influenced many young architects and sculptors. Max Bill, a Swiss designer trained at the Dessau Bauhaus, is a particularly severe practitioner and theoretician of a refined constructivist style; and, like Moholy-Nagy, he reestablished a second-generation Bauhaus, in this instance at Ulm, after World War II. *See* BAUHAUS; BILL, MAX.

Constructivism, which had its origin in geometrically abstract sculptures by Tatlin in 1913, was influenced by cubism in its inception and, in turn, exchanged influences with certain closely related movements. One of these was de Stijl, the Dutch painting and industrial-design style more accurately known as neoplasticism, headed by Piet Mondrian and Theo van Doesburg. The Abstraction-Création group of the early 1930s in Paris, to which Gabo and Pevsner belonged, received a certain impetus from constructivist methods, following the recognition of the mechanical aspects of that style by Ozenfant, Le Corbusier, and Léger in their purist movement of 1919–25. Many individual European and American artists in technique or concept felt some degree of constructivist influence: the English sculptors Henry Moore and Barbara Hepworth, the American Alexander Calder, and a number of post-World War II German artists (some of them students of Schlemmer and others at the Bauhaus) are cases in point. *See* ABSTRACTION-CREATION GROUP; DE STIJL; NEOPLASTICISM. *See also* SCHLEMMER, OSKAR.

Among the outstanding monuments of constructivism are Tatlin's *Monument to the Third Internationale* (1919–20), following his 1913 abstract reliefs; Lissitzky's constructions of about 1915–20; Rodchenko's painting, *Black on Black* (ca. 1915); Naum Gabo's *Constructed Head* (1916); Antoine Pevsner's *Torso* (1924–26; formerly Katherine S. Dreier Collection); and the later compositions by Pevsner and Gabo in plastic wire and translucent solids dating from the 1920s and 1930s. The principles of constructivism were actually totally manifest by about 1930, and followers of the style have since then simply exploited the implications of the method.

One of the leading sculptural and architectural styles of the 1920s, constructivism has had especially wide application in the field of industrial design. *See* INDUSTRIAL DESIGN.

BIBLIOGRAPHY. L. Lozowick, *Modern Russian Art*, New York, 1925; J. L. Martin, B. Nicholson, and N. Gabo, eds., *Circle: International Survey of Constructive Art*, London, 1937; M. Seuphor, *The Sculpture of This Century*, New York, 1960; C. Gray, *The Great Experiment: Russian Art, 1863–1922*, New York, 1962.

JOHN C. GALLOWAY

CONSULAR DIPTYCH. Elaborately carved folding writing tablets given as presents by consuls in the late Roman period. The inner surfaces were filled with wax for writing purposes. The reliefs on the outer surfaces are of great importance in the development of late Roman and Early Christian art.

CONTARINI, GIOVANNI. Italian painter (1549–1604). He was born in Venice. Originally a notary, Contarini turned to painting on the counsel of Alessandro Vittoria and taught himself by studying the works of Titian, Tintoretto, and particularly Jacopo Palma, whose influence is strong throughout his work. From 1579 to 1591 Contarini worked in Prague for Rudolph II and was knighted there; he then moved to Innsbruck and shortly thereafter returned to Venice, where he was employed at the Doge's Palace, among other places. His paintings *Doge Grimani Presented to the Virgin* and *Venetians Reconquering Verona* (both Doge's Palace) are thoroughly in the Venetian tradition with their coruscating light and vigorous figure style, derived from Tintoretto, in the context of hectic, almost baroque compositions. More original is the manneristic *Nativity of the Virgin* (Venice, Church of the Holy Apostles), in which the monumental figures are arranged in an oval movement against a steeply tipped space.

CONTE, JACOPINO DEL. Florentine painter (b. Florence, 1510; d. Rome, 1598). He was a pupil and an assistant of

Andrea del Sarto. Jacopino left Florence in 1538, perhaps on being commissioned to paint frescoes for the Oratory of S. Giovanni Decollato in Rome. These, the *Baptism of Christ* and *Preaching of the Baptist*, are mannerist in their complex spatial arrangements, reflecting Florentine draftsmanship in their clear, energetic contours and a strong Michelangelesque influence in figure conceptions and style of modeling. Jacopino's reputation as a portraitist won him commissions to paint the popes from Paul III to Clement VII. Many vigorous portraits, including one of Michelangelo, have been attributed to him.

BIBLIOGRAPHY. A. Venturi, *Storia dell'arte italiana*, vol. 9, pt. 6, Milan, 1933; F. Zeri, "*Me Pinxit*, 10: Salviati e Jacopino del Conte," *Proporzioni*, II, 1948.

CONTI, BERNARDINO DE'. Italian painter of Milan (fl. 1496–1522). Conti is said to have been born in Pavia, of a noble family. No documents of his life exist, but he is known from a dozen signed works. Some are Madonnas, dry copies of Leonardo da Vinci. The rest are portraits, equally dry and with archaic profile stiffness, but vivid tokens of aristocratic life. Most represent members of the most powerful families of the age. Among them are *Francesco Sforza Aged Five* (1496; Rome, Vatican Museums), *Portrait of a Cardinal* (1499; Berlin, former State Museums), *Fra Sisto della Rovere* (1501; formerly Berlin, Schloss), *Catellano Trivulzio* (1505; formerly Turin, private collection), and *Luigi Besozzi* (1506; Berlin, former State Museums). Undated portraits include *Alberigo d'Este* (Hannover Museum) and *Galeazzo Maria Sforza* (Milan, Brera). After 1506 or 1508 there are no signed paintings until

Contrapposto. Michelangelo, *Slave*. Academy, Florence.

Conversation piece. Eastman Johnson, *Family Group (The Hatch Family)*. Metropolitan Museum of Art, New York.

1522–23, when he painted two more Madonnas after Leonardo.

BIBLIOGRAPHY. W. Suida, *Leonardo und sein Kreis*, Munich, 1929.
CREIGHTON GILBERT

CONTOUR. Line that defines forms by delimiting them. Not merely an outline, contour is more expressive and may imply plasticity, perspective, and even texture.

CONTRAPPOSTO. Italian term denoting a pose in which the human figure is so balanced that the chest and shoulders face one direction and the hips and legs another. The Roman copy of Polycleitus's *Doryphoros* in Naples (ca. 450–440 B.C.) illustrates a moderate *contrapposto* of the classical period. In Hellenistic times the pose was exploited for dramatic effects. It was a *sine qua non* for the Renaissance artist and reached the limit of exaggeration in the work of Michelangelo and his imitators.

CONTRAST, COLOR. Optical effect in which a color appears to be intensified. The intensification effect is achieved by juxtaposing complementary colors. It is used frequently in contemporary painting.

CONTUCCI, *see* SANSOVINO, ANDREA.

CONVENTO. Church dwelling in the colonial architecture of Florida and the Spanish Southwest of the United States and of Latin America.

CONVERSATION PIECE (Conversation Group Portrait). Style of portrait painting that reached its fullest development in mid-18th-century England. The paintings normally consist of small-scale, full-length family portraits of middle-class people engaged in some everyday pastime in either an interior or exterior setting. The origins of the form cannot be readily distinguished from the group portraits popular in 17th-century Holland and early-18th-century France. Hogarth practiced this style of portraiture, especially early in his career, as did Gainsborough while he was at Ipswich. Among the other early exponents of the form are Philippe Mercier, Arthur Devis, and Francis Hayman. The fashion was continued in the late 18th century by Johann Zoffany, Francis Wheatley, and George Stubbs. *See* DEVIS, ARTHUR; GAINSBOROUGH, THOMAS; HAYMAN, FRANCIS; HOGARTH, WILLIAM; MERCIER, PHILIPPE; STUBBS, GEORGE; WHEATLEY, FRANCIS; ZOFFANY, JOHANN.

BIBLIOGRAPHY. S. Sitwell, *Conversation Pieces*, London, 1936.

CONWAY CASTLE. One of the great Welsh castles of Edward I, built in 1283–87 on a high narrow rock beside the river Conway. Forming part of a scheme that included a fortified town, Conway is a model of the highly developed medieval castle. Its long narrow shape was divided into two unequal baileys and defended by eight huge towers. Access to gateways at each end could be achieved only after climbing steep flights of stairs that were potentially exposed to heavy fire from the castle.

BIBLIOGRAPHY. S. Toy, *Castles, a Short History of Fortifications from 1600 B.C. to A.D. 1600*, London, 1939.

COOK, HOWARD. American painter, muralist, printmaker, and illustrator (1901–   ). Born in Springfield, Mass., he studied at the Art Students League, New York City, and was awarded a Guggenheim fellowship in 1932. He has traveled extensively throughout the world and has continually experimented with different techniques. His early work is realistic and fully modeled; his later work in collage is almost completely abstract.

BIBLIOGRAPHY. C. Zigrosser, *The Artist in America*, New York, 1942.

COOL (Coolen), WILLEM GILLISZ., *see* KOOL, WILLEM GILLISZ.

COOLIDGE, CHARLES ALLERTON, *see* SHEPLEY, RUTAN, AND COOLIDGE.

COOPER, SAMUEL. English portrait miniaturist (1609–72). He was probably trained by his uncle, John Hoskins, and may afterward have traveled abroad, since his chief works date from 1642. Cooper's reputation has always remained high. During his lifetime, Pepys called him "prince of limners" (*Diary*, 1668), and Cooper's patrons were the highest figures of both the Commonwealth and the Restoration. His portraits mark an advance in the art of miniature painting from the tight brushwork and shadowless outlines of the medieval illuminators to the broad and expressive modeling with color and light characteristic of oil painting. His best miniatures remain in the English Royal Art Collection and the collections of the Duke of Buccleuch and the Duke of Portland.

BIBLIOGRAPHY. A. G. Reynolds, *English Portrait Miniatures*, London, 1952.

COOSEMANS, ALEXANDER. Flemish still-life painter (b. Antwerp, 1627; d. there, 1689). A student of J. D. de Heem (1642), Coosemans became a master in 1645. His paintings, in the style of his teacher, frequently combine fruits, flowers, and crustaceans. His works have been confused with those of Aelbert Cuijp and Abraham Calraet.

BIBLIOGRAPHY. R. H. Wilenski, *Flemish Painters, 1430–1830*, 2 vols., New York, 1960.

COPE. Cloak or mantle worn by a priest over the alb as a protective outer garment during processions, solemn lauds, benedictionals, and so forth. Semicircular in form and without sleeves, it is fastened high on the chest with the morse. The cope is the richest of all ecclesiastic garments; its color varies according to the Church season. During Mass the chasuble is worn in place of the cope.

COPENHAGEN: MUSEUMS. Important public art collections in Copenhagen, Denmark, are located in the museums listed below.

Museum of Decorative Arts. Organized in the late 19th century, this collection is now housed in the old Fredericks Hospital, Copenhagen, designed by Eigtved in the 18th century. Its original purpose was to exemplify the applied arts as an impetus to contemporary craftsmanship. The scope of the museum has since been expanded to encompass a more general collection of decorative arts from all countries and periods. Examples of European textiles, porcelain, faïence, furniture, silverware, and other crafts have been added to the core of Danish applied arts. Outstanding in the group of tapestries is one from Tournai (ca. 1475) depicting a court scene. Chinese bronzes, porcelain, and stoneware from various periods are also well represented.

National Museum. Founded in 1807 by royal commission, the museum now has six departments concerned with art. Three departments of the vast collections are devoted to Danish art: the departments of Danish Antiquities (arts and crafts from the Old Stone Age through the Viking period, including the Gundestrup Caldron and King Harald's Stone from Jelling), the Middle Ages and Renaissance, and Danish Interiors. The Ethnographical Department is the oldest in the world and includes works from Africa, ancient America, Oceania, and other areas. The Department of Oriental and Classical Antiquities has two rare fragments of metope sculpture from the Parthenon in Athens. Finally, there is the Royal Collection of Coins and Medals.

BIBLIOGRAPHY. A. Roussell, ed., *The National Museum of Denmark*, Copenhagen, 1957.

Ny Carlsberg Glyptothek. In 1888 this museum was established as an independent institution by Carl and Ottilia Jacobsen. After 1906 the Danish government and the city of Copenhagen transformed the already famous Jacobsen Collection into a public museum. Especially known for its collections of Egyptian, Oriental, Greek, and Roman art (with the famous *Niobids* from the 4th century B.C. and excellent Roman portrait busts), the museum is also rich in French 19th- and early-20th-century paintings. The founder, Carl Jacobsen, also made the Glyptothek the largest collection of 19th-century French sculpture outside Paris, with works by Carpeaux, Rodin, Maillol, and so on. Jacobsen also gave works by Thorvaldsen's pupils to the museum.

BIBLIOGRAPHY. V. Poulsen, *Ny Carlsberg Glyptothek: A Guide to the Collections*, 7th ed., Copenhagen, 1962.

Rosenborg Palace. In the King's Garden, Copenhagen, once outside the East Gate but now within the city limits, this picturesque Danish Renaissance palace served as a residence for the kings of Denmark. It remains essentially unchanged from the time of its construction under Christian IV (1606–34) and the restoration of much of the interior in the 18th century. In addition to its own period décor, the palace exhibits in chronological order the acquisitions and accouterments of the Danish crown, including royal portraits and other pictures, furniture, robes, glassware, china, fabrics, enamels, and precious stones. Notable among these are the crown jewels, the royal orb, the sword of the realm, and the scepter.

BIBLIOGRAPHY. *Rosenborg Castle: A Guide to the Chronological Collection of the Danish Kings*, Copenhagen, 1949.

State Museum of Fine Arts. The building housing this collection was completed in 1896 to the plans of V. Dahlerup and E. W. Møller. It incorporates most of the Royal Collection of Pictures and the Royal Collection of Engravings. These collections were given impetus in the middle of the 17th century by Frederick III, who, like many other monarchs and princes of the time, began to purchase works of art on the open market.

Dutch and Flemish painting is stressed in the collection, which has representative works from most areas of European painting. The group of works by Lucas Cranach the Elder is the largest outside Germany and includes versions of *The Marriage of St. Catherine*, the *Crucifixion*, *The Judgment of Paris*, *Venus and Cupid*, a *Portrait of Martin Luther*, and several other portraits. Other notable works are a *Crucifixion* by Mantegna, *Christ and the Woman Taken in Adultery* by Tintoretto, *The Apostle Peter Finding the Tribute Money* by Jordaens, *The Judgment of Solomon* by Rubens, and a large group of landscapes by Jacob van Ruisdael. The comprehensive Royal Collection of Engravings boasts outstanding groups of Dürer woodcuts and engravings and Rembrandt etchings.

Since the donation of the Rump Collection in 1928, the museum has greatly developed its holdings in modern art. Matisse thought its representation of his work the best of any museum in Europe. Some of his better-known works there are *Portrait with a Green Strip* (1905), a *Self-Portrait* (1906), one of the series called *Le Luxe* (1907), and *The Violin* (1917–18). The original Fauve painters, with whom Matisse was associated, are particularly in evidence, with outstanding examples by Derain, Dufy, Braque, Vlaminck, and Marquet; these works were completed both during and after the period of Fauvism. A group of early Rouault nudes, paintings by Picasso, Modigliani, and Gris, and sculptures by Laurens, Despiau, Maillol, and Matisse are also notable in this section of the museum.

BIBLIOGRAPHY. Statens Museum for Kunst, *Catalogue of Old Foreign Paintings*, Copenhagen, 1951; Statens Museum for Kunst, *Moderns Udenlandsk Kunst, J. Rumps Samling etc.*, 3d ed., Copenhagen, 1958.

DONALD GODDARD

Thorvaldsen's Museum. In 1839 Albert Bertel Thorvaldsen, one of the leading neoclassical sculptors of Europe, bequeathed his entire art collection to his native city of Copenhagen. The monumental edifice that houses the collection was designed by G. M. Bindesbøll (1839–48). Homage is paid to the revered sculptor in the frieze on the exterior, which shows his reception in Copenhagen after a lifetime in Rome. Thorvaldsen's tomb occupies the central court. Around it are ranged galleries displaying the products of his prolific output, some of them casts. Danish

and other early-19th-century paintings, Italian paintings, Greek and Roman bronzes, vases, coins, and gems complete the collection.

BIBLIOGRAPHY. Thorvaldsens Museum, *Official Guide*, Copenhagen, 1949.

COPENHAGEN PORCELAIN. Copenhagen was first the scene of successful porcelain production when Louis Fournier, French potter and modeler, operated a soft-paste factory there between 1759 and 1765. His output was rococo in style under Vincennes-Chantilly influence. True porcelain (hard paste) was made later by Franz Müller, who founded the factory purchased by the crown in 1779. Müller's porcelain was bluish-gray in tone and decorated in a range of color limited to blue, purple, and iron red until 1780. The *muschel* pattern in underglaze blue is the best-known Copenhagen pattern. In the 1780s, when a fuller palette was used, neoclassical designs were made, with the *Flora Danica* for Catherine of Russia outstanding. Figures were made in the neoclassical style as well as more naturalistically.

BIBLIOGRAPHY. A. Hayden, *Royal Copenhagen Porcelain . . .*, London, 1911.

COPENHAGEN STOCK EXCHANGE, *see* STEENWINKEL FAMILY.

COPERSLAGERE, JACOB DE, *see* GERINES, JACQUES DE.

COPIES (Chinese Painting), *see* CHINA: PAINTING (COPIES).

COPING. Top course of a wall.

COPLEY, JOHN SINGLETON. American portrait and historical painter (b. in or near Boston, 1738; d. London, 1815). Born in New England shortly after his parents' emigration from Ireland, Copley was left fatherless at a very early age. When he was ten, his mother remarried, her new husband being the mezzotint engraver Peter Pelham, who encouraged Copley to become a painter. As he died in 1751, when Copley was only thirteen, Pelham may not have been a real instructor in the specifics of painting, but he was an important influence on the developing artist. Copley's next inspiration came from the paintings of John Smibert and the copies of old masters in Smibert's painting room. Copley began to paint about 1753, and his earliest paintings (*The Gore Children*, ca. 1755, Winterthur, Del., Winterthur Museum; *Galatea*, ca. 1754, Boston, Museum of Fine Arts) reflect the baroque influence of Smibert and those whom he influenced (Feke, Badger, and Greenwood). These works show Copley's early facility with the brush, although it is accompanied by a youthful naïveté.

In 1755 Copley came into contact with Joseph Blackburn, whose rococo lightness and coloring Copley quickly absorbed and surpassed (*Ann Tyng*, 1756; Boston, Museum of Fine Arts). At this time, too, he began to study anatomy, striving for accuracy, as shown in a volume of anatomical drawings in the British Museum, London. Removed from the artistic centers of Europe, he read such treatises on painting as C. A. Dufresnoy's *De arte graphica* and Roger de Piles's *The Art of Painting*. And Copley, like most American painters, utilized English mezzotints for fashionable poses (compare his *Mrs. Jerathmael Bowers*,

Copenhagen porcelain. Example of hard-paste ware by Franz Müller. Dansk Folke Museum, Copenhagen.

ca. 1767–70, New York, Metropolitan Museum, and James McArdell's mezzotint, ca. 1759, after Reynolds's *Lady Caroline Russell*). From all these influences Copley welded a personal style of great brilliance and power. His talent as a colorist and draftsman, for example, enabled him to produce a picture of aristocratic elegance and grace in the portrait of Mrs. Bowers, not merely a version of the Reynolds model.

Copley's independent style was achieved about 1757, and for the next seventeen years he painted portraits in America of penetrating realism combined with a magnificent handling of paint. Characteristic of his American portraiture at its best are such paintings as *Jacob Fowle* (ca. 1761; Washington, D.C., Corcoran Gallery of Art) and *John Hancock* (1765; Boston, Museum of Fine Arts). A type of portraiture that Copley often employed with success was the *portrait d'apparat*, the picture of an individual accompanied by the materials of his everyday life. Here, as in the *Paul Revere* (1768–70; Boston, Museum of Fine Arts), Copley's incisive realism and technical virtuosity are brilliantly displayed. Although oil was his usual medium, Copley also worked in pastels. Typical is his *Self-Portrait* of 1769 (Winterthur Museum), but as early as 1762 he had written the Swiss pastelist J. E. Liotard for help in procuring crayons and instructions for using them.

The letter to Liotard early indicated Copley's concern with the world of art beyond America. Three years later (1765) he sent a painting (*The Boy with the Squirrel*, Boston, private collection) to London, where it was included in the 1766 exhibition of the Society of Artists. Both West and Reynolds were excited by it, encouraged Copley in his art, and suggested that he come to Europe. He delayed until 1774, then sailed for London, never to return. After a short stay in London, he embarked on a grand tour to Italy. The effect of this Italian journey can be seen by comparing a double portrait done in Rome (*Mr. and Mrs. Ralph Izard*, 1775; Boston, Museum of Fine Arts) with one painted shortly before his departure from America (*Mr. and Mrs. Thomas Mifflin*, 1773; Philadelphia, Historical Society of Pennsylvania). Late in 1775 he returned to London.

Settling there, Copley was elected associate of the Royal Academy in 1776 and full academician in 1779. He continued his career as a portrait painter, but he also became a painter of history, the area in which his reputation in England was to lie. His English portraits retain the éclat of his earlier works, but not always with the forthrightness and honest realism that were such important elements of his American style. Yet in his best portraits done in England, for example, *Midshipman Augustus Brine* (1782; New York, Metropolitan Museum), Copley still displays the brilliance of his American paintings. In England he also began to paint larger group portraits, such as that of himself and his own family (*The Copley Family*, 1776–77; Washington, D.C., National Gallery) and *The Sitwell Family* (1786; Renishaw Hall). In these, Copley combined his keen perception and fine brushwork with a feeling for compositional arrangement.

It is this quality of composition that marks his major works in England: the depiction of contemporary events in modern dress rather than as classical allegories. Although

this speciality was introduced by West, it remained for another American, Copley, to achieve the greatest success in this vein. Copley's first modern-dress history painting, *Brook Watson and the Shark* (1778; versions in Washington, D.C., National Gallery and Boston, Museum of Fine Arts), was not a scene of great national significance, but rather a dramatic, sensational event concerning a single individual. The others of this genre, however, depicted events of importance concerning famous men or national heroes and were painted on a much larger scale. *The Death of the Earl of Chatham* (1779–81; London, Tate) was followed by *The Death of Major Pierson* (1782–84; Tate), *The Repulse of the Floating Batteries at Gibraltar* (completed 1791; London, Guildhall), and *The Surrender of the Dutch Admiral De Winter to Admiral Duncan* (completed 1799; Camperdown House). All four are large, dra-

Coppo di Marcovaldo, *Madonna and Child*. S. Maria dei Servi, Siena.

matic canvases, full of bravura and magnificently composed. For the finished paintings, which were exhibited and engraved, Copley made individual portraits of the people involved. These preparatory studies (drawing of *Lord Bathurst* for *The Death of Chatham*, Boston, Museum of Fine Arts; *Head of a Negro* for *Brook Watson and the Shark*, Detroit Institute of Arts) show the incisive portraiture and brilliant execution characteristic of his American paintings. The finished historical canvases, however, emphasize drama and composition at the sacrifice of the freshness of the earlier works.

Copley's works are represented in most major American museums. The most important collections are in the Museum of Fine Arts, Boston, and the Metropolitan Museum of Art, New York.

As a major force in English painting of the last quarter of the 18th century, and as the finest painter in colonial America, Copley occupies an important position. He brought to perfection the colonial American tradition of portraiture, and he successfully developed a new type of history painting that was to become widely used in the romantic era by such men as Géricault and Gros.

BIBLIOGRAPHY. F. W. Bayley, *The Life and Works of John Singleton Copley*, Boston, 1915; B. N. Parker and A. B. Wheeler, *John Singleton Copley*, Boston, 1938; J. T. Flexner, *John Singleton Copley*, Boston, 1948; E. K. Waterhouse, *Painting in Britain, 1530–1790*, Baltimore, 1953; J. D. Prown, *John Singleton Copley*, 2 vols., Cambridge, Mass., 1966.

DAMIE STILLMAN

COPPERPLATE. Usually refers to 16- or 18-gauge red copper employed in etching, engraving, and allied intaglio processes. Today, etchers use rolled copper plates, although hammered copper plates, if they were still available, would be more useful, especially in engraving.

COPPO DI MARCOVALDO. Italian painter of the Florentine school (fl. 1260–74). The art of this slightly older contemporary of Cimabue remained closely linked to the models provided by the immediate background of Byzantine tradition. With Giunta Pisano, Coppo must be considered the founder of the monumental tradition in Tuscan painting that lasted almost 300 years. He is first recorded in Florence in 1260 as living in the San Lorenzo quarter. From 1265 to 1274 he is mentioned as active in Pistoia.

Coppo's earliest known work is thought to be the *Madonna and Child* that he painted for the Sienese Church of S. Maria dei Servi in 1261. It shows his characteristic mode of interpreting the schematic formulas of Byzantine design by imbuing them with a sense of sculptural weight and thrust. This painting had an important influence on the course of Sienese painting of the later 13th century and on its principal master, Guido da Siena. Coppo painted another large, monumental *Madonna and Child* for S. Maria dei Servi in Orvieto, now in the National Museum of Umbria, Perugia.

His masterpiece, however, is the *Crucifix* in the Civic Museum in San Gimignano. Flanking its life-size figure of the dead Christ are six narrative scenes of the Passion; the side terminals contain the *Virgin and St. John* and the *Three Marys*, and the upper terminals the *Ascension* and a *Bust of Christ*. Coppo's most original achievement, the

interpretation of Byzantine patterns of lines and shadings in terms of light and shadow, may be seen particularly well in the Passion scenes. By means of this discovery he became the first Italian painter to suggest convincingly the physical reality of both figures and action.

The painted parts (figures of angels and saints, *The Annunciation*, and *The Three Marys at the Tomb*) of an altarpiece in S. Maria Maggiore in Florence, whose principal image is a painted wooden relief of the *Madonna and Child*, have been attributed to Coppo or to a close follower. A *Crucifix* by his son Salerno di Coppo is in the Cathedral of Pistoia.

BIBLIOGRAPHY. P. Bacci, "Coppo di Marcovaldo e Salerno di Coppo . . .," *L'Arte*, III, 1900; O. Sirén, *Toskanische Maler im XIII. Jahrhundert*, Berlin, 1922; G. Coor-Achenbach, "A Visual Basis for the Documents Relating to Coppo di Marcovaldo and His Son Salerno," *Art Bulletin*, XXVIII, 1946; C. Brandi, "Il restauro della Madonna di Coppo di Marcovaldo nella Chiesa dei Servi di Siena," *Bollettino d'Arte*, XXXV, 1950; J. White, *Art and Architecture in Italy, 1250–1400*, Baltimore, 1966.

HELLMUT WOHL

COPTIC ART. The art of Christian Egypt, particularly of the period between the 3d and 8th century, is called Coptic (from an Arabic corruption of the Greek word for Egypt). It is a provincial style of great force, as yet imperfectly understood, that resulted in part from the fusion of late-antique art with the formal traditions of ancient Egypt. Coptic art was tied closely to the religious and even the nationalistic convictions of its makers. The Coptic Church was Monophysite, believing in the single nature of the human and divine in Jesus Christ, and thus at odds with the official Byzantine Church; this belief largely determined the nature of Coptic iconography. The style tended to flourish in monastic centers up the Nile, away from sophisticated, Hellenized Alexandria. The Arab conquest of Egypt (mid-7th cent.) and the resulting supremacy of Islam severely reduced the production and creativity of Coptic artists.

Generally speaking, the plasticity of the Greco-Roman canon was abandoned in favor of simplified, often schematized, forms and outlines. Coptic wall painting, of which relatively few examples survive, is collaterally related to Early Christian and Byzantine painting, but tends to be formed of areas of solid color (yellow, red, and blue predominating) set in strongly drawn outlines. Notable examples are the frescoes at El-Bagawat and the Bawit Monastery. Subjects were often drawn from the Apocryphal Gospels. *See* BAGAWAT, EL-, FRESCOES; BAWIT FRESCOES.

Coptic figure sculpture preserved the bulky, dense forms of ancient Egypt; this tendency can be seen at an early stage in the famous goup of four Roman emperors on the exterior of St. Mark's in Venice. Architectural sculpture made considerable use of classical patterns but transformed them into comparatively rigid, linear forms. In all Coptic art there is a powerful drive toward abstraction and geometric shapes. This is apparent in textiles, in which the patterns are frequently woven in wool over linen. *See* RUGS, NEAR AND MIDDLE EASTERN.

Architectural forms were often severely simple, showing little of the vivacious contemporary development of the Byzantine style. Plain halls, defined by unarticulated and massive exterior walls somewhat reminiscent of pagan

Gonzales Coques, *Family Group*. National Gallery, London. This type of painting earned the artist the nickname "Little van Dyck."

Egyptian temple construction, terminated in triple chapels to form the standard Coptic church, as at Sohag. In this way an architecture was formed that reflected the ascetic desert monasticism from which much of Coptic culture sprang. Often, however, sanctuaries and residual areas were ingeniously vaulted in brick. The influence of Coptic art was felt chiefly in Nubia and Ethiopia. *See* SOHAG. *See also* DEIR BARAMUS; DEIR ES-SURIAN; DENDERA; SAQQARA, CHURCH OF.

BIBLIOGRAPHY. A. J. Butler, *The Ancient Coptic Churches of Egypt*, 2 vols., Oxford, 1884; A. J. Gayet, *... L'Art copte...*, Paris, 1902; S. Clarke, *Christian Antiquities in the Nile Valley...*, Oxford, 1912; C. R. Morey, *Early Christian Art...*, 2d ed., Princeton, 1953; P. C. Labib, *The Coptic Museum and the Fortress of Babylon at Old Cairo*, Cairo, 1956.

WILLIAM L. MACDONALD

COPY. Reproduction of a work of art not executed by the original artist. Although it is usually in the same material as the original, a copy can be of a different material, for example, the Roman bronze copies of Greek marble originals. Reproductions may also differ in size from the original, as is true of study copies. A reproduction is distinct from a replica, which is a copy executed by the original artist himself. *See also* CHINA: PAINTING (COPIES).

Coptic art. Portrait of a girl, mummy cover from Gayel, last half of 3d century. Encaustic on canvas. Louvre, Paris.

COQUES, GONZALES. Flemish painter of portraits, genre, and historical scenes (b. Antwerp, 1614/18; d. there, 1684). Coques was a disciple of Pieter Brueghel the Younger and David Ryckaert II. He became a master in 1641 and painter to the Count of Monterey, governor of the Low Countries, in 1671. It has been assumed that Coques traveled abroad before obtaining belated admission as master to the Guild of St. Luke; nothing more specific is known from these years than the existence of a painting, *Scholar and His Sister* (1640; Kassel, Gallery).

A series of allegorical paintings, the *History of Psyche*, was done for Prince Frederick Henry, Stadhouder of Holland, and paid for in 1648. They were less than a success. Coques, however, was by then known and appreciated as an outstanding artist in the field of single and group portraits, which were permeated with the flavor of courtly elegance in costume as well as in attitude. He began his career with adaptations from genre painting conspicuously influenced by the manner of Gerard Ter Borch, who introduced genre pieces and small-size portraits into Flanders about 1640. Furthermore, Coques's early works are still imbued with the tradition of Frans Francken the Younger or Hieronymus Janssens the Dancer.

Very soon, however, he must have been in contact with Van Dyck's works, especially those of the English period. From conscientiously depicting the milieu, he evolved toward the dignity and elegance of Van Dyck, although with the restriction of a smaller scale. It was with good cause that the nickname "Little Van Dyck" clung to him. The *Family of Burgomaster J. van Eyck* (Budapest Museum) and *Family Group* (London, National Gallery) are characteristic of this trend. The landscape backgrounds in Coques's paintings are often due to other hands, such as Peter Neefs, Lucas van Uden, and Jacques d'Arthois. Though often imitated, his best productions are of exquisite quality that assures the artist of a choice place among Flemish secondary masters.

BIBLIOGRAPHY. F. J. van den Branden, *Geschiedenis der Antwerpsche Schilderschool*, Antwerp, 1883; R. Oldenbourg, *Die flämische Malerei des XVII. Jahrhunderts*, 2d ed., Berlin, 1922.

ERIK LARSEN

CORBEL. Architectural term derived from the French *corbeau* and the Latin *corvus*, meaning "raven"; hence a beaklike projection. The corbel is a projecting element of a wall used to support roof beams, vaults, balconies, or even decorative elements. In the Palace of Diocletian, in Split, Yugoslavia, corbels support a decorative arcading.

The term corbel construction refers to the practice of projecting each horizontal course of masonry beyond the lower course until the apex is reached, as above the doorways of the tholos tombs in Aegean architecture. Corbeled vaults are found in Oeniadae, Assos, and Tiryns and in the beehive roof of the Treasury of Atreus in Mycenae. Although distinguished from true arch construction with its radiating voussoirs, corbel construction engages in arch action.

CORBEL TABLE. Course, as of masonry, supported on projecting corbels. The corbel table may form a decorative frieze, as an interlace of intersecting arcs springing from corbels, or be a simple projection resting on corbels. Ex-

amples of arcuated corbel tables are found in S. Ambrogio, Milan, and in Ely Cathedral; an example of corbels supporting a cornice is found in the apse of St-Pierre, Aulnay.

CORBETT, HARVEY WILEY. American architect (b. San Francisco, 1873; d. New York City, 1954). As early as the 1920s Corbett was a protagonist of the skyscraper. His firm of Corbett, MacMurray, and Harrison designed Rockefeller Center, New York. In the 1940s the war in Europe, with its bombings, altered the direction of his work away from skyscrapers, but in 1949 he returned to his early interests, proclaiming the City of the Future with great blocks of skyscrapers. In his exploitation of the New York zoning laws of 1925, he evolved the idea of the "envelope" to maintain light for adjoining buildings. In 1926 he urged cities to develop easy access to airports. His Bush Terminal Office Building (built in 1923) was one of New York's earliest modernistic structures. The base of his Metropolitan Life addition (1930–50) was so designed that with its setbacks it could have been carried 2,000 feet high.

CORBETT, MARIO. American architect (1901–   ). He was born in New York City. In his flat-roofed houses in California, stone walls bound large glass areas perforated with wooden paneling. In the house for Moritz Thomsen (1952) in Vina, Calif., the living area can be closed to the weather by sliding glass panels.

BIBLIOGRAPHY. H. R. Hitchcock and A. Drexler, eds., *Built in U.S.A.: Post-War Architecture*, New York, 1952.

CORBIE SCHOOL. One of the most illusive and debated "schools" of Carolingian manuscript illumination. It is difficult to ascribe any manuscripts, with certainty, to the abbey at Corbie. The school of Corbie itself, sometimes linked to the Franco-Saxon school, has also been disasso-

Corbel. Beaklike projection supporting other structural elements.

Corbel table. Decorative frieze or simple projection resting on corbels.

ciated from Corbie altogether and called instead the school of St-Denis. *See* SAINT-DENIS STYLE.

By far the most lavish of the debated productions of the Corbie scriptorium are the Psalter of Charles the Bald (Paris, National Library) and the Coronation Sacramentary (Paris, National Library). Both manuscripts, associated with Emperor Charles the Bald, are richly illuminated in an eclectic style suggestive of the Reims school illusionism and Tours school narrative monumentality. Franco-Saxon-style decorative elements are also evident. This very diversity of iconographic and stylistic elements has led to the proposal of a St-Denis provenance for supposed Corbie works.

BIBLIOGRAPHY. A. Goldschmidt, *Die deutsche Buchmalerei*, vol. 1, Munich, 1928.

CORBINO, JON. American painter (b. Vittorio, Sicily, 1905; d. Sarasota, Fla., 1964). He studied with DuMond and George Luks. Corbino painted darkly glowing compositions of animals and people in violent motion, somewhat in the manner of the baroque masters, especially Rubens.

BIBLIOGRAPHY. H. Salpeter, "Corbino: Artist on Horseback," *Esquire*, February, 1939.

CORCORAN GALLERY OF ART, WASHINGTON, D.C., *see* WASHINGTON, D.C.: MUSEUMS (CORCORAN GALLERY OF ART).

CORDED WARE. Pottery that has been decorated by the impression of a twisted cord against the damp clay. The cord is often applied in straight and parallel lengths to produce the appearance of horizontal bands or of vertical groovings. It can also be wrapped around the thumb and pressed in short, diagonal segments. This technique has been employed by many cultures; its use was especially widespread in the Danubian area of Central Europe during the late Neolithic and early Chalcolithic period.

BIBLIOGRAPHY. C. F. C. Hawkes, *The Prehistoric Foundations of Europe to the Mycenean Age*, London, 1940.

CORDELIAGHI (Cordella), *see* PREVITALI, ANDREA.

CORDERO, JUAN. Mexican painter (b. Teziutlán, Puebla State, 1824; d. Mexico City, 1884). Cordero studied at the academy in Mexico City, then in Rome (1844–53). Historical subjects, portraits (for example, *Dolores Tosta de Santa Anna*, 1855; Mexico City, Rafael Manso Collection), and murals in S. Teresa (1857) and S. Fernando (1859) churches constitute his *oeuvre*.

BIBLIOGRAPHY. J. Fernández, *Arte moderno y contemporáneo de México*, Mexico City, 1952.

CORDIER, CHARLES-HENRI-JOSEPH. French sculptor (b. Cambrai, 1827; d. Algiers, 1905). He studied in Paris with Rude. A trip to Africa awakened in him an interest in sculpting the different human types. He also produced large works, including a Christopher Columbus monument for Mexico.

CORDOBA, PEDRO DE. Spanish painter (fl. Cordova, ca. 1450–1500). Two signed paintings survive: an altarpiece, *Annunciation with Donors and Patron Saints*, in the Cathedral of Cordova, painted for a Canon of the Cathedral and completed on Mar. 20, 1475, according to an inscrip-

tion; and a *Nativity*, an earlier work, formerly in the López Cepero Collection in Seville, signed by Pedro as son of Juan de Córdoba. Now lost sight of is the signed *Christ Taking Leave of His Mother*, formerly in the Pacully Collection, Paris, one of a series apparently dating from the end of the century. Some critics consider the Cordova altarpiece the most important surviving indigenous Cordovan painting of the period.

BIBLIOGRAPHY. A. L. Mayer, *La pintura española*, 2d ed., Barcelona, 1929.

CORDOVA (Cordoba). City in southern Spain on the Guadalquivir River. Cordova was famous in the Middle Ages as a center of Islamic and Jewish culture and for the type of leatherwork to which it gave its name. Of the successive Iberian, Punic, and Roman towns on the site, only the last has left any considerable monumental remains, including parts of a temple and a bridge still in use, though much rebuilt. Smaller finds from the several periods can be studied in the Provincial Archaeological Museum. Cordova, a wealthy city in Roman times, was the birthplace of Seneca and Lucan.

With the fall of the Roman Empire the city's prosperity was destroyed. It rose again more gloriously under Islamic rule, when Cordova was first the seat of an emirate (founded in 715) and then the capital of the independent Umayyad caliphate (from 756). By far the most important monument of Islamic Cordova is the Great Mosque, or Mezquita Grande, which has been turned into the Cathedral. Begun about 785 and subsequently enlarged on three occasions, the Great Mosque exercised an incalculable influence on the Islamic religious architecture of Spain and North Africa. Of the other 490 mosques reputed to have existed in Cordova in the 11th century, only three towers survive in the churches of S. Juan, Santiago, and S. Clara.

Cordova's medieval Jewish community is recalled by the synagogue of 1315 and by the house of the philosopher Maimonides, which is maintained as the Municipal Museum. Of the Christian churches surviving from the Middle Ages, that of S. Andrés (1241; late Romanesque with Islamic influence) is probably the most noteworthy. The 16th-century Mudejar-style Church of the Carmelites contains an altarpiece by Juan de Valdés Leal (1658). Public buildings of interest include the Ayuntamiento (1594–1613) and the 16th-century Hospital de la Caridad, which now houses the Museum of Fine Arts and the Julio Romero de Torres Collection.

See also CORDOVA: MOSQUE; CORDOVA: PROVINCIAL ARCHAEOLOGICAL MUSEUM.

BIBLIOGRAPHY. V. Orti Belmonte, *Guía artística de Córdoba*, Cordova, 1929; L. Torres Balbás, *La mezquita de Córdoba y las ruinas de Madinat al-Zahra*, Madrid, 1952.

WAYNE DYNES

CORDOVA: MOSQUE. Umayyad mosque constructed about 785 by the fugitive 'Abd ar-Rahman I, who had refounded the Umayyad caliphate at Cordova (modern Córdoba), Spain. It was enlarged in 848, again in 961–965 when a minaret of stone was added, and again in 987. The mosque was converted to a church in later centuries, and a small Gothic chapel was inserted in one area. Between 1523 and 1607 a much larger chapel was erected within the very heart of the structure. The mosque is some 585 feet along its main north-to-south axis and about 410 feet in width. The open court is very much smaller than the covered area, which consists of a forest of columns which establish nineteen aisles with some thirty-two bays. Hundreds of stone columns carry horseshoe arches; a second set of arches is superimposed in order to give greater height to the beamed ceiling. Details of decoration in stone and marble are of amazing richness, and the gold mosaic decoration executed in the sanctuary area in 965 is well preserved.

See also UMAYYAD ARCHITECTURE (SPAIN).

BIBLIOGRAPHY. G. Marçais, *Manual d'art musulman*, vol. 1, Paris, 1926; K. A. C. Creswell, *A Short Account of Muslim Architecture*, Harmondsworth, 1958.

CORDOVA: PROVINCIAL ARCHAEOLOGICAL MUSEUM. Spanish collection. The Iberian, Roman, and Christian pieces housed in the museum are overshadowed by the remarkable collection of Islamic minor-arts objects, which includes metalwork, ceramics, and calligraphic slabs.

BIBLIOGRAPHY. S. de los Santos Gener, *Guía del Museo Arqueológico Provincial de Córdoba*, Madrid, 1950.

CORFE, CASTLE OF. Norman English castle with a stone keep dating from the time of Henry I (1100–35). Situated on a steep Dorset hilltop, it commands a strong defensive position overlooking the Purbeck area. Its keep consisted of a fore-building, a well-designed square hall trimmed by exterior pilaster strips, and a north chamber. Despite the walls of two outer baileys, it was almost completely destroyed in 1646 by Parliamentary cannon fire.

BIBLIOGRAPHY. A. Weigall, *The Grand Tour of Norman England*, London, 1927; H. Braun, *The English Castle*, London, 1936.

CORI: TEMPLE OF HERCULES. Doric tetrastyle temple in central Italy. It has a high podium and a deep colon-

Cordova. The Great Mosque, showing some of the horseshoe arches.

nade. The temple is dated to the time of Sulla (138–78 B.C.) by an inscription on the architrave of the cella door. Concrete was used in the supporting walls and in the pediment. The shafts were faceted for one-third of their height and then fluted.

BIBLIOGRAPHY. W. J. Anderson, R. P. Spiers, and T. Ashby, *The Architecture of Greece and Rome*, vol. 2: *The Architecture of Ancient Rome*, London, 1927.

CORINTH, LOVIS. German painter (b. Tapiau, East Prussia, 1858; d. Berlin, 1925). He attended the Gymnasium and art school in Königsberg, and in 1880 began study under Von Löfftz at the Munich Academy of Art. After completing his program in 1884, he visited Paris and worked with Bouguereau and Fleury at the Académie Julian. Corinth was influenced by various artists—among them Rubens, Millet, Manet, and Jongkind—and finally by expressionism, all of which combined in his style to form German impressionism, despite the ostensible roughness or heavy spontaneity of many of his paintings and prints. He left Munich for Berlin in 1900, and, associated with two other masters of late impressionism, Max Slevogt and Max Liebermann, he became one of the most influential painters in Germany.

As a member of the prestigious Berlin Secession, however, Corinth sided with that once-liberal group against the rising pressures of the new expressionist movements. He succeeded Liebermann in the presidency of the group in 1911; but he lost the election in 1913, when the dealer Paul Cassirer and a majority of liberals took the leadership and formed the "Free Secession."

Corinth came to recognize the artistic strength of the expressionists he had once stubbornly opposed, and certain of the Brücke artists evidently returned the admiration. His late style grew more colorful, at times showing an affinity with expressionism yet not fully approaching it. His last pictures are among his finest; the *Walchensee Landscapes*, done in the years just preceding his death in 1925, are characteristic. His graphic works also reflect a certain liberation of style, their restless transitions of light and dark possessing an expressive force. His *Apocalypse* (1921; lithograph) and *Adam and Eve* (1923; color lithograph) are examples. Corinth stands as a transitional figure between an academic impressionism, which he had begun to transcend at the time of his death, and expressionism, which he did not altogether reach.

BIBLIOGRAPHY. A. Kuhn, *Lovis Corinth*, Berlin, 1925; E. Waldmann, *Die Kunst des Realismus und des Impressionismus im 19. Jahrhundert*, Berlin, 1927; L. Justi, *Von Corinth bis Klee*, Berlin, 1931; G. von der Osten, *Lovis Corinth*, Munich, 1955.

JOHN C. GALLOWAY

CORINTH. Greek city located near the southwest end of the isthmus between the Peloponnesus and Megaris on the Greek mainland. The southern boundary of the ancient city was formed by its citadel, Acrocorinth, which is more than 1,800 feet high.

Corinth and the surrounding area were the scene of early and extensive prehistoric habitation. A period of prosperity and growth occurred in the Neolithic period (pre-3000 B.C.) and the Early Bronze Age (ca. 3000–2000 B.C.),

Lovis Corinth, *The Red Christ*, 1923. New Pinacothek, Munich.

Corinthian order. The most elaborate of the Greek styles.

but only with Dorian control of the Peloponnesus did Corinth begin to thrive.

From the 8th to the 6th century B.C., Corinth was under the rule of powerful clans, first the Bacchiadae and then the Cypselids (after the tyrant Cypselus). This period saw the rise of Corinth as a great sea power. Important colonies were founded in the west—such as Syracuse and Corcyra (Corfu)—and the trade contacts that were formed with the East, particularly Phoenicia, led to the rise of the "Orientalizing" style in Greek art, a development in which proto-Corinthian (725–650 B.C.) and Corinthian (680–550 B.C.) pottery played a major role.

The rise of Athens caused a decline in the prosperity of Corinth during the 5th and 4th centuries. It regained its importance in the Hellenistic period, as the leader of the Achaean League, but in 146 B.C. the Romans, led by the consul Mummius, sacked and totally desecrated the city. It lay deserted until 44 B.C., when Julius Caesar refounded it as a Roman colony.

The sack of Corinth by Mummius explains why most of the remains of the city visible today date from the Roman period. The most prominent monument of the pre-Roman period is the Doric Temple of Apollo (ca. 540 B.C.), of which seven columns still stand. South of the temple lay the area of the agora. The most remarkable building in this sector was the South Stoa (colonnade with shops, offices and so on), originally built in the 4th century B.C., but destroyed by Mummius and restored in the Roman period. It was the largest secular building in ancient Greece. In front of the South Stoa is the Roman bema (rostrum) before which St. Paul was called by the

Roman governor Gallio (Acts 18). Running northward out of the city from the agora is the Lechaeum road, which with its solid pavement and sidewalks is one of the outstanding examples of civil engineering in ancient Greece. Many other civic, commercial, and private buildings of the Roman period—including a theater, an odeum, and a private villa—and an early Christian church have been unearthed by the American excavations, which were begun in 1896 and are still under way.

BIBLIOGRAPHY. American School of Classical Studies at Athens, *Ancient Corinth: A Guide to the Excavations and Museum*, 6th ed., Athens, 1954.

JEROME J. POLLITT

CORINTHIAN ORDER. Essentially, a later variation of the Ionic order, differing from it only in the type of column capital and in some proportions. The Corinthian capital, an arrangement of tendrils and palmettes emerging from a base of acanthus leaves, was said to have been invented by the sculptor Callimachus in the late 5th century B.C. *See* CALLIMACHUS.

The earliest known examples, now lost, came from the cella of the Temple of Apollo at Bassae. Other early examples of its use in Greece are found in the Temple of Athena at Tegea (ca. 360 B.C.), the tholoi at Delphi (ca. 400 B.C.) and Epidaurus (ca. 350 B.C.), and the Choragic Monument of Lysicrates in Athens (334 B.C.). It is in structures belonging to the late Hellenistic and Roman periods, however (for example, the Olympieion in Athens), that we see the Corinthian style in full flower. *See* BASSAE; LYSICRATES, CHORAGIC MONUMENT OF, ATHENS; OLYMPIEION, ATHENS.

BIBLIOGRAPHY. D. S. Robertson, *A Handbook of Greek and Roman Architecture*, 2d ed., Cambridge, Eng., 1959.

Corneille de Lyon, *Portrait of Clément Marot*. Louvre, Paris.

CORNEILLE (Cornelis van Beverloo). Dutch painter (1922–   ). Born in Liège, Belgium, of Dutch parents, he studied drawing at the Academy of Fine Arts in Amsterdam but was self-taught as a painter. He was a founding member, with Appel, Jorn, and Constant, of the CoBrA group (1948); but, in the path of Klee and Miró, he followed a less violent and expressionistic direction. His delicately detailed and compartmented images, although abstract, sensitively evoke the light and forms of nature. *See* CoBrA Group.

CORNEILLE DE LYON (Corneille de la Haye). French portrait painter (b. The Hague? ca. 1500; d. Lyons, ca. 1574). He went to France from The Hague (his name may originally have been Corneliszen) and was established in Lyons by 1534, when he was Painter to Queen Eleanor. A painter at the court of the Dauphin in 1541, he was naturalized and made Painter to King Henry II in 1547 and to Charles IX in 1564. Corneille painted portraits of members of the court almost exclusively; only one burgher portrait is known, that of P. Aymeric (1534; French private collection).

There are no signed works by Corneille; all attributions are based on a group of portraits that were once in the R. de Gaignères Collection (1642–1715). Of these, only one is fully recorded, that of Charles de la Rochefoucault (Paris, Louvre). A great number of portraits are attributed to Corneille de Lyon, but only those closest to the Gaignères group and of the highest quality may be from his hand alone, as it is evident that he had a large workshop. It was visited in 1551 by the Venetian ambassador G.

Capelli, who marveled at the quantity of small portraits representing "all the court," and by Catherine de Médicis (1564), who praised the artist for his portrait of her. His sons Corneille II and Jacques and his sister (d. 1584) may have been active in his workshop.

In contrast to the case of Clouet and other French artists, no drawings or preparatory sketches by Corneille are known, and it is thought that he drew directly on his panels. His type of portraiture, ultimately derived from Joos van Cleve, was highly popular even outside France, notably in Germany, the Netherlands, and Italy. Characteristic are the small size, the uniform background (green or blue), and the successful combination of realism and courtly elegance. The heads, thinly painted though richly modeled, receive most of the attention, and the garments are summarily treated. Among the best portraits are *Clément Marot* (Louvre), *Catherine de Médicis* (Versailles, Museum), *Madeleine de France* (Blois, Museum of Ancient Art), and *Charles de Cossé-Brissac* (New York, Metropolitan Museum). Engravings signed CC, including a *Last Judgment* of 1547, *L'Epitomé des rois de France* of 1551 (69 engravings), and other engraved works have been attributed to him, though not without considerable disagreement among scholars.

BIBLIOGRAPHY. E. Moreau-Nélaton, *Les Clouet et leurs émules*, 3 vols., Paris, 1924; L. Dimier, *Histoire de la peinture de portrait en France au XVIe siècle...*, 3 vols., Paris, 1924–26.

PHILIPPE DE MONTEBELLO

CORNEILLE VAN CLEVE. French sculptor (1645–1732). He was a pupil of François Anguier. He worked at Versailles, under the supervision of J.-H. Mansart, mainly on the high altar of the chapel. Another work typical of his French classical manner is a marble group, *Loire and Loret*, in the Tuileries Garden.

BIBLIOGRAPHY. P. Francastel, *La Sculpture de Versailles*, Paris, 1930.

CORNEJO, PEDRO DUQUE, *see* DUQUE CORNEJO, PEDRO.

CORNELISZ., JACOB VAN OOSTSANEN (Jacob of Amsterdam). Dutch painter (b. Oostsanen, ca. 1470; d. Amsterdam, before 1533). His early work is derived from Geertgen, but his mature style was shaped by the technique of wood engraving and his 150 woodcuts show Dürer's influence. His religious scenes sometimes appear overcrowded. Perspective is not stressed, yet the textures of flesh and garments are clearly suggested. His backgrounds are striking: the *David and Abigail* in the National Museum in Copenhagen opens upon a densely wooded landscape; the *Nativity* of 1512, upon a seascape. His plebeian portraits set a tradition for Amsterdam. Cornelisz. made several versions of such stock themes as the Adoration of the Magi. He was a teacher of Jan van Scorel.

BIBLIOGRAPHY. J. Leymarie, *Dutch Painting*, Geneva, 1956.

CORNELIUS, PETER. German painter (b. Düsseldorf, 1783; d. Berlin, 1867). He studied at the Düsseldorf Academy, worked in Frankfurt am Main, and then, about 1811, went to Rome, where he became part of the Nazarene group of German artists. Like theirs, Cornelius's painting style was highly eclectic, deriving from various painters of the Italian Renaissance as well as from Northern artists, especially Dürer. The grandeur and energy of his com-

Peter Cornelius, *The Last Judgment*. Former State Museums, Berlin.

positions made Cornelius a leading German monumental painter of his time. His dramatic linearity growing into a sort of classicism can be seen in the cartoon of *The Four Horsemen of the Apocalypse* (ca. 1850; Berlin, former State Museums).

BIBLIOGRAPHY. C. Eckert, *Peter Cornelius*, Leipzig, 1906.

CORNELL, JOSEPH. American artist (1903–   ). Cornell was represented in the first American exhibition of the surrealists, at Julien Levy's gallery in New York (1932), and was associated with surrealist artists and writers during the 1930s and 1940s. His work has some affinity with surrealism and Dada, particularly with Marcel Duchamp, but is unique, consistent, and deeply personal. In his characteristic works, objects and cut-out pictures are arranged in small, stage-like boxes, which appear as microcosmic universes of poetic associations.

CORNELL UNIVERSITY: ANDREW DICKSON WHITE MUSEUM OF ART, *see* ITHACA, N.Y.: ANDREW DICKSON WHITE MUSEUM OF ART, CORNELL UNIVERSITY.

CORNER DELLA CA GRANDE PALACE, VENICE. Italian palace built for the wealthy Corner family after 1531. It was executed in a classically inspired style from a project by Jacopo Sansovino. The façade, rusticated on the ground floor with the Ionic and Corinthian orders on the first and second floors, respectively, is adapted to the character of the traditional Venetian house.

BIBLIOGRAPHY. E. Bassi, *Architettura del sei e settecento a Venezia*, Naples, 1962.

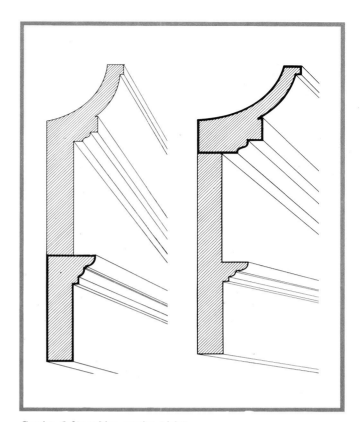

Cornice (left); raking cornice (right).

CORNETO (Tarquinia), TOMBS OF, *see* ETRUSCAN ART.

CORNFIELD WITH CYPRESS. Oil painting by Van Gogh in the Tate Gallery, London. *See* VAN GOGH, VINCENT WILLEM.

CORNICE. Projecting portion at the top of a wall. In classic and Renaissance architecture, it is the crowning or upper part of the entablature. The cornice in Greek architecture—consisting of bed molding, corona, and cyma—was elaborated according to a type, such as the Doric, Ionic, or Corinthian.

CORNICE, RAKING. Sloping cornice, as in the inclined cornice of the pediment in classical temples.

CORNUCOPIA (Horn of Plenty). Animal's horn, usually twisted, filled with fruit and flowers. It is a symbol of prosperity and abundance, especially in Roman times. In art the horn is usually placed in the hands of, or associated with, Plutus, Fortuna, Copia, or other similar deities. The Roman cornucopia is directly related to the Greek horn of Amaltheia.

CORO. Spanish choir, frequently situated west of the crossing, as in the Cathedrals of Burgos and Avila.

COROMANDEL LACQUER. Term once used to designate a class of Chinese screens with designs cut through several layers of lacquer to the wood foundation. The wood was then painted with various colors. The designs showed flowers, animals, birds, and lucky emblems; historical and legendary scenes; and landscapes, in restrained pure tones on black ground.

This technique was developed first for the Chinese market but proved to be popular among Westerners in the 18th and 19th centuries; it became · essentially an export art for the Chinese. Screens, chests, and panels utilizing the technique were transshiped from the Coromandel coast of southwest India; hence the misnomer "Coromandel."

CORONA. Projecting part of a cornice with a deep and usually plain vertical face. Its soffit is often recessed to form a drip. The corona in Greek architecture was frequently painted with a fret design.

CORONATION GOSPELS. Carolingian illuminated manuscript, in the Treasury, Vienna. *See* PALACE SCHOOL.

CORONATION OF MARY, *see* WOLFGANG ALTAR.

CORONATION OF NAPOLEON. Oil painting by David, in the Louvre, Paris. *See* DAVID, JACQUES-LOUIS.

CORONEL, RAFAEL. Mexican painter (1932–   ). Born in Zacatecas, Coronel was trained in Mexico City and has exhibited there since 1954. He has painted murals in the National Institute of Anthropology and History in Mexico City (1964). Coronel was one of Mexico's representatives at the São Paulo Bienal in 1965. Grotesque figures are his main theme.

COROT, JEAN-BAPTISTE-CAMILLE. French painter (1796–1875). Corot was apprenticed to a draper for seven years, but in 1822 his father settled an annual pension on him and allowed him to become a painter. Michallon, to whom Corot turned first, died too soon to give him more than the advice to study nature "naïvely and conscientiously." His second teacher, Victor Bertin, introduced him to the practices of classicist landscape composition. This was a highly formalized discipline, resting on the manipulation of stock types: elegantly contoured mountain ranges in the distance, overlapping planes in the middle, and looming trees silhouetted in the foreground—harmonious arrangements meant to be pictorially effective rather than true to visual experience. Despite its seeming sterility, the classicist "science" of composition gave to Corot that effortless assurance in the formal organization of landscapes which is one of his strongest qualities.

Corot traveled in Italy (1825–28) in deference to the accepted notion that the Italian countryside was the practical school of landscape painting. For nearly three years, he painted under the blue sky, sometimes among the ruins of Rome, more often in the open country of the Campagna and the Sabine or Albani mountains. There he taught himself the summary recording of landscape impressions by means of small oil sketches executed on the spot, with a consequent freshness and spontaneity. The companions of his Roman stay, Edouard Bertin and Caruelle d'Aligny, painted in a similar style. Corot surpassed them all in the exquisite simplicity and clarity of his compositions, which are harmonious without artifice; in the discreet ra-

diance of his colors, infinitely rich within a narrow range of hues; and in the quiet serenity of the spaces which open up in these small canvases (*Forum*, 1826; *Colosseum*, 1826; both Paris, Louvre). The outward results of this work were the two paintings exhibited at the Salon of 1827, a *Campagna Landscape* (lost) and *Narni Bridge* (Louvre), heavier, darker, and more conventional than the luminous studies on which they are based.

Back in France, he continued his restless voyaging in quest of landscape motifs. From 1829 to 1834 he shuttled back and forth between Normandy and Burgundy, with frequent, prolonged stays in the Forest of Fontainebleau. About 1830 such landscapes as *Chartres Cathedral* (1830; Louvre) become conspicuously light-filled. At the same time, he painted forest scenes that anticipate the Barbizon school and reflect familiarity with Constable's *Haywain* (notably, Corot's Salon picture of 1833, *Cart Fording a Stream in the Forest of Fontainebleau*).

A second voyage to Italy in 1834 produced studies of Volterra, Florence, Riva, and Venice, denser in tonality and more richly furnished compositionally than the landscapes of the earlier Italian stay. On returning to France, Corot undertook a number of large, composed views in the tradition of the "historical landscape" and more classical in conception than his previous work (*Hagar in the Desert*, Salon of 1835, New York, Metropolitan Museum; *Silenus*, Salon of 1838, Minneapolis, Institute of Fine Arts); they are not among his most successful works.

Corot's annual routine was to paint outdoors during the good-weather season and to return to his studio in the winter to translate his sketches into carefully arranged compositions with mythological or Biblical bywork, suitable for exhibition at the Salon. It was only in 1848 that he began occasionally to exhibit the sketches themselves. Yet it is quite evident that he was happiest when working spontaneously, from nature, and in small formats. He needed the stimulus of visual experience and was unfailingly true to the precise nuances of light or atmosphere. When he worked from memory, his work sometimes became labored and dully competent.

Recognition gradually came to Corot after 1840 with occasional government purchases and friendly press notices. In 1843 he visited Italy for the third time, returning with magnificent sketches of Tivoli, Lake Nemi, and the delightful nude *Marietta* (Fine Arts Museum of the City of Paris). Figure painting had always played a role in his work, and he had produced innumerable portraits of friends and relatives, particularly of children. From that time on, he frequently posed female figures in landscapes or in the studio. These quiet, portraitlike studies of pensive women, provided with musical instruments and decked out in fantastic dresses, remained unappreciated by Corot's contemporaries, even after the success of his landscape painting; today they are prized as being among his most powerful and beautiful works (*Shepherdess Reading*, ca. 1855, Winterthur, Reinhart Foundation; *Woman in the Studio*, ca. 1865, Louvre; *La Femme à la perle*, ca. 1868–70, Louvre).

The years between 1845 and 1855 mark a high point in Corot's realist landscape painting and, at the same time, a moment of transition. Some of the most accomplished plein-air sketches, still in the clear and luminous so-called "early" manner, date from this time (*La Rochelle*, 1852,

Jean-Baptiste-Camille Corot, *Memory of Mortefontaine*, 1864. Oil on canvas. Louvre, Paris.

New York, Stephen Clark Collection; *Breton Women at the Fountain*, Louvre). Yet it was also in these years that he painted the first of the misty dream-landscapes that long were considered his most characteristic and his best works. Silvery, crepuscular skies behind masses of half-transparent foliage, spreading over quiet ponds and distant buildings, and over foregrounds peopled with shepherds or flower-gathering children—these imagined landscapes at their best are poems of form and color, translations into a romantic language of the old constructed landscapes of classicism (*Memory of Castel Gandolfo*, ca. 1865, Louvre; *Memory of Mortefontaine*, 1864, Louvre). At worst, they are monotonous and facile. One particular quality of Corot's talent that they reveal is the gift for harmonious surface decoration. It is unfortunate that he was denied the opportunity of trying large-scale wall painting (his bathroom frescoes for M. Robert at Mantes, now in the Louvre).

Throughout his middle and later years, Corot continued his itinerant life, traveling from one corner of France to the other, venturing into Holland, Switzerland, and England. Success came in the 1850s; patronized by the government and by the emperor (and later hounded by dealers), Corot gradually became wealthy and was able to give large

sums to good causes, including the support of the family of Millet and of the aging Daumier. In response to pressing demands, he indulged in a somewhat repetitive mass production of poetic, vaporous landscapes. But at the same time he continued to paint, for his own amusement, landscapes in that more clearly defined and richly chromatic manner that he had first developed in Italy. Such late masterpieces as *The Belfry of Douai* (1871; Louvre) and *Interior of the Cathedral of Sens* (1874; Louvre) prove to what degree he preserved his keenness of observation and aristocratic refinement of tone and color until the very end.

After a decline in valuation in the early 20th century, Corot is once again regarded as one of the greatest artists of the 19th century and, with Constable, as one of the supreme masters of that visual realism, tinged with romantic feeling, which was a significant international current during the earlier part of that period. His paintings are to be found in all the principal museums of the world, particularly at the Louvre. Less well known than it should be is Corot's graphic work, his extremely original pen-and-pencil draftsmanship, his etchings and photo-clichés (a technique of drawing with a needle on a blackened pane of glass from which photographic prints can then be taken, as from a negative).

BIBLIOGRAPHY. A. Robaut and E. Moreau-Nélaton, *L'Oeuvre de Corot*, 4 vols., Paris, 1904–06; E. Moreau-Nélaton, *Corot; raconté par lui-même*, 2 vols., Paris, 1924; A. Schoeller and J. Diéterle, *Corot*, Paris, 1948; G. Bazin, *Corot*, Paris, 1951.

LORENZ EITNER

CORPORA, ANTONIO. Italian painter (1909–   ). After studies in his native Tunis, he lived in Florence, Paris, and Milan during the 1930s, working in a postimpressionist style and writing defenses of modern art, particularly in opposition to the conservative Novecento group. In Rome (1945) he joined with a neocubist group that included Guttuso and Frazzini, but turned to his own form of less formal abstraction after 1952. In his best works, which draw on a restrained automatism, highlights and ridges of paint emerge out of a general light and color field with a lyric intensity.

CORPUS CHRISTI COLLEGE, see CAMBRIDGE, ENGLAND; OXFORD.

CORREA FAMILY. Mexican painters (provenance uncertain): Juan (fl. ca. 1674–early 18th cent.), Juan (?), and Nicolás (fl. ca. 1695). Juan executed numerous paintings, especially for the Cathedral of Mexico, of a crowded and turbulent character. Probably a pupil of Antonio Rodríguez, he is best known for an *Assumption* in the Cathedral which displays iconographical elements peculiar to the Mexican baroque. To a second Juan, perhaps his son, are attributed certain pictures now located in Guatemala. Nicolás, a younger, less fecund member, painted simpler and gentler works such as the delightful *Virgin and Child with S. Rosalía* (1695) in the Academia de Bellas Artes in Mexico City.

BIBLIOGRAPHY. D. Angulo Iñiguez, *Historia del arte hispanoamericano*, vol. 2, Barcelona, 1950.

CORREGGIO. Italian painter of Parma, one of the greatest artists of the Renaissance (1489–1534). His real name was Antonio Allegri, but he was called by the name of the small town where he was born and always maintained a home. Early reports call him a pupil of Bianchi Ferrari in Modena, and in 1506 he was in Mantua, where he painted the four Evangelists in the funeral chapel (S. Andrea) of Mantegna, who died in that year. Back in Correggio, he painted the small Madonna with saints in a similar style; both show Mantegnesque composition and motifs but a softer, more up-to-date surface probably stimulated by Francia and Costa. These painters dominated the art of Ferrara and Bologna, which, like Mantua and Modena, are near Correggio.

He produced for S. Francesco, Correggio, his first major work, the altarpiece *Madonna with St. Francis* (1514–15; Dresden, State Art Collections, Picture Gallery). Still alluding to Mantegna and Francia, the work shows a fully mature command of broad moving forms and especially of intense light. A group of small works with somewhat Mantegnesque forms is also early, notably the Madonnas of Florence (Uffizi) and Modena (Este Gallery). Another group of small pictures shares more elaboration of color, details of costume, network of gestures, and pastoral overtones recalling Dosso. Chief of these are the *Nativity* (Mi-

lan, Brera), *Adoration of the Magi* (Brera), a *Madonna* (Madrid, Prado), and the *"Gypsy" Madonna* (Naples, Capodimonte).

Sometime between 1515 and 1520 Correggio must have gone to Parma to produce the work that first made him famous, the frescoes of the Camera di S. Paolo. Painted in a convent for the private apartment of the abbess, they are entirely secular. The pattern of the ceiling is a grape arbor with oval openings in which cupids appear. At the top of the walls is a row of monochromatic scenes with sixteen symbolic subjects, Adonis, Chastity, and so on. Most of the subjects are clear but the general program is not. In this very original work Correggio first states his art fully, showing a debt to the style of Leonardo but transforming it. His theme is the figure in light—gray, very soft, and tending to be sinuous. It is almost cloudy and intangible, and it absorbs the atmosphere and is absorbed by it, yet is always distinct and unified. Its psychology is that of smiling charm. This lightweight, sophisticated imagery, feathery and elegant, has been subject to drastic swings of taste, called the peak of art in the 18th century but regarded as decadent and pale in other eras.

The large figure over the fireplace of the Camera, *Diana*, is similar to his second major altarpiece, *Rest on the Flight into Egypt* (Uffizi). In an original theme, Correggio's new forms develop in a remarkable composition of softly sliding, asymmetrical diagonals. Asymmetry with night effects dominates the inventive *Christ Taking Leave of His Mother* (London, National Gallery). The dark *Four Saints* (New York, Metropolitan Museum), sometimes dated 1517, is relatively routine.

The S. Paolo frescoes led to the commission to fresco the dome of S. Giovanni Evangelista, Parma (1520–23). Correggio's aerial style was completely suited to the high hemisphere, where the flying Christ at the center flings himself into the sun, and rings of clouds and figures mingle below. Studies of figures in soft red chalk, with details of foreshortening, remind us that the body retains its form in this atmosphere. The dome had a huge influence on the baroque, but differs from baroque art in that it makes no point of suggesting effort and pressure; the figures are entirely at home, as are those in the lunettes below of St. John and the Coronation of the Virgin.

From the same church and probably the same time are *The Descent from the Cross* and *The Martyrdom of SS. Placidus and Flavia* (both Parma, Gallery), with fluttering scalloped robes in richer color. Related are the similarly colorful anthology piece *Adoration of the Child* (Uffizi), which may be a little earlier, and the brilliant nocturnal *Christ in the Garden* (London, Wellington Museum). Less surprising, though of supreme elegance, are *The Marriage of St. Catherine* (Paris, Louvre), *St. Catherine* (Middlesex, Hampton Court), and *Christ and Magdalene* (Prado). *The Education of Cupid* (London, National Gallery) is generally thought to be of these years, too.

The cupola led at once to the commission for frescoing the Cathedral dome (1524–30) on a far larger scale. *The Assumption of the Virgin* is surrounded by several rings of angels, and the figures now blend with each other, while

Correggio, *Antiope*, ca. 1524–25. Louvre, Paris.

their blowing robes interlock vibrantly. Many drawings exist, with hazy surfaces that nonetheless record exact anatomical detail.

More slowly during these years Correggio produced a series of famous altarpieces. *The Madonna with SS. Roche and Sebastian* (Dresden, State Art Collections) may be the first. The twining foreground figures lead up and back to the Virgin in the sky; the stress of the funneling movement is acute. *The Madonna with St. Jerome* (finished 1528; Parma, Gallery) develops the sliding diagonal with interlocking figures in a reduced, subtle form. *The Rest on the Flight* (*Madonna della Scodella*, 1524–30; Parma, Gallery) seems a synthesis of the two Madonnas above, with upward diagonal and luminous charm. *The Adoration of the Shepherds* (*The Night*, commissioned 1522, painted 1529–30; Dresden, State Art Collections) is the most vehement of his altarpieces, with sharp shadow, figures composed in an isosceles triangle on its side, and difficult spatial depth. *The Madonna with St. George* (Dresden, State Art Collections), with highly refined surface, is surprisingly classical. It was painted for the Cathedral of Modena.

After 1530 the artist left Parma and returned to his native town, but he worked especially for the Duke of Mantua. In his last years he did mainly a group of works for the Duke to present to Emperor Charles V. Representing the loves of Jupiter, they are a departure in theme and a new step in exploring forms. *Leda* (Berlin, former State Museums) uses a deep shadowy landscape in which small twining figures are absorbed. *Antiope* (Louvre), which is sometimes dated earlier than *Leda*, presents two figures in the same loose diagonal, softly absorbed in a wooded landscape. *Danaë* (Rome, Borghese) is presented as an interior, with a driving widening movement from left to right. The importance of space in these works is new. Still more surprising is the tall narrow *Ganymede* (Vienna, Museum of

Art History), in which the dog near us looks up a hazy mountain to the fluttering boy; it is a closed-down version of the Cathedral dome. Most original is *Io* (Vienna, Museum of Art History), in which the swooning figure, softly falling back to us, is engulfed by the pearly cloud. This figure is the concentrated essence and point of arrival of Correggio's art.

BIBLIOGRAPHY. A. E. Popham, *Correggio's Drawings*, London, 1957; A. A. Correggio, *Tutta la pittura del Correggio*, ed. P. Bianconi, 2d ed., Milan, 1960; S. Bottari, *Correggio*, Milan, 1961.
CREIGHTON GILBERT

CORRIDO. Popular Mexican form of political and social satire. Traditionally, the *corrido* is a forceful woodcut illustrating a strongly satirical ballad printed on gaily colored thin paper and sold cheaply. As a form of folk art, it reached a climax early in the 20th century with Posada, who developed a metal relief technique. He often portrayed the subjects as *calaveras* (skeletons), a familiar Mexican folk symbol. *Corridos* have also been employed in bitter topical commentary by the Taller de Gráfica Popular. *See* POSADA, JOSE GUADALUPE; TALLER DE GRAFICA POPULAR.

CORSINI PALACE, FLORENCE. Large baroque Italian palace, facing the Arno, constructed (1648–56) by Pier Francesco Silvani and Antonio Ferri. Two wings joined by a central building enclose a court with monumental stairs. The palace houses the most important private collection of paintings in Florence.

BIBLIOGRAPHY. V. Golzio, *Il seicento e il settecento*, Turin, 1950.

CORTE, JOSSE DE (Giusto Cort; Lecurt). Italian sculptor (b. Ypres, 1627; fl. Venice from 1657; d. 1679). His monumental group for the high altar of S. Maria della Salute in Venice is characteristic of late-baroque exuberance in its use of dramatic poses, but reveals the artist's Flemish background in the sharply delineated and delicate treatment of drapery and detail.

BIBLIOGRAPHY. R. Wittkower, *Art and Architecture in Italy, 1600–1750*, Baltimore, 1958.

CORTE, CASTELLO DI, MANTUA, *see* MANTEGNA, ANDREA; MANTUA: GALLERY AND MUSEUM OF THE DUCAL PALACE.

CORTESE, GUGLIELMO, *see* COURTOIS, GUILLAUME.

CORTESE, P. GIACOMO, *see* COURTOIS, JACQUES.

CORTILE. Interior court (Italian *corte*, "court"), often with surrounding passages and adjoining rooms. Such a *cortile* is found in the Renaissance Palazzo Pietro Massimi in Rome and the Doge's Palace in Venice. The open *cortili* of the Italian Renaissance were frequently several stories high, in contrast to the usually one-storied medieval cloister garth and the early Christian atrium.

CORTONA, DOMENICO DA, *see* BOCCADOR.

CORTONA, PIETRO DA (Pietro Berrettini). Italian painter and architect (b. Cortona, 1596; d. Rome, 1669). He went to Rome (ca. 1612–13) with his teacher, the Florentine

Cortile. Open interior court found in Italian Renaissance palaces.

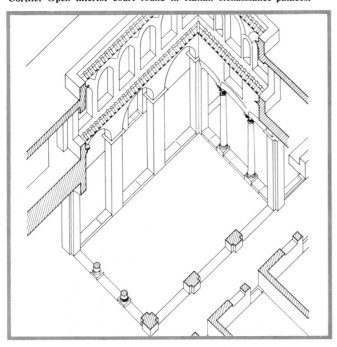

Pietro da Cortona, the portico and façade of S. Maria della Pace, modernized by the architect in 1656–57.

Andrea Commodi, and then worked with Baccio Ciarpi. Raphael, Polidoro, the Carraccis, and antique statuary, however, might well be considered his real masters. His background in classicism was further strengthened after 1623, when Marcello Sacchetti became his patron. Through him Cortona met Cardinal Francesco Barberini and Cassiano del Pozzo, assuring his success in Rome, where he remained except for a brief trip to Florence and Venice (1637) and a later sojourn in Florence (1640–47).

The classical leanings of his patrons and Cortona's early studies are reflected in such frescoes as those in Sta Bibiana, Rome (1524–26), with their archaeological details and frieze of figures extending across a stage of space in the foreground. Even here the voluminous forms, broad light effects, and sense of movement insinuate the stylistic innovations of his mature work, the ceiling frescoes in the Gran Salone of the Barberini Palace, Rome (1633–39), one of the first monuments of the full-blooded baroque style in Italy. Here an architectural framework of simulated stucco is filled with, and overlapped by, *mouvementé* figures and clouds, with a continuum of illusionistic space beyond, all of which creates an overwhelming effect of profusion and movement. This blending of elements was not repeated by Cortona; in his frescoes in the Pitti Palace, Florence (1640–47), he carefully separated the framework from the scenes it contains, a structural formula that is maintained in his frescoes in S. Maria in Vallicella, Rome (1647–51; 1655–56).

Cortona was the *principe* of the Academy of St. Luke from 1634 to 1638. During this period he engaged in a series of discussions with the classicist Andrea Sacchi, ostensibly about the number of figures that should appear in a painting. The argument was, in fact, basically concerned with style, that is, classical versus baroque. Cortona carried on a tradition of liberal taste that had been relatively continuous since the Carraccis, while Sacchi opposed Cortona's magnificence and set forth his own rigid classical doctrine. This dichotomy also appeared on the level of production; two opposing camps formed within the previously heterogeneous style of 17th-century Roman painting: Cortona's baroque and the classicism of such painters as Sacchi and Poussin.

BIBLIOGRAPHY. G. Ottonelli and P. Berettini, *Trattato della pittura e scultura . . .*, Florence, 1652; Cortona, *Mostra di Pietro da Cortona, 1956* (catalog), Rome, 1956; R. Wittkower, *Art and Architecture in Italy, 1600–1750*, Baltimore, 1958; G. Briganti, *Pietro da Cortona, o della pittura barocca*, Florence, 1962.

STEPHEN E. OSTROW

CORTONA AS ARCHITECT

Cortona's architecture is as important as his painting and, if anything, more original. His earliest architectural work may be the villa, now the Chigi Palace, at Castel Fusano (1626–30), but his ingenuity is seen first in the Villa del Pigneto near Rome, built for the Sacchetti family about 1630. The building, now destroyed, exhibited a monumental niche in the main façade and utilized curves in a plan that tied a complex system of stairs and terraces to the façade. Its antecedents include such monuments as the Temple of Fortuna at Palestrina (Praeneste), and it is probably correct to say that it was one of the most significant buildings of the period.

In 1634 Cortona began work in the crypt of the church of the Academy of St. Luke, of which he was *principe*, and

discovered the body of St. Martina. The following year a large new church, SS. Martina e Luca, was begun (finished 1650). The plan is a modified Greek cross, and the interior elevation is given a sculptural undulating surface by columns that articulate the crossing piers and reappear, apparently within the wall plane, in the apsidal ends. As in Borromini's works, the interior is white. The vaults are decorated by undulating geometric coffering of a novel type. Figural sculpture and painting are eliminated or play a subsidiary part in Cortona's architecture. In SS. Martina e Luca the architectural forms have roots in 16th-century Florence, but they are given new meaning. The façade, in two equal stories, is slightly curved and is decorated in a style consonant with the interior. The dome uses piled-up sculptural forms with an exuberance unique in Rome.

In his modernization of S. Maria della Pace (1656–57), Cortona joined his new façade with a city-planning scheme to rebuild the tiny piazza in front, forming a kind of theater. The outstanding element is the projecting segmental portico on paired columns, echoed by concave wings above to left and right that connect the church with the adjoining buildings. The upper façade seems to grow out of this shell, resulting in a theatrical interplay of curved forms that is surprising and delightful in the tiny context. *See* SANTA MARIA DELLA PACE, ROME.

The façade of S. Maria in Via Lata (1658–62) is by contrast relatively classicizing; it employs two orders with an open central arch derived from antique precedent. Cortona's dome for S. Carlo al Corso is his least successful work. Other projects, for the Louvre and for the Pitti Palace in Florence, among others, remained on paper. The latter would have had a garden theater echoing the ancient Palestrina complex. His restoration of the Palestrina sanctuary, published in 1655, had wide repercussions.

BIBLIOGRAPHY. R. Wittkower, *Art and Architecture in Italy, 1600–1750*, Baltimore, 1958.

HOWARD HIBBARD

CORTONA: SAN FRANCESCO. Italian church built in 1245 by Brother Elia, who was then head of the Franciscan order. It has the characteristic plan of the earliest Franciscan churches, with a nave terminating in three rectangular chapels, the central one the widest.

BIBLIOGRAPHY. G. Mancini, *Cortona, Montecchio Vesponi e Castiglione Fiorentino*, Bergamo, 1909.

CORTOT, JEAN PIERRE. French sculptor (b. Paris, 1787; d. there, 1843). He studied at the Ecole des Beaux-Arts in Paris and won the Prix de Rome in 1809. Cortot was a classicist sculptor who, although influenced by Canova, occasionally tended toward baroque excitement. The strictly neoclassical costume, attributes, and treatment of the figures of the *Triumph of Napoleon in 1809–10* (ca. 1833) on the Arc de Triomphe de l'Etoile are a cold counterpart to Rude's *La Marseillaise* on the same monument. The influence of Canova is more strongly seen in the *Messenger from Marathon* (1834; Paris, Louvre).

CORVEY (Korvey), MONASTERY CHURCH OF. Carolingian church in Corvey an der Weser, near Höxter, Germany. It was founded in 822 but was not completed until 885. The founding monks were from Corbie, Picardy, and were under the influence of St-Riquier. This meant con-

The Cosmatis, detail of the tomb of Cardinal Fieschi, S. Lorenzo fuori le Mura, Rome.

struction of a three-aisled church with transeptlike wings and eastern apses. As in St-Riquier, the most impressive feature of Corvey is the westwork (873–885).

The westwork consists of a massive blocklike front unit that incorporates the first aisle bays. The unit is capped by a low tower with a pyramidal roof. To the front of this central tower, but not rising quite so high, are two flanking staircase towers. The entire unit strongly resembles a fortress, a function for which the westwork was undoubtedly created. The one at Corvey is the best extant example of this notable feature of Carolingian architecture.

COSCI, see BALDUCCIO, GIOVANNI (COSCI).

COSGROVE, STANLEY MOREL. Canadian painter (1911–   ). He was born in Montreal and, after studying there, worked under Orozco in Mexico. A painter of figures, landscapes, and still life, he lives and teaches in Montreal.

BIBLIOGRAPHY. D. W. Buchanan, *The Growth of Canadian Painting*, London, 1950.

COSIMO, PIERO DI, see PIERO DI COSIMO.

COSINI, SILVIO. Italian sculptor (b. Poggibonsi, 1495; d. ca. 1547). The pupil of Andrea Ferrucci of Fiesole, he collaborated with him on the tombs of A. Strozzi and Maffei Volterrano. He then worked on the Medici Chapel, Florence, where he met and was influenced by Michelangelo. Some of his later works are in Pisa, Genoa, and Milan.

COSMAS AND DAMIAN, SS. Twin brothers of Arab origin (3d cent.). They practiced medicine in Cilicia without fee to win their clients to the Christian faith. Under Diocletian they miraculously survived tortures; finally their heads were cut off. Their three brothers were beheaded with them. Patrons of Florence and of the Medici, they are shown in art as doctors or apothecaries, often in furred robes and cylindrical hats. Their attributes are arrows, truss, knife, pharmacist's mortar, pestle, box of unguents, and spatula. Their feast is September 27. *See also* SAINTS IN ART.

COSMAS INDICOPLEUSTES. Byzantine illuminated manuscript, in the Vatican Library, Rome.

COSMATIS, THE. Italian marble workers (fl. largely in Rome and its environs from the beginning of the 12th to the 14th cent.). The term "Cosmati" is used to denote any craftsman of a number of Roman families who practiced the art of decorative marble inlay; it is derived from the repeated appearance of the name "Cosmas" among the extant inscriptions.

The marblework of the Cosmatis began to appear in Rome soon after 1100 during the "renaissance" of large-scale building and redecoration programs initiated during the reign of Paschal II (1094–1118). Cosmati work appears in architectural decoration (pavements, marble revetments or friezes, arcades), but it is more widely known in church furniture, where colorful marble designs embellish altars, chancel screens, episcopal thrones, pulpits, paschal candles, and funeral monuments.

Stylistically, Cosmati work is characteristically aniconic, although animal forms occasionally are included in the overall designs (altar, Rome, S. Cesareo), and several Cosmati tombs are elaborated by the addition of figural mosaics. In general, however, the designs are geometric and purely decorative, most frequently composed of a grid of white marble that encloses large rectangles and roundels of porphyry, serpentine (*verde antico*), or varicolored marble chips. Though Cosmati work preserved a high degree of stylistic unity for more than two centuries, earlier examples tend to be simpler in design and more monumental in conception; during the 13th century, Gothic influence appears in the elegant pointed designs and the patterns become more diverse and smaller in scale.

The sources of Cosmati work are not clearly understood. On the one hand, geometric mosaic and marble pavements appeared in Rome itself in the 5th century (S. Marco); brilliantly colored pavements were found in nearby Ostia during the same period. On the other hand, striking similarities occur between Roman Cosmati work and 11th- and 12th-century Byzantine church decoration (Hagia Sophia, Constantinople). It should also be mentioned that the strongly Byzantinized centers of southern Italy, such as Sicily, had a long tradition of marble decorative work that frequently exerted an influence on Cosmati work in Rome.

Cosmati work is fundamentally a two-dimensional system of surface decoration intended, by the juxtaposition of colored marbles, to enrich the appearance of the object it covered. Nonstructural in intent, Cosmati work characteristically follows and reinforces the structural boundaries

Francesco del Cossa, *The Annunciation*. State Art Collections, Picture Gallery, Dresden.

of the surface. Hence, pulpits are decorated with three major areas of marble that define the two staircases and the central parapet; in church pavements, the nave is set off from the aisles by a different design, and the most elaborate geometric patterns are reserved for the center of the nave, or the crossing.

The development of Cosmati decoration can best be traced in funeral monuments, all of which, however, date from the second half of the 13th century. In the earliest preserved, the tomb of Cardinal Fieschi in S. Lorenzo fuori le Mura, Rome, the antique sarcophagus is enclosed in a simple ciborium of mosaic-encrusted marble. Later, in Pietro Oderisi's tomb of Clement IV (1268; Viterbo, S. Francesco), marble encrustation of numerous infinitesimal patterns covers the entire structure. Finally, the Gothicizing sculptor Arnolfo di Cambio, in his tomb for Cardinal de Braye (1309; Bologna, S. Domenico), successfully employed Cosmati marblework as a backdrop for white marble sculpture.

While the greater part of the Cosmati work appears in Rome, examples of the art of the marble decorators appear as far south as the Campania, and north through Umbria. In addition, at the end of the 13th century, Pietro Oderisi went to England to execute the tomb of Edward the Confessor, and about six of his (and his assistant's) works may be seen in Westminster Abbey, London.

BIBLIOGRAPHY. G. Giovannoni, "Note sui marmorari romani," *Archivio della Società Romana di Storia Patria*, 1904; E. Hutton, *The Cosmati*, London, 1950; G. Bendinelli, "Intorno all'origine e per una nuova denominazione dei mosaici 'Cosmateschi,'" *Studies Presented to David Moore Robinson*, I, St. Louis, 1951.

PENELOPE C. MAYO

COSSA, FRANCESCO DEL. Italian painter of Ferrara (ca. 1435–77). Cossa is first recorded in a commission of 1456 for a work now lost. He lived a good part of his life in Bologna, where a stained-glass window on his design was produced in 1467. After working in Ferrara for the Duke's pleasure villa, Palazzo Schifanoia, or Scandiana (until 1470), he declined to continue when he was given no increase in fees and returned to Bologna, where, after completing his other chief works, he died of the plague.

A masterpiece, the *Allegory of Autumn* (Berlin, former State Museums), is probably an early work by him, though much disputed and thought to be by an otherwise unknown artist such as the many who are named in documents. It shows the influence of Mantegna and Piero della Francesca in its classically balanced weight and is similar to the 1467 window, but more urbane and "Hellenic." It was probably made for another ducal villa.

Cossa painted one wall at Schifanoia, with the March, April, and May sections of the cycle showing the influence of astrology on daily life. Symbols of the zodiac, triumphs of pagan divinities, and scenes of human occupations develop perhaps the liveliest and most representative imagery of secular art in the early Italian Renaissance. His handling, influenced by Tura, changes to blend with his Ferrarese collaborators, and is thus more tense and thin, with intricately twisted line, but retains a more sculptural mass than any of the others.

Cossa's major Bolognese works, after the Schifanoia wall, are *The Annunciation* (Dresden, State Art Collections, Picture Gallery), which is impassive and grandly cylindrical; three more stained-glass windows (Madonnas: Paris, Jacquemart-André Museum, and Berlin, Schloss Museum; and *St. John*, Bologna, S. Giovanni in Monte); the *Griffoni Altarpiece* (divided between London, National Gallery; Milan, Brera; and Washington, D.C., National Gallery); and the *Mercanzia Altarpiece* (Bologna, National Picture Gallery). The last two exploit the linear keenness of Schifanoia, with complex details in surfaces of faces and robes, but develop a majestic stony power and strong high-pitched color in broad areas.

BIBLIOGRAPHY. S. Ortolani, *Cosmè Tura, Francesco del Cossa, Ercole de' Roberti*, Milan, 1941.

CREIGHTON GILBERT

COSSIAU, JOHANNES (Jan Joost van Cossiau). Dutch landscape painter (b. Breda, ca. 1660; d. Mainz, 1732/34). Cossiau, who was a follower of Gaspard Dughet, was active in Paris. He painted idealized landscapes in the Italian manner with antique ruins and historical figures. He was director of the Aschaffenburg Museum.

BIBLIOGRAPHY. W. Bernt, *Die niederländischen Maler des 17. Jahrhunderts...*, vol. 1, Munich, 1948.

COSSIERS, JAN. Flemish painter of religious and mythological subjects, genre scenes, and portraits (b. Antwerp, 1600; d. there, 1671). After an apprenticeship with Cornelis de Vos, he traveled abroad, perhaps to Italy. He returned to Antwerp in 1628, settled down, and became a member of the Guild of St. Luke. In 1635 he worked at some decorations for the Joyous Entry of Cardinal Infant Ferdinand, and between 1635 and 1640 he collaborated at Torre de la Parada on paintings after sketches by Peter Paul Rubens. Cossiers made frequent use of Rubensian types in his religious canvases (*Adoration of the Shepherds*, Kassel, Gallery), but his color scheme is dark gray and conforms with the palette of the Caravaggio imitators. The series painted for the Béguinage at Mechlin and his genre scenes are reminiscent of Theodoor Rombouts and Geeraard Zegers; occasionally, he stands out in portraiture, as in *The Surgeon* (Antwerp, Royal Museum).

BIBLIOGRAPHY. F. J. van den Branden, *Geschiedenis der Antwerpsche Schilderschool*, Antwerp, 1883; R. Oldenbourg, *Die flämische Malerei des XVII. Jahrhunderts*, 2d ed., Berlin, 1922; A. von Schneider, *Caravaggio und die Niederländer*, Marburg, 1933.

COSTA, GIANFRANCESCO. Italian architect, painter and engraver (1711–73). Costa was active in Venice. Little is known about his work as architect and painter except that the Theater S. Benedetto, Venice, was restored after his design of 1755. His main work is a series of etchings, *Delizie del fiume Brenta* (1750–56).

BIBLIOGRAPHY. G. K. Nagler, *Die Monogrammisten...*, Munich, 1876–78.

COSTA, LORENZO. Influential Italian painter of Ferrara, also active in Bologna (ca. 1460–1535). From 1506 he was court painter in Mantua as Mantegna's successor. Between early work influenced by Ercole de' Roberti and late work influenced by Francia, he did his chief and most personal painting in Bologna.

BIBLIOGRAPHY. *Catalogo della Esposizione della pittura ferrarese del rinascimento*, 2d ed., Ferrara, 1933.

COSTA, LUCIO. Brazilian architect, historian, and city planner (1902–   ). With Oscar Niemeyer and Affonso Reidy, he inaugurated Brazil's modern architecture in their designs for the Ministry of Health and Education Building in Rio de Janeiro (1937–42). In other works, Costa's imaginative manipulation of ceramic screens to reduce sun glare is a hallmark of his style. His fan-shaped plan for Brasilia (1957) is his best-known work.

See also BRASILIA; RIO DE JANEIRO: MUSEUMS (MINISTRY OF HEALTH AND EDUCATION).

BIBLIOGRAPHY. P. L. Goodwin, *Brazil Builds, Architecture New and Old, 1652–1942*, New York, 1943.

COSTER, ADAM DE. Flemish painter of portraits and religious and historical subjects (b. Mechlin, 1586; d. Antwerp, 1643). Coster was active in Antwerp. He adopted the Caravaggio school's *maniera* and specialized in night scenes that are outstanding because of skillfully manipulated chiaroscuro and plastic handling of figures.

BIBLIOGRAPHY. F. J. van den Branden, *Geschiedenis der Antwerpsche Schilderschool*, Antwerp, 1883.

COSTIGAN, JOHN EDWARD. American painter (1888–   ). He was born in Providence, R.I., and is mostly self-taught. His paintings are thickly painted, somewhat impressionistic treatments of the figure and of woodland and farm scenes.

BIBLIOGRAPHY. R. Flint, "Costigan, American Pastoralist," *International Studio*, LXXX, March, 1925.

COSWAY, RICHARD. English miniaturist and portrait painter (b. Devonshire, 1742; d. London, 1821). He went to London to study under Thomas Hudson and established a practice as a painter of miniatures about 1760. He was elected associate of the Royal Academy of Arts in 1770 and full academician in 1771. In 1781 he married Maria Hadfield (1759–1838) who, as Maria Cosway, made her own name as a painter. Cosway quickly became an extremely fashionable man, had large numbers of sitters, and at one time was a close friend of the Prince of Wales. He evolved a delicate style of great elegance and at the end of the century was the most prominent miniaturist in the country. Examples of his works may be seen in the Victoria and Albert Museum, London, and in the Huntington Library and Art Gallery, San Marino, Calif. Cosway also practiced in oils, but his work in this medium cannot hold its own beside his work in pencil and water color.

BIBLIOGRAPHY. G. C. Williamson, *Richard Cosway*, London, 1917.

COTER (Coutere; Coultre), COLIJN (Colijn van). Flemish painter active in Brussels (ca. 1455–1538). His name is known from a panel in the Louvre, Paris, signed "Coliin de Coter pingit me in Brabancia Brussells." It has also been suggested that he is the "Painter Colin from Brussels" listed in the St. Luke's Guild of Antwerp in 1493. Only the evidence of his work provides some idea of his period of greatest activity. This is provided by two altar wings depicting Christ and Mary and donors. The donors, Philip the Fair and his wife Johanna, enable us to date the panels between 1496 and 1506.

Any other definite assertions about Colijn are difficult to make inasmuch as his work is totally and uninspiredly eclectic. The Louvre panel, *St. Luke Painting the Madonna*, is in all likelihood a copy of a lost work by the Master of Flémalle. Indeed, most of Colijn's work is either directly copied or derived from Flémalle and Rogier van der Weyden.

BIBLIOGRAPHY. J. Maquet-Tombu, *Colyn de Coter, peintre bruxellois*, Brussels, 1937.

COTES, FRANCIS. English portrait painter (b. London, 1726; d. there, 1770). He studied crayons under Knapton and began his career as a painter of portraits in pastel, but the bulk of his output was in oils. He quickly became fashionable. His style, which has a slightly French air, is at once graceful, sophisticated, and unaffected.

COTMAN, JOHN SELL. English landscape painter, chiefly in water color (1782–1842). Born in Norwich, he was educated at the grammar school there. He began sketching at an early age and in 1798 went to London. For a time he was employed by the printseller Rudolph Ackermann, probably in coloring aquatints. In 1799 he worked for the great connoisseur Dr. Thomas Monro and soon came into contact with Monro's protégé Thomas Girtin. He later joined Girtin's drawing society. Beginning in 1800 with a tour of Wales, he went on numerous sketching trips, the most significant being visits to Yorkshire in 1803, 1804, and 1805. The surrounding countryside, and especially the banks of the lovely river Greta, where he sketched in 1805, became the source of many of his happiest inspirations, for example, the celebrated *Greta Bridge* (London, British Museum).

Late in 1806, unsuccessful in the competitive world of London, Cotman returned to Norwich, then the center of a school of landscape painters led by John Crome ("Old Crome"). About the same time he fruitlessly turned to oil

John Sell Cotman, *Greta Bridge*. British Museum, London. A masterpiece of the artist's Greta period, 1805–10.

painting in an effort to improve his sales, persevering with it until 1810. He also tried teaching as a means of livelihood. Crome, however, was the established drawing master of Norwich, and there was hardly room for a competitor. At length Cotman resorted, with moderate success, to drawing and etching subjects of archaeological interest, many of which he published in series, for example, *Sixty Etchings of Norfolk Architectural Antiquities* (1818). In this he was encouraged by the wealthy Yarmouth banker Dawson Turner, an amateur botanist and antiquarian and a dominating personality who increasingly influenced the course of Cotman's life. In 1812 he persuaded Cotman to move to Yarmouth.

Turner's new interest in the architecture of Normandy led to Cotman's tours of the duchy in 1817, 1818, and 1820. The third visit yielded the famous sepia drawings of the rocky country around Domfront and Mortain. His chief occupation, however, was compiling a pictorial record of Norman architecture, and in the years immediately following he produced etchings based on his drawings. In 1822 the collection was published as *The Architectural Antiquities of Normandy*, with text by Turner.

After Crome's death, Cotman returned to Norwich (1823) and set himself up as a teacher of drawing, assisted by his son Miles Edmund Cotman. The "school" did not prosper, but in 1834 Cotman was appointed professor of drawing at King's College, London. In 1841 he visited for the last time Norwich, Yarmouth, old friends, and favorite sketching haunts. He produced a series of chalk drawings of surpassing quality.

The most comprehensive collection of Cotman's works is that of the Castle Museum at Norwich. The British Museum also owns many fine water colors and drawings.

Although he attained excellence in oil painting. Cotman was above all a water-colorist. Developing at first under the influence of Girtin, he soon evolved an original style culminating in the masterpieces of the Greta period (1805–10). In these he employed superimposed washes of nearly flat, discreetly harmonized color, without modeling, chiaroscuro, or linear emphasis. Configurations are suggested solely by masterly control of the shape and consistency of the washes. The effect is a kind of descriptive suggestion, a play of nature's patterns upon the artist's sensibilities. Cotman, however, renounces the active quest of a Girtin or a Turner for an intimate communion with nature. Thanks to their example, he inherited a lyrical vision from the start; but, instead of pursuing it, he froze it into a pattern of topographical precision. When at length he attempted to recapture the romantic vision, he lost his way in the thicket of vulgarity and commercialism that, though alien to his nature and understanding, the lack of a London reputation impelled him to cultivate. Thus, his later work appears uneven in quality and confused in direction, revealing many fruitless attempts to compromise with the popular taste for romantic crudities. Often such attempts led to clashes of discordant color and undigested incident. Nevertheless, at his best he shows no real waning of power. Sometimes he essayed a classical-pastoral idiom, perhaps influenced by Joshua Cristall, which in his hands became strangely abstract and exotic. The imaginary landscapes of his last years, however, painted in water color strengthened with a flour-paste medium of his own devising, indicate that he was at last finding a new, authentic path—bleak, tragic, and full of dim aspiration for the remote.

BIBLIOGRAPHY. A. P. Oppé, *The Water-Colour Drawings of John Sell Cotman*, London, 1923; S. D. Kitson, *The Life of John Sell Cotman*, London, 1937; V. Rienaecker, *John Sell Cotman*, Leigh-on-Sea, 1953; H. Lemaitre, *Le Paysage anglais à l'aquarelle, 1760–1851*, Paris, 1955.

DAVID M. LOSHAK

COTTE, ROBERT DE, *see* DE COTTE, ROBERT.

COTTET, CHARLES. French painter and etcher (b. Puy, 1863; d. Paris, 1925). In 1882 Cottet went to Paris, where he studied with Maillard and Roll and briefly with Puvis de Chavannes. He first exhibited in the 1889 Salon. Cottet traveled extensively in the Mediterranean and the Near East. Despite an early impressionist influence, his palette remained fundamentally dark. His composition is at times close to Gauguin's linear decorativeness. Cottet was best known for his somber paintings of scenes of Brittany peas-ant and maritime life. Their melancholy and sense of hovering death is best seen in his famous triptych *Au Pays de la mer* (1898; Paris, National Museum of Modern Art), in which the central panel, *Le Repas des adieux*, is flanked by *Ceux qui s'en vont* and *Celles qui restent.*

BIBLIOGRAPHY. J. Valmy-Baysse, *Charles Cottet: Sa vie, son oeuvre,* Paris, 1910.

COTTON GENESIS. Early Christian illuminated manuscript, from Alexandria, in the British Museum, London.

COUBINE, OTHON. French painter, sculptor, and graphic artist (1883–   ). He was born in Boskovice, Czechoslovakia, and studied in Prague and Antwerp. He traveled in France and Italy and settled in Paris in 1905. At the beginning of his career Coubine was influenced by the early forces in modern art, Van Gogh, Fauvism, and cubism. His mature style, however, has been a form of classical naturalism in which the subject, somewhat simplified, is painted with a structural solidity approaching monumentality. Coubine has painted portraits, figures, and still lifes but is best known for his landscapes.

BIBLIOGRAPHY. M. Raynal, *O. Coubine*, Rome, 1922; C. Kunstler, *Coubine*, Paris, 1929.

COUCY, CASTLE OF. Great castle in northern France, built (1225–40) by the lords of Coucy. From a high, triangular plateau they dominated the Aisne Valley and rivaled the king in power. On the adjacent slope is a large walled bailey, guarded by a series of towers on its north and west sides From the bailey's entrance towers in the east wall a bridge stretched to an extensive walled area enclosing the neighboring town. The castle and bailey covered an area of 10,000 square yards, and the castle itself was the greatest circular tower ever built (200 ft. high and 100 ft. in exterior diameter). It was defended from roof battlements equipped with stone corbels for the erection of wooden

Charles Cottet, *The Loggia of the Opéra Comique*, 1887. National Museum of Modern Art, Paris.

Castle of Coucy. Remaining walls and cylindrical tower of the stronghold built by the lords of Coucy, 1225–40.

hoarding. Subterranean passageways connected the castle with other buildings in the courtyard and provided a sallyport for counterattacks.

The castle's ingenious construction could be studied from its ruins until 1917, when a retreating German army destroyed it. The inner structure was composed of four stages of pointed arches, which, with the exception of the lowest stage, supported ogival vaults of twelve radiating ribs. These vaults roofed each of three great rooms, one above the other. The topmost was an audience hall with wooden galleries for spectators set within the piers of its arcade. Domestic buildings were added along two of the courtyard walls in the late 14th century. These were the halls of the Nine Heroes and the Nine Heroines and a chapel, where the spacious windows and elegant decorations indicated a new standard for seigneurial residential comfort.

BIBLIOGRAPHY. E. Lefèvre-Pontalis, *Le Château de Coucy*, Paris, 1909; F. Enaud, *Les Châteaux forts en France*, Paris, 1958; A. Tuulse, *Castles of the Western World*, London, 1958.

EMMA N. PAPERT

COUGHTRY, GRAHAM. Canadian painter (1931–). He studied in Montreal and Toronto and traveled in Spain and France. Originally a graphic artist, he turned to figure studies in oil and gouache in Toronto, showing the influence of Ben Shahn.

BIBLIOGRAPHY. R. Fulford, "Coughtry," *Canadian Art*, XVIII, 1961.

COULISSE. A groove in which a mobile piece, such as a drawer, slides. In theater terminology it refers to the groove in which a side scene moves, the side scene itself, or the interval between side scenes. Figuratively, it is a place behind the scenes. A fluting in a sword blade is also called a coulisse.

COULTRE, COLIJN VAN, *see* COTER, COLIJN.

COUNCIL HOUSE, *see* BOULEUTERION.

Coulisse. (1) Stage wing; (2) groove for sliding a mobile section; (3) support for a side scene; (4) side scene.

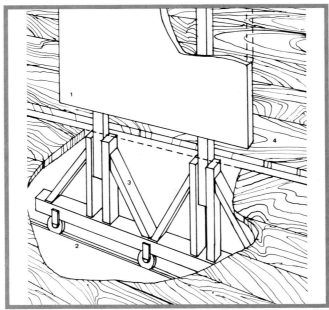

COUNCIL OF TRENT. Council (1545–63) called by Pope Paul III that brought into being the Catholic offensive against Protestantism known as the Counter Reformation. It is particularly important to the development of art in Catholic lands because of its strict rules governing religious art, particularly those reaffirming the veneration of images.

BIBLIOGRAPHY. H. Jedin, *A History of the Council of Trent*, New York, 1957.

COUNIHAN, NOEL. Australian painter and caricaturist (1913–). He was the leader of a group of left-wing realist painters who became prominent in Australia during and immediately after World War II. This group included the Polish-born Yosel Bergner (b. 1922) and the surrealist-realist Herbert McClintock (b. 1906).

COUNTER PROOF. In graphic arts, a working proof printed on paper from a freshly inked impression. The fresh impression is placed face upward, and a damped sheet of printing paper is placed upon it. Press pressure or burnishing by hand offsets the print from one sheet to the other.

COUNTER RELIEF, *see* RELIEF, COUNTER.

COURBET, GUSTAVE. French painter (b. Ornans, 1819; d. La-Tour-de-Peilz, Switzerland, 1877). Courbet studied at the polytechnic school of Besançon and in 1839 went to Paris, ostensibly to study law, but actually to take up painting. At Besançon he had taken lessons from Flageoulot, a pupil of David. In Paris, he boldly ignored the tenets of academic teachers (Steuben and Hesse). Instead, he taught himself the rudiments of painting, regarding himself as "the pupil of nature" and of the masters whose work he studied at the museum: Rembrandt, Veronese, the great Spaniards, and such moderns as Géricault and Delacroix. Gifted with enormous natural talent for painting and an instinctive sense of craftsmanship, Courbet rapidly evolved to technical and stylistic mastery, suffering none of the torments of self-doubt that normally beset young artists.

After unsuccessful attempts at narrative painting (*Walpurgis Night*; *Loth's Daughters*), he soon found more congenial expression of his talent in portraiture and landscape. A flavor of romantic sentiment still clings to his early works, particularly to the *Girl in a Hammock* (1844; Winterthur, Switzerland, Reinhart Foundation) and to the dramatized self-portraits that were the first manifestations of his artistic independence, such as *Self-portrait with Dog* (1842; Fine Arts Museum of the City of Paris), *Wounded Man* (1844) and *Man with Leather Belt* (ca. 1844; both Paris, Louvre), *The Lovers* (1845; Lyons, Museum of Fine Arts), and *Man with the Pipe* (ca. 1846; Montpellier, Fabre Museum). The essential features of his style already appear nearly fully formed in some of these. Of large and ruggedly simple conception, the figures are modeled in strong contrasts of light and shadow. The sensuous richness of the pigment, sometimes applied with the palette knife, betrays Courbet's relish for the physical substance of paint.

Gustave Courbet, *The Studio*, detail. Louvre, Paris.

The somber colors are most intense in the silky dark of the shadows.

From 1844 on, Courbet regularly exhibited at the annual Salons, excluded only in 1847. He avoided contemporary clichés of beauty and sentiment and asserted his personal vision. This independence of outlook, coupled with a confident grasp of the technical side of painting, made possible his rapid development, which was virtually complete by 1850. His studio in the rue Hautefeuille and his corner at the Brasserie Andler became rallying points for a coterie of enthusiastic followers. Art critics such as Champfleury and Baudelaire began to raise their voices on his behalf. At the Salon of 1849, his *After Dinner at Ornans* (Lille, Museum of Fine Arts) was greatly admired and received a Second Medal.

In 1850 Courbet found himself famous overnight; his *Stonebreakers* (formerly Dresden, State Art Collections, Picture Gallery) and *Funeral at Ornans* (Louvre) were the sensation of the Salon. Particularly the latter, a monumental treatment of a common genre subject, unleashed furious criticism. Courbet had intended to present the full reality of an actual scene (clergy and peasants surrounding an open grave, against a background of bleak landscape) without idealization or sentimentality. As a result, he was accused of crudity of feeling, shocking ugliness, and clumsiness in his treatment of figures. On the other hand, his sober honesty, masterly technique, and powerful realism of representation also found admirers. Courbet, who for several years had been involved in anarchist and socialist discussions, was hailed as a master of social realism. It is improbable that political reflection actually inspired the *Stonebreakers*, but Courbet gladly accepted the political interpretation of his work and considered himself a militant socialist in practice and thought (in 1863 he was to collaborate in the writing of Proudhon's *On Art and Its Social Significance*).

At the Salon of 1853, his *Wrestlers* and *Bathers* (both Fabre Museum) attracted notice and were attacked as "vulgar and trivial." In posing heavily corporeal figures in landscape settings, Courbet had difficulty in fusing their bodies with the enveloping space and light. This difficulty also mars his *Village Ladies* (1851; New York, Metropolitan Museum). A stay with the collector Bruyas at Montpellier (1853) gave Courbet an important patron and occasioned the autobiographical double-portrait *The Encounter* (Fabre Museum), a strange document of his artistic pride and a notable essay in open-air figure composition.

At the World's Fair of 1855, Courbet showed forty paintings in a pavilion of his own, inscribed "Le Réalisme." Among his new paintings were the *Grain Sifters* (Nantes, Museum of Fine Arts) and the immense "realistic allegory" *The Studio* (Louvre), in which he represented himself at work among his friends and models. With its symbolic accessories, the painting went beyond the bounds of realism, but in its magnificent suggestion of a vast shadowed interior filled with complex groups of firmly modeled, sharply characterized figures, it is one of the glories of 19th-century painting.

After 1855 Courbet turned increasingly to landscape, portraits, and nudes. The *Young Women at the Seine* (Salon of 1857; Fine Arts Museum of the City of Paris),

perhaps an allegory of idleness, and the *Return from the Conference* (1863; destroyed), a broad anticlerical satire, were among his last attempts at social themes. A passionate hunter, Courbet particularly specialized in forest interiors and hunting scenes (*Hunter's Picnic*, 1857, Cologne, Wallraf-Richartz Museum; *Battling Stags*, 1861, and *Deer in the Forest*, 1866, both Louvre). From this time date a number of large nudes and erotic compositions which earned him the epithet "flesh-maker" (*Venus and Psyche*, 1864; *Nude with Parrot*, 1866, Metropolitan Museum). Travels in the Jura and in Normandy resulted in a large number of broadly executed landscapes (*The Grotto*, 1864; Hamburg, Art Gallery) and beach scenes (*The Wave*, 1870; several versions). During the World's Fair of 1867, Courbet once again had his own pavilion, this time containing 120 works. The tone of his critics gradually changed from hostility to admiration. In Holland, Belgium, and Germany, he was enthusiastically acclaimed by a new generation of realist painters deeply influenced by him: Leibl, De Groux, and Munkácsy.

After the dethronement of Napoleon III in the war of 1870–71, Courbet served the Paris Commune as head of the arts commission. Having become implicated in the destruction of the Vendôme Column, he was imprisoned after the Commune's fall (1871). He used this time to paint still lifes (*Apples*, 1871; Munich, New Pinacothek). Condemned to pay for the reerection of the column, he fled to Switzerland in 1873. Though he continued to paint landscapes and portraits, the quality of his work declined during these last years.

Quite apart from his political activity, Courbet was a revolutionary force in 19th-century painting. He did not pioneer a new technique; his practice of modeling forms in graduated tones, proceeding from the dark underpaint to the highlights, was a conservative one, derived from Rembrandt and the Spaniards. Courbet's realism hinged on a new conception of the scope and aim of art rather than on a new technique. "Reality" to him meant palpable, material existence; truth and beauty resided in matter— physical experience, strongly savored, was his chief inspiration. He rejected abstract ideality and poetic effects that derived from verbal associations. Thus he helped to rid painting of the literary clichés, the artifices and escapisms that had threatened to smother it. Superbly plebeian, unafraid of modernity, and contemptuous of taste, he enabled a new generation of painters to concentrate on the problems of visual form. He was at his best painting the flesh of fruits or human bodies, the fur of animals, the texture of foliage and flowers. Under his hands, even the waves and clouds became tangible matter. He had a keen, sensuous relish for paint; the brilliance of his brushwork conceals the occasional crudities of his drawing. He attacked and conquered painting problems (as in his monumental *Funeral* and *Studio*) that were beyond the reach of his more cautious and learned contemporaries.

BIBLIOGRAPHY. G. Riat, *Gustave Courbet, peintre*, Paris, 1906; T. Duret, *Courbet*, Paris, 1918; G. Boas, *Courbet and the Naturalistic Movement*, Baltimore, 1938; F. Fosca, *Courbet*, Paris, 1940; G. Mack, *Gustave Courbet*, London, 1951.

LORENZ EITNER

COUR DE MARBRE, *see* VERSAILLES: PALACE.

Jacques Courtois, *The Battle.* Pitti Palace, Florence. A typically dynamic and picturesque work.

COURSE. Continuous band of masonry, as in brickwork. Several courses arranged in a recurring pattern are called a "bond."

COURSE, BELT (Stringcourse). Horizontal band, flush or projecting, running across the face of a wall.

COURTEYS. Family of French enamelers active from the mid-16th to the early 17th century in Limoges, when that city was the center of enameling in Europe. The Courteys, like their contemporaries Penicaud and Limosin, worked in the painted-enamel technique to produce pictures on the forms that they made of copper. The most important member of the family was the earliest, Pierre I (ca. 1520–91). He did large-scale panels for the façade of the Château de Madrid in the Bois de Boulogne, as well as a number of fine small classical forms. His pictorial style is related to the late mannerists of his time, and Roman decorative motifs were freely applied on borders.

COURT OF THE LIONS, *see* ALHAMBRA, GRANADA; MOORISH ARCHITECTURE (SPAIN).

COURT OF THE MYRTLES, *see* ALHAMBRA, GRANADA.

COURTOIS, GUILLAUME (Guglielmo Cortese; Il Borgognone). French history painter and engraver (b. Saint-Hippolyte, Doubs, Franche-Comté, 1628; d. Rome, 1679). A brother of Jacques Courtois, with whom he often collaborated, Guillaume studied with Pietro da Cortona. In 1657 Guillaume became a member of the Academy of St. Luke. He painted many altarpieces in Rome in his master's manner (S. Marco; St. John Lateran), decorated the chapel of the Altieri Palace, and painted *The Battle of Joshua* in the Quirinal Palace (1656–57). In addition, he painted a portrait of Alexander VII, engraved by Colignon.

BIBLIOGRAPHY. F. A. Salvagnini, *I Pittori Borgognoni Cortese,* Rome, 1937.

COURTOIS, JACQUES (P. Giacomo Cortese; Le Bourguignon; Il Borgognone). French painter (b. Saint-Hippolyte, Doubs, Franche-Comté, 1621; d. Rome, 1676). He was the pupil of his father, Jean Courtois. While in the Spanish army (1636–39) he executed on-the-spot sketches of landscapes and battle scenes. He settled in Rome in 1640 and Italianized his name as "Cortese." He was influenced first by Reni, Albani, and Pietro da Cortona, then by the Bamboccianti and Salvator Rosa, who determined his orientation toward battle pieces. His picturesque dynamism belies his French origin. Bernini praised the realistic horror of his combats, swirling in dust and morning vapor like a phenomenon of nature, which were different from the heroic Renaissance and Flemish bird's-eye-view formulas. Courtois's only pupil was Joseph-François Parrocel the Elder. His paintings and drawings are found in Besançon, Edinburgh, Epinal, Paris (Louvre), Nantes, Florence (Uffizi), and Chatsworth.

BIBLIOGRAPHY. G. Blondeau, "L'Oeuvre de Jacques Courtois, dit le Bourguignon des Batailles," *Réunion des Sociétés des Beaux-Arts des Départements,* 1914.

COUSIN, JEAN, THE ELDER AND THE YOUNGER. French artists: Jean the Elder, painter, stained-glass designer, geometer, and engraver (b. Sens, ca. 1490; d. Paris, ca. 1560/61); and his son Jean the Younger, painter, sculptor, and engraver (b. Sens, ca. 1522; d. Paris, ca. 1594). They constitute one of the outstanding families of French artists that remained relatively independent of the school of Fontainebleau, which dominated French 16th-century painting. Jean the Elder moved from Sens to Paris in 1538, although he made numerous visits back to his native city. Jean the Younger, who moved to Paris with his father, also

Jean Cousin the Elder, *Allegory of Charity*. Fabre Museum, Montpellier.

Guillaume Coustou, *Passage of the Rhine*. Royal Chapel, Versailles.

revisited Sens, most notably in 1563, when he worked on decorations for the entry of Charles IX. Both exemplify a craft consciousness that is essentially medieval (as opposed to the High Renaissance concept of individual genius), working as painters, geometers, tapestry and stained-glass designers, sculptors, engravers, and book illustrators.

The earliest known work of Jean the Elder is his *Eva Prima Pandora* (Paris, Louvre), painted in Sens before his departure from that city. While the physiognomy used has some precedence in Rosso's work, the landscape and grotto types and the dramatic contrasts of light and dark indicate a knowledge of Leonardo and of Dürer prints. Italian influences are even stronger in his tapestries with the *Life of St-Mammès* (1543; Langres, Cathedral), which, with their classical figures and perspective buildup by means of an architectural ensemble, speak strongly of the school of Raphael. Further Italianate inclinations are exhibited in his book on perspective, published in Paris in 1560.

Jean the Younger inherited his father's studio and excellent reputation and tended to perpetuate his style. Much of his activity seems to have been in the realm of portraiture, but these have survived only in the form of drawings (Paris, National Library, Cabinet des Estampes). His most famous known painting, *The Last Judgment* (Louvre), bears a thematic relation to the works of Caron, but the handling speaks more of Italian mannerist masters, such as Bronzino. A good indication of his crisp and elegant drawing style is the manuscript copy of his *Livre de fortune* (1568), which carries on the emblematic tradition of Alciati, and further exemplifies his reliance on Italian man-

nerist models. Also active in engraving (*Moses Showing the Serpent to the People*), stained glass (*Judgment of Solomon*, ca. 1586; Paris, St-Gervais), sculpture (base for the monument of Admiral Chabot, 1565–72; formerly Célestins de Paris), and book illustration (Ovid, *Metamorphoses*, Paris, 1570), Jean the Younger sustained the tradition of the versatile artist-craftsman to the close of the 16th century.

BIBLIOGRAPHY. J. Cousin, *Le Livre de Fortune*, ed. L. Lalanne, Paris, 1883; M. Roy, *Artistes et monuments de la Renaissance en France*, vol. 1, Paris, 1929; A. Blunt, *Art and Architecture in France, 1500–1700*, Baltimore, 1954; D. and E. Panofsky, "Roma Prima Pandora; Eva Prima Pandora; Lutetia Nova Pandora," *Pandora's Box*, New York, 1956.

STEPHEN E. OSTROW

COUSIN, LOUIS, *see* GENTILE, LUIGI.

COUSINS, HAROLD. American sculptor (1916–   ). Born in Washington, D.C., he studied at the Art Students League in New York, following war service, and with Zadkine in Paris in 1949. He began working in welded metals in the early 1950s. Cousins traveled widely in Europe and had one-man exhibitions in Amsterdam, Sweden, and Paris. His work was represented in Paris in the Salon de la Jeune Sculpture (1955–57) and in the Salon des Réalités Nouvelles. He works chiefly in bent, openwork metallic abstractions, distantly suggestive of natural forms.

BIBLIOGRAPHY. M. Seuphor, *The Sculpture of This Century*, New York, 1960.

COUSINS, SAMUEL. English engraver (b. Exeter, 1801; d. London, 1887). Almost forgotten today, Cousins was the first engraver to be named an academician at the

Royal Academy in London (1855). Most of his works are mezzotint portraits after Lawrence and historical plates in the 19th-century romantic tradition.

COUSTOU, NICOLAS AND GUILLAUME. French sculptors: Nicolas Coustou (b. Lyons, 1658; d. Paris, 1733) and Guillaume Coustou (b. Lyons, 1677; d. Paris, 1746). They were the sons of François Coustou and pupils of their father and of their uncle Antoine Coysevox, whose tradition they carried on. Nicolas was in Rome from 1683 to 1686 on the basis of his work *Cain Builds the City of Enoch*. He was elected to France's Royal Academy in 1693 for his bas-relief *Apollo Showing France the Bust of Louis XIV* (Paris, Louvre). Nicolas was professor at the Academy in 1702, rector in 1720, and chancellor in 1733. Extraordinarily productive, he collaborated closely with his younger brother Guillaume on statuary for the royal palaces of Trianon, Versailles, and Marly. During his stay in Rome he copied such antique statuary as the *Borghese Warrior* (Louvre) and the *Commodus* (Versailles Park). For Marly he did two statues of Meleager (1706), the *Seine* and the *Marne* (1712; now in Paris, Tuileries Gardens), *Diana, Endymion*, and *Mercury Putting Argus to Sleep* (1701). Guillaume executed the famous *Horses of Marly*, now in the Place de la Concorde, Paris, at the entrance of the Champs Elysées. Nicolas also executed for the portal of the Dôme des Invalides a lead St. Louis, various prophets for the chapels of SS. Gregory, Ambroise, and Jerome, as well as a *Louis XIV as Jupiter* (Louvre). For the equestrian statue of Louis XIV at Lyons (now in the City Hall) Nicolas did the Saône River and Guillaume, the Rhône.

Guillaume Coustou went to Rome on the strength of the piece *Reception of Joseph's Brothers at Pharaoh's Court* and collaborated with Pierre Legros on the *Triumph of Religion over Heresy*. In 1704 Guillaume became a member of the Royal Academy for his *Death of Hercules on the Funeral Pyre* (Louvre); he became professor in 1715, rector in 1733, and director in 1735. Among Guillaume's works are *Queen Maria Leczinska as Juno* (1730) for the Bosquet du Dauphin, a *Passage of the Rhine* for the Chapel at Versailles, cornices for the King's apartments at Trianon, and a lead and tin baldachino for the parks of Versailles. For the Invalides he did a *Mars*, a *Minerva*, and the *Louis XIV between Justice and Prudence* tympanum, the last of which is echoed in *Louis XIV between Truth and Justice* for the old chambers of the Parlement de Paris. For the Versailles Chapel, Guillaume executed religious groups such as the *Pietà of the High Altar* and *Jesus in the Temple*. The Coustous, like their uncle Antoine Coysevox, are typical of the classical side of the baroque.

W. MC ALLISTER JOHNSON

COUTANCES CATHEDRAL. Cathedral of Notre-Dame, in Coutances, France. It is possibly the finest extant example of 13th-century Norman Gothic architecture. Built following a fire in 1218, it was probably finished when Bishop Jean d'Essey was buried in the *chevet* in 1274. The nave chapels and axial Lady Chapel are 14th-century additions. Its *chevet*, with seven radiating chapels, recalls the plans of the Cathedrals of Amiens, Beauvais, and especially Le Mans. The tall double aisles of the *chevet* reflect the elevational schemes of Le Mans and Bourges. Throughout the interior there is a clarity of design and crispness of detail that is unmatched in the region. The octagonal crossing lantern interior is one of the finest in France.

BIBLIOGRAPHY. E. Lefèvre-Pontalis, "Coutances," *Congrès Archéologique de France, Caen*, LXXV, vol. 1, 1908.

COUTAUD, LUCIEN. French painter, graphic artist, and stage designer (1904–). He was born in Meynes and studied in Nîmes and Paris. His paintings are realistic in style and fantastic in subject. He has been well known for his sets and costumes since the late 1920s.

BIBLIOGRAPHY. H. Parmelin, *Cinq peintres et le théâtre*, Paris, 1956.

COUTERE, COLIJN VAN, see COTER, COLIJN.

COUTURE, THOMAS. French painter (b. Senlis, 1815; d. Villiers-le-Bel, near Paris, 1879). Couture studied with Gros and Delaroche in Paris and at an early age attracted attention with the *Jeune Vénitien après une orgie*, which he exhibited in the Salon of 1840. The climax of his popularity came in 1847, when he exhibited his masterpiece, *La Décadence des Romains* (Paris, Louvre), and won the medal for first place at the Salon. This led to his being appointed court painter to Napoleon III. Couture's style combined, within the academic formula, a Venetian sense of color with a very disciplined sense of design. He was also important as a teacher. Among his students were Manet and Anselm Feuerbach.

BIBLIOGRAPHY. J. C. Van Dyke, ed., *Modern French Masters*, New York, 1896; T. Couture, *Thomas Couture (1815–1879): Sa vie—son oeuvre . . .*, Paris, 1932.

COUTURIER, ROBERT. French sculptor (1905–). Couturier was born in Angoulême; his early training left little impression on him, but in 1928 he met Maillol and welcomed his instruction. Couturier has exhibited internationally and has taught at the Ecole Nationale des Arts Décoratifs. He abandoned classicism by 1944 and began producing attenuated, disembodied figures. In order to involve the surrounding space, he worked in bronze but later he returned to stone.

BIBLIOGRAPHY. J. Selz, *Modern Sculpture: Origins and Evolution*, New York, 1963.

COUWENBERGH, CHRISTIAEN VAN. Dutch genre, history, and portrait painter (b. Delft, 1604; d. Cologne, 1667). Couwenbergh was a pupil of Jan van Nes. He was in Italy before 1625, and by 1627 he was a member of the Delft guild. He worked for Prince Frederick Henry at the castle at Honselaersdijk (1638) and in The Hague (1647). In 1654 he settled in Cologne, where he worked as a portrait painter.

BIBLIOGRAPHY. J. G. van Gelder, "De Schilders van de Oranjezaal," *Nederlandsch Kunsthistorisch Jaarboek*, II, 1948-49.

COVARRUBIAS, ALONSO DE. Spanish sculptor and architect (1488–1570). Covarrubias was first active as a sculptor in various Castilian cities, creating the elaborate portal for the Church of La Piedad in Guadalajara (1526) and working in the Sigüenza and Toledo cathedrals. As royal architect (1534–53) he designed such buildings as the Alcázar in Toledo (1537) and the Archbishop's Palace in Alcalá (ca. 1540) in a conservative Plateresque style.

Miguel Covarrubias, *Self-portrait.* Fastlicht Collection, Mexico, D.F.

COVARRUBIAS, MIGUEL. Mexican draftsman and painter (1904–57). Born in Mexico City, Covarrubias began his career as a caricaturist and achieved success in the old *Vanity Fair* and *The New Yorker*. Through Adolfo Best-Maugard, he became interested in various art forms; this interest led to a lifelong enthusiasm for ethnology and archaeology, especially that of Mexico, and to an extraordinary collection of pre-Conquest art, later willed to the Mexico City National Museum of Anthropology.

Widely traveled, especially in more exotic regions, Covarrubias wrote and illustrated books on Bali, the Isthmus of Tehuantepec (*Mexico South*), and so on. His archaeological studies produced a monumental work (*The Eagle, the Jaguar, and the Serpent*) on pre-Conquest Mexico. It was left unfinished but was later published. Related to his studies of culture was a series of mural-scaled maps of the Pacific area for the 1939 San Francisco Fair, later transferred to New York City, as well as a map of Mexico's popular arts for the Museum of Popular Arts in Mexico City. He also designed theater sets in New York.

His era as director of the dance department of the Instituto de Bellas Artes was brilliant. He may be considered a gifted illustrator of cosmopolitan breadth, with facility and wit, rather than a painter per se.

BIBLIOGRAPHY. M. Helm, *Modern Mexican Painters*, New York, 1941; B. S. Myers, *Mexican Painting in Our Time*, New York, 1956.
JOSEPH A. BAIRD, JR.

COVERT, JOHN. American painter (1882–   ). Covert was born in Pittsburgh and studied there. He lived in Europe from 1909 to 1914. His few works were influenced by the Dadaism of Duchamp and the mechanism of Picabia, both of whom he knew.

BIBLIOGRAPHY. G. H. Hamilton, "John Covert: Early American Modern," *College Art Journal*, XII, Fall, 1952.

COVER TILE, *see* IMBREX.

COWICHAN INDIANS. Salishan group inhabiting southern Vancouver Island, British Columbia. The characteristic Cowichan art is wood sculpture. The outstanding forms are house posts involving human and animal forms, possibly with narrative content; and masks that often combine human and bird traits. The house posts are often well over life size.

Cowichan and other Salishan art is motivated in part by the drive to achieve or enhance "power" and to effect harmony between the world of real beings and that of supernatural spirits. Social factors, too, are instrumental in art production. Cowichan sculpture is represented in major eastern and northwestern ethnological museums.

See also SALISH INDIANS.

BIBLIOGRAPHY. P. S. Wingert, *American Indian Art: A Study of the Northwest Coast*, New York, 1949.

COX, DAVID. English landscape painter, principally in water color (1783–1859). Cox was born in Deritend, Birmingham. After a brief apprenticeship to a miniaturist named Fieldler, he worked at the Birmingham theater as assistant to James de Maria, the chief scene painter. He settled in London in 1804 and continued for a time to work at scene painting, but turned more and more to landscape in water color, in which he received lessons from John Varley. In 1805 he paid the first of many visits to North Wales. Cox joined the Old Water-Colour Society in 1812 and exhibited there throughout his career.

Like most water-colorists, Cox had to supplement his income by teaching. He published several manuals, the most important being *Treatise on Landscape Painting and Effect in Water Colour* (1814). He lived at Hereford (1814–27), where he taught drawing at a girls' school; returned to London (1827–41); and then retired to Harborne, a semirural suburb of Birmingham.

Cox was the last major figure of the English water-color school. Influenced by Varley, his early work tends toward careful flat washes and classical compositions. His later, more famous style is sketchy and atmospheric, often utilizing brilliant, broken color in scenes of wind-swept heaths and moors. Many characteristic water colors were painted on coarse wrapping paper. At times Cox is unduly repetitious, and his sentiment stereotyped, but at his best he forms an important bridge between John Constable and late-19th-century impressionism. Few artists have conveyed so vividly the effects of gathering storms and winds rising across upland country. After 1840, under the influence of William James Müller, he turned increasingly to oil painting. In his last works he becomes more dramatic, perhaps in emulation of Turner, dwelling upon themes of solitary figures grappling with the elements. The best public collection of his works is owned by the Birmingham Art Gallery.

BIBLIOGRAPHY. N. N. Solly, *Memoir of the Life of David Cox*, London, 1873; W. Hall, *A Biography of David Cox*, London, 1881; A. J. Finberg, *Drawings of David Cox*, London, 1906; F. G. Roe, *Cox, the Master*, Leigh-on-Sea, 1946; T. Cox, *David Cox*, London, 1947.
DAVID M. LOSHAK

David Cox, *A Windy Day*. Tate Gallery, London. A characteristic work by the last major figure of the English water-color school.

COX, JAN. Belgian painter and graphic artist (1919–   ). He was born in The Hague and studied in Antwerp and Ghent. He was a founding member of La Jeune Peinture Belge (Brussels, 1945) and a member of L'Art Contemporain group (Antwerp, 1949). He went to the United States in 1956. Cox is primarily concerned with the human form, and his most recent works are mystically symbolic, nearly surreal figure compositions.

BIBLIOGRAPHY. A. Corbet, *Jan Cox*, Antwerp, 1952.

COX, KENYON. American traditionalist painter (b. Warren, Ohio, 1856; d. New York City, 1919). He studied at the Pennsylvania Academy of Fine Arts (1876) and with Duran and Gérôme in Paris (1877).

In New York, Cox painted murals, such as *The Light of Learning*, that echoed the manner of Titian and Veronese in their use of rich colors, intricate rhythms, and ample forms. His learned and gracious designs ran counter to contemporary taste, for he felt that he could not find creativity within himself but only in academic study.

BIBLIOGRAPHY. K. Cox, *The Classic Point of View*, New York, 1911.

COXIE, MICHIEL I. Flemish painter (b. Mechlin, 1499; d. there, 1592). Coxie was a student of Bernard van Orley in Brussels. While in Rome (1531–34) he executed frescoes for Cardinal Enckevoort; in 1534 he became a member of the Academy of S. Luke. Back in Mechlin in 1539, he was made a master of the guild. From 1543 to 1563 he resided mostly in Brussels. Coxie was in demand in the major courts of Europe. His works, very numerous and mostly religious, are highly Italianate and hark back specifically to Raphael, so that Coxie was known as the Flemish Raphael.

BIBLIOGRAPHY. L. van Puyvelde, *La Peinture flamande au siècle de Bosch et Breughel*, Paris, 1962.

COYPEL, ANTOINE. French painter (1661–1722). He was born in Paris and at the age of eleven was a student at the French Academy in Rome, of which his father, Noël Coypel, was director. In Paris he won the Grand Prix (1676) and became academician and First Painter to Louis XIV's brother (1681) and to the future Regent (1688), professor (1692), director of the Royal Academy (1714), and First Painter to the King (1715); he was ennobled in 1717. He was the most manifest exponent of Italian baroque art found in France up to that time (*History of Aeneas*, Palais Royal, for the Regent, 1702–05, and the vault of the Chapel at Versailles, for Louis XIV, 1708–09). His bright color and light treatment of amorous classical themes, encouraged by Charles de La Fosse and Roger de Piles, led to the triumph of the rococo style in the next

Charles-Antoine Coypel, *Perseus Delivering Andromeda*, Louvre, Paris. A work anticipating the melodramatics of Greuze.

generation. His best works are 280 drawings (mostly in Paris, Louvre), showing the combined influences of Titian, Correggio, and Rubens, and done in a three-color crayon technique that anticipates Watteau.

BIBLIOGRAPHY. L. Dimier, *Les Peintres français du XVIIIe siècle . . .*, vol. 1, Paris, 1928.

COYPEL, CHARLES-ANTOINE. French painter, orator, and author (1694–1752). Born in Paris, he was the son of Antoine Coypel and a pupil at the Royal Academy in 1705. He became an academician and First Painter to the Duc d'Orléans (1715), Keeper of Louis XV's pictures (1722), professor (1733), rector (1746), and First Painter to the King and director of the Royal Academy (1747). He had apartments in the Louvre from 1722 until his death.

Though the least able painter among the Coypels, he affirms, through the influence of his academic pronouncements, the artistic principles that characterized the Louis XV period and that had been formulating since the time of Noël Coypel, his grandfather. In lectures his stress upon the expressive capacities in painting of "hyperbole, metaphor, comparison, apostrophe, combat of sentiments, explicit and implied description, repetition, antithesis, transition and amplification" evinces the literary tools of the playwright and explains his manifest fascination with the theater, a major preoccupation of the 18th century. He wrote *Les Folies de Cardenic*, a comedy performed before the King in 1721, which borrowed from Cervantes, and twenty-two scenarios for plays, *à l'Italienne*.

His concomitant activity in painting, whether in history or genre, bespeaks the comedy of manners. *Perseus Delivering Andromeda* (Paris, Louvre), *Rinaldo Protected by Love from the Fury of Armida* (Nantes Museum), and even *Little Girls Playing at Being the Lady* exaggerate Le Brun's principles of facial expression and anticipate in many respects the melodramatics of Greuze. Though Coypel is an able portraitist of actors and opera singers (*Adrienne Lecouvreur*, *Charlotte Desmares*, *LeKain*, and *Jelyotte*, all in the Louvre) he is most noted for his tasteful and witty interpretations of the *Histoire de Don Quichotte* (1714–51) in Gobelin tapestry designs.

BIBLIOGRAPHY. A. Fontaine, *Les Doctrines d'art en France . . .*, Paris, 1909; I. Jamieson, *Charles Antoine Coypel, premier peintre de Louis XV et auteur dramatique*, Paris, 1930.

GEORGE V. GALLENKAMP

COYPEL, NOEL. French history painter (1628–1707). Noël Coypel was born in Paris and was the sire of a line of influential artists, categorized under the reigns of Louis XIV (Noël Coypel, the father), the Regency (Antoine Coypel, the son), and Louis XV (Charles-Antoine Coypel, the grandson). Through a second marriage he is the father of Noël-Nicolas Coypel (1690–1734). He was early the pupil of a certain Poncet, in Orléans, then of Quillerier, in Paris. He became an academician in 1663. While director of the French Academy in Rome (1672–75), Coypel had become a disciple of Nicolas Poussin, but he later differed from Poussin in his partiality toward Flemish realism over the Italian "grand manner." As professor in the Paris Academy (1682), rector (1690), and director (1695–99), he generated the ascendancy of the more liberal principles of the "Moderns," or Rubenists. His tapestry designs, *The Triumph of the Gods* and *Zephyr and Flora* (shown in the Salon of 1699), demonstrate this tendency, while his earlier collaborative decorative works at Versailles, the Trianon, and the Invalides are more typical of Louis XIV classicizing academic principles.

BIBLIOGRAPHY. A. Dumont, "Documents sur les Dumont [sc.] et sur les Coypel," *Nouvelles Archives de l'Art français,* 1874–75; A. Dumont, "Documents nouveaux sur les Coypel et les Boullogne et sur les Dumont," *Nouvelles Archives de l'Art français,* 1877.

COYSEVOX, ANTOINE. French sculptor (b. Lyons, 1640; d. Paris, 1721). At eighteen, Coysevox was recommended by André Le Nôtre to Louis Lerambert, Guardian of the King's Antiquities. He fulfilled his apprenticeship and became court sculptor in 1666. From 1666 to 1671 he was in Alsace working for François Egon, Bishop of Strasbourg, on stucco work at Egon's Château Noir of Saverne (destroyed by fire in 1779). By 1676 Coysevox was definitively established in Paris and was received into the Royal Academy. From 1678 on, he worked at the head of stucco carvers in the Grande Galerie at Versailles on his most important ensemble. In the adjoining Salon of War he executed a stucco *tondo* of Louis XIV, the *Passage of the Rhine*, from designs of Charles Le Brun. Coysevox also did statues for the façade of the Marble Court at Versailles as well as for the Hôtel and Church of the Invalides in Paris. Among his more important works is a series of tombs, including that of the Marquis of Vaubrun, that of the Count d'Harcourt, and—most important of all—those of Cardinal Mazarin (1689–93; Paris, Institut de France), executed with Tuby and Le Hongre, and of the finance minister, Colbert, for St-Eustache. From 1694 on, Coysevox directed the School of Gobelins Tapestries with Le Clerc and Tuby. His statue of Louis XIV (1715) for the choir of Notre-Dame de Paris depicts the monarch offering himself to the Virgin, recalling the vow of Louis XIII to dedicate himself and his kingdom to her in return for a male heir.

Coysevox's preeminence under Louis XIV also prefigures many themes of the 18th century; besides the training of his nephews the Coustous, his other pupils, such as Le Lorrain and J.-L. Lemoyne, educated most sculptors of the 18th century. Coysevox's works for Marly, including the equestrians *Fame* and *Mercury* (1702; now in Paris, Place de la Concorde), herald the approach to naturalistic and mythological themes of the following century. Besides adaptations of antique statues, Coysevox was also largely responsible for the popularization in sculpture of the mythological travesty, such as the *Duchess of Burgundy as Diana* (1710; Paris, Louvre), which is similar in treatment to the paintings of Rigaud and Largillière. By contrast to such contemporary baroque sculptors as Bernini, Coysevox represents a formal and reserved classical style.

BIBLIOGRAPHY. A. Boinet, "Les Bustes de Coyzevox," *Gazette des Beaux-Arts,* series 3, II, 1920; G. Keller-Dorian, *Antoine Coysevox: Catalogue raisonné...,* Paris, 1920; A. Michel, *Histoire de l'art,* vol. 6, pt. 2, Paris, 1922; M.-E. Sainte-Beuve, "Le Tombeau du Marquis de Vaubrun...," *Gazette des Beaux-Arts,* series 5, XVIII, 1928.

W. MC ALLISTER JOHNSON

COZENS, ALEXANDER. English landscape draftsman and water-colorist (1717?–86). Born in Russia, he was the son of an English shipbuilder in the employ of Peter the Great. Virtually nothing is known of his early life in Russia and but little of his subsequent career. He was in England in

or before 1742 but may have returned to Russia. In 1746 he was in Rome. Soon afterward he was back in England, where he appears to have remained for the rest of his life, apart from a possible trip to the Continent in 1764.

Cozens earned his living principally as a drawing master, teaching at Christ's Hospital (1749–54) and later, from about 1763, at Eton, where Sir George Beaumont was among his pupils. He also taught privately, William Beckford being his most eminent pupil as well as his intimate friend. He did oil paintings as well as drawings and water colors, though only four small oils on paper are known to exist today. The richest assemblage of his works was formerly in the collection of the late Paul Oppé, who did much to revive interest in this almost forgotten artist.

Cozens published or projected numerous treatises on such subjects as the artistic classification of trees, skies, and the human head; he even planned a systematic dissertation on morality with literary and pictorial illustrations. Thus he truly belonged to the 18th-century Enlightenment. But another side of his personality is disclosed in his most famous treatise, the *New Method of Assisting the Invention in Drawing Original Compositions of Landscape* (ca. 1785). Here he advocates the use of what he calls "blots"; these were actually very free, imaginative landscape sketches in monochrome, based on preconceived general ideas but executed almost "automatically," and intended to serve as nuclei for more finished compositions. Several of these "blots" survive; their spontaneity and unity of design anticipate the romantic landscape of the 19th century and, even more, the expressionism of the 20th. His more finished drawings, also mainly monochrome, are both in-

Antoine Coysevox, stucco bust of Louis XIV. Grande Galerie, Versailles.

John Robert Cozens, *The Lake and Villa of Nemi*. Girtin Collection. An example of the "elegiac" trend in 18th-century landscape.

ventive and extremely varied. Cozens nevertheless remained a man of the 18th century in his eccentricity of sentiment, in his emphasis on the desolation and horror of nature rather than on its attractiveness (on loneliness rather than solitude), and most of all in his arrival at a highly personal expression by a theoretical rather than an emotional route.

BIBLIOGRAPHY. A. P. Oppé, "A Roman Sketch-Book by Alexander Cozens," *Walpole Society*, XVI, 1928; M. Hardie, "Alexander Cozens," *Collector*, XI, 1930; A. P. Oppé, *Drawings and Paintings by Alexander Cozens*, London (Tate Gallery), 1946; A. P. Oppé, *Alexander and John Robert Cozens*, London, 1952. DAVID M. LOSHAK

COZENS, JOHN ROBERT. English landscape painter in water color (1752–97). The son of Alexander Cozens, he was probably born in London. Even less is known of his life than of that of his father, who was probably his teacher. In 1776 he exhibited at the Royal Academy of Arts an oil painting, *Hannibal Crossing the Alps*, by means of which he unsuccessfully attempted to gain election as an associate. The picture has disappeared, however, and with one exception no oil painting accepted as his work survives today. Cozens visited Italy twice (1776–79 and 1782–83). The remainder of his working life appears to have been spent largely in working up the sketches made on these trips into finished water colors. In 1793 he became insane and from then until he died in 1797, he was cared for by Dr. Thomas Monro, the alienist and prominent amateur artist. The expenses were met by a subscription initiated by Sir George Beaumont. Through Dr. Monro, Cozens' influence was transmitted to Girtin and Turner, and through Beaumont it reached Constable, who thought him "the greatest genius that ever touched landscape."

Examples of Cozens' work are in many museums and private collections in England; the Victoria and Albert Museum, in London, and the collection of Mr. Tom Girtin have perhaps the richest selection. John Cozens was the greatest representative of what has been called the "elegiac" trend in 18th-century landscape, which his father originated. Less varied and less inventive than his parent, he excelled him in emotional depth and in the "sublime" grandeur of his effects, though these were obtained by a rather laborious technique and a severely limited palette. "Cozens was all poetry," wrote Constable. It was a poetry of melancholy solitude amid the wonders of nature. Cozens found his greatest inspiration beside the volcanic lakes of the Alban Hills, Lake Albano and Lake Nemi, a country full of classical recollections; but Cozens translated it into an ominous reflection of the forces he no doubt felt were alienating him from these and all other humanistic associations. The pregnancy of his vision is enhanced by extraordinary fidelity of atmosphere, which is the product of a brooding contemplation.

BIBLIOGRAPHY. C. F. Bell and T. Girtin, "The Drawings and Sketches of John Robert Cozens," *Walpole Society Annual Volume*, XXIII, 1934/35; A. P. Oppé, *Alexander and John Robert Cozens*, London, 1952.

DAVID M. LOSHAK

COZZA, FRANCESCO. Italian painter (b. Stilo, 1605; d. Rome, 1682). Cozza was initially a pupil of Domenichino. He executed numerous frescoes in the churches of Rome, where his essentially academic and neoclassic style is relieved by a graceful feeling for lyric composition and attractive luminous color. Typical of his large works is the ceiling of the Library in the Collegio Innocenziano,

Rome, where an enormous number of figures are drawn into a program with complex allegorical content.

BIBLIOGRAPHY. E. K. Waterhouse, *Baroque Painting in Rome*, London, 1937.

COZZARELLI, GIACOMO. Italian architect and sculptor of the Sienese school (1453–1515). A pupil of Francesco di Giorgio, with whom he worked at the Ducal Palace in Urbino, Cozzarelli was particularly in demand as a military architect and as a bronze caster. In the former capacity he built the fort at Montepulciano. The sculptural group of the *Pietà* in the Church of the Osservanza near Siena and other works in terra cotta have been attributed to him.

COZZARELLI, GUIDOCCIO DI GIOVANNI. Italian painter (fl. 1450–1516). In most of his prolific output, this Sienese artist imitated his contemporary Matteo di Giovanni. His most expressive and decorative work was reserved for manuscript illumination, book covers, and *cassone* panels.

CRABBE (Crabbe van Espleghem), FRANS. Flemish painter (b. ca. 1480; d. Mechlin, 1553). He entered the Mechlin guild in 1501 and was its dean in 1533 and 1549. No work by Crabbe is known today. Van Mander describes a Passion in water color by him in a style akin to that of Lucas van Leyden. Crabbe has been mistakenly identified with F. Minnebroer and the Maître à l'Ecrevisse.

BIBLIOGRAPHY. C. van Mander, *Dutch and Flemish Painters*, tr. with intro. by C. van de Wall, New York, 1936.

CRABETH, WOUTER PIETERSZ., THE YOUNGER. Dutch genre and religious painter (b. Gouda, ca. 1593; d. there, 1644). He was the son of the burgomaster of Gouda and the grandson of the glass painter Wouter Pietersz. Crabeth the Elder. Crabeth was a pupil of Cornelis Ketel in Amsterdam and perhaps of Abraham Bloemaert in Utrecht. In 1615 he traveled to France and Italy, where he was influenced by the work of Caravaggio. By 1628 he was back in Gouda. He was also active in Utrecht.

BIBLIOGRAPHY. G. J. Hoogerwerff, *De Bentvueghels*, The Hague, 1952.

CRACELURE (Crackle). Fine lines or cracks visible on the surface of old paintings that extend through all layers of paint to the support (canvas, wood, and so on). Cracelure is caused by differences in the drying speeds of the varnish and paint. It is considered a fine point in the connoisseurship of old paintings.

CRACKLE AND CRACKLE WARE. Network of cracks in ceramic glaze brought about by unequal rates of contraction of the clay body and of the glaze during the cooling period after firing. Crackle can be deliberately induced by changes in the glaze formula or by sudden chilling of the ware by means of cold water before firing or a current of cold air afterward. The Chinese exploited the decorative possibilities in crackle from the Sung Dynasty onward, and it was a feature in many types of ware, particularly *kuan* ware. During the Ch'ing dynasty, the Chinese were especially adept in producing elaborate crackles, which were filled with Indian inks for emphasis. Crackle also refers to a network of fine cracks sometimes visible on the surface of old oil paintings.

See also CRACELURE; KUAN WARE.

BIBLIOGRAPHY. E. Hannover, *Pottery and Porcelain*, vol. 2: *The Far East*, London, 1925.

CRACOW: ST. MARY. Polish Gothic church built of brick in the second half of the 14th century. It preserves a number of stained-glass windows of the period. St. Mary is chiefly known for the stupendous altarpiece (known as the Cracow Altarpiece) completed in 1489 by Veit Stoss; this work represents the culmination of the late Gothic tradition of wooden altarpieces staffed with naturalistic figures. *See* STOSS, VEIT.

BIBLIOGRAPHY. V. Stoss, *Wit Stwosz: Ołtarz krakowski*, ed. by S. Dettloff, et al., Warsaw, 1951.

CRADLING. Restoration technique used to prevent or remedy the warping of the panel in paintings executed on wood. Strips of wood, usually glued in layers at right angles to one another, are attached to the back of the panel. These act as equalizers to the stresses that cause warping.

CRAESBEECK, JOOS VAN. Flemish painter of genre scenes (b. Neerlinter, ca. 1606; d. Brussels, 1654). Craesbeeck was a baker at the castle of Antwerp when he met Adriaen Brouwer, who was imprisoned there in 1633. He fell under the master's spell and decided to become a painter. He was admitted as such by the Guild of St. Luke at Antwerp the following year, and at Brussels in 1651. At first, Craesbeeck closely followed Brouwer's style and specialized in small genre scenes animated by a few figures only. It is hard to tell whether pictures from that period are by Brouwer or by Craesbeeck. Later Craesbeeck experimented with larger compositions, chiaroscuro effects, and romanticism in the style of Rembrandt. In further opposition to Brouwer's customs, he introduced

Cradling. Method of counteracting warping in panel paintings.

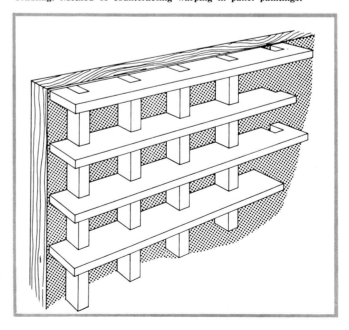

Edward Gordon Craig, design for Bach's *St. Matthew Passion*, 1901. The Arsenal, Paris.

female figures into scenes with a middle-class setting. *The Five Senses* (Antwerp, Royal Museum) is a representative work.

BIBLIOGRAPHY. K. Zoege von Manteuffel, "Joos van Craesbeeck," *Jahrbuch der Königlich Preuszischen Kunstsammlungen*, XXXVII, 1916; A. H. Cornette, *Introduction aux maîtres anciens du Musée Royal d'Anvers*, Antwerp, 1939.

CRAIG, EDWARD GORDON. English stage designer (b. Stevenage, 1872; d. Vence, France, 1966). Craig was the great pioneer of modern stage design. His exposition of a total and integrated conception of stage production has alternately been reviled and welcomed. During his early and brilliant career as an actor (1889–97) under Sir Henry Irving, he began to draw, eventually giving up acting to devote himself entirely to the reform of the theater. His earliest designs were for operatic productions (Handel and Purcell). The company in which his mother, the actress Ellen Terry, was the leading member then commissioned him to create designs for Ibsen's *Vikings at Helgoland* and Shakespeare's *Much Ado About Nothing* (1903). By 1905 Craig was well known throughout Europe; there he enjoyed his greatest success and influence. He received commissions from the Lessing Theater in Berlin; for Eleonora Duse's production of *Electra* in Italy; for the Abbey Theater in Dublin through his friend, the poet William Butler Yeats; and for a production of *Hamlet* (1912) by the Moscow Art Theater under Stanislavsky.

In these productions Craig broke the barriers of static, two-dimensional stage design. Using portable screens, abstracted but firm outlines of architectural or landscape forms, fluid lighting from above rather than from footlights, and rich but subdued colors, he created a total, three-dimensional setting, removing the theatrical experience to a world of poetic and dramatic imagination. Even costume designs were integrated into the whole. This totality and the towering epic forms often tended to subordinate the individual actor, a consequence of which some critics still disapprove.

Craig was also a prolific writer, concerned primarily with theatrical reform. His seminal work is *On the Art of the Theater*, first published in 1911. The two magazines he created, *The Page* (1898–1901) and *The Mark* (1908–29), presented old as well as new ideas. The disruption caused by World War I largely ended Craig's career as a theatrical designer, with the exception of productions for the Berlin and Danish state theaters (1926). He subsequently turned to writing and theatrical scholarship. Acclaimed but unsupported in his own country, he left England in 1929 and settled in Vence.

BIBLIOGRAPHY. J. Leeper, *E. Gordon Craig, Designs for the Theater*, Harmondsworth, Middlesex, 1948; D. Bablet, *Edward Gordon Craig*, Paris, 1962.

DONALD GODDARD

CRAIG, JAMES. Scottish architect (d. Edinburgh, 1795). In 1766 Craig won the competition for the planning of the New Town of Edinburgh. His plan was schematic and took little account of the conditions of the countryside. He laid out the first part, a parallelogram of streets with two squares. Each of the terminal squares on the main axis of the plan was intended to have a church. One square was named after the patron saint of England, St. George, the other, of Scotland, St. Andrew. Craig also designed some new buildings, but his masterpiece, the neoclassical Physicians' Hall, no longer stands.

BIBLIOGRAPHY. G. Hay, *The Architecture of Scottish Post-Reformation Churches, 1560–1843*, Oxford, 1957; J. Summerson, *Architecture in Britain, 1530–1830*, 4th rev. ed., Baltimore, 1963.

CRAM, RALPH ADAMS. American architect and writer (b. Hampton Falls, N.H., 1863; d. 1942). After training in New England, he became a partner of Charles Wentworth in 1890 and of Bertram Goodhue and Frank Ferguson between 1899 and 1914. Primarily an architect of colleges and churches, he was a philosophical leader of the 20th-century Gothic movement in America and a leading exponent of English Gothic styles, although he designed in other styles as well. He was responsible for the Swedenborgian Cathedral, Bryn Athyn, Pa. (1913- 28), erected largely according to medieval methods of construction with the workmen organized into pseudo-medieval guilds; and for the Cathedral of St. John the Divine, New York City, the planning of which he took over in 1907. He also constructed buildings for Princeton University, Williams College, Rice Institute, and the United States Military Academy at West Point. He wrote some twenty books on religion, architecture, sociology, and philosophy. *See* ST. JOHN THE DIVINE CATHEDRAL, NEW YORK.

See also CRAM, GOODHUE AND FERGUSON.

BIBLIOGRAPHY. R. A. Cram, *My Life in Architecture*, Boston, 1936.

CRAM, GOODHUE AND FERGUSON. American architectural firm of Ralph Adams Cram (1863–1942), Bertram Grosvenor Goodhue (1869–1924), and Frank W. Ferguson (1861–1926). In reaction to the Victorian Gothic, the firm brought a more elemental appreciation of Gothic modes into great popularity in both ecclesiastical and secular architecture between 1899 and 1914. It achieved recognition after winning the competition for the United States Military Academy at West Point, in 1903, with a collegiate Gothic design said to show the perfect union of Cram's austerity and Goodhue's exuberance. Favoring no particular Gothic mode, although Cram preferred English sobriety and Goodhue French flamboyance, the firm produced buildings in a variety of English and Continental medieval styles, including St. Thomas's Church in New York (1906) and the Rice Institute Administration Building in Houston (1910). *See* CRAM, RALPH ADAMS; FERGUSON, FRANK W.; GOODHUE, BERTRAM GROSVENOR.

BIBLIOGRAPHY. Cram & Ferguson, *The Work of Cram and Ferguson, Architects...* (Introduction by C. D. Maginnis), New York, 1929.

CRANACH, LUCAS, THE ELDER. German painter, engraver, and designer of woodcuts (b. Kronach, 1472; d. Weimar, 1553). He was called after his birthplace, Kronach, although his family name may have been Sunder or Müller. Very little is known about his early training, but it is generally assumed that Cranach studied first with his father in Kronach and then traveled in Bavaria. His earliest dated works are stylistically close to Altdorfer and the Danube school. About 1502 he appeared in Vienna, where he became known in the intellectual circles of the

Lucas Cranach, the Elder, *Eve.* **Uffizi, Florence.**

newly founded university and executed his first dated works. Late in 1504 Cranach was called to Wittenberg by the Saxon elector Frederick III (the Wise). There he became court painter to the first of three successive Saxon electors. He was highly esteemed in the court, both as an artist and as a loyal and valuable political servant. In 1537 he was elected Bürgermeister of Wittenberg. A close personal friend of the last Saxon elector, John Frederick (the Unfortunate), Cranach accompanied him into exile in 1550 after the Elector's defeat at the Battle of Mühlberg (1547).

In addition to his important relationship with the court, Cranach was a lifelong friend of Martin Luther. He portrayed the Reformer many times and painted the first Protestant paintings under Luther's direction.

Cranach's work falls roughly into three stylistic periods: an early period, closely associated with the Danube school; the early Wittenberg period, his most vigorous one; and the late Wittenberg period, characterized by a growing mechanical quality and subsequent crystallization of style. The works of the early period exhibit an intense interest in landscape and the expressionistic possibilities of the human figure. The chief early works are *Crucifixion* (1502; Vienna, Schottenstift), the *Portrait of Dr. Reuss* (1503; Nürnberg, German National Museum), and *Crucifixion* (1503; Munich, Old Pinacothek).

The early Wittenberg period witnessed the flowering of Cranach's graphic work. In *St. Christopher, Venus and Amor,* and *Rest on the Flight into Egypt* (all dated 1506) Cranach employed the new chiaroscuro technique in a most effective manner. The important paintings of this period are the *St. Katherine Altar* (Dresden, State Art Collections), *Portrait of Christoph Scheurl* (Nürnberg, German National Museum), and *Madonna under the Fir Tree* (Breslau Cathedral).

In the late Wittenberg period, Cranach established a large workshop that produced numerous repetitions of the master's works, mainly portraits, female nudes, and religious compositions peculiar to Lutheranism. In his last years his interest in painting waned as he became involved in the political events of the Reformation.

See also MASTER L Cz.

BIBLIOGRAPHY. M. J. Friedländer and J. Rosenberg, *Die Gemälde von Lukas Cranach*, Berlin, 1932; J. Jahn, *Lukas Cranach als Graphiker*, Leipzig, 1955.   DONALD L. EHRESMANN

CRANE, WALTER. English painter, illustrator, designer, and writer on art (1845–1915). Born in Liverpool, Crane was the son of a minor painter. He spent most of his early years at Torquay, in Devon. After his family moved to London, he was apprenticed (1859–62) to William J. Linton, the wood engraver. In 1862 he exhibited at the Royal Academy of Arts, whose policies he later opposed. Crane's painting, much of it allegorical, was influenced by the Pre-Raphaelites. In later life he became one of the leading spirits in the Arts and Crafts movement and also (following the example of William Morris) a militant socialist. His illustrations, especially of children's books, became immensely popular, and as a designer of wallpapers, textiles, and so on, he was a powerful influence in shaping contemporary taste on the Continent as well as in England.

BIBLIOGRAPHY. P. G. Konody, *The Art of Walter Crane*, London, 1902; W. Crane, *An Artist's Reminiscences*, London, 1907.

CRATER, *see* KRATER.

CRAVANT, CHURCH OF. Early French church of the Loire region, dated about 900(?). Cravant is especially noted for its patterned stonework, a type of masonry for which the region was particularly known. At Cravant the decorative patterns, as at St-Généroux, create an architectonic modality primarily associated with the First Romanesque of southern France.

CRAWFORD, LEONARD. Australian painter (1920–   ). His style is associated with the contemporary abstract school of painters in Melbourne. His geometric-abstract painting is characterized by a freedom of movement and a subtle scale of tone-color relationships. Crawford is mainly concerned with the expression of musical themes in plastic form.

CRAWFORD, RALSTON. American precisionist painter (1906–   ). He was born in Saint Catherines, Ontario, Canada, and lives in New York City. His family settled in the United States when he was four, at which time he was naturalized. He attended high school in Buffalo, N.Y., and was a sailor before studying at the Otis Art Institute in Los Angeles. In 1927 he worked for Walt Disney. He later studied at the Pennsylvania Academy of Fine Arts, Columbia University, and the Barnes Foundation. He had his first one-man show in 1939 in New York City. Crawford has taught at several schools, among them the Art School of the Brooklyn Museum and the University of Minnesota, and is currently a professor at Hofstra College, Hempstead, N.Y. In 1961 he had an exhibition of color lithographs at the Nordness Gallery in New York. Crawford depicts cityscapes, emphasizing hard edges and planes, often reducing values to two or three tones.

BIBLIOGRAPHY. R. B. Freeman, *The Lithographs of Ralston Crawford*, Lexington, Ky., 1962.

CRAWFORD, THOMAS. American sculptor (b. New York, 1814; d. London, 1857). He studied with Launitz, Frazee, and Thorwaldsen. His outstanding works are the huge *Freedom* crowning the dome of the United States Capitol and the equestrian *Washington* in Richmond, Va. Despite a certain tendency toward original adaptation of ideas taken directly from classical and early Renaissance art, Crawford reflected a derivative neoclassicism he learned in Italy.

CRAWHALL, JOSEPH. English painter (b. Morpeth, 1861; d. London, 1913). He studied with Aimé Morot in Paris. Crawhall was a superb water-colorist of animals and birds, which were accurately observed and effectively composed.

BIBLIOGRAPHY. A. Bury, *Joseph Crawhall: The Man and the Artist*, London, 1958.

CRAYER, GASPARD DE. Flemish painter of religious subjects and portraits (b. Antwerp, 1584 or 1582; d. Ghent, 1669). He was a pupil of Michiel Coxie in Brussels and became a master there in 1607 and in Ghent in 1664. De Crayer was strongly influenced by Rubens and followed the latter's evolution, without, however, going beyond Rubens's style of about 1630. His heavy shadows point to

Gaspard de Crayer, *Pietà with the Portraits of Burgomaster De Dongelberghe and His Wife*. Fine Arts Museum, Brussels.

Crayon engraving. François Boucher, *Study of a Male Head*. Albertina, Vienna.

Romanist reminiscences and constitute an acknowledgement of *tenebroso* techniques. The compositions are always well thought through and solid in technique; the color evolves from early hard local colors to a palette composed of pastel tones. In his portraiture there exists a valid point of departure with the signed *Pietà with the Portraits of Burgomaster De Dongelberghe and His Wife* (Brussels, Fine Arts Museum), whereas the much later *Cardinal Infant Ferdinand* (Madrid, Prado) lacks strong characterization.

BIBLIOGRAPHY. E. van Terlaan, "Un grand artiste méconnu: Gaspard de Crayer," *Gazette des Beaux-Arts*, XIII, 1926.

CRAYON. In the traditional sense, a small stick for drawing made of pigments (usually black or red) in a chalk medium, and therefore synonymous with chalk. More recently, crayon refers to the wax crayon that originally was a drawing tool in lithography.

CRAYON ENGRAVING. An intaglio (incised) print process that aims at rendering the quality of line of a chalk drawing. This technique, which emerged in the second half of the 18th century, is little practiced today. It grew out of the need to satisfy demands for reproductions of the drawings of Watteau, Boucher, and many others. Since it is a reproductive rather than an original technique, it has not attracted contemporary artists.

In essence, crayon engraving, or engraving in the chalk manner, is worked on a standard gauge metal plate in a fashion resembling both etching and mezzotint. A hard ground is laid on the surface of the plate as in etching. A pencil sketch may be transferred to the grounded plate by placing the sketch face down on the plate and running it through an etching press with light pressure. Next, various roulettes and a *mattoir* (a multi-pointed, butt-tipped instrument) are employed to pierce the ground in order to produce a simulation of a drawing. Areas that are to appear as darks in the final print will have many more and closer punctures than areas that are to be light or gray in value.

The plate is immersed in a bath of acid, then removed and stopped out at different intervals according to the tonal effects desired. Printing proceeds as in etching.

See also ETCHING; MEZZOTINT.

JULES HELLER

CREATION. The complete six-day cycle of creation described in Genesis, chapter 2. It has posed difficult problems for the artist. Only in the late Middle Ages did complete cycles in art become common, although there are earlier examples in which each day is given a separate scene (altar frontal, Salerno Cathedral; Vienna Genesis, 6th cent., Vienna, Austrian National Library). Byzantine mosaics presented the cycle on a monumental scale for the first time (Monreale Cathedral; Palermo, Palatine Chapel; both 12th cent.), and the culminating work is Michelangelo's frescoes for the Sistine Chapel ceiling (1508–12).

CREATION OF ADAM. Fresco painting by Michelangelo, in the Sistine Chapel, Rome. *See* MICHELANGELO BUONARROTI.

CREDI, LORENZO DI. Italian painter, sculptor, and goldsmith of the Florentine school (ca. 1458–1537). Vasari gives his real name as Lorenzo Sciarpelloni. Recorded as a painter in the studio of Verrocchio in 1480/81, Lorenzo remained an associate there until the master's death in 1488. He then acted as executor of Verrocchio's will and directed (until the intervention of Leopardi in 1490) the completion of Verrocchio's equestrian monument of Bartolommeo Colleoni in Venice. According to Vasari, Lorenzo also completed the Tomb of the Cardinal Forteguerri in the Cathedral of Pistoia, which Verrocchio had left unfinished at the time of his death. No independent sculptural works may be ascribed with any certainty to Lorenzo.

His activity as a painter can be reconstructed on the basis of a few documented works. In 1493 (not 1503, as is sometimes stated) he completed the altarpiece *Madonna and Child with Two Saints* (Paris, Louvre). Several works are documented in or about 1510: the *Nativity* (Florence, Uffizi), *St. Bartholemew* (Florence, Or San Michele), and an altarpiece, *Madonna and Child with Four Saints* (Pistoia, S. Maria delle Grazie). In 1523 he painted the *St. Michael* for the Florence Cathedral, now in the sacristy, and in the following year restored the equestrian frescoes by Paolo Uccello and Andrea del Castagno there.

Many panel paintings have been attributed to Lorenzo, but he does not seem to have worked in fresco. His hand may be seen in an altarpiece of the *Madonna and Child with Two Saints* (1478–85) in the Cathedral of Pistoia, executed in the studio of Verrocchio. A self-portrait in the National Gallery of Art in Washington, D.C., has the date 1456 inscribed on it as the year of the artist's birth (the authenticity of the inscription is questionable). His *Venus* in the Uffizi is, according to tradition, the only one of a series of paintings of pagan subjects not destroyed in the burning of the vanities of 1497. One of Lorenzo's finest works is the *Annunciation* in the Uffizi.

Both his paintings and his drawings show the influence of Verrocchio and, particularly, of the young Leonardo da Vinci. In his attention to detail and to glossy surfaces Lorenzo seems to have been influenced by Flemish painting. His style is often characterized by an exaggerated smoothness and a somewhat flaccid, fully rounded geometry. Several pupils worked in his manner and repeated many of his designs.

BIBLIOGRAPHY. B. Berenson, "Verrocchio e Leonardo, Leonardo e Credi," *Bollettino d'arte*, XXVII, 1933; G. Passavant, *Andrea del Verrocchio als Maler*, Düsseldorf, 1959.　　HELLMUT WOHL

CREMER, FRITZ. German sculptor (1906–　). Born in Arnsberg, he worked in Essen and studied with Gerstel in Berlin. He went to Vienna in 1940, and since 1945 he has been a professor at the Berlin Academy. Cremer has designed commemorative monuments at Auschwitz, Buchenwald, Mathausen, and Vienna since World War II. His work shows the influence of Barlach and Kollwitz.

CREMONA CATHEDRAL. One of the largest medieval monuments in Italy, erected between 1107 and 1190 in the Romanesque-Lombard style. It consists of a nave three bays long, two side aisles, two widely projecting transepts that are three bays long and are supplied with side aisles, a choir of two bays flanked by side aisles, three semicircular apses, and a crypt. It is vaulted throughout. The exterior is adorned with five turrets. The external galleries and a two-story entrance porch on the west front are characteristic of Lombard architecture. The interior is noted for frescoes by 16th-century Cremonese painters.

BIBLIOGRAPHY. A. Monteverdi, *Il duomo di Cremona, il battistero e il torrazzo*, Milan, 1911; A. K. Porter, *Lombard Architecture*, vol. 2, New Haven, 1916.

CREMONINI, LEONARDO. Italian painter (1925–　). He was born in Bologna and studied there and in Milan. Cremonini's paintings—of animals and, more recently, figures—combine somewhat expressionistic means with the classicism of controlled composition.

CRENELATION. Parapet having notches, called crenels, alternating with the solid portions, or merlons, associated with battlements. Crenelated molding, which has an indented or embattled pattern, is frequently found in medieval work. *See* BATTLEMENT.

CREPIDOMA (Crepis). Stepped platform of a Greek temple. Most frequently it consists of three steps, as in the Parthenon, Athens.

CRESILAS (Kresilas). Greek sculptor from Cydonia in Crete (fl. 450–425 B.C.). He made a figure of an Amazon for the famous contest described by Pliny (perhaps represented in copies by the "Capitoline type") and a portrait of Pericles, of which the type represented by the well-known herm in the British Museum must be a copy.

CRESPI, ANTONIO MARIA (Il Bustino). Italian painter (fl. 17th cent.). He was the son of the painter Benedetto Crespi, and like him nicknamed "Il Bustino" for their native town, Busto Arsizio, near Milan. With his father he painted a series of frescoes of the birth, martyrdom, and triumph of St. Lawrence in the parish church of Laino in Val d'Intelvi. His portrait of the Dominican Pio Rossi of Piacenza was engraved by G. B. Coriolano.

CRESPI, DANIELE. Italian painter (ca. 1600–30). He probably studied with Il Cerano and G. C. Procaccini in his native Milan, where he worked during his brief career. He also received commissions in Novara, Piacenza, and Pavia. Crespi's paintings reflect the popular and austere religious orientation of S. Carlo Borromeo of Milan in their simple, direct, and realistic presentation (*S. Carlo Borromeo at Supper*, ca. 1628; Milan, Sta Maria della Passione). His use of glancing overhead light to clarify forms, his realistic, popular types, and his economy of means (*Christ Carrying the Cross*, Milan, Brera) are reminiscent of Zurbarán.

BIBLIOGRAPHY. G. Nicodemi, *Daniele Crespi*, Busto Arsizio, 1930; R. Wittkower, *Art and Architecture in Italy, 1600–1750*, Baltimore, 1958.

CRESPI, GIOVANNI BATTISTA (Il Cerano). Italian painter and sculptor (b. Cerano, 1575; d. Milan, 1632). He made an early trip to Venice and Rome and finally settled in Milan, where he became director of Federico Borromeo's academy (1620). His early style, based on that of Gaudenzio Ferrari, was soon modified by the light and

Lorenzo di Credi, The Annunciation, with sculptured scenes from Genesis on the predella. Louvre, Paris.

Giuseppe Maria Crespi, *The Flea.* Uffizi, Florence.

of feeling, a psychological penetration that veers more toward genre than baroque drama. Even in such subjects as the *Massacre of the Innocents* (Uffizi), the intensity of the action is relieved by two women in the right foreground who, in their sorrowful withdrawal and stately dignity, add a note of individual and personal emotion to the rampant horror depicted in the rest of the canvas. This masterly analysis of the human element, which constitutes Crespi's greatest contribution, is applied to a variety of subjects, including genre (*The Flea*, Uffizi; *The Fair*, Milan, Brera); portraiture, both informal and formal (*The Artist in his Studio*, Hartford, Wadsworth Atheneum; *Chancellor Florius Senesius*, Boston, Museum of Fine Arts); and religious themes (*St. John of Nepomuk Confessing the Queen of Bohemia*, Turin, Sabauda Gallery). He also worked in fresco, using illusionistic space effects but refraining from the extremes of this technique as practiced by such artists as Cortona (*Assembly of the Gods*, Bologna, Palazzo Pepoli).

His painterly technique, human orientation, interest in genre, and exploration of a variety of subjects had a profound influence on the development of such 18th-century Venetian painters as Piazzetta (who was his pupil), Pietro Longhi, and Tiepolo.

BIBLIOGRAPHY. G. M. Crespi, *Giuseppe M. Crespi...* (catalog), ed. H. Voss, Rome, 1921; Bologna, Salone del Podestà, *Mostra celebrativa di Giuseppe M. Crespi* (catalog), ed. F. Arcangeli et al., 1948; M. Marangoni, *Arte Barocca*, new ed., Florence, 1953; C. Volpe, "Antefatti Bolognesi ed inizi di Giuseppe Maria Crespi," *Paragone*, no. 91, 1957; R. Wittkower, *Art and Architecture in Italy, 1600–1750*, Baltimore, 1958.

STEPHEN E. OSTROW

CRESSENT, CHARLES. French cabinetmaker and sculptor (b. Amiens, 1685; d. Paris, 1768). Contrary to guild regulations, Cressent achieved distinction as both a cabinetmaker and a brass founder. Working for the Regent and for Louis XV, he was one of the greatest exponents of the rococo style.

BIBLIOGRAPHY. M. J. Ballot, *Charles Cressent...*, Paris, 1919.

CRESTI, DOMENICO, *see* PASSIGNANO, DOMENICO.

CRETAN SNAKE GODDESS. Earth deity highly venerated in Crete during the Minoan period, usually depicted with one or more snakes around the body or arms. It was worshiped as the household goddess, the snake being revered as *Oikouros*, the guardian angel of the house. Two faïence statuettes of this goddess were found in the temple repository of the Palace of Cnossus, Middle Minoan III period (ca. 1600 B.C.). One of the figurines, thirty-five centimeters high, is considered the largest extant example of Minoan sculpture in the round. The goddess is clothed in the characteristic attire of that period, a tight bodice leaving bare the breasts and a bell-shaped skirt with an apron, and wears on her head a tall cylindrical hat entwined by the snake. Examples of this goddess may be found in the Heraklion Museum and the Boston Museum of Fine Arts.

BIBLIOGRAPHY. A. S. Marinatos, *Crete and Mycenae*, New York, 1960; R. W. Hutchinson, *Prehistoric Crete*, Baltimore, 1962.

CRETE. Long, narrow Mediterranean island, between Europe, Asia, and Africa, with a history of more than 8,000 years going back to pre-Neolithic times. Crete has been

color of Venetian painting, the full-bodied forms of Michelangelo, and mannerist spatial formulas (*S. Carlo Borromeo Blesses the Crosses*, 1602–04; Milan, Cathedral). Cerano did not move chronologically from mannerism to baroque but vacillated between them, achieving an emotional intensity typical of Milanese painting in the early 17th century (*Resurrected Christ with Saints*, ca. 1625; Meda, S. Vittore).

BIBLIOGRAPHY. A. dell'Acqua, "Per il Cerano," *L'Arte*, XLV, 1942, XLVI, 1943; G. Testori, "Inediti del Cerano giovine," *Paragone*, VI, July, 1955; E. Arslan, *Le pitture del Duomo di Milano*, Milan, 1960; M. Valsecchi, "Schede lombarde. III: Notizie sul Cerano," *Paragone*, XV, May, 1964.

CRESPI, GIUSEPPE MARIA (Lo Spagnuolo). Italian painter (1664–1747). Born in Bologna, Crespi rejected the lessons of his actual teachers, Canuti and Cignani, preferring those learned from the works of Lodovico Carracci, Guercino, Mastelletta, and Burrini. Correggio, Barocci, and the Venetians provided further models during his early travels (before 1690), which took him to Venice, Modena, Parma, Pesaro, and Urbino. He worked, for the most part, in Bologna, although with his spreading fame both Prince Eugenio of Savoy and Ferdinando of Tuscany became his patrons.

Crespi has been singled out as the only real genius of the late Bolognese school, a statement supported by his mastery of painterly technique and chiaroscuro in such works as *Cupid and Psyche* (Florence, Uffizi). These qualities are somewhat unique in late Bolognese painting, which continued to be dominated by the academicism of the Carraccis. All his paintings are permeated with a sincerity

settled since very early times, and it developed one of the greatest cultures of the ancient world. During the Neolithic period people lived in caves away from the sea and, even earlier, had developed a considerable culture, as shown by remains of pottery and implements excavated at various sites. To the Neolithic period belong two houses at Cnossus and a rock shelter nearby. Each house had two rooms with floors and hearths of clay and walls of large undressed limestone slabs. Settlements dating from the beginning of the Bronze Age, or Early Minoan I (3000–2800 B.C.), began to appear on slopes of hills, still away from the sea but accessible to it; later settlements were usually near the sea, since Crete was by then a naval power, able to protect itself.

The great Minoan civilization flourished uninterruptedly for 1,500 years, although the island suffered from time to time from fires, earthquakes, and tidal waves. It is divided into three main periods: Early Minoan (3000–2200 B.C.), Middle Minoan (2200–1580 B.C.), and Late Minoan (1580–1150 B.C.). Each main period is divided into three phases, I, II, and III, on the principle of its rise, maturity, and decline. The names of the nine periods are sometimes abbreviated to their initial letters and the numerals, for example, E.M. I, and so on.

Early Minoan houses had a few rooms, sometimes rectangular; the lower parts of the walls were made of stone, the upper parts of crude mud brick, and the walls were coated with stucco and painted red on top. Then a courtyard was added, which survived in later Minoan architecture. In the east, south, and center of Crete sites of Early Minoan II, or Copper Age, have been excavated, all accessible from the sea. No traces of the architecture of that period have been found, except in Mochlos, in eastern Crete, where stone houses were rectangular. *See* Mochlos.

At Vasiliki, an inland site a short distance from the sea on the east side of the island, two large houses, containing many fair-size rectangular rooms, were excavated. Sun-dried bricks, reinforced by wooden beams, formed the upper part of the walls. The lower part was of stone, and stucco covered the surface. Tombs of rough square stones, found on mountain peaks, in rock shelters, and in caves, had two chambers and thatched roofs. At Palaikastro, on the eastern coast, more chambers were added to the rectangular tombs, which were built like the houses; at Mesara, in southern Crete, tholoi, or circular tombs, with thick stone walls began to appear, and they remained in use for generations. Monolithic blocks formed the door jambs, with one solid block placed horizontally over them. In Cnossus, the lined chamber, or "beehive," tombs were rectangular, and elsewhere cist tombs, larnakes, and pithoi burials came into use. At Mallia, between the palace and the sea, a magnificent ossuary was excavated, containing many chambers filled with human skeletons and funerary furniture. Near it was the famous Chrysolakkos (gold pit), filled with gold ornaments, among them a masterpiece of the jeweler's art, a gold pendant with two bees and a honeycomb in embossed, granulated work (L.M.).

PALACES

In Middle Minoan I power began to concentrate in the north and center of the island, and the great palaces began to appear. Three major palaces have been discovered to

Crete. Vessel with cuttlefish. Archaeological Museum, Heraklion.

date, at Cnossus, Phaestos, and Mallia. All three follow the same pattern: all were built around a central court paved with flagstones; all had a theatral area to the north and one or more porticoes with upper galleries; all were oriented north to south; and all were about 80 feet wide and 170 feet long. The main ceremonial entrance was from the west, and the façade of the west wall was lined with recesses and shrines in an asymmetrical manner characteristic of Minoan architecture. There was also a ritual room; in Cnossus, it is known as the Tripartite Columnar Shrine. At Mallia it contains an altar, and at Phaestos it has a façade of piers and a central column.

East of the central court were the residential quarters with staircases. The living quarters of the palaces as well as the better houses were spacious, with painted murals showing nature or ceremonial scenes. They had bathrooms and toilets and provisions for adequate lighting and ventilation. The reception halls on the upper floors were elegant. Boxing, dancing, acrobatics, and bull-leaping were popular, and great athletic festivals took place in the central courts of the palaces.

Cnossus. Excavated by Sir Arthur Evans in the early 1900s, Cnossus was built around its palace, which covered three acres. It was destroyed many times and rebuilt with alterations. Little more than the ground floor was preserved after its final destruction. Evans reconstructed the palace and strengthened its walls with modern building materials.

In the famous Throne Room, entered by an anteroom with benches on two sides, the stone throne is preserved. On the lowest story is the Hall of the Double Axes, and near this, the Queen's quarters, with private bathroom and a series of small rooms including a toilet. A columned porch in the west court, decorated with scenes of the bull ring, led to the narrow Corridor of the Procession, with frescoes painted in bright colors, showing people bearing gifts. In the storage rooms hundreds of huge pithoi (clay jars) for storing olive oil were found, and beneath the floor, treasure pits still containing traces of gold. Small rooms for religious purposes were unearthed, two of them with stone pillars marked with the sacred symbol of the double ax, or labrys. In another room were pits containing cult objects of clay, faïence, and crystal: two-handled jars, snake goddess figurines, libation tables, shells, and two beautiful relief plaques—one representing a goat suckling its kids, the other, a cow with its calf. Toward the end of the Middle Minoan period, the palace was destroyed by earthquakes and was rebuilt on a more splendid scale. The present façade with its great gypsum orthostats was erected then, as well as the west porch with its rough column, the terraces to the south, and the lustral area. Basements with thick walls were built, and the servants' and craftsmen's quarters and the pottery stores were erected on that level. *See* Cnossus.

Mallia. The palace at Mallia, discovered in 1915 by the Greek archaeologist Joseph Hazzidakis, dates from the beginning of Middle Minoan I and is much smaller than the Cnossus palace. It has a central court and courts to the west and north. The ground plan is practically intact, and the central court is in a good state of preservation. The main reception rooms were on the upper stories. A large pillar crypt has two stone pillars marked with double axes, stars, and a trident.

The floor is covered with flagstones. A wide stone stairway led to a shrine with columns and to rooms on the next floor. Storage rooms and small workshops were in all parts of the palace, and in the southwest end were two rows of circular granaries. The residential quarters contained a men's hall with a light well and a queen's hall with attached bathroom and toilet, both opening on a columned portico facing the sea. The walls were painted and incised. The streets of Mallia were paved with stones, and a number of houses have been excavated. *See* Mallia.

Phaestos. The palace of Phaestos, above the plain of Mesara, dates from Middle Minoan I. It does not follow the rectangular plan of Cnossus and Mallia because of the uneven terrain. A paved court led to an entrance on the west façade, and there was a smaller court to the north, enclosed by porticoes, known as the Peristyle Court. A magnificent entranceway with a splendid stairway, 45 feet wide, with deep low steps, ascended to a double-porched propylon, whose outer portico was supported by a massive oval-shaped column in the center. Three oval columns at the rear supported the front of a very large light well. *See* Phaestos.

Other palaces. Besides the three major palaces, smaller ones have been found in Crete. The best known is the palace of Gournia, in northwestern Crete, on the Bay of Mirabello, excavated by the University of Pennsylvania from 1901 to 1904. Much smaller than the three major palaces, it is built on top of a hill. Great dressed limestone blocks form the base of the wall. The central court and a small bathroom had cement floors.

A fifth palace was discovered in Kato Zakro, on the eastern side of Crete, in 1965 by the Greek archaeologist Nicholas Platon. *See* Zakro.

At the beginning of the 20th century the Italian School of Archaeology discovered near Phaestos one of the loveliest sites in Crete, Hagia Triada, with a little palace known as the Royal Villa, similar to the major palaces and lavishly decorated with frescoes ranking among the finest in Crete. Beautiful steatite vases carved in low relief were found in the ruins. One, showing a festive procession of harvesters marching to the music of a sistrum player, is a masterpiece of Cretan relief sculpture. Another shows boxers in relief. Here also was found a hoard of nineteen bronze ingots, weighing more than 1,100 pounds, and a steatite beaker showing an officer presenting foreign envoys to a prince with long hair who has jewelry on his arms and neck and is wearing boots and a kilt. *See* Hagia Triada, Palace of.

About 250 yards northwest of the Cnossus palace is the Little Palace, also excavated by Evans. Much smaller than the three major palaces, it had a suite of connecting rooms, a main hall paved with gypsum and divided by a partition, and an adjoining lavatory. To the south the hall opened into a large square peristyle with three columns on each side, similar to the one in Phaestos. It also contained a three-pillar crypt, a lustral chamber, and a wide two-flight stairway leading to the second story. The lower part of the outer wall, the west side of which still stands, was of fine dressed masonry.

Northeast of the palace of Cnossus is a small rectangular Royal Villa on a terraced slope; it has a large partitioned hall and a light well with two columns. The lower part of the walls were gypsum-veneered, and the floor was covered with gypsum slabs. A heavy stone balustrade supported columns on either side of an opening through which steps led up to a raised platform. A purple stone pedestal lamp was found on the steps. The villa contained a large pillar crypt, living quarters with bathroom, and a stairway, with two landings, to second and third stories.

HOUSES

Many large, rich houses were built around the Cnossus palace. Among them were the House of Frescoes, where a number of frescoes were found stacked in a corridor, and the South House, which had living quarters, a lustral area, a toilet with a drain through the wall, a stairway leading to upper stories, and a pillar crypt with a conical stand for the double ax, the pillar in the middle supporting the main beam of the ceiling. Three silver bowls and a pitcher were found in this house, as well as many bronze tools, among them three saws and two double axes. In another house were found four big double axes of thin bronze, one about four feet wide, and a niche of another house had remains of sacral horns.

Remains of three very interesting houses were found at Tylissos, on Mt. Ida, west of Cnossus. One had a flagstone-paved hall, a pillar crypt, several small rooms, a toilet with drain, and a bathroom. A bronze ingot was found in a room, as were many big storage jars and three huge bronze caldrons. The second house had cult and

Crete. Sarcophagus from Hagia Triada, detail. Archaeological Museum, Heraklion.

storage rooms, living quarters with a bathroom, and a toilet with a drain through the wall. Many paintings decorated the walls.

Among the houses discovered at Mallia one of the better preserved was House Da, with a lustral basin next to the women's quarters, an upper story, and a spiral stairway, which was quite unusual at the time.

In 1932 Professor Spyridon Marinatos excavated a fine Minoan mansion in Amnissos, the Cnossus port, with massive walls of huge dressed limestone and orthostats marked with tridents and a star. This house had been destroyed by an earthquake or a tidal wave about 1500 B.C. Graceful wall paintings of lilies gave it the name Villa of the Lilies.

Excavations by the British School of Archaeology at Palaikastro from 1902 to 1906 revealed part of a small town with narrow winding streets and a considerable number of small houses. Other and larger houses have also been found at Palaikastro, as well as at many other sites, and remains of large buildings have been found southwest of Cnossus, at Archanes, Vathypetro, and Kahni Kastelli, where an olive press was discovered. See PALAIKASTRO.

In 1967 a joint expedition by several Greek and American institutions excavated a site on the small island of Thera, near Crete. Their diggings disclosed an entire city of the Late Minoan period. Buried by volcanic eruption about 1500 B.C., the city contains two- and three-story houses, some with painted frescoes. Well-preserved pottery from this site is decorated with sophisticated floral and spiral designs. It is speculated by seismologists that Thera may have been part of the lost continent of Atlantis, which might have included Crete and the Aegean archipelago.

FRESCOES

Colorful frescoes decorated walls and ceilings of Cretan palaces and houses. Two miniature frescoes from Middle Minoan III show a group of dancing girls outside the Cnossus palace and groups of spectators, the men painted in red, the women in white. Artistically executed frescoes with cult objects and floral and marine designs come from the Cnossus palace, as do the frescoes *Ladies in Blue*, showing women in gay costumes and many jewels; *Prince with the Plumed Headdress*, realistically executed in relief, showing a prince with very broad shoulders, a tiny waist, long hair, and elaborate headdress and necklace; *Cup Bearer*, a figure with an extremely narrow waist, carrying a tall rhyton; and the exquisite miniature fresco *Little Parisienne*, showing an elegant lady in profile, with upturned nose, large black eye, and black hair (L.M. II).

An example of Cretan monumental art is the Middle Minoan III life-size painted relief from the Cnossus palace depicting a charging bull. Another painted relief is the *Lady* from Pseira, near Mochlos, with her costume shown in great detail. The painted relief became quite popular in Late Minoan I. Best-known examples from Cnossus are the *Blue Bird* fresco and the *Saffron Gatherer*, showing a monkey in blue gathering white crocuses. Also of note is the frieze of red-legged partridges and the *Cat and Pheasant* fresco from the Royal Villa at Hagia Triada, showing two cats stalking a pheasant. The famous fresco of bull-leaping from the Cnossus Hall of the Double Axes (L.M. I) shows an acrobat somersaulting over a bull's back, a young girl standing at the tail end of the bull, and another girl acrobat grasping the charging bull by the horns.

POTTERY AND SCULPTURE

In Neolithic times pottery in Crete was monochrome, of coarse gray, brown, or black clay, completely unadorned. Later it was incised. With time the clay became polished, decorations appeared, and shapes became prettier. Pedestal vases came into use, an example of which is a beak-spouted yellowish jug from Hagios Onouphrios in southern Crete, with a lacework pattern painted in reddish glaze. Anthropomorphic and zoomorphic vases also appeared. A glazed yellow-brown teapot (E.M. II) shaped like a bird's head was found in Vasiliki and a steatite cover with a dog sketched on it in Mochlos. A bell-shaped vase showing a goddess with raised arms and flaring skirt and bowls with figures on them date from the Middle Minoan period. A shepherd and his flock are painted inside one such bowl.

In the Heraklion Archaeological Museum is the famous limestone sarcophagus from Hagia Triada. Painted on all four sides, it shows processions of men in red and women in white, a large offering table, bulls trussed for sacrifice, a lute player, goddesses in a chariot drawn by griffins, double axes, birds, and foliage. Cretan artists also exploited the grain of stone with startling effect, and their use of varicolored stones produced polychrome ware of great artistry. A jug of red-and-white stone from a Mochlos tomb (E.M. II) uses the natural colors of the stone to produce a marble-like effect.

By the end of the Early Minoan and during the Middle Minoan period the artistic Kamares ware had reached its highest development. It was decorated with geometric designs and floral and animal forms in brilliant colors: white, red, and orange, on black glazed backgrounds. Best examples of the Kamares ware of the Middle Minoan period are a vase from Cnossus, covered with rosettes and tendrils; the so-called "lily" vases; and, from Phaestos, a beak-spouted "mottled" vase with scroll designs in white and red paint on a dark background, and a beautiful "eggshell" cup with handle, the dark background painted with flower buds in red and white. To the Middle Minoan period belongs also the Vasiliki ware with various shades of brown and red painted on a black background. Later, white paint was also used in spiral patterns.

The largest figurine found in Crete (M.M. III) depicts the snake goddess with a tall cylindrical hat, bell-shaped skirt and apron, tight bodice with bare breasts, and snakes twining around her arms. Another faïence figurine shows a priestess holding a snake in each extended hand, a spotted cat sitting on her headdress. The great period of Cretan sculpture coincides with the period of the rebuilding of the great palaces, from Middle Minoan III to Late Minoan II. A perfectly executed steatite rhyton in the shape of a bull's head, found in the Little Palace of Cnossus, is inlaid with limestone and rock crystal and has gold-plated horns and nostrils inlaid with shell. See CRETAN SNAKE GODDESS.

Pottery of the Late Minoan period is very beautiful, with a light-brown background and floral, marine, and cult designs. A dolphin vase from Pachyammos is black glazed on a light background, and a vase from Palaikastro has an octopus with spread tentacles realistically executed. Toward Late Minoan II a new style of pottery appeared, but only in Cnossus, with less freedom of execution and more conventional designs: influences of Mycenaean art were becoming evident.

METALWORK AND OTHER ARTS

The Cretans had also developed the bronze-casting technique, and metalwork of Middle Minoan III and Late Minoan I shows great advances. Among the bronze objects found in the Mallia palace were a bracelet, a dagger, a great sword with crystal hilt, and a votive hatchet in the form of a panther. From Cnossus come fragments of a large statue, a bronze caldron, and a double ax as well as miniature cult objects, idols and figurines, horns, double axes, libation tables, sacred birds and trees, bulls, snakes, and bronze weapons of fine workmanship. A bronze cup from a Mochlos tomb has a design of ivy leaves, and from Tylissos comes a bronze statuette of a man in the attitude of prayer. The finest bronze statuette, now in Berlin (former State Museums), shows a female figure in full motion, bending down from the waist, her hand shading one eye. A bronze male figure wearing a peaked cap was discovered in Amnisos, and in a cave sanctuary at Psychro, in the Lasithi mountains, were found miniature bronze votive offerings, women's ornaments, an inscribed libation table, and a bronze blade wedged in a stalactite column.

Great quantities of faïence beads have been found in Crete along with many ivory objects, among them a magnificent table with flowers in relief, adorned with rock crystal and silver, and many artfully executed ivory and bronze figurines. Ivory figures from Palaikastro show children, a rare subject in Cretan art. A masterpiece of Minoan art is an ivory acrobat with curly hair of gold wire, from Cnossus. Gold and silver jewelry has been found, including many gold signet rings, one showing four women dancers and a diety in the background.

Engraved seals of an amazing variety have also been found: carnelian, steatite, chalcedony, hematite, amethyst, jasper, rock crystal, agate, and onyx as well as ivory. They are decorated with architectural features, buildings, human-and-animal figures, lions, griffins, fish, dolphins, birds, religious scenes, and animal hunts. Among the finest examples of Cretan glyptic art are a gold-mounted, light chalcedony cylinder seal, showing two men and a large mastiff; and a red carnelian seal with two ibexes and a dog, from Cnossus. A hoard of seals from Zakro depict mythological beings, bulls' heads, bats and winged griffins, women with birds' heads, lions, palm trees, and cities with walls and towers. Noteworthy among the ivory seals are the *Seated Monkey* from Trapeza, in eastern Crete, and two carved ivory seals from a tomb in southern Crete, one showing two lions surrounded by spirals, the other the figure of an ox. All are now in the Heraklion Museum. Many seals are also engraved with Minoan hieroglyphs and Linear B script.

WRITING

Thousands of inscribed tablets found in the destroyed buildings of Cnossus reveal that the Minoans kept records of their laws, customs, and everyday life. A long, but incomplete, inscription on the walls of a Roman theater in Gortyn, in the Mesara, contains property laws of the city during the 5th century B.C. The beautifully cut inscription is a fine example of the Greek script current in Crete at that time.

Writing was in use from prehistoric times in Crete. In the beginning of the Middle Minoan period the old hieroglyphic script was replaced by a linear script read from left to right, which developed into what is now known as Linear A. In the palace of Phaestos, a hieroglyphic inscription, known as the Phaestos Disk, was found. Made of clay, it is impressed on both sides. Inscribed stone vases, offering tables, and tablets have been found, and an inscribed clay figurine was discovered at Tylissos. Ink was also used for writing, and inscriptions in Linear A and in a spiral running inward have been found. Linear A script was followed by Linear B, found on clay tablets containing accounting records and furniture lists. Linear B script was deciphered in 1953 by Michael Ventris.

In 1400 B.C. Crete suffered a great catastrophe; its cities were destroyed and abandoned, heralding the decline of its civilization. After that, Greeks from the mainland settled in Crete, although Mycenaean Greeks had begun to settle there about 1500 B.C., and there was a revival of Cretan culture. But in the 7th century B.C. there was a new decline, which continued until Crete was finally occupied by the Romans.

BIBLIOGRAPHY. A. J. Evans, *The Palace of Minos*, 4 vols. in 6 and index, London, 1921–36; J. D. S. Pendlebury, *The Archaeology of Crete*, London, 1939; J. D. S. Pendlebury, *A Handbook to the Palace of Minos, Knossos*, London, 1954; L. Cottrell, *The Bull of Minos*, New York, 1958; S. Marinatos, *Crete and Mycenae*, London, 1960; J. W. Graham, *The Palaces of Crete*, Princeton, 1962; R. W. Hutchinson, *Prehistoric Crete*, Baltimore, 1962; F. Matz, *The Art of Crete and Early Greece*, New York, 1962; N. Platon, "A New Minoan Palace," *Archaeology*, XVI, 1963; N. Platon, *Crete*, Cleveland, New York, 1966.

LUCILLE VASSARDAKI

CREVE. Term employed in etching to describe a condition that arises when a number of closely drawn lines are undercut by acid during the biting process, causing the areas between the lines to break down. The *crevé* plate, when printed, does not produce a black, as would be expected, but a faint gray.

CRIOPHORUS. Term in ancient Greek art for a statue or figurine of a man carrying a ram. Hermes frequently was so represented. In Early Christian art, criophorus becomes a type of Christ the Good Shepherd.

CRISPIN AND CRISPINIAN OF ROME, SS. Brothers of a noble family and martyrs. Fleeing the Diocletian persecutions, they settled at Soissons, where they learned the shoemakers' craft. They made shoes free for the needy and won many of the poor to Christianity. Arrested by Maximian, they suffered numerous tortures and were finally beheaded. Crispin is usually represented as older than Crispinian. Their attributes include an awl, a needle, a knife, and leather. Their feast is October 25. *See also* SAINTS IN ART.

CRISPUS, *see* BRIOSCO, ANDREA.

CRISTALL, JOSHUA. English water-color painter (1767?–1847). Cristall was the son of a Scottish sea captain. He was an original member, and thrice president, of the Old Water-Colour Society. In earlier years he produced mainly classical landscapes. Later he turned to more naturalistic mountain scenery and rustic figure compositions that were less sentimental than usual for the period.

BIBLIOGRAPHY. R. Davies, "Joshua Cristall," *Old Water-Colour Society's Club*, IV, 1926.

Cristo de la Luz, Toledo, showing horseshoe arches on Visigothic capitals in the original mosque, built 999.

CRISTIANI, GIOVANNI, *see* GIOVANNI DI BARTOLOMMEO CRISTIANI.

CRISTO DE LA LUZ, TOLEDO. Spanish church consisting of two parts, a mosque of 999 and a Mudejar addition of the 12th century. The mosque was built on a square plan with four central columns, producing a scheme of nine compartments, each surmounted by a cupola. The horseshoe arches rest on Visigothic capitals. Frescoes may be seen in the apsidal 12th-century addition.

BIBLIOGRAPHY. *Ars Hispaniae,* vol. 3, Madrid, 1951.

CRISTOFANI, BUONAMICO, *see* BUFFALMACCO.

CRISTOFANO, FRANCESCO DI, *see* FRANCIABIGIO.

CRISTOFORO, EUSEBIO DI GIACOMO DI, *see* EUSEBIO DI SAN GIORGIO.

CRISTOFORO FINI, TOMMASO DI, *see* MASOLINO.

CRITIUS (Kritios) AND NESIOTES. Greek sculptors, probably Athenians, whose famous bronze group of the Tyrannicides, Harmodius and Aristogeiton, was set up in Athens in 477/76 B.C. These figures, known in Roman copies, became a symbol of democracy and enjoyed considerable fame in antiquity. They are the first masterpieces of freestanding sculpture in the early classical period, and show many of the stylistic features that differentiate the new era from the archaic period—particularly the portrayal of the human form in meaningful movement, with the concomitant changes in muscular tension and torsion.

Critius is also associated with a statue of a youth (the *Critius Boy* in the Acropolis Museum, Athens), another early example of experimentation in the rendering of the distribution of weight and the resulting adjustments in muscular balance.

BIBLIOGRAPHY. S. Brunnsaker, *The Tyrant-Slayers of Kritios and Nesiotes,* Lund, 1955; B. B. Shefton, "Some Iconographic Remarks on the Tyrannicides," *American Journal of Archaeology,* LXIV, April, 1960.

CRIVELLI, CARLO. Italian painter (fl. 1457–93). He was born in Venice but was active in small towns in the Marches and was perhaps the son of the painter Jacopo Crivelli. In Venice in 1457 he was jailed for adultery; he is not recorded again in that city. He was the chief artist of the rural Marches, with headquarters in Fermo and later in Camerino; he always signed himself "of Venice."

His earliest signed Madonna (Verona, Castelvecchio) shows that he had learned from the Squarcione group in Padua, especially from Schiavone, in the sharp line, polished surface, and ornamental fruit and marble, as well as in the facial type. The precision of his complex detail is more personal. His earliest dated altarpiece (1468; Massa, Town Hall) typifies them all. It is an elaborate polyptych with many panels of saints, obsolete in larger cities.

Crivelli's early style, up to about 1480, is blonde in tone and relatively light in weight, with neat and graceful lines of ornament and a marked delicacy (Madonnas, Richmond, Eng., Cook Collection; New York, Lehman Collection). The most ambitious of his early works (1473; Ascoli Cathedral) has a cutting line that evokes not only decoration but also muscular tension. This is most expressive in the many Pietàs (Detroit, Philadelphia, New York, and, the finest, Boston).

Crivelli's most famous works, *The Annunciation* (1486; London, National Gallery), commissioned to commemorate the freedom of the town of Ascoli Piceno, and the *Madonna of the Candle* (1493; Milan, Brera) were produced during his later phase. They are monumental in breadth, not only in scale, and darker in tone. Their weightiness combines with the brilliance of smooth execution, machined to a high polish, that no doubt has led to their popular appeal. But they are emotionally neutral in comparison with his earlier works. Their positive quality is apparent when a natural object such as a birdcage or a cucumber is evoked with startling reality and with no loss in the patterned precision. Crivelli's development, like that of other artists in extreme provincial isolation, merely reinforces and freezes the formal stylistic elements of his training, which at first he used in a relatively easygoing way with more references to the stimuli of experience.

BIBLIOGRAPHY. P. Zampetti, *Carlo Crivelli,* Milan, 1961.

CREIGHTON GILBERT

CRIVELLI, TADDEO. Italian miniaturist (ca. 1425–85). He was a member of the 15th-century school of Verona and Padua. Although his precise origins remain unknown (he may have come from either Milan or Mantua), his major works were executed for the D'Este family at Ferrara between 1452 and 1476. Of these, his style is best represented by the miniatures that he painted for the Bible of Borso d'Este (for example, no. I, folio 6, Modena, Este Library), in which the compositions are clearly, if somewhat theatrically, conceived. Most characteristic, however,

Critius and Nesiotes, *The Tyrannicides Harmodius and Aristogeiton*. Roman copy from Tivoli. National Museum, Naples.

Carlo Crivelli, *Madonna and Child*. Castelvecchio Museum, Verona. The painter's earliest signed Madonna.

is Taddeo's affinity for rich decorative designs that pervade all areas of the manuscript page and reveal a highly imaginative approach toward ornament and *drôleries*.

BIBLIOGRAPHY. G. Bertoni, *Il maggior miniatore della Bibbia di Borso d'Este: "Taddeo Crivelli,"* Modena, 1925; *La Bibbia di Borso d'Este*, facsimile with critical analysis by A. Venturi, Bergamo, 1961.

CRIVELLI, VITTORIO. Venetian painter (fl. 1481; d. 1501/02). He was the son of the painter Jacopo Crivelli and was active in small towns in the Marches. His work is a thinner, awkward echo of Carlo Crivelli, certainly a relative. No direct evidence proves Vittorio a brother or an assistant of Carlo, but the fact that he appears in legal documents only at a mature age may support the idea.

Vittorio produced numerous signed altarpieces and smaller works. Carlo's retention of old-fashioned methods in a backwater is part of his brilliant ornamentalism; Vittorio's, for a few more years, only a historical curiosity.

CROCE, BENEDETTO. Italian philosopher, statesman, historian, and editor (1866–1952). The major Italian philosopher of the 20th century, Croce formulated an influential theory of aesthetics based on intuition, influenced largely by the ideas of Giambattista Vico and Conrad Fiedler. Art is seen in *Aesthetic* (1901) as an aspect of theoretical activity, as a knowing of particulars, or intuition, whereas logic is a knowing of universals, or conception. In later books, such as *Aesthetic as Science of Expression and General Linguistic*, these categories, as well as those of practical activity, are more dynamically related, fol-

lowing Croce's exposure to Hegel. Croce's emphasis on the individual intuition and its expression is consonant with the autonomous philosophical nature of 20th-century art.

CROCKER ART GALLERY, SACRAMENTO, CALIF., *see* SACRAMENTO, CALIF.: E. B. CROCKER ART GALLERY.

CROCKET. Spur, carved in a plant form, projecting from the sloping sides of gables, spires, canopies, arches, and so on, frequently found in medieval work. The spires of

Crocket. Plant-form spur widely used in medieval architecture.

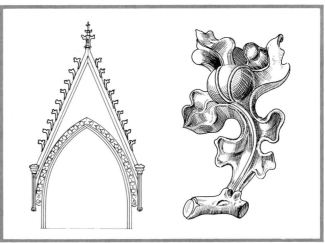

John Crome (Old Crome), *Moonrise on the Marshes of the Yare*. Tate Gallery, London.

Magdalen College, Oxford, the flèche of Amiens Cathedral, and the arches in St. John's Cley, Norfolk, are among Gothic examples. A crocket capital is one having a crocket form, as in the French Gothic example in Semur.

CRODEL, CARL. Franco-German painter and lithographer (1894–   ). Crodel was born in Marseilles and went to Germany at fifteen. He is a self-taught painter, but was influenced by Munch and Kirchner. He has produced woodcuts, colored lithographs, and several wall decorations, including one at the University of Jena, Germany.

CROME, JOHN (Old Crome). English landscape painter (b. Norwich, England, 1768; d. there, 1821). At fifteen he was apprenticed to a coach and sign painter. At twenty-two, he shared quarters with a printer's apprentice, Robert Ladbrooke, and together they began to paint landscapes. Crome's progress was hastened by the patronage of Thomas Harvey of Catton, a collector of taste, wealth, and wide acquaintance, who allowed the young painter to study and copy his paintings, which included works by Richard Wilson, Gainsborough, and Hobbema. He also introduced Crome to several wealthy Quaker families, who employed the young man as a drawing master.

As his gifts became known, Crome, a man of warm simplicity and a gift for friendship, gathered about him a group of disciples. In 1803, they formed the Norwich Society, which later became the Norwich School. Crome was elected president of the society in 1808, and during his lifetime exhibited about 300 paintings with the group. By his teaching and example he created the tradition of uniform excellence that characterized the history of this provincial school of painting.

Crome remains a great master of English landscape painting. Though he may have been inferior in drawing to Richard Wilson or Constable, his handling of color, tone, and mass gave Crome's landscapes atmospheric effects of breadth and expanse that are supremely his own and inimitable in their grand simplicity. He was always faithful to his uneventful corner of England, except for some paintings done while on a tour of the Lake District and two French views painted during his visit to Paris in 1814. Three of his greatest landscapes, *Mousehold Heath* (1815), *The Poringland Oak* (1818), and *Moonrise on the Marshes of the Yare* are presently in the Tate Gallery in London. The Victoria and Albert Museum and many other British museums own examples of his work.

See also NORWICH SCHOOL.

BIBLIOGRAPHY. C. H. C. Baker, *Crome...*, London, 1921; M. H. Grant, *Chronological History of the Old English Landscape Painters...*, vol. 5, London, 1959.

ALLAN MC NAB

CROME, JOHN BERNAY. English landscape painter (1794–1842). His early landscapes were in the Dutch 17th-century manner, but poverty forced him to turn out paintings in the style of his father, John Crome. Though at times mistaken for "Old Crome's" work, the son's paintings lack the touch, color, and atmosphere that were characteristic of the master.

CROMLECH. Flat stone, associated with primitive Western European architecture. The term sometimes refers to a large rough flat stone capping three or more upright monoliths, as at Lanyon, Cornwall, Maidstone, and other places in England, and in Wales, Ireland, northern France, Savoy, and other areas. In this sense the term is used interchangeably with dolmen. In another usage, cromlechs often include sacred circles of monoliths, as at Avebury and Stonehenge. *See* AVEBURY; DOLMEN; STONEHENGE.

CRONACA, IL (Simone del Pollaiuolo). Italian architect (b. Florence, 1457; d. there, 1508). According to Vasari, Cronaca studied in Rome. On his return to Florence he was involved from 1489 to about 1500 with the Palazzo Strozzi, where he executed the court and exterior cornice. Between 1495 and 1497 he directed work in the Sala del Consiglio of the Palazzo Vecchio. During this period he was elected *capomastro* of the Cathedral, and he was reelected in 1502. Although the documentation is confused, he apparently played a major role in the planning and execution of the sacristy and vestibule of Sto Spirito, completed about 1495. The construction of the Palazzo Guadagni (1502–04) has been attributed to him. His most important and original work is the church near S. Miniato, now called S. Francesco al Monte (ca. 1504). This spare and sober church with its emphasis on planes, their edges and junctures, had a profound influence on Michelangelo, who is said to have called it "la bella Villanella."

CROOS, ANTONIE JANSZ. VAN DER. Dutch landscape painter (b. ca. 1606; d. The Hague, after 1662). Croos was active in The Hague (1634–47) and Alkmaar (1649). In 1656 he was one of the founders of the painters' confraternity Pictura in The Hague. His work was strongly influenced by Jan van Goijen.
BIBLIOGRAPHY. W. Bernt, *Die niederländischen Maler des 17. Jahrhunderts...*, vol. 1, Munich, 1948.

CROOS, JACOB VAN DER. Dutch landscape painter (d. Amsterdam, ca. 1690). Croos was in Amsterdam in 1659 and in Alkmaar the following year. A young painter by this name, from Middelburg, was married in Amsterdam in 1654. His age was given as twenty-seven. Croos seems to have been a follower of Antonie Jansz. van der Croos and Jan van Goijen.

CROPSEY, JASPER FRANCIS. American painter (b. Rossville, N.Y., 1823; d. Hastings-on-Hudson, N.Y., 1900). He was a Hudson River school landscape painter who specialized in autumnal scenes in the Catskill Mountains. His idyllic views reveal the picturesque charm and naturalistic splendor of America's romantic virgin wilds.
BIBLIOGRAPHY. C. E. Sears, *Highlights among the Hudson River Artists*, Boston, 1947.

CROSATO, GIAMBATTISTA. Italian painter (1685/86–1758). Frescoes in his native Venice (S. Maria dei Servi) and Turin (Villa Regina and the Cistercian Santuario della Consolata) as well as scene paintings for the royal theater of Turin show Crosato's style to be abundant and effusive with the characteristic Venetian feeling for luminous color. He was elected a member of the Venice Academy in 1756.
BIBLIOGRAPHY. G. Fiocco, *Giambattista Crosato*, Padua, 1944.

CROSIER, *see* CROZIER.

CROSS, HENRI-EDMOND (Henri Delacroix). French painter (b. Douai, 1856; d. Saint-Clair, 1910). He studied at the Ecole des Beaux-Arts in Lille. His early paintings were realistic works and impressionistic scenes. As a founder of the Salon des Indépendants in 1884, Cross had become friendly with Seurat and Signac, and he was soon gradually applying the theories of Seurat's neoimpressionism in his own work but with important differences. A strong decorative tendency was evident in his early monochrome studies, which stressed the linear design.

While using the divisionist technique, Cross tried to obtain greater imaginative and expressive effects than those in Seurat's paintings; even his most divisionist paintings, such as *Grape Harvest* (1892; New York, The Hon. and Mrs. John Hay Whitney Collection), show few obvious rigidities of composition. In the early 1900s Cross achieved this aim in brightly colored, freshly painted landscapes and mythological subjects that were an important starting point for the Fauves.
BIBLIOGRAPHY. L. Cousturier, *H.-E. Cross*, Paris, 1932; J. Rewald, *Post-Impressionism: From Van Gogh to Gauguin*, New York, 1956.

CROSS. Device found in various forms in the art and symbolism of most ancient peoples, including the Sumerians, Babylonians, Phoenicians, Assyrians, Aztecs, and Greeks. The Egyptians had several cross-shaped hieroglyphs, the closest to the Christian in both form and meaning being the T shape surmounted by a loop. Amon-Ra, the god-man of Egyptian religion, is often depicted holding

Cross. Carolingian Cross of Lothair set with cloisons and cameos. Cathedral, Aachen.

such a cross as a symbol of eternal life. The role of Christ, and His relationship to the cross, is quite similar.

The cross of Christ's Crucifixion was very early (2d cent.) identified with the tree of life in the Garden of Eden, and then with all manner of wooden objects from the Old Testament: the roots of the tree of Jesse, the rod of Aaron, the rod of Moses, and so forth. But the Early Christians were careful to use the cross in a purely symbolic way, as a sign of redemption and salvation. Many variations occur on catacomb walls, including the Egyptian cross, the anchor, the trident, the T or Tau cross, and the figure of the orant with arms outstretched. Another dimension of symbolism is added in the Chi Rho sign, which combines the first two letters, the monogram, of Christ in Greek. After Emperor Constantine's vision and conversion in 313, this sign of the cross became his symbol and was emblazoned on his standards and monuments.

The earliest representation of a Crucifixion is a graffito on a wall of one of the Palatine buildings (2d cent.), in which mockery of the Christians is expressed by the depiction of the crucified figure with an ass's head. The Christians, however, refrained from representing the earthly Christ on the cross until the 5th century. By the 4th century the Crucifixion was represented by an empty Latin cross with a lamb, symbol of the purified Christ, above or below. Nonetheless, perhaps spurred by the growing popularity of the story of the true cross, the body of Christ on the cross was represented as early as the 5th century and frequently in the 6th century. The representation of the Crucifixion was finally accepted by the Council of Trullo (692). It was popular primarily in the art of Eastern Christianity and was also a main object of attack by the Iconoclasts. The figure on the cross is shown as the living, or triumphant, Christ wearing a long robe (8th cent. fresco in S. Maria Antiqua, Rome). *See* CRUCIFIX.

This representation was generally resisted during the early Middle Ages in the West, although the symbol of the cross itself was often used, in the form of reliquaries for remains of the true cross, on cross pages in illuminated manuscripts, and as sculptured monuments. The Irish Christians developed the monumental cross to a high artistic level, typically using a Latin cross with a circle joining the four arms (Cross of Muiredach in Monasterboice, Ireland, early 10th cent.). These huge stone monuments are richly carved with relief scenes and Celtic decorative motifs. Outdoor crosses remained popular, particularly in England, throughout the Middle Ages and until the 19th century. In market and wayside crosses, the cross itself was gradually overwhelmed by the architectural structures, which became shelters and meeting places. *See* CROSS, MARKET; CROSS, ROADSIDE. *See also* BEWCASTLE CROSS; RUTHWELL CROSS.

From the Romanesque period on, as the Passion of Christ became the major theme of Christian teaching, the Crucifixion was treated with increasing frequency in Western art. The greater emphasis on the humanity of Christ, His suffering and death, culminated in the dramatic spectacles depicted in paintings and sculptures of the Renaissance and baroque periods. Emblematic forms of the cross also proliferated during the medieval period. The cross was the symbol of the Crusaders, and the various orders of knights adopted their own versions: the Knights of Malta, the Knights Hospitalers, and the Teutonic Knights, among others. Concurrently, crosses became the most widely used emblems for heraldic devices. In addition to knightly orders and heraldic emblems, a great variety of different kinds of crosses are associated with religious orders, saints, Protestant groups, and theological concepts. The Papal cross has two shorter crossarms above the main crossarm. *See* CROSS, MALTESE; CROSS, ST. ANDREW.

Crosses have surmounted the domes of Eastern churches for many centuries, but were not widely used on the steeples, spires, and domes of Western churches until the 17th century. Processional crosses have been used since the 6th century. Altar crosses were not a necessary part of church furniture until the decree of Pope Innocent III in the 13th century. Churches have been built according to Latin- or Greek-cross plans since the 4th century, the former prevailing in the West, the latter in the East, although it is uncertain whether the original intention was symbolic or functional. *See* CROSS, LATIN; CROSS, GREEK.

BIBLIOGRAPHY. A. K. Porter, *The Crosses and Culture of Ireland*, New Haven, Conn., 1931; N. Laliberté and E. N. West, *The History of the Cross*, New York, 1960.   DONALD GODDARD

CROSS, GREEK. Type of cross with four arms of equal length. Aside from its use as a Christian symbol, it is an ancient ornamental motif. The Greek cross is the basis for the centralized plan in architecture of the Italian Renaissance.

CROSS, LATIN (Crux immissa). Type of cross in which the lower arm is longer than the other three. The most common form of Christian cross, it was the basis for the plan of church architecture in the Middle Ages.

CROSS, MALTESE. Type of cross with arms of equal length that widen from the center outward. The ends of the arms frequently have V-shaped notches. Called Maltese because it was used by the Knights of Malta, it is also known as St. John's cross.

CROSS, MARKET. Medieval roofed shelter used as a marketplace. Those in Salisbury and Chichester, England, were elaborate arcaded crownlike structures with buttresses and pinnacles.

CROSS, MONUMENTAL, *see* CROSS.

CROSS, ROADSIDE. Devotional cross or crucifix found throughout the countryside of Europe at conspicuous places along the roads, such as village entrances. Roadside crosses may be simple crosses, that is, without the figure of the crucified Christ; but more elaborate groupings, representing the Crucifixion or other Stations of the Cross, also exist.

CROSS, ST. ANDREW. Diagonally oriented, or X-shaped, Greek cross. It is the type of cross on which St. Andrew was martyred.

CROSS HATCHING. Method or technique of drawing or engraving in which shaded or modeled areas are represented by series of parallel lines crossing each other diagonally or at right angles. It is most frequently used in engraving.

CROSS VAULT, *see* VAULT.

CROWN DERBY. Type of fine china made at Derby, England, from about 1750 to 1848. Its name comes from the royal authorization given for its manufacture.

CROWS OVER THE WHEATFIELDS. Oil painting by Van Gogh, in the V. W. Van Gogh Collection, on permanent loan to the Municipal Museum, Amsterdam. *See* VAN GOGH, VINCENT WILLEM.

CROZIER (Crosier). An ecclesiastical staff, significant of authority and jurisdiction, conferred on bishops and mitered abbots and used by them in performing certain liturgical functions. Although its use in worship dates from about the 5th century, the crozier may have derived from the shepherd's crook, which it resembles. It was often exquisitely carved and jeweled, especially in the 11th and 12th centuries.

CRUCIFIX. Representation of Christ on the cross. The crucifix is distinct from the cross, which has no figure of Christ, and from the Crucifixion, which represents the entire scene and therefore has other figures, principally the Virgin and St. John the Evangelist. *See* CROSS.

CRUCIFORM. Resembling a cross. The term is applied in architecture to a crosslike plan, especially in medieval churches. The early Christian tomb of Galla Placidia, Ravenna, has a cruciform plan. The medieval cruciform plan

George Cruikshank, illustration for *Sketches by "Boz,"* 1836/37.

is supposed to have originated from such examples, as well as from early Christian basilicas whose bemas are seen as prototypes for the enlarged transepts forming one part of the medieval cross.

CRUIKSHANK, GEORGE. English illustrator and caricaturist (b. London, 1792; d. there, 1878). The second son of the caricaturist Isaac Cruikshank, he began working as a child in his father's studio, helping his mother and brother, Isaac Robert, print and hand-color lithographs and engravings. Cruikshank had little schooling and no formal art training. His natural gifts showed themselves early: drawings exist that he did at nine; at twelve he earned his first commission, etching for a lottery ticket.

Cruikshank began his career as a social and political caricaturist in 1811, when he did illustrations for the satirical magazine *The Scourge.* Between 1819 and 1821, he produced a series of colored etchings in *The Humorist,* a collection of comic stories in four volumes; and in 1824 he illustrated *Grimm's Popular Stories,* in two volumes.

In sixty-six years of work, Cruikshank, with unfailing energy and invention, illustrated more than 200 books. He was associated with the best authors and publishers of his time in the issuance of innumerable comic almanacs, miscellanies, table books, and yearbooks. A few of his productions are *John Gilpin* (1828), *Don Quixote* (1834), *Sketches by "Boz"* (1836/37), *Memoirs of Joseph Grimaldi* (1838), *Oliver Twist* (1839), and the *George Cruikshank Omnibus* (1842).

Cruikshank has a place in the great English satirical tradition of Gillray and Rowlandson. He was less savage, with a geniality and whimsicality they lacked, but his moral sense was as keen as Hogarth's. His genius, as with most comic artists, belongs to his age, yet his powers of sympathetic expression were such that the present-day picture of London life and manners among the lower and middle classes during the first part of the 19th century is unconsciously but inextricably colored by Cruikshank's warm-hearted depictions of them.

In 1847, Cruikshank illustrated a poem, "The Drunkard," and followed it with a set of eight etchings, *The Drunkard's Children,* illustrating, in the manner of Hogarth, the tragic consequences of alcoholism. By that time he had become a vociferous convert to the temperance movement. In 1862 he produced an oil painting, *Worship of Bacchus; or, the Drinking Customs of Society,* an enormous composition crowded with figures and moralizing incidents. The painting, later bought by popular subscription and given to the National Gallery, London, and the engraving from it, etched by Cruikshank himself, failed to gain the success he expected. As the Victorian age entered the prosperous assurance of its later years, the vogue for his productions began to pass, and Cruikshank's other attempts at painting met with little appreciation.

Books illustrated by Cruikshank continue to be popular with collectors of English colorplate books of the 19th century; examples are in the collections of most great libraries and museums in the United States and England.

BIBLIOGRAPHY. W. B. Jerrold, *The Life of George Cruikshank in Two Epochs...,* New York, 1882; A. M. Cohn, *A Bibliographical Catalogue of the Printed Works Illustrated by George Cruikshank,* London, 1914.

ALLAN MC NAB

CRUSIUS, CARL LEBERECHT. German engraver (b. Langenhessen, near Zwickau, 1740; d. Leipzig, 1779). He was the younger brother of Gottlieb L. Crusius. After a short apprenticeship at the Leipzig Academy, Carl worked with his talented brother on all forms of book illustration, including vignettes, signets, and illustrations. His grace of line, which distinguished him from his brother, gave way to a harsh classicism in his later work.

BIBLIOGRAPHY. G. K. Nagler, *Die Monogrammisten...*, Munich, 1876–78.

CRUX IMMISSA, *see* CROSS, LATIN.

CRUZ, DIEGO DE LA. Spanish sculptor, painter, or both (fl. ca. 1486–ca. 1500). He was a frequent collaborator of Gil de Siloe, but documentation and scholarship leave unsettled whether he actually assisted in the carving or was responsible only for the polychromy. He served as polychromist for Siloe's altarpiece of *The Tree of Jesse* (1477–88; Chapel of S. Ana, Burgos Cathedral), among others, but is not mentioned as collaborating on any of the unpainted alabaster works. In contracts for so-called independent works, he is called a painter.

BIBLIOGRAPHY. H. E. Wethey, *Gil de Siloe and His School*, Cambridge, Mass., 1936; B. Proske, *Castilian Sculpture, Gothic to Renaissance*, New York, 1951.

CRY, THE. Oil painting by Munch, in the Munch Museum, Oslo. *See* MUNCH, EDVARD.

CRYPT. Chamber partly or wholly underground (from the Greek *kryptos*, "hidden"). The Romans applied the term to underground structures such as sewers, *carceres* (stalls for horses and chariots in a circus), and tunnels. The early Christian *crypta* was a catacomb or a gallery of a catacomb. As a component of the church, the crypt developed from the *confessio*, a subterranean chapel containing the tombs of martyrs and saints, as in the early Christian Roman churches of St. Prisca, S. Prassede, S. Lorenzo fuori le Mura, and St. Peter's. The high altar of the church was located above the crypt as a fulcrum of the structure.

Crypt. A common component of early Christian churches in Rome.

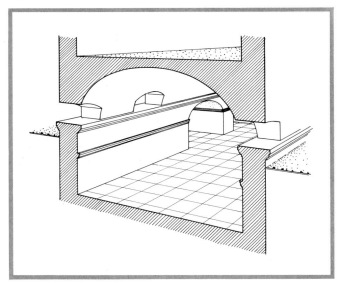

CRYPTOPORTICUS. Colonnade, portico, or gallery partly or wholly enclosed. In the Egyptian temple in Edfu the cryptoporticus consists of a row of columns walled to about mid-height. The cryptoporticus in the Palace of Diocletian in Split was a gallery more than 500 feet long and was used for exercises. The term is generally associated with galleries for private communication in Roman antiquity.

CRYSTAL. Specifically, works of minor arts such as plates, small vessels, figurines, and so forth, which are carved out of natural quartz crystal. Most objects are decorated with engravings, for example, the Susanna plate from Metz (9th century; London, British Museum). Crystal is also a general term for any cut or engraved glassware, which is more precisely called "flint glass."

CRYSTAL PALACE, LONDON, *see* PAXTON, SIR JOSEPH.

CSAKY, JOSEPH. Hungarian-French sculptor (1888–   ). Born in Hungary, he lived in Paris from 1908. In Hungary, he worked in decorative and industrial arts, especially ceramics. In France, he was strongly influenced by cubism, particularly Picasso's works; he turned to sculpture about 1910. His work was shown in the Salon d'Automne and the Salon des Indépendants. He has exhibited at the Léonce Rosenberg Gallery (Paris) and in the United States. Many of his works are in the Kröller-Müller Museum in Otterlo, Holland. His sculpture is related to that of de Stijl and to constructivism but has curvilinear elements breaking the straight plane.

BIBLIOGRAPHY. M. Seuphor, *The Sculpture of This Century*, New York, 1960.

CSOK, ISTVAN. Hungarian painter (1865–1961). Born in Puszta-Egeres, Csók was a pupil of Bouguereau and Fleury in Paris after studying in Budapest at the School of Decorative Art and in Munich. He worked in Paris and Hungary and exhibited at the Salons, winning a gold medal in 1900. In interior and exterior scenes he used dramatic light effects.

CTESIPHON PALACE, *see* CHOSROES, PALACE OF, CTESIPHON.

CUBA, NATIONAL MUSEUM OF, *see* HAVANA: NATIONAL MUSEUM.

CUBICULUM. Bed chamber in the Roman house, as in the House of Pansa, Pompeii. The term also denotes a chamber, or recess, to receive the dead, as the loculus of the catacombs; hence a tomb.

CUBISM. The cubist movement had its early development in the works of Picasso and Braque between 1907 and 1910 and, still under their leadership, underwent salient growth until 1914 with significant contributions by Juan Gris, Robert Delaunay, Fernand Léger, and Jacques Villon. Other painters, among them Albert Gleizes, Jean Metzinger, Auguste Herbin, Roger de La Fresnaye, Louis Marcoussis, Henry Le Fauconnier, André Lhote, André

Cubism. Pablo Picasso, *Standing Figure*. Museum of Fine Arts, Boston (Juliana Cheney Edwards Collection).

Derain, Marcel Duchamp, and Francis Picabia, in one or another measure adopted the cubist method before World War I. Some of them continued it, with individual modifications (as was the case with Picasso and Braque), into the 1960s. Cubism, rivaled only by the abstract expressionism of the German Blue Rider (Blaue Reiter) movement, has asserted the most penetrating influence imparted by any modern style upon post-World War I art.

The first cubist paintings by Georges Braque and Pablo Picasso reveal the intense effort to interpret landscape, figure, and still life in essentially geometric forms, especially the cylinder, cone, and pyramid. Both were inspired in 1907 by the posthumous retrospective show at the Salon d'Automne of Cézanne's firmly structured postimpressionist works and by that master's reference to seeking in nature certain geometric bases. It is evident, however, that Picasso, partly impelled by Negro African sculpture and otherwise independently intrigued by reducing form to simple volumes and planes, had anticipated this approach. He and Braque worked closely together after 1907, their canvases often resembling one another's even in detail. The designation "cubist" appears to have come from a remark made by Henri Matisse and reported by Louis Vauxcelles in the Nov. 14, 1908, *Gil Blas*, or to have been made by Vauxcelles himself, who had applied the similarly derisive name "Fauves" to Matisse and his associates in 1905. This skeptical term, however, was found not to be undesirable somewhat later and was "officially" accepted for the cubists by their spokesman, Guillaume Apollinaire.

The tendency of cubism from the date of Picasso's initial great painting, *Les Demoiselles d'Avignon* (1906–07; New York, Museum of Modern Art), until 1914 was the exploitation of the total structure of natural and man-made forms. The "analytic" phase of the style, occurring between 1910 and 1912, is remarkable for its geometric rendering of subjects from several simultaneous points of view, so that the spectator may at once see front, sides, and even elements from the back of forms. Planes are the dominant units of composition, sometimes overlapping, sometimes penetrating one another, and continuing interruptedly from one dimension of the canvas to another. The immediate similitude of subjects is decreased, although this never results in fully abstract forms; nor is it correct to assume that the subject loses its traditional importance to cubist artists, who, quite to the contrary, wished to re-create the underlying substance of things. It is interesting that while creating a revolutionary method of structure, the cubists used notably restrained color during the early and analytic stages of this style. Subdued browns, tans, pale blues and greens, and a wide span of grays composed their palette. It was not until the "synthetic" mode, from about 1913 through the early 1920s, that the cubists resorted to a fully chromatic pigmentation.

Picasso and Braque did not participate in the major group exhibitions of 1911 and 1912 that confronted the violently protesting public of Paris. Jacques Villon, at whose studio most of the cubists met during 1910 and 1911 for discussions of their program, organized the most controversial of cubist presentations, the famous Section d'Or (Golden Section) exhibition at the Galerie de la Boétie in October, 1912. The 200 works were so upsetting to the gallery visitors that a legislator formally denounced them in the Chamber of Deputies, demanding that official salons be closed to cubist paintings thereafter. The year 1912 was significant as well for the publication of the first cubist theoretical treatise, Albert Gleizes's and Jean Metzinger's *Du cubisme* (neither of these artists painted quite so cogently as he wrote). *See* SECTION D'OR.

At this time also *papier collé* and collage works were first created by Picasso and Braque—paintings into which they introduced shapes of paper such as newspaper clippings and printed letters and numerals. Picasso's fellow Spaniard Juan Gris became an expert practitioner of this method. In 1912 also appeared the mature Orphist, or "Orphic-cubist," paintings of Robert Delaunay, who advocated a more luminously colored, abstract variant of cubism and who exerted direct influence upon the German Blue Rider group and possibly upon the Italian futurists as well. Finally, Marcel Duchamp, for whom cubism provided the means to a distinctly personal manner related to futurism, painted his renowned *Nude Descending a Staircase* in that rich year. *See* COLLAGE; FUTURISM; ORPHISM; PAPIERS COLLES.

Braque, Picasso, Gleizes, Duchamp, and Picabia were included in the 1913 Armory Show in New York. Fernand Léger, an independent-minded but consistent cubist, developed his important series of *Contrasts of Forms* in 1913, and in that year the poet Apollinaire, the persistent literary advocate of cubism, published his important *Les Peintres cubistes*. The art of collage became more elaborate in 1913, and cubism underwent the mode called "synthetic." Complex analysis of volumed forms was deemphasized in favor of a more decorative, though still highly inventive, handling of flat planes and further departure from visual reality of objects. Picasso and other cubists were being frequently exhibited outside France.

By 1914 and the advent of World War I, cubism had become known to avant-garde painters and sculptors throughout Europe and in the United States. Almost no major artist of the generation of the cubists was completely untouched by this style (a notable exception is the Italian Giorgio de Chirico). Marc Chagall and Amedeo Modigliani, remarkably independent painters resident in Paris, were influenced briefly but distinctively by it; the Americans Macdonald-Wright, Morgan Russell, and Patrick Bruce were conditioned by Orphism. Wyndham Lewis, leader of the English vorticists and publisher of the journal *Blast*, also was influenced by cubism, although he renounced it and futurism alike. The Russians Larionov, founder of rayonism, and Malevich, the suprematist, were influenced by the more austere principles of Braque, Picasso, and Gris. Piet Mondrian, the Dutch cofounder of neoplasticism (de Stijl), based his experiments in geometric form upon lessons derived following 1910 from cubism. *See* DE STIJL; NEOPLASTICISM; RAYONISM; SUPREMATISM; VORTICISM.

Cubist sculpture began with Picasso's *Woman's Head* in bronze of 1909, a fully realized work related to the African primitive works that had in part inspired his 1907 *Demoiselles* and anticipated the first analytic paintings. His *Glass of Absinthe* (1914) clearly prefigures "assemblage" sculpture of much later times. Artists chiefly identifiable by 1914 as sculptors in the cubist style were Henri Laurens, Alexander Archipenko, Jacques Lipchitz, and

Cubist realism. Preston Dickinson, *Industry*. Whitney Museum of American Art, New York.

Raymond Duchamp-Villon. The last named died at the end of World War I; the others after about 1918 evolved styles largely independent of this influence.

By 1920 the cubists had ceased to maintain the closeness of professional exchange and friendship that from 1910 to 1914 had so strongly enriched the astonishing growth of the movement. Many of the Frenchmen had seen duty at the German front, and others had moved away from Paris. Independent amplifications of cubism were undertaken by Picasso, who in the early 1920s practiced various styles including a heavily neoclassical, figural one simultaneously with a brilliantly colored, flat-patterned technique; by Braque, who enriched his older methods and developed a certain grandness of composition more decorative than the older structure; by Gris, always strongly programmatic and who now painted strongly geometric, flatly conceived figural pieces; and by Léger, who, with Amédée Ozenfant and Jeanneret, founded the movement called purism, conditioned by architectural and machine forms. Other cubists who helped to develop the style during its analytic and synthetic years—the "high period"—similarly underwent changes of aesthetic. Picasso in the 1930s became increasingly expressionistic in manner, although seldom completely deserting his initial discipline. Braque continued to refine and to experiment more steadily. *See* PURISM.

Most of the central cubists were prolific and gifted printmakers as well as painters, with Picasso leading the group in this medium. Many of them illustrated books by their poet colleagues or by older writers. Picasso and Léger were especially active in designing the décor for contempo-

rary ballets and opera, and Picasso has remained an important contributor to modern sculpture.

Despite the obviously great talent of individual cubists, their combined gifts nonetheless required recognition and support outside the group. Early encouragement was given by the poets and critics Max Jacob, Guillaume Apollinaire, André Salmon, Maurice Raynal, Blaise Cendrars, and Paul Guillaume, as well as by the Americans Gertrude and Leo Stein; also by the dealers Berthe Weill, D. H. Kahnweiler, and Léonce Rosenberg in Paris, Alfred Stieglitz in New York, and Herwarth Walden of *Der Sturm* in Berlin. Many private collectors—French, Russian, German, British, Italian, and American—gave much needed affirmation to the cubists.

Cubism, strongest between 1907 and 1914 (and especially influential through its analytical and synthetic phases following 1910), has affected almost every major artist from its own time until the present, by no means excluding many gifted painters and sculptors who have deliberately rejected it. It is remarkably widely represented in private and public collections throughout Europe and the United States and is undoubtedly the movement associated by most persons with the term "modern art," as its co-founder, Picasso, is surely the best-known individual artist of the 20th century.

See ARCHIPENKO, ALEXANDER; BRAQUE, GEORGES; DELAUNAY, ROBERT; DERAIN, ANDRE; DUCHAMP, MARCEL; DUCHAMP-VILLON, RAYMOND; GLEIZES, ALBERT; GRIS, JUAN; LA FRESNAYE, ROGER DE; LAURENS, HENRI; LE FAUCONNIER, HENRI; LEGER, FERNAND; LHOTE, ANDRE; LIPCHITZ, JACQUES; MARCOUSSIS, LOUIS; METZINGER, JEAN; PICABIA, FRANCIS; PICASSO, PABLO; STIEGLITZ, ALFRED; VILLON, JACQUES. *See also* CUBIST REALISM.

BIBLIOGRAPHY. A. Gleizes and J. Metzinger, *Du "cubisme,"* Paris, 1912; A. H. Barr, Jr., *Cubism and Abstract Art*, New York, 1936; R. Goldwater, *Primitivism in Modern Painting*, New York, 1938; G. Apollinaire, *The Cubist Painters: Aesthetic Meditations, 1913*, New York, 1944; A. H. Barr, Jr., *Picasso: 50 Years of His Art*, New York, 1946; H. R. Hope, *Georges Braque*, New York, 1949; .D. H. Kahnweiler, *Picasso Sculptures*, London, 1949; Musée National d'Art Moderne, *Le Cubisme (1907–14)*, Paris, 1953; M. Raynal, *Modern Painting*, Geneva, 1956; R. Penrose, *Picasso: His Life and Work*, New York, 1958; J. Golding, *Cubism: A History and an Analysis, 1907–1914*, New York, 1959; G. Habasque, *Cubism*, Geneva, 1959; R. Rosenblum, *Cubism and Twentieth-Century Art*, New York, 1960; E. Fry, *Cubism* (Modern Artist and His World Series), New York, 1967.

JOHN C. GALLOWAY

CUBISM, FLAT-PATTERN. Term coined by R. H. Wilenski to apply to the paintings of synthetic cubism, in which spatial recession is denied by the organization of line, shape, and color. It originated between 1911 and 1914, with the introduction of collage and the emphasis on surface by Picasso and Braque, and culminated in the austere, architectural compositions of Ozenfant's purist still lifes.

CUBIST REALISM. American artistic movement of the 1920s known variously (and sometimes pejoratively) as immaculatism, precisionism, and sterilism. It arose primarily from experiments with abstraction shortly after the Armory Show by such artists as Charles Demuth and Charles Sheeler. Artists of the cubist realist group shared a common point of view more than a specific technical style. Basically cubist in approach, they organized industrial and architectural scenes or landscape and natural forms into impersonally handled, implicitly abstract compositions of simplified and geometric volumes, clean edges, and sharp images. *See* DEMUTH, CHARLES; SHEELER, CHARLES.

While the formal means of the movement derived mostly from cubism and purism, cubist realism, in choice of and attitude toward its subjects, is also related to the general 1920s reaction against abstraction, as seen in such a movement as the German New Objectivity. Among the other painters who worked in this manner are George Ault, Ralston Crawford, Preston Dickinson, Georgia O'Keeffe, Niles Spencer, and Joseph Stella. *See* AULT, GEORGE COPELAND; CRAWFORD, RALSTON; DICKINSON, PRESTON; O'KEEFFE, GEORGIA; SPENCER, NILES; STELLA, JOSEPH.

BIBLIOGRAPHY. M. W. Brown, "Cubist-Realism: An American Style," *Marsyas*, III, 1943–45; M. W. Brown, *American Painting from the Armory Show to the Depression*, Princeton, 1955; Minneapolis, Walker Art Center, *The Precisionist View in American Art*, Minneapolis, 1960.

CUBITT, JAMES, AND PARTNERS. English firm of architects founded by James Cubitt (1914–   ). The firm has established a wide practice, especially abroad and extending to the Far East. Its scope is varied: banks at Accra (1957), clubs at Umnkoroche (1959), factories at Rangoon (1959), houses at Leicester (1955), school and college at Kumasi (1953), and Stevenage (1958).

CUBITT, LEWIS. English architect (1799–1883). The only one of the three Cubitt brothers trained as an architect, he is credited with the designing of many of the houses built by his brother Thomas in Bloomsbury and Belgravia. His major work, in conjunction with Joseph Cubitt, was King's Cross Station (1851–52).

CUBITT, THOMAS. English architect (1788–1855). In 1815 Cubitt established the first modern building firm, employing all kinds of workmen to undertake large-scale speculative building schemes throughout London. The most important of his many enterprises of urban development were the squares of Bloomsbury and Belgravia.

CUEVAS, JOSE LUIS. Mexican draftsman and printmaker (1933–   ). He was born in Mexico City. Self-taught and precocious, Cuevas was given a one-man show at twenty. The greater part of his output, line drawings and wash drawings, explores social ills in the corrosive manner of Goya, Daumier, and Orozco. His typical themes involve inmates of hospitals, lunatic asylums, and brothels, and are usually done in India ink and gum arabic. Among the finest drawings by Cuevas are illustrations for a book on Kafka. Strongly expressionist, his art emphasizes hallucinatory distortions of form, suggestive linear rhythms, and disquieting conjunctions of light and shadow.

BIBLIOGRAPHY. P. Soupault and H. Flores-Sánchez, *La Personnalité de Cuevas: Le Peintre José Luis Cuevas*, Paris, 1955; "New Direction in Mexico," *Time*, LXXXI, March 29, 1963.

CUIJLENBURGH (Cuylenborch; Cuylenburgh), ABRAHAM VAN. Dutch painter of landscape, history, and religious scenes (b. Utrecht, ca. 1620?; d. there, 1658). If the date on a painting by Cuijlenburgh in the Schönborn Collection is correct, he was born before 1610. He may have been a pupil of Cornelis van Poelenburgh, whose

Aelbert Cuijp, *Portrait of a Bearded Man.* National Gallery, London.

work influenced him. Cuijlenburgh entered the Guild of St. Luke in Utrecht in 1639.

BIBLIOGRAPHY. H. Gerson, *Ausbreitung und Nachwirkung der holländischen Malerei des 17. Jahrhunderts*, Haarlem, 1942.

CUIJP (Cuyp), AELBERT. Dutch painter of landscapes, animals, and possibly portraits (b. Dordrecht, 1620; d. there, 1691). Cuijp studied in Dordrecht with his father, Jacob Gerritsz. Cuijp. Although many of his landscapes are painted in the Italianate style, Cuijp appears to have spent his entire life in Dordrecht with the exception of a few short visits to other Dutch cities. His Italianate style seems to have been derived from the work of other artists, such as Jan Both, who had visited Italy. Cuijp is best known for his noble landscape paintings.

Cuijp's earliest works are landscapes strongly influenced by the style of Jan van Goijen (*A River Scene with Distant Windmills*, mid-1640s, signed A cuÿp; London, National Gallery). These works of the 1640s make use of Van Goijen's color tonality as well as his general compositional scheme. Cuijp's Van Goijen–inspired river landscapes of his early period are replaced in the middle 1640s by works that seem to be inspired by older Utrecht painters. In such paintings as *On the River* (Rotterdam, Boymans-Van Beuningen Museum) the influence of Van Goijen, as well as older Utrecht painting, has been replaced by that of Jan Both. Possibly Cuijp had some personal contact with Both at Utrecht about this time. Cuijp's change in the rendering of light qualities, although his compositional format as a whole changes less dramatically, creates an effect that is quite different from the kind of Van Goijen–inspired tonal paintings he produced in the early 1640s. In works such as the *View of Nijmegen* (Indianapolis, Ind., Herron Art Institute), Cuijp seems to have followed the older compositional pattern of Van Goijen while using the new radiant lighting inspired by Utrecht and Jan Both.

Cuijp's activity as a portrait painter is difficult to define because of the lack of firmly attributed works. *Portrait of a Bearded Man; Bust* (signed and dated 1649; London, National Gallery), painted in the manner of his father, is one of the few portraits certainly by Cuijp. Toward the end of his life he seems to have stopped painting completely or to have executed works only occasionally. Cuijp's style influenced the work of Cornelis Saftleven, Lieven Verschuier, Ludolf Leendertsz. de Jongh, and others. His work was imitated during the 18th century by the brothers Abraham and Jacob van Stry.

BIBLIOGRAPHY. N. Maclaren, *National Gallery Catalogues: The Dutch School*, London, 1960; M. E. Houtzager et al., *Nederlandse 17e eeuwse Italianiserende Landschapschilders*, Utrecht, 1965; W. Stechow, *Dutch Landscape Painting of the Seventeenth Century*, London, 1966.
                                           LEONARD J. SLATKES

CUIJP (Cuyp), BENJAMIN GERRITSZ. Dutch painter of genre, history, and battle scenes (b. Dordrecht, 1612; d. there, 1652). Cuijp was a pupil of his half brother Jacob Gerritsz. Cuijp. Except for a short sojourn in The Hague (1643), he remained in Dordrecht. He was influenced by the work of Rembrandt and Leonard Bramer. Cuijp's battle paintings recall those painted by Adriaen van Ostade.

BIBLIOGRAPHY. J. Holmes, "The Cuyps in America," *Art in America*, XVIII, 1930.

CUIJP (Cuyp), JACOB GERRITSZ. Dutch painter of portraits, history, and animals (b. Dordrecht, 1594; d. there, after 1651). Jacob Gerritsz. Cuijp was the son of the Dordrecht glass painter Gerrit Gerritsz. Cuijp. He may have studied with the Utrecht painter Abraham Bloemaert. In 1617 Cuijp became a member of the Dordrecht painters' guild. In 1625 he was active in Amsterdam. Cuijp was the teacher of his half brother Benjamin Gerritsz. Cuijp as well as of his own son Aelbert Cuijp.

BIBLIOGRAPHY. E. Michel, "Une Famille d'artistes hollandais: Les Cuyp," *Gazette des Beaux-Arts*, 3d series, VII, 1892.

CUIJPERS, PETRUS JOSEPHUS HUBERTUS. Dutch architect (1827–1921). He worked in Amsterdam. Known for archaeological restorations of Dutch Gothic churches, Cuijpers also built many Neo-Gothic churches, using exposed brick. He is responsible for the Rijksmuseum and the Central Station, which were built in this style. *See* AMSTERDAM: MUSEUMS (NETHERLANDS NATIONAL MUSEUM).

BIBLIOGRAPHY. P. J. H. Cuypers, *Het Werk van Dr. P. J. H. Cuypers, 1827–1917*, Amsterdam, 1917.

CULLEN, MAURICE GALBRAITH. Canadian landscape painter (b. 1866, d. Quebec, 1934). In Paris, where he studied from 1889 to 1892, he became a follower of the impressionists. Returning to Canada, he used their pearly lights and bright colors in depicting his native landscape.

BIBLIOGRAPHY. Ottawa, National Gallery of Canada, *Catalogue of Painting and Sculpture*, vol. 3: *Canadian School*, Toronto, 1960 (15 illustrations).

CULT OBJECTS. Any of a variety of objects used by primitive and ancient peoples in the performance of religious rituals. These include fetish containers, totems, and masks, in primitive cultures; and votive images, lamps, and incense burners, in ancient cultures.

BIBLIOGRAPHY. S. Reinach, *Orpheus, A History of Religions*, New York, 1933.

CUMDACH. Construction used by the Irish clergy in the early Middle Ages as a shrine or reliquary to store the Gospel Books used in religious services. The scarcity of such books led to a superstitious reverence of the cumdach. One of the earliest (ca. 1000) contained the Gospel Book that reportedly belonged to St. Molaise (d. 563).

CUNEI. Wedge-shaped groups of seats (from the Latin *cuneus*, "wedge") formed by the radiating aisles of Greek and Roman theaters.

CUNEIFORM. Form of writing developed in Mesopotamia by the Sumerians; derived from the Latin word meaning "wedge-shaped." The cuneiform system of writing consists of characters made of four wedge-shaped strokes impressed into clay, brick, or stone. Its history runs parallel to that of Egyptian hieroglyphics.

In the 2d millennium B.C. an alphabet consisting of twenty-nine cuneiform signs was invented at Ras Shamra (the ancient Ugarit). The texts written in this script are couched in a language closely related to Hebrew and Phoenician. Babylonian and Assyrian writing used a large number of arbitrary cuneiform symbols for words and syllables; some of these symbols had originally been pictographs. An alphabetic system made it possible to spell out a word, but because the alphabet was Sumerian, a different language, there are many ambiguities. Outside Mesopotamia, cuneiform was used in Elam by the Hittites. The syllabary established for Old Persian, the writing of the Achaemenids, was a late use of cuneiform.

Cuneiform writing has been found at Nineveh, Telloh, Erech, Tel-el-Amarna, Susa, and Boghazkeuy. A group of several thousand tablets and fragments inscribed in Sumerian cuneiform of the first half of the 2d millennium B.C. exists. A great majority of these were excavated between 1889 and 1900 at Nippur, an ancient Sumerian site about 100 miles south of modern Baghdad. From Nippur comes one of the most human documents ever excavated in the Near East: a Sumerian cuneiform essay dealing with the everyday activities of a schoolboy, written by an anonymous teacher who lived about 2000 B.C.

The Istanbul Museum of the Ancient Orient, the British Museum, the Louvre, the Berlin former State Museums, Yale University, the University Museum of the University of Pennsylvania, and the Oriental Institute of the University of Chicago have collections of cuneiform writings. The Hilprecht Collection of the University of Jena (Frie-

Cuneiform. Writing system consisting of wedge-shaped forms.

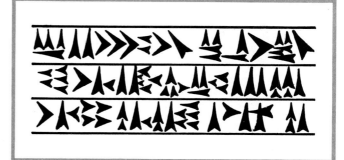

Currier and Ives, *Central Park, Winter: The Skating Pond.* Lithograph after a drawing by Charles Parsons; published 1862. Public Library, New York.

drich Schiller University) has a collection of 2,500 cunei-form tablets and fragments.

BIBLIOGRAPHY. S. N. Kramer, *From the Tablets of Sumer*, Indian Hills, Colo., 1956; H. Frankfort, *The Art and Architecture of the Ancient Orient*, 2d ed., Baltimore, 1959.   JEROME ROTHLEIN

CUNEO PERINETTI, JOSE. Uruguayan landscape painter (1889–   ). José Cuneo Perinetti studied in his native city of Montevideo and in Turin (1907–09) and visited Paris many times. He has worked in water color and in oil. He did an important series entitled *Moon* in the 1930s (for example, *Luna sobre el rancherío*; Montevideo, Octavio S. Assunção Collection).

BIBLIOGRAPHY. J. P. Argul, *El pintor José Cuneo, paisajista del Uruguay*, Montevideo, 1949.

CUNHA, MANOEL DA. Brazilian painter (b. Rio de Janeiro, 1737; d. there, 1809). Born a slave in the family of Canon Januario da Cunha Barbosa, Manoel first worked in the studio of João de Souza and was then sent to Lisbon, Portugal, to study art. On his return to Rio de Janeiro, Manoel became a tremendously prolific artist, painting murals and altarpieces in churches throughout the city, including the Chapel of Senhor dos Passos in the Church of the Carmelites, Santo Avelino, and the Santa Casa Hospital. Through his great reputation as a painter and his connections with highly placed patrons he was eventually freed from bondage. Manoel was Brazil's first portraitist, his masterpiece being a portrait of Count de Bobadela.

CUPID, *see* EROS.

CUPIDS, *see* PUTTO.

CUPOLA. Small dome or ceiling having a spherical form. Cupolas are found in the Roman Temple of Venus, Baalbek, in Sto Spirito, Florence, and in the Tempietto in the cloister of S. Pietro in Montorio, Rome, of the Renaissance. A large cupola is sometimes called a dome, but in St. Peter's, Rome, the smaller domes, though sizable, are called cupolas to distinguish them from the main dome.

CURIA. In general, the papal court and its functionaries. Specifically, it is the name of the town hall of ancient Rome built by Tullus Hostilius, replaced by Caesar, and later (ca. 625) converted into the Church of S. Adriano. It was restored to its antique form in 1937. The bronze doors from the Curia are now on the Lateran Basilica.

CURRIER AND IVES. The largest American firm of lithographic publishers in the 19th century. It was founded by Nathaniel Currier (1813–88), who was born in Roxbury, Mass. In 1857 he created the famous partnership with James Merritt Ives (1824–95), who was born in New York. Currier had been apprenticed to the Boston lithographic firm of William S. and John Pendelton at the age of fifteen; five years later he joined M. E. D. Brown in Philadelphia. In 1834, in New York City, Currier entered into an unsuccessful partnership of one year with Stodart and then established his own shop in 1836. In 1852 Ives joined Currier's firm as a bookkeeper. His congenial temperament and ability as an artist gained him the position of junior partner five years later.

From 1838 to 1872 the firm was located at 152 Nassau Street. It maintained a sales staff, published catalogs of its inventory, and had agents throughout the United States as well as in London. Subjects offered were described in one of the firm's sales letters of the 1870s: "Juvenile, Domestic, Love Scenes, Kittens and Puppies, Ladies Heads, Catholic Religious, Patriotic, Landscapes, Vessels, Comic, School Rewards and Drawing Studies, Flowers and Fruits, Motto Cards, Horses, Family Registers, Memory Pieces and Miscellaneous." The accompanying catalog contained 1,100 titles. Among the artists and lithographers most often connected with Currier and Ives were John Cameron, Otto Knirsch, Louis Maurer, Fanny Palmer, Napoleon Sarony, J. Schultz, C. Severin, and Franz Venino. The coloring of the prints was done by a staff of girls who worked in a production line from a model. Prints were also sent out for hand coloring. True chromolithography, printing in colors, was not used in the Currier and Ives shop; it was manufactured elsewhere, and did not appear until 1889.

Among the better known artists who produced designs for the firm were Louis Maurer (*Life of a Fireman* series), Thomas Worth (cartoons), Arthur Fitzwilliam Tait (sporting subjects such as *The Life of a Hunter: A Tight Fix*), Fanny Palmer (landscape and sporting prints such as *The Happy Family: Ruffed Grouse and Young*), George Henry Durrie (New England genre scenes including *Winter in the Country: Getting Ice* and *Home to Thanksgiving*), Charles Parsons (marine subjects and such others as *Central-Park, Winter: The Skating Pond*), and the marine artist James E. Butterworth.

Nathaniel Currier retired in 1880 and was succeeded by his son, Edward West Currier. James Ives remained with the firm until 1895 when he was succeeded by his son, Chauncey Ives, who purchased the business in 1902 and sold it in 1907.

BIBLIOGRAPHY. H. T. Peters, *Currier & Ives, Printmakers to the American People*, Garden City, N.Y., 1942.

KNEELAND MCNULTY

CURRIER GALLERY OF ART, MANCHESTER, N.H., *see* MANCHESTER, N.H.: CURRIER GALLERY OF ART.

CURRY, JOHN STEUART. American painter, lithographer, and illustrator (b. Dunavant, Kan., 1897; d. Madison, Wis., 1946). He studied in Kansas City and Chicago and at the Art Students League in New York and the Russian Academy in Paris. Curry painted realistic farm and rural subjects, often of an anecdotal nature. His *Baptism in Kansas* (1928, New York, Whitney Museum) won him prominence and helped establish the subject mat-

John Steuart Curry, *Baptism in Kansas*. Oil on canvas. Whitney Museum of American Art, New York.

ter of American regionalist painting of the 1930s. In 1932 he traveled with the Ringling Brothers circus, painting the animals and entertainers, as in the glowing red *Flying Codonas* (1932; Whitney Museum). Thereafter he again concentrated on the Middle Western scene, for example, *Wisconsin Landscape* (1940; New York, Metropolitan Museum).

BIBLIOGRAPHY. L. E. Schmeckebier, *John Steuart Curry's Pageant of America*, New York, 1943.

CURSIVE SCRIPT. In general, any handwriting in which the letters of the words are connected to one another. In medieval paleography, cursive is a type of rapid free-flowing handwriting, with connected letters, which was used by secular courts for records and documents. A more rigid, formal "book script" was used for religious manuscripts and other books.

BIBLIOGRAPHY. E. M. Thompson, *An Introduction to Greek and Latin Palaeography*, Oxford, 1912.

CURTAIN. Defensive wall of considerable height (20–30 ft. or higher) and thickness (6–9 ft. above plinth), constructed to encircle or otherwise protect a castle. Curtains ordinarily followed the contours of the ground on which they were built. Their development from simple 11th- and 12th-century structures to elaborate and extensive works incorporating towers occurred in the late 13th century, especially in England under Edward I. Caerphilly and Caernarvon castles offer the best examples.

BIBLIOGRAPHY. S. Toy, *The Castles of Great Britain*, 2d ed., London, 1954.

CURTIS, J. English engraver (fl. early 19th cent.). Curtis is known only through two celebrated colored engravings that appeared on the European auction market in 1908. The oval, delicately colored engravings of Louis XVI and Marie Antoinette, done after miniature portraits by Boze, bear the markings of Curtis and Boze, "Dufroe p," and the date 1802.

CURZOLA (Korcula) CATHEDRAL. The Cathedral of St. Mark in Curzola, Yugoslavia, built in the Romanesque style during the 13th century. A basilica with a nave, two aisles, and a semicircular apse, the building closely resembles earlier and contemporary churches in the Veneto. The tower (1438–65) uses an elaborate Gothic vocabulary.

CUSP. Triangular shape (from the Latin *cuspus*, "point") projecting from the soffit of an arch, as in medieval tracery. Formed by the intersection of two curves, cusping became increasingly elaborate in English Decorated and Perpendicular tracery, contrasting with its relative absence in late French Gothic.

CUSTOMS HOUSE, NEW YORK, see GILBERT, CASS.

CUVILLIES, FRANCOIS DE, THE ELDER. German architect and decorator (b. Soignies-en-Hainaut, 1695; d. 1768). He lived in Munich and entered the service of Maximilian Emanuel, elector of Bavaria, when he was very young, traveling with that court through northern Europe. After the Peace of 1715, the court returned to Munich, where Cuvilliés participated in the renewed building ac-

François de Cuvilliés the Elder, Amalienburg hunting pavilion, Munich.

tivity. The Elector sent him to Paris to study (1720–24) under Jacques François Blondel, so that his artistic formation is generally regarded as being purely French. From 1725 on he shared the honor of architect of the court of Munich with Joseph Effner. In 1745, when Maximilian succeeded to the electorate of Bavaria and when Effner died, he was named first architect. Although he differed from Effner, the elder partner's influence on Cuvilliés is great, since Cuvilliés's work consisted mainly in remodeling interiors, which he supplied with rich and fantastic designs related to the ostentatious designs of Effner.

In forty-three years' service, Cuvilliés executed many works; chief among them are the Amalienburg hunting pavilion of the Nymphenburg Palace, the gardens and buildings of the Munich Residenz, the Antiquarium, and the Opera. He also executed many private residences. Outstanding among them are the Palais Piosasque de Non, Palais Holnstein, Palais Portia, and Palais Fugger (1759), which illustrates his interest in the new classical trend after his second trip to France (1754–55). His last work was the façade of the Theatinerkirche (1765–68). The best known and perhaps greatest of his works is the iridescent Theater of the Munich Residenz. *See* NYMPHENBURG PALACE; RESIDENZ THEATER, MUNICH.

Cuvilliés adapted and popularized with great facility the style that grew out of the workshop of Jules-Hardouin Mansart. His infinite variations on the multiplicity of rococo forms made him an important source of the French style. His true importance is as chief promoter of this style in southern Germany and is determined as much by the widespread popularity of his published books of engravings as by his architectural works. He published nearly 500 plates during his lifetime; many were republished after his death by his son. These plates contained cartouches, trophies, ceiling designs, mirror and picture frames, panels, overdoors, ironwork, furniture, and fountains, as well as architectural projects and executed work.

BIBLIOGRAPHY. K. Trautmann, "Der kurfürstliche Hofbaumeister Franz Cuvilliés d. A. und sein Schaffen in Altbayern," *Monatsschrift des historischen Vereins von Oberbayern*, IV, 1895; J. Laran, *François Cuvilliés, dessinateur et architecte*, Paris, 1925; W. Braunfels, *François de Cuvilliés; ein Beitrag zur Geschichte der künstlerischen Beziehungen zwischen Deutschland und Frankreich im 18. Jahrhundert*, Würzburg, 1938.
DORA WIEBENSON

CUYLENBORCH (Cuylenburgh), ABRAHAM VAN, *see* CUIJLENBURGH, ABRAHAM VAN.

CUYP, *see* CUIJP.

CUZCO CATHEDRAL. Peruvian church begun in 1560. The architect in charge was Juan Antonio Veramendi from Viscaya, Spain. The Spaniard Francesca Becerra submitted his first plans in 1582 and new plans in 1598. By July, 1654, the work was complete except for the towers, which were delayed about three years or more. Because of the virtual identity with Becerra's Lima Cathedral, it is generally supposed that Becerra, together with Juan Correa, executed Cuzco Cathedral. Both churches are of the hall type, consisting of three naves of equal height; both have nonprojecting transepts without lantern; and the shapes of the piers and the large Doric entablature blocks are similar. The rectangular plan in both follows the type established in Spain in Seville Cathedral (1402), but at Lima there are pointed arches and groined vaults, while at Cuzco there are round arches. The interior is distinguished by its colossal proportions and austere simplicity. One may be led to recall the classicism of Herrera in the Escorial of 1567. At Cuzco one is immediately struck by the majestic space, which might have appeared slightly more vertical had pointed arches been used as first intended. The hard reddish-brown Andean stone, also used by the Incas, contributes to the grandeur.

The façade, designed in the mid-17th century, is broad in relation to the height of the towers. Brown Andean stone adds to the solemnity. Decoration is centered in the main portal, which is composed of several planes moving toward the middle. Over the doorway two steeply curving sections open to give space to the windows above. Heavily rusticated masonry emphasizes the two lesser entrances, whose rounded pediments enframe the coat of arms of Spain. The undecorated masses of the two towers are alleviated by open belfries. In spite of differences in detail and proportion, the general disposition of Cuzco's façade resembles that of Lima.

The famous cult image, known as *Christ of the Earthquakes*, is a crucifix reputedly presented to the city in the 16th century by Charles V of Spain. Tradition has it that the works of the organ, dated between 1600 and 1625, are of Flemish construction. The pipes of the two organs are grouped across the front in a manner common to Renaissance Europe. Gilded wooden scrollwork screens the upper open spaces. The Cathedral altar, overlaid in the new French rococo fashion of the third quarter of the 18th century, differs from the other furnishings. The retable of the Trinity (1655) is quite striking; like other sculptures in the Cathedral, it is a local product.

BIBLIOGRAPHY. H. E. Wethey, *Colonial Architecture and Sculpture in Peru*, Cambridge, Mass., 1949; P. Kelemen, *Baroque and Rococo in Latin America*, New York, 1951.

ABRAHAM A. DAVIDSON

CYCLADIC ART, *see* AEGEAN ART.

CYCLOPEAN MASONRY, *see* MASONRY, CYCLOPEAN.

CYLINDER SEALS, *see* SEALS: STAMP AND CYLINDER.

Cuzco Cathedral, façade, designed in the mid-17th century.

CYLIX, *see* KYLIX.

CYMA. Molding of double curvature (from the Greek *kyma*, "swollen," "wave"), S-shaped in profile. When the concave section is at the top, the molding is known as a *cyma recta*; when the convex section is above, it is called a *cyma reversa*.

CYMATIUM. Crowning molding of a cornice, usually in the form of a cyma. The Lesbian cymatium is a *cyma reversa*.

CYPRIAN OF CARTHAGE, ST. Bishop, martyr, and a Father of the Church (ca. 200–258). Born at Carthage, he was a pagan rhetorician who converted in 246. Chosen bishop of Carthage in 248, he fled the persecutions of Decius but continued to rule from exile. On his return,

Cymatium. Crowning molding in classical architecture.

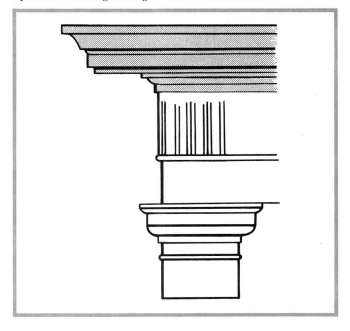

he reorganized the African church. Many had left the church because of plague and controversies. His short treatises and letters achieved great popularity. He is associated with St. Cornelius and was martyred in Carthage the day Cornelius's relics were transferred to Rome. His attribute is a sword. His feast is September 16. *See also* SAINTS IN ART.

CYPRUS. Mediterranean island near Asia on the sea route to the Aegean. Its location as well as its richness in copper (*kypros*) accounts for its widespread influence in the Levant and the eclectic character of its art style. Its neolithic pottery shows racial affiliations with Asia Minor (red polished ware) and the Levant (painted ware). Relations with early Phoenicia were superseded by those with Mycenae (after the 14th cent. B.C.), while proto-Doric elements and later Achaean ones arrived to colonize the island. Mycenaean pottery was imported and imitated locally. The dromos tomb of Mycenaean origin is found there also (13th cent. B.C.).

After the 12th century B.C. relations with the west ceased, while those with the east were reduced. A local style developed from the indigenous one and from the imitation of Mycenaean wares (10th cent. B.C.) without showing any influence from the Phoenician infiltration in the south (8th cent. B.C.). At that time seven rulers of Cyprus went to Sargon II in Babylon (713 B.C.) with offerings. In the 6th century B.C., Greek influence permeated the Hittite and Levantine zones of civilization in Cyprus, while Egyptianizing features and Phoenician influence appeared briefly. The Attic Greek style was patronized by Euagoras of Salamis (beginning of 4th cent. B.C.). Cyprus finally became a Ptolemaic Egyptian colony and followed Alexandrian trends.

Domestic architecture in the Neolithic period was similar to that in the Near East, consisting of round and oval houses. Later in the Copper Age, rectangular rooms were set around a courtyard, and a large palace at Enkomi (12th cent. B.C.) shows Mycenaean borrowings. At Vouni a palace was built later, in the Persian period and style (5th cent. B.C.) but with eclecticism in the choice of the elements (Hittite gateway, Mesopotamian *hilani*, Egyptianizing Hathor capital). *See* ENKOMI; VOUNI.

Temples seem to be hypaethral but appear occasionally with antecella and cella within one or two courts, as at Ajia Irini, Vouni, and Idalion. Mycenaean influence is conspicuous in the roof of the circular tomb (1600 B.C.) and later in the Mycenaean dromos tomb (13th cent. B.C.). *See* HYPAETHROS.

The faïence cups with a woman's head applied, which appear in graves in Cyprus (1300 B.C.) and other sites in the Near East, are perhaps copied after models produced locally at a shrine. Among the Phoenician elements is the motif, worked on a bronze support, of Aphrodite beckoning from a window, similar to the representation of Astarte in the Phoenician ivories. Fragments of fourteen metallic bowls found in Cyprus were dedicated by a governor of Hiram II of Tyre (ca. 738 B.C.). The occurrence of the so-called Cypriot palmette (reminiscent of the sacred volute tree of Mesopotamia) on a gold bracelet and on bronze bowls and stone capitals found in Cyprus can perhaps be explained as coming from its Phoenician workshops.

Tomb of Cyrus, Pasargadae, near Persepolis.

With the Christian era and the rise of Byzantium, Cyprus became part of the Byzantine empire. From the 7th century comes the rich Cyprus Treasure (New York, Metropolitan Museum), a series of silver plates with classically styled figures in repoussé, depicting events in the life of David. In 649 the island was captured by the Ummayads, with subsequent Islamic influence on its art.

In the Middle Ages the basic Byzantine and Islamic character of Cypriot art was modified by the Western European Gothic style imported by the Lusignan dynasty (1191–1489). *See also* BELLAPAIS ABBEY; FAMAGUSTA CATHEDRAL; NICOSIA CATHEDRAL.

BIBLIOGRAPHY. C. F. A. Schaeffer, *Missions en Chypre*, Paris, 1936; H. Bossert, *Altsyrien*, Tübingen, 1951; C. F. A. Schaeffer, *Enkomi-Alasia*, Paris, 1952.

ALEXANDER M. BADAWY

CYPSELUS, CHEST OF. Cedarwood chest once in the Temple of Hera in Olympia, Greece. It was probably a gift to the sanctuary from the Corinthian tyrant Cypselus or from one of his family in the late 7th or early 6th century B.C. Pausanias (5.17.5) describes the chest as being decorated with figures in ivory, gold, and wood. No trace of it remains today.

BIBLIOGRAPHY. J. G. Frazer, tr., *Pausanias's Description of Greece*, vol. 3, London, 1898.

CYRUS, TOMB OF, PASARGADAE. Small, square stone building, built by Cyrus the Great (559–530 B.C.) in the gardens of his palace in Pasargadae, the capital he founded near Persepolis, in southwest central Iran. The tomb is about 45 feet broad at the base and 42 to 43 feet high from the level of the ground to the roof. Six steps lead to a small doorway, 2½ feet high, facing east. The doorway leads into a chamber 9 feet wide, 11 feet long, and 8 feet high. The embalmed body of the king lay in a golden coffin, near which was a seat with feet of gold. Purple draperies and Babylonian carpets covered the walls. Two plates of cuneiform inscriptions proclaimed Cyrus founder of the Persian Empire.

BIBLIOGRAPHY. Kāvasjī Dīnshāh Kiash, *Ancient Persian Sculptures*, Bombay, 1889; A. Godard, *L'Art de l'Iran*, Paris, 1962.

CZECHOSLOVAKIA, NATIONAL MUSEUM OF, *see* PRAGUE: NATIONAL GALLERY.

D

DABBER. A round pad of felt, about 3 or more inches in diameter, wrapped in kid leather. The dabber is a do-it-yourself instrument used to apply etching ground to the warmed plate and especially to ground an intaglio plate in the traditional manner.

DABO, LEON. American painter (b. Detroit, 1868; d. New York City, 1960). He studied with La Farge and with Puvis de Chavannes and Whistler in Paris. He executed murals for two Brooklyn churches. His landscapes, misty and somewhat symbolic, are composed in broad bands of light and dark.

DADA. Movement in literature and the visual arts founded in Zurich, Switzerland, in February, 1916, by a brilliant and ironic group of international artists, including the Rumanians Tristan Tzara and Marcel Janco, the Germans Richard Huelsenbeck and Hugo Ball, the Alsatian Jean (Hans) Arp, and others. These individuals centered their activities at the Cabaret Voltaire, where Huelsenbeck and certain of the others served beer and doubled as musicians and dancers. The Cabaret Voltaire soon added a room as an art gallery, and Tzara (or others with the help of Tzara) selected the name Dada, meaning "hobbyhorse" (or, according to the *Oxford Concise Dictionary*, "an infantile sound"), more or less at random by opening a French lexicon with a paperknife. *See* ARP, JEAN.

The Dadaists were unified by a collectively antimilitarist, antiaesthetic attitude, impelled in part by the horrors of World War I but also, in the more professional sense, by boredom with cubism and other current modern styles as well as traditional art and literature in general. The review bearing the name of this movement specialized in what might be called a remarkably articulate inarticulateness—poems and articles of antilogical content that were sometimes hilarious, sometimes biting. The gallery of the Cabaret Voltaire exhibited works by Kandinsky, Klee, De Chirico, Max Ernst, Arp, Modigliani, and others. Not the least disquieting of their programs was frequent public display of consciously irrational behavior, such as mock fistfights and applause at illogical moments during plays.

The Zurich venture had in fact been anticipated by the independent activities of the French painters Marcel Duchamp and Francis Picabia after 1912 and, in 1915 or before, by the Americans Man Ray and Walter Arensberg, all of whom contributed to New York exhibitions and publications during World War I. Closer in spirit to the Zurich variety of Dada, however, was the Cologne association formed in 1919 by Max Ernst and Johannes Baargeld in collaboration with Arp. Arp and Ernst produced a series of collages known as *Fatagaga*, and one of their exhibitions was so controversial that it was closed by the police. *See* DUCHAMP, MARCEL; ERNST, MAX; PICABIA, FRANCIS; RAY, MAN.

Other 1919 Dada manifestations took place concurrently in Hannover, where Kurt Schwitters invented *Merzbilder* (junk pictures); in Paris, where André Breton, Louis Aragon, and Philippe Soupault were editing *Littérature* and were joined by most of the original Zurich group; and in Berlin, where Huelsenbeck published *Der Dada*. Arp worked independently as a painter and sculptor of increasingly abstract reliefs. A unifying principle, in addition to the antilogical character of the literature and art produced by the various individuals, was the group action of deliberately upsetting public behavior. *See* SCHWITTERS, KURT.

The Dada movement spread during the early 1920s through much of Europe; affiliated groups appeared in Holland, Belgium, Austria, and elsewhere. An international Dadaist exhibition was presented in 1922 at the Galerie Montaigne in Paris.

Dada was dissipated as an organized program by 1924, when some of its members led by André Breton founded surrealism. Several Dadaists contributed to the most imaginative and least pedantic aspects of surrealism, among them Ernst, Arp, and Man Ray, none of whom followed the central surrealist attitude of presenting fantastic content in the guise of a sometimes heavy-handed naturalism.

It is often alleged that Dada was a nihilistic, destructive movement, but it should be understood that many gifted artists advocated Dada. Among them were some of the

Dada. Georges Ribemont–Dessaignes, *Grand Musicien*, 1920. André Breton Collection, Paris.

most distinguished practitioners of surrealism and abstract art. The surrealist movement could hardly have developed without the collective and individual contributions of Dada. Further, the spirit of the Dadaists never completely disappeared, and the so-called Neo-Dada art of the late 1950s and 1960s in New York, including certain varieties of the "arts of assemblage," especially junk sculpture and some pop art, sustain the tradition.

BIBLIOGRAPHY. H. Ball, ed., *Cabaret Voltaire*, Zurich, 1916; R. Hülsenbeck, ed., *Dada Almanach*, Berlin, 1920; G. Hugnet, "L'Esprit dada dans la peinture," *Cahiers d'Art*, VII: 1-2, 6-7, 8-10, 1932; R. Motherwell, ed., *The Dada Painters and Poets: An Anthology*, New York, 1951; W. Verkauf, ed., *Dada: Monograph of a Movement*, Teufen, 1957; H. Richter, *Dada: Art and Anti-Art*, New York, 1965; New York, Museum of Modern Art, *Dada, Surrealism, and Their Heritage*, by W. Rubin, New York, 1968. JOHN C. GALLOWAY

DADDI, BERNARDO. Italian painter of the Florentine school (1290–1348). Bernardo Daddi was one of the leading painters of Florence during the first half of the 14th century. Nothing is known of his training, though the premises of his art are Giottesque. His name appears in a register of the Florentine guild of doctors and apothecaries for the years 1312 to 1320 and in another for the years 1320 to 1353.

In 1328 he painted the triptych for the Church of Ognissanti (now in Florence, Uffizi). A small portable triptych in the Bigallo Museum, Florence, is dated 1333; and the central panel of another, *Madonna and Child with Saints*, painted in 1334, is in the Academy in Florence. In 1335 he painted a panel, *The Vision of St. Bernard*, now lost, for an altar of S. Bernardo in the Palazzo Vecchio, Florence. Also lost are an altarpiece, *Three Dominican Saints*, which he painted for S. Maria Novella in 1338, and two altarpieces formerly in S. Maria a Quarto, one in the choir (dated 1340) and one on the main altar (dated 1341).

Bernardo's polyptych in the first cloister of S. Maria Novella is signed and dated 1344. In March and June, 1347, he received payments for the large splendid panel

Bernardo Daddi, *Martyrdom of St. Lawrence*. Fresco. Sta Croce, Florence. One of the many works attributed to the painter.

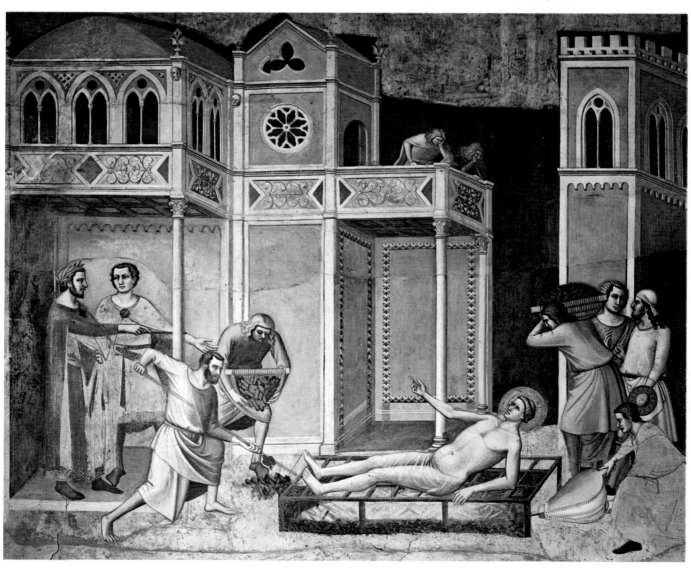

of the *Madonna and Child with Angels* in the tabernacle with reliefs by Andrea Orcagna in Or San Michele, Florence. A polyptych with the *Crucifixion, Eight Saints,* and smaller scenes from S. Giorgio a Ruballa, now in the collection of Major Gambier-Parry at Highnam Court, Gloucester, is dated 1348, the year of Bernardo's death.

Among the many works attributed to Bernardo Daddi are frescoes of the *Martyrdom of SS. Lawrence and Stephen* in Sta Croce, Florence, the lovely *Madonna and Child* panel in the Berenson Collection at Settignano, and many small portable altars elsewhere. He had a large shop and following, most of whom specialized, as he did, in small devotional panels and triptychs, though their production does not lack in works of monumental scale. Of all the Florentine painters of his time Bernardo shows the greatest affinity to Sienese painting, though no concrete link between his art and Siena has so far been established. In Florence he is most closely related to the St. Cecilia Master, an exponent, like Bernardo, of the miniaturist tendency in Florentine painting.

BIBLIOGRAPHY. G. Vitzthum von Eckstädt, *Bernardo Daddi*, Leipzig, 1903; O. Sirén, *Giotto and Some of His Followers*, 2 vols., Cambridge, Mass., 1917; R. Offner, *A Critical and Historical Corpus of Florentine Painting*, section 3, vols. 3 and 4, New York, 1930 and 1934.
HELLMUT WOHL

DADO. Tessera, or die; by extension, the face of a pedestal between its base and cornice. The term is also used to describe the lower portion of a wall when treated as a continuous band or pedestal, as in the painted dado of the throne room of the Mycenaean palace in Cnossus. When made of wood, the dado is known as a wainscot. *See* WAINSCOT.

DAEDALUS. Legendary Greek artist to whose handiwork the classical Greeks were fond of ascribing very ancient works of art—statues, temples, mechanical devices, and so on. He is associated with two strata of myths, the first associated with Minoan Crete; the second with early Greece. In Crete he was said to have invented the bronze cow for Pasiphaë, the labyrinth for the Minotaur, the thread for Ariadne, and finally the wings used by his son Icarus. In Greece his name was associated with ancient wooden statues, perhaps survivals from the Mycenaean period, and also with the first representations of walking figures (perhaps the first kouroi).

Under the influence of this tradition, modern students have come to refer to a 7th-century Cretan and Peloponnesian (therefore Dorian) type of statuette as "Daedalic."

BIBLIOGRAPHY. C. Picard, *Manuel d'archéologie grecque—La sculpture I: Période archaïque,* Paris, 1935.

DAGABA, *see* DAGOBA.

DAGNAN-BOUVERET, PASCAL ADOLPHE JEAN. French painter (b. Paris, 1852; d. Quincey, 1929). He studied with Gérôme and Corot. His early paintings were of classical subjects. Later he painted genre and religious scenes. Although academic in style, he sometimes displayed some originality in his color.

DAGOBA (Dagaba). Shrine in Buddhist architecture. It is related to the stūpa (a mound), the dāgoba being a mound containing the relics of saints.

Daguerreotype. Example of the type of photographic reproduction used by pioneer photographers.

DAGUERREOTYPE. Positive photographic reproduction made by the action of light on a silver-surfaced copper plate previously sensitized by iodine fumes. When the plate is placed in a camera obscura equipped with a lens, it is exposed and records the image before it; the exposure time depends upon the amount of sunlight available. The plate is developed by mercury vapor and fixed by a hypo bath. The process was invented in 1837 by Louis Daguerre and Isidore Niepce of Paris, and it was used by photographic pioneers to produce works of great artistic value.

BIBLIOGRAPHY. New York, Metropolitan Museum of Art, *. . . The Hawes-Stokes Collection of American Daguerreotypes by Albert Sands Southworth and Josiah Johnson Hawes,* New York, 1939.

DAHL, JOHANN CHRISTIAN. Norwegian painter (b. Bergen, 1788; d. Dresden, 1857). The most important Norwegian romantic landscape painter, Dahl studied at the Copenhagen Academy and after 1824 was professor at the Dresden Academy. In his late works he adopted a realistic style.

BIBLIOGRAPHY. A. Aubert, *Die nordische Landschaftsmalerei und Johann Christian Dahl,* Berlin, 1947.

DAHOMEY, *see* AFRICA, PRIMITIVE ART OF (WEST AFRICA).

DAHSHUR. Necropolis in the western desert south of Saqqara in Middle Egypt. There stand the two stone pyramids of Pharaoh Snefru (4th dynasty), the southern one rhomboidal in shape with its upper part at a steeper angle of incline (42°59′) than the lower (54°41′). There are also mastabas and the brick pyramids of Amenemhat II and

Salvador Dali, *The Sacrament of the Last Supper*, 1955. National Gallery, Washington, D.C.

Senusert III (12th dynasty), originally cased with limestone and topped with gray granite pyramidions. The jewelry of the royal ladies from Dahshur, masterpieces of craftsmanship, displays symbolic compositions woven around the cartouches of the Pharaoh.

See also EGYPT.

BIBLIOGRAPHY. J. de Morgan, *Fouilles à Dahchour*, Vienna, 1895.

DAIBUTSU OF KAMAKURA, *see* AMIDA BUDDHA, GREAT, OF KAMAKURA.

DAILEY, GARDNER A. American architect (1894–   ). Dailey was born in St. Paul, Minn. He began a private practice in San Francisco in 1926 and later did notable work on military buildings during World War II, particularly the U.S. Merchant Marine Cadet School (now San Mateo Junior College) at San Mateo, Calif., in 1942.

BIBLIOGRAPHY. New York, Museum of Modern Art, *Built in U.S.A., 1932-1944*, ed. E. Mock, 1944.

DAINICHI, *see* VAIROCANA.

DAIS. Raised platform, as in a lecture room or church. The dais was the elevated portion at the end of the medieval great hall where the master dined, as in Penshurst Place, Kent.

DAISENIN GARDEN. Japanese garden of the Daisenin, a subtemple of the Daitokuji in Kyoto. The Hōjō (living quarters of the chief abbot) of the Daisenin was built in the early 16th century, and its garden dates from about the same time. The garden occupies a narrow patch of ground along the north and east sides of the building. It is a dry garden, in which all the water elements, such as falls, streams, and ponds, are suggested by rocks and sand without introducing water. The only plants are a group of carefully trimmed sala trees, which symbolizes a distant hill.

BIBLIOGRAPHY. Tokyo National Museum, *Pageant of Japanese Art*, vol. 6: *Architecture and Gardens*, Tokyo, 1952; S. Horiguchi and Y. Kojiro, *Architectural Beauty in Japan*, 2d ed., Tokyo, 1957; Kokusai Bunka Shinkōkai, *Tradition of Japanese Garden*, Tokyo, 1962.

DALENS (Dalen), DIRCK. Dutch landscape painter (b. Dordrecht, ca. 1600; d. Zierikzee, 1676). Dalens was perhaps the pupil of Moses van Utenbroeck, whose influence can be seen in his earlier works. He became a master at The Hague in 1632 and painted four works for Prince Frederick Henry in 1648. He painted Arcadian landscapes, either with antique subjects or in the manner of Jan van Goijen.

BIBLIOGRAPHY. W. Bernt, *Die niederländischen Maler des 17. Jahrhunderts . . .*, vol. 1, Munich, 1948.

DALI, SALVADOR. Spanish painter, writer, book illustrator, stage designer, movie producer, and jewelry designer (1904–   ). Dali entered the art school of San Fernando Academy, Madrid, at age seventeen and was expelled in 1926. His student work was concerned with the cubist movement. About 1923, he became interested in the metaphysical aspects of works by Chirico and Carrà. Exhibitions of his work at Barcelona (1925) and Madrid (1926) aroused public attention because of his application of precise and serene draftsmanship to what has been called a new mythology of the Mediterranean.

He visited Picasso in Paris in 1928 as a self-styled cubist. The impact of Picasso's collages, Breton's theory of surrealism, Miró's biomorphic forms, and Tanguy's vast spaces caused Dali to reorient his artistic purpose. Shortly after meeting the practitioners of surrealism, he invited them all for a visit to Cadaqués, the birthplace of his father and Dali's favorite habitation.

His exploits have always received lavish publicity, and he has enjoyed great public attention. His abundant publications (*The Secret Life of Salvador Dali, Fifty Secrets of the Art of Magic*, and so on), purporting to reveal or explain the "real Dali" or the "true significance" of his art, are couched in impressively rich philosophical terminology, which he garbles in a species of abracadabra. Nevertheless, neither he nor his art can be dismissed. His evasiveness, nurtured by a canny intelligence, and the nonrational themes of his art are served by a high degree of technical skill.

Persistence of Memory (1931; New York, Museum of Modern Art) follows the Freudian inspiration of surrealism in depicting a hallucinatory dream world of painfully clear objects irrationally juxtaposed and individually deformed in an ensemble pregnant with hidden meanings. Dali put forward his so-called paranoiac method in an endless proliferation of enigmatic images within images, such as *Apparition of Face and Fruit Dish* (1931; Hartford, Wadsworth Atheneum).

Dali has since sought external inspirations for subject matter. *Atomic Leda and Swan* is his ambiguous response to the atomic age; the *Sacrament of the Last Supper* (1955; Washington, D.C., National Gallery) is a religious theme interpreted with the artist's own metaphysical symbolism.

BIBLIOGRAPHY. J. A. Gaya Nuño, *Salvador Dali*, Barcelona, 1950; A. R. Morse, *Dali: A Study of His Life and Work*, Greenwich, Conn., 1958; M. Jean and A. Mezei, *The History of Surrealist Painting*, New York, 1960; R. Descharnes, *The World of Salvador Dali*, New York, 1962.

EILEEN A. LORD

DALLAIRE, JEAN. Canadian painter (1916–). Born in Hull, Dallaire studied in Paris under Maurice Denis and André Lhote. His oil paintings are influenced by the surrealism of Jean Lurçat. He is also a muralist, tapestry designer, and film producer.

BIBLIOGRAPHY. Ottawa, National Gallery of Canada, *Catalogue of Paintings and Sculpture*, ed. R. H. Hubbard, vol. 3: *Canadian School*, 1960.

DALLAS, TEX.: MUSEUMS. Important public art collections in Dallas, Tex., are located in the museums listed below.

Museum for Contemporary Arts. Started in a rented room in a shopping center in 1957, the museum now occupies its own building. The frequently changing exhibits deal primarily with contemporary art. A permanent collection is being formed.

BIBLIOGRAPHY. E. Spaeth, *American Art Museums and Galleries*, New York, 1960.

Museum of Fine Arts. Originally formed in 1903, the museum was opened to the public in 1936. Some European paintings are on view, as well as a representative collection of Latin American art, including Tamayo's *El hombre*, commissioned by the museum. The American collection, ranging from Stuart to Wyeth, pays particular attention to Texas artists.

DALLE MASEGNE, *see* MASEGNE, JACOBELLO AND PIERPAOLO DALLE.

DALLIN, CYRUS E. American sculptor (1861–1944). He was active mainly in Boston. Dallin's most representative works are his equestrian portraits, many of Indian subjects. His *Anne Hutchinson* (Boston, State House) is well known. Numerous public works on the theme of the American Indian include *Signal of Peace* (Chicago, Lincoln Park) and *The Medicine Man* (1899; Philadelphia, Fairmount Park). At his best, Dallin worked in a substantially naturalistic manner devoid of the melodrama sometimes accorded themes of the "noble red man" by his contemporaries. On the other hand, his works reflect an unconvincing impressionist tendency that leaves his forms unsubstantial and lacking in individuality.

BIBLIOGRAPHY. W. H. Pierson and M. Davidson, eds., *Arts of the United States . . .*, New York, 1960.

DALL'OGLIO, EGIDIO. Italian painter (b. Cison di Valmarino, 1705; d. Venice, 1784). Dall'Oglio painted frescoes and oils for many churches in Venetia. Probably a pupil of Piazzetta, he painted in a mild and homely version of the master's style.

DALMASIO, LIPPO, *see* LIPPO DALMASIO DE' SCANNABECCHI.

DALMATA, GIOVANNI (Giovanni da Trau). Italian sculptor (b. probably Trau, ca. 1440; d. after 1509). With Mino da Fiesole, he worked on, and possibly designed, the tomb of Paul II, of which only fragments survive. His exaggerated but plastic forms retained their individuality despite collaboration in Rome with Mino and Andrea Bregno. He worked in Hungary and later, probably, in Venice.

BIBLIOGRAPHY. J. Pope-Hennessy, *Italian Renaissance Sculpture*, London, 1958.

DALMATIC. Sleeved, smocklike garment reaching below the knees. The dalmatic (Latin, *dalmatica*) originated in Egypt. In early Christian times it was transmitted to Rome, where it became a vestment for deacons. Eventually, the garment was universally adopted by deacons and certain other prelates and worn over the *alba*. Various-colored stripes on the dalmatic indicate different feast days.

DALMATIC OF CHARLEMAGNE. Byzantine vestment in St. Peter's Sacristy, Rome.

DALMAU, LUIS (Lluis). Spanish painter (fl. 1428–59). Probably born in Valencia, he was sent by Alfonso V to Castile in 1428; there he most likely saw a few Flemish paintings and may even have met Jan van Eyck. The King next sent Dalmau to Flanders in 1431 for the purpose of securing tapestry weavers for Valencia. He was still in Flanders when Jan van Eyck completed the *Ghent Altarpiece* (1432). Having returned home by 1436, he began

Luis Dalmau, *Enthroned Virgin and Child with Councillors*. Museum of Catalonian Art, Barcelona.

to receive a lifetime annual salary from the King in 1438.

At that time he was commissioned to paint an *Annunciation* (lost) for the Royal Castle in Játiva. His best extant work was commissioned by the city of Barcelona for its Town Hall Chapel—the *Enthroned Virgin and Child with Councillors* (1443–45; Barcelona, Museum of Catalonian Art). Painted in oil, it has an opacity that makes it less pleasing than the usual contemporary paintings produced in tempera on gold leaf in the International Gothic style. In conception it is a combination of the *Madonna of the Canon Van der Paele* and the *Ghent Altarpiece*. It has, in fact, been called an uninspired adaptation from the art of Van Eyck. Only the portraits of the councilors are

original. However, Dalmau had at the very least a complete understanding of the Eyckian style. As a result his art made possible the acceptance in Spain of Flemish influence, which subsequently played so prominent a role.

Dalmau was occupied with several other commissions during his stay in Barcelona. His son Antonio (1450–99) inherited the workshop after his father's death and eventually became a painter himself. Dalmau's influence is immediately apparent in several works by anonymous artists known as the Pedralbes Master and the Gerona Master.

BIBLIOGRAPHY. J. Gudiol i Ricart, *Spanish Painting*, Toledo, Ohio, 1941; E. Lafuente Ferrari, *Breve historia de la pintura española*, 4th ed., Madrid, 1953.

EILEEN A. LORD

DALOU, AIME-JULES. French sculptor (b. Paris, 1838; d. there, 1902). Aimé-Jules Dalou entered the Ecole des Beaux-Arts in Paris in 1854 and first exhibited in the Salon of 1861. After the Commune of 1870 he fled to England, where he exhibited in the Royal Academy, and returned to France only after the amnesty of 1879. Although he did many statues (*Lavoisier*, Paris, Sorbonne; *Delacroix*, Paris, Luxembourg Gardens), Dalou's fame rests on his monuments to the Third Republic, the most significant decorative plastic creations of that epoch. His masterpiece is the *Triumph of the Republic* (1880–99), executed for the Place de la Nation in Paris. His gigantic monument to Labor remained unfinished (sketches are preserved in the Fine Arts Museum of the City of Paris). Dalou's style, in which a vigorous realism is often misallied with allegory, owes much to Carpeaux and Rude.

BIBLIOGRAPHY. M. Dreyfous, *Dalou, sa vie et son oeuvre*, Paris, 1903.

DALWOOD, HUBERT. English sculptor (1924–   ). He studied engineering before World War II and then served in the British Navy. From 1946 to 1949, Dalwood studied at the Bath Academy of Art and worked in sculpture with Kenneth Armitage. In 1954 and following years, he had one-man exhibitions at Gimpel Fils in London. He has taught at the Newport School of Art and at the University of Leeds. Dalwood's style, which is related to that of Armitage, verges at times on abstraction but remains connected with figural imagery.

DALZIEL BROTHERS. English illustrators, engravers, and woodcutters (fl. 19th cent.). Four of the seven brothers were in the firm of Brothers Dalziel, founded by George Dalziel and Edward Dalziel in 1839. John Dalziel joined in 1852, and Thomas Bolton Dalziel in 1860. The firm, which produced woodcuts after the drawings of Gilbert, Rossetti, Ford Madox Brown, Tenniel, and others for large London publishers, flourished until 1893. It is possible that pupils or apprentices cut the blocks while the Dalziels acted mainly as contractors. Two of the brothers were outstanding. Edward, the seventh son (b. Wooler, 1823; d. Herne Bay, Kent, 1906), was an illustrator (Bryant's *Poems*, New York, 1857), in addition to his activities in the firm. Thomas, the fifth son (b. Wooler, 1817; d. Hampstead, 1905), was an outstanding engraver, especially of illustrations (*Pilgrim's Progress*, 1865).

BIBLIOGRAPHY. G. Dalziel and E. Dalziel, *The Brothers Dalziel*, London, 1901.

DAMASCENE. Technique for decorating metal, particularly steel swords, by etching or by inlaying a wavy pattern of lines with precious metals. This type of decoration originated with Arabian swords made in Damascus. Steel decorated in this pattern is known also as Damascus steel.

DAMASCUS. Capital and largest city of Syria, located in a fertile plain at the edge of the desert. The city is very ancient, having been independent from the reign of Solomon until the Battle of Issus in 333. Alexander's successors ruled it until 61 B.C., when Syria became a Roman province. Important under the Byzantines, the city, badly damaged by the Persians in 610–611, fell to the Arabs in 635. The Umayyads made it their capital soon after, but

Aimé-Jules Dalou, *Triumph of the Republic*. Place de la Nation, Paris.

this brilliant period ended in 750, when the Abbasids removed the seat of the caliphate to Baghdad. Fought over by Tulunids, Saljuks, and Crusaders, the city recovered under Nureddin from 1154 and under his successor, Saladin. In 1260 Damascus was sacked by the Mongols and in 1300 by the Tatars. It was a Turkish provincial capital from 1516 until 1918, when it passed to the French. Since World War II the city has enjoyed a precarious independence.

Near the Great Mosque and along the street called Straight are the remains of colonnades and triumphal arches, similar to those of Palmyra but much damaged. The lower courses of the surviving city walls also date from Roman times. The National Museum houses a distinguished collection of antiquities, including the interior of a Palmyrene tomb, the synagogue frescoes from Dura Europos, and a gateway from Qasr-al-Hair al-Gharbi. *See* DURA EUROPOS; ISLAM; PALMYRA.

The Umayyad Great Mosque (706–715) was built by Caliph al-Walid in the inner temenos of the ancient Temple of Jupiter. Its wooden flat-roofed three-aisled sanctuary, located on the south side of an open rectangular court, is bisected by a higher transept with a dome of much later date. The sanctuary façade on the *sahn* suggests the Chalke Palace in Constantinople. The splendid marble and mosaic ornament survives in part, revealing a late Hellenistic mosaic school in landscapes and fantastic architecture against gold grounds. The corner towers of the ancient temenos served as the first minarets in Islam, though the three present minarets are all of later date.

The Maristan (hospital) of Nureddin, begun in 1154, translates the cruciform plan, used by the great Saljuks in Persia for buildings in brick, into the local masonry technique. The stalactite half-vault of the portal and the similar vault in stucco over the antechamber are important.

The Tekiyeh, a monastery for dervishes built for Suleiman the Magnificent in 1554 on the remains of a 13th-century palace, is an excellent example of Ottoman architecture at its best, with the multiple lead-covered domes of its blocks of cells symmetrically flanking a mosque with twin minarets and a broad, eaved porch.

BIBLIOGRAPHY. K. Baedeker, *Palestine and Syria*, Leipzig and New York, 1906; E. Herzfeld, "Damascus, Studies in Architecture," 3 pts., *Ars Islamica*, IX-XII, 1942-46; K. A. C. Creswell, *A Short Account of Early Muslim Architecture*, Harmondsworth, 1958.

JOHN D. HOAG

DAMASCUS STEEL, see DAMASCENE.

DAMBRUN, JEAN. French illustrator and engraver (ca. 1741–after 1814). He generally produced small-format engraved book illustrations after designs by Kehl, Marillier, or Moreau le Jeune, and provided vignettes for almanacs depicting French society. His skill and the quality of his work place him among the masters of 18th-century illustration.

BIBLIOGRAPHY. M. Roux, *Inventaire du fonds français: graveurs du XVIIIe siècle*, vol. 5, Paris, 1946.

DAMER, ANNE SEYMOUR. English sculptor (b. London, 1748; d. there, 1828). She studied under Giuseppe Ceracchi and John Bacon and in 1767 married John Damer. Her husband died in 1776, and she thereafter devoted herself to sculpture; her artistic career was highly encouraged by her friend Horace Walpole. In her uneven *oeuvre* there are bust portraits of many distinguished people: George III, Lord Nelson, and Mrs. Siddons. Her best-known works are the stone heads representing the Thames and Isis rivers for Henley Bridge (1785).

DAMERY, WALTHERE. Flemish history and landscape painter (b. Liège, 1614; d. there, 1678). A student of Antoine Deburto, Damery painted many portraits during a trip to England (1639). Although first influenced classicistically by Bertholet Flémalle, later in Italy he was influenced by Pietro da Cortona. He painted an altarpiece for the Toulon Cathedral (1644) and the cupola of the Carmelite church on the Rue de Vaugirard in Paris.

BIBLIOGRAPHY. J. Philippe, *La Peinture liégeoise au XVIIe siècle*, Brussels, 1945.

DAMGHAN. Ancient capital of Iran, located in the Elburz Mountains. Prehistoric, Sassanian, post-Christian, and Islamic remains have been unearthed there. The finds include pottery, copper, silver and gold objects, seals, and clay and alabaster animal and human figurines, as well as ruins of a citadel, tombs, and a Sassanian palace with remains of mural paintings, stucco reliefs, and ornamental plaques.

BIBLIOGRAPHY. A. U. Pope, ed., *A Survey of Persian Art*, vol. 1, New York, 1938.

DAMINI, VINCENZO. Italian portrait and religious painter, probably born in Venice, who lived in London between 1720 and 1730. He is reputed to have been a pupil of Pellegrini and an excellent portrait painter, although none of his portraits are known. He and his pupil Giles Hussey painted the ceiling of the Lincoln Cathedral. They left London for a trip to France and Italy. Damini absconded with their money and seems to have gone to Aguila, where he left signed and dated religious paintings executed in the manner of Piazzetta.

DAMMARTIN (Dampmartin), DROUET DE. French sculptor and architect (d. Jargeau, 1413). Dammartin studied under Raymond du Temple (1365). Three years later he entered the service of the Duke of Berry in Bourges. In 1383 he became Master of Works for the Duke of Burgundy and directed the construction of the Chartreuse de Champmol in Dijon. He executed portal sculpture for the Ste-Chapelle in Dijon (1387); in 1396 he returned to the court of the Duke of Berry. His brother, Guy de Dammartin, and his son, Jean de Dammartin, were also architects.

DAMMARTIN (Dampmartin), GUY DE. French architect and sculptor (d. ca. 1398). Guy de Dammartin was a pupil of Raymond du Temple and was in the employ of Charles V and, after 1370, of Jean, Duke of Berry, who earlier employed Guy's brother, Drouet de Dammartin. After the great salon of the Palais Royal at Poitiers was destroyed by the English, he rebuilt it, beginning in 1388, in one of the richest programs of late Gothic architectural decoration and sculpture.

DAMMARTIN (Dampmartin), JEAN DE. French architect (d. 1454). Jean de Dammartin was supervising architect of the Le Mans Cathedral beginning in 1421. He built the transept there in the Rayonnant Gothic style. Beginning in 1432 he was master of the works at the Cathedral of Tours, where he completed the nave and the portal. His father, Drouet de Dammartin, and his uncle, Guy de Dammartin, were also architects.

DAN, see AFRICA, PRIMITIVE ART OF (WEST AFRICA: LIBERIA).

DANAE. Daughter of the legendary King Acrisius of Argos who was imprisoned by her father in a brass tower when an oracle predicted the King's death at the hands of a yet unborn grandson. Despite her seclusion, Danae was visited by Zeus, who appeared in the form of a shower of gold, and she became the mother of Perseus. Acrisius then attempted to do away with her and the infant by placing them in a chest that was thrown into the sea, but they were rescued by a fisherman. See PERSEUS.

BIBLIOGRAPHY. E. Hamilton, *Mythology*, Boston, 1942.

Danubian school. Albrecht Altdorfer, *St. George in the Forest.* **Old Pina-cothek, Munich.**

DANCE, GEORGE, THE ELDER. English architect (1695/1700–68). Dance served as clerk of the city works in London. His design for the Mansion House, London (built 1739–52), was accepted in 1737 in preference to the more sophisticated designs of other architects. The Mansion House displays a heavy-handed misuse of Palladian detail.

DANCE, GEORGE, THE YOUNGER. English architect (1741–1825). Clerk of the city works after his father, he designed Newgate Prison (1770–78) and planned several London squares, including Finsbury Square. His best designs, although unexecuted, were for the Port of London. His stylistic unconventionalities were taken over by his pupil John Soane.

DANCE OF DEATH. Common late medieval *vanitas* subject in which the living and the dead are contrasted (French, *danse macabre*; German, *Totentanz*). There are two types: (1) an actual dance scene in which the participants, representing the various stations of life, dance together with their dead counterparts; and (2) the cyclic representation in which the dance motif is absent and the dead counterpart is replaced by a skeleton. An example of the second type is Hans Holbein the Younger's *Dance of Death* (*Totentanz*) woodcut series, published in 1538.

BIBLIOGRAPHY. J. M. Clark, *The Dance of Death in the Middle Ages and the Renaissance*, Glasgow, 1950.

DANCE OF LIFE. Oil painting by Edvard Munch in the Munch Museum, Oslo. *See* MUNCH, EDVARD.

DANCER, THE, *see* JANSSENS, HIERONYMUS.

DANHAUSER, JOSEPH. Austrian painter (1805–45). Trained at the Vienna Academy by Peter Krafft (1824), he was influenced by his study of the Venetian masters (1826) and by his compatriot Friedrich Amerling. At his best in portraits, in which his coloristic gifts show up to advantage, he was esteemed by contemporaries for his sentimental or moralizing genre.

BIBLIOGRAPHY. A. Roessler, *Joseph Danhauser*, 2d ed., Vienna, 1946.

DANIEL. Old Testament figure whose experiences as a Jewish exile in Babylon are described in the Book of Daniel. In art, Daniel is usually shown safe among the lions, where he had been thrown by Darius the Mede, in a scene which is a prototype of the Resurrection of Christ. The description of the three youths in the fiery furnace, another Resurrection prefiguration, also comes from the Book of Daniel. Both scenes were frequently depicted in early Christian art.

DANIELL, WILLIAM. English engraver and painter (b. London, 1769; d. there, 1837). In addition to the aquatints he did with his brother Thomas Daniell, illustrating their trip to India (*Oriental Scenery*, London, 1808), William Daniell worked in stipple and etched an extensive series of soft-ground etching portraits after George Dance (for example, *Benjamin West*) as well as those done after his own drawings.

DANNECKER, JOHANN HEINRICH VON. German sculptor (b. Stuttgart, 1758; d. there, 1841). Like Pajou and Canova, under whom he worked in Paris (1783) and Rome (1785) respectively, Dannecker developed a sensuous neoclassic style, softly modeling his figures in pure white marble and placing them in pliable, picturesque exaggerations of classical poses. A well-known example of his work, in addition to his busts of Goethe and his friend Schiller, is the *Ariadne on a Panther* (1803).

DANSE, LA. Oil painting by Matisse in the National Museum of Fine Arts (Pushkin Museum), Moscow. *See* MATISSE, HENRI EMILE.

DANSE MACABRE, *see* DANCE OF DEATH.

DANTI, VINCENZO. Italian sculptor, goldsmith, painter, architect, and theoretician (b. Perugia, 1530; d. there, 1576). Although Danti was trained as a goldsmith, he earned fame as a sculptor. After executing the bronze statue of Julius III (1556) in Perugia, he went to Florence to work for Cosimo I. In 1561 he did the ground plan for the Escorial for Philip II; in 1567 his *Il primo libro* was published. An example of his manneristic sculpture is the marble *Honor Conquering Deceit* in the National Museum (Bargello), Florence.

BIBLIOGRAPHY. J. Pope-Hennessy, *Italian High Renaissance and Baroque Sculpture*, 3 vols., London, 1963.

DANUBIAN SCHOOL. Art of the Danubian Alps early in the 16th century. This school showed fantastically fearful interpretations of the German landscape. The important

Church of Daphni, Byzantine edifice with plan consisting of a cross within a rectangle, 11th century.

masters of the group were Albrecht Altdorfer, Lucas Cranach the Elder, Jorg Breu the Elder, Wolf Huber, and perhaps Mathias Grünewald. Regardless of the scene depicted, snarled trees and shaggy landscape forms dominate. Nature is seen as foreboding and inhospitable to man. Striking examples are Altdorfer's *St. George* (1511; Munich, Old Pinacothek), in which the figure of the saint is almost hidden in the luxuriant foliage of the seemingly menacing forest; and Cranach's *St. Jerome Penitent* (1502; Vienna, Museum of Art History), in which the ground is flinty and the tree twigs are sharply pointed. *See* ALTDORFER, ALBRECHT; BREU, JORG, THE ELDER; CRANACH, LUCAS, THE ELDER; GRUNEWALD, MATHIAS; HUBER, WOLF.

BIBLIOGRAPHY. M. J. Friedländer and J. Rosenberg, *Die Gemälde von Lucas Cranach*, Berlin, 1932; O. Benesch, *Der Maler Albrecht Altdorfer*, Vienna, 1939.

DANZIG: ST. MARY'S. Hall church in northern Poland. Begun in 1343, this brick building was enlarged and embellished with intricate net vaults at the end of the 15th century. Art works in St. Mary's Church include Memling's famous *Last Judgment* (ca. 1468–73) and a number of wood statues in late Gothic style.

BIBLIOGRAPHY. W. Drost, *Die Danziger Marienkirche*, Stuttgart, 1950.

DAPHNE. In Greek mythology, the daughter of a river god (Ladon or Peneus). She was loved by Apollo, whose advances she refused. When he pursued her, she prayed for help (to Zeus or Earth) and was changed into a laurel tree. Bernini's group in the Villa Borghese Museum and Gallery, Rome, is perhaps the most famous depiction of the myth.

DAPHNI, CHURCH OF. Byzantine church on the Eleusian Way just west of Athens, Greece. It dates from the end of the 11th century and is famous for its magnificent mosaics. In plan, the building consists of a cross set within a rectangle. The center space is covered by a high dome. On the east and west there are triple apses and double porches, respectively. Beautiful roundheaded windows are divided into hairpin-shaped openings by tall colonnettes in typical Byzantine fashion, and the superstructure is composed of clear geometric forms.

Inside the church the magnificently colored mosaics are ranged upon the upper walls and the surfaces of the various vaults. In the central dome is an imposing bust of Christ Pantocrator (All-Ruler). His terrible visage, isolated and majestic, looks down from a golden heaven. Ranged between the windows at the footing of the dome are sixteen prophets; below them are scenes from the life of Christ, ingeniously set in the half-cone shapes that support the architecture above. The Virgin and Child appear in the apse and are flanked by archangels in the presbytery. A score of other scenes and saints appear in the subsidiary spaces of the church, and below the mosaics the walls are sheathed in colored marbles.

The result is a sumptuous display of color and form that serves several ends. The structure of the architecture is covered; so the eye reads not the substance of the building but the brilliant scenes in mosaic or the smooth, continuous reflecting surfaces of the marble. The worshiper perceives an ascending hierarchy of Christian worthies, from the saints upon the walls, through the scenes from the New Testament, to the Christ on high. The most important scenes and holiest personages are in the vaults, floating above the human communicants below; in this way the figures and the architecture serve each other. Daphni is one of the foremost examples of the Byzantine ability to wed indissolubly the arts of architecture and mosaic.

In this art the figures are icons, literally venerable. The shapes used by the architect, especially the cross plan and the dome, are basic Christian symbols. This combination of two arts, when as at Daphni it produces a veristic spatial play among the figures upon the curving vaults, is the essence of Byzantine artistic genius. Daphni is chiefly valuable as a work of art in itself, and also because it records, with some local variations, the nature of many lost Byzantine works.

BIBLIOGRAPHY. E. Diez and O. Demus, *Byzantine Mosaics in Greece*, Cambridge, Mass., 1931; O. Demus, *Byzantine Mosaic Decoration*, London, 1948; O. Demus, "The Methods of the Byzantine Artist," *The Mint*, II, 1948; P. Michelis, *An Aesthetic Approach to Byzantine Art*, London, 1955.

WILLIAM L. MAC DONALD

DA PREDIS, *see* PREDIS, DA, FAMILY.

DARCIS, LOUIS. French stipple and line engraver (d. ca. 1801). His first work appeared in 1787. He is chiefly recognized for his success in engraving designs for Lavreince's *L'Accident imprévu* and *La Sentinelle en défaut* and for Carle Vernet's *Incroyables* and *Merveilleuses*.

BIBLIOGRAPHY. M. Roux, *Inventaire du fonds français: graveurs du XVIIIᵉ siècle*, vol. 6, Paris, 1949.

DARET, JACQUES. Flemish painter (b. ca. 1404). A native of Tournai, Daret is best known for his association with the Master of Flémalle (Robert Campin), to whom he was apprenticed in 1427, the same year as Rogier van der Weyden. In 1432 he completed his apprenticeship and was immediately chosen dean of the painters' Guild of St. Luke. Daret, who received all his training in the Master of Flémalle's workshop and worked only in Tournai for almost fifteen years, represents the direct continuation of the regional development of the Tournai school and the tradition of the Master of Flémalle.

His known work consists of four documented paintings, among them a copy of the Master of Flémalle's *Dijon Nativity*. The others are a *Visitation*, a *Presentation of Christ*, and an *Adoration of the Magi*, all of which were commissioned by the Abbot of St. Vaast for the exterior of a "Schnitzaltar" and completed by 1435.

DARET, JEAN. Flemish portrait and history painter (b. Brussels, 1613; d. Aix-en-Provence, 1668). A student of Van Opstal in Brussels, he later traveled to Italy, where he copied Guercino and Guido Reni. In 1637 he settled in Aix. During a brief trip to Brussels (1658–60) he took up engraving. Back in France he worked on the decoration of the Château de Vincennes. Daret's style betrays the influence of Guercino.

BIBLIOGRAPHY. R. H. Wilenski, *Flemish Painters, 1430–1830*, 2 vols., New York, 1960.

DARET, PIERRE. French engraver, painter, and writer (b. Paris, ca. 1604; d. Dax, Landes, 1678). Daret is associated with the group of 17th-century engravers who worked under the influence of Robert Nanteuil, the great portrait engraver. Among Daret's portraits are *Charles II of England*, *Equestrian Portrait of Louis XIII of France* (1643), and a series of seventy-six engravings of men in the Parisian circle of Louis Boissevin. In addition, Daret wrought numerous religious pages after J. Blanchard, E. Le Sueur, S. Vouet, and others, and copied Van Dyck as

Jacques Daret, *The Holy Family*. Museum of Fine Arts, Tournai.

well as G. Seghers in his hard, classical style. Le Blanc attributes 155 engravings to Daret, in addition to known book illustrations. He was admitted to the Academy in 1663 and in his late years did some writing; his *Life of Raphael* is essentially a free translation of Vasari.

D'ARGENTA, *see* VIGHI, GIACOMO.

DARIUS, PALACE OF, PERSEPOLIS, *see* PERSEPOLIS.

DARK, BERNARD FRANKLAND, *see* FARMER AND DARK.

DARMSTADT: HESSIAN LANDESMUSEUM. German museum founded in 1820. It is housed in a building by Alfred Messel (erected 1892–1906). The collection excels in German paintings from the 13th century to the present. Notable works are Stephan Lochner's *Presentation in the Temple* (1447), nine paintings by Lucas Cranach, works by 17th–18th-century artists such as Chodowiecki and Mengs, and romantic paintings by artists such as Schwind and Spitzweg. Among the late-19th-century painters represented, Böcklin, Feuerbach (*Iphigenia*), Thoma, Trübner, and Lenbach are outstanding. Besides those German works, examples from the Italian, French, Dutch, and Flemish schools round out the collection. They are supplemented by drawings and the graphic arts, among which works by Dürer, Rembrandt, and the romantic school deserve special mention. Otto Müller, Kirchner, and Heckel represent German 20th-century artists. Sculptures, especially from the Middle Rhine and southern Germany, and a representative collection of applied arts—furniture, textiles, metalwork, and so on—make the museum one of the outstanding smaller ones in western Germany.

BIBLIOGRAPHY. H. Jedding, *Keysers Führer durch Museen und Sammlungen*, Heidelberg, Munich, 1961.

D'ARONCO, RAIMONDO. Italian architect (b. Udine, 1857; d. 1932). Working in an Art Nouveau manner, he was one of Italy's leading modern architects at the turn of the century. The main pavilion of the Turin Exposition of 1902 and the Pavilion of Fine Arts at the Udine Exhibition of 1903 are among his major works.

BIBLIOGRAPHY. B. Zevi, *Storia dell'architettura moderna*, 2d ed., Turin, 1953.

D'ARTOIS, JACQUES, *see* ARTOIS, JACQUES D'.

DASBURG, ANDREW MICHAEL. American painter (1887–   ). He moved from Paris to the United States at an early age. He studied with Kenyon Cox and Birge Harrison at the Art Students League and with Robert Henri. Dasburg was one of the early group of American painters interested in European abstraction. The Armory Show impelled him toward cubism, which remained the dominant source of his style, despite brief experiments in about 1916 with orphism and synchronism. He later became more representational in manner but still retained a formally simplified approach to his subjects, particularly landscapes of the American Southwest.

DASWANTH, *see* MUGHAL PAINTING OF INDIA (AKBAR PERIOD).

Charles-François Daubigny, *Landscape near Pontoise*, 1866. Kunsthalle, Bremen. A work showing the painter's awareness of the properties of natural light.

DATHAN, JOHANN GEORG. German painter (b. Mannheim, 1703; d. there, after 1748). He painted portraits and historical scenes, combining the two in the *Allegory on the Marriage of Princess Marie Josephine of Poland with the Dauphin of France* (1748; Dresden, State Art Collections, Picture Gallery).

DAUBIGNY, CHARLES-FRANCOIS. French landscape painter and etcher (b. Paris, 1817; d. there, 1878). His family was artistic and he began his own career early, earning his living as a decorator of applied arts. He visited Italy in 1835, and on his return to Paris in 1836 he worked in the studio of the state restorer, Granet. He exhibited for the first time at the Salon of 1838, and from then on he was to exhibit landscapes regularly. For six months in 1840 he worked under Paul Delaroche, whom he left in order to concentrate on landscape. He worked in the forest of Fontainebleau for the first time in 1843; though he is generally considered a Barbizon painter, he preferred Valmondois and Auvers, near Paris.

His early reputation depended not only on his landscapes but to an even greater extent on his prints, and there is a prolific output, mainly of etchings, dating from 1838. The first prints are landscape souvenirs of his stay in Italy, but more important were his vignettes for *Chants et chansons populaires de la France* (1843). He also made prints after other masters, such as Jacob van Ruisdael and Claude Lorraine. Two albums of etchings (*Cahiers d'eaux fortes*)

established his position as a graphic artist and mark the development of his landscapes from a traditional style toward a greater naturalism.

He was established as a painter when the state bought his *View of the Seine* (1852; Nantes, Museum of Fine Arts) and when Louis Napoleon purchased *The Pond of Gylieu* (1853; Cincinnati Art Museum). His contact with Corot in 1852 led him to paint out of doors, in common with the other Barbizon artists. As a logical step, Daubigny in 1857 made his studio a boat, "Botin," from which he painted river scenes. He thus broke away from the classical tendencies of Corot, and he came closest of all the Barbizon painters to the work of the younger impressionists with his freshness of approach and direct choice of subject matter (for example, *Landscape near Pontoise*, 1866; Bremen, Kunsthalle). His more spontaneous works were critically received.

Daubigny traveled to England in 1866 and in 1870–71, during the Franco-Prussian War, in the company of Monet, whom he helped and with whom he traveled to Holland in 1871. His final years are marked by a continuing success which did not prevent his sympathy for the younger impressionists, whose looseness of handling most closely resembled his own late work. His paintings can be seen in the Louvre in Paris and elsewhere.

BIBLIOGRAPHY. L. Bourgès, *Daubigny, souvenirs et croquis*, Paris, 1900; L. Delteil, *Le Peintre-graveur illustré*, vol. 13, Paris, 1921; E. Moreau-Nélaton, *Daubigny, raconté par lui-même*, Paris, 1925; R. L. Herbert, *Barbizon Revisited*, New York, 1962.

MALCOLM CORMACK

DAUCHER, ADOLF. German sculptor (b. Ulm, ca. 1460; d. Augsburg, 1523/24). His early period spent in Ulm shows the influence of Jörg Syrlin the Elder. Later, in Augsburg, he and Hans Holbein the Elder became the chief exponents of the new Renaissance style. His main work is the choir stalls in the Fuggerkapelle in Augsburg.

BIBLIOGRAPHY. P. M. Halm, *Adolf Daucher und die Fuggerkapelle bei St. Anna in Augsburg,* Munich, 1921.

DAUCHER, HANS. German sculptor (b. ca. 1485; d. Augsburg, 1538). He was the son of Adolf Daucher. His early period was spent in Augsburg as an apprentice to Gregor Erhart. He later worked in Vienna and in 1537 was in the service of the Duke of Württemberg. Daucher was one of the foremost sculptors of miniatures during the German Renaissance.

BIBLIOGRAPHY. P. M. Halm, *Studien zur süddeutschen Plastik,* vol. 1, Augsburg, 1926.

DAULLE, JEAN. French portrait engraver (1703–63). Born in Abbeville, Daullé worked in Paris with Robert Hecquet. In 1735 he met Hyacinthe Rigaud, who engaged him to engrave his paintings and for whom he produced his best work—the portraits of Gendron, Countess de Caylus, and Rigaud. Daullé was a skilled but overworked craftsman.

BIBLIOGRAPHY. E. E. Delignières, "Catalogue raisonné de l'oeuvre gravé de Jean Daullé...," *Mémoires de la Société d'émulation d'Abbeville,* series 3, vol. 1, Abbeville, 1873.

DAUMIER, HONORE. French lithographer, painter, and sculptor (b. Marseilles, 1808; d. Valmondois, 1879). The son of a glazier, young Honoré Daumier was obliged to cut short his formal education and go to work. In Paris he became a messenger in a law court and later clerked in a bookstore. All the while he made drawings and frequently visited the Louvre. His parents, recognizing his gifts, placed him under the tutelage of the academician Alexandre Lenoir, who set Daumier to drawing plaster casts. Lenoir advocated the grand manner of representing noble themes drawn from history and mythology. Later, in his lithographs, Daumier was to poke fun at the pretentiousness of academicians.

In 1828 he became a student at the Paris Academy and at the same time began to make drawings for popular magazines. It was not until two years later, though, that he made his first political lithographs. He deeply resented the injustices of monarchy. He believed in a republican form of government and had faith in the essential goodness of the common man. Unlike Goya, he was not pessimistic. The precedent of the French Revolution inspired him, and the example of many of his contemporaries with similar convictions gave him comfort and encouragement. He accepted a position briefly for the politically satirical illustrated weekly *Silhouette*; and then, in 1831, he joined the staff of *Caricature*, which had been established the year before by Aubert and Philipon and was inspired by promises of political freedom and an end to repressive censorship by the "Citizen King," Louis-Philippe, after the Revolution of 1830. Daumier was eminently suited to Philipon's requirements of "indignation at heart and a verve at the end of his crayon."

In his lifetime Daumier was to execute more than 4,000 lithographs. His first works are rather tight and detailed. He frequently made sculptures and used them as models. In fact, between 1831 and 1833 he published a series of lithographs of politicians of the time and matched some forty-five of them with polychromed terra-cotta busts. About thirty-six of these exist today and have been cast in bronze.

By 1834 the offices of *Caricature* had been seized by government officials twenty-seven times. Philipon had been put in jail and fined, as had Daumier himself. In 1835 an attempt to assassinate the King led to an uncompromising check on the press, and *Caricature* died. Daumier began to contribute to a parent publication, *Charivari*, dedicated to the gentler pursuit of social satire. In the spirit of Balzac's *Comédie humaine*, Daumier reviewed all aspects of his society through a number of series of chosen examples. A partial list suggests the scope of his lithographic efforts for about a twenty-five-year period: *Bathers* (1839–42, 1864), *Bluestockings* (1844), *Professors and Pupils* (1845–46), *Divorcées* (1848), *Tragico-Classic Physiognomies* (1841), *Bohemians of Paris* (1841–42), and *Men of Justice*, depicting lawyers and judges (1845–49).

Daumier's manner of drawing became more spontaneous and expressive, more vivacious, and freer. Contour is often disengaged from the figure to suggest agitation and nervous energy. Duranty, the novelist and critic, said that Daumier would draw only when the idea, the subject, and the attitudes were well fixed in his mind, and that he never had to rework drawings. Others have attested to Daumier's phenomenal visual memory. Daumier averaged eight lith-

Honoré Daumier, *Servants' Habits*. Lithograph.

Honoré Daumier, *Circus Parade*. Louvre, Paris. The artist's paintings, like his lithographs, consist almost entirely of figures.

ographs per month. He found the work exhausting, a fact one would never guess from its freshness. His style is consistent and easily recognizable. He avoided all decorative elements, even in his paintings. His attitude is closest to that of Dickens. He often shows the subject as a victim of his own gullibility, the inflated image he has of himself, as an organism who is at once laughable, pathetic, and vulnerable. He ridicules the conventions of classical theater and shows lawyers as venal operators who are incapable of distinguishing between legal operations and social justice. He is gentler in his gibes at city folks in the country. He is amused by their perplexities and discomforts, introduced by such modern conveniences as the train.

With the abdication of Louis-Philippe in 1848, Daumier returned to political satire, but not with the passion of his earlier days. That same year he began to paint. He exhibited in the Paris Salon in 1849, 1851, 1861, and 1869. In 1855 he painted with the Barbizon group which included Millet, Daubigny, Théodore Rousseau, and Corot. The art public was generally unaware of his activities as a painter. He had his only comprehensive exhibition in 1878, when ninety-seven of his paintings were shown at Durand-Ruel in Paris. Like his lithographs, his paintings are composed almost entirely of figures. He tended to favor themes that are broader in their significance than the cartoons. The drawing technique and exaggerations typical of his caricatures were transferred to his painting in large meas-

ure. His style is related above all to the baroque as transformed by Delacroix, although his color suggests Rembrandt, whom he greatly admired. In the drawing *Soup* (Paris, Louvre), Daumier patterns the woman after the heroic proportions of Michelangelo's Cumaean sibyl on the Sistine Chapel ceiling. His pictures are usually small enough to hold in the hand. He indicated in his paintings of art lovers contemplating works of art that his ideal was a sympathetic connoisseur who expresses his affection for and interest in small pieces in the privacy of his study.

Daumier is never sentimental or trite. His ideal of womanhood is that of the laboring mother, the laundress with her child, the woman who valiantly accepts her burden. His workingman either endures the indignities and hardship of his labor or rebels to demand his rights and a decent living. Daumier's humanity is constantly on the move as a dynamic force. He shows the refugees not as an assemblage of individuals but as a glowing mass united in flight, with a will to live and push forward in the hope of a better and more productive life. Daumier was fascinated by the artifice of the theater, and in this respect he carried on the tradition of Watteau and prefigured Degas and the Picasso of the Blue Period. He recorded pathetic mountebanks and strong men at street fairs as well as scenes from Molière and audiences transfixed by some spectacle.

Daumier made several paintings of Don Quixote, with

whom he may have felt a sympathy, though an ironic one. He so resented being considered merely a draftsman of cartoons that he stopped such work altogether in 1860 and did none of it during the following three years. Toward the end of his life, his eyesight began to fail, and he was poor. Corot provided him with a place to stay in the country and a small stipend. Today, Daumier's reputation rests as much, if not more, on his paintings as on his matchless lithographs.

BIBLIOGRAPHY. A. Alexandre, *Honoré Daumier: L'Homme et l'oeuvre*, Paris, 1888; J. Adhémar, *Honoré Daumier*, Paris, 1954; O. W. Larkin, *Daumier: Man of His Time*, New York, 1966; R. Rey, *Honoré Daumier*, New York, 1966.

ROBERT REIFF

DAVANZATI PALACE, FLORENCE. One of the best examples of the type of town palace built by Florentine noble families in the 14th century. It is constructed of closely fitted cut stones along a narrow street, with arcades on the ground floor and ogival windows at regular intervals in the upper three stories. An open loggia at the top was added during the 15th century.

BIBLIOGRAPHY. L. C. Rosenberg, *The Davanzati Palace*, New York, 1922.

DA VANZO, JACOPO, *see* AVANZO, JACOPO.

DAVENPORT, IOWA: MUNICIPAL ART GALLERY. The collection includes European and American painting and sculpture of various periods, Japanese prints of the Ukiyo-e school, and a distinguished group of Mexican paintings of the colonial period.

BIBLIOGRAPHY. E. Spaeth, *American Art Museums and Galleries*, New York, 1960.

DAVENT, LEON. French etcher and engraver (fl. 1540–60). Part of the school of Fontainebleau, he followed the styles of Primaticcio, Rosso, Luca Penni, Leonard Thiry, and Giulio Romano. Only one print (1546) is signed with his name. The authorship of the many prints signed "L.D.," which are by more than one hand, has not yet been resolved.

BIBLIOGRAPHY. A. von Bartsch, *Le Peintre-graveur*, new ed., vol. 16, Würzburg, 1920.

DAVID. First king of the Judaean dynasty whose life is described in I and II Samuel and in I Kings 1–2:11. He is represented in art in a number of roles, but he is most commonly shown playing his harp, killing Goliath, or gazing upon the bathing Bathsheba. As an ancestor of Christ, he is one of the principal figures in the Tree of Jesse. David is symbolized by the harp and the crown.

DAVID, GERARD. Flemish painter (ca. 1460–1523). He was the last of the great Flemish primitives working in Bruges, and his works represent the final consolidation of the Flemish traditions of the 15th century. They show eclectic borrowing from contemporaries such as Memling and a return to the "founders"—Van Eyck and the Master of Flémalle.

David was born in Oudewater, Haarlem, and may have received his earliest training with Albert van Ouwater. He left his native land, according to conjecture, to join his countryman Geertgen tot Sint Jans in studies at Bruges. At any rate, David is mentioned in the official records there: first in 1483 as a member of the painters' guild, and then in 1484 as master of the same guild. In 1496 he married Cornelia Knoop, daughter of a prominent goldsmith and a miniaturist in her own right. Some time following his marriage he went to Antwerp, where in 1515 a Gerard of Bruges, assumed to be David, was listed in the painters' guild. He returned to Bruges (it is not known when) and remained there until his death.

Opinions differ concerning the number of works that can be authoritatively attributed to David. Some would accept only two works as adequately documented (an extreme view), while no less an authority than Max J. Friedländer accepts at least four and considers a total of fifty attributable to him. The two unquestionably accepted works are the *Justice Panels* (Bruges, Municipal Museum), one of which is dated 1498, and the *Virgin and Child with Angels and Saints* (1509; Rouen, Fine Arts Museum). These works, which might be considered as coming from David's "middle period," reveal an austere, extremely proficient painter greatly concerned with volume and space. Colors are rich and varied, and the use of light and shade is interesting and effective.

The *Justice Panels* illustrate the ancient legend (told by Herodotus) of the justice of King Cambyses. The panel

Davanzati Palace, Florence. Example of 14th-century Florentine palace architecture; loggia added in 15th century.

Gerard David, *Canon Bernardino de Salviatis and Three Saints*. National Gallery, London.

showing Cambyses having the dishonest judge, Sisamnes, arrested is especially interesting as one of the first northern paintings to employ Italian Renaissance motifs. Above Sisamnes's throne are *putti* holding flowered garlands, while to the left and right of it are cameolike plaques depicting classical legends. Memling had earlier used *putti* and garlands, but the cameos were quite new to Flemish painting.

David may have gotten the motif from Italian works in the possession of the large Italian colony in Bruges. The other panel depicts the punishment of Sisamnes, his being flayed alive. Both panels present solemn, ordered compositions with closely grouped figures in spatially open settings and with accurate details throughout (buildings in Bruges have been identified in the background).

The *Virgin and Child with Angels and Saints* shows the evolution of David's style. Within limited space the various figures are developed in full volume and achieve a heavy, monumental quality not present in the work of 1498. Between these dated works Friedländer places the *Canon Bernardino de Salviatis and Three Saints* (ca. 1501; London, National Gallery) and an altarpiece with the Baptism of Christ (ca. 1502–08; Bruges, Municipal Museum). The former has the austerity and stiffness of the *Justice Panels*, with an even greater opening out of space in the rich landscape behind the figures. Again David's ability to handle full volume is apparent, especially in his plastic use of light and shade. The *Baptism Triptych* shows the evolution of the landscape background into a full, convincing spatial unit within which the figures are well placed. Stylistic proximity to the *Canon Bernardino* work of 1501 is especially apparent in the donor figures on the wings. There are two dates for this work because the donor, Jan de Trompes, is depicted with his first wife, who died in 1502, on the inner wings; and with his second wife, whom he married in 1508, on the outer wings.

The fully mature style of David is seen in the *Marriage at Cana* (Paris, Louvre), commissioned by Jean de Sedano sometime after 1500. The panel is rich in its variety of color, texture, and form. Although the figures continue to be restrained in typical Davidian fashion, they are relatively more active than in his other works. The placement of the wine jars in the foreground, with their cast shadows and well-modeled forms, helps increase the depth recession of this interior space, while the colonnade behind Christ opens onto a city square (probably Bruges). Another late work, and possibly the high point of David's achievements, is the *Virgin and Child with Saints and Donor* (London, National Gallery). Unusually for David, the solemn conclave of fully plastic figures within the well-defined space is unified in a psychological rather than physical or compositional manner. Each figure kneels independently of the others on the carefully delineated floor space, and all flank the central figure of the Virgin holding the Child in an unbalanced symmetry. Yet, even as each figure is an isolated unit, the intense stares and solemn demeanors create a unity more binding than could any compositional means. Such details as the position and gesture of the Child and the rich brocade behind the seated Virgin refer back to Jan van Eyck. The total effect is one of grandeur, rarely achieved by David.

There are conflicting views concerning David's position and importance as an artist. On the one hand, he is seen by some critics as a not particularly inspired eclectic, full of conscious archaisms. In this view, he represents the last effort of Bruges to retain its glory in the face of the rising competition and cultural efflorescence of Antwerp. On the other hand, the admittedly archaistic, eclectic tendencies in David are interpreted quite differently by other authorities who see this artist attempting to return to the founders in order to build anew. This meant searching for new and valid means of representation, means that would bypass the nontangible transcendentalism of Rogier van der Weyden and his followers, whose art had dominated Flanders from the middle of the century on. It meant returning to the solidity of the "first generation," which would explain David's preoccupation with space and volume. According to this view, therefore, David can be considered a progressive force in the art of his time.

BIBLIOGRAPHY. E. Bodenhausen, *Gerard David und seine Schule*, Munich, 1905; M. J. Friedländer, *Die altniederländische Malerei*, vol. 6, Berlin, 1928; E. Panofsky, *Early Netherlandish Painting*, 2 vols., Cambridge, Mass., 1953.

STANLEY FERBER

DAVID, JACQUES-LOUIS. French painter (b. Paris, 1748; d. Brussels, 1825). Helped by his uncles, the architect Desmaisons and master mason Buron, and by his distant cousin François Boucher, David chose painting as a career and entered the studio of Vien in 1769. He competed for the Prix de Rome from 1771 to 1774, when he won the first prize, with *Antiochus and Stratonice* (Paris, Ecole des Beaux-Arts). In 1775 he left with Vien and his family for Rome, where he assiduously studied Roman antique art and abandoned the Boucher style of his *Combat of Minerva and Mars* (1771; Paris, Louvre) and *Death of Seneca* (1773; Paris, Fine Arts Museum of the City of Paris). In France again in 1780, he exhibited *Belisarius* (1781; Lille, Fine Arts Museum). Elected to the French Academy in 1783, he painted *Andromache Lamenting the Death of Hector* (Paris, Ecole des Beaux-Arts), a severe work with few figures. His neoclassicism appeared in such works as the *Oath of the Horatii* (1784; Louvre) and *Brutus, Having Condemned His Sons to Death* (1789; Louvre), both painted for Louis XVI, and *The Death of Socrates* (1787; New York, Metropolitan Museum), all republican and patriotic subjects filled with a moral urgency that appealed to men engaged in a growing revolution.

For the Revolution of 1789 David's Roman classicism changed to a realism tinged with classicism. In 1791 he began work on his huge (and unfinished, for he changed the actors as they gradually fell from power into disgrace) *Oath of the Tennis Court* (Versailles, Museum). David participated in the work of the Revolution, painting in 1793 its martyrs in *Lepelletier de St-Fargeau* (lost or destroyed) and the famous *Death of Marat* (Brussels, Museum of Modern Art). With the downfall of the dictator Robespierre, David was twice imprisoned in the Luxembourg (where he painted a rare landscape of the gardens in July, 1794, now in the Louvre). He was released in 1795 on his promise not to engage in politics.

He continued painting and teaching; the great artists of the new generation were his students: Gérard, Girodet, Gros, and, later, Ingres. The *Sabines* (Louvre), exhibited in 1799, seemed to exhort the dissident factions in France to make peace. This work strengthened his reputation throughout Europe.

David met Napoleon Bonaparte, then first consul, and proposed a painting of the general with a sword in his hand. Bonaparte preferred to be shown "calm on an angry horse," the subject of David's next great work in 1800 (various versions, Vienna, Museum of Art History, and elsewhere). When Napoleon was crowned emperor in December, 1804, David, First Painter to the Emperor, undertook the great *Coronation* (Louvre), an enormous canvas begun in 1805 and finished in 1807. He and his assistants executed a second version (Versailles, Museum) in 1822. In this scene the members of the new imperial court witness Pope Pius VII giving his benediction as the kneeling Empress Josephine is crowned by the Emperor himself.

Jacques-Louis David, *The Rape of the Sabines*. Louvre, Paris. A painting in the artist's later Greek classical style.

Members of the newly created royal family are shown participating in this event, together with marshals, ministers, and many others. A new realism stemming from Italian painting marks this work, in which numerous figures are gathered together in an expansive space. For Napoleon the painter also executed *The Distribution of the Eagles* (1810; Versailles, Museum) and other works, for which excellent drawings exist (Versailles, Museum; Lille, Fine Arts Museum; Louvre; and so on). David also executed fine portraits of Napoleon between 1797 and 1799 (Louvre) and in 1812 (Washington, D.C., National Gallery of Art) and, in 1805, of Pope Pius VII (Louvre) and of the Pope with Cardinal Caprara (Philadelphia, McIlhenny Collection).

David painted his family and his friends: a self-portrait in 1794; his in-laws M. and Mme Pécoul in 1784 and M. and Mme (née Emile Pécoul) Sériziat and their son in 1795 (all in the Louvre); his daughters Emilie Meunier and Pauline Jeanin (ca. 1812; private collections) and his wife Marguerite Charlotte (1813; Washington, D.C., National Gallery of Art); and, among his friends, Ambassador Meyer (1795), Antoine Mongez and his wife (1812), Alexandre Lenoir (1817), and the actor Wolf (1819–23), all in the Louvre. Elsewhere there are the fine portraits of the el-

egantly posed Madame Récamier in an austere *décor* (1800, unfinished; Louvre) and of Lavoisier and his wife (1788; New York, Rockefeller Institute), guillotined a few years after their sitting for the artist. (Though David took an active part in the Revolution, he did what he could to save the lives of his colleagues in such tumultuous times.) In the Frick Collection, New York, hangs the fine portrait of Comtesse Daru, painted in 1810.

David had worked for some time in a realistic Roman classical style, in which his observation was interpreted according to classical sculptural ideals. From 1797 to 1803 he began to adumbrate a "Greek" classical style; this appears in his *Sabines* and his *Leonidas at Thermopylae*, on which he worked intermittently until 1814 (signed 1814; Louvre). The Greek style was also championed by his students, who saw in it a chance to simplify painting. David published his ideas on the new style in the booklet he wrote for the exhibition of his *Sabines* in 1799; he stressed the importance of deriving inspiration from ancient art and of representing the nude in painting. In this Greek vein David later produced a number of somewhat sentimental pictures, which seem at variance with his early ones, but which in their softness and flatness nevertheless attempt to explore another path. Many of these works were executed in Brussels, where he was forced into exile in 1815, when as a stanch Bonapartist he refused to support the restored Bourbon king. Outstanding are his *Cupid and Psyche* of 1817 and his *Telemachus and Eucharis* of 1822 (Paris, private collections) and his *Mars Disarmed by Venus* of 1824 (Brussels, Fine Arts Museum). David continued to paint portraits of friends, among them Sieyès (1817; Cambridge, Mass., Fogg Art Museum). Meanwhile, exiled David charged Gros with carrying on the Davidian school and tradition in Paris.

David's importance lies not only in his art but in the wide influence he had in his own country and throughout Europe and even in the United States. As a teacher, he was not a rigid doctrinaire: he encouraged students to follow their particular bent. While his different styles borrow freely from Poussin, the Italians, and the antique, they reveal a renewed interest in the real representational world sculpturally and vigorously conceived. In his contemporary scenes his work is filled with a romantic exuberance which, breaking with antique ideals, inspired a new generation.

BIBLIOGRAPHY. R. Cantinelli, *Jacques-Louis David, 1748-1825*, Paris, 1930; M. W. Brown, *Painting of the French Revolution*, New York, 1938; K. Holma, *David, son évolution et son style*, Paris, 1940; D. L. Dowd, *Pageant-master of the Republic: Jacques-Louis David and the French Revolution*, Lincoln, Nebr., 1948; L. Hautecoeur, *Louis David*, Paris, 1954; N. Schlenoff, *Ingres, ses sources littéraires*, Paris, 1956; C. Sterling and H. Adhémar, *La Peinture au Musée du Louvre, Ecole française, XIXe siècle*, vol. 2, Paris, 1959; J. Lindsay, *The Death of the Hero: French Painting from David to Delacroix*, London, 1961.

NORMAN SCHLENOFF

DAVID D'ANGERS, PIERRE-JEAN.

French sculptor (b. Angers, 1788; d. Paris, 1856). He studied under Philippe-Laurent Roland and was in Paris by 1808. He was in Rome from 1811 to 1816, but successfully resisted the neoclassic idiom of Canova. Considering sculpture the "recorder of posterity," David d'Angers depicted his contemporaries in modern dress—among them Victor Hugo, Goethe, Lamartine, and Jefferson (1834; Washington, Capitol). He became a member of the Institut de France in 1826. In 1839 he left his models—68 statues, 47 bas-reliefs, and some 100 busts and 500 portrait medallions—to found a museum in Angers. His most important sculptural work is the pediment of the Pantheon in Paris (1835-37). His style marks the turn from classicism to vigorous realism. *See* ANGERS: FINE ARTS MUSEUM.

BIBLIOGRAPHY. H. Jouin, *David d'Angers...*, 2 vols., Paris, 1878; P.-J. David d'Angers, *Les Carnets*, vols. 1 and 2, Paris, 1958.

DAVIDSON, JO.

American sculptor (1883-1952). He studied at the Art Students League in his native New York City and at the Ecole des Beaux-Arts in Paris. Davidson's purpose was to create portraits of the outstanding personalities of the 20th century. A friendly and persuasive personality, he succeeded in making busts or figure portraits of more than 300 internationally recognized persons, including Tito, Gandhi, Franklin D. Roosevelt, Shaw, Gide, Pershing, Gertrude Stein, Gertrude Vanderbilt Whitney, Einstein, Chaplin, and Ben-Gurion. He worked in various media—terra cotta, marble, bronze. Davidson's portraits are, at their best, straightforward and interpretative of the personality of the sitter. Typically, he works in a basically naturalistic style, often with suppressed or exaggerated detail as he felt best fitted the character of his subject.

BIBLIOGRAPHY. J. Davidson, *Between Sittings*, New York, 1951; L. H. Kuhn, *The World of Jo Davidson*, New York, 1958.

DAVIE, ALAN.

British painter (1920–   ). He was born in Grangemouth, Scotland, and studied at the Edinburgh College of Art. He traveled and studied in France, Switzerland, Italy, and Spain in 1948-49. From a study of Klee in Switzerland, Davie learned that painterly means could be combined with ideas or symbols. His discovery of Jackson Pollock's symbolic paintings at the 1948 Venice Biennale gave him the technique. Davie's abstract paintings of the early 1950s stress geometrical elements of rich color and a vague symbolic meaning. In his recent work the symbolic imagery of forms with a ritualistic reference has become stronger.

BIBLIOGRAPHY. P. Heron, "British Painter Showing at the Catherine Viviano Gallery in New York," *Arts*, Apr., 1956.

DAVIES, ARTHUR BOWEN.

American painter, graphic artist, sculptor, and tapestry designer (b. Utica, N.Y., 1862; d. Florence, 1928). He studied at the Chicago Academy of Design, worked in Mexico as a draftsman from 1880 to 1882, and then studied further at the Art Institute of Chicago and the Gotham Art Students School and the Art Students League in New York. With the financial help of William Macbeth and Benjamin Altman he went to Italy in 1893. He was a member of The Eight. As president of the Association of American Painters and Sculptors, Davies was the instrumental organizer of the 1913 Armory Show, which was a monument to the catholicity

Pierre-Jean David d'Angers, *Philopoemen*, Louvre, Paris.

of his taste and to the wide range of his social contacts.

Davies's early paintings were landscapes, such as *Along the Erie Canal* (1890; Washington, D.C., Phillips Collection). His travels in Europe resulted in a variety of influences—lyrical Pompeian painting, Giorgione, the Pre-Raphaelites, Puvis de Chavannes, Marées, and Whistler—which, at his best, he assimilated with the more American romanticism of Ryder, as, for example, in *Every Saturday* (ca. 1896; Brooklyn Museum) or the more Venetian *Dancing Children* (1902; Brooklyn Museum). In the early 1900s, he began painting idyllic landscapes in which ethereal women, mythological figures, or unicorns move gracefully against a delicate background of rocks, trees, and water: for example, *Unicorns* (1906; New York, Metropolitan Museum) or *Leda and the Dioscuri* (1905; Art Institute of Chicago). The classical, friezelike arrangement of the figures is particularly evident in such a work as *Crescendo* (1910; New York, Whitney Museum). Davies's refined intellectuality produced such faint allegories as *The Jewelbearing Tree of Amity* (ca. 1912; Utica, Munson-Williams-Proctor Institute) as well as his later (1922) involvement with Gustav Eisen's theories of inhalation in Greek art.

For a while after the Armory Show, Davies worked in a personal and decorative version of cubism that geometrically fragmented the forms of figures, leaving their outlines intact, as in *Dancers* (after 1913; Detroit Institute of Arts). His last years were divided between the United States and travel in Europe, where he designed tapestries and supervised their execution at the Gobelins factory and painted subtly colored Italian landscapes such as *The Umbrian Mountains* (1925; Washington, D.C., Corcoran Gallery).

BIBLIOGRAPHY. Phillips Memorial Art Gallery, *Arthur B. Davies: Essays on the Man and His Art*, Cambridge, Mass., 1924; R. Cortissoz, *Arthur B. Davies*, New York, 1931.

JEROME VIOLA

DAVIES, THOMAS. English topographer and painter (ca. 1737–1812). A British army officer, he painted in Canada (1758–ca. 1790) and the northeastern United States an extensive series of decorative water-color landscapes of artistic, historical, and ethnological interest.

BIBLIOGRAPHY. F. St. George Spendlove, *The Face of Early Canada . . .*, Toronto, 1958.

DA VINCI, PIERINO. Italian sculptor and silversmith (b. Vinci, ca. 1530; d. Pisa, 1553). A nephew of Leonardo, Pierino da Vinci went to Florence about 1542 to work under Niccolò Tribolo (until 1548), thus coming under the influence of Michelangelo. Among his works are *Bacchus with Satyr* (Florence, Boboli Gardens), *Watergod with Putti* (Paris, Louvre), and religious and allegorical reliefs reflecting the *contrapposto* of Michelangelo without the *terribilità*.

BIBLIOGRAPHY. A. E. Brinckmann, *Barockskulptur*, Berlin, 1919.

DAVIOUD, GABRIEL JEAN ANTOINE. French architect (1823–81). A pupil of Leon Vaudoyer, he worked in Paris, where he was associated with Haussmann's rebuilding of the city. Davioud continued the eclectic style and lavish scale of the Second Empire in his Palais du Trocadero (now demolished) for the 1878 Exposition.

DAVIS, ALEXANDER JACKSON. American architect and draftsman (1803–92). Born in New York City, he joined with Ithiel Town in 1829 and the firm's revival-styled designs included the Connecticut State House (1827–31; now destroyed), in New Haven, freely derived from the Parthenon. After Town's death in 1844, Davis designed many academic buildings and mansions in the newer eclectic styles.

BIBLIOGRAPHY. R. H. Newton, *Town & Davis, Architects*, New York, 1942.

Arthur B. Davies, *Crescendo*. Oil on canvas. Whitney Museum of American Art, New York.

Stuart Davis, *Midi*, 1954. Wadsworth Atheneum, Hartford, Conn.

DAVIS, GLADYS ROCKMORE. American painter (1901–67). She was born in New York City and studied at the Art Institute of Chicago. She worked as a commercial illustrator. Her brightly colored gouaches, oil paintings, and pastels are of children, flowers, women, and ballet and stage subjects.

BIBLIOGRAPHY. American Artists Group, *Gladys Rockmore Davis*, New York, 1945.

DAVIS, STUART. American painter (b. Philadelphia, 1894; d. New York City, 1964). He studied with Robert Henri in New York from 1910 to 1913 and worked for *Harper's Weekly* and *The Masses*. A pioneer modernist, he exhibited five water colors at the Armory Show of 1913. The paintings he saw there, particularly those of the postimpressionists, were decisive in turning Davis away from realism toward a greater abstraction.

Such paintings as *Multiple Views* (1918) and *Yellow Hills* (1919; both New York, Downtown Gallery) are re-

lated to Gauguin and Van Gogh, but the water color *Cigarette Papers* (1921; private collection) shows what was to become the dominant influence of synthetic cubism. In these works, along with illusionistic painted textures, he introduced words not as cubist elements of reality but as a part of the total abstract structure of the picture. The famous *Eggbeater* series (1927–28) carried the surface disposition of generalized forms to a further degree, and when Davis went to Paris in 1928, he applied similar techniques to the painting of street scenes. For example, in *Place Pasdeloup* (1928; New York, Whitney Museum), the few remnants of traditional perspective are lost against the flat planes of bright color. After returning to the United States, he continued in this synthesizing style.

In 1933 Davis joined the Federal Art Project and later painted two murals for the WPA. Meanwhile his work had become almost totally abstract. In *Bass Rocks No. 1* (1939; Wichita Art Museum), the motif was reduced to lines set against areas of contrasting color. Naturalistic elements became completely subordinate to the needs of overall design. Davis's colors are bright and jumpy but calculated in effect, as seen, for example, in *Hot Stillscape for Six Colors* (1940; private collection), where areas of warm colors are dominant but not enough so as to form a spatial recession.

In 1944 Davis was given a retrospective show at the Museum of Modern Art in New York; subsequently he won many major prizes, the last of which was the 1964 gold medal for the best oil painting, given by the Pennsylvania Academy of Fine Arts. In the latter part of his career, Davis's works show a tendency toward straight-edged forms, though fewer in number than previously, combined with a bolder compositional use of words. He retained little of the social realism of his early days except for his general exuberance and the bits of everyday American life that found their way into his paintings as words or shapes.

Though based on cubism and the machine stylizations of Léger, Davis's paintings have a freshness of approach and a sense of humor completely his own, perhaps due to jazz, which was a constant source of his inspiration. Davis thought of his art as an integral part of the dynamic American scene and considered all his pictures, including those painted in Paris, as referential to that scene.

BIBLIOGRAPHY. J. J. Sweeney, *Stuart Davis*, New York, 1945; E. C. Goossen, *Stuart Davis*, New York, 1959; Smithsonian Institution, *Stuart Davis Memorial Exhibition*, Washington, D.C., 1965.

JEROME VIOLA

DAVRINGHAUSEN, HEINRICH MARIA. German painter and lithographer (1894–   ). He was born in Aachen and started his artistic career as a sculptor. He is a self-taught painter. He traveled in Spain in 1925–26. His early paintings were of Biblical subjects; later he painted figures, landscapes, still lifes, and portraits. Davringhausen's paintings have moved from expressionist formal distortion to an almost equally expressionist New Objectivity detailed style with tightly painted and constructed forms. The attention to detail lessened somewhat in the landscapes of the early 1920s, which have an ideal, dreamlike air. His portraits are more renderings of types than individuals, with facial treatment that is masklike in quality.

DAVY, JEAN. French architect (fl. ca. 1270–1320). Jean Davy was master of works at the Cathedral of Rouen beginning in 1278. He may have built the north portal (1280) and the early-14th-century Chapel of the Madonna.

DAWE (Dawes), PHILIPP. English engraver and mezzotintist (b. London, ca. 1750; d. there, ca. 1785). He was the father of George Dawe and Henry Edward Dawe. His genre, mythological, and epic scenes and portraits are done after Henry Morgan (his teacher) and other contemporaries, including Cosway, T. Hudson, and Van Dyck (for example, the *Birth of Christ*, after Singleton).

DAYES, EDWARD. English water-colorist and mezzotintist (b. London, 1763; d. there, 1804). From 1786 until his death, Dayes brought forth a steady production of portraits, landscapes, and street scenes. Many of his water colors are done in soft blue-gray tones accented with Chinese ink (*Procession and Service in St. Paul's*; London, Victoria and Albert Museum). He also illustrated poetic works, including those of Dryden. Thomas Girtin was his most outstanding pupil.

BIBLIOGRAPHY. A. M. Hind, *History of Engraving and Etching*, 3d ed., rev., London, 1923 (repr. New York, 1963).

DAY OF THE GOD. Oil painting by Gauguin, in the Art Institute of Chicago. *See* GAUGUIN, PAUL.

DEAMBULATORY, *see* AMBULATORY.

DEAN, JOHN. English mezzotintist and draftsman (b. London, 1750; d. there, 1798). A student of Valentine Green, Dean is identified through Green with the Romney school. In 1770 he set up his own shop, where he produced delicately colored but somewhat weak mezzotints after Rubens, Andrea del Sarto, and especially Romney.

BIBLIOGRAPHY. F. M. O'Donoghue, *Catalogue of Engraved British Portraits Preserved in ... the British Museum*, 6 vols., London, 1908–25.

DEANE, SIR THOMAS, *see* DEANE AND WOODWARD.

DEANE AND WOODWARD. Irish architects: Sir Thomas Deane (1792–1871) and Benjamin Woodward (1815–61). They worked in Dublin, Oxford, and London. They were closely connected with Ruskin during the fifties and built the Oxford University Museum, which included an interesting iron and glass court, in collaboration with him.

BIBLIOGRAPHY. K. Clark, *The Gothic Revival*, 2d ed., London, 1950.

DE ARTE ILLUMINANDI (On the Art of Illuminations). Fourteenth-century treatise on manuscript illumination, probably by an Italian illuminator. The only existing copy of it is a late-14th-century manuscript (Naples, National Museum, MS 12, E. 27), which is a version of the probably slightly earlier original. A very practical approach is taken in dealing with all aspects of decorating a manuscript except the writing itself. The principal topics are pigments, gilding, binders, and techniques of application.

BIBLIOGRAPHY. D. V. Thompson, Jr., and G. H. Hamilton (intro. and tr.), *An Anonymous Fourteenth-Century Treatise, De Arte Illuminandi*, New Haven, Conn., 1933.

DEATH OF GENERAL WOLFE. Oil painting by West, in the National Gallery of Canada, Ottawa. *See* WEST, BENJAMIN.

DEATH OF MARAT. Oil painting by David, in the Museum of Modern Art, Brussels. *See* DAVID, JACQUES-LOUIS.

DEATH OF PROCRIS. Oil painting by Piero di Cosimo, in the National Gallery, London. *See* PIERO DI COSIMO.

DEATH OF ST. FRANCIS. Fresco painting by Giotto, in Sta Croce, Florence. *See* GIOTTO DI BONDONE.

DEATH OF THE BUDDHA, KONGOBUJI, MT. KOYA. Japanese silk painting (1086). It represents the scene of the Buddha's death (Sanskrit, Nirvāṇa). In the center is the recumbent figure of the Buddha painted in brilliant gold and surrounded by groups of aristocratic-looking bodhisattvas and sorrowful weeping figures of monks and laymen. Even the animal kingdom is represented by a lion that writhes in grief. The Buddha's mother, Maya, hurries down from heaven on a cloud. It is the oldest and perhaps the best Japanese Nirvāṇa picture.

BIBLIOGRAPHY. Tokyo National Museum, *Pageant of Japanese Art*, vol. 1: *Painting*, pt. 1, Tokyo, 1952; T. Akiyama, *Japanese Painting* [Geneva?], 1961; National Commission for the Protection of Cultural Properties, ed., *Kokuhō (National Treasures of Japan)*, 6 vols., Tokyo, 1963–

DEATH OF THE VIRGIN. Oil painting by Caravaggio, in the Louvre, Paris. *See* CARAVAGGIO, MICHELANGELO MERISI DA.

DEBRET, JEAN-BAPTISTE. French painter (b. Paris, 1768; d. there, 1848). Debret studied at the Académie des Beaux-Arts in Paris. He was an ardent Bonapartist and, after Napoleon's fall, joined the Lebreton mission to Brazil (1816). He helped found the Academy of Fine Arts in Rio de Janeiro and painted court subjects (for example, *Desembarque da Princesa Leopoldina, 1822*; Rio de Janeiro, National Museum of Fine Arts). He returned to Paris in 1831 and published *Voyage pittoresque et historique au Brésil* with his lithographic illustrations.

BIBLIOGRAPHY. A. de Escragnolle Taunay, *A missão artística de 1816*, Rio de Janeiro, 1956.

DE BROSSE FAMILY. French architects, active in the late 16th and 17th centuries: Salomon de Brosse (1571–1626), Jean de Brosse (fl. after 1561; d. 1584), and Paul de Brosse (fl. 1617–44). The only significant member of the De Brosse family was Salomon, the most important French architect of his generation. His family, who were Protestants, moved to Paris after the Edict of Nantes (1598), and by about 1610 he had established himself as a successful architect. He then built three great châteaux: Coulommiers (1613) for Catherine de Gonzague, duchess of Longueville; Blérancourt (finished before 1619) for Bernard Potier; and the Luxembourg (1615) for Marie de Médicis. In 1618 he began to rebuild the Salle in the Palace of the Parisian Parlement and to reconstruct the Palace of the Parlement of Brittany at Rennes. In 1623 he rebuilt the Protestant Temple at Charenton. Salomon de Brosse's style marks the transition from the mannerist classicism of the 16th century to the baroque classicism of the 17th century. His main contribution to French architecture was that through his work he focused attention on designing in terms of mass rather than surface and pattern, as his contemporaries did. *See* LUXEMBOURG PALACE, PARIS.

BIBLIOGRAPHY. A. Blunt, *Art and Architecture in France, 1500–1700*, Baltimore, 1954.

DEBUCOURT, PHILIBERT-LOUIS. French genre painter and virtuoso of engraving (1755–1832). Born in Paris, he was notable for perfecting color engraving imitating water color and gouache. His early works reflect the boudoir genre of Baudouin and Lavreince, and in his middle period he became more satirical than provocative. He engraved mainly after Isabey, Carle, and Horace Vernet in his late years.

BIBLIOGRAPHY. H. Bouchot, *P.-L. Debucourt*, Paris, 1904.

Alexandre-Gabriel Decamps, *The Night Patrol at Smyrna*. Metropolitan Museum of Art, New York (Bequest of Catharine Lorillard Wolfe, 1887).

DECADENT ART. The term has two meanings. In one sense, it is derogatory, usually referring to the excesses of *fin de siècle* artificiality and oversophistication, and critical of the 19th-century sensibility that found expression in exotic or morbid themes and a precious style. The aesthetic movement, Art Nouveau, and symbolism have been so labeled.

In its other sense, decadent art is a surrogate for "degenerate art," a term used by the Nazi regime for modern art in general. Since all modern art expressed "political and cultural anarchy," galleries and museums had to be "purified" of it. The Munich exhibition of 1937, entitled "Entartete Kunst," was intended to demonstrate the blight of modernism. Such painters as Nolde, Klee, Beckmann, and Kokoschka were condemned by the Nazi regime. *See* DEGENERATE ART.

DECAMPS, ALEXANDRE-GABRIEL. French painter, etcher, and lithographer (b. Paris, 1803; d. Fontainebleau, 1860). Except for a short period of study with Abel de Pujol, Decamps was essentially self-taught. He began by painting small panels from nature and then learned etching and lithography. He entered the Salon of 1827 and in the same year traveled to Asia Minor. On his return to Paris he introduced Oriental subjects into French academic painting, and his work was received with much acclaim. His greatest popularity came in 1831, when he showed at the Salon *Night Patrol at Smyrna* (New York, Metropolitan Museum). Following a trip to Italy (1832–33), Decamps began to paint historical and religious subjects (*The Defeat of the Cimbri at Aquae Sextiae*, 1835; London, Wallace Collection).

BIBLIOGRAPHY. C. Clement, *Decamps*, Paris, 1886; P. du Colombier, *Decamps*, Paris, 1928.

DECASTYLE. Having ten columns in front. The Ionic Temple of Apollo Didymaeus, Miletus, has a double colonnade surrounding the cella to form a dipteral decastyle type.

DECATETRASTYLE. Denoting a temple with fourteen columns in front.

DECKER, CORNELIS GERRITSZ. Dutch painter of landscapes and interiors (b. before 1623; d. Haarlem, 1678). Decker was probably a pupil of Salomon van Ruysdael. He became a member of the guild in Haarlem in 1643. He collaborated with Adriaen van Ostade, who painted figures in Decker's work.

BIBLIOGRAPHY. A. Heppner, "Cornelis Deckers Innenraum-Darstellungen," *Adolph Goldschmidt zu seinem siebenzigsten Geburtstag*, Berlin, 1935.

DECORATED STYLE. Term applied to the middle, or second, phase of English Gothic architecture, from about 1270 to 1350. The style is distinguished by its rich treatment of vaulting portals and windows, as seen, for example, in the nave and choir of Exeter Cathedral. *See* EXETER CATHEDRAL. *See also* LICHFIELD CATHEDRAL.

DECORATIVE ARTS. Art forms with a primarily decorative rather than an expressive or emotional purpose. Thus where a painting, building, or sculpture may have a symbolic, emotional, expressive, or intellectual purpose as its reason for being, a decorative art work will be designed to embellish or decorate in a basically ornamental or even functional manner. Fabrics, ornamental brickwork, mosaic, marble, and other forms of inlay may be regarded as decorative arts. Painting and sculpture may, however, be used decoratively in architecture and, to that extent, be decorative arts.

Decorated style. Window of Magdalen College, Oxford University.

DE COTTE, ROBERT. French architect (1656–1735). He worked in Paris. After training in Jules-Hardouin Mansart's workshop, he succeeded Mansart as first architect. His career began about 1700 with commissions for hôtels and châteaux. After his appointment as first architect in 1708, he was called upon for ecclesiastical and royal architectural designs. His reputation extended into the provinces and throughout the Continent. Consulted by such prominent European architects as Neumann, he was in the fore of the new architectural movement with its emphasis on interior decoration, convenience, and comfort. De Cotte remained faithful to his early training in such designs as that for the façade of St-Roch, Paris (executed by his son Jules-Robert), which gives sinewy expression to the tradition of the Gesù in Rome with its planar treatment of heavy classical columns, entablatures, and pediment. His interior decoration, however, moved far beyond Mansart's work and places him as one of the originators of the rococo style.

BIBLIOGRAPHY. L. Hautecoeur, *Histoire de l'architecture classique en France*, vol. 3, Paris, 1950.

DE COUCY, ROBERT. French Gothic architect (d. 1311). He was master of St-Nicaise at Reims after 1263 and of Reims Cathedral after 1290. At the latter he was responsible for the upper part of the west façade and for the labyrinth in the nave, honoring the four architects who preceded him.

BIBLIOGRAPHY. L. Demaison, *La Cathédrale de Reims*, 3d ed., Paris, 1954.

DE CREEFT, JOSE. American sculptor (1884–   ). Born in Guadalajara, Spain, he was apprenticed at the age of twelve to a bronze foundry in Barcelona. He went to Paris (1905), where he studied at the Académie Julian and worked as a stonecutter. He went to the United States in 1928. Although an early exponent of direct handling of materials (he exhibited a "ready-made" of found objects in Paris in 1925), he is best known as a carver. His works exhibit solidity of form, often expressed in rounded volumes, and a sense for whimsical detail.

BIBLIOGRAPHY. C. Devree, *José de Creeft*, New York, 1960.

DE DIEGO, JULIO. American painter (1900–   ). Born in Madrid, he was trained to be a stage designer. He is mostly self-taught as a painter. De Diego went to the United States in 1924. He is best known for a series of semiabstract, symbolic war paintings, done during World War II (for example, *The Portentous City*, 1942–43; New York, Metropolitan Museum of Art). His most recent works deal with the destruction of the Spanish Armada.

BIBLIOGRAPHY. "Chicago's Versatile Spaniard, De Diego," *Art News*, XLII, May, 1943.

DEELEN (Delen), DIRCK VAN. Dutch painter of architecture and interiors (b. Heusden, 1605; d. Arnemuiden, 1671). Deelen, who was probably a pupil of Hendrik Aerts, entered the Middelburg guild in 1639 and later became burgomaster of Arnemuiden. His paintings recall the work of Hendrick van Steenwijck.

BIBLIOGRAPHY. W. Schmidt, "Dirk van Deelen und Adriaen Brouwer," *Zeitschrift für bildende Kunst*, IX, 1874.

DEERHURST: ST. MARY, see St. Mary, Deerhurst.

DEER MANDALA. Type of Japanese painting (Japanese, *Shika Mandara* or *Kasuga Shika Mandara*) made for the Kasuga Shinto Shrine in Nara. Deer mandalas represent a peculiarly Japanese blend of Buddhism and Shintoism, Japan's native religion. Deer of the Kasuga Shrine were venerated by the Fujiwara noblemen as their sacred guardians, and mandalas (diagrammatic representations of deities) were made for the purpose of worship. In the deer mandala, a deer stands in the center of the landscape background, which depicts the area around the Kasuga Shrine. The deer usually carries on its back a branch of the *sakaki* tree, sacred in Shinto, which in turn supports a mirror, the most sacred Shinto symbol. Small figures of Buddhist deities may be represented with the deer. In the late Heian and Kamakura periods, efforts to synthesize Buddhism and Shintoism were intensified, and Shinto gods were thought to be the manifestation of Buddhist deities on the soil of Japan. In order to express this alliance between two religions, a new iconography was created in painting and sculpture. Deer mandalas belong to this new religious art, and many fine examples were made from the late Heian period through the Muromachi. Important deer mandalas are found in the N. Miyaji Collection (Kamakura period), the Seika-dō Foundation (Muromachi period), and the Yōmei Bunko (Kamakura period).

BIBLIOGRAPHY. R. T. Paine and A. Soper, *The Art and Architecture of Japan*, Baltimore, 1955.
          MIYEKO MURASE

DEESIS. Greek term for the representation of the Enthroned Christ between Mary and St. John. It may be a separate representation or, as in the iconostasis of Byzantine art, the main group of the Last Judgment.

DEFRANCE, LEONARD. Belgian painter (b. Liège, 1735; d. there, 1805). He studied under Jan Baptiste Coclers and lived in Rome from 1753 to 1759. He first painted portraits and figures in the French neoclassic style. After 1773, influenced by the Dutch masters, he began to paint popular urban genre scenes that often stressed the light effects of open fires.

DEFREGGER, FRANZ VON. Austrian painter (b. Ederhof bei Stronach, Tyrol, 1835; d. Munich, 1921). He studied with Piloty in Paris and after 1878 was professor at the Munich Academy. In the last years of the 19th century, Defregger achieved great popularity in Munich as a painter of genre scenes from Tyrolean peasant life.

BIBLIOGRAPHY. A. Rosenberg, *Defregger* (Künstler-Monographien, no. 18), Bielefeld, 1897; H. Hammer, *Franz von Defregger*, Innsbruck, 1940.

DEGAS, HILAIRE GERMAIN EDGAR. French impressionist painter (b. Paris, 1834; d. there, 1917). He was

Deer Mandala. *Kasuga Mandara,* from the middle of the Kamakura period. Koyata Iwasaki Collection, Tokyo.

the eldest son of the banker Pierre-Auguste de Gas. Through a family friend, Valpinçon, he met his idol, Ingres. Degas was educated at the Lycée Louis-le-Grand, where he met Henri Rouart, who was to be a lifelong friend. By 1852 Degas had a studio of his own, and two years later he began to study with an Ingres student, Louis Lamothe. Soon after, he started classes at the Ecole des Beaux-Arts, Paris.

He went to Italy in 1854 and stayed five years. He lived with relatives in Florence and Naples and studied for a while in Rome. He returned to Paris in 1859, painted portraits of his friends, and did some pictures with historical subjects. About three years later, Degas came to know Manet and Edmond Duranty, a writer, critic, and friend of the impressionist group, who encouraged Degas to turn to contemporary themes. Degas was introduced to the artists and intellectuals who frequented the Café Guerbois. He soon earned his lifelong reputation for being haughty, sharply critical, and altogether formidable. Yet he had friends and many admirers who respected him.

During the Franco-Prussian War an illness affected his eyesight; it was to leave him almost totally blind in old age. In 1872 he went on a six-month vacation trip to Louisiana to visit members of his family who were in the cotton business. There he painted *The Cotton Exchange at New Orleans* (1873; Pau, Fine Arts Museum). This was the only work to be acquired by a museum in the artist's lifetime. He returned to Paris the following year and set up a studio in Montmartre. Degas did much to organize the first impressionist exhibition and showed ten works in it. He exhibited in all eight impressionist shows except the next to last. After 1893 he stopped showing altogether.

He made his first monotypes in 1876. In 1881 he began to use pastel and started to make his sculptures. Degas, himself an amateur photographer, was particularly interested in the action-sequence photographs of walking and running nude figures and of galloping horses taken by the Philadelphia photographer Muybridge, and these influenced his treatment of moving horses.

The members of the impressionist group drifted apart with growing acceptance of their work. Degas, troubled by failing eyesight, became something of a recluse. He had acquired a fine collection of art works including an El Greco, a Tiepolo, an Ingres, and a Delacroix, and even a Van Gogh, as well as paintings by Manet, Cézanne, Gauguin, and Corot. Degas collected his own pictures; he bought back some of his early works and frequently reworked them. The stature of his art was not assessed until after his death in 1917, when his works were auctioned off in Paris. Most of his art had been shielded from the general view in private collections or in his studio.

Degas developed his art by degrees. In order to learn, he copied old master paintings, for example, those of Titian, Veronese, Van Dyck, Velázquez, and Poussin, and he made several drawings of such diverse works as those of Rogier van der Weyden, Delacroix, Flaxman, and Guys, as well as of a Mughal miniature and an Assyrian relief. The copies are mostly incomplete, since he searched out only those details and fragments that impressed him. His first paintings, mostly portraits of his friends, are stiff and formal, recalling Ingres, Bronzino, Raphael, or Van Dyck, as well as the daguerreotype. After 1865, his figures be-

come more relaxed and appear as if they had been caught off guard by a camera eye. His historical works, such as *Young Spartan Girls Challenging Spartan Boys* (dated 1860; London, National Gallery), are, despite their themes, essentially nonclassical in conception. Degas abandoned academic themes after 1865 to depict the contemporary scene and reveal aspects of the modern. He had the example of Manet and painted the racetrack and the seashore. Here, as in nearly all his works, figures dominate. He showed them as active, organically functioning beings. He sought accuracy in capturing a pose unconsciously struck. He was not a plein-airist, and he preferred the use of line to the formless shapes of Monet, but like the plein-air painters Degas was very much concerned with the momentary aspect.

He considered a work as a product of the artist's imagination, as a synthesis which by artifice appears to be perfectly logical and natural. Naturalness and the look of spontaneity were achieved only through discipline and persistence. Many subjects of Degas's paintings are actively engaged in creating art or its complement through hard work. His ballet dancers, especially, are all elbows and flexing limbs, whether flopping in a chair exhausted or striking creative gestures. Whereas Renoir's women have an easy charm, Degas's milliners, laundresses, and dancers are posed so as to show the effort of their occupation. He adopted the oblique view derived from Japanese prints, giving a slanted, patterned appearance to the picture.

Like the other impressionists, Degas used broken color and favored spectrum colors. In his later work, particularly his pastels, light and color are stressed to the point that the modeling of the forms reduces figures to pattern. Contour is simplified to heighten the eloquence of significant gesture. Degas made sculptures for the study of movement, not for exhibition. He exhibited only one sculpture, in 1881, of a young dancer, done in wax but dressed in a real skirt and slippers. He also made many working drawings.

In the mid-1880s Degas turned more and more to pastel, which he applied as a crayon but also as a dampened powder spread on with a brush. At the last impressionist exhibition, in 1886, he exhibited a number of nudes, bathing, drying themselves, combing their hair, getting dressed, and so on. These late Degas works are luminous, frequently dazzling in the use of daring color, and yet grounded in reality, however generalized in effect and ultimately symbolic in meaning.

BIBLIOGRAPHY. P. A. Lemoisne, *Degas et son oeuvre*, 4 vols., Paris, 1946; D. C. Rich, *Degas*, New York, 1951; F. Fosca, pseud., *Degas*, Geneva, 1954; J. Rewald, *Degas' Sculpture*, New York, 1957; J. S. Boggs, *Portraits by Degas*, Berkeley, 1962.

ROBERT REIFF

DEGENERATE ART. Nazi Germany's epithet for all individualism in 20th-century art. In an attempt to destroy both the creation and appreciation of modern art, the state confiscated thousands of works from public museums and exhibited them viciously in Munich in 1937 as examples of degeneracy, pacifism, and non-Aryanism. The art of Cézanne, Gauguin, Braque, and Picasso as well as of most German expressionists was included.

BIBLIOGRAPHY. H. Lehmann-Haupt, *Art under a Dictatorship*. New York, 1954.

Edgar Degas, *The Bellelli Family*. Jeu de Paume, Paris. A large-scale group portrait from the artist's formative period.

DEGLER, JOHANN (Hans). German sculptor (d. 1637). Degler was active in Munich, in his native Weilheim, and later in Augsburg, where he constructed the choir and altar and two side altars of the Church of SS. Ulrich and Afra. His sculptures show his original and almost primitive power of fantasy.

DEGROUX, CHARLES, *see* GROUX, CHARLES DE.

DEHN, ADOLF. American painter and lithographer (1895–1968). He was born in Waterville, Minn., and lived in New York City. In 1914 he studied at the Minneapolis Institute of Fine Arts. Encouraged by the sale of his drawings, he went to New York, where he studied with Boardman Robinson. In 1921 he went abroad for seven years and was influenced by George Grosz and Julius Pascin. He exhibited his water colors for the first time in 1938. In 1939 and 1951 he received Guggenheim grants; he was awarded several prizes. Dehn taught summer sessions at the Colorado Springs Fine Arts Center. In 1946 he visited Haiti. Combining vigorous texture and an athletic

line with delicacy of tone, Dehn poked fun at Sunday painters, café society, habitués of Negro night clubs, and earnest prelates, and presented the landscapes of Minnesota, Haiti, Colorado, and other places with lyrical affection.

DE HOLLANDE, *see* AMSTEL, JAN VAN.

DEI, MATTEO DI GIOVANNI. Italian goldsmith and niellist (fl. 1439–55). A member of a Florentine family of goldsmiths that included Miliano di Domenico Dei, Matteo is first mentioned in the Florentine State Archives in 1439. A niello pax, *Coronation of the Virgin* (ca. 1470–75; Florence, National Museum), once attributed to Maso Finiguerra, has tentatively been identified as the pax commissioned from Matteo in 1455 for the Florence Cathedral.

BIBLIOGRAPHY. British Museum, Dept. of Prints and Drawings, *Nielli... Preserved in the British Museum...*, by A. M. Hind, London, 1936.

DEI, MILIANO DI DOMENICO. Italian goldsmith (fl. 1439–59). A member of a Florentine family of goldsmiths that included Matteo di Giovanni Dei, Miliano is first mentioned in the Florentine State Archives in 1439. In 1457 he was commissioned with Antonio Pollaiuolo and Betto di Francesco Betti to make the silver cross for the altar of S. Giovanni in the Florentine Baptistery (1457–59; Florence, Cathedral Museum). Miliano's contribution to the work, however, remains unidentified.

BIBLIOGRAPHY. H. Mackowsky, "Das Silberkreuz für den Johannisaltar im Museo di S. Maria del Fiore zu Florenz," *Jahrbuch der Königlich Preussischen Kunstsammlungen*, XXIII, 1902.

DEI, PIERO D'ANTONIO, *see* BARTOLOMMEO DELLA GATTA.

DEINEKA, ALEXANDER. Russian painter, graphic artist, and teacher (1899–   ). He was born in Kursk and studied at the Kharkov Art School and at the Moscow Vkhutemas from 1921 to 1924. Since 1924 Deineka has been an important graphic artist and illustrator for various periodicals, especially *The Atheist at the Bench*. He is also known for his patriotic posters, including the famous "We must ourselves become specialists." While Deineka's subjects are mostly standard scenes of Soviet realism—peasants, factories, and Russian history—his style is influenced by the emphasized silhouette and flat treatment of his illustrations and graphic work.

DEIR BARAMUS. Coptic monastery in the Wadi el-Natrun, between Cairo and Alexandria, Egypt. Founded in the 4th century, Deir Baramus retains some of the earliest fragments of any of the Coptic monasteries in this area. The *qasr* (used as a defensive tower against Bedouin marauders) seems to have served as the prototype for the more advanced examples in other monasteries of the wadi.

BIBLIOGRAPHY. H. G. Evelyn-White, *The Monasteries of the Wādi 'n-Natrūn*, 3 vols., New York, 1926-32.

DEIR EL BAHARI. Site named after a Coptic monastery on the top of a cliff in western Thebes, which overlooks a recess in the hills in which there are two unique mortuary temples.

Deir el Bahari. Mortuary temple of Queen Hatshepsut, 18th dynasty.

The temple of Pharaoh Mentuhotep (11th dynasty), in the southwest corner of Deir el Bahari, combines the pyramidal shape of a royal tomb of the Old Kingdom with a series of terraces. The latter consists of a lower terrace, at the front of which are pillared porticoes that support an upper terrace, with a peripteral gallery surrounding the pyramid base. Behind this are a peristyle court and a hypostyle hall leading to a chapel cut in the cliff. A formal grove of trees containing royal statues was at the front of the axial structure, which had no less than 250 columns and 172 pillars. From the court a sloping passage led to an underground chamber, where the impressive painted statue of Mentuhotep was found. The plan of the earlier girdle wall in the shape of a contemporary shield may have been a symbolic reminiscence of the final victory of the Theban dynasty over Herakleopolis.

The mortuary temple of Queen Hatshepsut (18th dynasty), in the northwest corner of Deir el Bahari, was probably inspired by that of Mentuhotep but is intended to be seen from the front only. It is oriented toward the Great Temple of Amun at Karnak. On the front of each stage of its terraced design there are twin porticoes flanking a central ramp. A chapel of Anubis (north) and another of Hathor (south) are cut out at the ends of the middle-level porticoes. Osiride pillars representing the Queen were at the front of the upper portico. Behind this stretches a hypostyle hall and at its rear is a deep sanctuary hewn out of the cliff. In its side walls are niches containing statues of Hatshepsut. An altar to Reʻ-Haarakhte is set in a northern courtyard.

The aesthetic significance of the temple derives as much from its unique architectural treatment, which integrated the temple with the natural environment of rocky vertical bastions and clefts (in three horizontal stages), as from the unique interest of the scenes carved in relief and painted on the walls of the middle porticoes. To the north, the theogamy of Hatshepsut's mother with Amun is depicted, and to the south, a trade expedition by sea to Pwenet (Somaliland) is shown with lively details of the ethnic characteristics of the natives, their architecture, and the fauna and flora of their country. The style of the reliefs shows the same classicism as the proto-Doric columns of the porticoes and the terraced design.

See also EGYPT.

BIBLIOGRAPHY. H. E. Winlock, *The Rise and Fall of the Middle Kingdom at Thebes*, New York, 1947; M. Werbrouck, *Le Temple d'Hatshepsut à Deir el Bahari*, Brussels, 1949; L. Dabrowski, "A Famous Temple Re-examined: Queen Hatshepsut's Temple at Deir el Bahari—and a Hitherto Unknown Temple," *The Illustrated London News*, CCXLV, Sept. 19, 1964.

ALEXANDER M. BADAWY

DEIR ES-SURIAN. Coptic monastery in the Wadi el-Natrun, between Cairo and Alexandria, Egypt. It contains the 9th-century Church of el-ʻAdra with frescoes and fine stucco decorations. The refectory and *qasr* (tower of refuge) date from the same period.

BIBLIOGRAPHY. H. G. Evelyn-White, *The Monasteries of the Wādi 'n-Natrūn*, 3 vols., New York, 1926-32.

DEJEUNER SUR L'HERBE (Luncheon on the Grass). Oil painting by Manet, in the Louvre, Paris. *See* MANET, EDOUARD.

Willem de Kooning, *Woman: Ochre*, detail, 1954–55. Oil on canvas. Martha Jackson Gallery, New York.

DE KOONING, WILLEM. Dutch-born American painter (1904–). A major abstract expressionist, he is a leader in the action group. Born in Rotterdam, he studied at the Rotterdam Academy of Fine Arts and then worked for a decorating firm. In 1926 he went to the United States. He did free-lance commercial art and murals during the late 1920s and early 1930s; he was with the Federal Art Project in 1935; and he collaborated with Fernand Léger on a mural for the French Line. De Kooning shared a studio with Arshile Gorky. De Kooning's earliest abstractions date from about 1930, but his greatest development occurred in the mid-1940s.

By about 1945 De Kooning had become a strong influence among avant-garde painters and a few critics in New York. He became internationally famous soon after his first one-man show at the Egan Gallery in 1948. His

Woman series of 1952–55, for which there are prototypes in the late 1940s, won astonishingly wide critical and popular attention. In 1958 he reinvestigated the nonobjective manner he had tentatively used about 1930 and had carried further in black-and-white enamel canvases in 1948. His violently brushed, brilliantly colored abstract expressionist paintings and collages of the late 1950s and early 1960s established him as a major contemporary artist. He has sometimes reverted to the *Woman* theme since 1962. He has taught at Black Mountain College and Yale University.

De Kooning has had one-man shows at the Sidney Janis Gallery, Boston Museum of Fine Arts School, Venice Biennale, and São Paulo Bienal. His works have been included in major group and international shows in New York (Museum of Modern Art; Whitney Museum of American Art), Pittsburgh (Carnegie International), Venice, and São Paulo.

BIBLIOGRAPHY. W. de Kooning, "What Abstract Art Means to Me," *Museum of Modern Art Bulletin*, XVIII : 3, 1951; C. Greenberg, " 'American-type' Painting," *Partisan Review*, XXII : 2, 1955; T. B. Hess, *Willem de Kooning*, New York, 1959; H. Janis and R. Blesh, *De Kooning*, New York, 1960.

JOHN C. GALLOWAY

DELACROIX, EUGENE. French painter (b. Charenton, 1798; d. Paris, 1863). He was related on his mother's side to artisans and artists (Oeben, Riesener) and on the side of his presumed natural father, Talleyrand, to the aristocracy of the old and the political power of the new France. The question of his paternity throws light on Eugène Delacroix's personality and career. In 1816 he entered the atelier of Guérin, an enlightened classicist through whose teaching many of the rising romantics had passed—Géricault, the Scheffer brothers, Cogniet, and Champmartin. More profitable than Guérin's lessons was Delacroix's self-training at the Louvre, where he copied above all Rubens and Veronese. His friend Soulier, and later the English painter Bonington, introduced him to water colors and British colorism, and awakened his interest in Shakespeare, Scott, and Byron, the literary sources of his romanticism.

At the Salon of 1822 his *Barque of Dante* (Paris, Louvre) —based on Dante's *Inferno*, Canto I—attracted notice. Influenced in feeling and style by Géricault's *Raft of the Medusa*, with borrowings from Michelangelo and Rubens, this immature but brilliantly promising work was condemned for its "exaggerations" by academics, and warmly praised by Gros. Talleyrand's hidden influence induced the government to buy the picture. In 1822 Delacroix began his *Intimate Journals*, which, together with his *Correspondence*, constitutes the most illuminating self-appraisal written by a modern painter.

The *Massacre of Chios* (Louvre), which scandalized Salon visitors in 1824, is a more forceful assertion of Delacroix's individuality than the *Barque of Dante*. The luminous sonority of its colors—Delacroix had recently come under Constable's spell—and its discordant composition shocked even progressive critics. As the dramatic interpretation of a contemporary event, an occurrence in the Greek War of Liberation, the *Massacre* goes beyond Géricault's *Medusa* (which influenced it). Its lustful dwelling on horror and its exaltation of sensuous beauty make it "a terrifying hymn in honor of doom and irremediable

suffering" (Baudelaire). The government again bought the picture, enabling Delacroix to visit England (May–August, 1825). With Bonington and Thales Fielding as mentors, he visited galleries, met Wilkie and Lawrence, saw Shakespeare acted, and read the English poets. On his return to France, his preoccupation with literature and a new interest in lithography led him to draw illustrations for Goethe's *Faust* (1827) and for *Hamlet* (1834/43).

At the Salon of 1827 Delacroix exhibited twelve paintings, including the orgiastic *Death of Sardanapalus* (Louvre), based on Byron's poem, an incoherent compilation of magnificent details—nudes worthy of Rubens, horses and jewels heaped round the pyre of the Assyrian who bears the features of Delacroix. Its romantic joy of destruction and fevered sensuality were his "Asiatic" defiance thrown to the Spartans of classicism; Delacroix paid for it with the loss of official favor.

A finer painting, the *Execution of the Doge Marino Faliero* (1826; London, Wallace Collection), marks the highest achievement of picturesque historical genre, not only for Delacroix but for the entire romantic movement. A pageant in Veronese's manner, it draws its powers of poetic suggestion from the musical enchantment of its colors. During this same fertile period Delacroix painted numerous Oriental genre pieces, odalisques, animal studies, still lifes, and two tumultuous medieval histories, the *Battle of Nancy* (1828–31) and the *Battle of Poitiers* (1830), precursors of the great *Battle of Taillebourg* (1837).

The Revolution of 1830 inspired Delacroix's one truly popular work, *Liberty Leading the People* (1831; Louvre), which was modern in conception, despite its allegory, and entirely free of romantic clichés. The silhouetted figures advancing over the barricade are more amply proportioned and broadly treated than those of earlier paintings; the colors are warmer and in a lower key; and the emotional impact of the scene is untinged by morbidity or literary allusion. A new phase in Delacroix's development began: a quieter and grander style, increased monumentality without lessening of animation, and subtler color harmony without loss of intensity.

In January–June, 1832, he visited Spain, Morocco, and Algiers as a member of De Mornay's embassy to the Moroccan Sultan. In Islamic Africa he discovered a survival of Homeric antiquity. The classical beauty and dignity he had vainly sought among the plaster casts of Guérin's studio Delacroix now encountered at every roadside under the African sky. He filled sketchbooks with notes on Arab life, costumes, weapons, horses, and landscape, gathering a store of pictorial motifs on which he drew for the remainder of his life. *Algerian Women in Their Harem* (1834; Louvre), the first and richest product of these impressions, shows the women in a dusky interior as a sumptuous tapestry of exotic greens, roses, reds, and dim gold, and at the same time gives them a troubling human intensity that challenges the spectator. This union of formal beauty and vital expression marks many of Delacroix's other Oriental subjects, notably *Fanatics of Tangier* (1838; private collection) and *Jewish Wedding* (1839; Louvre).

King Louis Philippe's government and subsequent ones favored Delacroix with commissions for architectural decorations, more numerous and important than fell to the lot

Eugène Delacroix, *Algerian Women in Their Harem*, 1834. Louvre, Paris. A painting inspired by the artist's North African sojourn.

of any other master of the century. The grand allegories in the Salon du Roi of the Palais Bourbon began the series (1833–36), followed by the decorations in the Library of the Palais Bourbon (1838–47) and the Library of the Luxembourg (1840–47), the ceiling of the Galerie d'Apollon at the Louvre (1850), and the decorations in the Hôtel de Ville (1852; destroyed 1871) and the Chapel of the Angels in St-Sulpice (1849–61). Delacroix was the last great muralist in the tradition of the baroque, unafraid of huge surfaces and capable of interpreting meaningfully the old themes of myth, religion, and history.

Delacroix's powers of monumental composition are manifest also in such large canvases as *The Justice of Trajan* (1840; Rouen, Museum of Fine Arts) and *Entry of the Crusaders into Constantinople* (1841; Louvre). Here, too, appears his mature technique of modeling form with interwoven strands or tight hatchings of contrasting colors that blend into vibrant harmonies when seen at a distance.

The late work of Delacroix continues the themes of his early years: Oriental subjects, dramatic lion or tiger hunts (1854, Louvre; 1855, Bordeaux, Museum of Fine Arts; 1858, Boston, Museum of Fine Arts; 1861, Chicago, Art Institute), romances from Tasso and Ariosto, religious subjects (*Christ on the Sea of Galilee*, 1853, New York, Metropolitan Museum; Baltimore, Walters Art Gallery; and elsewhere), and historical evocations and classical myths (*Medea*, 1862, Louvre; *Orpheus and Eurydice*, 1862, Montpellier, Fabre Museum). His compositional arrangements become larger, simpler, more serene; his execution, broader; and his palette, more complex in its nuances and accords of color. The specifically "romantic" flavor gives way to a conception too personal to be classifiable in any broad category. At the Salon of 1855 his work was exhibited along with that of his lifelong rival, Ingres. By that time the dichotomy of "classic" and "romantic" had largely lost all meaning; of the two, the "romantic" Delacroix was also the more traditional, the more gifted for monumental decoration, and the more deeply imbued with the spirit of classical epic or fable.

Often attacked for his supposed inability to draw, Delacroix is in fact one of the great expressive draftsmen of modern times. He not only left a substantial *oeuvre* of etchings and lithographs (L. Delteil, *Le Peintre-graveur*, vol. 3, Paris, 1908), but also proved in thousands of water colors and pen or pencil studies that line and tone were as important to him as color. His affinities with the baroque are particularly apparent in these drawings. The essence of his draftsmanship is the expression of energy, of motion and gesture, rather than the delineation of precise contour—hence his often untidy, rough, "incorrect" manner.

Delacroix left no coherent "school" at his death, but the suggestions contained in his work preoccupied painters later in the century, far beyond the confines of the so-called romantic movement. Traces of his influence are found in the work of the impressionists and neoimpressionists, even in Van Gogh, and, more recently, Picasso.

See also PARIS: MUSEUMS (DELACROIX MUSEUM).

BIBLIOGRAPHY. A. Robaut, *Oeuvre complet d'Eugène Delacroix*, Paris, 1885; E. Moreau-Nélaton, *Delacroix, raconté par lui-même*, 2 vols., Paris, 1916; E. Delacroix, *Oeuvres littéraires*, Paris, 1923; R. Escholier, *Delacroix: Peintre, graveur, écrivain*, 3 vols., Paris, 1926–29; A. Joubin, ed., *Journal d'Eugène Delacroix*, 3 vols., Paris, 1932; A. Joubin, ed., *Correspondance générale d'Eugène Delacroix*, 5 vols., Paris, 1936–38; W. Pach, *The Journal of Eugene Delacroix*, New York, 1937; H. Wellington, tr., *The Journal of Eugene Delacroix*, London, 1951.

LORENZ EITNER

DELACROIX, HENRI, *see* CROSS, HENRI-EDMOND.

DELAFOSSE, JEAN-BAPTISTE. French engraver (1721–75). Delafosse was a pupil of Fessard and was active in Paris. He distinguished himself in a number of engraving styles. For book illustration he made vignettes, *culs-de-lampe*, and other embellishments after Oudry, Gravelot, and Eisen, and he did portraits after Carmontelle. His most important works are clever prints, mostly after Carmontelle, which are worked in the size of the original. Delafosse had knowledge of a new color technique; he left the notes on this process to the Abbé of St-Non, for whom he had illustrated an extensive series, *Voyage pittoresque; ou, Description des royaumes de Naples et de Sicile* (5 vols., Paris, 1781–86). He became an art dealer toward the end of his life.

DELAMAIRE, RENE ALEXIS. French architect (1675–1745). He worked in Paris. Son of a master mason, he trained in De Cotte's workshop. Delamaire's style continues the freedom of planning and long, low elevations introduced by Jules-Hardouin Mansart. Delamaire's chief work is considered to be the remodeling of the complex of the Hôtels de Soubise and Rohan (1705–09). *See also* ROCOCO ART.

DELANO AND ALDRICH. American architectural firm of William A. Delano (1874–1960) and Chester H. Aldrich (1871–1940). It was founded in 1903, and was dissolved in 1940 on Aldrich's death. The firm specialized in private residences for the wealthy; in these there was usually a subtle blending of elements from the early Georgian of Sir Christopher Wren's time with the Regency style. Delano, through his friendship with Cornelius Vanderbilt III, received the commission for the Walters Art Gallery in Baltimore, Md., which the firm erected in an Italianate vein. Though they were not inclined to promote progressive architecture, Delano and Aldrich are to be admired for a fineness of detail: usually their high narrow doors are done with great finesse. The firm built the brick-faced James A. Burden residence at Syosset, Long Island, N.Y.; the Chapin School in New York City; and the Charles A. Lindbergh residence (1931) at Hopewell, N.J.

BIBLIOGRAPHY. W. L. Bottomley, "A Selection from the Works of Delano and Aldrich," *The Architectural Record*, LIV, July, 1923.

DELAPORTE, ROLAND, *see* ROLAND DE LA PORTE, HENRI HORACE.

DELARAM, FRANCIS. English engraver (b. London, ca. 1590; d. there, 1627). Of French origin, Delaram worked for a number of London publishers doing title pages and portraits of English nobility, bishops, and statesmen—some from life, for example, *Bishop John King*. His best work is a series of title pages for G. Wither's *Preparation to the Psalter* (London, 1619). His style is in the "hard" tradition of Simon van de Passe.

BIBLIOGRAPHY. F. M. O'Donoghue, *Catalogue of Engraved British Portraits Preserved in . . . the British Museum*, 6 vols., London, 1908–25.

DELAROCHE, PAUL. French painter (b. Paris, 1797; d. there, 1856). One of the most successful history painters of his time, he began his career as a student of Watelet and Gros. Delaroche made his debut in the Salon of 1822 to considerable acclaim, and by 1832 was a professor at the Ecole des Beaux-Arts. In 1834 he traveled to Italy to study Early Christian painting. On his return in 1837 Delaroche was given his most important commission, to decorate the half-dome of the Palais des Beaux-Arts in Paris. The work, *Apotheosis of Art*, was a great triumph, and from that time he was much sought after, particularly as a portrait painter (*Portrait of Pope Gregory XVI*, 1844; Versailles). His major works of history painting include *The Death of Queen Elizabeth of England* (1827; Paris, Louvre) and *The Murder of the Duke of Guise* (1835; Chantilly, Condé Museum).

BIBLIOGRAPHY. P. Colin, *La Peinture européenne au XIXe siècle: Le Romantisme*, Brussels, 1935.

DE LA SONNETTE, JEAN MICHEL AND GEORGES, *see* SONNETTE, JEAN MICHEL AND GEORGES DE LA.

DELATRE (Delattre), JEAN MARIE. French engraver in line and stipple (b. Abbeville? 1745; d. Fulham, near London, 1840). After arriving in Paris and working in Le Bas's workshop, he engraved portraits for the publishers Esnauts and Rapilly. Delatre was established in England shortly after 1770 and worked for Francesco Bartolozzi in the stipple manner, engraving plates after Cipriani, Hamilton, Angelica Kauffmann, Wheatley, and Stothard. He also engraved a series of small illustrations for Bell's *The Poets of Great Britain* (1777–92) and produced work, including portraits and vignettes, for various publishers. His work was not outstanding and he is not considered among the best of the Bartolozzi school.

BIBLIOGRAPHY. E. Delignières, "Un graveur de 95 ans. Delattre (Jean Marie) d'Abbeville, 1745–1840," *Réunion des Sociétés des Beaux-Arts*, XXVI, 1902.

DELAUNAY, ROBERT. French painter (b. Paris, 1885; d. Montpellier, 1941). He was a cubist and a founder of orphism in 1911–12. *See* ORPHISM.

Robert Delaunay, *Runners*, 1926. Delaunay Collection, Paris.

He studied theater design in 1902 and worked with the decorator Ronsin. Delaunay painted part time in Brittany and was influenced by the work of the Pont-Aven group. He carried out independent research in the color theories of Helmholtz, Chevreul, and the neoimpressionists. He was also influenced by Cézanne and Near Eastern decorative art.

The color of Delaunay's 1905 still lifes anticipates that of his later cubist works, but his first major paintings date from 1909–10, when he completed his famous series of *Cathedrals* and *Cities*. His *St-Severin* (1909; Philadelphia Museum of Art) and *Eiffel Tower* (1910; Basel, Art Museum) are documents of Delaunay's own early cubist style and reveal a strongly personal resolution of structural and spatial problems. An active member of the cubist circle after 1910, Delaunay was admired by the Munich Blue Rider group and exhibited his *City of Paris* (Paris, National Museum of Modern Art) in their 1911 exhibition. His principal concerns in 1910 and 1911 were dynamic movement —a kind of "simultaneity" not unrelated to futurist aesthetic—and color based upon delicate interpretations of the spectrum. Color became Delaunay's chief interest in 1912, when he produced his *Windows (Simultaneous Windows)* series. The name orphism was applied to his work by Guillaume Apollinaire, who wrote a poem on the *Windows*. Delaunay exhibited again with the Blue Rider group in Munich in 1912 and at the Galerie Barbazanges, as well as in the controversial cubist Section d'Or show at the Galerie de la Boétie.

He visited Berlin in 1913 and held a one-man show at Herwarth Walden's Der Sturm Gallery. Delaunay's essay *Sur la lumière* was translated by Paul Klee (an admirer of Delaunay) and published in *Der Sturm*. Delaunay's *Homage to Blériot* (Paris, private collection), an orphist work into which the artist introduced literal symbols of aeronautics, was done in 1914. From 1915 to 1920 he lived in Spain; he designed sets for the Diaghilev ballet *Cléopâtre* in 1918. Delaunay's home was a meeting place for the Parisian Dadaists after his return in 1921.

The Galerie Paul Guillaume held a retrospective of his work in 1922. In 1924 Delaunay undertook his *Runners* series and, in 1930, the *Multicolored Disks* (a restatement of his 1912 orphist aesthetic). He was instrumental in founding the first Réalités Nouvelles exhibition in 1939.

Delaunay's orphist development of the cubist style was a major contribution to 20th-century art, and his work was influential upon many artists. With his *Windows* and *Disks* works of 1912, he was one of the early practitioners of abstract art in France.

BIBLIOGRAPHY. Galerie L. Carré, *Robert Delaunay* (exhibition catalog), intro. J. Cassou, Paris, 1946; M. Seuphor, *L'Art abstrait; ses origines, ses premiers maîtres*, Paris, 1950; R. Delaunay, *Du Cubisme à l'art abstrait*, Paris, 1957; Musée National d'Art Moderne, *Robert Delaunay, 1885–1951* (exhibition catalog), Paris, 1957; R. Rosenblum, *Cubism and Twentieth-Century Art*, New York, 1960.

JOHN C. GALLOWAY

DELAUNE, ETIENNE. French printmaker (b. Paris, 1518/19; d. there, 1583). One of the finest engravers of ornament of the French Renaissance, he furnished designs for medalists and goldsmiths and worked in these crafts himself. His vigorous, delicately executed compositions are on a small scale comparable to that used by the German Little Masters.

DELEN, DIRCK VAN, see DEELEN, DIRCK VAN.

DELFF (Deltius), JACOB WILLEMSZ. II. Dutch portrait painter (b. Delft, 1619; d. there, 1661). He was the grandson of the portrait painter Jacob Willemsz. I Delff. He studied first with his father, the portrait engraver Willem Jacobsz. Delff, and then with his grandfather, Michiel Mierevelt. In 1640 Delff was still recorded at Delft, where he seems to have spent most of his life. Most of Delff's early works are strongly influenced by the manner of Mierevelt, as can be seen in his *Portrait of a Man* (1642; Rotterdam, Boymans–Van Beuningen Museum). However, some of his later works show the influence of the Amsterdam style of Bartholomeus van der Helst and the courtly style of Anthony van Dyck.

DELFF, WILLEM JACOBSZ. Dutch engraver and (allegedly) portrait painter (b. Delft, 1580; d. there, 1638). He was the son of Jacob Delff and studied with his father. It is not established, however, where Willem learned engraving, at which he was exceptionally skilled. It may have been in the workshop of Wierix under C. Goesius, which would explain the stylistic similarities between Hendrick Goltzius (Goesius's teacher) and Delff. Between 1600 and 1610 he worked mostly for publishers and book dealers. In 1613 Delff was admitted to the guild of Delft, and in 1618 he married the daughter of Michiel Mierevelt, whose portraits he copied with extraordinary mastery and with whom he worked for twenty years. Eventually Delff received the title "Engraver to the King of England." The major portion of his *oeuvre* is engraved portraits, and most of them are after Mierevelt.

BIBLIOGRAPHY. D. Franken, *L'Oeuvre de W. J. Delff . . .* (catalog), Amsterdam, 1872.

DELFT, MASTER OF. Netherlandish painter and designer of woodcut book illustrations (fl. Delft, ca. 1490–1520).

This master was named by Max J. Friedländer on the basis of a triptych in the National Gallery in London. His style is related to that of the Master of the Virgo inter Virgines, who also was active in Delft. *See* MASTER OF THE VIRGO INTER VIRGINES.

BIBLIOGRAPHY. M. J. Friedländer, *Die altniederländische Malerei*, vol. 10, Berlin, 1932.

DELFT: MUNICIPAL MUSEUM (Prinsenhof). Dutch collection. The Oranje-Nassau Museum was brought to this former Convent of St. Agatha from The Hague in 1959. Since this complex of buildings became the residence of the Prince of Orange after 1572, it now appropriately serves as a historical museum for the houses of Orange and Nassau, containing portraits of stadholders and paintings, prints, drawings, letters, proclamations, coins, and costumes connected with the Dutch princes. Also on view are plans, maps, photographs, and coins relating to the history of Old Delft.

DELFTWARE. Tin-glazed earthenware or faïence produced most notably in Delft from the second quarter of the 17th century on. The first record of faïence production in Delft dates from 1584 when the potter Herman Pietersz. moved from Haarlem. In 1611 when the Guild of St. Luke was founded in Delft, potters were among the first members, but it was not until the middle of the century that

Delftware. Polychrome faïence jug with Chinese-style decoration, beginning of 18th century.

a significant number of potters were active there. Ceramic production developed as local breweries declined and the capital, labor supply, and buildings made available were adapted to the new industry. The popularity of delftware grew as prosperity in the Netherlands increased and the Dutch East India Company, which imported Oriental porcelains, became more successful. Its decline began with the manufacture of true porcelain in Europe and was accelerated by the development of inexpensive wares in Staffordshire. Although referred to as "porceleyne," delftware was never an imitation of the porcelain body, but rather a high-fired earthenware that could be decorated under the glaze in a few colors such as blue, copper green, iron red, and yellow. During the 18th century a full range of color was achieved by applying other colors at a second firing in a muffle kiln.

Delft styles can be divided into two categories, depending on whether the inspiration is Oriental or European. Best known are the blue-and-white wares that imitate Wan Li and Ming designs. In polychrome, wares following the Chinese *famille verte* and the Japanese Arita (or Imari) patterns were introduced first in the 17th century. Occasionally Dutch figures were added to Oriental designs. European forms, inspired by metal designs first and later by porcelain, were used with decoration often inspired by contemporary painting. The heaviness of the delft body tended to affect both form and decoration so that boldness became characteristic of delft. A type of peasant ware evolved as a subcategory, in which one encounters rural figures, shoes, violins, and birdcages made with naïve charm. From the 17th century on several hundred potters have been identified by marks on their work, but it would be impossible to single out the best. In general, the earlier men are the most respected. During the 18th century there was a tendency for the potteries to be larger and in the control of financiers rather than of artists. By the 19th century the industry had all but disappeared until revivals or reproductions began to be made.

BIBLIOGRAPHY. E. Neurdenburg, *Old Dutch Pottery and Tiles...*, tr. with annotations by B. Rackham, London, 1923.

MARVIN D. SCHWARTZ

DELHI. City of India, comprising New Delhi and Old Delhi. Modern New Delhi, the capital of India, lies on the right bank of the Jumna River adjacent to the sites of a number of earlier cities. Vanished Indraprastha, ascribed to ancient Hindu kings, was the earliest such settlement. A Hindu ruler, Anangpal I, founded a city called Lal Kot or Dilli in the middle of the 11th century, and it was embellished by his successors until a Muslim invader seized the region in 1192. Following that event, it long served as the capital of Muslim kingdoms.

Qutb ad-Din Aibeg extended Dilli to the northeast under the name of Qutb. He began construction of the Qutb Minar about 1200 and erected the now ruined Quwaat ul-Islam Mosque. About 1303 Ala ad-Din Khilji erected a city called Siri on a circular plan at a site still farther northeast, and in 1321 Ghiyas-ud-Din Tughlak, founder of a new dynasty, established the city of Tughlakabad east of the earlier sites. His tomb, completed about 1326, survives. His son, Muhammad bin Tughlak, constructed Jahanpanah at a point between Siri and Qutb. In 1354 another Tughlak ruler, Firuz Shah, had work undertaken on Firuzabad, some miles north of the old cluster. *See* FIRUZABAD; GHIYAS-UD-DIN TUGHLAK, TOMB OF; QUTB MINAR.

Babur established the Mughal dynasty in Delhi in 1526, and Humayun, his son and successor, built the town of Din Panah south of Firuzabad. The mausoleum of Humayun, completed in 1556, stands in this area. For a brief period during Humayun's reign the area was taken over by Sher Shah Sur, who erected still another town, Shergah, on the site of Firuzabad. *See* HUMAYUN'S TOMB.

The Mughal ruler Shah Jahan built Shahjahanabad, the present Old Delhi, north of Firuzabad between 1644 and 1658. He embellished this splendid city with the great Jami Masjid (1644–58) and the Red Fort (1638–48). Within the red sandstone walls of the fort, mosques and royal structures are strewn in a parklike setting. The Red Fort and other structures of this city were plundered and damaged by the forces of Nadir Shah of Iran in 1739. *See* FORT, DELHI; JAMI MASJID, DELHI.

Structures of historic interest, other than those mentioned above, are numerous. They include, in the vicinity of the city, the tomb of Mubarak Shah Sayyid of 1434; the tomb of Isa Khan, erected about 1547 on a type developed by the Lodi kings; the tomb of Adham Khan of 1561, another version of the Lodi type of structure; and the mausoleum of Safdar Jang, completed in 1753, the last great monument of the Mughal period. *See* ADHAM KHAN, TOMB OF; ISA KHAN, TOMB OF; MUBARAK SHAH SAYYID, TOMB OF; SAFDAR JANG, MAUSOLEUM OF.

BIBLIOGRAPHY. R. C. Arora, *Delhi: The Imperial City*, New Delhi, 1953; A. Bopegamage, *Delhi*, Bombay, 1957.

DONALD N. WILBER

DELIN. (Del.). Latin abbreviation for *Delineat* or *Delineavit*, which means "drew it." The abbreviation is often found with the signature of a painter, an engraver, or other type of graphic artist.

DELITIO (De Litio; De Lisio; Delisio; Delisiis), ANDREA II. Italian religious and historical painter (fl. Guardiagrele, ca. 1473). In the Cathedral of Guardiagrele and in the Loggia of the Castle Orsini in Tagliacozzo are remains of frescoes by him. The Cathedral has a signed *St. Christopher*; the castle frescoes originally showed twenty-two heroes and heroines.

DELL, PETER, THE ELDER. German sculptor (ca. 1480–1552). He was born in Würzburg. One of a group of Franconian artists, Dell studied with Riemenschneider and Hans Leinberger. Most Franconian tomb monuments of his time are attributed to him, among them the *Epigraph of Bishop von Bibra* in Würzburg Cathedral.

BIBLIOGRAPHY. A. Feulner and T. Müller, *Geschichte der deutschen Plastik*, Munich, 1953.

DELLA BELLA, STEFANO, *see* BELLA, STEFANO DELLA.

DELLA CORNA, ANTONIO. Italian painter of Cremona (fl. 1478–94). Della Corna is known from two signed works, *St. Julian Killing His Parents* (1478; private collection) and an altarpiece (1494; Milan, Bagatti Valsecchi Collection), with sharp, bright, dynamic forms imitating Mantegna.

BIBLIOGRAPHY. Cremona, Museo Civico, Pinacoteca, *La pinacoteca di Cremona*, ed. A. Puerari, Florence, 1951.

DELLA PORTA, GIACOMO, *see* PORTA, GIACOMO DELLA.

DELLA PORTA, GUGLIELMO, *see* PORTA, GUGLIELMO DELLA.

DELLA QUERCIA, JACOPO, *see* QUERCIA, JACOPO DELLA.

DELLA RAGIONE PALACE, *see* PADUA.

DELL'ARCA, NICCOLO, *see* NICCOLO DELL'ARCA.

DELLA ROBBIA, *see* ROBBIA.

DELLAURANA, *see* LAURANA, LUCIANO.

DELLA VALLE, ANGEL. Argentine painter (b. Buenos Aires, 1852; d. there, 1903). Della Valle was trained in Buenos Aires and Florence. In 1883 he returned to Buenos Aires to paint scenes of Indian and Gaucho life (for example, *La vuelta del malón*, 1892; Buenos Aires, National Museum of Fine Arts). He was an influential teacher.

BIBLIOGRAPHY. M. L. San Martín, *Pintura argentina contemporánea*, Buenos Aires, 1961.

DELLO DI NICCOLO DELLI (Nicolao Fiorentino). Italian painter (b. Florence, ca. 1404; d. Valencia, 1470/71). Dello was trained and worked in Florence during a period of great artistic ferment, creating a now faded fresco *Jacob and Esau* in S. Maria Novella (ca. 1425–27). He traveled to Venice in 1427 and to Spain about 1433, where he was knighted and lived, except for a brief return to Italy, until his death. He was widely admired and studied in Spain.

The concerns of Dello's art remained those of the early Italian Renaissance. The genre qualities, picturesque architectural settings, and elegant figures of the northern Italian International Style, as well as the Florentine interest in perspective, are evident in the retable ascribed to him in the Old Salamanca Cathedral (before 1445). More advanced are the monumental nude figures and the *repoussoir* arrangement of the *Last Judgment* fresco in the same Cathedral (begun 1445). Dello's last documented work is the almost completely destroyed series of frescoes in the choir of the Valencia Cathedral (1469–70).

BIBLIOGRAPHY. C. R. Post, *A History of Spanish Painting*, vol. 3, Cambridge, Mass., 1930; G. Pudelko, "Minor Masters of the Chiostro Verde," *The Art Bulletin*, XVII, March, 1935.

DELORME, ANTONIE, *see* LORME, ANTONIE DE.

DE L'ORME (Delorme), PHILIBERT. French architect (1510/15–1570). The son of a master mason, Philibert de l'Orme went to Rome (ca. 1533), where he studied and measured the buildings of antiquity and moved in distinguished humanist circles. He also met Rabelais, who became his friend and admirer. Philibert began his career as an architect in his native Lyons in 1536. In 1540 he went to Paris and in 1547 was commissioned by Diane de Poitiers to build her château at Anet (completed ca. 1552). On the accession to the throne of Henry II, Philibert was appointed Superintendent of Buildings. He was the most influential artist in France during Henry's reign (1547–59). Among his royal commissions was the tomb of Francis I at St-Denis (begun 1547). At the King's death Philibert was dismissed by the queen mother, Catherine de Médicis, and replaced by her countryman Primaticcio.

Philibert was in disgrace for several years, and during this period he wrote two treatises, *Nouvelles inventions pour bien bastir et à petits frais* (1561) and *Architecture* (published in nine books, 1567). The latter is based on Vitruvius and Alberti but is of interest because of its personal approach, characterized by independence, national feeling, and sense, in combining theory and practice. Almost all Philibert's buildings have been destroyed and, with the exception of parts of Anet and the tomb of Francis I, are known only through his engravings.

The chapel and entrance gate of Anet are still *in situ*; the frontispiece of the main block is in the court of the Ecole des Beaux-Arts in Paris. The frontispiece is a fine example of the new monumental and correct classicism that Philibert introduced into French architecture. The chapel is the first important adoption in France of the Renaissance type of circular domed church. The entrance to Anet, probably built in 1552, is a uniquely original and imaginative structure. It is conceived as a composition of interacting rectangular blocks virtually devoid of classical elements ascending to a central slab with a clock flanked by consoles and niches. Benvenuto Cellini's bronze relief, now replaced by a copy, was in the lunette over the door. The gate is surmounted by the bronze figures of a stag and two hounds, which move when the hour strikes.

Toward the end of his life Philibert was once more in royal favor and prepared plans for the Tuileries and for the completion of the château at St-Maurs-des-Fossés for Catherine de Médicis (he had begun St-Maurs for Cardinal du Bellay in 1540). Through his works and engravings Philibert was the most influential figure in the creation of French classical architecture of the 16th century. The decorative part of the screen in St-Etienne-du-Mont in Paris (ca. 1545) with its pierced balustrades and spiral staircase has been attributed to him.

BIBLIOGRAPHY. A. Blunt, *Art and Architecture in France, 1500–1700*, Baltimore, 1954; A. Blunt, *Philibert de l'Orme*, London, 1958.
HELLMUT WOHL

DELOS. Small Greek island, one of the Cyclades. It played a major role in Greek history, from the Mycenaean period to the Roman Empire, as a religious center.

The earliest settlement on Delos, dating from the end of the 3d millennium B.C., was situated on Mt. Cythnos (ca. 370 ft. high) in the center of the island. During the middle Bronze Age (ca. 2000–1600 B.C.) the island seems to have been under Minoan influence, although the archaeological remains are very scant. In the late Bronze Age (ca. 1600–1100 B.C.), presumably under the domination of Mycenaean Greeks from the mainland, Delos blossomed into a religious center, devoted to a divine triad—two goddesses and a male child-god—which, in the 1st millennium, was identified as Artemis, Leto, and Apollo. In the wake of the Dorian invasions of Greece (ca. 1100 B.C.) another wave of mainland Greeks, the Ionians, came to Delos, and it seems to have been they who made Apollo the principal

Philibert de l'Orme, illustration for the treatise *Architecture* (Book IX).

god of the island. From this time on the island was always dominated by Ionian Greeks, especially by the island of Naxos (ca. 700–550 B.C.) and Athens (from the Peisistratid tyranny to the beginning of the Hellenistic period). From 315 to 166 B.C. Delos maintained its independence as part of an island confederacy. The Romans restored the island to Athens in 166 B.C., and it soon became an important trading point as well as a religious center. Mithridates of Pontus sacked Delos in 88 B.C.

Excavations on Delos were begun by the French in 1872 and still continue. The most important archaeological remains center in the Hieron (sanctuary) of Apollo, which is located in a level area northwest of Mt. Cythnos. Three temples of Apollo, one dating from the Archaic period (ca. 550 B.C.) and the other two, in their initial stages, from the 5th century B.C., have been excavated here. The sanctuary of Artemis was situated just west of these temples. The three other important archaeological areas on Delos are: (1) the area of the sacred lake north of the Hieron—here, around a small lake connected with the cult of Apollo, were many spacious Hellenistic and Roman structures, including a gymnasium, an agora, private houses, and an archaic terrace surmounted by the famous marble lions of Delos; (2) the area of the theater (2d cent. B.C.) south of the Hieron; and (3) the area southeast of the Hieron on the slope of Cythnos where a number of well-preserved Hellenistic houses and sanctuaries (dedicated mostly to Oriental deities) have been excavated. The private houses at Delos are especially noteworthy. They form, along with those of Olynthus, the basis of our knowledge of the domestic architecture of ancient Greece.

BIBLIOGRAPHY. Ecole Française d'Athènes, *Exploration archéologique de Délos...*, 26 vols., Paris, 1909–65; P. Roussel, *Délos*, Paris, 1925; H. Gallet de Santerre, *Délos primitive et archaïque*, Paris, 1958.
JEROME J. POLLITT

DELPHI. Site of the famous oracular shrine of Apollo situated on the south slope of Mt. Parnassus, about 2,000 feet above sea level, facing the Corinthian gulf.

Archaeological evidence as well as ancient tradition indicates that it was already a religious center in the Late Minoan and Mycenaean periods, perhaps consecrated to an earth divinity whom later generations remembered as Python (hence "Pythian" games, and so on), the snake whom Apollo slew when he took possession of the sanctuary. By the 7th century B.C. the cult of Dionysos had penetrated Delphi, and thenceforth Apollo shared the proprietorship of the sanctuary with Dionysos.

Delphi was the most important religious center in Greece. The oracles delivered by the priestess of Apollo had a deep influence on the politics, morality, and philosophy of all the Greek city-states. The number of famous monuments—buildings, statues, and paintings—set up at Delphi is so great that one could trace the entire history of Greek art through them.

Approaching Delphi along the main road from the east one came first to an outer sanctuary now known as the Marmaria (quarry). The most important remains in this area are parts of a 7th-century Temple of Athena Pronaia, one of the earliest Doric temples known; the Great Tholos (400 B.C.), an early example of the Corinthian order; and a gymnasium and running track (4th cent. and later).

Above the Marmaria was the famous Castalian Spring, and following the road westward one came to the walled precinct of Apollo. A winding road known as the Sacred Way led up the slopes to the actual Temple of Apollo, where the oracle was situated. The temple of which the foundations are now visible was built about 360 B.C. to replace one built in 513–505 B.C. by the Athenian clan, the Alcmaeonidae. The earlier temple, which was destroyed by an earthquake, was one of the first Doric temples for which marble was used.

Many smaller monuments clustered along the Sacred Way. These were principally of two types, treasure houses, or treasuries, erected by individual Greek cities and victory monuments. Famous examples of the former class are the Treasury of the Siphnians (525 B.C.), with its famous sculptured frieze, and the Treasury of the Athenians (ca. 510–500 B.C., now reconstructed). Notable among the victory monuments, which dated from all periods of ancient history, were the Stoa of the Athenians, commemorating the victory at Salamis; the Serpent Column (now in Istanbul), commemorating the Greek victory at Plataea; and the monument of the Roman general Aemilius Paulus, set up after his victory over the Macedonians at Pydna in 168 B.C. Situated on the slope above the temple were the Lesche (clubhouse) of the Cnidians, with its famous murals by Polygnotos, and a theater (4th cent. B.C.), and considerably farther up the slope was the well-preserved stadium where the quadrennial Pythian games were held. *See* POLYGNOTOS; SIPHNIAN TREASURY. *See also* CHARIOTEER OF DELPHI; SICYONIAN TREASURY.

BIBLIOGRAPHY. Ecole Française d'Athènes, *Fouilles de Delphes*, Paris, 1902– ; F. Poulsen, *Delphi...*, tr. G. C. Richards, London, 1920.
JEROME J. POLLITT

DELTIUS, JACOB WILLEMSZ. II, *see* DELFF, JACOB WILLEMSZ. II.

DE LUE, DONALD. American sculptor (1898–). Born in Boston, he studied there at the School of the Museum of Fine Arts and then was apprenticed to Robert Baker, an English sculptor living in Boston. De Lue went to Paris and Lyons to continue his studies. Returning to the United States, he acted as assistant to the sculptor Bryant Baker, Robert's brother, in New York City. De Lue opened his own studio in New York in 1938.

He has executed many sculptural commissions for buildings, for example, *Law* and *Justice* (both granite) for the United States Courthouse in Philadelphia, *The Alchemist* (limestone) for the Chemistry Building at the University of Pennsylvania in Philadelphia, and the *Triton Fountain* (marble) for the Federal Reserve Bank in Philadelphia, all of 1940. He executed six granite panels for the Harvey Firestone Memorial (1950) in Akron, Ohio, and six bronze shields and an American eagle (1953) for the Federal Reserve Bank in Boston.

Among his most famous works are the 22-foot figure in bronze for the United States Military Cemetery at Omaha Beach, St-Laurent, Normandy; the Boy Scout Memorial in Washington, D.C.; and *The Rocket Thrower*, a theme sculpture in bronze for the World's Fair of 1964–65 in New York. His style is heroic and monumental.

BIBLIOGRAPHY. C. L. Brummé, *Contemporary American Sculpture*, New York, 1948; J. F. Morris, ed., *Donald De Lue*, Athens, Ga., 1955.

DELVAUX, LAURENT. Belgian sculptor (b. Ghent, 1696; d. Nivelles, 1778). He was a pupil of the Ghent sculptor

Delphi. Remains of the shrine of Apollo.

Paul Delvaux, *Le Cortège*, 1963. Private collection, Brussels. A characteristic work by the Belgian surrealist painter.

J.-B. van Helderberghe, and at eighteen entered the Brussels atelier of P.-D. Plumier. In 1717 Delvaux went to London, where he collaborated on the tomb of the Duke of Buckingham (Westminster Abbey) and worked especially for the Duke of Bedford. In 1726 he went to Antwerp and Rome and then returned to Belgium. His most significant works are church pulpits: *Elie in the Desert* (1739–49) for Nivelles and the allegorizing pulpit of the birth of Christ, *Time Discovering Truth* (1741–45; Ghent, St. Bavon). His religious works show the influence of Bernini.

BIBLIOGRAPHY. G. Willame, *Laurent Delvaux...*, Brussels, 1914; M. Devigne, *Laurent Delvaux et ses élèves*, Brussels, 1928.

DELVAUX, PAUL. Belgian painter (1897–   ). He was born in Antheit and studied classics in Brussels. After switching to painting, he spent three years working at the Brussels Academy under Montald. His early work was influenced by the Belgian expressionists Permeke and Smet. Traveling through Italy and France, he discovered Chirico and surrealism, met Magritte, and became a surrealist about 1935. The strange atmosphere of his paintings is induced by nude women and clothed men wandering among classical ruins or down long streets, isolated, yet on some mysterious errand, as in *Phases of the Moon* (1939; New York, Museum of Modern Art).

BIBLIOGRAPHY. R. Gaffe, *Paul Delvaux*, Brussels, 1945; P.-A. De Bock, *Paul Delvaux*, Brussels, 1967.

DE MAESTRI, *see* ADRIANO FIORENTINO.

DE MAJO, WILLIAM. English graphic designer (1917–   ). Born in Vienna as a Yugoslav citizen, De Majo studied both business and art. He designs for such major British businesses as W. and A. Gilbey, Ltd., and has planned exhibits for such events as the 1951 Festival of Britain.

DE MARS, VERNON. American architect (1908–   ). Born in San Francisco, he studied at the University of California, where he now teaches. He is known for his work in housing, particularly for Chandler Farms, Arizona (1938). He collaborated on the design of the elegant apartment building 100 Memorial Drive, Cambridge, Mass. (1950).

BIBLIOGRAPHY. I. McCallum, "Machine Made America," *The Architectural Review*, CXXI, May, 1957 (*s.v.* De Mars in Section 2: "Genetrix").

DEMARTEAU, GILLES. French engraver (1722–76). He was born in Liège and went to Paris as a goldsmith. He began to engrave ornament plates and developed the method of reproducing drawings in the "crayon manner" to such perfection that they can be mistaken for originals. Much of his work was after drawings by François Boucher.

BIBLIOGRAPHY. L. de Leymarie, *L'Oeuvre de Gilles Demarteau l'aîné...*, Paris, 1896.

DEMETER (Ceres). Powerful fertility and harvest goddess of the ancient Greeks, she was worshiped as Ceres in Rome and presided over all aspects of the cultivation of grain. Demeter is shown as a tall, dignified matron with flowing robe and veil; she and her daughter Persephone were worshiped in the rites of the Eleusinian mysteries. The two goddesses often appear in Greek art accompanied by Triptolemus, a mortal whom Demeter sent abroad to spread the knowledge of agriculture and settled living.

DEMETER OF CNIDUS. Hellenistic statue (ca. 350 B.C.) in the British Museum, London. It was discovered on the

Charles Demuth, *Still Life*. A water color with all traces of brushwork removed and mottling obtained by blotting.

island of Cnidus in the Precinct of the Deities of the Underworld. The goddess is represented seated in a dignified pose. The figure is of massive proportions, and the body is enveloped entirely in a heavy himation with rich folds. The body is executed of inferior local marble; the head is of Parian marble. The face presents a refined and soft modeling; the expression is that of sadness, which is appropriate for Demeter, who is grieving for her daughter in the underworld. The deep-set eyes are reminiscent of the style of Scopas. The statue was executed by an early Hellenistic artist who was probably associated with Scopas.

BIBLIOGRAPHY. E. A. Gardner, *A Handbook of Greek Sculpture*, 2d ed., London, 1915; M. Bieber, *The Sculpture of the Hellenistic Age*, New York, 1955; G. M. A. Richter, *The Sculpture and Sculptors of the Greeks*, new rev. ed., New Haven, 1957.

DEMI-DOLMEN. Type of dolmen (prehistoric stone, tablelike structure), which lacks one of the supporting sides so that it resembles a simple lean-to. It consists of a large stone slab with one end resting on the ground; the other end is raised by a shorter slab. *See* DOLMEN.

DEMOISELLES D'AVIGNON, LES (Young Ladies of Avignon). Oil painting by Picasso, in the Museum of Modern Art, New York. *See* PICASSO, PABLO.

DEMOSTHENES. Hellenistic statue in the New Wing, Vatican Museums, Rome. A characteristic portrait of Hel-

lenistic art that is both psychologically and realistically interpretive, it was made by Polyeuctus in 280 B.C., some forty years after the orator's death in 322 B.C. The Vatican statue lacks the gesture of clasped hands described by Plutarch, which the copy in the State Museum of Fine Arts in Copenhagen has and which is also duplicated by a statuette in a private collection in New York. The facial features are authenticated by a small bronze bust from Herculaneum as well as by a silver medallion from Miletopolis (Berlin, former State Museums). The work is a tragic representation of a noble spirit and the best example of a standing portrait statue.

BIBLIOGRAPHY. G. M. A. Richter, *A Handbook of Greek Art*, London, 1959.

DEMUTH, CHARLES. American water-colorist (b. Lancaster, Pa., 1883; d. there, 1935). Sickly and lame as a boy, he was encouraged by his family to develop his interest in art. His father was a talented amateur photographer, and his aunt and grandmother were water-colorists. He studied at the School of Industrial Art in Philadelphia, and at the age of twenty-two entered the Pennsylvania Academy of Fine Arts to study under Marin's teacher, Thomas Anschutz. Demuth spent the year 1909 in Paris, where he saw Rodin's water colors, Japanese prints, and the art of Cézanne and Toulouse-Lautrec. He finished his studies in Philadelphia and in 1914 returned to Paris, where he saw and was influenced by the cubist art of Gleizes

Dendera. Open façade of the Temple of Hathor.

and Metzinger. In 1915, in New York City, he came to know Marcel Duchamp, who became a lifelong friend. Demuth joined the gallery of Alfred Stieglitz in New York City. His most productive years were those between 1914 and 1920. Developing diabetes in 1920, he retired to his home town and spent summers from 1930 to 1934 in Provincetown, Mass.

His best-known water colors are those he did from 1914 on of tender spring flowers, acrobats, vaudeville entertainers, café and bar scenes, and illustrations of such stories and plays as Zola's *Nana*, Henry James's *The Turn of the Screw*, and Wedekind's *Erdgeist*. The illustrations were freely developed and were not meant for publication. The figure studies are imbued with a nervous energy and a winsomeness. He favored a fragile, often pulsating pencil line, which moved independently of the movements of the figures and the folds of their costumes. Filmy washes and stains of color complement rhythms rather than define form. In his flower studies, Demuth emphasized delicacy, evanescence, and succulence. He often removed all trace of brushstrokes and obtained a mottled texture by blotting up washes of water color. He turned to tempera in 1919, when he did most of his architectural landscapes. Among these is his abstraction of a Wrenlike church steeple in a manner that recalls Feininger. He reduced forms to facets of light and used intersecting diagonals to suggest shafts of light and shadow. In 1920 he turned to oil paint to compose several studies of factories and other industrial sites. These last works link him with such precisionist artists as Preston Dickinson and Charles Sheeler. *See also* CUBIST REALISM.

BIBLIOGRAPHY. A. C. Ritchie, *Charles Demuth*, New York, 1950.
ROBERT REIFF

DENDERA. One of the most ancient sites in Upper Egypt, on the western bank of the Nile at a loop in the river. Its name is derived through the Greek Tentyra from the Egyptian Enet-ta-ntore. It is renowned for its well-preserved Temple of Hathor, which was built on the site of an older temple by the last Ptolemies and Augustus (1st cent. B.C.) and decorated by other Roman emperors. A massive girdle wall in brick (ca. 954 by 921 ft.) surrounds the Temple of Hathor and its two mammisis (temples dedicated to the birth of the deity's son, who is destined to be the reigning Pharaoh), a sacred lake, a rear Temple of Isis, and a later Coptic church.

The Temple of Hathor proper is within a rectangular enclosure oriented perpendicularly to the river bank (nearly north-south). There is no pylon or columned portico in front of the great vestibule. The open façade, characteristic of the late temples, consists of columns and intercolumnar screen walls, and fronts on three other rows of columns. All the columns are Hathoric; those in the vestibule are the largest of the type (ca. 47 ft. high; capitals ca. 17 ft. high). The screens are covered with scenes in low relief of a particular style, emphasizing modeling, and represent the ritual procession of the king to the temple.

On the walls the successive Roman emperors are shown presenting offerings, and on the ceiling are astronomical subjects. The hypostyle is a rather small room with six columns flanked by two rows of three chambers. From the two sides of the following chamber rise a straight staircase (east) and a newel staircase (west) to the terrace. A second antechamber fronts on a large dark sanctuary for the sacred boat, which is surrounded by various rooms and a kiosk. Windows are either apertures in the ceiling (vestibule) or in the side walls, and are closed with gratings in the shape of Hathoric colonnettes. Within the thickness of the outer walls there are twelve independent crypts below ground level, accessible by means of trap doors on a high aperture in the wall and shut with sliding slabs. Their walls are decorated with colored reliefs representing the ritual objects kept in these apartments. On the terrace is a shrine to Osiris, the rear room of which had a representation of a circular zodiac on its ceiling (Paris, Louvre).

The mammisis are two small temples set at right angles to the main one and dedicated to the nativity of the son of Hathor, who is to be the reigning king. The one nearer the temple is the earliest known and was built by Nectanebo. The second dates from the time of the Roman emperors and features a sanctuary surrounded on three sides by a peripteron with plant columns, capitals with bas-reliefs, and intercolumnar screen walls.

Between the mammisis is a Coptic church (5th cent.) built of stone on a rectangular plan. It has remarkable decorative carvings, a narthex with a rounded niche at each end, a nave with two aisles, and a trefoil sanctuary, which is probably the most refined example in Coptic architecture. The brick structures south of Nectanebo's mammisi are healing baths similar to the Greek *abaton*. The rectangular lake southwest of the temple has four stairways descending along its sides to the bottom and an inner staircase leading down to a lower level.

See also EGYPT.

BIBLIOGRAPHY. E. Chassinat, *Le Temple de Dendara*, 6 vols., Cairo, 1934–52; M. Alliot, *Le Culte d'Horus à Edfou*, 2 vols., Cairo, 1949–54; F. Daumas, *Les Mammisis de Dendara*, Cairo, 1959.
ALEXANDER M. BADAWY

DENEYN, PIETER, *see* NEYN, PIETER PIETERSZ. DE.

DENGESE, *see* AFRICA, PRIMITIVE ART OF (CENTRAL AFRICA: CONGO-LEOPOLDVILLE).

Maurice Denis, *Homage to Cézanne*, 1900. National Museum of Modern Art, Paris.

DENIS, MAURICE. French painter (b. Granville, 1870; d. Paris, 1943). He spent his entire life in St-Germain-en-Laye. At the Lycée Condorcet he met Lugné-Poë, Roussel, and Vuillard, and he met them again in 1888 at the Académie Julian. He became a member of the Nabis and defined its aesthetics in an article in *Art et critique* (1890), where he counseled: "Remember that a picture—before being a horse, a nude, or some sort of anecdote—is essentially a flat surface covered with colors arranged in a certain order" (1890).

Through Sérusier, who returned from Brittany in 1888, Denis was introduced to the message of Gauguin, whose ideas on symbolism and its offspring, synthetism, were taking shape. Denis's unmodeled forms and subtle contours reveal also the influence of the Art Nouveau style. In 1892 he received his first commission, to decorate the ceiling of Henri Lerolle's home. Meanwhile the Académie Julian group (Denis, Sérusier, Bonnard, Vuillard, Roussel, Piot, and Ranson) began to react against impressionism, which nevertheless these men admired. Denis's keenness for ideas led him to treat his subjects with more complex significance than simple landscape or still life, as in *The Muses* (1893; Paris, National Museum of Modern Art).

In 1895 and 1897 Denis made trips to Italy, where he admired Quattrocento frescoes and those by Raphael in the Vatican Stanze. This led to a more vigorous modeling of forms and a more traditional use of perspective. A profoundly religious artist, Denis turned to his faith for themes. An intellectual and poetic concept, symbolism suited his demands that a picture not only should be a material representation of the external world but also should express and suggest thoughts or states of mind (*Ave Maria with Red Slippers*, 1898). In 1900 he painted what is perhaps his most famous work, *Homage to Cézanne* (Paris, National Museum of Modern Art), a continuation of Fantin-Latour's paintings on the same theme. Around a still life that belonged to Gauguin, Denis grouped a number of his friends who admired the master of Aix. The predominating importance given to Redon is characteristic of Denis.

Denis was one of the most important theorists of his time. His painted work is a reflection of his attitude, which gradually caused him to devote himself exclusively to religious art. Yet there was a strange contradiction between Denis's work and his ideas. One of the first to stress the all-important principle that a work of art should find its justification in itself, Denis reestablished the primary importance of the subject.

BIBLIOGRAPHY. F. Fosca, *Maurice Denis*, Paris, 1924; S. Barazzetti-Demoulin, *Maurice Denis*, Paris, 1945; P. Jamot, *Maurice Denis*, Paris, 1945.   ARNOLD ROSIN

DENIS (Dionysius) OF PARIS, ST. Bishop and martyr (3d cent.). A missionary sent to Gaul by Pope Fabian, he became the first bishop of Paris. Beheaded with his companions Rusticus and Eleutherius, St. Denis took his head in his hands and walked 2 miles to Montmartre, the place of burial. From the 9th century he has been identified with Dionysius the Areopagite, first bishop of Athens, who was converted by Paul. The legends were fused. St. Denis usually appears with his head in his hands. His attributes are a miter and prison chains. His feast is October 9. *See also* SAINTS IN ART.

DENMARK, MUSEUMS OF. See under the names of the following cities:

Aarhus. Art Museum.

Copenhagen. Museum of Decorative Arts; National Museum; Ny Carlsberg Glyptothek; Rosenborg Palace; State Museum of Fine Arts; Thorvaldsen's Museum.

DENNER, BALTHASAR. German painter and miniaturist (b. Hamburg, 1685; d. Rostock, 1749). He studied in Danzig and at the Berlin Academy. Denner's first success was with portrait miniatures, and he was soon extremely popular in the courts of Europe, including Denmark, where he was invited in 1712, and London, where he worked from 1721 to 1728. The reason for Denner's success was his extremely minute realism, and the miniaturist's concern for meticulous detail was carried over into his paintings of genre, flowers, and still life. His miniature portrait heads of aged people also enjoyed a great vogue.

DENON, DOMINIQUE VIVANT. French diplomat, amateur draftsman, and engraver (b. Givry, 1747; d. Paris, 1825). He cultivated the arts and women, was universally popular, and produced about 500 works. Accompanying Napoleon Bonaparte to Egypt, he recorded the expedition in his *Voyage de la Haute et Basse Egypte* (1802), for which he made the drawings. For this work alone his name would endure. He was named director of the National Museums by Napoleon, a post he kept throughout the Empire period. He is also remembered for his series of engravings after the collection of self-portraits in the Uffizi Gallery, Florence, and for his portraits of women encountered in his diplomatic travels.

BIBLIOGRAPHY. A. de La Fizelière, *L'Oeuvre originale de Vivant Denon*, 2 vols., Paris, 1872–73.

DENTICULE. Member in which dentils, or denticles, are cut.

DENTIL. Toothlike cube in Ionic and Corinthian cornices. The word is derived from the Latin *dentes*, meaning "teeth." Such rectangular blocks, usually in the bed mold of a cornice, have been assumed to represent originally the ends of wooden joists carrying a flat roof.

DENTONE, GIOVANNI (Zuan da Milano). Italian sculptor (fl. Padua, 16th cent.). He was a student of Antonio Lombardo and Cristoforo Solari. Dentone's major work is a marble group of Admiral Capello and St. Helena in SS. Giovanni e Paolo, Venice. He also executed one of the nine large miracle reliefs in the Chapel of S. Antonio, Padua, entitled *The Miracle of the Slain Wife* (1524).

BIBLIOGRAPHY. W. G. Waters, *Italian Sculptors*, London, 1926.

DENVER, COLO.: DENVER ART MUSEUM. Collection established in 1923. The museum encompasses the South Wing, which contains the Kress collection of Renaissance paintings and sculpture, as well as European and Mediterranean art; the Oriental Museum, with objects from Eastern countries ranging from China to Persia; and Chappell House, with a distinguished collection of North American Indian art and examples of Spanish Colonial religious folk art of the Southwest in the form of *santos*. The Schleier Gallery houses special exhibitions, and the Living Arts Center has exhibits illustrating the technical aspects of art such as color and form.

In the painting collection there are many portraits, including those of Augustus, grand duke of Saxony, and his wife Anne by Lucas Cranach the Younger; one of Rubens by Van Dyck; a rare example of a Corot portrait, *La Femme à la pensée*; and one of Renoir's many portrayals of his son, *Portrait of Coco*. There are period rooms and a 16th-century wool tapestry by Lucas van Leyden. The museum owns the largest collection of bullfight art in the United States, including Goya etchings.

BIBLIOGRAPHY. E. Spaeth, *American Art Museums and Galleries*, New York, 1960.

DEODATO ORLANDI. Italian painter of the school of Lucca (fl. 1288–1301). He is mentioned in documents of 1288, the date of the signed *Crucifix* in the National Picture Gallery, Lucca, and of 1301, when he signed a *Crucifix* in the Church of S. Miniato al Tedesco and a polyptych in the National Museum of St. Matthew, Pisa. All three works illustrate the gradual dissolution of the Byzantine style.

DEPARTURE, THE. Oil triptych by Beckmann, in the Museum of Modern Art, New York. *See* BECKMANN, MAX.

DE PISIS, FILIPPO, *see* PISIS, FILIPPO DE.

DEPOSITION. Removal of Christ from the Cross; also called Descent from the Cross. The Deposition appears in Byzantine art after the 9th century and in Western art after the 10th (for example, in the Codex Egberti). The scene portrays Joseph of Arimathaea, usually standing on a ladder, lowering the upper part of Christ's body while Nicodemus removes the nails and supports His legs.

DE QUESNOY, JEROME, THE ELDER, *see* DUQUESNOY, JEROME, THE ELDER.

DE QUESNOY, JEROME, THE YOUNGER, *see* DUQUESNOY, JEROME, THE YOUNGER.

DERAIN, ANDRE. French Fauvist painter (b. Chatou, 1880; d. Garches, 1954). Following his regular education

André Derain, *Pinewood at Trez.* Ca' Pesaro, Venice.

at the Collège Chaptal, Derain took painting classes at the Académie Carrière (1898) and the Académie Julian (1904) in Paris. He was a brilliant student, and in 1905 the dealer Ambroise Vollard, introduced to him by Matisse, bought almost all his works and gave him a contract. In that year Derain also participated in the controversial Fauvist show at the Salon d'Automne and at the Galerie Berthe Weill, which in 1906 purchased several of his pictures.

Derain's Fauvist style of 1905–07, which he exemplified in a prolific series of landscapes done during visits to the south of France and London, was the most vigorous phase of his career. His painting is characterized by brilliant (sometimes pure) color, rapid and broken brushwork, and almost spontaneous composition. His 1906 landscapes and occasional portrait studies are among the most typical Fauvist pictures (*London, Big Ben*, New York, Robert Lehman Collection; *Hyde Park*, Paris, private collection; *Landscape at Collioure*) and relate his style closely to that of Friesz, Matisse, and Vlaminck.

Derain received a contract from Kahnweiler in 1907. During that year and 1908 he met frequently with Picasso, Braque, and other cubist painters and poets. He came under their influence and that of Cézanne, whose 1907 posthumous exhibit had impelled him to restudy the problems of structure and space. His *Still Life with Two Jugs* (1910; Paris, private collection) is a major document of this period of influence.

In 1912 Derain began what is called his "Gothic period," in which he combined cubist and neoclassic manners, especially in figure compositions and portraits (*The Two Sisters*, 1914, Copenhagen, State Museum of Fine Arts; *Portrait of Paul Poiret*, 1915, Grenoble, Museum of Painting and Sculpture; *The Drinker*, 1913–14, Tokyo, Kabutoya Gallery). In 1918 he gave his first one-man show at the Galerie Paul Guillaume. After this his style became increasingly neoclassic, and the earlier Fauvist spontaneity and the more immediate influences of cubism disappeared. His *Pierrot and Harlequin* (1924; Paris, private collection) is characteristic. Derain received the first prize at the Carnegie International in Pittsburgh in 1928 for *La Chasse*. His painting did not undergo a significant change of direction after the 1920s.

He was also prolific as an illustrator and a stage designer. As early as 1902 he illustrated books by Vlaminck, and in 1909 he did drawings for Apollinaire's *L'Enchanteur pourrissant*. After World War I he illustrated works by Breton, Dalize, Salmon, Reverdy, Rabelais, and others. His stage décor included designs for Diaghilev, Poulenc, and Roland Petit. Derain also produced a number of sculptures, especially in 1939.

One of the most prolific and talented of the French Fauves, Derain made a significant contribution, particularly between 1905 and 1912, to early modern painting.

BIBLIOGRAPHY. E. Faure, *A. Derain*, Paris, 1923; "Pour ou contre André Derain," *Chroniques du Jour*, VIII, 1931; D. Sutton, *André Derain*, New York, 1959; J.-P. Crespelle, *The Fauves*, Greenwich, Conn., 1962.   JOHN C. GALLOWAY

DERBY PORCELAIN. Derby porcelain was made in the English town of Derby from about 1750 to 1848 and again from 1876 to the present. One of the great English porcelains, it was made of soft paste in the 18th century. The earliest dated piece is a 1750 creamer in the Victoria

Derby porcelain. Figurine of King Lear, 18th century. Victoria and Albert Museum, London.

and Albert Museum, London. Early production consisted mainly of figures. In 1756 a new factory was opened, and domestic wares were produced. At the time Derby was aptly referred to as "second Dresden" because of the dominant Meissen influence. French influence was more apparent when the neoclassical style superseded the rococo after 1770, and Derby was combined with a Chelsea company. After 1811 bone porcelain was manufactured in Empire and rococo revival styles. Since 1876 the company has produced high-quality porcelain in conservative designs.

BIBLIOGRAPHY. G. Savage, *Eighteenth Century English Porcelain*, New York, 1952; F. B. Gilhespy, *Derby Porcelain*, London, 1961.

DER HAROOTIAN, KOREN. Armenian-American sculptor (1909–   ). Born in Ashodavan, he arrived in the United States at the age of twelve and settled in Worcester, Mass. Largely a self-taught painter, he moved to Jamaica and in 1938 began to carve. While visiting England he sculpted animals; now back in the United States, he does both animals and human figures, generally in stone. He was chosen in 1950 by the Fairmount Park Association in Philadelphia to execute sculptures for the Ellen Phillips Samuel Memorial, and from 1951 to 1953 he carved *The Inventor* (8½ ft. tall, granite) for this commission. He is represented in the Whitney Museum in New York by *Eagles of Ararat* (1955–56; serpentine marble).

He is an exponent of direct carving and frequently contrasts passages of rough and polished surfaces. His style is realistic.

BIBLIOGRAPHY. R. Pearson, *The Modern Renaissance in American Art*, New York, 1954; L. Goodrich and J. H. Baur, *American Art of Our Century*, New York, 1961.

Descent of Amida, Reihokan, Mount Koya, detail of the silk painting, showing the great Amida Buddha.

DERUET (De Ruet; Drevet), CLAUDE. French portrait and history painter (b. Nancy? ca. 1588; d. there, 1660). He was a student of Claude Henriet. In Italy Deruet worked in Tempesta's studio, mostly on battle scenes, and mastered engraving. In 1619 he worked for Henry II of Lorraine and later for Louis XIII. In 1626 he decorated the Church of the Carmelites in Nancy, for which Claude Lorraine, his student, painted the landscape backgrounds. Deruet's historical works are naïve and provincial; his portraits, often allegorical, are stiff and archaic but not devoid of charm.

BIBLIOGRAPHY. F.-G. Pariset, "Claude Deruet," *Gazette des Beaux-Arts*, series 6, XXXIX, 1952.

DESBOUTIN, MARCELLIN. French painter and engraver (b. Cérilly, 1823; d. Nice, 1902). At an early age he copied the wood engravings of Tony Johannot and wrote verse. He was a pupil of the sculptor Etex and of the painter Thomas Couture. After traveling in Holland and England, Desboutin settled in Italy at Ombrellino, where he studied painting, heliogravure, and photography. He returned to Paris to stay in 1872 and became engaged in writing plays, painting, selling pictures, and executing the drypoint portraits for which he is famous. His sitters, who also counted as friends, included Edmond de Goncourt, Berthe Morisot, Manet, Degas, Puvis de Chavannes, Jules Jacquemart, Renoir, Roger Portalis, and Zola.

BIBLIOGRAPHY. N. Clément-Janin, *La Curieuse vie de Marcellin Desboutin, peintre-graveur-poète*, Paris, 1922.

DESCENT FROM THE CROSS. Oil painting by Rubens, in the Cathedral of Antwerp, Belgium. *See* RUBENS, PETER PAUL.

DESCENT OF AMIDA, REIHOKAN, MOUNT KOYA. Japanese silk painting (12th cent.). It represents the Buddhist theology of Raigō, in which the Amida Buddha with his entourage descends to earth to receive the soul of the dying into his Western Paradise of eternal bliss. At the heart of this large picture is the great Amida Buddha, brilliant in gold color, accompanied by a stately group of thirty-one Bodhisattvas, some playing celestial music and some in deep religious devotion. The figures, outlined in red and richly dressed, are friendly and approachable gods, announcing the advent of salvation to the believers.

BIBLIOGRAPHY. Tokyo National Museum, *Pageant of Japanese Art*, vol. 1: *Painting*, pt. 1, Tokyo, 1952; T. Akiyama, *Japanese Painting* [Geneva?], 1961; National Commission for the Protection of Cultural Properties, ed., *Kokuhō (National Treasures of Japan)*, 6 vols., Tokyo, 1963–

DESCENT OF THE GANGES, *see* MAMALLAPURAM.

DESCHAMPS, JEAN AND PIERRE. French architects of the second half of the 13th and the early 14th century. Their work, centered in south-central France, consists of an academic revival of Gothic architecture from the north, especially that of Amiens, St-Denis (the nave), and Soissons. Jean, the elder of the two (and possibly Pierre's father), built the *chevet* chapels of Clermont-Ferrand Cathedral (begun ca. 1250) and was buried there in 1295. The *chevet* was completed according to his plans by Pierre. Jean seems also responsible for Limoges Cathedral (begun in 1276) and the *chevet* of Narbonne Cathedral (begun after 1286). The Cathedrals of Toulouse (begun 1276) and Rodez (begun in 1277) are attributed to him with less certainty.

BIBLIOGRAPHY. H. Stein, *Les Architectes des cathédrales gothiques*, Paris, 1909.

DESCOURTIS, CHARLES MELCHIOR. French engraver (b. Paris, 1753; d. there, 1820). He was a pupil of Jean François Janinet, whose successful formula for printing aquatints in color he adopted. Among his most popular works are four subjects after Nicolas-Antoine Taunay: *Village Fair*, *Village Wedding*, *The Quarrel*, and *The Tambourine*.

BIBLIOGRAPHY. C. E. Russell, *French Colour-prints of the XVIIIth Century: The Art of Debucourt, Janinet, and Descourtis*, London, 1927.

DESERT PALACE. Type of winter palace built by the caliphs of Damascus in the desert at the northern end of the Dead Sea. The most important examples are Qusayr 'Amra and Mshatta, both in Jordan. The former is famous for the mythological scenes executed in the Hellenistic manner that extensively decorate the palace. *See* MSHATTA PALACE; QUSAYR 'AMRA.

DESIDERIO, MONSU, *see* NOME, FRANCOIS DIDIER.

DESIDERIO DA FIRENZE. Italian sculptor and bronze founder (fl. Venice, 1532–45). In 1545 he was mentioned in a document as assistant to Tiziano Minio in casting a baptismal font for the Baptistery of S. Marco in Venice.

DESIDERIO DA SETTIGNANO (Desiderio di Bartolommeo di Francesco detto Ferro). Italian sculptor (b. Settignano, near Florence, ca. 1430; d. there, 1464). Descend-

Desiderio da Settignano, *The Young St. John the Baptist*. **National Museum, Florence.**

ment in S. Lorenzo, Florence, completed in 1461. Authentic but chronologically less secure are the fragments of a marble ciborium, now in the National Gallery of Art, Washington, D.C., identified with a ciborium made for S. Pier Maggiore; a polychrome wood statue of Mary Magdalen in Sta Trinità, completed by Benedetto da Maiano; and a frieze of cherubim heads on the exterior of the Pazzi Chapel, once ascribed to Donatello. To Desiderio have been attributed also a number of exquisitely cut low reliefs, of which the outstanding are the Madonnas in the Arconati-Visconti Collection, Paris, the Sabauda Gallery, Turin, the National Museum (Bargello), Florence, and the Philadelphia Museum of Art; *St. Jerome Kneeling before a Crucifix* in the National Gallery of Art, Washington, D.C.; and *The Young St. John the Baptist* in the Bargello. Several female portrait busts, the most likely of which is the inspired marble bust in the Bargello, and a number of portrait busts of children and of the infant St. John the Baptist have also been attributed to the master.

Desiderio was an expert draftsman and a sculptor of consummate skill who combined strength of design with a virtuoso's command of the marble-cutting technique. His skill as a carver yielded effects ranging from pure surface lyricism to rich polychromy achieved through strong undercutting and the use of the drill. Generally resolute in the subordination of figural content to decorative values, he nevertheless was capable of expressing moods as widely divergent as the ecstatic joy of the angels in the S. Lorenzo tabernacle, the melancholy of St. Jerome in the Washington relief, and the sprightly charm of youth in the left putto of the Marsuppini tomb.

BIBLIOGRAPHY. L. Planiscig, *Desiderio da Settignano*, Vienna, 1942; J. Pope-Hennessy, *Italian Renaissance Sculpture*, London, 1958; I. Cardellini, *Desiderio da Settignano*, Milan, 1962; A. Markham, "Desiderio da Settignano," book review, *Art Bulletin*, XLVI, June, 1964; C. Seymour, *Sculpture in Italy, 1400–1500*, Baltimore, 1966.   DARIO A. COVI

DESIGN. The arrangement of the visual elements of an object or a work of art. In painting and sculpture, line, form, space, light, and color are among the elements that must be controlled in a consistent system, or through design, to create the desired image. In architecture and the decorative arts, design involves integrating functional necessity and a system or vocabulary of ornament. The degree to which the decoration or the function determines the appearance of a building or an object is dependent upon the approach of the designer. Design is the vehicle of expression for the designer, and it reveals the basic concepts of man, varying with each era. The other definition of the word "design" as a preliminary sketch for a work of art is less important in contemporary usage. More commonly, it refers to the arrangement of visual elements and most often to that arrangement in decorative objects. Today, a designer is one responsible for such things as furniture, tableware, and packaging.

Among the earliest known man-made objects are paleolithic utensil handles carved in ivory or bone. In these, animal forms are realistically rendered in positions dictated by the shape of the handle, which was determined by functional needs. The craftsman producing the handle visualized the required form as a familiar animal he rendered faithfully. Another approach in prehistoric times—one associated with neolithic man by some but not all prehis-

ed from a family of stone masons, he was essentially a marble carver and in 1453 matriculated in the Stone and Wood Carvers' Guild of Florence. Although nothing is known of his training, he appears particularly close to Bernardo Rossellino and was indirectly influenced by Donatello. In 1453 Desiderio acted as joint assessor with Antonio Rossellino for the narrative reliefs carved by Andrea di Lazzaro Cavalcanti for the pulpit in S. Maria Novella, Florence; in 1461 he competed for the commission of the *Madonna della Tavola* in the Cathedral at Orvieto.

Only two works by Desiderio are closely datable: the marble tomb of Carlo Marsuppini (d. 1453) in Sta Croce, Florence, and the marble Tabernacle of the Holy Sacra-

torians—involves the use of geometric patterns as decoration. These patterns are either simplifications of familiar images or repetitions of the patterns of one medium in another, as when inscribed lines suggesting woven straw are the decoration of a ceramic jar. Contemporary primitive peoples have continued these two approaches; and, to some degree and at any moment when aesthetic principles have been involved, the development of forms determined by the function of an object and admiration for the natural qualities of the materials used has produced objects and an architecture parallel with the art of earliest times. For many contemporary designers in the applied arts, prehistoric and primitive art is a great source of inspiration. Oriental art has parallel principles that explain its importance to designers of the modern movement.

In the West, including ancient Egypt, there was a tendency to develop vocabularies of ornament consistent for a large variety of objects and for architecture, too. The shapes of objects were determined by the scheme of ornament more than by the immediate functional requirements. Wherever possible, architectonic concepts were applied to the design of small objects. In ancient Egypt, as in ancient Greece and Rome, chests were often conceived as buildings in miniature, and chairs and beds might be animalized by the designing of supports as animal legs. In Egypt decorative motifs were derived from the papyrus tree; in Greece and Rome other natural sources were exploited and idealized for extensive use in the classical style. For this classical style the material used was rarely a factor influencing the design. For example, ceramics were made to look like metal or stone with the surface polished and painted to limit any possible suggestion of the character of clay. In the part of the world where Rome dominated, classical ornament remained influential long after classical concepts were replaced by new approaches to design. *See* CERAMICS; FURNITURE.

In Early Christian, Byzantine, and medieval art, classical ornament persisted in forms determined by tradition and function, but it was treated more abstractly. By the 12th century, when Gothic art emerged, revivals of classical designs preceded the introduction of the Gothic vocabulary of ornament in the decorative arts. The return of the use of the classical vocabulary at the advent of the Renaissance was accompanied by changes in the concepts of design. The vocabulary of ornament remained basically the same through a series of radical changes in style from the Renaissance to the neoclassical period.

The 19th century marked the beginning of historical analysis of design and a critical approach, which involved a continuous search for the principles of design in nature and history. The 19th-century designer sought new vocabularies of design by adapting decorative motifs of the past to suit the new requirements of mass production and of appealing to a mass audience. Reactions against mass production with its traditional ornament brought revivals of the crafts by reformers such as William Morris and, ultimately, new attempts at design without ornament at the beginning of this century. *See* MORRIS, WILLIAM.
See also INDUSTRIAL DESIGN.

BIBLIOGRAPHY. G. Warren, *The Romance of Design*, New York, 1926; W. D. Teague, *Design This Day . . .*, New York, 1940.

MARVIN D. SCHWARTZ

DESJARDINS (Van Den Bogaert), MARTIN. French sculptor (b. Breda, 1640; d. Paris, 1694). He was apprenticed in Antwerp in 1651 to Caspar Pieter Verbruggen I, and then went to Paris to study with Jacques Buirette. Desjardins worked at the Collège Mazarin, the Invalides, and the Sorbonne. He was elected to the Royal Academy in 1671 and was rector there in 1686. His greatest work, in a solid French classic style, was the bronze statue of Louis XIV (1686) for the Place de la Victoire, fragments of which are preserved in the Louvre in Paris.

BIBLIOGRAPHY. L. Dussieux, ed., *Mémoires inédits sur la vie et les ouvrages des membres de l'Académie royale de peinture et de sculpture*, vol. 1, Paris, 1854; A. Michel, *Histoire de l'Art*, vol. 6, pt. 2, Paris, 1922.

DESKEY, DONALD. American industrial and interior designer (1894–   ). A native New Yorker, Deskey was one of the early practitioners of modern, streamlined design in the United States, ranging from bowling-ball racks, printing presses, vending machines, and oil burners to factory and domestic interiors. He has made important contributions to space heating, the use of basement space, and the accommodation of machinery to industrial architecture, and is noted principally for his designs for the interior of the Radio City Music Hall in New York (1932) and for the interior and furnishings of the R. H. Mandell House in Mount Kisco, N.Y., the latter done in collaboration with the architect Edward Durrell Stone.

DESMAREES, GEORGES. Swedish painter (b. Osterby, 1697; d. Munich, 1776). A pupil of Marten Mijtens, he studied in Nürnberg, Augsburg, Venice, and Rome. Desmarées was in Bonn, Kassel, and Würzburg briefly, but worked for the Bavarian court in Munich from 1730 on, internationalizing the elegant 18th-century French portrait style in the manner of G. B. Piazzetta and of Rosalba Carriera.

BIBLIOGRAPHY. A. Feulner, *Bayerisches Rokoko*, Munich, 1923.

DE SMET, GUSTAVE, *see* SMET, GUSTAVE DE.

DES MOINES, IOWA: DES MOINES ART CENTER. Museum established in 1948, housed in a building designed by Eero Saarinen. The collection includes some antiquities and Chinese and Renaissance pieces, but specializes in 20th-century American painting, with works by Calder, Shahn, Feininger, Knaths, Rothko, and Stamos.

BIBLIOGRAPHY. E. Spaeth, *American Art Museums and Galleries*, New York, 1960.

DESPIAU, CHARLES. French sculptor (b. Mont-de-Marsan, 1874; d. Paris, 1946). In 1891 he went to Paris and worked under Hector Lemaire at the Ecole des Arts Décoratifs and then with Barrias at the Ecole des Beaux-Arts. Despiau began to exhibit in 1902. Rodin invited him to join his atelier, and he was the master's collaborator from 1907 until 1914. A trip to Germany during the Occupation of World War II was criticized by his countrymen. He followed the quiet pursuit of a gentle, almost classical, art. His *Paulette* (1907) and *Young Girl from Landes* (1909) are in the Paris National Museum of Modern Art, and *Mme Schulte* and *Assia* (1938) are in the New York Museum of Modern Art. His best work is in the sensitive feminine portrait. The limited success of his art rests on nuance and understatement.

BIBLIOGRAPHY. C. Despiau, *Despiau* [by] W. George, New York, 1959.

DESPLACES, LOUIS. French engraver (b. Paris, 1682; d. there, 1739). He produced a considerable number of tasteful but undistinguished plates in the style of Gérard Audran. His best works are after the painter Jouvenet. Many of Desplaces' models were Italian baroque painters.

BIBLIOGRAPHY. H. Cohen, *Guide de l'amateur de livres à gravures du XVIIIe siècle*, 6th ed., Paris, 1912.

DESPORTES, ALEXANDRE-FRANCOIS. French painter (b. Champaigneulles, 1661; d. Paris, 1743). He was a pupil of the Fleming Nicasius Bernaerts and of François de Troy. Collaboration with Claude Audran III led to Desportes' decorative embellishments of the châteaux of La Muette, Chantilly, and Compiègne and of the Hôtel de Bouillon, as well as to Gobelins tapestry designs (*Les Indes* series, 1735). He was court portraitist to Jean Sobieski in Poland in 1695, then Painter of the Royal Hunt to Louis XIV, executing opulent still lifes with dead game and animated portraits of the royal dogs. His landscape sketches anticipate the plein-air methods of the Barbizon school and the impressionists. His art links the 17th-century Flemish baroque tradition of hunting and still-life painting with the decorative formality of the 18th-century French Regency style.

BIBLIOGRAPHY. L. Hourticq, "L'Atelier de François Desportes," *Gazette des Beaux-Arts*, 5th series, II, 1920.

DESPREZ, JEAN LOUIS. French architect, engraver, and theatrical designer (1743–1803). He lived in Rome, Paris, and Stockholm. A pupil of Jacques François Blondel, Desprez is best known for his work in Sweden, where he lived from 1784, designing theater sets and architectural projects in which he was able to work in a variety of styles.

DE STAEL, NICOLAS, *see* STAEL, NICOLAS DE.

DE STIJL. Dutch purist art movement ("stijl," pronounced "style"; de Stijl means "the Style"). It involved painters, sculptors, designers, and architects whose works and ideas were pooled and disseminated through the periodical *De Stijl* between 1917 and 1931. Its editor, Theo van Doesburg, was the initiator and coordinator of the group. *See* DOESBURG, THEO VAN.

The movement began on June 16, 1917, with the first issue of the periodical. The founders and contributors to the first number were the painters Piet Mondrian, Vilmos Huszar, Bart van der Leck, and Gino Severini; the architects J. J. P. Oud, Jan Wils, and Robert van't Hoff; the sculptor George Vantongerloo; and the poet A. Kok. They were joined later by others, including the architect Gerrit Rietveld. *See* HOFF, ROBERT VAN'T; LECK, BART VAN DER; MONDRIAN, PIET; OUD, JACOBUS JOHANNES PIETER; RIETVELD, GERRIT THOMAS; SEVERINI, GINO; VANTONGERLOO, GEORGE; WILS, JAN.

A program was established in the first number of *De Stijl*, stating that the periodical would articulate a new sense of beauty that was to be communicated to the aesthetically immature members of society. In developing a

Charles Despiau, *Paulette*, 1907. National Museum of Modern Art, Paris. An art of nuance and understatement.

universal visual language, the plastic artists were to subordinate their individuality in order that "they will serve a general principle far beyond the limitations of individuality" (*De Stijl*, vol. 1, no. 1, p. 1). Thus, from the beginning, de Stijl was committed to its fundamental tenets that art is a social and universal activity and that all the plastic arts are interdependent.

Design principles based upon the most astringent minimum of artistic means eventually evolved. Colors were reduced to the primaries and white, gray, and black; form was limited to the rectangle; and composition was based upon the asymmetrical arrangement of perpendicularly oriented planes, flexible space loosely defined by all these visual elements.

In 1924 Van Doesburg published sixteen points of a new architecture in his "Toward a Plastic Architecture" (*De Stijl*, vol. 6, nos. 6 and 7, pp. 78–83), a statement of greater clarity, but less influence, than Le Corbusier's *Vers une architecture* (1923). Van Doesburg called for the banishment of all preconceived architectural forms and the fresh, analytical statement of the problem. Architecture should evolve from the elemental factors of function, mass, plane, time, space, light, color, and material in the most economical and direct manner possible. Monumentality in architecture, according to Van Doesburg, should be replaced by an architecture based exclusively upon the relationship of one thing to another. He called for an architecture of open, dynamic spaces generated by the requirements of the plan, with undecorated, interlocking volumes loosely organized within an asymmetrical framework. Finally, he argued that architecture was the summation of all the plastic arts, that painting and sculpture must be absorbed into architecture.

De Stijl was fundamentally an aesthetic, not a materialistic, movement that aimed to create a universal form language which could be manipulated independently of the personal emotions of the artist. It made a major contribution to modern art by introducing this language to the Bauhaus, where the aesthetic was combined with the practical, seen, for example, in the work of Marcel Breuer. *See* BAUHAUS.

Because of de Stijl's objective quality and social orientation, its principles were immediately applicable to the needs of a modern democratic-technological society. Since the 1920s a de Stijl aesthetic has so completely permeated our man-made environment that it is an integral part of virtually all quality graphic, industrial, and architectural design.

See also NEOPLASTICISM.

BIBLIOGRAPHY. H. L. C. Jaffé, *De Stijl, 1917–1931*, Amsterdam, 1956; T. M. Brown, *The Work of G. Rietveld, Architect*, Utrecht, 1958; R. Banham, *Theory and Design in the First Machine Age*, London, 1960.

THEODORE M. BROWN

DESVALLIERES, GEORGES OLIVIER. French painter, decorator, and designer (b. Paris, 1861; d. there, 1950). He studied in Paris with Elie Delaunay and Gustave Moreau, whose symbolic paintings greatly influenced him. Desvallières' subjects from the early 1900s were primarily sacred or mystical, done with originality and religious fervor. He became interested in church decoration through Maurice Denis and completed several projects, including one for a church in Pawtucket, R.I. In 1919 he founded, with Denis, the Ateliers d'Art Sacré. He also designed stained-glass windows.

BIBLIOGRAPHY. R. Huyghe, *La Peinture française: Les Contemporains*, Paris, 1939.

De Stijl. Vilmos Huszar, *Composition*. 1916.

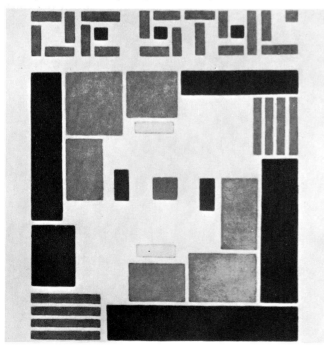

Detmold, Grotto of the Holy Sepulchre. *Descent from the Cross.* Early German Romanesque sculpture, ca. 1115.

DETAILLE, EDOUARD. French painter of military subjects (b. Paris, 1848; d. there, 1912). He was a student of Meissonier. Detaille made his debut in the Salon in 1867 and received early recognition for *Maneuver Rest on a Field at St-Maur* (1869), which was highly praised by Gautier. From his experiences in the Franco-Prussian War Detaille drew his most famous paintings (for example, *The Defense of Champigny*, 1879) and a very popular series of drawings illustrating a text by J. Richard, *L'Armée française* (1883). Detaille executed several important murals in Paris; the most notable was the *Vers la gloire* (1905) in the apse of the Panthéon. His style is particularly notable for the great care he took in rendering details of costumes and weapons and for its historical authenticity; these make his work an important source for the study of the military history of his time.

BIBLIOGRAPHY. M. Vachon, *Detaille*, Paris, 1897.

DETENTE. Term applied by French art historians to late Gothic art, when idealism had begun to replace profusion of detail and intricacy. P. Vitry, in *Michel Colombe et la sculpture française de son temps* (1909), was especially responsible for its use. *Détente*, meaning relaxation, is a term that is most suited to the French art of this early-16th-century period between Gothic and Renaissance expression—between the Gothic concern with death and heaven and the Renaissance concern with life and earthly glory.

DETMOLD: GROTTO OF THE HOLY SEPULCHRE. German chapel in the Teutoburg Forest near Detmold in

Westphalia. The Externsteine is a strange rock formation; a natural grotto here was turned into a chapel, at the entrance of which is a relief carved out of the living rock. The relief, 18 feet high, is a fine example of early German Romanesque sculpture on a monumental scale. It dates from about 1115, and depicts a *Descent from the Cross*.

The relief is in a stiff and angular style. Its linear, nonplastic technique is strongly reminiscent of the decorative linear style of Barbarian art. There is no indication of influence from the developing schools of French Romanesque sculpture in Burgundy and Languedoc, thus pointing out the *retardataire*, isolated nature of German Romanesque sculpture.

BIBLIOGRAPHY. E. Panofsky, *Die deutsche Plastik des XI. bis XIII. Jahrhunderts*, 2 vols., Munich, 1924.

DETROIT: DETROIT INSTITUTE OF ARTS. The present building was opened in 1927 after the city took over the ownership and operation of the former Detroit Museum of Art. All of the world's great schools of art are well represented.

The jewel of the collection is a small room that contains early Flemish paintings, including Jan van Eyck's *St. Jerome in His Study* (1442), once owned by Lorenzo de' Medici, and works by Rogier van der Weyden, Gerard David, and Michiel Sittow. Adjoining it is another room filled with later Flemish paintings, including the masterpiece *The Wedding Dance* by Pieter Brueghel the Elder, a copy of which, long thought to be the original, hangs in Antwerp.

A rich Italian section, filled with Renaissance furniture, contains not only a rare bronze of *Judith* by Andrea del Verrocchio but also a painting of the *Adoration with Two Angels* by him and his famous pupil, Leonardo da Vinci. There are works by Giovanni Bellini (*Madonna and Child*), Botticelli, Chardin, Claude, Constable, Courbet, J.-L. David, Donatello (*Coat of Arms of the Minerbetti Family*), Van Dyck, Pieter de Hoogh, Della Robbia, Fragonard, Gainsborough, Ghiberti (*Madonna and Child*), Van Gogh, Goya, El Greco, Guardi, Hals, Hogarth, Holbein, Murillo, Pisano, Poussin (*Selene and Endymion*), Raphael, Raeburn, Rembrandt, Reynolds, Rodin, Rubens (*Meeting of David and Abigail*), Ruisdael, Sassetta, Tiepolo, Tintoretto, Titian (*Portrait of a Man Holding a Flute*), Velázquez, and Veronese.

The ancient world and the Orient are well represented in pottery, textiles, sculpture, and metalwork. *Early Autumn* by Ch'ien Hsüan is one of the great 13th-century Chinese paintings in the United States.

The American section is the most complete west of the Appalachians. There are four rooms from Whitby Hall, an 18th-century house near Philadelphia. Paintings and sculpture range from Allston to Whistler: outstanding are four paintings by Copley; excellent examples of Smibert, Earl, and C. W. Peale; works of the Hudson River school; and Sloan's *McSorley's Bar*, Eakins's *Portrait of Robert M. Lindsay*, and George Caleb Bingham's *The Trappers' Return*.

The frescoes in the Garden Court were executed by Diego Rivera in 1932–33.

BIBLIOGRAPHY. J. D. Morse, *Old Masters in America*, Chicago, 1955; E. Spaeth, *American Art Museums and Galleries*, New York, 1960.

JOHN D. MORSE

Arthur Devis, *Portrait of a Lady*. Tate Gallery, London.

DEUTSCH, NIKOLAUS, *see* MANUEL-DEUTSCH, NIKOLAUS.

DEUTSCHMANN, JOSEPH ADAM. German sculptor (b. Imst, 1717; d. Passau, 1787). He worked in the studio of Joseph Matthias Gotz and took it over in 1742. Deutschmann produced religious figures in wood, and some in ivory, in the popular theatrical style of the day.

DEVATA. Divine being or god in Buddhism and Hinduism. Devatā most often refers to all the inferior gods.

DEVAUX, MARTIN, *see* VAUX, MARTIN DE.

DEVERELL, WALTER HOWELL. English painter (b. Charlottesville, Va., 1827; d. London, 1854). Deverell was closely associated with the Pre-Raphaelite circle, although he was never formally a member of the Brotherhood. His early death cut short what might have become a distinguished artistic career. His best-known painting, *The Pet* (London, Tate Gallery), gives evidence of a concern with purely pictorial problems, such as broad handling, composition, and light, not shared by all the Pre-Raphaelites. His last paintings, however (left unfinished at his death), suggest a development toward the more normal Victorian concern with anecdote and morality.

BIBLIOGRAPHY. R. Ironside and J. Gere, *Pre-Raphaelite Painters*, London, 1948.

DEVERIA, ACHILLE. French draftsman, lithographer, illustrator, and painter (b. Paris, 1800; d. there, 1859). As a pupil of Louis Lafitte he was made to copy the engravings of Edelinck and Robert Nanteuil. Until 1831 Devéria was known as an illustrator whose work was engraved by lesser artists. He began his lithographic work as early as 1819 with political subjects, changing, from 1823 on, to portraiture (for example, *Victor Hugo*, 1829). He was made librarian of the Cabinet des Estampes in 1848, and then Conservator in 1859 just before his death. To the Cabinet he contributed an important system of iconographic classification that he had worked on all his life. His portraits are precise, lively delineations with minimum shading.

BIBLIOGRAPHY. M. Gauthier, *Achille et Eugène Devéria*, Paris, 1925.

DEVI. Hindu goddess, the consort of Siva and daughter of Himavat (the Himalaya Mountains). Devī is identified with Pārvatī and Umā; her terrible aspects are Durgā and Kālī. *See also* MAHADEVI.

DEVIL. In theology, head of the fallen angels; in general, the personification of evil and sin in Christianity. He is represented in art in a variety of forms: the snake in the Fall of Man; a dragon; or a half-human, half-animal creature with a bird's feet and bill, animal horns, scaly flesh, and bat wings, or a combination of these. In the early Middle Ages, the devil appears as the Tempter of Christ, usually in the person of a dark-skinned angel. In the high and late Middle Ages, he appears in Last Judgment scenes in his half-animal form. He figures in such subjects as the Temptation of St. Anthony and *ars moriendi*, reaching a high point in the art of Jerome Bosch. Italian artists of the Renaissance and baroque periods tended to portray the devil in human form.

BIBLIOGRAPHY. J. Levron, *Le Diable dans l'art*, Paris, 1935.

DEVIL'S WORK. Older Western designation for the finely cut openwork found in some 17th-century Chinese ceramics. The Chinese term for this work is *ling-lung*, referring to the tinkling sound produced by the thin, delicately cut, and often reticulated jade ornaments. Much of the openwork porcelain imitated jade.

DEVIS, ARTHUR. English portrait painter (b. Preston, 1711; d. there, 1787). He specialized in the small conversation piece and may be said to have set the pattern for it before the arrival of Zoffany in England about 1758. Devis traveled a good deal through the north and west of England, where his sitters were members of the landed gentry and the professional classes rather than of the aristocracy. He usually painted on a small scale and never overcame a slight stiffness in the presentation of his groups, which nevertheless have great charm. He probably studied under Tillemans, and this may account for a Dutch reminiscence in his style.

BIBLIOGRAPHY. S. H. Pavière, *The Devis Family of Painters*, Leigh-on-Sea, 1950.

DEWING, THOMAS WILMER. American figure painter (b. Boston, 1851; d. New York, 1938). He studied with Boulanger and Lefebvre in Paris and with Duveneck in Munich. Later he was made an academician and became a member of the Ten.

His pictorial repertoire includes portraits and figure pieces of women. *The Recitation* (1891) reveals his poetic expression of a delicate female nobility. His women are never pretty; they are, rather, beautiful and dignified, frequently slim and tenuous. In their spirit of refinement, his forms are serenely quiet and genteel. His intimate oils possess a precious, jewellike tonality and charm of brushstroke that is never obvious.

BIBLIOGRAPHY. E. Tharp, "T. W. Dewing," *Art and Progress*, V, 1914; N. C. White, "The Art of Thomas W. Dewing," *Art and Archaeology*, XXVII, June, 1929.

DE WINT, PETER. English landscape painter (b. Stone, Staffordshire, 1784; d. London, 1849). The son of a Dutch-

Peter de Wint, *Cornfield. Ivinghoe, Buckinghamshire.* Tate Gallery, London.

American doctor who had settled in England, De Wint was apprenticed in 1802 to the engraver John Raphael Smith, with whom he remained until 1806. A fellow apprentice was the painter William Hilton, a full academician of the Royal Academy of Arts, who became De Wint's intimate friend and whose sister he married in 1810. After leaving Smith, De Wint frequented the house of Dr. Thomas Monro, the famous patron and amateur artist. He also received some informal teaching from John Varley and in 1809 enrolled in the Royal Academy schools. In 1810 he was elected an associate of the Old Water-Colour Society, and in the following year, a full member. He became a successful teacher in London, and took numerous sketching trips to various parts of the country, especially to Lincolnshire and Yorkshire. Only once did he go abroad—to Normandy in 1828; like Cox, he was too insular to have much use for foreign scenery.

Of all the greater English water-colorists, De Wint was most purely a *painter*—the richest colorist. His harmonies are often dark, dominated by shades of plum and purple. Influenced by Girtin and Cotman, he handled the brush with greater freedom than either, and, unlike most of the water-colorists, he also painted in oil throughout his career. His domesticated romanticism foretells the more cerebral complacency and ruralism of much later 19th-century landscape painting. The most comprehensive collection of his work is in the Victoria and Albert Museum, London.

BIBLIOGRAPHY. Sir W. Armstrong, *Memoir of Peter De Wint*, London, 1888; W. S. Sparrow, "The Life and Work of Peter De Wint," in C. Holme, ed., *Masters of English Landscape Painting*, London, 1903; A. P. Oppé, *The Water-colours of Turner, Cox and De Wint*, London, 1925.

DAVID M. LOSHAK

DEXILEOS STELE. Attic grave relief, dated in the beginning of the 4th century B.C. The stele stood in the cerameicus in Athens. An inscription on the relief records that the deceased, Dexileos, fell in battle in 394 B.C. in the war against Corinth. Dexileos is represented on horseback striking a fallen enemy with his spear. The composition of the relief breathes classical purity, which is attained by the contrast between the diagonal planes of the horse and the figure on the ground and the perpendicularity of Dexileos's body. The representation of this tombstone found several adaptations in antiquity and set a type that became particularly popular under the Roman emperors. A copy of the work is in the Villa Albani, Rome.

BIBLIOGRAPHY. E. A. Gardner, *A Handbook of Greek Sculpture*, 2d ed., London, 1915; G. M. A. Richter, *The Sculpture and Sculptors of the Greeks*, rev. ed., New Haven, 1957.

DEYSTER, LOUIS DE. Flemish painter of historical and religious scenes and etcher (before 1656–1711). A native of Bruges, the artist abandoned his artistic career in his later years in order to take up the manufacture of violins and organs. His style is based on Italian neoclassic (primarily Roman) prototypes, translated into a Flemish idiom via Anthony van Dyck.

BIBLIOGRAPHY. H. Fierens-Gevaert, *La Peinture à Bruges*, Brussels, 1922.

DHARMA. Sanskrit term (Pali, *dhamma*) meaning "law." Dharma is the Buddhist law or teaching.

Fra Diamante, *St. Jerome in the Desert with SS. John the Baptist and Ansanus* (attrib.). Fogg Art Museum, Cambridge, Mass.

DHARMACAKRA. Mudrā, or symbolic position of hands, in Buddhist art. It is the attitude of teaching or turning the Wheel (cakra) of the Law (dharma). Both hands are against the chest, the right turned palm outward and the left in, the fingers counting off the Noble Eightfold Path.

DHARMAPALA. Name, meaning "Defender of the Law," applied to Tantric divinities of northern Buddhism, usually eight in number. The Dharmapālas are ferocious but not malignant. They are represented in princely dress.

DHYANA. Sanskrit word referring to the process of concentration of mind in order to experience the ultimate truth. From dhyāna are derived Zen (Japan) and Ch'an (China) Buddhism. *See* ZEN.

DHYANI-BODHISATTVA. Celestial Bodhisattva dwelling in the Arūpadhātu heaven in the body of absolute completeness, in a state of reflected spirituality. The Dhyāni-Bodhisattvas are considered to be five or eight in number. The former group, thought of as emanations from the five Dhyāni-Buddhas, are the creators of the world.

DHYANI-BUDDHA. First *kaya* (body) in the Buddhist trinity, who dwells in the Arūpadhātu heaven in abstract form of perfect purity. The accepted group of five Dhyāni-Buddhas is thought to have originated from Adi-Buddha, from which there evolve the five Dhyāni-Bodhisattvas.

DIACONICON (Diaconicum). Place in which church vessels are kept by deacons; a sacristy. The diaconicon in Greek churches corresponds to the Western sacristy and is generally placed on the south side of the bema, opposite the prothesis.

Diaz de la Peña, *Storm in the Forest of Fontainebleau*. Fitzwilliam Museum, Cambridge, England.

DIADEM. Type of headdress commonly worn in ancient Greece by women and youths. The diadem (Greek, *diadein*, "to bind around") consisted of a simple band, of metal or of woven textile, worn around the forehead. An example is found on the *Diadumenus* by Polycleitus. It is also a heraldic term for the part of the crown that supports the cross or globe at the top.

DIADUMENUS (Diadoumenos). In Greek antiquity, an athlete binding a fillet about his head, over which the victor's wreath was to be placed. The act of tying on the fillet was often represented by Greek sculptors; hence the name is given to any statue of an athlete thus occupied. The most famous example of the diadumenus is the figure by Polycleitus, of which Hellenistic and Roman copies exist in the National Museum, Athens, the Prado, Madrid, the British Museum, London, the Metropolitan Museum, New York, and elsewhere.

DIAMANTE, FRA. Italian painter (1430–after 1498). He was a close follower of Fra Filippo Lippi, with whom he collaborated from 1452 to 1469 on the great fresco cycles of the Cathedrals of Prato and Spoleto. After the death of Lippi in 1469 Fra Diamante completed the apse mosaics in Spoleto, and his hand may be seen in large parts of the *Coronation* and the *Death of the Virgin*. The development of Fra Diamante's individual style is unclear because, as yet, not a single work can be attributed to him on the basis of documents. On the basis of stylistic evidence, however, the *SS. Gerolamo, Tecla, and John the Baptist* (Cambridge, Mass., Fogg Art Museum) has been generally attributed to his hand; it reveals primarily the influence of Lippi, but is more stilted than the work of that master. The perspective recession is uncertain, the poses are somewhat late Gothic and artificial, and the composition is essentially static. Fra Diamante's use of color (as in the Prato, Spoleto, and Fogg works) is bright and clear, with an emphasis on rose and yellow tonalities, yet it lacks the important vibrating quality of light seen in the work of Lippi. In essence, Fra Diamante's style is that of a successful, if not inspired, reduction of Fra Filippo Lippi's monumental work.

BIBLIOGRAPHY. M. Pittaluga, "Fra Diamante collaboratore di Fra Filippo Lippi," *Rivista d'arte*, XXIII, 1941; M. Pittaluga, *Filippo Lippi*, Florence, 1949.

PENELOPE C. MAYO

DIAMANTI PALACE, FERRARA. Italian palace, begun about 1492. Some 12,600 blocks of marble, each finely chiseled to a point, revet the walls from base to cornice. The building was begun by Biagio Rossetti for Sigismondo d'Este and completed after 1565 for Cardinal Luigi d'Este. Today it houses the Municipal Picture Gallery, the Boldini Museum, and the Municipal Collection of Modern Art. *See* FERRARA: MUSEUMS.

DIANA, *see* ARTEMIS.

DIANA. Stone sculpture by Goujon, in the Louvre Museum, Paris. *See* GOUJON, JEAN.

DIANA, BARTOLOMMEO (Benedetto Rusconi). Venetian painter (fl. 1482–1525). Diana is known by three signed works—altarpieces in the Venice Academy and Crema Cathedral and a *Christ Blessing* (London, National Gallery)—as well as by the *Miracle of the True Cross* (Venice, Academy), part of the series by Gentile Bellini and others, which early writers attributed to Diana. All dating after 1500, these works show solid, traditional forms modified, however, by a special bluish light of much sensitivity; the Venice altarpiece has Raphaelesque mannerisms. All the important documents are after 1500, too, including a reference to a competition against Carpaccio that Diana won in 1507.

The early work is often reconstructed by reference to a group of airy but stiff Bellinesque works, but without firm bases. Carpaccio's forms and light, without his narrative qualities, are the chief inspiration for Diana.

BIBLIOGRAPHY. B. Berenson, *The Venetian Painters of the Renaissance*, 3d ed., New York, 1897; A. Venturi, *Storia dell'arte italiana*, vol. 7, pt. 4, Milan, 1915.

DIANA, BATHS OF, NIMES, *see* NIMES.

DIANA, TEMPLE OF, *see* EPHESUS; NIMES.

DIAPER. Overall pattern formed by repeating one or more elements or by connecting an array of such elements.

DIAPHRAGM ARCH, *see* ARCH, DIAPHRAGM.

DIASTYLE. Denoting columns in Greek architecture that are rather widely spaced. The term is sometimes used to designate intercolumniation when the space between two columns is equal to three column diameters.

DIAZ DE LA PENA, NARCISSE VIRGILE. French painter of landscape and figure composition (b. Bordeaux, 1808; d. Menton, 1876). Diaz de la Peña began his career in 1825 as a porcelain painter together with Jules Dupré;

both became members of the Barbizon group. Diaz also trained for a short period under the painter Souchon. His early works—influenced by his training as a decorator and by his admiration for Delacroix, which was lifelong—were romantic in spirit, even looking back to the 18th century, and reflect the bohemianism of the period. *The Courtesans* (ca. 1835–40) and *The Descent of the Bohemians* (1844; both Boston, Museum of Fine Arts) exemplify this period.

Diaz met Rousseau in the forest of Fontainebleau in 1837 and by the 1840s was a friend of all the major Barbizon painters. Influenced by the Dutch masters and Constable, Diaz's landscapes are painterly with an exuberant handling, which reflected his personality. His large circle of acquaintances included the younger impressionists, particularly Renoir, Monet, Sisley, and Pissarro.

Throughout Diaz's career his style was divided: on the one hand, compositions of mythological and nude female figures, consisting mainly of Venus and Cupid and nymphs painted in a style reminiscent of Prud'hon and Correggio (*Nymphs and Amorini*, 1857; Paris, Louvre); and, on the other, landscapes of the forest of Fontainebleau, which he exhibited regularly at the Salon. Diaz painted with the other members of the Barbizon group in the forest of Fontainebleau and remained faithful to it as a site. His motifs are often clearings in the dense woodland treated realistically and with an impressive grasp of form (*The Forest of Fontainebleau*, 1858; Toledo, Ohio, Museum of Art).

Toward the end of his life Diaz's landscapes became richer and heavier in feeling (*Storm in the Forest of Fontainebleau*, 1871; Cambridge, Fitzwilliam Museum). His thicker impasto influenced Monticelli, the other-worldly nature of his subject pictures was developed in the work of Fantin-Latour, and his interest in transient light effects can be compared with the impressionists. Representative examples of Diaz's work are in the Louvre, Paris; the Metropolitan Museum, New York; the Wallace Collection, the Victoria and Albert Museum, and the National Gallery, all in London; and in Reims, Glasgow, Boston, and elsewhere.

BIBLIOGRAPHY. T. Silvestre, *Histoire des artistes vivants*, Paris, 1856; R. L. Herbert, *Barbizon Revisited*, New York, 1962.

MALCOLM CORMACK

DIAZ DE LEON, FRANCISCO. Mexican painter (1897–   ). Díaz was born in Aguascalientes. In 1917–19 he studied at the Academy of San Carlos. A founder and director of the open-air painting schools, he was an influential teacher as well as painter. Under his auspices an exhibition of children's pictures was given in Paris, exciting the interest of Picasso.

Since the early twenties his greatest contribution has been in graphic arts, especially prints. Díaz revived the art of woodcut and encouraged engraving and lithography. His prints are marked by crisp line and textural richness. As a member of the short-lived Group of Seven, Díaz was active in the literary society of Mexico City. With Fernández Ledesma he edited *Mexican Art and Life*.

BIBLIOGRAPHY. M. Helm, *Modern Mexican Painters*, New York, 1941.

DIAZOMA. Greek word for the horizontal passageway dividing rows of seats in a theater or stadium, as in the theater in Epidaurus.

DI CHIRICO, GIORGIO, *see* CHIRICO, GIORGIO DE.

DICKERSON, ROBERT. Australian painter (1924–   ). He was a boxer before he became a painter. His paintings and drawings, notable for their intense humanism, are associated with the contemporary figurative school in Australia. They display a powerful monumentality, executed with effective economy of means.

DICKINSON, EDWIN. American painter (1891–   ). He was born in Seneca Falls, N.Y., and now lives in New York City. He studied with William M. Chase, Frank DuMond, and Charles W. Hawthorne. In many of his sombre monochromes he combines figures with still life as emerging, half-revealed, from the soft focus of deep shadow.

BIBLIOGRAPHY. D. C. Miller, "Edwin Dickinson," in J. I. H. Baur, ed., *New Art in America*, New York, 1957.

DICKINSON, PRESTON. American painter (b. New York City, 1891; d. Spain, 1930). He studied with Ernest Lawson at the Art Students League. Between 1910 and 1915 he was in Europe, mostly Paris, studying paintings in museums.

Dickinson's early work was influenced by Japanese prints and by Cézanne; elements of Oriental principles of pattern and design remained an important aspect of his style for most of his later career. However, his personal use of late Cézanne and early cubist formal treatment involved emotional depiction more than aesthetic analysis. This approach is evident in a city scene, one of his favorite subjects, the later *Old Quarter, Quebec* (1927; Washington, D.C., Phillips Collection), in which buildings and sky are fragmented into strong patterns.

In the early 1920s Dickinson was associated with the precisionist, or cubist realist, style in American painting. But unlike such a precisionist as Sheeler, whose forms are at least theoretically inherent in the subject, Dickinson used industrial and urban shapes as the starting point for exercises in pure painting. The shifting planes and ambiguous space of *Industry* (before 1924; New York, Whitney Museum) or *Factory* (1924; Columbus Gallery of Fine Arts) owe more to cubist technique than to the abstract beauties of modern machinery. *See* CUBIST REALISM.

In the late 1920s Dickinson, along with other European and American artists, shared in the trend away from abstraction and back toward the object. Nevertheless, in his late oil still lifes, he manages to combine both the recognizable object and the incorporation of most of its accidental characteristics into the total composition, as in *Plums on a Plate* (1926; New York, Museum of Modern Art) or the richly colored *Still Life with Yellow Green Chair* (1928; Columbus Gallery of Fine Arts).

BIBLIOGRAPHY. Minneapolis, Walker Art Center, *The Precisionist View in American Art*, Minneapolis, 1960.

JEROME VIOLA

DICKINSON, WILLIAM. English engraver and mezzotintist (b. London, 1746; d. Paris, 1823). Primarily a portrait engraver, Dickinson worked mainly after well-known English and French painters. He spent his later years in

Paris. Among his better-known engravings are *Sir Joshua Reynolds* (1774) and *Napoleon I* (1815), after Gérard.

DIDARGANJ CHAURY BEARER. Stone sculpture of a female figure (5 ft. 3 in.) found at Patna, Bihar State, India. It is one of the finest early Indian sculptures. The date of the Dīdargañj figure is controversial. Because of its highly polished surface, some consider it to be Mauryan (ca. 324–ca. 185 B.C.), but stylistically it resembles other sculptures of the 1st century of the Christian era.

BIBLIOGRAPHY. H. R. Zimmer, *The Art of Indian Asia*, vol. 2, New York, 1955.

DIDIER, MARTIN. French enameler (fl. 1599). He has been identified as the artist signing himself "M.D.P.P." or "Pape" and as a follower of Léonard Limousin. Didier appeared on a list of 1599 as an artist of the King, but otherwise little is known of him. Works attributed to him in the museum in Lyons, the Dutuit Collection in Paris, and the Museo Civico in Bologna include fine examples of grisaille that show Limoges at its best.

BIBLIOGRAPHY. J. Labarte, *Histoire des arts industriels...*, 2d ed., vol. 3, Paris, 1875.

DIE. Tool for embossing, consisting of a small metal block with a letter or design engraved in it. The object to be embossed, usually of leather or cloth, but sometimes of metal (as in the case of die-struck coins), is then impressed with the die, either by steady hand pressure or by striking with a hammer.

BIBLIOGRAPHY. R. Banham, *Theory and Design in the First Machine Age*, London, 1960.

DIEBENKORN, RICHARD. American painter (1922–). Diebenkorn was born in Portland, Ore. He attended Stanford University in Palo Alto, Calif., and the University of California before studying and teaching at the California School of Fine Arts in San Francisco. He was deeply influenced by David Park as well as by Clyfford Still, Mark Rothko, and Hassel Smith. The freedom of brushstroke and the color relationships of his early abstract expressionist paintings were incorporated into the new figurative style that he evolved from 1955 onward. Simple interior settings with landscape views and figures are reworked repeatedly in terms of broad perspective patterns of brushstroke and modulations of color.

DIENTZENHOFER FAMILY. German architects of the Bohemian and south German schools (fl. 17th and 18th cents.). The Dientzenhofers, originally from the district of Aibling in Upper Bavaria, were the creators of the baroque style in Bohemia. They were also of decisive importance for the development of German baroque architecture after their activity spread to Franconia and other parts of Germany.

Georg Dientzenhofer (1643–89) was the first member of the family to settle in Prague. He is recorded there in 1682 as an assistant of Abraham Leuthner. Georg's known buildings are all in Franconia. He designed the façade of St. Martin at Bamberg (1681–91) and the chapel near Waldsassen (1685–89), an important building with a trefoil plan and circular towers at the angles (symbolizing the Trinity), surrounded by arcades and surmounted by three bulbous domes.

Christoph Dientzenhofer (1655–1722), Georg's younger brother, was the leading Bohemian architect of his time. His main works are the nave of St. Niklas on the Kleinseite in Prague (1703–11), where both the interior walls and the façade are composed in continuous undulating curves, and the Church of St. Margaret (1719–21) attached to the Benedictine monastery of Břevnov (Breunau) near Prague, whose nave is formed by four intersecting ovals and whose façade is remarkable for the curving of its corners. Christoph's work is based largely on the curvilinear and circular interpenetrating schemes of Guarino Guarini, who was in Prague in 1679.

Kilian Ignaz Dientzenhofer (1689–1751), Christoph's son, was the leading master of the late baroque in Bohemia. In contrast to the prevailing late baroque tendency toward greater lightness, Kilian Ignaz's style is characterized by an increased sculptural massiveness. Its development may be traced from the relatively supple design of the Villa Amerika in Prague (1720) to the robust strength of the Sylva Tarouca Palace in Prague (ca. 1749).

In his church designs Kilian Ignaz used a great variety of curvilinear schemes: an oval plan at Naměcké-Verneřovice (1719); a circle at Nicov; an octagon with concave outer and convex inner sides at Heřmanice; an oval with niches on the longitudinal sides at Vižňov; and elliptical chapels with upper galleries leading diagonally toward a dome at the Benedictine abbey church of St. Niklas in the Altstadt at Prague (1732–37). His church at Ruprechtice is an octagon with straight sides, and the Chapel of St. Mary of the Morning Star near Křinice has a star-shaped plan. He also designed the domed crossing and the chancel of St. Niklas on the Kleinseite (1737–52). The excessively complex and basically unresolved character of his style is most clearly apparent in the Church of the Magdalen at Karlovy Vary (1732–36), where he combined a transversely set elongated octagon with concave sides and an oval domed central bay with a choir and transverse elliptical bays at the organ end.

Johann Dientzenhofer (1663–1726), the younger brother of Georg and Christoph, was in Italy in 1699–1700 and then worked chiefly in Franconia. The influence of Borromini's S. Giovanni in Laterano is evident in his design for the rebuilding of the Cathedral of Fulda (1704–12). In the Benedictine abbey church of Banz (1710–18), which has a plan of intersecting transverse ovals and a complex interpenetration of spatial forms, there is a strong relationship to the Bohemian works of his brother Christoph. Johann built for the elector Lothar Franz von Schoenborn the magnificent Pommersfelden Castle (1711–18) in which, despite the participation of other architects, his sculptural Franconio-Bohemian style prevails. *See* FULDA: ABBEY CHURCH.

BIBLIOGRAPHY. E. Hempel, *Baroque Art and Architecture in Central Europe*, Baltimore, 1965.
HELLMUT WOHL

DIEPENBEECK, ABRAHAM VAN. Flemish painter (b. 's Hertogenbosch, 1596; d. Antwerp, 1675). He was active in Antwerp, where he achieved considerable renown as a painter on glass. He made numerous models for engraving, and became a painter rather late in life. Since definite information is lacking, he is presumed to have followed the styles of Rubens and Van Dyck.

DIEPRAAM, ABRAHAM (Arent Diepraem?). Dutch genre painter (b. Rotterdam, 1622? d. there, 1670?). Houbraken mentions an Abraham Diepraem who was a pupil of Hendrik Martensz. Sorgh and the glass painter W. J. Stoop, and after a trip to France, Adriaen Brouwer. A number of paintings signed "A. Diepraem" and dated from 1648 to 166(8?) show the influence of Brouwer. Brouwer died in 1638, however, and it is unlikely that a painter born in 1622 could have had him for his third master. Houbraken also noted that he knew Diepraem in Dordrecht in 1674 and that he died later in Rotterdam.

BIBLIOGRAPHY. N. Maclaren, *National Gallery Catalogues: The Dutch School*, London, 1960.

DIEST, WILLEM VAN. Dutch painter of seascapes and sea subjects (b. The Hague? before 1610; d. after 1663 and before 1666). Little is known of Diest's early life and training. His style is related to the "gray" manner of such painters as Simon de Vlieger, and his renderings of scenes with a quiet sea recall the style of Hendrick Dubbels. Diest's son Jeronimus was also a painter.

BIBLIOGRAPHY. F. C. Willis, *Die niederländische Marinemalerei*, Leipzig, 1911.

DIETRICH, CHRISTIAN WILHELM ERNST. German painter and etcher (b. Weimar, 1712; d. Dresden, 1774). Dietrich was in Italy in 1742. He painted historical scenes, genre, and landscapes in the style of earlier masters, including Rembrandt and Rosa. He also produced a large number of etchings after the manner of Rembrandt.

DIETTERLIN, WENDEL. German architect, painter, and etcher (1550–99). Dietterlin was born in Strasbourg. The first collected edition of his major work, *Architectura*, was published in 1598. It consists of 209 etched plates, divided into five books according to the five orders, in which columns, cornices, windows, doors, fountains, tombs, and other architectural forms are depicted in a richly ornamental style.

BIBLIOGRAPHY. D. Guilmard, *Les Maîtres ornemanistes, dessinateurs, peintres, architectes, sculpteurs et graveurs...*, 2 vols., Paris, 1880–81.

DIETZ, ADAM FERDINAND. German sculptor (b. Bohemia, 1709; d. near Bamberg, 1777). Dietz was trained probably in Prague. From 1736 on he worked in Franconia. Most of his works were elegant and witty sandstone statues for princely parks.

BIBLIOGRAPHY. H. Kreisel, *Der Rokokogarten zu Veitshöchheim*, Munich, 1953.

DIEZ, ROBERT. German sculptor (b. Pössneck, 1844; d. Dresden, 1922). He studied with Johannes Schilling. In his sculptures and monuments Diez departed from the neoclassic tradition and returned to Renaissance realism, with influence from the neobaroque compositions of his day.

DIGHTON, ROBERT. English painter, caricaturist, and writer (b. London, ca. 1752; d. there, 1814). Dighton is best known for a series of full-length caricatures of well-known people of his time—politicians, officers, actors, and others—executed with an unusually sure but capricious hand. The British Museum in London owns an extensive collection of etched caricatures, and the Victoria and Albert Museum has some aquatints and lithographs.

DIJCK (Dyck), ABRAHAM VAN. Dutch painter of portraits and genre (b. ca. 1635; d. Amsterdam, 1672). Van Dijck must have been a pupil of Rembrandt, probably in the second half of the 1650s. He painted elderly men and women in the manner of Rembrandt and Nicolaes Maes. His small genre paintings follow Gabriel Metsu and Quiringh van Brekelenkam.

BIBLIOGRAPHY. Matthiesen Gallery, *Rembrandt's Influence in the 17th Century*, London, 1953.

DIJCK (Dyck), FLORIS CLAESZ. VAN. Dutch still-life painter (b. Haarlem? 1575; d. there, 1651). He visited Italy and was friendly with Il Cavaliere d'Arpino (Giuseppe Cesari). In 1610 Van Dijck entered the Guild of St. Luke in Haarlem. He belonged to the group of the earliest Dutch painters of independent still-life subjects.

BIBLIOGRAPHY. I. Bergström, *Dutch Still-Life Painting in the Seventeenth Century*, New York, 1956.

DIJON. Capital of the Côte-d'Or Department in eastern France. In the 11th century Dijon became the capital of the Duchy of Burgundy, but it was not until the 14th century that it began to achieve fame. Until the 18th century the city enjoyed great prosperity. Among the most distinguished artists who worked for the Dukes of Burgundy were Claus Sluter and his nephew Claus de Werve; some of their works are in the Fine Arts Museum. The Cathedral of St-Bénigne dates essentially from the 13th century. The architecture of the Chartreuse de Champmol was executed by Jean de Marville between 1381 and 1389. At the Chartreuse is the superb Well of Moses by Sluter. Dijon is also an important university town. *See* DIJON: FINE ARTS MUSEUM; SAINT-BENIGNE; SAINT-MICHEL.

DIJON: FINE ARTS MUSEUM. French collection occupying the former palace of the Dukes of Burgundy. Together with Melchior Broederlam's altarpiece of 1399, the Guard Room contains masterpieces of late Gothic sculpture including the magnificent tomb of Philip the Bold by Claus Sluter and Claus de Werve and the tomb of John the Fearless (originally in the Chartreuse de Champmol), by Jean de la Huerta and Antoine Le Moiturier. The early Netherlandish paintings displayed include the *Nativity* by the Master of Flémalle. There are also small groups from the Venetian and Flemish schools and a representative collection of French paintings from the 16th to the 19th century. Sculptors represented include Coysevox, Caffieri, Houdon, Rude, and Pompon de Saulieu.

BIBLIOGRAPHY. *Catalogue historique et descriptif du Musée de Dijon*, Dijon, 1883; P. Quarré, *Catalogue des sculptures, Musée des beaux-arts de Dijon*, Dijon, 1960.

DIKKA. Tribune in the Muslim mosque, from which the imam reads passages from the Koran and recites prayers. *See also* MIMBAR.

DILLENS, JULIEN. Belgian sculptor (b. Antwerp, 1849; d. Brussels, 1904). His teachers were his father, the painter Henri Dillens, and Simonis. Before winning the Prix de Rome in 1877, he worked with Rodin and Belleuse on sculptures for the Bourse in Brussels. Italian Renaissance sculpture exercised the most profound influence on his work, which, after his stay in Italy, was flowing and lyrical, particularly in his tomb figures.

DILLER, BURGOYNE. American abstract painter (b. New York City, 1906; d. there, 1965). He studied at Michigan State College, at the Art Students League in New York City, and, briefly, with Hans Hofmann. He first worked as an expressionist, then turned to Cézanne and to cubism, before committing himself to neoplasticism. In 1934 he became a disciple of Mondrian, the first in the United States. In addition to one-man gallery shows in New York City, he was represented in the New York Museum of Modern Art's 1951 exhibition of American abstract art. He was a member of the American Abstract Artists.

Like the other followers of the de Stijl movement, Diller favored primary colors and black and white in strict vertical-horizontal compositions. He employed the grid, which he transformed and made personal by enriching it with interrupting intersections and multiplication.

BIBLIOGRAPHY. E. De Kooning, "Diller Paints a Picture," *Art News*, LI, 1953; L. Campbell, "The Rule That Measures Emotion," *Art News*, LX, 1961.

DILLIS, GEORG. German painter (1759–1841). Dillis traveled widely as royal gallery inspector. His luminous water colors and oil sketches of landscapes mark him, with Constable, as a precursor of 19th-century plein-air naturalism. He helped found major Munich painting collections.

BIBLIOGRAPHY. W. Lessing, *Johann Georg Dillis als Künstler und Museumsmann, 1759–1841*, Munich, 1951.

DILLON, GERARD. Irish painter (1916–   ). Dillon was born in Belfast. Self-taught, he began painting in 1939 and paints somewhat naïve, strongly designed landscapes, figures, and still lifes. He has also experimented with painting-collage combinations.

DINANDERIE. Name for medieval art work in copper, brass, and bronze. *Dinanderie* was introduced in the Middle Ages when the town of Dinand (now Dinant) on the Meuse was a center of copper working because of its location and favorable trade position. At the height of its prosperity Charles the Bold destroyed the city (1466); its population of 60,000 had included 8,000 copper metalworkers. According to one theory, *dinanderie* began in northern Europe during the reign of Charlemagne. Since the Bronze Age had lingered in the north, working copper and its alloys had a continuous tradition there. Predominantly ecclesiastical work, *dinanderie* followed the architectural styles in vogue from the 8th to the 15th century.

BIBLIOGRAPHY. British Museum, *Guide to the Medieval Room . . .*, Oxford, 1907; J. T. Perry, *Dinanderie . . .*, London, 1910.

DINE, JIM. American painter (1935–   ). He studied at the University of Cincinnati, the Boston Museum of Fine Arts School, and Ohio University. He lives in New York City. His work appeared in the Venice Biennale of 1964. The ambiguities between art and reality that appear in the work of Jasper Johns are taken up in a more direct and aggressive way by Dine. Pictures drawn on the canvas, objects, such as tools, hung from the canvas, and the canvas itself are played against each other in a startling and often humorous manner.

DINGLINGER, JOHANN MELCHIOR. German goldsmith and jeweler (b. Biberach-an-der-Riss, Württemberg, 1664; d. Dresden, 1731). Son of a Biberach cutler and swordsmith, Dinglinger was trained by his maternal uncle, J. G. Schopper, a goldsmith of Ulm. In 1693, with his brothers Georg Christoph and Georg Friedrich, he went to Dresden, where in the same year he became a master goldsmith. Appointed goldsmith to the Saxon court of Augustus the Strong in 1698, he created the numerous works in the baroque style now in the Dresden Grünes Gewölbe, including a gold and painted-enamel coffee service set with jewels (1701) and the *Court of the Great Mogul*, which consists of more than 160 figures of enameled gold (1701–08).

BIBLIOGRAPHY. E. von Watzdorf, *Johann Melchior Dinglinger*, 2 vols., Berlin, 1962.

DINKELSBUHL: ST. GEORGE. The most important work of Niclaus Eseler the Elder, built between 1448 and 1492, and one of the most beautiful late Gothic hall churches in Germany. Like its sister Church of St. George in Nördlingen, it is a perfect hall-church form, having a long nave and aisles with graceful piers that soar upward to the intricate net vaulting. *See* NORDLINGEN: ST. GEORGE.

BIBLIOGRAPHY. F. Mader, *Stadt Dinkelsbühl* (Die Kunstdenkmäler von Bayern, vol. 5: *Mittelfranken*, pt. 4), Munich, 1931.

DINTON, CHURCH OF. Romanesque English church whose south doorway alone remains. The original church may have been the model for Lund Cathedral, Sweden, which, according to archaeological investigations, had an 11th-century Anglo-Saxon type plan. The chancel and south arcade are 13th century, and the rest mainly Perpendicular. *See* LUND CATHEDRAL.

BIBLIOGRAPHY. N. Pevsner, *The Buildings of England*, vol. 19, Harmondsworth, 1960.

DINWIDDIE, JOHN EKIN. American architect (1902–59). He was born in Chicago and studied architecture at the University of Michigan. After working as an architectural designer in New York City (1927–30), he went into private practice in San Francisco (1930–53), where he executed a number of homes. From 1953, he was dean of the School of Architecture at Tulane University.

DIOCLETIAN, BATHS OF, ROME. Roman baths (thermae) begun by Diocletian and Maximian. Completed A.D. 305, they were dedicated the next year. These baths, the

Baths of Diocletian, Rome, ca. A.D. 300. Reconstruction by Edmond Paulin, 1890.

Theater of Dionysos, Athens.

largest in the Empire, were close in plan to those of Caracalla. An enclosure wall with arcades two stories high surrounded the entire conglomeration of buildings having as their principal nucleus the tepidarium. The baths were rectangular in plan and conformed to a strict symmetry and axiality. In the center of the east side was the frigidarium, framed at either side by vestibules; beyond them were the apodyteria. Two large open palaestrae surrounded by colonnades occupied the center of the north and south sides. The baths were entered through four entrances, all on the east side. The tepidarium was restored by Michelangelo in the 16th century as the Church of S. Maria degli Angeli. Part of the building is now occupied by the National Museum of Rome. See ROME: MUSEUMS (NATIONAL MUSEUM OF ROME). See also THERMAE.

BIBLIOGRAPHY. S. B. Platner, *The Topography and Monuments of Ancient Rome*, Boston, 1904; G. T. Rivoira, *Architettura romana*, Milan, 1921; W. J. Anderson, R. P. Spiers, and T. Ashby, *The Architecture of Greece and Rome*, vol. 2: *The Architecture of Ancient Rome*, London, 1927.

DIOCLETIAN, MAUSOLEUM OF AND PALACE OF, *see* SPLIT (SPALATO): PALACE OF DIOCLETIAN.

DIONYSIUS. Russian painter (fl. 1466–1502). In 1466–67, Dionysius painted the frescoes in the Borovski Monastery, Novgorod, and in 1482 he painted those in the Uspensky Cathedral (Cathedral of the Dormition), Moscow. In 1484, assisted by his two sons, he began the paintings in the Volokolamski Monastery, Novgorod. A 16th-century inventory found there lists eighty-seven icons by him, of which two have survived. Between 1500 and 1502, he decorated the Church of the Birth of the Virgin, Moscow; these frescoes are the only ones by him extant. Completely covering the church walls, they represent New Testament episodes and are painted in light colors unique in the Russian wall decoration of the period. Dionysius ranks second only to Rublev in the Moscow school.

DIONYSIUS OF FOURNA. Byzantine monk active in the 18th century. He is the author of the *Painter's Guide*,

which set down rules for the style and technique of painting. Some scholars believe that the *Painter's Guide* reflects a much earlier original. The best edition of the *Guide* is in Greek, edited by P. Keramaeus (St. Petersburg, 1909).

BIBLIOGRAPHY. C. Diehl, *La Peinture byzantine*, Paris, 1933.

DIONYSIUS THE AREOPAGITE (Pseudo-Dionysius). Early Christian theologian active in the 5th century. His writings, four in number, show a synthesis of Christian dogma and Neoplatonic thought; as such they form the basis for much of later Christian mysticism. His first book, the *Celestial Hierarchy*, is the principal source for the representation of the nine orders of angels in medieval art. Arranged according to their rank from highest to lowest, the orders are seraphim, cherubim, thrones, dominations or dominions, virtues, powers, principalities or princedoms, archangels, and angels.

DIONYSOS, *see* BACCHUS.

DIONYSOS, THEATER OF, ATHENS. Ancient theater on the south slope of the Acropolis. It was built within the sacred precinct of Dionysos Eleuthereus, whose cult was introduced into Athens in the 6th century B.C. The festival of the god included dances and choirs, dialogue and mime, which gave birth to antique drama.

To the original earthen terrace, supported by a sustaining wall (a few stones may still be seen), wooden levels and probably benches were added in the early 5th century B.C. During the second half of the 5th century extensive changes were made to accommodate the new drama of Sophocles, Euripides, and Aristophanes. The stone auditorium in its final dimensions dates from about 330 B.C., though important changes were made in the Hellenistic period and at the time of Nero, in the 1st century of the Christian era, when the striking sculptures representing the legend of Dionysos were made for the stage.

BIBLIOGRAPHY. *Das Dionysos-Theater in Athen . . .* (Leipzig, Staatliche Forschungsinstitute, Forschungsinstitut für klassische Philologie und Archäologie, antike Theater-Bauten, hft. 5–9), Stuttgart, 1935–1950; I. C. Hill, *The Ancient City of Athens, its Topography and Monuments*, Cambridge, Mass., 1953.

DIORAMA. Method of showing paintings so that spectacular scenic effects are produced. It was invented by Daguerre and Bouton and first exhibited in 1822. The viewer, looking through an opening, sees the painting go through a series of magical changes caused by skillful lighting techniques. The term also applies to a building used for such exhibitions.

DIOSCORIDES MANUSCRIPT. Name given an important illuminated manuscript made at Constantinople in 512 (Vienna, Austrian National Library). It contains full-page illuminations that are a link between Greco-Roman and Byzantine painting styles.

The manuscript, apparently based on an earlier original, shows in its first folio a number of classical compositions, featuring the portraits of famous physicians. Further on, there are portraits of the author (Dioscorides) conversing with feminine figures who symbolize Discovery, Attention, and so on, again classical in inspiration. Finally, there are pictures of medicinal plants, many of which were already known in Alexandria and Pergamon, on which later herbals were based. One miniature apparently represents the Byzantine princess Juliana Anicia for whom this manuscript was made.

It is predominantly late antique in style, although certain new elements (for example, the use of gold and of brilliant colors) indicate the newer Byzantine methods.

BIBLIOGRAPHY. S. de Vries, ed., *Codices Graeci et Latini*, vol. 10: P. Dioscorides, *Codex Aniciae Julianae picturis illustratus...*, Leyden, 1906; C. Diehl, *Manuel d'art byzantin*, 2d ed., rev., 2 vols., Paris, 1925–26.

DIOSCURI. In Greek religion and mythology, the sons of Tyndareus (Zeus in some versions) and Leda. They are better known as Castor and Polydeuces (Latin, Pollux). They play a role in many myths, especially that of the expedition of the Argonauts. In art they are represented as cosmic horsemen, bringers of rescue and luck, with stars (the constellation Gemini) as their attributes.

DIPRE, NICOLAS. French painter (fl. Avignon, 1495–1531). He is known as the author of a fragment in the Museum of Carpentras, which has permitted the attribution to him of a series of predella panels. Dipre's style is marked by typically Provençal adaptation of Flemish and Italian features absorbed into architecturally conceived compositions, with forms simplified and solidly modeled. His figures have large heads and stocky bodies.

BIBLIOGRAPHY. C. Sterling, "Nicolas Dipre," *Gazette des Beaux-Arts*, XXII, October, 1942.

DIPTERAL. Denoting a temple having a double peristyle, or two rows of columns surrounding the cella. The word is derived from the Greek *dipteras*, meaning "double-winged." The Temple of Zeus Olympieios in Athens is a notable example of the Hellenistic era.

DIPTYCH. Generally, a diptych (from the Greek, meaning folded together) is any pair of small or moderate-size rectangular wood, ivory, or metal panels hinged together; specifically, a type of two-winged retable, usually with painted scenes. Frequently, the donor appears on one panel adoring the religious personages on the other, as, for example, on the *Wilton Diptych* (ca. 1400; London, National Gallery).

DIPYLON GATE, ATHENS. Most important gate of Athens, Greece, located in the northwestern part of the city wall. Through the gate passed religious processions on the Sacred Way to Eleusis and commercial traffic to and from the port of Piraeus. The chief cemetery of the city, the Cerameicus, lay just outside the gate; monuments, both funereal and honorific, lined the road. The gate was double, as the name indicates, one gate inside the other with a 130-foot courtyard separating them. Thus, attack at this point was doubly difficult. The success of the system is evidenced by the failure of Philip V of Macedonia to enter Athens even after he had broken through the heavily defended first gate and fought his way into the courtyard. If, as most scholars believe, Pausanias entered Athens by the Dipylon Gate, his opening chapters describe some of the important monuments in the vicinity.

BIBLIOGRAPHY. W. Judeich, *Topographie von Athen*, 2d ed., Munich, 1931.

DIPYLON VASE. Large Geometric amphora (height, 5 ft.) in the National Archaeological Museum, Athens. The

Dioscorides Manuscript. Full-page illumination. Austrian State Library, Vienna.

Dipylon vase. Large amphora with Geometric decoration. National Archeological Museum, Athens.

amphora was discovered in a tomb near the Dipylon Gate, Athens, where it served as a tomb marker. Representative of a whole series of Geometric vases, the amphora is ascribed to the Dipylon Master and is considered a masterpiece of ripe Geometric style (800–750 B.C.). The entire surface is divided into horizontal bands decorated with friezes of animals, meanders, and various Geometric motifs. The focal point is the scene of prothesis represented on the upper part of the vase. The human figures, drawn in silhouette, are reduced to abstract decorative forms. A sense of order and discipline, characteristic of most Geometric vases, pervades the decoration of the amphora.

BIBLIOGRAPHY. R. M. Cook, *Greek Painted Pottery*, London, 1960; J. M. Davison, *Attic Geometric Workshops* (Yale Classical Studies, vol. 16), New Haven, 1961.

DIRECT PAINTING, SCHOOL OF. School of painting in the United States contemporary with French impressionism. Initiated by Edward W. Redfield, it is characterized by its *alla prima* technique, that is, by bold modeling of shapes and an effort to capture momentary atmospheric effects.

BIBLIOGRAPHY. J. Lipman, *American Primitive Painting*, New York, 1942.

DISCOBOLUS. Any representation, but usually in Greek sculpture, of an athlete about to throw the discus. The original discobolus (Greek, discus thrower) is the 5th-century work by Myron, famous for its expression of transitory movement. The best copy of Myron's *Discobolus* is in the Terme Museum in Rome. The discus thrower is sometimes shown in more relaxed poses.

DISEASES SCROLL. Japanese *emaki* (12th cent.). Originally it was one scroll illustrating fifteen unusual diseases and deformities, but now it is divided among several collections, the major portion being in the Sekido Collection. Together with the scrolls illustrating Hungry Demons and Hells, it forms a group of *emaki* reflecting the Buddhist teaching of the Six Roads of Reincarnation (the Roads of Heaven, Men, Asuras, Beasts, Hungry Demons, and Hells), through which all living beings pass without beginning and without end. The artist of this scroll treated the phenomena of various diseases objectively, with a touch of humor, but never with sadism or excessive ugliness. *See* HUNGRY DEMONS SCROLL.

BIBLIOGRAPHY. *Nihon emakimono zenshū (Japanese Scroll Paintings)*, vol. 6: *Jigoku zōshi, Gaki zōshi, Yamai zōshi*, Tokyo, 1960; H. Okudaira, *Emaki (Japanese Picture Scrolls)*, Rutland, Vt., 1962; National Commission for the Protection of Cultural Properties, ed., *Kokuhō (National Treasures of Japan)*, vol. 4: *The Kamakura Period*, Tokyo, 1966.

DISEGNO. Italian word for drawing or design, evolved as a philosophical concept during the Renaissance. In the time of Giotto, drawing was considered the basis of good art not only in the simple meaning of the word but also in a meaning that attributed to the artist greater powers than those of manual labor. For later Florentines such as Cennini and Ghiberti, drawing was a function of imagination and reason in realizing form. Alberti is more explicit about rational processes when he makes mathematics and the example of nature the components of *disegno*. With the impact of Neoplatonic philosophy and Michelangelo's mysticism, the idealistic side of these rather practical ideas was

taken up with great fervor by the mannerist theoreticians. *Disegno* became the vessel of Godlike creativity in the artist. A special term, *disegno interno*, signified the perfect form as it was contained in the mind. Thus the meaning of *disegno* came full circle to be made a tool of academic usage in the late 16th century. In the 17th century its functional aspects were once again stressed as it was championed by academic theorists as the basis of good art.

BIBLIOGRAPHY. L. Venturi, *History of Art Criticism*, rev. ed., New York, 1964.

DISPUTE OVER THE SACRAMENT. Fresco painting by Raphael, in the Papal Apartments of the Vatican, Rome. *See* RAPHAEL.

DISTEMPER. Aqueous painting medium composed of water, powdered color, and size (glue) or casein. This combination is quick-drying and opaque. Although it was widely employed by the ancients for wall painting, its contemporary value for artists is mainly for poster colors, which are applied to small areas. When mixed with whiting, distemper is termed calcomine, or cold water paint, and is used by house painters for interior wall and ceiling surfaces.

BIBLIOGRAPHY. R. Mayer, *The Artist's Handbook of Materials and Techniques*, New York, 1940.

DISTYLE IN ANTIS. Denoting a temple or porch front with two columns between antae, end piers resembling pilasters. The megaron in Tiryns is an early example of the use of distyle-in-antis columniation.

DIVINO, EL, *see* MORALES, LUIS DE.

DIVISIONISM, *see* NEOIMPRESSIONISM.

DIWAN. Council chamber, courtroom, or audience hall, as in Indian architecture.

DIWAN-I-AM, *see* FORT, DELHI.

DIWAN-I-KHAS, *see* FORT, DELHI.

DIX, OTTO. German painter (1891–   ). He was born in Untermhausen and lives in Hemmenhofen, West Germany. His father was a railway worker. Dix was an apprentice to a decorative painter for four years before studying under Richard Müller at the Dresden School of Arts and Crafts. From 1914 to 1918 he served in the army. He returned to Dresden and then went to Düsseldorf to study. From 1922 to 1925 he taught at the Düsseldorf Academy. In the 1920s he acquired his reputation as a critic of society and of war. In 1924 he published *War*, a book with many illustrations. In 1927 he was given a professorship at the Dresden Academy but was dismissed in 1935 by the Nazis and forbidden to exhibit. He was jailed in 1939 in Dresden allegedly for plotting against the life of Adolf Hitler. Toward the end of World War II he was a prisoner of the French. When the war ended he returned to his post at the Dresden Academy, only to move to West Germany shortly afterward.

Before 1920 Dix had painted in a variety of styles, from impressionism and a Hodler-like decorative abstraction to cubism and finally, as an expression of anarchic

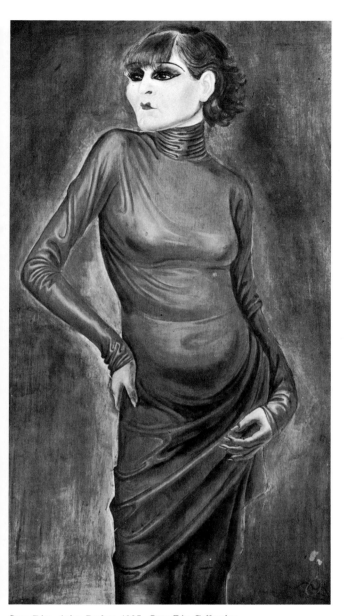

Otto Dix, *Anita Berber*, 1925. Otto Dix Collection.

revolt, to Dada. In the mid-1920s he and George Grosz were leaders in the Neue Sachlichkeit (New Objectivity) movement, a reaction against all that was lyrical, personal, and mystic in expressionism although it retained many expressionist techniques. Artists turned to contemporary themes and to a treatment relatively more realistic. The brutalities of gas and trench warfare had horrified Dix, and he revealed them with unrelenting intensity in his pictures. He found the graphic clarity of such German romantics as Runge and the hyperrealism of Cranach and Hans Baldung-Grien and of contemporary primitives sympathetic to his need for power of statement, and he imitated them.

In his well-known *Parents of the Artist* (1921; Basel, Public Art Collections), he combines tortured, nervous contours with sickly color to create an effect of exaggerated realism that both fascinates and repels. *The Procuress* (color lithograph, 1923) recalls Grosz in the quality of its satire and in its bitterness. His portrait of Dr. Mayer-Hermann (1926) in the Museum of Modern Art, New York, is merciless in its blunt naturalism. After World War II Dix rejected his veristic approach for a personal interpretation of religious themes in a manner that is decidedly expressionist and reminiscent of Nolde.

BIBLIOGRAPHY. B. S. Myers, *The German Expressionists*, New York, 1957.

ROBERT REIFF

DIXEY, JOHN. Irish-American sculptor (b. Dublin, ca. 1770; d. New York, 1820). Dixey studied and exhibited at the Royal Academy in London. After additional training in Italy he went to the United States about 1789, worked in Philadelphia, and then settled in New York. His works include a statue called *Justice* for the New York City Hall.

DIXON, JOHN. Irish engraver and mezzotintist (ca. 1740–1800). Dixon worked in London copying the paintings of his contemporaries Reynolds, Ramsay, Gainsborough, Pine, Stubbs, and others. He often used drypoint to finish his plates, for example, the *Duke of Leinster*, after Reynolds. About 1780 he gave up his profession when he married a wealthy woman.

BIBLIOGRAPHY. A. M. Hind, *A History of Engraving and Etching . . .*, 3d ed., rev., London, 1923 (repr. New York, 1963).

DIXON, NICHOLAS. English portrait miniaturist (fl. London, 1665–1708). He has been wrongly called "Nathaniel" and has been confused with John Dixon, a mezzotint engraver. Nicholas Dixon was well enough established by 1673 to be appointed court painter to Charles II, to succeed Samuel Cooper, and to be made Keeper of the King's Picture Closet. Dixon's portraits show the soft modeling of Hoskins, whose pupil he may have been; they are further characterized by certain mannerisms copied from Lely, for example, the eye as a long oval. The quality of his work fell off about 1680, probably because of the disastrous failure of a lottery scheme. Ultimately bankrupt, he was forced to mortgage seventy miniatures to the Duke of Newcastle, thirty of which remain in the collection at Welbeck Abbey. Dixon's signature of 1708 on this transaction is the last dated reference to him.

BIBLIOGRAPHY. A. G. Reynolds, *English Portrait Miniatures*, London, 1952.

DJESER'S COMPLEX AT SAQQARA. Unique ensemble of funerary monuments around a stepped pyramid at Saqqara, Egypt, built for the first time in stone by Pharaoh Neterikhet, later called Djeser (3d dynasty). The pyramid consists of a series of six superimposed square mastabas. It has accretions of layers with slanting courses built around a core, a construction system followed in all subsequent pyramids. A stairway descended from the north to the bottom of a large vertical shaft where the burial chamber was built in granite; an aperture was left in its ceiling, which was blocked with a granite stopper after the funeral. Other underground chambers and passages were arranged rather irregularly, some lined with blue faïence tiles imitating reed partitions. In the mastaba along the south side of the enclosure, possibly containing the canopic jars with

Djeser's complex at Saqqara. The stepped pyramid and one of the surrounding dummy buildings with engaged columns, ca. 2650 B.C.

the internal organs of the Pharaoh, there were similar tiled rooms with panels in low relief representing Neterikhet performing the rites of the Heb-Sed jubilee.

Within the rectangular enclosure, which has recessed paneling, several courtyards are arranged around the pyramid. These have dummy buildings whose façades have only engaged columns imitating prototypes built of plant stems. The interior was filled in with rubble and sand. This complex was intended for the celebration of the jubilee of the Pharaoh. Besides the ribbed ceiling and engaged columns, such elements as the cavetto cornice, with straight profiles, and the kheker frieze are interpreted in stone for the first time. *See* Cavetto; Kheker Frieze.

See also Egypt.

BIBLIOGRAPHY. J.-P. Lauer, *La Pyramide à Degrés*, 3 vols., Cairo, 1936–39; J.-P. Lauer, *Histoire monumentale des pyramides d'Egypte*, vol. 1, Cairo, 1962.

ALEXANDER M. BADAWY

DOBELL, SIR WILLIAM. Australian portraitist (1899–). He became widely known in 1944, when his right to win an award was challenged unsuccessfully in the courts by a faction of academic painters. This affair became a landmark in the history of Australian art; because of it, Dobell was considered the nominal leader of the modern art movement in Australia. His works, which display sharp cynicism, are not advanced in terms of contemporary art trends but are greatly influenced by Hogarth, Renoir, Gainsborough, and other masters. In 1948 Dobell received further awards for portraiture and landscape painting; he was knighted in 1966.

BIBLIOGRAPHY. J. Gleeson, *William Dobell*, London, 1964.

DOBLIN, JAY. American industrial designer (1920–). He was born in New York. As an associate of Raymond Loewy for thirteen years, Doblin designed vending machines for Coca Cola, refrigerators for Frigidaire, electric razors for Schick, pens for Eversharp, and other products. He has taught industrial design at Pratt Institute in Brooklyn and at his own Studio D in New York City, and is now director of the Institute of Design at the Illinois Institute of Technology in Chicago.

DOBSON, FRANK. English sculptor (1887–1963). Born in London, he studied at the Leighton School of Art and the City and Guilds School there. Dobson first worked with the London group of young painters who were influenced by the new European art movements, especially cubism. After 1918 he turned to sculpture. In his first cubist period the figure was conceived in rhythmic angles, but his style later developed toward an abstract classicism, related to Maillol, dominated by flowing lines and buoyant volumes. He produced many portraits of literary and stage figures, taught at the Royal College of Art (1946–53), and was elected to the Royal Academy in 1953.

BIBLIOGRAPHY. T. W. Earp, *Frank Dobson, Sculptor*, Hove Brighton, England, 1945.

DOBSON, JOHN. English architect (1787–1865). He established a practice in Newcastle and dominated building in the northern counties. He was one of the early engineer-architects—his works include Newcastle Central Railway Station—and a town planner of great perception.

BIBLIOGRAPHY. M. J. Dobson, *Memoir of John Dobson of Newcastle-on-Tyne*, London, 1885.

DOBSON, WILLIAM. English painter (b. 1611; d. London, 1646). Little is known about Dobson's brief career, and practically nothing is known about his early training and experience. The first certain work from his hand is dated 1642, only four years before his death. He is associated almost exclusively with portraits of the Royalist commanders during the Civil War. These were painted between October, 1642, and April, 1646, while Charles I and his army were at Oxford. Dobson could hardly avoid the influence of Van Dyck, but his painting exhibits a remarkably independent personality, which is more virile and direct in both handling and characterization than is Van Dyck's normal English style. Dobson was certainly the most distinguished native-born English painter of the 17th century.

BIBLIOGRAPHY. M. Whinney and O. Millar, *English Art, 1625–1714*, Oxford, 1957.

DOBUJINSKY, MSTISLAV. Russian-American stage designer (b. Novgorod, 1875; d. Massapequa, N.Y., 1957). A landscape painter and illustrator, he is best known as a designer for the ballet. He studied at the academy in St. Petersburg and later (ca. 1902) became part of the group of artists active there, which included Benois, Bakst, and Diaghilev. Dobujinsky was a leading designer for the Moscow Art Theater of Stanislavsky and the Russian Ballet of Diaghilev. He left Russia in 1923, worked in Lithuania and London, and finally settled in the United States in 1939, where he designed productions for the Metropolitan Opera, the City Center Opera, and the Theater Guild. His work was highly decorative, making use of colorful, arabesque forms.

DOCCIA PORCELAIN. Italian porcelain produced since 1737 by the Ginori family in a factory near Florence. Most distinctive of its output are the large statuary groups produced after 1770. In the 19th century the factory began to reuse molds from various 18th-century Italian factories, causing much confusion in dating objects.

BIBLIOGRAPHY. A. Lane, *Italian Porcelain*, London, 1954.

DOCUMENTARY RELIEFS. Carved reliefs whose primary function is to record the activities and often the glories of a ruler or domain. The documentary relief is particularly associated with the art of the ancient Near East.

DODECASTYLE. Having twelve columns in front, as in the Doric telesterion in Eleusis, a prostyle dodecastyle example.

DOELENSTUCK, *see* MARKSMEN'S GUILD PIECES.

DOERNER, MAX. German painter (b. Munich, 1870; d. there, 1939). He studied at the Munich Academy and began teaching there in 1911. He painted portraits and landscapes and taught, experimented, and wrote on the techniques of painting.

DOES, JACOB VAN DER. Dutch painter of landscape, genre, and portraits (b. Amsterdam, 1623; d. Sloten, 1673). Van der Does was a pupil of Nicolaes Moejaert before traveling to Rome. In Rome (ca. 1645–50) he belonged to the group of Northern painters, and was nicknamed "Tamboer." He was the father and teacher of Simon van der Does.

BIBLIOGRAPHY. G. J. Hoogewerff, *De Bentvueghels*, The Hague, 1952.

DOES, SIMON VAN DER. Dutch painter of landscapes, animals, and some portraits (b. Amsterdam, 1653/54; d. Antwerp, after 1718). Van der Does was the pupil of his father, Jacob, whose style he imitated. He worked mainly in The Hague, but was active for short periods in London, Brussels, and Antwerp.

BIBLIOGRAPHY. W. Bernt, *Die niederländischen Maler des 17. Jahrhunderts...*, vol. 1, Munich, 1948.

DOESBURG, THEO VAN (C. E. M. Kupper). Dutch abstract painter, writer, and critic (b. Utrecht, 1883; d. Davos, Switzerland, 1931). As a young man Van Doesburg trained to be an actor, but turned to painting by 1900. He made a living selling pictures he copied from those in the Rijksmuseum. In 1913 he published a volume of poems called *Full Moon*. He became interested in the

William Dobson, *Endymion Porter*. Tate Gallery, London.

modern art movement and wrote articles about it and about the art of Asia.

By 1916 he had begun to render naturalistic representations, such as landscapes and cows, into their geometric counterparts. He maintained that this was an attempt to achieve total harmony through reduction to forms that were universal and timeless. In 1917 he wrote an article on Mondrian, who read it and sought out its author. Soon afterward Mondrian and Van Doesburg joined with Bart van der Leck, the architects Rietveld, Oud, and Wils, and the sculptor Vantongerloo to form the de Stijl group and to publish an influential review of the same name. It came out in 1917 and went through eighty-seven issues until 1931, the year Van Doesburg died.

De Stijl was noted internationally, largely through the propagandizing efforts of Van Doesburg, who traveled throughout the Continent lecturing. In 1921 he met Mies van der Rohe and Le Corbusier, and from 1921 to 1923 Van Doesburg taught at the Bauhaus in Weimar. In 1923 he organized a comprehensive exhibition of de Stijl art in Paris. That same year, under the name of J. K. Bonset, Van Doesburg participated in the Dada movement in Holland and helped publish a journal, *Mechano*. With the entry of new members such as El Lissitsky and Jean Arp into de Stijl, there was a relaxation and broadening of the original precepts, which led Mondrian to break with the group in 1925. By 1924 Van Doesburg coined the term "elementarism," and he explained its ideas in a manifesto in *De Stijl* in 1926 and later, in 1930, in a magazine, *Art concret*, which he published under the name Aldo Camini with Jean Hélion. In 1928 Van Doesburg collaborated with the Arps in designing L'Aubette, a restaurant in Strasbourg.

His art, like Mondrian's, developed from cubism. Limiting himself to primary colors, black, and white, and to horizontal and vertical rhythms, Van Doesburg sought to purge his art of all that was chance, personal, and fantastic. He sought an ethic that expressed honesty, clarity, discipline, purity, and constructiveness, an art that was self-sufficient and complete in itself and not an interpretation of something else. Unlike Mondrian, he did not employ a grid; and although by 1924 he used a freer geometry and made the diagonal an essential part of his art,

Theo van Doesburg, *Composition (The Cow)*. Gouache. Museum of Modern Art, New York.

Carlo Dolci, *Madonna del Dito*. Villa Borghese Museum and Gallery, Rome.

his aesthetic philosophy remained fundamentally unchanged.

BIBLIOGRAPHY. H. L. C. Jaffé, *De Stijl, 1917–1931: The Dutch Contribution to Modern Art*, Amsterdam, 1956.   ROBERT REIFF

DOGE LOREDANO, PORTRAIT OF. Oil painting by Bellini, in the National Gallery, London. *See* BELLINI, GIOVANNI.

DOGE'S PALACE, VENICE, *see* VENICE.

DOGON, *see* AFRICA, PRIMITIVE ART OF (WEST AFRICA: MALI).

DOGTOOTH (Tooth Ornament). Type of ornament shaped like a four-leafed flower, the center of which projects in a cusped form. It is said to derive its name from its resemblance to the dogtooth violet. The dogtooth was frequently used in English medieval architecture, for example, in Lincoln Cathedral, Binham Priory, and Dunstable Priory.

DOHACHI (Nin'ami Dohachi). Japanese potter (1783–1855). A descendant of a long line of Japanese potters, Dōhachi was influenced by Ninsei. He is noted for his bold, colorful, overglaze decoration on Kyoto-type wares. *See* NINSEI.

BIBLIOGRAPHY. R. A. Miller, *Japanese Ceramics*, Rutland, Vt., 1960.

DOIDALSAS. Greek sculptor from Bithynia, in northwest Asia Minor (fl. ca. 250 B.C.). His most famous work was the "Crouching Aphrodite," known through many Roman copies (for example, Paris, Louvre). Its naturalistic pose, experimental composition, and opulent, even sensual rendering of the flesh is an early example of many of the general tendencies of Hellenistic sculpture.

BIBLIOGRAPHY. M. Bieber, *The Sculpture of the Hellenistic Age*, rev. ed., New York, 1961.

DOLCI, CARLO. Italian painter (1616–86). He studied in his native Florence with Matteo Rosselli and Jacopo Vignali. Dolci achieved early success, and his fame spread to Venice and England. He remained in Florence except for a trip to Innsbruck (1672), where he painted portraits of Claudia Felicitas (Vienna, Museum of Art History; Florence, Uffizi) when she married Leopold I. His paintings are marked by an excess of sweetness, extreme piety, delicate coloring, and miniature-like finish; these qualities remain constant in his vast production of saccharine devotional images, such as the *Madonna del Dito* (Rome, Borghese Gallery; Vienna, Museum of Art History; Naples, National Museum), and allegorical figures, such as *Sincerity* (Vienna, Museum of Art History). His few portraits indicate that he might have achieved greatness in that field; the *Self-portrait* in the Uffizi is an example.

BIBLIOGRAPHY. F. Baldinucci, *Notizie de' professori del disegno . . .*, 6 vols., Florence, 1681–1728.

DOLMEN. Primitive structure consisting of two or more upright stones capped by a large horizontal monolith, as in the Constantine Dolmen, Cornwall, and at Pierre-Couverte, Saumur, France. The term is interchangeable with cromlech in describing such megaliths. *See* CROMLECH.

See also CARNAC: DOLMENS; DEMI-DOLMEN.

DOME. Structure, generally a surface of revolution, used to roof an area. The dome is characterized by tangential and radial stresses and, like the arch and vault, produces a diagonal thrust depending on its shape. Thrust is sometimes relieved by massive piers, ties, and apses: Michelangelo's dome of St. Peter's in Rome has a girdle of iron chains to keep it from spreading.

Assyrians used spheroidal and ellipsoidal domes, as indicated in the wall slab from Nineveh. The Greeks used corbeled domes, building them by overlapping rings of masonry. When true domes were built in Rome is problematical. That of the Pantheon, constructed about A.D. 120–124, has a diameter of 142 feet; its lower courses are corbeled with horizontal courses, and its upper section is possibly arched. Corbeling reduced the need for centering and may not reflect an ignorance of dome action. The nymphaeum of the Baths of Gallienus, the so-called Temple of Minerva Medica (A.D. 266), has a decagonal plan with small pendentives.

The dome of the early Christian Mausoleum of Galla Placidia in Ravenna (ca. 450) is filled with amphorae, and, recalling vault construction of the Circus of Maxentius in Rome, that of S. Vitale in Ravenna (526–547) has hollow cylindrical jars fitted together to lighten the weight of the dome.

Sassanian 4th- and 5th-century domes in Sarvistan and Firuzabad had ovoid sections, the transitions at the corners from a square plan to a circle being effected by squinches. Domes on pendentives were built in Byzantine times, the Byzantines taking over Roman construction in

brick and concrete and erecting their domes on circular, polygonal, and square plans. The pendentive, whose origins have been ascribed to early times, as far back as the Chaldeans, is a triangular segment formed when a dome is sliced at the sides to make a square plan. The Church of Hagia Sophia in Constantinople (532–537) has a pendentive dome 107 feet in diameter. *See* SQUINCH.

The dome of the Cathedral of Pisa has an elliptical plan; the Baptistery, a conoid form thrusting through a spherical shell. The octagonal dome of the Cathedral in Florence, begun about 1420 by Brunelleschi, has an inner and an outer shell framed by meridional ribs.

A dome whose pendentives are part of the same sphere is called a simple dome. When the dome is cut at the upper level of the pendentives and is raised on a base or drum, it is known as a compound dome. That of the Mausoleum of Galla Placidia is a simple dome; most of the monasteries on Mt. Athos have compound domes. Melon domes are those subdivided into convex lunes, or scalloped sections, as in the churches of St. Theodore and SS. Sergius and Bacchus in Constantinople.

The Renaissance made wide use of the dome on a square base. It elaborated the high drum, typically piercing it with windows and surrounding it with a peristyle. False domes (the name refers to the outer shell) were sometimes superimposed upon an inner dome to increase the effective height of the dome. S. Maria dei Miracoli, Venice, is an example of such a double dome. St. Paul's in London has a triple dome, consisting of a cone superimposed on an inner dome and enveloped by a raised exterior dome.

Dome. The octagonal dome of the Cathedral of Florence by Filippo Brunelleschi.

Islamic and Indian domes follow another path. The śikhara of the Indian Dravidian temple was often bulbous, like that of the Buddhist dāgoba. Surmounting the *adhistana*, or base, it had a *griva*, or drum, on which the dome rested, in turn surmounted by a pinnacle, or *stūpikā*. The outline of characteristic Indian domes was obtained by revolving one half of a four-centered arch about a vertical axis, giving it a pointed form, as in the tomb of Salim Chisti in Fatehpur Sikri. Bulbous domes were also common, notable among them that of the Taj Mahal in Agra.

Domes today are built of ribs, as in steel construction; compounded of triangles or hexagons in a system indicated by Viollet-le-Duc in his *Discourses on Architecture* and developed by Buckminster Fuller; made of comparatively flat layers of tile; or poured monolithically in reinforced concrete, such domes being called shells and being generally plain or ribbed.

MILTON F. KIRCHMAN

DOMELA (Domela-Nieuwenhuis), CESAR. Dutch sculptor and painter (1900–   ). He was born in Amsterdam and studied in Berlin and Switzerland. Domela began as a painter and exhibited abstract paintings with the Berlin November Group in 1923. In 1924 he went to Paris, where he met Van Doesburg and Mondrian and became a member of de Stijl. Domela's early geometric works are more closely related to Van Doesburg's elementarism (in the use of the diagonal) than to Mondrian's more austere neoplasticism. By 1930, influenced by Gabo and Pevsner, Domela

César Domela, *Neoplastic Lozenge, Composition No. 10.* Municipal Museum, The Hague.

was making constructions in glass, metal, and other materials. He participated in the Cercle et Carré (1930), Abstraction-Création, and the Salon des Réalités Nouvelles. He has had many one-man shows in Paris for his sculptures, which have also been shown at the Municipal Museum (Stedelijk), Amsterdam. His works combine pure form with curvilinear suggestions of Art Nouveau, displaying highly finished surfaces in the metal and stone abstractions. His later sculptures, also nonobjective and composed of various substances, are of rhythmic, Arp-like, biomorphic shapes.

BIBLIOGRAPHY. *Réalités Nouvelles* (exhibition catalogs), Rouen, 1947–   ; H. L. C. Jaffé, *De Stijl, 1917–1931*, Amsterdam, 1956.

DOMENECH MONTANER, LUIS. Spanish architect (1850–1923). He was a local imitator of Gaudí. The bold and even coarse extravagance of Domenech Montaner's Palacio de la Música Catalana (1908) in his native Barcelona, however, lacks Gaudí's integrity.

BIBLIOGRAPHY. H. R. Hitchcock, *Architecture, Nineteenth and Twentieth Centuries*, 2d ed., Baltimore, 1963.

DOMENICHINO (Domenico Zampieri). Italian painter (1581–1641). He was born in Bologna. After studying in the studio of Calvaert, he transferred to the Carracci Academy, where Lodovico Carracci then reigned supreme. Domenichino traveled to Modena, Reggio Emilia, and Parma, and in 1602 went to Rome, where he assisted Annibale Carracci on the frescoes for the Farnese Gallery. By 1604 Domenichino had received the patronage of Monsignor G. B. Agucchi, which assured him commissions in Rome. He worked there except for a trip to Bologna and Fano (1617–21) and prolonged stays in Naples (1631–34 and 1635–41).

His early Roman works show the influence of Annibale Carracci, as in the *Scourging of St. Andrew* fresco (1608) in S. Gregorio Magno, Rome. He soon moved in a more severely classical (Raphaelesque) direction, paying closer attention to the expression of the individual figures and to the achievement of tightly knit spatial and surface organization in the *St. Cecilia* frescoes (1615–17) in S. Luigi dei Francesi, Rome. This greater degree of classicism can be measured by comparing his *Communion of St. Jerome* (1614; Rome, Vatican Museums) with the Agostino Carracci work (early 1590s; Bologna, National Picture Gallery) upon which it is based (for example, compare the treatment of the *putti* in the two paintings).

Domenichino was severely criticized by the proponents of the baroque style in Rome, especially by Lanfranco. After blending Titianesque elements into his style in such works as the *Hunt of Diana* (ca. 1617–21; Rome, Borghese), he deliberately tried to be more baroque in his *Four Evangelists* for the pendentives of S. Andrea della Valle in Rome (1624–25), making the work of Correggio and Michelangelo his models for achieving a sense of dynamic movement and illusionistic foreshortening. This trend was bound to continue in his frescoes in the Cappella del Tesoro, or di S. Gennaro (1631–34, 1635–41), in the Cathedral in Naples, that city being a stronghold of such baroque artists as Ribera. In such scenes as the *Eruption of Vesuvius* (1633) and *S. Gennaro Protects Naples from the*

Domenichino, *Portrait.* State Art Collections, Dresden.

Saracens (1637) he binds the action into a unified and moving whole that belies the classicism of his earlier years.

Nonetheless Domenichino has been considered the classicist par excellence of 17th-century Italy by critics as dissimilar as Poussin and Stendhal. It is in landscape painting, however—the late *Landscape with St. John Baptizing* (Cambridge, Fitzwilliam Museum), for example—that his influence is most strongly felt, especially in the work of Claude Lorraine.

BIBLIOGRAPHY. L. Serra, *Domenico Zampieri detto il Domenichino*, Rome, 1909; J. Pope-Hennessy, *The Drawings of Domenichino . . . at Windsor Castle*, London, 1948; M. V. Brugnoli, "Gli affreschi dell'Albani e del Domenichino nel palazzo di Bassano di Sutri," *Bollettino d'arte*, XLII, 1957; E. Borea, "Domenichino a Fano," *Arte antica e moderna*, no. 8, 1959; E. Borea, "La restaurata cappella di Santa Cecilia in San Luigi dei Francesi," *Bollettino d'arte*, XLVI, 1961; L. Salerno, "A Domenichino Series at the National Gallery, the Frescoes from the Villa Aldobrandini," *Burlington Magazine*, CV, May, 1963; H. Hibbard, "The Date of the Aldobrandini Lunettes," *Burlington Magazine*, CVI, April, 1964; E. Borea, *Domenichino*, Milan, 1965; D. Posner, "Domenichino and Lanfranco: The Early Development of Baroque Painting in Rome," *Essays in Honor of Walter Friedlaender*, New York, 1965.
STEPHEN E. OSTROW

DOMENICO DA CORTONA, *see* BOCCADOR.

DOMENICO DEL BARBIERE, *see* BARBIERE, DOMENICO RICOVERI DEL.

DOMENICO DELLA PACE, *see* BECCAFUMI, DOMENICO.

DOMENICO DI BARTOLO GHEZZI. Italian painter of the Sienese school (ca. 1400–before 1447). He is believed to have been a pupil of Taddeo di Bartolo. Domenico is documented as a painter between 1428 and 1444. His earliest known work is the *Madonna of Humility with Musical Angels* in the Pinacoteca in Siena (1433), painted in a style showing the influence of Masaccio, Jacopo della Quercia, and Luca della Robbia. In 1434 Domenico designed the pavement graffito of the *Emperor Sigismund Enthroned* in the Siena Cathedral. A small panel of the *Madonna and Child* in the Johnson Collection in the Museum of Art, Philadelphia, is dated 1437, and the polyptych *Madonna and Child with Saints and Five Scenes from the Life of St. John the Baptist* in Perugia dates from 1438. Domenico's frescoes (1441–44) in the Ospedale della Scala, representing the founding, history, and activities of the hospital, are the most important monumental 15th-century fresco cycle in Siena and are impressively influenced by the innovations of the early Renaissance in Florence.

BIBLIOGRAPHY. M. L. Gengaro, "A proposito di Domenico di Bartolo," *L'Arte*, XXXIX, 1936; C. Brandi, *Quattrocentisti senesi*, Milan, 1949.

DOMENICO DI MICHELINO. Italian painter of the Florentine school (1417–91). Domenico was a follower of Fra Angelico. His work may be reconstructed on the basis of his fresco representing Dante, signed and dated 1465, in the Cathedral of Florence.

BIBLIOGRAPHY. A. M. Ciaranfi, "Domenico di Michelino," *Dedalo*, VI, January, 1926; L. Collobi Ragghianti, "Domenico di Michelino," *La Critica d'arte*, VIII, January, 1950.

DOMENICO FIORENTINO (Dominique Florentin), *see* BARBIERE, DOMENICO RICOVERI DEL.

DOMENICO VENEZIANO (Domenico di Bartolomeo di Venezia). Italian painter (ca. 1400–62). He is first documented with a letter from Perugia dated Apr. 1, 1438, addressed to Piero di Cosimo de' Medici; in it Domenico exhibits a knowledge of Florentine painting and its leading masters and requests a recommendation for commissions to execute in Florence. His biography prior to this date is at present totally unknown. Attempts to attribute to him works that would have been executed before 1438 have not met with success. His knowledge of Florentine art, however, does seem to indicate his presence in Florence before the date of the letter. According to Vasari, Domenico's first work in Florence was the fresco at the Canto dei Carnesecchi. In 1439–45 he is documented at S. Egidio in Florence, where he executed a group of three frescoes (lost) with his assistants Piero della Francesca and Bicci di Lorenzo. Vasari states that Domenico also worked with Piero della Francesca on a group of frescoes at the Casa Santa in Loreto (lost), probably in the 1440s, but the source is not precise. The biographer also indicates a trip to Venice in 1445. Domenico then remained in Florence until his death.

The problem of tracing Domenico's career is complicated by the lack of knowledge concerning early work or training. There may have been a connection with Fra Angelico. His first certain work is the *Carnesecchi Tabernacle* (ca. 1438–40; London, National Gallery). The signed fresco of the enthroned Madonna already indicates the influence of Masaccio. The Olivieri portraits (Boston, Isabella Stewart Gardner Museum, and New York, Metropolitan Museum) have been attributed to Domenico and are usually dated in the early 1440s. The Madonnas in the Berenson collection and the National Gallery, Washington, D.C., were both painted at about this time. His major work, the altarpiece for S. Lucia dei Magnoli in Florence (1440–45; Florence, Uffizi), reveals his debt to earlier masters but also underscores his own contribution in the use of color and in the treatment of space and the human figure. The predellas (Washington, National Gallery; Cambridge, Fitzwilliam Museum; Berlin, former State Museums, Picture Gallery) run the full gamut of the artist's expressive means. His last work, the fresco SS. *Francis and John the Baptist* in Sta Croce in Florence, approaches in its nervous treatment the late works of Castagno. The *Adoration of the Magi* (Berlin, former State Museums, Picture Gallery) has been considered an early work (prior to 1438) as well as a fairly late work (after 1450). The latter proposal must assume an artistic retrogression.

Although Domenico is often given credit for introducing oil painting in Florence, there is no reason to believe that he was solely responsible. His major contribution to 15th-century Italian painting is in his lyrical use of color associated with solid sculptural forms.

BIBLIOGRAPHY. M. Salmi, *Paolo Uccello, Andrea del Castagno, Domenico Veneziano*, Rome, 1936, 2d ed., Milan, 1938; L. Berti, *Catalogo della Mostra di Quattro Maestri del primo Rinascimento* (exhibition catalog), Florence, 1954.
JOHN R. SPENCER

DOME OF THE ROCK (Omar Mosque), JERUSALEM. Earliest surviving masterpiece of Muslim architecture. The mosque was probably begun in 688–689 and completed

Domenico Veneziano, *Sacra Conversazione, with the Madonna and Child and SS. Francis, John the Baptist, Zenobius and Lucy*. Uffizi, Florence.

in 691–692 for the Umayyad caliph 'Abd al-Malik. It stands on the Haram as-Sharif, the ancient temple area over a bare rock, the *sakhra*, traditional site of the offering of Abraham, from whom the Arabs claim descent. It is also sacred as the place from which Muhammad was believed to have made his night journey to heaven. Moses, Mary, and Jesus are all mentioned in the foundation inscription, and the circular inner arcade echoes in the rhythm of its columns and piers those of the Holy Sepulchre. The building may therefore have been intended to express the hopes of Islam to gather to itself the two faiths it was supplanting.

The outer structure is built in the shape of an octagon, oriented so that its four portals correspond almost exactly to the cardinal points. It is sheathed in marble to the windowsills, above which there are now glazed tiles that replaced glass mosaics. Through the roof of the octagon rises the gilded wooden dome on a high cylindrical drum. Inside, an octagonal arcade divides the space around the dome into two ambulatories. The architrave separating the columns and piers from the arches suggests a 4th-century Roman prototype. Throughout the building the semicircular arch is consistently used. Only the arches of the inner arcade seem slightly pointed, probably because the marble sheathing was added at a much later time. The magnificent metal grille separating the inner domed space from the rest of the shrine was added by the Crusaders.

The ornament throughout is extremely rich in the marble encrustation, in the hammered bronze plates covering all wooden parts, and in the glass mosaic. The mosaic vine scrolls within the drum of the Dome may have been renewed in the 11th century, but those of the outer octagon are original. They combine formalized plant motifs of apparent Sassanian origin with illusionistic presentations in a Hellenistic tradition. Above the arches of the inner side of the octagonal arcades runs the great dedicatory inscription in archaic Kufic, the first monumental inscription in Islam and the beginning of a great tradition.

The Dome of the Rock is an eclectic composition blending Eastern (Sassanian) and Western (Byzantine) traditions into a new whole, at this early stage already surprisingly distinct from either of its models.

BIBLIOGRAPHY. E. T. Richmond, *Moslem Architecture*, London, 1926; K. A. C. Creswell, *A Short Account of Early Muslim Architecture*, Harmondsworth, 1958; O. Grabar, "The Umayyad Dome of the Rock in Jerusalem," *Ars Orientalis*, III, 1959.

JOHN D. HOAG

DOMICAL VAULT, see VAULT, DOMICAL.

DOMINGUES, AFFONSO. Portuguese architect (fl. ca. 1380–1400). He was the first architect of the monastery church of Batalha (begun 1386). It was built on the order of King João I in fulfillment of a vow made before the battle of Aljubarota (1385) in which he defeated the armies of Spain. The building, with its marked verticalism and its vertically accentuated decoration, shows relationships to English Perpendicular buildings of the 14th century.

BIBLIOGRAPHY. M. Tavares Chicó and M. Novais, *A arquitectura gótica em Portugal*, Lisbon, 1954.

DOMINGUES, DOMINGO. Portuguese architect (fl. ca. 1300–20). He was the architect of the large early-Gothic cloister at the Cistercian abbey of Alcobaça. Begun in 1308, the two-storied cloister was completed in 1311 by Diogo Dias.

BIBLIOGRAPHY. M. Tavares Chicó and M. Novais, *A arquitectura gótica em Portugal*, Lisbon, 1954.

DOMINIC OF GUZMAN, ST. Founder of the Dominicans, or Order of Friars Preachers (1170–1221). Born in Caleruega, Spain, he studied philosophy and theology at Palencia. After preaching at Toulouse against the Albigensians, he obtained permission from the pope to found an order to defend the faith against heresy. He held a General Chapter of the order in Bologna, where he died. He is pictured wearing a white habit and hooded black cloak. His attributes are a lily (allusion to his devotion to the Virgin), a star (which appeared on his forehead at baptism), a dog (of the Lord, *Domini canis*) with a torch in its mouth, and a rosary (tradition wrongly credits him with initiating devotion to it). His feast is August 4. *See also* SAINTS IN ART.

DOMITIAN, PALACE OF, ROME. Ancient Roman palace on the Palatine hill. The Domus Domitiana was built on a rectangular platform during Domitian's reign (81–96) by his architect Rabirius. According to ancient writers, the structure was unsurpassed in grandeur and lavish decoration. The palace consisted of (1) the throne room, or vestibule, of great size (97 by 118 ft.), which was sumptuously decorated and had a barrel vault divided by transverse rib arches; (2) the triclinium, or dining room, which was rectangular and had a banded barrel vault; (3) the private apartments, which were at a lower level accessible by a staircase; and (4) a rectangular building, found on the lower level, which had two colonnades and a semicircular apse on one of its shorter sides (this structure has been identified by Rivoira with a basilica). Axiality, a Roman architectural feature, was maintained in the design of the palace.

BIBLIOGRAPHY. G. T. Rivoira, *Roman Architecture . . .*, Oxford, 1925; W. J. Anderson, R. P. Spiers, and T. Ashby, *The Architecture of Greece and Rome*, vol. 2: *The Architecture of Ancient Rome*, London, 1927.

DOMITILLA CATACOMB, ROME. One of the two most ancient and the largest of Early Christian catacombs (the other being that of Priscilla), located in Rome near the Via Ardeatina. It originated in the late 1st or early 2d century as a burial ground for the wife of a martyred Roman consul. The catacomb contains a large number of wall paintings. *See also* CATACOMB PAINTING.

BIBLIOGRAPHY. O. Marucchi, *Le catacombe romane*, 3d ed., Rome, 1932.

DOMJAN, JOSEPH. Hungarian-American painter and printmaker (1907–   ). Born in Budapest, he studied at the Budapest Academy of Arts. He escaped from Hungary in 1957 and now lives in New Jersey. Domjan has developed a unique kind of color woodcut, rich in color and texture. His subjects include flowers and Hungarian folk art themes. He has exhibited in many countries.

BIBLIOGRAPHY. N. Kent, "Joseph Domjan, Master of the Woodcut," *American Artist*, XXIII, 1959.

DOMUS. Roman private house, usually consisting of a public portion centered in the atrium and a private section centered in the peristyle. The House of Pansa, Pompeii, exemplifies the developed *domus*. It had a *prothyrum*, or entrance passage, leading from the street to the atrium, an open court surrounded by cubicula, alae, and exedrae, for servants and guests. An open room, the tablinum, separated atrium from peristyle, which was also reached through a fauces, or passage. The peristyle was itself surrounded by a triclinium, or dining room, alae, or recesses for conversation, and cubicula, or bedrooms. An oecus, or reception room, led to a xystus, or garden.

DOMUS AUREA, ROME, *see* GOLDEN HOUSE OF NERO, ROME.

DONATELLO (Donato di Niccolo di Betto Bardi). Italian sculptor (b. Florence 1382/83 or 1386; d. there, 1466). Nothing is known of his training. From 1404 to 1407 his name appears among the assistants employed by Ghiberti on his bronze doors for the Florence Baptistery. Between 1406 and 1408 Donatello received payments for marble statues that he carved for the Porta della Mandorla of the Florence Cathedral. In 1408–09 he executed for a buttress of the Cathedral a marble figure of *David*, now in the National Museum (Bargello), Florence. In 1412 he enrolled in the Company of St. Luke as a goldsmith and stone carver.

A period of intensive activity followed. He executed a marble statue of *St. John the Evangelist* for the façade of the Cathedral (1408–15), now in the Cathedral Museum; a marble figure of *St. Mark* for Or San Michele (1411–12); a marble statue of *St. George*, much praised for its sense of movement and its terrifying spirit—with a relief of *St. George Slaying the Dragon*, the first example of the technique of *rilievo schiacciato* (flat relief) for which Donatello became famous—also for Or San Michele (1415–17), now in the Bargello; five marble statues of *Prophets* for the Campanile (1415–36), now in the Cathedral Museum, of which one, *Abraham and Isaac*, is largely the work of an assistant; a marble *Marzocco* for the staircase of the quarters of Pope Martin V in S. Maria Novella (1419), now in the Bargello; and marble relief busts of a *Prophet* and a *Sibyl* for the Porta della Mandorla (1422).

From 1425 to 1433 Donatello shared a studio with the architect-sculptor Michelozzo; and during this period he executed, probably with the help of Michelozzo, a bronze statue of *St. Louis* and its marble tabernacle for Or San Michele, completed shortly after 1423, later removed to Sta Croce and now in the Museo dell'Opera di Sta Croce, Florence. He also made a gilt bronze reliquary bust of *S. Rossore* for the brothers of the Convent of Ognissanti, completed in 1427, now in the National Museum of St. Matthew, Pisa; collaborated with Michelozzo on the tomb of Baldassare Cossa (Antipope John XXIII) in the Baptistery (ca. 1425–27), the bronze effigy of which is a striking essay in character analysis; executed a bronze relief, *The Feast of Herod*, and seven bronze statuettes for the baptismal font in S. Giovanni, Siena (1416–29); carved the marble relief, *The Assumption of the Virgin*, for Michelozzo's tomb of Cardinal Rainaldo Brancacci in S. Angelo a Nilo, Naples (1427–28); executed a bronze tomb slab of Bishop Giovanni Pecci (d. 1426) in Siena Cathedral; and was commissioned with Michelozzo to carve a marble balustrade of singing angels for the exterior of Prato Cathedral (1428). Before or while carrying out the last assignment, Donatello visited Rome (1430–33), where he was responsible for the marble *Tabernacle of the Sacrament*, now in the Sagrestia dei Beneficiati in St. Peter's, and the bronze tomb slab of Giovanni Crivelli in S. Maria in Aracoeli (1432–33). After his return from Rome he completed the Prato balustrade, carved a marble *cantoria* for the Cathedral of Florence (1433–38), now in the Cathedral Museum, and, probably during this period, executed the limestone *Annunciation* tabernacle in Sta Croce, the bronze *David, Bust of a Youth*, and *Atys-Amorino* in the Bargello, each of which is replete with classical reminiscences, and executed the bronze doors and stucco decorations of the Old Sacristy in S. Lorenzo, which reveal the artist's mastery of illusionistic means.

Late in 1443 Donatello transferred his studio to Padua, where he executed the bronze crucifix and high altar of S. Antonio (1444–50); the bronze equestrian monument of Erasmo da Narni (Gattamelata) in the Piazza del Santo (1447–53); and the polychrome wooden statue *St. John the Baptist* in S. Maria dei Frari, Venice (1452–53). The high altar of S. Antonio marks a pivotal point in Donatello's career, as he attains a subtle balance between the ideal and the realistic and between the calm and the dramatic. The altar consists of seven bronze life-size statues, twenty-one bronze reliefs, and one limestone relief, originally arranged within an architectural framework. The frame has long since disappeared, and the sculptures have been rearranged, with obvious impairment to the unity of the original grouping.

Donatello returned to Florence in 1453 and there executed a bronze statue of *St. John the Baptist* for Siena Cathedral, for which the payment of export duty is recorded in 1457; a wooden statue of *St. Mary Magdalen* in the Baptistery, unflinching in its portrayal of a penitent sinner; a marble statue of *St. John the Baptist as a Youth* (*Giovannino Martelli*), in the Bargello, remarkable for its penetration of the psychology of an inspired saint; a bronze group, *Judith and Holofernes*, ordered by the Medici family for its palace and transferred to the Palazzo della Signoria, before which it now stands; and two bronze pulpits in S. Lorenzo, completed after the master's death under the supervision of Bertoldo di Giovanni. The last are among the most complex iconographic and stylistic achievements of the 15th century.

Donatello also executed marble reliefs of the *Madonna and Child* in the former State Museums, Berlin, and the Museum of Fine Arts, Boston; *The Ascension and the Delivery of the Keys to St. Peter* in the Victoria and Albert Museum, London; and *The Feast of Herod* in the Fine Arts Museum, Lille. The bronze relief of *The Lamentation* is in the Victoria and Albert Museum, London. Numerous other works have been attributed with more or less certainty to Donatello, or stem from his workshop or immediate circle.

Donatello was the undisputed giant among Quattrocento Florentine sculptors and the most influential master of the early Renaissance in Italy. He grew out of the Gothic

tradition of the cathedral workshop and, through the force of his own personality and his knowledge of the antique, he became one of the most individualistic masters of the period. Dedicated to the proposition that an artist must be able to feel deeply and translate these feelings into plastic form, he invested his work with a sense of life and with a spirit that has been aptly described as "terrible." As a vehicle for such expression he evolved a technique of low-relief carving and modeling of both expressive and illusionistic capabilities. He approached his subject now with the aim of an idealist and again with the goal of a realist and achieved a range of performance extending from almost pure classical beauty to brutal ugliness. He can be said to have made ugliness an artistic form.

BIBLIOGRAPHY. H. Kauffmann, *Donatello*, Berlin, 1935; U. Middeldorf, "Donatello. By H. Kauffmann," *Art Bulletin*, XVIII, 1936; H. W. Janson, *The Sculpture of Donatello* (incorporating the notes and photographs of the late Jenö Lányi), 2 vols., Princeton, 1957, 2d ed., 1 vol., 1963; J. Pope-Hennessy, *Italian Renaissance Sculpture*, London, 1958.   DARIO A. COVI

DONATO DI SAN VITALE. Italian painter (fl. by 1367; d. before 1388). Donato worked with Caterino in Venice on a cross for S. Agnese (1367) and a *Coronation of the Virgin* (1372), now in the Querini-Stampalia Collection in Venice. The latter is modeled on the composition and figure style of Paolo Veneziano, and retains the characteristic Byzantine use of gold, dark modeling, linear drapery patterns, and rich ornamentation.

DONDUCCI, GIOVANNI ANDREA, see MASTELLETTA.

DONGEN, KEES VAN (Cornelius Theodorus Marie van Dongen). Dutch painter (1877–1968). He was born in Delfshaven. As an adolescent he painted and drew realistic works and was soon influenced by the French impressionists. In 1897 he settled in Paris and made sketches for several satirical papers. A habitué of Montmartre life, he responded enthusiastically to Fauvism, for he was a natural colorist. He juxtaposed tones in wide parallel bands with little concern for depth. His already brilliant style was perfectly suited to his vigorous sensualism, achieving richness with direct, simple, and concentrated means. Eager to experience sensations, Van Dongen cared little for drawing and composition. Typical of this period is *Reclining Nude* (1904–05), a daring work of colors contrasted to obtain the desired effect.

At the end of World War I Van Dongen was the fashionable portraitist of Parisian society. He made few concessions to his sitters, neither flattering them nor concealing their physical or moral flaws. He created the "Van Dongen" type, the princess of the international set, thin, pallid, with red lips, scantily clad in transparent tulle and adorned with glittering jewels. Yet his vision remained that of a strong personality and an incomparable colorist. His interpretations of Anatole France, the Countess de Noailles (Amsterdam, Municipal Museum), and the politician Charles Rappoport are pitiless. Among his paintings of Parisian life is *Aux Champs-Elysées* (1920; private collection). He became a French citizen in 1929.

When Van Dongen turned to landscape, he painted for

Kees van Dongen, *The Countess de Noailles*. Municipal Museum, Amsterdam.

pleasure, without artifice or any display of virtuosity, employing a few direct and telling forms reduced to the essential. Unfortunately, these moments of freedom were rare.

Van Dongen was a member of Die Brücke and had affinities with German expressionist art. He was still active but no longer the painter of the superb *Femme à l'aigrette* (1908) at the time of his death. In his later work all his sensuality, pessimism, dexterity, and verve seem to have disappeared.

BIBLIOGRAPHY. B. Dorival, *Twentieth-Century French Painters*, 2 vols., New York, 1958; J. Levmarie, *Fauvism*, Geneva, 1959; R. Nacenta, *School of Paris*, London, 1960.   ARNOLD ROSIN

DONJON, see KEEP.

DONNER, GEORG RAPHAEL. Austrian sculptor (b. Essling, 1693; d. Vienna, 1741). His earliest works are in Salzburg, for example, figures in the staircase of Schloss Mirabell. In the early 1730s he worked for the archbishop's court in Pressburg. From 1734 on he worked in Vienna, and in 1739 he became court sculptor to the Emperor. His preference for lead sculpture, obviating the sharp highlights of bronze, was one aspect of his pioneering of a more classical style, independent of architectural frame-

Donatello, *St. George*, from Or San Michele, ca. 1415–17. Marble. National Museum, Florence.

works and aiming at clarity and balance of form. These qualities appear most clearly in his figures for the *Mehl-marktbrunnen* (1738–39), now in the Austrian Baroque Museum in Vienna.

BIBLIOGRAPHY. K. Blauenstainer, *Georg Raphael Donner*, Vienna 1947.

DONOR. Person who gives or donates a work of art to the church. In art the donor was first represented by an inconspicuous figure kneeling at the edge of the religious scene. By the late Middle Ages, as a trend toward naturalism developed, the donor's figure assumed greater importance until, in Renaissance painting, the donor competed with the religious personages for size and position. Jan van Eyck's *Madonna with Chancellor Rolin* (ca. 1436; Paris, Louvre) is an example of the latter trend.

DONZELLO, PIERO DEL. Italian painter (b. Florence 1452; d. there, 1508/09). He was apprenticed in the work shop of Giusto d'Andrea. After 1481 Piero and his brother accompanied Giuliano da Maiano to Naples, where they were to collaborate in the decoration of a royal palace designed by Giuliano. Subsequently, Piero fulfilled several important commissions for Ferdinand II there. His last years were spent producing minor works in Florence.

DOOMER, LAMBERT. Dutch landscape and portrait painter (b. Amsterdam, 1622/23; d. Alkmaar, 1700). He was probably a pupil of Rembrandt about 1642. Doomer traveled frequently in France, Germany, and England, and made many topographically important landscapes. Rembrandt's influence is especially strong in Doomer's drawings, but it is also apparent in his paintings.

BIBLIOGRAPHY. T. Wortel, "Lambert Doomer te Alkmaar," *Oud-Holland*, XLVI, 1929.

DORDRECHT: DORDRECHT MUSEUM. Dutch museum. Highlighting the fine collection of 19th-century Dutch paintings are works by Jacob and Willem Maris, Josef Israels, Mauve, and Van Gogh. The 17th-century painters Hoogstraten, Bol, the Cuijps, Maes, and Aert de Gelder are also represented.

DORE, GUSTAVE PAUL G. French graphic artist, illustrator, painter, and sculptor (b. Strasbourg, 1832; d. Paris, 1883). Doré enjoyed both critical acclaim and popular recognition in the 19th century for his drawings, caricatures, and book illustrations. Today his fantastic-realistic creations, which are grouped with those of the romantic academicians, are far less appreciated and are prized by only a small group of collectors.

Doré arrived in Paris in 1847. His acquaintance with the publisher Philipon yielded a commission for a weekly lithograph caricature for *Journal pour rire* (from 1848 on). From an early age Doré had been making sketches for classic works of literature, and with encouragement from Paul Lacroix he began translating his sketches into woodcuts. His woodcut illustrations to Rabelais's *Gargantua* (1854) and Balzac's *Droll Stories* (1855) quickly made him famous. After a trip to Spain with Gautier and Dalloz in 1855, Doré settled down to producing a large output of woodcut illustrations, among them those for Sue's *Wandering Jew* (1855), with his first woodcut illustrations in large

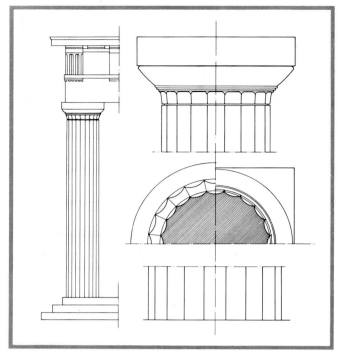

Doric order. The oldest and simplest of the Greek orders.

format; Dante's *Inferno* (1861); *Don Quixote* (1865); and the Bible (1865), by far his most ambitious and successful project.

In the early 1870s Doré took up painting and sculpture, and his book illustration production fell off. His etchings, which he began to produce in 1872, were simply notes on painting and not even reproduction etchings. In general, his efforts in painting and sculpture were not so successful as those in graphics. He was basically an illustrator, and his fantastic dream-world images, similar in style to those of Grandville and Töpffer, were best suited to black-and-white media. His paintings show a poorly developed sense of color and lack the spontaneity of his illustrations. He is seen at his best in original sketches, many of which are in the Doré Gallery in London.

After 1862 he no longer drew on the woodblock but only made sketches, which were transferred to the block by photographic means. This accounts for the fact that his best illustrations (for the Bible of 1865, for example) were done after that time. At the height of his popularity he employed as many as forty assistants, and eventually his large-size woodcuts achieved a kind of virtuosity that he offered as a substitute for paintings.

BIBLIOGRAPHY. E. Ollier, *The Doré Gallery... with Memoir of Doré...*, London, 1870; G. Pauli, *Die Kunst des Klassizismus und der Romantik*, Berlin, 1925; J. Valmy-Baysse, *Gustave Doré...*, Paris, 1930. JULIA M. EHRESMANN

DOREN, HAROLD VAN, *see* VAN DOREN, HAROLD.

DORFSMAN, LOUIS. American corporate designer (1918–   ). He studied at Cooper Union in his native New York City and in 1946 started as a staff designer in advertising and promotion for the CBS radio network. Since 1959 he has been Creative Director of Sales Promotion and Advertising for the CBS television network, in

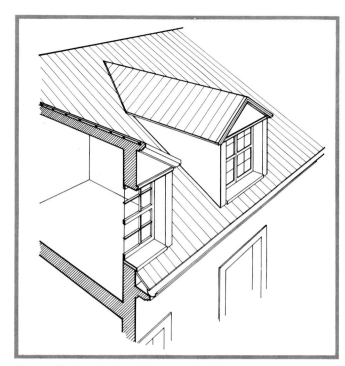

Dormer. Roof projection with a vertical window.

which capacity he oversees and originates most of the design for all phases of advertising and promotion.

DORIANS. Group of Greek-speaking tribes whose iron-using culture supplanted the great Mycenaean kingdoms at the end of the Bronze Age (ca. 1100 B.C.). They were concentrated chiefly in the Peloponnesus, Crete, and Magna Graecia; hence much art and architecture belonging to these areas is often, especially in the archaic period, called Doric.

BIBLIOGRAPHY. J. L. Myres, *Who Were the Greeks?*, Berkeley, 1930.

DORIA PALACE, *see* GENOA; ROME: MUSEUMS (DORIA PAMPHILI GALLERY).

DORIC ORDER. Type of architecture that evolved in the Dorian and western regions of ancient Greece. The oldest of the Greek orders, Doric is characterized by its relative simplicity and strength. The Doric column has no base, is short in proportion to its diameter, and is grooved by flutes, which meet in a sharp edge or arris. The entablature is distinguished by its triglyphs, grooved rectangles that suggest the ends of timber beams resting on the architrave. *See* ARCHITRAVE; ARRIS; ENTABLATURE; TRIGLYPH.

The Doric architectural order is essentially an indigenous product of Greece. The forms of the Doric column bear close affinities to Mycenaean columns, and these Mycenaean columns in turn are descendants of the wooden columns used in Minoan palaces. The transfer of the Doric column form from wood to stone in the early archaic period, however, was probably influenced by the fluted columns (so-called proto-Doric) of Egypt. In the earliest Doric temples triglyphs were perhaps originally ornamental coverings that protected the exposed ends of wooden crossbeams,

and metopes were panels inserted to close off the spaces left vacant between these beams. *See* METOPE.

The plan of the cella of the Doric temple is apparently derived from the Mycenaean megaron, in which the shrine of a protective deity was usually installed. Many classical temples occupied sites where Mycenaean shrines had once stood. The complex of buildings at Thermon in Aetolia gives us an idea of how an early shrine may have developed into a temple. Here an early (perhaps 10th cent. B.C.) building known as Megaron B was surrounded by a U-shaped peripteron of wooden columns. On the same site, about 640–620 B.C., a Temple of Apollo, the earliest Doric temple of which the plan is known, was built. Although it is not certain whether Megaron B was, in fact, a temple, there is clearly a lineal connection between it and the Apollo temple. Other important early Doric temples were the Heraeum of Olympia (late 7th cent. B.C.) and the temple of Athena Pronaia at Delphi (ca. 630–620 B.C.). Hence it is clear that the characteristic form of the Doric order first took shape in the second half of the 7th century B.C. *See* OLYMPIA.

From the 6th to the 4th century B.C. the Doric temple underwent subtle morphological changes that serve as criteria for dating. The later temples are wider in proportion to their length than the archaic temples; the later columns are more slender, and their capitals have a more vertical profile as compared with the compressed, predominantly horizontal profile of the earlier capitals.

Doric structures of which substantial portions still stand are: the so-called Basilica (540 B.C.), Temple of Ceres, and Temple of Poseidon at Paestum; the Temple of Apollo at Corinth (540 B.C.); the Treasury of the Athenians at Delphi (510–490 B.C.); the Theseum (begun 449 B.C.), the Parthenon (447–432 B.C.), and the Propylaia (437–432 B.C.) in Athens; the Temple of Concord at Akragas (ca. 440 B.C.); and the Temple of Apollo at Bassae (450–400 B.C.). The most important temples of the 4th century, those of Athena at Tegea (370–355 B.C.), Zeus at Nemea (330 B.C.), and Apollo at Delphi (the "sixth temple," 360 B.C.), are less well preserved. *See* BASSAE; PARTHENON, ATHENS; THESEUM.

In the Hellenistic period the popularity of the Doric order waned, for its subtlety failed to appeal to the grandiose taste of the time. Although elements of the Doric system were used to decorate private and public buildings well into Roman times, the order never regained its early popularity.

BIBLIOGRAPHY. W. B. Dinsmoor, *The Architecture of Ancient Greece*, 3d ed., London, 1950; D. S. Robertson, *A Handbook of Greek and Roman Architecture*, 2d ed., Cambridge, Eng., 1959.

JEROME J. POLLITT

DORIGNY, MICHEL. French painter, decorator, and engraver (b. St-Quentin, 1617; d. Paris, 1685). He was the pupil and son-in-law of Simon Vouet, whose decorative works he engraved (for example, the *Palais Royal* series, 1674). An academician and professor (1663), Dorigny collaborated with Le Sueur, Bourdon, and Le Brun under Levau to decorate the Ile St. Louis. He alone executed the works for the Château de Vincennes.

DORMER. Bedroom; also a dormer window. A dormer window is set in a sloping roof, usually that of a bedroom;

hence the name. The term is also applied to the architectural roof projection of which the window is an element.

DORMITION OF THE VIRGIN. The death of the Virgin Mary, given only in apocryphal sources. Medieval legend attributes the death to a longing for her Son and places it twelve years after His crucifixion. In art the subject was first represented and received its most usual form in early Byzantine times. The Virgin is usually shown lying on a bed surrounded by Christ and the Apostles.

BIBLIOGRAPHY. G. Ryan and H. Ripperger, trs., *The Golden Legend of Jacobus de Voragine*, London, New York, 1941.

DORMITORY, *see* DORTER.

DOROTHY OF CAPPADOCIA, ST. Virgin and martyr (d. 304). Arrested at Caesarea by the governor, she refused to sacrifice to gods. She was given to two formerly Christian women to be persuaded but reconverted them. Placed on a rack, St. Dorothy was tortured. Theophilus, a man of law, taunted her to send him fruits or roses from the garden of paradise. A child brought them to him upon her death, and he was converted. Her attributes are a crown of flowers, a rose, and a child with a basket of flowers. Her feast is February 6. *See also* SAINTS IN ART.

DORPAT (Tartu) CATHEDRAL. The Cathedral of Ss. Peter and Paul at Dorpat, Estonia, was built in the Hanseatic late Gothic brick style during the 14th and 15th centuries. The structure burned in 1624 and has remained

Alceo Dossena, *Madonna and Child*. Victoria and Albert Museum, London.

a ruin, of which the octagonal nave supports and remnants of the façade survive.

DORTER (Dormitory). Monks' sleeping hall located in the upper story of the east wing of a cloister. The dorter is usually constructed with two vaulted aisles, creating some of the most interesting architectural spaces in medieval building.

DORYPHOROS, *see* POLYCLEITUS.

DOSIO, DORASTANTE MARIA. Italian sculptor and silversmith (fl. 2d half of 17th cent.). A native of Florence, Dosio was active in Bologna, where he created a bronze statue of Pope Alexander VII (1660; Palazzo Comunale, Sala Farnese). He also worked in the Church of S. Giacomo Maggiore there.

DOSIO, GIOVANNI ANTONIO. Italian architect and sculptor of the Roman school (1533–1609). A native Florentine, Dosio moved to Rome in 1548 and was apprenticed to Raffaele da Montelupo from 1549 to 1552. Dosio's major activity in Rome was the study of antique sculpture and architecture. His drawings of Roman antiquities are among the most important sources for our knowledge of the topography of the ancient city. Dosio worked chiefly as a sculptor until 1575 and thereafter as an architect. In 1576 he moved back to Florence and designed several palaces there and elsewhere.

DOSSENA, ALCEO. Italian sculptor and forger (1878–1936). As a young man, Dossena was employed as a restorer of marble balustrades and columns in his native Cremona and neighboring towns. Dossena's own pieces were purported to be examples of the *oeuvre* of artists who lived from the 4th century B.C. to the 17th century. No sculpture of Dossena is modeled precisely after an original, but each is a remarkable re-creation of the technique and idiom of a master or his school. After World War I Dossena's works were accepted by connoisseurs as Greek *korai*, as examples of the schools of Verrocchio, Donatello, Antonio Rossellino, and others, and even as originals in the manner of Simone Martini, who was known only as a painter. Examples of sculptures thought to have been fabricated by Dossena's workshop are the *Velia*, which was accepted for a time by the Cleveland Museum of Art as an authentic, archaic style Athena; a *Kore* formerly in a Swedish museum; and more recently a *Diana* in the Etruscan manner, which is owned by the City Art Museum, St. Louis.

BIBLIOGRAPHY. National Art Galleries, Inc., *Sculptures by Alceo Dossena*, New York, 1933.

DOSSERET. Thick block set above a capital, as in Byzantine architecture. The dosseret resembles a deep abacus with splayed sides. It is sometimes assumed to have originated in the section of an entablature placed above columns. An early Christian example of the dosseret is in the basilican Church of S. Apollinare in Classe, Ravenna.

Dosso, *Circe*. Villa Borghese Museum and Gallery, Rome. A small work in the tradition of Giorgione.

DOSSO (Dosso Dossi; Giovanni Luteri). Italian painter of the Ferrarese school (ca. 1490–1542). He worked all his life for the court there, making stage sets, designs for majolica, and the like, as well as paintings, but these works are lost. He traveled to Rome, Florence, Venice, and perhaps Spain for the Duke of Ferrara. Dosso probably studied in Venice with Titian.

A hypothesis about the character of Dosso's early work has recently been confirmed by *The Feast of Cybele* (1514; London, National Gallery), part of the Duke's program of mythologies in which Titian also took part. It shows the romantic haze and rich landscape of later work, but firm dumpy figures in the Costa tradition. Later dated works are chiefly formal altarpieces, the *Madonna and Three Saints* (1522, Modena Cathedral) being followed by less interesting ones in 1532 and 1540.

Dosso's originality appears in his secular works, which are mainly small. In his maturity their brushwork is sketchy, in dry wisps, and their color shadowy and acid, with overtones of dream, pastoral, and magic. They are a spe-

Gerrit Dou, *The Quack*. Boymans–Van Beuningen Museum, Rotterdam.

cial phase of the Giorgione tradition. The most notable are *Circe*, *Apollo* (both Rome, Borghese), and *Jove and Virtue* (Vienna, Lanckoronski Collection). Some more informal religious works share their qualities, for example, *John the Baptist* (Florence, Pitti Palace), *St. George* (Dresden, State Art Collections), *St. Jerome* (Vienna, Museum of Art History), *Holy Family* (Middlesex, Hampton Court), and even the large nocturnal altarpiece (Ferrara Gallery).

Small decorative pictures such as the *Nymph and Satyr* (Pitti Palace), *Dido* (Rome, Doria Pamphili), and *Bacchus* (Modena, Este Gallery) have a unique suggestion of sensuous humanism. Wispy landscapes recur in all of these. Dosso's art is in tension between this sketchy moodiness and the formal classical figure; an intermediate stage is in the one preserved, though damaged, large fresco cycle at the castle in Trent (1530–32).

BIBLIOGRAPHY. H. Mendelsohn, *Das Werk der Dossi*, Munich, 1914; A. Morassi, "Pictures at the Court of Bernardino Clesio at Trento," *Bollettino d'arte*, XXIII, December, 1929; R. Longhi, *Officina Ferrarese, 1934* . . . (*Opere complete di Roberto Longhi*, vol. 5), Florence, 1956.

CREIGHTON GILBERT

DOSSO, BATTISTA DEL. Italian painter of the Ferrarese school (fl. 1517–53). He was the brother and lifelong assistant of Dosso. Battista's reflected fame rests on debates as to whether he may have painted some of the weaker works in Dosso's style. The best documented, *Allegory of Peace* (Dresden, State Art Collections, Picture Gallery), strongly recalls his period in Raphael's shop.

"DOTTED PRINT" TECHNIQUE, *see* MANIERE CRIBLEE.

DOTTI, CARLO FRANCESCO. Italian architect (ca. 1670–1759). He worked in Bologna. His masterpiece is the Sanctuary of the Madonna di S. Luca (1723–57). The façade resembles the illusionist painting of contemporary Bolognese artists, and the interior is related to Pietro da Cortona's architectural work.

BIBLIOGRAPHY. R. Wittkower, *Art and Architecture in Italy, 1600–1750*, Baltimore, 1958.

DOU, GERRIT (Gerard). Dutch painter of history, genre, and portraits (b. Leyden, 1613; d. there, 1675). The son of the Leyden glass painter Douwe Jansz., Dou received his first training in his father's profession. His father's workshop was close to Rembrandt's house, and in February, 1628, Dou became one of Rembrandt's first pupils. He remained in Rembrandt's studio until Rembrandt departed for Amsterdam in 1631/32. Dou became one of the first members of the newly founded Leyden painters' guild in 1648. He seems to have spent nearly his entire life in his native city, and even declined an invitation by Charles II to visit England.

Dou's early style was strongly influenced by Rembrandt's early Leyden manner. Rembrandt's rather fine technique of the late 1620s, and his more moderate sense of dark-and-light pattern, apparently suited the young Dou, who had already received some artistic direction from the meticulous technique required by his father's craft. Among Dou's earliest works, probably painted between 1628 and 1631 while he was still in Rembrandt's studio, are two oval panels, *An Old Man* and *An Old Woman* (Kassel, State Picture Collections), which have sometimes been identified, perhaps for romantic reasons, as portraits of Rembrandt's father and mother. These two works were executed completely under the impact of Rembrandt's early manner.

Typical of Dou's mature period is his anecdotal rendering of *The Quack* (1652; Rotterdam, Boymans–Van Beuningen Museum). Rembrandt's influence can still be felt in various sections of the composition, but it is the impact of early-Leyden-period Rembrandt rather than his more mature Amsterdam style. Dou's position as leader of the Leyden "fine painters" (*fijnschilders*) technique was established with works such as this one. His meticulous rendering continued in his later works, such as the *Young Woman at Her Toilet* (1667; Boymans–Van Beuningen Museum), and set the entire tone for the later members of the "fine painters' group." Among his most important pupils and followers in this manner were Frans van Mieris the Elder and Gabriel Metsu. Dou's nephew Dominicus van Tol was also his pupil and painted in his style.

BIBLIOGRAPHY. W. Martin, *Gérard Dou*, Paris, 1911; W. Martin, *Klassiker der Kunst: Gérard Dou*, Stuttgart, Berlin, 1913; N. Maclaren, *National Gallery Catalogues: The Dutch School*, London, 1960.

LEONARD J. SLATKES

DOUANIER, LE, *see* ROUSSEAU, HENRI.

DOUFFET (D'Ouffet; Doufeet; Douffeit), GERARD. Flemish painter of history, genre, and portraits (b. Liège, 1594; d. there, 1661/65). He received his first training with the Liège painter Jan Tauliers before entering the workshop of Rubens in 1612–14. Douffet traveled to Italy

Thomas Doughty, *In Nature's Wonderland*, 1835. Detroit Institute of Arts. Luminosity with strong contrasts of light and shadow.

soon after leaving Rubens's studio. Little is known of Douffet's earliest activity in Rome. In 1620 he was living there, in the parish of S. Maria del Popolo, with the French painters David le Riche and Moïse le Valentin. In Rome Douffet seems to have been influenced by the style of Caravaggio as well as by northern followers of Caravaggio such as Dirck van Baburen. Douffet also visited Naples, Pesaro, and Venice. He was back in Liège in the spring of 1623.

Nothing certain is known of Douffet's Italian period. However, before he left for Italy he supposedly executed a copy (now lost) of Rubens's *Judith and Holofernes* from Cornelis Galle's print. Nothing of Rubens's influence is apparent in the *Miracle of the True Cross* (Munich, Bavarian State Picture Galleries), a painting which was executed by Douffet in 1624 for the Monastery of St. Lawrence in Liège. This large canvas exhibits a somewhat restrained combination of Caravaggio's style and elements borrowed from his Roman associate Le Valentin. There is an unusual French classical quality to Douffet's compositions. His form of Caravaggism was nearly unique in

Flanders at that time. His large canvas *Pope Nicolas V at the Grave of St. Francis* (Bavarian State Picture Galleries) also shows some affinities with the work of Domenichino, especially in the use of architectural elements. Douffet had many pupils and was the founder of the Liège school.

BIBLIOGRAPHY. A. von Schneider, *Caravaggio und die Niederländer*, Marburg an der Lahn, 1933; J. Philippe, *La Peinture liégeoise au XVIIᵉ siècle*, Brussels, 1945.   LEONARD J. SLATKES

DOUGHTY, THOMAS. American painter (b. Philadelphia, 1793; d. New York City, 1856). Doughty was a successful leather dealer whose hobby, painting, gradually became more important, especially when he sold some of his early works, mostly topographical views of country estates. By 1820 he had left his business in order to paint landscapes, an art in which he was self-taught. In 1822 Doughty had his first public exhibition, eight paintings shown at the Pennsylvania Academy of Fine Arts, Philadelphia. In 1824 he again exhibited eight works, including two illustrations of scenes from Cooper's *Pioneers*. He was abroad twice: in 1837, when he was briefly in England, and in 1845, when he traveled in England, Ireland, and France.

Douris, detail of a cup showing the quarrel between Odysseus and Ajax. Museum of Art History, Vienna.

One of the first American painters to devote himself to landscape, Doughty was an early and important member of what was later called the Hudson River school. He was not, however, entirely free from European influences; he often composed his pictures around a sort of slowly winding recession in which compositional elements are piled on each other as they move into the picture space, a technique apparently derived from 17th-century Dutch painters, as in *The Raft* (1830; Providence, Rhode Island School of Design, Museum of Art). The debt to Holland is clear in the later *Landscape after Ruisdael* (1846; Brooklyn Museum), which also shows a trace of the structure of Poussin. Another often recurring characteristic is a strong luminosity, probably ultimately owed to Claude Lorraine, which organizes the picture in strong contrasts of light and dark, for example, *In Nature's Wonderland* (1835; Detroit Institute of Arts) and *In the Catskills* (1836; Andover, Mass., Phillips Academy, Addison Gallery of American Art).

In Nature's Wonderland is a perfect expression of Doughty's attitude toward landscape. His unaffected love of nature led him to record faithfully the appearance of idyllic country scenes. This approach, contemplative and poetic, left the obviously sublime or grandiose view for other hands

and permitted the vital creative power of nature to speak in more pastoral tones. Nature's great power, more than the mere size of mountains or trees, dwarfs the figures, which occasionally appear in the middle ground.

Doughty painted in a hard, firmly drawn style, with an emphasis on naturalistic detail that was sometimes enough to dispel the painting's quiet mood. His contribution to the development of American painting lay in his recognition of the American landscape itself as a viable subject for painting.

BIBLIOGRAPHY. F. A. Sweet, *The Hudson River School and the Early American Landscape Tradition*, Chicago, 1945.

JEROME VIOLA

DOUGHTY, WILLIAM. English painter and engraver (b. York, ca. 1755; d. Lisbon, 1782). He studied with Sir Joshua Reynolds, and after an unsuccessful career in Ireland as a portrait painter, settled in London, in 1779. Doughty was more successful as an etcher and mezzotintist, both after painted portraits and after his own designs, for example, his portrait of the poet Thomas Gray.

BIBLIOGRAPHY. A. C. Whitman, *Masters of Mezzotint*, London, 1898.

DOURA EUROPOS, *see* DURA EUROPOS.

DOURIS. Attic vase painter (fl. ca. 500–470 B.C.). His extant works number more than 200. He was a great draftsman, and his work is prized principally for its brilliance of composition. In some cases, however, on a cup in Vienna showing the quarrel between Odysseus and Ajax, for example, this great technique was combined with a feeling for dramatic narrative.

BIBLIOGRAPHY. E. Pfuhl, *Masterpieces of Greek Drawing and Painting*, tr. J. D. Beazley, New York, 1955.

DOUVEN, BARTHOLOMEUS. Dutch-German portrait and history painter (b. Düsseldorf, 1688; d. after 1726). The son of the painter Johan Frans van Douven, Bartholomeus was a pupil of Adriaen van der Werff, whose influence can be seen in his work. Douven was active as a court painter in Cologne and Düsseldorf. A painting in the State Picture Collections in Kassel by Douven is dated 1726.

BIBLIOGRAPHY. W. Bernt, *Die niederländischen Maler des 17. Jahrhunderts...*, vol. 1, Munich, 1948.

D'OU VENONS-NOUS?..., see WHENCE DO WE COME?....

DOUWERMANN, HEINRICH. German sculptor (fl. Lower Rhine, ca. 1500–50). He is traceable as a woodcarver in Cleve, Kalkar, and Xanten, where he carved his masterpiece, the *Marienaltar*, in 1535. His style is primarily late Gothic, with some use of Renaissance motifs.

BIBLIOGRAPHY. R. Hetsch, *Die Altarwerke von Heinrich Douwermann*, Munich, 1937.

DOVE, ARTHUR GARFIELD. American painter (b. Canandaigua, N.Y., 1880; d. Centerport, N.Y., 1946). After graduating from Cornell University in 1903 Dove became a magazine illustrator, a job at which he worked periodically until 1930, when the patronage of Duncan Phillips enabled him to become a full-time painter. In 1908 he went to France for almost two years.

At his first one-man show, in 1912 at Stieglitz's gallery, Dove exhibited the Paris-oriented canvases he had painted in Europe, but he also included ten abstract oils that he had done in 1910. They are like the first abstractions of Kandinsky, which were painted at almost exactly the same time. But Dove seldom used abstraction as an end in itself. His paintings are based on an image of reality, often a landscape or an aspect of the weather, purified of nonessential detail and composed on the picture surface, but always present. This is readily seen in his work up to 1920, for example, *Plant Forms* (1915; New York, Whitney Museum), in which simplified vegetable shapes plainly reveal their natural origin.

In the 1920s Dove became concerned less with arranging organic forms and more with the power of color and form to produce a visual equivalent to an experience or a feeling. *Fog Horns* (1929; private collection), with concentric circular shapes of resonant color set in a seascape, re-creates the dull sound of horns in a foggy harbor. To the same period belong Dove's constructions, witty arrangements of materials that represent a crystallization of a subject's personality or outstanding features. Thus, in *Portrait of A. S.* (1925; New York, Museum of Modern Art) the important characteristics of Alfred Stieglitz are exhibited in terms of a lens, a mirror, steel wool, and a clock spring. In the

Arthur G. Dove, *Plant Forms*, 1915. Whitney Museum of American Art, New York.

constructions, as in the paintings, the same attempt to create a plastic version of an experience can be seen.

Dove's later paintings became increasingly abstract and were often restricted to geometric forms. Even limited means, however, were sufficient for Dove to express his lyric delight in the oneness of man with the forces of nature. Though influenced by the synchromists in his color, Dove is almost unique in modern American art in his ability to fuse, consistently and successfully, an abstract mode of expression and a personal, nearly mystical, view of the world.

BIBLIOGRAPHY. R. Goldwater, "Arthur Dove," *Perspectives*, II, Winter, 1953; F. S. Wight, *Arthur G. Dove*, Berkeley, Los Angeles, 1958.

JEROME VIOLA

DOVE. Symbol of the Holy Spirit in Christian art, spoken of in the Acts of the Apostles but not officially sanctioned until 536 at a council in Constantinople. The dove appears in representations of the Trinity (Rome, Lateran mosaics) and the baptism of Christ (Sarcophagus of Junius Bassus, Rome, St. Peter's) as early as the 4th century. The dove appears in the Pentecost by the 10th century (Pontifical of Winchester, Rouen) and by the 13th century in the Annunciation. Saints often have the dove as an attribute, particularly the God-inspired Evangelists and Church Doctors.

DOVER CASTLE. As the coastal key to England, the castle has been much added to and reconstructed, and the total conception is one of complicated building periods. Harold's fortress from before the Norman Conquest is visible as ditches. There were considerable rebuildings (1168–74), and curtain walls survive. Maurice the Engineer was the engineer, and his staircase design appears only here and at Newcastle. Between 1180 and 1196 the keep, curtain, and adjacent towers were built. The keep follows the square-towered type (as in Kenilworth) but it was out of date by the time of its erection. More defense works were added (1230–40), including three great gates. Later alterations were of a domestic character. King's Gate and Palace Gate were rebuilt in 1800. The most notable part of the interior is the Romanesque chapel in the east angle of the keep.

BIBLIOGRAPHY. Ministry of Works, *Ancient Monuments and Historic Buildings*, vol. 2, London, 1917–58.

DOWNING, ANDREW JACKSON. American horticulturalist, landscape architect, and author (1815–52). Born in Newburgh, N.Y., he became one of his country's first architectural critics, a key figure in the reaction against the Greek revival and a leading proponent of the improvement of rural architecture. His books were arbiters of taste.

BIBLIOGRAPHY. R. Lynes, *The Tastemakers*, New York, 1954.

DOWNMAN, JOHN. English painter (b. near Exeter, ca. 1750; d. Wrexham, 1824). He is best known for his small portrait drawings in pencil and wash or crayons. He painted some subject pictures, including illustrations to Shakespeare. He worked mainly in London, but practiced in Exeter in 1807–08. He was elected associate of the Royal Academy of Arts in 1795.

BIBLIOGRAPHY. G. C. Williamson, *John Downman*, London, 1907.

DOYLE, RICHARD. English illustrator (b. London, 1824; d. there, 1883). Doyle, whose precocity brought him to the attention of *Punch* at the age of nineteen and whose ripe imagination and technical virtuosity made him one of the most famous of English satirical illustrators, began drawing under the instruction of his father, Iren Doyle. By the age of sixteen he had completed *Dick Doyle's Journal* (1840; London, British Museum), a sketchbook of 161 pages of brilliant ink and wash drawings of keenly observed people and situations. The Victoria and Albert Museum, London, acquired a similar youthful work of thirty-two fantastic and humorous drawings, the *Book Full of Nonsense by Dick Kitcat*. After 1843 Doyle was a regular contributor to *Punch*. His book illustrations include those for Dickens's *Cricket on the Hearth* (1846) and Thackeray's *Rebecca and Rowena* (1850). Between 1865 and 1870 Doyle turned almost exclusively to illustrating books of fairy tales, and between 1868 and 1883 he produced many water colors, mostly of fantastic subjects.

BIBLIOGRAPHY. F. G. Kitton, *Dickens and His Illustrators*, London, 1899; D. Hambourg, *Richard Doyle: His Life and Works*, London, 1948.

DRAGON. Mythological animal, which is a composite of various animals. In Christian art the dragon is generally a symbol of evil (for example, St. George and the dragon), but in Chinese art it is a symbol of vitality. The dragon is usually portrayed with deer horns, ox ears, serpentine body, tiger paws, and hawk talons.

DRAKE, JOHANN FRIEDRICH. German sculptor (b. Pyrmont, 1805; d. Berlin, 1882). He studied with Rauch in Berlin and was in Italy in 1836. He was known for his public monuments and portraits of famous men, executed in the prevailing neoclassic style.

DRAPERY. General term for the material clothing a figure that is full enough to hang in folds. Drapery is one of the principal sources for the analysis of style because of the infinite variety of fold types and the changes in handling them from one period to the next. The soft and angular styles of late Gothic art of the North, for example, are characterized by their treatment of drapery.

DRAVIDIANS. Aboriginal people of India, shorter and darker than the Aryans, and numerous in the south. The term "Dravidian" also refers to certain languages in this area, including Tamil, Telugu, and Kanarese. Geographically, Drāviḍa extends from Madras to Cape Comorin.

DRAWING, HISTORY OF. The history of drawing reaches back to prehistoric pictographs, but in modern art history it begins at that fine point when the influence of antique and Eastern art was overshadowed by fresh, unprejudiced observation, sometime during the 13th century. The *Pattern Book* (1230–35) of Villard de Honnecourt (Paris, National Library) is one of the first examples, but the Western tradition of drawing clearly comes from Italy.

Except for manuscript *drôleries*, drawings (that is, studies, sketches, and cartoons) from before the 15th century are rare. Dating from the 14th century are Taddeo Gaddi's study for a *Presentation of the Virgin in the Temple* (Paris, Louvre) and the drawings of Giovannino de' Grassi and of the artists of the court of Charles IV in Prague. More drawings are extant from the 15th century, for example, those of Pisanello and Stefano da Verona in Italy and the Master of the Amsterdam Cabinet and Schongauer in the North.

In the 16th century drawing was rapidly developed. Michelangelo spoke of the drawing as the soul of the painting, and he, Raphael, Holbein, and Clouet all used it as an exploratory step. In contrast, Leonardo, Dürer, and the latter's followers in Germany and the Netherlands developed the drawing as a work of art in itself. Whatever their philosophy, many Renaissance and mannerist draftsmen shared the discoveries of wash, charcoal, crayon, and chalk techniques, which in practice paralleled the development of painting from the basically linear to the basically painterly.

In many respects drawing was most fully developed in the 17th century. In Holland the Flemish influence was outgrown, and the Dutch developed free of an academic tradition. Rembrandt was the greatest Dutch draftsman, but Rubens, Van Dyck, Teniers, and many others realized the full, spontaneous potential of the drawing. Callot in France did much the same in a more delicate, academic style. Except for some 16th-century artists of the Danube school, Claude Lorraine and Poussin were the first to develop the landscape drawing.

During the 18th century the Italians and French dominated drawing, Tiepolo in wash drawing and Watteau, Boucher, and other rococo artists in other forms. In the 19th century there were many styles of drawing, from the linear pencil studies by Ingres to the charcoal patches of Seurat; Delacroix, Daumier, Degas, Toulouse-Lautrec, Menzel, and many others worked in an expressive and lyrical manner. The drawings of such modern artists as Picasso, Matisse, Klee, and Kollwitz have achieved even greater independence as works of art in themselves.

See also DRAWING, TYPES OF.

BIBLIOGRAPHY. H. Leporini, *Die Stilentwicklung der Handzeichnung XIV. bis XVIII. Jahrhundert*, Vienna, 1925; C. de Tolnay, *History and Technique of Old Master Drawings*, New York, 1943.

JULIA M. EHRESMANN

DRAWING, TYPES OF. Reduced to its simplest definition, a drawing is a sheet on which an artist has drawn with some form of marking material. The materials for drawing, both the surface and the instrument that leaves the line, have great variety, but a drawing, in contrast to all forms of the graphic arts processes, is a unique creation of the artist, one in which the artist has placed his mark directly on the surface. Drawings can serve many purposes, but in general they can be grouped around one of four types by use: sketch, study, cartoon, and drawing.

The sketch serves the artist as a kind of memory. He uses it to capture impressions, record details, help plan a painting, sculpture, or work of architecture, and develop a visual idea. Sketches range from a few characteristic lines to an elaborate page indicating textures, lights and darks, and even the frame.

The study is used to further define individual forms, for instance, to explore the movement, posture, anatomy, or modeling of a figure. This may be done as an independent exercise or as a means of clarifying the various parts or the entire composition of a larger work. Studies are also made of the work of earlier masters, as part of the learning process (particularly in academic training), or as a means of reinterpreting the qualities of an earlier style. Watteau, for example, made studies of Italian masters, contemporary costumes, and life studies for paintings.

The cartoon has a more specific purpose and proportion. It is a full-scale drawing, usually made on a grid, intended to be reproduced on another surface and in another medium. The cartoon is most closely associated with mural painting, although cartoons have been preparatory drawings for tapestries and small objects of art. Among the most famous extant cartoons are seven by Raphael for a series of tapestries (London, Victoria and Albert). *See* CARTOON.

The fourth category is the drawing as a work of art in itself. Pastel portraits, Chinese brush drawings, and drawings by a number of modern masters fall into this category. They are intended to be complete works of art.

The materials of drawing vary perhaps more than the types of drawing. In the past the surface was wood, stone, parchment, and vellum; today it is generally paper. Since so much of the surface of a drawing is exposed, the choice of it is as important as the choice of coloring material. Papers vary in the texture of the surfaces from crinkled to almost glossy, the absorbent qualities, and the color. Thus a pen-and-ink drawing on a highly absorbent, colored paper differs from one on nonabsorbent, white paper.

There are five broad categories of drawing media: pen, brush, metal point, pencil, and broad line drawings. The first includes pen and ink—usually Chinese or India ink; tusche, bister, sepia, and modern nonbrown inks were developed after the 16th century. Brush drawings are drawings made with the brush and include Chinese brush drawing, dry brush, and wash drawings. The metal points are silverpoint, gold point, and lead point, all forerunners of pencil drawings (either natural or artificial graphite). The broad line media include crayon, chalk, pastel, and charcoal. *See* BRUSH DRAWING; CHALK DRAWING; CHARCOAL DRAWING; GOLD POINT DRAWING; INK DRAWING; PASTEL DRAWING; PENCIL DRAWING; PEN DRAWING; SILVERPOINT DRAWING. *See also* DRAWING, HISTORY OF.

BIBLIOGRAPHY. J. Meder, *Die Handzeichnung, ihre Technik und Entwicklung*, rev. 2d ed., Vienna, 1923; C. de Tolnay, *History and Technique of Old Master Drawings*, New York, 1943.
JULIA M. EHRESMANN

DREAM, THE. Oil painting by Rousseau, in the Museum of Modern Art, New York. *See* ROUSSEAU, HENRI.

DREIKONIGENSCHREIN, COLOGNE CATHEDRAL. Gilded copper and silver reliquary shrine made for the Cathedral of Cologne, Germany, in the late 12th and early 13th century. It is in the form of a Romanesque basilica and reproduces in miniature the sculptural program of the choir of the Cathedral. Begun in 1181 by Nicolas de Verdun, with additions made in 1198 and 1220, the Dreikönigenschrein is perhaps the most important reliquary shrine of the Middle Ages.

BIBLIOGRAPHY. H. Schnitzler, *Der Dreikönigenschrein*, Bonn, 1939.

DRESDEN. Industrial city in East Germany and former capital of the Kingdom of Saxony. Until its nearly complete destruction in the bombing raid of February, 1945, Dresden boasted one of the finest monumental ensembles in Europe. In view of the magnitude of the task, rebuilding efforts have been concentrated on the Old City, notably on the Zwinger.

Dresden was founded in the 12th century as a fortified town guarding the Elbe passage; in the following century a stone bridge was built across the river. Among the few noteworthy medieval buildings are the castle of the Hausmannsturm and the two-aisled Franziskanerkirche. The town hall dates from 1549-50. The modern phase of building in Dresden did not begin until after the Thirty Years' War, when Wolf Caspar von Klengel introduced the baroque style. His fine Opera House (1664–67) was destroyed by fire not long after completion. Klengel was succeeded by Johann Georg Starcke, who was entrusted with the building of an imposing palace, the Grosser Garten (1679–83). The reign of Augustus the Strong (1694–1733), despite its political failures, represented the culmination of Dresden's architecture. M. D. Pöppelmann's Zwinger became the central focus of a group of spectacular buildings along the river. These included two splendid churches, the Protestant Frauenkirche and the Catholic Hofkirche. The Frauenkirche (1725–43; destroyed), by Georg Bähr, was a high-domed square with rich corner pinnacles. The Roman architect Gaetano Chiaveri built the Hofkirche (begun 1737), which contains many altars and statues. Other important features of central Dresden included the Japanese Palace (begun 1715) and the Augustus Bridge (1728). Unlike most of the city palaces, a number of fine examples have survived in the countryside; among these are the Pillnitz (1720–24; architects Pöppelmann and others), Gross-Sedlitz and Moritzburg (both begun 1723; architects Zacharias Longuelune and Pöppelmann), and Ubigau (1724–26; architect J. F. Eosander von Göthe).

The dismantling of the fortifications in the early 19th century gave a renewed impulse to building. The influential architect and theorist Gottfried Semper came to Dresden in 1836, and the following year he began the Opera House in Neo-Renaissance style; after a fire in 1896 it was rebuilt with enrichments, and the building became a typical example of the German equivalent to Victorian architecture.

See also DRESDEN: STATE ART COLLECTIONS; LIEBFRAUENKIRCHE; ZWINGER PAVILION.

BIBLIOGRAPHY. E. Hempel, *Gaetano Chiaveri, der Architekt der katholischen Hofkirche zu Dresden*, Dresden, 1955; F. Löffler, *Das alte Dresden, Geschichte seiner Bauten*, Dresden, 1955; B. Geyer, *Die Stadtbild Alt-Dresdens, Baurecht und Baugestaltung*, Berlin, 1964.
WAYNE DYNES

DRESDEN: STATE ART COLLECTIONS. German museum. The most famous of the Dresden State Collections is undoubtedly the picture gallery of old masters with its treasures of German, Dutch, Italian, French, and Spanish painters of the 15th to the 18th century. Connected with this is the picture gallery of modern masters with important paintings of the 19th and 20th centuries.

The Dresden Picture Gallery, the basis of all the Dresden art collections, was originally the Kunstkammer. Founded in 1560 by Prince August, it was a collection in which all kinds of curiosities and rarities were gathered, as was the case in most of the princely German courts of the 16th century. These collections are often referred to as Chambers of Marvels, since their essential contents were not works of art but, rather, wonderful things and curiosities of all kinds. The Dresden collection included objects of various kinds of precious and other metals, complicated clocks, mathematical instruments, and horns as well as bronze sculpture from Italy, Chinese porcelains, graphic works, and even some paintings.

The Dresden art museum really dates from 1721, occupying a wing in the princely palace until it was dismantled in 1942. The Picture Gallery itself dates from 1722, when all the important paintings from the Kunstkammer, the princely palaces, and the various churches were brought together in one place. After various alterations the Picture Gallery was transferred in 1855 to a gallery building in the Zwinger Palace, built after plans by Gottfried Semper. The paintings remained there until the end of August, 1939, just before the beginning of World War II, when they were removed for safekeeping.

The most important portion of the famous paintings of the Dresden Picture Gallery began to come in after the death of August the Strong, under his son August III, with such works as Vermeer's *The Procuress*, Rubens's *Boar Hunt*, and paintings by Tintoretto and Van Dyck. From Paris came various treasures, such as Rembrandt's *Self-Portrait with Saskia* and *Adoration of the Kings*. In 1745 one hundred paintings were acquired, including Titian's *Tribute Money*. Raphael's *Sistine Madonna* was acquired in 1754. In 1853 fifteen important paintings were acquired from the former collection of Louis-Philippe of France. Other important acquisitions followed during the latter part of the 19th century.

Important works by modern masters were acquired in the late 19th and the early 20th century. The Dresden gallery, like many others in Germany, came under fire during the Hitler regime; forty-one paintings were removed from it, including works by Nolde, Kokoschka, Hofer, Grosz, and the various masters of Die Brücke. Graphic works and sculptures by modern German artists also suffered severely at this point.

Many of the treasures of the Dresden gallery were dispersed among forty-five castles and estates, a number of which were damaged during the last part of the war. Two hundred and six pictures were destroyed, most of them during the air attack on Dresden on Feb. 13, 1945, and the published catalog of 1963 indicates more than 500 lost pictures whose fate remains unknown. Some of these losses were the result of the confusion attending the collapse of the Nazi regime and the fact that a number of storage places were left without guards. Many paintings were taken back to the Soviet Union by the occupying Russian armies in East Germany, where they were taken care of and apparently restored. Ultimately, most of these were returned to the German Democratic Republic.

Since World War II the various buildings of the Dresden State Collections have been rebuilt. Thus the picture gallery of old masters is now in the Semper Building in the Zwinger Palace; the painting gallery of modern masters, on the second floor of the Albertinum. The sculpture collection will ultimately be housed in the latter building. All the other Dresden collections, including the graphics, coins, and applied arts, will eventually be placed in the former Residenz Palace.

BERNARD S. MYERS

DRESDEN PORCELAIN, *see* MEISSEN PORCELAIN.

DREVET, CLAUDE (17th cent.), *see* DERUET, CLAUDE.

DREVET, CLAUDE. French engraver (b. Loire, 1697; d. Paris, 1781). The last of the Drevet engravers, he studied under his uncle, Pierre Drevet, but was also influenced by his cousin, Pierre Imbert Drevet, and he carried on the tradition of engraved portraiture for which the family is famous. In 1739 he was given the use of the apartment in the Louvre which had been jointly held by his uncle and cousin. Actually Claude Drevet engraved only fourteen plates: five religious subjects and nine portraits. He combined the sureness of his uncle's hand with the artistry of his cousin, but he chiefly promoted the considerable work of his relatives.

BIBLIOGRAPHY. A. Firmin-Didot, *Les Drevet*, Paris, 1876.

DREVET, PIERRE. French engraver (b. Loire, 1663; d. Paris, 1738). The father of Pierre Imbert Drevet and the uncle of Claude Drevet, he studied engraving under Germain Audran in Lyon and then under Gérard Audran in Paris. His friendship with Hyacinthe Rigaud probably explains his specialization in portraiture. He became his own publisher in 1692, and was accepted as an academician by the Royal Academy in 1707. In 1726 he and his son were given the privilege of the apartment in the Louvre formerly used by Bérain. His work is a marvel of technical virtuosity, displaying infinite craftsmanship in the handling of decorative accessories such as lace, fur, and other materials. He was above all a portrait delineator of the first order.

BIBLIOGRAPHY. A. Firmin-Didot, *Les Drevet*, Paris, 1876.

DREVET, PIERRE IMBERT. French engraver (b. Paris, 1697; d. there, 1739). The son of Pierre Drevet and the cousin of Claude Drevet, he was taught by his father and worked with him throughout his life. He was received into the Royal Academy, and in 1726 was given the use of an apartment, with his father, in the Louvre. In 1729 he was named royal engraver. His work is considered superior to his father's; an engraved portrait of Bossuet is recognized as his *chef-d'oeuvre*, unequaled in technical brilliance. Unfortunately he was afflicted with a mental disorder, which accounts for the fact that many of his plates were finished by his father. Their authorship is therefore uncertain.

BIBLIOGRAPHY. A. Firmin-Didot, *Les Drevet*, Paris, 1876.

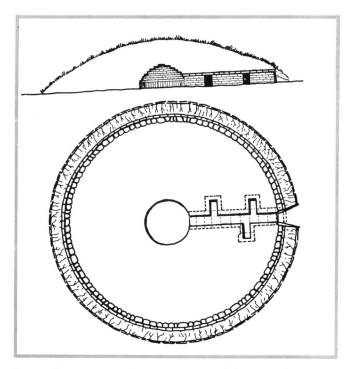

Dromos. Passageway to the inner chambers of Aegean tombs.

DREYER, BENEDICTUS. German woodcarver (fl. Lübeck, 1510–55). Dreyer was the chief master of manneristic late Gothic sculpture in Lübeck. His masterpiece, *St. Michael* (ca. 1515; Lübeck, Marienkirche), shows his painterly technique, which, quite characteristically, is free from detailed ornamentation.

BIBLIOGRAPHY. H. Deckert, "Studien zur hanseatischen Skulptur im Anfang des 16. Jahrhunderts," *Marburger Jahrbuch für Kunstwissenschaft*, I, Marburg, 1924.

DREYFUSS, HENRY. American industrial designer (1904–   ). Born in New York City, he has been cited as one of the half-dozen men who have most shaped industrial design in the United States since 1930. Working with such giants of American industry as the Bell Telephone Company, he has convinced manufacturers of the importance of good design in earning profits. At twenty, he apprenticed himself to designer Norman Bel Geddes, whose dynamic personality and radical stage designs made a lasting impression on him. Three years later, Dreyfuss himself was in demand as a stage designer. After traveling in Paris and North Africa, he opened his first industrial design office in 1929 in New York.

For him and for other pioneer designers, the Depression of the 1930s became a boon. For the first time, manufacturers actively sought out designers who could help sell goods by making them more attractive and efficient. For General Electric, in 1933, he designed a refrigerator whose motor was in the bottom instead of sitting on top; and for the New York World's Fair of 1939 he planned the interior of the Perisphere, making a scale model of the "city of tomorrow." Dreyfuss's work for the Crane Company has led a trend toward built-in plumbing fixtures. In graphic design, he has influenced such well-known magazines as *Time*, *Reader's Digest*, and *McCall's*. He has designed Hoover vacuum cleaners, Eversharp pens, Royal typewriters, bowling equipment for American Machine and Foundry, and gas stations for Cities Service Company.

Keeping his office relatively small, Dreyfuss stresses teamwork and research, and to every design problem he applies a five-point yardstick: utility and safety, maintenance, cost, sales appeal, and appearance.

BIBLIOGRAPHY. H. Dreyfuss, *Designing for People*, New York, 1955; H. Dreyfuss, *Ten Years of Industrial Design*, a series of privately printed volumes including a pictorial record of his work from the early years to 1957.   ANN FEREBEE

DRIELENBURG, WILLEM VAN. Dutch painter of landscapes and cityscapes (1632–after 1677). Drielenburg, a native of Utrecht, may have been a pupil of Abraham Bloemaert there. His landscapes, however, are strongly influenced by the work of Jan Both. In 1666 Drielenburg was listed in the records of the painters' college in Utrecht. In 1668 he moved to Dordrecht, where he is last mentioned in 1677. Arnold Houbraken was his pupil.

BIBLIOGRAPHY. W. Bernt, *Die niederländischen Maler des 17. Jahrhunderts...*, vol. 1, Munich, 1948.

DRINKERS, THE, *see* BORRACHOS, LOS.

DROLERIES. Type of subject matter common in all forms of Gothic art, but particularly in illuminated manuscripts and in carved wooden choir stalls. *Drôleries* are playful and sometimes satiric scenes that fill otherwise unadorned portions of works of art. In the most typical, men and animals play interchangeable roles, such as men hunting animals and animals hunting men.

DROLLING, MARTIN. French portraitist and genre painter (b. Oberbergheim, near Colmar, 1752; d. Paris, 1817). He studied in Schlestadt, in Strasbourg, and in Paris at the Ecole des Beaux-Arts, and exhibited at the Salons of 1793 to 1817. During the Empire he worked for the Sèvres porcelain factory. He prolonged the aesthetic authority of Chardin through his fondness for familiar interiors, in which meticulously painted utensils glint in half light. His sentiment, however, is anecdotal, sometimes trite, like Greuze's. Charmingly mischievous boys play pranks surreptitiously, and the innocence of *The Little Milkmaid* (ca. 1795; Strasbourg, Museum of Fine Arts) is implicit. He resuscitates the memory of the Le Nains, but he also pleasingly relieves the near-Gothic introspection of their peasant scenes with the effects of the intervening Age of Reason.

BIBLIOGRAPHY. H. Haug, *Natures: Catalogue de la collection du Musée des Beaux-Arts de Strasbourg*, Strasbourg, 1954.

DROMOS. Long, narrow passageway leading to the inner chamber of an Aegean tomb. The Aegean dromos was occasionally filled with earth, emptied, and filled again. The dromos of the Treasury of Atreus, Mycenae, approximately 20 feet wide by 115 feet long, led to a doorway with downward-tapered columns, beyond which was a large beehive-shaped chamber. *See also* THOLOS.

DROOGHSLOOT (Droochsloot), JOOST CORNELISZ. Dutch painter of historical subjects, cityscapes, portraits, and village scenes (b. Utrecht? 1586; d. there, 1666). Nothing is known of Drooghsloot's training; however, the influence of Abraham Bloemaert is apparent in his landscapes. The influence of the Brueghel tradition as well as of such painters as Bernard van Orley and Sebastiaen Vrancs might indicate that he traveled to Antwerp. He entered the Utrecht guild in 1616.

BIBLIOGRAPHY. A. P. de Mirimonde, "Deux portraits de J. C. Droochsloot par lui-même," *Oud-Holland*, LXXIII, 1958.

DROP ARCH, *see* ARCH, DROP.

DROUAIS, FRANCOIS-HUBERT. French painter (1727–75). He was born in Paris and was successively the pupil of his father, Hubert Drouais, and of D. Nonotte, C. A. Van Loo, Natoire, and Boucher. Provisionally accepted in the Academy in 1755, he was court painter in 1756, academician in 1758, counselor in 1774, and a protégé of Mme du Barry. François-Hubert Drouais was a characteristic 18th-century portraitist of high fashion; his court beauties and actresses in mythological guise manifest both faults of mannered superficiality and virtues of graceful charm, and are masterfully composed. They are conceived primarily as splendid personalized adjuncts to interior decoration. Though Diderot's condemnation of his portraits (at Salons from 1755 to 1775) may bear some truth, his elegant portraits of children (*Charles-Philippe of France and His Sister*, 1763; Paris, Louvre) sustain a refreshing French tradition that endured from the 15th century to Renoir.

BIBLIOGRAPHY. L. Réau, *Histoire de la peinture française au XVIIIe siècle . . .*, 2 vols., Paris, 1925–26; J. Seznec and J. Adhémar, *Diderot salons*, vol. 1, Oxford, Eng., 1957.

DROUAIS FAMILY. Three generations of French 18th-century painters: Hubert Drouais (b. near Pont-Audemer, Normandy, 1699; d. Paris, 1767); François-Hubert Drouais (1727–75); and Jean-Germain Drouais (b. Paris, 1763; d. Rome, 1788).

Hubert was a pupil of F. de Troy in Paris and did copy work after Belle, Oudry, Van Loo, and Nattier. He was admitted to the Royal Academy as a portraitist in 1730. His specialty was miniature, pastel, and oil portraits of fashionable actresses. Though appreciated in his own time, he was eclipsed by the vogue for the works of his son, François-Hubert, who was the best known of the family. *See* DROUAIS, FRANCOIS-HUBERT.

Jean-Germain was the son of François-Hubert. He studied with his father and with N. G. Brevet and J.-L. David. He won the Prix de Rome in 1784, and after manifesting brilliant promise as a history painter, he contracted malaria and died at the age of twenty-five.

BIBLIOGRAPHY. P. Dorbec, "Les Drouais," *Revue de l'art ancien et moderne*, XVI, 1904 and XVII, 1905.

DRUIDIC. The practices of the Druids, religious and political leaders of the Celts in ancient Gaul, Britain, and Ireland. During the 19th century the term "druidic" was mistakenly applied to such architectural works as Stonehenge and Carnac. Although these structures were used by the Druids for ceremonial purposes, they were actually constructed by Megalithic peoples during the 2d millennium B.C.

BIBLIOGRAPHY. G. E. Daniel, *The Prehistoric Chamber Tombs of France*, London, 1960.

DRUM. Cylindrical section of a column shaft. A drum is also the lower section of a dome or roof which it supports, such a drum being cylindrical, square, or polygonal. The Philippeion in Olympia has a cylindrical drum supporting a conical roof.

DRYAD. A wood nymph thought by the ancient Greeks to inhabit a tree and to be dependent on it for her life. Dryads, who were also known as hamadryads, were long-lived but not immortal: they died when their trees withered or were felled by axes. Grateful dryads could grant wishes to those who spared their tree abodes, but they could also cause harm to those who injured their pride.

DRYPOINT. An intaglio (incised) graphic process similar to etching. Its prime characteristic is a soft velvety line that, like the engraved line, tapers to a point at its ends. The anonymous Master of the Housebook (German, 15th cent.) is one of the early masters of this technique. If an engraved line may be described as cold and an etched line characterized as warm and fluid, then a drypoint line depicts the heat of the aesthetic moment. All the nuances of touch and pressure—the slightest scratch, the deepest furrow—are simply and directly transmitted from the artist, through his tool, to the plate.

A drypoint needle is worked directly upon a plate without benefit of ground. The needle, though it cuts into the plate, does not remove any of the metal; it merely displaces it, creating a furrow. The metal thrown up on either side of the furrow is called the burr and is responsible for the soft quality of the line. In the course of printing an edition of drypoints, the burr will be worn down and eventually break off, leaving a pale version of the original.

The needle should be made of the finest steel and be kept well sharpened. The plate is preferably of standard gauge copper, although many other metals and plastics may be employed. The use of copper allows maximum freedom for the drypoint lines and permits the printing of a fairly large edition. Most artists work directly upon the plate, without tracing the main lines of their compositions, and thus achieve a certain linear freedom. Etching ink is applied and the printing proceeds as in etching.

See also ETCHING.

BIBLIOGRAPHY. J. Heller, *Printmaking Today*, New York, 1958; A. M. Hind, *A History of Engraving and Etching*, 3d ed., rev., London, 1923 (repr. New York, 1963).   JULES HELLER

Drypoint. *Woman*, by Fiorenzo Giorgi. Private collection, Verona, Italy.

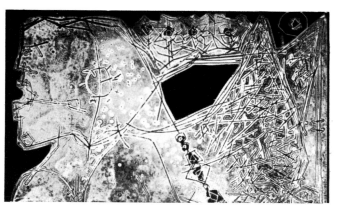

DRYSDALE, GEORGE RUSSELL. Australian regional painter (1912–). He was born in England, but received his early training at the George Bell School, in Melbourne. Later he studied in London and Paris. He is an outstanding and penetrating interpreter of the vast Australian outback and its inhabitants. His figures are highly stylized and elongated.

BIBLIOGRAPHY. G. Dutton, *Russell Drysdale*, London, 1964.

DUBAN, JACQUES FELIX. French architect (1797–1870). He worked in Paris and was associated with the rationalist (Neo-Greek) school. He is best known for the Seine façade of the Ecole des Beaux-Arts, designed in an original manner that rises above the eclectic modes of the Second Empire style.

BIBLIOGRAPHY. L. Hautecoeur, *Histoire de l'architecture classique en France*, vol. 6, Paris, 1955.

DUBBELS, HENDRICK JACOBSZ. Dutch painter of sea subjects (b. Amsterdam, 1620/21; d. there, 1676). Dubbels's early works have the cool gray tonality of Simon de Vlieger, who was living in Amsterdam from 1638. According to Arnold Houbraken, Dubbels was the teacher of Ludolf Bakhuisen in about 1650. In 1663 he was listed as a shopkeeper. Dubbels also painted a few winter landscapes (Madrid, Prado).

BIBLIOGRAPHY. F. C. Willis, *Die niederländische Marinemalerei*, Leipzig, 1911.

DUBLE, LU. American sculptor (1896–). Born in Oxford, England, Lu Duble studied at the Art Students League, the National Academy of Design, and the Cooper Union Art School, all in New York City. She also studied under Archipenko, De Creeft, and Hofmann. In 1937–38 she was awarded a Guggenheim Fellowship. She has taught at Bennett College in Greensboro, N.C., and at the Dalton School in New York.

At the Metropolitan Museum's "American Sculpture 1951" (a national competitive exhibition), she showed *Dark Mother* (plaster, 14 inches). In the Whitney Museum of American Art, she is represented by *Cain* (1953).

Her style is expressionistic. *El Penitente* (plaster model for bronze), for example, is reminiscent of Ernst Barlach.

BIBLIOGRAPHY. Sculptor's Guild, *Fourth Outdoor Sculpture Exhibition, 1942*, New York, 1942; J. I. A. Baur, *Revolution and Tradition in Modern American Art*, Cambridge, Mass., 1951.

DUBLIN: CUSTOMS HOUSE. Georgian structure in Ireland. Built around two courtyards, the Dublin Customs House displays a handsome domed façade that overlooks the Liffey River. It was erected between 1781 and 1791 by James Gandon, a pupil of Sir William Chambers.

DUBLIN: MUSEUMS. Important public art collections in Dublin, Ireland, are located in the museums listed below.

Municipal Art Gallery. It shares with the National Gallery in London, the Sir Hugh Lane Collection, which includes such paintings as Renoir's *Les Parapluies*, Manet's *Eva Gonzalès*, and Daumier's *Don Quixote and Sancho Panza*. Among the gallery's permanent possessions works by the Barbizon, French impressionist, and modern European schools are represented, as is a wide variety of works by Irish painters and sculptors.

National Gallery. Qualitatively one of the finest museums

François-Hubert Drouais, *Child with a Doll*. Painting Museum, Grenoble.

of Europe, containing important works from all schools of painting. New building construction and renovation have enlarged and modernized the exhibitions. In the collections are works by Fra Angelico, Michelangelo, Perugino, Titian, Tintoretto, El Greco, Murillo, Mantegna, Goya, Poussin, Rembrandt, Frans Hals, Hogarth, Reynolds, and Gainsborough, as well as a representative Irish group. Among the most notable treasures are Fra Angelico's *The Attempted Martyrdom of SS. Cosmas and Damian Under the Proconsul Lysias*, Titian's portrait of Baldassare Castiglione, Mantegna's *Judith with the Head of Holofernes*, and Rembrandt's *Shepherds Resting at Night* and *Portrait of a Young Woman*.

National Museum. Includes the national collections of antiquities and fine arts (except painting). Of special interest are the rich assortment of prehistoric gold objects and the relics of the Early Christian period, such as shrines, bells, croziers, brooches, and other items of artistic metalwork. Among the important exhibits are the Tara Brooch, Ardagh Chalice, Lismore Crozier, Shrine of St. Patrick's Bell, and Cross of Cong.

Trinity College Library. Part of the oldest Irish institution of higher learning, this library now holds, among its 5,000 manuscripts, the world's foremost collection of early Irish illuminated manuscripts. The building was designed by Thomas Burgh and constructed between 1712 and 1732. Acquisition of the Ussher Library in 1661 brought into the collection its renowned masterpiece, the Book of Kells, an elaborately illuminated Gospel book of the 8th century.

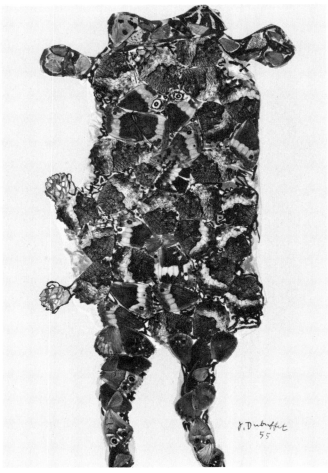

Jean Dubuffet, *Personnage au Chapeau*, 1955. Thompson Collection, Pittsburgh.

It is on display in the Long Room, along with other outstanding productions of the Irish monasteries. These include the 7th-century Book of Durrow, the oldest extant example, the 8th-century Book of Dimma and Book of Mulling, and the 9th-century Garland of Howth and Book of Armagh. A new building, connected to the old library by a basement extension, opened in 1967.

BIBLIOGRAPHY. F. Henry, *Early Christian Irish Art*, Dublin, 1954.

DUBOIS (Bosschaert), AMBROISE. French history, portrait, and decorative painter (b. Antwerp, 1543; d. Fontainebleau, 1614). A leading painter of the second school of Fontainebleau, Dubois came to France as a youth (1568?) and may have lived a number of years in Troyes. He entered the service of Henry IV in 1592 and became a French citizen in 1601. In 1606, he was made Painter to the Queen, Marie de Médicis, and in 1608, Custodian of the Royal Collection. Dubois, whose style betrays the influence of Dubreuil but is more mannered, was a master of decoration. At Fontainebleau he painted Heliodorus's history of Theagenes and Chariclea and collaborated with D'Hoey in the decoration of the Chapelle-Haute. At the Louvre he decorated the queen's apartment with a suite of scenes from Tasso's *Clorinda*. His magnum opus, now destroyed, was the Galerie de Diane at Fontainebleau. As-

pects of this sumptuous composition are preserved by water colors of Percier and Fontaine (Paris, Library of the Institute of France). In his baroque disposition of space and his opulent but ordered decorations, Dubois prefigures such masters as Simon Vouet and Le Brun.

BIBLIOGRAPHY. S. Béguin, *L'Ecole de Fontainebleau*, Paris, 1960.

DUBOIS, GUILLEM (Guilliam). Dutch landscape painter (b. ca. 1610; d. Haarlem, 1680). Dubois's early works show the influence of Alexander Keirinckx and, perhaps, even reminiscences of Gillis van Coninxloo. In the 1640s he had a Hercules Seghers phase. In 1652 Dubois traveled through Germany with Cornelis Bega and Theodoor Helmbreker. Adriaen van de Velde painted figures for him.

BIBLIOGRAPHY. W. Stechow, *Dutch Landscape Painting of the Seventeenth Century*, London, 1966.

DU BOIS, GUY PENE. American painter (b. Brooklyn, 1884; d. Boston, 1958). He was a student of Chase, Henri, and Miller and went to Paris in 1905 to study with Steinlen. On his return he wrote for various newspapers and magazines. Du Bois's early paintings were dark genre scenes in the realist Ashcan spirit. Gradually his figures became more tightly painted and assumed a solidly sculptural, simplified form, for example, *Opera Box* (1926; New York, Whitney Museum). His subject was the social life of the rich, which he treated satirically. In the 1930s he began to paint portraits and figures in an academic style. He wrote several monographs on American artists.

BIBLIOGRAPHY. G. P. Du Bois, *Artists Say the Silliest Things*, New York, 1940.

DUBOIS, PAUL. French sculptor and painter (b. Nogent-sur-Seine, 1829; d. Paris, 1905). He first studied law, then received his artistic training with Toussaint and from 1858 at the Ecole des Beaux-Arts in Paris. He lived in Italy from 1859 to 1862. His early genre sculptures, such as the *Florentine Singer* (1865; Paris, Louvre), were influenced by Rude and especially by the Renaissance bronzes of Donatello and Verrocchio. Dubois was generally interested in a revival of Renaissance treatment. His most famous monument, the tomb of General Lamoricière (1876–78) in Nantes Cathedral, is based on French tombs of the 16th century. He also executed portrait busts and painted portraits.

DUBREUIL, TOUSSAINT. French history painter (b. Paris, ca. 1561; d. there, 1602). The leading painter of the second school of Fontainebleau, Dubreuil studied with Médéric Fréminet, father of Martin Fréminet. As Painter to King Henry IV, Dubreuil was active at Fontainebleau: he restored Primaticcio's Galerie d'Ulysse and painted *The Labors of Hercules* in the Pavillon des Poesles and views of the royal residences in the Galerie des Cerfs.

At the Louvre he painted the ceiling of the Petite Galerie, where his *Battle of Titans* became famous (the gallery burned in 1661). He decorated the Château de Saint-Germain-en-Laye, mostly with mythological subjects, and designed a set of tapestries on the story of Diana, basing it on an earlier series possibly drawn by Jean Cousin the Elder.

Little of Dubreuil's work remains except for a few panels from Saint-Germain. He was an able organizer; since most of his decorations were executed by assistants, we may judge him fairly only from numerous drawings, for the most part in the Louvre. These betray such varied influences as Primaticcio, Niccolò dell'Abbate, and Michelangelo and show the mark of a highly sensitive, personal painter. In the feeling for substance and clarity that permeates his basically mannerist compositions may be found the roots of French 17th-century painting.

BIBLIOGRAPHY. S. Béguin, "Toussaint Dubreuil, peintre de Henri IV," *Art de France*, IV, 1964.   PHILIPPE DE MONTEBELLO

DUBROEUCQ, JACQUES.
Flemish sculptor and architect (b. Mons, 1500/10; d. there, 1584). Dubroeucq was in Rome before 1535; Giovanni da Bologna was his pupil (1544–50). His early works are his best, but they survive in fragments, such as the reliefs from the rood screen of St. Waltrudis in Mons (1545–48; screen destroyed in 1797). Schloss Binche, the first Netherlandish palace done directly from French models, was his architectural masterpiece; it was executed for Maria of Hungary between 1545 and 1549 and destroyed in 1554. Dubroeucq's atelier also copied the sculptures of Germain Pilon. Gifted with a strong plastic and rhythmic sense, he may be placed between the Renaissance and baroque styles.

BIBLIOGRAPHY. R. Hedicke, *Jacques Dubroeucq . . . von Mons*, Strasbourg, 1904.

DUBROVNIK.
Late medieval city, surrounded by 15th-century walls, on the Dalmatian coast of Yugoslavia. Preserved intact are an old city, churches, monasteries, palaces, houses, and a harbor. The local gallery contains works by painters of that area, especially those of the 15th and early 16th centuries. *See* RECTOR'S PALACE.

DUBUFFET, JEAN.
French painter (1901–   ). A native of Le Havre, he went to Paris in 1928. He studied briefly at the Académie Julian but was mainly self-taught. Dubuffet developed a visionary approach to art. For several years he was forced to give up painting in order to provide for his family, and he became a wine dealer. He resumed his art in 1940, using extraordinary mixtures of ashes, sand, and cinders bound by a congealing thick varnish. The resultant clotted crust is engraved or incised with line. Dubuffet's style is called *l'art brut*, or "raw art;" and he consciously invents antiaesthetic, quasisurrealist images. Scrawls and childlike figures populate his brown-toned, densely pigmented compositions. Typical canvases are *Eyes Closed* (1954; New York, Pierre Matisse Gallery) and *Paris Montparnasse* (1961; Paris, private collection).

Dubuffet in 1948 founded the Société de l'Art Brut and assembled hundreds of crude works by prisoners, fortune-tellers, and the insane. He has been represented in one-man shows at the Galerie Rive Gauche and the Galerie Drouin in Paris, the Pierre Matisse Gallery and the Museum of Modern Art in New York, and elsewhere; and has exhibited at the Venice, Pittsburgh, and other major internationals. Dubuffet's art, impossible to classify precisely, relates to French *tachisme*, Dada-surrealism, and expressionism.

BIBLIOGRAPHY. D. Cardier, *The Drawings of Jean Dubuffet*, New York, 1960; L. Pippard, "Ernst and Dubuffet," *Art Journal*, XXI, Summer, 1962; P. Selz, *The Work of Jean Dubuffet*, New York, 1962.   JOHN C. GALLOWAY

DUC, JOSEPH LOUIS.
French architect (1802–79). He worked in Paris. He was a pupil of Percier and a Prix de Rome winner. His huge all-metal Colonne de Juillet (1831–40) is one of the major examples of the modified Greek style characteristic of rationalist (Neo-Greek) architecture.

BIBLIOGRAPHY. P. Sédille, *Joseph Louis Duc*, Paris, 1879.

DUCAL PALACE,
see MANTUA; URBINO; VENICE.

DUCCIO DI BUONINSEGNA.
Italian painter of the Sienese school (1255/60–1319). Duccio was the first and greatest of a number of painters who, in the first half of the 14th century, created in Siena what was perhaps the most profoundly lyrical of all schools of painting. He was born in Siena, the son of Buoninsegno di Lucchese. One of his nephews, the son of his brother Bonaventura, was the painter Segna di Bonaventura. Duccio is first recorded in 1278 as a painter of twelve chests for safeguarding the public records of the commune. In 1279 he was paid for decorating the cover of one of the official registers, or the *biccherna*. Duccio received other payments for painting the covers of *biccherna* (for which the commune commissioned all its leading painters during the 14th and 15th cent.) in 1286, 1291, 1292, 1294, and 1295. None of these has survived. In 1295 he was a member of a municipal commission charged with recommending the site for a proposed fountain. From a document of 1304 it appears that he was the owner of a vineyard at Castagneto, near Siena. In 1313 he was living in the San Quirico quarter of Siena, near the Cathedral.

Of his three major documented works, one (an altarpiece of the *Maestà* commissioned for the chapel in the Palazzo Pubblico, Siena, in 1302) has been lost. The second, ordered by the Company of the Laudesi of S. Maria Novella in Florence on Apr. 15, 1285, is a large *Madonna and Child Enthroned with Angels* (Florence, Uffizi), known as the *Rucellai Madonna*. Attributed by Vasari to Cimabue, it was recognized as Duccio's only in the 20th century, long after the contract had been discovered, in 1790. The Virgin, with the Infant Christ on her lap, is seated on a luxurious throne supported at either side by three kneeling angels. The frame, which, as in all panels of the time, forms an integral part of the painting and is continuous with it, is decorated with medallions containing the busts of prophets and saints. The style of the *Rucellai Madonna* is primarily linear; its Byzantine background has been interpreted with an entirely new sense of immediacy and spatiality. It is as if Byzantine ritual had been transformed into romance and poetry.

Duccio's third major commission is the most extensive of his works: the altarpiece of the *Maestà* now in the Museo dell'Opera Metropolitana in Siena. He signed the contract for its execution in 1308, agreeing not to take on other jobs before it was completed. On June 9, 1311, the finished altarpiece was transferred from Duccio's studio to the high altar of the Cathedral in a solemn and elaborate procession. The *Maestà* was painted on two sides. The front contained the large, courtly *Madonna and Child Enthroned Surrounded by Saints and Angels*, surmounted, on either side of the Madonna, by small half-length figures of apostles; a predella, the *Infancy of Christ*, with seven

scenes interspersed with small figures of prophets; and eight pinnacles surmounted by busts of angels dedicated to scenes from the last days of the Virgin, two of which (the *Assumption* and the *Coronation*) have been lost.

The back consisted of twenty-six scenes from the *Passion of Christ* (reading from left to right in two zones composed, save for the *Entry into Jerusalem* in the lower zone and the *Crucifixion* in the upper one, of two superimposed rows of panels); a predella of ten panels, the *Early Life of Christ* (two of which, the *Baptism* and the *First Temptation*, have been lost); and eight pinnacles containing episodes after the Resurrection. The inscription on the base of the Virgin's throne reads: MATER SANCTA DEI—SIS CAUSA SENIS REQUIEI—SIS DUCIO VITA—TE QUIA DEPINXIT ITA (Holy Mother of God, grant peace to Siena and life to Duccio who has painted you thus).

The *Maestà* was removed from the high altar of the Cathedral in 1506; in 1795 its two sides were split and shown separately in one of the chapels there. By 1881, when the altarpiece was installed in the museum, a number of its panels had been destroyed and dispersed. Three panels are in the National Gallery in London; four, in the National Gallery of Art in Washington, D.C. (one of which, the *Nativity* from the front predella, is flanked by the two small figures of prophets); one, in the Frick Collection in New York; and one, in the Rockefeller Collection in New York. Five busts of angels (one each in Wellesley, Mass., the Stoclet Collection in Brussels, and the Johnson Collection in Philadelphia, and two in the Loeser Collection in Florence) by assistants of Duccio seem to have belonged to the *Maestà*. The narrative, coloristic, and compositional subtlety of its panels parallels, on an intimate scale, the approximately contemporary innovations of Giotto in the Arena Chapel and sets the course of Sienese painting for at least 150 years.

Duccio's *oeuvre* includes the early, small *Madonna of the Franciscans*, the *Madonna and Child*, and two later, many-compartmented polyptychs with the *Madonna and Child with Saints and Angels* (all in Siena, National Picture Gallery). Other *Madonna and Child* panels are in the Museo dell'Opera Metropolitana in Siena and in the National Gallery of Umbria in Perugia; an exquisite small triptych with the *Madonna and Child* in the center is in the National Gallery in London. Other works associated with Duccio are in the Archiepiscopal Museum in Utrecht, the Art Museum in Bern, the Frick Collection in New York, the Museum of Fine Arts in Boston, and elsewhere. Duccio is presumed to have designed the large, round stained-glass window in the Siena Cathedral containing the *Coronation*, the *Assumption and Dormition of the Virgin*, *Four Saints*, and the *Four Evangelists*.

Duccio's several immediate followers include Segna di Bonaventura, Ugolino da Siena, and the Master of the Badia ad Isola. He was an innovator in his experimentations with perspective and in his adoption of the decorative delicacy and narrative liveliness of the Gothic style of France and Burgundy. His greatest achievement was the creation of a new Sienese school of painting through the fresh interpretation and the transformation of the Byzantine tradition.

BIBLIOGRAPHY. C. H. Weigelt, *Duccio*, Leipzig, 1911; E. Cecchi, *Trecentisti senesi*, Rome, 1928; C. H. Weigelt, "The Problem of the Rucellai Madonna," *Art in America*, XVIII, 1929–30; E. Carli, *Duccio di Buoninsegna*, Milan, 1962; J. White, *Art and Architecture in Italy, 1250–1400*, Baltimore, 1966.

HELLMUT WOHL

DU CERCEAU FAMILY. French architects and decorators (fl. 16th and 17th cent.). Jacques Androuet du Cerceau the Elder (ca. 1520–after 1584) is known only through his books of architectural engravings. None of the small number of buildings he designed has survived. The larger part of his engravings are decorative and can be traced back to Italian originals. His first books were *Arcs* (1549), *Temples* (1550), and *Vues d'optique* (1551). In 1559 he published the *Livre d'architecture* containing fifty designs of town houses composed of one or more simple blocks, often with elaborate surface decoration, and on the inside divided into apartment units. Jacques the Elder's best-known book is *Les Plus excellents bâtiments de France* (1576 and 1579), an important source of information on French 16th-century architecture. He designed two châteaux: Verneuil (ca. 1565–1600) and Charleval (begun in 1573 for Charles IX but abandoned almost immediately). His fantastic and almost excessively involved ornamental style influenced French architecture for some time.

Baptiste du Cerceau, Jacques the Elder's brother, was a mannerist architect in the tradition of Bullant. He built the Hôtel d'Angoulême (1584; now the Hôtel de Lamoignon) in Paris for Diane de France.

Jacques du Cerceau the Younger (ca. 1550–1614) designed the Hôtel de Mayenne (begun in 1605 for Charles, duc de Mayenne), which was based on the 16th-century Hôtel Carnevalet.

Jean du Cerceau (ca. 1585–after 1647), Baptiste's son, was the most important designer of Parisian town houses during the reign of Louis XIII. Among his works are the Hôtel de Sully (1624–29) and the Hôtel de Bretonvilliers (1637–43; demolished in the 19th cent.). *See* SULLY, HOTEL DE, PARIS.

BIBLIOGRAPHY. A. Blunt, *Art and Architecture in France, 1500–1700*, Baltimore, 1954.　HELLMUT WOHL

DUCHAMP, GASTON, *see* VILLON, JACQUES.

DUCHAMP, MARCEL. French painter (1887–1968). He was born in Blainville, Normandy, and was the brother of the artists Suzanne Duchamp, Jacques Villon, and Raymond Duchamp-Villon. As a youth he attended school in Rouen. After moving to Paris, he worked as a librarian at the Bibliothèque Ste-Geneviève and, with some training at the Académie Julian, taught himself to paint. Duchamp's strongest early influence was Cézanne, as is revealed in such early canvases as *Chapel at Blainville* (1904) and *Portrait of the Artist's Father* (1910), both in the Philadelphia Museum of Art, Arensberg Collection.

A certain brilliance attended Duchamp's efforts from the very first; and a notable independence of intellect kept him from aligning himself totally with any programmatic movement. He and Francis Picabia, whose aims resembled his own, worked in 1911 and 1912 in a method closely re-

Duccio di Buoninsegna, Madonna and Child Enthroned with Angels (known as the Rucellai Madonna). Uffizi, Florence.

Marcel Duchamp, *Nude Descending a Staircase II*, 1912. Philadelphia Museum of Art (Louise and Walter Arensberg Collection).

Raymond Duchamp-Villon, *Seated Woman*. Yale University Art Gallery, New Haven, Conn.

lated to analytic cubism. Duchamp's renowned *Nude Descending a Staircase II* (Arensberg Collection) also implies, although not distinctly, a connection with Italian futurism. In any case, his deeper purposes were antirepresentational, despite the fact that the titles of his works were meaningful to him and were often lettered on the picture surface.

By 1913 Duchamp was clearly prefiguring the Swiss-based Dada movement of 1916. His paintings became increasingly whimsical in character and sometimes depicted curious and useless machines (*Chocolate Grinder No. 1*, 1913); in 1915 and 1916 he arrived at the use of unconventional materials and techniques, as in *Water Mill within Glider* (Arensberg Collection), in which he used oil paint combined with wire on a lunette-shaped glass sheet.

In 1916 Duchamp also created his astonishing "readymades," satirically formed assemblages of such everyday items as combs, shovels, balls of twine, and bicycle wheels. This style, with notable variants and with occasional regressions to compositions on glass (which he sometimes cracked for special effects), continued into the early 1920s. He signed some works "Rrose Sélavy," a word play on "arroser c'est la vie" (to water, that's life).

Duchamp's personal and professional activities in connection with Dada and abstract art were central to the ultimate acceptance of both by a large audience. The *succès de scandale* of his *Nude Descending a Staircase* and its sale along with that of his other three entries in the controversial New York Armory Show of 1913 had prepared the way for Duchamp's visiting the United States two years later. With Man Ray, Picabia, and Alfred Stieglitz, Duchamp founded the review *291*, followed in 1917 by his journal *The Blind Man* and *Rong-Wrong*. He and Katherine S. Dreier founded the important Société Anonyme in New York in 1920, the year in which he exhibited his notorious *L.H.O.O.Q.*, the Mona Lisa with a mustache and beard. In those high days of Dada, Duchamp's verbal as well as painterly lucidity marked him as one of the international leaders of the movement, even while he remained a singularly independent personality.

True to his own Dadaist vow to annihilate painting, Duchamp in 1923 ceased working on his *Bride Stripped Bare by Her Bachelors, Even* (Philadelphia Museum of Art, Dreier Bequest) and turned to chess, writing a study of the game in 1926, and to experiments in optical theory and occasional organization of surrealist exhibitions and publications. He published an occasional "suitcase" during the 1930s, each case containing sketches and notes relating to his major works including the *Bride Stripped Bare*. He also helped to edit the surrealist publication *Minotaure* and was instrumental in organizing the International Surrealist Exhibition in Paris in 1938. He was cofounder of the review *VVV* (1940–42). The special March number of *View* was devoted to Duchamp. He was again active in arranging a surrealist show, the 1947 International at the Galerie Maeght in Paris, where he designed two special rooms.

Duchamp had spent most of his life after 1915 in New York City. He was a constant influence upon younger artists, more because of his presence than because of his activities; and yet his existence long kept alive the unrestrictive, liberating tradition of Dada.

See also DADA.

BIBLIOGRAPHY. A. H. Barr, Jr., ed., *Fantastic Art, Dada, Surrealism*, New York, 1936; K. S. Dreier and Matta Echuarren, *Duchamp's Glass: An Analytical Reflection*, New York, 1944; S. Janis, *Abstract and Surrealist Art in America*, New York, 1944; K. Kuh and D. C. Rich, *20th-Century Art, from the Louise and Walter Arensberg Collection*, exhibition catalog, Chicago, 1949; R. Motherwell, *The Dada Painters and Poets: An Anthology*, New York, 1951; W. Verkauf, ed., *Dada: Monograph of a Movement*, Teufen, 1957; H. Richter, *Dada: Art and Anti-Art*, New York, 1965.

JOHN C. GALLOWAY

DUCHAMP-VILLON, RAYMOND. French sculptor, cubist architect, and physician (b. Damville, 1876; d. Cannes, 1918). He was the brother of Jacques Villon and Marcel Duchamp. After studying medicine for three years, he became a sculptor in 1898. Exhibiting frequently in Paris salons, he joined with the cubists in 1912. His design for a cubist house dates from that year. His work was in the New York Armory Show of 1913. During service in World War I he contracted blood poisoning and died.

The Museum of Modern Art, New York, owns a cast of his great *Horse* (1914) and *Lovers* (1913), the Yale University Art Gallery, New Haven, has *Seated Woman* (1914), and the Guggenheim Museum, New York, has *Cat* (1913). Duchamp-Villon was one of the first to evolve the modern sculptural metaphor.

BIBLIOGRAPHY. C. Giedion-Welcker, *Contemporary Sculpture*, New York, 1955.

DUCHATEL (DUCHASTEL), FRANS. Flemish painter (1625–ca. 1694). Born in Brussels, the artist was a painter of portraits and plein-air compositions. He also painted military scenes in the manner of Adam Frans van der Meulen, with whom he had worked in Paris. His early apprenticeship was served under David Teniers the Younger, and Teniers's influence prevailed in Duchatel's renderings of figures.

BIBLIOGRAPHY. R. Oldenbourg, *Die flämische Malerei des 17. Jahrhunderts*, 2d ed., Berlin, 1922.

DUCK, JACOB. Dutch painter of genre and etcher (b. Utrecht? ca. 1600; d. there, 1667). He was a pupil of Joost Cornelisz. Drooghsloot in Utrecht and in 1621 was still reported as a pupil. He was a master in the Utrecht Guild of St. Luke from 1626 to 1632. In 1629 Duck presented a painting, *Musical Company*, to the Hiobsgasthuis in Utrecht. He remained in Utrecht until 1646; between 1656 and 1660 he was active in The Hague. Duck is best known for genre interiors, often with soldiers, such as *The Winecellar* (signed J. Duck; Amsterdam, Rijksmuseum). Paintings such as *Woman Ironing* (signed JA. Duck; Utrecht, Centraal Museum) suggest some relation to certain Leyden painters—Gerrit Dou, Willem van Mieris, and Gabriel Metsu—but the exact nature of the relationship has not been defined.

BIBLIOGRAPHY. F. Schlie, "Jacob Duck," *Repertorium für Kunstwissenschaft*, XIII, 1890.

DUCLOS, ANTOINE JEAN. French engraver and etcher (b. Paris, 1742; d. there, 1795). A pupil of Saint-Aubin, Duclos executed historical plates, even of contemporary events, and produced series of technically accomplished vignettes and book title pages (etched), especially after Gravelot, C. Eisen, C. P. Marilliet, and Moreau.

BIBLIOGRAPHY. H. Cohen, *Guide de l'amateur de livres à gravures du XVIIIe siècle*, 6th ed., Paris, 1912.

DUCREUX, BARON JOSEPH. French portraitist (b. Nancy, 1735; d. Paris, 1802). He was sent to Vienna in 1769 to portray the imperial family. He then became First Painter to Marie-Antoinette and, later, portraitist of the French Revolution, the Directorate, and the Consulate. Though his portraits are good likenesses, they lack the psychological vivacity of his master, Maurice-Quentin de La Tour.

BIBLIOGRAPHY. P. Dorbec, "Joseph Ducreux," *Gazette des Beaux-Arts*, 3d series, XXXVI, 1906.

DUDOK, WILLEM MARINUS. Dutch architect-planner (1884–   ). He was born in Amsterdam. Trained as a military engineer, he served in the army until 1913, when

Willem Marinus Dudok, the "Bijenkorf," Rotterdam, 1929.

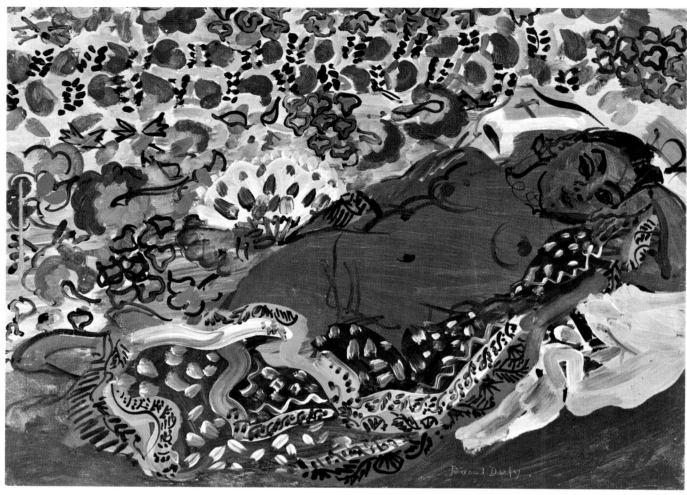

Raoul Dufy, *L'Hindoue*, 1928. Galerie Louis Carré, Paris. The artist painted in a sketchy, arabesque style.

he became the municipal engineer of Leyden. In 1915 he became director of public works for Hilversum and since 1927 has been its city architect. Although he worked independently of de Stijl, he was greatly influenced by the work of Frank Lloyd Wright. Of particular importance are his masterplan of Hilversum, Municipal Baths, Dr. H. Bavinck School (all 1921); Slaughterhouse (1923); Netherlands Student House, Cité Universitaire, Paris (1927); and "Bijenkorf," Rotterdam (1929). His masterpiece is the Hilversum Town Hall, designed in 1924 and executed between 1928 and 1931.

BIBLIOGRAPHY. W. M. Dudok, *Willem M. Dudok*, Amsterdam, 1954; R. F. Jordan, "Dudok and the Repercussions of his European Influence," *The Architectural Review*, CXV, April, 1954.

DUFRESNE, CHARLES. French painter, decorator, and graphic artist (b. Millemont, 1876; d. Seyne-sur-Mer, 1938). He studied in Paris and lived in Algiers from 1910 to 1912. Dufresne painted exotic landscapes and fantastic scenes in a colorful Fauvist-cubist style.

DUFRESNOY, CHARLES ALPHONSE. French history painter and theoretician (1611–68). He was born in Paris but lived mostly in Rome from 1634, in learned pursuit of Nicolas Poussin's precepts. His Latin poem, *De arte*

graphica (1667), which embodied both classical and Venetian doctrines, was useful to Roger de Piles in support of the "Moderns," or Rubenists.

BIBLIOGRAPHY. L. Demonts, "Deux peintres de la première moitié du XVIIe siècle: Jacques Blanchard et Charles-Alphonse Dufresnoy," *Gazette des Beaux-Arts*, 5th series, XII, 1925.

DUFY, RAOUL. French painter and decorator (b. Le Havre, 1877; d. Forcalquier, Basses-Alpes, 1953). He studied art first in Le Havre. In 1892 he met Georges Braque and Othon Friesz, fellow art students. He admired Boudin and Delacroix. By 1900 he had gone to Paris to study at the Ecole des Beaux-Arts and felt the impact of the art of the impressionists, of Van Gogh, and of Cézanne. He exhibited for the first time at the Salon des Indépendants in 1903, and three years later he had his first one-man show. By 1904 he was painting harbor scenes in bright color in a manner that led him to join Matisse, Marquet, and Van Dongen as a Fauve. He was deeply impressed by *Luxe, Calme et Volupté* by Matisse, shown at the Salon d'Automne in 1905.

While living with Braque at L'Estaque in 1909, Dufy changed his style, and his palette became more somber. His painting at this time stemmed from late Cézanne and was related to the earliest phase of cubism. He began to make woodcuts as illustrations for books. In 1910 he printed some of these on dress fabrics. The brilliant colors printed on silks so delighted him that he abandoned his cubist manner and began to develop a fashionably decorative style to which he adhered for the rest of his life. Furthermore, he found a ready market for his fabric designs.

By 1920, however, Dufy had abandoned this profitable project and devoted himself completely to painting, drawing, and lithography. He traveled to Morocco and Venice, and lived much of the time on the French Riviera. He did many water colors. In 1936–37 he designed a mural painting (200 ft. by 32 ft.) on the theme of scientific progress for the Electricity Building for the Paris World's Fair. In 1952 he won first prize at the Venice Biennale. A large retrospective was given him in Paris in 1953.

In a sketchy manner, with fragmented brush strokes and flourishes of arabesques, Dufy depicted the carefree world of fashion, luxury, and pleasure. He painted resort centers, such as Nice and Trouville; spectacles, such as parades, horse races, and symphony concerts; and intimate corners of a music room or a studio. With disarming simplicity and yet with breadth and imagination he applied bright, rich color thinly on a white surface so it appeared as luminous as colored glass. He tended to avoid browns and grays but took obvious pleasure in juxtaposing large blocks of deep ultramarine and emerald green with scarlet, lemon yellow, orange, and white. On these tones, he superimposed and integrated a linear pattern, a drawing that defined his subjects. Elegant, often facile, unpretentious, and charming, Dufy's art glorifies the civilized life and French taste and sensibility.

BIBLIOGRAPHY. P. Courthion, *Raoul Dufy*, Geneva, 1951.

ROBERT REIFF

DUGENTO. Italian term meaning two hundred, used as an abbreviation for twelve hundred. It designates the art, and by extension the whole culture, of the 13th century in Italy. The term Dugento painting now replaces the obsolete designation "Italian primitive."

DUGHET, GASPARD (Gaspard Poussin; Le Guaspre). French landscape painter (1613–75). He was the son of a Parisian, Jacques du Ghets, who was established in Rome; Gaspard was born, lived, and died in Rome. The adoption of the nickname "Poussin" is based upon his lifelong admiration for the work of Poussin, whom his sister married. Dughet's development has never been definitely established. He is traditionally believed to have been Poussin's pupil between 1630 and 1633, but his early style (ca. 1630–45) reflects the inspiration of Elsheimer and Brill in its preference for storm scenes and for strong light and dark contrasts manneristically composed. This tradition was most likely suggested to him in his youth in Rome by Salvator Rosa, for large decorative works in the Colonna and Doria palaces overflow with dynamic movement, intuitive perspective, and picturesque figural motifs, which were merely accessory to the romantic mood. Between 1640 and 1647 he traveled to Milan, Naples, Perugia, and Florence. In Florence, Pietro da Cortona urged him to execute a fresco in the Pitti Palace. In the late 1640s, when Poussin began to paint idealized classical landscapes, Dughet's style became more calm and more cautiously composed. Simultaneously, a softening light, inspired by Claude Lorraine, pervades his views of the Roman campagna.

After this brief period of adjustment, Dughet's own personality asserted itself from 1655 until his death. From the compromise between the sobering classic style of Poussin and the romantic ideality of Claude, his latent dynamism recurs but is more heroically rendered than in his youth. Powerfully rich compositions of surging vitality emerge, relating him more to the Italian baroque temperament than to the French rationality of the period. The young Dutch and Flemish artists residing in Rome were strongly influenced by his more dramatic interpretation of the vast panoramas that were almost veristically observed from his various houses in Rome, Tivoli, and Frascati. The vogue for his works among English travelers had a marked influence upon the "picturesque" style of Richard Wilson and was carried out in garden arrangements in the 18th century. Dughet's vision of nature ultimately contributed to the efflorescence of French impressionism.

Aside from his frescoes in S. Martino ai Monti and at S. Vitale, in Rome, nothing can positively be assigned to him. The works attributed to him remain questionable as possible imitations of his mature style by Jean-François Millet, Lemaire, and other pupils who were inspired by his direct observation of immense and chaotic nature. Works ascribed to him are in Paris (Louvre), Besançon, Narbonne, Nîmes, London (National Gallery), Derbyshire (Chatsworth), and in the collection of Dennis Mahon, as well as in the National Gallery of Scotland at Edinburgh, the Dresden Gallery, the Pitti Palace in Florence, the Metropolitan Museum of Art in New York, and Oberlin College in Oberlin, Ohio.

BIBLIOGRAPHY. L. Pascoli, *Vite de' pittori, scultori, ed architetti moderni...*, vol. 1, Rome, 1730; F. Baldinucci, *Notizie de' professori del disegno da Cimabue in qua...*, rev. ed., vol. 5, Florence, 1847; L. E. Dussieux, *Artistes français à l'étranger*, Paris, 1876; K. Gerstenbers, "Gaspar Dughet, called Poussin," *Monatshefte für Kunstwissenschaft*, XV, 1922; E. K. Waterhouse, *Baroque Painting in Rome...*, London, 1937.

GEORGE V. GALLENKAMP

Gaspard Dughet, *Story of Elijah*, detail. Fresco. S. Martino ai Monti, Rome.

DUIJNEN (Duynen), ISAAK VAN. Dutch still-life, fish, and animal(?) painter (b. ca. 1630? d. between 1677 and 1681). Little is known of this painter. An artist of this name sold a painting of two cows in The Hague in 1651. If this is the same Van Duijnen, his birth date must be put at about 1630. Duijnen apparently came from Dordrecht, but he is recorded as having entered the Guild of St. Luke in The Hague in 1665. His fish paintings are similar to those painted by Abraham van Beijeren.

BIBLIOGRAPHY. I. Bergström, *Dutch Still-Life Painting in the Seventeenth Century*, New York, 1956.

DUIJSTER (Duyster), WILLEM CORNELISZ. Dutch painter of interiors, musical and guard groups, and several portraits (b. Amsterdam, 1599/1600; d. there, 1635). He was probably a pupil of Pieter Codde. His brother-in-law Simon Kick painted in a similar manner. Contemporary sources held Duijster in high esteem.

BIBLIOGRAPHY. R. H. Wilenski, *Dutch Painting*, New York, 1955.

DUISBURG: LEHMBRUCK MUSEUM. German collection of works by the sculptor Wilhelm Lehmbruck, including sculptures, paintings, and graphics. The museum also contains sculptures and paintings by other 20th-century artists.

DUJARDIN (Du Jardin), KAREL. Dutch painter of landscape, genre, and history (b. Amsterdam, ca. 1622; d. Venice, 1678). Dujardin was possibly the son of the painter Guilliam du Gardin, and he occasionally signed his works "du Gardin." He may have studied with Claes Berchem, whose influence can be seen in works such as *Landscape with Cattle and a Sleeping Youth* (The Hague, Mauritshuis Art Gallery; signed "K. Du Jerdin 1646"). Dujardin is also possibly identical with the "Carel du Gardin" who was reported as a "coopman" (merchant) in Amsterdam in 1650 and who was preparing at that time for a journey to Paris. Dujardin was in Italy for a few years between 1640 and 1650 and was a member of the Northern artists' association in Rome; he was back in Amsterdam in 1652. About 1655 he moved to The Hague, where in 1656 he

Karel Dujardin, *Landscape with Cattle and Flute Player*. Fine Arts Museum, Brussels.

was one of the charter members of the artists' confraternity Pictura. In 1659 he returned to Amsterdam, where he remained until 1675, when he traveled to Italy and North Africa.

His style after 1650 developed along the lines of the Italianate manner of Berchem. Dujardin's landscapes with animals, such as *Landscape with Cattle and Flute Player* (Brussels, Fine Arts Museum; signed K. Dujardin fec.), are related to the work of Paulus Potter.

BIBLIOGRAPHY. E. Brochagen, "Karel Dujardins späte Landschaften," *Bulletin, Musées Royaux des Beaux-Arts*, VI, 1957; M. E. Houtzager et al., *Nederlandse 17e eeuwse Italianiserende Landschapschilders*, Utrecht, 1965.　　LEONARD J. SLATKES

DUKE AND DUCHESS OF URBINO. Oil painting by Titian, in the Uffizi Gallery, Florence. *See* TITIAN.

DUKE OF RUTLAND PSALTER. Thirteenth-century Gothic illuminated manuscript in Belvoir Castle, Leicester, England.

DULONGPRE, LOUIS. Canadian painter (b. France, 1754; d. Saint Hyacinthe, Quebec, 1843). After serving with French forces in the American Revolution, Dulongpré settled in Montreal. He was a prolific portrait painter in oil and pastel, and executed some religious paintings.

DUMANDRE, HUBERT. French sculptor (b. Tenery, 1701; d. Madrid, 1781). Dumandre was active chiefly in Spain. He executed the Bath of Diana (1746) in the garden of the Palacio S. Ildefonso at La Granja and, together with Pitue, the tomb of Philip V and his wife in the Colegiata at La Granja.

BIBLIOGRAPHY. O. Schubert, *Geschichte des Barocks in Spanien*, Esslingen, 1908.

DU MAURIER, GEORGE. English illustrator, engraver, and writer (b. Paris, 1834; d. London, 1896). Although he was French by birth and was trained in both Paris and Antwerp, Du Maurier is thought of as a fashionable and very British satirist. He moved to London in 1860 and shortly after joined the circle of well-known contributors to *Punch*—Tenniel, John Leech, and Cruikshank. He caricatured the worlds of high society and the arts.

BIBLIOGRAPHY. M. H. Spielmann, *History of "Punch" . . .*, London, 1895.

DUMONSTIER FAMILY. French artists of the 16th and 17th centuries. The eldest was Geoffroy, whose three sons were Etienne, Pierre, and Come. A nephew, also well known, was Daniel. Other members of the family (for example Daniel's children, Pierre II and Nicolas) were minor painters.

Geoffroy (ca. 1510–60) was Painter to the Court of Francis I and to Henry II. He worked at Fontainebleau (1538–40) with Rosso, whose style he assimilated. A number of engravings are attributed to him, as well as a few drawings, among which are designs for stained-glass windows. He is recorded also as being a painter of miniatures.

Etienne (1540–1603) was Painter and *valet de chambre* to Henry II, Francis II, Charles IX, Henry III, Catherine de Médicis, and Henry IV. He was quite highly esteemed during his lifetime and was actually paid more for his

Dumonstier family. Daniel Dumonstier, *Portrait of an Old Woman*. Art Museum, Rennes.

services to the Queen than even François Clouet. He and his brother Pierre were sent on a mission to Vienna at the court of Maximilian II. A drawing in the National Library in Paris, representing the Emperor and the Empress, is attributed to him.

Pierre (ca. 1545–1610) is called "the uncle" to distinguish him from Pierre II, son of Daniel. The National Library in Paris has two signed drawings by him. His portraits of Le Gagneur and Jean de Beaugrand (engraved by De Leu) continue the French tradition of portraits done in pencil, sometimes in three colors. He is the author of a beautiful portrait of the Maréchal de Biron in the Bonnat Museum, Bayonne.

Come (ca. 1550–1605) was Painter and *valet de chambre* to the Queen Mother and to the Queen of Navarre. He spent his late years in Rouen. No certain works by his hand are known.

Daniel (1574–1646) was by far the most famous Dumonstier, partially because so much of his *oeuvre* was preserved, by virtue of the fact that he almost always signed and inscribed his paintings. He, too, served as Painter and *valet de chambre* to various kings. Daniel's portraits, though less sensitive and acute than Pierre's, have immediate appeal. He mixed pencil with pastel, creating a rich effect, and his works are sometimes confused with those of Pourbus, to which they owe a great deal. His portrait of Brulard was engraved by L. Gaultier.

BIBLIOGRAPHY. E. Moreau-Nélaton, *Les Clouet et leurs émules*, vol. 1, Paris, 1924.

PHILIPPE DE MONTEBELLO

DUMOUCHEL, ALBERT. Canadian painter and graphic artist (1916–   ). He studied graphic art and sculpture in Montreal and now teaches at the Ecole des Beaux-Arts there. He paints abstract oils and water colors and is a printmaker.

BIBLIOGRAPHY. Ottawa, National Gallery of Canada, *Catalogue of Paintings and Sculpture*, ed. by R. H. Hubbard, vol. 3: *Canadian School*, 1960.

DUNBLANE CATHEDRAL. Part of the tower of this Scottish cathedral is 12th century, but the rest was built largely between 1237 and 1258. The nave and choir are in pure early English style. The west door, of tripartite design, is of particular monumentality.

BIBLIOGRAPHY. J. H. Cockburn, *The Medieval Bishops of Dunblane and Their Church*, Edinburgh, 1959.

DUNFERMLINE ABBEY. Norman rebuilding of this Scottish church probably dates from about 1150. The nave, west front, and fragments of the monastic buildings remain. The nave style derives from Durham but with tunnel vaults rather than ribs. The 13th-century choir has been destroyed.

BIBLIOGRAPHY. D. Macgibbon and T. Ross, *The Ecclesiastical Architecture of Scotland*, 3 vols., Edinburgh, 1896–97.

DUNKER, BALTHASAR ANTON. Swiss landscape painter and etcher (b. Saal, 1764; d. Bern, 1807). Dunker, who was more distinguished as an etcher than as a painter, made book illustrations and other miscellaneous prints, many of which deal with French customs and manners before the French Revolution. He worked after Roos, Van der Does, Hackert, and Schutz.

DUNLAP, WILLIAM. American painter and art historian (b. Perth Amboy, N.J., 1766; d. New York, 1839). He studied with West and Davey in London (1784–87) and returned to New York, where he painted miniatures, historical themes, portraits, and landscapes in the Hudson River school tradition. Later he became a founder and a vice-president of the National Academy.

His careers in art, commerce, the theater, literature, history, the army, and teaching demonstrate his versatility. His *History of the Rise and Progress of the Arts of Design in the United States* (1834) was a study of 18th- and early-19th-century American artists. It consisted of a collection of biographical data and critical opinion that considered the personality of the artist and his subject matter. His paintings were straightforward, academically competent, and sympathetic.

BIBLIOGRAPHY. W. Dunlap, *Diary of William Dunlap*, 3 vols., New York, 1930.

DUNWEGE, VICTOR AND HEINRICH, see BAEGERT, DERICK.

DUOMO. Italian cathedral. The term originated from the use of large cupolas or domes in the construction of cathedrals.

DUPLESSI-BERTAUX, JEAN. French historical engraver and painter (1750–1820). He lived in Paris. Although he studied under Vien and Lebas, his real master was Jacques Callot. He preserved a historical record of his time in hundreds of tiny vignettes that made him known to his contemporaries as "the Callot of our time."

Jules Dupré, *The Great Oak*. Louvre, Paris. The artist abandoned academic landscape painting techniques early in his career.

DUPLESSIS, JOSEPH SIFFRED. French portraitist (b. Carpentras, 1725; d. Versailles, 1802). He was a pupil of his father, of Brother Imbert, and of Pierre Subleyras. He became portraitist to Louis XVI and after the French Revolution was director of the Versailles galleries. His unpretentious interpretations of Benjamin Franklin (New York, Metropolitan Museum) and Gluck (Vienna, Museum of Art History) strongly contrast with the courtly portraits by Roslin and Tocqué.

BIBLIOGRAPHY. J. Belleudy, *J. S. Duplessis, peintre du roi, 1725–1802*, Chartres, 1913.

DUPRE, GIOVANNI. Italian sculptor (1817–82). His sculptures include *Dying Abel* (Florence, Gallery of Modern Art), *Sappho* (1857; Rome, National Gallery of Modern Art), *Monument to Cavour* (Turin), and *Giotto* (Florence, Uffizi). Dupré blended realism with classicism to express extreme pathos. He presented his ideas on art in his essays, *Ricordi*.

BIBLIOGRAPHY. M. Salmi, *L'arte italiana*, 3d ed., vol. 3, Florence, 1946–47.

DUPRE, JULES. French landscape painter and lithographer (b. Nantes, 1811; d. L'Isle-Adam, 1889). At an early age Dupré worked in his father's porcelain factory and was later sent to paint porcelain at his uncle's factory in Paris. He was for the most part self-taught; his slight formal artistic training was received from Jean-Michel Diébolt, an animal painter, but this schooling left few traces in his work, which, at its best, was marked by an original craftsmanship.

His first important exhibition was at the Salon of 1831 to which he sent seven landscapes, the subject on which he concentrated throughout his life. The prime sources of these early landscapes were Diaz and the 17th-century Dutch painters, whose immediacy of approach to nature he admired. In 1834 Dupré traveled to England, where he saw the work of many British landscape painters and was especially affected by Bonington's and Constable's freshness as well as by the peculiarities of English weather. The rendering of misty air and atmosphere became an increasingly important concern and, in his late paintings, threatened to overshadow the natural subject. This may have been partly a result of his admiration for comparable effects in Corot. He was, for a period, a close friend of Théodore Rousseau and worked with him at Barbizon.

Dupré's landscapes may be roughly divided into two parts: poetic and romantic descriptions of scenery; and rural genre subjects approaching the sentimental. Unlike the English painters who were, by and large, content simply to record their impressions of a natural scene, Dupré often invested his subjects with an emotion and a sense of brooding largely of his own invention. This overly dramatic interpretation was at odds with his decorative and sober compositional structure. The subjects and his manner of painting them tended, in his later landscapes, to become repetitious and uninspired.

He began with a small-stroked, relatively tight style that changed into a broader treatment with formal generalization and a stronger use of the palette knife and thick layers of paint to create his emotional effect. Dupré's importance lies in his early abandonment of the academic techniques of landscape painting.

BIBLIOGRAPHY. J. W. Mollett, *The Painters of Barbizon*, 2 vols., London, 1890; G. Hediard, *Jules Dupré*, Le Mans, 1892.

JEROME VIOLA

DUQUE CORNEJO, PEDRO.
Spanish sculptor, painter, and architect (b. Seville, 1677; d. Cordova, 1757). He was the pupil of Pedro Roldán. Called by Philip V to the court, he was in Madrid from approximately 1740 to 1746. He abandoned the traditional Sevillian quietude of pose, using instead poses of dynamic moment comparable to those employed by Bernini, as in the *Magdalen* (1716–19; Granada, Sagrario de la Cartuja). He worked in marble with the same ease as in polychromed wood and was active until his death, when he had just completed the outstanding choir stalls (1748–57) for Cordova Cathedral.

His altarpiece (ca. 1730) for the Novitiate Chapel of S. Luis in Seville combines architecture, sculpture, and painting. Shapes as fantastic as any devised for rococo arabesques are executed in gilded wood as frames for paintings and statuary that almost lose their specific identity in the overall luxuriance. The result strongly suggests a "Moorish baroque" style in that the extravagant geometric pattern of the architectural setting dominates the ensemble and forces an optical illusion of two-dimensionality upon the whole.

BIBLIOGRAPHY. P. Quintero, "Sillas de coro españoles," *Boletín Sociedad Española de Excursiones*, XVI, 1908; R. Aguilar, "Bosquejo histórico de la ejecución de la sillería del coro de la catedral de Córdoba," *Boletín Real Academia de Bellas Artes de Córdoba*, XVII, July–December, 1946; G. Kubler and M. Soria, *Art and Architecture in Spain and Portugal and Their American Dominions, 1500–1800*, Baltimore, 1959.

EILEEN A. LORD

DUQUESNOY (Du Canoi: Quesnoy), FRANCOIS (Il Fiammingo; Francois Flamand).
Flemish-Italian sculptor (b. Brussels, 1594; d. Livorno, 1643). An important 17th-century baroque sculptor, François studied with his father, Jérôme the Elder. About 1618 he went to Rome, where he assisted Bernini in the creation of the tabernacle of St. Peter's. He was befriended by Poussin, who greatly influenced his style in a classical direction. His works fall into two groups: monumental works in bronze, such as his masterpiece, a statue of St. Susanna in S. Maria di Loreto, which shows a strong classicism; and smaller works in ivory and terra cotta that were influential in his native country. His small sculptures were avidly collected and even forged as early as the late 17th century. Likened to that of his 16th-century countryman Giovanni da Bologna, Duquesnoy's style is a fusion of the Italian baroque of Bernini and the 17th-century classicism of Poussin.

BIBLIOGRAPHY. M. Franselot, *F. du Quesnoy: Sculpteur d'Urbain VIII*, Brussels, 1942; R. Wittkower, *Art and Architecture in Italy, 1600–1750*, Baltimore, 1958.

DUQUESNOY (De Quesnoy; Quesnoy), JEROME, THE ELDER.
Flemish sculptor (b. Quesnoy, before 1570; d. Brussels, 1641). He was the father of the sculptors François Duquesnoy and Jérôme Duquesnoy the Younger. Jérôme Duquesnoy the Elder is traceable after 1600 in Brus-

Jérôme Duquesnoy the Younger, *The Magdalene Meditating*. Fine Arts Museum, Brussels.

sels, where all his major works were executed. Among his best-known sculptures are the tabernacle in St. Martin, Aalst (Alost), with reliefs of caryatids (1600/04); four garden statues in the Labyrinth, Brussels (1605); and a fountain with a statue of St. Michael and satyrs as ornaments, for which he received payments in 1617 and 1622. In 1619 Jérôme the Elder was commissioned to make the designs for the famous Manneken Fountain behind the Hôtel de Ville in Brussels. Its execution is usually identified with his sons François and Jérôme the Younger. The elder Duquesnoy was a forerunner of the late Renaissance style.

BIBLIOGRAPHY. E. de Busscher, "Les Du Quesnoy," *Annales de la Société Royale des Beaux-Arts de Gand*, XIII, 1873; H. Gerson and E. H. ter Kuile, *Art and Architecture in Belgium, 1600–1800*, Baltimore, 1960.

Dura Europos. Ezra as depicted in the wall paintings of the synagogue. Copy painted on the site (1933–35) by H. J. Gute. Yale University Art Gallery, New Haven, Conn.

DUQUESNOY (De Quesnoy; Quesnoy), JEROME, THE YOUNGER. Flemish sculptor (b. Brussels, 1602; executed in Ghent, 1654). Jérôme Duquesnoy the Younger was the son of Jérôme Duquesnoy the Elder and the brother of François Duquesnoy. In 1622 he probably followed François to Rome. He then went to Madrid to work for Philip IV, but no work from that period has survived. Among his works are the tomb of the Bishop Villain (Tournai Cathedral) and four apostles (1644–46) for St. Gudule of Brussels. From 1643 to 1654 he took over his brother's commission for the tomb of Bishop Antoine Triest (Ghent, St. Bavon), which is his masterpiece. Jérôme was influenced by his brother's smaller sculptures, especially in ivory, and reflects that style, but with notable coarseness and superficiality. Unfortunately, Jérôme's work is known really only from the last decade of his life, and the confusion between him and his brother that prevailed in the 18th century hinders secure attributions.

BIBLIOGRAPHY. E. Marchal, *La Sculpture et les chefs-d'oeuvre de l'orfèvrerie belges*, Brussels, 1895.

DURA (Doura) EUROPOS. Ancient Syrian religious center (founded ca. 300 B.C.; destroyed ca. A.D. 260). On the Euphrates River, midway between Aleppo and Damascus, and hence strategically located, Dura Europos contains buildings belonging to thirteen different religions. It was founded by a certain Nicanor, probably a relative of the Hellenistic king of Syria, Seleucus. Its buildings include a Christian church dated about 225, a Mithraic temple, the oldest known synagogue, and buildings consecrated to various syncretic sects. The site of a Roman citadel, Dura was coming under the influence of Palmyra, which was in the process of losing its connection with Parthia and becoming ever more dependent on Rome, when it was destroyed by the Sassanians.

Temples at Dura were dedicated to local variations of Zeus. Gods on horseback and camelback, and patrons of camel riders and caravans, appear on stone bas-reliefs and as terra-cotta figurines. Solar gods worshiped at Palmyra are shown wearing Parthian and Roman military uniforms. Some terra cottas, intaglios, and fragments of pottery and a marble statuette of Aphrodite with her tortoise betray Greek workmanship and probably date to early in Dura's history.

Most remarkable are the religious wall paintings, rendered in a stiff, schematized manner betraying an insular Greco-Iranian origin. In the best-preserved temple, the temple of the Palmyrene gods, a colossal figure in Iranian dress is depicted standing beside a miniature chariot drawn by horses. This cult figure stands on a highly stylized mountain range, represented by rows of half ovals piled one upon the other. To his left are two standing armed male figures, probably worshipers or divine acolytes. In the Temple of Zeus Theos, a similar scene occupied the whole of the back wall of the naos, while the side walls of both the naos and the pronaos were decorated with scenes of sacrifice. All the figures are shown in rigid frontality, with no movement suggested.

The little Christian building features themes of salvation: Christ saving Peter from the waters, Christ saving a paralytic, David and Goliath. The synagogue, in spite

Asher Brown Durand, *Ariadne*. Engraving after a painting by John Vanderlyn. New York Public Library.

of ancient Jewish prohibitions against the making of images, is lavishly decorated with scenes from the Old Testament. In the miracle of the crossing of the Red Sea, the Jews are shown in a highly ordered military formation. In the war between David and Saul, the horses look like equestrian statues on Roman coins. There is a constant play between the Greek and Iranian world: in a temple scene, the men wear Persian costumes, but the architecture is of Greek origin. The posture of Ezra is thoroughly Greek in the anatomical disposition, in the rendering of the asymmetrical sides of the body, and in the foreshortening of the leg; but the fusing of the scroll with the figure and the elongation of the body are unclassical.

See also EAST CHRISTIAN ART AND ARCHITECTURE (SYRIA); JEWISH ART.

BIBLIOGRAPHY. M. Rostovtzev, *Dura Europos and its Art*, Oxford, 1938; Yale University, *The Excavations at Dura-Europos: Final Reports, 4-5-6-8*, New Haven, Conn., 1943-59.

ABRAHAM A. DAVIDSON

DURAMEAU, LOUIS-JEAN-JACQUES. French painter (b. Paris, 1733; d. Versailles, 1796). He was a pupil of J. B. Pierre. Though at first a history painter, he later spe-

cialized in decoration (the ceiling of the Galerie d'Apollon, Paris, Louvre). He was in Rome in the mid-1760s and then became an academician (1774), a painter to Louis XVI (1778), and a director of the Salon exhibitions (1791). His impressionistic technique was admired by Diderot.

DURAN, CHARLES-AUGUSTE-EMILE (Carolus-Duran). French painter (b. Lille, 1838; d. Paris, 1917). Duran studied in Paris between 1859 and 1862 and in Italy until 1866. He entered the Salon of 1866 with *L'Assassine*, which brought him immediate fame and was purchased by his native city of Lille. After a trip to Spain, where he came under Velázquez's influence, he returned to Paris and began to specialize in portraits (*Equestrian Portrait of Sophie Croizettes*, 1873 Salon), which greatly increased his popularity. In 1904 he was made director of the French Academy in Rome. During his early career Duran was associated with Courbet and Ribot, and like Courbet, worked in the realistic style. Later he became more academic (*Triumph of Marie de Médicis*, 1878; ceiling painting in Paris, Louvre).

BIBLIOGRAPHY. A. Alexander, *Carolus-Duran*, Paris, 1903.

DURAND, ASHER BROWN. American painter and engraver (b. Jefferson Village, N.J., 1796; d. there, 1886). Apprenticed to the engraver Peter Maverick, Durand learned so quickly that in five years he was a partner in the business. He had meanwhile studied at the American Academy of Fine Arts. After his engraving of Trumbull's *Declaration of Independence* made him sufficiently popular, he became an independent and very successful engraver and illustrator.

In the early 1830s he was commissioned by Luman Reed to paint a series of portraits of American presidents. Reed's patronage was influential in turning Durand from engraving to painting. Among his works of this period is *Mrs. Durand and Her Sister* (1831; Newark Museum), a conventional portrait in the English tradition except for the importance given to the landscape background. At the same time he did such historical subjects as *The Capture of Major André* (1833; Worcester Art Museum). In 1840 Durand went to Europe with Kensett, Casilear, and Rossiter. He admired Claude Lorraine, the Dutch landscape painters, and Salvator Rosa and on his return to America began to paint landscapes. Among his few excursions into the sort of romantic, allegorical landscape identified with Thomas Cole were *The Morning of Life* and *The Evening of Life* (both 1840; New York, National Academy of Design). Generally, however, Durand represents the realistic aspect of the Hudson River school, in which untamed landscapes were replaced by views implying the civilizing effect of man on nature. (See illustration.)

Albrecht Dürer, *Knight, Death, and the Devil*, 1513. Engraving.

In line with his training as an engraver, Durand painted his early scenes in a detailed manner, for example, *Rutland, Vermont* (1838–40; Detroit Institute of Arts); but in *Kindred Spirits* (1849; New York Public Library), a kind of landscape portrait of Thomas Cole and William Cullen Bryant, a reverence for the beauty of nature transcends the particularized painting. Durand's later paintings are marked by a freer handling, a greater richness of color, and an increasing concern for the rendering of space and light, as in *Catskill Clove* (1866; New York, Century Association).

Durand was one of the first American artists to advocate the direct painting of landscape scenes out of doors, and in his *Letters on Landscape Painting*, published in *The Crayon*, he constantly stressed the depiction of the real as opposed to the painting of ideal subjects. A founder of the National Academy of Design, he was its president from 1846 to 1862.

BIBLIOGRAPHY. J. Durand, *The Life and Times of A. B. Durand*, New York, 1894.

JEROME VIOLA

DURAND, JEAN NICHOLAS LOUIS. French architect (1760–1834). He worked in Paris. A pupil of Etienne-Louis Boullée, he taught at the Ecole Polytechnique. His published lectures, synthesizing practice and theory of the preceding forty years in France, were influential in the spread of the romantic classical style throughout Europe. *See* CLASSICISM, ROMANTIC.

BIBLIOGRAPHY. A. Rondelet, *Notice historique sur la vie et les ouvrages de Jean Nicholas Louis Durand*, Paris, 1835.

DURANDUS (Duranti), WILLIAM (Gulielmus), THE ELDER. Bishop of Mende (1230–96). Durandus was the author of many writings on canon law and liturgy. His most famous work is a compendium of liturgical knowledge, *Rationale divinorum officiorum*. It is one of the principal sources for the understanding of double meanings in the symbolism of Christian art.

DURER, ALBRECHT. German painter, engraver, and designer of woodcuts (b. Nürnberg, 1471; d. there, 1528). Dürer is the most famous and perhaps the greatest of all German visual artists. His father, Albrecht the Elder, was a goldsmith, and Dürer received his earliest artistic training in his father's workshop. In 1486 he was apprenticed to the Nürnberg painter Michael Wolgemut, and he worked under him for four years, receiving instruction in panel painting and in the technique of woodcut illustration, a specialty of the Wolgemut shop. There, in 1493, woodcuts for the profusely illustrated Schedel's *Neue Weltchronik* were produced. Contributing to the woodcut production was Wolgemut's stepson Wilhelm Pleydenwurff, and it is probable that he influenced the young Dürer.

Soon after Easter of 1490 Dürer left the Wolgemut workshop and began his *Wanderschaft*. His route during the first year is unknown. There is speculation that he traveled in the region of the Middle Rhine, possibly in search of the now legendary Master of the Housebook. Early in 1492, he appeared in Colmar, Alsace, seeking the famous engraver Martin Schongauer, who had, however,

Albrecht Dürer, *The Nativity*. Old Pinacothek, Munich.

died several months before. From Colmar Dürer traveled to Basel, where he remained until the fall of 1493. He then sojourned in Strasbourg until his return to Nürnberg in May, 1494. The following autumn Dürer made his first trip to Italy, returning to Nürnberg in the spring of 1495. Little is known about this trip, but it appears that it was restricted to Venice and its immediate surroundings.

Until 1505 Dürer remained in Nürnberg, establishing his workshop and widening his contacts with learned Humanistic circles. In the summer of 1505 he made his second trip to Italy and remained there until January, 1507. This extremely important period of contact with Italian High Renaissance art is documented by ten letters that Dürer wrote to Pirckheimer from Italy, revealing his appreciation of Italian art and, above all, of the respected position Italian artists held in the new Renaissance society. He made the acquaintance of several Italian artists, among them the elder Bellini.

When he returned to Nürnberg in 1507, he came as an artist of considerable fame. In 1517 he received the patronage of the Kaiser Maximilian, which lasted until the Kaiser's death in 1520. Hoping to gain the patronage of the new emperor Charles V, Dürer went to the Netherlands in the spring of 1520. He met the Emperor, received an offer of patronage (which never materialized), and traveled on to the Low Countries, where he met a number of Flemish artists, among them Quentin Metsys. He returned to Nürnberg in 1521 and spent the remainder of his life there, devoting himself less to art and more to writing and publishing various theoretical works, such as the work on fortifications published in 1526 and his famous treatise on the proportions of the human body published soon after his death.

The development of Dürer's art is generally seen as a series of periods divided by the significant travels: the early period, before the *Wanderschaft*; the *Wanderschaft*; the first Italian trip and the years up to the second Italian trip; the second Italian trip and the mature period through the Netherlandish trip; and finally the late period.

Works that belong to the early period of Dürer's apprenticeships are few. Most important are the silverpoint *Self-Portrait* (1484; Vienna, Albertina), the pen drawing *Madonna with Two Angels* (1485, Berlin, former State Museums), and the crayon drawing *Young Woman with Falcons* (ca. 1489; London, British Museum). All show a precocity remarkable for an artist so young, and all are executed in the style that prevailed in the Wolgemut workshop—that of the German late Gothic tradition strongly influenced by Netherlandish painting.

Works from the *Wanderschaft* are extremely difficult to ascertain. With the exception of a signed wood block, *St. Jerome and the Lion*, which was made as the title page of *Epistolare beati Hieronymi* (Basel, 1492), no signed or documented works exist. Stylistic studies have, however, attributed many woodcut illustrations published in Basel and Strasbourg to Dürer's hand. Among these are illustrations to *Ritter vom Turn* (Basel, 1493) and to Sebastian Brandt's *Das Narrenschyff* (Basel, 1494). Several drawings such as the *Wise Virgin* (1493; Albertina) and *Young Couple Walking* (Hamburg, Art Gallery) belong to this period, for they show the considerable influence of Martin Schongauer and the Master of the Housebook.

During his first trip to Italy, Dürer was particularly impressed by the works of the Pollaiuoli and Mantegna. The pen drawing *The Death of Orpheus* (1494; Hamburg, Art Gallery) reflects a similar Mantegna work and is considered by many to be a work of the first Italian trip. On his way home he executed many water-color sketches of remarkable spontaneity and observation. Notable among these are the *Castle of Trent* (London, British Museum) and the *Wehlsch Pirg* (Oxford, Ashmolean Museum). After his return, Dürer concentrated chiefly on woodcut production. The great woodcut series of the *Apocalypse*, the *Large Passion*, and the *Life of the Virgin* date from this period. The engraving *Adam and Eve* (1504) and the painted *Paumgartner Altar* (1502–04; Munich, Old Pinacothek) and *Adoration of the Magi* (1504; Florence, Uffizi) reveal the confrontation with Italian Renaissance ideals of form that Dürer had struggled with just before his second Italian trip.

Dürer's mature period begins with the second trip to Italy. The conflict between the late Gothic and Renaissance styles so evident in works previous to this period was replaced by a complete synthesis of the two styles in a manner more sure and successful than that of any other Northern artist. While in Venice he created what is perhaps his painting masterpiece, *Feast of the Rose Garlands* (Prague, National Gallery). Back in Nürnberg he concentrated mainly on engravings—such as the three "master" engravings, *Knight, Death, and the Devil* (1513), *St. Jerome in His Study* (1514), and *Melancholia* (1514)—and above all on portraiture, painted and engraved. Examples are the *Portrait of Holzschuher* and the *Portrait of Muffel* (both 1526; Berlin, former State Museums) and the engraved portraits of Albrecht von Brandenburg (1523), Friedrich der Weise (1524), Melanchthon (1524), and Erasmus (1524).

The late period, the last two years of his life, followed the disastrous Peasants' War of 1525 and the complications of the Reformation. It was a period of intense religious concern, and consequently Dürer's art shows a modification of the Renaissance equilibrium of his mature period. It was a period of incipient mannerism, and Dürer's last painting, called the *Four Apostles* (1526; Munich, Old Pinacothek), which was given by the artist to his native city, is the embodiment of the volatile and dynamic Christianity of Luther expressed in a style of mixed late Gothic and Renaissance tendencies. *See* NURNBERG: MUSEUMS (ALBRECHT DURER HOUSE).

BIBLIOGRAPHY. H. W. Singer, *Versuch einer Dürer Bibliographie*, 2d ed., Strasbourg, 1928; H. Tietze and E. Tietze-Conrat, *Kritisches Verzeichnis der Werke Albrecht Dürers*, 2 vols., Augsburg, 1928, Basel, 1937, Leipzig, 1938; F. Winkler, *Die Zeichnungen Albrecht Dürers*, 4 vols., Berlin, 1936–39; H. Wölfflin, *Die Kunst Albrecht Dürers*, 6th ed., Munich, 1943; E. Panofsky, *Albrecht Dürer: The Life and Art*, 4th ed., Princeton, 1955; F. Winkler, *Albrecht Dürer*, Berlin, 1958.

DONALD L. EHRESMANN

DURET, FRANCISQUE JOSEPH. French sculptor (b. Paris, 1804; d. there, 1865). He began to study with Bosio in 1818 and went to Italy in 1824. His early work included such realistic genre subjects as the bronze *Dancing Neapolitan Fisherman* (1833; Paris, Louvre). His later work was increasingly influenced by the taste for the antique mode.

DURGA. Terrible aspect of the Hindu goddess Devī, consort of Siva. Durgā (meaning "inaccessible") is usually

Durham Cathedral, the nave, vaulted between 1128 and 1135.

represented with eight or ten arms, mounted on a lion or tiger and slaying the demon buffalo Mahiṣa.

DURGA, TEMPLE OF, AIHOLE, see AIHOLE.

DURHAM CATHEDRAL. Romanesque cathedral in northern England, grouped together on a rock with a castle and monastery. The cathedral was begun in 1093, the chancel was vaulted by 1104, and the nave vault was up by 1135. The 12th-century plan is chancel with aisles, transepts and central tower, nave with aisles, and west towers. About 1170–75 a galilee was added in front of the west portal and at a lower level on the edge of the ravine. In 1242 a curious east transeptal arrangement, known as the Chapel of the Nine Altars, was added. The architect for this opus was probably Richard of Farnham.

The effect of the 12th-century interior is one of overwhelming power and of unsurpassed Anglo-Norman proportions. The chancel was begun first and with its apse was complete by 1104. Its aisles are vaulted with cross-ribs, and Bilson proved that the main space was also vaulted. Durham thus is believed by some historians to possess the earliest rib vaults of western Europe. (Others believe the priority belongs to Sant'Ambrogio in Milan.) Although the nave is later, vaulted between 1128 and 1135, it has certain innovations, such as the oblong vault bays and the special feature of transverse arches behind the galleries, which is in essence the so-called Gothic flying buttress.

The greatest post-Romanesque addition to the cathedral was the Chapel of the Nine Altars, particularly the great Joseph window in its north side (ca. 1280–90). It marks a point of departure from the Anglo-French Gothic toward the lushness of the English Decorated style. The decoration of these parts ranges from the conventional stiff-leaf foliage of about 1250 to a naturalistic display of figure carving on the capitals, derived from the Lincoln Angel Choir and probably dating after 1280.

The Neville Screen was begun in 1372 and finished in 1380. The choir stalls, dated 1665, are remarkable examples of Gothic survival decoration. The carver was John Clement, who probably also carved the Parclose Screens of the same date. The Bishop's Throne is part of Bishop Hatfield's monument, erected by him before 1381. Steps lead up above his chantry to the throne in the center of a screen.

South of the cathedral are the cloisters and adjacent buildings. The undercrofts of the refectory and the dormitory may belong to the 1070s. The cloister proper is 12th century, the arcades having been rebuilt by 1418. South of the transept are the parlor and chapter house. The latter was complete by 1140 and is a rib-vaulted room of two square bays with a rebuilt apse, whose ribs rest on caryatids, a motif unique to England. Beyond the west range is the dormitory, of impressive splendor (194 ft. long, 39 ft. wide), built between 1398 and 1404. The kitchen, built between 1366 and 1370 by John Lewyn, is a remarkable medieval room with a unique vault.

BIBLIOGRAPHY. J. Harvey, *The English Cathedrals*, London, 1950; N. Pevsner, *The Buildings of England*, vol. 9, Harmondsworth, 1953.

JOHN HARRIS

DURIEUX, CAROLINE. American lithographer and painter (1896–). Born in New Orleans, she studied at Newcomb College there as well as at Tulane University, Louisiana State University, and the Pennsylvania Academy of the Fine Arts under Henry McCarter and Arthur B. Carles. In Europe she studied lithographic printing methods at Desjobert's. Durieux has worked for extended periods in Havana, Mexico, and South America. In 1951, collaborating with Dr. Harry Wheeler of Louisiana State University and his wife Naomi, she began experimentation on the electron print, a method of reproducing drawings with inks containing radioactive isotopes. A further extension of this medium has led to color electron prints and color *cliché-verres*. Her works, often penetrating satires of the social scene, are in many public and private collections. *See* CLICHE-VERRE.

BIBLIOGRAPHY. C. Zigrosser, *Caroline Durieux, 43 Lithographs and Drawings*, Baton Rouge, 1949.

DURRIE, GEORGE HENRY. American portrait and landscape painter (b. Hartford, Conn., 1820; d. New Haven, Conn., 1863). He studied with Nathaniel Jocelyn and painted portraits in Connecticut, New Jersey, New York, and Virginia. He later turned to genre landscape painting. His seasonal views, reproduced by Currier and Ives, possess an intimate nostalgia and a decorative brilliance.

BIBLIOGRAPHY. Wadsworth Atheneum, *George Henry Durrie, 1820–1863, Connecticut Painter of American Life*, Hartford, Conn., 1947.

DURROW, BOOK OF. Illuminated 7th-century manuscript, in Trinity College Library, Dublin. *See* CELTIC ART; HIBERNO-SAXON ART.

DUR SHARRUKIN, see KHORSABAD.

DUR UNTASHI, see CHOGA-ZAMBIL.

Cornelis Dusart, *Dutch Kermesse*. Fine Arts Museum, Brussels.

DUSART (Du Sart; Dusaert), CORNELIS. Dutch painter, draftsman, and etcher (b. Haarlem, 1660; d. there, 1704). Dusart, who was a pupil of Adriaen van Ostade, entered the guild of Haarlem in 1679 and was elevated to commissioner in 1692. He was primarily a genre painter; because of his talent and because of his association with Van Ostade (Dusart finished a large number of canvases begun by his teacher), his paintings were long confused with Van Ostade's. Dusart's paintings can be distinguished, however, by their exaggerated satire and color range, which are closer to Jan Steen than to Van Ostade. Dusart was a close friend of the art patron Dingeman and was also on close terms with the engraver J. Gole, who finished many of Dusart's plates.

BIBLIOGRAPHY. W. Bernt, *Die niederländischen Maler des 17. Jahrhunderts...*, Munich, 1948.

DUSART, FRANCOIS. Flemish sculptor (d. 1661). Born in Arquinghem, Dusart worked in Rome from 1620 to 1630 as an assistant to Duquesnoy. From 1641 he was active chiefly in Holland, where he executed his major works, standing figures of the four Princesses of Orange and Elector Friedrich Heinrich (Berlin, Charlottenburg Castle), which were commissioned by Friedrich's wife, Louise Henriette of Orange.

BIBLIOGRAPHY. F. H. Hofmann, *Die Kunst am Hofe der Markgrafen von Brandenburg...*, Strasbourg, 1901.

DUSSELDORF: MUSEUMS. Important public art collections in Düsseldorf, Germany, are located in the museums listed below.

Art Museum. Founded in 1913, the museum is now housed in the so-called Ehrenhof, erected in 1925–26. It is outstanding for its collection of German paintings of the romantic school (by Blechen, C. D. Friedrich, Richter, and others) and of the Düsseldorf school (by Bendemann, Feuerbach, and others). The Art Museum also has works by such 20th-century artists as Baumeister, Heckel, Kandinsky, Kirchner, Nolde, and Schmidt-Rottluff. Compared with these notable works, the collection of paintings of the Italian, Netherlandish, and Spanish schools is of secondary importance.

About 70,000 drawings and works of graphic art are in the collection. They range from Rhenish miniatures to works by the 20th-century expressionists. The sculptures—from a late Romanesque crucifix to pieces by such 20th-century artists as Archipenko, Barlach, Lehmbruck, and Marini—again demonstrate the wide variety of the museum's holdings. About 8,000 pieces of ceramics in a part of the building known as the Hetjens Museum include rare pieces from classical antiquity, the medieval period, and the 17th and 18th centuries as well as some works by Picasso.

LOTTE PULVERMACHER-EGERS

Jagerhof Museum. The museum, formerly a princely hunting lodge and residence from the mid-18th century, houses cultural and historical objects related to the city of Düsseldorf as well as the outstanding ceramics collection of Dr. Heinrich Schneider. This collection, one of the richest of Meissen ware, contains porcelain by such famous masters as Böttger and Höroldt, parts of princely table service sets, and small animal figures by Kaendler, including his "monkey orchestra" (*Affenkonzert*).

BIBLIOGRAPHY. H. Jedding, *Keysers Führer durch Museen und Sammlungen*, Heidelberg, Munich, 1961.

DUSSELDORF SCHOOL. Elector Carl Theodor established an art academy in Düsseldorf in 1767 that eventually became one of the most important centers of 19th-century German romantic painting. In the early 19th century, Peter Cornelius dominated the school. His style combined classic and romantic trends with a keen sense of the monumental and a precise draftsmanship. Painters from the Düsseldorf school are especially known for their grandiose wall paintings and illustrations of editions of Goethe. Wilhelm von Kaulbach and Wilhelm von Schadow also belonged to the Düsseldorf group. The latter, together with Cornelius, joined the Nazarenes in Rome in the second decade of the 19th century. *See* CORNELIUS, PETER; KAULBACH, WILHELM VON; SCHADOW, WILHELM VON.

BIBLIOGRAPHY. G. Pauli, *Die Kunst des Klassizismus und der Romantik*, 2 vols., Berlin, 1925; W. R. Deusch, *Malerei der deutschen Romantiker und ihrer Zeitgenossen*, Berlin, 1937.

DUTARY, ALBERTO. Panamanian painter and draftsman (1932–   ). Dutary studied in his native Panama City and Madrid. He has exhibited in Madrid (1957; Sala Seral), Washington (1961; Pan American Union), Venice (1962), and San Salvador (1961). His art is figurative, with imaginative and psychological tendencies (for example, *Ternura*; Panama City, Arias Collection).

BIBLIOGRAPHY. University of Kansas, Museum of Art, *Pintores centroamericanos* (exhibition catalog), Lawrence, Kans., 1962.

DUTCH NEW GUINEA, *see* OCEANIC ART (MELANESIA).

DUTCH SCHOOL. Before the 16th century no national school of painting existed in Holland, although many notable painters of Dutch origin, such as Dirk Bouts and Gerard David, contributed to the development of 15th-century Flemish painting. The beginnings of a Dutch school were made in the 16th century by Lucas van Leyden, Jan van Scorel, and Maerten van Heemskerck, who drew upon German, Italian, and native sources to produce the Netherlandish Renaissance. The flowering of the Dutch school occurred in the 17th century with such painters as Rembrandt, Hals, Vermeer, and Ruisdael. During the 17th century, centers of painting were established in all major Dutch cities; the most important were Haarlem, Amsterdam, and Delft. The Dutch school became known especially for its landscape, genre, marine, and still-life paintings. By the 18th century, the school was in a general decline. *See* HALS, FRANS FRANSZ.; HEEMSKERCK, MAERTEN VAN; LEYDEN, LUCAS VAN; REMBRANDT HARMENSZ, VAN RIJN; RUISDAEL, JACOB ISAACKSZ. VAN; SCOREL, JAN VAN; VERMEER, JOHANNES REYNIERSZ.

BIBLIOGRAPHY. W. Martin, *Dutch Painting of the Great Period, 1650–97*, London, 1951; R. H. Wilenski, *Dutch Painting*, New York, 1955.

DUVENECK, FRANK. American painter, etcher, sculptor, and teacher (b. Covington, Ky., 1848; d. Cincinnati, Ohio, 1919). Duveneck early found work painting decorations in a tight style for churches in Kentucky.

In 1870 he went to Munich, where he acquired the broad painting style after the manner of Rembrandt, Hals, and Velázquez. Duveneck practiced the style himself and later, as an influential teacher, imparted it to his American students. The *Head of an Old Man in a Fur Cap* (1870; Cincinnati Art Museum) illustrates the transition between his early hard technique and his later loose handling of paint. His famous *Whistling Boy* (1872; Cincinnati Art Museum), sketchy except for the face, already shows his mastery of the new mode. In 1873 Duveneck returned to the United States and painted portraits in Cincinnati. By 1875 he was back in Munich and opened his school there in 1878. *The Turkish Page* (1876; Philadelphia, Pennsylvania Academy of Fine Arts) was a concession to the prevailing taste for exotic subjects, but *The Cobbler's Apprentice* (1877; Cincinnati Art Museum) shows Duveneck characteristically concentrating on the single figure loosely but powerfully painted in broken planes of light and dark.

In 1879 Duveneck and his students, known as the "Duveneck boys," went to Italy, where he spent the next few years alternating between Florence and Venice. Two paintings of this period, *The Blacksmith* (ca. 1879) and *Girl in a Black Hood* (1879; both Cincinnati Art Museum), exhibit the fluid Munich style. Later works done in Italy show a change to a less sharp, smoother treatment. Such paintings as *Italian Courtyard* (1886) and *Girl in a White Waist* (ca. 1887; both Cincinnati Art Museum) are still, however, essentially realistic. In 1880 Duveneck became interested in etching, and some of his prints, oddly, were confused by some with the work of Whistler. His stays in Venice produced a group of atmospheric, thinly painted marines, such as *Red Sail in the Harbor at Venice* (ca. 1884; Cincinnati Art Museum). Duveneck continued teaching after his return to the United States in 1888 and joined the faculty of the Art Academy of Cincinnati in 1900. The few paintings of his later years show both his Munich and his Italian styles. Duveneck's paintings and his teach-

Frank Duveneck, *Whistling Boy*. Cincinnati Art Museum.

ing illustrate the change from interest in detailed Düsseldorf painting to interest in the looser Munich style, which was the most important influence on American painting in the early 20th century.

BIBLIOGRAPHY. N. Heermann, *Frank Duveneck*, Boston, 1918; Cincinnati Museum Association, *Exhibition of the Work of Frank Duveneck*, Cincinnati, 1936.

JEROME VIOLA

DUVET, JEAN. French engraver (1485–ca. 1561). Duvet trained as a goldsmith and lived mainly in Langres and Dijon and possibly in Geneva. His early engravings (*Annunciation*, 1520) demonstrate an accurate knowledge of Correggio and Raphael, indicating that he made a trip to Italy. Moving in the direction of mannerism with a strong medieval flavor (*Unicorn Series*, 1540s), Duvet's work culminates with the *Apocalypse Series* (published 1561). Although he relies on Dürer in the latter, Duvet makes no attempt at naturalism of space and scale or compositional clarity in his literal interpretation of the supernatural text. His prints show parallels with early Florentine mannerism and foreshadow French art of the late 16th century.

BIBLIOGRAPHY. A. E. Popham, "Jean Duvet," *Print-Collector's Quarterly*, VIII, 1921; A. Blunt, *Art and Architecture in France, 1500–1700*, Baltimore, 1954

DUYCKINCK FAMILY. American painters and glaziers (fl. New York, 17th–18th cent.). Evert Duyckinck I (b. Holland, 1620/21; d. New York, 1700–03), a limner and glazier, arrived in New Amsterdam about 1638. Gerrit, his son (baptized New York, 1660; d. there, ca. 1712), was also a limner and glazier as well as a glass stainer.

Gerardus I, Gerrit's son (baptized New York, 1695; d. there, ca. 1746), and Gerardus II, Gerrit's grandson (baptized New York, 1723; d. there, 1797), were portrait painters, gilders, japanners, and dealers in paints and glass. Gerardus II also advertised as a teacher of painting and drawing. Evert Duyckinck III (b. Holland, 1677; d. New York, 1724/27), a grandson of Evert I, was a portrait painter.

BIBLIOGRAPHY. W. P. Belknap, *American Colonial Painting: Materials for a History*, Cambridge, Mass., 1959.

DUYNEN, ISAAK VAN, *see* DUIJNEN, ISAAK VAN.

DUYSTER, WILLEM CORNELISZ., *see* DUIJSTER, WILLEM CORNELISZ.

DUYTS, JAN DEN. Flemish painter (1629–76). The artist, born in Antwerp, was a painter of religious and mythological compositions who worked in the style of the late followers of Rubens. From his signed works we can establish that he found Van Dyck's attractive formulas more tasteful than Rubensian dynamism and forcefulness.

BIBLIOGRAPHY. R. Oldenbourg, *Die flämische Malerei des XVII. Jahrhunderts*, 2d ed., Berlin, 1922.

DYCE, WILLIAM. British painter (b. Scotland, 1806; d. London, 1864). He studied at the Royal Academy, London, and in Rome. Back in Scotland by 1830, he found no market for his religious compositions and turned to portraiture. He became concerned, as were most cultivated men of the age, with the lack of design in British manufacturing and studied and wrote on the problem of art education for the workingman. His ideas, character, and administrative ability so impressed the Prince Consort and the committee formed to improve the industrial arts that he was made head of the first government school of design. In spite of his doubts as to the suitability of fresco to the English climate and temperament, Dyce was one of the artists chosen to decorate the rebuilt Houses of Parliament; his frescoes, on the Arthurian legends, were unfinished when he died. His work can perhaps be considered the product of his vast learning rather than of inspiration; Dyce was never able to completely achieve the grand manner that he attempted to bring to English painting.

DYCK, ABRAHAM VAN, *see* DIJCK, ABRAHAM VAN.

DYCK, ANTHONY VAN. Flemish painter of portraits, religious and mythological scenes, and occasionally water colors representing landscapes (b. Antwerp, 1599; d. Blackfriars, near London, 1641). The artist, a pupil of Hendrik van Balen, had a studio of his own as early as 1615, but he became a free master of the Guild of St. Luke only in 1618. Between 1618 and 1620, he seems to have collaborated closely with Peter Paul Rubens.

Van Dyck made his first trip to England in 1620. He returned to Antwerp for a few months in 1621, and left the same year for Italy, where he remained until 1627. He returned to Antwerp toward the end of 1627, visited Holland in 1628–29, returned again to Antwerp, and stayed there until 1632, when he again set out for London, going by way of Holland. Knighted and appointed "Principalle Paynter in ordinary to their Majesties at St. James's" the same year, he settled down to become an extremely popular portrait painter. His English sojourn was briefly interrupted twice: in 1634–35 and in 1640–41, when he returned to Flanders.

In spite of earlier studies, Van Dyck's youthful style is still difficult to define, primarily because a complex of authentic works is lacking. The problem of Van Dyck's collaboration with Rubens and the degrees of influence sustained has by no means been solved: the young artist seems to have progressed by leaps and bounds, in search of a suitable style and manner. His early compositions were far removed from the later, elegantly melancholic productions that established his reputation.

The earliest works are characterized by a quest after artistic personality. Van Dyck essays himself a naturalist, influenced by Jacob Jordaens's broad brushstroke fused with Caravaggesque violence and contrasts. The *Self-Portrait* (Vienna, Academy) must have been painted about 1614, to judge from the age of the model. It is freely done, and there are rhythmic qualities in the execution that far surpass the probably contemporary *Apostles* (Munich, Bamberg, Paris). Further series of kindred subjects date probably from between 1616 and 1618 (Earl Spencer, Dresden, the former Boehler series).

With respect to composition, *Drunken Silenus* and *The Martyrdom of St. Peter* (both at Brussels, Fine Arts Museum) as well as the *Martyrdom of St. Sebastian* (Paris, Louvre) have been assigned to Van Dyck's pre-Rubensian years. This assumption is based on the similarity of their execution to that of the above-mentioned studies of apostles. Three canvases, for which there is documentary evidence concerning Van Dyck's authorship, were probably painted about 1618–20, because of their more advanced style: *Two Saint Johns* (signed), *Christ Crowned with Thorns* (destroyed), and *The Descent of the Holy Ghost* (all in Berlin, former State Museums, Picture Gallery). These are also the years of the painter's collaboration with Rubens, when he produced painted copies, drawings, and grisailles after the older master. It is also said that Van Dyck had a hand in, among others, *Le Coup de lance* (Antwerp, Fine Arts Museum) and *Bacchanal* (Berlin, former State Museums, Picture Gallery).

From about 1617 to 1621 Van Dyck's new portrait style evolved—fresh, distinguished, and already acknowledging Venetian influences. Highlights from this period are the artist's self-portraits (Munich, Pinacothek; Leningrad, Hermitage; New York, Metropolitan Museum); the companion pieces, *Frans Snyders* and *Margaretha De Vos*, a portrait of Snyders's wife (New York, Frick Collection); and *Cornelis van der Geest* (London, National Gallery). Of the approximately 130 works currently ascribed to these years, many must be considered to be erroneous attributions.

Information concerning Van Dyck's Italian sojourn is very sketchy. Since he was already an accomplished painter whose eyes had been opened to Italian form and colors while he was still in Antwerp, there is no doubt that he was altogether prepared to dip into the treasure trove that the country offered him. He assiduously studied the Ve-

Anthony van Dyck, *The Artist with Sir Endymion Porter*, ca. 1635. Oil on canvas. Prado, Madrid.

netians, above all Titian and Veronese; the eclectics; Guido Reni, Francesco Albani, and Raphael. The *Chatsworth Sketchbook* bears witness to his efforts to transcribe entire compositions and details destined for later use. In spite of occasional borrowings, however, Van Dyck never yielded to slavish Italianism. The forms and ideas of his compositions were amalgamated in a manner that remained altogether personal and Flemish. The same holds true of color and technique; though he was familiar with the Venetian palette as seen through Rubens's eye, he adapted it in sonorous hues characteristic of his own vision. While perfecting his mastery of the *fa presto* technique, he reverted

occasionally to the customary fatty pigmentation. The prime religious composition of the period is the *Virgin of the Rosary* (Palermo, Congregazione della Madonna del Rosario), whose construction proceeds both from Titian's *Assumption* and from Rubens's Grenoble altarpiece.

The portraits *Sir Robert* and *Lady Shirley* (Petworth, Sussex, England, Lord Leconfield's Collection) were done in 1622 in Rome. *Cardinal Bentivoglio* (Florence, Pitti) was probably done a year later.

In Genoa Van Dyck excelled himself. Portraits executed for the local aristocracy hail back to Rubensian examples, to which Van Dyck brought increased stateliness, elegance, pomp, and a touch of arrogance (*Marchesa Brignole Sale and Her Son*, Washington, D.C., National Gallery).

The artist's productions after he went back to Antwerp are cast in the mold of a matured conception. He painted numerous religious canvases, in which he abandoned Rubens's classicism and arrived at personal solutions. His formal language becomes calm and measured, his palette mostly monochromatic. But the personages are permeated with feeling and inspire a sense of devotion. The *Crucifixion* (Mechlin, Church of St. Rombout) and the *Erection of the Cross* (Courtrai, Church of Notre-Dame) rank high among works commissioned for churches and convents. The same slow rhythm typifies historical and mythological scenes such as *Rinaldo and Armida* (Baltimore, Museum of Art). Rubens's absence, to which much of the increased demand for Van Dyck's handiwork appears to have been due, also intensified the demand for his portraits. Among the most expressive, firmly modeled, and gracefully elegant likenesses of these years are *Anna Wake* (1628; The Hague, Mauritshuis) and *Maria Louisa de Tassis* (Vaduz, Liechtenstein Collection).

Van Dyck was settled in London by the end of 1632, and he elaborated a style that became the foundation for British portrait painting for the next 200 years. His historical subjects (for example, *Cupid and Psyche*, Buckingham Palace, Royal Collections) are less important than his refined likenesses, but they are transcribed with nobility and show no affectation or mannerism. In England, Van Dyck became a painter of distinction: his draftsmanship was precise, his coloring was precious, and his conception was courtly. There he fashioned a world, establishing an artistic model that English aristocracy finally resembled.

The King, the Queen, and the royal family sat for him repeatedly (for example, *Charles I à la chasse*, Paris, Louvre; *Queen Henrietta Maria*, Berkeley, Windsor Castle; *The Three Royal Children*, Berkeley, Windsor Castle). In these portraits, as well as in numerous portraits of lesser English nobility, the essence of Van Dyck's artistry comes to the fore, conveying the tone of an eclogue before some impending tragedy. Landscape and figure are fused; models are endowed with fascination rather than with verisimilitude. He keeps his distance rather than, like Rubens, approaching life too intimately and directly. Even though, technically speaking, Van Dyck's English productions are often executed perfunctorily and with extensive studio help, they constitute the apex of his work—beautifully decorative superficiality rather than deeply felt psychology.

Van Dyck excelled also as a draftsman and engraver. The series of portraits called *Iconographie*, part of which was etched by him, is a document of great importance.

BIBLIOGRAPHY. A. Michiels, *Van Dyck et ses élèves*, Paris, 1881; J. Guiffrey, *A. van Dyck*, Paris, 1882; L. Cust, *Anthony van Dyck*, London, 1900; L. Cust, *Van Dyck*, London, 1906; H. Rosenbaum, *Der junge Van Dyck*, Munich, 1928; G. Gluck, *Van Dyck, Des Meisters Gemälde*, Stuttgart, 1931; M. Delacre, *Le Dessin dans l'oeuvre de Van Dyck*, Brussels, 1934; G. A. Adriani, *A. van Dycks italienisches Skizzenbuch*, Vienna, 1940; M. Mauquoy-Hendrickx, *L'Iconographie d'Antoine van Dyck*, Brussels, 1956; L. van Puyvelde, *Van Dyck*, 2d ed., Brussels, 1959; H. Vey, *Die Zeichnungen Anton van Dycks*, 2 vols., Brussels, 1962; E. Larsen, "A Presumed Portrait of John Milton by Anthony van Dyck," *Pantheon*, XXIV, September-October, 1966.

ERIK LARSEN

DYCK, FLORIS CLAESZ. VAN, *see* DIJCK, FLORIS CLAESZ. VAN.

DYING GAUL, THE. Marble statue representing the figure of a wounded Gaul in the Capitoline Museum, Rome. It is a Roman copy of a famous work from Pergamon (ca. 200 B.C.). The original statue probably formed part of a larger bronze group dedicated by Attalus I (r. 241–197 B.C.) to celebrate his victory over the Gauls. It had stood in the center of the sanctuary of Athena. The Gaul is represented lying on his shield awaiting death. He is wounded under the right breast; the flow of the blood from the wound is plastically rendered. The head sinks forward. The expression of agony in the face is characteristic of Pergamene "baroque" art. The nationality of the figure is established by the necklace around the neck and the rough streaks of hair. Anatomical details are rendered realistically.

BIBLIOGRAPHY. E. A. Gardner, *A Handbook of Greek Sculpture*, 2d ed., London, 1915; M. Bieber, *The Sculpture of the Hellenistic Age*, New York, 1955.

DYING LIONESS. Detail from the famous Assyrian relief *Lion Hunt* (London, British Museum), which formed part of a continuous frieze adorning the interior of King Assurbanipal's palace at Nineveh (7th cent. B.C.). The frieze was a pictorial narration of the king's achievements, the hunt symbolizing his prowess as a hunter. Considered a masterpiece of animal sculpture, the lioness, shown in low relief with bared fangs, is pierced by three arrows. She still has enough strength to raise herself on her forefeet, although her hind legs are paralyzed and trail on the ground. The artist obviously had a good knowledge of anatomical detail. The realistic treatment and liveliness of form show a superior technique in the art of portraying animals in violent movement and is an advance over most earlier, static forms.

DYING SLAVE, THE. Marble sculpture by Michelangelo, in the Louvre, Paris. *See* MICHELANGELO BUONARROTI.

DYNAMIC SYMMETRY. Theory propounded by the American artist and writer Jay Hambidge (1867–1924) concerning the underlying principles of good design. Dynamic symmetry operates on the same principles that govern living organisms, human proportions, and plant growth. Whereas static symmetry has fixed proportional relationships, dynamic symmetry is based on a series of compound relationships mathematically measurable in terms of areas rather than linear patterns.

Hambidge derived his ideas from his measurements of ancient Egyptian and Greek works of art, particularly Greek vase decoration, which he claims were made in full knowledge of these principles. As developed in several books, Hambidge's theory was received skeptically by many but also had an influence on a number of writers and artists, which included George Bellows and José Clemente Orozco. *See* BELLOWS, GEORGE WESLEY; OROZCO, JOSE CLEMENTE.

BIBLIOGRAPHY. J. Hambidge, *The Elements of Dynamic Symmetry*, 3d ed., New York, 1967.

E

EADWINE PSALTER. Carolingian illuminated manuscript, in the British Museum, London.

EAGLE. Bird whose strength and soaring flight have inspired men since ancient times to use it as an emblem of military, national, and imperial power. It was especially popular in classical antiquity and during neoclassic revivals such as the Napoleonic and American Federal periods. During the Middle Ages the eagle represented St. John the Evangelist in Christian symbolism.

BIBLIOGRAPHY. G. Ferguson, *Signs and Symbols in Christian Art*, complete and unabridged ed., New York, 1961.

EAKINS, THOMAS COWPERTHWAITE. American portrait and genre painter (b. Philadelphia, 1844; d. there, 1916). Eakins was a student at the Pennsylvania Academy of the Fine Arts from 1861 to 1866, and at the same time he also studied anatomy at Jefferson Medical College. Going to Paris in 1866, he studied at the Ecole des Beaux-Arts for three years under Gérôme and also worked briefly under Léon Bonnat, a portraitist, and A.-A. Dumont, a sculptor. Because of ill health, Eakins went to Spain in 1869–70, and there he was influenced strongly by the works of Velázquez and Ribera. These two influences, as well as that of Rembrandt, were to be the most important effects of his stay in Europe. In July, 1870, Eakins returned to Philadelphia, where he spent the rest of his life.

Between 1876 and 1886 Eakins taught at the Pennsylvania Academy schools, becoming professor of anatomy in 1879 and director in 1882. In 1886 he resigned his post, largely as a result of a controversy over nude models. He then taught without payment at the Philadelphia Art Students League, organized by his pupils, and from 1888 to 1894 he taught at the National Academy of Design in New York. During the mid-1880s he did protographic studies of motion, predecessors of the motion pictures.

Eakins's paintings reveal the same insistence on realism that had brought about his resignation from the Pennsyl-

Thomas Eakins, *The Oarsmen*, detail. Philadelphia Museum of Art.

vania Academy schools. He combined this emphasis with a marvelous quality of light, bright in his early works (*Max Schmitt in a Single Scull*, 1871; New York, Metropolitan Museum), richer and much more mellow during the rest of his career (*Between the Rounds*, 1899; Philadelphia Museum of Art). His interest in anatomy is evident in much of his work, but it is especially striking in the large group portraits of medical schools, *The Gross Clinic* (1875; Philadelphia, Jefferson Medical College) and *The Agnew Clinic* (1898; Philadelphia, University of Pennsylvania). From the mid-1880s Eakins began to concentrate more on portraits, incisive character studies (*Miss Van Buren*, 1889; Washington, D.C., Phillips Collection) which brought him no commercial success. Among the most important collections of his works are those of the Philadelphia Museum of Art and the Metropolitan Museum.

Working independently of contemporary European movements, Eakins was an uncompromising realist whose canvases reflect his passionate concern with people, character, and light.

BIBLIOGRAPHY. L. Goodrich, *Thomas Eakins, His Life and Work*, New York, 1933; M. McHenry, *Thomas Eakins, Who Painted*, Oreland, Pa., 1946; F. Porter, *Thomas Eakins*, New York, 1959.

DAMIE STILLMAN

EAMES, CHARLES. American architect and industrial designer (1907–   ). Born in St. Louis, Mo., he was educated at the Washington University School of Architecture. Best known for his "Eames chairs," among the first successful molded plywood and molded plastic chairs to be mass produced in the United States, he has also designed toys, movies, houses, packaging, exhibitions, and an array of consumer and industrial products.

By 1930, he had begun working with Eliel and Eero Saarinen, and ten years later he married Ray Kaiser, who has been his regular collaborator ever since. World War II saw him designing motion picture sets for Metro-Goldwyn-Mayer, as well as special equipment for the United States Navy. After the war, Eames's interest in cinema broadened to include the making of his own films. He has produced a number of highly original and experimental one- and two-reel films for schools, for the government, and for such companies as IBM and ALCOA.

His travels in behalf of design have taken him around the world. He was a guest of the German State Department as part of its cultural evaluation program; and for the Indian government, Eames and his wife made recommendations on problems of design and environment. Eames has been especially active in design education as both consultant and teacher in various universities; for example, he established the design department at Cranbrook Academy. He has been awarded nearly every outstanding design prize.

ANN FEREBEE

EANNATUM: STELE OF THE VULTURES. Limestone stele (Paris, Louvre), excavated at Lagash (Telloh), which commemorates Lagash's victory over the neighboring city of Umma. Now fragmentary, it was approximately 6 feet high and 4 feet wide. The victory is represented on one side as a human contest, on the other as a divine conquest. The four registers of the historical side show Eannatum, who ruled Lagash in the late Early Dynastic III period (ca. 2450–2350 B.C.), and his warriors with the dead enemy. At the bottom are sacrificial and libation scenes.

On the two registers of the mythological side, an enormous figure, possibly the god Ningirsu, clasps a net filled with the enemy. Other small deities and part of a chariot are also preserved.

See also TELLOH.

BIBLIOGRAPHY. A. Parrot, *Tello,* Paris, 1948.

EARL, HARLEY. American industrial designer (1893–   ). In 1937 the Los Angeles-born designer took charge of the General Motors Company's newly created styling sec-

Charles Eames, Case Study House, Santa Monica, California, 1949.

tion, eventually playing a large role in the trend toward the low, rounded, sleek silhouette of the American automobile of the 1950s.

EARL, RALPH. American portrait and landscape painter (b. Worcester Co., Mass., 1751; d. Bolton, Conn., 1801). Ralph Earl grew up in the interior of Massachusetts and Connecticut, and most of his career was tied to the cities and small towns of this region. Shortly before the Revolution, he set himself up as a portrait painter in New Haven, but during the first years of the war he traveled with Amos Doolittle to the sites of the early battles, making drawings of Lexington and Concord, which were engraved by Doolittle. Early in 1778 Earl was forced to flee to England because of his loyalist sentiments. He remained there until 1785, painting portraits in London and Norfolk and exhibiting at the Royal Academy (1783–85). From 1786 on, Earl traveled about painting portraits and a few landscapes in New York City, on Long Island, in western and central Massachusetts, and especially in Connecticut. He worked in the larger cities such as New Haven, New London, and Hartford, but also in many smaller towns, among them Stamford, Litchfield, Windsor, and Woodstock.

Throughout his career, Earl's style changed very little. His early work (*Roger Sherman*, ca. 1775–77; New Haven, Yale University Art Gallery) is characterized by strong, clear outlines and a feeling for shape and color, but paintings done in England (*William Carpenter*, 1779; Worcester Art Museum) are equally tight. After his return to the United States, Earl's work became somewhat subtler and more elegant, but it still retained the honesty and the sensitivity to line, shape, and color that mark his early work. Full-length portraits in an interior or landscape setting are most characteristic of his work. *Chief-Justice and Mrs. Oliver Ellsworth* (1792; Hartford, Wadsworth Atheneum) is of the first type, while *Mrs. William Mosely and Son Charles* (1791; Yale University Art Gallery) illustrates the portrait in a landscape. The sharpness and clarity of the landscape here is also characteristic of Earl's few pure landscapes (*Looking East from Denny Hill*, ca. 1796–98; Worcester Art Museum).

One of the largest collections of his work is in the Litchfield, Conn., Historical Society, but he is also well represented at Yale University and at Worcester.

A self-taught painter whose works reveal a strong feeling for line and pattern as well as a somewhat archaic naïveté, Earl is one of the most distinguished painters to flourish in a post-Revolutionary Connecticut that produced many artists. He was the brother of James Earl and the father of Ralph E. W. Earl, both portrait painters.

BIBLIOGRAPHY. Yale University Art Gallery, *Connecticut Portraits by Ralph Earl,* New Haven, 1935; F. F. Sherman, "The Painting of Ralph Earl," *Art in America,* XXVII, October, 1939; W. Sawitzky, *Ralph Earl,* New York, 1945.

DAMIE STILLMAN

EARLOM, RICHARD. English mezzotint and stipple engraver (b. London, 1743; d. there, 1822). He studied stipple engraving under G. B. Cipriani, a pupil of Bartolozzi, but presumably taught himself the art of mezzotinting, for which he is best known. In 1777 he executed for the publisher Boydell a series of lightly mezzotinted reproductions

Ralph Earl, *Chief-Justice and Mrs. Oliver Ellsworth*, 1792. Wadsworth Atheneum, Hartford, Conn.

of Claude Lorraine's sepia drawings in the Duke of Devonshire's collection known as the *Liber veritatis*. The set was very popular and was republished several times. Earlom excelled in large mezzotints, particularly in those after Snyders's market still lifes, Zoffany's *The Royal Academy*, Van Huysum's fruit and flower pieces, and Wright's *A Blacksmith's Shop*. The soft velvety tones, laid over an etched outline, make these among the finest mezzotints ever produced.

BIBLIOGRAPHY. J. E. Wessely, *Richard Earlom*, Hamburg, 1886.

EARLS BARTON CHURCH. Church in Northamptonshire in central England, on the road between Northampton and Peterborough. Its plan is unique in that the tower space forms the body of the church with only a small projecting chancel. Similar plans occur at Barton-on-Humber and at Broughton, both of which have west extensions.

Earls Barton is early 11th century, and the plan a pre-Conquest peculiarity. The tower is of lofty, narrow Saxon proportions. It is ornate and of a type with horizontal emphasis rather than the type with little decoration and small windows. Earls Barton is the extreme example of the use of pilaster strips, or lesenes, where the surface is a network of stone strips and arcades—a conscious imitation of earlier timber construction.

BIBLIOGRAPHY. N. Pevsner, *The Buildings of England*, vol. 22, Harmondsworth, 1961.

EARLY CHRISTIAN ART AND ARCHITECTURE. This survey is limited to artistic developments in the Latin West and its related areas; developments in the Greek East are treated in the articles on Byzantine art and architecture and on East Christian art and architecture.

The subject of the sources and origins of Early Christian

Early Christian art. Marble sarcophagus of Junius Bassus, 4th century. Vatican Grottoes, Rome.

art has been one of the most controversial in the realms of archaeology and art history. Almost until the beginning of the 20th century, Rome was considered the germinal center of the new Christian art. By far the most numerous early examples of Christian art extant were from the Roman ambient, and these were studied by pioneers in the field. However, with the publication of the works of Josef Strzygowski early in this century, the Near and Middle East were put forth as the creative centers around which the new art coalesced. It has only been in the past three or four decades that a more accurate viewpoint has been developed, establishing the fact that it was a synthesis of Eastern and Western sources that gave rise to the new art.

Generally speaking, the style of Early Christian art represents a continuous breakdown of the late-antique, Hellenistic illusionism prevalent in the Mediterranean orbit during the 2d and 3d centuries A.D. The degeneration of illusionism can be clearly traced through three monuments. The Column of Trajan (117) presents a narrative sequence of action against a continuous landscape background such as occurs in the *Odyssey Landscapes*, but with a tendency to increased use of conventional, undifferentiated symbols. The Column of Marcus Aurelius (175), although imitative of Trajan's Column, already shows significant changes. The narrative sequence is no longer continuous, scenes tend to stand as isolated events, and there is an uninteresting repetition of motifs. The Arch of Septimius Severus (203) has reliefs (quite damaged) which show figures of increased frontality, squatness, and lack of detailed finish, and a limited light-dark relief pattern. This was the stylistic heritage of Early Christian painting and sculpture. *See* MARCUS

AURELIUS, COLUMN OF, ROME; SEPTIMIUS SEVERUS, ARCH OF, ROME; TRAJAN, COLUMN OF, ROME.

In architecture the situation was somewhat different. The earliest Christian congregations in Rome seem to have met secretly in private homes and in times of persecution to have hidden in the catacombs. With the Peace of the Church and official recognition under Constantine the Great, the Christians needed assembly halls large enough to house their growing congregations and to provide for liturgical needs. No single building type existed which answered these needs. The Roman basilica was a large assembly hall of varied uses—law courts, military exercise fields, military barracks, and so forth—but in and of itself, it did not answer those liturgical needs of the faith which were to determine the type of church to be erected.

If the specific church were associated with a martyr or the site of his martyrdom, or with Christ's life, it took a central-plan form (no doubt derived from the pagan *heroöan*, which was related to the worship of gods or godlike emperors). If the same church were associated with a large, permanent congregation, or were the goal of pilgrimages, a large assembly hall had to be attached. Of this latter type were Constantine's Church of the Nativity, Bethlehem, and Church of the Holy Sepulchre, Jerusalem, both of the early 4th century. Both were large, basilican-plan churches culminating in a circular or octagonal shrine over the sacred spot to which the church was dedicated. Another form of Early Christian church architecture was the "T" basilica. This type was specifically associated with Rome and Constantine's imperial house. Old St. Peter's and St. Paul's outside the Walls (423) were enormous five-aisled basilicas, with long, continuous transepts, and single apses. The churches were covered with open-timber roofs and contained galleries. The transept ends were set off by a columnar screen which served to set aside for liturgical purposes the two compartments thus created. See BETHLEHEM; HOLY SEPULCHRE, JERUSALEM; ST. PAUL'S OUTSIDE THE WALLS, ROME; ST. PETER'S (OLD), ROME.

The variety of architectural solutions during the formative Constantinian period belies any such generic term as "Constantinian basilica" or "Early Christian basilica." Other Constantinian structures, varied in type, include the five-aisled "standard" basilica at Orléanville, North Africa (ca. 320); the small-scale double church with a "U" plan at Aquileia in northern Italy (ca. 319); and the enormous double basilica in Trier, Germany. By the middle of the 4th century a certain standardization as well as a concurrent variety was apparent. S. Lorenzo Fuori le Mura and S. Sebastiano, both in Rome, are large basilican churches associated with martyr's tombs. As such, they helped to standardize the basilican type, but differed from preceding churches in their ambulatory-like structures around the apse (to accommodate the pilgrims to the martyr's tomb), which were probably derived from Roman funerary structures. In the same period were built S. Costanza, Rome, followed in the 5th century by S. Lorenzo, Milan (ca. 410–70), and S. Stefano Rotondo, Rome (468), all three central-plan structures with martyr associations. See SAN LORENZO FUORI LE MURA, ROME; SANTO STEFANO ROTONDO, ROME; SANTA COSTANZA, ROME; TRIER.

During the same period (4th–5th cent.) there appeared two other church types which were to play a dominant role in the development of church architecture. In Rome, a series of "normal" basilicas, the basic form of Western European development, were erected. S. Pudenziana (ca. 370), S. Sabina (ca. 420–30), and S. Maria Maggiore (mid-5th cent.) are three-aisled basilicas with open-timber roofs, columnar arcades, triforia, and clerestory windows. The same type appeared also in the old St. Martin at Tours (ca. 466–70). The second significant type, the cross-plan church, although it did not originate in the Latin West, appears in Milan in the Basilica Apostolarum (ca. 382), supposedly built by St. Ambrose. It has a Latin-cross plan with an elongated nave. The other cross-plan church in the West was at Gerazzah, North Africa. The Prophets, Martyrs, and Apostles Church there (ca. 464–65) had a Greek-cross plan (equal arms) inscribed within a square, a type especially significant for later Byzantine developments. See ST. MARTIN, BASILICA OF, TOURS; SANTA MARIA MAGGIORE, ROME; SANTA PUDENZIANA, ROME; SANTA SABINA, ROME. See also TEBESSA, MONASTERY OF.

In the 6th century, building activities were primarily confined to Ravenna and the southeastern coastlands of Italy, where a simple regional three-aisled basilican type prevailed. These churches were characterized by an eastern apse with a polygonal exterior, flanked by square side chambers, and a narthex with flanking tower. In addition to the Ravenna churches of this type, the Cathedral of Parenzo (ca. 540) and Sta Maria delle Grazie at Grado (ca. 550) might be mentioned. At the same time, Eastern, Syrian influences entered southern France and made themselves felt in such buildings as the Crypt of St-Laurent, Grenoble, and the Baptistery of St-Jean, Poitiers. During the 7th and 8th centuries a revival of the Constantinian "T" basilica occurred in Rome, parallel to a similar revival in Carolingian architecture. With this return to Constantinian models, a Christian architectural tradition had been achieved, and under the impetus of the Carolingian dynasty a new synthesis, based on Western traditions and Byzantine achievements, heralded the Christian architecture of the Middle Ages. See GRADO CATHEDRAL; PARENZO CATHEDRAL; RAVENNA; SAINT-JEAN, BAPTISTERY OF, POITIERS; SAINT-LAURENT, GRENOBLE.

Painting, both monumental and manuscript, follows the stylistic course outlined at the beginning, but with more frequent intrusions from the East than are witnessed in architecture. The earliest Christian catacomb paintings of the 2d and 3d centuries show an abbreviated symbolic imagery in a degenerating, late-antique style. Iconographic motifs are limited and largely restricted to themes of deliverance—from sin, from misery, from death. Such is the imagery found in the catacombs of Priscilla (2d cent.), Calixtus (2d cent.), Domitilla (3d cent.), and Peter and Marcellinus (3d cent.). Catacomb painting continued through the 6th century with an increase in iconographic themes and an almost corresponding degeneration of the late-antique style. See CATACOMB PAINTING.

The earliest extant mosaics in Rome are the 4th-century works in the Lateran Baptistery and S. Costanza. They consist of decorative bird and flower patterns which give an overall "carpet" effect, suggestive of Eastern influence (the mosaics at Antioch). Figural mosaic is seen in the apse of S. Pudenziana, a completely classical composition replete with Christian symbolism. The earliest extant complete mosaic cycle, of Old Testament subjects, is found in S. Maria Maggiore (432–40). Stylistically, these mosaics relate to 5th-century manuscript illumination, as in the Vatican Vergil (ca. 420). This work, with its gradual color modeling, its graded, tinted skies, and its delicate coloring, reproduces in the highest fashion the late-antique, Alexandrian style. Although not a Christian work, the Vatican Vergil stands at the foundations of medieval book illumination. Another related manuscript, probably of a slightly later date, is the Quedlinburg Itala (Berlin, former State Museums). This fragment of Old Testament text, written in uncials, is among the earliest extant manuscript fragwents with illuminated initials. See UNCIAL.

During the 6th century the uncertain conditions in the West were reflected by the variety of styles in Christian painting. In Ravenna the Byzantine style of Justinian reigned supreme, but elsewhere in Italy the situation was not so stable. Mosaics at SS. Cosmas and Damian, Rome, show a continuation, although diminished, of antique illusionism. In the same city, the frescoes in S. Maria Antiqua, S. Saba, and S. Maria in Via Latina show little suggestion of volume and great emphasis on expressive power. This style, with its heavy contours and flatness, is strongly suggestive of Syrian and Eastern influences—influences parallel to those affecting architecture in southern France at the same time.

Existing evidence indicates that by this time manuscript production had shifted from Rome, and new centers were in full operation. Therefore, the Codex Purpureus (Munich, Staatsbibliothek) has been assigned on stylistic and iconographic grounds to a northern Italian or Provençal scriptorium. The manuscript consists of two illuminated folios of the 6th century inserted into a 9th-century codex. The opaque overlaying of paint is still somewhat suggestive of the Vatican Vergil, but a certain lack of finesse, a harshness, and iconographic peculiarities militate against a Roman origin.

The Cambridge Gospels, or St. Augustine's Gospels (Cambridge, Fitzwilliam Museum), of the mid-6th or perhaps 7th century, present a similar problem. According to legend, this was the Gospel book that St. Augustine of York brought with him from Rome on his mission to Britain. Scholars are divided as to whether it is an expert English copy of a 6th-century Italian original, or an original 6th-century Italian work. Style, paleography, and iconography are all uncertain, so that the manuscript has been given to an Italo-Gallic school working in Provence, and to a southern Italian scriptorium, perhaps continuing the tradition of Cassiodorus's *Vivarium*. A similarly confusing situation exists in relation to the Ashburnham Pentateuch (Paris, National Library). The most fully illustrated and impressive of Early Christian (Latin) manuscripts, it is dated 6th or 7th century and is of very uncertain provenance. Experts differ in giving it a Spanish, northern Italian, or southern French provenance, but all agree on its dependence on an Eastern (Syrian or Greek) prototype. In light of the strong Syrian influences in architecture and wall painting at this time, some see it as the product of Syrians or Greeks working in the West during the late 6th century.

Sculpture and the decorative arts seem not to have been widely practiced during the Early Christian period. The Biblical stricture against graven images seems to have been felt most strongly in sculpture, where the relation to pagan idols was the most obvious. And in the first centuries of the Christian era, the Church had not yet accumulated enough wealth to order the magnificently executed and decorated church utensils which were to become so important a part of the art of the Middle Ages. Except for the 5th-century wooden doors of S. Sabina, extant sculpture is limited to sarcophagi and ivory plaques. The sarcophagi follow the pattern of late-antique illusionism degenerating into the now familiar crude, squat, almost nonclassical forms. There is a greater emphasis on decorative surface pattern and linearity at the expense of a fully plastic, sculpturesque treatment. A similar stylistic movement is discernible in the ivory carving of the time. The consensus is that just as manuscript production shifted from Rome, so did the centers of carving. Milan, Catalonia, and Provence have been proposed as carving centers for the sarcophagi and ivories. An Italo-Gallic school working in or near Marseilles has been strongly advanced, but Milan, specifically, seems to have been responsible for five-part jeweled and decorated ivory plaques, which in all probability derived from a Byzantine-Alexandrian prototype.

By the end of the 7th and the beginning of the 8th century, Early Christian art had taken on a new aspect. The impact of the Barbarian art of the various migratory peoples who had settled in northern Europe and pushed into the Mediterranean littoral added an anticlassical, nonfigural aspect to the earliest Christian developments. The results of the merging of these two streams are first seen in the Irish monastic scriptoria, where the first of the great new Christian manuscripts were produced. *See* BARBARIAN STYLE. *See also* CELTIC ART; HIBERNO-SAXON ART.

In France, under the aegis of the Frankish kings, a similar process occurred, which resulted in Merovingian art. In Spain, the Visigoths had established their own rather isolated culture, giving rise to art forms more Barbarian than Christian but uniquely beautiful in their own right (for example, the gold Visigothic crowns now displayed in Paris and Spain). *See* MEROVINGIAN ART; VISIGOTHIC ART.

At the beginning of the 9th century, the Carolingian dynasty arose in France and quickly established a firm central authority in western Europe. Under the leadership of Charlemagne, and with the astute help of English, Spanish, and Italian artisans and scholars, a new art and culture was created which was no longer Early Christian. The development of Carolingian art became the starting point of the art of the Christian Middle Ages in Europe.

BIBLIOGRAPHY. J. Strzygowski, *Orient oder Rom...*, Leipzig, 1901; J. Wilpert, *Roma sotterranea: Le pitture delle catacombe romane*, 2 vols., Rome, 1903; A. Grabar, *Martyrium: Recherches sur le culte des reliques et l'art chrétien antique*, 2 vols., Paris, 1946; C. R. Morey, *Early Christian Art*, 2d ed., Princeton, 1953; A. Grabar and C. Nordenfalk, *Early Medieval Painting...*, New York, 1957; R. Krautheimer, *Early Christian and Byzantine Architecture*, Baltimore, 1965.   STANLEY FERBER

EARLY ENGLISH ARCHITECTURE.

Style of English medieval architecture succeeding the Norman style at the end of the 12th century. It was popular until the last quarter of the 13th century, when the Decorated style became dominant. In contrast with the latter, the Early English style gives the impression of simplicity and emphasizes delicacy of line through slender columns, abundant use of sharply pointed arches, and long, narrow lancet windows without mullions.

BIBLIOGRAPHY. G. F. Webb, *Architecture in Britain: The Middle Ages*, Baltimore, 1956.

EARLY MINOAN ART, *see* CRETE.

EARTHENWARE.

Simple type of pottery fired at low temperature. Its color is that of the clay employed, often brownish red, yellowish, or buff. The structure is coarse-grained and porous, but it can be waterproofed by glazing and refiring, a refinement that also provides decoration. It retains heat well but chips easily and is most commonly used in brickmaking and for objects of daily use.

BIBLIOGRAPHY. G. Savage, *Pottery through the Ages*, Baltimore, 1959.

EASEL PAINTING.

Type of oil painting first popular in the Renaissance. The artist works on the painting as it stands before him on an easel, which is usually a three-legged structure with a cross rest that can be adjusted according to the size of the canvas. Small in format and portable, easel paintings were suitable for private devotion and for collectors. Easel painting reached its height in 17th-century Holland, where the majority of works depicted landscapes, still lifes, and all manner of genre scenes appealing to a broad middle-class public. It has continued as the most popular format into the 20th century.

BIBLIOGRAPHY. I. Bergström, *Dutch Still-Life Painting in the Seventeenth Century*, New York, 1956.

EAST CHRISTIAN ART AND ARCHITECTURE.

Any discussion of East Christian art invokes one of the bitter controversies of art history and archaeology: the precedence of the Middle East (Armenia, Syria, and elsewhere) as opposed to that of the West (Rome and Greece) in the development of Early Christian and Byzantine art. Until the end of the 19th century it had been assumed that Christian art originated in Rome and the Roman ambient. Byzantine art ranked merely as a semi-Oriental barbarization of Roman art, and other provincial developments were considered to a greater or lesser degree continuations of the Roman tradition.

With the publication of Josef Strzygowski's works early in the 20th century, greater emphasis was placed on the Middle East and Hither Asia (specifically, Armenia and Syria) as areas providing a generating force in Christian art. Strzygowski, however, soon tied his art-historical research to racial views, interpreting certain developments as racial products rather than as the results of sociocultural intermingling. Furthermore, to advance his theories, he tended to date key monuments earlier than did other scholars. Strzygowski thus lost most of his serious art-historical following, but his investigations had served to increase the vistas of the forces at work in the creation of a Christian art.

To examine East Christian art, this article considers those areas of the Middle East where Christian art developed independently of Byzantine and Roman Early Christian art, or where it was open to other influences independent of or simultaneous with influences from Rome and Constantinople. This takes in areas that are frequently considered provincial Byzantine, but which also show an older, somewhat independent tradition of development. Each country is presented alphabetically; interrelationships are shown where they exist. In most cases, because of the isolated and relatively primitive nature of these areas, little is preserved; it is often necessary to rely on the evidence of any single medium that remains.

ARMENIA

This area is central to the argument of Middle Eastern precedence in Christian art. No small part of its importance rests on two significant facts: it was the first nation to officially adopt Christianity as its state religion (303); and, geographically, it was a buffer state between the Roman and Persian empires. It was alternately tied to each, though it was sometimes independent politically, but was almost always culturally related to Persia. Because of the lack of documentary material for the earlier centuries, the age of many important monuments is debatable. Hence the position of Armenia as innovator or recipient of art forms is still open to some question.

The evidence of masonry technique and analogous style indicates that the earliest existing churches of Armenia date from the late 5th and the 6th centuries and show a strong dependency on Syrian models. The essential question in these and subsequent churches concerns the use of the masonry dome, which may have developed out of the structural principles of Persian fire temples. The fire temples, made of sun-dried brick, no longer exist, but reconstructions assume domed vaulting. The same form of sun-dried brick construction was also prevalent in Mesopotamia in pre-Christian times. Whether this structural technique was adapted to stone and first used in churches in Armenia is a moot point. However, this form of domed construction

was widespread in the Near East at the time of Christ and could have entered Christian architecture from any one of numerous areas.

The discussion of Armenian architecture of the 7th century rests upon firmer ground. The Cathedral of Echmiadzin still stands, while the church at Zwarthnot, probably of the same date, is now in ruins. Excavations and reconstructions of the latter church show it to have been a central-plan building of the same type as the church at Ani, which dates to the year 1000. An ambulatory in quatrefoil plan encircles the central nave area, which was domed. The dome rests on four freestanding piers. This is the church type most prevalent in Armenia and is also seen in the 10th-century church at Achtamar on Lake Van. The church at Thalin (T'alin) is of uncertain date. It has barrel-vaulted side arms and nave, with a dome over the central bay. It is a domed basilica type, such as the Byzantine church at Meriamlik (possibly as early as the 6th cent.). This type was extremely important in the evolution of mid-Byzantine architecture; hence, priority in its development assumes great pertinence in deciding the influences at play in the growth of the mid-Byzantine church. The Thalin church has been dated 6th–7th century, or as late as the 11th century, which would make it derivative of Constantinopolitan churches. Since the dating of Meriamlik is also uncertain (6th–8th cent.), the role of Armenia in important Byzantine architectural developments remains a reasonable possibility. *See* ACHTAMAR ON LAKE VAN, MONASTERY CHURCH OF; ECHMIADZIN: CATHEDRAL.

Significant Armenian sculpture is found at Achtamar on Lake Van. Low reliefs, carved in the building stones of the church, show strong Syrian influences. The figural sculpture here is strongly intermixed with decorative foliate forms along the façade, but little formal or architectural unity is attained. Armenian painting and illumination do not date prior to the 8th century and appear to be dependent on Byzantine, Syrian, and Iranian influences. Existing wall paintings at T'alish, Mren, and Thalin seem to postdate these 7th-century churches. They do show, however, that Armenian painting depicted a full New Testament picture cycle at an early date (although derived from other sources). Manuscript illumination is strongly indebted to Byzantine and Syrian models, but with a marked Oriental influence from Iran. The best extant manuscripts are from the 9th and 10th centuries and are especially under the influence of the Macedonian style. Among the most noteworthy of these are the Gospel Book of Queen Mlqé (ca. 862; Venice, S. Lazzaro) and the Trebizond Gospels (11th cent.; Venice, S. Lazzaro), the latter done perhaps by a Greek artist. *See* MACEDONIAN STYLE.

EGYPT

Although a part of the Roman Empire from as early as the time of Julius Caesar, Egypt developed a distinct, Eastern form of Christian art, primarily owing to a mixture of local pre-Roman tradition and Syrian influence. Coptic art, the product of Egyptian Christianity, was influential in manuscript illumination, wall painting, and textiles. *See* COPTIC ART.

Surviving works show Egyptian or Eastern forms that seem to have been indigenous to Christian architecture in the area from the very first centuries after Christ. Thus, the so-called "White Convent" at Sohag, of the 4th or 5th century, displays a triconch apse and a dome on drum over the crossing. (The triconch apse was adopted by Justinian in his renovation of the Church of the Nativity, Bethlehem.) A similar disposition is found in the so-called "Red Convent," of the same period, in Upper Egypt. Other Christian buildings in Egypt, such as those at Ptolemais and Hermopolis, are in a "standard" Early Christian basilican tradition. *See* SOHAG.

The church at Sohag has relief sculptures, dating from the 5th through the 7th century, that show knowledge of, and dependence on, classical motifs, but these are transformed by Syrian influence into highly expressive, linear, nonplastic works. The best extant Coptic frescoes are located at Bawit. Dating from the 6th century, they show a diminished antique influence and an increase in frontality, rich and strong colors, and heavy, dark contours. Coptic silk textiles show the two elements that vie with each other in Egyptian art. One group of textiles, probably produced in Alexandria or Antinoë, is replete with classical motifs and style. The other group, probably produced in Upper Egypt, is more striking in its linear and coloristic expressivity and reflects Syrian influences. The major early Christian ivory-carving center of Alexandria is not considered here, for despite its Egyptian location, the city was stylistically and culturally one of the most firmly entrenched areas of Early Christian and Byzantine Hellenism. *See* BAWIT FRESCOES.

PALESTINE
This area must be considered because of its production of lead, clay, and glass ampullae, and because of its importance as a crossroad of East and West. Here, pilgrims from the West encountered Syro-Palestinian developments in art, which were given special sanction by being located in the Holy Land; and they carried Syro-Egypto-Palestinian ideas back to the West. Hence, Palestine was one of the major gates through which Eastern art entered the West. Among the ideas and concomitant art that traveled west from Palestine were those of monasticism, a product of Egyptian-Syrian Christianity.

The ampullae were small flasks used by pilgrims to carry home sanctified oil from the Holy Land pilgrimage sites. For the most part they date from the 5th century. On them are depicted the earliest extant representations of the Crucifixion. Many of them are now collected in the treasuries of Monza and Bobbio. In general, Palestinian art was under Roman, Byzantine, or Syrian influence, or a combination of these. It offers no distinctive developments of its own. *See* BOBBIO, ABBEY OF; MONZA CATHEDRAL, TREASURY OF.

SYRIA
The foregoing discussion has already implied the extreme importance of Syria in the development of East Christian art, as it was in the general evolution of Christian art. The depiction of Christ as dark, bearded, and with long, dark hair (the prevalent type in Christian art) is of Syrian origin. Old and New Testament narrative picture cycles, so important in later Christian art, seem also to have originated in Syria. Some theories even give Syria credit for the beginnings of the twin-tower façade in church architecture.

Architecture. Syrian Christian architecture dates from as early as the 4th century. The Church of Constantine at Antioch (333) is an octagonal central-plan building with

East Christian art. *The Descent of the Holy Spirit*, from the Rabula Gospels. Laurentian Library, Florence.

an ambulatory and exedrae. In the martyrium tradition, it may stand behind the 5th-century Eastern revival of this type. A similar central plan is seen in the 4th-century church at Kaoussie, a tomb monument over the grave of St. John the Theologian to which four long arms were added in a cross plan to accommodate pilgrims.

The 5th century was one of great building activity in Syria, and the variety of church types indicates the rich imagination brought to bear on the problems of a Christian architecture. At Kalat Seman, the church had a cross plan with four equal arms converging on a central, vaulted octagon (generally similar to the church at Kaoussie). At Shabbak, the three-aisled, columnar basilica (ca. 460) displays the typical Syrian hewn-stone construction plus a rich use of strongly classical decorative profiles to articulate the wall surfaces. The space within the church is cubic, emphasizing the mass of the structure. A similar impression is given by the mid-5th-century church at Roueiha, where diaphragm arches across the nave (nonsupporting in view of an open-timber roof) serve to emphasize the cubic compartments of the interior space. Kalb Louzeh (ca. 480), also similar to Shabbak, has two squat towers flanking an enclosed porch on the façade. Some scholars tend to see this development behind the evolution of the twin-tower façade in the West, but there is insufficient evidence on this question. *See* KALAT SEMAN: CONVENT OF ST. SIMEON STYLITES; KALB LOUZEH, CHURCH OF; ROUEIHA, CHURCH OF.

The Cathedral of Bosra (now in Iraq), of about 526, created a new church type that may have provided one of the sources of Justinianian architecture. An outgrowth of Roman imperial audience halls, Eastern martyria, and im-

East Christian art. Detail of a mosaic from Antioch, with phoenix motif. Louvre, Paris.

perial palatine chapels, the Cathedral is a large, domed(?), central-plan structure with ambulatory and gallery. The central vaulting rests on a drum supported by a continuous circular arcade. Whether the vaulting was a true dome or a cloister vault has not been ascertained, but the disposition of space and parts certainly relates it to Justinianian building. The 6th-century church at Resâfah (Resapha), a three-aisled columnar basilica with barrel-vaulted aisles, was a type that influenced such North African churches as those at Tebessa in Algiers and Tabratha in Cyrenaica.

See also KASR-IBN-WARDAN.

Illuminated manuscripts. Syrian illumination was of the utmost significance in the evolution of Christian art. A number of outstanding early manuscripts are extant, including the important Rabula Gospels (586; Florence, Laurentian Library). Written and illuminated by the monk Rabula, at the Monastery of St. John in Zagba, it is strongly suggestive of Greek and Byzantine prototypes. But the richness of its decorative elements (arcades, floral, plant, and bird motifs) and the originality of its iconography place it at the forefront of Syriac illumination. The earliest extant painted Crucifixion scene appears in this manuscript, as do numerous other themes important to the evolution of Christian iconography. The "Fountain of Life" depicted in the Rabula Gospels reappears in the Armenian Echmiadzin Gospels (989), another Syriac manuscript, and was a feature of many Carolingian manuscripts, especially those of the Ada school. Other 6th-century manuscripts showing strong Syrian influence, if not of actual Syrian production, are the Rossano Gospels (Rossano, Cathedral Treasure), with the typically dark, bearded

Christ of Syria, and the Sinope Codex (Paris, National Library). The latter, related to the Rossano Gospels, shows an even greater emotional expressivity of linear design than the previously mentioned works. The Vienna Genesis (ca. 4th–6th cent.; Vienna, National Library) is the most "classical" in appearance of the East Christian illuminated manuscripts. It has a rich painterly quality against a background of dyed purple vellum. Although its provenance (like its date) has been vigorously debated, its direct storytelling quality and use of continuous narrative seem to indicate a Syrian provenance (other suggestions place it in Ravenna, Anatolia, and Constantinople).

Frescoes. Behind Syrian manuscript illumination loom the early Syrian fresco cycles, best exemplified by those of the Christian Chapel at Dura Europos (before 250). These Gospel episodes, some narrative, others not, show perhaps for the first time in Christian painting a full depiction of Christ. In addition, the scenes at Dura Europos show greater scope and detail in their storytelling than do the contemporaneous catacomb paintings in Rome. Stylistically, they show the strong frontality, linearity, and rhythmical repetition that were hallmarks of the Eastern ascendancy over late Hellenistic art. *See* DURA EUROPOS. *See also* JEWISH ART.

Antioch mosaics. No discussion of East Christian or Syrian art would be complete without mention of the great city of Antioch. An important cultural center and the stronghold of Greek art and thought, the city reached the epitome of its prosperity in the 5th and 6th centuries. Of Antiochene art, the most significant remains are the hundreds of mosaic pavements unearthed in recent years. It is in a chronological survey of these mosaics, ranging from the 2d to the 6th century A.D., that one can see the gradual but inevitable transition of Hellenistic forms and composition to the Oriental mode which came to dominate the non-Byzantine East. This is clearly seen in the treatment of the Hellenistic *emblemata* (figural scenes, separately made and then set into the floor). The earliest pavements show elaborate figure scenes which gradually are reduced to a bust in a medallion and are finally eliminated in favor of overall "carpet patterns" or geometric designs.

See also BYZANTINE ART AND ARCHITECTURE; EARLY CHRISTIAN ART AND ARCHITECTURE.

BIBLIOGRAPHY. J. Strzygowski, *Orient oder Rom ...*, Leipzig, 1901; A. Gayet, *... L'Art copte...*, Paris, 1902; L. Bréhier, "L'Art du Moyen age est-il d'origine orientale?" *Revue des Deux Mondes*, LXXIV, 1909; J. Strzygowski, *Die Baukunst der Armenier und Europa*, Vienna, 1918; S. Der Nersessian, *Armenia and the Byzantine Empire...*, Cambridge, Mass., 1945; A. Grabar, *Martyrium: Recherches sur le culte des reliques et l'art chrétien antique*, 2 vols., Paris, 1946; C. R. Morey, *Early Christian Art*, 2d ed., Princeton, 1953.

STANLEY FERBER

EASTER COLUMN, *see* HILDESHEIM.

EASTER ISLAND. Easternmost of the Polynesian islands, Easter Island is best known for the monumental volcanic stone carvings of heads and figures located on its slopes. These huge sculptures probably represent the actual or legendary first inhabitants of the island as well as cult heroes. Some, 30 feet high, are of solemn countenance and are rendered in strong planes and contained volumes.

Easter Island. These huge sculptured heads dot the island's slopes.

The antiquity of these objects remains problematical. It appears likely that they date from no earlier than the 15th century, by which time most aboriginal Polynesian settlement had been completed. Because of sparse vegetation, driftwood has been used for most recent sculpture, in which the distinctive works are skeleton-like ancestor figures.

See also OCEANIC ART (POLYNESIA); POLYNESIA.

BIBLIOGRAPHY. K. Routledge, "The Bird Cult of Easter Island," *Folk-Lore*, XXVIII, December, 1917; S. Chauvet, *L'Ile de Pâques et ses mystères*, Paris, 1935; A. Métraux, *Ethnology of Easter Island* (Bernice P. Bishop Museum, Bulletin 160), Honolulu, 1940.

EASTLAKE, SIR CHARLES LOCK. English painter and art historian (b. Plymouth, 1793; d. Pisa, 1865). He studied in London under Benjamin Robert Haydon and at the Royal Academy schools. After a visit to France in 1814, he achieved a success with *Napoleon on Board the Bellerophon* (Plymouth Art Gallery). From 1817 to 1830 he lived in Rome, where his mind was set on history painting. *The Spartan Isadas* (Derbyshire, Chatsworth), which he sent to the Royal Academy in 1827, was much praised. He was more widely known, however, for his romanticized scenes from Italian peasant life and, later, for *Christ Lamenting over Jerusalem* (London, Tate Gallery), which made a popular engraving. From 1842, when he accepted the post of secretary to the Fine Art Commission, Eastlake was less a painter than a public figure. He became, successively, librarian to the Royal Academy (1842), keeper of the National Gallery (1843–47), president of the Royal Academy (1850), and director of the National Gallery (1855). Among his many writings perhaps the most valuable is *Materials for a History of Oil Painting* (1847).

KENNETH L. GARLICK

EASTMAN, SETH. American painter of Indian life (b. Brunswick, Maine, 1808; d. Washington, D.C., 1875). After graduating from West Point he was stationed at Fort Crawford, Wis., and Fort Snelling, Minn. There he made sketches, later transformed into paintings and illustrations, of the Chippewa and Sioux Indians. His original combination of factual observation and pictorial romanticism constitutes a valuable record of Indian life and landscape.

BIBLIOGRAPHY. J. E. McDermott, *Seth Eastman, Pictorial Historian of the Indian*, Norman, Okla., 1961.

EAVES. Lower parts of a roof projecting beyond the face of the wall below.

EBAUCHE. French term for a rough draft or outline sketch. The *ébauche* is used as a preparatory study for any type of art work.

EBBO GOSPELS. Carolingian illuminated manuscript, in the Municipal Library, Epernay, France.

See also REIMS SCHOOL.

EBERLEIN, GUSTAV HEINRICH. German sculptor (b. Spiekershausen, 1847; d. Berlin, 1926). He studied in Nürnberg and Italy. His early mythological statues add some naturalism and a rococo softness to academicism. His later works, especially the public monuments, often show a baroque complication of figure and movement.

BIBLIOGRAPHY. A. Rosenberg, *Eberlein* (Künstler-Monographien, LXVI), Bielefeld, 1903.

EBERSWALDE GOLD HEAD. Prehistoric metalwork of about 1000 B.C., in Eberswalde, Germany.

EBERZ, JOSEF. German painter (b. Limburg an der Lahn, 1880; d. Munich, 1942). He was a pupil of Halm and Stück at Münden and studied in Karlsruhe, Düsseldorf, and Stuttgart. His early paintings are religious scenes, sometimes emphasizing an arabesque curve, as in the *Sacred Heart of Jesus* (1913) for the Konviktkirche in Ehingen. The characteristic outlining of figures slightly visible in that painting developed into a linearity and spatial flattening, as in *Christ's Farewell to the Women* (1914; Mannheim, Municipal Art Gallery). His colors grew warmer and brighter, and his emphasis on emotion resulted later in strongly expressionistic landscapes and figures.

BIBLIOGRAPHY. L. Zahn, "Der Maler Josef Eberz," *Jahrbuch der Jungen Kunst*, XIV, 1920.

ECBATANA (Hamadan). Capital of Cyaxares the Mede, who captured Nineveh in 612 B.C., located on the route from the west to the plateau of northern Iran. It was connected by a road to Susa. The court spent the hot summer months there. Herodotus's report (I, 101) of the seven concentric enclosure walls at successive levels, each colored differently, may be a misinterpretation of the seven stories of a ziggurat. *See* SUSA.

BIBLIOGRAPHY. R. Ghirshman, *Iran*, Harmondsworth, 1954.

ECCE HOMO. Latin for "Behold the man," the words spoken by Pilate in presenting Christ to the Jews (John 19:5). In representations of this theme, rare before the 15th century, the poignant figure of Christ, wearing the crown of thorns, the purple robe, and often holding a mock scepter, stands before the crowd which demands His crucifixion.

ECHAVE IBIA, BALTASAR DE. Mexican painter (b. early 1590s; d. ca. 1650). Born in Mexico City, he was the son of Baltásar the Elder and was probably trained by his father. His pictures, which feature landscape and a peculiar blue, suggest Andalusian influences of about 1600.

BIBLIOGRAPHY. J. Fernández, *Arte mexicano de sus origenes a nuestros días,* 2d ed., Mexico City, 1961.

ECHAVE Y ORIO, BALTASAR DE. Mexican painter (b. Spain, ca. 1548; d. Mexico, 1619/23). The first of three generations of artists, Echave the Elder arrived in Mexico in 1573. Although basically mannerist, his paintings also reflect the early baroque. His son was Baltásar de Echave Ibia.

BIBLIOGRAPHY. D. Angulo Iñiguez, *Historia del arte hispanoamericano,* vol. 2, Barcelona, 1950.

ECHINUS. Convex form below the abacus of the Greek Doric capital. The world is derived from the Greek *echinos,* meaning "sea urchin." A similar form is found in the Ionic capital, where it is often ornamented with egg and dart, which was sometimes painted on. The capitals in the ancient Palace of Cnossus, with their bulbous echinus cushions, are symptomatic of the later Doric form.

ECHMIADZIN: CATHEDRAL. Religious center of the Armenian Church, in southwestern Russia, founded before 484. Little or nothing is known of the original structure. The present building, mostly dating from about the year 1000, is a square central-plan structure with four exedrae (niches), one protruding from each side. It is divided into nine bays by four central piers supporting the central dome.

ECHMIADZIN: ST. HRIPSIME. Armenian church built in A.D. 618, exhibiting the typical plan of the area. The austere cube of heavy masonry has a central dome of ribbed vault construction over the crossing. The four arms end in apses and have niches at the angles between them. Square sacristies in the corners complete the rectangular plan.

ECHOPPE. A specially prepared etching needle with the point cut to a bevel, providing extremely fine lines that taper and swell when the tool is rotated. In the hands of fine craftsmen, such as Callot and others in the 17th century, the tool creates effects that exceed those obtainable with an engraved line.

ECHTERNACH SCHOOL. One of the main centers of late Ottonian manuscript illumination, located at the abbey of Echternach in Luxembourg. Flourishing from about 1025 to about 1055, the school produced many notable works. Among its most famous manuscripts are the Codex Aureus Epternacensis (ca. 1035; Nürnberg, Germanic National Museum), the Book of Pericopes of Henry III (ca. 1040; Bremen, State Library), and its major achievement, the Codex Aureus of Speyer (ca. 1046; El Escorial, Spain, Library).

The Echternach school was stylistically rather rigid and academic when contrasted with the vitality achieved by earlier Ottonian centers. But the hieratic and schematic rendering of figures and decorative elements is also an indication of the developing Romanesque style.

ECKERSBERG, CHRISTOPHER WILHELM. Danish painter (b. Schleswig, 1783; d. Copenhagen, 1853). He studied at the Copenhagen Academy with Abildgaard and, more important, in David's atelier in Paris. He spent from 1813 to 1816 in Rome, and the basic clarity and realism of his Roman view *S. Maria in Aracoeli* (Copenhagen, State Museum of Fine Arts) is a good example of his fundamentally sober style. A similarly detailed fidelity to the appearance of his subject can be seen in such a portrait as *The Daughters of M. L. Nathanson* (1820; Copenhagen, State Museum of Fine Arts). His landscapes, especially the later marines, were important in the development of Danish painting in the first half of the 19th century.

BIBLIOGRAPHY. E. Hannover, *Maleren C. W. Eckersberg...,* Copenhagen, 1898; C. W. Eckersberg, *C. W. Eckersberg i Paris...,* comment. by H. Bramsen, Copenhagen, 1947.

ECLECTIC ART. Term characterizing a method used by artists to select, and subsequently to incorporate into their own style, qualities admired in the art of others. Although this sometimes conscious, often subconscious, practice was traditional in the Renaissance, the term has been used to disparage post-Renaissance art, especially that of the Carracis. The implication was that the selecting artist lacked originality and genius.

ECOLE DE MEDECINE, PARIS, *see* GONDOIN, JACQUES.

ECOLE DE PARIS. Group of foreign painters who settled in Paris after 1918 without becoming part of the then-current movement in French art. Marc Chagall, Moise Kisling, Amedeo Modigliani, and Julius Pascin were all members of the Ecole de Paris. The term is falsely applied to the whole artistic output in Paris at that time. *See* PARIS, SCHOOL OF.

BIBLIOGRAPHY. M. Raynal et al., *History of Modern Painting,* vol. 3: *From Picasso to Surrealism,* Geneva, 1950.

ECOLE DES BEAUX-ARTS, PARIS, *see* BEAUX-ARTS, ECOLE DES, PARIS.

ECOLE MILITAIRE, PARIS, *see* GABRIEL, ANGE-JACQUES.

ECORCHE. Anatomical figure or mannequin with the skin removed to show the arrangement of muscles; used as a model by artists. A common type of *écorché* was derived from a model by the mannerist sculptor Cigoli.

ECOUEN, CHATEAU D', *see* BULLANT, JEAN.

ECSTASY OF ST. THERESA. Marble sculpture by Bernini, in S. Maria della Vittoria, Rome. *See* BERNINI, GIAN LORENZO.

ECTYPUM. In the broadest sense, any copy of an original work of art. Specifically, ectypum refers to a cast used in numismatics and classical archaeology. It is made from a mold taken from the original inscription or coin.

EDELFELT, ALBERT. Finnish painter (b. Borgå, 1854; d. there, 1905). The son of the architect Carl Albert Edelfelt, he studied in Helsinki, at the Antwerp Academy, and with Gérôme at the Ecole des Beaux-Arts in Paris. Fundamentally academic in style, his early works were genre and historical scenes. Later portraits and figures, especially of women, were influenced by the academic impressionism of Bastien-Lepage. His last works were freer in treatment, looser, and less detailed. He is also important in Finnish art for his involvement with the design workshop of Borgå.

BIBLIOGRAPHY. B. O. Hintze, *Albert Edelfelt*, 3 vols. in 1, Helsinki, 1942-44.

EDELINCK, GERARD. French engraver (b. Antwerp, 1640; d. Paris, 1707). He learned his trade from his countryman Cornelis Galle, but decided to join his younger brother in Paris in 1666. There he and other Flemings were befriended by Philippe de Champaigne, at whose atelier Edelinck met a number of illustrious artists, including Nanteuil, whose daughter he married. He was received into the Academy in 1677 and was also placed in charge of the drawing class at the Gobelins. His facility with the burin was remarkable; he apparently engraved with ease, requiring little if any correction. His portraits, for which he is best known, were executed with finesse and honesty. He made engravings after Philippe de Champaigne, Le Brun, Nanteuil, Rigaud, and others.

BIBLIOGRAPHY. H. Delaborde, *Gérard Edelinck*, Paris, 1886.

EDFU. Site in Upper Egypt, south of Luxor on the west bank of the Nile, marked as the scene of a mythological fight between Horus and his uncle Seth, god of evil. It has a well-preserved temple, the Temple of Horus, which

Edfu. Open façade in the great court of the Temple of Horus.

was built by the Ptolemies (237–57 B.C.) on the site of an earlier one. It is a typical cult temple of the late period.

The Temple of Horus is enclosed within a girdle wall with a rectangular outline (N–S) and is carved with religious scenes. At its front is a lofty two-towered pylon, once provided with four tall flagstaffs erected in special recesses in the façade. In each tower a newel staircase, lighted by slot windows, rises to the terrace.

Behind the pylon stretches a courtyard with a columned portico. The rear side is an open façade of the vestibule with composite columns and intercolumnar screens carved with scenes representing Ptolemy IX (146–117 B.C.) making offerings. This king is also shown performing various rites in the murals, which are set out in four registers (panels) according to the usual Ptolemaic arrangement. The hypostyle hall, with twelve composite columns and lighted by windows in the walls and ceiling, is preceded by two rooms and flanked by two others.

From the antechamber there are two staircases to the terrace, the eastern one of the newel type for the ascending procession and the western one with straight flights for the descending. The large sanctuary intended for the sacred boat is surrounded by an ambulatory with ten rooms lit by apertures in the ceiling. In the floor of two corner rooms there are trapdoors to the crypts built within the thickness of the walls above ground level. At the top of the outer face of the temple there are gargoyles in the shape of the foreparts of lions with spouts between their forelegs. The walls are carved with four registers of religious scenes, mainly episodes from the myth of Horus and Seth. A cylindrical well with a spiral staircase located outside the girdle wall to the east was used as a Nilometer.

The mammisi (temple dedicated to the birth of the deity's son, who is destined to be the reigning Pharaoh) is set at right angles to the west side of the temple and is built on a socle; it features a peripteron, with composite columns topped by cubical abaci, on the front of which is carved the awkward figure of the god Bes. The carving in the temple is characteristic of the late style: small figures, bold relief, and smooth plump modeling.

In the mounds west of the temple the remains of the successive strata of the town—Islamic, Coptic, Greco-Roman, and Egyptian—have been uncovered, yielding a rich assortment of household objects.

BIBLIOGRAPHY. E. Chassinat and Marquis de Rochemonteix, *Le Temple d'Edfou*, 12 vols., Cairo, 1892-1934; E. Chassinat, *Le Mammisi d'Edfou*, 2 vols., Cairo, 1910-39; H. Henne, *Rapport sur les fouilles de Tell Edfou*, 5 vols., Cairo, 1924-35; B. Bruyère and J. Michalowski, *Tell Edfou (Rapports des Fouilles Franco-Polonaises)*, 3 vols., Cairo, 1937-51.

ALEXANDER M. BADAWY

EDINBURGH. Capital of Scotland, situated on the Firth of Forth. A Roman fortress once existed on the heights of Castle Rock. The dominating mass of medieval Edinburgh Castle, built on those heights, is a focal point of the city. Holyrood Abbey, founded in 1128 and now in ruins, was connected with the castle by the Royal Mile. The houses built along this road formed the burgh, chartered in 1329, which became an important trading center. During the 17th century the timber houses were rebuilt in stone and enlarged, often with projecting upper floors over arches or pillars. *See* EDINBURGH: CASTLE.

In the 18th century the ravine below the old city was bridged, and the New Town was laid out on a rectangular plan (1767) by James Craig. Many buildings were designed by Craig, Robert Adam, and William Chambers. The present main street of the city, Princes Street, marks the beginning of the New Town, and beyond it are 18th-century squares and streets. There are numerous historic monuments in both the old and new portions of the city—for example, St. Giles's Church, originally Romanesque, reconstructed in the 14th century and enlarged in the 15th century; Holyrood Palace, begun in 1500; and Magdalene Chapel, Cowgate (1540), with the only medieval stained glass surviving in Scotland. Parliament House (1632–39), containing a great hall with a hammer-beam roof, was incorporated in the Law Courts between 1808 and 1840. George Heriot's Hospital (1629–50), a quadrangular building by William Wallace, is partly Gothic and partly Renaissance in style.

Fine examples of 16th- and 17th-century residences remain. John Knox's house, dating from the 16th century but since restored, is built of stone and plaster with timber galleries. Huntly House (1570) is now a city museum. Gladstone's Land, Lawnmarket (ca. 1620), is six stories high with the upper floors projecting over an arcaded ground floor, an external stone stair, and, in the interior, several walls and ceilings with paintings. The University of Edinburgh was begun by Robert Adam in 1785 and continued by W. H. Playfair after 1816.

During the 19th century the New Town expanded markedly, its architects working mainly in a neoclassic Greek style. In this period W. H. Playfair designed Regent, Carlton, and Royal terraces; and on an artificial hill called the Mound he constructed the Royal Institution and the National Gallery of Scotland. See EDINBURGH: MUSEUMS.

BIBLIOGRAPHY. E. J. Macrae, *The Heritage of Greater Edinburgh*, Edinburgh, 1947; G. Scott-Moncrieff, *Edinburgh*, London, 1947.

EDINBURGH: CASTLE.

The main group of buildings is known as the Citadel. St. Margaret's Chapel (ca. 1090) is Romanesque, but much restored. The remains of David's Tower (1367) are in ruins. The visible parts of the castle are 16th century and later.

The King's Lodging (1615), an example of early Scottish renaissance, is much restored. Its sculptures were executed by William Wallace, the King's master mason. The great hall with a fine timber hammer-beam roof is early 16th century. These parts of the castle form a quadrangular composition with the National War Memorial (1927). Slightly northwest is the Governor's House within the outer defense works. It was erected in the early 18th century. The New Barracks adjacent are from later in the century.

BIBLIOGRAPHY. Ministry of Works, *Ancient Monuments and Historic Buildings*, vol. 3, London, 1917–58.

EDINBURGH: MUSEUMS.

Important public art collections in Edinburgh, Scotland, are located in the museums listed below.

Corporation Museums. Five museums operated by the city and royal burgh of Edinburgh, for the preservation and exhibition of local antiquities relating to the history of Scottish life and culture. They are located in different parts of the city and are open daily to the public, upon payment of a small admission fee. They comprise Canongate Tolbooth, Huntly House, Lady Stair's House, Lauriston Castle, and the Museum of Childhood.

Canongate Tolbooth was the burgh courthouse and prison for more than 300 years. Built in 1591, on the site of an even older "Tolbuith," it has recently been restored and houses the J. Telfer Dunbar Highland Dress and Tartan Collection and other local material.

Huntly House is the largest of the Corporation Museums. It contains the principal collections of local history and topography. Some parts of the building date from 1517, but the main portion was constructed in 1570 and restored in 1931. A large collection of Sir Walter Scott mementos and manuscripts is on display here. It also contains exhibits relating to the trade guilds and houses an original copy of the National Covenant of 1638.

Lady Stair's House is a reconstructed Edinburgh town house dating from 1622 and restored in 1907. The furnishings re-create the atmosphere of 17th-century life, and the collections include miscellaneous remains associated with the Stair family, local history, relics from demolished historical buildings, and a comprehensive survey of Scottish pottery. An important collection of Robert Burns material and manuscripts is also exhibited.

Lauriston Castle is a fine country mansion situated on large grounds overlooking the Firth of Forth. The great house and its contents were given to the nation by its owners in 1926. The rooms contain excellent pieces of French and English 18th-century furniture, Flemish tapestries, and other decorative arts. Also on view is a special collection of Derbyshire Blue John (vases, urns, and other types of decorative pieces that are carved from a kind of fluorite).

The Museum of Childhood attempts to present the child's world as completely as possible. Toys, games, hobbies, articles from home and school, and materials dealing with the child's health and welfare are some of the sections of its collections, which are still in the process of being expanded. A large group of children's portraits is on view; the collections of costumes and children's books are currently being enlarged.

BIBLIOGRAPHY. *Museums and Galleries in Great Britain and Northern Ireland*, London, 1955.   ALLAN MC NAB

National Gallery of Scotland. Museum erected between 1850 and 1858 to the design of W. H. Playfair. The collection surveys the Continental schools as well as British and especially Scottish art. The early Italian paintings include triptychs by Bernardo Daddi and the school of Jacopo di Cione as well as a *Holy Family* by Filippino Lippi. Notable later Italian works are Tintoretto's *Venetian Family Presented to the Madonna*, Bassano's *Adoration of the Magi*, and Tiepolo's *Finding of Moses*. The highlight of the Flemish school is undoubtedly Hugo van der Goes's altarpiece, originally from the Trinity Church (ca. 1474). The Spanish school is represented by El Greco, Zurbarán, Velázquez, and Goya, the Dutch by Hals, Rembrandt, Ruisdael, Steen, and others. The outstanding Dutch work is Vermeer's rare religious painting *Christ in the House of Mary and Martha*. The major French paintings are by Poussin, Watteau, Chardin, Boucher, Corot, Pissarro, Degas, Monet, Gauguin, and Van Gogh. Works of the English school include Reynolds's *The Waldegrave*

Ladies, examples by Hogarth, Zoffany, and Constable, and Gainsborough's lovely *Mrs. Graham*. Works of the Scottish school include incomparable Raeburns and a representative survey of 17th-century portraiture.

The most impressive exhibition is composed of a group of paintings from Bridgewater House, lent by Lord Ellesmere. It includes several paintings by Raphael, Titian, and Rembrandt, and others by Lotto, Tintoretto, Claude Lorraine, and Hobbema. Titian's *Diana and Actaeon* and *Diana and Callisto* are unmatched for brilliance. Towering above all else, however, is the series of seven paintings depicting the sacraments which were created by Poussin for Fréart de Chantelon (1644–48).

BIBLIOGRAPHY. C. Thompson, *A Short Guide*, Edinburgh, 1956.

JOHN HARRIS

Royal Scottish Museum. The art and ethnography collections, which form but a part of the museum, are extraordinarily varied, though easel paintings are excluded. The European collections include furniture, textiles and tapestries, coins, and arms and armor. Outstanding among the extensive holdings of primitive art are the Benin bronzes. The Egyptian Hall documents the civilization of the Nile Valley from earliest times to the Coptic period. The Asian collections are highlighted by the Tibetan painted tankas.

BIBLIOGRAPHY. *The Royal Scottish Museums... 1854–1954*, Edinburgh, 1954.

EDITION. In the area of fine prints, a particular number of impressions of the same visual image, each of which is an original. The number of prints in a contemporary edition is usually noted in pencil in the lower margin as the denominator of a fraction; the numerator is the number assigned to that particular print (for example, 10/50 designates the 10th of 50 impressions).

EDLINGER, JOSEPH GEORG VON. German painter (b. Graz, 1741; d. Munich, 1819). Edlinger studied in Vienna and began to work in Munich (1770), where he became court painter in 1781. Primarily a portraitist, Edlinger drew on the directness of the rococo style rather than on its elegance. He was also influenced by the vigorous brushwork and realism of Hals and Rembrandt.

EDO CASTLE, TOKYO. Japanese castle that once stood where the imperial palace is now located. The original structure was built in 1457 and later became the seat of the Tokugawa shogunal government. Extensive improvements and enlargements were started in 1600 and continued for twelve years. Edo once represented the perfected form of Japanese castle architecture. It was destroyed by fire toward the end of the Edo period, however, and only some gates, the watchtowers, and the stone wall remain from the original castle. The interior of the buildings was decorated with paintings (now lost) done in 1623 by Tannyū and his pupils. *See* TANNYU.

E-DOKORO. Official staff of painters of Japanese imperial courts, large Buddhist monasteries, or the shogun's government.

EDO PERIOD, *see* JAPAN.

EDSON, ALLAN AARON. Canadian painter (1846–88). He studied with Léon Pelouse in France and traveled widely in Europe. His oils and watercolors, exclusively of the Montreal area and Rocky Mountain landscapes, were exhibited widely in Canada, London, and Paris.

EDZARD, DIETZ. German painter (1893–1963). Born in Bremen, Edzard studied with the impressionist Trübner at Karlsruhe in 1914 and had his first exhibition in Berlin two years later. His early paintings have the elongated proportions and linear qualities of Modigliani, and he subsequently developed a rigid, melancholy expressionist style. Moving to Provence, Edzard produced some of his best work in landscapes somewhat in the manner of Utrillo. He settled in Paris permanently in 1928 and adopted the semi-impressionist style that was to become his trademark. After that, his principal theme was the women of Paris, fashionable or picturesque, all painted with loose brushwork and tonal sweetness and portrayed with vague pleasantness. The popularity of this mode led also to commissions for advertising.

BIBLIOGRAPHY. D. Edzard, *D. Edzard*, introd. G. Muehsam, New York, 1948.

EECKHOUT, GERBRANDT VAN DEN. Dutch painter of genre, history, and portraits (b. Amsterdam, 1621; d. there, 1674). He was the son of the goldsmith Jan Pietersz. van den Eeckhout. He entered Rembrandt's studio at the age of fourteen (1635) and remained there about five years. According to Arnold Houbraken, Eeckhout was Rembrandt's "best pupil who adheres to his master's manner

Gerbrandt van den Eeckhout, *The Bathers*. Rijksmuseum, Amsterdam.

till the end of his life." Eeckhout was also one of Rembrandt's closest friends.

Eeckhout's early works are sometimes close to the style of another Rembrandt pupil, Govert Flinck, but his later works become more individual and personal. Besides the influence of Rembrandt, Eeckhout seems also to have had some contact with Rembrandt's Leyden associate, Jan Lievens. Eeckhout painted several large corporation group portraits for the Amsterdam wine merchants (1657; London, National Gallery).

BIBLIOGRAPHY. Matthiesen Gallery, *Rembrandt's Influence in the 17th Century*, London, 1953; Leyden, Stedelijk Museum, *Rembrandt als Leermeester*, Leyden, 1956.

EESTEREN, CORNELIS VAN. Dutch architect and planner (1897–   ). Born in Alblasserdam, he worked and taught in Holland and Germany. In the 1920s he was a member of de Stijl and executed some historically important projects in collaboration with Theo van Doesburg. He is director of the Department of Town Planning, Amsterdam.

BIBLIOGRAPHY. H. L. C. Jaffé, *De Stijl, 1917–1931*, Amsterdam, 1956.

EEUWOUTS, HANS, *see* EWORTH, HANS.

EGARA: CATHEDRAL COMPLEX, *see* TARRASA: CATHEDRAL COMPLEX.

EGAS, ENRIQUE. Spanish architect (ca. 1455–1534). Egas was the last great Spanish Gothic architect. Like Juan Guas, he applied Renaissance decorative forms to basically Gothic schemes, and he is considered the founder of the Plateresque style. Egas's buildings include the Colegio de Santa Cruz at Valladolid (1480–92), the Hospital Real in Santiago de Compostela (1501–11), the Hospital of Santa Cruz in Toledo (1504–14), and the Capilla Real at Granada (1506–17).

EGBERT, GOSPEL LECTIONARY OF, *see* CODEX EGBERTI.

EGELL, PAUL. German sculptor (b. 1691; d. Mannheim, 1752). After working under Permoser in Dresden, Egell settled in Mannheim and became court sculptor to the Elector. Increasingly intense in expression and antinaturalistic (particularly in his clay sketches), he developed a rococo style of religious sculpture that owed little to Rome (though he probably went there in 1744) and had considerable influence on such pupils as Ignaz Günther.

BIBLIOGRAPHY. A. Feulner, "Zum Werk Paul Egell's," *Zeitschrift des deutschen Vereins für Kunstwissenschaft*, 1934.

EGESTA, *see* SEGESTA.

EGG AND DART (Egg and Tongue). Egg-shaped molding alternating with a dart.

EGGERS, BARTHOLOMEUS. Dutch sculptor (b. Amsterdam, 1630; d. there, 1692). A student of Pieter Verbruggen and Erasmus Quellinus, he is best known for his tomb monuments, such as that of Admiral Wassenaer van Obdam (1667, Amsterdam, Jacobskirche), and for the eleven marble statues of the Brandenburg electors (1686–87) executed for the alabaster hall of the old royal palace in Berlin.

BIBLIOGRAPHY. A. W. Weissman, *Geschiedenis der Nederlandsche bouwkunst*, Amsterdam, 1912.

EGGSHELL PORCELAIN. Paper-thin variety of porcelain, translucent enough to resemble milk-white glass. Produced in China since the Ming period, it was made by paring down the clay body until the finished ware appeared to consist only of two layers of glaze. During the Ch'ing dynasty, eggshell wares were often painted with *famille rose* enamels for export purposes. Especially prized in this category are "ruby back" plates, which have wide under-rims of deep-pink enamel. *See* FAMILLE-GROUP PORCELAINS.

BIBLIOGRAPHY. W. B. Honey, *The Ceramic Art of China and Other Countries of the Far East*, London, 1945; G. Savage, *Ceramics for the Collector*, London, 1949.

EGMONT, JUSTUS VAN. Flemish painter (b. Leyden, 1601; d. Antwerp, 1674). Egmont was active in Italy and Paris, and later in Brussels and Antwerp. He painted portraits and historical scenes. After 1618 he was a pupil of Rubens, and he helped his master with the execution of the Medici series. Later, he became court painter to Louis XIII and to Louis XIV, as well as a founder of the French Academy of Painting in 1648. His collection of paintings by contemporaries was justly famous.

BIBLIOGRAPHY. C. Leurs, ed., *Geschiedenis van de Vlaamsche Kunst*, vol. 2, Antwerp, 1939.

EGYPT. The art of Egypt follows closely its political history because the major demand for artistic production came from the court and the clergy. Various styles of art reached their climaxes during the 4th, 12th, and 18th dynasties. The major periods of Egyptian history are as follows:

Paleolithic	18000–5000 B.C.
Neolithic	5000–4000 B.C.
Predynastic	4000–3200 B.C.
Archaic (Dynasties I and II)	3200–2778 B.C.
Old Kingdom (Dynasties III–VI)	2778–2280 B.C.
First Intermediate (Dynasties VII–XI)	2280–2050 B.C.
Middle Kingdom (Dynasties XI–XII)	2050–1778 B.C.
Second Intermediate (Dynasties XIII–XVII)	1778–1570 B.C.
New Kingdom (Dynasties XVIII–XX)	1570–1080 B.C.
Decadent (Dynasties XXI–XXIV)	1080–751 B.C.
Late (Dynasties XXV–XXX)	751–332 B.C.

The country was described by Herodotus as a "gift of the river," and its art can share, to a large extent, this description. The wild rushes, papyrus, lotus, and reeds—as well as clay—played a creative role in the earliest architecture and sculpture, which provided the prototypes for later stages. Periodic inundation dictated the location of settlements, on high ground along the river banks, and brought on the invention of irrigation. The navigable waterways, allowing for easy traffic and interchange of materials and influences, inspired the artist with a sense of regularity and rhythm. The radiant sun fostered outdoor life and encouraged painted low relief and simple architectonic masses. Plenty of good stone answered the needs of the religious and funerary programs for monuments of eternity, which were carried out by an autocratic ruler and a powerful clergy. Egypt was renowned for its religiosity, and the primary purpose of art was to achieve perfection in construction and clarity in representation in conjunction with the rites of the cult or with the afterlife of the deceased, be it stellar, solar, or Osirian. Art was permeated with religious symbolism, and the harmonic systems that governed its designs constituted but one method of expressing it in a consistent way through the ages. *See* OSIRIS.

ARCHITECTURE

From prehistoric Egypt, only those settlements of huts built of plant stems sunk into the gravel on the outskirts of the valley of the Nile are preserved; the vast majority, being nearer the river, are irretrievably lost beneath the silt deposits. The development of the use of clay, first as a coating for plant stems and mats, gradually in the form of blocks, and ultimately as bricks, was completed by the beginning of the historic period, when Egypt was unified, hieroglyphs were invented, and copper implements were common. By that time the typical constructional elements had been invented: battered walls (a result of the use of slippery clay), doorjambs, lintels, and sills (as in the Predynastic house model from Amra). *See* BATTER.

Invaluable information about the prototypes of stylistic elements can be derived from the numerous representations on archaic labels and palettes (moldings and tablets). The cavetto cornice and torus molding that top all monumental structures derive from the upper edges of reed partitions and their bindings, which follow the edges of the façades. The kheker frieze originates in the edges of uprights that are bound into ornamental bundles. The peculiar vault with irregular profile is the stylized form of the vaulted roof of a theriomorphic hut of reeds, imitating the profile of a crouching jackal. The ribbed vault of brick imitates an archaic construction with bundles of reeds bent into reinforcing arches. Fluted and ribbed shafts of columns are the stylized forms of bundles of reeds used as supports. These forms and elements are copied in stone, probably directly from their prototypes in plant stems, in the mortuary complex of Neterikhet Djeser (3d dynasty) at Saqqara. *See* CAVETTO; DJESER'S COMPLEX AT SAQQARA; KHEKER; TORUS.

Plant forms were further stylized and adapted to more rational construction with the monolithic palmiform, papyriform, and lotiform columns, made of hard stone, in the mortuary temples of the 5th and 6th dynasties at Abusir and Saqqara. Later plant columns were built of courses of masonry and reached colossal proportions. The stylized bundles of their shafts (Middle Kingdom and 18th dynasty) were smoothed into cylinders with slight entasis (19th dynasty), and their slender proportions deteriorated into massive ones (20th dynasty). They were entirely covered with scenes of offerings and texts. The Amarna interlude under Akhenaten saw the invention of capitals loaded with bunches of pendent ducks and flowers. In the last stages of Egyptian art, composite capitals had several rows of volutes, striking a note of rich diversity in the open columnar façades of Ptolemaic temples and Roman kiosks. *See* ENTASIS; KIOSK; VOLUTE.

Houses and urbanization. Though the typical elements of the small house are known from the Predynastic period through the model from Amra, no further evidence is found until the 3d dynasty, at Saqqara. The tripartite plan of the small brick house is corroborated by the study of the so-called Royal Pavilion in the complex of Neterikhet Djeser. In the 4th dynasty, near the tomb of Khentkawes at Giza, a pyramid town for the priests of the necropolis was built of uniformly planned houses set side by side between two east–west streets. The plan of each unit is labyrinthian but still shows a northern court and a separation of private from reception rooms. The latter were vaulted and were accessible from the ceremonial street running along the south façade.

Evidence concerning royal castles is found in three fortified enclosures from the 2d dynasty (at Hierakonpolis and Abydos) and from a comparative study of the architectural hieroglyphs for "castle" with the palace façade shown with recessed paneling. The so-called "soul houses," clay models of houses set above the graves of the First Intermediate period, include various types: a simple rectangular enclosure with an awning or a columned portico along the rear, longer side; a group of rooms with a columned portico in front, located behind a court containing bins, oven, and water basin; or a two-storied similar arrangement with a stairway rising along a side wall to a recessed portico on the first floor and to the terrace, where awnings were set up. Ventilators opened to the lower bedrooms.

The remains of the workmen's city of Sesostris II at Illahun (El Lahun) show a successful urban housing project. An enclosure wall, probably square (ca. 1,270 ft. to a side) and oriented to the cardinal points of the compass, surrounded rows of uniformly planned houses set side by side and back to back along secondary streets running east and west. An internal wall running north and south divided the town into two areas, with the western part being about two-fifths the size of the eastern. Aside from the huge mansions (ca. 130 by 180 ft.) built in two rows along both sides of an east–west street in the northernmost sector, at least four types of houses were used. The plan features units, each of which consists of a north court with a south columned portico at the front of a columned hall (reception) and the private apartments. Wooden columns support the ceilings. A similar, though smaller, urban project is that at Amarna East.

Much can be learned about town and country houses at Thebes in the New Kingdom from the representations painted on the walls of private tombs. There is even a sectional view of a three-storied house, belonging to Thutinefer, which has an independent stairwell, a basement with looms, a high ground floor, an upper floor, and a terrace with bins and lines for drying fish. The typical country house is depicted as two-storied, with windows set high up in the walls. It stands at the rear of a garden containing an artificial pond, and the entire complex is surrounded by an enclosure wall. Ventilators open onto the terrace in order to catch the cool winds from the north. There are smaller rest houses for short stays in the country. Models show that four-storied houses were built at least as early as the New Kingdom and on into Greco-Roman times. *See* THEBES.

Town planning. Among the physical factors that shaped town planning were (1) the annual flooding of the Nile, which made necessary the location of settlements on the tops of mounds and stimulated the early invention of an orthogonal system of irrigation canals, probably fostering a regular plan for towns and necropolises; (2) the flatness of the alluvial valley; (3) the prevailing north wind, which together with the bright sun led to the orientation of the planned towns to the cardinal points of the compass; and (4) the lack of water supply, which dictated the building of the towns near the river banks.

Human factors also had their influences. Religion played a most important role in Egyptian life, and the temple was the focus of the city. Communities of artisans and priests, attached to the pyramids and necropolises of the Old Kingdom, were settled in special pyramid towns on the edge of the Western Desert, which were dependent on the high priests or the Pharaoh. Fortified trade outposts were built along the Nile south of the First Cataract as a result of the expansion of Egyptian trade and the exploitation of the mines in Nubia during the Old Kingdom and especially in the Middle Kingdom.

The main types of towns were the irregular and the preplanned, with the latter being subdivided into orthogonal, axial, and mixed layouts. The irregular town grew organically in the vicinity of a waterway. Houses were added along narrow streets without any set alignment, and levels of occupation rose with the piling up of detritus (debris), as in the modern Orient. The orthogonal type of layout had regular plots or blocks of houses set along streets which crossed at right angles and were oriented within a square enclosure, as in the workmen's towns at Illahun (Sesostris II) and Amarna East (Akhenaten). Houses were built on standard patterns, set side by side and back to back, with an east–west orientation so as to take advantage of the sunrise in the bedroom and kitchen and the sunset in the living room. This type was probably known from early dynastic times, being represented in one form of the hieroglyph for "town" with a circular enclosure around a checkerboard pattern of streets.

The axial plan featured two arteries that crossed at right angles and connected the gateways of a fortified town within a rectangular enclosure (Sesebi in the Sudan), a fortress on flat land in Nubia (Kuban, Buhen, and Ikkur), or on rocky ground (Semna, Kumma, Uronarti, and Askut). This type was represented in a second form of the hieroglyph for "town" with a circular enclosure and two crossing arteries. The mixed type was characterized by an orthogonal pattern of quarters, further arranged according to private initiative so that secondary streets and alleys were "doglegged" or cul-de-sac (Amarna, Naukratis, and Karanis).

Temples. The embryo of the cult temple can be recognized in the tripartite plan of the Archaic shrine of Khentiamentiu at Abydos. The strictly symmetrical plan of this cult temple is projected at right angles to the riverbank. Its walls and columns are covered with religious scenes in low relief, stuccoed and painted to offer visual instruction to the illiterate masses. Cult temples growing by accretion attained extensive proportions at Thebes. Most of the structures were built on top of earlier remains or on hallowed ground. An exceptional plan is that of the temple dedicated to Sobek and Haroeris ("Hor-wer" in Egyptian) at Kom Ombo: it has two cellae and twin halls along two parallel axes. Sun temples are different, since the god worshiped in them was the sun, through the intermediary of an obelisk as at Abu Gurab (5th dynasty), a benben stone as at Heliopolis, or numerous offering tables and an altar set in courtyards as at Amarna. *See* AMARNA PERIOD; CELLA; HELIOPOLIS; OBELISK.

The mortuary temples, which developed from the chapels abutting archaic tombs where the funerary rites were performed, assumed huge proportions and had a terraced layout (valley portal, causeway, and funerary temple) in the Old Kingdom. *See* ABUSIR; GIZA; SAQQARA.

Chapels of private mastabas evolved and were built within the superstructure. At the same time, the number of rooms increased and the walls were covered with carved scenes representing everyday life. In the unique Temple of Mentuhotep at Deir el Bahari, some of the elements are grouped in a terraced design with pillared porticoes surrounding a dummy pyramid, while the tomb itself is hewn from the rock at the back of the temple. Later, small pyramids of brickwork surmounted the porticoed entrance to the funerary chapel above the private tomb, as at Abydos and Deir el Medina. Large mortuary temples at Thebes West, dedicated to Amun, usually include a temple-palace to accommodate the Pharaoh during the visit to Amun's statue. *See* ABYDOS; DEIR EL BAHARI; MASTABA. *See also* MEDINET HABU; RAMESSEUM.

Cult temple. The temple is the "castle of the god" who was embodied in the small cult statue of gilded wood set within a naos (shrine). The representative temple, as exemplified by those built by Rameses II and Rameses III at Karnak, is laid out symmetrically along a longitudinal axis. Its tripartite plan (three transverse parts) consists of (1) a pylon (monumental two-towered gateway); (2) a courtyard, usually having columned porticoes along one or more of its sides; (3) a hypostyle (columned) hall with a central nave, bordered by tall columns and flanked by two lower aisles; and (4) at the rear a sanctuary with a naos and several subsidiary chambers. The levels of the floors of the various parts are higher toward the rear, while their ceilings become correspondingly lower. This gradual reduction in the height of the apartments, combined with a reduction in the lighting, tends to impress the worshiper with the hallowed mystery of the sanctuary. All the walls and columns are usually of stone, carved and painted with scenes and hieroglyphs related to the rituals performed in the various rooms. The layout conforms to a system of harmonic design that controls the growth of the structure by accretion, whereby the later courtyards and pylons added in front are larger than the earlier ones according to set proportions. *See* KARNAK. *See also* LUXOR.

Tombs. The tomb was designed to preserve the body of the deceased and allow his soul to fulfill its destiny in the afterlife: if as a star, a ramp or a stairway was provided, rising from the burial chamber toward the circumpolar stars; if with the sun god, a stairway and an offering place (false door, offering table, and serdab) were included to the east; if as an Osiris, the underground apartments were equipped like houses. The superstructure, called a mastaba, may possibly imitate the mound above prehistoric graves or the primeval mound of creation. The burial chamber was cut deeper and deeper in an attempt to elude violators. Funerary boats were set to the north to be used by the deceased in his travels across the sky. See SERDAB.

Pharaohs of the 3d dynasty built stepped pyramids as tombs, probably as monumental staircases to the sky. In the 4th dynasty, the truly geometric pyramid was a huge solar monument in conjunction with a mortuary temple built against its eastern face. Nevertheless, it retained its northern entrance, and in one case it had two channels rising from the burial chamber in the direction of the circumpolar stars and of Orion. In the 5th and 6th dynasties, the pyramids were much smaller and less carefully built. Pyramid texts were carved on the walls of the inner apartments, which follow a standard plan. See CHEOPS, PYRAMID OF.

In the Middle Kingdom, the pyramid embodied numerous devices against robbers (a doubling-back layout, blind corridors, portcullises sliding sideways in the ceilings, false blockings, and a massive chamber sarcophagus). It was large, but built economically with a filling of coarse stone or brick within compartments formed by radiating and encircling retaining walls (Dahshur, Hawara, and Lisht). Private tombs were cut in the rock of the cliffs overlooking the towns of Middle Egypt; they consisted of a chapel with a columned portico and hall and a shaft tomb (Beni Hassan, Bersha, and Meir). The old mastaba tomb still occurred. In the New Kingdom the Pharaohs were buried in corridor tombs hewn deep in the cliffs of western Thebes. The walls were painted, or occasionally carved, with religious scenes. Private people had similar, but smaller, tombs with painted murals representing scenes from everyday life. In the Late period shaft tombs were surmounted by funerary chapels. See BENI HASSAN; DAHSHUR; LISHT.

Military architecture. Archaic hieroglyphs represent the square or oval plans of fortified towns with external buttresses and the elevations of independent cylindrical towers (contemporaneous models) and with battered (sloping) walls topped by balconies with battlemented parapets. The only access was provided by a rope ladder leading to an aperture just beneath the balcony. The fortified enclosures of brick from the 2d dynasty (Hierakonpolis and Abydos) have one or more gateways, each with an angled approach. Oval fortified towns with pairs of semicircular buttresses at the gateway were seen by the Egyptians in Asia (painting at Deshasha, 6th dynasty). A fortified settlement at Buhen dates from the 4th dynasty. Small forts in Middle Egypt are represented in the tombs of the nobles as having a lower glacis (sloping wall), one or two doorways, battlements, and projecting balconies. See HIERAKONPOLIS.

With the colonization of Nubia (12th dynasty), a chain of fortresses along the river banks and the islands of the Nile was built to control the mining districts and the trade routes. Two types show adaptation to the conditions of the terrain: a rectangular plan built on flat land with a double enclosure wall, a ditch on three sides, and a longitudinal main street crossing secondary ones; and an irregular layout erected on rocky ground with long spur walls, towers, and buttresses. The numerous representations on the walls of the temples of the Empire period

(Karnak, Medinet Habu, and Abu Simbel) show Asian fortified towns conquered by the Egyptians. They had complicated systems of concentric walls built around a citadel. Perhaps an echo of this style is found in the fortified enclosure of the Medinet Habu temple (Rameses III) and its two monumental gateways. See ABU SIMBEL.

Harmonic design in Egyptian architecture. The huge monuments of Egyptian architecture could not have achieved their rhythm and aesthetic regularity without conforming to certain rules that governed the relative proportions of width and length in both plan and elevation. This is more obvious in a temple that grew by accretion, with the addition of front courtyards and pylons of gradually increasing size during the course of a millennium, as at Karnak. Analysis of numerous examples of architectural design proves that the harmonic system was based on the use of proportions expressed by a square representing the unit 1 and by triangles constructed on the square. Amulets have been found that illustrate the architect's square and triangles.

SCULPTURE

The main objective of Egyptian sculpture, whether religious or funerary, is accurate and complete representation. This results from the conception, essentially religious in origin, that the statue or relief is to accommodate the soul of the god or the deceased. Naturalism pervades the style, characterized in its design by the law of frontality, whereby a frontal representation is achieved, symmetrical in the Archaic period, and nearly so in later times. Various materials are used: hard and soft stones; wood, usually stuccoed and painted; and inlaid eyes. The statue is life-size or smaller. Wooden statues are made of several parts jointed together (Ka-aper). Statues of beaten copper sheets are known (Pepi I). See FRONTALITY, LAW OF.

There evolve standard types: the striding male with his left foot forward and with both arms along his sides or with his left arm extended and holding the staff of authority; and the female standing with both arms stretched along her body or with left arm bent across her bosom and her feet together. Seated figures are nearly frontal, with both arms on the knees or the left arm bent across the bosom. Scribes, even those of princely origin, are represented squatting, ready to write. Pharaohs are occasionally represented kneeling, but only when they are presenting an offering to a deity. Group statues appear in the 4th dynasty, carved from one block or from the bedrock. In such groups the heads of standing and seated figures are on the same level, which accounts for the variation in the size of the bodies. The owner of the statue is shown in heroic size. Gestures conveying affection are shown between husband, wife, and children or between a Pharaoh and a goddess (Mycerinus). Besides the frontal statues, there are exceptional smaller ones representing individuals, usually carrying a burden, or groups such as wrestlers, a lady having her hair dressed, or a seated figure with another one on its lap—not all of which do conform to the law of frontality. See SCRIBES, EGYPTIAN.

New subjects, such as servants at work, appear from the 4th dynasty on. For religious reasons the figure is complete, but there is an exception in the case of the so-called "reserve heads" from the reign of Cheops. These were placed at the bottom of the shaft leading to the burial chamber

Egypt, sculpture. Relief with traces of paint depicting offering bearers carrying supplies to the deceased, ca. 2450 B.C. Kestner Museum, Hannover.

of private tombs. In the Amarna period similar heads are found (Nefertiti, princesses—possibly trial pieces). Busts are known (Ankhhaf). Colossi of Pharaohs, such as the mummiform Osiris, stand before the pillars of mortuary temples (New Kingdom) or, as rulers seated on their thrones, abut the pylons of cult temples (Luxor and Karnak) and rock-cut temples. The purpose of the latter certainly involved political propaganda. *See* ABU SIMBEL.

Architectural statuary deteriorated in quality in the Late period (25th dynasty). The few cult statues known are usually small figures of wood, gilded and painted and having inlaid eyes. The style of royal statuary evolved along with the concept of royalty. The Pharaoh was shown as a god in the 4th dynasty, with far-gazing eyes, serene features, and an idealized figure (Chephren). Later in the Old Kingdom the features are more human, less stylized (Sahure and Pepi II). Statues of private persons echo the trend toward idealization of the Memphite school with simplified planes and features (reserve heads) or with more naturalistic modeling and well-built stocky figures. In the Middle Kingdom the elongated forms of the figures, the rigidity and slender limbs, characteristic of the statues of the First Intermediate period, are retained, though with better aesthetic results. The realistically drawn features of the Pharaohs reflect the concerns of a human monarch (Sesostris III and Amenemhat III). Statues of private people show similar trends. Elaborate models of workshops and companies of soldiers included numerous wooden figures.

In the New Kingdom the general trend was to achieve elegance of proportions and sophistication in the stylization of the features, often verging on mannerism. Portraiture is, however, still an aim in itself. Heavy wigs and elaborate folds of flowing dresses, through which the forms of the body appear, lend a delicate touch to the modeling. Pharaohs are shown as energetic rulers well practiced in sports and warfare. The unique interlude under Akhenaten is characterized by a servile trend to establish the deformed figure of the Pharaoh as a model for all human figures. From clay models of heads with realistic features, there is evidence of the use of plaster casts. Early Ramesside statuary is still an artistic achievement (Rameses II). *See* AMARNA PERIOD.

In the Decadent period modeling was done in metal (gold and bronze) inlaid with gold threads (21st and 22d dynasties) and shows full faces on sturdy bodies. The Kushite style (25th dynasty) emphasizes the muscles. The Saitic revival (26th dynasty) was based on the art of the Old Kingdom and does not display originality. The hardest rocks were finished to a high polish and realism in portraiture is outstanding.

Low relief. As early as the Archaic period, palettes show the peculiar composite or vertical projection that is typical of Egyptian graphic arts. The aim was to present as full a picture as possible, combining flattened front and side views of a subject, with the body raised above the representation of its outlines. Animals are always seen in side view. The standing human figure shows the profile of the head, with an eye in front view; the upper part of the body in front view, with one breast in profile and a side view of both arms; and the lower part, from the waist down, in side view in striding posture. The female figure does not show so long a stride. Frontal views occur only for gods and foreign prisoners. True side view was used to represent statues and the Pharaoh seated in the jubilee kiosk.

The initial draft was done in red ochre lines corrected with black lines. Proportional squares helped in the copying and enlarging from models. The scenes carved on the palettes are narrative, representing hunts and wars. They are without ground lines and are carved in bold flat relief, sometimes with an emphasis on the modeling of the muscles, as in Mesopotamian sculpture. The later mace heads and palettes (beginning of 1st dynasty) record historical events in several registers (panels) separated by ground lines and show most of the characteristics of Egyptian graphic composition: arrangement by registers, heroic size of the Pharaoh, alignment of figures, flattening out of bodies, and hieroglyphic texts allied with the elements of the scene (Na'rmer palette). Scenes in low relief, carved on slab stelae, represent the deceased facing to the right while seated at his funerary meal in front of a table bearing rows of offerings. See STELE.

In the Old Kingdom a hieroglyphic text integrated into the composition gives the names and titles of the deceased as part of a funerary formula. This essential element of the funerary equipment is set in the east face of the superstructure of the mastaba of the rich; later it is found in the upper part of the false door in the chapel. Other scenes are gradually introduced—offering bearers from the various estates and aspects of daily life—with the purpose of ensuring a supply of food and other necessaries for the deceased in case the daily funerary service should fail. The scenes are set side by side, following a logical sequence, in registers above a dado. The deceased is shown standing in heroic size on both doorjambs of the entrance to the chapel and on the false door, supervising the various activities of his relatives and servants. Hieroglyphs name these activities, or a short dialogue occasionally forms part of the composition. The style is naturalistic, showing stocky figures with strong muscles. The whole is painted, but details and elements intended to be seen through water are usually not carved, but added with brushstrokes.

Toward the end of the 5th dynasty a bolder type of relief appears. In the mortuary temples of the Pharaohs of the Old Kingdom, war, hunting, and other scenes similar to those in the mastabas are carved on the inner walls and causeway with a striking naturalism (prisoners in the pyramid of Sahure') or even realism (Unas's famine). Scenes on the walls of the chapel in the sun temple of Neuserre' represent the personification of the seasons, foundation ceremonies, and jubilee festivals.

The style in the rock tombs of the First Intermediate period in Middle Egypt, which is characterized by angular elongated figures, stiff limbs, and even the absence of a ground line, influences that of the Middle Kingdom, in spite of the vitality of the Memphite school in Lower Egypt. Low relief in Thebes (11th dynasty) displays a broad treatment, and many characteristics were inherited from the First Intermediate period. In the mortuary temple of Mentuhotep at Deir el Bahari are scenes of war, desert hunts, Nile boats, and the royal griffin trampling on his enemies. Sunken low relief occurs on the sarcophagi of Kawit and 'Ashyt. In the rock tombs of Meir (12th dy-

nasty) the naturalistic traditions of the Old Kingdom appear in scenes from everyday life carried out in simplified relief. Painting tends to replace relief. In the raised relief on the pillars of the peripteral chapel of Sesostris I at Karnak, the quality of the draftsmanship and carving is of the highest.

The low relief on the temples of the New Kingdom does not betray any influence from the foreign domination of Egypt during the Second Intermediate period. Idealism in the figures themselves is allied to realistic portraiture. The canon of proportions called for slenderer figures. Aesthetic beauty is achieved with simple attitudes and harmonious gestures, helped by perfect technique. Religious scenes are set in registers on the inner walls and columns of the temples, while huge compositions of scenes of war and victory are carved in sunken relief on the external walls. The reliefs of Akhenaten at Amarna show the same realism as his statuary, though allied with aesthetic elegance in the slim limbs, carried out mostly in sunken relief. That brief period introduces diversity and suppleness in forms (tomb of Horemheb) as well as naturalistic proportion and emotional expressions (Seti I). The narrative quality of later historical scenes is enhanced by the expression of the element of time in the composition and movement in Ramesside battle scenes (Karnak). Kushite scenes introduce the representation of men leading horses and the characteristic round shape for the head. Saitic reliefs copy, in the so-called Neo-Memphite scenes, whole tombs from Memphis. These are found as far south as Kawa. Some of the Neo-Memphite reliefs have suppleness of form and show attempts at foreshortening, mannerisms that permit us to regard them as forerunners of Hellenistic relief in Egypt.

See MEMPHITE STYLE. See also BETH SHAN.

PAINTING

The earliest mural painting, in a Predynastic tomb at Hierakonpolis, shows some of the characteristics of later representations, albeit on a primitive level: the victorious ruler striking kneeling prisoners with his mace, the imaginary ground line, and the flattening out of forms. It is painted in black, red, and yellow ochres. As a rule, paint is applied to the stone walls or bedrock after a thin coat of plaster or mud has been applied. In the Archaic period the façades of the mastabas were painted to imitate variegated hangings of mats or rugs stretched vertically on a wooden framework, a theme found in later mastabas of the Old Kingdom. The scenes carved on the walls of the chapels were painted with slightly conventionalized colors (blue and blue-gray for mud, reddish brown for men, yellow for women, blue for water, red for dried reed and wood, and green for plants). Painted murals emerged as a significant form as early as the 3d dynasty (Hesyre'), although occurring only occasionally and having less impact than in the 6th dynasty. A unique technique of colored pastes occurs, inlaid in scooped-out areas in stone and finished with brushstrokes (chapel of Neferma't at Meydum, 4th dynasty).

Pigments of the primary colors and, occasionally, green were used in the Old Kingdom. In the First Intermediate period secondary colors, such as pinks and several hues of yellows, contrasted with reds on a dark blue background, were also employed. The colors were mixed in a gum medium. Besides the use of contrasting secondary colors, mural painting in the First Intermediate period is characterized by lively gestures, angular figures, and the abstraction of shapes into patterns. Painting replaces relief, even in the chapels of the princesses of Mentuhotep (11th dynasty) and more so in the rock tombs in Middle Egypt. In the Middle Kingdom, the number of figures increases, and one theme stretches over more than one register. Modeling, shading, and texture of materials are indicated with brushstrokes. The new subject of wrestling, with innumerable poses of a pair of wrestlers, and representations of local sports are added to the earlier repertory and are characterized, as before, by an excellent feeling for animal life, for example, in hunting scenes.

In the New Kingdom mural painting reaches its apex. The repetition of slender figures tends to be monotonous. Ethnic and perspective conventions occur. Graded colors are used to pass from one hue to another in the representation of animals, but seldom in figures (Queen Nefertari, 19th dynasty). The painter renders a humorous touch (banquet scenes), as well as tragic sadness (funerals), but never laughter. Realistic trends at Amarna are shown in representations of the details of the nostrils, corners of the lips, toes, and ankles, as well as of plant life. Painted pavements imitate an artificial pool framed by water plants and animals. Ramesside painting declines rapidly toward academism and unimpressive coloring against a characteristic yellow background. In palaces, decorative friezes of garlands of stylized flowers run along the tops of the walls, from which project elegant necks of wood or clay birds.

MINOR ARTS

Even in Predynastic Egypt, crafts produced objects of aesthetic value. Pottery forms and, later, pottery paintings representing geometric patterns, plants, animals, figures, and boats with numerous oars all have a lively charm. Vessels carved of the hardest rocks, theriomorphic flints, palettes (some with animals in opposed positions as in Mesopotamian themes), jewelry, and furniture show many of the traits that persisted in the later crafts.

In the Archaic period, the traditional imitation of the fore and hind legs of a bull or a lion for the legs of furniture, initiated in the Predynastic period, is well established. The bracelets of the queen of King Djer, made of beads of gold and semiprecious stones, rosettes, and a *serekh*, combine taste with symbolism. There are also alabaster disks inlaid with animal figures, gaming pieces of ivory, and vessels of hammered copper sheet and schist. The last, imitating thin metallic forms, indicate the appreciation of art in everyday life. Pottery and stone vases show a diversity of elegant forms.

In the Old Kingdom, the simple crafts of the earlier period tend to disappear and are replaced by others employing elaborate decoration, consisting of elements derived from feathers, plants, and animals (furniture and jewelry of Hetepheres). The emblematic papyrus and the Upper Egyptian heraldic plant, intertwined to symbolize the unification of Egypt, appear in openwork in the side panels of chairs. Enameled faïence tiles imitating matwork line the walls of underground chambers in the mortuary complex of Neterikhet (Djeser).

In the Middle Kingdom, blue faïence is shaped into vessels, animal figurines, and scarabs. Vases in the form of two trussed geese are carved in blue marble. Copper mirrors with papyriform handles, daggers, and an openwork brazier show the versatility of craftsmen in metal. The refined elegance of the pectorals, diadems, and necklaces worked in chased gold, niello, and repoussé is allied with their symbolic implications, "to be read," or interpreted, and speaks for the unique ability of the jewelers of the 12th dynasty. *See* NIELLO; REPOUSSAGE.

In the New Kingdom, alabaster is carved into vases, canopic jars, and lamps of a heavy style (Tutankhamen). Of greater aesthetic value are the ceramic lotiform cups and bottles, the figurines, and the variegated inlays for architecture and furniture. Glass objects are much favored, especially those in the characteristic "mosaic" technique. Furniture displays artistic technique in openwork panels, carved in wood on thrones and beds, and in incrustation with faïence, ivory, and metals in caskets, or even in miniature paintings representing war scenes (casket of Tutankhamen). Headrests, staffs, fans, and musical instruments are all adorned with masterpieces of carving. Originality as well as ability is evidenced in the various unguent containers, mirror cases, combs, and ointment spoons with handles in the shape of female figurines. Bronze is evident only from the 18th dynasty on. Jewelry is heavier than in the 12th dynasty, and although original, it does show occasional Asian influence. A leather tent with a checkered design (21st dynasty) and a tapestry (18th dynasty) are worthy of notice. *See* EMBROIDERY; FURNITURE (EGYPT); GLASS; IVORY; JEWELRY, HISTORY OF.

BIBLIOGRAPHY. J. Capart, *Egyptian Art*, London, 1923; J. Capart, *Documents pour servir à l'étude de l'art égyptien*, Paris, 1927–31; W. S. Smith, *History of Egyptian Sculpture and Painting in the Old Kingdom*, 2d ed., Cambridge, Mass., 1949; J. Vandier, *Manuel d'archéologie égyptienne*, 3 vols., Paris, 1952–58; A. Badawy, *A History of Egyptian Architecture*, 2 vols., Giza, 1954–66; A. Mekhitarian, *Egyptian Painting*, Geneva, 1954; W. Wolf, *Die Kunst Ägyptens*, Stuttgart, 1957; W. S. Smith, *The Art and Architecture of Ancient Egypt*, Baltimore, 1958; L. Dabrowski, "A Famous Temple Reexamined: Queen Hatshepsut's Temple at Deir el Bahari—and a Hitherto Unknown Temple," *The Illustrated London News*, CCXLV, Sept. 19, 1964; A. Badawy, *Ancient Egyptian Architectural Design: A Study of the Harmonic System* (University of California Publications, Near Eastern Studies, No. 4), Berkeley, 1965; A. Badawy, *Architecture in Ancient Egypt and the Near East*, Cambridge, Mass., 1966.   ALEXANDER M. BADAWY

EGYPT: CAIRO MUSEUM, *see* CAIRO: EGYPTIAN MUSEUM.

EHRENBERG, WILHELM SCHUBERT VON. Flemish painter (1630–ca. 1670). Born in Antwerp, he was a painter of architectural scenes, among which the *Church of the Jesuits in Antwerp* (destroyed by fire in 1718) stands out. His works are permeated with baroque pathos and a feeling for display.

BIBLIOGRAPHY. A. H. Cornette, *De Vlaamsche Schilderkunst in de XVIIe Eeuw*, Antwerp, 1939.

EHRENSTRAHL, DAVID KLOCKER. Swedish painter (1628–98). Born in Hamburg, he studied in Amsterdam and went to Sweden in 1652. He spent the years from 1655 to 1661 in European study. Often called the Father of Swedish painting, David Klöcker Ehrenstrahl worked in two styles: official (decorations, allegorical portraits) and intimate (genre, portraits, still life, landscape, wildlife). The second group constitutes his finest painting—directly observed, fresh, and dignified.

BIBLIOGRAPHY. A. Sjöblom, *David Klöcker Ehrenstrahl*, Malmö, Sweden, 1947.

EIBESDORF: KIRCHENBURG. German church in Romania. It is one of many fortified churches (*Wehrkirchen*) built in the 14th century in the Siebenbürgen region of Romania by Saxon-German colonists who began developing the area in the 12th century. The church is noted for its west tower.

BIBLIOGRAPHY. G. Oprescu, *Die Wehrkirchen in Siebenbürgen*, Dresden, 1961.

EICHENBERG, FRITZ. American graphic artist (1901–   ). Born in Cologne, Germany, Eichenberg studied at the Kunstgewerbeschule in Cologne and the Akademie für Graphische Künste und Buchgewerbe in Leipzig. He worked as an illustrator in Germany and went to the United States in 1933. He has taught widely and in 1956 was made head of the graphic arts department of Pratt Institute in Brooklyn. Large collections of his works are owned by the New York Public Library, the Art Institute of Chicago, and several other institutions. In his commercial work and in the more than sixty books he has illustrated, his most effective medium is wood engraving. With a meticulous technique he has created vivid, if conservative, illustrations that achieve strong effects with tightly knit parallel cuts.

BIBLIOGRAPHY. F. Eichenberg, *American Artist-Printmakers*, New York, 1959.

EICHENS, FRIEDRICH EDUARD. German engraver (b. Berlin, 1804; d. there, 1877). After studying with Buchhorn, Eichens studied in 1827 with Forster and then traveled extensively in Italy. In 1833, he returned to Berlin, where he became a teacher at a government school. His works include a *Shakespeare Gallery* and a series after E. G. Kaulbach's frescoes in the former Berlin State Museums.

BIBLIOGRAPHY. A. Apell, *Handbuch für Kupferstichsammler . . .*, Leipzig, 1880.

EIDLITZ, LEOPOLD. American architect (1823–1908). Born in Prague, he arrived in the United States in 1843 and for a time worked for Richard Upjohn. An exponent of a German Romanesqueoid style, as exemplified in his St. George's Church in New York (1848), Eidlitz was progressive enough, despite his revivalist bent, to make the American Exchange Bank (1857–59) New York's first fireproof commercial structure.

EIERMANN, EGON. German architect (1904–   ). Born in Karlsruhe, he is one of the most distinguished architects in postwar Germany. He has designed a number of religious, commercial, and industrial works. Notable are St. Matthew's Church in Pforzheim (1953); Concert Hall of the South-German Radio in Stuttgart (1952); "Burda-Moden" Publishing House in Offenburg (1954); and a textile factory in Blumberg (1951).

BIBLIOGRAPHY. G. Hatje et al., *New German Architecture*, New York, 1956.

EIFFEL, GUSTAVE-ALEXANDRE. French engineer (b. Dijon, 1832; d. Paris, 1923). Educated in Paris at the Ecole Polytechnique and Ecole Centrale des Arts et Manufactures, Eiffel made important contributions in iron and steel construction. After working for engine manufacturers, he was on his own by 1866 as a consulting engineer. In 1867 he was listed as a builder with workshops for metal construction at Lavallois-Perret. Eiffel was called to verify calculations on the strength of steel arches being constructed for the main building of the International Exhibition of 1867. He constructed bridges in France, Spain, Portugal, Hungary, Romania, Egypt, Peru, and Bolivia. The Garabit viaduct over the Truyère near Ruines in southern France, his most outstanding bridge, reaches about 400 feet above the river and has an arch span of about 540 feet. He did the Bon Marché in Paris with the architect Boileau in 1876.

The inner structure of the Statue of Liberty in New York Bay is the work of Eiffel. The precision of his calculations made it possible to prefabricate parts and assemble them on the site. The Eiffel Tower, begun in 1887 and completed for the Exposition Universelle of 1889, is his most famous work. About 985 feet high, it was also prefabricated. A large outcry from Parisian artists against the tower failed to prevent its construction, but it was not until the 1900s that it was popular. Eiffel's last twenty years were spent working on problems of aerodynamics.

BIBLIOGRAPHY. M. Besset, *Gustave Eiffel*, Paris, 1957.

MARVIN D. SCHWARTZ

Gustave-Alexandre Eiffel, the Eiffel Tower, Paris, constructed 1887–89.

EIFFEL TOWER, *see* EIFFEL, GUSTAVE-ALEXANDRE.

EIGHT, THE. Ultimately a part of the Ashcan school, The Eight was an association of American painters formed in protest against the monopoly that the National Academy held on aesthetic taste and exhibition space. The precipitating spark was the rejection by the 1907 Academy jury of a painting by George Luks, an act symptomatic of the official hostility toward newer tendencies in American art. The protest, which crystallized around the dynamic personality of Robert Henri, culminated in the first and only exhibition of The Eight at the Macbeth Gallery in New York City in 1908. *See* HENRI, ROBERT; LUKS, GEORGE BENJAMIN.

The men who formed the core of the group around Henri, the ones whose realistic urban genre subjects provoked most of the public outcry, were George Luks, William Glackens, Everett Shinn, and John Sloan. They were originally newspaper artists, whom Henri had met in Philadelphia about 1891, before they moved to New York. Allied to these five by dissatisfaction with the Academy were the impressionist Ernest Lawson; Maurice B. Prendergast, technically the most advanced of all; and the gentle painter of romantic fantasies, Arthur B. Davies. What brought these varied men together was not a common style or technique, but simply a more free and open attitude toward painting than that forcefully advocated by the Academy. It is only against the background of the early-20th-century American art world that the work of The Eight could appear radical. In reality, their painting styles, with the exception of Prendergast, were *retardataire* by contemporary European standards. The most important influences on the early art of the realist members were Hals and Manet, seen through the work of Henri. *See* DAVIES, ARTHUR BOWEN; GLACKENS, WILLIAM JAMES; LAWSON, ERNEST; PRENDERGAST, MAURICE BRAZIL; SHINN, EVERETT; SLOAN, JOHN.

Because they took their subjects from the slums and from fringe elements of society, much was made, especially later, of the "social consciousness" of the realists. This, too, was more apparent than real, although it was the absence of the ideal and the all too strong presence of the immediately perceivable, but hitherto unpainted, city scenes that aroused the harshest criticism. Far from being social reformers, however, the realists were aiming only at a heightened artistic vitality. This meant the use of all possible subjects, with no arbitrary social distinctions. Despite these aims, the sentimentalism of the period is readily seen in many of their paintings. A few years after their exhibition, the eight painters, briefly united mostly by friendship, went their different aesthetic ways. However, they were subsequently absorbed into the larger grouping known as the Ashcan school, and their idea of independence and liberalism became a permanent theme in American artistic life. *See* ASHCAN SCHOOL.

BIBLIOGRAPHY. Brooklyn Institute of Arts and Sciences, *The Eight*, Brooklyn, N.Y., 1943; M. W. Brown, *American Painting from the Armory Show to the Depression*, Princeton, 1955.

JEROME VIOLA

EIGHT ECCENTRICS OF YANG-CHOU, *see* YANG-CHOU, EIGHT ECCENTRICS OF.

The Eight. John Sloan, *Backyards, Greenwich Village*. Whitney Museum of American Art, New York.

EILSHEMIUS, LOUIS MICHEL. American painter (b. near Newark, N.J., 1864; d. New York City, 1941). He was educated in Geneva and Dresden and at Cornell University. Eilshemius studied painting in New York from 1884 to 1886, at the Art Students League and with Robert L. Minor, and at the Académie Julian in Paris from 1886 to 1887. From 1888 until the early 1900s he traveled in Europe, Africa, the South Seas, and the southern United States. Eilshemius's career began in his twenties with the exhibition of his paintings at the National Academy of Design. This was the first, and only, recognition given him by the official art world during his lifetime.

Many of Eilshemius's early paintings were quiet, sensitively brushed landscapes, comparable in feeling to the Hudson River school in the United States or, in restrained massing of tonal values, to the Barbizon painters in France (for example, *Delaware Water Gap Village*, ca. 1886; New York, Metropolitan Museum). He was also skilled, however, in the evocation of mood through the figure, as in *Mother Bereft* (ca. 1888; Joseph H. Hirshhorn Collection). His native strain of visionary poetry began to appear toward the end of the century; the lack of recognition and the isolation which it caused only served to confirm Eilshemius in the practice of his personal theme: the dreamy and lyrical relationship of the human figure, particularly the female nude, to the surrounding landscape. The floating nymphs and the forest and stream of *Afternoon Wind* (1899; New York, Museum of Modern Art) are, in the relatively firm painting of forms, closer to his early style than to the soft, fluid touches of pigment which he later used.

Despite the contrary evidence of his thorough academic training, Eilshemius has often been called a "primitive" painter, presumably because of the seemingly naïve treatment of his subjects, as in *Figures in Landscape* (1906; New York, Whitney Museum), and his antinaturalistic distortions of anatomy and perspective, as in *Early American Story* (1908; Philadelphia Museum of Art). But the approach as well as the distortions must often be considered part of the attempt to produce a mood or an emotion:

Louis Michel Eilshemius, *Figures in Landscape*, 1906. Whitney Museum of American Art, New York.

sad, as in *The Funeral* (1916, Newark Museum); eerie, as in *The Haunted House* (ca. 1917; Metropolitan Museum); or simply "poetic," as in *The Dream* (1917; Washington, D.C., Phillips Collection).

Discovered for the avant-garde by Marcel Duchamp at the 1917 Independents' exhibition, Eilshemius was given one-man shows by the Société Anonyme in 1920 and 1924, although he had stopped painting about 1921.

BIBLIOGRAPHY. W. Schack, *And He Sat Among the Ashes*, New York, 1939.

JEROME VIOLA

EINBECK, KONRAD VON. German architect and sculptor (fl. Halle, late 14th–early 15th cent.). For the Moritz-kirche in Halle he produced a group of stone sculptures, among them *St. Moritz* (1411) and a relief, *Adoration of the Magi*. These works are noted for their somber expressionism and complex treatment of form.

BIBLIOGRAPHY. E. Hohmann, "Meister Conrad von Einbecke, ein Bildhauer des 15. Jahrhunderts," *Das Bild*, VI, 1936.

EINDHOVEN: VAN ABBE MUNICIPAL MUSEUM. Dutch collection. In addition to a group of 20th-century Dutch and Belgian paintings, the museum contains works by Picasso, Braque, Chagall, Delaunay, Léger, Dufy, Kandinsky, Manessier, Dubuffet, Tapiès, and others.

EINFUHLUNG, *see* EMPATHY.

EINSIEDELN, ABBEY OF. Benedictine abbey in Switzerland. It was founded in 934. The Carolingian structure of 984 was replaced by four subsequent pilgrimage churches.

Built between 1704 and 1770 and designed by Caspar Moosbrugger, it is the most splendid baroque shrine in Switzerland. The present church (begun 1719) forms the east–west axis of a large rectangle containing four courts. Above the galleries of the church interior is a unique large octagon vault and two smaller but increasingly steep cupolas. The main altar is at the exact center of the whole monastic complex. The sculptural decoration, the stuccowork, and the ceiling painting are mainly the work of the Asam brothers. An important medieval library is housed in the monastery.

BIBLIOGRAPHY. L. Birchler, *Die Kunstdenkmäler des Kantons Schwyz*, vol. 1, Basel, 1927.

EINSTEIN TOWER, POTSDAM, *see* MENDELSOHN, ERIC.

EIRENE. The personification of Eirene (Greek, meaning peace) is found occasionally in early Greek literature, but it is not represented in art until after the Peloponnesian War. The most famous of these representations was the *Eirene Holding the Infant Ploutos* (wealth), by Cephisodotus, of which there is an excellent Roman copy in the State Antiquities Collection, Munich. *See* CEPHISODOTUS.

EISEN (Keisai Eisen). Japanese Ukiyo-e printmaker (1790–1848). Eisen first studied painting from a Kanō master but later changed to wood-block printing. He is best known for his voluptuous women in languid poses and for his landscapes reflecting the influence of European painting. He often collaborated with Hiroshige. *See* HIROSHIGE; KANO SCHOOL.

EISEN, CHARLES. French draftsman, painter, and engraver (b. Valenciennes, 1720; d. Brussels, 1778). He learned drawing and engraving from his father, and in 1742 he entered the atelier of Lebas in Paris. His wit and ability brought him to the attention of the court, where he became royal painter and draftsman, with Mme de Pompadour as his pupil. He etched and engraved a variety of subjects, but is best remembered for his book illustrations, which in their elegant charm, light manner, and gentle eroticism typify the courtly tastes of the period. Such books as La Fontaine's *Contes* (1762), Dorat's *Baisers* (1770), and Montesquieu's *Temple de Cnide* (1772) are among the most elegant of French illustrated books.

BIBLIOGRAPHY. P. de Baudicour, *Le Peintre-graveur français continué . . .*, vol. 2, Paris, 1861.

EISHI (Hosoda Eishi). Japanese Ukiyo-e printmaker (1756–1815). Born to a family of feudal lords, Eishi studied painting with a Kanō master. In the early 1780s he renounced the title of lord and became a professional print designer, but from 1799 on he devoted himself to painting. He specialized in portrayals of delicate women marked by aristocratic grace and nobility. *See* KANO SCHOOL.

BIBLIOGRAPHY. L. V. Ledoux, *Japanese Prints, Sharaku to Toyokuni, in the Collection of Louis V. Ledoux*, Princeton, 1950.

EITOKU (Kano Eitoku). Japanese painter (1543–90). Eitoku was probably trained by his father, Shōei, and his grandfather, Motonobu. He was regarded as the genius of his time and was a prolific artist; yet an extremely small number of his works have survived. In 1576 he painted the walls of Azuchi Castle, the seat of the military ruler Nobunaga. After the untimely death of Nobunaga, Eitoku was patronized by the succeeding ruler, Hideyoshi, for whom he decorated Osaka Castle and Jurakudai Palace. All these large projects were destroyed in wars soon after completion, but their magnificent beauty was highly praised in the literature of the period. The screen paintings *Cypress* (Tokyo National Museum) and *Chinese Lions* (Imperial Collection) are good examples of his work, characterized by stiff, vigorous brushstrokes, and a sweeping arrangement of gigantic forms, executed in a decorative manner, against a brilliant gold-leaf background. *See* MOTONOBU; SHOEI.

BIBLIOGRAPHY. T. Akiyama, *Japanese Painting* [Geneva?], 1961; J. E. H. C. Covell, *Masterpieces of Japanese Screen Painting: The Momoyama Period (late 16th Century)*, New York, 1962.

EKKEHARD AND UTA STATUES, *see* NAUMBURG CATHEDRAL.

EKOI, *see* AFRICA, PRIMITIVE ART OF (WEST AFRICA: NIGERIA); NIGERIA.

EKPHRASIS. The Greek term conventionally used by modern critics to denote a rhetorical description of a work of art in ancient Greek and Roman literature. Ancient writers do not appear to use the term in this sense until about the 3d century of our era. It is through such descriptions that we catch a glimpse of what the composition, detail, and subject matter of some of the great paintings of antiquity may have been. The most significant examples of such descriptions are to be found in various works of Lucian (2d cent.), in the *Eikones* (Pictures) of the Elder and the Younger Philostratus (early and late 3d cent.,

respectively), and in the *Descriptions* of Callistratus (early 4th cent.?) and of Paulus (6th cent.).

The accuracy of many of these *ekphraseis* has been questioned. They have, however, served as inspirations to later artists. Botticelli's *Calumny of Apelles* is perhaps the best-known painting inspired by an *ekphrasis*.

BIBLIOGRAPHY. J. J. Pollitt, *The Art of Greece, 1400–31 B.C.*, Englewood Cliffs, N.J., 1965; J. J. Pollitt, *The Art of Rome, ca. 753 B.C.–337 A.D.*, Englewood Cliffs, N.J., 1966.

ELAM. Earliest name of the western Iranian plateau and its culture of Sumero-Semitic origin (3d millennium). Elam invented a script similar to that of Sumer and adopted the cylinder seal. Gold and lapis lazuli were imported from Afghanistan to Mesopotamia through Elam, which also exported copper and livestock. Wars between Mesopotamia and Elam provided the latter with Mesopotamian works of art, which influenced native crafts. The prehistoric emphasis on decoration (4th millennium) persisted, however, in Elam and later in Persia. Sumerian types of statues, seals, vessels, and steles were imitated in Elamite Susa (3000–2000 B.C.) and later inspired a local style (1300

Eitoku, *Chao-fu and the Ox.* National Museum, Tokyo.

B.C.). Both the capital, Susa, and Choga-Zambil were cities laid out on an oval plan. There was a ziggurat with three stairways at Choga-Zambil, and this feature as well as the orthogonal system of streets points to strong Mesopotamian influence. *See* CHOGA-ZAMBIL; SUSA.

BIBLIOGRAPHY. H. Frankfort, *The Art and Architecture of the Ancient Orient*, Baltimore, 1954.

ELCHE, THE LADY OF. Iberian female bust of the 3d century B.C., in the Prado, Madrid. Carved of soft limestone and painted, it is about 22 inches high. The finest example of Iberian sculpture, the bust shows Hellenizing influence and was perhaps executed by a Greek artist. The figure wears an un-Greek headdress which projects at the sides in two elaborately carved hemicycles that frame the face.

BIBLIOGRAPHY. A. García y Bellido, *Ars Hispaniae*, vol. 1: *Colonizaciones púnica y griega, El arte ibérico, El arte del las tribus célticas*, Madrid, 1947.

ELECTION, THE. Oil painting by Hogarth, in the Sir John Soane Museum, London. *See* HOGARTH, WILLIAM.

ELECTROTYPE. Most important modern method of graphic reproduction. A mold is made of an original etching, halftone, or type layout, after which it is immersed in a bath containing copper salts. By means of galvanic action, a layer of copper is deposited on the immersed mold. When the mold is removed, a copper duplicate is left, which is then employed for printing.

ELEMENTARISM, *see* DOESBURG, THEO VAN.

ELENBAAS, VALDEMAR HANSEN. Dutch painter and graphic artist (1912–   ). Born in Rotterdam, he studied painting first, in 1932, and became a graphic artist only in 1947, as a lithographer. Influenced by Picasso, he works mostly with color woodcuts, using simple cutout forms. The Colomba Prize for graphics was awarded him at the Venice Biennale of 1952.

ELEOUSA MADONNA. Type of Madonna and Child in Byzantine art that reveals a human warmth between the Mother and Child. Its name is derived from the Greek word *eleusa*, which means "maternal love." The Eleousa Madonna provides a contrast to the hieratic Hodegetria Madonna type (also Byzantine). *See* HODEGETRIA MADONNA.

BIBLIOGRAPHY. C. Diehl, *Manuel d'art byzantin*, 2d ed., rev., 2 vols., Paris, 1925–26.

ELEPHANTA. Island, originally called Gharapuri, in the harbor of Bombay, Maharashtra State, India. It is noted for its large Hindu rock-cut cave temples dedicated to the god Siva. The main temple was created in the middle of the 7th century during the Rāṣṭrakūṭa dynasty. It is the last great achievement of architectural sculpture in western India. It was badly desecrated by the Portuguese in the 16th century.

The plan of the temple at Elephanta was inspired by the Dhūmar Leṇā temple at Ellora. Both depart from the rock-cut tradition in that they have three portals, one at the front and one at each wing. This arrangement provided space for ceremonial processions and for an opening for light, which cast interesting shadows on various parts of the interior. The cave at Elephanta, however, does not have the cruciform arrangement of the one at Ellora. The main

Elephanta. Columns with cushion capitals in the sanctuary hall of the main cave temple.

shrine is pushed to the side of the temple so that *pradakṣinā* (circumambulation) is impossible. The Elephanta temple has two liṅgam shrines (shrines containing stylized phallic symbols that are emblems of the god Siva). Each is detached from the wall, permitting *pradakṣinā*, and has four entrances guarded by *dvārapālas* (door guardians).

The room in which the sanctuaries are contained is 130 feet square and opens toward the Himalayas. The columns in the room have a cushion capital and show the final development of a type already seen at Ellora. They are covered with a thin layer of stucco, which gives the interior a marblelike shine.

The most important feature of the Elephanta cave can be seen at the southern wall of the temple. Three large recesses, divided by pilasters, contain some of the most magnificent sculptural reliefs produced in India. The panel to the left contains the figure of Siva Ardhanārī (representing the male and female principles of Siva); the panel to the right represents the marriage of Siva and Pārvatī. The central panel is by far the most magnificent. It is a 23-foot-high triple bust of Siva Maheśvara (Siva in his manifestation as the Great Lord). The image to the left of the beholder is that of a male, and the one to the right is a female. The meaning of this work has been summed up as a central transcendent essence of creation with the divine generative force manifested in the complementary poles of the male and female. The female embodies the world-mothering principle; the male, the aspect of destruction.

See also INDIA.

BIBLIOGRAPHY. S. Kramrisch, *The Hindu Temple*, 2 vols., Calcutta, 1947; H. R. Zimmer, *The Art of Indian Asia*, 2 vols., New York, 1955; B. Rowland, *The Art and Architecture of India*, 2d ed., Baltimore, 1959.

ELIZABETH S. BERGER

ELEPHANTINE. Granite island in the Nile opposite Aswan, called Yeb, which formed the southern boundary of Egypt in the 11th dynasty. It has a fortified harbor dating to the 12th dynasty, temples to the deified governor Hekayeb of the Old Kingdom and to the local goddess Satet, and a Nilometer staircase. Its most significant monument, destroyed since it was recorded by the French scholars of Napoleon, was a peripteral temple built by Amenhotep III. It consisted of a cella, surrounded by an ambulatory with pillars, and two front bud papyriform columns set on a parapet wall above a socle to which a stairway led.

See also EGYPT.

EL ESCORIAL: MUSEUMS. Spanish collections. Thirty miles northwest of Madrid, in the foothills of the Guadarrama Mountains, stands the vast complex of the Monastery of S. Lorenzo el Real. Begun in 1563 by Philip II, it combined in one grandiose project a royal necropolis, monastery, church, and personal retreat for the King. It contains many art works and at least 7,500 relics of saints.

The original plans were drawn by Juan Bautista de Toledo. Following his death, in 1568, Juan de Herrera took over the task until it was completed in 1584. The plan of the church, in the shape of a Greek cross, was based on Bramante's first design for St. Peter's in Rome. Besides the high altar, with a retable about 98 feet high covering the entire east wall, the church contains forty-two other altars adorned with paintings and sculpture by Spanish and Italian masters of the time of Philip II. Flanking the high altar are the funeral monuments of Charles V and Philip II, featuring naturalistic sculptured figures of the monarchs and their families by Pompeo Leoni. In the trascoro is Cellini's white marble Christ on a black marble cross (1562).

As successive Spanish kings continued to furnish and embellish the immense interior spaces, the exuberance and florid decorative effects of mannerist and baroque trends counteracted the basic somberness. Walls and vaults were decorated by fresco painters brought from Italy, including Granello and Castello in the late 16th century and Luca Giordano in the late 17th. Under Philip III the Panteón de los Reyes was completed; under Philip IV notable additions were made to the great picture collection; and under Charles II a new altar dedicated to a Miraculous Host was built in the sacristy, for which Claudio Coello painted *Charles II Adoring the Host* (1685–89).

Despite severe damage by fires in 1671 and 1872 and by military vandalism in 1808, and despite the removal of works of art for various reasons, El Escorial remains an important art center. In the library is a collection of manuscripts dating from the 10th through the 16th century, including rare Arabic manuscripts, as well as ivories, enamels, and goldsmith's work of high quality. In the sacristy and chapter halls are noteworthy paintings by the Spanish masters El Greco, Ribera, Zurbarán, Velázquez, Sánchez Coello, Pantoja de la Cruz, and Carreño de Miranda, as well as works by Veronese, Tintoretto, Jacopo Bassano, Titian, Jacopo Palma, Rubens, Bosch, and Patinir. There are also Spanish and Flemish tapestries from cartoons by Goya, Rubens, Teniers, and others.

BIBLIOGRAPHY. J. de Sigüenza, *Fundación del monasterio de El Escorial*, Madrid, 1605, new ed., Madrid, 1963; A. Ximénez, *Descripción del Real Monasterio de San Lorenzo del Escorial*, Madrid, 1764; A. Calvert, *The Escorial*, London, 1907; J. A. Gaya Nuño, *El Escorial*, Madrid, 1947.   MADLYN KAHR

ELEUSINIAN RELIEF. Large Greek dedicatory relief from Eleusis (5th cent. B.C.), in the National Archaeological Museum, Athens. It represents Demeter and the Kore (Persephone), with the boy Triptolemos in the center. Demeter, a matronly figure, is represented giving ears of wheat to Triptolemos; she is draped in the heavy Doric peplum, which falls in straight vertical folds and recalls the similar treatment of drapery in early classical figures. The treatment of the Kore's drapery, however, is close to the Parthenon pedimental figures and, therefore, indicates that this work was executed at about the same time as the Parthenon sculptures (ca. 430 B.C.). Successful Roman copies of this famous classical work are in the Louvre, Paris, and the Metropolitan Museum, New York.

BIBLIOGRAPHY. E. A. Gardner, *A Handbook of Greek Sculpture*, 2d ed., London, 1915.

ELEUSIS: HALL OF MYSTERIES. Greek building dedicated to the cult of Demeter and Persephone. The Hall of Mysteries (Telesterion) served as a hall of initiation rather than as a temple. It was constructed on a site on which a series of sacred buildings had stood since the Mycenaean period. In the second half of the 6th century B.C., in the time of the Peisistratids (ca. 550–510), the early Telesterion was built entirely of porous limestone. The archaic structure consisted of a square hall with a prostyle porch; the interior contained five rows of five columns each. (Remains of this building are preserved on the south wall.) The

Eleusinian relief, 5th century B.C. National Archaeological Museum, Athens.

Elgin Marbles. Metope representing the battle of the Centaurs and Lapiths, from the Parthenon. British Museum, London.

southwest corner of the Peisistratid hall was occupied by the so-called palace (anaktoron), the name given to a room that served as the repository of the cult objects (hiera). The archaic Telesterion was destroyed by the Persians in 480 B.C.

The 5th-century Telesterion was designed by Ictinus, the architect of the Parthenon, and was completed by Metagenes, Xenocles, and Koroibos, who modified Ictinus's plan. It consisted of a vast square hall (ca. 168 by 170 ft.). The interior had forty-two columns arranged in six rows of seven columns each, with a superposed colonnade. An oblong central lantern, through which the hall was lighted, was placed on top of the building. The anaktoron was

placed in the center of the hall under the lantern. Along the four walls of the Telesterion were arranged tiers of eight steps, which served as seats. The mysteries were enacted in the middle of the hall in the presence of large crowds of worshipers. Access to the hall was given by six doorways, two on each side except the west. The walls were built of gray-blue Eleusinian stone. *See also* ELEUSINIAN RELIEF.

The Periclean Telesterion did not have a portico. This was added in 336–326 B.C. by the architect Philon, and it was called the Philonian Stoa. The Stoa, built of Pentelic marble, was prostyle and dodecastyle with Doric columns. The Telesterion underwent reconstruction during the Roman period; it was partially destroyed by the Kostovoks (Costoboci) in A.D. 170.

See also LESSER PROPYLON, ELEUSIS.

BIBLIOGRAPHY. W. B. Dinsmoor, *The Architecture of Ancient Greece*, 3d ed., London, 1950; A. W. Lawrence, *Greek Architecture*, Baltimore, 1957; G. E. Mylonas, *Eleusis and the Eleusinian Mysteries*, Princeton, 1961.

EVANTHIA SAPORITI

ELEVATION. Orthographic projection on a vertical plane. An elevation in architectural drawing is obtained by placing one of the faces of a building parallel to a vertical plane and projecting lines orthographically, that is, at right angles, to that plane. A front elevation shows the front face so projected; a side elevation, the side; and a rear elevation, the rear face.

See also PERSPECTIVE.

ELGIN CATHEDRAL. Scottish cathedral developed in three stages: up to 1230, to 1250, and after 1270. The plan includes west towers and portal, nave with aisles, tower crossing and transepts, choir and aisles, and presbytery and chapter house. Most of the west and east parts are in ruins.

ELGIN MARBLES. Name given to a group of Greek sculptures, especially those from the Parthenon, collected (beginning in 1801) by Lord Elgin, the British ambassador to Turkey. The sculptures were purchased from Lord Elgin by the British government in 1816, and they are now in the British Museum in London. Besides the Parthenon sculptures, the collection also includes one of the caryatids from the Erechtheum, a number of additional architectural members from both the Parthenon and the Erechtheum, and numerous other sculptured reliefs and fragments.

Lord Elgin was granted permission to collect antique marbles in Greece by the Turkish government at Constantinople. The actual removal was mostly directed by a Sicilian painter, Lusieri, whom Lord Elgin had hired in Italy at the suggestion of Sir William Hamilton. The conditions under which the marbles were removed and the tragic destruction to which they had been subjected in the century prior to their removal are all set forth in the *Report from the Select Committee of the House of Commons on the Earl of Elgin's Collection* (London, 1816).

The Elgin collection includes most of the fragments of the pediments of the Parthenon, fifteen metopes, and substantial portions of the east, north, and south friezes from the exterior of the cella. A few pedimental fragments, a number of metopes, mostly badly damaged, and the west frieze are still *in situ*; there are also fragments in the Acropolis Museum in Athens, the Louvre in Paris, and other museums.

Although any complete study of the Parthenon must take account of all the known fragments, the essential outline of the stylistic development of the Parthenon sculpture can be seen in the Elgin collection alone. The metopes of the collection, for example (447–442 B.C.), representing the battle of the Centaurs and the Lapiths, reflect the early development of the "ripe classical" style of Greek sculpture and reveal an increasingly brilliant inventiveness in composition. The frieze (442–437 B.C.), which represents the lively movements of the Panathenaic procession and, on the east side, a convocation of the gods, marks a classic moment in Greek sculpture when a perfect union of reality and ideality, of movement and arrest, and of the spiritual and secular was achieved. Perhaps the best illustration of these qualities is the procession of horsemen from the north section of the frieze, now reassembled in the British Museum. In the two pediments (437–432 B.C.) the Parthenon sculptors sought to heighten the effects of drama and animation by emphasizing contrasts of light and shade and by giving a wind-blown effect to the drapery of the figures. The east pediment represented the birth of Athena; the west, the struggle of Poseidon and Athena for the rulership of Athens. Some of the most famous Elgin marbles come from these groups. These include, from the east, heads of the horses from the chariots of the sun and moon, a reclining male figure conventionally called Theseus, and the famous group commonly known as the Three Fates; and, from the west, the colossal torso of Poseidon, part of which is in Athens and part in the British Museum. See FATES.

BIBLIOGRAPHY. London, British Museum, Dept. of Greek and Roman Antiquities, *The Sculptures of the Parthenon*, introd. and commentary by A. H. Smith, London, 1910; A. H. Smith, "Lord Elgin and His Collection," *Journal of Hellenic Studies*, XXXVI, 1916.

JEROME J. POLLITT

EL GRECO, see GRECO, EL.

ELIASZ. PICKENOIJ (Pickenoy), NICOLAES. Dutch painter of individual and group portraits (b. Amsterdam, 1590/91?; d. there, between 1654 and 1656). He was the son of a coat-of-arms cutter whose family came from Antwerp, and was probably a pupil of Cornelis van der Voort. Eliasz. Pickenoij's works were influenced by Frans Hals as well as by the Rembrandt school. He was probably the teacher of Bartholomeus van der Helst.

BIBLIOGRAPHY. J. Six, "Nicolaes Eliasz. Pickenoy," *Oud-Holland*, IV, 1886.

ELIGIUS OF NOYON, ST. Bishop and artisan (b. Chaptelat, near Limoges, ca. 590). A farrier, he cut off the leg of a restive horse the more easily to shoe him, and when the work was finished the leg was restored by the owner (Christ disguised). A goldsmith and master of the mint under Clotaire II and Dagobert I, he was famous for masterpieces in metal, especially reliquaries. He founded monasteries and churches with the fortune he made. Dagobert I made him bishop of Noyon. His attributes are tongs, hammer, wedding ring, and a horse's severed foot. His feast is December 1. See also SAINTS IN ART.

EL JIB, see GIBEON.

ELKAN, BENNO. German sculptor (b. Dortmund, 1877; d. London, 1960). After early training in painting in Munich and Karlsruhe, he turned to sculpture, continuing his studies in Paris with Bartolomé and then in Rome. Elkan created portraits, funerary monuments, and other works, and during the Nazi persecutions in the early 1930s settled permanently in England. His last great work is a massive sculptured menorah in bronze, given to the parliament of Israel by the British government.

Ellora. Cave XVI (the Brahmanical Kailāsa temple).

ELLIOTT, CHARLES LORING. American portrait painter (b. Scipio, N.Y., 1812; d. Albany, 1868). After working for his father, an architect, Elliott moved to New York and studied with Trumbull and Quidor. His early bust portraits are romantically painted, but because of the growing impact of the camera his later work became photographically realistic and less successful.

BIBLIOGRAPHY. T. Bolton, "Charles Loring Elliott," *Art Quarterly*, V, Winter, 1942.

ELLORA (Elura). Village about 18 miles northwest of Aurangābād in Maharashtra State (formerly in Hyderabad), India. It is the site of a group of thirty-four rock-cut shrines in a ridge of low hills. The shrines, popularly called caves, are cut into the living rock of the west side of the ridge and are numbered consecutively from south to north. Three religions are represented: Buddhism, Hinduism, and Jainism. *See also* INDIA.

The southernmost group, Caves I to XII, are Mahāyāna Buddhist and are the oldest at Ellora, having been started in the 5th or 6th century A.D. and continued into the middle of the 7th. Cave X, the Viśvakarmā chaitya hall, is the last rock-cut example of the type in India, following in general the design of the earlier chaitya halls, such as those at Ajaṇṭā, but with innovations, particularly in the façade, which is two-storied and lacks the impressive horseshoe-arch window of the earlier examples. The other Buddhist caves are all vihāras; nos. XI and XII, which are large, multipillared, and three-storied caves, are particularly impressive.

The Brahmanical (Hindu) caves, nos. XIII to XXIX, created in the 7th to the 9th century, occupy a section of the ridge north of the Buddhist group. They reflect, in their magnitude and beauty, the return to dominance of the Hindu religion after the previous centuries of Buddhist emphasis. Most impressive is Cave XVI, the Kailāsa temple, dedicated to Śiva and representing Śiva's paradise on Mt. Kailāsa. Unlike the earlier rock-cut shrines of Ellora, which were hollowed out of the rock, the Kailāsa was created as a freestanding monolithic temple by the removal of the rock around it. All the other Brahmanical temples are pillared shrines hollowed out of the cliff in the usual manner. The sculptured figures of the Brahmanical caves are among the finest in India. *See* KAILASA TEMPLE, ELLORA.

The Jain caves, nos. XXX to XXXIV, of the 9th and 10th centuries, are the northernmost group. They follow, in general, the form of the Brahmanical temples; one, Cave XXX, is a smaller version of the great Kailāsa temple.

BIBLIOGRAPHY. H. R. Zimmer, *The Art of Indian Asia*, 2 vols., New York, 1955; P. Brown, *Indian Architecture*, vol. 1: *Buddhist and Hindu Periods*, 4th ed., Bombay, 1959; R. S. Gupte and B. D. Mahajan, *Ajaṇṭā, Ellora, and Aurangābād Caves*, Bombay, 1962.

CHARLES D. WEBER

ELMES, HARVEY LONSDALE. English architect (1814–47). Elmes was a major Greek revival architect. At an early age he won the important competition for St. George's Hall and the Assize Courts, Liverpool. This work was begun in 1842, but because of Elmes's poor health it was completed by Robert Rawlinson and C. R. Cockerell in 1854. *See* ST. GEORGE'S HALL, LIVERPOOL.

ELMO, ST., *see* ERASMUS OF GAETA, ST.

ELMSLIE, GEORGE G., *see* PURCELL AND ELMSLIE.

ELNE CATHEDRAL. French church, situated in the Department of the Pyrénées-Orientales. Begun toward the middle of the 11th century, interrupted, and later resumed in a consistent style, Elne Cathedral is an excellent example of the Romanesque style of Roussillon, with its predominantly Catalan and Lombard features. Much of the original construction is still to be seen in the Cathedral. The cloister is one of the few that have come down to us virtually intact, except for the loss of the upper galleries. Only the south gallery is Romanesque, dating from the last quarter of the 12th century.

BIBLIOGRAPHY. *Roussillon Roman*, text by M. Durliat, La Pierrequi-Vire (Yonne), 1958.

ELPHEGE, ST., *see* ALPHEGE, ST.

ELSHEIMER, ADAM (Adamo Tedesco). German painter (b. Frankfurt am Main, 1578; d. Rome, 1610). He first studied with Philipp Uffenbach, a *retardataire* follower of Grünewald, in Frankfurt, but also was influenced by the landscape painting of the nearby Frankenthal colony (Gillis von Coninxloo, for example). In Venice by 1598, Elsheimer worked with the German painter Hans Rottenhammer the Elder. By 1600 Elsheimer was in Rome, where he became part of the Netherlandish circle that had formed around Paul Bril. Elsheimer remained there until his death, slowly producing small paintings on copper panels.

Elsheimer's works during his Venetian period show the influence of Rottenhammer's figure style and Tintoretto's light and color, as in the *Baptism of Christ* (ca. 1600; London, National Gallery). The somewhat illogical proportions of figures and spatial definition and the minute landscape details give way to a simpler and clearer style under the influence of Roman classicism, as exemplified in *Paul and Barnabas at Lystra* (ca. 1600–04; Frankfurt am Main, Städel Institute and Municipal Art Gallery). Here, light and shadow are used to separate the figures from the classical architectural background. There is a stronger sense of unifying rhythmic relationships among the figures and a logical outlining of the foreground space. Caravaggio's *tenebroso* also formed part of the Roman influence, and Elsheimer adapted it for his own dramatic purposes in such works as *The Riddle of Ceres* (ca. 1606–08; Madrid, Prado).

Elsheimer's greatest contribution, however, was in the field of ideal landscape, where he harmonized the northern romantic vision with the Italian sense of clarity and unity (*Aurora*, ca. 1604–10; Brunswick, Herzog-Anton-Ulrich Museum). In such night scenes as *Moonlit Landscape with the Flight into Egypt* (ca. 1606–09; Paris, Louvre), he not only took full advantage of the nocturnal mood but also experimented with the inclusion of several sources of natural and nonnatural light. The blend of figures and landscape, the romantic exploration of the theme of classical ruins, the idyllic mood, and the clear organization that distinguish the *River Scene with the Round Temple at Tivoli* (ca. 1608–10; Prague, National Gallery) had a profound influence on the development of 17th-century landscape painting, so broad as to include the classicist Poussin, the baroque Rubens (a close friend of Elsheimer in Rome), and most of all, Claude Lorraine.

BIBLIOGRAPHY. W. Drost, *Adam Elsheimer und sein Kreis*, Potsdam, 1933; W. Drost, *Adam Elsheimer als Zeichner*, Stuttgart, 1957; F. Saxl, "Elsheimer and Italy," *Lectures*, vol. 1, London, 1957.

STEPHEN E. OSTROW

ELSINORE: KRONBORG CASTLE, *see* HELSINGOR: KRONBORG CASTLE.

ELTZ AN DER MOSELLE. German castle located a short distance north of Cochem an der Moselle, Rhineland-Palatinate. The ancestral home of the counts of Eltz, it consists of a composite of buildings dating from the 13th to the 16th century erected on top of a lofty rock picturesquely situated among wooded hills. It is notable for its fine state of preservation.

EL 'UBAID, *see* AL-'UBAID.

ELURA, *see* ELLORA.

ELVIRA HOUSE, MUNICH, *see* ENDELL, AUGUST.

ELY CATHEDRAL. English Romanesque cathedral erected on the site of an earlier church. The east end to the

Adam Elsheimer, *Landscape with Figures*. Uffizi, Florence. Idealized landscapes of this kind influenced much 17th-century landscape painting.

transepts and crossing was begun about 1083. By the early 12th century the building was completed to the west end with tower and porch. Then came the galilee. The chancel and aisles were rebuilt and lengthened in 1234–52 and in 1321–28. The Lady Chapel was built from 1321 to 1349. The crossing, rebuilt in the form of an octagon from 1323 to about 1330, is a stroke of genius; the idea was probably Alan of Walsingham's. The remarkable timber work over the crossing and the octagonal timber lantern were probably designed by William Hurle; the lantern was finished by 1342. In the cloister is the prior's door of about 1140, with a lavish allover effect of ornamentation.

BIBLIOGRAPHY. N. Pevsner, *The Buildings of England*, vol. 10, Harmondsworth, 1954.

ELZEVIR. Any book produced by the publishing and printing Elzevir family between 1540 and 1712 in the Low Countries. A typical Elzevir is an unusually small format edition of the classics, or of such standard works as those of Erasmus, characterized by its minute but clear and beautiful type. Elzevirs are sometimes decorated with engravings and are highly prized collectors' items.

BIBLIOGRAPHY. K. Schottenloher, *Das alte Buch*, 3d ed., Brunswick, 1956.

EMAIL BRUN. Technique for decorating copper most commonly in use during the 12th and 13th centuries. The surface to be decorated was coated with a linseed oil varnish made hard by heating. The designs were cut through the varnish to the bare metal, and these exposed parts were then gilded. *Email brun* frequently decorated the bottom or rear side of liturgical objects.

BIBLIOGRAPHY. M. Creutz, *Geschichte der Metallkunst*, vol. 2, Stuttgart, 1909.

EMAKI (Emakimono), *see* MAKIMONO.

EMBARKATION FOR CYTHERA. Oil painting by Watteau, in the Louvre, Paris. *See* WATTEAU, JEAN-ANTOINE.

EMBARKATION OF THE QUEEN OF SHEBA. Oil painting by Claude Lorraine, in the National Gallery, London, *See* LORRAINE, CLAUDE.

EMBERRES, GIL DE, *see* SILOE, GIL DE.

EMBLEMA. Archaeological term referring to (1) the central design in some mosaic pavements, especially those of Hellenistic times; and (2) a metal ornament, in the form of an animal, a mask, or a medallion, affixed to the exterior or the interior of a metal art object such as a bowl, vase, or cup. These metal emblemata sometimes became detached and today are often found in museums independently of the objects they once decorated.

BIBLIOGRAPHY. E. Pernice, *Die hellenistische Kunst in Pompeji*, vol. 6: *Pavimente und figürliche Mosaiken*, Berlin, 1938.

EMBLEM BOOKS. Books with illustrations, usually woodcuts, having explanatory captions or text that describe various proverbs and fables. They were common in the 16th and 17th centuries (for example, *Emblematus libellus*, 1552). Emblem books were an important source for much of the profane subject matter of the Renaissance and baroque periods.

EMBLEMS, CHINESE, *see* MARKS, CHINESE.

EMBOSSING. Technique for producing raised designs, usually on metal but also on leather and textiles. The object to be embossed is impressed with a die; in the case of metal, it is hammered from the back. In textiles the same effect can be produced by various weaves.

EMBRASURE. Small slitlike opening in the walls of a castle or fortification through which projectiles are launched toward an attacking enemy. Usually the sides of the embrasure widen diagonally outward to give maximum view from the inside without allowing a dangerously large opening.

BIBLIOGRAPHY. A. H. Thompson, *Military Architecture in England During the Middle Ages*, London, 1912.

EMBRIACHI. Venetian family active in the 15th century producing small panels of sculptural relief in ivory and bone. Series of the panels were incorporated into altarpieces and small chests. Minnesinger poetry provided inspiration for profane work, which was characteristically International Gothic in style. The most ambitious effort of the Embriachi is an altarpiece at the Certosa in Pavia.

BIBLIOGRAPHY. J. von Schlosser, "Die Werkstatt der Embriachi in Venedig," *Jahrbuch der Kunsthistorischen Sammlungen des Allerhöchsten Kaiserhauses*, XX, pt. 1, 1899.

EMBROIDERY. The art of ornamenting textiles, fabrics, and other materials with needlework. It is a method of decorating by sewing on a finished piece of cloth, which differentiates it from ornamentation woven into the fabric. About 300 different embroidery stitches are used, and these generally fit into four categories: flat, looped, chained, and knotted. In embroidery the entire surface may be covered with the stitching or the ground fabric may be ornamented by the sparing use of stitchery.

The history of embroidery begins in the Neolithic era. Although no textiles survive, bone needles have been unearthed at several neolithic sites, including one inhabited by the Swiss lake dwellers. It is difficult to distinguish between embroidery and tapestry in representations in stone, but there is reason to believe that, traditionally, elegant materials were embroidered.

The oldest surviving cloth is from ancient Egypt, a Middle Kingdom linen fragment with patterns sewn on in blue, red, green, and black (Cairo Museum). The technique employed, instead of being a simple embroidery stitch, is one that involves sewing on the warp threads of the ground rather than on the finished cloth. The cloth has a pattern of rows of lotus flowers and papyrus inflorescences that relate to patterns found in representations of clothing in Egyptian wall reliefs.

No cloth has survived from the Babylonian and Assyrian civilizations; in representations of people in the monumental reliefs, however, patterned cloth is shown, and this might have been embroidered. Homer describes the richest type of embroidery as the work of Helen of Troy. Centuries later, in the classical era, the importance of the peplum made every five years to shield the goddess Athena was mentioned widely and was quite elaborately sewn with metal threads. Examples of Greek cloth dating from the 4th and 3d centuries B.C. have been found in

Crimea. In these the stylization of the figures has a naïveté unrelated to the classical style and also unlike the fragment of the Hellenistic centaur (Lyons, Historical Museum of Fabrics), which is in the classical pictorial tradition. The centaur is done in the stem-and-chain stitch.

Between the 2d and the 6th century of our era many varying cultures were active in the civilized world; in the few examples of embroidery surviving from the period the richness of that moment in history is seen. The continuing Greco-Roman tradition had ramifications as far off as Turkestan and Mongolia. In Egypt wonderfully stylized examples have survived. The Middle Eastern world is represented by Sassanian work, which reflects strong Roman influence. Oriental fragments show evidence of the unbelievably rich separate tradition in silk embroidery; this is best represented in the embroidery of A.D. 621 depicting the Buddhist paradise, preserved in the Chūgūji at Nara, Japan. Peru produced some of its most interesting needlework, including embroidery, in this period. Arabic and Oriental influences were felt in Europe at the time when Byzantium emerged. A band of gold embroidery preserved in Ravenna, which relates closely to the ivories there, shows the Byzantine tradition in its early phase, and a 12th-century robe, the so-called dalmatic of Charlemagne, in the Treasury of St. Peter's, Rome, suggests the grandeur of the full-blown style with its distinctive stylization of figural and floral motifs.

The decorative arts in general and miniature painting in particular had a strong relationship to embroidery from the 2d to the 15th century, so that there is a similar approach in medieval needlework. In the Christian world needlework was produced in monasteries by both men and women specialists. According to documents, royal and noble ladies also were fine embroiderers. The finest work produced in the 10th to the 12th century was English, and it reflected a strong connection with the miniature tradition of the British Isles at that time; a prime example is the maniple of St. Cuthbert (909–916; Durham Cathedral). The Bayeux tapestry is not a tapestry but an embroidery, executed in the late 11th century either by Norman or English craftsmen (Bayeux, Museum of Queen Mathilde). The richness of the European work of the time is demonstrated by the imperial mantle (11th or 12th cent.) in the Metz Cathedral and by the vestments of the Norman kings of Sicily (12th cent.) in the Treasury in Vienna, decorated with pearls and enamel plaques. One of the robes of the Norman kings has a Kufic inscription that shows Arabic influence in Palermo, where it was made. *See* BAYEUX.

The 13th century marked the beginning of a number of national styles, most important of which was the English. The opus Anglicum, or English embroidery, was treasured everywhere in the period. It was at its height from 1250 to 1350 and is particularly well done, with decorative schemes that matched those of the other decorative arts of the time. Ironwork connections have been pointed out, for example. The cope from Syon House (14th cent.; London, Victoria and Albert) is a fine example of English embroidery. These national styles were essentially Gothic, and in the French and German work one can begin to discern a shift in embroidery from being a part of the miniature and craft tradition to approaching the work of painters of the period. In the *Treatise on Painting* by Cennino Cennini of the 14th century, painters designing for embroiderers are discussed. In the 15th century this is seen as a prominent element in both Flemish and Italian work. The most famous example is the part played by Antonio del Pollaiuolo in designing the embroideries for the Florentine Baptistery; the embroideries are in the Cathedral Museum in Florence. At this time the less monumental and more decorative embroideries seemed to reflect Eastern influences. Chinese and Arabic silks were used, and in Spain the Moorish influence was significant.

In the 16th century the spread of mannerism throughout Europe led to more pictorial work in embroidery; but for clothing and small objects, patterns related to Near Eastern imports were done as well as decorative designs that were inspired by classical motifs. As a desire for rich ornamentation was satisfied in many varied ways, architectural patterns, swags, and the like were also used. A section from a bed hanging (New York, Metropolitan Museum), with a fruit motif applied in a rich variety of stitches and natural color combined with gold on a dark-purple satin ground, suggests the richness typical of the era. Samplers played a significant role from the 16th century on. The publication of pattern books, such as Shorleyker's *A Scholehouse for the Needle*, made domestic work easier to do, and the introduction of steel needles resulted in a new range of stitches.

Most significant for the 17th century was the development of pictorial techniques for small objects. An example of this is stump work, a method of building up relief in needlework for pictures. English stump work is particularly fine. In other types of embroidery the ideas of the 16th century were continued. Wool embroidery, called crewel, was developed extensively, with Near Eastern foliate patterns a prime inspiration in design. These are found at their best in bed hangings and exist in many American and English collections. Classical motifs continued to be important in the grandest expressions of the time. Also included in the category of needlework were the overall patterns on canvas that came into fashion, such as the flame stitch, a continuous zigzag most often used for upholstery.

In the 18th century there is little that is new in the field of embroidery. Most of the changes in design were the effects of changes in taste that resulted in alterations in scale, but for the most part the same repertory of motifs was used.

The most significant factors of change came in the 19th century, when a decline in the craft tradition began. From the 1830s to the 1870s there was no interest in really fine craftsmanship, but then a reaction began and schools of embroidery were instituted. Modern work of importance is being done by a small group of craftsman, some of whom work in the contemporary style while others are more interested in reviving 17th-century design.

BIBLIOGRAPHY. M. Symonds and L. Preece, *Needlework through the Ages*, London, 1928; M. Schuette and S. F. C. Müller, *A Pictorial History of Embroidery*, New York, 1964.

MARVIN D. SCHWARTZ

EMERSON, WILLIAM RALPH. American architect (1833–1918). He was born in Illinois. A student of Jona-

Empire style. Table with sphinxlike legs. Private collection, Milan.

than Preston, Emerson began working in the 1870s and contributed considerably to the development of the "shingle style." In his best private houses there is a flow and continuity of masses and a plastic relation between walls and roof.

EMILIA. Region in north-central Italy. Before the Roman annexation in the late 3d century B.C. Emilia was an area of Etruscan colonization served by Greek trading posts on the Adriatic coast. Roman vestiges have survived in Rimini, the starting point of the Via Aemilia. The most characteristic monuments of Emilia come from the Middle Ages; there are, for example, Early Christian and Byzantine works in Ravenna; Romanesque cathedrals in Ferrara, Modena, Parma, and Piacenza; and Gothic buildings in Piacenza and Bologna. Ferrara in the 15th century was one of the most important centers of the Renaissance. In the following century cultural hegemony passed to Bologna, where the Carracci Academy played an important role in the development of baroque painting. *See* BOLOGNA; ETRUSCAN ART; FERRARA; MODENA; PARMA: CATHEDRAL AND BAPTISTERY; PIACENZA CATHEDRAL; RAVENNA.

BIBLIOGRAPHY. C. Ricci, *L'arte in Italia*, vol. 3: *Emilia e Romagna*, Bergamo, 1911; Touring Club Italiano, *Emilia e Romagna*, 4th ed., Milan, 1957.

EMPATHY (Einfuhlung). Term coined by Edward Titchener in 1909 as a translation for the German aesthetic term *Einfühlung*, to convey the idea of the artist's projection of self into objects as a result of his response to imagery.

EMPEROR OTTO, STATUE OF. Gothic equestrian statue of Otto I, in the market square at Magdeburg, Germany.

EMPIRE STYLE. The second phase of neoclassicism in the decorative arts, named for the Napoleonic empire (1804–14) but actually beginning in the Directoire era, or about 1795 in France. It persisted until 1850. The word "Empire" is used in America and France; the same style is called Regency in England and Biedermeier in Austria and Germany. The style spread wherever western European fashion was respected, and it varied less than earlier styles. Ancient Greek and Roman forms served as the models for the design of Empire-style objects, which were kept as faithful to the antique as possible. Chairs followed the lines of the Greek klismos, vases duplicated ancient Roman forms, and chests of drawers and tea sets followed in spirit by being adaptations of Greco-Roman forms. *See* BIEDERMEIER STYLE.

One key factor of the style is that it was a reaction to the earlier neoclassicism of Robert Adam. Since the first phase of the style was flat and linear with delicate patterns and pale colors, this phase was heavy and massive with strong contrasting patterns and bold colors. In furniture, smooth and shiny dark woods, preferably mahogany or rosewood, were used and gold-colored brasses were applied in bold classical patterns. Plain heavy columns often served as supports, but occasionally simple gilt caryatid figures were used. The same system of bold designs and strong contrasts evolved in silver and ceramics. Gold was used extensively in ceramics, and in silver the borders contrasted strongly with the plain center surfaces.

Credit for initiating the Empire style belongs to the architects responsible for the royal apartments of Napoleon: Charles Percier (1764–1838) and Pierre Fontaine (1762–1853). Their designs were published in *Recueil de décorations intérieures* in 1801 and 1812. *See* PERCIER AND FONTAINE.

Popular suggestions of Empire-style designs appeared all over Europe in the first few decades of the 19th century. George Smith and Thomas Hope in England and Giuseppe Soli and Giocondo Albertolli in Italy borrowed freely from French publications for their own collections of designs. One factor that affected the style profoundly was a general spirit of democratization over Europe and the United States, which, in an effort to provide high style for everyone, inspired shoddy production. With the Empire style came a universal desire to be in style. No longer were fine provincial creations that mastered the necessary economic limitations produced for the middle classes. This second phase of neoclassicism marked the beginning of extensive efforts to make cheap imitations of fine objects.

The great examples of the Empire style are Malmaison outside of Paris, the early rooms at the White House in Washington, D.C., and the Bartow-Pell mansion in the Bronx, N.Y.

See also FURNITURE.

BIBLIOGRAPHY. S. Faniel, ed., *Le XIXe siècle français* (Collection Connaissance des Arts, 1), Paris, 1957; R. Edwards and L. G. G. Ramsey, eds., *The Connoisseur Period Guides to Houses...*, vol. 5: *The Regency Period, 1810–1830*, London, 1958; M. Praz, *Gusto neoclassico*, 2d ed., Naples, 1959.

MARVIN D. SCHWARTZ

Enamel. Byzantine bracelet, 9th century. Gold and cloisonné. Archaeological Museum, Thessalonika.

EMPOLI, JACOPO DA, *see* CHIMENTI, JACOPO.

EMPOLION. Wooden or bronze block at the center of a column drum joint holding the centering pin, as used in Greek architecture.

EMULSION. Type of painting medium in which two liquids are suspended in one another with the aid of an emulsifying agent. Egg yolk, for example, was used to keep oil emulsified in water in an early Renaissance oil painting medium.

BIBLIOGRAPHY. M. Doerner, *The Materials of the Artist and Their Use in Painting,* New York, 1934.

ENAMEL. The history of enamels has a somewhat mysterious beginning. Prototypes of enamel in the form of frit or glass inlaid on ceramics and metal were known in ancient Egypt and Assyria, but no true enamel has been found in these cultures. In Mycenae gold ornaments with enamel in hollows punched in the upper surface are known from the period between 1425 and 1300 B.C. The technique seems to have been of short-lived popularity. In the 12th century in Cyprus a type of enamel made from broken fragments of glass set in cloisons was made. It is strange to encounter innovation in as remote an area as Cyprus at that time, but there is no evidence of the source of the idea in a more important center. The process is found a little later in the 10th and 9th centuries B.C. in northern Syria and then not again until the 6th century B.C. in Greece, and a little later in Etruria. In both these centers the enamel is contained in filigree, a variation not used in medieval and modern times. *See* CLOISONNE.

Filigree enamel was regularly made in Greece until Hellenistic times. White, deep blue, deep green, and pale greenish blue were the enamel colors favored in Greece. The Romans rarely used enamel; they preferred inlays of stone and glass. In western Europe, in the 3d and 4th centuries A.D., probably under Celtic influence, champlevé

enamel was used with brightly colored enamels set in bronze. Enamels have also been found in eastern parts of the Roman Empire from the 3d century A.D. In the West interlace designs in bronze and gold with fantastic animals were set off by the addition of enamel. *See* CHAMPLEVE ENAMEL; FILIGREE.

The use of enamels continued through the Merovingian and Carolingian periods with some influence from Byzantium. In Byzantium, since flat, linear compositions were favored, the cloisonné technique was particularly suitable to the pictorial representations desired on various religious objects. Literary documents suggest the importance of cloisonné in Byzantium from the 6th century on, and there are a few actual examples that may be dated that early, although most are later. The Byzantine enamelers flourished from the 9th to the 12th century. In the West a number of centers of enamel work emerged, which produced gold cloisonné combining the flat patterns of Byzantium with some of the lively geometric conceptions of the Celts and Saxons.

With the advent of the Romanesque style (ca. 1000) broader, more generalized representations in champlevé became more prominent. Copper was used more than silver and gold for reliquaries in the champlevé technique, with enamels more frequently opaque than translucent. In general, the Western craftsman tended to be bolder in design and possibly less refined in technique than his Byzantine counterpart. In the 12th-century work of Godefroy de Claire at Liège, and of the prolific and influential Mosan school in general, comes the beginning of new refinements in the West. Brilliant yellows, blues, and greens with white highlights are used in a new technique related to the instructions of Theophilus in *De diversis artibus* for separating colors by the use of a quill pen instead of the traditional cloisons. Limoges, long a center of metalworkers, having served as the mint for the Merovingian kings, emerged as a second center of enameling to provide ritual vessels needed in many new churches then under construction. There was a continuous development which resulted in the 13th-century introduction of basse-taille, in which relief figures are covered with translucent enamel. In the 14th century the plique-à-jour ("open to the light") technique was introduced and was practiced in France and Italy. In this process a miniature stained-glass effect was obtained by enclosing areas of translucent glass pastes in a web of cells without any backing. *See* GODEFROY DE CLAIRE; MOSAN ART.

At Limoges, toward the end of the 15th century, enameling once more became important with the introduction of the technique that has come to be known as "Limoges," that of painted enamels whose objective is to create a picture in enamel. Several generations of enamelers achieved prominence at Limoges, beginning with the Pénicauds and then the Limousins and Reymonds, all of whom created objects and pictures in painted enamels on classical forms such as pitchers or bowls or in frames decorated with classical motifs. For the enamelers of the 16th century the medium had become pictorial, and High Renaissance compositions of both north and south were inspiration for the pictures. Often engravings were used as models, but the finest enamelers were capable of being original. They worked a great deal in grisaille, applying whites in varying degrees of thickness on a black or dark-blue ground to achieve the effect of relief. Whether polychrome or grisaille, luminosity is the foremost quality of painted enamels. *See* LIMOUSIN; PENICAUD FAMILY; REYMOND FAMILY.

Enamel techniques do not seem to have been transmitted to the East in ancient times, when they were first important in the West. The technique was introduced into China in the 14th century by Arabian craftsmen. There is said to have ·been a succession of enamelers from the Near East who set up shops to do cloisonné as they crossed Asia. Although examples of Chinese enamels exist from the Ming period, most of them date from the 18th and 19th centuries, with traditional bronze forms used as the bases of colorful and extremely well-executed cloisonné designs. Chinese painted enamels are a result of 17th- and 18th-century influences from Europe and were in the main a part of the export wares made in China for the European trade.

On the European scene changes of importance came in the 18th century with the introduction of the simpler painted enamel ground usually decorated with colors not fused to the surface. The technique was used for rococo objects made at centers that also produced porcelains. The English factories at Chelsea and Battersea were the most prominent. Their products are generally small bibelots in pastel colors with floral designs or scenes used as decoration. In Europe after 1840 a revival in enameling was initiated in the art-school movement of Gottfried Semper, promoted in Great Britain by Prince Albert, and later associated with the teachings of William Morris. Traditional designs and techniques in the academic tendency predominated, but subsequently experiments in both technique and design were introduced. This movement had its influence throughout western Europe and in North America.

In the 20th century there have been important new developments in the technique of enameling. Besides working in traditional methods, contemporary enamelers are experimenting with new ones for the large-scale architectural panels that are now in favor. At no time since the 18th century has enameling been practiced as extensively as in the 1950s and 1960s. The medium is ideal for flat compositions in the modern idiom.

BIBLIOGRAPHY. W. Burger, *Abendländische Schmelzarbeiten*, Berlin, 1930; K. Bates, *Enamelling: Principles and Practice*, Cleveland, 1951; Cooper Union for the Advancement of Science and Art, Museum for the Arts of Decoration, *Enamel: An Historic Survey to the Present Day*, New York, 1954; R. A. Higgins, *Greek and Roman Jewellery*, London, 1962.
MARVIN D. SCHWARTZ

ENCAUSTIC. A broad term (from the Greek *enkaustikos*, "burning in") applicable to ceramic enamels and tiles, but most often used to describe methods of painting in hot, pigmented wax. The Greco-Egyptian mummy portraits from Fayoum demonstrate the lively coloring and opportunity for sculptural modeling permitted by the wax. They also illustrate the excellent survival qualities conferred by heat applied during the painting process and immediately thereafter.

BIBLIOGRAPHY. F. Pratt and B. Fizel, *Encaustic Materials and Methods*, New York, 1949.

ENCEINTE. French term used by writers in the field of medieval military architecture to denote the space enclosed by the walls of a fortified area. In the description of a castle or fortress, the word can be used to include the keep, its courtyard, inner bailey, outer bailey, and any other structures surrounded and protected by an extensive wall. It can also be applied to a town surrounded and defended by fortified walls.

ENDELL, AUGUST. Self-taught German architect (1871–1925). Endell was born in Berlin. He was director of the Breslauer Kunstakademie from 1918 until his death. His most influential work was the Elvira Photographer's Studio (Elvira House) built in Munich (1897–98), an exuberant Art Nouveau design, bearing a fantastic dragonlike decoration on its façade.

ENDYMION. In Greek mythology a beautiful youth, a king of Elis; or in other versions, a Carian shepherd who was loved by Selene (the moon). Either by her devising or his own wish, he was lulled into everlasting sleep. Symbolizing death as an eternal sleep, he is often represented on Roman sarcophagus reliefs.

ENGEBRECHTSZ. (Engelbrechtsz.), CORNELIS. Netherlandish painter of history and portraits (b. Leyden, 1468; d. there, 1533). Nothing certain is known of his early life. It has been suggested that he had his initial training in Brussels either with Colijn de Coter or with one of his followers. Engebrechtsz. is first mentioned in 1499 as a member of the Leyden musketeers' guild, and he appears to have remained a member until 1522.

Nothing certain by Engebrechtsz. can be dated before 1508. This date has been suggested for a triptych, *Lamentation over the Body of Christ* (Leyden, State Museum "de Lakenhal"). His later works, after 1520, show certain affinities to the conservative mannerist trend usually associated with the Antwerp mannerist group. Engebrechtsz. was the teacher of his three sons, Pieter Cornelisz. (called

Cornelis Engebrechtsz., *Lamentation over the Body of Christ.* Central panel of the triptych. State Museum "de Lakenhal," Leyden.

Kunst), Cornelis Cornelisz., and Lucas Cornelisz. He may also have taught Lucas van Leyden and Aertgen Claesz. van Leyden.

BIBLIOGRAPHY. E. Pelinck, "Cornelis Engebrechtsz, de herkomst van zijn kunst," *Nederlandisch Kunsthistorisch Jaarboek*, II, 1948–49; Amsterdam, Rijksmuseum, *Middeleeuwse kunst der Noordelijke Nederlanden* (catalog), Amsterdam, 1958.

ENGLISH SCHOOL. Until the 18th century painting in England was dominated by foreigners. Holbein the Younger, for example, was the most sought-after painter in the 16th century. The native painters of this period, such as Nicholas Hilliard and Isaac Oliver, were chiefly miniatur-ists. In the 17th century Dutch and Flemish painters predominated in the market and at the royal court: Van Dyck worked in England from 1632 to 1640; Sir Peter Lely, a Dutchman, worked there in the 1640s; and a German painter, Sir Gottfried Kneller, was particularly successful as a court painter in the second half of the century.

In the 18th century an indigenous school of painting began to flourish with Hogarth and Hayman; it came to its golden age in the second half of the century with Reynolds and Gainsborough. This English school soon gained international recognition, drawing pupils from abroad, particularly from America (for example, John Singleton Copley and Benjamin West). *See* GAINSBOROUGH, THOMAS; HAYMAN, FRANCIS; HOGARTH, WILLIAM; REYNOLDS, SIR JOSHUA.

The 19th century saw a further development of the English school with Cozens, Turner, and Constable. Pre-Raphaelite influences, as well as French-inspired trends, dominated the English school during the second half of the 19th century. *See* CONSTABLE, JOHN; COZENS, ALEXANDER; PRE-RAPHAELITE MOVEMENT; TURNER, JOSEPH MALLORD WILLIAM.

BIBLIOGRAPHY. R. Redgrave, *A Century of British Painters*, rev. ed., London, 1947; E. K. Waterhouse, *Painting in Britain, 1530–1790*, Baltimore, 1953.

DONALD L. EHRESMANN

ENGOBE, *see* SLIP.

ENGRAVING. Intaglio (incised) print process; cutting lines into a metal plate by pushing a cutting tool across the surface. (The term is also used when the material incised is an end-grain block of wood.) The same term describes a print pulled from a copper plate or end-grain wood block. The engraving process results in a strong, clean line that, under magnification, shows pointed ends.

In line engraving a linear composition is drawn directly or traced on a copper plate, and cutting is begun. Engraving tools are called burins. They are further classified as standard gravers, tint tools, and scorpers. Each tool cuts a particular kind of line as it is pushed forward, and a ribbon of copper unfurls slowly in front of it. The traditional hallmark of the engraved line, the pointed end, derives from the very act of engraving, since the burin enters the material at a relatively small attack angle that is in-

Engraving. Example of a wood-block print.

creased as it goes along and then diminished to remove the sliver of copper from the line.

A proof may be struck off on an etching press, and corrections may be made with the scraper and burnisher. It is not unusual in modern engraving for many intaglio procedures to be used in one plate, for example, etching, engraving, softground etching, and aquatint. Printing proceeds as in etching.

See also ETCHING; WOOD ENGRAVING.

BIBLIOGRAPHY. S. W. Hayter, *New Ways of Gravure*, New York, 1949; J. Heller, *Printmaking Today*, New York, 1958.

JULES HELLER

ENKOMI. Important city of the 2d millennium B.C., capital of Alasia, the ancient Cyprus. It flourished between 1600 and 1200 B.C. On the eastern coast of Cyprus, Enkomi was a fortified city with a well-protected port. A center of metallurgical industries, especially bronze, it suffered from floods, earthquakes, and enemy invasions and disappeared about 1050 B.C.

Excavations have revealed walls, streets, buildings, workshops, bronze foundries and copper mines, a great Achaean palace, a rich necropolis, and a wealth of objects of Achaean, Mycenaean, Rhodian, Syro-Phoenician, Philistine, Egyptian, and other influences, evidence of Cyprus's far-flung trade with many lands and peoples.

Among the finds were painted pottery, faïence, bronze and iron tools and implements, statuettes and figurines, gold and silver vases, jewelry and diadems, cylinder seals, engraved ivory objects, engraved glass beads, and inscriptions in Cypro-Mycenaean characters.

BIBLIOGRAPHY. C. F. A. Schaeffer, *Enkomi-Alasia: Nouvelles missions en Chypre, 1946–1950* (publication of the Mission archéologique française and the Mission du Gouvernement de Chypre à Enkomi), Paris, 1952; H. Frankfort, *The Art and Architecture of the Ancient Orient*, Baltimore, 1954.

LUCILLE VASSARDAKI

ENNEASTYLE (Nonastyle). Denoting a temple front of nine columns, as in the Doric order Telesterion in Eleusis, a prostyle enneastyle example. With its colonnade encircling the cella, the so-called basilica in Paestum is peripteral enneastyle.

ENRIQUE. Spanish architect (d. 1277). Enrique is mentioned in documents of 1261 and 1277 (death notice) as master builder of Burgos Cathedral. He served in a similar capacity at León Cathedral. The design of the *chevet* (before 1243) and of the transept façades of Burgos (completed 1257) have been attributed to him in the past.

BIBLIOGRAPHY. V. Lampérez y Romea, *Historia de la arquitectura cristiana española en la edad média*, vol. 2, Madrid, 1909.

ENRIQUEZ, CARLOS. Cuban painter (1900–   ). Enríquez studied briefly in New York and Philadelphia (1924) and later in Europe. A romantic *Landscape with Wild Horses* (1941) is in the Museum of Modern Art, New York.

BIBLIOGRAPHY. L. Kirstein, *The Latin American Collection of the Museum of Modern Art*, New York, 1943.

ENRYAKUJI. Japanese Buddhist temple at Mt. Hiei, northeast of Kyoto. The monastery was started as the headquarters of the Tendai sect by the priest Saichō (known also as Dengyō Daishi) sometime between 782 and 805, and it gradually developed into a large monastery consist-

James Ensor, *Masks* (*Intrigue*), detail, 1890. Museum of Fine Arts, Antwerp. Masks are an important element in the artist's work.

ing of many buildings. The central building, the Komponchūdō, was erected at the beginning of the monastery's history as a small structure consisting of three separate building blocks; these were later combined to form one large unit. The present structure of the hall, which is the best example of a main hall in Tendai monasteries, is the reconstruction of 1640. Since then it has been repaired regularly every thirty or forty years. *See* TENDAI.

BIBLIOGRAPHY. R. T. Paine and A. Soper, *The Art and Architecture of Japan*, Baltimore, 1955.

ENSCHEDE: TWENTHE MUSEUM. Dutch museum founded in 1929. Its collections include prehistoric objects from the eastern Netherlands, works of medieval art, and paintings dating from the 14th to the 19th century.

ENSHU (Kobori Enshu). Japanese architect and garden designer (1579–1647). He was also a great tea master, and

taught the shogun the art of the tea ceremony while holding a high official position as a supervisor of the shogun's construction works. Many buildings and gardens are attributed to Enshu, but some were actually executed by his followers, such as Katagiri Sekishū, Kentei, and his brother Kobori Masaharu. The Bōsen in the Kohō-an and the Mitsu-an in the Ryūkō-in of the Daitokuji in Kyoto are among Enshu's works. He also designed gardens for the abbot's living quarters (*hōjō*) in the Nanzenji in Kyoto and for the Chokunyū-ken in the Kohō-an of the Daitokuji. *See* KOHO-AN GARDEN.

BIBLIOGRAPHY. J. B. Kirby, *From Castle to Teahouse: Japanese Architecture of the Momoyama Period*, Rutland, Vt., 1962.

ENSINGEN, ULRICH VON, *see* ULRICH VON ENSINGEN.

ENSOR, JAMES. Belgian painter and printmaker (b. Ostend, 1860; d. there, 1949). Ensor was an outstanding pre-

cursor of the German expressionists and a master of one of the unique styles of the postimpressionist era. His art was fully developed by about 1900, although he painted actively during the 20th century. Almost all his life was spent in Ostend, where his parents owned a curio shop. The souvenirs that he saw while he was a child, particularly grotesque masks and marionette figures, exerted a strong influence upon the imagery of his paintings and graphic works.

Ensor took drawing lessons from a local artist named Van Cuick and in 1877 attended the Brussels Academy of Fine Arts. He returned to Ostend in 1879. From the first, Ensor was a draftsman of remarkable talent. His early works are characterized by a personally assimilated influence of baroque art, and he later underwent the stimulus of Van Gogh. By 1880 Ensor's style had become individualized by its biting line and expressionistlike broken pigment. The avant-garde group known as The Twenty (Les Vingt), founded in 1883, quickly admitted Ensor, and he showed in their first exhibition in 1884. They were to expel him in 1889, however, because, despite their progressiveness, they considered his treatment of religious themes too blasphemous, as in his renowned *Entry of Christ into Brussels* (1888; Antwerp, Fine Arts Museum), in which Christ is a tiny figure all but lost in the milling, self-centered public that surrounds him.

Ensor became well known for his etchings, the first of which date from 1886, and he was recognized by most avant-garde painters throughout Europe by about 1896, when he was given a large one-man exhibit in Brussels. *La Plume* in 1899 devoted a special number to him, and in 1900 he was given a one-man show in Paris. In that year he was inspired by the African Negro figures and masks which he saw at the Royal Museum of Central Africa in Tervueren, near Brussels; their weirdness reinforced his early penchant for puppets and masks.

King Albert conferred a baronetcy upon Ensor in 1930, and the Galerie des Beaux-Arts in Paris honored him with a one-man show. The artist, however, made mistrustful by his earlier troubles, was to become a recluse whose bitterness sometimes touched profundity. As early as 1915 and 1921 he had already declared his own originality to be greater than that of the impressionists and postimpressionists and referred to his priority in the discovery of new treatment of light and liberation of the imagination.

Ensor was a brilliant printmaker, and he frequently worked over his etchings and engravings with pencil or color. *The Artist's Father Dead* (1887), *The Plague of Elephants* (1888), *Skaters* (1889), and an etching of 1889 after his 1888 canvas, the *Entry of Christ into Brussels*, are characteristic in their remarkable fluency of line and command of the medium. By 1905 he had ceased to make prints, but it is generally felt that his work in this field influenced many major 20th-century artists of expressionist and surrealist leanings, including Klee, Chagall, and Nolde.

Ensor's oil-painting style, like that of his graphics, was mature by the late 1880s. It changed little in fundamentals during the remainder of his long life. His use of twisted, deliberately groping line and his smeary, broken pigmentation declared a highly individualized expressionist attitude; and the disquieting, although sometimes humorous, im-

agery of his canvases clearly anticipated Dada and surrealist themes. Among the outstanding paintings are his early *Lamp Boy* (1880; Brussels, Fine Arts Museum), *Woman Eating Oysters* (1882; Antwerp, Fine Arts Museum), *Skeletons Warming Themselves by a Stove* (1889; Dallas, private collection), and *Masks* (*Intrigue*, 1890; Antwerp, Fine Arts Museum). Ensor also painted views of Ostend and still lifes, remarkable for the grisly textures and suggestions of double imagery which he gave to marine forms.

With his contemporary Edvard Munch, Ensor was an expressionist ahead of his time. Not the least important of his achievements, however, was his deliberately anti-aesthetic abuse of the painting's surface, a device that enhanced his ironic and at times consciously unlovely choice of themes. He was one of the very first artists to be attracted to primitive African art and was an outstanding precursor of early 20th-century art.

BIBLIOGRAPHY. A. Croquez, *L'Oeuvre gravé de James Ensor*, Paris, 1935; F. Fels, *James Ensor*, Geneva, 1947; L. Tannenbaum, *James Ensor*, New York, 1951; P. Haesaerts, *James Ensor*, New York, 1959.　　　　　JOHN C. GALLOWAY

ENTABLATURE. Upper portion of an order of architecture, supported by columns. Usually divided into three sections, the entablature consists of an architrave, the lowest part spanning the columns; a frieze, or middle section, often enriched with ornament and sculpture; and a cornice, or crowning part. In Asiatic Ionic architecture the frieze is frequently omitted. The Greek entablature is assumed to have originated from wood construction.

ENTASIS. Greek architectural term, meaning "a stretching." Entasis is the slight convex bulge in the shaft of

Entasis. Slight bulge in a column shaft.

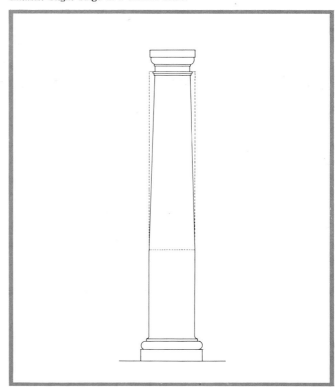

columns. This tapering, especially identified with Greek Doric columns, is commonly interpreted as a refinement to correct an optical illusion arising from parallel cylindrical columns.

ENTEMENA, VASE OF. Silver vase (Paris, Louvre) excavated at Lagash (Telloh). Approximately 14 inches high, it is made from a single piece of metal. It stands on a copper base. Around the body, a lion-headed eagle holding two animals in its claws is engraved four times. The animals are two lions, two stags, two lions, and two goats, in that order. The stags and goats are also held in the mouths of the lions. Above this design, over a chevron border, are crouching calves. On the neck is an inscription: "For Ningirsu, warrior of Enlil, Entemena, king of Lagash, for Ningirsu has made this vase of pure silver . . . at this time Dudu was priest of Ningirsu." Entemena ruled in the Early Dynastic III period (ca. 2450–2350 B.C.).

See also TELLOH.

BIBLIOGRAPHY. A Parrot, *Tello*, Paris, 1948.

ENTOMBMENT OF CHRIST. Scene following the Descent from the Cross, described in each of the four Gospels. It is represented in Byzantine art at an early date, then transmitted to the West, where it appears first in a manuscript of the Reichenau school. Initially, only Joseph and Nicodemus were present with the body of Christ before a rock-cut tomb, but in the 13th century other figures, including Mary and St. John, were added.

ENTRY INTO JERUSALEM. Principal introductory scene in the Passion cycle (Matt. 21:7). In art, Christ is represented mounted on an ass (sidesaddle in Byzantine art, astride in Early Christian) and riding from left to right toward the gates of Jerusalem. This scene is found in most large Passion cycles in Western art from the 11th to the 14th century.

BIBLIOGRAPHY. K. Künstle, *Ikonographie der christlichen Kunst*, vol. 1, Freiburg im Breisgau, 1926.

EOTTES, HANS, *see* EWORTH, HANS.

EPAZOJUCAN MONASTERY FRESCOES. Mexican murals, executed in 1556. The figures in the murals have an elongation somewhat reminiscent of Flemish painting. In spite of an appealing awkwardness, a plaintiveness close to Rogier van der Weyden can be detected in some of the participants in *The Road to Calvary*. Gillet found that the figures of the women and St. John in the *Pietà* resemble those of Gerard David. He has claimed that the mountains are derived from Bosch and Patinir. But the hypothesis of a Flemish source has yet to be substantiated.

BIBLIOGRAPHY. L. Gillet, "L'Art dans l'Amérique latine," in A. Michel, ed., *Histoire de l'art*, vol. 8, no. 3, Paris, 1929; G. Kubler, *Mexican Architecture of the Sixteenth Century*, vol. 2, New Haven, 1948.

EPHESUS. Ancient Greek colony in Ionia, in western Asia Minor, near Selçuk, Turkey, later the capital of the Roman province of Asia. Ephesus was one of the wealthiest cities of antiquity. Little remains of the famous Sanctuary of Artemis, the goddess of fertility; some of the massive sculptured column bases can be seen in the British Museum in London. Within the Hellenistic wall lie the impressive remains of the town, which had a regular plan and was crossed by a colonnaded main street. Of Roman date are the library, theater, and stadium. Two large Early Christian churches, badly damaged, have been preserved: St. Mary, where the Council of 434 was held; and St. John, which was sumptuously rebuilt under Justinian. Near the Church of St. John is the 14th-century Mosque of Isa Bey, which has stalactite decorations.

BIBLIOGRAPHY. *Forschungen in Ephesos*, 5 vols., Vienna, 1906–53; J. Keil, *Ephesos, ein Führer . . .*, 5th ed., Vienna, 1964.

EPICTETOS. Attic vase painter (fl. ca. 520–500 B.C.). He was an early practitioner of the red-figured style who specialized in the decoration of large cups. Several of the inner *tondi* on these cups are among the greatest examples of linear draftsmanship in all ancient art. His work was that of a conservative perfectionist rather than that of an experimenter.

BIBLIOGRAPHY. G. M. A. Richter, *Attic Red-Figured Vases, A Survey*, New Haven, 1958.

EPIDAURUS, THOLOS OF. The most beautiful circular building in Greece. Built between 360 and 320 B.C., it was designed by Polycleitus the Younger. The tholos measured 66 feet in diameter; it consisted of a peristyle of twenty-six Doric columns resting on a stylobate and of a circular cella, which had a zone of fourteen freestanding Corinthian columns carrying an entablature of cyma-profiled frieze, the earliest example of this type. The interior was lighted by two windows on either side of the doorway. The cella floor was paved with alternating black-and-white rhomboidal slabs. The metopes of the exterior colonnade were decorated with great rosettes carved in relief. The ceiling had marble coffered plaques decorated in the center with carved floral designs. A subterranean labyrinth, found below the floor, was perhaps used for the snake cult of Aesculapius. The tholos had a sloping roof crowned with a floral acroterion. Fragments of this beautiful structure are housed in the Archaeological Museum, Epidaurus.

BIBLIOGRAPHY. P. Kavvadias, *Die Tholos von Epidauros*, Berlin, 1909; W. B. Dinsmoor, *The Architecture of Ancient Greece*, 3d ed., London, 1950; A. W. Lawrence, *Greek Architecture*, Baltimore, 1957.

EPINAOS. Open vestibule at the rear of a Greek or Roman temple. *See also* POSTICUM.

EPISCENIUM. Upper story (Greek, *episkēnion*) of the structure containing the skene of the Greek theater. Usually behind the proscenium colonnade, it became a feature of the Hellenistic theater.

EPISTYLE. Greek name for architrave, from the Greek *epistylion*, meaning "upon column." *See also* ARCHITRAVE.

EPITAPH. Generally, any tomb marking with a funeral inscription. Specifically, an epitaph is a type of tomb marking that differs from the tomb monument in being a small rectangular relief showing the deceased adoring some religious personage, or scene, together with the inscription.

EPSTEIN, JACOB. British sculptor, illustrator, and watercolorist (b. New York City, 1880; d. England, 1959). His first art works were drawings made of people of the East

Side of New York City, many of whom were actors. These were used as illustrations for a book on the East Side by N. Hapgood. Epstein studied at the Art Students League, in New York City, under George Grey Barnard while working in a bronze foundry in 1901. He went to Paris and attended the Ecole des Beaux-Arts from 1902 to 1906, where he worked under Thomas. He also attended the Académie Julian and received occasional criticism from J. P. Laurens. In 1906 he went to England, subsequently became a British citizen, and spent almost all of his life thereafter in that country.

In 1907 Epstein received the first of several important and highly controversial commissions, the Strand Sculpture series symbolizing the stages of life. These works were later destroyed. By 1908 he had begun to make portraits, first using his wife as his subject. In 1911 he was awarded the commission for a tomb for Oscar Wilde, and his sculpture created a scandal. In the same year he also met Henri Gaudier. He returned to Paris in 1912, where he met Brancusi and Modigliani, who briefly influenced his work (*Mother and Child*). Epstein's production of this time reflected his interest in primitive sculpture (*O Cursed Be the Day I Was Born*, 1912). He went back to England in 1912, feeling that he could not work in Paris.

In 1913 he executed *Rock Drill* (a result of his brief ardor for machinery), using as a model a pneumatic drill and a visored robot. After this work Epstein quickly recognized that his strength lay in portraits and figure sculpture. In 1917 he began his first statue of Christ; its portraitlike naturalism horrified the public. His many sculptures on religious themes include his most powerful works, *Visitation* (1926; London, National Gallery), *Genesis* (1931; A. C. Bossom Collection), *Behold the Man* (1935), *Consummatum est* (1937), and *Madonna and Child* (1927; a cast of this is in the cloister of the Riverside Church, New York City). His direct carving in stone differed from his modeling in its blockishness, hard angles, and archaic form, as in *Night* (1930), *St. James Park Station* (1932), and *Sun God* (1932).

It was as a reader of human character in portraits that Epstein made his greatest contribution. His brilliant series of busts includes *Bernard van Dieren* (1915–27), *Dolores* (1921–23), *The Ninth Duke of Marlborough* (1923–25; Blenheim), *Joseph Conrad* (1924), *Paul Robeson* (1928), *Einstein* (1933; London, Tate), and *Haile Selassie* (1936). His loosely textured, rhythmically modeled forms are imbued with great emotional power and physical strength. Epstein surmounted unbelievable critical adversity and helped to raise British sculpture out of mediocrity.

BIBLIOGRAPHY. J. Epstein, *Let There Be Sculpture*, New York, 1940.

ALBERT ELSEN

EQUESTRIAN. Any representation of a person mounted on a horse; for example, the equestrian statue of Marcus Aurelius (Rome, Capitoline). Lysippus, who produced equestrian statues of Alexander and his generals, appears to have originated this form in sculpture.

BIBLIOGRAPHY. O. Grossmann, *Das Reiterbild in Malerei und Plastik*, Berlin, 1931.

EQUIPOISED SCULPTURE. In constructivist sculpture, the ideal of freeing the work from its earthbound context,

Jacob Epstein, *The Glory of Christ*. Private collection.

thereby creating a volume seemingly independent of the laws of gravity and different from our usual way of seeing things. Gabo particularly has made an effort to achieve this by suspending or revolving abstract constructions to display the self-sufficient operation of forces within the work.

ERASMUS OF GAETA, ST. (St. Elmo). Martyr (d. ca. 301). According to legend, he was arrested while bishop of Antioch by pagan persecutors under Diocletian, but was rescued and transported by an angel to Italy. Later, preaching in Italy, he was again miraculously saved, this time from lightning. Thus sailors, seeing the natural phenomenon of blue luminous flashes around the mastheads before and after storms, attributed them to him, calling them St. Elmo's fire, and invoked him to protect their ships in a storm. Artists gave him the windlass as an attribute, but the meaning was misunderstood and a new legend resulted. The saint came to be pictured reclining, with his abdomen opened, and his attribute became not a marine implement but an instrument of torture used by executioners to extract and wind up his intestines. After he was martyred in Formia, his relics were moved to Gaeta. His feast is June 2. *See also* SAINTS IN ART.

ERBSLOH, ADOLF. German painter and graphic artist (b. New York City, 1888; d. Irschenhausen, Germany, 1947). He studied in the academies of Karlsruhe and Munich. In 1909 he was a founding member of the Neue Künstlervereinigung, and from 1916 to 1920 he was a member of the Munich Neue Sezession. In his expressionist paintings of figures, landscapes, and flowers, Erbslöh combined expressive and emotional color with Jugendstil tendencies toward decorative effects.

ERECH, *see* WARKA.

ERECHTHEUM (Erechtheion), ATHENS. Ionic temple on the north side of the Acropolis in Athens, Greece. It was dedicated to Athena Polias, Cecrops, and Erechtheus. Construction began in 421 B.C., was interrupted during the Syracusan expedition, and was resumed in 409 B.C. The temple is built of Pentelic marble and is complicated in plan. It was constructed on two levels and had three porticoes of different designs. It consists of a main block built on stylobates with a prostyle hexastyle porch of six Ionic columns at the east end. A prostyle tetrastyle portico was placed at the west end of the north flank. The central doorway of the north porch offers the finest example of Greek design. On the south side is the Caryatid Porch, named after the six female statues that support the marble roof. The interior was divided by cross walls into four chambers dedicated to (1) Athena Polias and probably (2) the ancient Athenian king Buteo, (3) Hephaestus, and (4) Poseidon-Erechtheus. The frieze of the entablatures consisted of blocks of black Eleusinian marble, upon which figures in white marble were attached by clamps. Outside the west end are the grave of Cecrops, the snake-legged first king of Attica, and the Pandroseum, or sanctuary of Pandrosos, daughter of Cecrops and first priestess of Athena, where the olive tree given to Athens by Athena stands.

See also ELGIN MARBLES.

BIBLIOGRAPHY. W. J. Anderson, R. P. Spiers, and W. B. Dinsmoor, *The Architecture of Greece and Rome*, vol. 1: *The Architecture of Ancient Greece*, London, 1927; L. D. Caskey, H. N. Fowler, et al., *The Erechtheum*, 2 vols., Cambridge, Mass., 1927.

EVANTHIA SAPORITI

EREMITANI, CHURCH OF THE, PADUA. Italian church built for the Augustinians in the 13th century. It has been restored after its virtually complete destruction by bombing in 1944. Only fragments remain of the important frescoes depicting the legend of St. James, painted by Andrea Mantegna between 1448 and 1455, which were its chief glory. These paintings, with their bold perspec-

tives, solidly modeled figures, and archaeologically correct classical references, brought northern Italian painting up to the level of the most progressive achievements of the contemporary art of Florence.

BIBLIOGRAPHY. P. Verzone, *L'architettura religiosa dell'alto medio evo nell'Italia settentrionale*, Milan, 1942; A. Mantegna, *Mantegna . . .*, ed. E. Tietze-Conrat, London, 1955.

ERFURT: CATHEDRAL COMPLEX. The Cathedral of this chief city of Thuringia in central Germany was founded on a hill by St. Boniface in 752. The present building is largely late Gothic, incorporating some Romanesque remains. Inside are a 12th-century candlestick and a large Gothic altarpiece (Erfurt was a center of Gothic panel painting). There are also a number of original stained-glass windows. The adjacent Severikirche (13th-14th cent.) is a hall church with five aisles; within is a remarkable font of 1467.

BIBLIOGRAPHY. K. Mertens, *Der Dom zu Erfurt*, Berlin, 1955; K. Mertens, *Die St. Severikirche zu Erfurt*, Berlin, 1959.

ERGOTIMOS, *see* CLEITIUS AND ERGOTIMOS.

ERHART, GREGOR. German woodcarver (d. Augsburg? 1540). From 1494 he worked mainly in Augsburg, where he operated a large and influential workshop with Adolf Daucher. Erhart's *oeuvre*, defined mainly by stylistic comparison, shows a close affinity to the work of Multscher. The high altar of the church of Blaubeuren (1493–94) is Erhart's main work.

BIBLIOGRAPHY. G. Otto, *Gregor Erhart*, Berlin, 1943.

ERIDU (Abu Shahrein). Eridu, the present-day Abu Shahrein, in southern Iraq, is mentioned as the oldest city in the ancient Near East in the Babylonian myth of creation. The excavations were carried out by the Iraqi archaeological expedition under Lloyd and Safar (1946–49) at a temple of the Ubaid and Uruk periods (4100–3200 B.C.), probably dedicated to the water god Enki, and at a series of houses and a cemetery of the Ubaid period. The archaeological finds include material that is the earliest known in southern Mesopotamia. The temple shows a steady development through a number of stratified levels, and some of the plans show a definite relationship to contemporary temples at Tepe Gawra in northern Mesopotamia. A stratified sequence of Eridu, Hajji Muhammad, Early Ubaid, and Late Ubaid pottery was produced by excavations in the temple levels. There is disagreement among scholars about whether the first two types are of the Ubaid period or earlier. *See* TEPE GAWRA.

BIBLIOGRAPHY. S. Lloyd, "The Oldest City: A Pre-Sumerian Temple Discovered at Prehistoric Eridu," *Illustrated London News*, CCX, May 31, 1947; F. Safar, "Eridu, a Preliminary Communication on the First Season's Excavations, January–March, 1947" (introd. S. Lloyd), *Sumer*, III, July, 1947; S. Lloyd and F. Safar, "Eridu, a Preliminary Communication on the Second Season's Excavations, 1947–48," *Sumer*, IV, September, 1948; "The Oldest City of Sumeria: Establishing the Origins of Eridu," *Illustrated London News*, CCXIII, Sept. 11, 1948; F. Safar, "Eridu, a Preliminary Report on the Third Season's Excavations, 1948–49," *Sumer*, VI, 1950.

ERIXSON, SVEN ("X : et"). Swedish painter (1899–   ). He traveled in France, Spain, and Italy and in 1943 was appointed professor at the Royal Academy of Fine Arts in Stockholm. Erixson paints the life of the people in brightly colored sophisticated primitivism inspired by European expressionism, Swedish folk art, and medieval frescoes. His decorative work includes several murals (Stockholm Crematory), tapestry cartoons, and stage sets (*Aniara*).

BIBLIOGRAPHY. J. P. Hodin, *Sven Erixson*, Malmö, Sweden, 1947.

ERNI, HANS. Swiss painter and graphic artist (1909–   ). Erni first studied in his native Lucerne and then at the Académie Julian in Paris and at the Berlin Academy. In 1930 he discovered the art of Picasso and Braque. He became part of the Abstraction-Création group in Paris in 1933 and painted for a while in a purely abstract style. During the early 1940s his art went through a rather literal surrealist phase. Most of his work since has been concerned with humanistic themes—with the contemporary issues of scientific advance, man in a technological society, racial prejudice, the struggles of underdeveloped countries, and the prevalence of war.

In treating such themes Erni has developed a wide range of media (oils, mosaic, fresco, lithography, ceramics), styles, and subject matter. Many murals in Switzerland and elsewhere treat the human situation on a heroic scale with abiding optimism, as the *In Health There is Freedom* for the United Nations at the Brussels World's Fair (1958). The clinical realism with which figures and their surroundings are depicted follows in the tradition of Swiss 19th-century painting; it sometimes descends to sentimentality, especially in Erni's magazine illustrations and other commercial work. In many paintings the realistic tableau is overlaid with patterns of pure line that seem to suggest a more universal meaning in the realm of abstract or scientific thought, or in some cases in classical mythology. Erni's strongest works, however, are his simplest statements, such as the sketchy portrayal of the Sharpeville massacre in South Africa (1960; private collection).

BIBLIOGRAPHY. C. J. Burckhardt, *Hans Erni*, Zurich, 1964; C. Roy, *Hans Erni*, Lausanne, 1964.

DONALD GODDARD

ERNST, JIMMY. American painter (1920–   ). Ernst was born in Cologne, Germany. The son of the surrealist painter Max Ernst, he received brief training in Germany in typography and graphics before going to the United States in 1938. Ernst's earlier abstractions depict linear structures set in an uncertainly lit, pulsating, ambiguous space, for example, *A Time for Fear* (1949; New York, Museum of Modern Art) and *Personal History* (1949; New York, Whitney Museum). For a while he experimented with similar forms painted in various tones and textures of black, as in *Blue and Black* (1956; Chicago, Art Institute). The linear structures have more recently become an irregular network, punctuated at points by areas of glowing color and at times hinting at an architectural image. In 1959 Ernst completed a large interior mural for the Continental Bank Building in Lincoln, Nebr.

BIBLIOGRAPHY. A. C. Ritchie, *Abstract Painting and Sculpture in America*, New York, 1951; A. C. Ritchie, *The New Decade*, New York, 1955.

ERNST, MAX. German painter and sculptor (1891–   ). Born in Brühl, near Cologne, he studied philosophy at Bonn University; he was self-taught as a painter. He exhibited at the first Herbstsalon in Berlin in 1913, and in 1914 visited Paris, where he met Jean Arp. In 1919 Ernst and Baargeld, joined by Arp, established the Dada move-

ment in Cologne. Ernst was an early practitioner of collage and coeditor of Dada journals. In 1920 the police closed one of his special exhibitions. Ernst joined Tzara, Eluard, and others in Dadaist manifestations in the Tyrol. Again in Paris in 1922, he illustrated books for Eluard and was active in the development of *frottage* and automatic writing. *See* FROTTAGE.

Ernst joined the surrealists in 1924, exhibiting in their first major show at the Galerie Pierre, Paris, and in the same year created, with Joan Miró, the décor for *Romeo and Juliet*. A true innovator who demanded of himself new formal approaches for new ideas, Ernst grew tired of the orthodox, unimaginative style of the central group of surrealists and left the movement in 1938 (they were to disclaim him, in turn, in the 1950s). He lived in the United States from 1941 to 1949, when he returned to Paris. In 1950 he had an important one-man show at the Galerie Drouin, and in 1954 he received first prize at the Venice Biennale.

Ernst has always met the challenge of both techniques and fantasy of theme. With Schwitters, he was one of the most imaginative practitioners of collage, and he was possibly the first artist to use *frottage*, or rubbings over textured surfaces. Among Ernst's most characteristic paintings, some of them distinctly surrealist in content and others essentially abstract, are *The Elephant of the Celebes* (1921; London, Penrose Collection), *Men Will Make Nothing of It* (1923; Penrose Collection), *Vision Evoked by a Night View of Porte Saint-Denis* (1927; Brussels, private collection), *The Whole City* (1937; Paris, private collection), *A Little Calm* (1939; artist's collection), and *Mother and Children on the Terrestrial Globe* (1953; Mannheim, Municipal Art Gallery). Ernst was among the most inventive and prolific contributors to the development of both Dada and surrealism and is one of the most original members of those groups.

ERNST AS SCULPTOR

His first reliefs, which are related technically to the somewhat earlier cubist assemblages of Picasso, date from the 1916–19 period. His *Fruit of a Long Experience* (1919), a construction relief of painted wood and metal, is characteristic of this phase. It relates generally to Arp's painted fluid-form reliefs in wood being done more or less concurrently, but it is more complex and satirical in expression.

An untitled carved object in wood, complete with bells, irrelevant additions of other kinds, and an attached hatchet, was one of the sensational three-dimensional works exhibited by Ernst at the renowned Cologne Dadaist show of 1920. This composite sculpture bore a list of instructions as to how to respond to it, one possibility being to attack it with the hatchet. Ernst's sculptures of the middle 1920s, especially those after he joined the surrealists in 1924, consist largely of combinations of plaster with cork, wood, and canvas; most of them are also painted.

While the playful tone of Dada never completely left Ernst's sculpture, an increasing attention to formal completeness and actual sculptural volumes and line occurred after about 1932. His *Oedipus* (1934, plaster; cast in bronze in 1960) and *Lady Bird* (*Femme Oiseau*, 1935; Houston,

Max Ernst, *The Eye of Silence*. Detail. Washington University, St. Louis, Mo.

De Menil Collection) are examples of a serious plastic direction still bearing the wry stamp of Dadaist verbal satire. To this same phase belongs *Lunar Asparagus* (1935; New York, Museum of Modern Art).

Ernst worked frequently with sculpture during his sojourn in the United States between 1941 and 1949, his principal development being a continued and sensitive articulation of actual sculptural statement as distinguished from his earliest, verbally conditioned creations. While many American and European sculptors were exploiting the assemblage of "found objects" during the 1940s, Ernst conceived bronze figural pieces in which modeled forms resemble to some extent discarded materials. To this period belong *Moon Man* (New York, Slifka Collection), *The King Playing with the Queen* (New York, Museum of Modern Art), and *The Table Is Set* (Houston, De Menil Collection).

Ernst's sculpture has seen even more significant growth since his return to Europe in 1949. Disklike faces with radically simplified features, powerfully reduced, compressed volumes suggesting torsos, and schematically arcuated limbs project figural images in which formal, sculptural values clearly take precedence over any programmatic satire. *The Parisian Woman* (1950), *Are You Niniche?* (1956), *Daughter and Mother* and *Bosse-de-nage* (both 1959; New York, Galerie Chalette) are bronzes of a strength and directness that compare most favorably with the quality of Ernst's painting of the same period. Among his recent works are *A Chinaman Fargone* and *The Spirit of the Bastille* (both 1960).

BIBLIOGRAPHY. M. Ernst, *Oeuvres de 1919 à 1936, Cahiers d'Art*, Special Number, Paris, 1937; P. Eluard and M. Ernst, *Misfortunes of the Immortals*, New York, 1943; M. Ernst, *Beyond Painting, and Other Writings by the Artist and His Friends*, New York, 1948; J. Bousquet and M. Tapié, *Max Ernst*, Paris, 1950; W. Verkauf, ed., *Dada: Monograph of a Movement*, Teufen. 1957; P. Waldberg, *Max Ernst*, Paris, 1958; W. S. Lieberman, *Max Ernst*, New York, 1961; M. Ernst, *Max Ernst: Life and Work*, ed. J. Russell, New York, 1967.   JOHN C. GALLOWAY

EROS (Cupid). Greek god of love. Eros was considered to be the son of Aphrodite or perhaps to have sprung from Chaos. His name signified desire, and he was shown as a gracefully winged, handsome boy, equipped with arrows or a flaming torch.

As Cupid, the son of Venus and Mars, he occupied a minor place among the Roman gods. After the 4th century B.C. his representations became increasingly childlike and playful, resulting in the cupids and *amorini* of the Roman period. In this form cupids were represented in Pompeian wall painting as carrying on arts and crafts. Their popular charm was revived in Renaissance painting and sculpture. *See* AMORINO.

EROTES. Followers of the cult of Eros in ancient Greece. They were sometimes represented in reliefs carrying garlands in a procession. The term is also applied to small, putto-like figures.

ERRI, AGNOLO AND BARTOLOMMEO. Italian painters in Modena. Agnolo (fl. 1448–63) and Bartolommeo (fl. 1460–76) were brothers, members of a large family of artists. Their only extant work is the *Modena Altarpiece* (1462–66; Modena, Este Gallery), the most notable Modenese painting surviving from the period. It is an elabo-rate Gothic polyptych, much influenced by Zoppo in its tight intricacy. The predella shows narratives in a Renaissance space, which has led to the plausible attribution to the Erris of two sets of small panels of the lives of St. Vincent Ferrer (Vienna, Este Collection) and St. Dominic (in nine museums), thought by others to be by Domenico Morone.

BIBLIOGRAPHY. A. Venturi, *Studi dal Vero*, Milan, 1927; R. Pallucchini, *I dipinti della Galleria Estense di Modena*, Rome, 1945.

ERRICO, ANTONIO D', *see* TANZIO DA VARALLO.

ERTLE, SEBASTIAN. German sculptor (b. Uberlingen, ca. 1570; fl. to 1612). A student of Hans Morinck, Ertle participated in the decoration of the Magdeburg Cathedral (1595/97–1612). He ran a large workshop in Magdeburg, where he was the leading figure in the renewal of a sculptural tradition.

ES, JACOB FOSSENS VAN. Flemish painter of still life (d. Antwerp, 1666). He was active in Antwerp and became a free master there in 1617. His breakfast pieces are of simple composition, sometimes reminiscent of Pieter Claesz.; in later life, he tended toward the more decorative Jan Davidsz. de Heem conception. His palette stresses clear yellows and grays.

BIBLIOGRAPHY. F. J. van den Branden, *Geschiedenis der Antwerpsche Schilderschool*, Antwerp, 1883.

ESCALANTE, JUAN ANTONIO (Juan Antonio de Frias y Escalante). Spanish painter (b. Cordova, 1633; d. Madrid, 1670). He studied under Francisco Rizi de Guevara and was greatly influenced by the Venetian school, specifically through a knowledge of works by Titian, Tintoretto, and Veronese purchased by King Philip IV.

In his brief life Escalante far surpassed his teacher and developed a brilliant ease of execution in the baroque grand manner, which he personalized with a debonair and delicate use of the brush and an efflorescent palette. This is exemplified in the *Annunciation* (signed and dated 1663; New York, Hispanic Museum). In his most individualized works, such as the *Dream of St. Joseph* (ca. 1665; New York, Chrysler Collection), he expresses a young man's idealistic fancy; Escalante could project onto his canvas an airy, tender conviction. Under the direct influence of Rubens, he painted in a more robust rhythm (*The Conversion of St. Paul*, Madrid, Cerralbo Museum).

BIBLIOGRAPHY. E. Lafuente Ferrari, "Escalante en Navarra y otras notas sobre el pintor," *Príncipe de Viana*, II, September, 1941; E. Lafuente Ferrari, "Nuevas notas sobre Escalante," *Arte Español*, 1944; E. Lafuente Ferrari, *Breve historia de la pintura española*, 4th ed., Madrid, 1953.

ESCOMB, CHURCH OF. Remarkable English survival from the time of the Venerable Bede (d. 735). It must be seen against the background of the flowering of Christianity and art in Northumbria about the 7th century. The two main centers were Monkwearmouth and Jarrow. The former church was completed by 675. Its uncommonly tall proportions appear at Escomb, which has a long nave, a narrow square-ended chancel, and a dividing arch showing long and short work—a technique that can be seen on the angles of the church. There are some original windows, small with deep splays. There are inserted windows of the 13th century and of the 19th century. Masonry of the

Eskimo art. Doll with wooden body and carved ivory head, from Alaska. Museum of the American Indian, New York.

early church is said to have come from the Roman Vinovia.

BIBLIOGRAPHY. N. Pevsner, *The Buildings of England*, vol. 9, Harmondsworth, 1953.

ESCORIAL, *see* EL ESCORIAL.

ESCUTCHEON.

In general, any shieldlike form used for decoration, frequently bearing monograms, initials, or heraldic devices. In heraldry, it is the only surface upon which heraldic devices may be emblazoned.

BIBLIOGRAPHY. C. Boutell, *Heraldry*, rev. ed., New York, 1954.

ESELER, NICLAUS, THE ELDER.

German architect (fl. 1439–92). Eseler was the leading southern German master of the final and definitive development of the late Gothic hall church with ambulatory. His principal works are St. Michael in Schwäbisch Hall (1439–42), St. George in Nördlingen (until 1459), and St. George in Dinkelsbühl (1448–99). His son Niclaus Eseler the Younger (d. 1509) continued his father's projects.

ESHERICK, JOSEPH.

American architect (1911–). Born in San Francisco, Esherick has worked principally in California. Besides residences, he has built some large complexes, among them the Child Study Center of the University of California at Berkeley, where a rectangular administrative and testing wing containing observation galleries faces two complete nursery schools.

BIBLIOGRAPHY. J. Esherick, "Special School: Nursery for Teaching, Research, Testing," *Architectural Record*, CXXXIII, May, 1963.

ESHNUNNA, *see* TELL ASMAR.

ESKI DJUMA, *see* SAINT PARASKEVI CHURCH, SALONIKA.

ESKIMO ART.

The art of the Eskimo is a compact testimony to man's insistence on creating beauty, even in a rigorously unsympathetic environment. The scarcity of traditional materials and the cultural isolation of many localities resulted in the concinnity of the aesthetic and the utilitarian. The majority of Eskimo carvings in the round and engraved reliefs, the favorite artistic expressions of this arctic people, appear on weapons and utensils. In certain localities, however, elaborate masks and small sculptures were created for ceremonial use; some ancient nonrepresentational forms remain obscure in purpose.

The vast region occupied by scattered Eskimo villages is frequently treated by archaeologists as tripartite: the northwestern area, comprising parts of Siberia and northwestern Alaska; the southwestern area, which includes the insular Aleut culture and sections of peninsular Alaska; and the eastern zone, consisting of the Canadian Arctic, Labrador, part of Newfoundland, and Greenland. Throughout most of this expanse the Eskimo had access to the coast, and sea mammals provided not only much of his sustenance but clothing and bone or ivory for art work as well.

The Eskimo's housing reflects an ingenious solution to the demands of adequate shelter in a threatening climate. Circularly planned domical huts, popularly called igloos, were built in the most severe areas. They were made of snow-and-ice blocks and entered through a protective tunnel. In parts of Alaska, a rectangular plan with rounded corners was adopted. These huts were also of snow blocks, but they were partly constructed of natural stone and were insulated with a layer of earth. The oppressive arctic winds of the extreme north were effectively diverted by the domical, or domoidal, design.

The ancient societies of the northwest region included the Old Bering Sea, Okvik, Ipiutak, Punuk, Birnirk, and post-Punuk cultures. The Old Bering Sea culture has yielded puzzling winglike forms of nonrepresentational character, finely engraved with curvilinear and dot-and-circle motifs. Most northwestern sites have yielded weapons or implements with smallish ivory and bone carvings in the round or engraved reliefs of animal, human, and geometric themes. Some objects date from many centuries before the Christian era.

The southwestern region witnessed the Early, Middle, and Late Aleut cultures, the earlier phases of which produced small carvings, not unrelated to those of the northwestern Eskimo, and stone lamps. The wooden mask, which was to reach spectacular expression in the Late Aleut culture and to persist into recent times, first appeared during the Middle period. Modern spirit masks of the Kuskokwim River district of Alaska are astonishingly grotesque and asymmetrical of feature. During ritual dances they are enlivened by mobile appendages such as feathers and thin wooden slats.

The eastern area developed the Dorset, Thule, and Inugsuk cultures, beginning at about the time of Christ and continuing until about 1800. The Inugsuk culture reflects in its art what is probably the first significant contact between Europeans and American aborigines. Bone and wooden ornaments, including chessmen, are likenesses of medievally clothed Norsemen who settled in Greenland during the Middle Ages. The wooden mask, its features exaggerated and twisted and often comical in expression, is important in more recent eastern Eskimo art.

Eskimo art, though it varies considerably from west to east, is typically direct and economical in conceptualization and execution and compact and clear in statement. The Kuskokwim and related Aleut ceremonial masks, as well as Greenland mask forms, are exceptions to the general rule of simplification. Recently, small carvings in the round have been produced in various Eskimo areas, partly in response to commercial demands. In some the traditional vigor has been sacrificed to schematic streamlining.

See also BERING SEA CULTURE; IPIUTAK CULTURE; NORTH AMERICAN INDIAN ART (ESKIMO); PUNUK CULTURE.

BIBLIOGRAPHY. H. B. Collins, *Prehistoric Art of the Alaskan Eskimo*, Washington, 1929; H. Himmelheber, *Eskimokünstler*, Eisenach, 1953; K. J. Birket-Smith, *The Chugach Eskimo*, Copenhagen, 1953; H. Schaefer-Simmern, *Eskimo-Plastik aus Kanada*, Kassel, 1958.
JOHN C. GALLOWAY

ESPANOL, PEDRO, *see* BERRUGUETE, PEDRO.

ESPINOSA, JERONIMO JACINTO. Spanish history and portrait painter (b. Cocentaina, 1600; d. Valencia, 1680). Espinosa studied with his father, Jerónimo Rodríguez, with Nicolas Borrás, and then with Francisco Ribalta, whose leading disciple he became. Espinosa's very expressive, naturalistic altarpieces abound in the churches of Valencia. His masterpiece is *The Communion of Magdalen* (1665), in the Provincial Museum of Fine Arts, Valencia.

BIBLIOGRAPHY. J. Rico de Estasen, *El Padre Borrás y Jerónimo J. de Espinosa...*, Alicante, 1952.

ESQUILINE HILL, *see* ROME.

ESQUISSE. Any preparatory sketch or rough draft for an illustration, layout, or design. The term is most commonly used in reference to the minor arts.

ESQUIVEL, ANTONIO MARIA. Spanish painter (b. Seville, 1806; d. Madrid, 1857). Esquivel started his studies in Seville as an imitator of Murillo and continued them at the Academy of S. Fernando, Madrid, in 1831. After making a living from sales of genre scenes and Murillo copies, he became one of the leaders of the romantic movement in Spain. He is noted particularly for his portraits.

ESSELENS, JACOB. Dutch landscape painter (b. Amsterdam, 1626; d. there, 1687). Esselens is listed in contemporary documents as both painter and merchant. He appears to have traveled frequently to Italy, England, and Scotland, and he made many drawings on these trips. He painted in the manner of Frederick de Moucheron and Johannes Glauber. His coastal landscapes recall the works of Simon Jacobsz. de Vlieger. Esselens also painted some winter landscapes and a few portraits.

BIBLIOGRAPHY. S. J. Gudlaugsson, "Een figuurstudie van Jacob Esselens te Besançon," *Oud-Holland*, LXVI, 1951.

ESSEN: FOLKWANG MUSEUM. German collection especially noted for its 19th- and 20th-century art. Established in 1922 upon the merger of the Municipal Museum of Essen (founded in 1905) and the Folkwang Museum of Hagen (founded in 1902), it is now housed in a modern building (1956–60). The collection begins with romanticism and classicism, as represented by Carus, Hackert, Koch, Richter, and Schinkel, and includes later 19th-century painters such as Böcklin, Feuerbach, Klinger, Marées, Thoma, and Trübner. It excels in works by German expressionists such as Baumeister, Beckmann, Corinth, Max Ernst, Feininger, Heckel, Kirchner, Klee, Kokoschka, Marc, Modersohn-Becker, Nolde, Schlemmer, and Schmidt-Rottluff. Non-German artists represented are Cézanne, Corot, Daumier, Gauguin, Léger, Manet, Matisse, Renoir, Van Gogh, Munch, Picasso, and Mondrian. The collection also includes works from antiquity (Egypt, Greece, and Rome), 14th- to 18th-century sculptures, modern sculptures by Arp, Barlach, Lehmbruck, Rodin, and Moore, works of applied arts (14th–19th cent.), and some non-European ceramics.

BIBLIOGRAPHY. H. Jedding, *Keysers Führer durch Museen und Sammlungen*, Heidelberg, Munich, 1961.
LOTTE PULVERMACHER-EGERS

ESSEN: MINSTER. Unusual German church preserving some of the important parts constructed during the time of the abbesses Matilda (971–1011) and Theophano (1039–58). The beautifully disposed west façade, with a large central tower flanked by two small stair towers, is preceded by a forecourt. The extraordinary western choir is a copy of three sides of the interior of Charlemagne's Palatine Chapel at Aachen. The early church, basilican in form with double transepts and choirs, was turned into a rib-vaulted hall church in a rebuilding that began about 1275. A 10th-century crypt at the east end, extended beyond the apse in the mid-11th century for use as the funerary chapel of Theophano, still exists.

No less remarkable than the building itself is its treasury, which contains many precious objects, including a seated *Virgin and Child* (973–82) in lindenwood covered with sheets of gold; a processional cross of the abbess Matilda in gold and gilded copper sheets with jewels and enamels over a wooden core; and a cover of the Gospel Book of the abbess Theophano with gold repoussé plaques and jewels framing an Ottonian ivory.

BIBLIOGRAPHY. K. Wilhelm-Kästner, *Das Münster in Essen*, Essen, 1929; W. Zimmermann, *Das Münster zu Essen*, Essen, 1956; L. Grodecki, *L'Architecture ottonienne*, Paris, 1958; H. Jantzen, *Ottonische Kunst*, rev. ed., Hamburg, 1959.
EDWARD P. LAWSON

ESSLINGEN, DOMINICAN CHURCH OF. South German Romanesque church. It is one of a group of churches of the mendicant orders that were somewhat *retardataire* stylistically. A three-aisled, basilican church with a single east apse, it originally had a flat wooden roof but was vaulted in 1271. The church has a basically Romanesque structural system, that is, a nave separated from the aisles by a simple colonnade, no gallery, and simply articulated walls. There is a ratio of nave bay to aisle bay of 1:1. Inasmuch as the building was late, the arches and window openings were pointed in the Gothic manner. The exterior is simple and, as with other churches of the mendicant orders of the time, is devoid of towers. The interesting architectural feature of this church is the manner in which the choir is walled off from the side aisles and appears to be an extension of the sanctuary into the nave.

BIBLIOGRAPHY. G. G. Dehio and G. von Bezold, *Die kirchliche Baukunst des Abendlandes...*, 7 vols., Stuttgart, 1887–1901.

Villa d'Este, Tivoli, the Organ Fountain.

ESTE, VILLA D', TIVOLI. Private residence built for the cardinal of Ferrara, Ippolito II d'Este, who was made governor of Tivoli in 1550. The principal designer was Pirro Ligorio, antiquarian, architect, and garden planner. The old monastic property was converted into an elegant villa with an important collection of classical sculpture, largely during the 1560s. The extraordinary fountains and reflecting pools are fed by large conduits from Monte Sant'Angelo and the Cascade of Tivoli. Modifications and reworkings continued to the 19th century, with an important change in the character of the gardens resulting from the growth of vegetation. The exterior of the residence is unfinished; interior frescoes were executed under the direction of Muziano, Zuccari, Agresti, and Nebbia.

BIBLIOGRAPHY. D. Coffin, *The Villa d'Este at Tivoli*, Princeton, 1960.

ESTERHAZY CASTLE, KISMARTON. Castle built for the Esterházy family in Kismarton, Hungary (now Eisenstadt, Austria). The medieval structure was rebuilt in baroque style for Prince Pál Esterházy, palatine of Hungary, by Carlo Martino Carlone in 1663–72. Its façade is faced with giant Tuscan pilasters; the side toward the courtyard is decorated with stucco. The castle was enlarged under the direction of the Viennese architect Karl Ritter von Moreau in 1801–05. Here and at the Esterházy Castle at Fertöd in Hungary (begun in 1720 by Erhard Martinelli for Prince Miklós József Esterházy and completed in 1763) much of the music of Haydn, who was the conductor of the Esterházy family orchestra from 1761 to 1790, was first performed.

BIBLIOGRAPHY. A. Hekler, *Ungarische Kunstgeschichte*, Berlin, 1937; E. Hempel, *Baroque Art and Architecture in Central Europe*, Baltimore, 1965.

ESTERRI D'ANEU: SANTA MARIA. Three-aisled, groin-vaulted basilica (now in ruins) of the 11th century in Lérida province, Spain. The fragmentary fresco from the semidome of the central apse (Barcelona, Museum of Catalan Art), by the Master of Pedret (fl. ca. 1130), represents the Virgin and Child enthroned, adored by the three Magi and flanked by the archangels Michael and Gabriel, who hold scrolls as they present the prayers of the faithful. (The same subject was depicted by the Master of Pedret in the apsidal fresco from S. Juan de Tredós, in The Cloisters, New York.) Below, Elijah and Isaiah kneel before the four fiery wheels and two standing seraphim, who place hot coals in the mouths of the prophets. Striking resemblances to the apsidal frescoes of S. Vincenzo at Galliano in Lombardy lead to the conclusion that the Spanish fresco was derived from such a north Italian source, which in turn derived from Byzantine art. The freshness of the brushwork and the originality of the iconography place this fresco high on the list of monumental 12th-century paintings.

See also PEDRET: SAN QUIRCE.

BIBLIOGRAPHY. C. L. Kuhn, *Romanesque Mural Painting of Catalonia*, Cambridge, Mass., 1930; C. R. Post, *A History of Spanish Painting*, vol. 1, Cambridge, Mass., 1930; *Ars Hispaniae*, vol. 6: *Pintura e imaginería románicas*, Madrid, 1950.

EDWARD P. LAWSON

ESTEVE, AGUSTIN. Spanish painter (b. Valencia, 1753; d. Madrid, after 1809). He was Pintor de Cámara in Madrid and studied at the Academy of S. Fernando there. There are portraits by him in public and private collections in Spain, as well as drawings for portrait commissions.

BIBLIOGRAPHY. A. L. Mayer, *La pintura española*, 2d ed., Barcelona, 1929.

ESTEVE, MAURICE. French painter (1904–   ). Born in Culan, Estève studied in Paris at the informal academies. His early paintings were influenced by Cézanne and cubism. His recent works are abstractions with broad interlocked planes of bright, subtly worked color.

BIBLIOGRAPHY. P. Francastel, *Estève*, Paris, 1956.

ESTEVE Y VILELA, RAFAEL. Spanish engraver (b. Valencia, 1772; d. there, 1847). He began his studies at the Valencia Academy in 1785; after 1802 the king of Spain attached him to the royal house. Esteve's considerable fame was based upon etched portraits of the royal family and monumental etchings after Italian baroque painters.

ESTHETICS, *see* AESTHETICS.

ESTRADA, JOSE MARIA. Mexican portrait painter (fl. mid-19th cent.). Estrada was a distinguished provincial painter of a group of quietly dignified portraits of men and women of his native Jalisco. His works are stylistically related to those of the New England limners of the mid-18th century. Estrada's clarity, rectitude of lineament, and gracefully elegant attitude toward his sitters resulted in images of a genteel, regional sobriety that are memorable in a period of empty academism.

BIBLIOGRAPHY. J. Fernández, *Arte mexicano de sus orígenes a nuestros días*, 2d ed., Mexico City, 1961.

ETAMPES, NOTRE-DAME-DU-FORT. French Gothic church dating from after 1125, with later alterations. Its irregular plan is a result of its location within a royal palace complex. Of special interest are the Gothic jamb statues of the south portal (ca. 1150), which are related to the west façade figures of Chartres and St-Denis.

BIBLIOGRAPHY. W. Stoddard, *The West Portals of Saint-Denis and Chartres*, Cambridge, Mass., 1952.

ETCHING. One of the major intaglio (incised) graphic arts processes used in the reproduction of black-and-white designs. The design is bitten into a metal plate by means of acid. Etching allows a more freely drawn line than does engraving. Under magnification the etched line shows nearly square ends; the engraved line has pointed ends.

First, an acid-proof ground must be laid on a metal plate, preferably standard-gauge copper. The ground is a mixture containing asphaltum. The etcher has the choice of working directly on the grounded plate with an etching needle or of tracing his drawing on the plate before etching. The etching needle need not be sharp; it must merely penetrate the ground to reveal the copper.

The plate is then immersed in acid, which wears away the metal in the places where the ground is scratched away. After the lightest areas have been bitten they are stopped out with an acid resist, and the plate is placed in the bath again and again to obtain the darker lines and values.

Etching ink is rolled or dabbed all over the surface, and the plate is put through the etching press. After studying the proof, the artist may make alterations by laying other grounds, scraping, or burnishing. A plate may be reworked many times to achieve what, in the final print, appears to be spontaneity or freshness of approach.

BIBLIOGRAPHY. London, British Museum, *A Guide to the Processes and Schools of Engraving*, rev. ed., London, 1933; J. Heller, *Printmaking Today*, New York, 1958.

JULES HELLER

ETCHMIADZIN, see ECHMIADZIN.

ETERNAL CITY, THE. Oil painting by Blume, in the Museum of Modern Art, New York. See BLUME, PETER.

ETHOS. Greek word, roughly translatable as "character," especially the quality of moral elevation and nobility of character that was attributed by critics in antiquity to the paintings of Polygnotos. He achieved it partly through the formal beauty of his paintings and partly through his preference for calm, meditative scenes—often the prelude to or aftermath of some great event. See POLYGNOTOS.

ETIMASIA. In Byzantine art, a peculiar type of Last Judgment scene in which an empty throne replaces Christ as Judge. The back of the throne bears a cross, and on its seat are an open evangeliar and a purple mantle. It is empty to symbolize the invisible power of Christ.

BIBLIOGRAPHY. F. van der Meer, *Maiestas Domini: Théophanies de l'Apocalypse dans l'art chrétien*, Rome, 1938.

ET IN ARCADIA EGO . . ., see SHEPHERDS IN ARCADIA.

ETOWAH MOUNDS. Prehistoric earthworks in Cartersville, Ga. A number of mounds, which were evidently crowned by temples or residences, were excavated by Moorehead in the 1920s in the Etowah River area in Georgia. Carvings in both stone and shell taken from the Etowah area are represented in the Phillips Academy collection in Andover, Mass.

An imaginative, assured primitive style is present in these works. Especially imposing is a seated stone figure possibly representing a chief. More than 2 feet high, it possesses the power of mass common to pre-European stone art throughout North America, although certain archaeologists relate Etowah art to that of contemporaneous Mexico. A generally similar style may be seen in mound art taken from other Georgia sites and from Tennessee, Oklahoma, and Alabama.

See also MOUND BUILDERS; NORTH AMERICAN INDIAN ART (EASTERN UNITED STATES AND CANADA).

BIBLIOGRAPHY. W. K. Moorehead et al., *Etowah Papers*, New Haven, 1932; A. D. Krieger, "An Inquiry into Supposed Mexican Influence on a Prehistoric 'Cult' in the Southern United States," *American Anthropologist*, XLVII, October–December, 1945.

ETRURIA, *see* ETRUSCAN ART.

ETRUSCAN ART. The Etruscans inhabited the Italic peninsula in the early part of the 7th century B.C. They occupied an area called Etruria, which stretched from the Ligurian Alps and lower Po Valley down to the mouth of the Tiber on the Tyrrhenian Sea. They were called Etruscans by the Romans, Tyrrhenians by the Greeks, and Rasenna by themselves. Ancient writers centralized the Etruscan nation in twelve cities. The south of Etruria developed earlier than the north and comprised great ancient cities located near the sea: Veii, Caere (Cerveteri), Tarquinia (Corneto), and Vulci. These cities have well-preserved ruins. The cities of inland northern Etruria were Clusium (Chiusi), Cortona, Perusia (Perugia), Arretium (Arezzo), Faesulae (Fiesole), and Volaterrae (Volterra). Their development was rather *retardataire*. Two more cities, Vetulonia and Populonium (Populonia), were situated on the Tyrrhenian shore. The climax of the Etruscan power was reached in the 7th and 6th centuries B.C.; during that period Etruria dominated almost the whole of Italy, from the Po Valley to Campania. Etruria lost its independence to Rome in 241 B.C., and its history came to an end a short time before the Christian era. See CAERE; TARQUINIA; VEII.

The enigma of the origin of the Etruscans remains unsolved, but various theories have been proposed. Herodotus (*Histories*, I, 94) assigned to them an Eastern origin in the belief that the Etruscans, led by Tyrrhenus, came from Lydia (Asia Minor). Dionysius of Halicarnassus, a Greek historian of the 1st century B.C., maintained that the Etruscans were autochthonous people. In modern times scholars have followed one or the other of these theories, but a third was added in the 19th century, assigning to the Etruscans a northern origin, the Alps. The best-known and most frequently accepted theory is the one supporting the Eastern origin.

The Etruscan language still has not been deciphered. It does not conform to the great family of Indo-European languages, but the Etruscan alphabet does bear analogies to the Greek alphabet. It is possible that the Etruscans borrowed the Greek alphabet when they were still in their native land in Anatolia. Also, a definite relationship has been established between the Etruscan language and the

Etruscan art, sculpture. Deceased couple on a terra-cotta sarcophagus from Caere, ca. 510 B.C. National Etruscan Museum, Villa Giulia, Rome.

language that was spoken in ancient times on the island of Lemnos. An inscription found on Lemnos from 600 B.C. bears a resemblance to the Etruscan alphabet. The Etruscan language, therefore, can be read, but its meaning still remains unknown. It was spoken in Tuscany until the beginning of the Christian era. About 10,000 inscriptions discovered during excavations were engraved or painted on mirrors, cistae, sculpture, and paintings. A glossary of about thirty words with their meanings has been formulated.

Etruscan art received its first impetus from the indigenous culture of Tuscany, known as Villanovan, which had existed there since 1000 B.C. It was also influenced by Eastern art, and after the end of the 7th century B.C. by Greek art. Certain scholars consider Etruscan art a mere reflection of Greek art and find it completely lacking in originality. An opposing view claims that Etruscan art has its own unique characteristics of a particularly local flavor. Probably the truth lies in between. In spite of outside influences, Etruscan art developed its own personality and unique character.

From the 7th century on, Etruria established its own artistic productivity. There is no consistent development in Etruscan art. Periods of stagnation and setbacks were followed by startling innovations. Interest in Etruscan art was aroused in the 17th century when the first tombs were discovered at Tarquinia. The earliest excavations began in 1728 on the site of Volterra. In the 18th century such renowned Etruscan cities as Caere, Vulci, Chiusi, Orvieto, and Tarquinia were brought to light.

Architecture. The Etruscans were great architects, and their architecture was very influential on Roman architecture. They adhered to a strictly geometric pattern for the layout of their towns. Their cities were built on hills and were fortified by strong and massive surrounding walls that were formed of large blocks of local stone, generally volcanic tufa, and were laid in a regular pattern. The arch, an Etruscan invention that influenced Roman architecture, was used to build city gates, such as the Porta dell'Arco at Volterra (the most ancient of all surviving Etruscan gateways), Porta Marzia and Porta Augusta in Perugia (somewhat later), which are rich in architectural details, Porta Sanguinaria at Ferentinum, and Porta Saracinesca at Signia. *See also* PORTA DEL BOVE, FALERII.

The Etruscan temple stood on a podium and consisted of a portico in the front, which was supported by two rows of columns, and of three contiguous and parallel rooms in which the statues of the gods were placed. The foundations and podiums of the temples were made of stone; wood or brick was used for the superstructure, and therefore few remains of Etruscan temples have survived. The temples were decorated with painted terra-cotta antefixes and figural friezes that encircled the upper part of the building. Excavations of Etruscan cities have uncovered very few private dwellings.

The only Etruscan city that has been systematically excavated is Marzabotto (near Bologna), which was founded about the end of the 6th century B.C. Marzabotto was laid out on a regular town plan. It was divided into two parts by a main street that ran straight from north to south and was intersected by three streets running from east to west. The town had regular blocks of houses. The houses consisted of an atrium with an impluvium in the center to receive rain water and living quarters arranged around the atrium. This type of house served as the model for the Roman house. The better Etruscan houses had loggias and, at times, pillared halls. A number of funerary urns in the shape of houses show a variety of forms of Etruscan houses.

The tombs reproduced the homes of the living. As a rule, they were situated outside the walls of the city. The early tombs were great mounds (tumuli) of earth and stone. The burial chamber was built inside the tumulus and was surmounted by a vault or a dome formed by the superimposition of stone blocks that slightly overlapped one another. From the 7th century on, couches were placed all around the room and the dead were laid on them. Later, the burial rooms increased in number, thus giving the impression of a complete house, in which life could continue after death. The Etruscans were also concerned with building well-constructed sewers, aqueducts, forts, and bridges, as were the Romans later. *See also* NORCHIA: ROCK-CUT TOMBS.

Sculpture. The Etruscans worked primarily in clay and bronze, rarely in stone. There is very little marble sculpture in Etruria. Among the finest achievements of Etruscan metalwork is the almost intact bronze chariot from Monteleone near Spoleto (mid-6th cent. B.C.; New York, Metropolitan Museum). The front of the chariot represents Thetis giving Achilles his weapons. One side panel shows a combat scene and the other side panel shows a man in a chariot drawn by two winged horses. One of the best-known Etruscan bronzes is the chimera from Arezzo (5th cent. B.C.; Florence, Archaeological Museum). Another important bronze is the Capitoline she-wolf (end of 6th cent. B.C.; Rome, Capitoline Museums).

In portraiture the aim of the Etruscan artist was to perpetuate after death the image of a living person. The figure of the deceased, usually in a half-reclining position, was modeled on the lid of the funerary urn or sarcophagus. The faces of the two figures (husband and wife) on the terra-cotta sarcophagus from Caere (ca. 510 B.C.; Rome, National Etruscan Museum) have been smoothed out to attain a certain degree of idealization. In contrast, the faces of the elderly married couple on the lid of a terra-cotta urn from Volterra (Volterra, Guarnacci Museum) present in stark realism all the signs of old age.

Etruscan art reached its climax in the 6th century B.C. The Etruscan sculptor used the traditions of Greek archaic art to produce many original works. This is clear in the life-size terra-cotta statues that decorated the roof of the Temple of Apollo at Veii and that probably came from the workshop of the artist Vulca (end of 6th cent. B.C.). The most famous sculpture from this temple is the statue of Apollo (National Etruscan Museum). Although it was modeled after the Greek kouroi statues, it shows a departure from them. Its Etruscan characteristics are apparent in the slight inclination of the figure forward, the enigmatic expression of the face, the depiction of inner tension, and the deliberate stylization of the folds of the garment clinging tightly to the body.

During the 5th century the Etruscan artists resisted the influence of the forms of Greek classical art and their sculpture is *retardataire*. They continued to work in clay. The terra-cotta head from Veii, called the Malavolta head (2d half of 5th cent. B.C.; National Etruscan Museum), displays a fine sensitivity. Another beautiful work is a pair of painted terra-cotta winged horses (originally harnessed to a chariot, which is missing). This group (4th–3d cent. B.C.; Tarquinia, National Museum) was found at Tarquinia and was probably from the Ara della Regina Temple.

Hellenistic art, because of its dramatic and picturesque context, appealed to the Etruscans, who then created works of great beauty. An example is the figure of a young god, reflecting portraits of Alexander the Great, which had adorned the "Scasato" Temple at Falerii (3d–2d cent. B.C.; National Etruscan Museum). These works, however, when compared with Greek prototypes, show technical inferiorities. Among the finest examples of Etruscan portraiture from the Hellenistic period are the bronze portrait head of a young boy (3d cent. B.C.; Florence, Archaeological Museum) and the bronze head known as the Elder Brutus (3d–2d cent. B.C.; Rome, Capitoline Museums); both works reveal the extraordinary likeness of a given person. The purely Etruscan character can be seen at its best in the sarcophagi and funerary urns decorated with figural representations in high relief. A good example is the small urn from Volterra (1st half of 2d cent. B.C.; Volterra, Guarnacci Museum).

Painting. The greatest achievement of Etruscan art lies in the realm of painting. The Etruscans decorated the walls of their tombs with frescoes. There are over sixty painted tombs at Tarquinia, twenty at Chiusi, and many at Caere, Veii, Orvieto, and Vulci. The oldest painted tombs were found at Caere; they were decorated with Orientalizing motifs. In its early painted tombs of about 530 B.C., Tarquinia established the prototype for all Etruscan wall paintings in tombs. These tombs reveal a distinctive local character in their execution. Since Greek original paintings do not exist, these Etruscan works are extremely important for the study of archaic painting. The Etruscan artists painted on a fresh *enduit* that covered the surface of the rocky wall of the burial chamber. The colors employed were simple at first; later, polychromy was used with bright tones. The choice of subjects was varied, consisting of mythological and religious themes and scenes of daily life. In the wall paintings of the 6th century the style is schematic and illustrates the stylization and naïveté of archaic art. Among the earliest wall paintings are four terra-cotta slabs from Caere (ca. 550 B.C.; London, British Museum; Paris, Louvre) with mythological themes. The figures are stocky and of heavy proportions, drawn with firm outlines; color has been carefully applied.

Among the most important painted tombs found at Tarquinia are the Tomb of the Bulls (530–520 B.C.), the oldest tomb at Tarquinia, decorated with scenes representing the story of Achilles and Troilos; the Tomb of the Augurs (520–510 B.C.), with mourning scenes and athletic contests; the Tomb of Hunting and Fishing (510–500 B.C.), with one of the largest landscape scenes preserved in ancient painting; and the Tomb of the Triclinium (480–470 B.C.), one of the finest tombs of the first half of the 5th century, with representations of dancers and musicians. A number of painted tombs from the 4th century B.C. offer a good example of the continuity of the old traditions of painting that was further developed by the use of chiaroscuro, a technique the Etruscans borrowed from the Greeks, which enabled them to shade their colors. The most important of the later tombs is the recently discovered Tomb of the Ogre in Tarquinia, dating from the 2d century B.C., with representations of the underworld. The head of Hades in this tomb is the culmination of the art of Etruscan wall

Etruscan art. Fresco with dancers, Tomb of the Lionesses, Tarquinia.

painting in the late period. Etruscan painting, as distinguished from Greek, is notably morbid in expression.

Minor arts. From the beginning the Etruscans made jewelry. They worked in ivory and gold; the gold jewelry was decorated with filigree and granulation. They also excelled in the technique of metal engraving; mirrors, cistae, and other metal objects, the majority found in the tombs, were richly engraved. *See* JEWELRY, HISTORY OF.

BIBLIOGRAPHY. M. Pallottino, *Etruscan Painting*, Geneva, 1952; S. von Cles-Reden, *The Buried People*, London, 1955; M. Pallottino, *The Etruscans*, Baltimore, 1955; R. Bloch, *The Etruscans*, New York, 1958; L. Banti, *Die Welt der Etrusker*, Stuttgart, 1960.

EVANTHIA SAPORITI

ETRUSCAN MUSEUM, *see* ROME: MUSEUMS (NATIONAL ETRUSCAN MUSEUM OF THE VILLA GIULIA; VATICAN MUSEUMS: MUSEO GREGORIANO ETRUSCO).

ETTY, WILLIAM. English painter (b. York, 1787; d. London, 1849). Early in his career he studied with Lawrence. Though Etty spoke most reverently of Venetian art, his large canvases, for example, *The Combat* (1825; London, National Gallery), recall the grand manner of Bologna or Rome. Between 1825 and 1830 he completed a trilogy of great canvases of *Judith* and *Benaiah Slaying the Two Lionlike Men of Moab*. English patrons were awed and even repelled by these bombastic machines, which were purchased in 1831 by the Royal Scottish Academy, Edinburgh. His glowing colors occasionally suggest Rubens. Some of Etty's most successful pieces were studies of nudes made during his attendance at the Royal Academy.

BIBLIOGRAPHY. T. S. R. Boase, *English Art, 1800–1870*, Oxford, 1959.

EU: SAINT-LAURENT D'. Gothic collegiate church in Normandy, begun with the nave in 1186, but altered before its completion, about 1225. The *chevet*, burned in 1426, was rebuilt between 1455 and 1584 and offers one of the most magnificent examples of the Flamboyant style of late Gothic architecture in Normandy.

BIBLIOGRAPHY. A. Legris, *L'Eglise d'Eu et la Chapelle du Collège*, Paris, 1913.

EUCHARIST. Central act of Christian worship, embodied in the Mass of the Roman Catholic Church and in the Holy Communion of Protestant churches. It is the sacramental commemoration of the Last Supper, at which Christ broke bread to symbolize His body broken for mankind and offered wine to symbolize the salvation through the shedding of His blood. The most important Old Testament Eucharist prototypes are the meeting of Melchizedek and Abraham and the Passover service.

EUDES DE MONTEREAU, *see* MONTREUIL, EUDES DE.

EUHEMERISM. Theory propounded about 300 B.C. by the Greek writer Euhemerus that the gods were originally noble men, who after their death were worshiped as divinities by their grateful subjects. The theory was influential in the art of late antiquity and the Renaissance, when pictorial cycles of great inventors and benefactors, including the pagan gods, were developed.

BIBLIOGRAPHY. J. Seznec, *The Survival of the Pagan Gods*, New York, 1953.

EUPHRANOR. Greek sculptor, painter, and art theoretician (fl. ca. mid-4th cent. B.C.). Ancient writers such as

Euphronios, Heracles wrestling with Antaeus, detail of a krater from Caere. Louvre, Paris.

Pliny, Vitruvius, and Pausanias speak of him as one of the outstanding artists of his century, but except for a part of his *Apollo Patroos*, found in the Athenian Agora, his works have not survived.

EUPHRONIOS. Attic vase painter (fl. ca. 510–500 B.C.). He was one of the most powerful painters of the early red-figured style. His most famous and exemplary work, a krater in the Louvre, Paris, showing Heracles wrestling with Antaeus, reveals a striving for monumental effect and psychological expressiveness, as well as extensive realistic interest in the delineation of anatomy.

BIBLIOGRAPHY. G. M. A. Richter, *Attic Red-Figured Vases, A Survey*, New Haven, 1958.

EUROPA. In Greek mythology the daughter of King Agenor of Sidon. While playing with her friends on the shore near Tyre, she was seen by Zeus, who fell in love with her. He descended from the skies as a white bull with golden horns and carried Europa off through the sea to the island of Crete. There, Europa bore Zeus three sons—Minos, Rhadamanthus, and Sarpedon—who later became heirs to the throne of Crete by Europa's marriage to Asterius.

BIBLIOGRAPHY. E. Hamilton, *Mythology*, Boston, 1942.

EURYDICE, *see* ORPHEUS.

EURYTHMIA. Greek term used to describe a work of art that possessed beauty of proportion, grace of composition, or a particularly harmonious balance of line.

EUSEBIO DI SAN GIORGIO (Eusebio di Giacomo di Cristoforo). Umbrian painter (b. Perugia, ca. 1467/70; d. there, soon after 1540?). Although as Vasari says, he was probably a pupil of Perugino, Eusebio was equally, if not more, influenced by Pinturicchio. One of Eusebio's earliest and best works, the *Adoration of the Magi* (1505; Perugia, National Gallery of Umbria), is basically Pinturicchiesque in style, but was inspired by Perugino's *Adoration* (1504; Città della Pieve). The influence of Raphael became important later. Eusebio's altarpiece of 1512, the *Madonna and Saints* in the Church of S. Francesco at Matelica, is Raphaelesque. Eusebio ranks with Lo Spagna as one of the more important members of the school of Perugia.

BIBLIOGRAPHY. W. Bombe, "Eusebio da San Giorgio," *Repertorium für Kunstwissenschaft*, XXXIX, 1916.

EUSTACE OF ROME, ST. Martyr (2d cent.). Originally called Placidus, he was a general under Trajan. While hunting, he saw a crucifix shining like the sun between the horns of a stag. Converted by this miracle, he was baptized with his wife and two sons, taking the name Eustace, Greek for Placidus. Hadrian had the family roasted alive, but Eustace's body was found intact and buried. His attribute is a stag's head bearing a crucifix. His feast is September 20. *See also* SAINTS IN ART.

EUSTACHIO, FRA. Italian miniature painter (1473–1555). A Dominican monk who was influenced by the paintings of Fra Bartolommeo, Fra Eustachio worked mainly in his native Florence in the High Renaissance style. His classical ornament and the patterns of borders have been more greatly admired than the figures in the works he did for the

Library of S. Marco and the Cathedral, both in Florence.

BIBLIOGRAPHY. C. J. Labarte, *Histoire des arts industriels . . .*, 2d ed., 3 vols., Paris, 1872-75.

EUSTON ROAD GROUP. Group of English painters, active between 1937 and 1939, who adopted the realistic side of postimpressionist art. Among them were Graham Bell, William Coldstream, and Claude Rogers. *See* COLDSTREAM, WILLIAM. *See also* PASMORE, VICTOR.

EUSTYLE. Having well-spaced columns. The term designates a system of column spacing devised by Hermogenes of Priene and by Vitruvius. It is sometimes used to describe column arrangement when the space between two columns is 2¼ diameters.

EUTHYCRATES. Greek sculptor (fl. late 4th and early 3d cent. B.C.). A son of Lysippus, Euthycrates apparently imitated his father's principles of proportion but otherwise cultivated a more austere style (Pliny 34, 66). Some scholars hold that the "Alexander statuette" in Naples (National Archaeological Museum) is based on Euthycrates' statue of Alexander the Great hunting.

EUTHYMIDES. Attic red-figured vase painter (fl. ca. 510–490 B.C.). As illustrated by an amphora in Munich (State Antiquities Collection) showing a group of revelers, his most original artistic efforts were directed toward the convincing delineation of figures in movement through foreshortening and subtle contours. In general, his vases are notable for their free, deft draftsmanship and spirited sense of humor.

BIBLIOGRAPHY. J. C. Hoppin, *Euthymides and His Fellows*, Cambridge, Mass., 1917.

EUTYCHIDES. Greek sculptor from Sicyon, a pupil of Lysippus. His famous *Tyche of Antioch*, dedicated between 296 and 293 B.C., is known through Roman copies. This figure of the goddess of fortune is perhaps the best-known example of personification in Greek art, and displays a talented pupil's application of the compositional principles of Lysippus.

BIBLIOGRAPHY. M. Bieber, *The Sculpture of the Hellenistic Age*, rev. ed., New York, 1961.

EVANGELIAR. Type of illustrated manuscript whose text consists primarily of excerpts from the four Gospels. Many evangeliars have been extremely important in the development of art because of their illuminations. The Ada Gospels (ca. 800; Trier, City Library) is an excellent example.

BIBLIOGRAPHY. D. Diringer, *The Illuminated Book*, London, 1958.

EVANGELISTS, THE FOUR. Matthew, Mark, Luke, and John, authors of the four Gospels. The earliest symbols show the Evangelists as four scrolls or books in the angles of a Greek cross, then as four rivers flowing from a rock upon which stands the Lamb of Christ. Next they appear as the four creatures of Ezekiel: cherub or man for Matthew, lion for Mark, bull for Luke, and eagle for John. Later the heads and feet of these forms are combined with human bodies holding books or scrolls, Matthew having the only human face.

EVANS, SIR ARTHUR. English archaeologist (b. Hemel Hempstead, 1851; d. near Oxford, 1941). He was famed for his excavations of the Palace of Minos at Cnossus, Crete, and for his research and writings on Minoan civilization. Evans was educated at Harrow, Oxford, and Göttingen. In 1884 he was appointed curator of the Ashmolean Museum at Oxford, which post he held until 1909, when he became extraordinary professor of prehistoric archaeology at the university. Among his many honors and awards were his election to the Royal Society in 1901, knighthood in 1911, and the Copley Medal of the Royal Society in 1936. His chief publications were *Cretan Pictographs and Prae-Phoenician Script* (1895), *Scripta Minoa* (vol. 1, 1909; vol. 2, ed. by J. L. Myres, 1952), and the famous *The Palace of Minos* (1921–36).

Originally drawn to Crete in 1894 to confirm a theory about the interpretation of some pictographic materials, Evans became interested in the traces of ancient ruins that were visible there. After highly involved negotiations, he purchased the site of Cnossus and commenced excavations there in March, 1900. Almost immediately he hit upon ancient ruins, remains unlike any found before. Evans had discovered Minoan civilization.

The excavations uncovered a huge palace of many levels and hundreds of rooms. Because some of the buried buildings had several contemporary levels, Evans had to shore up higher stories in order to explore lower ones, and he restored the original elements that had supported the upper stories in ancient times. Theodore Fyfe, a British architect assisting the excavators, took charge of the early phase of this operation, rebuilding wooden pillars, masonry walls, and window openings in the style and location indicated by Evans and his lieutenants. This policy eventually produced the highly restored site of today, which, however, may give a distorted impression of what the archaeologists actually found there. Evans continued working at Cnossus until 1935, supervising restorations, preparing the publication of his findings, and overseeing new excavation campaigns as further discoveries were made. *See* CNOSSUS.

In recent years Evans's methods of excavation and his conclusions based thereon have come under attack; other scholars have rushed to his defense. The controversy is not yet resolved, but, whatever the outcome, most scholars will continue to consider Evans one of the great archaeologists of the early 20th century.

BIBLIOGRAPHY. A. J. Evans, *The Palace of Minos*, 4 vols. in 6, London, 1921–36; J. Evans, *Time and Chance*, London, 1943.

EVANTHIA SAPORITI

EVENEPOEL, HENRI. Belgian painter (b. Nice, 1872; d. Paris, 1899). He studied first in Brussels, then in Paris, for a time with Moreau. Evenepoel painted street scenes and café life, but his finest works are his remarkably unsentimental studies of children and his portraits, powerful full-length figures, solidly set against a wall or on the sidewalk, for example, *L'Espagnol à Paris* (1898–99; Ghent, Fine Arts Museum), which recalls Manet. In 1897 his health forced him to go to Algeria for a year. There his color brightened, and his pictures of Arab outdoor life are more strongly composed than his earlier, impressionistic Paris scenes.

BIBLIOGRAPHY. P. Lambotte, *Henri Evenepoel* (Belgian Artists: Collection des artistes belges contemporains), Brussels, 1908; L. Haesaerts and P. Haesaerts, *Henri Evenepoel, 1872–1899*, Brussels, 1932.

Allart van Everdingen, *Waterfall in Scandinavia*. Bavarian State Picture Gallery, Munich.

EVERDINGEN, ALLART VAN. Dutch landscape painter and graphic artist (b. Alkmaar, 1621; d. Amsterdam, 1675). According to Arnold Houbraken, writing in 1719, Van Everdingen was first a pupil of Roelant-Jacobsz. Savery, presumably in Utrecht, and later of Pieter Molijn in Haarlem. About 1640 he traveled to Sweden and Norway. Early in 1645, while still living in Alkmaar, he entered the Haarlem painters' guild. He eventually settled in Amsterdam, where he became a citizen in 1657.

His relationship with Savery is best seen in Van Everdingen's fifty-seven etchings of animals illustrating Hendrick van Alcmar's *Reynard the Fox*. However, Savery's alpine landscapes also seem to have provided Van Everdingen with a predisposition toward mountainous landscapes, which he developed further under the impact of the Scandinavian topography. Van Everdingen's *Waterfall in Scandinavia* (1650; Munich, Bavarian State Picture Gallery) is considered typical of the new type of landscape that he introduced into Dutch painting. This picture is representative of the style that influenced the work of Jacob van Ruisdael.

Van Everdingen also painted a few seascapes. Ludolf Bakhuysen, the painter of sea subjects, was his pupil. His brother Cesar van Everdingen was also a painter.

BIBLIOGRAPHY. W. Stechow, *Dutch Landscape Painting of the Seventeenth Century*, London, 1966.

LEONARD J. SLATKES

EVERDINGEN, CESAR PIETERSZ. VAN. Dutch painter of portraits, history, and allegory (b. Alkmaar, 1616/

17?; d. Amsterdam, 1678). The date of Van Everdingen's birth is uncertain; in 1637 he is said to have been about twenty. However, in 1661 he give his age variously as forty-four and as forty. The latter statement is obviously inaccurate, for he entered the Alkmaar painters' guild in 1632.

According to Arnold Houbraken, writing in 1719, Van Everdingen studied with the Utrecht painter Jan van Bronckhorst. However, Van Everdingen's style shows somewhat closer affinities to the artists of the Haarlem school, such as Pieter de Grebber, than to the Utrecht followers of Caravaggio. Van Everdingen was also active in the Hague between 1648 and 1650 and executed several works for the Oranjezaal of the nearby Huis ten Bosch. In 1651 he became a member of the Haarlem Guild of St. Luke and held several official positions in that organization, including dean (1655 and 1656). He was living in Amsterdam in 1661 but returned to Alkmaar shortly afterward. In his later years he occasionally signed his works "Cesar Bovetius van Everdingen." He was the brother of Allart van Everdingen.

BIBLIOGRAPHY. V. Bloch, "Pro Caesar Boetius van Everdingen," *Oud-Holland*, LIII, 1936; N. Maclaren, *National Gallery Catalogues: The Dutch School*, London, 1960.

LEONARD J. SLATKES

EVERGOOD, PHILIP. American painter (1901–   ). He was born in New York City and has lived in Southbury, Conn., since 1960. His father was a landscape artist. Evergood graduated from Eton in 1919, then studied with Henry Tonks in England, and, in 1923, with George Luks in the United States. He had his first one-man show in 1927. In 1931 he married Julia Cross, and in the same year went to Spain and discovered El Greco.

After 1932, reacting to the Depression, he featured themes of social protest, more as an affirmation of faith in humanity than as a call for political action. He combines the blunt, forthright character of a primitive in drawing with free fantasy in use of color and a sophistication in treatment of subject. He admires the art of Rowlandson, Hogarth, and Goya. He was given a retrospective exhibition in 1960 at the Whitney Museum of American Art in New York.

BIBLIOGRAPHY. J. I. H. Baur, *Philip Evergood*, New York, 1960.

EVREUX: CATHEDRAL OF NOTRE-DAME. Little remains today of the Romanesque cathedral that was burned twice in the 12th century. The choir and radiating chapels were finally rebuilt by Mathieu des Essarts, who was bishop from 1299 to 1310. During the 14th century many chapels were added to both the choir and nave. During the 15th and 16th centuries the transepts were completed, and the Cathedral was finally consecrated on Mar. 19, 1548.

Evreux is famous for its 14th-century stained glass. In the clerestory windows in the choir the figures exhibit the finest degree of elegance in draftsmanship and are warm in tonality. The whole illuminates the nave with a pearly clarity. Bishop Jean du Prat (1328–34) gave the window in the choir in which he is shown kneeling at the feet of the Virgin holding the Child. Geoffroi Fae (1335–40), his successor, gave many windows, notably those of the Annunciation and the Coronation of the Virgin which flank Du Prat's window. More windows were added during the first half of the 14th century, and all of them are exquisite in style and show a clear relationship to the stained-glass artists of Rouen.

During the second half of the 14th century the style showed a developing realism that reflected the influence of Parisian craftsmen. Portraits and perspective enhanced the sense of reality. Outstanding among the windows executed in this manner are two presented by Bishop Bernard Cariti (1376–83). In the 15th century Bishop Guillaume de Centiers presented the beautiful window (the fifth clerestory window on the north side of the nave) in which he appears kneeling before the Virgin, with additional figures of St. Catherine, the Virgin, and the Angel of the Annunciation.

Architecturally the choir far surpasses the nave in the beauty of its soaring unity. It has a lovely quality of airiness, thanks to the grace of the glazed triforium and the elegantly proportioned clerestory windows.

There are a number of finely carved Renaissance screens connected with the ambulatory chapels. The woodcarved stalls and ironwork in the choir are also noteworthy.

The most striking features of the exterior are the late-15th-century openwork spire surmounting the high tower over the crossing and the rich tracery of the transepts (1511–31). The one to the north is a fine example of the Flamboyant Gothic style.

BIBLIOGRAPHY. M. Aubert, *Gothic Cathedrals of France and Their Treasures*, London, New York, 1959.

ALDEN F. MEGREW

EWER. Type of wide-mouthed pitcher with an extended lip. Ewers are frequently made of silver or pewter and are richly decorated (for example, the one by Cellini with scenes of the battle between the Lapiths and Centaurs).

EWORTH (Eeuwouts; Eottes; Ewoutz), HANS. Flemish-English portrait painter (b. Antwerp, ca. 1515; d. England, after 1573). Master of the Antwerp guild in 1540, Eworth immigrated to England about 1543. He painted for the English nobility and Queens Mary and Elizabeth. His richly colored and precisely painted portraits, while Flemish in execution, show strong English influence in their allegorical presentation. Notable are the portrait of Mary Tudor (Antwerp, Fine Arts Museum) and a religious work, rare for this artist, *The Wise and Foolish Virgins* (1570; Copenhagen, State Museum of Fine Arts). Because of an error in the interpretation of the monograms, a number of Eworth's portraits were once attributed to Lucas de Heere.

BIBLIOGRAPHY. *Le Siècle de Brueghel: La Peinture en Belgique au XVIe siècle*, exhibition catalog, Brussels, 1963.

EXCUDIT. Mark placed on prints, usually to indicate the person or firm that printed the plates. When it is unaccompanied by a name, it may mean that the printer himself executed the plates. The abbreviations "excud." and "exc." are also used.

EXECIAS. Attic vase painter, the greatest master of the black-figured style (fl. ca. 550–525 B.C.). The subjects of his paintings have a restrained dignity and an emphasis on psychological tension rather than overt action which is elsewhere unknown in archaic art. An amphora in the

Evreux, Cathedral of Notre-Dame, side view showing flying buttresses, transept and crossing tower.

Execias, black-figured amphora showing Achilles and Ajax gaming. Vatican Museums, Rome.

Vatican showing Achilles and Ajax gaming is a famous and characteristic work.

BIBLIOGRAPHY. W. Technau, *Exekias*, Leipzig, 1936.

EXECUTION OF THE CITIZENS OF MADRID. Oil painting by Goya, in the Prado Museum, Madrid. *See* GOYA Y LUCIENTES, FRANCISCO JOSE.

EXECUTION OF THE EMPEROR MAXIMILIAN. Oil painting by Manet, in the Municipal Art Gallery, Mannheim. *See* MANET, EDOUARD.

EXEDRA. Stone or marble seat, usually semicircular; also a rectangular or semicircular recess. The Argives set up the characteristic large semicircular niche, or exedra, filled with statues in Delphi after the victory at Oenoe in 456 B.C. In Greek buildings exedrae were usually recesses or alcoves with raised seats. Palestrae, or gymnasiums, had exedrae for lecturers. The Romans applied the term to any semicircular or rectangular recess with benches, as in the Forum of Augustus, Rome. Roman thermae, or baths, had exedrae that were used for discussion. The term is also applied to an apse or a niche in a church, as in Hagia Sophia, Constantinople.

EXETER CATHEDRAL. Cathedral in southwestern England, begun in 1275. The two transept towers are Norman, and their singular position suggests influences from the Burgundian orbit. The nave walls from the crossing as far as the west front and from the crossing eastward to the pulpitum are also Norman. A rectangular chapter house was added in 1224–44; it was roofed in 1265–78; and its upper parts were rebuilt about 1413. Its adjacent cloister, built about the same time and rebuilt in 1377, has been destroyed except for an early doorway in the east bay of the south aisle.

Then comes the great rebuilding period for which a unique series of fabric rolls exists. The Lady Chapel was "new constructed" in 1280; the east end of the chancel was glazed in 1302; and the whole of the east end was completed by 1310. In 1330, work had started on the nave, and the west front was raised by 1342. The nave, however, was not vaulted until 1353, and to this period belongs the splendid series of realistic and naturalistic bosses. The west front was rebuilt to the Norman scale and proportions, but in addition a screen was flung across the lower stories in the form of a reredos. This has a series of tiered canopies with figural sculpture in a 1330–40 style. The rood screen, richly frivolous with depressed ogee arches and ogee cresting, was built in 1320–40. The presbytery sedilia, in an elaborate and spatially intricate late-13th-century style, have canopies with small star vaults and ogival gables. The minstrel's gallery, with angels carrying musical instruments in small recesses, is mid-14th century. The choir stalls, mostly by Sir George Gilbert Scott in the 1870s, retain their misericords by John of Glastonbury, dating from the mid-13th century and being the earliest such series in England. The Bishop's Throne, one of the highlights of the Cathedral, has woodwork that was probably executed by Thomas of Winton in 1313.

The most notable monuments are of Bishop Stafford (1419), with an early type of tomb chest; and the Speke and Oldham chantries (1518–19) at the east ends of the north and south chancel aisles. The Cathedral is in effect the style of the Master of Exeter of about 1250–60, employing luxurious decorative idiosyncrasies, complicated tierceron vaults, original and Francophile tracery forms, multishafted piers, and a broad, impressive, wholly English nave proportion. Although this master's identity is unknown, his personal style makes Exeter one of the most surprising of English cathedrals.

BIBLIOGRAPHY. J. Harvey, *The English Cathedrals*, London, 1950; N. Pevsner, *The Buildings of England*, vol. 5, Harmondsworth, 1952.

JOHN HARRIS

EXONARTHEX. Outer narthex or vestibule, particularly in basilican and Byzantine churches. Generally, the exonarthex denotes the outer passage of a double narthex, as in Hagia Sophia, Constantinople.

EXOTICISM. The tendency to search for new and unusual forms from cultures other than one's own. Early examples are the chinoiserie and the turquerie of the 17th and 18th centuries in western Europe. The Prince Regent's Pavilion at Brighton (1810) began the long list of 19th-century monuments displaying exoticism. In the 18th century, artists had traveled mainly to record what they saw; in the 19th, they sought out alien cultures for direct inspiration. Delacroix visited North Africa for this purpose, and Gauguin's famous sojourn in Tahiti was similarly motivated. Matisse derived much of his inspiration from Islamic ornamental motifs, and American painters have either directly, as in Morris Graves's work, or indirectly, as in Mark Tobey's, sought inspiration in the art of the Far East.

BIBLIOGRAPHY. H. Honour, *Chinoiserie: The Vision of Cathay*, London, 1961.

EXPRESSIONISM. Movement in early 20th-century art most clearly typified by the painting and graphic art of two German groups, the Bridge (Die Brücke), founded in Dresden in 1905, and the Blue Rider (Der Blaue Reiter), an outgrowth of the Munich New Artists' Association, dating from 1911. The term "expressionism" is much wider in application, however, and is often attached to the styles or individual paintings or sculptures by German artists even loosely affiliated with the two groups just mentioned. It has also been applied to the works of non-German artists (Rouault for example) whose methods denote one degree or another of similarity to the aesthetic of the Bridge or the Blue Rider. Certain critics have gone so far as to designate as "expressionist" almost all kinds of avant-garde 20th-century art, with confusing results.

The first German group to manifest an explicit style was the Bridge, organized by Ernst Ludwig Kirchner (1880–1938). His first associates, some of them like Kirchner studying architecture in Dresden, were Erich Heckel, Fritz Bleyl, and Karl Schmidt-Rottluff, soon joined by Emil Nolde, Max Pechstein, Cuno Amiet, and Axel Gallén. Under the informal leadership of Kirchner, the Bridge artists first met to discuss the purposes and nature of their program: the appeal to all German (and, by extension, other) artists to join in revolt against vitiated academic painting and sculpture; to establish a new, vigorous aesthetic linked with the Germanic past but charged with modern emotion and form; and hence to form a "bridge" between artists and cogent spiritual sources. The Bridge artists first exhibited at an improvised gallery in a Dresden lamp factory in 1906, then in 1907 at the Richter Gallery. Two "Albums" were produced in those years, amounting to brief manifestos—the Bridge had no complicated program—in the form of woodcuts. A related document, *Chronik der Brücke*, was published by Kirchner in 1913. *See* AMIET, CUNO; BLEYL, FRITZ; HECKEL, ERICH; KIRCHNER, ERNST LUDWIG; NOLDE, EMIL; PECHSTEIN, MAX; SCHMIDT-ROTTLUFF, KARL.

Until 1911, these artists lived and worked in close communion; they then moved to Berlin, where, until the outbreak of World War I, they still retained some identity as a group. (Nolde had withdrawn a year after joining in 1906.) Der Sturm Gallery of Herwarth Walden and the Sonderbund exhibition in Düsseldorf included selections of Brücke works during this period, and the group was also represented at Arnold's Gallery in Berlin and in the New York Armory Show of 1913. Among additional artists who had joined the Bridge before it disbanded were Otto Müller and the Dutch Fauvre Kees van Dongen. *See* DONGEN, KEES VAN; MULLER, OTTO.

Although Kirchner and his associates lacked a formal aesthetic plan, they were impelled by commonly felt sources, and allowing for distinctive personal approaches, they shared several traits of style in a general way. Among the older influences were northern European medieval and Renaissance sculptures, prints, and paintings (including the

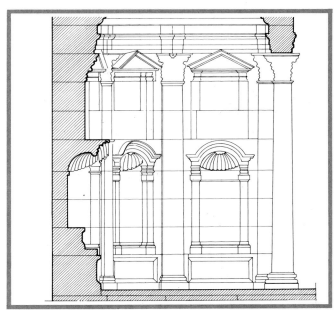

Exedra. A recess or alcove with raised seats first found in Greek and Roman architecture.

art of Dürer, Schongauer, Cranach, and Grünewald). Recent sources were Van Gogh, Gauguin, Edvard Munch, James Ensor, the stylized decorative mode of the turn of the century known as Art Nouveau or Jugendstil, and the color theories of several 19th-century scientists, as well as those of Georges Seurat and Paul Signac, the French neoimpressionists. A special and salient influence was that of primitive art, particularly the wood carvings of Negro Africa and the South Pacific.

The Bridge also found stimulus in the contemporaneous French movement known as Fauvism (as mentioned above, Van Dongen, a Fauve, actually belonged to the Bridge; and Pechstein, visiting Paris in 1907, brought back to Dresden direct word of the exciting French association). These two groups in fact shared a number of stylistic elements, although the Germans were more intense in their handling of color and texture and the choice of expressionist themes was more provocative and emotionally rooted. Like the Fauves, the Bridge artists worked rapidly with the brush and, characteristically, preferred rough or broken textures. Their form, however, was more angular and often more crowded within the picture space than that of their French contemporaries. Printmaking, particularly the woodcut, was far more common in the art of the Bridge than in the Fauvist program. Georges Rouault, the only Fauve who frequently interpreted religious themes, shared that characteristic with several of the Bridge artists, particularly Emil Nolde; and his forceful technique is held by many students of modern painting actually to be expressionist rather than Fauvist. *See* ROUAULT, GEORGES.

Several German painters, printmakers, and sculptors may reasonably be identified with the Bridge manner of expressionism, at least in some degree or particular, although they did not belong to the group. Paula Modersohn-Becker and Christian Rohlfs, older artists who were in a sense protoexpressionists, developed independently.

Max Beckmann and George Grosz, both of whom were to leave Germany for the United States during the Nazi regime, are usually identified with the New Objectivity movement of the 1920s, though they were influenced by the Bridge style. Karl Hofer and the distinguished graphic artist Käthe Kollwitz are clearly expressionist and are not greatly removed from the Bridge aesthetic and spirit. The sculptors Ernst Barlach and Wilhelm Lehmbruck were distinguished for strongly personal expressionist styles, but were independent of any movement. The Austrians Oskar Kokoschka and Egon Schiele, generally related to the Bridge expressionists in intensity and to some extent in actual style, are outstanding representatives of expressionism outside Germany. The movement found some response in the Low Countries and in the United States. *See* BARLACH, ERNST; BECKMANN, MAX; GROSZ, GEORGE; HOFER, CARL; KOKOSCHKA, OSKAR; KOLLWITZ, KATHE; LEHMBRUCK, WILHELM; MODERSOHN-BECKER, PAULA; ROHLFS, CHRISTIAN; SCHIELE, EGON.

The second expressionist group, the Blue Rider, was headed by the Russian Wassily Kandinsky (1866–1944); since 1896 he had resided in Munich, first attending the Academy of Art, then in 1901 founding his own school and becoming prominent in artists' organizations including the Neue Künstlervereinigung (New Artists Federation), out of which the Blue Rider was formed in 1911. Kandinsky's associates included Franz Marc, Alexey von Jawlensky, Gabriele Münter, August Macke, and Heinrich Campendonk; and in the first Blue Rider exhibition on December 18, 1911, at the Thannhäuser Gallery, Munich, the Frenchmen Robert Delaunay and Henri Rousseau, the Austrian composer Arnold Schönberg, the Russian brothers David and Vladimir Burliuk, and a very few other artists were also represented. The second Blue Rider show, held in 1912 at the Goltz Gallery, Munich, added Paul Klee, Alfred Kubin, Natalie Gontcharova, Larionov, and several Parisians, including La Fresnaye, Braque, and Picasso.

Kandinsky, Marc, Jawlensky, Macke, and Klee were the most active and characteristic of the Blue Rider association. The name was selected because of Kandinsky's and Marc's liking for the color blue and their respective admiration of riders and horses. Although the Blue Rider artists were more directly conversant with French developments (including cubism) and on the whole more involved with formal theories than were the Bridge painters, they were not unemotional. The difference was that, in the purely visual sense, Blue Rider painting at once discloses its complexity of color and structure. Kandinsky was in fact both intellectual and emotional, a Moscow University graduate in law before he turned to art but deeply interested in music and literature. Marc sought a metaphysic that would resolve his disciplined painterly attitude and his philosophical view of nature, particularly animals. *See* JAWLENSKY, ALEXEY VON; KANDINSKY, WASSILY; KLEE, PAUL; MACKE, AUGUST; MARC, FRANZ.

Kandinsky's contribution to expressionism in particular and to the history of modern art in general was his discovery of abstract or nonobjective painting in 1910, following his astonishing development away from an earlier

naturalistic style. His first abstraction evolved from a progression of landscape and figural studies which gradually and almost systematically became reduced syntheses of natural forms.

Franz Marc and August Macke died in World War I, but by 1914 each had sensitively contributed to the force of the Blue Rider movement, especially with respect to color. Both were to some extent influenced by cubism, particularly the Orphist works of Delaunay. Even more evidently encouraged by Orphism was Paul Klee, who was not to reach full development until after World War I, but whose remarkably ingenious techniques in mixed media and liberation of unconscious imagery were to make him one of the major artists of the century.

Like the Bridge, the Blue Rider as a group was largely dispersed by the advent of the war. Kandinsky, who was in Russia during the revolution, turned to a geometrically based extension of his all-important abstract style. Klee developed a whimsical protosurrealist style and content which won favor among avant-garde artists everywhere. Kandinsky and Klee were grouped with Jawlensky as professors at the German Bauhaus in Weimar, directed by the architect Walter Gropius; and, in 1924, they were joined by Lyonel Feininger, long sympathetic with the earlier Blue Rider, to form the Blue Four, which exhibited in Europe, the United States, and Mexico. Kandinsky and Klee were exceptionally influential as teachers, but when the ascendancy of the Nazis in Germany in 1933 closed the Bauhaus, Kandinsky went to Paris and Klee returned to his native Switzerland. Both remained strongly influential upon later avant-garde movements in Europe and America. *See* FEININGER, LYONEL.

Kandinsky's evolvement of abstract style, generally known as early "abstract expressionism," is related to all subsequent nonobjective art, including the New York developments of the 1940s and 1950s. Although Kandinsky was familiar with the French movements of the first decade of the century and was confirmed in his own aesthetic by both Fauve and cubist practices, it is significant that his first abstractions are substantially indebted to neither of those styles. Other Blue Rider painters were greatly influenced by the color of Delaunay's Orphism, although Klee, Marc, Jawlensky, and Macke were painters of salient originality.

With the death of Klee in 1940 and Kandinsky in 1944, the direct confluence of the Blue Rider aesthetic was terminated. It thereafter obtained in the work of younger artists everywhere who worked in the abstract-expressionist style. Kandinsky and Klee were also influential as theorists—Kandinsky especially being a prolific writer on art.

All the Blue Rider artists exhibited extensively during their lifetimes. Major exhibitions of their works were also held at the Royal Scottish Academy, Edinburgh, in 1960 and at the Leonard Hutton Galleries and the Guggenheim Museum, New York, in 1963. The combined influences of the Dresden Bridge and the Munich Blue Rider have rivaled those of cubism as the most abiding forces in 20th-century art. *See also* CAMPENDONK, HEINRICH; KUBIN, ALFRED; MUNTER, GABRIELE.

BIBLIOGRAPHY. W. Kandinsky, *Concerning the Spiritual in Art*, New York, 1947; W. Grohmann, *Paul Klee*, New York, 1954; W. Haftmann, *The Mind and Work of Paul Klee*, New York, 1954; C. L. Kuhn, *German Expressionism and Abstract Art; the Harvard*

Ernst L. Kirchner, *Portrait of Doctor Bauer*. Woodcut.

Karl Schmidt-Rottluff, membership card of the Bridge (Die Brücke) group, 1911. Woodcut print.

Collections, Cambridge, Mass., 1957; B. S. Myers, *The German Expressionists: A Generation in Revolt*, New York, 1957, 1963; P. Selz, *German Expressionist Painting*, Berkeley, 1957; W. Grohmann, *Wassily Kandinsky*, New York, 1958; H. M. Wingler, *Oskar Kokoschka*, Salzburg, 1958; M. Brion, *Kandinsky*, London, 1961.

JOHN C. GALLOWAY

EXPULSION FROM THE TEMPLE. One of the intermediary scenes in the Passion (Mark 11:15–17). Its representation appears to be of Byzantine origin; it emerges only rarely in Western medieval art—the Paliotto in S. Ambrogio, Milan, of about 835 is one example. After Giotto's Arena Chapel frescoes (1310), the Expulsion became more common in Western art and was utilized during the Reformation as a symbol for Luther's program of religious reform.

BIBLIOGRAPHY. K. Künstle, *Ikonographie der christlichen Kunst*, vol. 1, Freiburg im Breisgau, 1926.

EXTERNSTEINE, *see* DETMOLD: GROTTO OF THE HOLY SEPULCHRE.

EXTRADOS, *see* ARCH.

EXULTET ROLL. Scroll-like illuminated manuscript produced in southern Italy from the 10th to the 13th century. The roll had pictures that were arranged upside down in relation to the interspersed text. This arrangement permitted the pictures to be viewed by the congregation when the exultet roll was used during a church service. After a portion of the roll had been read by the priest, he allowed it to fall over the front of the pulpit; the pictures then appeared right side up to the congregation.

BIBLIOGRAPHY. M. Avery, *The Exultet Rolls of South Italy*, Princeton, 1936.

EX-VOTO. From the Latin, meaning "out of thankfulness," the term is applied to works of art, usually painted or sculptured, presented by a donor to a divinity as a sign of gratitude for some particular blessing. Ex-voto tablets generally bear only an inscription and have no pictorial representations.

EYCK, HUBERT VAN, *see* VAN EYCK, HUBERT.

EYCK, JAN VAN, *see* VAN EYCK, JAN.

EYRE, WILSON. American architect (1858–1944). His houses of the 1880s in Philadelphia featured brick and half-timbered exteriors. Their plans were striking, with long rooms of varied and irregular shapes strung out on either side of halls from which stairs rise within grilled enclosures.

BIBLIOGRAPHY. H. R. Hitchcock, *Architecture: Nineteenth and Twentieth Centuries*, 2d ed., Baltimore, 1963.

EZEKIEL, VISION OF. The vision of Ezekiel (Ezek. 1) reveals the Lord enthroned, surrounded by four fantastic beasts: one with the head of a man; another, of an ox; the third, of a lion; and the fourth, of an eagle. Each creature sprouted four wings and had four faces. The scene was taken over in Byzantine art as a source for the Christ in Majesty (Majestas Domini), and it was transmitted to Western art in the Carolingian period. The vision is rarely represented in a scene by itself.

BIBLIOGRAPHY. W. Neuss, *Das Buch Ezechiel in Theologie und Kunst bis zum Ende des XII. Jahrhunderts*, Münster, 1912.

EZRA (Zorah): ST. GEORGE. Church of A.D. 516 in what is now southern Syria. In plan it is an octagon inscribed in a square, with the eastern apse and its subsidiary chambers drawing a longitudinal axis through the main central feature. This is an octagonal arcade upon which a timber or masonry dome once rested (the building has been much damaged and altered). Between the octagon and the outer wall there is an ambulatory, or aisle, that circles the central, higher feature. Perhaps on the site of a pagan temple, St. George is an early example of the type of building made famous slightly later by S. Vitale in Ravenna and other buildings of Justinian.

BIBLIOGRAPHY. H. C. Butler and E. B. Smith, *Early Christian Churches in Syria*, Princeton, 1929; J. W. Crowfoot, *Early Churches in Palestine*, London, 1941.

F

FABBRI, AGENORE. Italian sculptor (1911–). Born in Barba, he studied at the academy in Pistoia and later worked in the ceramic shop of T. Mazzotti in Liguria. He produces brightly polychromed terra-cotta sculpture in a style closely related to that of Marini and Manzù.

BIBLIOGRAPHY. A. Fabbri, *Agenore Fabbri Scultore*, ed. R. Carrieri, Milan, 1950.

FABIANI, MAX. Austrian architect (1865–1947). He worked in Vienna. Otto Wagner's pupil and assistant, he is represented by his 1897 office building, which demonstrates through the classical geometry of its façade the influence of his master and the peripheral position of Viennese architects in relation to Art Nouveau. Fabiani is also known for his major role in rebuilding Ljubljana, Yugoslavia, after the 1895 earthquake and for his work on the first master plan for that city (1900).

BIBLIOGRAPHY. L. Hevesi, *Osterreichische Kunst im 19. Jahrhundert*, vol. 2, Leipzig, 1903.

FABRE, JAIME. Spanish architect (fl. ca. 1290–1340). Fabré was a native of Mallorca, where he directed the work at the Dominican church (probably begun according to his plans in 1296) until 1317. That year he took over direction of the work at the Cathedral of Santa Cruz in Barcelona, where he worked until 1339. He was master of works at Gerona and Narbonne cathedrals.

BIBLIOGRAPHY. V. Lampérez y Romea, *Historia de la arquitectura cristiana española en la edad media*, vol. 2, Madrid, 1909.

FABRIANO, GENTILE DA, *see* FRANCESCO DI GENTILE DA FABRIANO; GENTILE DA FABRIANO (GENTILE DI NICCOLO DI GIOVANNI DI MASSIO).

FABRITIUS (Maes; Maesse; Maessen), BARENT. Dutch painter of portraits, history, and genre (b. Middenbeemster, 1624; d. Amsterdam, 1673). Barent Fabritius was the younger brother of the painter Carel Fabritius, whose surname he also adopted about 1650. In 1641 Fabritius was living in Middenbeemster and, like his brother, was recorded as a carpenter. In 1643 he was living in Amster-

Barent Fabritius, *Willem van der Helm and His Family*, 1656. Rijksmuseum, Amsterdam.

dam. It is not certain whether Fabritius was ever a direct pupil of Rembrandt; however, he seems to have developed his style under the impact of Rembrandt, perhaps through contact with the works of his brother, who was in Rembrandt's workshop, rather than directly. Fabritius apparently lived in Amsterdam until 1652, when he returned to Middenbeemster.

Subsequently, he may have gone to Leyden as early as 1656, for his portrait of a Leyden architect, *Willem van der Helm and His Family* (Amsterdam, Rijksmuseum), was painted during that year. Fabritius became a member of the Leyden guild in 1658, but later settled in Amsterdam, about 1669/70. There he seems to have been friendly with Nicolaes Maes, a former Rembrandt pupil.

Fabritius's earliest known work is the *Self-Portrait* (Frankfurt am Main, Städel Art Institute and Municipal Gallery) of 1650, which shows the impact of Rembrandt's manner of the later 1640s. The same influences can be seen in his *Girl Plucking a Duck* (in the New York art market in 1956; drawing in a private Swiss collection), which derives in both style and composition from Rembrandt's *Young Girl at a Half-Open Door* (Chicago, Art Institute) of 1645. However, his *Self-Portrait as a Shepherd* (Vienna, Academy of Fine Arts) shows the dominant influence to be the work of his brother Carel. The influence of his brother's style is tempered by that of his friend Nicolaes Maes in the *Slaughtered Ox* (1652?; Rotterdam, Boymans–Van Beuningen Museum). At other times the influence of another Rembrandt pupil, Gerbrandt van den Eeckhout, is apparent in Fabritius's work.

BIBLIOGRAPHY. W. R. Valentiner, "Carel and Barent Fabritius," *Art Bulletin*, XIV, 1932; D. Pont, *Barent Fabritius, 1624–1673*, Utrecht, 1958; N. Maclaren, *National Gallery Catalogues: The Dutch School*, London, 1960.   LEONARD J. SLATKES

FABRITIUS, CAREL. Dutch painter of genre, portraits, and history (b. Middenbeemster, 1622; d. Delft, 1654). Fabritius was the son of a schoolmaster, Pieter Carelsz. He seems to have received his early training as a carpenter (*faber*) and apparently adopted his surname from that occupation. His brother Barent, also a painter, used the same surname, and their father is also known to have used it on at least one occasion. The father was probably an amateur artist, and it is possible that Fabritius received some early training from him.

Along with Samuel van Hoogstraten, he is listed as a pupil of Rembrandt at Amsterdam, either late in 1641 or early in 1642. This date is confirmed by a number of stylistic influences in his earliest work, *The Raising of Lazarus* (Warsaw, Alexander Church), which shows the influence, especially in its color and light effects, of Rembrandt's *Night Watch* (Amsterdam, Rijksmuseum), which was completed in 1642. In 1643 Fabritius returned to Middenbeemster, but probably visited Amsterdam frequently. In 1650 he was said to be living in Delft, and in 1652 he was a member of the Delft painters' guild. It is possible that at this time Fabritius had some contact with the young Johannes Vermeer, although its exact nature is uncertain.

Aside from being a very individual portrait painter ([*Self?*] *Portrait*, Rotterdam, Boymans–Van Beuningen Museum; *Portrait of Abraham de Potter*, 1648, Rijksmuseum), Fabritius seems to have indulged in various perspective investigations. It is likely that his *View of Delft, with a Musical Instrument Seller's Stall* (1652; London, National Gallery) was once part of a perspective box or peep show. This assumption is supported by his early contact with Hoogstraten, who is known to have built similar devices, and by his probable carpentry training.

Unlike many Rembrandt pupils Fabritius, after leaving the master's studio, produced a very individual style and a sense of light color which was no longer dependent upon Rembrandt. Whatever his relationship to Vermeer, Fabritius presents a painting style and an interest in space and light that must be taken into consideration in any evaluation of the development of the school of Delft in general and of Vermeer specifically.

BIBLIOGRAPHY. C. Hofstede de Groot, *Jan Vermeer van Delft en Carel Fabritius*, Amsterdam, 1907; H. F. Wijnman, "De Schilder Carel Fabritius," *Oud-Holland*, XLVIII, 1931; W. R. Valentiner, "Carel and Barent Fabritius," *Art Bulletin*, XIV, 1932; K. E. Schuurman, *Carel Fabritius*, Amsterdam, 1947.

LEONARD J. SLATKES

FACADE. General architectural term designating that part of the exterior of a building which can be called the front, usually the site of the principal entrance. However, some buildings, such as Gothic churches, have multiple façades. In this case, there is a main façade on the west end of the nave and additional façades on the north and south ends of the transept.

FACET CUBISM. The early phase of cubist art in which, through emphasis on the interplay of the planes, the visual effect of faceted jewels is produced. Facet cubism is seen in some works by Braque and Picasso.

BIBLIOGRAPHY. R. Rosenblum, *Cubism and Twentieth-Century Art*, New York, 1961.

FA-CH'ANG, *see* MU-CH'I.

FACING. Any material used to cover the outer surface of a wall. Usually the wall requiring facing is constructed of inferior material, such as brick. Marble or stone facing is then applied to give a more sumptuous appearance. This was a common construction technique in Roman times.

Facet cubism, Pablo Picasso, *Portrait of Ambroise Vollard*, detail. Pushkin Museum, Moscow.

FACSIMILE. Exact copy of any work of art, but usually restricted to copies of works of graphic art. In the latter case, a drawing, engraving, etching, or similar work is reproduced by a mechanical process, such as heliogravure. For example, a drawing reproduced in line engraving is a facsimile.

BIBLIOGRAPHY. J. T. Arms, *Handbook of Print Making and Print Makers*, New York, 1934.

FACTURA. Type of cubism developed in Russia during the first decades of the 20th century. It explores textures and multiple planes of vision through the use of collage and dissection of objects into their component parts. Factura had its greatest influence on the Constructivists. *See* CONSTRUCTIVISM.

BIBLIOGRAPHY. L. Moholy-Nagy, *Vision in Motion*, Chicago, 1947.

FADER, FERNANDO. Argentine painter (b. Mendoza, 1882; d. Córdoba, 1935). Fader studied in Munich. He was the most influential impressionist painter in Argentina. *Shawls from Manila* (Buenos Aires, National Museum of Fine Arts) is typically colorful.

BIBLIOGRAPHY. J. L. Pagano, *Historia del arte argentino*, Buenos Aires, 1944.

FADINO, *see* ALENI, TOMASO.

FADRUSZ, JANOS. Hungarian sculptor (b. Bratislava, 1858; d. Budapest, 1903). He began as a locksmith and became a creator of massive historical monuments with boulderlike heroic figures. Outstanding among them are the Matthias Corvinus monument at Cluj and the no longer extant Maria Theresa monument, formerly at Bratislava.

Faenza ware. Majolica or tin-glazed earthenware, dish with young gentleman. Louvre, Paris.

FAENZA WARE. Majolica or tin-glazed earthenware manufactured in the Italian town of Faenza. The ware was painted with metallic colors applied directly to the unfired, opaque-glaze surface. A high-temperature firing fused the bright colors to the white glaze. Popular subjects for painting were mythological, Biblical, and genre scenes, known collectively as the "Istoriato style." Although Faenza's creative peak was reached during the 16th century, the city has continued to make ceramics to the present day.

BIBLIOGRAPHY. W. B. Honey, *European Ceramic Art from the End of the Middle Ages to about 1815*, 2 vols., London, 1949-52; G. Savage, *Pottery through the Ages*, Harmondsworth, 1959.

FAES, PETER VAN DER, *see* LELY, SIR PETER.

FAGUS WERKE, ALFELD, *see* GROPIUS, WALTER.

FAIENCE. Earthenware covered with an opaque white glaze made of a combination of lead and tin. It is a type of tin-glazed earthenware also called "delftware." The name "faïence" is applied more commonly on the Continent than in England or the United States. It is a French word derived from the Italian city of Faenza, which was a center of majolica production and export in the 16th century. Evidently the corruption faïence had become a synonym for pottery in France, just as majolica, a corruption of Majorca, the Spanish source, had become its synonym in Italy a century earlier. The name has been incorrectly applied to a glass-covered colorful substance made in ancient Egypt and to a light early-Persian ceramic ware. One common extension of its meaning is found in *faïence fine*, a French term referring to the white or

cream-colored lead-glazed earthenware introduced in Staffordshire in about 1750. *See* DELFTWARE; FAENZA WARE.

Faïence is made of more highly refined clay than majolica so that it can be shaped more delicately. It was developed in the 17th century by potters copying Chinese porcelain and was made in the 18th and 19th centuries in both Oriental and Occidental shapes. The thin body and the white glaze were achieved by firing at a high temperature, so that at first the colored decoration over the white glaze was restricted to the so-called high-temperature colors made of iron, manganese, copper, and cobalt. A broader range of color was used early in the 18th century after the introduction of an overglaze decorating technique, possibly achieved by firing a second time at lower temperature.

In the 17th century, Delft was the largest producer of faïence, although Nevers was as important for Chinese and Near Eastern designs. In about 1680, Rouen, which had been a center of the manufacture of French majolica, began producing faïence based on metal models or designs of local origin. Rouen influenced Moutiers and Nevers as well as potteries in Germany, Spain, and Scandinavia. In the 18th century there were significant producers of faïence all over Europe developing local traditions and generally following contemporary fashion. Perhaps most unique is the Scandinavian form of bishop's hat bowl. The less expensive faïence was more simple in design than porcelain, but equally fashionable. Its manufacture was gradually discontinued in the 19th century as the lighter lead-glazed earthenwares produced by English factories surpassed it in economy and popularity.

BIBLIOGRAPHY. E. Hannover, *Pottery and Porcelain*, 2 vols., London, 1925; W. B. Honey, *European Ceramic Art ...*, 2 vols., London, 1949-52.

MARVIN D. SCHWARTZ

FAIRWEATHER, IAN. Australian painter (1890–   ). Born in Scotland, he studied painting at the Slade School in London. In 1934 he went to Australia, where he is widely known for his restless and adventuresome personality. His art reflects the influences of Jacob Epstein's sculpture, Oriental calligraphy, and Australian aboriginal art.

FAITH, ST., *see* FOY OF CONQUES, ST.

FAITHORNE, WILLIAM, THE ELDER. English engraver and pastel artist (b. London, 1616; d. there, 1691). Working in the monumental baroque style of Nanteuil, Faithorne gained a considerable reputation, which toward the end of his life was diminished by the mediocre work of his many workshop assistants. He studied with the publisher Robert Peake, under whom he served for the Royalist cause in the Civil War (from 1642 on). During Faithorne's subsequent imprisonment he developed his technique in portraits of fellow inmates. His greatest growth came when he visited Paris (1649–50), under the patronage of Michel de Marolles, and studied with Nanteuil himself, whose growth from mannerist to the monumental Faithorne paralleled throughout his career. Faithorne's greatest portraits, done between 1660 and 1680, are works with monumental gestures, skillfully modeled skin tones,

William Faithorne, *Catherine, Infanta of Portugal*. Albertina, Vienna.

Etienne-Maurice Falconet, *Bather*. Marble. Louvre, Paris.

and delicate rendering of texture. His best prints are scarce and sought after; his cipher is "FF."

BIBLIOGRAPHY. L. Fagan, *Descriptive Catalogue of the Engraved Works of W. Faithorne*, London, 1888.

FAKES, *see* FORGERY.

FALCA, ALESSANDRO, *see* LONGHI, ALESSANDRO.

FALCA, PIETRO, *see* LONGHI, PIETRO.

FALCK, JEREMIAH. German engraver (b. Danzig, ca. 1619; d. Hamburg, ca. 1663). Falck's portraits and historical plates, executed in an elegant style very close to Bloemaert's, earned him a considerable reputation in his lifetime. He made several celebrated plates for the Amsterdam Reynst Kabinet; *Louis XIII* (1643), after Justus van Egmont, is considered his best work.

BIBLIOGRAPHY. J. C. Block, *Jeremiah Falck, sein Leben und seine Werke . . .*, Danzig, 1890.

FALCONE, ANIELLO. Italian painter (b. Naples, 1607; d. there, 1656). One of the earliest and certainly the greatest of specialists in battle paintings, he probably never saw a military engagement. The unsettled social conditions of 17th-century Naples contributed to his great popularity, but he also sent many paintings to France, Belgium, and Spain.

BIBLIOGRAPHY. F. Saxl, "The Battle Piece without a Hero. Aniello Falcone and His Patrons," *Journal of the Warburg and Courtauld Institutes*, III, 1939-40.

FALCONET, ETIENNE-MAURICE. French sculptor (1716–91). Born in Paris, Falconet entered the atelier of Jean Baptiste Lemoyne at eighteen and later did eight statues (destroyed) for St-Roch, Paris, which served as a transition from small to monumental works. From 1757 to 1766, Falconet directed the National Manufactory of Sèvres, producing editions of many of his own small allegorical groups in biscuit. He was received into the Royal Academy in 1754. In 1766 he and his pupil Marie-Anne Collot went to Russia to execute a colossal statue of Peter the Great ordered by Catherine II. He left Russia in 1778, returning to Paris in 1780 via Amsterdam and The Hague. In the last decade of his life he produced no sculpture, although his prolific literary works were published in six volumes (Lausanne, 1781). His style is that of the transition to neoclassicism under Louis XVI, but rather vigorous.

BIBLIOGRAPHY. L. Réau, "Documents inédits sur Falconet," *Bulletin de la Société de l'Histoire de l'Art Français*, 1918–1919; L. Réau, *Etienne-Maurice Falconet*, Paris, 1922; H. Dieckmann and J. Seznec, "The Horse of Marcus Aurelius: A Controversy between Diderot and Falconet," *Journal of the Warburg and Courtauld Institutes*, XV, 1952.

FALCONETTO, GIOVANNI MARIA. Italian architect and painter of the school of Verona (1468–before 1540). Giovanni Maria Falconetto was the most distinguished member of a Veronese family of architects and decorators active during the 15th and 16th centuries. Both in his architecture and in his painting he tried to imitate with meticulous exactness the art of antiquity. As a painter he shows certain affinities with Pisanello and Liberale on the one hand and with Mantegna on the other. He is said to have been a pupil of Melozzo da Forlì. In 1497–99 he worked on the frescoes in the S. Biagio Chapel in the Church of SS. Nazaro e Celso in Verona. In 1503 he worked as a painter in the Calcasoli Chapel of the Cathedral in Verona; the frescoes in the Maffei and Emili chapels there are also attributed to him. These works are most interesting for their richly ornamented architectural perspective settings. In architecture, the Loggia in Verona and the Casino (1524), the Porta Savonarola (1530), and the Porta S. Giovanni (1528) in Padua are among his works.

BIBLIOGRAPHY. G. Zorzi, "Altri disegni di vari artisti riguardanti monumenti antichi nelle raccolte palladiane di Vicenza e di Londra," *Palladio*, VI, 1956; C. Semenzato, "Gian Maria Falconetto," *Bollettino del Centro Internazionale di Studi d'Architettura Andrea Palladio*, III, 1961.

FALGUIERE, JEAN-ALEXANDRE-JOSEPH. French sculptor and painter (b. Toulouse, 1831; d. Paris, 1900). Falguière studied with Jouffroy at the Ecole des Beaux-Arts in Paris and won the Prix de Rome in 1859. His works combine the classicism of his training with a strong realism. Both are apparent in an early work, the bronze *Victor of the Cockfight* (1864; Paris, Louvre), as is also the influence of Italian Renaissance sculpture. His main works are strongly personalized portraits, statues, and monuments. Falguière's keen interest in the depiction of movement can be seen in his realistically rendered nude statues of classical subjects.

FALLINGWATER. Country house in Bear Run, Pa., built by Frank Lloyd Wright in 1936 for Edgar J. Kaufmann. Situated on the bank of a woodland stream, the house has several levels of reinforced concrete balconies with parapets, which are boldly cantilevered over the stream at a point where it spills into a rock ravine below. The cantilever anchors are massive piers of the same rock as the bank ledge from which they rise. The balconies, which overhang each other, carry the living space and sun terraces, these two areas being separated by a wall of glass doors. The other walls are formed by the piers. The main effect of the exterior is a dynamism of vertical piers and horizontal balconies, which is enhanced by the contrast between the rock and concrete. See WRIGHT, FRANK LLOYD.

BIBLIOGRAPHY. "New and Unpublished Work of F. L. Wright," *Architectural Forum*, LXVIII, 1938; J. Joedicke, *A History of Modern Architecture*, New York, 1960.

FAMAGUSTA CATHEDRAL. The ruined Cathedral of Famagusta, in Cyprus, is one of the most bizarre buildings of the late Middle Ages. It was erected by the Greek citizens of the town in the late 14th century in the Gothic style, which the Frankish rulers of Cyprus favored, but it is surmounted by a dome. The semicircular apses are covered with semipointed domes, the nave has quadripartite vaulting, and Gothic pinnacles adorn the exterior. It is one of the largest structures of Greek provenance.

BIBLIOGRAPHY. J. A. Hamilton, *Byzantine Architecture and Decoration*, 2d ed., London, 1956.

FAMILLE-GROUP PORCELAINS. The terms *famille rose*, *famille verte*, *famille noire*, and *famille jaune* were first employed by the French student of porcelain Albert Jacquemart in his pioneer work of the mid-19th century. Jacquemart arbitrarily classified groups of Chinese enam-

eled porcelains according to the predominant color employed in the background. His descriptions are still encountered today in European literature on Chinese ceramics when porcelains of the K'ang-hsi (1662–1722) and later periods are discussed. See CHINA: CERAMICS.

The so-called *famille verte* class distinguished by Jacquemart covered porcelains decorated with brilliant copper green, but yellow, purple, and blue also occur in translucent form. Iron red was the only opaque color used in the production of *famille verte*. The *famille noire* group was actually only a variant of *famille verte* since the copper green was applied over a dull black background. The *famille rose* class eventually became the most popular and best known in Europe. The rose-pink enamel used as the background color in this group was derived from gold, known in Europe as "purple of Cassius" after the name of the German developer. Depending on the temperature at which it was fired, the gold varied from pale pink to brown red or violet. The Chinese refer to *famille rose* colors as *yang-tsai*, or "foreign colors," since they were brought to China by way of India. A dated plate of 1721 in the British Museum, London, indicates that the *famille rose* class was produced during the reign of K'ang-hsi, but it became more common in the reign of Yung-cheng (1723–35). All the colors employed in the *famille rose* group are opaque by contrast with the translucent enamels of the *famille verte* group. Thus a more meticulous style of painting was developed for the *famille rose* group. The subject matter of this class of wares was occasionally devoted to European themes in the 18th century.

BIBLIOGRAPHY. M. Beurdeley, *Porcelain of the East India Companies*, London, 1962.

MARTIE W. YOUNG

FAMILY OF CHARLES IV. Oil painting by Goya, in the Prado Museum, Madrid. See GOYA Y LUCIENTES, FRANCISCO JOSE.

FANCELLI, LUCA. Italian sculptor and architect (b. Florence, 1430; d. Mantua, 1495). Although little is known of Fancelli's early career in Florence, he is thought to have executed Brunelleschi's plans for the Pitti Palace. By 1450 he was in Mantua in the employ of Lodovico Gonzaga. He is best known as Alberti's personal envoy for the planning and construction of the churches of S. Sebastiano and S. Andrea in Mantua. The reputation he gained from these two works perhaps led to commissions for a group of minor buildings which have been attributed to him. The most notable of these are the Palazzo Arrivabene and the *Domus nova* of the Gonzaga Castle in Mantua. Although Fancelli was quite active, his work for Alberti has completely overshadowed his own career.

BIBLIOGRAPHY. A. Venturi, *Storia dell'arte italiana*, vol. 8, pt. 1, Milan, 1923.

FANCELLI FAMILY. Italian sculptors (17th cent.). Originally Florentine, they were active in Rome, where several were associated with Bernini. Carlo I had four sons who were sculptors: Antonio, Giacomo Antonio, Cosimo, and Francesco. The last had sons and grandsons who carried on the tradition. Giacomo Antonio (1619–71) and Cosimo (1620?–88) stand out. The former seems to have been an assistant to Bernini in about 1630, was active in the decoration of St. Peter's in the 1640s, and executed the representation of the Nile on Bernini's *Four Rivers* fountain (ca. 1650). Cosimo was the sculptural executant for Pietro da Cortona and decorated most of that architect's buildings. The *Angel with the Sudarium* on the Ponte S. Angelo (1668–69) is his. Like Ercole Ferrata, he tended toward a classicizing simplicity of form.

BIBLIOGRAPHY. R. Wittkower, *Art and Architecture in Italy, 1600–1750*, Baltimore, 1958.

FAN CH'I. Chinese painter (1616–after 1692). His *tzu* was Hui-kung. A native of Chiang-ning in Kiangsu Province, he is usually considered by the Chinese to be the second most prominent member of the so-called Eight Masters of Nanking, ranked only behind the leader of the school, Kung Hsien. He painted both figures and flowers, subjects which Kung Hsien never attempted, as well as delicate and charming landscapes. Fan Ch'i patterned himself, according to Chinese sources, after the Sung-dynasty master Liu Sung-nien and can be considered a traditionalist who refined an earlier style. *See* KUNG HSIEN; LIU SUNG-NIEN.

BIBLIOGRAPHY. A. Lippe, "Kung Hsien and the Nanking School, II," *Oriental Art*, IV, 1958.

FANG, *see* AFRICA, PRIMITIVE ART OF (CENTRAL AFRICA: GABON).

FANG, *see* CHINA: PAINTING (Copies).

FANG TS'UNG'I (Fang Fang-hu). Chinese painter (fl. 2d half of 14th cent.). One of the most important followers of Kao K'o-kung, he entered a Taoist monastery and spent most of his life on Lung-hu Mountain in his native Kiangsi. His recognition came rather late in his life, partly because of his lack of contact with other painters. His best-known works are all in the National Palace Museum Collection now in the Sun Yat-sen Museum, Formosa. *See* KAO K'O-KUNG.

FAN K'UAN. Chinese painter (fl. late 10th cent.–ca. 1030). A native of Hua-yuan, Shensi Province, Fan K'uan was probably the leading exponent of what has been termed the "monumental" style in the early Sung landscape tradition. Not much is known of his life since he did not hold any official position in the government. He was greatly admired by Mi Fu, the major critic of the early 12th century, who placed Fan K'uan at the top of the landscape painters and considered him the equal of the great Ching Hao. Like Ching Hao, Fan K'uan was something of a Taoist recluse. His landscape style is preserved in one magnificent painting, *The Travelers among Mountains and Streams*, in the Sun Yat-sen Museum on Formosa. The work is unsigned, but it has been largely accepted by most scholars as being close to Fan K'uan, if not by him. The giant, stark cliff of the mountain dominates the vision of the painter, and the scale of the small figures near the bottom of the painting emphasizes the sense of monumentality. Conceived in a heroic mode and executed with absolute clarity, the painting seems to epitomize the lucid vision of the Northern Sung landscape masters. *See* CHING HAO; MI FU.

BIBLIOGRAPHY. O. Sirén, *Chinese Painting, Leading Masters and Principles*, vol. 1, New York, 1956.

MARTIE W. YOUNG

FANLIGHT. Arched window, generally with radiating subdividing members resembling a fan. Set above windows and doors, fanlights were popular in 18th-century American Colonial architecture, especially elliptical ones above an entrance door flanked on either side by narrow sidelights or windows.

FAN PAGODA, *see* K'AI-FENG.

FANTASTIC ART. Any art that is eccentric, grotesque, or perversely or irrationally imaginative in character. It belongs to no period or country. It excludes art that is merely visionary, as is the case in many religious paintings. A Tantric Buddhist god with many arms seems strange and thus fantastic to a Christian but not to a Tibetan. On the other hand, the visionary art of William Blake is so personal in nature as to be considered fantastic. *See* BLAKE, WILLIAM; TANTRA.

Unless the element of the fantastic is induced and encouraged, it rarely seems fantastic to its creator. The images of the Gorgon Medusa, gargoyles on Gothic cathedrals, the demon guardian Niō by the Japanese sculptor Unkei, Goya's *The Sleep of Reason Produces Monsters*, the Casa Zuccari in Rome, Gaudí's Church of the Sacred Family in Barcelona, the German film *The Cabinet of Dr. Caligari*, and much of the art of the surrealists are fantastic because the artists willed them to be so. Unkei's temple guardians were made frightful so as to ward off evil spirits. Goya wished to communicate his hatred of man's cruelty and senseless bestiality toward his fellow creatures in his aquatints of war atrocities and did so through distortion. The architect of the Casa Zuccari cast the frames of the door and windows as faces with gaping mouths out of a spirit of fun. Hogarth employed the irrational situation to make apparent a rational one, just as he exaggerated folly or immorality to drive home the need for reforms. *See* GAUDI I CORNET, ANTONI; GOYA Y LUCIENTES, FRANCISCO; HOGARTH, WILLIAM; UNKEI.

It was the surrealists and their immediate predecessors, the Dadaists, who made a wholly conscious attempt as a group to demean reason, law, and morality. The surrealists sought to reveal another reality, that of the subconscious, which they considered a "sur-reality." They turned to their dreams for subject matter and revealed their obsessions and phobias. They permitted imagination full play but were, however, quite consciously seeking the fantastic element and fantastic relationships within a picture. Seeking a sharp-focus realism to express himself, the celebrated surrealist Salvador Dali eloquently brought together improbable combinations of objects. Marc Chagall allowed his figures to defy gravity, to float above a city as if in a somnambulant state. He freely invented combinations, such as a mermaid with the head of a fish and the body of a woman. The French artist Jean Dubuffet treats the human figure in such a manner that the result is fantastic: he flattens out the forms, distorts the whole with contours which are calculatedly crude, and substitutes a gritty texture for that of flesh and earth colors for flesh tones, so that the figure ultimately resembles a land mass seen from a height. *See* CHAGALL, MARC; DADA; DALI, SALVADOR; DUBUFFET, JEAN; SURREALISM.

The reasons for the fantastic in art vary considerably.

Ignace-Henri-Jean-Théodore Fantin-Latour, *Hommage à Eugène Delacroix*. Louvre, Paris.

In some cases the expression is so personal as to defy analysis, while in others the fantastic has a utilitarian role: to frighten away evil spirits or, as in a depiction of hell, a warning to reform.

BIBLIOGRAPHY. A. H. Barr, Jr., ed., *Fantastic Art, Dada, Surrealism*, New York, 1936; R. Callois, *Au Coeur du fantastique*, Paris, 1965.

ROBERT REIFF

FANTIN - LATOUR, IGNACE - HENRI - JEAN - THEODORE.

French painter of portraits, flowers, and allegories (b. Grenoble, 1836; d. Buré, 1904). He received his first instruction from his father, who was a portrait painter. In 1850 he began studying under Lecoq de Boisbaudran at the Ecole de Dessin, and in 1854 he was at the Ecole des Beaux-Arts. The previous year he had begun his large number of copies after old masters in the Louvre, particularly Veronese, Titian, Rubens, Rembrandt, De Hoogh, and Chardin. He met Degas in 1851 and later became a friend of Manet and Whistler.

The strongest influences on him during this period were Courbet, whose "school of realism" he attended in 1861, and Delacroix. His respect for the latter was embodied in his major group portrait, *Hommage à Eugène Delacroix* (Salon of 1864; Paris, Louvre), in which admirers such as Manet, Whistler, Baudelaire, and Fantin-Latour are grouped around a portrait of the master. He later produced a series of group portraits of friends from the literary and musical world in a similar vein, for example, *Atelier aux Batignolles* (1870; Louvre), featuring the younger revolu-

tionary artists, Renoir, Bazille, Monet, and Zola, around their hero, Manet; and *Autour du piano* (1885; Louvre), with lovers of Wagner around Emmanuel Chabrier.

In 1862 he produced his first work with a musical subject, *Tannhäuser on Venusberg*, inspired by the opera by Wagner, his favorite composer. Like many of his allegorical works, it exists in more than one medium, lithograph (1862) and painting (1864). In 1864 he began to produce flower paintings, which were much admired and which provided a constant source of income. He also produced lithographs illustrating, for example, Jullien's books on Wagner (1886) and on Berlioz (1888).

Fantin-Latour's early portraits are marked by a quiet realism derived from his study of the old masters. There is an obvious affinity with the Dutch painters in the quietness of his groups and still lifes, while his later portraits are painted with a dark tonality. The figures are arranged with dignity and an insistent realism that was undoubtedly influenced by photography (*La Famille Dubourg*, Salon of 1878; Louvre). His work shows something of Manet's and Courbet's directness, but he never became an impressionist, though he was their friend. From the 1870s he enjoyed an academic success, and his respect for the past and the power of official art prevented him from developing his modern tendencies. His musical pictures looked backward in feeling to the romantic movement, with their evocation of the music of Wagner and Berlioz, and were increasingly divorced from contemporary trends, though his lithographic technique was to be an influence on the drawings of Seurat.

Cosimo Fanzago, cloister of S. Martino, Naples, begun 1625.

His works can be best seen in the Louvre, and there are examples in most major European and American museums.

BIBLIOGRAPHY. G. Hédiard, *Fantin-Latour: Catalogue de l'oeuvre lithographique du maître*, Paris, 1906; Mme Fantin-Latour, *Catalogue de l'oeuvre complet (1849–1904) de Fantin-Latour*, Paris, 1911; F. Gibson, *The Art of Henri Fantin-Latour*, London, 1924; Smith College, Museum of Art, *Henri Fantin-Latour, 1836–1904: An Exhibition*, Northampton, Mass., 1966. MALCOLM CORMACK

FANTONI, ANDREA. Italian sculptor and engraver (b. Rovetta, 1659; d. Bergamo, 1734). The son of Grazioso Fantoni, Andrea was a member of the very important Fantoni family of sculptors. He was a student of Pietro Rame, a German artist who lived in Brescia. His most important works are in the Church of S. Martino at Alzano Maggiore, where he executed the pulpit and designed the furniture for the sacristy. The bas-reliefs of the pulpit represent scenes from the Old and New Testaments and are in rococo style.

BIBLIOGRAPHY. R. Wittkower, *Art and Architecture in Italy, 1600–1750*, Baltimore, 1958.

FANZAGO (Fanzaga), COSIMO. Italian architect and sculptor (1591–1678). He was a leading artist in the baroque school of Naples. From 1612, when he is documented as a master of sculpture, until his death, Fanzago produced an enormous *oeuvre* of churches, palaces, fountains, pulpits, altars, and religious statues. His highly decorative style is exuberant in its profusion of fleshy, organic forms and is most frequently given to pictorial fantasy. In Fanzago's important cloister (1625 and later) at S. Martino in Naples, for instance, the architecture is graceful and elegant, recalling the most classical designs of Tuscan arcades. The doors leading into the cloister, however, are fully baroque in decoration, with spiral volute forms, half-length figures of saints in twisted and dramatic positions inside oval recesses, and garlands of heavy fruit. Architecturally, Fanzago's churches always show some attempt to enforce a central plan; hence, most frequently a mannerist tension is set up between the axes. Most characteristic of Fanzago's style, however, are his subordination of structure to curvilinear surface designs and his late baroque spirit of inventiveness, as in the trompe l'oeil cupolas of S. Lorenzo in Lucina, Rome.

BIBLIOGRAPHY. P. Fogaccia, *Cosimo Fanzago*, Bergamo, 1945; R. Wittkower, *Art and Architecture in Italy, 1600–1750*, Baltimore, 1958. PENELOPE C. MAYO

FARA (Shuruppak). Fara, the ancient Mesopotamian city of Shuruppak, 12 miles south of Nippur, in southeastern Iraq, and originally situated on the Euphrates River. In Sumerian legend it was the abode of Utnapishtum. Shuruppak was excavated by the Deutsche Orient-Gesellschaft in 1902–03 and by the University Museum of the University of Pennsylvania, Philadelphia, in 1931. The finds date chiefly from the late protoliterate, Early Dynastic, and Ur III periods. Pottery, stone vessels, and seals come from the earliest level and are divided from the succeeding occupations by a sterile flood deposit. Clay tablets with drawings and seal impressions from the houses excavated are Early Dynastic II in date, and a number of cuneiform literary tablets belong to the Early Dynastic III period. Both mat and sarcophagus burials were found in the Early Dynastic levels. A circular granary of the Early Dynastic period was reused in the Ur III period for mass burials.

BIBLIOGRAPHY. A. Deimel, *Die Inschriften von Fara*, 3 vols., Leipzig, 1922–24; E. Heinrich, *Fara...*, Berlin, 1931; E. Schmidt, "Excavations at Fara, 1931," *The Museum Journal [of] the Museum of the University of Pennsylvania*, XXII, Sept.-Dec., 1931.

FARFA BIBLE. Eleventh-century Mozarabic illuminated manuscript, in the Vatican Library, Rome.

FARINA, PININ. Italian auto designer and coach builder (1895–1966). Born in Turin, he received his education in the local coachworks and set up his own small workshop for motor car bodies before World War I. After World War II he created the sensual, smoothly curved, teardrop forms that became known as the "Italian look" in automobiles. Although he was praised as one of the first of the old custom school of Italian designers to "industrialize," his custom designs for some of his early racers are far more felicitous than the designs he developed after the war for the Nash, a mass-produced American car. Among his most successful designs are the 1947 Cisitalia, the Cis-Alpina, the Alfa Romeo line, and the Ferraris.

FARINATI, PAOLO. Italian painter of Verona (1524–1606). He painted chiefly narrative pictures in large sets for churches. Somewhat influenced by his slightly younger townsman Paolo Veronese, he is more intimately attached to a Roman tradition, which is responsible for his massive, muscular figures in twisted poses. Their somewhat classicizing imitation of Michelangelo causes them to resemble the works of Daniele da Volterra in Venetian fresh air. Numerous drawings by Farinati survive.

BIBLIOGRAPHY. A. Venturi, *Storia dell'arte italiana*, vol. 9, pt. 4, Milan, 1929.

FARMER AND DARK. English architectural firm founded by Frank Quentery Farmer (1879–1955) and Bernard Frankland Dark (1903–   ) in 1934. It has teams in the Middle East doing mainly industrial work, such as the Kuwait power stations (1957). It has built several schools (Sutton Coldfield, 1958) and office buildings (Max Factor, Bournemouth, 1960). The firm works on the principle of groups and smaller teams.

FARNESE BULL. Group sculpture in the National Archaeological Museum, Naples. The original group was set up in Rhodes. The group in Naples was made in the early

3d century of our era for the Baths of Caracalla and was a copy of a work of the 1st century B.C. executed by the artists Apollonios and Tauriskos of Tralles, who worked in Rhodes. The work has undergone several restorations in modern times. The group represents the Punishment of Dirce as she is being tied to a bull by her stepsons, Zethus and Amphion. The figure of Antiope is a Roman addition. The group is pyramidal in structure and recalls in its composition the *Laocoön* group. The violent movement of the figures and the twisting of the bodies create a disturbing effect that is characteristic of late Hellenistic art.

BIBLIOGRAPHY. E. A. Gardner, *A Handbook of Greek Sculpture*, 2d ed., London, 1915; M. Bieber, *The Sculpture of the Hellenistic Age*, New York, 1955.

FARNESE HERACLES. Statue of Heracles found in the Baths of Caracalla, now in the National Archaeological Museum, Naples. The Roman copy was executed in the 1st century B.C. by Glycon, an Athenian artist of the Neo-Attic school who worked in Rome. The original was a famous work by Lysippus. Heracles is represented bearded as an old man standing and leaning heavily on his club, which is covered with a lion skin. The Greek hero is shown as tired and exhausted after his superhuman tasks. In his right hand he holds the Apples of the Hesperides. The figure is massive, with an excess of musculature, and is considerably removed from the Lysippean original. Remains of this type can be found in all media: a good example is offered by a bronze statuette of Heracles in the Walters Art Gallery, Baltimore.

BIBLIOGRAPHY. E. A. Gardner, *A Handbook of Greek Sculpture*, 2d ed., London, 1915; M. Bieber, *The Sculpture of the Hellenistic Age*, New York, 1955.

FARNESE PALACE, ROME, see SANGALLO FAMILY.

FARNESINA PALACE, ROME, see PERUZZI, BALDASSARE.

FASCES. Ax carried before Roman magistrates in ancient times as a symbol of their judicial powers. It was so arranged in a bundle of twigs or rods that only its head projected.

FASCIA. Flat projecting band (from the Latin *facies*, "face"), broader than a fillet. The term also denotes a stringcourse or belt course; a band of facing material, as in architectural trim; and the plain vertical face of a cornice. As a flat band, the fascia describes the subdivisions in classical architraves; Ionic and Corinthian architraves are often subdivided into two or, more commonly, three such bands.

FASOLATO, AGOSTINO. Italian sculptor (fl. Padua, 18th cent.). In 1753 he executed two pilasters with bas-reliefs of putti and ornaments in the choir of S. Antonio. In his *Fall of the Angels* in the Papafava Palace he achieved the feat of carving sixty small figures from one piece of marble.

FASOLO, GIOVANNI ANTONIO. Italian painter of Vicenza (1530–72). A close follower of Veronese, he is most notable for his large group portraits (museums of Vicenza, Sarasota, and San Francisco), including the naïve but vivid fresco series of the Villa Coldogno.

Fatehpur Sikri. Marble-covered tomb of Salim Chisti, ca. 1571.

FASSBENDER, JOSEPH. German painter and graphic artist (1903–). He was born in Cologne and studied there. Fassbender paints freely composed linear abstractions which include references to organic forms—for example, the Klee-influenced augmented monotype *Prophetenfisch* (1948; Amsterdam, Municipal Museum). More recently, his pictures have displayed a more open treatment of space, often including a vague feeling of landscape, as in *Coniectura* (1958–59; Hamburg, Art Gallery).

BIBLIOGRAPHY. G. Aust, *Joseph Fassbender*, Recklinghausen, Germany, 1961.

FATAGAGA, see DADA.

FATEHPUR SIKRI (Fathpur Sikri; Futtehpore Sikri). Indian town some 25 miles west of Agra, in Uttar Pradesh. The emperor Akbar undertook the construction of a new capital city in 1571. The Jami Masjid, begun in that year, was the largest and most important structure of Fatehpur Sikri. It comprises a rectangular area 542 by 438 feet, most of which is occupied by the vast central courtyard. Access to the courtyard is through three monumental portals, of which the most impressive is the Boland Darwaza, erected about 1603. The many covered halls surrounding the courtyard are embellished on their interior surfaces with carved, painted, and inlaid ornament of great brilliance and variety. Salim Chisti's tomb is a structure of modest size set within the courtyard of the Jami Masjid. Square in plan, the tomb consists of the small central chamber crowned by a dome that is encircled by wide verandas. It was originally built of red sandstone in about 1571, but in about 1670 this fabric was clad in white marble, featuring pierced screens and decorative carving.

See also MUGHAL ARCHITECTURE OF INDIA.

BIBLIOGRAPHY. P. Brown, *Indian Architecture*, vol. 2: *Islamic Period*, 4th ed., Bombay, 1959.

FATES (Horae). Marble group (ca. 435 B.C.) of three seated female figures from the east pediment of the Parthenon, now in the British Museum, London. The rich draperies of the figures with their multiple cascading folds are harmoniously combined with the bodies, which they articulate. In this group, classical art reached its zenith.

BIBLIOGRAPHY. E. A. Gardner, *A Handbook of Greek Sculpture*, 2d ed., London, 1915.

Giovanni Fattori, *Cavalryman*. Gallery of Modern Art, Milan. Scenes of military life were the artist's specialty.

FATHER'S CURSE, THE. Oil painting by Greuze, in the Louvre Museum, Paris. *See* GREUZE, JEAN-BAPTISTE.

FATHPUR SIKRI, *see* FATEHPUR SIKRI.

FATIMID ARCHITECTURE OF CAIRO. Egypt was in the possession of rulers of the Fatimid dynasty from 969 until 1171, and most of the surviving Muslim monuments of the period are in Cairo, although there are a few of lesser importance in Upper Egypt. Immediately after the conquest of Egypt in 969 by Gawhar, the general of this new line, he ordered the building of Cairo (al-Qahira) to the north of al-Fustat as an extensive fortified enclosure. In 970 Gawhar had construction started on the al-Azhar Mosque. It was rebuilt many times and later renowned as a university; the few elements of this period indicate the earliest use of a transept in an Egyptian mosque. The al-Hakim Mosque, named after a Fatimid ruler, was erected between 990 and 1012. Square in plan, with a vast open court, it had five sanctuary aisles of seventeen arches each. *See* AL-AZHAR MOSQUE, CAIRO; AL-HAKIM MOSQUE, CAIRO.

At the end of the 12th century Cairo was enclosed by massive walls of cut stone. A long section of the wall and three gateways, Bab an-Nasr, Bab al-Futuh, and Bab Zuweila, survive in good condition and reflect the influence of Byzantine fortifications. Badr al-Gamali, responsible for the walls of the city, erected the al-Guyushi Mosque in 1085 in the Moqattam Hills east of Cairo; it contains the tomb

of the founder and a magnificent stucco mihrab. The mausoleum of Sayyida Ruqayya of 1132 featured a beautiful wooden mihrab, which is now on display in the Museum of Islamic Art, Cairo. In 1125 al-Ma'mun, grand vizier of al-'Amir, erected the Mosque of al-Aqmar, which featured one of the earliest uses of stalactites in Egypt. In addition to these more important structures of the period, numerous smaller mausoleums and shrines remain in good condition. *See* MIHRAB; STALACTITE.

During this period there was an increased use of cut-stone masonry in bands of contrasting color, the monumental entrance was developed, domes were fluted on the exterior and the interior, and the first steps toward the evolution of the stalactite pendentive were taken. The architecture of the period is less notable for structural innovations than for ornamentation, marked by influences from earlier work in North Africa and Syria. Decorative Arabic inscriptions and arabesques were featured, as were panels and mihrabs in stucco and carved woodwork. In general, the decoration was lighter in character and design than were the rather solid monuments of the period.

BIBLIOGRAPHY. K. A. C. Creswell, *The Muslim Architecture of Egypt*, vol. 1, Oxford, 1952.   DONALD N. WILBER

FATIMID GLASS AND CRYSTAL, POTTERY, TEXTILES, *see* ISLAMIC GLASS AND CRYSTAL (FATIMID PERIOD); ISLAMIC POTTERY AND TILES (FATIMID PERIOD); ISLAMIC TEXTILES (FATIMID PERIOD; PAINTED AND PRINTED ABBASID AND FATIMID TEXTILES).

FATTORE, IL, *see* PENNI, GIOVAN FRANCESCO.

FATTORI, GIOVANNI. Italian painter and etcher (b. Leghorn, 1825; d. Florence, 1908). One of the early Italian impressionists, Fattori studied with Baldini in Leghorn, then after 1847 in Florence, until, in a Bohemian phase, he dropped his formal schooling and associated himself with the Macchiaioli. When French troops were in Florence in 1859, Fattori began to paint the scenes of military life that were to become his specialty. In 1869 he was appointed professor at the Florence Academy. Fattori was a sharp observer of nature, but his paintings, although in the energetic tradition of late French realism and early impressionism, are notably lacking in color sense. He also executed landscapes, genre paintings, and portraits (for example, *Le macchiaiole*; Rome, National Gallery of Modern Art). *See* MACCHIAIOLI.

BIBLIOGRAPHY. G. Delogu, *Italienische Malerei . . .*, Zurich, 1939.

FATTORINO, BARTOLOMMEO DEL, *see* BARTOLOMMEO, FRA.

FAUCES. Term used in Roman architecture (from the Latin, meaning "throat"). The fauces is a passage, usually leading from an entrance to the atrium or from the atrium to the peristyle of the private house, or *domus*.

FAUN, HOUSE OF THE, POMPEII. Oldest house in Pompeii (2d cent. B.C.–A.D. 79) and the most remarkable for size and beauty. It is named after a bronze statuette of a dancing faun (Naples, National Archaeological Museum) found in its impluvium. The house occupies an entire insula (315 by 115 ft.) abutting on the north side of the Street of Fortune and had two entrances. It contained a *prothyron* (entrance passage), a Tuscan atrium with a coffered ceiling, and a smaller tetrastyle atrium. A large peristyle in the center of the house occupied nearly the entire width of the two atria. At the end of the house there was a large garden surrounded by porticoes. Several wine amphorae found in the house indicate that it was the residence of a wine merchant. The house yielded, among other finds, the Alexander Mosaic (Naples, National Archaeological Museum). The decoration of the house belongs to the first Pompeian style; it is executed in the incrustation technique, and the walls are painted to resemble slabs of different marbles. *See* ALEXANDER MOSAIC.

BIBLIOGRAPHY. A. Mau, *Pompeii, Its Life and Art*, New York, 1899; L. Curtius, *Die Wandmalerei Pompeijs*, Leipzig, 1929.

FAUNUS. Ancient and popular Roman deity, equivalent to the Greek Pan. Characterized as a good spirit of the countryside, especially the woodlands, he was thought to ensure the fruitfulness of cattle and to predict the future to votaries who slept in the cult precincts. His festival, in early December, was marked by joyous dancing and merrymaking.

FAUTRIER, JEAN. French abstract painter (1898–1964). He was born in Paris of parents from Béarn and brought up in England. He studied at the Royal Academy in London and at the Slade School. His first one-man show was

Jean Fautrier, *The Jewess*. National Museum of Modern Art, Paris.

held in Paris in 1927, and André Malraux helped him get a commission to illustrate Dante. During World War II he was active in the French Resistance, and while in hiding, over a period of two years, he painted *Hostages*, a series of abstractions, which was exhibited in 1945. In sympathy with the Hungarian freedom fighters, in 1956 he painted a triptych, *The Partisans*. In 1957 he was given a large retrospective exhibition at the Sidney Janis Gallery in New York and later exhibited widely. In 1960 he won the International prize for painting at the Venice Biennale.

Fautrier's art is linked with that of Wols, Michaux, Soulages, Hartung, and others in a broad movement called "Art Informel," which finds its ancestry in surrealism, Dada, and the art of Paul Klee. It features varieties of psychic improvisation and advances the aesthetic of irrational, lyrical abstractionism. In a characteristic work, Fautrier masses impasto, usually in broad, coarse strokes, as *haute pâté* with a palette knife. He surrounds this island of thick, clotted pigment with a band of a contrasting, thinly washed-on glaze. Gray and pale blue are predominating colors. These small works seem limited and austere, modest and yet forthright and bold.

BIBLIOGRAPHY. M. Ragon, *Fautrier*, Paris, 1957. ROBERT REIFF

FAUVISM. First of the several avant-garde movements in art that appeared between the turn of the 20th century and World War I. Although it was not launched as the result of a definitive program, Fauvism did possess certain collectively shared traits: brilliant, often pure color; rapidly brushed texture, patchlike or with spots of white canvas left bare; ostensibly improvised or random composition; and strongly subjective handling of themes or natural forms. In most Fauve pictures the space is flatly designated. Landscapes, figure compositions, portrait studies (usually informal in arrangement), and still lifes in this exciting style were abundantly created between 1903 and 1908, with 1905–07 being the high phase of Fauve maturation. After 1908 most of these artists developed in other directions, one or two of them turning to cubism, others retaining semblances of Fauvism but refining them (sometimes to less bold clichés of the earlier values).

The first exhibition at which they showed as a (still unnamed) group was the controversial Salon d'Automne held in Paris in 1905. Two such annuals had already been held, in 1903 and 1904; but although certain pre-Fauve painters had participated, their works had not been collectively shown in special rooms, and the full impact of the new style had not been received. By 1905, however, Henri Matisse (1869–1954) had become the leader of a loosely organized group whose turbulent, vividly hued pictures were placed together. The effect was shocking; the exhibition met with public hostility; it was then that the critics called the painters Fauves, or "wild beasts." With Matisse, the exhibitors included Georges Rouault, Othon Friesz, Albert Marquet, André Derain, Maurice Vlaminck, Henri Manguin, Louis Valtat, Kees van Dongen, Charles Camoin, Raoul Dufy, and Georges Braque. Several of these men had studied under the same teacher, Gustave Moreau, at the Académie Carrière, where they had received basically traditional instruction. Moreau, however, had been a stimulating, though academic, master, and the Fauves-to-be were not dissuaded by him from seeking excitement in the still scandalous works of the postimpressionists. While Matisse and most of the others were fully conversant with the paintings of the great masters at the Louvre, by about 1900 they were increasingly stimulated by what they had seen of the work of Seurat, Signac, Van Gogh, and Gauguin (the Gauguin show at the 1903 Salon d'Automne had a collective effect upon the movement). Cézanne's work, in so far as it was known to the Fauves, was by no means passed by; but the bright color of other postimpressionists appealed more strongly to Matisse and his contemporaries, who also owed something to the Nabis.

The years 1905 to 1907, the zenith of Fauvism, produced a rich complex of canvases which still appear brilliant and modern. Matisse's interiors and landscapes at Collioure and the renowned portrait of Mme Matisse (1905; Copenhagen, State Museum of Fine Arts) brought to vivid maturation his daring palette of saturated greens, vermilions, and blues. He continued in 1906–07 with equally brilliant compositions, some of them with arabesque structuring suggesting the flowing patterns of Gauguin and even the decorative style called Art Nouveau. A younger and especially daring exponent of Fauvist extravagance of color and dashing brush texture was Maurice Vlaminck. André Derain and Georges Braque painted brilliantly, but with a certain discipline of composition that suggests the lesson of Cézanne. Othon Friesz, Van Dongen, and Raoul Dufy also colored their landscapes and figure compositions with powerful planes or passages of ultramarine, vermilions, greens, oranges, and yellows. Marquet, Camoin, Valtat, and Puy were to varying degrees more reserved in their tonalities, offsetting resonant notes of pure hues by distributing them among grayed zones.

Fauvist subjects, like certain aspects of Fauvist style, followed those of impressionist and postimpressionist sources. The beach, the landscape, carnivals, interiors, and, somewhat less commonly, figure compositions and portrait studies were the principal themes. Georges Rouault, who has sometimes been classified as a French expressionist rather than as a Fauvist, chose more serious subjects: sinister judges, women of the night, somber clowns or acrobats.

The Fauvist movement has been compared to the German expressionist movement, and it is true that these styles share certain traits: they both stemmed in part from the reaction of vital-minded young artists against a prevailing, outmoded academic art in their respective countries; they both projected brilliant coloration and spontaneous brushwork; and each manner was indebted in its way to the same late-19th-century sources, especially to Van Gogh. It has been said, however, that the Frenchmen were, traditionally enough, more involved with the formal aspects of pictorial organization, whereas the German expressionists were more emotionally involved with their subjects. It is also significant that Kees van Dongen, Dutch in origin, was an honorary member of the Brücke, exhibiting with them as well as with the Fauves. Finally, both the French and German movements materialized in 1905, although the Fauves individually had developed the style before then.

The Fauvist movement as such had dissipated by 1908, even though Matisse created some of his strongest works after that year. The Fauves did not continue to exhibit as a group; but it was due to their collective energies that the Salon d'Automne, remarkably controversial in 1905, soon became an acceptable institution in the Parisian art scene. Braque left the circle to become the cofounder, with Picasso, of cubism; Derain, after briefly undergoing cubist influence, became a widely popular painter in a somewhat neoclassic manner; Raoul Dufy developed a peculiarly dashing post-Fauvist mode that soon became fashionable among commercial illustrators and fabric designers; and Vlaminck, one of the most consistently Fauvist of the association, turned to brown-and-gray–toned works of a systematized vivacity. Rouault continued his comparatively independent line of development, repeating his somber themes and turning more and more to religious expression. Of all the Fauves, Matisse found the greatest liberation of style and the most long-lasting inventiveness and vigor. Although Derain worked in sculpture from time to time, Matisse was the only Fauve who significantly contributed to that medium.

Fauvism. Henri Matisse, *La Gitane*, 1905. Musée de L'Annonciade, Saint-Tropez.

Fayoum portraits. Example of a mummy portrait of a youth. State Antiquities Collection, Munich.

The Fauvist movement has major importance in the history of early-20th-century art: first, for being the primary avant-garde manifestation among various revolutionary happenings in art before World War I; second, for its specific liberation of color and texture; and, finally, for synthesizing some of the formally significant aspects of postimpressionism and bringing them inextricably into the total aesthetic of modern painting. *See* BRAQUE, GEORGES; CAMOIN, CHARLES; DERAIN, ANDRE; DONGEN, KEES VAN; DUFY, RAOUL; FRIESZ, ACHILLE EMILE OTHON; MARQUET, ALBERT; MATISSE, HENRI EMILE; PUY, JEAN; ROUAULT, GEORGES; VLAMINCK, MAURICE.

BIBLIOGRAPHY. G. Coquiot, *Les Indépendants, 1884-1920*, Paris, 1920; G. Diehl, *Les Fauves*, Paris, 1948; G. Duthuit, *The Fauvist Painters*, New York, 1950; A. H. Barr, Jr., *Matisse: His Art and His Public*, New York, 1951; C. Greenberg, *Henri Matisse*, New York, 1953; M. Raynal, *Modern Painting*, Geneva, 1956; J. P. Crespelle, *The Fauves*, New York, 1962.

JOHN C. GALLOWAY

FAVRAN (Faveran), JAUME. Spanish architect (fl. 1321-30). Jaume Favran is recorded as architect of the new Gothic choir of the Cathedral of Gerona, which had been begun in the last years of the 13th century.

FAYDHERBE, LUCAS. Flemish sculptor (b. Mechlin, 1617; d. there, 1697). Faydherbe worked in Rubens's studio. A painterly quality shows in the reliefs he designed for the Church of Onze Lieve Vrouwe van Hanswijk, Mechlin, for which he was the architect (1663). His great marble monument of Bishop Cruesen in the Mechlin Cathedral is reminiscent of Michelangelo, though Faydherbe never traveled to Italy.

FAYOUM (Fayum) PORTRAITS. Scattered throughout the museums of the world is a series of portraits in full-faced or three-quarter view, painted on gesso-covered wood panels, which seldom reveal more than the head and shoulders. All come from Egypt, mostly from the Fayoum, an oasis that opens out from the western side of the Nile Valley south of Cairo. There, between the 1st and the 3d century of our era, a group of Hellenized Egyptians, and probably foreigners, adopted the practice of mummification and used these portraits to cover the faces of the deceased. Although close dating is impossible, they are important for the study of ancient painting because they range in style from the impressionistic technique often found at Pompeii to the huge-eyed frontal "soul-portrait" that points to a much later development in Byzantine art.

BIBLIOGRAPHY. H. Zaloscer, *Porträts aus dem Wüstensand*, Vienna, 1961.

FAZZINI, PERICLE. Italian sculptor (1913–   ). Born in Grottammare, Italy, he studied privately in Rome in the late 1920s, working on reliefs and on portraits in an idealized naturalistic style. In the 1940s he did figural works with principal attention to synthesis of rhythmic body movements, as in *The Gymnast, Crouching Figure*, and *Acrobats*. There was a further simplification of his style in the 1950s, with movement and formal values superseding the importance of the figure itself. He had one-man shows in Rome and in New York at the Iolas Gallery. He has been represented in international expositions in São Paulo, Antwerp, and Venice. He lives in Rome.

BIBLIOGRAPHY. R. Lucchese, *Pericle Fazzini*, Rome, 1952.

FEASTS, ECCLESIASTICAL. The number of official church holidays has varied greatly over the ages. They may be divided into three groups: those commemorating Christ, such as Sunday, Christmas, Epiphany, Easter, the Ascension, and Corpus Christi; those commemorating the Virgin Mary, such as Presentation in the Temple, Birth, and Assumption; and those commemorating the saints. Feasts are also grouped as Sundays; movable feasts, such as Easter and Pentecost, with variable dates; and immovable feasts such as Christmas, Epiphany, various feasts of the Virgin Mary, and feasts of other saints, with fixed dates.

BIBLIOGRAPHY. A. A. McArthur, *The Evolution of the Christian Year*, London, 1953.

FEATHERWORK. Ornamentation of garments and other objects by means of feathers that are tied, sewn, or woven onto a foundation of sturdier material. The most outstanding examples are the elaborate ceremonial mantles and headdresses produced from the brilliantly colored plumages of tropical birds. These were made by the Indian civilizations of both Mexico and South America, and by the Polynesian peoples of Hawaii and New Zealand. Innumerable overlapping feathers were attached to fabrics of network or to wickerwork frames in large, geometric patterns—a technique known also as "feather mosaic."

BIBLIOGRAPHY. W. T. Brigham, *Hawaiian Feather Work*, Honolulu, 1899; F. S. Dellenbaugh, *The North-Americans of Yesterday*, New York, 1901; G. C. Vaillant, *The Aztecs of Mexico*, Harmondsworth, 1956.

FECAMP, ABBEY OF. Fécamp was one of the first Benedictine chapters to undergo a revival of the rule; it was initiated by the Italian reformer William of Volpiano when he arrived in Normandy from Dijon early in the 11th century. The ultimate result was a great Romanesque church, burned in 1168(?) and rebuilt during the next 100 years, being completed only in 1297. A typical example of Norman Gothic, it is overshadowed, however, by such buildings as the Cathedral at Coutances and St-Laurent at Eu. Fécamp illustrates the slow, uncertain adoption of features from the Ile-de-France in the 13th century, as it retains a long side-aisle bay for each vaulted nave bay.

BIBLIOGRAPHY. R. de Lasteyrie, *L'Architecture religieuse en France à l'époque gothique*, vol. 2, Paris, 1927.

FEDDES VAN HARLINGEN, PIETER. Dutch painter and etcher of portraits, history, city- and landscapes; also poet (1586–ca. 1634). Feddes was born in Harlingen. Little is known of his background and training. His graphic work contains many late mannerist overtones, possibly because of his provincial training. He painted and etched portraits of the counts of Nassau and etched fifty-three portraits for the book *Martini Hamconii Frisia*, published in 1620.

BIBLIOGRAPHY. K. Bauch, "Beiträge zum Werk friesischer Künstler: I, Pieter Feddes," *Oud-Holland*, XLIII, 1926.

FEDERAL ART PROJECT. Part of the Public Works of Art Project, established in the United States in 1933, to alleviate the Depression. In 1935 a special section of fine arts was formed under Edward Bruce in the Treasury Department, and assistance to artists on relief was reorganized as the Federal Art Project under the direction of Holger Cahill. A national program was set up to decorate not only Federal buildings in Washington but also newly erected post offices and schools throughout the country. Holger Cahill reported that five months after the Federal Art Project had been organized, it was employing 5,300 artists on 360 project units in 43 states. While employment figures fluctuated considerably, it is estimated that the project had on its rolls upward of 4,000 artists for a period of eight years.

Although some of the work, especially the murals, was of poor quality, the project was instrumental in providing for the public thousands of handicraft articles and in extending the knowledge of art, socially as well as geographically, through educational programs in underprivileged areas. The artists of the project completed 22,000 drawings for the Index of American Design, thus establishing the first comprehensive record of the decorative and folk arts in the United States.

Among the more noteworthy of the murals executed in Washington were those by Henry Varnum Poor, William Gropper, and John Steuart Curry; these have a boldness of conception, as opposed to the usually more detailed murals of such artists as George Biddle, who did decorations for the Department of Justice. Elsewhere, memorable work was done by Ben Shahn for the Community Center in Roosevelt, N.J., and by Frank Mechau for the Fine Arts Center of Colorado Springs, Colo. The subjects varied greatly. Cameron Booth's *Street in Stillwater* is a portrayal of a small, contemporary Midwestern town, while Peppino Mangravite's mural in the post office of Hempstead, Long Island, shows an early American Indian settlement. Some of the work of Louis Guglielmi presents a haunting evocation of the depersonalized dwellers of Brooklyn. The Federal Art Project also has significant ties with abstract expressionism; Gorky, De Kooning, Rothko, and Pollock were all employed on the project, and it is questionable whether they would have been able to continue their artistic careers without that financial assistance. *See* BIDDLE, GEORGE; CURRY, JOHN STEUART; DE KOONING, WILLEM; GORKY, ARSHILE; GROPPER, WILLIAM; GUGLIELMI, O. LOUIS; MECHAU, FRANK; POLLOCK, JACKSON; POOR, HENRY VARNUM; ROTHKO, MARK; SHAHN, BEN.

BIBLIOGRAPHY. E. M. Benson, "Art on Parole," *American Magazine of Art*, XXIX, November, 1936; H. Cahill, "Artists in War and Peace," *The Studio*, CXXX, July, 1945; E. P. Richardson, *Painting in America*, New York, 1956.

ABRAHAM A. DAVIDSON

FEDERIGHI, ANTONIO (Antonio di Federigo dei Tolomei). Italian architect and sculptor (d. 1490). He directed work on the façade of Orvieto Cathedral, and from 1456 until his death he was *capomastro* of Siena Cathedral and carved for the Loggia della Mercanzia three statues of saints and a marble bench with reliefs, which reflect the mixed influences of Jacopo della Quercia and of antiquity.

FEI, PAOLO DA GIOVANNI. Sienese painter (fl. 1372–1410). He may have been a student of Andrea Vanni. In his early works Fei displays a graceful fluidity of line reminiscent of the Gothic lyricism of Simone Martini. Later, as in his best-known work, *The Nativity of the Virgin* (Siena, Academy), the influence of Bartolo di Fredi appears in the more rigid and mannered gestures, the bright coloration, and the profusion of decorative drapery folds.

FEININGER, LYONEL. American painter (1871–1956). Feininger became a student of music in New York in 1880; he was taken by his parents to Germany in 1887 to study the violin. Determined, however, to become an artist, he studied at the Hamburg Arts and Crafts School and at the Berlin Academy of Fine Arts (1890–91). In 1892 and 1893 he was in Paris and studied at the Aca-

Lyonel Feininger, *Small mask.* Private collection.

démie Colarossi. Living in Berlin until 1906, he worked as an illustrator and cartoonist for German, French, and American journals and newspapers.

In 1911 he met Delaunay and other French cubists in Paris; and cubism, especially its Orphist manner, became a persistent influence upon Feininger's style (early documents of his development are the 1912 *Bicycle Riders,* the 1913 *Sidewheeler,* and the 1914 *Allée*). His prismatic, clear-cut sheafing of planes and his deft handling of light were strongly personal adaptations of Delaunay's more lyrical Orphist style. Feininger's early pictures, which anticipate the development of his whole career, also resemble characteristic works by the futurists and by Franz Marc in his semiabstract phase. Feininger exhibited with the Munich Blue Rider (Blaue Reiter) group and at the Berlin Herbstsalon in 1913.

He was appointed to the faculty of the Bauhaus at Weimar in 1919 and remained with that school most of the time until, after it had moved to Dessau, it was closed by the German government in 1933. During that period he formed the Blue Four group with Kandinsky, Klee, and Jawlensky (formerly with the Blue Rider in Munich) and gave one-man shows at the Anderson Gallery in New York and the Berlin State Gallery. Outstanding works from this period are Feininger's *Viaduct* (1920) and *The Steamer Odin, II* (1927; both New York, Museum of Modern Art), *Church of the Minorites* (1926; Minneapolis, Walker Art Center), and *Towers at Halle* (1931; Cologne, Wallraf-Richartz Museum). He worked almost exclusively in water color and in graphic media from his earliest period.

Feininger resettled permanently in the United States in 1937, his work having been officially proscribed by the Nazi regime. He lived in New York and Connecticut, painting murals for the New York World's Fair in 1939 and holding a large retrospective show at the New York Museum of Modern Art in 1944. Feininger's style was brought to full maturation with water colors such as *Dawn* (1938; New York, Museum of Modern Art), *The River* (1940; Worcester Art Museum), and *Yacht* (1952; private collection). The last-named work reveals a new, although consistent, attention to looser handling of light and definition of major shapes. Additional important exhibitions of Feininger's works were held in 1950 at the Galerie Jeanne Bucher, Paris, and at Curt Valentin's, New York.

Feininger's major work belongs to the stream of development of French cubism and German abstraction. His style is notable for its delicacy and great finish.

BIBLIOGRAPHY. H. Klumpp, *Abstraktion in der Malerei: Kandinsky, Feininger, Klee,* Berlin, 1932; D. C. Miller, ed., *Lyonel Feininger,* exhibition catalog, Museum of Modern Art, New York, 1944; E. Scheyer, *Lyonel Feininger: Caricature and Fancy,* Detroit, 1964.

JOHN C. GALLOWAY

FEI-PO (Flying White). Term in Chinese painting usage that refers to a technique in which the hairs of the brush are allowed to separate as the brush is drawn across the surface. The stroke is thus not a solid black but appears streaked in appearance, with the surface of the paper or silk showing through, and the total visual effect is one of rapidity and slight randomness. The technique apparently was developed first in calligraphy and was adapted to painting as one of the variants of the "broken-ink" (*p'o-mo*) style. *See* P'O-MO.

BIBLIOGRAPHY. F. van Briessen, *The Way of the Brush: Painting Techniques of China and Japan,* Rutland, Vt., 1962.

FEKE, ROBERT. American portrait painter (ca. 1706/10– after 1750). Feke was born in Oyster Bay, L.I. His life can be documented only during a ten-year period, from 1741 to 1750; during this decade he produced a series of elegant and lustrous portraits that mark him as the finest American painter before the middle of the 18th century. Feke's activities before 1741 are completely obscure. In 1741 he was established in Boston as a portrait painter, signing in that year the group portrait *Isaac Royall Family* (Cambridge, Harvard Law School). This work testifies to his acquaintance with the paintings of Smibert, for its pose and treatment are based upon Smibert's *Bishop Berkeley and His Entourage* (1729; New Haven, Yale University Art Gallery). In 1742 Feke married in Newport and settled there, though he made various painting trips to other cities—to Philadelphia in 1746 and 1750 and to Boston in 1748. Nothing is known of him after 1750, except that he may have gone to the West Indies.

Inspired by Smibert's baroque manner, Feke went on to paint portraits epitomizing aristocratic elegance (at least as understood in the Colonies) and characterized by lustrous silks and luminous colors. Like many Colonial painters, he extensively utilized English mezzotints as his prototypes, but his portraits have a sparkle and power that mark them as accomplished works of art. Characteristic of his work are the *Portrait of an Unknown Woman* (perhaps Mrs. John Vinal, ca. 1748; Brooklyn Museum) and the even more sparkling male portraits *Isaac*

Winslow (ca. 1748; Boston, Museum of Fine Arts) and *General Samuel Waldo* (1748–50; Brunswick, Me., Bowdoin Museum of Fine Arts), all three of which display Feke's adroitness with fabrics. Feke could also be successful in much simpler portraits, such as the *Rev. Thomas Hiscox* (1745; private collection). Despite this facility with paint, Feke's work still shows the qualities of a self-taught artist, albeit a sensitive and talented one.

In addition to the institutions mentioned above, Feke's portraits can be found in a number of American museums, including those of New York (Metropolitan Museum of Art), Cleveland, Toledo, Detroit, and Providence.

BIBLIOGRAPHY. H. W. Foote, *Robert Feke: Colonial Portrait Painter*, Cambridge, Mass., 1930; Whitney Museum of American Art, *Robert Feke*, New York, 1946; W. P. Belknap, *American Colonial Painting: Materials for a History*, Cambridge, Mass., 1959.

DAMIE STILLMAN

FELDER, HANS, THE ELDER. German architect (fl. ca. 1460–1500). Felder is recorded from 1461 to 1471 in Lucerne and later in Zurich. His main works are the Church of St. Wolfgang near Cham (1473), the choir of St. Oswald in Zug (begun 1478), the Wasserkirche in Zurich (1479–84), and the chapels at Walenwil and Crespen (1485).

FELICITAS, ST. Roman matron and martyr (d. 2d cent.). Under Marcus Aurelius she was killed after having witnessed the martyrdom of her seven sons, whom she had encouraged to refuse to sacrifice to idols. The story is based on that of the Maccabees, whose mother was named Felicitas. She is shown in art with her sons. Her attributes are a sword with seven heads on the blade, or heads on a platter, and a widow's veil. Her feast is November 23; July 10 is the feast of Felicitas and her sons. *See also* SAINTS IN ART.

FELIN, JEAN DE. French architect (fl. ca. 1502–29). In 1502 Jean de Félin replaced his father, Didier de Félin, as chief architect of the new Pont Notre-Dame in Paris. Between 1506 and 1510 he worked at the sanctuary of St-Aspais in Melun, a building in pure Gothic style. He became royal master of the works in 1519 and was replaced in this post by Jacques Aratre in 1529.

FELIPE DE BORGONA, *see* BIGARNY, FELIPE DE.

FELIXMULLER, CONRAD. German painter (1897–   ). Felixmüller was born in Dresden and was a pupil of Bantzer and Dorsch at the Dresden Academy. He traveled widely and received many prizes for his work. His portraits, figure paintings, landscapes, and religious pictures are done in an expressively realistic style.

FELLHEIMER AND WAGNER. American architectural firm of Alfred T. Fellheimer (1875–1959) and Steward Wagner (1886–1958), specializing in railroad stations. Fellheimer and Wagner designed several important stations during the 1920s: in Boston, North Station (begun 1927); in Buffalo, Central Station (1927–29); and in Cincinnati, their best work, Union Station (1929–33), conspicuous for its enormous 200-foot entrance arch.

BIBLIOGRAPHY. C. L. V. Meeks, *The Railroad Station, an Architectural History*, New Haven, Conn., 1956.

FENESTELLA. Small glazed opening in an altar or shrine for viewing relics within. The term also denotes a small niche on the south side of an altar above a piscina or credence, as well as an opening for a bell in the top of a gable.

FENESTRATION. Arrangement of windows. The term is applied to the size, type, and disposition of windows in architectural design.

FENESTRATO. Combination of windows grouped to form a unit. The term is applied particularly to Venetian examples in which a window group divided by mullions or colonnettes is regarded as a single window.

FENG-HSIEN TEMPLE, *see* LUNG-MEN.

FERBER, HERBERT. American sculptor (1906–   ). Born in New York City, he graduated in 1929 from Columbia University, where he had studied dentistry and oral surgery. From 1927 to 1930 he studied sculpture at the Beaux-Arts Institute of Design, New York City. He began to exhibit sculpture in 1930 at the National Academy of Design, Washington, D.C., and later had several one-man exhibitions. His *. . . and the bush was not consumed* (1951) adorns the façade of the Millburn, N.J., synagogue. The Museum of Modern Art, New York, owns *Portrait of Jackson Pollock* (1949); the Albright-Knox Gallery, Buffalo, owns *Green Sculpture II*; the Whitney Museum, New York, owns his *Sunwheel* (1956); and the collection of Mr. and Mrs. Victor Riesenfeld contains *Mercury* (1955). Ferber is one of the most inventive of the openwork sculptors in soldered metal. This inventiveness appears also in his space design and in his often aggressive shape formation.

BIBLIOGRAPHY. E. C. Goossen, "Herbert Ferber," in *Three American Sculptors*, New York, 1959.

FERENCZY, KAROLY. Hungarian painter (b. Vienna, 1862; d. Budapest, 1917). He studied in Naples, at the Académie Julian in Paris, and in Munich. At first Ferenczy's paintings were naturalistic, influenced by Bastien-Lepage. After the late 1890s his style loosened, and he began to use richer and higher color.

FERETORY. Shrine for relics carries in processions, such as Memling's Gothic shrine of St. Ursula in St. John's Hospital, Bruges.

FERGUSON, FRANK W. American architect (1861–1926). He joined Cram and Wentworth about 1889 and became a major partner when the firm was reorganized as Cram, Goodhue and Ferguson about 1899. As construction engineer and chief of building operations, he designed very little, but was instrumental in realizing some of the firm's designs, notably the Cathedral of St. John the Divine in New York City. *See* CRAM, GOODHUE AND FERGUSON.

FERGUSON, WILLIAM GOWE. Scottish-Dutch still-life painter (b. Scotland, 1632/33; d. there? 1695 or later). Ferguson is listed in Utrecht from 1648 to 1651. In 1649 he was mentioned as a painter and citizen of that city. He was also active in The Hague (1660–68) and Amsterdam (1681). Ferguson traveled in France and Italy. His works show the influence of Jan Weenix and Willem van Aelst.

BIBLIOGRAPHY. A. P. A. Vorenkamp, *Bijdrage tot de geschiedenis van het Hollandsch stilleven in de zeventiende eeuw*, Leyden, 1934.

FERNANDES, MATEUS. Portuguese architect (fl. after 1480; d. 1515). Fernandes's career is identified exclusively with the monastery of Batalha, where he is first mentioned in 1480 and appears as master of the works from 1490 until his death. He was one of the early masters of the Manueline style and is believed to have designed the portal of the Capelas Imperfeitas and the vaulting of the chapel of John II and Queen Leonor. *See* BATALHA: CHURCH OF THE MONASTERY; MANUELINE STYLE.

BIBLIOGRAPHY. R. dos Santos, *O estilo Manuelino*, Lisbon, 1952.

FERNANDES, VASCO. Portuguese painter (ca. 1480–1543). The leading painter of the Renaissance school of his native Viseu, Fernandes worked throughout the Beira region of Portugal and seems also to have worked briefly in the atelier of Jorge Afonso in Lisbon (1514). Works attributed to him with reasonable certainty are the *Lamego Altarpiece* (1506–11; Lamego, Regional Museum), a *Pietà* triptych (ca. 1520–30; Richmond, Cook Collection), the *Pentecost* (1535; Coimbra, Sta Cruz), and a *Calvary* and *St. Peter Enthroned* (ca. 1530–40; both Viseu Museum). In the altarpiece the elegant figures and the detailed and highly accomplished landscape reveal a strong Flemish influence. The *Pentecost* shows mannerist tendencies in its poses, its elongated figures, and its spatial compression, but it also exhibits a new monumentality of form. This quality is carried further in the *Calvary* and *St. Peter Enthroned*, with their heavy and imposing figures and draperies, their symmetrical compositions, and their impressive use of deep space as a foil for the figures.

BIBLIOGRAPHY. R. dos Santos, *L'Art portugais*, Paris, 1953.

FERNANDEZ (Hernandez), ALEJO. Spanish painter (ca. 1475–1543). He arrived in Seville in 1508 from Cordova—probably his birthplace—where he had been established as early as 1498. It is thought he was of German extraction, being the brother of the sculptor known as Jorge Fernández Alemán (the second surname meaning "German"). This supposition is supported by a hybrid German-Flemish stylistic influence. However, his style may be explained by a relationship to a group of Portuguese artists who developed a manner derived from Quentin Metsys. Fernández's use of *sfumato* and linear perspective also demonstrates a knowledge of Venetian painting.

His synthesis of influences served to open up the possibilities in Andalusia for greater freedom of expression than was permitted by the fixed formulas of the late-15th-century Hispano-Flemish manner. The stimulating impact of his art challenged younger artists to master the style with more sophisticated ease. His primitive quality is shown in *Virgen del Buen Aire* (*Virgin of the Favor-able Winds*), painted for the chapel of the Trade House in Seville (1520; Seville, Alcázar). In this, as in most of his works, he creates a mood of dulcet lyricism.

A number of artists continued his style and linked it to the subsequent mannerism in Andalusian art. Among them was Alejo's son Sebastián, who painted an altarpiece for the seminary in Osuna.

BIBLIOGRAPHY. D. Angulo Iñiguez, *Alejo Fernández*, Seville, 1946; C. R. Post, *A History of Spanish Painting*, vol. 10, Cambridge, Mass., 1950.

EILEEN A. LORD

FERNANDEZ, AUGUSTIN. Cuban painter (1929–). Fernández lives in Paris. He paints large, organic forms, sometimes using rounded relief protrusions of machinelike metal forms, in a manner that is often ominous and erotic.

FERNANDEZ (Hernandez), GREGORIO. Spanish sculptor and architect (1565/66–1636). Born in Galicia, he may have trained in Valladolid under Francisco del Rincón, a disciple of Juan de Juni. Later Fernández worked for the Italian Milan Vimercati, a former assistant of Pompeo Leoni. Fernández was a prolific artist and there are many extant works by him.

He worked in polychromed wood in a style of baroque realism, creating a strong sense of immediacy in the figures. Specializing in cult images and *pasos* (single or group sculptures to be carried in processions), he became expert in creating postures and facial expressions appropriate to an instantaneous dramatic impact. *The Dead Christ* (1605; Madrid, Capuchinos del Pardo) and *The Veronica* from a *paso* of *Christ Carrying the Cross* (1614; Valladolid Museum) illustrate this ability. His polychromy is usually harsh, his drapery heavy and angularly mannered in the folds, and his textures, with the exception of flesh, are often arbitrarily unrelated to reality.

He executed many notable altarpieces, including the high altar (1624–34) in the Plasencia Cathedral. The architecture of these altarpieces was habitually composed of tiered rectangular panels flanked by columns, single or in clusters, with pediments to isolate the main panel or to cap the top. Pediments also joined the reliefs, since Fernández tried to avoid gradations of planes. His reliefs consist of figures in the round and others half-rounded (*en cabochon*, beetle-shaped with flat backs), attached to a painted backdrop in an appliqué technique.

BIBLIOGRAPHY. R. de Orueta, *Gregorio Hernández*, Madrid, 1920; E. García Chico, *Gregorio Fernández*, Valladolid, 1952; M. E. Gómez-Moreno, *Gregorio Fernández*, Madrid, 1953.

EILEEN A. LORD

FERNANDEZ LEDESMA, GABRIEL. Mexican painter (1900–). He was born in Aguascalientes. In his writings and paintings he has been inspired by folk art and has used themes such as native dances, death customs, toys, and animals. As editor of *Forma*, an art review, he was among the first to direct attention to the Mexican renaissance.

BIBLIOGRAPHY. V. Stewart, *45 Contemporary Mexican Artists*, Stanford, 1951.

FERNANDEZ MURO, JOSE ANTONIO. Argentine painter (1920–). Born in Madrid, José Antonio Fernández Muro settled in Buenos Aires in 1938. His early work is

Gregorio Fernández, the high altar of Plasencia Cathedral.

in the Fauve tradition. More recent paintings are geometric abstractions, often including embossed rubbings from industrial materials. He is a notable colorist. His work has been widely shown, for example, at the Venice Biennale in 1956.

BIBLIOGRAPHY. M. L. San Martín, *Pintura Argentina contemporánea*, Buenos Aires, 1961.

FERNKORN, ANTON DOMINIK VON. Austrian sculptor (b. Erfurt, 1813; d. Vienna, 1878). He began his training in Munich but worked from 1840 on in Vienna. Fernkorn was a direct inheritor of the classicizing influences of Thorwaldsen and Schwantaler, but his works, infused with a baroque and fiery spirit, stand by themselves. The *Lion of Aspern*, near Vienna, and *Prince Eugène*, Vienna, a monumental equestrian piece, best illustrate Fernkorn's dramatic and personal handling of the classical type.

BIBLIOGRAPHY. F. Novotny, *Painting and Sculpture in Europe, 1780–1880*, Baltimore, 1960.

FERRAMOLA, FLORIANO. Italian painter of Brescia (ca. 1480–1528). His leading works are the vivid if naïve secular frescoes from the Casa di Corte, influenced by Luini and Bergognone (London, Victoria and Albert; Brescia, Gallery). He collaborated with the young Moretto da Brescia on the Brescia Cathedral organ shutters (Lovere Cathedral).

BIBLIOGRAPHY. Brescia, *La pittura bresciana del rinascimento*, 2d ed., Bergamo, 1939.

FERRARA. City in north-central Italy. The history of Ferrara is closely linked to the fortunes of the house of Este; in the 15th and 16th centuries the Este family maintained one of the most splendid courts in Europe. The Cathedral, begun about 1135, has a tripartite façade, punctuated by loggias, and is Romanesque below and Gothic above. The three portals and the porch were decorated by Master Nicolaus, one of the most important Italian Romanesque sculptors. The upper part of the porch bears a Gothic statue of the Madonna by Cristoforo da Firenze and relief sculpture representing the Last Judgment. On the south flank stands the majestic campanile, erected between 1412 and 1594. Except for the apse, which was built (1498–99) by Biagio Rossetti, the interior of the Cathedral represents a reconstruction of the 17th and 18th centuries.

The Este Castle, begun in the 14th century and completed in 1570, rises imposingly from its moat. The castle has a square plan with four massive corner towers connected by high curtain walls. Under Borso d'Este (d. 1471) the city was embellished with palaces, notably the Schifanoia Palace, with its famous astrological frescoes by Francesco del Cossa, and churches, including the Certosa. At this time a vigorous local school of painting appeared in Ferrara, personified by Cosimo Tura, Francesco del Cossa, and Ercole de' Roberti. *See* FERRARESE SCHOOL; SCHIFANOIA PALACE.

The reign of Ercole I (1471–1505) was the golden age of Renaissance Ferrara. The brilliant architect and city planner Biagio Rossetti laid out the Herculean Quarter, which, with its broad streets and stately palaces, effectively doubled the area of the city. Thanks to the efforts of Ercole and Rossetti, Ferrara could justly boast of being the first modern city in Europe. Perhaps the two finest buildings erected by Rossetti are the Palace of Ludovico il Moro, executed for the Duke of Milan, and the Diamanti Palace, which takes its name from its rusticated façade. Under Alfonso I (1505–34), Ariosto's patron, a new school of painting appeared, represented by Garofalo, Ortolano, and the Dosso brothers. The splendor of the Ferrarese court continued until the death of Alfonso II (1597), when the establishment of papal rule signaled the beginning of a period of decline. *See* DIAMANTI PALACE.

The National Archaeological Museum contains material from Spina. The Municipal Picture Gallery documents the evolution of Ferrarese painting from the 14th through the 16th century. Attached to the Cathedral is a small but significant museum. *See* FERRARA: MUSEUMS.

BIBLIOGRAPHY. G. Agnelli, *Ferrara e Pomposa*, 3d ed., Bergamo, 1906; P. E. Arias and N. Alfieri, *Il Museo Archeologico di Ferrara*, Ferrara, 1955; R. Longhi, *Officina Ferrarese, 1934...* (...Opere complete di Roberto Longhi, vol. 5), Florence, 1956; B. Zevi, *Biagio Rossetti*, Turin, 1960.   WAYNE DYNES

FERRARA: MUSEUMS. Important public art collections in Ferrara, Italy, are located in the museums listed below.

Municipal Picture Gallery. The gallery, located in the Diamanti Palace, comprises twenty rooms of Ferrarese paintings, including works by Cosimo Tura, Ortolano, and Dosso Dossi. Attached is the small Boldini Museum, which contains paintings and documents of Ferrara's leading 19th-century artist, Giovanni Boldini.

National Archaeological Museum. The Palace of Ludovico il Moro was restored (1932–35) to house material from the Etruscan city of Spina, which had intensive traffic with Greece. The finds (6th–3d cent. B.C.) from the necropolis of this Hellenized commercial center include one of the finest collections of painted vases in Italy, as well as bronzes, amber, and gold- and silverwork.

BIBLIOGRAPHY. N. Alfieri and P. E. Arias, *Spina: Guida al Museo Archeologico in Ferrara*, 2d ed., Florence, 1961.

FERRARESE SCHOOL. Northern Italian school of the Renaissance. In the 15th century it was composed of a group of Ferrarese artists who developed a vigorous local tradition. The most important were Cosimo Tura, the founder of the school, Francesco del Cossa, Ercole de' Roberti, Lorenzo Costa, and Francia, a Bolognese in Costa's circle.

Ferrarese school. Ercole de' Roberti, detail of a predella depicting the miracles of St. Vincent Ferrer. Palazzo di Schifanoia, Ferrara.

In the 16th century Ferrarese painting was largely molded by influences from the High Renaissance art of Venice and Rome. Dosso, whose somewhat romantic style is especially indebted to Giorgione and Titian, was the most outstanding master of the later school. Others in the circle were his brother Battista del Dosso, Ortolano, and Garofalo. *See* COSSA, FRANCESCO DEL; COSTA, LORENZO; DOSSO; DOSSO, BATTISTA DEL; FRANCIA; GAROFALO; ORTOLANO; ROBERTI, ERCOLE DE'; TURA, COSIMO.

BIBLIOGRAPHY. B. Berenson, *The Italian Painters of the Renaissance*, rev. ed., London, 1952.

FERRARI, AGOSTINO. Italian painter (fl. late 14th cent.). He is known from a *Crucifixion* with many figures, signed and dated 1376, in the Church of S. Antonio di Combo in Bormio (Valtellina).

BIBLIOGRAPHY. F. M. Valeri, "Note d'arte valtellinese," *Rassegna d'arte*, VI, September, 1906.

FERRARI, DEFENDENTE. Italian painter of Piedmont (fl. 1509–47). Ferrari is known from unimportant legal documents of his active years in the small town of Chivasso, Piedmont, and one documented and nine other signed works, mainly altarpieces. The chief ones are at S. Giovanni d'Avigliano (two, one of 1511), Ivrea Cathedral (1521), the Rosminian monastery (1523), Oldenburg, Germany, Museum (1528), and S. Antonio in Ranverso (1531). All show a strong influence from northern painters in the general tradition of Rogier van der Weyden, with some infusion of provincial Gothic ornamentalism and more of Italianate classic balance. The typical Madonna type is narrow-faced but graceful. The attribution of the painting in Turin Cathedral, with vivid scenes of the stories of SS. Crispin and Crispinian, is questioned.

BIBLIOGRAPHY. Turin, Mostra d'arte al Palazzo Carignano, *Gotico e Rinascimento in Piemonte* (catalog), Turin, 1939.

FERRARI, ETTORE. Italian sculptor (b. Rome, 1849; d. there, 1929). He studied at the Academy of St. Luke and later became president of the Fine Arts Academy, Rome. He was particularly concerned with the representation of historic and patriotic figures. His style is romantic in feeling and at times sentimental; but his modeling shows attention to detail and his best work has buoyant charm.

BIBLIOGRAPHY. A. R. Willard, *History of Modern Italian Art*, 2d ed., London, 1900; F. Sapori, *Modern Italian Sculpture*, Rome, 1949.

FERRARI, GAUDENZIO. Italian painter of Lombardy (ca. 1480–1546). He worked in many small cities west of Milan, especially Vercelli and Varallo, until 1539, when he became Milan's leading artist. Early influenced by Leonardo and Bramantino, Ferrari developed his own style tending toward realistic folk art, with swirling robes, crowds, and action to evoke stormy scenic drama. The result resembles late Gothic wood sculpture in Germany.

His works are numerous and include large fresco cycles at S. Maria delle Grazie, Varallo (1513), S. Cristoforo, Vercelli (1532), S. Maria dei Miracoli, Saronno (1534), and S. Maria della Pace, Milan (1545). Throughout his life he decorated a number of chapels at the Sanctuary of Sacro Monte, Varallo, achieving an extraordinary effect with the frescoes providing a panoramic background for

Gaudenzio Ferrari, fresco decoration with angels in glory, in the dome of S. Maria dei Miracoli, Saronno, Italy.

realistic sculpture groups. He also painted many nervous, vivid altarpieces and narrative pictures.

BIBLIOGRAPHY. E. Halsey, *Gaudenzio Ferrari*, London, 1908; Vercelli, Museo Borgogna, *Mostra di Gaudenzio Ferrari*, Milan, 1956.

FERRARI, GIOVANNI ANDREA DE. Italian painter (b. Genoa, 1598; d. there, 1669). He studied with Bernardo Castello and Bernardo Strozzi. He was the head of a large studio, but in the latter part of his life he was incapacitated by illness. His last dated work is the *Madonna del Carmine* (1635) in the Church of the Carità at Alassio.

BIBLIOGRAPHY. E. Falletti, "Inediti giovanili di Gio. Andrea de Ferrari e proposte per una cronologia," *Commentari*, VII, 1956.

FERRARI, GREGORIO DE'. Italian painter (1647–1726). He was an important figure in the formation of the great decorative style in late Genoese fresco painting. His style, represented in the sparkling fantasies painted for the Balbi-Gropallo Palace in Genoa (1684) and the ethereal *Death of St. Scholastica* (ca. 1700; Genoa, S. Stefano), is essentially a brilliant fusion of Pietro da Cortona's grand manner with the luminous color and supple linear qualities that De' Ferrari learned from studying the works of Correggio in Parma in 1669–73. In its combination of grace, delicate effects of lighting, and languid charm, De' Ferrari's art is clearly a part of the development of the rococo movement in Italy.

BIBLIOGRAPHY. A. Griseri, "Per un profilo di Gregorio de Ferrari," *Paragone*, VI, July, 1955; R. Wittkower, *Art and Architecture in Italy, 1600–1750*, 2d ed., Baltimore, 1965.

FERRARI, LORENZO DE'. Italian painter (1680–1744). The son of the early-rococo Genoese artist Gregorio de' Ferrari, Lorenzo carried his father's decorative style to brilliant heights in his exquisite designs for the gallery of the Cataldi Palace (now Camera di Commercio, Via Garibaldi). Scenes from Vergil's *Aeneid* set into a lavish program of *tondi*, lunettes, and ceiling frescoes are all enmeshed in a rich gilded stucco framework. The fundamental strength and *élan* of Lorenzo's airy illusions are characteristic of the native vivacious Genoese rococo style and stand in contrast to the more effeminate charm of the French rococo, a style also represented in numerous contemporary Genoese monuments.

BIBLIOGRAPHY. O. Grosso, *Dimore genovesi: I palazzi, le ville, i castelli*, Milan, 1956; R. Wittkower, *Art and Architecture in Italy, 1600-1750*, 2d ed., Baltimore, 1965.

FERRATA, ERCOLE. Italian sculptor (1610-86). He was active in Naples and Rome. In the 1650s he was a trusted assistant of Bernini. Ferrata's chief works, in the classicizing baroque style, are *St. Agnes on the Pyre* (1660) and the *Stoning of St. Emerentiana* (finished by L. Retti), both in S. Agnese in Agone, Rome. He had a large, influential studio.

BIBLIOGRAPHY. R. Wittkower, *Art and Architecture in Italy, 1600-1750*, 2d ed., Baltimore, 1965.

FERREN, JOHN. American painter (1905–   ). Born in Pendleton, Ore., he lived in Europe from 1929 to 1938. He studied in Paris, Florence, and Spain and was at first interested in sculpture, which he left for painting about 1931. A certain sculptural interest is still apparent in the solidly modeled abstract shapes of his compositions from the late 1930s. In the 1940s Ferren painted figures in clean, bright colors and flat designs. His later abstractions, somewhat based on natural appearance, are open in formal structure and high in color, for example, *The Garden* (1954; New York, Whitney Museum). In his most recent paintings thick coiling lines of bright pigment are organized against rectangular fields of flat color.

BIBLIOGRAPHY. A. C. Ritchie, *Abstract Painting and Sculpture in America*, New York, 1951.

FERRER, MIGUEL, *see* TORO, OSVALDO LUIS, AND FERRER, MIGUEL.

FERRI, CIRO. Italian painter and draftsman (1634-89). He was born in Rome. A student of Pietro da Cortona, Ferri was Cortona's most competent and closest follower. Working primarily in Rome and Florence and often entrusted with the completion of decorative schemes begun by his master, he is famed today as a continuator of Cortona's high baroque style.

FERRISS, HUGH. American architect, writer, and illustrator (1889-1962). He was born in St. Louis and studied at Washington University. In 1915 he began to practice in New York. He is best known for his vision of the 20th-century city, *The Metropolis of Tomorrow*, published in New York in 1929.

FERRO, GREGORIO DE. Spanish painter and illustrator (b. Santa María de Lamas, 1742; d. Madrid, 1812). He studied with Mengs at the Madrid Academy and was named director of the academy in 1804. Most of his works are devotional paintings in the style of Mengs for churches in Madrid and Toledo. His illustrations were usually engraved by others (*Viaje de España*, 1772).

FERROCONCRETE, *see* CONCRETE, REINFORCED.

FERRUCCI, ANDREA. Italian sculptor (b. Fiesole, 1465; d. Florence, 1526). Originally a decorative carver, he is considered one of the best sculptors of the early 16th century. Some of his works are the font in the Cathedral of Pistoia, a bust of Marsilio Ficino in the Cathedral of Florence, and the tomb of Antonio Strozzi in S. Maria Novella in Florence.

BIBLIOGRAPHY. W. G. Waters, *Italian Sculptors*, 2d ed., London, 1926.

FERRUCCI, FRANCESCO DI SIMONE (Francesco del Tadda). Italian sculptor and architect (b. Fiesole, 1437; d. Florence, 1493). A member of a family of marble carvers, he was decisively influenced by Desiderio da Settignano and later by Andrea del Verrocchio. He brought to bear a command of fine ornament and a feeling for strong plastic forms, as his monument to Alessandro Tartagni (d. 1477) in S. Domenico, Bologna, shows.

FERSTEL, HEINRICH VON. Austrian architect (1828-83). He worked in Vienna. One of his most important buildings is the Neo-Gothic Votivkirche, designed in 1858. His style illustrates the Austro-Germanic tendency toward richer and more Gothicizing forms, as well as European tendencies toward creative eclecticism.

BIBLIOGRAPHY. H. Tietze, *Wien*, Leipzig, 1923.

FESZEL, FRIGYES. Hungarian architect (1821-84). He worked in Budapest. A student at the Munich Academy, Feszel shows in much of his work the influence of the contemporary architecture of Berlin and Vienna in its tendency toward ornateness and Gothicism.

FETE CHAMPETRE. Term referring to subject matter innovated between 1716 and 1720 by Jean-Antoine Watteau, representing the pleasures of country life enjoyed by Paris society during the Regency. The term at this time is synonymous with *fêtes galantes*. Watteau was struck by the poetic affinity between the pastoral revery of Giorgione's *Concert champêtre* (Paris, Louvre) and the charm of the informal afternoon theatricals, emulating the Italian theater, that were held in the park of Montmorency by his patron, P. Crozat. Such a work as *Les Amusements champêtres* (London, Wallace Collection) reveals the immemorial nostalgia for nature experienced by urbanists. Ultimate sources are Theocritus's *Bucolics* and Vergil's *Eclogues* visually transposed into murals in Pompeian villas, Botticelli's *Primavera* (1478; Florence, Uffizi), and others. Echoes occur in Manet's *Déjeuner sur l'herbe* (1863; Paris, Louvre) and Picasso's *Demoiselles d'Avignon* (1907; New York, Museum of Modern Art).

BIBLIOGRAPHY. E. Pilon and F. Saisset, *Les Fêtes en Europe au XVIIIe siècle*, St-Gratien, 193?; R. H. Wilenski, *French Painting*, rev. ed., London, 1949.

FETI (Fetti), DOMENICO. Italian painter (b. Rome, 1589; d. Venice, 1623). After studying with Cigoli in Rome (1604-13), Feti went to Mantua to become court painter to Duke Ferdinando and remained there for nine years. He made a brief trip to Venice to collect paintings for the Duke in 1621, and transferred to that city in 1622.

There is little evidence of Cigoli's teachings in Feti's

Domenico Feti, *The Veil of Veronica*. National Gallery, Washington, D.C. (Samuel H. Kress Collection, 1952).

early style; he was influenced to a greater extent by the *Caravaggisti* and Rubens. His *Image of the Virgin Supported by Angels* (Baltimore, Walters Art Gallery), painted for S. Lorenzo in Damaso, Rome, is one of the few paintings documented during his Roman period. Although it is based on a painting by Rubens for the Chiesa Nuova (Grenoble, Museum), there are elements of Caravaggesque light, which can also be seen in his *Six Sainted Martyrs* series (Mantua, Ducal Palace), one of which is signed and dated 1613, the year in which he went to Mantua. There, Feti once more fell under the spell of Rubens, as well as of Tintoretto, combining the flickering light effects of the latter with a rich and painterly surface, as in the *Miracle of the Loaves and Fishes* (Mantua, Ducal Palace). His last years were devoted to small easel paintings, such as the *Flight into Egypt* (ca. 1621–23; Vienna, Museum of Art History). With increasing painterliness he fused figures with atmospheric landscapes, laying the groundwork for 17th-century Venetian painting.

The best measure of Feti's later stylistic development and the continuation of influences from his early years in Rome may be found in a series of parables painted for the Duke of Mantua between 1618 and 1622. The imagery, couched in popular terms, is the kind that appealed to Feti, nourished as he was on the example of Caravaggesque genre. A comparison of the *Mote and the Beam* (York, Art Gallery; Rome, Vici Collection), painted before his Venetian sojourn in 1621, with the *Good Samaritan* (Dresden, State Art Collections, Picture Gallery; Boston, Museum of Fine Arts; New York, Metropolitan Museum), painted after, reveals how the example of Vene-

tian painting led him to accentuate painterly and *mouvementé* qualities, to lighten his palette, and to devote greater portions of the canvas to landscape. These effects were further developed by Johann Liss (in Venice ca. 1620–29) and characterized the dominant trend in Venetian art of the 17th century.

BIBLIOGRAPHY. D. Feti, *Domenico Feti . . .* (catalog), ed. R. Oldenbourg, Rome, 1921; G. Paccagnini, "Dipinti di Domenico Feti a Mantova," *Studi in onore di Matteo Marangoni*, Pisa, 1957; *La pittura del seicento a Venezia* (catalog), 2d ed., 1959; P. Askew, "The Parable Paintings of Domenico Fetti," *Art Bulletin*, XLIII, 1961.

STEPHEN E. OSTROW

FETISH. Work of primitive art which is thought to house a spirit. Native worshipers believe that veneration of the fetish will placate the spirit it contains.

FETIYE CAMI, CONSTANTINOPLE, *see* St. Mary Pammakaristos, Constantinople.

FETTI, DOMENICO, *see* Feti, Domenico.

FETTI, GIOVANNI DI FRANCESCO. Italian sculptor and architect (fl. Florence, 1355–86). It is known from documents dating from 1355 to 1386 that he participated in the construction of the Cathedral of Florence. In 1377 he was confirmed as *capomastro*. In 1381 he became *capomastro* for the Loggia dei Lanzi, and between 1384 and 1385 he participated in the figural decoration there after drawings by Agnolo Gaddi.

FEUCHTMAYER, JOSEPH ANTON. Bavarian sculptor (b. Linz, 1696; d. Mimmenhausen, 1770). Feuchtmayer was the scion of a family of stuccoists of Wessobrunn. He supplied ornamental sculpture of exceptional quality for many churches in southern Germany and northern Switzerland. His figures convey religious excitement through complex movement, a richly broken surface, and considerable anatomical elongation.

BIBLIOGRAPHY. W. Boeck, *Joseph Anton Feuchtmayer*, Tübingen, 1948.

FEUERBACH, ANSELM. German painter (b. Speyer, 1829; d. Venice, 1880). One of the leading German Romantic painters, Feuerbach began his career as a student of Wilhelm von Schadow and J. W. Schirmer at the Düsseldorf Academy in 1845. From 1848 to 1850 he was in Munich, where he studied intensively the Dutch and Flemish masters in the Pinacothek. He was in Paris between 1851 and 1853, studying for a time with Thomas Couture, and was strongly influenced by Delacroix and Courbet. In 1855 he went to Italy with the poet Scheffel, stopping first in Venice and then in Rome, where he remained until 1873, when he was called to teach history painting at the Vienna Academy. In 1876 he returned to Venice.

Before his sojourn in Italy, Feuerbach's art differed little from that of other students of Couture (*Hafis in der Schenke*, 1852; Mannheim, Municipal Art Gallery). Once there, however, he quickly developed a powerful neoclassical style, under the stimulus of antique art and Italian High Renaissance painting, which put him at the forefront of the second generation of German Romantic painters working in Rome. Many of the masterpieces of this Italian period are notable for their powerful female figures and nudes, most of them inspired by two Italian women, Nanna Risi and Lucia Brunacci. These works include *Iphigenia* (1871), *Judgment of Paris* (1870; both Hamburg, Art Gallery), and *Battle of the Amazons* (1871; Nürnberg, Galerie).

BIBLIOGRAPHY. E. Voigtländer, *Anselm Feuerbach: Versuch einer Stilanalyse*, Leipzig, 1912; H. Uhde-Bernays, *Feuerbach*, Leipzig, 1914; E. Heyck, *Feuerbach*, Bielefeld, 1925; U. Christoffel, *Anselm Feuerbach*, Munich, 1944.

DONALD L. EHRESMANN

FIAMBERTI, TOMMASO. Lombard sculptor (fl. 1st quarter of 16th cent.; d. Cesena, 1525). Born in Campione, he worked in Ancona, Cesena, Forlì, and Ravenna. His single signed work is a tomb in S. Maria dei Servi, Forlì, executed with Giovanni Ricci in 1502; it was modeled after the tomb of Barbara Manfredi in S. Biagio, executed by Francesco di Simone Ferrucci.

FIAMMENGHINO, IL, *see* ROVERE, GIOVANNI MAURO DELLA.

FIAMMINGO, IL, *see* DUQUESNOY, FRANCOIS.

FIASELLA, DOMENICO (Il Sarzana). Italian religious, historical, and portrait painter (b. Sarzana, 1589; d. Genoa, 1669). He was the son of the goldsmith Giovanni Fiasella and the pupil of Aurelio Lomi. A facile but uneven painter, Domenico used soft, harmonious colors in his religious, Biblical, mythological, and allegorical compositions, some done in the manner of Raphael.

FIBULA. Type of brooch or clasp used to fasten garments, especially the tunic, at the shoulder. Fibulae were an important art form among barbarian tribes during the migration period, when they were made of elaborately decorated precious metals, either enameled or inlaid with semiprecious stones. Fibulae are the main source for the study of barbarian ornament.

BIBLIOGRAPHY. W. von Jenny and W. F. Volbach, *Germanischer Schmuck des frühen Mittelalters*, Berlin, 1933.

FICQUET, ETIENNE. French engraver (b. Paris, 1719; d. there, 1794). He was the pupil of G. F. Schmidt and J.-P. Le Bas. Ficquet has left 352 known plates, among the earliest and best of which are a series depicting distinguished literary personages of France. He worked in a neat and delicate style. His portraits of Rubens and Van Dyck appear in Descamp's *Vie des peintres flamands et hollandais*.

FIDENZA, *see* BORGO SAN DONNINO, FIDENZA.

FIELD, ROBERT. Canadian painter (b. England, ca. 1769; d. Jamaica, 1819). He lived in the United States (1794–1808) and in Halifax (to 1817). Trained as an engraver at the Royal Academy School, London, he was the most competent painter of oil portraits and miniatures on Canada's eastern seaboard, where he influenced many other painters.

BIBLIOGRAPHY. H. Piers, *Robert Field . . .*, New York, 1927.

FIELDING, ANTHONY VANDYKE COPLEY. English painter (b. East Sowerby, Yorkshire, 1787; d. Worthing, 1855). He received his first lessons in painting from his father. Fielding traveled throughout the British Isles and settled in London in 1809. There he studied with John Varley. Fielding was a very popular and prolific watercolorist. He began with landscapes of Wales and the Lake country. After 1814, because of his wife's health, he was periodically at the shore, where he began his production of seascapes. His vast output necessitated much repetition, and he often reduced his water colors to a formula of circular or ovoid composition. He was president of the English Water Colour Society from 1831 to 1855.

FIELIUS, JAN, *see* TILIUS, JAN.

FIENE, ERNEST. American painter and graphic artist (b. Eberfeld, Germany, 1894; d. Paris, 1965). After coming to the United States in 1912, he studied at the National Academy of Design and the Art Students League. He taught for many years in New York. His early works were strongly composed, realistic landscapes and urban subjects; he later showed a tendency toward abstraction in city scenes.

FIESOLE, FRATE GIOVANNI DA, *see* ANGELICO, FRA.

FIESOLE, MINO DA, *see* MINO DA FIESOLE.

FIESOLE. Town 3 miles northeast of Florence, Italy. Fiesole was originally an Etruscan city known as Faesulae. Dating from the Etruscan period are the walls and the ruins of a temple. The Roman theater has a cavea of the 1st century B.C. Next to the theater is a museum containing Etruscan and Roman antiquities excavated in and near Fiesole.

In Christian times Fiesole became the seat of an episcopal see. Its cathedral, S. Romolo, of Tuscan Romanesque style, was built in 1028; it was enlarged in 1256 and in the 14th century. Adjoining the Cathedral is a typical Tuscan campanile of about 1213. The Palazzo Pretorio dates from the 14th century.

The slopes around Fiesole are dotted with fine examples of early Renaissance villas, among them the Villa Palmieri and the Villa Medici (Poggio a Caiano). Begun by Giuliano da Sangallo and restored by Michelozzo, the Villa Medici was decorated by Franciabigio, Pontormo, and Andrea del Sarto. Near Fiesole is the Badia, rebuilt by Brunelleschi. *See* BADIA, THE. *See also* SANGALLO FAMILY.

FIGARI, PEDRO. Uruguayan painter (b. Montevideo, 1861; d. there, 1938). Figari was successful as a journalist, lawyer, public official, and writer (for example, *Arte, estética, ideal*, 1912). His painting was inspired by Uruguayan collections of Vuillard, but his style is his own after 1921. Uruguayan life is his theme, as in *Pericón* (Montevideo, National Museum of Fine Arts).

BIBLIOGRAPHY. Comisión Nacional de Bellas Artes, *Exposición Pedro Figari*, Montevideo, 1945.

Fibula. An important art form among the barbarian tribes. Example from the Museum of Medieval Art, Rome.

FIGHTING TEMERAIRE, THE. Oil painting by Turner, in the National Gallery, London. *See* TURNER, JOSEPH MALLORD WILLIAM.

FIGINI AND POLLINI. Italian architectural firm of Luigi Figini (1903–   ) and Gino Pollini (1903–   ). Original members of the Gruppo 7, they were among the first architects to work in Italy in a contemporary mode. The firm became known in 1933 with its Artist's House at the Fifth Triennale in Milan. The firm designed the main plant of the Olivetti Company in Ivrea (1939–42), along with other elements in the Olivetti complex, and the Church of the Madonna of the Poor in Milan (1952).

FIGLINE MASTER. Italian painter (fl. early 14th cent.). The name given to this artist derives from the location of a *Maestà* ascribed to him. He has also been identified with the Master of the Fogg Pietà. Although he probably worked with Giotto at Assisi, the Figline Master followed a different path, one that made him a leading exponent of an art deeply influenced by the French Gothic style. His work eschews the volumetric monumentality of Giotto for angular, emotionalized forms within tableaulike, linear compositions.

BIBLIOGRAPHY. L. Marcucci, "Dal 'Maestro di Figline' a Giottino," *Jahrbuch der Berliner Museen*, V, 1963.

FIGUEIREDO, CRISTOVAO DE. Portuguese painter (fl. 1515–40). One of the leading painters of the school of Lisbon and a student of Jorge Afonso, Figueiredo entered the Lisbon Guild in 1515 and was painter to the Infante Cardinal Dom Afonso in 1531. Figueiredo worked at times in collaboration with Francisco Henriques and with Garcia Fernandes. His major work is the retable of Sta Cruz in Coimbra (1522–30). A *Deposition*, once part of this altarpiece, is preserved in the National Museum, Lisbon. In 1533–34 Figueiredo worked at Lamego in the Convent of Ferreirim and in 1538–39 at Batalha on a retable (now lost). The portraits of donors in Figueiredo's works are justly admired for their realism and striking harmonies of gray and black. His religious works, often triangular in composition, are dramatic and colorful and are unusually painterly for this time.

BIBLIOGRAPHY. R. dos Santos, *L'Art portugais*, Paris, 1953.

FIGURATIVE ART. Art containing some degree of representational form or recognizable images. It contrasts with the term "nonfigurative," which indicates a nonrepresentational art. The figurative quality of a Kokoschka painting may thus be contrasted with the nonfigurative quality of a Kandinsky painting.

FIGURINE. Any small sculptured figure or group of figures executed in clay, porcelain, or similar vitreous substances. Figurines are frequently decorated with gold or colors. Greek Tanagra figurines of the 4th century B.C. are examples.

FIJI ISLANDS, *see* OCEANIC ART (MELANESIA).

FILARETE (Antonio di Piero Averlino). Italian sculptor and architect (after 1400–after 1464). Born in Florence, he may have been trained in sculpture in Ghiberti's workshop.

Filarete, façade of the Ospedale Maggiore, Milan.

In 1433 (or 1438) Filarete began, for Pope Eugene IV, the bronze central doors for Old St. Peter's in Rome, which were set in place in 1445 and moved to the present structure in 1619. Filarete was expelled from the papal territories prior to 1449 and went to Florence, Venice, and finally in 1450 to Milan.

Under the patronage of Francesco Sforza he executed reliefs for a tower (since destroyed) on the Sforza Castle in Milan, was briefly appointed architect of the Cathedral of Milan, and in 1457 received a commission to design and execute a new hospital for the city of Milan, the Ospedale Maggiore. Although it was not finished until the 18th century and although Filarete's elevations were altered, this hospital represented a new concept in sanitation and comfort. Its plan, itself an architectural innovation, established the basic organization for hospitals until the 18th century and prefigured the plan of the Escorial. During the construction of the Ospedale Maggiore, Filarete designed a cathedral for Bergamo and composed a treatise on architecture. He resigned from the Ospedale Maggiore in August, 1464, but no further documentation of his life or work is known to exist.

BIBLIOGRAPHY. M. Lazzaroni and A. Muñoz, *Filarete*, Rome, 1908; H. Roeder, "The Borders of Filarete's Bronze Doors," *Journal of the Warburg and Courtauld Institutes*, X, 1947; J. R. Spencer, "La datazione del trattato . . .," *Rivista d'arte*, ser. 3, XXXI, 1956; J. R. Spencer, "Filarete and His Central-plan Architecture," *Journal of the Society of Architectural Historians*, XVII, 1958; H. Saalman, "Early Renaissance Architectural Theory and Practice in Antonio Filarete's Trattato . . .," *Art Bulletin*, XLI, 1959.

JOHN R. SPENCER

FILIGREE. Delicate form of jeweler's ornament composed of gold or silver wire drawn out to great fineness and then twisted, braided, or shaped into a variety of circular and geometric forms. The filigree pattern is attached to the underlying metal ground with a combination of solder and borax applied by a blowpipe. The finest examples of filigree work are seen in Greek and Etruscan jewelry, medieval reliquaries, and the production of India.

Filigree. Leech-type earring. National Museum, Taranto.

FILIPPI, SEBASTIANO, THE YOUNGER (Bastianino).
Italian religious painter (b. Ferrara, 1532; d. there, 1602).
The son and pupil of Camillo Filippi, Sebastiano was a
painter of the Lombard school. At eighteen he went to
Rome, where he became a disciple of Michelangelo, whose
style he imitated with uneven success.

FILIPPO DA VERONA. Italian painter (fl. 1509–15). He
is known from signed frescoes at S. Antonio, Padua; Madonnas in the museums of Bergamo, Fabriano, and Turin;
and a *St. Jerome* (London, private collection). His mechanical Bellinesque compositions are influenced by Carpaccio
and later by Raphael.

BIBLIOGRAPHY. B. Berenson, *The Venetian Painters of the Renaissance*, 3d ed., New York, 1897.

FILIPPO DI MATTEO TORELLI. Florentine miniaturist
(1409–68). He is first mentioned as receiving payment for
a miniature of St. Gregory in 1436. His most important
work was the decoration of a series of choir books for
S. Marco (1446–54; Florence, Museum of San Marco). He
was only responsible for the decoration; Zanobi Strozzi is
known to have done the actual miniature work. Filippo also
did a page of the Gloria for the Book of S. Giovanni Gualberto (Venice, Cini Collection). His last work was an
Evangelarium (1465–68; Florence, Laurentian Library),
which was completed after his death by Ser Ricciardo di
Nanni. Filippo was known as a great decorator; his innovations became the vogue in the mid-15th century.

BIBLIOGRAPHY. M. L. D'Ancona, *Miniatura e miniatori a Firenze
dal XIV al XVI secolo*, Florence, 1962.

FILLET. Flat, narrow molding. Usually without enrich-
ment, fillets are often used to separate other moldings and
to terminate the molded profiles of cornices. They also
separate the concave flutes, or vertical grooves, in column
shafts, as in Ionic and Corinthian architecture.

FIN DE SIECLE. French term meaning end of century.
Specifically, it denotes a period in French art at the end
of the 19th century marked by various styles of enervation
and private reverie. It is characterized by the decorative
eroticism of Art Nouveau, the pallid visions of Puvis de
Chavannes, the more somber waterscapes of Monet, the
decadent opulence of Gustave Moreau, and the mysticism
of the Rose Croix group. *See* ART NOUVEAU; MONET,
CLAUDE-OSCAR; MOREAU, GUSTAVE; PUVIS DE CHAVAN-
NES, PIERRE; ROSE CROIX MOVEMENT.

BIBLIOGRAPHY. S. Hunter, *Modern French Painting*, New York,
1956; N. Pevsner, *Pioneers of Modern Design from William Morris
to Walter Gropius*, rev. ed., Baltimore, 1964.

FINE ARTS. General term for the group of arts that in-
cludes architecture, sculpture, painting, and some minor
arts. Fine art, as distinct from applied, industrial, and
commercial art, is not primarily utilitarian.

FINELLI, GIULIANO. Italian sculptor (b. Carrara, 1601;
d. Rome, 1657). In 1622 he became Bernini's first assistant.
Algardi's influence is strong in Finelli's tomb of Giulio
Antonio Santorio in St. John Lateran, Rome (early 1630s).
Soon after, in Naples, his work became coarser.

BIBLIOGRAPHY. R. Wittkower, *Art and Architecture in Italy, 1600–
1750*, Baltimore, 1958.

FINIAL. Terminal or crowning element, often of floral
form (from the Latin *finis*, "end"). It is used in steles,
pediments, gables, roofs, and pinnacles. Characteristic of
medieval architecture, finials often terminate the pinnacles
of flying buttresses.

FINIGUERRA, MASO (Tommaso). Italian goldsmith,
draftsman, niellist, engraver, and intarsia designer (b. Florence, 1426; d. there, 1464). Although he seems to have
worked mostly from the designs of others, Finiguerra was
considered the master of niello by his contemporaries
and later by Vasari and Cellini, and he was highly regarded
for his other talents. However, none of the many works
attributed to him in various media can be completely
authenticated; they are assigned on the basis of his supposed relationships with other artists.

He probably worked as an assistant to Ghiberti in the
last years of completing the east door of the Florence Baptistery. Attributed to him are niello plates depicting scenes
of the Creation, which come to us in the form of sulphur
casts (London, British Museum). These borrow directly
from Ghiberti's door panels. A silver pax with a niello
of the Crucifixion (Florence, National Museum), which
may be identical with one made by Finiguerra for the
Florence Baptistery (1452–55), also shows the influence of
a Ghiberti relief of the subject. Other influences, particularly of the figure style of Fra Filippo Lippi, appear in
sulphur casts of scenes from the Passion (British Museum;
Paris, Louvre).

It seems likely that Finiguerra collaborated with Antonio
del Pollaiuolo for several years (1459–64). In this relationship it is probable that Pollaiuolo created most of the
original designs and Finiguerra engraved and finished the
niello plates. To this collaboration belong a pax with the
Crucifixion (Louvre) and one with the Coronation of the

Virgin (Florence, National Museum), in which Pollaiuolo's incisive and vigorous style of draftsmanship are in evidence.

There is clear evidence that Finiguerra also designed five intarsia panels in the Sacristy of the Florence Cathedral (1463–64) under the supervision of Giuliano da Maiano. The influence of Baldovinetti is seen in the stiff *Presentation of Christ* and *St. Zenobius* panels; of Pollaiuolo, in the lively *Annunciation, Amos*, and *Isaiah* panels.

Vasari credited Finiguerra with the invention of engraving on copper, as a development out of engraving for niello. In any case, he was certainly one of the first to produce engravings. Those on the planets (British Museum) attributed to him have a childish quality in their drawing and in their crowding of multitudes of figures and other elements.

An important volume of drawings, the *Florentine Picture Chronicle* (British Museum), is usually credited to Finiguerra. Presenting a Biblical history of the world, it

Maso Finiguerra, *Adam and Eve.* **Engraving. Uffizi, Florence.**

provides a source for the study of many 15th-century motifs. The volume is incomplete, and Finiguerra may have been working on it at his death.

BIBLIOGRAPHY. J. G. Phillips, *Early Florentine Designers and Engravers*, Cambridge, Mass., 1955.   DONALD GODDARD

FINSONIUS (Finson; Fynson), LODOVICUS (Louis). Flemish painter of religious subjects and portraits (b. Bruges, ca. 1580; d. Arles, 1632 or 1618). He followed Abraham Janssens and Rubens's style of 1614–18 in the classicist manner, featuring firmly modeled bodies. Furthermore, a prolonged Italian sojourn and work done in Naples under the direction of Caravaggio decisively influenced Finsonius's style. He settled in Aix-en-Provence, where he contributed to the collection of the humanist Peiresc. Finsonius was responsible for a lasting impression of unmitigated Caravaggesque realism upon the contemporary Provençal school. There exist altarpieces by Finsonius signed "Ludovicus Finsonius Belga Brugensis," such as the *Resurrection* (1610; Aix, Church of St. John); portraits; and attributions of copies or imitations after Caravaggio.

BIBLIOGRAPHY. A. von Schneider, *Caravaggio und die Niederländer*, Marburg, 1933; Milan, Palazzo Reale, *Mostra del Caravaggio e dei caravaggeschi, catalogo...*, 2d ed., Florence, 1951.

FIORE, ERNESTO DE. Italo-German sculptor (b. Rome, 1884; d. São Paulo, 1945). He studied painting at the Munich Academy (1903–04), and his painting was influenced by Hodler. The sculpture of Maillol attracted Fiore, and he turned to sculpture about 1910. He became a German citizen in 1914 and settled in Berlin. His characteristic works, although related to the aesthetic of Maillol in general interpretation, bear resemblance to the simplified, restrained expressionist forms of Gerhard Marcks and Georg Kolbe, as in the nude, *The Soldier* (1918; Hamburg). Fiore left Germany in 1936 for Brazil. His work was shown at the Venice Biennale in 1950.

BIBLIOGRAPHY. A. C. Ritchie, *Sculpture of the 20th Century*, New York, 1952.

FIORE, JACOBELLO DEL, *see* JACOBELLO DEL FIORE.

FIORENTINO, DOMENICO, *see* BARBIERE, DOMENICO RICOVERI DEL.

FIORENTINO, FRANCESCO, *see* BANCHI, FRANCESCO DI ANTONIO.

FIORENTINO, NICCOLO (Niccolo de Forzone Spinelli). Italian goldsmith and medalist (b. Florence, 1430; d. there, 1514). He was a member of a Florentine family of goldsmiths and the son of Forzone Spinelli. Niccolò is thought to have engraved seals for Charles the Bold of Burgundy in 1468, and in 1484 he repaired the silver seal of the Arte de' Giudici e Notai of Florence. Niccolò made a number of Renaissance medals characterized by their powerful portraiture. These include *Silvestro Daziari* (1485; Vienna, State Collection of Medallions), *Lorenzo de' Medici* (ca. 1490; Florence, National Museum; London, British Museum; Paris, National Library; Vienna, State Collection of Medallions; New York, Metropolitan Museum), and *Alfonso I d'Este* (1492; London, Paris, Vienna). A large number of medals have been attributed to him, including a group of portraits of members of the French court, such as *Charles VII* (ca. 1494–95; New York, Paris), which

Niccolò Fiorentino, *Giovanna Tornabuoni*, from the Medici collection of medals. National Museum, Florence.

were probably made at Florence rather than in France; a Roman group (1480–86); a Savonarola; and a literary heroes group. Many of these attributions have been questioned. Although it is certain that Niccolò visited Flanders, there is no evidence that he made medals there.

BIBLIOGRAPHY. British Museum, Dept. of Coins and Medals, *A Corpus of Italian Medals of the Renaissance before Cellini*, by G. F. Hill, 2 vols., London, 1930.   CLARE VINCENT

FIORENTINO, NICOLAO, see DELLO DI NICCOLO DELLI.

FIORENZO DI LORENZO.
Italian painter (b. Perugia, ca. 1440; d. there, 1522–25). Registered in the painters' guild from 1463 on, he introduced into Umbrian painting the plastic tendencies of Verrocchio and the Florentines before entering the orbit of Perugino and Pinturicchio.

His development may be followed in his only signed work, the niche frame of *The Madonna with SS. Peter and Paul* (1487) from S. Francesco al Prato, and such attributed works as the triptych of *The Madonna with Angels, Saints, and Donors* from the Confraternita della Giustizia, the altarpiece of *The Adoration of the Shepherds* from Monteluce, and the fresco of *The Mystic Marriage of St. Catherine* (1498) from S. Giorgio, all in the National Gallery of Umbria, Perugia. A series of eight panels (one dated 1473) of the miracles of St. Bernardino of Siena, in the National Gallery of Umbria, may be from his workshop or circle.

BIBLIOGRAPHY. R. van Marle, *The Development of the Italian Schools of Painting*, vol. 14, The Hague, 1933.

FIORENZUOLA, GIOVANNI.
Italian goldsmith (fl. Rome, early 16th cent.). He was born in Milan. Cellini is reported to have been in Fiorenzuola's studio in 1519. Fiorenzuola worked in an excessively rich ornamental style, revealing much interest in northern motifs. He was commissioned to make a set of silver tableware for the papal household. In 1528 he was Consul of the Goldsmiths in Rome.

BIBLIOGRAPHY. S. Churchill, *The Goldsmiths of Italy*, London, 1926.

FIRENZE, FRATE GIOVANNI DA, see ANGELICO, FRA.

FIRING.
Application of heat to pottery for the purpose of driving out moisture and thereby making the clay objects durable. Firing or burning is usually done in a kiln, although even an open fire can be used to bake earthenware. The characteristics of the ware produced depend not only on the clay employed but also on the temperature level of the heat applied. The final stage, brought about by intense heat, is complete vitrification, at which point the clay particles become a homogeneous substance similar to glass.

BIBLIOGRAPHY. W. B. Honey, *The Art of the Potter*, London, 1946; B. H. Leach, *A Potter's Book*, 4th ed., New York, 1949.

FIRST CHURCH OF HARTFORD, CONN., see HARTFORD, CONN.: FIRST CHURCH.

FIRUZABAD.
Ancient town south of Shiraz, in southwestern Iran. It was founded in the 3d century by Ardashir

Firuzabad. Palace of Ardashir I, roofed with domes built on squinches.

I, first king of the Sassanian dynasty. Firuzabad was built on a circular plan, and from the air one can see the outline of the walls and the lines of its two radial avenues.

Near the site is the ruined palace of Ardashir I, constructed of plaster-coated rubble masonry. Its plan shows a rectangular outline subdivided into two squares. The front one consisted of the reception apartments with a central vestibule (in the form later called a liwan) roofed by a catenary vault, which was flanked on either side by two liwans, and a transverse row of three square rooms, roofed with domes built on squinches. The rear square had a court with a central liwan surrounded by contiguous vaulted rooms. The façade was decorated with two tiers of blind arcades and vertical recesses on the sides.

Two bas-reliefs were cut in the rock faces of the gorge near the town. One depicts the victory of Ardashir over Artabanus V, the last Parthian king; the other shows the investiture of Ardashir by Ahura Mazda.

BIBLIOGRAPHY. R. Ghirshman, *Iran: from the Earliest Times to the Islamic Conquest*, Harmondsworth, 1954; R. Ghirshman, *Persian Art: The Parthian and Sassanian Dynasties*, New York, 1962.

DONALD N. WILBER

FISCHER, HANS. Swiss painter, graphic artist, and illustrator (1909–58). Born in Bern, he studied in Geneva, in Zurich, and in Paris with Fernand Léger. Fischer illustrated several books, including the *Fables* of La Fontaine.

FISCHER, JOHANN MARTIN. Austrian sculptor (b. Bebele, 1741; d. Vienna, 1820). He worked mainly in Vienna, where he was professor of anatomy from 1786 at the Academy of Sculpture. He renovated Georg Raphael Donner's fountain in the Neuer Markt, Vienna, and was a close follower of this baroque sculptor. Fischer infused an early strain of classicism into his work.

BIBLIOGRAPHY. F. Novotny, *Painting and Sculpture in Europe, 1780–1880*, Baltimore, 1960.

FISCHER, JOHANN MICHAEL. German architect (1691–1766). He worked in Munich. Beginning his career as a bricklayer, he came to Munich from Bohemia in 1717. He was architect of more than 50 abbeys and churches. In his masterpiece, the abbey church of Ottobeuren (1744–67), he concentrated in the interior on a lavish series of interconnecting spaces and an architectural vocabulary used strictly as ornament.

BIBLIOGRAPHY. P. Heilbronner, *Studien über Johann Michael Fischer*, Munich, 1934.

FISCHER, KARL VON. German architect (1782–1820). He worked in Munich. He is responsible for the layout of the Karolinenplatz (1808) and for the National Theater (1810–18), both designed in the romantic classical style of urban planning similar to that of Friedrich Weinbrenner's Karlsruhe Marktplatz.

FISCHER, THEODORE. German architect (1862–1938). Born in Schweinfurt, he studied in Munich, where he became the city's building administrator. He worked in a simplified Romanesque revival form, for example, the Church of the Redeemer in Munich (1899–1901), the Garrison Church at Ulm (1908–11), and the Art Gallery at Stuttgart (1911).

Johann Bernhard Fischer von Erlach, Karlskirche, Vienna.

FISCHER VON ERLACH, JOHANN BERNHARD. Austrian architect (1656–1723). The son of a sculptor, he lived in Vienna. He was in Italy between 1670 and 1687 and is generally believed to have had contact with Bernini's workshop in Rome. In 1687 Fischer von Erlach appeared in Vienna, and two years later he was appointed architectural tutor to Joseph I, king of Hungary; when Joseph became emperor in 1705 he made his tutor Oberinspector, a position that was reconfirmed by Charles VI when he became emperor in 1711. Besides his architectural work, Fischer prepared over a period of eighteen years a treatise on historical architecture (published in English as *A Plan of Civil and Historical Architecture . . .*, London, 1730), one of the earliest books to consider the history of architecture as comprising Oriental, Egyptian, and Near Eastern buildings as well as the classical antiquities of Greece and Rome and to present this history in terms of illustrations instead of verbal descriptions.

His earliest works are the hall and chapel (1689–91) of the castle at Vranov (Frain) in Moldavia; the chapel is related to Guarini's work in spatial complexity, and the hall is an example of the great Austrian baroque. His most important palaces are the Palais Trautson in Vienna and Schönbrunn Castle. Typical of his style is the ground-story rustication that raises the architecture of the upper floors above the spectator, so that the building is viewed as a spectacle. The complexity and drama in the buildup of horizontals and verticals, the dramatic shifts in axes, views, and lighting effects, and great structural daring contribute to this effect. His Hofbibliothek (Austrian National Library) in Vienna carries out a complex spatial arrangement by means of differentiated vaulting zones, screens, and light. *See* SCHONBRUNN CASTLE.

Although he was not a prolific ecclesiastical architect, his most important work is the Karlskirche in Vienna, begun in 1716 and completed by his son after Fischer's death. A unique combination of architectural motifs and iconography, this church shows a universality in its ambitions and forms similar to that advocated in Fischer's treatise. Built as the result of a vow made by Charles VI during a plague, the church was designed as a monument, and its plan was centralized in the tradition of memorial and pilgrimage churches. The varying aspects of this oval, freestanding church illustrate again Fischer's emphasis on dramatic effects.

Fischer von Erlach was one of the most famous architects in Europe in his time. His work, through style and iconography, illustrates the scope of imperial ambitions of the Viennese Emperor. As an architect, Fischer possessed an interest in universal knowledge and scientific understanding of the past that is typical of his age and relates him to such contemporaries as Sir Christopher Wren and Nicodemus Tessin the Younger.

BIBLIOGRAPHY. G. Kunoth, *Die historische Architektur Fischers von Erlach*, Düsseldorf, 1956; H. Sedlmayr, *Johann Bernhard Fischer von Erlach*, Vienna, 1956; H. Keller, "Rückblick auf das Fischer von Erlach-Jahr," *Kunstchronik*, X, July, 1957.

DORA WIEBENSON

FISCHER VON ERLACH, JOSEPH EMANUEL. Austrian architect (b. Vienna, 1693; d. there, 1742). He was the son and pupil of Johann Bernard Fischer von Erlach. After travels to Rome, Leyden, Paris, and England, Joseph worked with his father and completed a number of his projects, including the Hofbibliothek (Austrian National Library, 1722–35) and the Karlskirche (1716–23/24), both in Vienna. Joseph was appointed court architect after his father died in 1723, and designed extensions for the Hofburg and the Winter Riding School (1729–35) in Vienna. *See* HOFBURG, VIENNA.

BIBLIOGRAPHY. T. Zacharias, *Joseph Emanuel Fischer von Erlach*, Vienna, 1960.

FISEN, ENGLEBERT. Flemish painter (1655–1733). Born in Liège, Fisen painted religious scenes and portraits. He studied portraiture with Carlo Maratta in Italy. Back in Liège, Fisen drew inspiration from the tradition set down by Bertholet Flémalle.

BIBLIOGRAPHY. J. Helbig, *L'Art mosan, depuis l'introduction du christianisme jusqu'à la fin du XVIIIe siècle*, vol. 2, Brussels, 1911.

FISHER, ALVIN. American landscape, portrait, and genre painter (b. Needham, Mass., 1792; d. there, 1863). He studied painting with John R. Penniman and traveled in England, France, and Switzerland. A member of the Hudson River school, Fisher displays a clarity and charm of organization in his romantic landscapes of New England scenery.

BIBLIOGRAPHY. C. E. Sears, *Highlights among the Hudson River Artists*, Boston, 1947.

FISHER, EDWARD. English engraver (b. Dublin, 1722; d. London, ca. 1785). Working mainly in mezzotint, Fisher did a considerable number of portraits and a few other subjects. His best plates are large reproductions of Reynolds's paintings. Although Fisher's work shows refinement and purity, he is a less powerful engraver than his contemporaries MacArdell and Houston.

BIBLIOGRAPHY. M. C. Salaman, *Old English Mezzotints*, London, 1910.

FISKER, KAY. Danish architect (1893–   ). Born in Copenhagen, Fisker studied at the Copenhagen Art Academy and has been on its faculty since 1924. A key figure in developing Danish architecture during the 1930s, he designed, together with C. F. Møller and Povl Stegmann, the University of Aarhus (1933–47).

FITZGERALD, LIONEL LEMOINE. Canadian painter (1890–1956). His entire life was spent in Winnipeg. After local study, he attended the Art Students League, New York City, studying with Miller and Robinson. Fitzgerald was associated briefly with the "Group of Seven." He painted prairie landscapes and still lifes in oil, and is known for his drawings.

BIBLIOGRAPHY. Ottawa, National Gallery of Canada, *L. L. Fitzgerald, 1890–1956: A Memorial Exhibition*, Ottawa, 1958.

FITZWILLIAM MUSEUM, CAMBRIDGE, ENGLAND, *see* CAMBRIDGE, ENGLAND: FITZWILLIAM MUSEUM.

FIXATIVE. Liquid containing a mild binding medium, such as glue, sprayed onto charcoal, pastel, or chalk drawings to prevent them from rubbing off. It is generally applied with a mouth-operated spray.

FLABELLUM. Fan used by ladies in antiquity to cool themselves. In Christian times it was used to keep the flies away from holy objects during Mass. Most often the flabellum was made of peacock feathers, but sometimes it was composed of lotus leaves or thin pieces of wood.

FLAGELLATION, THE (Christ at the Column). The scourging of Christ before the Crucifixion, mentioned in all four Gospels and represented in art since medieval times. Christ is shown bound to a column, and whip marks are visible on His body. His tormentors, usually three, and spectators are often present. Although the texts say nothing of the column, it is a frequent iconographical subject.

FLAGG, ERNEST. American architect (1857–1947). Flagg was born in New York City. An Ecole des Beaux-Arts graduate in 1888, whose best-known works are stylistically called Beaux Arts, he designed the Singer Office Tower in New York (1907), the Corcoran Art Gallery in Washington, D.C. (1897), and buildings for the United States Naval Academy in Annapolis, Md.

FLAMAND, FRANCOIS, *see* DUQUESNOY, FRANCOIS.

FLAMBE. Ceramic glaze of lavender-red or purple splashed with opalescent blue in a manner suggesting flame. In the 18th century *flambé* was produced in China and Japan by the application of a reddish copper glaze to biscuit porcelain or stoneware. The ware was then subjected to low-temperature firing in a reducing atmosphere. Upon cooling, the formation of minute surface crystals contributed a blue, variegated appearance caused by the reflection of light.

BIBLIOGRAPHY. A. L. Hetherington, *Chinese Ceramic Glazes*, 2d rev. ed., South Pasadena, Calif., 1948.

FLAMBOYANT STYLE. In architecture, a term (from the French *flambeau*, "flame") used to describe the late Gothic form of the 15th and 16th centuries that is characterized by double curves in its tracery, giving it a flame-like appearance. The double curvature—when used for ogee arches—gave the name. The form was strongly influenced by the English curvilinear style and appeared in Europe toward the end of the 14th century. Basically an atectonic form, it was mainly developed for extravagant decorative purposes in the tracery of façades and windows, but it was also used in the complex rib-vaulting systems of the period, completely negating the functional purpose of ribs. Examples are St-Maclou, Rouen; Brou; St-Germain-l'Auxerrois and St-Etienne-du-Mont (interior), Paris; Notre-Dame-de-Lépine, near Châlons-sur-Marne; and the towers of the Cathedrals of Antwerp and Vienna. *See* ANTWERP: CATHEDRAL OF NOTRE-DAME; BROU; OGEE; SAINT-MACLOU, ROUEN.

See also BIARD, PIERRE, THE ELDER; GOTHIC ART (ARCHITECTURE).

FLAMENG, FRANCOIS. French painter and engraver (b. Paris, 1856; d. there, 1923). Son of the artist Leopold Flameng and a student of Cabanel, Hédouin, and Jean-Paul Laurens, this academic artist began showing at the Salon of 1873 and won the Grand Prix in the year of the Paris Exposition (1889). His portrait, history, and genre paintings were in great demand, and he fulfilled several large commissions, including decorations for the Sorbonne

and the Opéra Comique in Paris and others in London, New York, and Moscow.

FLANDES, JUAN DE. Flemish painter (fl. from 1496; d. Palencia? ca. 1519). One of the Flemish court painters to Queen Isabella, Juan de Flandes was established in Spain by 1496. His extant works are predella fragments from a retable for the chapel of the University of Salamanca (1505), twelve panels from the high altar retable in the Palencia Cathedral (ca. 1508), and some of the forty-seven panels of a polyptych done for Isabella, depicting the lives of Christ and the Virgin, now in the Prado, Madrid. He seems to have been influenced primarily by Gerard David and, in the manner of many Flemish artists of the day, by Italian painting. The spatial breadth and compositional clarity of his work, the adjustment between two and three dimensions, are not found in the picture-plane-oriented Spanish painting of the period.

BIBLIOGRAPHY. E. Bermejo, *Juan de Flandes*, Madrid, 1962.

Hippolyte Flandrin, *Figure Study*, Louvre, Paris. The artist began his career as a student of Ingres.

FLANDRIN, HIPPOLYTE. French painter (b. Lyons, 1809; d. Rome, 1864). The greatest religious mural painter in 19th-century France, he began his career as a student of Ingres in Paris in 1829. In 1832 Flandrin traveled to Italy, where he was strongly influenced by 15th-century painting. He sent several paintings to the Salon, such as *St. Clair Healing the Blind* (1837; Nantes Cathedral), which attracted great attention. After his return to Paris in 1838 Flandrin received many major commissions for church murals, including frescoes in the Chapel of St-Jean in St-Séverin, Paris (1840–41); choir frescoes in St-Germain-des-Prés, Paris (1842–46); frescoes in St-Paul, Nîmes (1847–49); and frescoes in St-Vincent-de-Paul, Paris (1849–53). The success of these murals earned Flandrin the title "the second Fra Angelico." In later life he executed many well-received portraits, particularly of young women, such as *Jeune fille à l'oeillet* (Paris, Louvre), which was exhibited in the Salon of 1859. Flandrin's style was similar to that of the German Nazarenes; he combined certain monumental elements from his classical background with features derived from 15th-century painting.

BIBLIOGRAPHY. L. Flandrin, *Hippolyte Flandrin: Sa vie et son oeuvre*, Paris, 1902.   JULIA M. EHRESMANN

FLANNAGAN, JOHN. American sculptor (b. Fargo, N. Dak., 1895; d. New York City, 1942). From 1914 to 1917 he studied painting at the Minneapolis Institute of Arts with Robert Koehler. He was a seaman from 1917 to 1922. Aided by Arthur B. Davies, Flannagan returned to painting and began wood carving, a medium he dropped in 1928. His work in stone began in 1926. Poverty caused him to use fieldstone. He made two visits to Ireland, in 1930 and in 1932–33. After 1934 he began to work in metal, showing at the Weyhe Gallery. The Museum of Modern Art, New York, owns *Triumph of the Egg* (1937) and *Dragon Motif* (1933). The Minneapolis Institute of Arts has his *Not Yet* (1940). Flannagan's strength was in direct stone carving of animals and birds and in his use of the theme of birth.

BIBLIOGRAPHY. New York, Museum of Modern Art, *The Sculpture of John B. Flannagan*, ed. D. C. Miller, introd. C. Zigrosser, New York, 1942.

FLASHED POTTERY. Pottery whose surface has been discolored as a result of being touched by the flames of the firing process. In most cases a flashed surface is considered a defect, but it has also been utilized to decorate the faces of ornamental, or flashed, bricks. Flashing can be avoided by the use of "saggers," clay containers in which individual ceramic pieces are placed to protect them from the flames of a kiln.

FLATIRON BUILDING, NEW YORK, *see* BURNHAM, DANIEL HUDSON.

FLATMAN, THOMAS. English portrait miniaturist, poet, and member of the Bar (b. 1637; d. London, 1688). He was educated at Oxford and Cambridge. His portrait style is based on the broad manner of Samuel Cooper, but his colors are harsher and his figures less rounded than those of the master. Among Flatman's best likenesses are the fine self-portrait in the Victoria and Albert Museum, London, and the portrait of Abraham Cowley in the Alan Evans Collection, England.

FLAT-PATTERN CUBISM, *see* CUBISM, FLAT-PATTERN.

FLAXMAN, JOHN. English sculptor and draftsman (b. York, 1755; d. London, 1826). The son of a molder and dealer in casts of antique sculpture, Flaxman grew up surrounded by the Greek and Roman art that was to be of tremendous influence on his style. A precocious boy, his talent was recognized and encouraged by his father's more prominent clients. At twelve Flaxman won first prize at the Society of Arts. At fifteen he studied and exhibited at the Royal Academy, where he did not get along with Sir Joshua Reynolds, the Academy president. Although he achieved fame early, he was not able to earn a sufficient income until, in 1775, he went to work for Wedgwood producing wax models from which pottery molds were made. His taste for the antique made him the ideal artist for Wedgwood's neoclassical jasper wares.

An important part of Flaxman's work was the funeral monuments he made after 1780. They are in churches all over England, including St. Paul's and Westminster Abbey in London, and are mainly simple classical reliefs with elements of sentimentality that increased as he got older. Flaxman was probably best known in his own time for the outline drawings he did as illustrations for the *Iliad*, the *Odyssey*, the plays of Aeschylus, and Dante, which were engraved by Piroli. In these drawings, linear sculpturesque figures reflect his dependence on ancient and High Renaissance models. Flaxman went to Rome in 1787; he stopped providing models for Wedgwood but took over the supervision of the Wedgwood studio in Rome, where designs from the antique were adapted for pottery by a staff of artists. While in Rome Flaxman was commissioned to do several marble groups, the *Fury of Athamas* (Ickwith, England) and *Cephalus and Aurora*.

His return to London in 1794 marked the beginning of an uneventful but successful mature period; his admirers included Canova, Goethe, and Ingres. He was made an associate of the Royal Academy in 1797, and in 1800 a full academician. In 1810 a chair of sculpture was created for him at the Royal Academy, where he was a valuable teacher. His published lectures show that he was interested in medieval art as well as classical. Flaxman's style was naïve and sentimental, but he was one of the foremost exponents of the neoclassical style in the British Isles. The British Museum, University College, London, and the Royal Academy have some of his best sketches.

BIBLIOGRAPHY. W. G. Constable, *John Flaxman*, London, 1927.
                                                         MARVIN D. SCHWARTZ

FLECHE. Slender church spire, usually of wood, placed at the crossing of nave and transepts and commonly containing the Sanctus bell. The word means "arrow" in French. The flèches of the Cathedrals of Amiens and Notre-Dame, Paris, are notable examples.

FLEGEL, GEORG. German painter (b. Olmütz, 1563; d. Frankfurt, 1638). Flegel was one of the earliest still-life painters in Germany. He began as a landscape painter working in the style of the Flemings of the Frankenthaler school. Examples of his painting are *Still Life* (1589; Kassel, State Picture Collections) and *Still Life with Candle* (Karlsruhe, State Art Gallery).

BIBLIOGRAPHY. W. J. Müller, *Der Maler Georg Flegel und die Anfänge des Stillebens*, Frankfurt, 1956.

FLEMALLE, BERTHOLET. Flemish history painter (b. Liège, 1614; d. there, 1675). A student of Gerard Douffet, Flémalle traveled to Italy in 1638. He worked for Ferdinand II de' Medici in Florence and later at Versailles; he was back in Flanders by 1647. In 1670 Flémalle worked at the Tuileries in Paris and was elected to the Royal Academy of Fine Arts. His style is derived from Roman classical baroque and from Poussin.

BIBLIOGRAPHY. J. Philippe, *La Peinture liégeoise au XVIIᵉ siècle*, Brussels, 1945.

FLEMALLE, MASTER OF, see MASTER OF FLEMALLE.

FLEMISH SCHOOL. In the strictest sense, the term Flemish should be applied only to paintings produced in Flanders after the division of the Netherlands in the second half of the 16th century. This created the Dutch cultural area in the north and the Flemish in the south. Painting in Flanders before this time is more precisely called the "early" or "old" Netherlandish school, although the use of "Flemish" to denote the art of the Van Eycks is not yet obsolete.

The foundation for the great flowering of the Flemish school of the 17th century was laid in the second half of the 16th century by a group of Flemish painters who had studied in Italy: Pieter Brueghel the Elder, Jan Gossaert, and Frans Floris. These painters combined the older Netherlandish tradition with Italian High Renaissance and mannerist elements. The great period of the Flemish school was during the 17th century, when Rubens made Antwerp one of the leading centers of European painting. His tradition was carried on by his many students, among whom numbered Van Dyck, Snyders, Teniers, and Brouwer. The Flemish school declined in the 18th century. In 1830 the kingdom of Belgium was established, and a new, nationalistic art arose. *See* BROUWER, ADRIAEN; BRUEGHEL, PIETER, THE ELDER; DYCK, ANTHONY VAN; FLORIS, FRANS; GOSSAERT, JAN; RUBENS, PETER PAUL; SNYDERS, FRANS; TENIERS, DAVID, THE ELDER; VAN EYCK, HUBERT; VAN EYCK, JAN. *See also* ANTWERP SCHOOL.

BIBLIOGRAPHY. E. Heidrich, *Vlämische Malerei*, Jena, 1913; E. Fromentin, *Masters of Past Time*, New York, 1948.

DONALD L. EHRESMANN

FLESH TINTS. Those colors used in art to reproduce the colors of the nude human body. It is also an obsolete term referring to a particular artist's rendering of the nude, for example, the "flesh tints" of Rubens.

FLEURON. Ornament in the form of a flower, as in the middle of the abacus of Corinthian capitals such as those in the tholos of Epidaurus in ancient Greece.

FLEURY. French village, site of the Abbey of St-Benoît-sur-Loire, an important center of learning and manuscript production in Carolingian times. The initial impetus for St-Benoît seems to have come from the Reims school. *See* SAINT-BENOIT-SUR-LOIRE (ABBEY OF FLEURY).

Fleury was particularly noted for the copying of antique scientific illuminated manuscripts. These manuscripts were copied in a late-antique naturalistic manner but with much of the nervous, line-drawing quality of Reims-school manuscripts. Among the most noted of this category of manuscripts produced by the scriptorium in Fleury are an Aratus manuscript of the mid-9th century, now in the British Museum, London; a manuscript with selections from Bede, Aratus, and others, in the National Library, Paris; and the Bern Physiologus, with its remarkable illuminations of flowers, animals, and rocks, in the Art Museum, Bern.

FLIGHT, CLAUDE. English painter and designer (1881–1955). He was born in London. His paintings and designs for posters and textiles show geometric forms in bold rhythmic patterns, based on the discoveries of the cubists. He has written several books on cutting and printing from linoleum blocks, a technique particularly suited to his style.

BIBLIOGRAPHY. C. Flight, "Claude Flight, by Himself," *Drawing and Design*, V, December, 1925.

FLINCK, GOVERT. Dutch painter of history, genre, and portraits (b. Cleves, 1615; d. Amsterdam, 1660). He was taken to Leeuwarden by the painter Lambert Jacobsz. to study in his studio. There Flinck met Jacob Backer, whom he seems to have followed to Amsterdam about 1632. Both painters entered Rembrandt's workshop, and Flinck appears to have remained there until 1635. From 1636 on Flinck worked independently. However, such portraits as his 1637 *Samuel Menasseh ben Israel* (The Hague, Mauritshuis Art Gallery) still show the influence of Rembrandt. He continued to work in this Rembrandtesque manner until the 1640s, when his style became somewhat more fashionable, following the manner of painters such as Cornelius Johnson and Bartholomeus van der Helst.

In 1656/57 Flinck received a commission for the decoration of the new town hall in Amsterdam, which was to consist of eight large scenes representing the revolt of the Batavians. Although drawings for several of the compositions exist (Hamburg, Art Museum), Flinck died before he could complete the paintings. The commission was then given to several other painters, including his former teacher Rembrandt.

BIBLIOGRAPHY. J. W. von Moltke, *Govaert Flinck*, Amsterdam, 1965; Städtisches Museum Haus Koekkoek, *Govert Flinck*, Cleves, 1965.

LEONARD J. SLATKES

FLORENCE (Firenze). Chief city of Tuscany, in central Italy. Despite the destruction of World War II, the remarkable fusion of Gothic and Renaissance elements in the building fabric of Florence and its wealth of painting and sculpture of the highest quality assure it the foremost place among Italy's "cities of art." Roman and Carolingian Florence are known only through archaeological investigations, and the true beginning of the city's importance may be dated from the establishment of the commune in 1115. Florence reached its apogee as a cultural center under the Medicis, who ruled first through the republic (15th cent.) and then as grand dukes of Tuscany (until 1737). *See* FLORENTINE SCHOOL.

The oldest of Florence's monumental buildings is the octagonal Baptistery of S. Giovanni, consecrated in 1059 and enlarged in the 13th century. The exterior is decorated in geometric patterns of green-and-white marble, a feature typical of the Florentine Romanesque style. There are three pairs of bronze doors, the first set by Andrea Pisano

(1330–36) and the other two pairs by Ghiberti (1st half of 15th cent.). Within are Byzantinizing mosaics and sculpture by Donatello and Michelozzo. The basilica-type Church of S. Miniato al Monte (11th–13th cent.) has a raised presbytery over an 11th-century crypt. Within the church is the Chapel of the Cardinal of Portugal (1461–66), with decorations by Antonio del Pollaiuolo, Baldovinetti, Luca della Robbia, and Antonio Rossellino. Other buildings preserving significant elements from the Romanesque period are SS. Apostoli, S. Pietro Scheraggio, S. Jacopo sopr'Arno, and S. Salvatore al Vescovo. *See* BAPTISTERY OF SAN GIOVANNI; SAN MINIATO AL MONTE.

The Gothic style, imported from across the Alps, began to appear in Florence toward the middle of the 13th century. The Dominican Church of S. Maria Novella (begun in 1278) is a Gothic basilica, whose rib-vaulted nave and aisles are terminated by a transept and a straight-ended choir flanked by rectangular chapels. The façade was completed in early Renaissance style by Leon Battista Alberti. Within are frescoes by Orcagna, Spinello Aretino, Masaccio (*The Trinity*), and Domenico Ghirlandajo. In the adjacent monastery the Chiostro Verde was frescoed by Uccello, the Spanish Chapel by Andrea da Firenze. The Franciscan Church of Sta Croce was begun at the end of the 13th century, probably by Arnolfo di Cambio. The austere timber-roofed nave concludes in the beautiful triadic composition of the east end. The church contains frescoes by Giotto (Bardi and Peruzzi chapels), Agnolo and Taddeo Gaddi, Bernardo Daddi, Giovanni da Milano, and Maso di Banco, as well as sculptures by Donatello (*The Annunciation*), Desiderio da Settignano, and Antonio Rossellino. Other works, including Cimabue's *Christ Crucified*, are displayed in the former refectory, now a museum. The Pazzi Chapel, a freestanding architectural unit, was begun by Brunelleschi and completed by other hands. *See* PAZZI CHAPEL; SANTA CROCE; SANTA MARIA NOVELLA.

The Cathedral of S. Maria del Fiore was begun in 1296, after a design by Arnolfo di Cambio, and continued on an enlarged scale by Francesco Talenti (after 1357). The crossing is surmounted by Brunelleschi's famous dome, actually an octagonal cloister vault (1418–34). Among the works preserved in the interior are a Michelangelo *Pietà* and frescoes by Uccello and Andrea del Castagno. The campanile was designed by Giotto in 1334. Or San Michele, originally the grain market, was turned into a church in the late 14th century. The exterior bears sculptures commissioned by the guilds of Florence from Ghiberti, Nanni d'Antonio di Banco, Donatello, and others; within is Orcagna's imposing marble tabernacle. The Bargello, or Palazzo del Podestà (begun in 1254), is an irregular three-story building with a tall crenelated tower. The largest of Florence's medieval civic buildings is the Palazzo Vecchio, begun in 1298 in the Gothic manner and enlarged in the 16th century. Diagonally opposite the Palazzo Vecchio is the Loggia dei Lanzi, by Benci di Cione and Simone di Francesco Talenti (late 14th cent.), which contains sculpture by Cellini, Giovanni Bologna, and others. The picturesque Ponte Vecchio, the oldest of Florence's bridges, was built in 1345. *See* FLORENCE: CATHEDRAL OF SANTA MARIA DEL FIORE; LANZI, LOGGIA DEI; OR SAN MICHELE; PONTE VECCHIO; VECCHIO, PALAZZO.

The appearance of the Renaissance style in Florence is personified by the architect Brunelleschi. His Hospital of the Innocents constitutes a radical break with the preceding Gothic style. The Basilica of S. Lorenzo (1422–46) with its Old Sacristy is perhaps Brunelleschi's most representative building. The New Sacristy of S. Lorenzo and the adjacent Laurentian Library were built by Michelangelo in the 16th century. Brunelleschi's late style is represented by the central-plan Church of S. Maria degli Angeli (unfinished) and the Basilica of Sto Spirito. The 15th century witnessed the erection of a series of splendid Renaissance palaces, of which the most notable are Alberti's Rucellai Palace and Michelozzo's Medici-Riccardi Palace. The chief remaining work of Masaccio in Florence is his fresco cycle in the Brancacci Chapel of S. Maria del Carmine (other scenes by Masolino and Filippino Lippi). *See* HOSPITAL OF THE INNOCENTS; MEDICI-RICCARDI PALACE; RUCELLAI PALACE; SACRISTY, NEW, OF SAN LORENZO; SACRISTY, OLD, OF SAN LORENZO; SAN LORENZO.

Bartolommeo Ammanati, Bernardo Buontalenti, and Giorgio Vasari were active as architects in 16th-century Florence. Ammanati is remembered for his enlargement of the 15th-century Pitti Palace (1570) and for the harmonious design of the Ponte Sta Trinità (1569; destroyed in World War II and since rebuilt). Vasari designed the Uffizi Palace (1560–85), a landmark in the field of secular architecture, to house the city's administrative offices. *See* PITTI PALACE; UFFIZI PALACE.

The baroque buildings of Florence are less numerous and less conspicuous than those of earlier periods. The architect Matteo Nigetti was responsible for the large Cappella dei Principi at S. Lorenzo (begun in 1604), the Church of SS. Filippo e Giacomo, and the façade of the Church of Ognissanti (1637). Two fine ensembles of baroque interior decoration are the frescoes in the Pitti Palace (Francesco Furini, Giovanni di San Giovanni, Pietro da Cortona, and Ciro Ferri) and the Medici-Riccardi Palace (Luca Giordano). *See* OGNISSANTI, CHURCH OF.

Florence boasts two noteworthy 20th-century buildings of the International Style: Pier Luigi Nervi's stadium (1932) and G. Michelucci's Central Station (1935).

Among Florence's museums and galleries the following deserve special mention: Uffizi Gallery (13th–18th-cent. paintings; ancient sculpture), with the attached collection of drawings and prints; Museum of S. Marco (Fra Angelico); Gallery of the Academy (Tuscan primitives; Michelangelo); Archaeological Museum (Etruscan and Roman finds); National Museum (sculpture); and Cathedral Museum (painting and sculpture from the Cathedral). *See* FLORENCE: MUSEUMS.

The Casa Buonarroti (so-called House of Michelangelo), purchased by the artist himself for his nephew Leonardo, became a museum in 1858. It is noteworthy for two early works of the master, the so-called *Madonna della Scala* (Madonna of the Stairs) and the *Battle of the Centaurs and Lapiths*. There are also two wax models of the *David*, miscellaneous Michelangelo drawings, and objects relating to the history of the family, especially the portrait of Michelangelo by Daniele da Volterra.

In November 1966 an unprecedented flooding of the Arno River into Florence caused the destruction of countless books and manuscripts, serious damage to such works of art as the world-famous Ghiberti bronze Baptistery doors, and even the destruction of such works as the great Cimabue *Christ Crucified* in Sta Croce.

See also BIGALLO, LOGGIA DEL; BOBOLI GARDENS; CORSINI PALACE; DAVANZATI PALACE; PIAZZA DELLA SIGNORIA; PONTE ALLE GRAZIE; QUARATESI PALACE; STROZZI PALACE.

BIBLIOGRAPHY. G. Boffitto and A. Mori, *Piante e vedute di Firenze*, Florence, 1926; W. and E. Paatz, *Die Kirchen von Florenz*, 5 vols., Frankfurt am Main, 1952–55; E. Sandberg-Vavalà, *Studies in the Florentine Churches*, vol. 1– , Florence, 1959– ; Touring Club Italiano, *Firenze e dintorni*, 5th ed., Milan, 1964.

WAYNE DYNES

FLORENCE: CATHEDRAL OF SANTA MARIA DEL FIORE.

Italian church erected on the site of the earlier Church of S. Reparata from the design of Arnolfo di Cambio (1296–1301). The original designer was succeeded as architect for the building first by Giotto (1334–36) and then by Andrea Pisano (1336–49). In 1357 the plan was expanded, and the nave vaulting was begun by Francesco Talenti. The exterior was further ornamented with marble in harmony with the original detail. In 1366 the forms for the choir and dome were decided upon, and this plan has since been adhered to. The three apses were completed between 1407 and 1421. In 1418 Brunelleschi was chosen to execute the dome (1420–34). The church was consecrated in 1436, but the lantern of the dome, also designed by Brunelleschi, was not completed until 1462. The unfinished old façade was removed in 1588, and the present façade was erected between 1875 and 1887.

The church, which is larger than all previous churches in Italy, has an interesting plan. The central crossing is an octagon—recalled in the octagonal dome—from three sides of which open apses (included within five sides of the octagon) and from the fourth projects the nave, flanked by spacious side aisles. The building is 556 feet long and 342 feet wide (across the octagon); the dome is 300 feet high, and the lantern is 352 feet high. The nave is characteristic of Gothic churches in Italy. It is divided into four large square bays with quadripartite vaults. The three apses are covered by octagonal half-domes, and each has a vaulted chapel about 20 feet square, enclosed by the outer wall. The interior is sparsely decorated with frescoes by Renaissance artists, including an equestrian monument to John Hawkwood by Uccello (1436) and one to Niccolò da Tolentino by Andrea del Castagno (1456). There are also stained-glass windows and a reliquary casket by Lorenzo Ghiberti (1440), sculptures by Donatello and Luca della Robbia, and an unfinished *Pietà* by Michelangelo.

The campanile, begun by Giotto and carried on by Andrea Pisano and Francesco Talenti, was completed in 1387. It is a separate structure 292 feet high, built in four stories and decorated with geometric patterns of colored marble, like the church itself, and with sculpture by Donatello, Andrea Pisano, and Luca della Robbia.

After the disastrous flood of November 1966, restoration work disclosed the ruins of the earlier church, and it was decided to excavate and reopen S. Reparata. A layer of reinforced concrete will be placed under the floor of the Cathedral to form a ceiling for the church below. Access to S. Reparata will be through two staircases leading from the upper church.

BIBLIOGRAPHY. V. Crispolti, *Santa Maria del Fiore alla luce dei documenti*, Florence, 1937; W. and E. Paatz, *Die Kirchen von Florenz*, vol. 3, Frankfurt am Main, 1952; E. Lavagnino, *L'arte medioevale*, 2d ed., Turin, 1960.

RAYMOND LIFCHEZ

FLORENCE: MUSEUMS.

Important public art collections in Florence, Italy, are located in the museums listed below.

Archaeological Museum. One of the richest archaeological collections in Italy, the museum is particularly important for the study of Etruscan civilization. Prominent are objects from such sites as Tarquinia (cinerary urns), Vetulonia (tomb furniture), Chiusi (enthroned mother goddess), and Luni (terra-cotta pediments from a temple). The Egyptian antiquities include a statue of the pharaoh Haremheb, a fine Middle Kingdom basalt bust, and numerous steles. Among the Etruscan and Roman bronzes are several pieces of the first importance, such as the funerary portrait statue known as *L'Arringatore*; the *Idolino*, a fine copy of a 5th-century Greek original; and the famous *Chimera of Arezzo*. The splendidly painted François Vase, a Corinthian krater of about 570 B.C., is preeminent among the ceramics.

BIBLIOGRAPHY. A. de Agostino, *Il Museo Archeologico Centrale dell'Etruria*, Florence, 1959.

Cathedral Museum (Museo dell'Opera del Duomo). This collection consists chiefly of sculpture from the Cathedral and its campanile. The most important pieces are the *Madonna* by Arnolfo di Cambio and *St. John the Evangelist* by Donatello, both for the Cathedral façade, the fragments from the Porta della Mandorla, Donatello's *Prophets* for the campanile, and the two singing galleries by Donatello and Luca della Robbia.

BIBLIOGRAPHY. F. Rossi, *Guida del Museo dell'Opera di S. Maria del Fiore*, Florence, 1948.

Gallery of the Academy. The gallery contains a number of important works by Michelangelo: the marble *David*, the four unfinished *Slaves*, and the *St. Matthew*. There is also a considerable collection of paintings by Tuscan primitives and by artists of the 15th and 16th centuries.

BIBLIOGRAPHY. U. Procacci, *The Gallery of the Academy of Florence*, 2d ed., Rome, 1951.

Museum of San Marco. Situated in the former Dominican Monastery of S. Marco, the museum includes the series of cells frescoed by Fra Angelico and assistants (1437–45), a landmark in Italian painting. Most of the other works of Fra Angelico surviving in Florence have been grouped in the adjoining pilgrims' hospice.

BIBLIOGRAPHY. L. Berti, *The Museum of San Marco in Florence*, Milan, 1961.

National Museum (Bargello). The Palazzo del Bargello (or Palazzo del Podestà), consisting of three connected structures built between 1254 and 1356, houses a collection of unique importance for the study of Tuscan sculp-

Florence, Cathedral of S. Maria del Fiore.

ture. Pre-Renaissance work is represented by the figures from the Arca of St. Dominic in Bologna, which came from Nicola Pisano's workshop. The core of the collection is a splendid sequence of Florentine 15th-century masterworks. In fact, the history of Renaissance sculpture *tout court* begins with two bronze reliefs executed by Lorenzo Ghiberti and Brunelleschi in 1403 in competition for the second pair of doors for the baptistery. In these two works, both depicting the sacrifice of Isaac, the artists succeeded in recapturing the beauty of the human form in the antique sense. The most important sculptor of the early Renaissance was Donatello, whose *St. George* of 1416 from Or San Michele was the first life-size figure to be executed in the full round since Roman times. Also by Donatello are a marble and a bronze *David*, the *Marzocco* (a lion symbolizing Florence), and the mysterious bronze *Atys-Amorino*. Luca della Robbia's *St. Peter Predella* is an outstanding example of this elegant master's work. From the middle of the 15th century come works by Desiderio da Settignano (*Panciatichi Madonna*, *The Young St. John the Baptist*), Antonio Rossellino (bust of Matteo Palmieri), and Agostino di Duccio (two Madonnas). Bertoldo's bronze battle relief is one of the first works of modern times to reveal a thorough understanding of Roman narrative art. A worthy conclusion to the 15th-century cycle is Andrea del Verrocchio's forceful *David*.

The High Renaissance collection is dominated by Michelangelo. The museum has his unfinished *Pitti Tondo*, the youthful *Bacchus*, the ethereal *Apollo*, and the somber *Brutus*. Among works by Cellini are the bust of Cosimo I and the models for the *Perseus*. Two masterworks by Giovanni Bologna are shown: the *Medici Mercury* and the allegorical group of *Florence Triumphing over Pisa*. The 17th century is more sparsely represented with works by Francesco Mochi, Gian Lorenzo Bernini (bust of Costanza Buonarelli), and others.

The museum also has an extensive collection of the minor arts. Exhibited are arms and armor (9th–19th cent.), ivories (including the 5th-cent. diptych of Ariadne), Renaissance majolica, medals, and textiles.

BIBLIOGRAPHY. G. Sangiorgi, *Collection Carrand au Bargello*, Rome, 1895; F. Rossi, *Il Museo Nazionale di Firenze*, 3d ed., Rome, 1951.　　　　　　　　　　　　　　WAYNE DYNES

Palazzo Vecchio (Palazzo della Signoria). Begun in the 13th century and extended in the Renaissance, the palace preserves a number of splendidly decorated rooms from the 15th and 16th centuries. These include the Salone dei

Florence, museums. National Museum (Bargello), the Great Hall.

Cinquecento, frescoed by Vasari and assistants and displaying Michelangelo's *Victory*; the *studiolo* of Francesco I, revetted with stuccoes and paintings by mannerist artists; the Sala dell'Udienza and Sala dei Gigli with ceilings by G. da Maiano and portals by B. da Maiano; the apartments of Leo X and of the Elements, decorated by Vasari; and the apartment of Eleonora of Toledo with the chapel frescoed by Bronzino. Tuscan sculpture and paintings of the 14th to the 16th century are also on display.

BIBLIOGRAPHY. G. Sinibaldi, *The Palazzo Vecchio in Firenze*, 2d ed., Rome, 1950.

Pitti Palace Museums. The Pitti Palace was erected in the second half of the 15th century and later enlarged. At present it houses the Galleria Palatina, the Museo degli Argenti, and the Galleria di Arte Moderna. Formed from various grand ducal collections, the Galleria Palatina Collection consists mainly of paintings of the 16th and 17th centuries. Among them are outstanding works by Raphael (*Madonna del Granduca* and *Madonna of the Chair*), Titian (*Concert* and *Man with a Glove*), Fra Bartolommeo (*Pietà*), Reni (*Cleopatra*), and Rubens (*Four Philosophers*). Adjacent to the gallery are the former royal apartments with decorative paintings by Susterman and others as well as furniture of the neoclassic period. The Museo degli Argenti contains an extensive collection of objects in gold- and silverwork, precious stones, crystal, and ivory. The Galleria di Arte Moderna exhibits 19th-century paintings from the neoclassic, purist, and Macchiaioli schools, as well as some 20th-century works.

See also PITTI PALACE.

BIBLIOGRAPHY. R. Chiarelli, *La Galleria Palatina a Firenze*, Rome, 1956.

Uffizi Gallery. Although it makes no claim to provide a comprehensive survey of the history of art, by virtue of the extraordinarily high quality of the paintings shown—the sequence of Tuscan works is of unique importance—the Uffizi ranks as one of the world's great museums. It is housed in a building designed by the artist-historian Giorgio Vasari in the mid-16th century for the administrative offices (*uffizi*) of the Medici government.

The three monumental Madonna compositions by Cimabue, Giotto, and Duccio that are exhibited in the first room of paintings constitute an impressive "overture" to the gallery and at the same time afford an understanding of the situation of central Italian painting in the years before and after 1300. Cimabue sums up the experience of 13th-century Florentine art in fusing the imported *maniera greca* with a vigorous local trend of Romanesque derivation. In the clarity and simplicity of its plastic forms Giotto's *Ognissanti Madonna* shows the revolutionary advance made by this artist, who opened the way to the painting of modern times. Duccio's *Rucellai Madonna*, more conservative but almost equally impressive, provides the foundation for an understanding of the development of 14th-century Sienese painting. In Florence the 14th century was dominated by the many followers of Giotto, including the St. Cecilia Master (*St. Cecilia Altarpiece*), Bernardo Daddi (triptych), and the mysterious figure known as Giottino (*Lamentation*). Somewhat more independent of the master's example are the more formalistic artists of the period after the Black Death, including Orcagna (altarpiece of *St. Matthew with Scenes from His Life*) and Giovanni del Biondo (*St. John the Evangelist*).

The Sienese 14th century is represented by paintings of Pietro Lorenzetti (*Madonna and Child* of 1340; *Beata Umiltà Polyptych*), Ambrogio Lorenzetti (scenes from the life of St. Nicholas and *Presentation in the Temple*), and above all by a consummate example of mellifluous linearism, the *Annunciation* (1333) by Simone Martini, assisted by Lippo Memmi. A polyptych by Giovanni da Milano reveals a fusion of north Italian and Florentine ideals of the mid-14th century.

The first quarter of the 15th century saw the appearance of the International Gothic Style in Florence as represented by Lorenzo Monaco. His *Adoration of the Magi* and *Coronation of the Virgin* are pleasing because of their brilliant, enamel-like colors and detailed observation of reality. Other artists of this trend are Starnina (*The Thebaid*) and the Umbrian Gentile da Fabriano (*Adoration of the Magi*).

Masaccio's magnificent *Madonna with St. Anne* develops the heritage of Giotto in accordance with the new Renaissance principles of perspective and humanistic idealization of the human form. Uccello's fascination with perspective is evident in his large *Battle of San Romano*, which retains much of the charm and color of medieval narrative painting. Fra Angelico's *Coronation of the Virgin* combines the variety of the International Style with a new seriousness achieved through the application of Renaissance principles of composition. A more intimate Renaissance trend emerges in the work of Domenico Veneziano (*Madonna with Saints*), Baldovinetti (*Annunciation*), and especially Fra Filippo Lippi (two Nativities). The two scenes of the *Labors of Hercules* by Antonio del Pollaiuolo show the interest in movement that emerged toward the end of the 15th century, while at the same time they document the increasing attraction to themes derived from classical mythology. This attraction is fully displayed in two lyric masterworks by Botticelli, *Primavera* (Spring) and the *Birth of Venus*. The achievement of the early Renaissance is perhaps best summed up in Piero della Francesca's severe portraits of the Duke and Duchess of Urbino, with the triumphal processions in a landscape depicted on the reverse sides of the panels. The most important foreign school of the 15th century, that of Flanders, is represented by two outstanding paintings, Rogier van der Weyden's *Entombment* and Hugo van der Goes's *Portinari Altarpiece*.

Two youthful works by Leonardo, the *Annunciation* and the *Adoration of the Magi*, inaugurate the High Renaissance. The angel painted by Leonardo in the *Baptism of Christ* of his teacher Verrocchio permits one to evaluate the advance made in painting by the great polymath. A personal interpretation of the High Renaissance was achieved by the introspective Andrea del Sarto (*Madonna of the Harpies*). Michelangelo's *tondo*, the *Doni Holy Family*, is a worthy example of his monumental conception of the human form, and Raphael's *Leo X with Cardinals Giuliano de' Medici and Ludovico de' Rossi* is one of the master's most successful essays in psychological portraiture. The German school of the 16th century comes to the fore in important works by Dürer (*Adoration of the Magi*), Cranach (*Adam and Eve*), and Altdorfer (scenes from the life of St. Florian). The mannerism of the later 16th century is variously revealed in paintings of Salviati (*Carità*), Rosso Fiorentino (*Moses Defending the Daughters of Jethro*), Bronzino (*Lamentation*), Pontormo (*Supper at Emmaus*), and Parmigianino (*Madonna of the Long Neck*). Titian (*Venus of Urbino*) and Veronese (*Annunciation*) represent the illusionistic colorism of Venice at its height.

The 17th century is ushered in by Caravaggio's provocative *Bacchus*. There are other important paintings of the Bolognese (the Carraccis, Reni, Guercino) and Neapolitan (Caracciolo, Mattia Preti, Cavallino) 17th-century schools. Italian painting of the 18th century is documented by works of G. M. Crespi, Piazzetta, Canaletto, Guardi, and Pietro Longhi. The art of the Low Countries in the baroque period may be seen in paintings by Honthorst, Rubens, Rembrandt (*Portrait of a Rabbi*), and Jacob van Ruisdael. French masters include Claude Lorraine (*Port Scene*), Chardin (*Boy Playing Cards*), Nattier (portraits), Largillière, and Rigaud. The Uffizi Gallery also possesses a considerable group of self-portraits, which are shown separately.

The collection of antique sculpture, which played an important part in the formation of neoclassic taste in the 18th and 19th centuries, contains mostly Roman copies of Hellenistic works (*Medici Venus, Niobe, Knife Grinder, The Wrestlers*, torso of a satyr). The gallery also displays tapestries of Brussels and Florentine manufacture. The famous Gabinetto dei Disegni e Stampe, attached to the Uffizi, contains more than 100,000 prints and drawings, including numerous examples by the great Tuscan masters.

BIBLIOGRAPHY. *The Uffizi Gallery: Catalogue*, Florence, 1948; E. S. Vavalà, *Uffizi Studies*, Florence, 1948; G. Pacchioni, *The Uffizi Gallery*, Rome, 1955; F. Rossi, *Art Treasures of the Uffizi and Pitti*, New York, 1956; L. Becherucci, *The Treasures of the Uffizi Gallery*, Milan, 1957; G. Mansuelli, ed., *Galleria degli Uffizi: Le sculture*, 2 vols., Rome, 1958–61.   WAYNE DYNES

FLORENTIA, RAPHAEL DE, see RAFFAELLINO DEL GARBO.

FLORENTIN, DOMINIQUE, see BARBIERE, DOMENICO RICOVERI DEL.

FLORENTINE SCHOOL. Leading school of Italian painting from the 13th to the 16th century. It was most significant in the development of Renaissance art. Among important names associated with the school are, in the 13th century, Cimabue; in the 14th century, Giotto and Orcagna; in the 15th century, Masaccio, Andrea del Castagno, Uccello, Fra Angelico, Fra Filippo Lippi, Botticelli, Domenico Ghirlandajo, Antonio del Pollaiuolo, and Verrocchio; and, in the 16th century, Leonardo, Michelangelo, Lorenzo di Credi, Andrea del Sarto, Sodoma, and Bronzino. *See* ANGELICO, FRA; BOTTICELLI, SANDRO; BRONZINO, AGNOLO; CASTAGNO, ANDREA DEL; CIMABUE; CREDI, LORENZO DI; GHIRLANDAJO, DOMENICO; GIOTTO DI BONDONE; LEONARDO DA VINCI; LIPPI, FRA FILIPPO; MASACCIO; MICHELANGELO BUONARROTI; ORCAGNA, ANDREA; POLLAIUOLO, ANTONIO DEL; SARTO, ANDREA DEL; SODOMA; UCCELLO, PAOLO; VERROCCHIO, ANDREA DEL.

BIBLIOGRAPHY. B. Berenson, *Italian Painters of the Renaissance*, 2d ed., London, 1952.

FLORENTIN Y TORRIGIANI, PEDRO, see TORRIGIANI, PIETRO.

FLORIS, FRANS (Frans de Vriendt). Flemish painter (b. Antwerp, 1516; d. there, 1570). The son of a sculptor, Floris began his training in his father's workshop. Later he came in contact with Lambert Lombard, whose Romanized northern paintings probably introduced him to the achievements of the Italians. Between 1542 and 1547 Floris went to Italy. In Rome he drew from antique sculpture and recorded many of the nude giants in Michelangelo's recently finished *Last Judgment* (1541; Vatican, Sistine Chapel). Michelangelo's language of forms and the rich colors of the Venetians figure prominently in the works of Floris, such as his signed and dated *Last Judgment* (1565; Vienna, Museum of Art History). According to Karel van Mander, Floris had more than 100 students. Through them the northern mannerist style that Floris evolved remained the strongest current in Flemish history painting until the end of the 16th century.

BIBLIOGRAPHY. M. J. Friedländer, *Die altniederländische Malerei*, vol. 13, Leyden, 1936.

FLORIS DE VRIENDT, CORNELIUS (Cornelis). Flemish architect and sculptor (1514–75). He was trained in Antwerp; in 1538 he went to Rome, where he remained nine years. His most important building is the Town Hall of Antwerp (1561–66), in which Gothic and Renaissance forms are combined in a design profusely embellished with sculptural decoration. Floris's importance is due to his importation to Flanders of Roman grotesque ornament, on which he published a book of engravings in 1556.

BIBLIOGRAPHY. H. Gerson and E. H. ter Kuile, *Art and Architecture in Belgium, 1600–1800*, Baltimore, 1960.

FLOTNER, PETER. Swiss-German ornamental sculptor, draftsman, and woodcarver (b. Thurgau, ca. 1490; d. Nürnberg, 1546). Flötner spent his early period in Ansbach and then traveled, spending time in Italy, where he closely studied Italian Renaissance ornament. In 1522 he moved to Nürnberg and remained there for the rest of his life. He produced many models for plaquettes (a kind of low relief sculpture) and also carved architectural ornaments and small decorative sculpture. Among his important works are the wood decorations for the Hirschvogelhaus (1534), decoration for the Tuder House (1533–44), and the plaquettes from Blei (Berlin, former State Museums). In addition to their high aesthetic quality, his works are important as early examples of German Renaissance ornament.

Flötner owes his fame to a set of forty Moresque patterns issued without title by Rudolf Wyssenbach in Zurich in 1549. Flötner introduced into Germany a style—Saracenic in origin and transmitted to Europe through Venice—which subsequently played an important role in German design. Among his book illustrations are nine woodcuts for *Der Hungern Chronica*, printed in Vienna (1534), and 329 woodcuts adapted from the 1499 *Hypnerotomachia*, from the Como Vitruvius, and from Serlio, for Walter Rivius's book on architecture and perspective, published in Nürnberg (1547).

BIBLIOGRAPHY. K. Lange, *Peter Flötner*, Berlin, 1897; London, British Museum, Dept. of Prints and Drawings, *Catalogue of Early German and Flemish Woodcuts . . .*, by C. Dodgson, vol. 1, London, 1903; E. F. Bange, *Peter Flötner*, Leipzig, 1926.

FLUTE. Groove used to articulate a column or pilaster. In the Greek Doric and early Ionic, the flutes were separated by a comparatively sharp arris; in later Ionic and Corinthian, by a fillet, or flattened molding.

FLYING MERCURY. Bronze sculpture by Bologna, in the National Museum, Florence. *See* BOLOGNA, GIOVANNI.

FLYING WHITE, *see* FEI-PO.

FLY RIVER, *see* OCEANIC ART (MELANESIA).

FO, *see* BUDDHA.

FOGG ART MUSEUM, CAMBRIDGE, MASS., *see* CAMBRIDGE, MASS.: MUSEUMS (FOGG ART MUSEUM).

FOGGINI, GIOVANNI BATTISTA. Italian sculptor and architect (b. Florence, 1652; d. there, 1725). The pupil of V. Dandini and J. Giorgi, Foggini was sent by Cosimo III de' Medici to Rome in 1673 to copy antique statuary under Ercole Ferrata. Foggini's major works are the reliefs (ca. 1679) in the Corsini Chapel of S. Maria del Carmine in Florence, depicting Andrea Corsini and the Battle of Anghiari. He restored the interior of S. Ambrogio in Florence from 1716 to 1719. Foggini was also active in Pisa and Pistoia. He employed a rather dry baroque mode.

BIBLIOGRAPHY. K. Lankheit, "Il giornale del Foggini," *Rivista d'arte*, XXXIV, 1959.

FOGOLINO, MARCELLO. Northern Italian painter (fl. 1519–48). He was active first in his native Vicenza, then in the Udine area, and, after being exiled for murder, in Trent. His early masterpiece, the *Adoration of the Magi* (Vicenza Museum), is Carpaccio-like in narrative, light, and clear forms. Later he retained his anecdotal zest while his style of execution was first dominated by Pordenone and then, in Trent, by Romanino, with whom he worked on the castle frescoes of soldiers and hunters.

BIBLIOGRAPHY. A. Morassi, "I pittori alla corte di Bernardo Clesio a Trento, III: Marcello Fogolino," *Bollettino d'arte*, XXIII, February, 1930.

FOHR, KARL PHILIPP. German painter (b. Heidelberg, 1795; d. Rome, 1818). Fohr began his training as a student at the Heidelberg Academy and studied for a short time at the Munich Academy. In 1813 he went to Rome and in 1816 joined the Nazarenes. He is best known as a painter of landscapes similar in style to those of Joseph Koch, for example, *Landscape with Shepherd* (1818; Darmstadt, Schlossmuseum). Collections of Fohr's water colors and drawings are in Frankfurt am Main and Darmstadt.

BIBLIOGRAPHY. K. F. von Hardenberg and E. Schilling, *Karl Phillip Fohr*, Freiburg, 1925; W. R. Deusch, *Malerei der deutschen Romantiker . . .*, Berlin, 1937.

FO-HSIANG-KO, *see* LUNG-HSING-SSU, CHENG-TING.

FOIL. In tracery, a lobe or petal-shaped opening that, when arranged with other foils, meets in points or cusps, as in Gothic arches and windows. The word is derived from the Latin *folium*, meaning "leaf." Tracery is often identified according to the number of such foils, the terms "trefoil," "quatrefoil," and "cinquefoil" referring to three-, four-, and five-leafed forms, and is thus characterized as foliated.

FOKKE, SIMON. Dutch etcher and engraver (b. Amsterdam, 1712; d. there, 1784). Employed chiefly by booksellers to make vignettes and portraits, Fokke also designed theater sets and single-page engraved portraits. He supplied his own designs to Wagenaar's *Vaderlandsche Historie* (1749–50).

FOLIATED, *see* FOIL.

FOLIGNO, *see* NICCOLO DI LIBERATORE DA FOLIGNO.

FOLK ART. Broad designation for the artistic expression of folk cultures. Folk art is produced in every part of the world, and probably has been since the emergence of civilization, although little visual proof is available from earlier than the 18th century. The most clear-cut and fully developed folk environments are rural or peasant communities that are usually isolated geographically from the principal centers of culture and are therefore able to develop a continuous tradition. Other groups isolated in different ways also produce folk art. Some ethnic groups in large cities continue to practice the traditional forms of art, as do strongly traditional religious groups such as the Hassidic Jews and Pennsylvania Mennonites. Men working at certain professional skills, such as sign painting, bottlemaking, or carpentry, also produce forms of folk art.

The isolation required for the production of folk art must exist within an over-all context of culture on a "high" level, however. The folk environment is not comparable to the primitive environment since the former draws on the forms of the sophisticated environment; in art this is evident in the adaptation of motifs, symbols, and even styles. Similarly, folk art cannot be considered a decadent form of sophisticated art, inasmuch as it has its own vital traditions.

Although they may echo or even ape sophisticated art, the folk arts play a different role in their own society. High culture demands a divisione of labor; the fine arts are produced by artists for an elite or dominant class. Each work is the expression of a complex intellectual development conveyed through institutions. Folk art, although it may in some wealthy communities be subject to a similar division of labor, is usually an expression of the ideals, beliefs, needs, and tastes of the entire community. Art is more intimately related to everyday life and therefore appears in a more practical guise. Artistic attention is lavished on the form or the decoration of such useful objects as plows, boat prows, cradles, ox yokes, weathervanes, carts, and quilts. Most members of the community produce art in some form although artists with special skills and reputations are also active. Much of the most interesting folk art, no less closely connected with the life of the group, is produced for religious ceremony and worship and for such special occasions as festivals and such seminal events as birth, marriage, and death.

The traditional nature of folk art is evident in its tendency to retain motifs, symbols, and decorative patterns through many generations. It is, however, a constantly renewed traditionalism in which images that have lost their original meaning and have been transformed into purely decorative motifs may be reintroduced with a new meaning. Unhindered by dogma, the folk artist may improvise and adapt images and themes to his own experience. Religious scenes especially are often presented in the trappings of local customs. The local environment also provides the artist with materials, which reflect the spirit of improvisation and may include rags, twine, paper, leaves, flowers, fruit, dough, or anything that is available in addition to the standard materials.

There is no universal folk style, although certain qualities seem to prevail. The most important perhaps is simplification. Line, modeling, color, volume, and space are treated in a simple, straightforward manner rather than as integral aspects of the complex problems of representation. This is true even when a realistic or illusionistic representation is attempted. There is therefore a tendency toward abstraction and toward the surface ornamental quality that has often been noted. In rendering a narrative scene, the folk artist is likely to distort or magnify important forms or to combine different scenes and spaces in one picture. Despite the ornamental and literal quality of much folk art, there are many objects and images that have an emotional expressiveness of great power, such as masks and votive images.

BIBLIOGRAPHY. P. L. Ducharte, *Art Populaire*, Paris, 1931; J. Kipman, *American Folk Art*, New York, 1948; H. T. Bossert, *Folk Art of Europe*, New York, 1953; H. T. Bossert, *Peasant Art of Europe and Asia*, New York, 1959; P. Toschi, *Guida allo studio delle tradizioni popolari*, Turin, 1962; L. E. Fischer, *Colonial American Craftsmen*, 10 vols., New York, 1967; H. J. Hansen, ed., *Europas Volkskunst*, Oldenburg/Hamburg, 1967 (Eng. tr. *The Folk Art of Europe*, New York, 1968). DONALD GODDARD

FOLLY. Imaginative and exotic structure designed to ornament parks and gardens during the mid-18th century in England. Among the various types of buildings constructed were classical temples and theaters, antique "ruins" or arches, hermit cells, Gothic lodges, Chinese bridges, and Arab mosques and "alhambras." The picturesque pagoda erected in Kew Gardens, near London, remains as an example of these pavilions and summerhouses.

BIBLIOGRAPHY. N. Pevsner, *An Outline of European Architecture*, 6th (Jubilee) ed., Baltimore, 1960.

FON, *see* AFRICA, PRIMITIVE ART OF (WEST AFRICA: DAHOMEY).

FONDUTI, AGOSTINO DEI (Il Padovano). Italian ceramic sculptor (fl. 15th cent.). Called "Il Padovano" because he spent so much time in Padua, he was actually born in Crema. In 1483 he contracted to decorate the terra-cotta frieze in the nave and transept of S. Maria presso S. Satiro, in Piacenza. The next year, along with Giovanni Battaggio, he did the decorative work on the Landi Palace, Piacenza. One of his last known works is the statue of an apostle in S. Celso, Milan.

FONOYLL, RAYNARD. English architect (14th cent.). Fonoyll was the English mason who from 1331 to 1341 was in charge of building the south cloister of the Cistercian Monastery of Santas Creus in the Catalan province of Tarragona. In 1352 he began the Church of S. Maria at Montblanch, Spain.

BIBLIOGRAPHY. J. Harvey, *The Gothic World, 1100–1600*, London, 1950.

FONT. Vessel containing water for baptismal rites (from the Latin *fons*, "fountain" or "spring"). Unimportant in

Eastern churches, fonts were used extensively in the West, especially after the 9th century, when baptism by aspersion, or sprinkling, became more common. (Other forms of baptism are immersion and infusion, in which water is poured over the candidate's head.) Fonts were made of stone, marble, and sometimes lead.

FONTAINE, JACQUES-FRANCOIS-JOSEPH, see SWEBACH, JACQUES-FRANCOIS-JOSEPH.

FONTAINE, PIERRE, see PERCIER AND FONTAINE.

FONTAINEBLEAU, CHATEAU OF. Former royal residence near Paris. The forest of Fontainebleau was a favorite resort of French kings from the 12th century onward. The present vast edifice, which is only loosely organized around three courtyards, faithfully reflects the imprint of the kings who took special interest in it. Of the first château only the turret in the Cour Ovale survives.

The most brilliant period of Fontainebleau was during the reign of Francis I (1515–47), who established Italian Renaissance art in France. In 1528 his architect Gilles Le Breton began construction of the new wings. Two Italian artists, Primaticcio and Rosso Fiorentino, were invited to take charge of the interior decoration. With its stuccoes and paintings, the Galerie François I (1533–44) remains unsurpassed for richness, contrast, and wealth of invention. Another outstanding achievement of Francis I was the Chapelle Royale, completed in 1545.

In the succeeding reigns of Henry II, Francis II, and

Château of Fontainebleau. Chapel of the Holy Trinity, 1529.

Charles IX, work continued at Fontainebleau, though much retarded by the turmoil of the wars of religion. At the end of the 16th century, however, the building campaign of Henry IV completed and consolidated the various parts that had been begun in the course of the century. Fontainebleau saw a new phase of activity in the mid-18th century, when the court architect J.-A. Gabriel built the Gros Pavillon for Louis XV. Somewhat later (1780–85) are the apartments decorated in Pompeian style for Queen Marie Antoinette. During the French Revolution Fontainebleau was largely stripped of its interior furnishings; shortly thereafter, however, Napoleon commissioned replacements from the designers Percier, Jacob, and Thomire. The park of Fontainebleau, which blends into the adjacent forest, consists of three main parts: the Jardin de Diane, the English park, and the French garden of Louis Levau.

Fontainebleau has given its name to two schools of painting. In the 16th century a distinctive French type of mannerism known as the *école de Fontainebleau* developed around the painters who had been commissioned to decorate the château. The Barbizon school of landscape painters, whose members frequented the forest in the 19th century, is also sometimes called the school of Fontainebleau. *See* BARBIZON SCHOOL; FONTAINEBLEAU, SCHOOL OF. *See also* FONTAINEBLEAU TAPESTRY.

BIBLIOGRAPHY. J.-J. Champollion-Figeac and R. Pfnor, *Monographie du palais de Fontainebleau*, 3 vols., Paris, 1863–85; L. Dimier, *Fontainebleau*, Paris, 1908; C. Terrasse, *Fontainebleau*, Paris, 1951; A. Bray, *Le Château de Fontainebleau*, Paris, 1956.

WAYNE DYNES

FONTAINEBLEAU, SCHOOL OF. A 16th-century French school promoted by Francis I (reigned 1515–47) and his successors, who, because of a dearth of good French artists, imported Italians and Flemings to decorate the château at Fontainebleau. The first major French Renaissance movement, it revived the tradition of architectural decoration in France. The style is essentially mannerist, characterized by elegance and preciousness. The Italians Rosso Fiorentino (1494–1540), Primaticcio (1504–70), and Niccolò dell'Abbate (1512–71), among others, originated the Fontainebleau tradition.

A second school, related in style to the first but less forceful and somewhat academic, probably began under Henry IV in 1589. Its main exponents were Ambroise Dubois (1542/43–1614), Toussaint Dubreuil (1561–1602), and Martin Fréminet (1567–1619), who continued the palace decorations. Influences from the second school were important for the young Poussin and for 17th-century European art in general.

The Barbizon group of the 19th century is also sometimes called the school of Fontainebleau because of its association with the forest. *See* BARBIZON SCHOOL.

BIBLIOGRAPHY. A. Blunt, *Art and Architecture in France, 1500–1700*, Baltimore, 1954; S. Béguin, *L'Ecole de Fontainebleau*, Paris, 1960.

SARAH B. LANDAU

FONTAINEBLEAU TAPESTRY. The tapestry works at Fontainebleau, near Paris, were set up in the 1530s (both 1530 and 1535 are claimed to be the founding dates) by Francis I and operated by him and his son and successor, Henry II, until the latter's death in 1559. Francis established the workshop as one of his many acts of patronage of the arts at a moment when French tapestries were at a low ebb. Weavers were evidently gathered from Paris and Flanders, and designs were provided by the Italian mannerist artists at Fontainebleau. The resulting tapestry manufacture produced work of quality, thus reviving the art in France. The Fontainebleau studio was run by Jean and Pierre LeBries, the latter identified as the Pierre Le-Bryain mentioned in Paris in 1547. Cartoons were the responsibility of Claude Baudoin, an assistant first of Rosso Fiorentino and then of Primaticcio, the chief court painters. Francis I's sudden decrease in orders from the Brussels workshops in 1538 is interpreted as an indication that the local shop was in full production by then.

Among the tapestries that have survived, the series in the Austrian State Collections in Vienna are the most interesting. This group is simply a reproduction of the frescoes of the Galerie François I of Fontainebleau by Rosso Fiorentino and Primaticcio, including the stucco decorations that framed the pictures and the corbel table and beams. The elongated mannerist figures are well executed in a colorful and confusing juxtaposition of realistic garlands of fruit and classicistic decorative elements. Echoes of Raphael seem to resound in both compositions and decorative schemes. Du Cerceau, a court architect who published engravings in the spirit of the Roman arabesques that inspired Raphael and Primaticcio, may well have assisted in designs for a tapestry now in the Gobelin Museum, or for another which French and Company owned in 1928. In 1551 Henry II established a tapestry workshop in the Maison de la Trinité, where orphans and destitute children were taught weaving, eliminating the need for continuing the previous studio.

BIBLIOGRAPHY. H. Göbel, *Wandteppiche*, pt. 2, Leipzig, 1928; H. Wescher, "Fontainebleau and the French Renaissance Tapestries," *Ciba Review*, VI, 1948.

MARVIN D. SCHWARTZ

FONTAINE DES INNOCENTS, *see* FOUNTAIN OF THE INNOCENTS.

FONTANA, ANNIBALE. Italian sculptor and gem cutter (1540–87). First mentioned in Palermo in 1570 as a Milanese marble sculptor, Fontana may have studied in Rome. He was back in his native Milan by 1577, doing work in crystal, bronze, and silver as well as marble at S. Maria presso S. Celso. His Michelangelesque mannerist figures were praised by such contemporaries as Lomazzo and Borghini.

BIBLIOGRAPHY. E. Kris, "Materialien zur Biographie des Annibale Fontana und zur Kunsttopographie der Kirche S. Maria presso S. Celso in Mailand," *Kunsthistorisches Institut in Florenz, Mitteilungen*, III, 1930.

FONTANA, CARLO. Italian architect (1634–1714). After an apprenticeship with Bernini, Rainaldi, and Pietro da Cortona, Fontana emerged in Rome as an independent master of the late baroque with S. Biagio in Campitelli (now rebuilt). His masterpiece, the façade of S. Marcello al Corso (1682–83), is concave with an illusionistic niche, but shows the trend toward classicism. His largest commission, the church and college in Loyola, Spain, was executed by others. He was important as a chapel architect: the Ginetti Chapel, S. Andrea della Valle (1671), and the Cybo Chapel, S. Maria del Popolo, both in Rome,

are splendid examples of the use of polychromy. His production of tomb, altar, fountain, and festival designs was enormous. He is also the author of *Templum Vaticanum* (1694).

BIBLIOGRAPHY. R. Wittkower, *Art and Architecture in Italy, 1600–1750*, Baltimore, 1958.

FONTANA, DOMENICO. Italian architect (b. Melide, 1543; d. Naples, 1607). He was the brother of the engineer Giovanni Fontana and the uncle and teacher of Carlo Maderno. His career in Rome centered around Pope Sixtus V (1585–90), for whom he had earlier designed the Villa Montalto. Sixtus put Fontana in charge of his vast city-planning schemes, which included a new aqueduct (Acqua Felice) and fountains, new streets linking the Roman basilicas, new palaces (Lateran; Vatican), and the erection of obelisks. Fontana was a great organizer, but his style is dry and unimaginative. After the death of Sixtus, Fontana's enemies forced his exile to Naples, where he designed the Royal Palace. His masterpiece is probably the large Sistine Chapel of S. Maria Maggiore, which houses papal tombs.

BIBLIOGRAPHY. R. Wittkower, *Art and Architecture in Italy, 1600–1750*, Baltimore, 1958.

FONTANA, LUCIO. Italian painter (1899–1968). Fontana moved to Milan from his native Argentina in 1905 and later became a stoneworker there. It was only in 1927 that he began to study painting at the Brera Academy in Milan. From the beginning of his artistic career (1930) Fontana created abstract works that, in the traditional sense, are almost not art, in which shapes and scrawled incised lines appear as spontaneous gestures against roughly painted backgrounds. In 1934 he became part of the Abstraction-Création group in Paris. He spent the war years and some time thereafter (1939–46) in Argentina and at the end of that period issued his *White Manifesto*. It called for a new conception of art (Spazialismo), freed from the materialistic objectivity of the past, and enunciated the need for common cause with scientists in exploring new concepts and creating new materials for their expression. "Motion, evolution, and development" are the basic conditions of matter, and dynamism.

From this period on, Fontana's canvases appear as expanding voids of space, against which holes punched in the surface and shadow-casting projections create a strange spatial ambiguity suggesting infinity. This approach became regularized until 1951, when new irregular elements were added: knife slashes, swirling strokes of paint, larger jagged holes, and colored stones. He also began to get away from the restrictions of the picture format, creating sculptures and entire environments by using neon lights in otherwise black rooms. After 1959 a new refinement was seen in Fontana's work. Luminous, smooth metallic surfaces are penetrated by gashes that powerfully articulate the sculptural form.

Fontana's works have been exhibited in leading museums, including the Stedelijk (Amsterdam), the Tate Gallery (London), and the Museum of Modern Art (New York). He won a top prize at the 1966 Biennale in Venice.

BIBLIOGRAPHY. *Fontana: With an Introduction by Michiel Tapié and the White Manifesto 1946 (Spazialismo)*, New York, 1962.

DONALD GODDARD

FONTANA, ORAZIO. Italian majolica painter (fl. 1542–71). He was the eldest son of the majolica painter Guido Durantino, the grandson of Nicola Pellipario, and the brother of Camillo Fontana. Orazio first worked in his father's *bottega* in Urbino. His Renaissance *istoriato* style has been determined from a series of seven signed examples dated from 1541 to 1544. These include two dishes, *View of the City of Urbino* (1541; London, Victoria and Albert Museum) and *Rape of Helen* (1543; Montpellier, Fabre Museum). About 1565, he had a *bottega* of his own in Urbino. Such workshop pieces as a table service for Guidobaldo II, Duke of Urbino (1565–71; Florence, National Museum; London, Victoria and Albert Museum), include floridly ornate wine coolers, large platters, and salts, all decorated in rich polychrome colors with *istoriato* scenes surrounded by Raphaelesque grotesques on a white ground.

BIBLIOGRAPHY. G. Liverani, "Un piatto a Montpellier marcato da Orazio Fontana ed altri ancora," *Faenza*, XLIII, 1957.

FONTANA, PROSPERO. Italian painter (1512–97). Born in Bologna, he studied under Innocenza da Imola, then worked with Perino del Vaga in Genoa (1528) and Vasari in Florence and Rome, where he also collaborated with Taddeo Zuccari (ca. 1540). A year with Primaticcio in France (1560) rounded out his exposure to the mannerist tradition. While this background usually manifested itself stylistically, as, for instance, in Parmigianino's influence in his *S. Alessio* (1576; Bologna, S. Giacomo), Fontana also borrowed whole motifs; Raphael's *Transfiguration* appears in his *Beata Diana d'Andalò* (1545; Bologna, S. Domenico). His brand of Bolognese mannerism typifies all that the Carraccis opposed in their reform (compare his 1580 *Crucifixion* in S. Giuseppe, Bologna, with Annibale's 1583 version in S. Nicolò).

BIBLIOGRAPHY. R. Galli, "Alcuni documenti sul pittore Prospero Fontana," *L'Archiginnasio*, XVIII, 1923.

FONTENAY, ABBEY CHURCH OF. Cistercian monastery on the Côte d'Or, France. It was founded in 1119 by Raynard de Montbard as a daughter-foundation of Clairvaux. A second, completely preserved church was begun in 1139 and consecrated by the Cistercian pope Eugene III in 1147. Except for its considerable size, Fontenay furnishes the ideal example of the Burgundian Cistercian oratory. The simple façade was originally preceded by a porch. A single entrance leads into the nave with its eight rectangular bays flanked by transverse barrel vaults above the side aisles. Four rectangular chapels and a large rectangular apse are attached to the spacious transept. The broken barrel vault rests directly on the arcades, but the fenestration of the end walls makes up for the lack of a clerestory. The complete lack of figural decoration in the church, as well as in the cloister and chapterhouse, follows St. Bernard's anti-Cluniac precepts.

BIBLIOGRAPHY. M. Anselme Dimier, *Recueil de plans d'églises cisterciennes*, vol. 1, Grignan, 1949.

FONTEVRAULT, ABBEY OF. Founded in 1100 by Robert d'Arbrissel, the abbey of Fontevrault, France, has one of the finest of the domed churches. The church was dedicated by Pope Calixtus II in 1119, when only the apse was complete. The wide nave consists of four bays and is aisleless. Each bay is surmounted by modern domes resting on the original pendentives. There are many fine capitals executed in the Poitevin-Angevin style. This is the burial place of Henry I and Richard I of England, though their tombs have been destroyed. The tombs of Eleanor of Aquitaine and Isabella of Angoulême, however, are noteworthy. Of special interest is the 12th-century abbey kitchen with its curious octagonal shape and strange chimneys.

BIBLIOGRAPHY. K. J. Conant, *Carolingian and Romanesque Architecture, 800–1200*, Baltimore, 1959.

FONTHILL ABBEY, *see* WYATT, JAMES.

FOPPA, CRISTOFORO, *see* "CARADOSSO," CRISTOFORO FOPPA.

FOPPA, VINCENZO. Italian painter (1427/30–1515/16). He lived in youth and old age in Brescia, but in maturity he was in Pavia as court painter to the Duke of Milan. His major works include a *Crucifixion* (1456; Bergamo, Gallery), a fresco cycle in S. Eustorgio, Milan (ca. 1468), the *Bergamo Polyptych* (Milan, Brera), *The Martyrdom of St. Sebastian* (Brera), and the frescoes in S. Maria del Carmine, Brescia. A major lost work was the fresco *Justice of Trajan* in Milan.

Much influenced by Mantegna in modeling and perspective, Foppa is original in his sketchy technique, gray tones, and landscapes. His style dominated painters of the Lombard towns until Leonardo's arrival.

BIBLIOGRAPHY. C. J. Ffoulkes and R. Majocchi, *Vincenzo Foppa of Brescia*, London and New York, 1909; F. Wittgens, *Vincenzo Foppa*, Milan, 1948.

Vincenzo Foppa, *The Martyrdom of St. Sebastian*. Castello Sforzesco Museum, Milan.

FORAIN, JEAN LOUIS. French painter and illustrator (b. Reims, 1852; d. Paris, 1931). A local artist saw some drawings of the youthful Forain and suggested that he continue his studies in Paris. When he was fifteen he went to Paris, and four years later he studied for a year with Carpeaux at the Ecole des Beaux-Arts. This was his only formal training; he developed his art largely by observing the work of others. Carpeaux did encourage him to leave the studio, find a blind beggar, and paint him. Forain said that at that point he discovered the streets.

He was friendly with Monet and Degas, and his painting prior to 1900 reflects the influence of the impressionists, notably Degas; yet compared to him, Forain lacked originality and conviction. In 1873 he took up etching and began his career as an illustrator. By 1886 he had completed twenty-eight etchings. These reveal the influence of several masters: Goya, Manet, Degas, and Felicien Rops. These etchings, like the early paintings, seem immature when compared with his later work. Forain ceased to make etchings for twenty-two years after 1886 and turned to lithography. He made his living as a cartoonist and caricaturist for newspapers and journals. Two hundred and fifty of these sketches were collected and brought out in a single volume, *Comédie Parisienne*.

In his cartoons he followed the lead of Daumier, Gavarni, Steinlen, and Guys to become a social critic. He lampooned the superficialities of the Parisian *bourgeoisie*. Most of his criticism, however, was centered on the gross injustices of the law courts. Like Daumier, he sought to reveal the disparity between true social justice and justice based exclusively on legal distinctions, but his art seems forced and melodramatic compared to that of the older master. He is never consumed with Daumier's demonic glee at exposing the legal profession as corrupt and hypocritical. Forain, rather, emphasizes the cruelty wrought by injustices.

When Forain returned to etching in 1908, he produced ninety-five etchings and three monotypes in less than a year. He continued to make prints, but never with such intensity. Marcel Guerin's *catalogue raisonné* (Paris, 1912) lists eighty-nine lithographs produced between 1890 and 1910. It is estimated that between 1910 and 1931 Forain turned out another forty etchings and seventeen lithographs. His late graphic work is preponderantly religious. He turned to the New Testament for his subject matter and to Rembrandt for his inspiration and example.

BIBLIOGRAPHY. C. Kunstler, *Forain*, Paris, 1931.

ROBERT REIFF

FORD, EDWARD ONSLOW. English sculptor (1852–1901). The highlights of Ford's career are his public monuments—such as the Shelley Memorial, University College, Oxford, and that of Lord Strathnairn, Knightsbridge—and his lifelike portrait busts of Millais, Huxley, and many others. He was one of the first English sculptors to produce replicas of his own work.

FORESHORTENING. Reduction in size of objects as they recede from the eye, or point of sight. In conventional perspective, objects lying in the picture plane are not foreshortened, those lying in front of the picture plane—that is, between the eye and the picture plane—are en-

Jean Louis Forain, *The Petitioner*. National Gallery, Washington D.C.

larged, and those lying behind the picture plane are foreshortened. Foreshortening, a concomitant of perspective drawing, was used in ancient art, such as the Pompeian frescoes, but developed as a science in Renaissance art.

FORGE, THE. Oil painting by Louis Le Nain, in the Louvre Museum, Paris. *See* LE NAIN BROTHERS.

FORGERY. The practice of forgery, that is, deliberate manufacture of an art object with the intent to deceive the purchaser as to date and authorship, is as old as the interest in collecting. A forgery is distinct from an imitation, which can be made by the master's pupils, or from a later copy produced without fraudulent intent. Forgeries can be of several types: copies of existing works of art, works in the style of a particular master or period but not direct copies, or pastiches made from fragments of original works of art.

The earliest records reporting forgeries date from Roman times. Phaedrus (*Fabulae Aesopiae* V, prologue) mentions sculptors who affixed the names of Praxiteles and Myron to their own statues with the hope of deceiving a collector of Greek objects. But most antique forgeries were directed toward deception of material, particularly the counterfeiting of gold, silver, and gems in jewelry. Little is known about the practice of forgery in the Middle Ages, but in the Renaissance forgery again appears to have increased. Both contemporary work and work by antique artists were forged. Vasari records that Ghiberti forged antique medals and that others falsified antique intaglios. The most famous example of Renaissance forgery mentioned by Vasari is that of Michelangelo, who is said to have made a marble cupid and "antiqued" it by burying it in a vineyard. An interesting example of a Renaissance artist forging a work by a contemporary was the *Christ Healing a Lame Man*, a fake Dürer painted by Luca Giordano.

A great increase in forgery occurred in the 18th century coincident with the new interest in archaeology. Soon after the excavations of Pompeii and Herculaneum forged Roman paintings appeared, the most notable examples by Giuseppe Guerra, a pupil of Solimena. The height of archaeological forgery occurred in the 19th century, when nearly every major excavation was followed by a series of forgeries. One famous example was the Tiara of Saïtapharnes, a solid-gold headdress with scenes from the *Iliad* and an inscription stating that it was a gift to the Scythian king Saïtapharnes. The tiara was purchased by the Louvre as an original work of the 3d century B.C. The controversy over its authenticity was settled in the early 20th century, when a resident of Odessa admitted that the tiara was his creation. One of the greatest forgers of the 19th century was Alceo Dossena, who was expert in fabricating Greek, Etruscan, and Roman works of sculpture as well as works by such early Renaissance sculptors as Desiderio da Settignano and Mino da Fiesole. *See* DOSSENA, ALCEO.

The forgers of our day are even more adept. They are frequently aware of the many techniques employed to detect forgeries and are able to make it nearly impossible to detect their fraudulent products by purely scientific means. Only very acute stylistic analysis can detect these modern forgeries. The most famous of modern forgers was H. van Meegeren, who created incredibly convincing forgeries of Vermeer and other Dutch old masters. Forgers have kept up with the changes in collecting taste, and many forgeries of modern artists such as Van Gogh and Braque have appeared.

BIBLIOGRAPHY. A. Fürtwängler, *Neuere Fälschungen von Antiken*, Berlin, 1899; M. J. Friedländer, *Genuine and Counterfeit*, New York, 1930; R. G. Reisner, *Fakes and Forgeries in the Fine Arts: A Bibliography*, New York, 1950; F. Arnau, *3,000 Years of Deception in Art and Antiques*, London, 1961.

DONALD L. EHRESMANN

FORMENT, DAMIAN. Spanish sculptor (ca. 1475–1540). Born in Valencia, Damián Forment appears to have trained in Florence, then worked in his native city for nine years before locating his studio in Saragossa in 1509. His early works, such as the high altarpiece (1509–12) in the Church of El Pilar, Saragossa, despite their Gothic frames, show in the statues and reliefs a knowledge of Donatello and Ghiberti. Later Forment used the Gothic frame in one of the first mannerist works in Spain, the high altarpiece (1520–34) in Huesca Cathedral. He most often worked in alabaster but sometimes used polychromed wood.

BIBLIOGRAPHY. M. Abizanda y Broto, *Damián Forment*, Barcelona, 1942; J. M. Azcárate, *Ars Hispaniae*, vol. 13: *Escultura del siglo XVI*, Madrid, 1958.

FORMERET. Half-rib formed at the wall side of a medieval vault. Called a wall rib in English architecture, the formeret enclosing the lateral vaulting compartment came into frequent use in 13th-century England, as in Southwark Cathedral.

FORMOSA (Taiwan): SUN YAT-SEN MUSEUM. Collection of the Republic of China. Located in suburban Taipei, the museum houses the most significant items of the former Imperial Chinese treasures. Its 240,000 objects represent nearly 6,000 years of Chinese art. More than 3,000 objects are shown at a time in a constantly changing series of exhibits. These include important paintings of the T'ang, Sung, Yüan, and Ming periods, such as Fan K'uan's *The Travelers among Mountains and Streams*, Kuo Hsi's *Early Spring*, and Wen Tung's *Bamboo*; calligraphy, such as copies and stone rubbings of the work of Wang Hsi-chih; twenty-six magnificent Sung porcelains from the imperial pottery of Ju-chou; and outstanding groups of jades, metalwork, and tapestries. The collection was previously housed in Peking in the National Palace Collection and the National Central Museum.

FORNER, RAQUEL. Argentine painter (1902–   ). Born in Buenos Aires, Raquel Forner is an expressionist painter who uses symbolic themes, as in *Those Who Saw the Moon*, a series of paintings of the 1960s. Her training was in Buenos Aires and in Paris with Friesz. She has exhibited widely since 1937, and her work is owned by the Museum of Modern Art in New York. Among her many prizes is the grand prize of the National Salon in Buenos Aires (1955).

BIBLIOGRAPHY. G. Giani, *Raquel Forner*, Milan, 1960.

FORSTER, LUDWIG. Austrian architect (1797–1863). Förster worked in Vienna. His work reflects the change in taste about the mid-19th century toward elaboration of ornament, richness of forms, and emphasis on color. He is also known for his competition-winning design for the layout of the Vienna Ringstrasse.

FORT, AGRA. Indian fortress-palace on the western bank of the Jumna River. Begun by the emperor Akbar in 1564, it is encircled by massive walls of red sandstone nearly 1.5 miles in circuit, with the splendid Delhi Gate providing access on the west side. Some 500 structures of red sandstone in the architectural styles of Bengal and Gujarat were built within the enclosure, but most were demolished less than a century later. Surviving is the Jahangiri Mahal, a residential palace which represents a transitional stage from Hindu to Muslim palace architecture.

BIBLIOGRAPHY. P. Brown, *Indian Architecture*, vol. 2: *Islamic Period*, 4th ed., Bombay, 1959.

FORT, DELHI. Indian fort situated on the eastern bank of the Jumna River, in Old Delhi. Its towering walls of red sandstone enclose an area 3,200 feet long and 1,800 feet wide. It was completed in 1648 during the reign of Shah Jahan, after ten years of continuous building.

A section of the enclosure displays several separate royal structures in a parklike atmosphere. Nearest to the western entrance gate of the fort is the Diwan-i-Am, or Hall of Public Audience. Built as the principal structure of the palace area, it is 500 feet long and 300 feet wide and features a vast hall containing an elevated recess lined in marble from which Shah Jahan dispensed justice. Farther to the east is the lovely Moti Masjid, or Pearl Mosque, erected in 1657 by Aurangzeb, son of Shah Jahan. It is a mosque in miniature, all of white marble and crowned by three delicate domes.

Just south of the Pearl Mosque is the Diwan-i-Khas,

Delhi Fort. Domes of the Moti Masjid rising above the red sandstone walls.

or Hall of Private Audience, a pavilion of white marble set on a raised platform. The throne was placed in the central chamber, whose roof was supported by thirty-two pillars, with all wall and ceiling surfaces covered with ornamental patterns executed in semiprecious stones and in gold and silver. Just south of the Diwan-i-Khas is the Rang Mahal, or Colored Palace, once the living quarters of the imperial seraglio. Latticework screens in the great windows along the eastern side offer a splendid view over the countryside.

BIBLIOGRAPHY. R. C. Arora, *Delhi: The Imperial City*, New Delhi, 1953.   DONALD N. WILBER

FORT-SAINT-ANDRE, VILLENEUVE-LES-AVIGNON. French fort, situated on a hill overlooking the Rhone River. A fine example of medieval fortification, it was built in the second half of the 14th century by John the Good and Charles V. An imposing entrance gate with twin crenelated towers and spacious rooms with ogive vaults give access to the precincts of the Benedictine abbey, founded in the 10th century, of which remnants still stand.

BIBLIOGRAPHY. H. Chobaut, *Avignon et le Comtat Venaissin*, Grenoble, 1950.

FORTUNA, TEMPLE OF, PRAENESTE, *see* PRAENESTE.

FORTUNA VIRILIS, TEMPLE OF, ROME. Rectangular Roman Ionic temple, situated in the Forum Boarium. The temple is variously called the Temple of Fortuna Virilis and the Temple of Mater Matuta. It is dated in Caesar's time on the basis of an inscription on the architrave of the cella door. The temple is tetrastyle, prostyle, and pseudoperipteral with a portico two columns deep; it is raised on a podium. Engaged columns decorate the external walls of the cella on three sides. This temple provides the first

example of a cornice supported by consoles, a style which was used in other Roman temples in the 1st century B.C. The large cella extends the full width of the portico.

BIBLIOGRAPHY. W. J. Anderson, R. P. Spiers, and T. Ashby, *The Architecture of Greece and Rome*, vol. 2: *The Architecture of Ancient Rome*, London, 1927.

FORTUNE, WHEEL OF. Late medieval allegorical subject in which various personages, frequently kings and the upper clergy, are mounted upon the spokes of a wheel. The entire grouping is turned by a blindfolded female figure who personifies fortune. Her power to put one figure on top of the wheel and another on the bottom symbolizes the changeableness of human existence. The motif appeared first in the *Hortus deliciarum* of Herrade of Landsberg (ca. 1175).

FORTUNE MOUND, ARK., *see* MOUND BUILDERS; NORTH AMERICAN INDIAN ART (EASTERN UNITED STATES AND CANADA).

FORTUNY Y CARBO, *see* FORTUNY Y MARSAL, MARIANO JOSE MARIA BERNARDO.

FORTUNY Y MADRAZO, MARIANO. Spanish-Italian painter, stage designer, sculptor, photographer, and inventor (b. Granada, 1871; d. Venice, 1949). The son of the Spanish painter Mariano Fortuny y Marsal, he was brought up in Venice and lived there throughout his life. Although he studied painting in Paris, he was largely self-taught. His style in painting echoes in a lush Beaux-Arts manner the sensuality of the Venetian tradition, particularly of the rococo period. Fortuny is perhaps better known as the highly successful inventor of a technique for embossing patterns on fabrics and metals and as the creator of a method of indirect lighting that is widely used in theaters and galleries throughout the world.

FORTUNY Y MARSAL (Fortuny y Carbo), MARIANO JOSE MARIA BERNARDO. Spanish painter (b. Reus, 1838; d. Rome, 1874). Fortuny began his studies at the Barcelona Academy (1852) under Lorenzale and Mila. He created many religious works but was also influenced by the lithographs of Gavarni. He won the Prix de Rome in 1858 and, accompanying the Spanish army, began a lifetime of travel in 1859 by covering the Moroccan war. Through the French dealer Goupil, his small, facile, genre-like paintings of the *ancien régime* brought him international success, and all of his work thereafter commanded fabulous prices. In other paintings he produced lively, if superficial, representations of Spain, particularly of Granada, and other stops in his travels.

BIBLIOGRAPHY. F. Pompey Salgueira, *Fortuny* (Temas españoles no. 72), Madrid, 1953.

FORUM. Public place in ancient Rome. The forum was an open area surrounded by buildings. Corresponding to the Greek agora, the Roman forum was used as a marketplace and a civic center. The Forum Romanum, the oldest and most important forum, was placed in the valley between the Capitoline and Palatine hills. Used in early times as a hippodrome and for contests, it developed into a complex of temples, tribunals, porticoes, and colonnades, adorned with statues and pillars of victory.

FORUM OF TRAJAN, ROME, *see* TRAJAN, FORUM OF, ROME.

FORUM PACIS (Forum of Vespasian), ROME. Roman forum which covered the area at the southeast end of the imperial forums. Construction was begun in A.D. 71 by Vespasian. Before the 4th century, the forum was called Templum Pacis. The only architectural remnant is a building into which the Church of SS. Cosmas and Damian was later built. *See* SACRAE URBIS, TEMPLUM, ROME.

FORUM ROMANUM, ROME, *see* ROMAN FORUM, ROME.

FOSCARI PALACE, VENICE. Fifteenth-century Italian palace, an important example of the Venetian Gothic of its time. It was the establishment of Doge Francesco Foscari (d. 1475), who ruled the republic for thirty-eight years.

BIBLIOGRAPHY. G. Lorenzetti, *Venice and Its Lagoon*, Rome, 1961.

FOSSANO, AMBROGIO DA, *see* BERGOGNONE, AMBROGIO DA FOSSANO.

FOSSANOVA, MONASTERY OF. Cistercian monastery near Rome, built between 1179 and 1208. As a religious center, its importance derives from the fact that St. Thomas Aquinas died there (1274).

Architecturally, Fossanova is an example of how the Cistercians carried their variant of Burgundian (Cluniac) architecture into Italy. The monastery was abandoned in 1812, and many of its buildings fell into disrepair and ruin. However, the church preserves an unusual staged crossing tower (partially Renaissance) of stone, which seems to suggest the type of staged wooden belfries used by the Cistercians in France. There are also vestiges of an exterior low front porch, common to French and German Cistercian churches and ultimately derived from Burgundian types. Like all Cistercian architecture, Fossanova is severe, bare of decorative ornament, and imposing in its austerity.

BIBLIOGRAPHY. C. Ricci, *Romanesque Architecture in Italy*, London, 1925.

FOSTER, MYLES BIRKET. English painter and engraver (b. North Shields, Northumberland, 1825; d. Weybridge, Surrey, 1899). He was apprenticed to Ebenezer Landells, a wood engraver who was a pupil of Thomas Bewick. Foster did drawings for the *Illustrated London News* and other periodicals and also illustrated many books. His first independent success, after leaving Landells in 1846, were drawings for *Evangeline*, published in 1850. In the 1850s he illustrated the works of many important authors, including Goldsmith, Scott, Milton, and Wordsworth. He then left illustration for the eventually popular water colors of landscapes, seasides, and rural subjects, which retained the detailed execution characteristic of his early training.

BIBLIOGRAPHY. H. M. Cundall, *Birket Foster, R. W. S.*, London, 1906.

FO-TO, *see* BUDDHA.

FOUCQUET, JEAN, *see* FOUQUET, JEAN.

FOUGERON, ANDRE. French painter (1913–). Mainly a self-taught artist, he was born in Paris, where he took night courses during 1927–28. He executed small pieces of sculpture and colored lithographs and completed several large decorations, including one for the Students' Sanatorium in Hilaire-du-Touvet, Isère. His search for expressive form and color was similar to that of Pignon and Gischia, except that his style was more realistic. His art is related to some of Picasso's later strong figural canvases. Fougeron's *Les Parisiennes au marché* (1940), shown at the Salon d'Automne that year, was the point of departure for the French neorealistic-socialist school, and it is in this definite style that Fougeron has continued to work. In 1946 he was awarded the Prix National.

BIBLIOGRAPHY. R. Nacenta, *School of Paris*, London, 1960.

FOUJITA, TSOUGOHARU (Tsuguji Fujita). Japanese painter (1886–1968). Born in Tokyo, Foujita lived most of his life in Paris and became a naturalized citizen of France. Sharp, precisely drawn lines and a sensitive, poetic color harmony characterize his work, all of which is European in manner. There are examples in the National Museum of Modern Art in Paris.

BIBLIOGRAPHY. G. Bauër and R. Rey, *Foujita*, Paris, 1958.

FOUNDING. General term designating the entire process of casting in metals. The foundry is the site of casting. *See* CAST AND CASTING.

Tsougoharu Foujita, *Girl's Head*, 1947. Private collection, Paris.

FOUND OBJECTS, *see* OBJETS TROUVES.

FOUNTAIN. In art, a structure incorporating an artificially produced jet of water. Usually it involves the combination of architectural elements and some sort of basin to collect water. Fountains without architectural elements, imitating natural grottoes or waterfalls, became popular in the baroque period. Since the late Middle Ages, figures have become popular as components of fountains.

FOUNTAIN OF LIFE. Christ's power of salvation represented allegorically as a fountain flowing inside a temple. Frequently, the waters of this fountain nourished animals (as in the Godescalc Gospels, ca. 761). At a later date the water became the blood of Christ (as in the *Ghent Altarpiece*, ca. 1432).

FOUNTAIN OF THE INNOCENTS. Stone relief sculpture (most of which is now in the Louvre) executed by Goujon for the Hospital of the Innocents, Paris. *See* GOUJON, JEAN.

FOUNTAINS ABBEY. Possibly one of the two (the other, Rievaulx) earliest important surviving Cistercian abbeys in Europe, coeval with the mother house at Clairvaux. The church nave and transepts were begun about 1135. The east end was begun anew about 1205–10, and with the eastern transepts was complete by 1257. The north transept tower was built about 1539. The monastic buildings are of the perfect Cistercian English pattern. The north–south range of the great cellar and the dorter is part late Norman and part dating about 1200. The cloister to the east, which may have been built of wood, is gone. South of this is the refectory, of the 13th century, and in the east range is the chapter house, built before 1170.

BIBLIOGRAPHY. N. Pevsner, *The Buildings of England*, vol. 17, Harmondsworth, 1959.

FOUQUET (Foucquet), JEAN. French painter (ca. 1420–before 1481). Born in Tours and trained in Paris in workshops of miniaturists in the employ of the Duke of Bedford, Fouquet advanced far beyond his Gothic origins to blend in a new and characteristically French way the classical idealization and balance of the Italians with the analytic representation of observed reality introduced by the great Flemings. His was the earliest visit to Italy by a great northern painter that can be dated with certainty.

As a young man he was in Rome to paint the portrait of Pope Eugene IV, who died early in 1447. This important commission indicates that by 1446 he must have been accomplished and well known as a portraitist. His *Portrait of Charles VII* (Paris, Louvre) may have helped to establish this reputation. Frontal, dry, archaic in conception and execution, this painting at the same time introduced something new in royal portraiture: the three-quarter view. It was probably painted in 1444, following the truce of Arras, when the inscription on the frame, "très victorieux roi," would have been appropriate.

He was back in Tours in 1448, and soon after he probably started to work for important personages at the court of Charles VII, then established in Tours. The Book of Hours of Etienne Chevalier, which may be dated about

1450, is replete with references to his Italian trip. Architectural details suggest that Fouquet visited Florence as well as Rome; his illumination of the Visitation, for example, clearly recalls the Florence of Brunelleschi. Forty miniatures from this book, cut away from the text, are now in the Condé Museum in Chantilly; two are in the Louvre; one is in the British Museum in London; and three are in private collections. They show an interest in anatomy, volume, and perspective that reflects the achievements of the most progressive Italian painting of the time. Certain affinities to the work of Fra Angelico in particular may be discerned. But what Fouquet learned from the Florentines he adapted freely in accord with his own bent; his perspective was not scientific, but empirical. He was an experimenter of singular originality in his approach to problems of space representation, both in interiors and in varied rural and urban open-air settings. No less striking is his skill and inventiveness in other aspects of the painter's art: the depiction of figures in action, of genre scenes and still-life elements, of landscapes organized in depth, and of reflected light. His ability to employ light and shade not only to build the relief of the object but to relate the object to its environing space would alone have placed him in the forefront of painting anywhere in Europe in the middle of the 15th century.

While in his miniatures Fouquet seems to enjoy the challenge of every kind of subject, in his known easel paintings he is concerned almost exclusively with the depiction of the human figure. The *Melun Diptych*, apparently painted close to the time of the Chevalier Book of Hours, portrays in the left wing (Berlin, former State Museums) the donor, the same Etienne Chevalier, being presented by St. Stephen to the Virgin and Child, who are represented on the right wing (Antwerp, Fine Arts Museum). Consistent with tradition, the divine figures are treated in a more abstract and sculptural manner than the human ones. Fouquet's paintings, which appear to portray sculptured figures, stem from the experience of a French artist who grew up among churches rich with statues.

There are two medallions in the then-new technique of painting in enamel which were made by Fouquet, probably at the time of the *Melun Diptych*, as decorations for its frame: a *Self-Portrait* (Louvre) and *The Believing and the Unbelieving Receiving the Holy Ghost* (Berlin, Charlottenburg Castle). Also close in date is a fragment from a panel painting, *Head of a Monk* (Tours, Museum of Fine Arts).

The Munich Boccaccio can be dated from its frontispiece, which shows the trial of the Duke of Alençon at Vendôme in October, 1458. This manuscript includes ten miniatures by the master and eighty small ones probably executed in his workshop after his designs, illustrating *Les Cas des nobles hommes et femmes malheureux* (Munich, Staatsbibliothek). Closely corresponding to these in style are the fifty-one illustrations for *Les Grandes chroniques des rois de France*, which likewise show evidence of workshop collaboration (Paris, National Library). Here Fouquet's epic style finds full scope in the depiction of battle scenes, triumphal entries, and other historic events that call forth his mastery in the composition of dramatic crowd

Jean Fouquet, *Portrait of Charles VII*. Louvre, Paris.

scenes with focused action. His adherence to close observation reveals itself in the strict domination of settings and costumes, which are contemporary rather than historical. Many of the figures may be portraits as well; most of the kings show the features of Charles VII and the emperors those of Sigismund of Austria.

The *Portrait of Guillaume Juvenal des Ursins* (Louvre), the preparatory drawing for that portrait (Berlin, former State Museums, Print Cabinet), and another portrait drawing, that of a papal legate (New York, Metropolitan Museum), date from about 1460. In 1469/70 Fouquet was commissioned to paint the frontispiece for the statutes of the newly founded Order of St. Michael (Paris, National Library), and between 1470 and 1476 he did nine miniatures, identified as his in a contemporary note, for the *Antiquités judaïques* (Paris, National Library). It is on the basis of stylistic comparison with these illuminations that the whole of the master's *oeuvre* has been reconstructed. In these mature studies of battles and deeds of heroism, Fouquet puts the observer in the midst of the scene. Following the Gothic tradition, he continues to mix with minutely observed architecture fantastic features designed to indicate strangeness in time and place.

In 1475 Louis XI named him "Peintre du Roi." From about this time date five detached miniatures from the *Ancient History until Caesar and the Feats of the Romans*. Three somewhat questionable ones from the *Livy of Rochechouart*, or *Livy de la Sorbonne* (Paris, National Library), could not have been begun before 1477. This work may have been interrupted by the death of the master, which took place before 1481.

In the course of his development, the earlier concern with detail has given way to a broader and looser style, and the color has become less strongly contrasted and less brilliant. In the *Nouans Pietà* of about 1475 (Nouans, parish church), though the subordinate figures show workshop collaboration and the panel has been cut down and painted over, the figure of the Virgin, with its sculptural volumes and expressive power, presents a worthy summation of Fouquet's personal style in the fullness of maturity. It is marked by the monumentality that signalized his work from first to last.

Though he had a busy workshop, including perhaps his two sons, François and Louis, Fouquet established no school. His influence is seen more in book illustration than in easel painting, but even here there is more evidence of superficial imitation than of an ability to carry on the advances he had introduced, which apparently were not fully understood by his followers.

BIBLIOGRAPHY. H. Focillon, "Le Style monumental dans l'art de Fouquet," *Gazette des Beaux-Arts*, XV, January, 1936; K. Perls, *Jean Fouquet*, London, 1940; C. Sterling, "Klaus Perls, Jean Fouquet, 1940, and Paul Wescher, Jean Fouquet und seine Zeit, 1945," book review, *Art Bulletin*, XXVIII, June, 1946; P. Wescher, *Jean Fouquet and His Time*, London, 1947. MADLYN KAHR

FOUQUIERES (Fouquiere; Fouquier), JACQUES. Flemish painter and engraver of landscapes (b. 1580/90; d. Paris, 1659). He first followed and interpreted the conceptions of Josse de Momper and Paul Bril. His later works anticipate Jacques d'Arthois's decorative style and often feature a large tree in the center of the composition.

BIBLIOGRAPHY. W. Stechow, "Drawings and Etchings by Jacques Fouquier," *Gazette des Beaux-Arts*, XXXIV, December, 1948.

FOUR APOSTLES. Oil painting by Dürer, in the Bavarian State Picture Galleries, Munich. *See* DURER, ALBRECHT.

FOWLER, CHARLES. English architect (1791–1867). He contributed a form of utilitarian Italianesque revival, closely following Charles Barry's impetus, but mostly in market buildings: Hungerford Market, London (1831–33), and Exeter Lower Market (1835–36). His skillful use of iron components was advanced for its date.

FOX INDIANS, *see* SAUK AND FOX INDIANS.

FOYATIER, DENIS. French sculptor (b. Bussière, 1793; d. Paris, 1863). He studied with Joseph Chinard in Lyons and in Paris. A statue of a young faun won him the Prix de Rome in 1819. His works were mostly powerful personifications and mythological figures done in a neoclassic style.

FOY (Faith) OF CONQUES, ST. Martyr (ca. 290–ca. 303). She was born at Agen, converted by a nurse, and baptized by St. Caprais. Governor Dacian tried to persuade her to recant, but she refused. When executioners placed her nude on a flaming gridiron, a dove bringing her a martyr's crown let fall a rain of dew, which extinguished the fire; she was then decapitated. Her relics are in a famous gold and jeweled reliquary (10th cent.) in the church at Conques, which shows her as a grown woman. (St. Foy should not be confused with St. Faith of SS. Faith, Hope, and Charity.) Her attributes are a gridiron, sword, and dove. Her feast is October 6. *See also* SAINTS IN ART.

FRACTIONAL CONCEPT. Manner of depicting objects that is common in primitive art and certain phases of modern art. Various views of an object are incorporated into a single view; for example, a face may be shown frontally, while the eye is seen in profile.

FRAENKEL, ITZHAK. Israeli painter and stage designer (1900–   ). Born in Odessa, U.S.S.R., he immigrated to Israel in 1919 after studies at the Odessa Art School and the Ecole des Beaux-Arts in Paris. The founder and director of the Art Academy in Safad, he has won numerous prizes in Israel and has had his work shown internationally, including at the Venice Biennale in 1948.

FRAGONARD, JEAN-HONORE. French genre, landscape, portrait, and history painter; draftsman, decorator, and etcher (b. Grasse, 1732; d. Paris, 1806). He was taken to Paris about 1738. He became a clerk to a notary (1747–48) who, struck by the boy's drawing talents, advised formal instruction with an artist. Boucher at first rejected him as unformed, but Chardin accepted him briefly (1750) to lay out his palette, and set him to copying prints. Though Fragonard was not interested in his master's subject matter, Chardin's cautious methods founded in him a reserve

Jean-Honoré Fragonard, *Young Girl Reading*, ca. 1776. National Gallery, Washington, D.C. (Gift of Mrs. Mellon Bruce, 1961).

of good technical habits to offset his natural impetuosity. On his own, he studied paintings in Paris churches and often copied them from memory. The fruit of this initiative was Boucher's acceptance of him as pupil and collaborator (1750–54). Though Fragonard was not a student in the Royal Academy, Boucher authorized him to compete for the Prix de Rome, which he won in 1752 with *Jeroboam Sacrificing to the Idols* (Paris, Ecole des Beaux-Arts).

In 1753, Charles André Van Loo, director of the Academy school, recommended that Fragonard be admitted. From 1754 to 1755 he did history painting, which was exhibited at Versailles with works of fellow students. In December, 1755, he arrived in Rome as pensioner at the French Academy. His bewilderment at the grandeur of High Renaissance masters occasioned a lapse of ability, so that at first the director, C. J. Natoire, doubted his credentials. The current eclectic academic attitude fortunately permitted him freedom in finding his own temperamental preference. The stylistic as well as the major thematic elements of his *oeuvre* were set through his study of Barocci, Pietro da Cortona, Solimena, Tiepolo, Feti, and Lys during the next few years, as well as through the influences of the landscape painter Hubert Robert and the amateur etcher and archaeologist Abbé Jean Claude Richard Saint-Non. A sojourn at the Villa d'Este at Tivoli and trips to Venice, Naples, Pompeii, and Sicily afforded him subjects for landscape drawings with antique architectural motifs. Saint-Non's suite, *Voyage pittoresque*, commemorates the reciprocal rewards of this association. The styles of Rembrandt and other Dutch and Flemish 17th-century landscape painters are reflected in the works of these formative years. Returning to Paris in 1761, Fragonard was given quarters in the Louvre. P.-F. Basan published engraved views of Rome and Naples drawn by him and Hubert Robert.

Though he was never a full-fledged academician, his dramatic interpretation, *The High Priest Corésus Sacrificing Himself to Save Callirhoé* (Paris, Louvre), begun in 1761 and submitted in 1765, occasioned his immediate acceptance as an associate at the Royal Academy. Louis XV ordered that the painting be translated into tapestry at the Gobelins.

Fragonard then entirely abandoned this grand manner, not only because of his fundamental indifference, but also because of his dissatisfaction at the dilatory payment for the work. After 1767 he no longer exhibited at the Salon. It was deplored that, instead of working for glory and posterity, he was satisfied to shine in boudoirs; that, instead of conducting himself in a manner befitting *sieur Fragonard, peintre du Roi, officier de l'Académie*, he was content to be simply "Frago," as he then signed his works. Henceforth, he catered to a private clientele. Amorous scenes, rustic landscapes, and decorative panels were the bulk of his production and the basis of his reputation. A typical work is *The Swing* (*L'Escarpolette*, 1767; London, Wallace Collection). The joyfulness of these scenes of dalliance precludes vulgarity. Good fortune again smiled on him in the patronage of an enormously rich amateur, Bergeret de Grancourt. His influence in parvenu society instantly gave Fragonard entree as decorator. Among many decorating commissions in ensuing years, most prominent were those for the *hôtel* of the dancer La Guimard, for Mme de Pompadour (at Bellevue), for Mme du Barry (at Louveciennes), and for Louis XV (Versailles, dining room).

In 1773–75 he made an extensive tour of Italy with his wife and M. de Bergeret, returning to France by way of Austria and Germany. Later, Bergeret brought suit against him for withholding drawings made during the trip, claiming that they belonged to him since he had financed the entire trip.

In the 1780s Fragonard's painting became an almost mystical adulation of sentimental love; without doubt, this reflects indirectly the influence of Jean-Jacques Rousseau and anticipates in fervid, poetic fashion the end of the era. Paradoxically, though his art is quintessential of the declining old regime, he welcomed the objective principles of the French Revolution even though it deprived him of clientele and prestige. In 1792 the Revolutionary committee that selected models for the Gobelins factory rejected his *Corésus and Callirhoé* (Louvre) because "the subject evokes only superstitious ideas." This rejection manifests the triumph of republican ideals evident in the neoclassic art of Jacques-Louis David. Despite the disillusionment of finding his expressive genius anathema to the new order, Fragonard was much indebted to David for his friendship during these years. Through David he became both president and curator of painting of the new Conservatory of the Musée du Louvre. By imperial decree, however, in 1805 he and other artists were deprived of their apartments in the Louvre.

Fragonard cared little for making an imprint upon posterity. Because he rarely dated his works, and because he began and ended a virtuoso, an analysis of his stylistic development is difficult. There is great diversification of technique and variety of media found in the works of this deliciously sensuous painter. Whether working in oils, water-color and ink washes, chalks, or Chinese ink, his genius for catching joyful human emotion in impromptu sketches makes him the most dazzling interpreter of this light-hearted era. With brilliant but sure spontaneity he consummates sentiently the reverie of Watteau. His total work includes about 500 paintings, 1,000 drawings, illustrations, and etchings, which are to be found in museums in Besançon, Boston, Cincinnati, Cleveland, Detroit, London (Wallace Collection), New York (Metropolitan Museum and Frick Collection), Paris (Louvre and Banque de France), Washington (National Gallery of Art), and elsewhere.

BIBLIOGRAPHY. P. Bergeret de Grancourt, *Bergeret et Fragonard: Journal inédit d'un voyage en Italie 1773–1774, précédé d'une étude par M. A. Tornézy*, Paris, 1895; A. de Montaiglon and J. Giuffrey, *Correspondance des directeurs de l'Académie de France à Rome avec les surintendents des bâtiments . . .*, vol. 11, Paris, 1901; L. Guimbaud, *Saint-Non et Fragonard, d'après des documents inédits*, Paris, 1928; E. L. de Goncourt and J. A. de Goncourt, *French XVIII Century Painters*, New York, 1948; J. Seznec and J. Adhémar, *Diderot Salons*, Oxford, Eng., vol. 1, 1957; vol. 2, 1960; J.-H. Fragonard, *The Paintings of Fragonard*, complete ed. by G. Wildenstein, London, 1960.

GEORGE V. GALLENKAMP

FRAME, PLATFORM. Type of wood construction, also called "western frame," in which each floor is a platform, the wall studs being one story high. Used generally in two-story dwellings, the platform frame, with studs and posts of equal height at each story, is intended to equalize wood shrinkage.

FRANCAVILLA, PIERRE, *see* FRANQUEVILLE, PIERRE.

FRANCE, MUSEUMS OF. See under the names of the following cities:

Aix-en-Provence. Granet Museum.
Ajaccio. Fesch Museum.
Albi. Toulouse-Lautrec Museum.
Amiens. Museum of Picardy.
Angers. Fine Arts Museum.
Antibes. Grimaldi Museum.
Autun. Rolin Museum.
Avignon. Calvet Museum.
Bayonne. Bonnat Museum.
Besancon. Fine Arts Museum.
Biot. Fernand Léger Museum.
Bordeaux. Fine Arts Museum.
Caen. Fine Arts Museum.
Chantilly. Condé Museum.
Colmar. Unterlinden Museum.
Dijon. Fine Arts Museum.
Grenoble. Museum of Painting and Sculpture.
Le Mans. Fine Arts Museum.
Lille. Fine Arts Museum.
Lyons. Fine Arts Museum; Guimet Museum; Textile Museum.
Marseilles. Fine Arts Museum.
Montauban. Ingres Museum.
Montpellier. Fabre Museum.
Nantes. Fine Arts Museum.
Nice. Chagall Museum.
Orleans. Fine Arts Museum.
Paris. Carnavalet Museum; Cernuschi Museum; Cluny Museum; Cognac-Jay Museum; Delacroix Museum; Fine Arts Museum of the City of Paris; Guimet Museum; Jacquemart-André Museum; Jeu de Paume Museum; Louvre Museum; Luxembourg Museum; Marmottan Museum; Moreau Museum; Museum of French Monuments; Museum of Man (Musée de l'Homme); National Library and Collection of Medals (Bibliothèque Nationale and Cabinet des Médailles); National Museum of Modern Art; Orangerie; Rodin Museum.
Pau. Fine Arts Museum.
Reims. Fine Arts Museum.
Rouen. Fine Arts Museum.
Saint-Germain-en-Laye. Museum of National Antiquities.
Strasbourg. Fine Arts Museum; Notre-Dame Museum (Musée de l'Oeuvre Notre-Dame).
Toulouse. Museum of the Augustinians.
Tours. Fine Arts Museum.
Troyes. Fine Arts Museum.
Valenciennes. Fine Arts Museum.
Versailles. Museum.

FRANCESCA (Franceschi), *see* PIERO DELLA FRANCESCA.

FRANCESCHI, FRANCESCO DE'. Venetian painter (fl. 1443–68 or 1445–56). Many documents bearing this name, not certainly referring to one person, appear in legal records. Franceschi's art is known from one altarpiece (Padua, Municipal Museum) with Peter and other saints, once signed and dated 1447. It shows the influence of Jacobello del Fiore and other International Gothic artists but also exhibits strong interest in plain plastic modeling inside the gilded linear ornament. The most important attributed work is the *St. Mammas Altarpiece,* now in sections in the museums of Verona, Budapest, and Yale University.

BIBLIOGRAPHY. B. Berenson, *The Venetian Painters of the Renaissance,* 3d ed., New York, 1897; L. Testi, *La storia della pittura veneziana,* vol. 2: *Il divenire,* Bergamo, 1915.

FRANCESCHINI, BALDASSARE (Il Volterrano). Italian painter (b. Volterra, 1611; d. Florence, 1689). Assisting Giovanni da San Giovanni on frescoes at the Pitti Palace in Florence (1635–36), Franceschini developed an even airier style of subtle contrasts than his master's in his *Practical Joke of the Priest Arlotto.* His later work in the Pitti Palace and SS. Annunziata in Florence emulates the weightier baroque manner of Pietro da Cortona.

FRANCESCHINI, MARCANTONIO. Italian painter (1648–1729). Born in Bologna, Franceschini was trained in the school of Cignani, from whom he learned monumentality of form and expressive gesture. He was elected head of Bologna's Accademia Clementina and received numerous important commissions, among them the decoration of the Sala del Consiglio Comunale in Naples (1737; destroyed). He worked also in Modena and Piacenza, and in Rome he executed the cartoons for the mosaics in St. Peter's. The interior of the Church of Corpus Domini in Bologna was decorated in collaboration with Enrico Haffner; it exhibits lavish scenic effects combined with delicate tonal gradations and an occasional sentimentality of expression. Basically, his style represents the highly decorative current in Bolognese art, capable of freshness and charm, beauty of color, and mastery of line, if sometimes lapsing into the superficiality of mannered gestures and conventional compositions.

BIBLIOGRAPHY. R. Wittkower, *Art and Architecture in Italy, 1600–1750,* Baltimore, 1958; F. Arcangeli et al., *Maestri della pittura del seicento emiliano, catalogo critico,* 2d ed., Bologna, 1959.

FRANCESCO CAPRIANI, see VOLTERRA, FRANCESCO DA.

FRANCESCO DA FAENZA (Francesco di Pietro Bitini?). Romagnol painter (b. 1400/10; d. Faenza, 1450/51). He is known principally as the cosigner, with Castagno, of frescoes (dated 1442) in the S. Tarasio Chapel in S. Zaccaria, Venice. Francesco remains an artist to whom no specific work has been successfully assigned.

BIBLIOGRAPHY. C. Grigioni, "Il pittore Francesco da Faenza collaboratore di Andrea del Castagno a Venezia," *L'Arte,* XXV, 1922.

FRANCESCO D'ANTONIO DEL CHERICO. Italian painter of miniatures (fl. 1463–85). Working at S. Marco, Francesco produced several antiphonaries for the Florence Cathedral (1463–71) in collaboration with the more conservative Zanobi Strozzi. In later decorated editions of Plutarch, Petrarch, and Books of Hours and other religious works, he approximates the vigorous style of Pollaiuolo.

FRANCESCO DA TOLENTINO. Italian painter (fl. 1525–30). All knowledge of this painter's style is based on two works preserved in S. Maria a Parete di Liveri at Nola. On the basis of these works, which reveal Francesco da Tolentino as a lesser master working in the manner of Pinturicchio, several frescoes, including those in S. Maria Nuova in Naples, have been attributed to him.

FRANCESCO DA VOLTERRA. Italian painter (fl. 1343–71/73). Only one work can be attributed to him with any certainty: the *Madonna with Child and Angels* (Modena, Este Gallery) which is signed "Francesco di Neri da Volterra." It is known that Volterra worked largely in Pisa, and this painting reveals that he was strongly influenced by the art of Taddeo Gaddi and Andrea da Firenze.

FRANCESCO DA VOLTERRA (16th cent.), *see* VOLTERRA, FRANCESCO DA.

FRANCESCO DI ANTONIO DI ANGELUCCIO. Italian painter and miniaturist (fl. Perugia, early 15th cent.; d. 1463). He probably can be identified with a "Francesco" whose name is listed in the Porta Sole at the end of the 14th century as the painter of works in the Monastery of S. Giuliana. The painting of the arms of the Visconti in the Palazzo del Popolo at the turn of the century is attributed to him along with Ottaviano Nelli da Gubbio and Cristoforo di Nicoluccio. He is also most probably to be identified with the miniaturist "Francesco di Antonio," who is known to have been active in Umbria between 1419 and 1446. Francesco painted the arms of Pope Eugene IV in 1445.

BIBLIOGRAPHY. U. Gnoli, *Pittori e miniatori nell'Umbria*, Spoleto, 1923.

FRANCESCO DI CRISTOFANO, *see* FRANCIABIGIO.

FRANCESCO DI DOMENICO, *see* VALDAMBRINO, FRANCESCO DI.

FRANCESCO DI GENTILE DA FABRIANO. Fabrianese painter (fl. second half of 15th cent.). No documents or dated works help establish the chronology for this artist. The eclecticism that characterizes Francesco's *oeuvre* is at least partly the result of diversities in the works attributed to him. The few signed pieces extant indicate only two facts clearly—that there was an influence, probably early, of the International Gothic Style and an influence, probably late, of Carlo Crivelli.

BIBLIOGRAPHY. L. Serra, "Francesco di Gentile da Fabriano," *Rassegna Marchigiana*, XI, 1933.

FRANCESCO DI GIORGIO (MARTINI). Italian architect, painter, and sculptor (b. Siena, 1439; d. there, 1501). He was active in Siena, Urbino, Milan, and Naples. There is no documentation for the family name Martini. Francesco's career as a painter and as a sculptor indicates the influence of Vecchietta; no master is known for his training in architecture, although he seems to have drawn on Florentine and ancient Roman models.

Francesco's most important work as architect was carried out for the dukes of Urbino, Federigo da Montefeltro and his son Guidobaldo. Although it is difficult to determine precisely his contributions to the Ducal Palace at Urbino, the major part of its construction from 1472 must have been under his direction. Between 1472 and 1477 he directed the construction of the Church of S. Bernardino outside Urbino and of the Ducal Palace in Gubbio. In 1484 he sent plans to Ancona for the Palazzo degli Anziani and accepted the commission for S. Maria del Calcinaio in Cortona. In 1486 he provided plans and

a model for the Palazzo del Comune in Iesi. Of uncertain date are a group of fortresses constructed for the dukes of Urbino in their territory.

In 1490 he was in Milan to advise on the construction of the dome of the Cathedral, and during the summer of that year he traveled with Leonardo da Vinci to Pavia to advise on the construction of the Cathedral in that city. In 1491 he was among the large group of artists who submitted designs for the façade of the Cathedral of Florence. From 1492 he was in the service of Duke Alfonso of Calabria in Naples, although he returned frequently to Siena. On November 25, 1495, he successfully exploded a mine beneath the walls of the Castelnuovo in Naples, permitting the Aragonese troops to storm the breach and recapture the important fortress from the troops of Charles VIII of France. The later years of his life were spent in Siena, where he served primarily in an advisory role.

Francesco di Giorgio's reputation rests on his work as an architect; his fortifications were the first to provide an adequate defense against cannon fire, and his architectural forms are important in the development of the High Renaissance. He also translated Vitruvius and composed an original architectural thesis.

BIBLIOGRAPHY. C. Promis, ed., *Trattato di architettura civile e militare di Francesco di Giorgio Martini...*, 2 vols., Turin, 1841; A. S. Weller, *Francesco di Giorgio*, Chicago, 1943; R. Papini, *Francesco di Giorgio, architetto*, 2 vols., Florence, 1946.

JOHN R. SPENCER

FRANCESCO DI GIORGIO AS SCULPTOR AND PAINTER

His chief works in sculpture are four bronze *Angels* in Siena Cathedral (1489–97); the *Lamentation*, bronze reliefs in the Carmine, Venice (ca. 1476); the *Flagellation*, in the National Gallery of Umbria, Perugia; and the so-called *Discord*, known only in stucco casts in the Victoria and Albert Museum, London, and the Chigi-Saracini Collection, Siena. These show mastery of representation and movement and a predilection for agitated design.

Francesco's painted *oeuvre* may be reconstructed on the basis of the signed *Nativity* (1475) and the documented *Coronation of the Virgin* (1471) in the Pinacoteca at Siena, where there are several other works attributed to him. In painting, and to a lesser extent in sculpture, he followed Sienese traditions.

BIBLIOGRAPHY. J. Pope-Hennessy, *Italian Renaissance Sculpture*, New York, 1958.

FRANCESCO DI NICCOLO. Florentine goldsmith (fl. mid-14th cent.). He worked with his pupil, Leonardo di Ser Giovanni, on the left wing of the *S. Jacopo Altar* for the Pistoia Cathedral. The altar, which represents scenes from the Book of Genesis and the life of the Virgin, was executed between 1361 and 1364.

BIBLIOGRAPHY. F. Rossi, *Italian Jeweled Arts*, New York, 1954.

FRANCESCO DI PIETRO BITINI, *see* FRANCESCO DA FAENZA.

FRANCESCO DI STEFANO, *see* PESELLINO, FRANCESCO.

FRANCESCO DI VANNUCCIO. Italian painter (fl. by 1367; d. before 1403). The spare figure style and linear stylization of Francesco's one signed work, a small proces-

Francesco di Giorgio (Martini), *The Coronation of the Virgin*. Pinacoteca, Siena.

sional panel (Berlin, former State Museums) with the *Crucifixion* on one side and the *Enthroned Virgin* on the other, as well as of other paintings assigned to him, are reminiscent of similar qualities in the work of his Sienese predecessors Lippo Memmi and Simone Martini.

FRANCESCO D'UBERTINO, *see* BACCHIACCA.

FRANCESCO FIORENTINO, *see* BANCHI, FRANCESCO DI ANTONIO.

FRANCESCO NAPOLETANO. Italian painter (fl. ca. 1500). A naïve follower of Leonardo da Vinci's Milanese phase, he is known from a signed altarpiece (Zurich Art Gallery) and an almost identical Madonna (Milan, Brera). Attempts to identify other works and to link him with documents mentioning painters of his name from Naples have not been persuasive.

BIBLIOGRAPHY. W. Suida, *Leonardo und sein Kreis*, Munich, 1929.

FRANCESCO TORBIDO, *see* TORBIDO, FRANCESCO.

FRANCHEVILLE, PIERRE, *see* FRANQUEVILLE, PIERRE.

FRANCHI, ROSSELLO DI JACOPO, *see* ROSSELLO DI JACOPO FRANCHI.

FRANCHOYS, LUCAS, THE YOUNGER. Flemish painter of religious, historical, and mythological scenes as well as portraits (1616–81). Franchoys was born in Mechlin. Although he was originally a disciple of Rubens, the artist closely followed in the footsteps of Van Dyck, whose influence was to remain preeminent in the works of Franchoys.

BIBLIOGRAPHY. H. Gerson and E. H. ter Kuile, *Art and Architecture in Belgium, 1600–1800*, Baltimore, 1960.

FRANCHOYS, PIETER. Flemish painter of religious and historical subjects and of portraits (b. Mechlin, 1606; d. there, 1654). He was at first a pupil of his father, Lucas Franchoys the Elder, and then studied under Geerard Zegers in Antwerp. He was active in Mechlin, Antwerp, and Paris.

The artist excelled in portraiture. His work alternately reflects the influence of Anthony van Dyck and the Caravaggesque influences transmitted through the Brussels and Liège *tenebrosi*. A Van Dyckian manner and "speaking gestures" are apparent, for example, in *Portrait of a Drinker* (Brussels, Museum of Fine Arts), which is signed and dated 1639. However, his use of color—heavy shadows, brown local color, and heavily rouged cheeks—distinguishes him sharply from his Antwerp colleagues. The essence of his style can be seen clearly in the elegant *Portrait of a Man* (Frankfurt am Main, Städel Art Institute and Municipal Gallery).

BIBLIOGRAPHY. R. Oldenbourg, *Die flämische Malerei des 17. Jahrhunderts*, 2d ed., Berlin, 1922.

FRANCIA (Francesco Raibolini). Italian painter of Bologna (fl. 1482; d. 1517). He was first a goldsmith and also worked in sculpture, but his preserved works are nearly all paintings belonging to the Ferrarese tradition.

His earliest works are often associated with the goldsmith's technique, especially the *St. Stephen* (Rome, Borghese Gallery) with its shining, folded textures.

His mature style is emergent in the Bologna Gallery altarpiece (1494) and complete in the 1495 *Madonna* (Budapest, formerly Palffy Collection). These works are softened with blue and gray tones, much like those in the work of Lorenzo Costa, and in general suggest adherence to the new modeling qualities of Leonardo and Perugino.

These qualities, with goldsmith's ornament showing only in the architectural backgrounds, remain constant through a series of altarpieces and a very large number of Madonnas. Notable among the former are those of S. Giacomo Maggiore, Bologna (1499), and *The Assumption* (1504; Berlin, former State Museums). There and in the unusual frescoes in S. Cecilia, Bologna, with graceful groups of standing figures and huge pale landscapes, the proportions of the figures are elongated as in the works of Ercole de' Roberti. The strong combination of full, round forms and soft surface in these works made them much admired by 19th-century collectors, since they seemed primitive in the sense of elementary simplicity but not in toughness.

Several portraits are brighter and firmer, such as the early *Bartolommeo Bianchini* (London, National Gallery) and a remarkable late work, *Federigo Gonzaga as a Child* (1510; New York, Metropolitan Museum). Other late works include repetitious Madonnas done with assistance from his large workshop.

BIBLIOGRAPHY. G. C. Williamson, *Francesco Raibolini called Francia*, London, 1901.   CREIGHTON GILBERT

FRANCIA, FRANCOIS LOUIS THOMAS. English water colorist (1772–1839). Francia was born in Calais and was one of the better minor painters of the English water-color school. At his best (under the influence of his friend Girtin), he painted dramatic and romantic landscapes in rich dark tones. Later, he was also influenced by Cotman. For a time he painted in water color for the Duchess of York and also gave drawing lessons to Bonington.

BIBLIOGRAPHY. R. H. Wilenski, *English Painting*, 4th ed., London, 1964.

FRANCIA, GIACOMO AND GIULIO. Bolognese painters: Giacomo (before 1486–1557), Giulio (1487–1540). They were sons of Francesco Francia. A large number of altarpieces is known; some are signed in collaboration, some by Giacomo only, but none by Giulio. These show a mechanical continuation of their father's work, modified by a more modern emphasis on deep shadow. Some of the many small Madonnas of the Francia school are no doubt also by them.

BIBLIOGRAPHY. A. Venturi, *Storia dell'arte italiana*, vol. 7, pt. 3, Milan, 1914.

FRANCIABIGIO (Francesco di Cristofano; Francesco Giudini or Giudici). Italian painter (b. Florence? 1482/83; d. there, 1525). His first works, close to Ridolfo Ghirlandajo or Piero di Cosimo, have Quattrocento angularities and hard forms and dispersed and active figure arrangements—all features that never quite disappear from his art. Through association with Albertinelli, probably as an assistant, and through assimilation after 1500 of the Florentine art of the young Raphael, Franciabigio moved a

Francia, *Portrait of Evangelista Scappi*. Uffizi, Florence.

little closer to the monumental style. Most Raphaelesque is his *Madonna del Pozzo* (ca. 1508; Florence, Academy). In 1513 he worked in competition (says Vasari) with Andrea del Sarto in the forecourt of the Annunziata. Franciabigio's *Marriage of the Virgin* was unveiled at the same time as Andrea's *Birth of the Virgin*, and Franciabigio destroyed part of his composition in angry chagrin. Franciabigio's figures were evidently a little "old-fashioned"—still a little awkward and impetuous in movement, and scattered in arrangement.

From Raphael's developed style he then adopted not so much its weight and classical solidity as its large movement and dramatic gesture. The *St. Job Altar* (1516; Florence, Uffizi) shows fewer figures, which loom with pathos in a smoky Sartesque background, and a certain rigidity or impulsiveness in forms and poses and in light-and-dark contrasts, suggesting also mannerist effects. After Andrea left for France (1518), Franciabigio was called to finish the Chiostro dello Scalzo grisailles, of which he painted the *Benediction of St. John by Zachary* and the *Meeting of Christ and St. John*. They are effective, though startling in the awkward, plastic bulk of the figures. His 1519 *Madonna and Child with St. John* (Vienna, Museum of Art History) is again close to Del Sarto. Franciabigio worked with Del Sarto and Pontormo on the decoration of the Medici villa at Poggio a Caiano, in which the rich architectural background and triumphal movement and figure types of his *Triumph of Cicero* reflect the Roman grand manner and combine well with his narrative impulsiveness.

From this time, the conflict of stylistic elements in his art becomes more evident than their cohesion.

Franciabigio painted many portraits, the earlier of which resemble those of Ridolfo Ghirlandajo, the equally successful contemporary Florentine portraitist. Franciabigio's portraits later tend to be drier objective records.

BIBLIOGRAPHY. G. Vasari, *Le vite*, ed. G. Milanesi, vol. 5, Florence, 1878; A. Venturi, *Storia dell'arte italiana*, vol. 9, pt. 1, Milan, 1925; I. Fraenckel, *Andrea del Sarto...*, Strasbourg, 1935; S. J. Freedberg, *Painting of the High Renaissance in Rome and Florence*, 2 vols., Cambridge, Mass., 1961.   ALTHEA BRADBURY

FRANCIS, SAM. American painter (1923–). Francis was born in San Mateo, Calif., and studied there with David Park and Clyfford Still. Francis has become one of the leading members of the second generation of abstract expressionists. Based in Paris since 1950, he has carried out mural commissions in Tokyo, Bern, New York, and elsewhere. From his better known paintings featuring an amorphous flow of soft forms, he has moved to more violent, centrifugal, and sparse works using acid colors.

FRANCIS I. Oil painting by Clouet, in the Louvre Museum, Paris. *See* CLOUET, FRANCOIS.

FRANCIS OF ASSISI, ST. Founder of the Order of Friars Minor (1182–1226). Born at Assisi, he renounced his inheritance, after a dissipated youth, for a mystic marriage with Poverty. He founded an order whose first rule was approved orally by Innocent III. St. Francis had a vision of Christ on the cross as a seraph, received the stigmata, and preached to the birds; the last two events are common subjects in Renaissance art. Counter Reformation art shows him as an ascetic, often with a skull. His attributes are a gray or brown habit belted by a triple-knotted cord (for Poverty, Chastity, Obedience), a crucifix, stigmata, and a skull. His feast is October 4. *See* CLARE OF ASSISI, ST. *See also* SAINTS IN ART.

FRANCIS OF SALES, ST. Bishop of Geneva, Counter Reformation leader, and Church Doctor (1567–1622). Born at the castle of Sales, Savoy, France, he studied in Annecy, Paris, and Padua. After ordination in 1593, he won fame for reconverting the province of Chablais from Calvinism by preaching and through works of mercy. Later, as coadjutor bishop of Geneva, he organized the teaching of the catechism. In Annecy in 1610, with Jeanne, baroness of Chantal (St. Jane Frances de Chantal), he founded the Order of the Visitation. He may be shown with pierced heart surrounded by a crown of thorns or with a cross in glory. His feast is January 29. *See also* SAINTS IN ART.

FRANCISQUE, *see* MILLET, JEAN-FRANCOIS (FRANCISQUE).

FRANCK, KAJ. Finnish glassware and ceramic designer (1911–). A graduate of the Industrial Art Institute (1932) in Helsinki, Franck also studied in Germany, Italy, France, and England. A leader in modern design, he created the designs for the familiar tall cylinder glassware pitcher. He has been art director for the Notsjö glass factory since 1946 and has also designed furniture, fabrics, light fittings, and other objects.

FRANCKE, MASTER, see Master Francke.

FRANCKEN, FRANS, THE ELDER. Flemish painter of religious and allegorical compositions (b. Herenthals, 1542; d. Antwerp, 1616). He studied with Frans Floris, became a citizen and a member of the Guild of St. Luke in Antwerp in 1567, and remained active in Antwerp all his life. Francken's style is representative of cold classicism along with the use of many colors and the occasional adjunction of numerous bearded figures. In his earlier works, such as the *Altarpiece of the Schoolmakers* (unveiled in 1587; Antwerp Cathedral), traces of Floris—pale colors and crude execution—were still prominent. Later, he diminished the size of his productions, turned to small-figured compositions, and aimed at increased detail expressed through an intense palette. The monogrammed *Adoration of the Magi* (Brunswick, Gallery) exemplifies this trend.

BIBLIOGRAPHY. J. Gabriels, *Een Kempisch schilder-geslacht-de Franckens*, Hoogstraten, 1930.

FRANCKEN, FRANS, THE YOUNGER. Flemish painter of religious and historical subjects, genre, landscapes, and "gallery pictures" (b. Antwerp, 1581; d. there, 1642). He studied with his father, Frans Francken the Elder, and was received into the Antwerp Guild of St. Luke in 1605. The artist was the best-known and most popular member of the Francken family. His large-size altarpieces, such as *The Martyrdom of the Four Crowned Saints* (1624; Antwerp, Fine Arts Museum), are conceived in the Romanist style. The numerous small mythological and religious scenes are equally archaic in manner, but are distinguished for their terse draftsmanship. Later, thinly and fluidly painted genre pictures are attractive in color scheme; sometimes, especially when historical subjects are involved, they approach the Rubensian style. In his so-called gallery pictures, the artist depicts well-known contemporaneous collections (for example, in Vienna and Munich, and in the Borghese Gallery, Rome).

BIBLIOGRAPHY. R. Oldenbourg, *Die flämische Malerei des 17. Jahrhunderts*, 2d ed., Berlin, 1922; F. C. Legrand, *Les Peintres flamands de genre au XVIIe siècle*, Brussels, 1963.

FRANCO BOLOGNESE. Italian illuminator (fl. early 14th cent.). A prominent figure in the leading Italian school of manuscript illumination, that of Bologna, Franco was praised by Dante in the Purgatory section of *The Divine Comedy*. Franco was influenced primarily by Giotto in the several manuscripts attributed to him.

FRANCO-CANTABRIAN STYLE. Style of paleolithic art known from the cave art of central and southern France and northern Spain. It was a creation of the Upper Paleolithic period, and its development can be traced from the Châtelperronian phase through the Gravettian to the Magdalenian in caverns such as those of Altamira, Castillo, and Pindal in northern Spain, Niaux and Pair-non-Pair in southwestern France, and Font-de-Gaume, Combarelles, and Lascaux in west-central France. Its best expression is to be found in the now-famous paintings of Lascaux, which were the product of the Aurignacio-Périgordian culture (once called late Aurignacian), and in the well-known paintings of Altamira, which date to the time of the Mag-

dalenian culture. These famous polychrome murals are dominated by the representation of animals vital to the hunting society of the Upper Paleolithic. *See* Altamira, Caves of; Aurignacian Art; Lascaux; Magdalenian Culture.

FRANCO-FLEMISH STYLE. Term used to designate the style of manuscript illumination and panel painting employed primarily in the court of the dukes of Burgundy during the last decades of the 14th and first decades of the 15th century. The style combines the delicate, linear sophistication of the French approach, typified by the school of Paris at the close of the 14th century, and the more robust, vital realism of the north, typified by the art of Flanders. The difference in approach of the two areas arose from Flemish contact with German art, across the Rhine, as opposed to French contact with Italian painting to the south. The Franco-Flemish style in illumination is exemplified by the work of Jan Hennequin and in panel painting, by the works of Melchior Broederlam. *See* Broederlam, Melchior; Hennequin, Jan.

BIBLIOGRAPHY. G. Bazin, *L'Ecole franco-flamande, XIV–XV siècles*, Geneva, 1941.

FRANCOIS, CLAUDE, see Luc, Frere.

FRANCOIS, JEAN CHARLES. French engraver (b. Nancy, 1717; d. Paris, 1769). Credited with the invention of an engraving technique that imitated crayon drawing, François received a pension and court position from the king. He had, as well, a considerable reputation as a portraitist. His more important plates are for *Histoire des philosophes modernes* (1761–69).

BIBLIOGRAPHY. A. M. Hind, *A History of Engraving and Etching . . .*, 3d ed., rev., London, 1923 (repr. New York, 1963).

FRANCOIS, MAITRE, see Maitre Francois.

FRANCOIS VASE. Archaic Greek black-figured volute krater (ca. 570 B.C.) in the Archaeological Museum, Florence. It was found outside Chiusi by Alphonse François. The vase is signed by the potter Ergotimos and the painter Cleitius. It is entirely decorated with horizontal friezes of mythological narrative scenes, such as the wedding of Peleus, the return of Hephaestus, and a chariot race. The decoration is a fine example of Early Attic vase painting. *See* Cleitius and Ergotimos.

BIBLIOGRAPHY. J. D. Beazley, *The Development of Attic Black-Figure*, Berkeley, Calif., 1951.

FRANCO-SAXON STYLE. Manner of Carolingian manuscript illumination practiced in the last half of the 9th century. Its center, although not known, is thought to have been in the north of France, at St-Denis or at St-Amand, near Tournai. The style is noted for its clear "classical" initial letters and its refined use of interlace. *See* Saint-Denis Style.

FRANCUCCI, INNOCENZO, see Imola, Innocenzo da.

FRANKENTHALER, HELEN. American painter (1928–   ). Frankenthaler lives in her native New York City. Early training with Tamayo at the Dalton School was followed by studies at Bennington College with Paul Feeley and at the Art Students League. Since her first contact with the art of Pollock and De Kooning in 1950, she has painted in an abstract style. In the early 1950s she innovated the staining technique, using thinned paints on unsized cotton duck, which has been taken up by Kenneth Noland, Morris Louis, and a number of other artists. In 1959 Frankenthaler had a one-man show at the Jewish Museum in New York and represented the United States at the São Paulo Bienal.

FRANKENTHAL PORCELAIN. Regarded as one of the seven finest 18th-century German porcelains, Frankenthal was produced between 1755 and 1799. The factory was founded by Paul Antoine Hannong from Strasbourg. Its output, in a creamy-white hard paste with a thin glaze, consisted of flamboyantly rococo useful wares and a wide variety of figures.

BIBLIOGRAPHY. W. B. Honey, *German Porcelain*, London, 1947.

FRANKFURT AM MAIN. Great transport, trade, and banking city in West Germany. The natural advantages of the site attracted settlement as early as Neolithic times, when the *Bandkeramik* people—so-called for their band-patterned pottery—established themselves where the relatively easy river crossing created an inevitable center of a major north-south route through Central Europe. Romans, Celts, Alamanni, and Franks in turn took possession of this strategic ford. In 794 Charlemagne made Frankfurt his headquarters and the place of election and coronation of emperors of the Holy Roman Empire.

The famous Old Town, the largest surviving medieval city of Germany, was almost completely demolished by air raids in 1944; only one wooden Renaissance building escaped destruction. The oldest of the city's surviving edifices is the 12th-century Chapel of the Saalhof, a complex of buildings on the site of the palace built by Louis the Pious in 822. Some old buildings have survived in Sachsenhausen, on the south bank of the Main River, where the House of the Teutonic Order (damaged and restored), its church, and several of the old watchtowers may still be seen.

The New Town (or Inner Town) dates from the expanded city of 1333, whose outer ring of walls, torn down on Napoleon's order during the French occupation in 1805, may be followed now in the form of parkways. Only one tower remains of the forty-two that were part of the ramparts.

Among the rebuilt edifices of the Old Town is St. Leonard's Church, a 13th-century Romanesque basilica transformed in the 15th century into a hall church; the original Romanesque doors are noteworthy. The Carmelite cloister, with 13th- to 16th-century elements, has also been rebuilt, as has the "Römer" or old Town Hall, a group of buildings of varied styles and dates, unified in the late 19th century by a Gothic façade with steep step gables. The red sandstone Cathedral of St. Bartholomew, whose 15th-century tower long dominated Frankfurt's skyline, was badly damaged and restored; the emperors were crowned here. Its fine 14th-century carved pews and 15th-century murals escaped destruction, but only one of the stained-glass windows was saved.

The 15th-century Cloth Hall is now a municipal museum. In Goethe's birthplace, a 16th-century house rebuilt and restored to a semblance of its appearance in Goethe's time, and in the adjoining Goethe Museum, memorabilia are displayed. The Museum of Industrial Arts contains, besides goldsmith work and decorative arts, reminders of the city's importance as an early center of printing: the home of Gutenberg and Egenolf. There are important paintings in the Städel Art Institute and Municipal Gallery. Sculpture of all periods is shown in the adjoining Municipal Sculpture Collection (Liebieghaus). *See* FRANKFURT AM MAIN: MUSEUMS.

BIBLIOGRAPHY. M. Merian, *Topographiae Germaniae*, 1st ed., 8 vols., Frankfurt am Main, 1642–72; H. Voelcker, ed., *Die Stadt Goethes. Frankfurt am Main im XVIII. Jahrhundert*, Frankfurt am Main, 1932. MADLYN KAHR

FRANKFURT AM MAIN: MUSEUMS. Important public art collections in Frankfurt am Main, Germany, are located in the museums listed below.

Municipal Sculpture Collection (Liebieghaus). Founded in 1907 in the private villa of Baron Liebieg and enlarged in 1909, the Liebieghaus contains 1,200 works of sculpture of all civilizations up to about 1800. Among the earliest works are a statuette from Sumer (ca. 2500 B.C.) and Egyptian works from the Old Kingdom (including grave reliefs from Abusir, ca. 2600 B.C.) and from the Middle and New Kingdoms (including frescoes from Queen Hatshepsut's temple at Deir el Bahari, ca. 1440 B.C.). Greek and Roman antiquities include Roman marble copies of Greek originals by Myron, Polycleitus, and Praxiteles and Roman portrait busts. German sculpture ranges from Romanesque times through the 18th century; French works range from the 12th through the 15th century; and Italian art is represented by works of the school of Giovanni Pisano as well as of the circle that included Donatello, Ghiberti, Rossellino, and Andrea della Robbia. Among the small bronze statuettes are copies of the *Venus Callipygus*, the *Apollo Belvedere*, and the *Farnese Hercules*. A collection of ivories, from a 9th-century book cover to a wing of a 14th century French diptych, round out the works of Western art.

The Far East is represented by Chinese Han figures, statuettes and horses of the T'ang period, Buddha figures from India (ca. 700), and works from Siam (13th cent.) and Cambodia (11th cent.).

BIBLIOGRAPHY. H. Jedding, *Keysers Führer durch Museen und Sammlungen*, Heidelberg, Munich, 1961.

LOTTE PULVERMACHER-EGERS

Stadel Art Institute and Municipal Gallery. The Art Institute was founded in 1817, the Municipal Gallery in 1906; they are housed in the gallery building erected in 1878 by Oskar Sommer. The museum, which contains about 2,250 paintings, ranks foremost among German picture galleries. Its European paintings are from almost all schools, ranging from the Middle Ages through the present. Among the early German works are the charming little *Garden of Paradise* (ca. 1410) by an anonymous artist from the Upper Rhine, Altdorfer's *Adoration of the Magi*, Baldung-Grien's *Holy Night*, and Tischbein's *Goethe in the Campagna* (1787). The later German artists include those of the romantic period (C. D. Friedrich, Blechen, and Schwind), 19th-century painters (Böcklin, Feuerbach, Menzel, Marées, and Trübner), and the expressionists (Beckmann, Kirchner, Marc, Nolde, and Purrmann).

French works from the 16th to the 18th century include *Noli me tangere* by Claude Lorraine and a stormy landscape with Pyramus and Thisbe by Poussin. There are numerous works by Degas, Manet, Monet, Renoir, Rousseau, and Sisley. Among the Italian paintings, from the 13th to the 18th century, are works from the school of Cimabue, Renaissance masters, and 18th-century painters such as Canaletto, Longhi, and Piazzetta. Early Flemish art is represented by Jan van Eyck's *Lucca Madonna* (1435–40) and Petrus Christus's *Madonna* (1475). All the leading 17th-century masters from Holland and Flanders are collected (for example, Rembrandt, Aert de Gelder, Fabritius, Van Goijen, Hobbema, Ruisdael, Teniers, and Rubens). Among the very few Spanish paintings, Velázquez's *Cardinal Borja* and Murillo's *Peach Eaters* are notable.

The collection includes about 19,000 drawings from nearly all the European schools: from Germany, by artists such as Master E. S.,) Dürer, and Holbein to masters of romanticism and expressionism; from France, examples by Claude Lorraine, Poussin, Watteau, Boucher, and Fragonard; from Italy, master drawings by Mantegna, Raphael, Titian, Tintoretto, and Tiepolo; and from the Netherlands (besides two rare silverpoint drawings by Jan van Eyck), drawings by Brueghel, Van Dyck, Rubens, and Rembrandt. The highlights of the collection of about 65,000 works of graphic art are the complete *oeuvre* of Schongauer, Dürer, and Rembrandt. Beckmann and Kirchner are the best-represented modern graphic artists.

The sculpture collection covers mainly works of the

Antonio Frasconi, illustration from Pablo Neruda's poem *Bestiary*. Woodcut.

19th and 20th centuries, especially by German artists (Barlach, Hildebrand, Klimsch, Klinger, Kolbe, Lehmbruck, Sintenis) and by French artists (including Degas, Despiau, Maillol, Meunier, Renoir, and Rodin).

BIBLIOGRAPHY. H. Jedding, *Keysers Führer durch Museen und Sammlungen*, Heidelberg, Munich, 1961.

LOTTE PULVERMACHER-EGERS

FRANQUEVILLE (Francavilla; Francheville), PIERRE. French sculptor (b. Cambrai, 1548/53; d. Paris, 1615). He spent four years from 1566 with a wood sculptor in Innsbruck. He went to Tuscany in 1574, where he became one of the best pupils and collaborators of Giovanni Bologna. In 1589 Franqueville executed six marble saints after Bologna's models for S. Marco in Florence. About 1594 Franqueville went to Pisa to execute a fountain with a statue of Cosimo I. He aided Bologna in replacing the doors of the Cathedral of Pisa from 1595. In 1604 Franqueville went to Paris and did three bas-reliefs for the pedestal of the equestrian statue of Henri IV by Bologna and Pietro Tacca (destroyed 1792). He continued in favor under Louis XIII. Four *Slaves* from the same monument (Paris, Louvre) were finished in 1618 by Bordoni. Franqueville's style is similar to that of his master, but somewhat colder and drier.

BIBLIOGRAPHY. A. Durieux, *Les Artistes cambraisiens...*, Paris, 1874.

FRA PARAVICINO. Oil painting by El Greco, in the Museum of Fine Arts, Boston. *See* GRECO, EL.

FRARE, IL, *see* BIANCHI FERRARI, FRANCESCO.

FRARI, I, VENICE, *see* SANTA MARIA DEI FRARI, VENICE.

FRASCONI, ANTONIO. Uruguayan painter and printmaker of Italian parentage (1919–   ). Frasconi was born in Montevideo and attended the Escuela Industrial de la Construcción. He received formal art training at the Círculo de Bellas Artes in Montevideo, where he had his first one-man exhibition of drawings at the age of twenty-six. He came to the United States in 1945 on a scholarship to the Art Students League. In 1947 he won a second scholarship, to the New School for Social Research, New York City, where he studied under Kuniyoshi and Camilo Egas. Frasconi prefers to work on wood, and produces bold, dramatic compositions, both in color and black and white, some in series, such as *Some Well-known Fables* (1950). He has also done commercial illustrations.

BIBLIOGRAPHY. Print Club of Cleveland, *The Work of Antonio Frasconi*, Cleveland, 1952.

FRASER, JOHN ARTHUR. Canadian painter (1838–98). He was born in England, and trained in the Royal Academy Schools, London. Fraser lived in Toronto and Montreal from 1856 to shortly before his death. He helped organize the Ontario Society of Artists and the Royal Canadian Academy, and painted oil and water-color landscapes.

FRASER RIVER STYLE. British Columbian stone art dating from pre-Christian times and probably well matured long before the arrival of Europeans on the Northwest Coast. It is related in certain particulars, the interpretation of the human face, for example, to the later and better-known wood-carving styles of this general region. There are also connections between Fraser River stone sculpture and that of the Columbia River Valley.

Mortars, figurines, and totemic objects are typical Fraser River forms, but the outstanding object is the figure of a seated person holding with outstretched arms a shallow bowl. Such carvings have been discovered in many parts of the Fraser River area. The Fraser River style is well represented in the Vancouver City Museum, the Provincial Museum, Vancouver, and the University of British Columbia Anthropological Museum, Vancouver. It is notable for its strong influence on the Northwest Coast wood sculpture, which succeeded it.

See also COLUMBIA RIVER STYLE; NORTH AMERICAN INDIAN ART (ARCTIC; NORTHWEST COAST); NORTHWEST AMERICA, ART OF.

BIBLIOGRAPHY. P. S. Wingert, *Prehistoric Stone Sculpture of the Pacific Northwest*, Portland, Ore., 1952; W. Duff, *Prehistoric Stone Sculpture of the Fraser River and Gulf of Georgia* (Anthropology in British Columbia, No. 5), Vancouver, 1956.

FRAUENBURG (Frombork) CATHEDRAL. German Gothic cathedral of the Bishopric of Ermland (Warmja), formerly in East Prussia and since 1945 in Poland. It was built between 1329 and 1388 (the choir was dedicated in 1342). The Cathedral is one of the major examples of East Prussian architecture. A hall church with eight bays, it is striking for the huge gable on the main façade, finished in 1388.

BIBLIOGRAPHY. G. Dehio, *Handbuch der deutschen Kunstdenkmäler*, vol. 2, Berlin, 1922.

FRAUENKIRCHE, DRESDEN, *see* LIEBFRAUENKIRCHE, DRESDEN.

FRAZEE, JOHN. American sculptor (b. Rahway, N.J., 1790; d. Rhode Island, 1852). He was at first self-trained but then studied at the American Academy of Fine Arts. His stone-cutting shop, in which Launitz became a partner, produced mantelpieces and tombstones. Frazee is best judged by such direct and unaffected portraits as those of John Marshall and Joseph Wright. He contributed to a typically American style by avoiding the neoclassicism prevalent at the time.

BIBLIOGRAPHY. J. Frazee, *Autobiography, John Frazee* (Marsh Papers, New Jersey Historical Society), Newark, 1944.

FREAKE MASTER. American portrait painter (fl. New England, 1670–80). Among the enigmas of American painting is the identification of a highly sensitive painter of portraits in New England in the last half of the 17th century. This artist is best represented by two paintings of members of the Freake family, *Mrs. Elizabeth Freake and Baby Mary* and *John Freake* (both 1674; Worcester Art Museum). Painted with fairly thick brushstrokes, the portraits are in the medieval tradition of Elizabethan England, with emphasis on the costume, the pattern, and the line. They are flat, two-dimensional studies, with no interest in volume or realistic spatial relationships. Instead, it is the linear grace and delicacy that arrest the viewer. The details of lace and pattern are beautifully and sensitively rendered. The artist was a limner who was attuned to the beauty of line and pattern, and was very perceptive in the arrangement of his composition. The latter fact can be ascertained from X-ray shadowgraphs that show the artist's alteration of his canvas, not to correct errors in draftsmanship but rather to achieve a more satisfying compositional arrangement. The artist's feeling for paint is expressed by the rich color.

Related to the two Freake paintings are three portraits of children of the Gibbs family, *Margaret Gibbs, Robert Gibbs*, and *Henry Gibbs* (all 1670; privately owned). Although there are differences between these three portraits and those of the Freake family, it is very likely that all five paintings are by the same hand, though certain scholars feel that the works may be by two different artists (see, for example, V. Barker, *American Painting*, New York, 1950). The Gibbs portraits feature a small child standing on a floor of large squares that appears to recede into the background, though, as in the Freake paintings, there is really almost no interest in space. The concern with line and pattern, with the elegance and delicacy of costume, is very similar in the Gibbs and Freake groups, and both groups also exhibit the artist's difficulty with hands. The Gibbs portraits are somewhat more thinly painted, and there are no indications of alterations by the artist as in the Freake works, but the five portraits convey the same feeling of provincial Elizabethan portraiture with its delight in flat pattern and graceful lines tempered by a distinct naïveté.

Another group of children's portraits, of members of the Mason family, shows some resemblance to the Gibbs portraits, but there are important differences. As the Mason portraits bear the same date (1670) as the Gibbs paintings, the Mason canvases must represent the work of another artist, not earlier work by the Freake (or Gibbs) master. *See also* MASON LIMNER.

BIBLIOGRAPHY. L. Dresser, *XVIIth Century Painting in New England*, Worcester, Mass., 1935.

DAMIE STILLMAN

FREDENTHAL, DAVID. American painter (b. Detroit, 1914; d. Rome, 1958). He studied with Zoltan Sepeshy and Boardman Robinson, and painted murals for the Detroit Naval Armory and the New York World's Fair of 1939–40. He gained prominence as a war artist correspondent for *Life*. His work features pronounced humanitarian themes with a linear, graphic realism.

FREER GALLERY, WASHINGTON, D.C., *see* WASHINGTON, D.C.: MUSEUMS (FREER GALLERY).

FREIBERG: GOLDEN DOOR, MARIENKIRCHE. Main portal of the Cathedral of Freiberg in Saxony, Germany. So named after its original gilding, it is the first complete statue portal in Germany. Dating from about 1230, the portal contains eight jamb figures, archivolt figures, and a figural tympanum with the Adoration of the Magi. In style the Golden Door is a somewhat provincial German adaptation of the French model.

FREIBURG, SWITZERLAND, *see* FRIBOURG, SWITZERLAND.

Freiburg im Breisgau, Cathedral, apse with net-vaulted choir.

FREIBURG IM BREISGAU: CATHEDRAL. German
Gothic basilican church, constructed in red sandstone.
The only remaining Romanesque parts are the lower sec-
tions of the transepts and side towers of the early 13th
century. The nave was begun about 1235. The use of
plain walls, rather than triforium galleries, above the clustered piers is typical of the transitional phase of Upper
Rhine Gothic. The apse was begun in 1354 by Johannes
Parler and the net-vaulted choir in 1359 by John of
Gmünd, although it was not completed until 1510–13.
Most astonishing is the unity of design achieved in the
single western tower (1275–ca. 1340). The transitions from
the square base to the octagonal middle section and then
to the pierced, openwork spire are almost imperceptible.
The spire itself, based on those of the Cologne Cathedral,
is the first of this distinctly German type to be completed.

BIBLIOGRAPHY. H. Jantzen, *Das Munster zu Freiburg*, Burg, 1929.

FREIBURG IM BREISGAU: MUNICIPAL COLLEC-
TIONS (Augustinermuseum). German museum founded in
1861 as the Municipal Collection of Antiquities (Städtische
Altertümer Sammlung). It is housed in a former monastery that dates partially from the 14th and 18th centuries.
The collection offers an excellent survey of medieval and
baroque art from the Upper Rhine in painting and sculpture as well as in the applied arts. Most outstanding are
paintings by the so-called Master of the Housebook (*Passion Altar*), Schongauer, Hans Baldung-Grien, and Matthias Grünewald (*Miracle of the Snows*); sculptures such
as a 12th-century *Crucifix*, a *Madonna on the Throne* (originally in Freiburg Cathedral), and various figures of saints

from the environs of Lake Constance and neighboring Alsace; 13th- to 16th-century stained-glass windows; and colorful tapestries with holy scenes. These works are supplemented by liturgical objects from the same periods.

BIBLIOGRAPHY. H. Jedding, *Keysers Führer durch Museen und
Sammlungen*, Heidelberg, Munich, 1961.

FREMIET, EMMANUEL. French sculptor (b. Paris, 1824;
d. there, 1910). He studied with his uncle, François Rude.
Frémiet started as an anatomical and zoological painter
and sculptor. He first concentrated on animal groups, influenced by Barye's naturalism but usually not as violent.
An exception is his well-known *Gorilla Carrying Off a
Woman* (1887; Nantes, Museum of Fine Arts). He is best
known for his large-scale equestrian statues of medieval
and Renaissance historical figures, in which great attention to accurate detail is combined with the clear rendering of personality in both rider and horse, for example,
Joan of Arc (1874) in the Place des Pyramides, Paris.

BIBLIOGRAPHY. J. de Biez, *E. Frémiet . . .*, Paris, 1910; P. Faure-
Frémiet, *Frémiet*, Paris, 1934.

FREMIN, RENE. French sculptor (b. Paris, 1672; d. there,
1744). A pupil of François Girardon and Antoine Coysevox, Frémin was in Rome from 1695 to 1698, and was
elected to the Royal Academy in 1701. As court sculptor
to Louis XIV, he did decorative works for the chapel at
Versailles (1705–17). Frémin went to Madrid (1721–38)
and became court sculptor to Philip V in 1727, executing
allegorical fountains for the Park of La Granja in San
Ildefonso. His style is transitional from the 17th to the
18th century.

BIBLIOGRAPHY. L. Dussieux et al., *Mémoires inédits sur la vie et
les ouvrages des membres de l'Académie royale de peinture et de
sculpture*, vol. 2, Paris, 1854.

FREMINET, MARTIN. French history painter (b. Paris,
1564; d. there, 1619). An important painter of the second
school of Fontainebleau, Fréminet probably studied with
his father, Médéric Fréminet, who was also the teacher
of Toussaint Dubreuil. In Italy, in 1592, Martin Fréminet
came in contact with Il Cavaliere d'Arpino and with P.
Thomassin, who engraved his *Christ with the Instruments
of the Passion* in 1615. In Rome Fréminet fell under the
spell of Michelangelo and his disciples. In Turin he painted
mythological decorations for the Duke of Savoy and a
St. Martin. Back in Paris, in 1603, he was made painter
to King Henry IV and the drawing teacher of Louis XIII.

Fréminet's major work is the decoration of the Chapel
of the Trinity in Fontainebleau, recently restored. Paintings of the Fathers of the Church and the Evangelists are
in the Museum of Fine Arts, Orléans. Fréminet's style,
reminiscent of Pellegrino Tibaldi's, is characterized by
dissonant colors and tormented forms.

BIBLIOGRAPHY. S. Béguin, *L'Ecole de Fontainebleau*, Paris, 1960.

FRENCH, DANIEL CHESTER. American sculptor (1850–
1931). One of America's most popular artists in the 19th-
century figural style, he studied with John Quincy Adams
Ward in New York and with the anatomist-sculptor Rim-
mer in Boston. French visited Paris in the 1880s and was
influenced by various tendencies then in vogue in France.
His *Minute Man* (1875; Concord, Mass.) had already at-

tracted acclaim from American patriotic factions. A number of commemorative monuments, especially in cemeteries, represent French's style. These reveal a prodigious technical facility depending largely upon late-19th-century French tendencies, as in the *Melvin Monument* at Sleepy Hollow Cemetery in Concord. *Death and the Sculptor* of 1893 (the Milmore monument) at Forest Hills, Boston, and the seated *Lincoln* in the Lincoln Memorial in Washington, a not especially distinguished work, are among his most popular sculptures. French's style was dominated by the more sensitive, if not actually more original, expression of Saint-Gaudens.

BIBLIOGRAPHY. S. Brinton, "Recent Sculpture of Daniel Chester French," *International Studio*, LIX, 1916; L. Taft, *The History of American Sculpture*, rev. ed., New York, 1930.

FRENCH, JARED. American painter and sculptor (1905–). Born in Rutherford, N.J., he studied with Boardman Robinson and Thomas Hart Benton. French's realistic, somewhat surreal paintings are usually of stylized figures in a landscape.

BIBLIOGRAPHY. D. C. Miller and A. H. Barr, Jr., eds., *American Realists and Magic Realists*, New York, 1943.

FRENCH, LEONARD. Australian painter (1928–). He began studying in Melbourne and went to England, Ireland, Holland, and Belgium in 1950, where he was influenced by the Belgian painter Permeke. He next experimented with the cubism of Léger and Delaunay, adapting the latter's circle motif as an important and permanent element in his art. In developing his symbolic style, French often employed literary themes (for example, the Homeric myths).

After a trip to the Far East in 1961 he emerged as one of the leading Australian painters, abandoning coldly mechanized forms in favor of a warm, rich decorativeness used to symbolize universal concepts of birth, struggle, death, and rebirth. Among his fully developed works are a series of five paintings on themes from the Book of Genesis (1960) and a series based on the life of the English Jesuit martyr Edmund Campion (1961). Both series show his characteristic use of gilt and heavily glazed enamels with subtle modulation of rich dark tones. His art achieves a massive splendor of color and scale, combining various ancient and modern influences.

ALAN MC CULLOCH

FRENCH GUINEA, *see* AFRICA, PRIMITIVE ART OF (WEST AFRICA: GUINEA COAST).

FRENCH SCHOOL. Loosely, French painting from the 17th through the 19th century, covering diverse periods and styles linked by national traits. Some consider that the school began with Simon Vouet (1590–1649) and came into its own with the founding of the French Royal Academy of Painting and Sculpture (1648). In the 17th century Poussin and Claude Lorraine were the leading painters in the dominant neoclassical style, which gave way in the 18th century to the rococo under Watteau and later Fragonard. The Revolution brought another neoclassical period, with David and Ingres, followed by a romantic movement led by Delacroix. The styles of the latter half of the 19th century include Courbet's realism, the individ-

uality of Corot and Manet, and the last thoroughly French movement, impressionism. Since then French painting has assumed a more international character. *See* COROT, JEAN-BAPTISTE-CAMILLE; COURBET, GUSTAVE; DAVID, JACQUES-LOUIS; DELACROIX, EUGENE; FRAGONARD, JEAN-HONORE; IMPRESSIONISM; INGRES, JEAN-AUGUSTE-DOMINIQUE; LORRAINE, CLAUDE; MANET, EDOUARD; NEOCLASSICAL ART; POUSSIN, NICOLAS; REALISM; ROCOCO ART; ROMANTICISM; ROYAL ACADEMY OF PAINTING AND SCULPTURE, FRANCE; VOUET, SIMON; WATTEAU, JEAN-ANTOINE.

BIBLIOGRAPHY. R. H. Wilenski, *French Painting*, rev. ed., London, 1949; W. Friedländer, *David to Delacroix*, Cambridge, Mass., 1952; A. Blunt, *Art and Architecture in France, 1500–1700*, Baltimore, 1954.

FRESCO. Technique of wall painting on freshly spread moist plaster. The pigments are applied in a water medium, which allows them to penetrate and combine chemically with the plaster. This results in a painted surface that does not peel as a result of moisture. This technique is also called buon fresco or true fresco to distinguish it from fresco secco.

FRESCO SECCO. Type of wall painting designed to imitate true fresco. In fresco secco (dry fresco) freshly moist plaster is not used. Instead, the wall is saturated with baryta water, and then pigment in a glue and water medium is applied to the relatively dry plaster. Of great antiquity, the fresco secco technique lacks both the durability and the clarity of true fresco.

FRESNAYE, ROGER DE LA, *see* LA FRESNAYE, ROGER DE.

FRET (Key Pattern). Ornament composed of short straight lines commonly intersecting at right angles to form a continuous pattern, as in the swastika ornament of ancient Greek architecture and in the Renaissance example from the Grimani Palace, Venice. *See also* MEANDER.

FREUDENBERGER (Freudenberg), SIGMUND. Swiss painter and graphic artist (b. Bern, 1745; d. there, 1801). After Boucher and Greuze had promoted his studies in Paris (1765), Freudenberger studied the Dutch "Little Masters." He turned from painting portraits to making rural and city scenes for Parisian engraving firms. In 1773 he returned to Bern, where his highly popular subject matter narrowed to local genre.

BIBLIOGRAPHY. W. Hugelshofer, ed., *Schweizer Kleinmeister*, Zurich, 1943.

FREUNDLICH, OTTO. German sculptor (1878–1943). He was born in Pomerania, Germany, and died in a Nazi concentration camp in Poland. He first studied art history under Wölfflin, then undertook sculpture in Munich, Florence, and Paris. Between 1910 and 1919 he exhibited in France, Cologne, Amsterdam, and Berlin. He lived in Paris, following visits to Germany, from 1924 until the late 1930s. He was given a retrospective showing at the Galerie Jeanne Bucher in Paris in 1938; by that time his style had become increasingly abstract. His art is notable for its independent assertion of abstract aesthetic, related to cubism and constructivism, and for occasional primitive

Caspar David Friedrich, *Shipwreck of the "Hope" in the Ice*. Art Gallery, Hamburg.

influences (as in the *Monumental Head* of 1926, reminiscent of Easter Island stone images).

BIBLIOGRAPHY. C. Giedion-Welcker, *Contemporary Sculpture*, New York, 1955; M. Seuphor, *The Sculpture of This Century*, New York, 1960.

FREYSSINET, EUGENE. French bridge and highway engineer (1879–1962). His masterwork, and one of the important pieces of the century, was the airship hangars at Orly (1916; destroyed during World War II). The structures were a pioneering design of shell reinforced concrete made of folded parabolic arches, spaced apart to admit light, anticipating the work of Robert Maillart and Pier Luigi Nervi.

BIBLIOGRAPHY. "Eugene Freyssinet" [Obituary], *The Architectural Review*, CXXXII, October, 1962.

FRIAR BALA. Colossal Indian stone sculpture (over 8 ft. high) in the Archaeological Museum, Sārnāth, Uttar Pradesh. The earliest dated representation of Sākyamuni Buddha, it is inscribed as a dedication of Friar Bala in the third year of Kanishka's reign (1st or 2d cent. A.D.). The sculpture is typical of other examples, small and large, all probably made in Mathurā.

BIBLIOGRAPHY. B. Rowland, *The Art and Architecture of India*, 2d ed., Baltimore, 1959.

FRIAS (Frias y Escalante), JUAN ANTONIO DE, *see* ESCALANTE, JUAN ANTONIO.

FRIBOURG (Freiburg), SWITZERLAND. Founded in 1178 on an impregnable rock above the Sarine River and admitted to the Confederation of Swiss City-States in 1481, Fribourg is one of the most picturesque medieval cities north of the Alps. Surrounded by a well-preserved wall of the 14th and 15th centuries, with towers up to 90 feet high and river fortifications, the tightly knit roofline of the city is interrupted only by the bulk of the St. Nicolas Cathedral. The nave, which was partially built in 1343 and completed in the 15th century, is preceded by an immense tower with 14th- to 16th-century bells. The complex early 17th-century system of ribs above the single apse contrasts with the simplicity of the quadripartite nave vaults. The south portal shows excellent statuary of the second half of the 14th century (the Virgin, the Magi, St. Nicolas, and others). Many of the Cathedral furnishings are preserved, among them a large *Crucifixion* of the early 15th century, a holy sepulchre of 1442, and a rich treasury.

The Loreto Chapel (1647–50), an early baroque interpretation of the Sanctuary of the Holy House in Loreto, Italy, and the Visitanerinnenkloster, with its centrally planned church covered by complex Gothic vaults (1653–56), were built by H. F. Reyff. Fribourg is rich in official buildings ranging from the 16th to the 19th century such as the Town Hall, the Chancellerie d'Etat, and the Prefecture.

BIBLIOGRAPHY. Société Française d'Archéologie, *Congrès Archéologique*, Paris, 1953; M. Strub, *Les Monuments d'art et d'histoire du Canton de Fribourg*, 3 vols., Basel, 1956–64.

FRANCOIS BUCHER

FRIDAY MOSQUE. Type of mosque first built in Persia under Abbasid rule (750–1258). Such mosques are huge square or rectangular structures that are open in the center and are designed to accommodate large numbers of Muslim warriors as they assemble on Fridays to pray. The mosques are the symbol of the combination of the Muslims' military and religious ardor at the height of their power. *See also* JAMI MASJID.

BIBLIOGRAPHY. K. A. C. Creswell, *Early Muslim Architecture*, 2 vols., Oxford, 1932–40.

FRIEDLAENDER, JOHNNY. German graphic artist (1912–   ). Born in Pless, Upper Silesia, Friedlaender studied painting with Otto Mueller and Carl Mense at the Breslau Academy and first exhibited in Dresden at the age of eighteen. He thereafter turned to printmaking. In 1937 he settled in Paris, where he still lives, and became part of the Resistance during World War II. In his work he achieves a wide variety of effects by combining etching techniques. Friedlaender sticks to a few basic themes—birds, fish, women, and so on—creating pencil-thin linear patterns that somewhat resemble those of Klee, but without the latter's qualities of fantasy and automatism.

BIBLIOGRAPHY. Cincinnati Art Museum, *The Etchings of Johnny Friedlaender*, Cincinnati, 1956.

FRIEDRICH, CASPAR DAVID. German painter (b. Greifswald, 1774; d. Dresden, 1840). After studying at the Copenhagen Academy under Juel and Abildgaard (1794–98), he settled permanently in Dresden. His earliest works are careful, topographical landscape drawings, precisely outlined with the pencil and lightly washed with sepia. In Dresden, Friedrich knew his Pomeranian compatriot, the painter Runge, and befriended the poet Tieck. In solitary rambles among the Saxon hills and along the coast of the Baltic, he explored landscape motifs that were to remain his lifelong preoccupation: rocky beaches, barren mountain ranges, trees reaching into the sky.

Only in 1807 did he begin to paint in oils. His altarpiece *Cross in the Mountains* (1808; Dresden) is a bold attempt to replace traditional religious subject matter with landscape symbolism. Like Runge, Friedrich sought to invent a new pictorial language for the expression of Romantic feeling. Unlike Runge, he dispensed with familiar figural iconography and concentrated wholly on landscapes interpreted both lyrically (as experience recalled) and symbolically (as emblems of man's fate). *Monk at the Seashore* (1808; Berlin, former State Museums), exhibited in 1810, brought him fame. Poets such as Kleist and Arnim recognized in it the image of the Romantic individual's isolation. Other symbolical landscapes followed: *Ruined Cloister in the Snow* (1819; Berlin, former State Museums)

and *Shipwreck of the "Hope" in the Ice* (1822; Hamburg, Art Gallery), which are expressions of his pessimism and obsession with death; *Landscape with Rainbow* (1809; Weimar Museum) and *Men Observing the Moon* (1819; Dresden, State Art Collections), which exemplify his treatment of natural phenomena as magical apparitions. The Napoleonic wars inspired him to insert veiled patriotic allusions into several of his landscapes (*Chasseur in the Forest*, 1812; *Arminius's Tomb*, 1813; Bremen, Art Gallery).

Friedrich's landscapes are constructed of observed elements. Sweeping horizontals dominate these often bleakly naked settings within which human figures play a subordinate role. Main features, such as trees, ruins, or sails, are usually silhouetted against atmospheric backgrounds. The dryly smooth execution and the cold, acidulous colors contrast oddly with the emotional poignancy of mood that pervades these landscapes. Friedrich's insistence on sharp contour and the heroic bareness of his compositions betray his debt to classicism. But his observation of light and atmosphere is precise and personal. Throughout his work, tight control and Romantic sentiment, stylistic artifice and intimate observation of nature are held in precarious balance.

Appointed to the Dresden Academy in 1816, Friedrich was an influential teacher; his disciples included Kersting, Dahl, and Carus. He is considered with Runge the greatest of the German Romantic painters. The majority of his works are to be found in Berlin (former State Museums) and in Dresden, Munich, Weimar, and Hamburg.

BIBLIOGRAPHY. C. D. Friedrich, *Bekenntnisse* (Eberlein ed.), Leipzig, 1924; H. von Einem, *Caspar David Friedrich*, Berlin, 1938; F. Nemitz, *Caspar David Friedrich*, Munich, 1949; F. Bauer, *Caspar David Friedrich*, Gütersloh, 1961.

LORENZ EITNER

FRIES, HANS. Swiss painter (b. Fribourg, ca. 1465; d. Bern? 1523). He was the most important Swiss painter of his time. During his *Wanderjahre* Fries studied the painting of the Netherlandish, Ulm, and Augsburg schools. From 1497 he worked in Fribourg, where in 1506 he produced his most important painting, *The Sermon of St. Antonius*, for the Franziskanerkirche. It is close in style to the work of Holbein the Elder.

BIBLIOGRAPHY. A. Kelterborn-Haemmerli, *Die Kunst des Hans Fries*, Strasbourg, 1927; J. Gantner and A. Reinle, *Kunstgeschichte der Schweiz*, 4 vols., Frauenfeld, 1936–62.

FRIESEKE, FREDERICK CARL. American painter (b. Owosso, Mich., 1874; d. Mesnil-sur-Blangy, France, 1939). He studied in Chicago and New York and with Constant, Jean-Paul Laurens, and Whistler in Paris. Frieseke painted mostly outdoor scenes and sunlit interiors, emphasizing a Renoir-derived depiction of light.

FRIESZ, ACHILLE EMILE OTHON. French painter and illustrator (b. Le Havre, 1879; d. Paris, 1949). He studied from 1896 to 1899 in Le Havre with Charles Lhullier, in whose classes he met Dufy and Braque. In 1899 he went to Paris, where he studied with Léon Bonnat at the Ecole des Beaux-Arts and with Gustave Moreau. In Moreau's studio he met Matisse, Marquet, and Rouault.

Until this time, Friesz was painting in a manner based upon impressionist style, but he was one of the earliest converts to the new pictorial and coloristic methods of Matisse and he exhibited in the Fauve Salon d'Automne in 1905. His Fauve works were composed of fluid, separated strokes, as in *La Fête foraine à Rouen* (1905; Montpellier, Fabre Museum). For Friesz, as for other artists of the group, the intense color and loose design of Fauvism was a phase through which he passed on the way to a more classical concern for architectural composition and firm spatial construction. The large and relatively darker canvas *Le Travail à l'automne* (1908; Oslo, National Gallery), with its stylized forms and decorative arabesques of figures and landscape, marks the transition to his new interests. Similar tendencies are evident in *Le Printemps* (1909; Fine Arts Museum of the City of Paris), although here the composition is derived from Matisse's *Joie de vivre*.

The natural influence on most of Friesz's post-Fauve paintings was Cézanne, as can be seen in the severe and simplified landscape forms of *Cassis* (1909; Zurich, Art Gallery). Significant for the development of his style is the fact that Friesz was most impressed by the paintings of Giotto during a trip to Italy in 1909. Giotto acted as a historical confirmation of his interest in the strong composition of plastically rendered volumes, for example, *Nu* (1924; Toulon, Museum of Fine Arts) and the tightly brushed, Cézannesque landscape *Méounes* (1925; Paris, National Museum of Modern Art). Friesz's later works are more thickly painted and show the increasing ease with which he reconciled the depiction of mass and space with the modern respect for the picture plane, as in the figure painting *Baigneuses à Annecy* (1932; Fine Arts Museum of the City of Paris) or the mature view *Saint-Cirq-Lappie* (1946; Geneva, Museum of Art and History).

BIBLIOGRAPHY. A. E. O. Friesz, ... *Friesz: Oeuvres (1901–1927)*..., Paris, 1927; M. Gauthier, *Othon Friesz*..., Geneva, 1957.

JEROME VIOLA

FRIEZE. Sculptured or ornamented band; also the middle section of an entablature. Ornamented and sculptured friezes are frequent in the architecture of the ancient Near East. Notable Greek sculptured friezes are on the west portico of the Theseum, Athens, depicting the Battle

E. Othon Friesz, *Baigneuses*, 1948. National Museum of Modern Art, Paris. One of the artist's post-Fauve paintings.

William Powell Frith, *The Derby Day*, 1858. Tate Gallery, London.

of the Centaurs and Lapiths, and the Panathenaic procession of the Parthenon. The Doric frieze is composed of triglyphs, or channeled elements, alternating with metopes, or rectangular spaces often filled with sculpture.

FRIGIDARIUM. Cooling room in Roman thermae (from the Latin *frigidarius*, "cooling"). It was usually located in the main structure of the thermae and contained a piscina for cold baths. The frigidarium adjoined a tepidarium, a warm room intermediate in temperature between the frigidarium and the calidarium, or hot room.

FRIS, JAN (Johannes). Dutch painter of still lifes (b. ca. 1627; d. after 1673). Little is known of Fris's early activity or training. He was married in Amsterdam in 1649, and two years later he became a citizen of that city. There are dated works by Fris recorded for the years 1665, 1669, and 1673. His brother Pieter also painted still lifes.

BIBLIOGRAPHY. A. P. A. Vorenkamp, *Bijdrage tot de geschiedenis van het Hollandsch stilleven in de zeventiende eeuw*, Leyden, 1934.

FRISCH, JOHANN CHRISTOPH. German painter and etcher (b. Berlin, 1738; d. there, 1815). He studied with Christian Bernhard Rode in Berlin and was in Rome in 1765. Frisch painted historical subjects and portraits and did palace decorations in Germany.

FRISIUS, SIMON WEYNOUTS (Simon de Vries). Dutch graphic artist, draftsman, and illustrator (b. Harlingen, ca. 1580; d. The Hague, 1629). In 1598 and 1599 Frisius was reported in Paris. He was active in The Hague from 1614. He is also known to have traveled in Germany, France (Paris, 1620), Czechoslovakia (Prague), Russia, and Spain. He made prints after, and in the style of, Lucas van Leyden and numerous other Dutch and foreign artists.

BIBLIOGRAPHY. F. W. H. Hollstein, *Dutch and Flemish Etchings, Engravings, and Woodcuts, ca. 1450–1700*, vol. 7, Amsterdam, 1952.

FRITH, WILLIAM POWELL. English narrative painter (b. near Ripon, 1819; d. London, 1909). He studied at Sass's Academy, Bloomsbury, and at the Royal Academy of Arts schools, and began his career by exhibiting historical and literary pieces in the convention of the time. He was elected associate of the Royal Academy in 1845 and full academician in 1853, but it was not until 1854, with *Ramsgate Sands* (purchased by Queen Victoria), that he found the kind of subject matter that made his reputation. This work was followed by *The Derby Day* (1858; London, Tate Gallery) and *The Railway Station* (1862; Egham, Royal Holloway College). All three paintings were popularized in engravings. Frith's crowded scenes from contemporary life are painted with immense skill and animation. Much of his later work is considerably inferior to the three major successes. He also published *My Autobiography and Reminiscences* (1887) and *Further Reminiscences* (1888); these writings are valuable sources of anecdote for Victorian painting.

FROMBORK CATHEDRAL, see FRAUENBURG CATHEDRAL.

FROMENT, NICOLAS. French painter (b. Uzès; fl. 1450–90 in the south of France). He was painter to the great patron King René of Anjou. Two documented works establish Froment's position. The earlier of them is the triptych of the *Raising of Lazarus*, signed and dated 1461 (Florence, Uffizi). The harsh realism of the painting suggests that the artist may have been influenced in his youth by Netherlandish painters working in Avignon. The depiction of the donor and attendants on the reverse of a wing, however, represents Provençal portraiture at its best, with its sculptural approach to form and tendency toward abstraction, traits that are equally noteworthy in the Virgin before whom the donor kneels in obeisance. The fact that the cityscape in the background of the obverse of one of the wings is constructed according to rational perspective has led to the assumption that it was painted in Florence. On the basis of similar perspective construction, the *Legend of St-Mitre* (ca. 1470; Aix-en-Provence, St-Sauveur) has been attributed to Froment.

The second documented work, Froment's masterpiece, is the triptych of the *Burning Bush* (Aix-en-Provence, St-Sauveur), for which there is a record of payment by the donor, King René, in 1476. This painting shows Flemish influence in its overall program and close scrutiny of nature, but is Provençal in its compositional strength and simplification; the fine landscape, too, is recognizably Provençal. King René and his queen, Jeanne de Laval, are depicted on the wings with relentless realism; on the reverse of the wings is an Annunciation in grisaille in the Flemish manner. The small diptych of King René and his wife in the Louvre has also been attributed to Froment.

BIBLIOGRAPHY. E. Harris, "Mary in the Burning Bush: Nicolas Froment's Triptych at Aix-en-Provence," *Journal of the Warburg Institute*, I, April, 1938; C. Jacques (Sterling), *La Peinture française: Les Peintres du moyen âge*, Paris, 1942; M. Laclotte, *L'Ecole d'Avignon: La Peinture en Provence aux XIVe et XVe siècles*, Paris, 1960.

MADLYN KAHR

FROMENTIN, EUGENE. French painter and art critic (b. La Rochelle, 1820; d. St-Maurice, 1876). The author of the influential *Les Maîtres d'autrefois* (1876), Fromentin was also a painter of importance. He worked in a style similar to that of Alexandre-Gabriel Decamps and was particularly noted for his scenes of North African life.

BIBLIOGRAPHY. E. S. A. Fromentin, *Oeuvres complètes...*, biography... by M. Revon, Paris, 1937.

FRONTALITY, LAW OF. One of the basic laws in ancient Egyptian sculpture; representation of figure frontally and nearly symmetrical around a vertical axis passing from the nose to the navel. Absolute symmetry occurs in some standing figures from the Archaic period and later in some standing female figures.

The standing male figure usually was represented with the left foot forward, as if striding, and both arms at the sides, the left hand sometimes holding a baton. The seated figure was frontally symmetrical except for the position of the hands or arms. There were always exceptions to the law of frontality in statues of figures in motion, such as those of servants carrying loads, mothers carrying children, and dancers, and in figures at rest—turning the head, sitting askew, or holding a child. In animals the head was usually shown frontally, turned at right angles to the body.

In painting and relief sculpture the typical standing figure is composite: the head is seen in side view, the upper part of the body faces the viewer, the hips and the lower part of the body are in side view, and the legs are shown in striding position. Exceptions to this rule occurred in the representation of statues, deities (side view), and foreign prisoners (frontal) within these paintings and reliefs. Animals were shown in side view with the legs striding, though birds would have their wings outstretched. In the New Kingdom there was a tendency to show bending figures in side view. *See also* EGYPT.

BIBLIOGRAPHY. A. Badawy, "La Loi de frontalité dans la statuaire égyptienne," *Annales du Service des Antiquités de l'Egypte*, LII, Cairo, 1954.

ALEXANDER M. BADAWY

Nicolas Froment, *The Raising of Lazarus*. Uffizi, Florence.

FRONTE NUOVO DELLE ARTI, *see* NEW ART FRONT.

FROTTAGE. Semiautomatic technique by which patterns are made by placing paper or canvas on a figured surface, such as heavily grained wood, a rough fabric, or embossed ceramic tile, and then rubbing the paper or canvas with crayon, pencil, or a roller coated with paint to get an impression. The surrealist Max Ernst developed the technique in 1925 and used it to make a series of drawings entitled *Natural History*. He was enchanted by the suggestions of images such as faces, clouds, and contours of distant hills and of the human figure to be found by studying these tracings of natural structures. Ernst composed several of these patterns on a single ground and gained further surprising effects through their juxtaposition.

FRUEAUF, RUELAND, THE ELDER. German-Austrian painter (b. Salzburg? ca. 1440; d. Passau, 1507). He was active in Salzburg and later in Passau. Frueauf's style shows close affinities to the older Salzburg tradition, combined with influences from Netherlandish painting. His main works are the four panels of the *Passion* (1490–91; Vienna, Museum of Art History) and the *Resurrection of Christ* (Munich, Old Pinacothek).

BIBLIOGRAPHY. L. Baldass, *Conrad Laib und die beiden Rueland Frueauf*, Vienna, 1946.

FRY, EDWIN MAXWELL. English architect (1899–   ). His ideas were molded by partnership with Gropius. He is influential in tropical planning and has a large practice

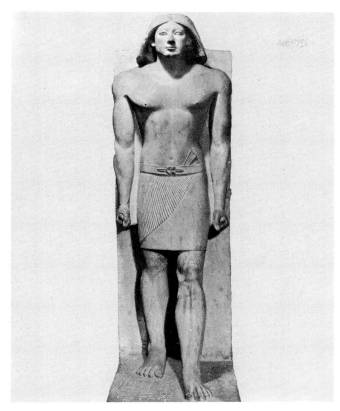

Law of frontality. Statue of the priest Ranofer. Egyptian Museum, Cairo.

in the Middle East and Gold Coast. His most recent projects, Ahmadi General Hospital, Kuwait, and a primary school at Lagos (1960), confirm this tropical tendency.

FRY, ROGER. English art critic and artist (1866–1934). Born in London, Fry went to King's College, Cambridge, to study science in 1884, but was encouraged in his interest in art by several friends. After leaving Cambridge he started to paint and tried to reconcile this interest with his further scientific studies, but in 1891 he went to Italy, to paint and study the old masters. After another trip in 1894 he began to exhibit at the New English Art Club and to develop as a connoisseur in art. He also began to lecture, with great success. He wrote articles for the *Athenaeum* and in 1901 became its regular art critic. He also published a small book on Bellini, two long articles on Giotto, and an edition of Reynolds's discourses. He took part in the establishment of *The Burlington Magazine* and had a considerable reputation as a scholar and expert. In 1905 he became director of the Metropolitan Museum in New York City.

In 1906 Fry saw Cézanne's work for the first time and regarded him as a great painter who had reconciled the brilliant color of the impressionists with the structural coherency of the old masters. From then on his interest in modern art was intense, and he wrote many articles about it. In November, 1910, he organized the sensational exhibition of modern French painters at the Grafton Gallery, under the title of postimpressionists. It aroused intense emotions on all sides. Fry seems to have gained confidence and vitality from the attacks leveled against him and became the champion of modern art instead of the austere scholar. He was closely identified with the London Bloomsbury group of Virginia Woolf, Duncan Grant, Clive Bell, and others. In 1913 he founded the Omega Workshops, which made furniture, pottery, fabrics, and other articles in a very avant-garde style. The aim behind the workshops, which employed many modern designers, was not unlike that of Morris and the Arts and Crafts movement.

After World War I Fry began to develop his aesthetic ideas; like Clive Bell he believed that form and color can have an aesthetic effect no matter what they represent. Thus the idea of "pure form" was evolved. This rather austere philosophy did not in any way affect the brilliance of Fry's analysis of actual works of art, where he was always at his best. His two most famous books are *Transformations* and *Vision and Design*, which were collections of essays and articles. Most of his later publications are in the form of lectures he gave; as books they tend to lack structure, though the lectures themselves were vivid, persuasive, delightful, and immensely popular. In 1933 he became Slade Professor at Cambridge. His paintings were strongly influenced by Cézanne and the impressionists but are very timid and careful in comparison. They are chiefly landscapes, treated in a naturalistic and rather learned style. It is, however, as a critic that Fry achieved importance.

BIBLIOGRAPHY. E. M. Forster, *Abinger Harvest*, New York, 1936; V. Woolf, *Roger Fry, A Biography*, London, 1940.

RICHARD L. ORMOND

FUDO MYO-O. Japanese term for a Buddhist deity (Sanskrit, Acala or Achala), considered a messenger of the Buddha. He is also regarded as the defender of the Buddha's Law and is a special favorite of the Shingon sect in Japan. Fudō Myō-ō holds a very important place in the arts of the Japanese Mikkyō (esoteric Buddhism). The Fudō is shown holding a sword to cut down the evils of the world and a rope to bind them. His face is frightening, with large, bulging eyes and two fangs protruding from his mouth. He is often seated on a rock, symbolizing his character as the "immobile one." His body may be shown in different colors, such as yellow (*Yellow Fudō* in the Onjōji, 9th cent.), red (*Red Fudō* at Mt. Kōya, 9th cent.), or blue (*Blue Fudō* in the Shōren-in, 11th cent.). *See* FUDO MYO-O IN MYOOIN, MOUNT KOYA; MIKKYO; SHINGON.

BIBLIOGRAPHY. E. D. Saunders, *Mudrā: A Study of the Symbolic Gestures in Japanese Buddhist Sculpture*, New York, 1960; E. D. Saunders, *Buddhism in Japan*, Philadelphia, 1964; D. Seckel, *The Art of Buddhism*, New York, 1964.

FUDO MYO-O IN MYOOIN, MOUNT KOYA. Japanese silk painting (9th cent.). It is commonly known as the Red Fudō, since the body and dress are painted in shades of red and the figure is seated against an orange-red background of flames. The ferocious-looking deity Fudō Myō-ō is a manifestation of Dainichi (Sanskrit, Vairocana). In his left hand he holds a sword entwined with a dragon, symbol of his might, and in his right, a rope, which restrains evil. Youthful attendants symbolize subjugating power and sustaining virtue. *See* VAIROCANA.

BIBLIOGRAPHY. Tokyo National Museum, *Pageant of Japanese Art*, vol. 1: *Painting*, pt. 1, Tokyo, 1952.

FUGA, FERDINANDO. Italian architect (b. Florence, 1699; d. Naples, 1782). His first important Roman commission was the Palazzo della Consulta (1732–37), a late baroque building of virtuoso detail with an open stairway of great originality in its court. Contemporary with it is the rebuilding of the Church of the Orazione e Morte, Rome, with an unusual façade. His Corsini Palace, Rome (1736 on), is a large complex with a typically grand 18th-century stairway. His masterpiece is perhaps the façade of S. Maria Maggiore, Rome (1741–43), an open design of lyrical character. After Galilei's death in 1737 Fuga was the leading architect of Rome, and his manner became ever more classical (for example, the Coffee House, Quirinal Gardens, 1741–44). After 1751 he worked in Naples, building the huge Albergo de' Poveri (1752) and the Church of the Gerolamini (1780).

BIBLIOGRAPHY. R. Wittkower, *Art and Architecture in Italy, 1600-1750*, Baltimore, 1958.

FU-GEN, *see* SAMANTABHADRA.

FUGEN BOSATSU IN THE NATIONAL MUSEUM, TOKYO. Japanese silk painting (12th cent.). Fugen, symbol of wisdom and a guardian of the followers of the Lotus Sūtra, is seated on a white elephant in an attitude of deep religious devotion. The immaculate white bodies of Fugen and the elephant are boldly contrasted with his elegant dress and saddle, decorated in green, yellow, orange, blue, and thinly cut gold strips. The quiet elegance and subtle mood of the painting epitomize the aristocratic and sophisticated taste of the Fujiwara court nobles.

BIBLIOGRAPHY. Tokyo National Museum, *Pageant of Japanese Art*, vol. 1: *Painting*, pt. 1, Tokyo, 1952; National Commission for the Protection of Cultural Properties, ed., *Kokuhō (National Treasures of Japan)*, 6 vols., Tokyo, 1963–

FUHR, XAVER. German painter, graphic artist, and teacher (1898–). He was born in Neckarau and is self-taught. Although Fuhr is generally expressionist in orientation, his style also emphasizes linear constructive elements. Since World War II he has taught in the Munich Academy.

FUJITA, TSUGUJI, *see* FOUJITA, TSOUGOHARU.

FUKIEN WARE, *see* SWATOW WARE.

FUKU JO-JU, *see* AMOGHASIDDHI.

FULDA. Important Carolingian center, east of Cologne and northeast of Mainz. A scriptorium located by some at Fulda may have been the source of the Ada Gospels. The abbey church, consecrated in 819, has been overlaid with 18th-century construction. Excavations have established that the edifice had a nave separated from the two aisles by ten columns, representing a reversion to the Early Christian basilica. To the east the nave ended in a semicircular apse, and to the west it ended in a large continuous transept that protruded far beyond the lateral walls of the aisles. Also found at Fulda were carved capitals of rather coarse execution. *See* ADA GROUP; FULDA: ABBEY CHURCH.

BIBLIOGRAPHY. R. Hinks, *Carolingian Art*, London, 1935; R. Krautheimer, "The Carolingian Revival of Early Christian Architecture," *Art Bulletin*, XXIV, 1942.

FULDA: ABBEY CHURCH. Church of the great Benedictine abbey of Fulda, Germany, founded in 744 by St. Boniface. The abbey was one of the most important centers of northern European civilization in late Carolingian and Ottonian times. The church was replaced by the present baroque Cathedral of Fulda by Johann Dientzenhofer between 1704 and 1712, but the new structure contains a number of the actual elements of the 9th-century abbey church, maintains the proportions, and, with its high, thin towers, echoes the feeling of the former church.

An early structure, built in 751, was replaced between 791 and 819 by a double-apsed basilica based on Old St. Peter's in Rome. The most impressive basilica north of the Alps, it was the leader in the Carolingian revival of Early Christian architecture. It even seems that Fulda's nave and its great continuous transept, which forms a T-shaped basilica with its semicircular apse, were based on the measurements of Old St. Peter's. This type of basilica construction was strongly associated with Christian Imperial Rome and was adopted by the Carolingians as an expression of the imperial claims of their dynasty.

In 754 the interment of the remains of St. Boniface himself occasioned the rebuilding program that produced for the Apostle of the Germans a building similar to that in which the Prince of the Apostles was buried. During the rebuilding program begun by Ratgar and finished under Eigil, the church of 751 was greatly enlarged and provided with a western transept and apse constructed in Roman style. Under it an elaborate martyrium was constructed to contain the remains of St. Boniface. At the west, another raised but smaller apse was provided, dedicated to the Saviour and Mary. The church was completed by the western cloister, or atrium, in 922. Between 937 and 948, the eastern part of the church was reconstructed, and two round towers, flanking the eastern apse, were added.

BIBLIOGRAPHY. R. Krautheimer, "The Carolingian Revival of Early Christian Architecture," *Art Bulletin*, XXIV, 1942; L. Grodecki, *L'Architecture ottonienne*, Paris, 1958; D. Groszmann, "Kloster Fulda und seine Bedeutung für den frühen deutschen Kirchenbau," in *Das erste Jahrtausend...*, ed. K. Böhner et al., text, vol. 1, Düsseldorf, 1962.

ERNEST P. LAWSON

FULDA: CATHEDRAL, *see* FULDA: ABBEY CHURCH.

FULDA: ST. MICHAEL'S. Carolingian church built between 820 and 822 in Fulda, Germany. This building, erected by Abbot Hrabanus Maurus as a cemetery church, was one of the few central-plan structures of the time and the only circular one. It was consciously modeled after the rotunda of the Church of the Holy Sepulchre in Jerusalem and followed the *martyrion* tradition.

As a round building it differed from other Carolingian central-plan structures such as Germigny-des-Prés, the Palatine Chapel in Aachen, and Stephen's Chapel in Werden. Whereas these other structures set no particular pattern for future development, St. Michael's set a style for round chapels that continued through Gothic times.

BIBLIOGRAPHY. J. Schalkenbach, "Die Wiederherstellung der Michaelskirche zu Fulda," *Deutsche Kunst und Denkmalpflege*, Vienna, 1938.

FULDA PORCELAIN. First manufactured in 1764, this porcelain was characterized by a good-quality paste used

Buckminster Fuller, the geodesic dome of the United States pavilion at Expo 67, Montreal, Canada.

for the usual rococo and neoclassical figures and table-wares. Lasting until 1790, the output was impressive, varied, but not revolutionary, and shows Meissen influence.

BIBLIOGRAPHY. H. H. Josten, *Fulder Porzellanfiguren*, Berlin, 1929.

FULHAM WARE. Light gray and also red stoneware manufactured by John Dwight in Fulham, near London, after 1671, the year in which he was granted a patent to produce "transparent earthenware." His jugs and wine bottles were often decorated with a stamped design in a manner similar to that used on German stoneware of the period. They were made from a highly refined mixture of clay and pounded flint and were given a hard salt glaze of blue or brown, sometimes mottled. The factory also produced fine portrait busts, statuettes, and plaques.

BIBLIOGRAPHY. W. E. Cox, *The Book of Pottery and Porcelain*, vol. 2, New York, 1944; G. Savage, *Pottery through the Ages*, Baltimore, 1959.

FULLER, BUCKMINSTER. American architectural theoretician (1895–   ). Born in Fulton, Mass., Fuller has applied his own system of geometry to the problems of mass shelter, thus producing revolutionary concepts of structure. He is noted for designs of highly efficient technologically based products, such as the dymaxion house and auto and the geodesic dome. His prefabricated, self-supporting domes, each made of a frame that is a network of aluminum tubes covered by a plastic membrane, are remarkably light (ca. 8¼ pounds per square yard). Of fragile appearance, they are quite resistant. They have been used for hangars, theaters, showrooms, gymnasiums, markets, factories, and offices. Prominent examples are the United States pavilion at Expo 67 in Montreal, Canada, the Alcoa branch office in Cleveland, Ohio, and the Union Dome in Baton Rouge, La. The Union Dome, made of folded and externally braced hexagons of steel sheet, is 384 feet in diameter (the world's largest). Except in the military field, Fuller's innovations have not been widely used; however, he has received many honors for his designs. Among these are the gold medal of the American Institute of Architects and, in 1968, the gold medal for architecture of the National Institute of Arts and Letters.

BIBLIOGRAPHY. I. McCallum, *Architecture USA*, New York, 1959; R. B. Fuller, *Ideas and Integrities*, Englewood Cliffs, N.J., 1963.

THEODORE M. BROWN

FULLER, GEORGE. American painter (b. Deerfield, Mass., 1822; d. Boston, 1884). He studied with H. K. Brown in Albany and attended the Cowles Art School, the Art Students League, and the Raphael Colin School in Paris. In New York City he painted portraits and landscapes, but he soon settled in Deerfield as a tobacco farmer. In 1875, however, he again became a full-time painter. A member of the Society of American Artists, he helped to perfect the mezzotint etching technique.

The portrait of *Winifred Dysant* illustrates his somber introspection and poetic nostalgia. With murky impressionistic mists, he creates a twilight mood of dream and imagination. His figures possess an intrinsic charm and spirituality that recall the work of Hunt and Rossetti.

BIBLIOGRAPHY. J. B. Millet, *George Fuller*, New York, 1886.

FULLER AND LAVER. American architectural team of Thomas W. Fuller (1822–98) and Augustus Laver (1834–

98). They were English-born architects who designed, though not in partnership, the High Victorian Gothic Parliament House in Ottawa, Canada (1859–67). They later joined forces to design the New York State Capitol in Albany (1868; subsequently modified) and the Municipal Buildings in San Francisco (ca. 1878) in the Second Empire mode.

FULVIA ET AEMILIA BASILICA, ROME, *see* Aemilia Basilica, Rome.

FUNCTIONALISM. Design concept or attitude in architecture, furniture, and other applied arts that stresses the practical use of the object in determining form. Functionalism is therefore opposed to ornate traditional forms in that even the choice of materials is affected by the object's function. Functionalism became prevalent in the first quarter of the 20th century.

BIBLIOGRAPHY. J. M. Richards, *An Introduction to Modern Architecture*, Baltimore, 1956.

FUNERAL AT ORNANS, THE, *see* Burial at Ornans, The.

FUNGAI, BERNARDINO. Italian painter (1460–1516). Although Fungai was probably trained by a Sienese artist (Giovanni di Paolo or Benvenuto di Giovanni), much of his early work is Florentine in its discreetness for form and Umbrian in its use of deep, gently rolling landscapes. These qualities are evident in the *Adoration of the Child* in the Chiusi Cathedral and in *St. Catherine Receiving the Stigmata* in the House of St. Catherine, Siena. More hieratical are two versions of the *Assumption* in Siena, at S. Girolamo (1487) and at the National Picture Gallery. In later works, such as the *Coronation of the Virgin* in S. Maria dei Servi in Siena, Fungai, like Signorelli, presents an array of figures, but with harsh modeling and outlines and in the context of an angular, patterned composition.

BIBLIOGRAPHY. R. van Marle, *The Development of the Italian Schools of Painting*, vol. 16, The Hague, 1937.

FUNHOF, HINRIK. German painter (fl. Hamburg, from 1475; d. 1484/85). He took over the workshop of Hans Bornemann in Hamburg in 1475 and created altarpieces for churches in Lüneburg and Hamburg. Judging by his delicate and elongated forms it is conjectured that he had been apprenticed to Dirk Bouts in the Low Countries.

FU PAO-SHIH. Chinese painter (1904–   ). A native of Kiangsi Province, he studied at the Imperial Academy in Japan. He became a professor at the Nanking Central University art department in 1935 and has since remained a central figure in contemporary Chinese art. His style of painting is quite individual and distinctive; he relies on close-textured brush and subtle color harmonies in grays and greens. His subject matter tends to be traditional, featuring the Chinese landscape or scholars at study, but there is a haunting quality to his paintings created through his use of mists, color relationships, and slight distortions of form. Fu Pao-shih is also widely known for his scholarly writings on Chinese art history and theory.

FURIES, THE. Frightful creatures of ancient Greek legends sent to inflict secret punishment on criminals who had somehow escaped official justice. Known as Erinyes or Eumenides, they were described as having bloody eyes, swift wings, and snaky locks. Their pursuit of Orestes for the murder of his mother Clytemnestra is an example of their tireless vengeance.

FURINI, FRANCESCO. Italian painter (ca. 1600–46). Born in Florence, he initially studied under Matteo Rosselli but was largely influenced by the baroque classicism of Guido Reni. In Rome, Furini collaborated with Giovanni da San Giovanni, another student of Rosselli, on the frescoes of the Casino Bentevoglio. Furini's works, such as the *Fides* (1635; Florence, Pitti Palace), are characterized by a use of highly elegant gestures and Leonardesque *sfumato* to set off the flesh tones, which are composed of minute gradations. His figures, tending toward graceful elongation with an emphasis on undulating contours, are bathed in a cool, dispassionate light with bluish overtones. Basically, his style returns to the mannerist period in its hypersensitivity toward color, and his works, while evoking an atmosphere of mystery, verge on morbidity.

BIBLIOGRAPHY. E. Toesca, *Francesco Furini*, Rome, 1950; R. Wittkower, *Art and Architecture in Italy, 1600–1750*, Baltimore, 1958.

FUR MOSAIC. Pattern made up of small pieces of fur in contrasting colors that have been sewn together to make garments or rugs. The technique is especially successful when furs of deep pile are employed because the long hairs conceal the seams that join the pieces. Almost any fur can be used, varying from relatively inexpensive lambskin to luxurious combinations of winter and summer ermine.

FURNESS, FRANK. American architect (1839–1912). He was born in Philadelphia. A student of Richard M. Hunt, Furness designed private homes, banks, and public buildings in his native city. Their façades are strongly plastic, with virile and uniquely personal detail; Viollet-le-Duc's influence can be noted. Louis Sullivan worked in Furness's office in 1873.

FURNITURE. Objects used in the home, such as beds, chairs, tables, and chests, have been a part of every recorded civilization. They have generally been made of wood, and the techniques of construction and ornamentation have not changed much through the centuries, although differences in cultures have affected the type and the amount of furniture used. Tenon and dowel, dovetailing, and joining by tongue and groove were known in ancient Egypt as they are today, and inlay and carving vary in design rather than technique from age to age.

Egypt. The history of furniture is best begun toward the end of the 4th millennium B.C. with evidence from Egypt. In the painted tomb reliefs of the Old Kingdom are representations of couches, chairs, stools, and tables. Designs are simple, seemingly dictated by functional requirements. The decoration follows three themes: animal elements, plant forms, and architectural moldings. Very little actual furniture is preserved from the early period. There are animal legs from a couch of the 1st dynasty in Stockholm (Egyptian Museum). A couch, chair, table, and canopy in Boston (Museum of Fine Arts) have been reconstructed from evidence found at Giza in the Tomb of Hetepheres I, a queen of the 4th dynasty. This furniture is made of wood sheathed in gold, with rich inlays adorning the solid panels. More elaborately ornamented later Egyptian furniture was very similar in general line to the early examples. An interesting exception was the very plain furniture, evidently for workmen's use, uncovered in the excavations of the necropolis at Thebes. The chairs from this group are similar in design to the ceremonial pieces. *See* EGYPT (MINOR ARTS). *See also* IVORY.

Assyria. The rich detail on Assyrian reliefs gives us a good idea about their furniture, which has entirely disappeared. Tables and thrones reminiscent of Egyptian examples have trumpet-shaped legs with feet probably cast in bronze. In a relief from Kuyunjik (Nineveh) of the mid-7th century B.C., Assurbanipal and a queen are in a setting that includes furniture that appears to be richly inlaid.

Greece. Greek furniture is known mostly from illustrations on vases and relief sculpture, since it, too, has largely disappeared. Conservatism was an important characteristic of its design, and the range of forms continued to be limited. The couch, or *kline*, was used for eating as well as resting, and a number of them would be gathered for a banquet. It was at our table height from the floor, with shorter stools and tables used with it. Generally it had a curving headrest on which cushions might be placed; its legs would be animal-shaped, rectangular with leaf ornamentation, or turned. Stools, both folding and stationary, were a common Greek furniture form. A group of terracotta statuettes of people at work (Boston, Museum of Fine Arts) shows a variety of stools, as do many vase paintings, where turned and animal legs are depicted. There is an expressive contrast between the folding and stationary stool in a relief representing a dog and cat fight on a statue pedestal of about 500 B.C. in Athens (National Museum). A turned wooden leg of Greek manufacture, but found in Egypt, is in New York (Metropolitan Museum).

The important Greek innovation in furniture was the graceful side chair known as the *klismos*. Mentioned in Homer and common in archaic times, the *klismos* varied in design until the 5th century B.C., when it became standardized as a plain form with legs curving out and a curved open back topped with a simple deep panel. The table, used by the Greeks primarily for eating, was portable and was generally small and light. One common type has a rectangular top and is supported by two legs at one end and a third at the other, sometimes reinforced with a fairly high stretcher. The legs are either plain or animal-shaped. Round tables were also known, and one of these of the Hellenistic period survived in Egypt (Brussels, Cinquantenaire Museum). In Greece the chest varied in size from the small container for jewelry to examples large enough to hide several people. The simple rectangular box was made as a framework with panels, and often the stiles formed legs. The lids, as in Egyptian examples, were either flat or gabled, and the form was decorated with architectural ornament. Bronze and marble were used for furniture in ancient Greece, although wood was the most important material and the one that most influenced design.

Rome. The tradition of Greek design was carried on and revitalized by the Romans after the 1st century of our era. A greater use of metal and marble is suggested in the furniture that has survived. Using the same vocabulary of ornament, the Romans made more elaborate furniture and more complex designs. Even so elemental a detail as a turned leg is more complicated when Roman. The headboard of the couch became more elaborate and broader. It seemed to take on the thickness of the first layer of cushions to provide an area for extra decorative detail. Long rectangular tables with solid carved rectangular supports at both ends were introduced in Roman times, as were a variety of smaller tables. The latter included some that had bases that could be folded together, such as the table with bronze legs and a marble top in Naples (National Archaeological Museum). The most singular innovation in furniture design was the introduction of the cupboard. Although none has survived, the cupboard is represented in a fresco from Herculaneum. Roman furniture was often quite elegant. Rich inlays in complex designs are described in the contemporary literature. Roman patricians occasionally paid unbelievably high prices for unusual objects in the decorative arts, including furniture, so there is no doubt that the finest craftsmanship was applied to furniture for appreciative patrons.

Middle Ages: Romanesque and Gothic. From the time of the fall of Rome to the Gothic era very little furniture has been preserved, and few documents illustrate it. It would appear that there were few changes in form and some rather basic changes in ornament. Basically Greco-Roman motifs are flattened and schematized in decorative schemes of the Middle Ages. The Throne of Maximianus (546–556; Ravenna, Archiepiscopal Museum) shows how the throne form was simplified in shape to accommodate a group of ivory panels set into the wooden carcass. The folding stool of King Dagobert I (d. 638; Paris, National Library) has griffin legs of Roman inspiration with detail handled more broadly than it would have been in imperial days. The conservatism and dependence on Roman models is evident in small chests that have been preserved, which often have a great vitality because of the novelty of their approach to the traditional. Occasional representations in manuscripts and reliefs suggest that strong simple furniture, decorated in great simplifications of Roman motifs, became typical of the Romanesque period. Turned post chairs, not unlike Pilgrim-style American examples, appear in 12th-century French sculpture and are known in the Scandinavian region in 13th-century examples. What has survived of the Romanesque style has come from areas where the style lingered. The chests and cupboards are essentially simple, with flat geometric patterns carved in circular designs or arcades that contain areas of a piece. *See* THRONE OF MAXIMIANUS.

The emergence of the Gothic style in architecture did not bring about a revolution in furniture design. The 12th and 13th centuries were a period of rich production with design inspired by the classical, but what we know seems more influenced by a renaissance of classical knowledge than by the new style. The Gothic style first affected furniture design in the 14th century. It was the style of northern Europe in the 15th century, when the pointed arch was ubiquitous. Thus, in the main, Gothic furniture was made at the time the Renaissance style was emerging in Italy. Gothic furniture is depicted in the paintings of the 15th-century Flemish masters, who were great realists. Interior scenes show a variety of form in the tables, chairs, cupboards, and chests represented. The case pieces generally consist of a frame tenoned and doweled together, with enclosing panels often decorated. Carved traceries are one motif, and the linenfold another, frequently used. One unfamiliar form is the small cupboard on tall legs with a shelf below. Both the top and the shelf were used for display. For beds, most often the hangings covered the form.

Renaissance. Like the Gothic, the Renaissance style in furniture began in the 14th century. Although the pointed arch is found in throne and frame designs, Greco-Roman moldings and capitals appear in the furniture represented in 14th-century paintings by Giotto and the Lorenzettis. In the main, the difference between north and south in the 15th century was in vocabulary of ornament, with Italians favoring a revival of the Greco-Roman, which they conceived of as including some of what we consider medieval. The form that has survived best is the chest, or cassone, which was elaborately decorated. In the 15th century painted panels or gilded reliefs, representing mythological scenes, were often the main decoration. *The Dream of St. Ursula* (Venice, Academy) by Carpaccio and *The Birth of the Virgin* (Florence, S. Maria Novella) by Ghirlandajo give a good idea of the simplicity and elegance of the Italian interior.

High Renaissance. By the 16th century the classical was better understood and more successfully used. In furniture there is a greater variety of form and more elaborate decoration. The most notable innovation in form was the introduction of the chest of drawers. Known first in Tuscany, the early chest has four tiers of drawers and is often on a lion's-paw base. The cassone in the 16th century was most frequently of rich dark wood carved with classical architectural motifs and scenes. The cassapanca, a combination bench and chest, was carved with figures and architectural motifs that might well reflect the influence of High Renaissance masters. Chair forms consisted of a variety of folding forms and a development of the stool, a side chair with solid carved panels replacing the legs and a carved back. This chair, called a sgabello, often has an octagonal seat.

Mannerism. Although the effects of mannerism are hard to discern in Italian work of the 16th century, furniture of the court of Henry II of France is essentially Italian mannerist. The French court attracted a number of important Italian mannerist painters who formed a court style that affected all the arts. The Henry II style is best expressed in the grotesques published by the architect Jacques Du Cerceau. These designs, in which classical motifs form overall patterns in surprising juxtapositions, influenced cabinetmakers who carved the Du Cerceau suggestions on panels of large case pieces. An outstanding furniture maker of the period was Hugues Sambin of Dijon, to whom cabinets have been attributed on the basis of their resemblance to his published folio of 1572. French furniture of the period included conservative designs in which the single Renaissance element was the portrait medallion carved on the front. Simple columnar legs on both tables

and narrowly proportioned armchairs seem a French peculiarity. *See* Du Cerceau Family; Sambin, Hugues.

Baroque. The advent of the baroque style at the very beginning of the 17th century brought with it a new and more creative approach to design. Whereas the High Renaissance and mannerist designer worked within an established vocabulary of ornament, the baroque designer could create new motifs by working in the spirit of the classical. In France during Louis XIII's reign (1610–43) the degree of change was limited. The spiral-turned and vase-shaped legs were used on forms that were not very different from what had been done before. Contrasting color by using ebony and walnut in case pieces is one result of the new approach.

For the early years, or before 1650, the Netherlands was an important influence. Hans Vredeman de Vries and Crispin van de Passe published books of designs that were frequently followed. One form particularly associated with the Netherlands is the *Kast*, or armoire, with heavy cornice and three engaged columns across the front. The use of contrasting-colored woods and building up the surface of the doors by adding moldings are elements that show the baroque taste for movement in design. Chairs with back and seat upholstered and frames that often have turned stiles and legs are another development of the early 17th century. Essentially conservative although reflecting the new taste, Dutch design was an important influence in northern Europe in the 17th century, as can be seen in the furniture of the German, Scandinavian, and English areas. Dutch designs exploited the talents of the finest craftsman without giving him impossible challenges so that the results were kept within middle-class taste and purchasing power. *See* Passe, Crispin van de, the Elder; Vredeman de Vries, Hans.

The style associated with Louis XIV is extreme in every sense. Completely new and unfamiliar designs calling for the use of unusual materials resulted in furniture that must have been a shock to see and pay for. Louis XIV's interest in the arts dates from his majority (1659). The cabinetmaker most characteristic of the French court of the time was André-Charles Boulle. Boulle created unusual forms elaborately inlaid in metal and veneered in tortoise shell or ebony. Designs for panels of inlay were often inspired by the work of Jean Berain, who published engravings of ornamental fantasies. *See* Boulle, André-Charles.

The Oriental began to play an important role in furniture design in the late 17th century. Lacquerwork from the Orient was used along with chinoiserie designs both in court and middle-class work. Caning, another import from the East, was used in elaborately carved frames by the Portuguese, Spanish, and then the Dutch and English. The influence of the French court on European furniture design was important. In England during the reigns of Charles II, James II, and William and Mary, furniture design was elaborate. Rich marquetry and veneers of French inspiration were used within the limitations prescribed by the English market. At the same time, on the American scene, a group of dated pieces made in New England are essentially 16th-century Renaissance in form. Although following Tudor designs, the cupboards are made of oak stained to simulate walnut with applied turned parts blackened to look like ebony, so that in coloring, at least, they are baroque. In all areas away from the centers of fashion, old styles tended to persist with minor concessions to new styles.

Rococo. French court design continued to dominate in the 18th century with the introduction of the rococo style. This innovation was characterized by a general lightening of proportion and a more whimsical use of classical motifs. By using curving surfaces the bulky appearance in large case pieces was minimized. The lavish use of ormolu mounts also tended to disguise the size of large chests. Smaller forms, tables and cabinets for special uses, were made in quantity. The rococo began at the end of the reign of Louis XIV but was most important during the reign of Louis XV. Among the large number of favored cabinet-makers for the court was Jean François Oeben, whose desk for the King (now in the Louvre) is the epitome of rich rococo design. The extremes of rococo design are to be seen in the engravings of Gilles Marie Oppenord and J. A. Meissonier. *See* OEBEN, JEAN FRANCOIS.

The lightening of form and the creation of more intimately scaled furniture became fashionable all over Europe. In England this new style, called Early Georgian, was first expressed in designs in walnut and mahogany. These were essentially simple, with minimal carving or inlay decoration. The curving animal leg, the cabriole, the pad or claw and ball feet, is typical of this style.

By the middle of the 18th century more exuberant designs with the more complex patterns of French inspiration were in vogue. This phase of the English rococo is best known in the publication of Thomas Chippendale, a fashionable London cabinetmaker. Chippendale transformed the French court style into one for middle-class use.

His book, *The Gentleman and Cabinet-Maker's Director*, first published in 1754, boasted of having designs in the French, Gothic, and Chinese taste, all the facets of rococo whimsey. American cabinetmakers knew the book but tended to simplify even more to achieve their distinctive style. Surveying the many facets of the rococo, in a collection like that at the Metropolitan Museum of Art, New York, reveals that small-scale and curving lines are two constant characteristics. Decorative schemes vary from the most complex inlay patterns used with applied ormolu mounts to simpler designs in which carving is the typical means of decoration. *See* CHIPPENDALE, THOMAS.

Neoclassicism. The reaction to the rococo began as an English phenomenon in the work of Robert Adam. Adam had established his architectural office in London before 1760, and was doing houses in the new style. He designed furniture appropriate to the new interiors, employing a repertory of ancient Roman motifs. The scale remained small, and the designs became linear, precise, and even lighter. He preferred painted or light woods in flat simple shapes. The degree of Adam's invention is difficult to determine. His concept of neoclassicism had been evolved during a stay in Rome, where the idea of reviving the classical was being explored by a group that was more intellectual than artistic and included men such as Winckelmann, Gavin Hamilton, Mengs, and Vien. Adam had the talent to use the Roman ideas in fine designs. The important change in furniture form was the introduction of special dining-room pieces. *See* ADAM BROTHERS.

The French court turned to the neoclassical very shortly after Adam introduced it. Before the end of the reign of Louis XV the straight lines and more classical forms of

Furniture. Rococo pieces upholstered in Beauvais tapestry after a design by François Boucher. Louvre, Paris.

the new style, called Louis XVI, began to appear, and cabinetmakers such as Jean Henri Riesener changed to it. For the court, a revival of Boulle designs was included in this reaction to the rococo. The popularization of the neoclassical in England was stimulated by publications of furniture designs in the new taste. Published posthumously, George Hepplewhite's *Cabinet Maker and Upholsterer's Guide* (1788) is a compendium of neoclassical design featuring a variety of small forms and chair backs that are shield-shaped. Following Adam and the French cabinetmakers, Hepplewhite used ancient motifs in contemporary forms. *See* Hepplewhite, George; Riesener, Jean Henri.

A second phase of the style involved a more purist approach to ancient designs and is closely related to Napoleon's interest in promoting himself as continuing and reviving the ancient Roman Empire. Napoleon chose to live with furniture that revived ancient forms. His designers, Percier and Fontaine, reused the *klismos* and pedestal tables of Roman design and adapted other forms to the same idiom in developing a second phase of the neoclassical. Another important change was the use of plain dark wood with ornamentation in gold. Either ormolu mounts were added or carved areas were gilded. This style, which is called Empire, began about 1795. In the 1802 edition of Thomas Sheraton's *The Cabinet-Maker and Upholsterer's Drawing Book* are both the Adam style and the more Roman ideas. By 1810 the more archaeologically inspired neoclassicism was made heavier in proportion and achieved great popularity all over the Continent and in England. In Germany and Austria the style is called Biedermeier and in England, Regency. On the American scene Sheraton design was most influential and is best exemplified in the work of Duncan Phyfe. *See* Biedermeier Style; Empire Style; Percier and Fontaine; Phyfe, Duncan; Sheraton, Thomas.

Revival styles. About 1812 the more Napoleonic design of a refugee from France, Charles Honoré Lannuier, began to be fashionable, although the earlier style continued in popular favor for some time. Since it was closely connected to the court of Napoleon at the moment when theorists began relating the style and ideas of an era, the Empire style went out of fashion in France soon after Napoleon's regime was overthrown. It was replaced by a series of revival styles that might be explained as attempts at restoring the old order. Rococo designs were revived by the 1820s, and adaptations of Louis XIII and Louis XIV furniture forms were introduced a short time later. Interest in the Gothic, which had begun in the 18th century as a facet of rococo whimsey, became moralistic in the 19th-century essays of such men as the English architect Augustus Pugin. *See* Pugin, Augustus Welby Northmore.

Generally called "early Victorian," the revival styles, popular between 1830 and 1860, were adaptations of early models to suit the needs of the 19th century. The approach is explained in an American book, *The Architecture of Country Houses* (New York, 1851), by A. J. Downing: "Furniture in *correct* taste is characterized by its being designed in accordance with recognized styles." It goes on to characterize the many styles that can be used. *See* Downing, Andrew Jackson.

One important change in the 19th century involved the techniques of manufacture. Papier-mâché, bentwood, and iron furniture were produced in the popular styles of the moment, and the introduction of a modified mass production affected the more usual furniture. For the first time quantities of shoddily made, inexpensive furniture were offered for sale. The reaction was twofold. First there were attempts at improving the education of the artisans involved, and then there were attacks against the system. The latter, beginning with the writings of Carlyle and Ruskin, argued for a return to small-scale production in the hands of craftsmen. This point of view is best expressed by the English theorist, artist, and craftsman William Morris. In 1861 he founded the firm of decorators Morris, Marshall, and Faulkner, which produced the kind of furniture he thought correct. He desired designs to be forthright and forms to be well built. He and his circle used the whole history of design for inspiration, although case pieces generally were derived from Gothic prototypes. The architect Sir Charles Eastlake published a book on interior decorating, using Morris's ideas, that was influential enough for the style to be frequently called the Eastlake style. Under Morris's and Eastlake's influence diverse sources were exploited. *See* Eastlake, Sir Charles Lock; Morris, William; Ruskin, John.

Art Nouveau and after. Toward the end of the 19th century and the beginning of the 20th a style that seemed to have centered around Nancy for its best work, Art Nouveau, appears. Elongated, precious forms, carved in floral motifs and handsomely inlaid, were characteristic of this style. Its height was reached between 1900 and 1910 but some of the designers working in the style continued longer. *See* Art Nouveau.

The real break with the tradition of using the history of design came about the time of World War I, in the Netherlands with the de Stijl group and in Germany with the Bauhaus. Both sought to use the new aesthetics in painting and sculpture for furniture design. Their tradition is followed in architect-designed furniture by Le Corbusier, Ludwig Mies van der Rohe, and Eero Saarinen and in the spectacular innovations of Charles Eames. *See* Bauhaus; De Stijl; Eames, Charles; Le Corbusier; Mies van der Rohe, Ludwig; Saarinen, Eero.

BIBLIOGRAPHY. G. M. A. Richter, *Ancient Furniture . . .*, Oxford, 1926; A. Feulner, *Kunstgeschichte des Möbels . . .*, Berlin, 1927; L. A. Boger, *The Complete Guide to Furniture Styles*, New York, 1959.

MARVIN D. SCHWARTZ

FURSTENBERG, THEODOR CASPAR VON. German mezzotintist (d. Mainz, 1675). Fürstenberg spent most of his life as a church official at the Cathedral of Mainz, but he developed a very fine technique and style. His plates, signed T.C.B.D.F., are rare. Among them are the *Portrait of Archduke Leopold William of Austria* (1656) and *Christ with Crown of Thorns*, after Dürer.

BIBLIOGRAPHY. C. J. Davenport, *Mezzotints*, London, 1904.

FURSTENBERG PORCELAIN. First made in 1753, it is still being produced today. Its best period was between 1768 and 1795. Among the finest products were comedy figures and miners by Simon Feilner and rococo wares in relief patterns that concealed imperfections in the body.

BIBLIOGRAPHY. Kestner Museum, *Fürstenberger Porzellan aus drei Jahrhunderten*, Hannover, 1956.

FUR TRADERS DESCENDING THE MISSOURI. Oil painting by Bingham, in the Metropolitan Museum of Art, New York. *See* BINGHAM, GEORGE CALEB.

FUSELI, HENRY (Johann Heinrich Fussli). Swiss-English writer, painter, and draftsman (b. Zurich, 1741; d. Putney Hill, England, 1825). Fuseli led a rich life that included a great variety of activities. He was brought up in an artistic and intellectual environment, studied theology, and for a while served in holy orders. In the early 1760s, however, he joined a group of young political reformers whose activities so irritated the local authorities that in 1763 he was obliged to leave Zurich. After a stay of some months in Berlin, Fuseli went to London (1764), where, except for a period of nine years in Italy, he spent most of the rest of his life. Much of Fuseli's time during his first years in London was given to writing and translating. In 1765, for example, he translated Winckelmann's *Reflections on the Paintings and Sculptures of the Greeks.*

With the encouragement of Sir Joshua Reynolds, Fuseli decided in the late 1760s to devote his career primarily to painting. He left England for Italy in 1769 and did not return until 1779. Most of his time abroad was spent in Rome. His chief model for study was Michelangelo, but he ranged widely through Italian 16th-century mannerist art. The basic qualities of his style took form during his Continental sojourn and remained fairly constant throughout his career. He had a penchant for heavily muscled figures which were cast in poses suggesting violent and rather hysterical activity, accentuated by a low viewpoint for the spectator and exaggerated contrasts of light and shadow. He also quickly settled on his favorite themes, which were usually dramatic and highly literary. His preferred sources were Shakespeare, Milton, Dante, and the Nibelungenlied.

Fuseli began to exhibit at the Royal Academy of Arts in 1774, when he sent his *Death of Cardinal Beaufort* from Rome, but it was not until 1788 that he achieved the rank of associate academician. He was elected full academician in 1790. During the late 1780s and 1790s he was engaged

Henry Fuseli, *La Petite Fée*. Museum, Basel.

primarily on two projects, John Boydell's Shakespeare Gallery (opened 1789) and Fuseli's own Milton Gallery (opened 1799). In the latter year he was also appointed professor of painting at the Royal Academy. The discourses on painting which he delivered to the Academy were published in 1801. During the last years of his life, Fuseli enjoyed considerable prestige in his profession. Among his admirers were William Blake, Sir Thomas Lawrence, and the sculptor John Flaxman.

Fuseli's art was generally neglected from shortly after his death until early in the present century, when interest in his work revived. The force of his imagination cannot be denied, but, like his younger contemporary Blake, his technical equipment and execution were not always equal to his ideas. His reputation rests mainly on his drawings. Historically, the intense, highly wrought character of his art occupies an important place in the early phase of the romantic movement.

BIBLIOGRAPHY. J. Knowles, *The Life and Writings of Henry Fuseli*, 3 vols., London, 1831; A. Federmann, *Johann Heinrich Füssli, Dichter und Mahler*, Zurich, 1927; P. Ganz, *Die Zeichnungen Hans Heinrich Füsslis*, Bern, 1947; F. Antal, *Fuseli Studies*, London, 1956.
ROBERT R. WARK

FUSINA, ANDREA. Italian sculptor (fl. Milan, 1495–1525). Fusina served as an engineer and sculptor for the Cathedral of Milan, producing for it a figure of Judas Maccabeus which draws heavily on the antique in pose, dress, proportions, and expression. A number of tombs in Lodi, Monza, and Milan are also attributed to him.

FUSSLI, JOHANN HEINRICH, see FUSELI, HENRY.

FUSSLI, JOHANN MELCHIOR. Swiss designer and engraver (b. Zurich, 1677; d. there, 1736). He studied with J. Meyer in Zurich and with S. Blesendorf in Berlin. After 1697 Füssli was very active in Zurich as a designer for engravers and as an etcher for book illustrations (he did 750 plates in a Bible printed by J. J. Scheuchzers) and for Zurich periodicals.

BIBLIOGRAPHY. C. J. Benziger, *Geschichte des Buchgewerbes im fürstlichen Benediktinerstifte U. L. F. v. Einsiedeln*, Einsiedeln, 1912.

FUSTAT, see AL-FUSTAT.

FUSUMA. In Japanese architecture, panels resembling *shoji* made of opaque paper pasted on both sides of a wood frame. By the removal of *fusuma* panels, several rooms can be converted into one room. *See* SHOJI.

FUTTEHPORE SIKRI, see FATEHPUR SIKRI.

FUTURISM. Italian movement in early modern painting and sculpture. It was announced in a manifesto written by the poet-critic Filippo Tommaso Marinetti and published on February 20, 1909, in the Parisian journal *Le Figaro*. Marinetti, projecting the explosive attitudes of a group of intellectuals and artists in Milan, Rome, and Florence, proclaimed the glories of speed, physical aggressiveness, war, and the modern machine; and, negatively, he decried Italy's lingering affinity with its past archaeological wonders and the tourism that was its chief cultural

asset. Marinetti held that the *Victory of Samothrace* was less beautiful than a hurtling automobile, that violence should become in poetry what it was in a modern machine.

The 1909 manifesto was reinforced by an April, 1910, counterpart setting forth the technical manifesto of futurist painters. Its author, Umberto Boccioni, had become, with Marinetti, a leading strategist of early futurism. Boccioni also held one of the first significant one-man shows representing the movement (in Venice, 1910), although most of the pictures were in the Italian divisionist or neoimpressionist style and were not yet fully indicative of futurist connections with cubism. Boccioni's "Technical Manifesto" exhorted painters to interpret the "whirling life of steel" rather than imitate nature, to revolt against prevalent norms of good taste. Also signed by Luigi Russolo, Carlo Carrà, Gino Severini, and Giacomo Balla, this document declared the superiority of science and "universal dynamism" as the latter might be rendered in sensations of an antiharmonious mobility in paintings. *See* BALLA, GIACOMO; BOCCIONI, UMBERTO; CARRA, CARLO; RUSSOLO, LUIGI; SEVERINI, GINO.

Important developments occurred in the futurist painting style between 1910 and 1912; and by late 1911 the signers of the "Technical Manifesto" of 1910 had achieved a faceted, rhythmic expression related generally to analytic cubism, with which they were by now familiar, but obviously more concerned with movement. Modern machines including the automobile, the streetcar, and the locomotive were becoming familiar subjects in futurist canvases, although many distinctive works interpreted the simultaneous movements of the human or animal figure. Futurist color, especially as applied by Severini and Boccioni, was more chromatic than the characteristically restrained tonality of analytic cubism of 1910–11; but the futurist method of fragmenting form into sequential or intersecting planes appears to be directly indebted to the French style. The renowned painting by Marcel Duchamp of France, *Nude Descending a Staircase* (1912), occupies a problematic position in the relation of cubism to futurism and in all probability discloses an interchange of influences. *See* DUCHAMP, MARCEL.

The canvases of Severini, who had lived in Paris since 1906 and was responsible for the publication of Marinetti's first manifesto, were closest to the cubist method. Russolo, whose basic interest was music rather than painting and who invented the cacophonous *intonarumori* (an organlike sound machine upon which its maker actually performed concerts), was the least orthodox of the futurists in the technical sense, although his works fit broadly into context. Balla, who as an advocate of Italian pointillism, or divisionism, had been the teacher of Boccioni and Severini at the turn of the century, often approached abstraction; and it is not incorrect to consider as abstract the basic concerns of Boccioni for translating speed and sequence of action of his subjects rather than their similitude.

The year 1912 was important for theoretical as well as artistic works by the futurists. In April, Boccioni published *La scultura futurista*, in effect another technical manifesto; and in May, Marinetti issued his "Technical Mani-

Futurism. Umberto Boccioni, *Unique Line of Continuity in Space.* Bronze. Gallery of Modern Art, Milan.

festo of Futurist Literature," which proposed a radically free use of words. Many paintings of this year were shown with earlier futurist works in the first Parisian exhibit of the Italians, at the Galerie Bernheim-Jeune. This collection, with certain withdrawals and additions, was also sent to the Herwarth Walden (Der Sturm) Gallery, Berlin; the Sackville Gallery, London; the Salle Giroux, Brussels; the Biesing Gallery, The Hague; the Audretsch Gallery, Amsterdam; and the Thannhäuser Gallery, Munich. Boccioni also showed sculptures in the 1912 Salon d'Automne in Paris. To the names of the artists most prominently figuring in the development of early futurist style—Boccioni, Carrà, Balla, Severini, Russolo, Sant'Elia—should be added those of Leonardo Dudreville, Ugo Giannattasio, Ardengo Soffici, Mario Sironi, and Ottone Rosai, all of whom contributed to the movement shortly after its formulation. *See* ROSAI, OTTONE; SIRONI, MARIO; SOFFICI, ARDENGO.

The strongest, most characteristic futurist paintings were created between 1910 and 1915. The futurists as a group strongly supported Italian intervention on the side of the Allies in World War I; several of them were jailed for their assiduous public demonstrations, and newspaper clippings of headlines referring to battles and other military activities were introduced into futurist collages in 1914. After 1915, when many futurists went to the front, the movement lost the cohesiveness it had enjoyed; and the death of Boccioni in 1916 during cavalry maneuvers was an especially severe interruption in the logical extension of the general style, particularly in sculpture.

Boccioni, whose bronzes and plaster works characterize the futurist aesthetic for the third dimension, was in advance of his time both ideationally and technically in his dynamic projection of figural shapes in space. As early as in his 1912 manifesto he advocated the manipulation of sculptural planes by means of a motor, although he never actually motorized his works. He also declared that various nontraditional substances might legitimately be added to conventional ones; thus, anticipated only by Picasso, he proposed what was later called the "art of assemblage."

Futurist architecture was not as such significantly practiced during the high years of the movement; but Antonio Sant'Elia, like Boccioni a victim of the war, brilliantly projected modern futurist cities as well as individual structures for power plants and related technological units.

During 1915 and 1916, certain futurists deviated from the principal style and founded "metaphysical painting." Carlo Carrà was a leader of this method and exhibited canvases of this kind in both Italy and France. Severini, who had continued to live in Paris throughout the development of the movement, reflected an increasingly close affinity with cubism until after 1920, and in 1921 he published *Du cubisme au classicisme*, turning thereafter to a series of *Harlequins* in neoclassic style. Giacomo Balla remained an orthodox futurist over a longer period than any of his colleagues, although he did not exhibit characteristic works until 1912. He occasionally painted in the original futurist manner until after 1930, and in the early 1950s he joined a belated action to restore to futurism in Italy something of its initial force. Marinetti, who framed the first futurist manifesto and, with Boccioni, gave the group its great early stimulus, became a Fascist senator after World War I. It is not incorrect to hold that futurism

continued until the mid-20th century, but the main currents were established by the end of the war. *See* PITTURA METAFISICA.

Futurism, whatever may have been its debt to cubism in the procedural sense, was concerned with sequential mobility of forms in space to a greater extent than had been any modern program. It influenced certain American painters, notably Joseph Stella, who had studied it at firsthand before 1920 in Europe, and to a lesser degree, Lyonel Feininger. George Grosz in his little-discussed Dadaist phase, as well as Hans Richter, was touched by futurist method. The interchange of influences between the futurists and cubists and the impact of futurism upon certain of the German Blue Rider (Blaue Reiter) artists in Munich is still problematical. *See* FEININGER, LYONEL; GROSZ, GEORGE; STELLA, JOSEPH.

Important exhibitions of futurist art were held in 1958 at the Art Institute of Chicago (Winston Collection); in 1959 at the Barberini Palace in Rome, sponsored by the Ente Premi Roma; in 1960 at the Sede della Famiglia Artistica Milanese, Milan, and in a special gallery at the 30th Venice Biennale; and in 1961 in the United States (New York, Museum of Modern Art, and elsewhere).

BIBLIOGRAPHY. Bernheim-Jeune Gallery, *Les Futuristes italiens*, exhibition catalog, Paris, 1912; U. Boccioni, *Pittura, scultura futuriste*, Milan, 1914; J. T. Soby and A. H. Barr, Jr., *Twentieth-Century Italian Art*, New York, 1949; U. Apollonio, *Pittura italiana moderna*, Venice, 1950; R. Carrieri, *Avant-garde Painting and Sculpture in Italy (1890-1955)*, Milan, 1955; M. Drudi Gambillo and T. Fiori, eds., *Archivi del futurismo*, 2 vols., Rome, 1958-62; R. T. Clough, *Futurism*, New York, 1961; J. C. Taylor, *Futurism*, New York, 1961. JOHN C. GALLOWAY

FUTURISTS, RUSSIAN. Loosely defined group of young writers, artists, and thinkers formed, in 1910, under the leadership of the artist D. Burliuk and the poet V. Mayakovski. Ideologically they embraced the manifestoes of Italian futurists (1909–10) without actually producing futurist works of art. The rayonist movement (ca. 1913) did incorporate some futurist principles. *See* BURLIUK, DAVID; RAYONISM.

BIBLIOGRAPHY. G. H. Hamilton, *The Art and Architecture of Russia*, Baltimore, 1954.

FYLFOT, *see* SWASTIKA.

FYNSON, LOUIS, *see* FINSONIUS, LODOVICUS.

FYT, JAN. Flemish painter of still lifes and, more rarely, of flowers (b. Antwerp, 1611; d. there, 1661). He was a pupil of Frans Snyders and became a member of the Guild of St. Luke in 1630. He traveled in Paris, Italy, and Holland. Fyt was, next to Snyders, one of the most important painters of animals in Flanders. His earlier works are mostly large-size scenes depicting the huntsman's bag, with occasional figures by Erasmus Quellinus, Theodoor van Thulden, or Jacob Jordaens. A spotted dog is often included. From the period of his maturity, the 1650s, date smaller still-life paintings, such as the one at the Prado in Madrid, which stress the opposition of light and shadow, and which feature cool color schemes and impasto treatment. Compositions consisting solely of fruit or flowers or both occur infrequently; they are loosely treated in an independent manner.

BIBLIOGRAPHY. W. Bernt, *Die niederländischen Maler des 17. Jahrhunderts . . .*, vol. 1, Munich, 1948; E. Greindl, *Les Peintres flamands de nature morte au XVIIe siècle*, 2d ed., Brussels, 1964.

G

GAAL, BARENT, *see* GAEL, BARENT.

GABBIANI, ANTONIO DOMENICO. Italian painter (1652–1726). Born in Florence, he was primarily a follower of Carlo Maratta. The numerous works executed for Gabbiani's Florentine patron, Cosimo III (such as the decoration of the cupola of S. Frediano, Florence, 1701–18), show a clarity of design and a precise handling of form, although the coloration tends to be dull and monochromatic. Gabbiani is also known for his etchings, in which fine sensitive strokes reveal his mastery of line.

GABLE. Triangular wall enclosed by the sloping planes of a roof. Although the term is usually associated with more steeply pitched roofs, as in Gothic gables, it is also applied to classical pediments and to walls framed by gambrel roofs.

GABO, NAUM. Russian-American sculptor, painter, and teacher (1890–   ). He was born in Brainsk, Russia. In 1910 he was a gymnasium graduate at Kursk and then became a medical student at the University of Munich. In 1911 he began the study of the natural sciences and in 1912 went to a Munich engineering school. In 1911–12 he attended the art history lectures of Heinrich Wölfflin in Munich. In 1912 he visited Venice and Florence. He returned to Moscow and saw the Shchoukin and Morosov collections of advanced art. When the war began in 1914 he went to Oslo, where his brother, Antoine Pevsner, joined him in 1916. In 1915 Gabo made his first constructions. *See* CONSTRUCTIVISM.

From 1917 to 1920 he was again in Russia, where he taught with Kandinsky, Tatlin, and Malevich at the Moscow School of Art. Reacting against the use of art as a political instrument, a practice championed by Tatlin and Rodchenko, Gabo and Pevsner published their *Realistic Manifesto* in Moscow during 1920. That same year Gabo had his first public exhibition and produced his *Kinetic Sculpture* as a demonstration of his ideas about movement. From 1922 until 1932 he lived in Berlin. With his brother he did stage sets for Diaghilev during 1926–27 and lectured

Naum Gabo, *Linear Construction Variation*, 1942–43. Plastic and nylon thread. Phillips Collection, Washington, D.C.

at the Bauhaus in 1928. In 1931 he returned to architectural design in a theater project that he had begun in 1919, when he worked out ideas for radio stations in Russia.

From 1932 to 1935 he was in Paris and joined the Abstraction-Création group. He went to London in 1935, later editing the magazine *Circle* with Ben Nicholson and J. L. Martin. In 1936 Gabo's sculpture appeared in the New York Museum of Modern Art show "Cubism and Abstract Art." He went to the United States in 1938 and had several exhibitions. In 1939 he went to Cornwall, England, and remained there until 1946. He joined the Design Research Unit in 1944.

In 1946 Gabo took up residence in the United States, and in 1953–54 he was a professor at the Harvard University Graduate School of Architecture. He did a number of architectural commissions, such as that for the U.S. Rubber Company, Rockefeller Center, New York City (1956). In 1957 he did his famous sculpture for the Bijenkorf Building, Rotterdam.

The Museum of Modern Art, New York, owns *Head of a Woman* (1916), *Column* (1923), and *Spiral Theme* (1941). The Guggenheim Museum, New York, has *Construction Space "Arch"* (1937) and *Variations of Spheric Theme* (1937). *Construction Suspended in Space* (1951–52) is in the Baltimore Museum of Art. Gabo gave to sculpture the feel and precision of modern science, effectively fusing art and its technological environment in materials invented in the 20th century. His transparent, light-catching forms gave a new elegance and aesthetic range to modern sculpture.

BIBLIOGRAPHY. New York, Museum of Modern Art, *Naum Gabo* [*and*] *Antoine Pevsner*, introd. H. Read, text R. Olson and A. Chanin, New York, 1948; N. Gabo, *Gabo, Constructions, Sculpture, Paintings, Drawings,* [*and*] *Engravings*, with introd. essays by H. Read and L. Martin, Cambridge, Mass., 1957.

ALBERT ELSEN

GABON (Gaboon; Gabun), *see* AFRICA, PRIMITIVE ART OF (CENTRAL AFRICA: GABON).

GABRIEL (Archangel). One of seven archangels, ranking after Michael. As God's messenger, Gabriel announced to Daniel the return of the Jews from captivity, foretold the birth of Samson, and announced the birth of John the Baptist to Zacharias and the conception of Christ to the

Virgin. In art he is shown clad in alb and dalmatic (15th cent.), carrying the knobbed stick of a messenger, a scepter, a lily, an olive branch or lighted taper, or a scroll with the first words of the angelic salutation. His feast is March 24. *See* MICHAEL (ARCHANGEL); RAPHAEL (ARCHANGEL). *See also* SAINTS IN ART.

GABRIEL, ANGE-JACQUES. French architect (1698–1782). He worked in Paris. Taught by his father, Jacques-Jules, he employed traditional forms, but his genius lay in the choice of forms and their arrangement. First architect of the king, Gabriel was responsible for the Ecole Militaire, for which he designed many projects from 1750 on, and for work at Versailles, Fontainebleau, and the Louvre. The publication of Le Roy's book on the ruins of Greece coincided with Gabriel's adoption of a purer, more "Greek" style, first expressed in the Petit Trianon. His efforts were always toward simplicity, renouncing the picturesque effects and extravagant details of the preceding generation. His prominent position in the Academy extended his influence. *See* PETIT TRIANON, VERSAILLES.

BIBLIOGRAPHY. Comte de Fels, *Ange-Jacques Gabriel, premier architecte du roi*, Paris, 1912.

GABRIEL, JACQUES-JULES. French architect (1667–1742). He lived in Paris. A pupil of Jules-Hardouin Mansart, he replaced De Cotte in 1734 as first architect of the king. More an engineer than an architect, Gabriel constructed many of the bridges in Paris as well as many buildings, and is now best known for his role in transmitting Mansart's training to his son, Ange-Jacques.

GABRIELINO INDIANS. The Gabrielino (Gabrieliño) Indians, neighbors of the Chumash, lived in pre-European times in Los Angeles County and on the Channel Islands off the California coast. Their small steatite carvings of

Ange-Jacques Gabriel, Petit Trianon, Versailles, garden façade.

marine subjects are notable for their simplified naturalism and excellent finish.

See also CHUMASH INDIANS; NORTH AMERICAN INDIAN ART (CALIFORNIA).

BIBLIOGRAPHY. G. G. Heye, *Certain Artifacts from San Miguel Island, California*, New York, 1921; D. B. Rogers, *Prehistoric Man of the Santa Barbara Coast*, Santa Barbara, Calif., 1929.

GABRON, WILLEM. Flemish painter of still life (b. Antwerp, 1619; d. there, 1678). The artist traveled for many years in Italy, and adapted Willem Claesz. Heda's style of breakfast pieces to Italian developments. Gabron's major work, a still life signed and dated 1652, is in the Herzog-Anton-Ulrich Museum in Brunswick, Germany.

BIBLIOGRAPHY. F. J. van den Branden, *Geschiedenis der Antwerpsche Schilderschool*, Antwerp, 1883.

GABUN (Gabon), *see* AFRICA, PRIMITIVE ART OF (CENTRAL AFRICA).

GADDI, AGNOLO. Italian painter of the Florentine school (fl. after 1369; d. 1396). Agnolo Gaddi was the son and pupil of Taddeo Gaddi. On his father's death Agnolo's moral education, according to Vasari, was entrusted to Jacopo da Casentino; for instruction in painting he was sent to Giovanni da Milano.

In 1369 Agnolo was working in the Vatican, apparently as an assistant to his brother Giovanni. There are records of several payments made to Agnolo for the design of reliefs for the Loggia dei Lanzi in Florence (1383, 1384, 1386) and of statues for the Cathedral of Florence (1387, 1389, 1395) and also for gilding and painting statues for the latter (1390). In 1394 and 1396 he was paid for the cartoons for stained-glass windows in the Cathedral.

Agnolo's only documented work on panel is the altarpiece with *SS. Giovanni Gualberto and Miniato and Scenes from the Passion* (Florence, Chapel of the Crucifix, S. Miniato al Monte), begun in 1393 and left unfinished at his death. His frescoes in the Cappella della Cintola in the Cathedral of Prato, the *Story of the Virgin and Her Girdle*, were painted from 1392 to 1395. The other fresco cycle traditionally attributed to Agnolo, the *Legend of the True Cross* in the choir of Sta Croce, Florence, is thought to have been painted about 1380. Both fresco cycles were executed with the help of assistants.

Many panel paintings have been attributed to Agnolo, though there is a wide variety of opinions regarding the exact extent of his *oeuvre*. The panels on which there is general agreement include the *Madonna of Mercy* (Florence, Academy), *Assumption of the Virgin* (Rome, Vatican Museums), *Mystic Marriage of St. Catherine* (Philadelphia Museum of Art), *Coronation of the Virgin* (London, National Gallery), *Crucifix* (Sesto Fiorentino, S. Martino), *Crucifixion* (Florence, Uffizi), *Pentecost* (Fiesole, Bandini Museum), *Last Supper* (Altenberg, Lindenau Museum), and *SS. Michael, James, and Julian* (New Haven, Yale University Art Gallery).

Agnolo's style is the last direct descendant, through his father, Taddeo, of the tradition of Giotto, though it was influenced by his contacts with sculptors, as is suggested by the sharpness, brilliance, and clarity in his shaping of relief by means of color and value. His work has been considered the purest example of the technique of Giottesque painting as it is described by Cennino Cennini. In his frescoes Agnolo often shows a marked inventiveness in illusionistic effects.

BIBLIOGRAPHY. R. van Marle, *The Development of the Italian Schools of Painting*, vol. 3, The Hague, 1924; R. Salvini, *L'arte di Agnolo Gaddi*, Florence, 1936.

HELLMUT WOHL

GADDI, GADDO (Gaddo di Zanobi). Italian painter and mosaicist (ca. 1250/59–ca. 1327/30). He was the father of Taddeo Gaddi and the first of the Gaddi family, which was prominent in Florentine painting for more than a century. Vasari states that Gaddo was seventy-three years old in 1312, while documentary evidence implies that he lived until 1327/30. Further information given by Vasari states that Gaddo and Cimabue were friends, that he was a contemporary of Giotto and a fellow worker of Andrea Tafi, who worked on the mosaics in the Baptistery, Florence. Vasari also informs us that Gaddo was called to Rome by Clement V in 1308 and makes various arbitrary attributions to Gaddo in Rome, Arezzo, Pisa, and Florence.

Although there have been serious attempts to identify Gaddo with the Isaac Master, the most recent scholarly evidence attributes to Giotto the Assisi frescoes in question. Gaddo has been credited with the mosaic *Coronation of the Virgin* in the Cathedral in Florence (1282–ca. 1290), medallions of saints in S. Maria Maggiore in Rome (1297), and the façade mosaics of the founding of S. Maria Maggiore (1298–1300). In the Florence Baptistery mosaics that may reasonably be attributed to Gaddo, he works in a massive Byzantine style that reflects the influence of Cimabue. *See* ISAAC MASTER.

BIBLIOGRAPHY. F. J. Mather, *The Isaac Master: A Reconstruction of the Work of Gaddo Gaddi*, Princeton, 1932; M. Meiss, *Giotto and Assisi*, New York, 1960.

DONALD NOLAN

GADDI, TADDEO. Italian painter of the Florentine school (ca. 1300–66). He was the son of Gaddo Gaddi and the father of Agnolo Gaddi. Taddeo was the most constant and close follower of Giotto, by whom he was trained and with whom he is said to have been in collaboration for twenty-four years. He is generally thought to have been an assistant to Giotto on the altarpiece of the *Coronation of the Virgin* (Florence, Medici Chapel, Sta Croce) and was perhaps chiefly responsible for its execution.

In 1332 Taddeo received the commission to decorate the Baroncelli Chapel in Sta Croce with frescoes of scenes from the *Life of the Virgin*. Finished in 1338, these large compositions show that while he retained Giotto's method for the shaping of individual forms, Taddeo departed from it in his tendency to multiply and proliferate his figural, architectural, and background repertoire. A highly finished silverpoint drawing of the *Presentation of the Virgin* (Paris, Louvre) is perhaps a study for (or after) the fresco of this subject in the Baroncelli Chapel. In September, 1334, Taddeo completed the portable triptych of the *Crucifixion, Nativity, and Other Scenes* (Berlin, former State Museums) in which he shows a certain affinity with the art of Bernardo Daddi.

In 1340 and 1341 Taddeo was working in S. Miniato al Monte, Florence, and in S. Francesco, Pisa. In 1353 he was awarded the commission for a large polyptych, *Ma-*

Agnolo Gaddi, *The Resurrection of Drusiana*, from the fresco cycle *Legend of the True Cross*, in the choir of Sta Croce, Florence.

donna and Child with Saints (Pistoia, S. Giovanni Fuorcivitas). His last dated work is the *Madonna and Child* (1355; Florence, Uffizi).

In 1359, 1363, and 1366 he was a member of a commission of artists named by the board of the Florentine Cathedral workshops. In 1363 he received a payment for a fresco (now lost) in the Mercanzia. His works on panel are believed to include a series of quatrefoils with scenes from the *Life of Christ* and the *Legend of St. Francis* painted for the cupboard door in the sacristy of Sta Croce (now in the Florentine Academy, with panels also in Berlin and Munich). These show particularly well the close relationship between painting and relief sculpture at this time (in fact, both Taddeo's master, Giotto, and his son and pupil, Agnolo, worked as designers of sculpture).

One of Taddeo's most remarkable works, painted near the end of his life, is the somber and impressive recently cleaned *Pietà* (New Haven, Yale University Art Gallery). The beautiful and grave *Madonna and Child* (Florence, S. Lorenzo alle Rose) is from the same period. Other works

by Taddeo are in New York (Metropolitan Museum), Bern, Pisa, and elsewhere.

BIBLIOGRAPHY. O. Sirén, *Giotto and Some of His Followers*, 2 vols., Cambridge, Mass., 1917; R. van Marle, *The Development of the Italian Schools of Painting*, vol. 3, The Hague, 1924; R. Offner, *Studies in Florentine Painting*, New York, 1927; J. White, *Art and Architecture in Italy, 1250–1400*, Baltimore, 1966.

HELLMUT WOHL

GADDO DI ZANOBI, see GADDI, GADDO.

GADROONS, FALSE. Western term used at one time to describe the variant forms of the lotus-petal design when employed as a decorative motif around borders by the Chinese. Sometimes the forms are simply called gadroons, the reference being to the similar notched or carved molding found in the West.

GAEL (Gaal), BARENT. Dutch genre, landscape, and animal painter (b. Haarlem, 1630s; d. Amsterdam? after 1681). He painted numerous works, which he usually signed, showing the influence of his teacher, Philips Wouwermans. Gael collaborated with Isaak Koene and Jan Wijnants. Gael's landscapes are close to the style of Claes Molenaer and Roelof van Vries.

BIBLIOGRAPHY. W. Bernt, *Die niederländischen Maler des 17. Jahrhunderts...*, vol. 1, Munich, 1948.

GAESBEECK, ADRIAEN VAN. Dutch painter of genre and portraits (b. Leyden, 1621/22; d. there, 1650). In 1636, at the age of fourteen, Gaesbeeck enrolled at Leyden University. His name appears again in the university records in 1649. He was recorded in Leyden in 1644 and entered the Leyden painters' guild in that year. His painting *Gerrit Dou's Studio* (Amsterdam, Rijksmuseum) suggests that he studied with Dou. Gaesbeeck's work is also influenced by the color and dark-and-light patterns of Rembrandt.

BIBLIOGRAPHY. Leyden, Stedelijk Museum, *De Lakenhal*, 2d ed., Leyden, 1951.

GAETANO, IL, see PULZONE, SCIPIONE.

GAG, WANDA. American printmaker, author, and illustrator (1893–1946). Born in New Ulm, Minn., she studied in St. Paul and Minneapolis and at the Art Students League in New York City. Gág wrote and illustrated a number of books, including *Millions of Cats* (1928). Her lithographs and woodcuts, often drawn in a rhythmic style, depict material with a folk-tale quality.

BIBLIOGRAPHY. W. Gág, *Growing Pains*, New York, 1940.

GAGGINI, ANTONELLO. Italian sculptor (b. Palermo, 1478; d. there, 1536). The leading Sicilian sculptor of his day, he worked in Messina (1498–1508) and Palermo (1509–36), where he created many monumental works in a style approaching that of the High Renaissance, characterized by massive forms, voluminous draperies, and pliant sentimentality. In his major work, sculptural decorations for the tribune of the Palermo Cathedral, he directed the creation of seventy-five figures and many reliefs, a number of them now in the National Museum of Sicily, Palermo.

Taddeo Gaddi, *Madonna and Child*, 1355. Uffizi, Florence.

GAGGINI (Gagini), BELTRAME. Italian sculptor (fl. Genoa; d. ca. 1476). Gaggini, from Bissone in Lombardy, is known principally as the father of a family of artisans who in the course of the 15th and 16th centuries migrated to the south of Italy and to France and Spain, where they carried the new Renaissance style.

GAGGINI, DOMENICO, see GAGINI, DOMENICO.

GAGGINI, GIOVANNI. Italian sculptor (b. Bissone; d. 1517). Active in Genoa after 1449, Giovanni worked with his father, Domenico Gagini, until the latter's departure from Genoa in 1465. Giovanni is particularly known for his architectural sculpture, the principal examples of which are doorway frames made for Genoese palaces. The reliefs are shallow-cut, delicate, and harmonious renderings of decorative motifs and religious scenes in a sophisticated early Renaissance style.

GAGGINI, PACE. Italian sculptor (fl. 1493–1522). A brother of Giovanni Gaggini, Pace was also an architectural sculptor. He worked on the façade of the Certosa of Pavia (1493), with Antonio Tamagnini in Genoa, with Rivarolo (1497), and on commissions for the French (1506–07). His style is coarser and less harmonious than that of his brother.

GAGINI (Gaggini), DOMENICO. Italian sculptor (fl. Genoa and Palermo; d. Palermo, 1492). He was the father of Giovanni and Pace Gaggini. In 1448 Gagini was received by the Cathedral of Genoa as master of marble carving, and from 1448 to 1465 he worked on the façade for the Chapel of St. John the Baptist in the Cathedral. In 1465 he went to Palermo, where he was active from 1468 on in a workshop that evidently specialized in sculpture for export. Gagini was perhaps influenced by Francesco Laurana, and it is possible that the two were partners. Gagini's style is Gothic with a heightened psychological feeling, as in the Solemi baptismal font (1468).

BIBLIOGRAPHY. G. di Marzo, *I Gagini e la scultura in Sicilia nei secoli XV e XVI*, 2 vols., Palermo, 1880–83; A. Venturi, *Storia dell'arte italiana*, vol. 6, Milan, 1908; M. Accascina, "Aggiunte a Domenico Gagini," *Bollettino d'arte*, XLIV, 1959.

GAGNON, CLARENCE A. Canadian painter (1881–1942). He studied under William Brymner in Montreal, where he later settled. He was in Paris in 1904–05, and then traveled extensively in Europe and came under the influence of the work of J. W. Morrice. Gagnon painted French-Canadian landscapes in oil and illustrated French-Canadian literature.

BIBLIOGRAPHY. A. H. Robson, *Clarence A. Gagnon*, Toronto, 1938.

GAI, ANTONIO. Italian sculptor (b. Venice, 1686; d. there, 1769). The foliate grillwork of Gai's bronze gates for the Loggetta in Venice, as well as his portrait busts, exhibits a fussy classicism and a predilection for expressive surface effects.

GAILLARD, RENE. French engraver and etcher (b. ca. 1719; d. Paris, 1790). He was erroneously called Robert Gaillard in old bibliographies. René Gaillard produced a considerable number of portraits, historical subjects, and landscapes. His earliest work is dated 1749 and, like most of his early prints, is in small format of poor quality. When he took up a large format, he developed a distinguished delicate style that successfully imitated the soft flesh tones of the French portraitists whom he copied. The works of Schenau succeeded those of Boucher as primary models for these portraits. Gaillard also produced landscapes and historical prints.

BIBLIOGRAPHY. R. Portalis and H. Béraldi, *Les Graveurs du dix-huitième siècle*, Paris, 3 vols., 1880–82.

GAILLON, CHATEAU OF. Elaborate Renaissance château in northern France, Department of Eure. It was built between 1501 and 1509 on the irregular foundations of the 13th-century fortress (demolished by the English in 1424). Gaillon was constructed for Cardinal Georges d'Amboise, a famous minister of Louis XII; the design of its first building stage was influenced by the late Gothic châteaux of the Loire region. In the second phase of its building, Italian workmen were employed to enrich the courtyards with loggias and carved panels in the classical style of the Renaissance. Painting and fine relief sculpture, including Michel Colombe's *St. George* (Paris, Louvre), ornamented the chapel. The château was surrounded by elegant and extensive formal gardens. Since the château was largely destroyed during the Revolution and subsequently remodeled, its previous splendor can only be studied in the Du Cerceau drawing of the estate. Two of its Italian fountains and some other fragments still survive, as well as a great gate with short, flat pilasters and a classical entablature and balustrade ornamenting its severe surface.

BIBLIOGRAPHY. E. Chirol, *Le Château de Gaillon*, Rouen, 1952; A. Blunt, *Art and Architecture in France, 1500–1700*, Baltimore, 1954; R. Dutton, *The Châteaux of France*, London, 1957.

EMMA N. PAPERT

GAINSBOROUGH, THOMAS. English painter (b. Sudbury, Suffolk, 1727; d. London, 1788). In 1740 he went to London to study painting and remained there until 1748. His closest associations were with two older artists, Francis Hayman and the French engraver Hubert Gravelot; Gainsborough may have been apprenticed to Gravelot. The work of these two artists, together with Gainsborough's own devotion to Dutch landscape painting (especially the pictures of Wijnants and Jacob van Ruisdael), supplied the components of his early style. Landscapes figure prominently among his first paintings, and he retained a strong inclination toward this art form throughout his life, although the bulk of his work is portraiture.

On his return to Suffolk, Gainsborough settled in Ipswich. There he built up a practice in portraiture, specializing in the small-scale full-length portrait of the conversation-piece variety. In this he followed closely the form established by Hayman, but always with a distinctive touch of poetry and elegance that probably reflects the influence of 18th-century French art channeled through Gravelot. The masterpiece of Gainsborough's Ipswich period is the portrait of Mr. and Mrs. Robert Andrews (London, National Gallery).

In 1759 Gainsborough moved to Bath, where he remained until 1774. Even before leaving Suffolk he had abandoned the conversation-piece portrait to concentrate on full-scale heads and half-length portraits. In Bath the full-scale portrait, which later was extended to full-length size, became his primary concern, and he gradually perfected this form. The major artistic influence in accomplishing the transformation was the work of Van Dyck. In landscape, too, new influences made themselves felt during the 1760s when Gainsborough studied Rubens; richer color and greater formal complexity resulted in his own work.

In 1768 he was invited to become a founder-member of the new Royal Academy of Arts in London, but his relations with the Academy were rather stormy. He quarreled openly with the hanging committee concerning the display of his paintings at the 1773 and 1784 exhibitions, and he ceased to exhibit at the Academy after 1784. In 1774 he moved to London, where he remained for the rest of his life. He and Reynolds were acknowledged as the foremost portrait painters of the day, and Gainsborough received a large number of commissions. Although he now devoted more and more of his time to portraiture, he continued to paint landscapes. These, however, became increasingly detached from direct observation of nature and were more idealized and poetic in character.

In his later years Gainsborough gave considerable attention to what he and his contemporaries called "fancy pictures," mildly sentimental genre subjects, usually bucolic in character but with figures definitely dominating the landscape. He attached great importance to these works, charging more for them than for landscapes or portraits.

Gainsborough has remained one of the perennially attractive figures in British art, in contrast to his contemporary rival Reynolds. Gainsborough was a more spontaneous painter, and his compositions, though effective, are much less sophisticated and complicated. The range of characterization in his portraits is more restricted, but he excels in simple control of the medium and sheer beauty in manipulation of paint on canvas. For Gainsborough the painting itself as a sensually appealing and decoratively attractive object always comes first.

His paintings are widely scattered in public and private collections throughout Great Britain and America. The great vogue for British portraits at the beginning of the 20th century brought many fine Gainsboroughs to the United States, particularly the large, full-length canvases of his maturity. Probably the most spectacular collection is in the Henry E. Huntington Library and Art Gallery, San Marino, Calif., the home of Gainsborough's best-known painting, the *Blue Boy*. In England the major concentrations are in London, in the National Gallery, the Tate Gallery, and the Royal Collection.

Gainsborough's drawings are among the most attractive produced by any British painter. Occasionally the drawings may be directly related to paintings, but more often they are completely independent works of art, executed for the artist's own pleasure. Landscapes predominate over figure studies. The technique is usually free and open; the strong rhythmic quality evident in all Gainsborough's work is even more pronounced here than in his paintings. There are fine groups of his drawings in the British Museum, London, and in the Morgan Library, New York.

BIBLIOGRAPHY. W. T. Whitley, *Thomas Gainsborough*, London, 1915; M. Woodall, *Gainsborough's Landscape Drawings*, London, 1939; E. K. Waterhouse, *Gainsborough*, London, 1958.

ROBERT R. WARK

Thomas Gainsborough, *Talk in a Park*. Louvre, Paris. An English variant of the rococo style.

GAKU. Japanese term for a horizontal tablet painted with a pictorial or calligraphic subject and hung against an open transom over sliding doors. A *gaku* was sometimes placed high on a wall, or, in the interior, over the main entrance to a house or on a back wall facing the entrance. It was framed or bordered but not under glass.

GAKUO ZOKYU. Japanese priest-painter (fl. mid-15th cent.). Gakuō faithfully preserved the Shūbun style in ink landscape painting. Paintings bearing his signatures are most often done in rich, velvety ink varying in tone from dark black to soft gray, suggesting that he was also influenced by the works of Hsia Kuei of Sung China. *See* HSIA KUEI; SHUBUN.

GALATEA. Sea nymph in Greek mythology, the daughter of Nereus and Doris. According to Philoxenus and Theocritus, she was pursued by the one-eyed Cyclops Polyphemus, though she was in love with Acis. When Polyphemus killed Acis, Galatea turned the latter into the Sicilian river that bears his name. Galatea's story is popular in literature and art. The sea nymph Galatea should be differentiated from the Galatea in the legend of Pygmalion, king of Cyprus, who made a beautiful statue of a woman, Galatea. *See* PYGMALION.

GALBE. French term denoting curvature or contour, derived from the Italian word *galbo* or *garbo*. It can be used to delineate the entasis, or swell, of an architectural column or the silhouette of a capital or a console. It can also be employed to describe profile drawings of pottery that attempt to show the shape, curve, and outline of a particular piece. In addition, it has been applied to descriptions of the human profile, both bodily and facial.

Galilee. Type of porch usually located at a cathedral entrance.

GALGAL. Type of primitive, basically prehistoric, burial chamber consisting of a dolmen, or crude stone sepulchre, covered by a large mound of earth. In England it is known as a barrow; in archaeological terminology, tumulus. Galgals are found all over the world. *See* BARROW; DOLMEN; TUMULUS.

GALGARIO, FRA, *see* GHISLANDI, GIUSEPPE.

GALICIA, JOSE LUIS. Spanish painter and printmaker (1930–   ). He is the self-taught son and grandson of painters and one of the excellent Spanish printmakers, working in all techniques. His color lithographs are especially good. He has exhibited in many countries and now lives in his native Madrid.

GALILEE. Type of porch associated especially with English medieval churches. The galilee was usually placed at the entrance of a cathedral and was variously used as a chapel for penitents and as an accessory room.

GALILEI, ALESSANDRO. Italian architect (b. Florence, 1691; d. Rome, 1737). His first important work was the large, classicizing Corsini Chapel in St. John Lateran, Rome (1732–35), a Greek cross with dome whose baroque character derives solely from the soft polychromy and sculptural ornament. His chief commission, the façade of St. John Lateran (1733–36), came as the result of the greatest architectural competition held up to that time. Galilei had been in England, but the character of the façade is essentially Roman and severely classical at a time when a late baroque style was favored. Its antecedent is Maderno's façade for St. Peter's, but the relationship of mass to space has been reversed. His façade for S. Giovanni dei Fiorentini (1734) is comparatively *retardataire*. *See* LATERAN, THE, ROME (SAN GIOVANNI IN LATERANO).

BIBLIOGRAPHY. R. Wittkower, *Art and Architecture in Italy, 1600–1750*, Baltimore, 1958.

GALIMBERTI, FRANCESCO. Italian painter and engraver (b. Venice, 1755; d. Vienna, 1803). A follower of Tiepolo, he was prominently employed by Doge Michiel on frescoes and portraits. He also worked as an engraver, reproducing the works of other artists with Giovanni Dal Pian, with whom he moved to Vienna in 1797.

GALIZZI, GIOVANNI. Italian painter (fl. 1543–65). He lived in Venice but was active in country churches near his native Bergamo. His altarpieces of 1543 and 1547 are remarkable parallels, with provincial schematization, of the sketchy and colorful style of the young Tintoretto.

BIBLIOGRAPHY. B. Berenson, *The Venetian Painters of the Renaissance*, 3d ed., New York, 1897.

GALLA PLACIDIA, MAUSOLEUM OF, RAVENNA. Traditional name for a mid-5th-century Italian building, perhaps originally an Oratory of St. Lawrence. It stands next to S. Vitale and contains Early Christian mosaics of the highest importance. In plan the building forms a cross; at the intersection of the arms of the cross rises a square tower within which there is a domical vault. The exterior walls of the cross arms are treated with blank arcades

Mausoleum of Galla Placidia, Ravenna. Lunette mosaic of Jesus the Good Shepherd, mid-5th century.

foreshadowing later medieval styles. The interior is intimately scaled, fairly dim yet luminous. This effect is achieved because the vertical walls are sheathed in colored marbles and the vaults with mosaics of colored glass and gold. Sarcophagi, one traditionally that of the late Roman empress Galla Placidia, are placed in three of the four arms of the cross. These arms are barrel-vaulted; all point toward and open into the higher, domed central space.

The mosaics are undimmed by time. The barrel vaults are sheathed in gloriously rich colors defining forms that imitate the starry firmament and the living, growing things of the earth. The half-circular panels, or lunettes, formed by the barrel vaults and their end walls are decorated with representations in mosaic of martyrs and of Jesus the Good Shepherd. In the latter a youthful Christ, clad in robes of gold and blue, is seated in a schematized and idealized landscape somewhat reminiscent of landscapes in Hellenistic-Roman wall paintings. Christ holds a golden staff in the shape of a cross, and on either side of Him three sheep regard His face. On the four side walls of the central tower are pairs of apostles at whose feet are chalices, fountains, and doves. In the highest vault, that of the central dome, the symbols of the four Evangelists appear in the lower corners where the dome rises from the square tower. Above them are concentric rings of eight-pointed stars encircling a golden cross.

The visual effect of all this is desubstantiation of the physical reality of the building. The marbles and, particularly, the mosaics reflect and return the light; the walls and vaults become sheaths of color. In program, the building clearly shows an important step in the gradual development of the Byzantine system of a graded, hierarchical presentation of symbols and figures, with the most important and efficacious elements in the highest positions. In this sense, the mosaics of Galla Placidia are somewhat tentative, but as works of art they are bold and powerful.

BIBLIOGRAPHY. A. Grabar, *Byzantine Painting*, Geneva, 1953; G. Bovini, *Chiese di Ravenna*, Novara, 1957; F. W. Deichmann, *Frühchristliche Bauten und Mosaiken von Ravenna*, Baden-Baden, 1958.
WILLIAM L. MACDONALD

GALLATIN, ALBERT EUGENE. American painter, collector, and writer (b. Villanova, Pa., 1881; d. New York City, 1952). He studied law briefly. Gallatin's interest in art in general, and later in abstract painting in particular, led him to establish in 1927 the Gallery of Living Art at New York University, a museum that pioneered in the exhibition of 20th-century painting. The collection was moved to the Philadelphia Museum of Art in 1943. Gallatin's nonobjective paintings derive from constructivism and the careful balance and composition of cubist still lifes, for example, *Composition* (1942; Philadelphia Museum of Art). Among his writings are monographs on Whistler, Beardsley, Vermeer, Lachaise, Demuth, and Braque.

BIBLIOGRAPHY. A. E. Gallatin, *Paintings*, New York, 1948.

GALLE, PHILIP. Dutch engraver and print publisher (b. Haarlem, 1537; d. Antwerp, 1612). As an engraver for the Antwerp publisher Hieronymus Cock, and as an independent printmaker and publisher, Galle made engravings after the work of Pieter Brueghel as well as such Italianized Flemings as Frans Floris, Maerten van Heemskerck, Maerten de Vos, and Jan van der Straet. Galle's engravings show delicate and dense linear schemes.

GALLE FAMILY. Flemish engravers and print publishers (fl. 17th cent.). Making their headquarters in Antwerp for over 125 years, this family engraved and published an enormous number of prints. Philip Galle was the oldest member of the family. His elder son, Theodore (ca. 1571–1633), continued the publication of Jan van der Straet's drawings. Philip's younger son, Cornelis I (b. Antwerp, 1576; d. there, 1633), preferred to engrave after Rubens. *Judith Beheading Holofernes*, after a Rubens painting of about 1600 (now lost), is his chief work. He also engraved after Van Dyck, Agostino and Annibale Carracci, Guido Reni, and others. Theodore's son Johannes (b. Antwerp, 1600; d. there, 1676) contributed least to the graphic production of the family. Cornelis II (b. Antwerp, 1615; d. there, 1678), son of Cornelis I, made over 300 prints, including many portraits after Rubens, Van Dyck, and Velázquez. *See* GALLE, PHILIP.

GALLEGOS (Gallego), FERNANDO. Spanish painter (fl. 1467–1507). Following Jorge Inglés, Gallegos is the first satisfactorily documented artist who employed the Hispano-Flemish style in Castile. He is, however, not a mere imitator; he imposes a unique, interpretative quality upon the style. The highly subjective note in his work is usually referred to as a Spanish attribute; certainly it creates a mood of fervent spirituality that is characteristic of his countrymen.

In two signed but undated works agreed to be of his extreme youth, a *Crucifixion* and a *Pietà* (Madrid, Weibel Collection) primitivistic distortion of the figures is redeemed by technical precision and harmoniously patterned panoramic landscapes. He made rapid progress thereafter, as demonstrated in the undated *Enthroned Virgin and Child*, the central panel of a triptych in the St. Anthony Chapel of the New Cathedral, Salamanca. It is believed that he executed this work shortly after the 1467 *Altarpiece of S. Ildefonso* in the Zamora Cathedral. It would thus appear that in his late twenties he achieved an impressively mature manner imbued with a grave dignity. The Christ Child is still somewhat wooden. However, in the monumental figure of the Madonna, Gallegos has captured the essence of matronly beatitude; her head is reminiscent of Botticelli's Venus.

There are many paintings associated with his workshop in which Gallegos must have personally intervened. Notable among them are the *Main Altarpiece of S. Lorenzo* (ca. 1500; Toro Cathedral) and the *Via Crucis* and *Last Judgment* (ca. 1480–88; Richmond, Cook Collection), both from the Cathedral of Ciudad Rodrigo.

Francisco Gallegos, either a brother or son of Fernando and probably his collaborator, continued the style. In 1503 Pedro Bello painted wings for the Zamora altarpiece of Fernando Gallegos in a weak imitation of the master. *See* GALLEGOS, FRANCISCO.

BIBLIOGRAPHY. C. R. Post, *A History of Spanish Painting*, vol. 10, Cambridge, Mass., 1950; E. Lafuente Ferrari, *Breve historia de la pintura española*, 4th ed., Madrid, 1953.

EILEEN A. LORD

GALLEGOS (Gallego), FRANCISCO. Spanish painter (fl. early 16th cent.). He was either the son or the brother of Fernando Gallegos and probably collaborated with him at times. Francisco's only documented work is the *Altarpiece of S. Catalina* in the Old Cathedral, Salamanca. His work, which is much weaker than Fernando's, is garish in color and features rather squat figures, some almost caricatures.

BIBLIOGRAPHY. J. A. Gaya Nuño, *Fernando Gallego*, Madrid, 1958.

GALLERY. Architectural term with several definitions; it may be any long, narrow room or a covered, often arcaded, passageway. Long, narrow passageways connecting different parts of a building, particularly in Elizabethan and Jacobean houses, are called galleries. The long gallery, a room extending the entire length of one side of a house or palace, and usually facing the gardens, was particularly popular in 17th- and 18th-century France and England (Hatfield House, Hertfordshire; Galerie des Glaces, Versailles). Long rooms used to display works of art (Farnese Gallery in the Farnese Palace, Rome) are the forerunners of modern exhibition galleries. Balconies overlooking a large room, sometimes used to accommodate musicians, and covered, arcaded passageways along a street may also be referred to as galleries. In church architecture galleries are the passageways over the side aisles; such passages under the eaves are known as dwarf galleries. Open, arcaded galleries also appear on church exteriors, particularly in medieval Italian and German churches.

GALLI FAMILY, *see* BIBIENA FAMILY.

GALLINA, LODOVICO. Italian portrait and religious painter (b. Brescia, 1752; d. Venice, 1787). He began as a pupil of A. Dusi in Brescia, and then went to the Academy in Venice (1770), where he studied with A. Zucchi and F. Maggiotto, won first prize for a copy after Titian (1774), and later became a member (1784). Though he did various religious frescoes, he is noted particularly for his many fashionable portraits.

GALLO, GIOVANNI. Italian graphic artist (fl. Lombardy, 16th cent.). He is known for three colored woodcuts, after designs by Marco Pino, which are signed "Johannes Gallus": *Descent from the Cross, Holy Family,* and *Perseus as Slayer of Medusa.* Some scholars have identified Gallo as the Lyons artist Jean Salomon, and Nagler has attributed a number of other woodcuts to him.

BIBLIOGRAPHY. G. K. Nagler, *Die Monogrammisten...*, repr., vol. 2, Nieuwkoop, 1966.

GALLO-ROMAN STYLE. Opulent and highly civilized style of ancient Gaul during the period of Roman rule. The fusing of Celtic imagination with Rome's classical heritage resulted in an art often called provincial Roman. It imitated Rome in the construction of its buildings and aqueducts and in the sculpture and mosaics used for decoration. The Gallic or Celtic tradition is more evident in small bronze statuettes or bronze jewelry with enamels.

BIBLIOGRAPHY. O. Brogan, *Roman Gaul*, Cambridge, Mass., 1953; M. Pobe, *The Art of Roman Gaul*, Toronto, 1961.

GALQUE, ADRIAN SANCHEZ, *see* SANCHEZ, ADRIAN.

GALUCCI, NICCOLO D'ANDREA DI PASQUALE, *see* NICCOLO DA GUARDIAGRELE.

GAMARRA, JOSE. Uruguayan abstract painter (1934–   ). Born in Tacuarembó, José Gamarra studied in Montevideo and Rio de Janeiro, and has lived in São Paulo and Paris. He has exhibited widely (for example, at the Biennial of Young Artists in Paris in 1963). He paints impasto abstract signs on toned grounds, suggesting neolithic art.

GAMBARA, LATTANZIO. Italian painter of Brescia (1530–74). A pupil and son-in-law of Romanino, he was more influenced by Antonio Campi, echoing his standardized Parmigianinesque mannerism. A successful artist, he produced various fresco cycles, notably in the nave of Parma Cathedral.

GAMBIER ISLANDS, *see* OCEANIC ART (POLYNESIA).

GAMBREL. Roof comparable to a gable type, but having its slope broken so that the lower sides are steeper than the upper ones. The steeper slope is sometimes curved. Common in early American architecture, the gambrel is associated with 18th-century Dutch colonial houses. Examples were also to be found in the colonies in the 17th century, presumably derived from English sources.

GAMITZER FAMILY, *see* JAMNITZER FAMILY.

GAND, *see* GHENT.

GANDARA, ANTOINE DE LA. French painter and graphic artist (b. Paris, 1862; d. there, 1917). He studied with Gérôme from 1876 to 1881. Gandara painted landscapes and Parisian scenes, but he was most popular for his cool-toned aristocratic portraits.

GANDHARA. A region, not precisely defined, in modern Pakistan and northeastern Afghanistan. It consisted principally of the valley of the Kabul River, from the Khyber Pass eastward to the Indus River, and of nearby parts of the Indus River Valley; and it included at times additional areas around the Indus River and the hilly districts of Swat and Buner, all now in Pakistan, and the valley of the Kabul River west of the Khyber Pass in Afghanistan. The region is famous for its ancient Buddhist art, particularly its sculpture.

Gandhāra lay on the ancient trade route between India and the West, which brought not only economic prosperity but also repeated invasions from the West and from north India. It appears first in recorded history as part of the Achaemenid empire. Gandhāra fell to Alexander the Great in his campaign of 327–326 B.C., and then it was successively dominated by Alexander's successor, Seleucis, the Mauryas of India, the Bactrian Greeks, the Sakas (Scythians), the Parthians, and the Kushans. Some Parthian remains have been found, but the bulk of the art is from the Kushan period, from the 1st century A.D. until the region was overrun and laid waste by the White Huns about 460. The art which developed in Gandhāra combined, iconographically and stylistically, elements from both India and the West.

The Western element in Gandhāran art was formerly thought to have stemmed from a Greek heritage implanted in the region by Alexander's occupation, and the sculpture became known as Greco-Buddhist. More recent studies have shown that the major Western influence actually came from the art of the contemporary Roman world, primarily as it existed in the eastern Roman provinces. This Roman provincial art retained a Hellenistic legacy, which helps to account for the Greek element in Gandhāran art.

Unfortunately, practically all the examples of Gandhāran sculpture scattered throughout the world are without records of locale or of associations among themselves or with other objects. Reign dates inscribed on a few objects are not readily converted into the Gregorian calendar. Consequently, there are many differing viewpoints concerning the chronological arrangement within the Kushan period of the various types of Gandhāran sculpture.

The most extensive excavations have been those of Sir John Marshall at a number of sites in the vicinity of the ancient city of Taxila, 20 miles northwest of modern Rawalpindi. The most important are at Sirkap and Jandial. At Sirkap, dating from pre-Kushan and early Kushan times, there are the foundations of a royal palace, a large conglomerate of rooms containing the king's quarters, a harem, and an audience chamber, and the so-called Shrine of the Double Eagle, a square stūpa base decorated with engaged columns and relief niches of three types, a Greek pediment, a chaitya hall, and a torana. At Jandial, of the Parthian period, there is an interesting temple with a flat roof and a central tower, which was probably a Zoroastrian fire temple.

There are other significant examples of Gandhāran architecture at two sites near Peshawar: at Takhti-i-Bāhi, the remains of a Buddhist vihāra, consisting of a series of open courts surrounded by cells for the monks, assembly halls, and a cluster of stūpas; and at Shāh-jī-kī-Dherī, the square base of an enormous stūpa, which originally contained a wooden tower rising to a height of 700 feet, built by the great Kushan ruler Kanishka. A relic box containing several inscriptions, which unfortunately do not fix its date, was found in the stūpa. *See* KANISHKA RELIQUARY.

There is another well-known reliquary, a round gold box found at Bimaran in Afghanistan, studded with rubies and decorated on the sides with figures in relief under arcades, in the manner of Roman sarcophagi from Asia Minor.

The sculpture of Gandhāra is Mahāyāna Buddhist, consisting mostly of full-round figures of the Buddha and Bodhisattvas and reliefs depicting scenes from the life of Buddha, his death and entrance into nirvāṇa (the *Mahāparinirvāṇa*), and the distribution of relics of Buddha. There are a few representations of Jātakas, of Indian deities such as Panchika and Hāritī, and of figures borrowed from the West, such as centaurs, river gods, and Atlantes. Most impressive are the full-round standing figures of Buddha, usually in the gesture of reassurance, heavily robed in the manner of Roman senators, haloed, the head sometimes reminiscent of the *Apollo Belvedere*, with a wavy topknot covering the ushnīsha; and mustached Bodhisattvas, heavyset, jeweled, and robed in the manner of a local raja. *See* MAHAYANA.

Gandhāra. Head of a monk, from Hadda, Afghanistan. Stucco. Musée Guimet, Paris.

All the sculpture, both relief and full-round, was used in conjunction with architecture, the full-round figures being placed in wall niches and the relief carvings forming wall panels and stair risers. The early sculpture was carved in a gray schist; after the 3d century, stucco replaced stone. Originally the sculpture was painted or gilded.

It has been suggested that the Buddha image had its origin in Gandhāra, as the result of a local, Greek-inspired taste for anthropomorphism, and that then the concept spread to the workshops of Mathurā and other parts of India. It is more likely that the Buddha image appeared simultaneously in Gandhāra and Mathurā as the result of the requirements of the increasingly popular Mahāyāna form of Buddhism.

Actually the art of Gandhāra had very little impact upon the art of India. Its greatest legacy was its contribution to the Buddhist art of Central Asia, China, and Japan, as the Mahāyāna phase of Buddhism was spread by missionaries and traders from Gandhāra, passing first through the Khyber Pass, then north over the mountains, and then eastward across the Tarim Basin and into China.

See also BAMIYAN.

BIBLIOGRAPHY. B. Rowland, "A Revised Chronology of Gandhāra Sculpture," *Art Bulletin*, XVIII, Sept., 1936; H. Buchtal, "The Western Aspects of Gandhāra Sculpture," *Proceedings of the British Academy*, XXXI, 1945; H. Deydier, *Contribution à l'étude de l'art du Gandhāra*, Paris, 1950; J. H. Marshall, *Taxila*, 3 vols., Cambridge, Eng., 1951; H. Ingholt, *Gandhāran Art in Pakistan*, New York, 1957; B. Rowland, *The Art and Architecture of India*, 2d ed., Baltimore, 1959; Asia Society, New York, *Gandhāra Sculpture from Pakistan Museums*, text by B. Rowland, 1960.

CHARLES D. WEBER

GANDHARVA. Heavenly singer or musician who attends the banquets of the Indian gods; depicted in Hindu art.

GANDOLFI FAMILY. Italian artists from Bologna (fl. Emilia, 18th–19th cent.). The painter and engraver Gaetano Gandolfi (1734–1802) was the leading member of the family. He studied with his brother, Ubalde (1728–81), and with Lelli and Menozzi in Bologna, and later came under the influence of Tiepolo in Venice. Noted as a brilliant colorist, he did many works in and around Bologna, including frescoes for the cupola of S. Maria della Vita. Gaetano's son, Mauro (1764–1834), primarily an engraver and water-colorist, gained great renown. He worked throughout Europe and, in 1816, visited the United States to engrave book illustrations for the American painter John Trumbull. Mauro's son, Democrito (1797–1874), was a sculptor.

GANESA. Elephant-headed son of the gods Siva and Pārvatī. Ganeśa, whose name means "Lord of Hosts," is the Hindu god of wisdom, remover of obstacles, and patron of writers. He is often depicted with four arms holding the attributes of a rosary, a rice bowl, an elephant goad, and his own severed tusk. His mount is a rat.

GANGA. Hindu goddess of the sacred Ganges (Gangā) River.

GANGHOFER, JORG. German architect (d. 1488). Jörg Ganghöfer was appointed municipal architect of Munich in 1468 and in that year began work on the Frauenkirche. Its roof was more or less in place by 1478, but it was not completed until after Ganghöfer's death. His approach to architecture was that of a builder. The Frauenkirche is a hall church with three naves. It is completely plain inside as well as outside.

GANJIN IN TOSHODAIJI, NARA. Japanese lacquer sculpture (8th cent.). One of the finest portrait sculptures of Japan, it represents the Chinese T'ang priest Chien-chên (Japanese, Ganjin; d. 763), who initiated a proper ordination ceremony in Japan. After a series of unsuccessful attempts to reach Japan, he arrived there in 753, though by then he had become blind. The statue, done in hollow dry-lacquer technique, portrays him as an old, blind priest. The quiet execution of the facial features and drapery folds expresses his profound spiritual quality as well as his determination.

BIBLIOGRAPHY. Tokyo National Museum, *Pageant of Japanese Art*, vol. 3: *Sculpture*, Tokyo, 1952; *Masterpieces of Japanese Sculpture*, introd., text, and comment. by J. E. Kidder, Jr., Rutland, Vt., 1961.

GANKU. Japanese painter (1756–1838). He was largely self-taught, but his works show the influence of Shen Nanp'ing in the careful handling of depth, and of Okyo in the naturalistic representation of animal life. He founded the Kishi school of painting, which became a strong rival of the Maruyama and Shijō schools. See OKYO; SHEN CH'UAN (SHEN NAN-P'ING).

BIBLIOGRAPHY. R. T. Paine and A. Soper, *The Art and Architecture of Japan*, Baltimore, 1955.

GANO DA SIENA. Italian sculptor and architect (fl. early 14th cent.). A follower of Agostino di Giovanni and Agnolo di Ventura, he created two tombs in the Collegiate Church of S. Maria Assunta in Casole d'Elsa, near Siena.

These show, in a simplified and crude manner, the influence of Giovanni Pisano.

GANOSIS. Process used in the ancient world, especially in Greece, to protect the finish of painted sculpture from the injurious effects of light and weather. It employed a mixture of oil and fine wax. Frequent applications of this coating were made by highly trained artisans. In Rome, the technique was used for the waterproofing of painted wall surfaces.

BIBLIOGRAPHY. G. M. A. Richter, *The Sculpture and Sculptors of the Greeks*, rev. ed., New Haven, 1957.

GANYMEDE. Son of King Tros of Troy, a mythological youth whose beauty and grace attracted the love of Zeus. He was carried off to Olympus by the eagle of Zeus, or perhaps by the god himself in the form of an eagle. In ancient art, Ganymede is usually shown in his role of cupbearer, nude but for a Phrygian cap, and either being wooed or being transported by an eagle.

BIBLIOGRAPHY. G. M. A. Richter, *A Handbook of Greek Art*, London, 1959.

GARAVAGLIA, GIOVITA. Italian engraver (b. Pavia, 1790; d. Florence, 1835). A pupil of Faustino Anderloni, Garavaglia enjoyed academic and popular adulation during his lifetime; it culminated in his election as professor of engraving at the Florence Academy in 1833. Most of his plates are after Italian baroque painters, especially Reni.

BIBLIOGRAPHY. G. Campori, *Lettere artistiche inedite*, Modena, 1866.

GARAY, EPIFANIO. Colombian painter (b. Bogotá, 1849; d. Villeta, 1903). Garay studied in Paris with Bouguereau and others, and then returned to Colombia to help establish the national art school. His *oeuvre* consists of oil portraits (e.g., *Lady with a Fan*, 1893; Bogotá, National Museum), religious scenes, and murals.

BIBLIOGRAPHY. Academia Colombiana de Bellas Artes, *Iniciación de una guía de arte colombiano*, Bogotá, 1934.

GARBE, HERBERT. German sculptor (b. Berlin, 1888; d. France, 1945). He studied in the School of Applied Arts, Munich, and in the Berlin Academy. One of the leaders of the movement toward abstraction in German sculpture, he worked with the architect Mies van der Rohe in the 1920s.

GARBHAGRIHA (Garbha Grha). Sanskrit term meaning "womb chamber." It is the innermost shrine room within the tower of the Indo-Aryan type of Hindu temple.

GARBO, RAFFAELLINO DEL, see RAFFAELLINO DEL GARBO.

GARDELLA, IGNAZIO. Italian architect (1905–). Born in Milan, Gardella has been professionally active since the 1930s, during which time he designed a tuberculosis clinic in Alessandria (1935–38). One of his recent works is the imaginative dining and recreational hall of the Olivetti factory in Ivrea—a three-story hexagonal building nested into the side of a hill.

GARDEN OF LOVE. Oil painting by Rubens, in the State Art Collections (Picture Gallery), Dresden. *See* RUBENS, PETER PAUL.

GARDENS. Gardens, large and small, fall into one of two categories: formal and organic, or landscape, gardens. The purpose of the formal garden is to organize nature by laying out trees, bushes, shrubs, flowers, and paths along a regular, even geometric, and often enclosed plan. In the landscape garden, the elements of the garden are arranged as though they had grown there in a kind of accidental paradise. Both try to transfer nature to man's domain.

The formal garden is the older by more than a millennium; it first appeared in Egypt. The Babylonians advanced the formal garden by using terraces in the fabled Hanging Gardens. Greeks first made public gardens, and Romans continued the public and private formal garden on a broad scale. During the Middle Ages, the greatest innovations were made in the East, especially by the Byzantines and Arabs, who added fountains, ornamental trees, and bird cages. In the West the cloister and court gardens of the Middle Ages were transformed during the Renaissance into far more complex geometric schemes, which were part of a coordinated architecture of house and grounds. Later, the great baroque gardens of European nobility were less confined and were planned along vanishing lines (paths) that culminated in some particular point of interest. The gardens at Vaux-le-Vicomte, by Le Nôtre, exemplify the masterful coordination of separate gardens—some with grottoes, some with statuary, hedges, and so on—into an overall grand system. *See* VAUX-LE-VICOMTE, CHATEAU OF.

The organic or landscape garden was an 18th-century English development, an extension of certain ideas of English intellectuals, among them Pope and William Kent. The gardens at Chiswick House in London are in this tradition. In the 19th century, although no new concepts of the garden were developed, all forms were appreciated. During the 20th century there has been much Western interest in the Japanese garden, which achieves great beauty with economy of means and often with a spiritual approach. *See* JAPAN: ARCHITECTURE (MUROMACHI PERIOD; EDO PERIOD).

BIBLIOGRAPHY. M. L. Gothein, *Geschichte der Gartenkunst*, 2 vols., Jena, 1914; J. C. Shepherd and G. A. Jellicoe, *Italian Gardens of the Renaissance*, New York, 1925. JULIA M. EHRESMANN

GARDET, GEORGES. French sculptor (b. Paris, 1863; d. there, 1939). He studied in Paris with A. Millet and Frémiet and won fame as a sculptor of animals, which were often combined in compositions with human figures. He produced both decorative and monumental works, and several of his designs were executed in porcelain.

GARDNER (Isabella Stewart) MUSEUM, BOSTON, see BOSTON: MUSEUMS (ISABELLA STEWART GARDNER MUSEUM).

GARELLI, FRANCO. Italian sculptor (1909–). Born in Diano d'Alba, Garelli was trained as a doctor. He now teaches at the Albertina Academy of Fine Arts in Turin. One of his works decorates a modern building in Turin and is well integrated with the architecture. His abstract metal sculpture is dramatically composed of masses and voids.

GARGALLO, PABLO. Spanish sculptor (b. Mailla, 1881; d. Reus, 1934). Gargallo studied drawing and sculpture in Barcelona. He first visited Paris in 1906 and on his second visit in 1911 saw Picasso's cubist paintings. He in turn introduced Picasso to metal sculpture. In 1914 he returned to Barcelona, and in 1917 he was appointed to teach at the Escuela Superior de Artes Oficios. He stayed there until 1923, when he returned to Paris.

His early sculpture was realistic—for example, the head of Picasso in stone (1912; Barcelona Museum)—but his style changed when he turned to ironwork. Examples are *The Prophet* (1933; Paris, National Museum of Modern Art), which is a perforated bronze figure of solids and voids, and the wrought-iron *Picador* (1928; New York, Museum of Modern Art).

Gargallo is important as one of the first sculptors of the 20th century to work in iron.

BIBLIOGRAPHY. P. Courthion, *Gargallo, sculptures et dessins*, Paris, 1937; H. Read, *A Concise History of Modern Sculpture*, London, 1964.

GARGOYLE. Projecting waterspout, usually placed on the upper part of a building. Early medieval gargoyles were frequently simple open channels, but early-13th-century and later examples were elaborated into grotesque beasts and droll monsters, as in the Ste-Chapelle, Paris.

GARNIER, CHARLES. French architect (1825–98). He worked in Paris. Trained in the Ecole des Beaux-Arts, he won the Rome prize in 1848. A pupil of Louis Hippolyte Lebas and, briefly, of Viollet-le-Duc, he developed his interest in both Greek and Roman archaeology; although his creative work was not influenced by these studies, his writings include archaeological monographs.

His career began with his most important work, the Paris Opéra (1861–75). He was able to equal the baroque luxuriousness of this building only in his Casino at Monte Carlo of 1878. In both these works the neobaroque style exemplifies the taste for lavish display, ornamentation, and monumentality of the mid-19th century. His other buildings, less famous, are also quieter in design. *See* OPERA, L', PARIS.

BIBLIOGRAPHY. C. Moyaux, *Notice sur la vie et les oeuvres de M. Charles Garnier*, Paris, 1899.

GARNIER, FRANCOIS. French still-life painter (b. before 1627; d. before 1658). He was the father-in-law and teacher of Louise Moillon. His two known works are dated 1637 and 1644 (*Gooseberries* and *Cherries*; Paris, Louvre). In French still-life development, he adhered to the Flemish tradition of opposing bright and cool tones. The sloping table, his own contrivance, anticipates devices of Georges Braque.

BIBLIOGRAPHY. C. Sterling, *Still Life Painting from Antiquity to the Present Time*, new rev. ed., tr. J. Emmons, New York, 1959.

GARNIER, TONY. French architect (1867–1948). He worked in Lyons. He is best known for his Cité Industrielle project, which he designed while he was a *pensionnaire* at the French Academy in Rome. His later work reflects the progressive use of reinforced concrete and the paring away of superfluous ornament and the academic tinge of his early projects.

BIBLIOGRAPHY. G. Veronese, *Tony Garnier*, Milan, 1947.

Pablo Gargallo, *The Prophet*, 1933. Museum of Modern Art, Paris.

GAROFALO (Benvenuto Tisi). Italian painter of Ferrara (1481–1559). A pupil of Boccaccio Boccaccino, he first painted small Madonnas like those of his teacher, but after the first of several Roman trips he developed a mature style, which changed little thereafter. It is Raphaelesque in stylish outward elements, poses, and types, but local in intense color and landscape tone.

Besides numerous altarpieces and smaller Holy Families, a Mantegnesque ceiling painting may be by him (Ferrara, Seminario). His masterpiece is the harp covered with decorative figures that was made for Lucrezia d'Este (Modena, Este Gallery). After losing the sight of one eye he continued painting, but he became wholly blind in 1550. He worked at times with Dosso.

BIBLIOGRAPHY. G. Mazzariol, *Il Garofalo, Benvenuto Tisi*, Venice, 1960.

GARTNER, FRIEDRICH VON. German architect (1792–1847). He worked in Munich and Athens. After studying at the Munich Academy he traveled in Europe and England, later becoming professor of architecture at his own school and, in 1841, director. His Munich work reflects the writings of Jean Nicholas Louis Durand in its combination of utilitarian austerity and emphasis on rhythm and in the play of solid against void. He worked generally in an Italianate or medievalizing and romantic manner, with emphasis on color and material, as seen in such buildings as his Wittelsbach Palace and his Ludwigskirche; in the latter he introduced the Rundbogenstil, or round-arched style. He is responsible for the Old Palace in Athens

(1835–41), which is one of the early buildings in the Greek-revival style in that city. *See* RUNDBOGENSTIL.

BIBLIOGRAPHY. H. Moninger, *Friedrich von Gärtner's Originalpläne und Studien...*, Munich, 1882.

GARUDA. Mythical bird on which the Hindu god Vishnu rides. Garuda's face is white, his wings red, and his body golden. He is the enemy, and often the conqueror, of nāgas.

GASPARE DAGLI OCCHIALI, *see* VANVITELLI, GASPARE.

GASPARI, ANTONIO. Italian architect and architectural painter (1670–1730). Lacking in architectural individuality, he is connected, among other work, with the building of the cloister of S. Giorgio Maggiore and the completion of the Palazzo Pesaro in Venice.

GASPARI, GIOVANNI PIETRO. Italian painter (1720–85). Born in Venice, he was the most distinguished member of a family of scenographic and perspective painters that originated with his father, Francesco Antonio. He executed numerous works in Germany, particularly Bavaria, in collaboration with his brother Giovanni Paolo Gaspari. Nominated to the Academy of Venice in 1782, he painted for it a *Prospettiva* (now hanging in the Gallery of the Academy) that closely follows the manner of both Bibiena and Piranesi.

BIBLIOGRAPHY. C. Donzelli, *I pittori veneti del Settecento*, Florence, 1957.

GASSEL, LUCAS (Helmont). Flemish landscape painter and engraver (ca. 1500–1556/70). Born in Helmont, Gassel resided mostly in Brussels. His style is reminiscent of Herri Met de Bles and Patinir. His landscapes, of which very few remain, are generally the settings of Biblical scenes.

BIBLIOGRAPHY. R. H. Wilenski, *Flemish Painters, 1430–1830*, 2 vols., New York, 1960.

GASUR, *see* NUZI (JORGAN TEPE).

GATCH, LEE. American abstract painter (1902–68). Born near Baltimore, he studied with John Sloan and Leon Kroll in New York. In 1924 he went to France and studied with André Lhote and Moïse Kisling. He had his first one-man show at the New Art Circle, New York City, in 1927. His art was represented in the Venice Biennales of 1950 and 1956. In 1960 he was given a retrospective exhibition at the Whitney Museum of American Art in New York.

In the early 1930s his art was influenced by Paul Klee, who was then little known. Gatch painted small, semiabstract landscapes in which natural forms are reduced to geometric patterns without losing their organic character or the scenes their sense of light and atmosphere. Mystical, pantheistic overtones are implied. A series begun in 1960 combined flagstone with paint and collage.

BIBLIOGRAPHY. P. T. Rathbone, *Lee Gatch*, New York, 1960.

GATES OF PARADISE. Bronze sculpture by Ghiberti; east door to the Baptisterv of Florence. *See* GHIBERTI, LORENZO.

GATTAMELATA, IL. Bronze equestrian sculpture by Donatello, in the Piazza del Santo, Padua. *See* DONATELLO.

GATTI, BERNARDINO (Il Sojaro). Italian painter of Cremona (ca. 1495–1576). He developed under the local im-

Charles Garnier, Paris Opéra, 1861–75. An example of the mid-19th-century revival styles.

Antoni Gaudí i Cornet, interior of the Palacio Güell, Barcelona.

pact of Pordenone's work and that of Correggio in nearby Parma. As a result he always worked more in a "prebaroque" style of heavy movement than in the mannerist patterns of his time. He is best known through his collaboration with Pordenone (frescoes, 1543; Piacenza, S. Maria in Campagna) and his continuation of a project left unfinished by Parmigianino (Parma, Steccata).

BIBLIOGRAPHY. Cremona, Museo Civico, Pinacoteca, *La Pinacoteca di Cremona*, ed. A. Puerari, Florence, 1951.

GAU, FRANZ. French architect (1790–1853). He worked in Paris. A pupil of Debret and Louis Hippolyte Lebas, he did archaeological research in Egypt. His major work is the Neo-Gothic Church of Ste-Clothilde, in which the extensive use of iron was structurally advanced for its time.

GAUDIER (Gaudier-Brzeska), HENRI. French sculptor (1891–1915). Gaudier was killed in action in World War I, but his output, necessarily limited by his premature death, revealed a talent of the first rank. His marble *Torso* is at once suggestive of Hellenistic sensuousness and abstract attention to the quality of movement. He was influenced by discussions with Roger Fry and Ezra Pound; his art has been an acknowledged inspiration to Henry Moore. Although his work was exhibited in London during 1914, Gaudier did not receive extensive attention until after his death. In 1918 more than 100 of his graphic works and sculptures were shown at the Leicester Galleries. His style is personal and sensitive; a blending of figural and non-

figural qualities suggests that he might have become a pioneer of abstract sculpture in our time.

BIBLIOGRAPHY. M. Seuphor, *The Sculpture of This Century*, New York, 1960.

GAUDI I CORNET, ANTONI. Spanish architect (b. near Reus, Catalonia, Spain, 1852; d. Barcelona, 1926). In the 1870s Gaudí associated himself with Juan Martorell, who admired French Gothic architecture. But Gaudí was neither a strict revivalist nor an advocate of the international school of the 1920s. All his life a fervid Catalonian nationalist, he evolved an extraordinarily personal style sometimes vaguely reminiscent of Mudejar architecture, sometimes of Art Nouveau. An apartment house, the Casa Milá (1905–14; Barcelona), with its undulating façade has been likened to the rocks of the Pyrenees.

No straight lines are apparent in the building; even many of the window areas show partial curves. The total effect of its complex composition of supporting elements suggests natural forms, such as caves and grottoes, while its balconies are covered with wrought iron strewn about like seaweed. The galleries of the Güell Park (1900–14; Barcelona) are reminiscent of a natural cavern: columns resembling stalagmites lean inward in places to support a bizarrely irregular vaulted roof.

Undoubtedly, Gaudí's masterpiece is the well-known but unfinished Church of the Sagrada Familia in Barcelona, on which he worked for many years, principally from 1903 to 1926. Although only the transept of this extraordinary building was completed, its exotic forms dominate Barcelona's skyline with their extravagant modulations, which may be compared with the slightly earlier Güell city mansion.

Basically Gaudí's art may be regarded as a personal expression dominated by Gothic structural techniques, which were extended by forms translated into characteristically Spanish, even Moorish, richness.

BIBLIOGRAPHY. H.-R. Hitchcock, *Gaudí*, New York, 1957; G. Collins, *Antonio Gaudí*, New York, 1960; J. L. Sert and J. J. Sweeney, *Antoni Gaudí*, New York, 1961.

GAUGUIN, PAUL. French postimpressionist painter, sculptor, ceramicist, and printmaker (b. Paris, 1848; d. Hiva-Hoa, Marquesas Islands, 1903). Gauguin's father, Clovis Gauguin, a journalist from Orléans, fled to Peru with his family in 1851, when Louis-Napoléon came into power. He died en route, and his widow and two children stayed in Lima with relatives for four years. The Gauguins then returned to France and settled in Orléans, where Paul went to school. At the age of seventeen he went to sea as a navigating cadet in the merchant marine. In 1871 he entered Bertin's stockbroking offices in Paris and became a successful financier. He married Mette Sophia Gad, a Danish minister's daughter, in 1873.

In 1873 Gauguin began to paint and to collect impressionist paintings. He owned works by Pissarro, whom he had befriended, and by Manet, Renoir, Monet, Sisley, and Cézanne. In 1876 Gauguin had a picture accepted for the Paris Salon. The following year he made his first sculptures. He became more and more absorbed in art. Gauguin exhibited in the last four impressionist exhibitions. In 1883 there was a crash in the financial world, and Gauguin left business to take up painting full time.

Paul Gauguin, *Fatata te Miti (By the Sea)*. National Gallery, Washington, D.C. (Chester Dale Collection, 1962).

Gauguin's early painting is tentative and cautious, reminiscent of Pissarro while he was under the influence of the Barbizon painters. In his paintings of the early 1880s Gauguin loosened and broadened his stroke, giving the whole a tremulous rhythmic character. His color, while still cautious, contained hints of what was to develop. He massed areas of color and took liberties in stressing color accents, such as shadows that are bright blue and a red roof that all but jumps out of its context. The treatment of color approaches the arbitrary. At that time Gauguin was unable to sell any pictures, and his funds began to dwindle. Exhibitions he arranged in 1884 in Rouen and the following year in Copenhagen were financially disastrous. In 1885 Gauguin took his son Clovis to Paris, leaving his wife with their four other children in Copenhagen. He lived in direst poverty and took a job fixing posters on walls.

Despite adversity, Gauguin remained optimistic, proud, vain, and credulous. He made his first trip to Brittany in 1886 and his second in 1888. In between, he and Charles Laval sailed to Panama to work on the canal. They both caught fever, but before returning to Paris, they went to Martinique, where they painted.

In February, 1888, Gauguin went to Pont-Aven in Brittany, where he met Emile Bernard, who had some ideas that Gauguin was to develop and refine. They are fundamental to the philosophy of the movement that has come to be known as "synthetism." A reaction to Courbet's realism and an urge to extend impressionism led Bernard to explore new dimensions. Bernard and Gauguin both sought new expressive power. They argued for an art that had the same eloquence, directness, and universality as a symbol, a compression of sensations that sacrifices details and specific references for an intense, concentrated synthesis of impressions, ideas, and experiences. *See* SYNTHETISM.

Gauguin moved away from the fractured light of the impressionists, their aim of fixing the fleeting vision, and their avoidance of literary allusions. In *Jacob Wrestling with the Angel* (1888; Edinburgh, National Gallery of Scotland) Gauguin used intense, unnatural color. There is no indication of a light source in the scene: instead, the color seems to emit its own light. A priest in the lower right corner relates the Biblical story of Jacob and the angel, and a row of peasant women in starched caps listen. They are submissive and reverential. In the upper right quarter are the wrestling figures of the angel and Jacob.

They are separated from the women by a tree, thrown diagonally across the picture. The Biblical characters are at once the mental image of the women and actual beings in their midst. Gauguin communicates the aura of naïve mysticism with free, curvilinear rhythms, but mostly through the use of color, about which he wrote: "By means of skillful harmonies we create the symbol, and color, which like music is vibration, achieves what is vaguest and most universal in nature: her inmost force."

In *Jacob Wrestling with the Angel*, Gauguin surrounded color areas with contours reinforced by line, just as enamel is reinforced by wire in cloisonné. Gauguin noticed the similarity himself and made use of the term "cloisonnisme," a term which has since been applied somewhat loosely as a synonym for synthetism. In the same eventful year, 1888, Gauguin had his first one-man show and went to Arles to visit Van Gogh for a two-month period, a visit that ended disastrously for their friendship.

In 1889 Gauguin returned to Pont-Aven and then went to Le Pouldu, where his art took on its final, simplified form, with intensified color and backgrounds reduced to rhythmically curved shapes, as seen, for example, in *The Yellow Christ* (1889; Buffalo, N.Y., Albright-Knox Art Gallery), an important work of this period. Back in Paris, he organized an exhibition of the "Symbolist and Synthetist Group" at the Café Volpini.

In 1891 he sailed to Tahiti, having managed to sell enough work in an auction to finance the trip. He arrived in June and stayed until July, 1893. He found the European colony at Papeete offensive and moved some 25 miles south, where he lived in a native hut. He was enchanted by the beauty and mystery of the place. He had not gone to escape, but to find the genuine, the untouched, the pure. He idealized the "savage" as one who is guided by instinct, one who is close to nature and the source of true creation. Gauguin soon discovered that the natives were subject to a strict social code and that they, too, had tyrannical gods, whom they feared. *Manao Tupapau* (1892; New York, A. Conger Goodyear Collection) shows a nude native girl in the grip of such fears. The color is bright and vibrant. It has timbre and yet mellowness and subtlety. The harmonies are evocative. By this time, Gauguin had rejected complementaries. He became fond of juxtaposing reds and oranges, blues and greens, purples and fuschias. He used indigo as black. His figures stand, lie, and move lethargically in a somnambulistic state of reverie.

On returning to Paris, he became a celebrated figure, living flamboyantly and dressing in garish clothing. During a visit to Pont-Aven his ankle was broken in a street fight. It never healed properly and was later to cause him considerable pain.

He went back to Tahiti in July, 1895. He kept a journal, *Noa-Noa*, which was published in 1897 by *La Revue Blanche*. After his daughter died in 1897, he painted *D'Où venons nous?—Que sommes nous?—Où allons nous?* (Boston, Museum of Fine Arts). Depressed by bad health, poverty, and his daughter's death, he attempted suicide in 1898. In 1901 he left for the Marquesas. He painted some of his freshest, most imaginative works at this time despite fits of severe depression. His last picture was a snow scene of Brittany.

BIBLIOGRAPHY. C. Estienne, *Gauguin*, Geneva, 1953; L. Hanson and E. Hanson, *Noble Savage*, New York, 1954; R. Goldwater, *Paul Gauguin*, New York, 1957; J. Rewald, *Gauguin Drawings*, New York, 1958; H. R. Rookmaaker, *Synthetist Art Theories: Genesis and Nature of the Ideas of Art of Gauguin and His Circle*, Amsterdam, 1959; P. Gauguin, *Noa-Noa*, Oxford, England, 1961; C. Gray, *Sculpture and Ceramics of Paul Gauguin*, Baltimore, 1963; L. Skykorva, *Gauguin Woodcuts*, London, 1963.
ROBERT REIFF

GAUHAR SHAD, MOSQUE OF, MESHED. Iranian mosque of the Timurid period. An outstanding example of Muhammadan architecture of the 15th century, it was built by Gauhar Shad, wife of Shah Rukh. Unusual mosaic polychrome designs in relief decorate its various surfaces—domes, minarets, and portals. Blues, greens, and yellows, mingling with black and white in decorative friezes and exquisite floral arrangements, produce a dazzling effect.

BIBLIOGRAPHY. A. U. Pope, ed., *A Survey of Persian Art*, vol. 2, New York, 1939.

GAUL, AUGUST. German sculptor (b. Grossauheim, 1869; d. Berlin, 1921). After simultaneously working with a goldsmith and studying drawing at the Hanau Academy (1886–88), Gaul attended the Berlin School of Arts and Crafts and then the Berlin Academy. He worked in the studio of Reinhold Begas and, having been awarded the Prix de Rome, visited Rome (1897–98).

Gaul is primarily known as Germany's best animal sculptor. Among his works are a fountain with ducks at Charlottenburg, a bear balanced on a ball for the Wertheim stores, a fountain with a bison for Königsburg, and a

G. B. Gaulli, *Triumph of the Name of Jesus.* Church of the Gesù, Rome.

fountain with penguins for a private villa in Wannsee, near Berlin. He had a fresh approach to representations, searching for the natural form of the animal and simplifying it in the manner of Adolf Hildebrand.

GAUL AND HIS WIFE. Statuary group representing a Gaul killing his wife and himself (ca. 240–200 B.C.), now in the National Museum of Rome. It is the marble copy of a bronze original which was dedicated by King Attalus I of Pergamon to commemorate his victory over the Gauls. Both figures are on a single base, characteristic of Asian works of the 3d century B.C.

BIBLIOGRAPHY. M. Bieber, *The Sculpture of the Hellenistic Age*, New York, 1955.

GAULLI, GIOVANNI BATTISTA (Baciccio; Baciccia). Italian painter (b. Genoa, 1639; d. Rome, 1709). He went to Rome in about 1660 and there produced his first public work, the *Virgin and Child with SS. Roch and Anthony* (Rome, S. Rocco). Between 1672 and 1685 he carried out his best-known cycle of decorative paintings, the frescoes on the ceiling of the Gesù, an extraordinary mingling of painting and stucco which is one of the major monuments of Roman baroque art. His last two major canvases, *St. Francis Xavier Baptizing an Eastern Queen* and *St. Francis Xavier Preaching in the East*, are in S. Andrea al Quirinale. Also a distinguished portraitist, probably the finest working in Rome during the 17th century, Gaulli painted portraits of seven popes.

BIBLIOGRAPHY. R. Enggass, *The Paintings of Baciccio: Giovanni Battista Gaulli, 1639–1709*, University Park, Pa., 1964.

Gavarni, lithograph from the series *Oeuvres Nouvelles de Gavarni.*

Mosieu Emile Johbias, s'il vous plait, avocat à la Cour Royale
C'est moi M'sieu

GAUTAMA (Chinese, Ch'iao-ta-ma; Japanese, Kudon). Family name of the Buddha.

GAVARNI (Guillaume Sulpice Chevalier). French lithographer, water-colorist, and painter (b. Paris, 1804; d. there, 1866). At the age of ten he learned the rudiments of drawing from an architect named Dutillard. At fourteen he worked with Jecker, a mathematical instrument maker, and studied higher mathematics. He later became a student at the Conservatoire des Arts et Métiers, where he learned to design machinery. Meanwhile he drew for his own amusement and sold some drawings to a print dealer, Mlle Naudet. She introduced him to the publisher Blaisot, for whom, in 1824, Gavarni executed his first album of lithographs, entitled *Etrennes de 1825: Récréations diabolico-fantasmagoriques*, using the name "H. Chevalier." In the same year he attached himself to an architectural etcher, Jean Adam, who had him etch the bridge and harbor facilities at Bordeaux. From the end of 1825 Gavarni worked for two years for a surveyor at Tarbes, in the Pyrenees, where he made innumerable sketches of the people and landscape. He returned to Paris in May, 1828, after making some costume studies for another publisher, La Mesangère.

His pseudonym was acquired through an error at the Salon of 1829, when the title of his landscape *Gavarnie* was assumed to be his name. Liking the sound of the word, he began to sign his work "Gavarni." He was soon attracting the notice of collectors and publishers. His interest in costumes led to a position on the staff of the publication *La Mode*, where, in 1830, his work aroused considerable interest. From 1833 to 1835 he published *Le Journal des Gens du Monde*, which ended in financial embarrassment and a term in prison at Clichy. He next began to publish lithographs in *Charivari*, where much of Daumier's work first appeared. Such series as *Fourberies des femmes en matière de sentiment* (1840), *Les Lorettes* (1841–43), and *La Boîte aux lettres* (1837–39) exercised his ability to depict both the sentimental and comical foibles of his favorite subject—women. From 1847 to 1851 he was in England, where he produced lithographs for London and Paris periodicals. On his return to France he contributed to the newspaper *Paris* the series *Masques et visages*, which included such subseries as *Les Propos de Thomas Vireloque* (1852), *Les Partageuses* (1852), and *Bohèmes* (1853).

Gavarni's designs are not caricatures. They are sensitively drawn pictures of persons in the human drama. The legends are witty and often provocative, and the subject matter ranges from sluts and gamins to the cultured and urbane. Gavarni produced some 8,000 pictures, including about 3,000 lithographs. The remainder are etchings, drawings, and various compositions reproduced for publication.

BIBLIOGRAPHY. J. Armelhault and E. Bocher, *L'Oeuvre de Gavarni*, Paris, 1873; J. Adhémar and J. Lethève, *Inventaire du fonds français, après 1800*, vol. 8, Paris, 1954. KNEELAND MC NULTY

GAY, WALTER. American genre painter (b. Hingham, Mass., 1856; d. Barbizon, France, 1937). In Paris he studied painting with Léon Bonnat at the Ecole des Beaux-Arts and at home painted genre themes in a hard, academic manner. Late in his career he executed decorative scenes of 18th-century interiors.

GAZA: ST. SERGIUS. No longer extant Byzantine church of the 6th century, situated in what was southwestern Palestine. Its mosaics, which were described in detail by a contemporary of the artist, showed the Virgin and Child in the apse and New Testament scenes in the upper parts of the building.

BIBLIOGRAPHY. R. W. Hamilton in *Palestine Exploration Fund, Quarterly Statement*, 1930.

GEBEL, MATTHES. German sculptor and medalist (d. Nürnberg, 1574). He was the most important medalist of Nürnberg from 1523, when he attained citizenship, until 1553. Gebel's output included portraits of important figures such as Dürer. He worked in a northern realistic style; his profile portraits were Gothic in his first years and Renaissance after 1527.

BIBLIOGRAPHY. G. Habich, *Die deutschen Medailleure des 16. Jahrhunderts*, Halle, 1916.

GEBEL EL 'ARAQ, KNIFE OF. Carved ivory handle of a predynastic knife (close of the 4th millennium B.C.) named after the locality in Upper Egypt where it was found. The low relief on one face of the knife handle represents a bearded man poised between two standing lions—a characteristic motif of Mesopotamian art. Below are dogs and desert animals. On the other side there are two rows of pairs of men fighting with clubs. Beneath are two Mesopotamian boats on one side of a waterway in which drowning people can be seen; there are three Egyptian boats on the opposite side of the waterway. No groundline appears.

BIBLIOGRAPHY. G. Bénédite, "Le Couteau de Gebel el-'Arak," *Monuments Piot*, XXII, Paris, 1916.

GEBHARDT, EDUARD VON. German painter (b. St. Johannis, Estonia, 1883; d. Düsseldorf, 1925). Von Gebhardt studied in Russia, Belgium, and Holland and devoted himself primarily to religious painting. Both the Dutch masters and Pinturicchio contributed to his style, which protested the romanticism of the Nazarene group.

GEDDES, ANDREW. British painter (b. Edinburgh, 1783; d. 1844). Geddes, whose father was a man of taste and a collector, attended the University of Edinburgh and started his career in the Excise Office. In 1807 he entered the Royal Academy of Arts schools. Sir David Wilkie was a fellow pupil with whom he had a lifelong friendship. Returning to Edinburgh in 1810, Geddes started painting portraits; these were to be his best and most characteristic works. Although he settled in London in 1814, he frequently visited Edinburgh and also toured the Continent. A regular exhibitor at the Royal Academy, he was elected an associate in 1832. His portraits—those of Wilkie, Sir Walter Scott, and other Scottish figures are best known—possess great charm and technical assurance. He occasionally painted large pictures in the grand manner and was a highly skilled etcher, producing about forty etchings, which are greatly prized by collectors.

GEDDES, NORMAN BEL. American industrial and stage designer (1893–1958). Bel Geddes was born in Adrian, Mich. A giant of the American design world, he is perhaps as memorable for his tempestuous and eccentric personality as for his brilliant stage and product designs. He was at-tracted to industrial design only after years of success in the theater, and lent a sense of glamour to a fledgling profession. He participated in 234 theatrical productions, and his stage sets for such plays as *Lysistrata*, *The Miracle*, and *The Eternal Road* are remembered as outstanding features of those productions.

Bel Geddes introduced the present-day method of lighting theater stages by lamps with lenses. He also designed the Graham-Paige automobile of 1928, the Philco radio of 1930, a puncture-proof tire for Firestone, an electric typewriter for IBM in 1946, and interiors for the Pan American China Clipper of 1934. He streamlined the Union Pacific train in 1931, made a sheet steel, all-white enamel stove for Standard Gas in 1932, and designed the ice theater for Rockefeller Center in 1937. His exhibit for the General Motors Futurama at the New York World's Fair of 1939 contained 500,000 model buildings, 50,000 cars, and 10 million trees. In all, he designed several thousand products for leading industrial manufacturers.

He has been called a modern counterpart of the 15th-century master craftsman. Blending beauty, utility, and profit, his often grandiose schemes were sponsored by the most conservative industrialists.

BIBLIOGRAPHY. N. Bel Geddes, *Horizons*, Boston, 1932; N. Bel Geddes, *Magic Motorways*, New York, 1940; G. Seldes and H. Dreyfuss, "Norman Bel Geddes," *Industrial Design*, V, June, 1958.

ANN FEREBEE

GEEL, JACOB VAN. Dutch landscape painter (b. 1584/ 85; d. in or after 1638). From 1615 to 1618 Geel was an officer of the Guild of St. Luke in Middelburg, where he is often documented between 1616 and 1625. In 1628 he is listed as a "foreign" member of the Delft guild. Geel belongs to the transitional group of landscape painters, and his development is similar to that of such painters as Alexander Keirinckx and Gillis d'Hondecoeter.

BIBLIOGRAPHY. C. Müller and J. Q. van Regteren Altena, "Der Maler Jacob van Geel," *Jahrbuch der Preussischen Kunstsammlungen*, LII, 1931.

GEERTGEN TOT SINT JANS (Gerard of Haarlem). Dutch painter (ca. 1465–ca. 1495). Of the many Haarlem painters, including Ouwater and Bouts, who went to Flanders to study and work, Geertgen was probably the most original. Some evidence indicates that he may have been an apprentice in Bruges, while other evidence, including style, places him close to his compatriot Albert van Ouwater, in Leyden. The latter relationship is further borne out by the fact that Geertgen entered the monastery of the Order of St. John in Haarlem (Ouwater's home) as a lay brother. In his short life he made rapid progress as a painter, and he can be credited with producing at least a dozen works, which vary in size and approach to such a degree that a Geertgen chronology is extremely difficult to postulate.

Considered the earliest of Geertgen's *oeuvre* is a tiny (4 in. by 2 ¾ in.) *Madonna*, in Milan, painted on vellum. Placed early because of its illuminated, miniature-like quality, it shows definite Boutsian influence. His *Holy Family and Their Kin* (Amsterdam, Rijksmuseum) was probably painted under the influence of Ouwater's *Raising of Lazarus*. This influence is especially apparent in the architec-

Geertgen tot Sint Jans, *The Nativity*. National Gallery, London.

Aert de Gelder, *Hermanus Boerhaave and His Family.* Rijksmuseum, Amsterdam (on loan from the collection of Baron Schimmelpennick van der Oye).

tural setting and disposition of figures. Geertgen's true forte—the treatment of landscape as continuous space—becomes noticeable in such works as the *Raising of Lazarus* (Paris, Louvre) and the *Adoration of the Magi* (Prague, National Museum). The three distinct "grounds"—fore-, middle-, and distant—begin to be unified into a continuity of space. This development culminates in a refined, lyrical manner in the *St. John the Baptist in the Wilderness* (Berlin, former State Museums). The serene, lyrical landscape is seemingly presented for its own sake. The figure of the Baptist, although spatially and visually contained within the landscape, seems almost extraneous to it.

Geertgen's greatest achievement comes in a *Nativity* (London, National Gallery). It is a true night scene with the sources of light visible within the panel. The Child radiates a golden light, which illuminates the Virgin and the surrounding angels. A secondary reflected glow half reveals the ox and the ass. Joseph, in a corner and out of range of the Child's radiant light, holds a candle shielded behind one hand which faintly illuminates his features in the prevailing gloom. A break in the back wall of the manger reveals a landscape lit by a silvery radiance, which emanates from the angel announcing the birth to the shepherds. The cold brilliance of the angel's light dominates the feeble, warm glow of the shepherds' campfire. In his use of visible sources of light and in the attendant style of his modeling, Geertgen foreshadows the use made of chiaroscuro by Caravaggio and Georges de La Tour more than a century later.

BIBLIOGRAPHY. L. Baldass, *Geertgen van Haarlem*, Vienna, 1921; E. Panofsky, *Early Netherlandish Painting*, 2 vols., Cambridge, Mass., 1953.

STANLEY FERBER

GEESE OF MEDUM. Egyptian fresco painting, in the Egyptian Museum, Cairo.

GEEST, WIJBRANDT SYMONSZ. DE. Dutch portrait painter (b. Leeuwarden, 1592; d. there, after 1660). De Geest probably received his early training from his father. He may have also studied with Abraham Bloemaert in Utrecht before traveling through the southern Netherlands and France to Italy. De Geest spent four years in Rome and belonged to the northern artists' group. In 1622 he married Hendrikje van Uylenburgh, the sister of Rembrandt's wife, Saskia.

BIBLIOGRAPHY. G. J. Hoogewerff, *De Bentvueghels*, The Hague, 1952.

GEIAMI (Shingei). Japanese painter (1431–85). The son of Nōami, he inherited from his father the position of art critic and cataloger of the shogunal collection. His painting *Viewing a Waterfall* (1480; Nezu Museum), which he gave to his pupil Shōkei, suggests Geiami's indebtedness to Sesshū. *See* NOAMI; SESSHU TOYO; SHOKEI.

BIBLIOGRAPHY. T. Akiyama, *Japanese Painting* [Geneva?], 1961.

GEIGER, NICOLAUS. German sculptor and painter (b. Laningen, 1849; d. Berlin, 1897). He studied in Munich and was in Italy from 1877 to 1879 and afterward in Paris and Vienna before settling in Berlin. He produced statues and public monuments with an increasing tendency toward the incorporation of naturalistic elements.

GEKKEI (Matsumura Gekkei), *see* GOSHUN.

GELASIAN SACRAMENTARY. Illuminated Merovingian manuscript, located in the National Library, Rome. *See* MEROVINGIAN ART.

GELDER, AERT (Aart) DE. Dutch painter of history, portraits, and landscapes (b. Dordrecht, 1645; d. there, 1727). In about 1660 De Gelder was a pupil of Samuel van Hoogstraten, a former Rembrandt student. Shortly afterward, about 1661, De Gelder entered Rembrandt's studio in Amsterdam. As the master's last important pupil, De Gelder is responsible for continuing the Rembrandt tradition into the 18th century. His technique is very closely based on the late, broad manner of Rembrandt in the 1660s. His color also remains true to the warm hues of the great painter's last works. On his return to his native Dordrecht, De Gelder was friendly with the artist and artist's biographer Arnold Houbraken. In his early works De Gelder shows his dependence not only on Rembrandt himself but also on some of Rembrandt's earlier students. De Gelder's 1669 *Beneficence of Scipio* (German art market, 1940) is almost a variation on the composition of Gerbrand van den Eeckhout's painting (Toledo, Ohio, Museum of Art; New York Historical Society).

Most interesting among De Gelder's later works is a series of twenty-two paintings representing the Passion of Christ. The completed series remained in the artist's possession until his death, and twelve of the paintings were eventually sold in Amsterdam in 1770. Only twelve of the series have come down to us (seven in Aschaffenburg, Museum; three in Munich, Old Pinacothek; two in Amsterdam, Rijksmuseum). In the realm of group portraiture, De Gelder's late *Hermanus Boerhaave and His Family* (ca. 1722; Amsterdam, Rijksmuseum, on loan from the collection of W. A. A. J. Baron Schimmelpennick van der Oye) brings Rembrandt's late portrait manner to the very edge of an 18th-century rococo style. Even in this late work, however, De Gelder's indebtedness to his great teacher is still apparent.

BIBLIOGRAPHY. K. Lilienfeld, *Arent de Gelder, sein Leben und seine Kunst* (Quellenstudien zur hollandischen Kunstgeschichte, 4), The Hague, 1914; K. Lilienfeld, "Neues über Leben und Werk Aert de Gelders," *Kunstchronik und Kunstmarkt*, XXX, 1918/19; J. Rosenberg, S. Slive, and E. H. ter Kuile, *Dutch Art and Architecture, 1600–1800*, Baltimore, 1966.

LEONARD J. SLATKES

GELDER, NICOLAES VAN. Dutch painter of still lifes (b. Leyden? ca. 1623/36; d. between 1675 and 1677). Little is known of Van Gelder's early life and training. He was active in Stockholm in 1661; however, he is recorded as being back in Leyden in 1666. He seems to have gone to Amsterdam shortly afterward.

A *Still Life* (1664; Amsterdam, Rijksmuseum), which is signed by Van Gelder, is related to the works of Pieter de Ring and other Leyden followers of Jan Davidsz. de Heem. In Amsterdam, Van Gelder was influenced by the works of Willem van Aelst. That Van Gelder was still alive in 1675 is proved by a signed *Still Life* (1675; Leyden, Stedelijk Museum).

BIBLIOGRAPHY. A. P. A. Vorenkamp, *Bijdrage tot de geschiedenis van het Hollandsch stilleven in de zeventiende eeuw*, Leyden, 1934; W. Bernt, *Die niederländischen Maler des 17. Jahrhunderts...*, vol. 1, Munich, 1948.

GELDORP, GOLTZIUS. Flemish painter of portraits and, occasionally, of religious and historical subjects (b. Louvain, 1553; d. Cologne, 1618). He studied with Frans Francken the Elder and Frans Pourbus the Elder in Antwerp, and settled in Cologne in 1579 as painter to the Duke of Terra Nova. *A Female Saint in Ecstasy* (The Hague, Royal Museum) is characteristic of his religious style. The portraits are almost without exception on panel. They are mostly half figures, featuring strong brown tonalities, with the whites of collars and cuffs turning into bluish shades. These works are solid and dry, and Geldorp is undeserving of the title "the Miereveld of Cologne," which is often used to describe him. *Lucretia Pellicorne* (1608; Amsterdam, Rijksmuseum) can be considered a fair example of Geldorp's manner in portraiture.

BIBLIOGRAPHY. W. Bernt, *Die niederländischen Maler des 17. Jahrhunderts...*, vol. 1, Munich, 1948.

GELLEE (Gelee), CLAUDE, *see* LORRAINE, CLAUDE.

GELLONE, SACRAMENTARY OF, *see* MEROVINGIAN ART.

GEMITO, VINCENZO. Italian sculptor (b. Naples, 1852; d. there, 1929). Twice winner of the grand prize at the Universal Exposition in Paris (1867 and 1889), he is best known for his appealing bronze statues of models from everyday life, although he also executed models of classical subjects. His work blends naturalism and an ability to portray and even exaggerate character with delicacy and attention to fine detail.

BIBLIOGRAPHY. A. R. Willard, *History of Modern Italian Art*, 2d ed., London, 1900; F. Sapori, *Modern Italian Sculpture*, Rome, 1949.

GENEVA. City in southwest Switzerland, at the tip of Lake Geneva. At first a Celtic and Helvetic settlement, Geneva became Roman in the 1st century B.C. and an important Burgundian city in the 5th century, and it was finally overcome by the Ostrogoths and later the Franks. Eventually it became a major city in the kingdom of the Arelate and joined the Confederation of Swiss City-States in 1526. Made a bishopric in A.D. 400, Geneva acquired fame through Calvin's theocratic government (1533–64) and was for three centuries a haven for refugees adhering to the Reformation. These groups became important in the watchmaking and jewelry industry. In the 18th century Geneva offered asylum to Rousseau and Voltaire. Geneva's university was founded in 1559, and its museums in the early 19th century.

The Cathedral of St. Peter is built on the foundations of a Roman temple and 6th- and 10th-century basilican structures. It was rebuilt (early 12th cent.) and completed in the early Gothic style (ca. 1232); its vaulting system underwent changes into the 14th century. Vézelay, the Cistercian abbey of Pontigny, and the Lyons Cathedral choir influenced the massive interior, which is decorated with figured capitals of the middle and last third of the 12th century. In 1406 the Chapel of the Maccabees, which may have contained the *Geneva Altarpiece* of Konrad Witz, was added to the south aisle. The colonnaded west façade by Alfieri (1752–56) is a major example of classicism in Switzerland.

The nearby St. Mary Magdalen (14th–15th cent.) is built on a Roman substructure. St. Gervais has an 8th–9th-century crypt which was restored in the 15th century. In addition to a baroque church, there are a number of Neo-Byzantine, Neo-Romanesque, and Neo-Gothic structures.

The late-15th-century Town Hall near the Cathedral has a Renaissance ramp by Bogueret (1556–78). In the hill section of old Geneva are the 13th-century Tavel House and a large number of 15th- to 17th-century houses. Rows of 18th-century burgher house façades dominate the city. Their courts of honor are closed off by high walls with excellent baroque or rococo portals. A dozen classicist structures by Eynard, Vaucher, Callet, and others are of high quality. Le Corbusier's apartment building on Rue Adrien Lachenal (1931–32; so-called "Glass-house") contrasts favorably with the large building complex of the League of Nations in the Ariana Gardens. Begun in 1930 after the plans of Broggi, Nénot, Flegenheimer, Lefèvre, and Vogo, the League of Nations structure follows neoclassicist lines.

A statue of Rousseau by J. Pradier (*Ile Rousseau*) and the Monument of the Reformation (1909–17) by Laverrière, Landowski, Bouchard, and others dominate their respective sites. The Museum of Art and History contains important works by Konrad Witz and others. *See* GENEVA: MUSEUM OF ART AND HISTORY.

In the vicinity of Geneva is Carouge, planned in 1782 by King Victor Amadeus II of Sardinia (Savoy) as a rival to Geneva. Built under the direction of the architect Elia, this city, with its rational grid plan, apartment rows, and centrally located churches, remains unfinished. At Nyon, Roman remains and a large porcelain collection are housed in the castle. The abbey church of Bonmont, above Nyon, represents probably the finest Cistercian oratory with a standardized plan.

BIBLIOGRAPHY. C. Martin, *St. Pierre, ancienne cathédrale de Genève*, Geneva, 1910; Société Française d'Archéologie, *Congrès Archéologique*, Paris, 1953.

FRANÇOIS BUCHER

GENEVA: MUSEUM OF ART AND HISTORY. Swiss collection housed in a building of 1903–10 by Camoletti. The exhibits commence with prehistoric, Roman, and barbarian finds from the area of Geneva. The Egyptian and ancient Near Eastern collection includes a statue of Ramses II and several Luristan bronzes. There are Greek and Italian vases as well as Greek sculptures and bronzes. Applied and decorative arts (stained glass, church furniture, arms, coins, woodwork, and so on) range from the early medieval period to the 18th century. Although there are few paintings from before the 19th century, the treasure of the museum is the *St. Peter Altarpiece* by Konrad Witz, of which the two wings, with paintings on both sides, have been preserved. Geneva's close connection with France during the 18th century is reflected in the presence of paintings by Vigée-Lebrun and Liotard as well as in several portrait busts by Houdon. The modern collection includes works by Corot, Rodin, Hodler, Vallotton, Van Gogh, Gauguin, Rouault, Dufy, and Chagall.

BIBLIOGRAPHY. *Le Musée d'art et d'histoire de Genève, 1910-1960: Album du cinquantenaire*, Geneva, 1960.

GENEVIEVE OF PARIS, ST. Patron saint of Paris (ca. 422–ca. 500). Born at Nanterre, she was drawn toward the religious life by St. Germain of Auxerre. She settled in Paris and encouraged citizens to pray and to resist Attila and the Huns, who in the end bypassed the city. During the famine she provided the inhabitants of Paris with food. In the 14th century she was confused with Marguerite, a shepherdess. Geneviève is often shown as a nun. Her attributes are a crook or distaff, a medal engraved with a cross (gift of St. Germain), or a flaming candle. Her feast is January 3.

See also SAINTS IN ART.

GENGA, GIROLAMO. Italian painter and architect (b. Urbino, ca. 1476; d. there, 1551). He was a pupil and an assistant of Signorelli and then of Perugino. Genga's first documented works date from about 1504 in Urbino; he did paintings, theater designs, and festival décor in Urbino, Siena, Cesena, and Rome, and worked for the Sforza in Pesaro. After 1523 he was principally engaged in architecture, most importantly the Villa Imperiale at Pesaro, to which he also contributed painted décor. His painting style curiously combines the Quattrocento's tight scientific-mechanistic movement, bright colors, and hard (to the point of caricature) delineation of facial type with an already mannered adaptation of High Renaissance compositional elements.

BIBLIOGRAPHY. G. Vasari, *Le vite...*, ed. G. Milanesi, vol. 6, Florence, 1878; A. Venturi, *Storia dell'arte italiana*, vol. 9, pt. 5, Milan, 1932.

GENIUS. A general deity common among the ancient Etruscans, Romans, and Greeks. The genius (Latin for "creator") created and maintained life, accompanied an individual throughout his existence as his protector and tutelary spirit, and strove to influence his destiny for the good. The equivalent among the Greeks was the daemon. At first, only humans had genii, but after Etruscan times, localities, such as streets, baths, and theaters, came to have them, too. Genii are usually represented as snakes and winged figures. Their Christian counterparts are guardian angels.

GENJI SCROLL, *see* TALE OF GENJI SCROLL.

GENNARI, BENEDETTO, II. Italian painter (b. Cento, 1633; d. Bologna, 1715). With his father he joined Guercino in Bologna (1649) and produced works which have often been wrongly attributed to that master. He went to Paris in 1672, and in 1674 he went to England, where he painted portraits of Charles II and other members of the royal family (now Middlesex, Hampton Court). Returning to Bologna in 1690, he was much in demand for portraits and other works. The influence of Dutch realism can be seen in his meticulous treatment of materials and textures. Gennari was also one of the founders of the Accademia Clementina in Bologna.

GENOA. Chief city of Liguria, in northern Italy. Although Genoa preserves a number of significant monuments, notably in the field of secular architecture, on the whole its artistic patrimony does not measure up to the city's historical commercial importance (12th–16th cent.). The walls of 1155 enclosed an amphitheaterlike area focusing on the port; surviving portions of this circuit of walls include the Porta Soprana (Porta di S. Andrea) and the Porta dei Vacca. The Cathedral of S. Lorenzo, begun in 1118 and continued through the 14th century and later, combines Romanesque and Gothic forms. In the façade the use of banded marble indicates Pisan influence, while the splayed portals are of French derivation. The installation of the Cathedral Treasury (1954–56) by F. Albini is an uncompromising and influential example of modern design. The nearby Piazza S. Matteo, with the Doria houses and the Church of S. Matteo (1278), provides a harmonious ensemble of medieval architecture.

In 1550 the Via Nuova (now the Via Garibaldi) was opened. This monumental street is flanked on both sides by festive palaces designed by G. Alessi and his followers. These include the Palazzo Bianco (civic collections of painting and sculpture), the Palazzo Rosso (also housing an art collection), the Palazzo Municipale, the Palazzo Podestà, and the Doria, Parodi, and Cambiaso palaces. The Via Balbi offers palaces of similar character, including that of the university, with its picturesque flights of stairs descending a hill into the *cortile*. Alessi built a number of villas in Genoa's environs—the Cambiaso (1548), the Pallavicini delle Peschiere (1560), and the Scassi (1560). The Palazzo del Principe (1st half of the 16th cent.) contains frescoes by Perino del Vaga. The Church of S. Maria Assunta del Carignano by Alessi (1552), whose interior is dominated by a central dome, is the most important of Genoa's 16th-century ecclesiastical structures. *See* ROSSO, PALAZZO, GENOA.

In the first half of the 19th century the extensive activity of the neoclassic architect C. Barabino left an impress on the city. His works include the Via Carlo Felice (now Via XXV Aprile), the opera house, and the Accademia Ligustica di Belle Arti. Since World War II Genoa has developed rapidly, and the city's skyline is marked by tall buildings of functional character.

See also GENOA: GALLERY OF THE PALAZZO BIANCO.

BIBLIOGRAPHY. P. P. Rubens, *Palazzi moderni di Genova*, Antwerp, 1652 (facsim. repr. Novara, 1956); W. Suida, *Genua*, Leipzig, 1906; O. Grosso, *Genova*, Bergamo, 1926; Touring Club Italiano, *Liguria*, 4th ed., Milan, 1952; E. Cozzani, *Genova*, 2d ed., Turin, 1961.

WAYNE DYNES

GENOA: GALLERY OF THE PALAZZO BIANCO. Italian collection consisting mainly of paintings. The gallery in the baroque Palazzo Bianco is an exemplary modern installation (1950), in which are exhibited works by Luca Cambiaso, Pontormo, Palma Vecchio, Gérard David, Rubens, Van Dyck, and others. There are also the fragments of the sculptural tomb of Margaret of Brabant by Giovanni Pisano.

BIBLIOGRAPHY. *Catalogo provvisorio della Galleria di Palazzo Bianco*, 4th ed., Genoa, 1961.

GENOELS, ABRAHAM (Archimedes). Flemish painter of landscapes (b. Antwerp, 1640; d. 1723). He worked in Paris for Charles Le Brun, returned in 1672 to Antwerp in order to secure membership in the Guild of St. Luke, and subsequently journeyed to Rome for a lengthy sojourn (1674–82). His style is Italianizing and reveals the influence of Nicolas Poussin.

BIBLIOGRAPHY. Y. Thiéry, *Le Paysage flamand au XVIIe siècle*, Paris, 1953.

GENOVESE, IL, *see* CARLONE, GIOVANNI ANDREA.

GENOVESE, GAETANO. Italian architect (1795–1860). He worked in Naples. His two major monuments are the richly decorated throne room in the palace at Caserta, designed for Ferdinand II, and the sympathetic alterations and additions to the royal palace in Naples, both in the romantic classical style.

BIBLIOGRAPHY. C. Sasso, *Storia de' monumenti di Napoli e degli architetti che li edificavano*; vol. 2, Naples, 1858.

GENRE. Broadly, and particularly in painting, any subject matter other than history or landscape; usually applied to scenes from everyday life executed in a realistic manner. Practiced since antiquity, genre has traditionally been held in low esteem as a subject, because it is based on life rather than on the ideal. It was especially popular with the Dutch and Flemish masters in the form of interior scenes and still lifes.

GENTILE (Gentiel), LUIGI (Louis Primo or Primont; Louis Cousin). Flemish history and portrait painter of the Roman school (b. Brussels, 1606; d. Rome, 1667/68). For thirty years he lived in Rome, where he became a member of the Academy of St. Luke and acquired such patrons as Pope Alexander VII. His surname was earned by his gentility of behavior and elegant style.

BIBLIOGRAPHY. L. van Puyvelde, *La Peinture flamande à Rome*, Brussels, 1950.

GENTILE DA FABRIANO (Gentile di Niccolo di Giovanni di Massio). Italian painter (b. Fabriano, ca. 1370; d. Rome, 1427). He makes his first documented appearance in Venice in 1408, with an already established reputation, and was then active in Brescia, Perugia, Fabriano, Florence, and Siena.

Gentile's major importance in the history of art lies in his role as leading proponent of International Gothic Style in Italy. The sources of his art would seem to be in the painting of such Lombard artists as Giovannino de' Grassi and Michelino da Besozzo, with later influences from Taddeo di Bartolo. Parallels, if not influences, also exist between his work and that of Masolino and Ghiberti. Gentile's impact on Italian art can be most clearly seen in Venice, northern Italy, and Umbria. His closest follower, Pisanello, continued the art of the master well into the 15th century. Gentile also provided an impetus to keep Sienese painting close to the traditional forms of the Middle Ages until late in the 15th century.

In 1408 he was in Venice to receive payment for two paintings (lost). His fresco for the Sala del Maggior Consiglio in the Doges' Palace (ca. 1409) was destroyed in 1479. By 1414 he was in Brescia with his students decorating a chapel in the Broletto (destroyed) for Pandolfo Malatesta. On November 21, 1422, he matriculated in the Florentine guild. In May, 1423, he signed the altarpiece for Palla Strozzi and in May, 1425, that for the Quaratesi family. In June, 1425, he was engaged on a fresco in Siena, the *Madonna de' Notai* (lost). He received payment in October of the same year for a fresco, *Madonna and Child*, in the Cathedral of Orvieto. In October, 1426, he was again in Siena, completing the *Madonna de' Notai*, and by January, 1427, he had taken up residence in Rome, where he received payment for frescoes executed in the Lateran through the month of July.

· OPVS · GENTILIS · DE · FABRIANO · · M · C · C · C · C · XX · III · MENSIS · MAII ·

Gentile's existing early works were all executed prior to his arrival in Florence. The earliest of these, *Madonna and Child Enthroned with St. Nicholas and a Donor*, is signed on the frame and has been dated about 1390–95 on stylistic evidence. The figures and plants together with the decorative elements argue strongly for Gentile's dependence at this date on Lombard models. The major work of this period is the *Valle Romita Polyptych* (Milan, Brera). This imposing altarpiece, dismembered and now restored, came from an Observant Franciscan monastery in Fabriano. Although it would appear to date from about 1400, some scholars consider that it could have been executed as late as 1410. Here the major influences on Gentile's formation are most manifest—Lombard miniature and panel painting with indirect influences from the Franco-Flemish school as well as the direct influence of Sienese painting through Taddeo di Bartolo. Stylistic hesitation is emphasized by the different modes of presentation of the enthroned Madonna or the saints and by the small panels above each saint. The forward-looking aspects of these small panels occur again in a *St. Francis Receiving the Stigmata* (private collection) and in the badly damaged *Madonna and Child Enthroned* (New York, Metropolitan Museum). Of a more traditional nature are the *Madonna and Angels* (Perugia, National Gallery of Umbria), the early *Madonna and Child* (Washington, D.C., National Gallery), and the *Adoration of the Magi* (Pisa, National Museum). Within this period Gentile's work is characterized by a variety of styles and a vacillation between the stylistic choices possible.

Gentile is perhaps best known for major works completed in Florence between 1422 and 1425. Of these the large *Adoration of the Magi* (Florence, Uffizi) most clearly represents a synthesis of his early training. The painting was executed on commission from Palla Strozzi and was originally placed on the altar of the family chapel in Sta Trinità. Gentile very knowingly made use of the architectural frame to enclose the incidents in the travels of the Magi and to focus attention on the major elements of the scene. It is, in a sense, a long courtly procession with all the richness of materials and variety of human and animal types so dear to painters in the International Style. The panel shimmers with gold leaf, the bosses on the bridles stand out in low relief, and color is used lavishly in a glowing display. Yet within this richness some details indicate a growing interest in naturalism and in perspectival problems that is more typical of 15th-century Florentine art. In the predella panels in particular, the architectural setting and genre details of the *Presentation* and the lyric landscape of the *Flight into Egypt* seem to point toward the future. The second great altarpiece of this period, the *Quaratesi Altarpiece* (now dismembered), was painted for a chapel in S. Niccolò Oltrarno, by coincidence the parish church of Masaccio. The standing saints on the wings (Uffizi) draw heavily on Gentile's earlier training, while the *Enthroned Madonna* (London, National Gallery) can be more fruitfully compared to the work of Masolino or to Masaccio's *Madonna and St. Anne* in the Uffizi. In the predella, Gentile again allowed himself freedom of experimentation, particularly manifest in the panel now in the National Gallery, Washington, D.C. From this same period come two of Gentile's most handsome Madonnas, one in the National Gallery, Washington, and the other, an especially striking example, in the Jarves Collection at Yale University, New Haven, Conn.

Of Gentile's late works there remain only two damaged frescoes and a few sketchily indicated figures in a drawing by Borromini. The *Madonna and Child* in the Cathedral of Orvieto (executed October–December, 1425) depends largely on Gentile's Florentine experience for the solidity and mass of its forms. The frescoes of saints in niches for the Lateran would probably have been similar, but the only indication of Gentile's Roman work, an attributed fresco in Velletri (from SS. Cosmas and Damian, Rome), represents a regression toward the decorative and linear traditions of his youthful work.

BIBLIOGRAPHY. R. van Marle, *The Development of the Italian Schools of Painting*, vol. 8, The Hague, 1927; L. Grassi, ed., *Tutta la pittura di Gentile da Fabriano*, Milan, 1953.

JOHN R. SPENCER

GENTILE DA FABRIANO, FRANCESCO DI, *see* FRANCESCO DI GENTILE DA FABRIANO.

GENTILESCHI (Lomi), ARTEMISIA. Italian painter (b. Rome, 1597; d. Naples, after 1651). She studied with her father, Orazio, as well as with Tassi before 1612, and left Rome with the former to travel in Tuscany (ca. 1621–ca. 1626). After returning to Rome, she was in Naples by 1630, in London in 1638–39 (where her father died), and back in Naples before 1647, where she probably remained until her death.

Artemisia Gentileschi, *Judith and the Woman Servant with the Head of Holofernes*. Pitti, Florence.

Gentile da Fabriano, *Adoration of the Magi*. In the predella panels: *The Nativity, The Flight into Egypt*, and *The Presentation*. Uffizi, Florence.

There are few secure attributions to Artemisia, and her works, especially during the early Roman period, are often confused with Orazio's. In general her paintings are coarser and more vigorous than her father's, although they partake of the same genre-oriented Caravaggism as his Roman works. For example, her *Miracle of S. Carlo Borromeo* (before 1620; Florence, Cecconi Collection) is, except for the figure of the saint, essentially a family scene. While in Rome, Artemisia also experimented with a series of night scenes, pushing Caravaggesque *tenebroso* to new extremes and paralleling similar works by Honthorst. Examples are *David and Goliath* (Rome, Corsini Collection) and *Lot and His Daughters* (Rome, Borghese Gallery). The effect of her Tuscan sojourn can be seen in *Judith and the Woman Servant* (Florence, Corsini Collection and Pitti Palace), in which great care is taken with details of clothing and still-life elements, and a harder, more linear quality is apparent.

Artemisia's true powers emerge in *Judith Decapitating Holofernes* (Florence, Uffizi; Naples, Capodimonte), in which the abrupt foreshortening and brutal violence, as well as the vigor of the painterly surface, belie any sense of "a woman's touch" in her art. This style, which she inculcated into Neapolitan painting, became, if anything, more painterly under the influence of Van Dyck in London (compare her pre-London *Self-Portrait* in the Prado, Madrid, with her *Self-Portrait* in the Spencer Collection, London). A painting from her last period, *The Birth of St. John the Baptist* (Prado), part of a series she did in conjunction with Massimo Stanzione, exemplifies the manner in which her art influenced the development of Neapolitan painting. Its sense of "actuality," couched in terms of genre, its atmospheric effects of light, implied vigor of the forms, and moderately painterly surface are qualities that make her work, along with that of Ribera, one of the sources for such romantic *Caravaggisti* in Naples as Stanzione and Cavallino.

BIBLIOGRAPHY. R. Longhi, "Gentileschi, padre e figlia," *L'Arte*, XIX, 1916; *Milan, Mostra del Caravaggio e dei caravaggeschi* (catalog), Florence, 1951.

STEPHEN E. OSTROW

GENTILESCHI (Lomi), ORAZIO. Italian painter (b. Pisa, ca. 1563; d. London, 1639). Orazio first studied with his brother Aurelio and then went to Rome at an early age, remaining there until 1620. He then traveled to Ancona and Fabriano, settled briefly in Genoa (1621–24), and moved to Paris (1625) and finally to London (1626), where he worked for the English court until his death. His "Florentine" manner of precise, flowing contours (*Angel Gabriel*, Turin, Albertina) acquired Caravaggesque overtones during his Roman experience (*St. Francis Supported by an Angel*, ca. 1600; Rome, Corsini Collection). He was especially influenced by Caravaggio's early manner (though not his *tenebroso*) with its anecdotal realism and textural descriptiveness (*St. Cecilia and an Angel*, ca. 1606; Corsini Collection). Even before he left Rome this Caravaggism diminished (*St. Peter Nolasco Carried by Angels*, Rome, S. Adriano), a tendency which was accentuated when he went to northern Italy and came within the Venetian orbit (*Annunciation*, ca. 1623; Turin, Sabauda Gallery).

The style that Orazio brought to England is best exemplified by his *Lot and His Daughters* (London, Spencer Collection). The accent here is on clear if complex contours, bathed in light, the inherent grace of which nullifies the "vulgar" overtones of the subject. Much the same submersion of realistic detail in a network of flowing line can be seen in his famous *Rest on the Flight into Egypt* (ca. 1626; Paris, Louvre; Vienna, Museum of Art History). The influence of Van Dyck in England is the final ingredient of Orazio's stylistic development. In his *Finding of Moses* (Madrid, Prado; Castle Howard), painted for Philip IV in 1630, Orazio not only softened outlines but completely eliminated all hints of anything not imbued with courtly elegance.

Orazio is typical of the *Caravaggisti* in that he selected certain aspects of the master's manner to graft onto his own style; his Caravaggism is neither complete nor permanent. He was at heart an eclectic, who stretched over a framework of Tuscan *disegno* the threads of Caravaggesque, Venetian, and northern (Van Dyckian) influences. But for all this, he formed a basis for that type of northern genre realism which is dependent on grace of form and subtlety of light effect; he was, in short, a forerunner of such painters as Vermeer.

BIBLIOGRAPHY. R. Longhi, "Gentileschi, padre e figlia," *L'Arte*, XIX, 1916; C. Gamba, "Orazio Gentileschi," *Dedalo*, III, 1922; D. R. de Campos, "Una 'Giuditta,' opera sconosciuta del Gentileschi nella Pinacoteca Vaticana," *Rivista d'arte*, XXI, 1939; A. M. Crinò and B. Nicolson, "Further Documents Relating to Orazio Gentileschi," *The Burlington Magazine*, CIII, 1961.

STEPHEN E. OSTROW

GENTILI, ANTONIO (Antonio da Faenza). Italian goldsmith (1519–1607). He was active in his native Rome (1550–67) with Orazio Marchesi and Gabriele Gerardi. His greatest masterpieces, commissioned by Cardinal Alessandro Farnese, were executed for St. Peter's and consisted of a silver and gold altar cross and two chased silver candlesticks wrought for the main altar. In 1585, he was appointed Master of the Pope's Mint.

GENTILI FAMILY. Family dynasty of Italian majolica painters from Castelli (Abruzzi). The founder of the dynasty was Bernardino II (d. 1683), who studied under Francesco di Giovanni Grue. The family line continued through the 18th century in Bernardino's two sons, Giacomo I (1668–1713) and Carmine (1678–1763); Carmine studied under Carlantonio di Francesco di Giovanni Grue and later taught his own sons, Giacomo il Giovane (b. 1717) and Bernardino III (1727–1813), both of whom specialized in genre and pastoral scenes, reflecting the light, rococo taste of the century.

BIBLIOGRAPHY. V. Balzano, *L'arte abruzzese*, Bergamo, 1910.

GEOMETRIC STYLE. Term used to describe the style of Greek vase painting and miniature sculpture prevalent from about 900 to 725 B.C. The essential characteristic of the style is the use of rectilinear patterns, sometimes completely abstract, sometimes stylized versions of human and animal forms. Athens, with its monumental Dipylon amphorae, was the foremost producer of Geometric painted pottery. *See* DIPYLON VASE.

BIBLIOGRAPHY. G. M. A. Richter, *A Handbook of Greek Art*, 3d ed., London, 1963.

Orazio Gentileschi, *SS. Valerian, Tiburtius, and Cecilia*. Brera, Milan.

GEORGE, SIR ERNEST. English architect (1839–1922). He was mainly a domestic architect who presumably popularized the Netherlands style for the 19th century. Melcombe, in Dorset, and Batsford, in Gloucestershire, are his major houses, and the Royal Academy of Music, in Marylebone, his chief public commission. Sir Edwin Lutyens was one of his pupils.

GEORGE GISZE, PORTRAIT OF. Oil painting by Holbein the Younger, in the former State Museums, Berlin. *See* HOLBEIN, HANS, THE YOUNGER.

GEORGE OF CAPPADOCIA, ST. Martyr. While an officer in the Roman army, he passed through a city terrorized by a dragon to whom the inhabitants had offered one sheep and one youth chosen by lot each day. George vanquished the dragon and rescued the king's daughter. After terrible tortures, he was martyred under Diocletian at Diospolis, formerly Lydda, Persia. He has been confused with George, patron saint of England. His attributes are a broken lance, sword, and a princess with a dragon on a "leash" (her girdle). His feast is April 23.
See also SAINTS IN ART.

GEORGE WASHINGTON, PORTRAIT OF. Oil painting by Stuart, in the Museum of Fine Arts, Boston (on permanent loan from the Boston Athenaeum). *See* STUART, GILBERT.

GERARD, BARON FRANCOIS-PASCAL-SIMON. French painter (b. Rome, 1770; d. Paris, 1837). In 1782 he studied with the sculptor Pajou and in 1786 with J.-L. David. He was a fine portraitist: *Isabey and His Daughter* (1785) and *Marquise Visconti* (1810) are both in the Louvre, Paris. During his lifetime he was occupied with portraits of the nobility (Versailles, Museum, and elsewhere). In allegorical and history painting he produced the neoclassic *Love and Psyche* (1798; Louvre) and the large *Battle of Austerlitz* (1808; Versailles, Museum). Gérard's cold, smooth, and dry style set the standard for official art for a long time; he was much imitated and copied.

BIBLIOGRAPHY. C. Lenormant, *François Gérard, peintre d'histoire...*, Paris, 1846; F. Gérard, *Oeuvre du Bon François Gérard, 1789–1836*, texte par H. Gérard, 3 vols. in 4, Paris, 1852–57; H. Gérard, ed., *Correspondance de François Gérard...*, Paris, 1867.

GERARD, IGNACE-ISIDORE, *see* GRANDVILLE, SEAN.

GERARD OF HAARLEM, *see* GEERTGEN TOT SINT JANS.

GERHAERT VON LEYDEN, NIKOLAUS, *see* GERHARD, NIKOLAUS, FROM LEYDEN.

GERHARD, HUBERT. Dutch sculptor, bronzeworker (b. s'Hertogenbosch, Netherlands, ca. 1540; d. Munich, 1620). Gerhard traveled in Italy and studied under Giovanni Bologna. He spent from 1581 until the end of the 16th century in the service of Duke William V of Bavaria. At the time of the Duke's abdication in 1598, Gerhard joined the service of the Fugger family of Augsburg, working particularly on their castle at Kirchheim, for which he executed the first monumental bronze fountain north of the Alps. After 1613, he became active at the court of Archduke Maximilian III of Hapsburg at Innsbruck. Hubert Gerhard was probably the most important of the northern Renaissance bronzesmiths.

BIBLIOGRAPHY. Y. Hackenbroch, *Bronzes, Other Metalwork and Sculpture in the Irwin Untermyer Collection*, New York, 1962.

GERHARD, NIKOLAUS, FROM LEYDEN (Nicolaus von Leyden; Nikolaus Gerhaert von Leyden; Nicolaus Lerch). Netherlandish-German sculptor (b. ca. 1420/30; d. Wiener Neustadt, ca. 1473). He was the chief master of late Gothic sculpture in the Upper Rhine. In Trier he created the tomb monument of Archbishop von Sierck (1462), in Strasbourg the votive relief of Canon von Büsang (1464), and in Vienna the grave plaque of Friedrich IV (1473).

BIBLIOGRAPHY. L. Fischel, *Nicolaus Gerhaert und die Bildhauer der deutschen Spätgotik*, Munich, 1944.

GERHARD OF COLOGNE. German architect (fl. ca. 1250–75). Gerhard was the first architect of the Cathedral of Cologne. The choir with its glazed Rayonnant Gothic triforium was completed under his guidance in 1258. He is also credited with the designs of the Cathedral of München-Gladbach (1256–75) and the Cistercian church at Altenburg (begun in 1255). Gerhard studied the High Gothic cathedrals of France as a young man and was responsible for the continuation of the French trend of stylistic development in German architecture of his time.

BIBLIOGRAPHY. P. Frankl, *Gothic Architecture*, Baltimore, 1962.

GERICAULT, THEODORE. French painter (b. Rouen, 1791; d. Paris, 1824). The son of wealthy parents, he was financially independent throughout his life, a fact which helps to explain the experimental and fragmentary character of much of his work. Frustrated heroic ambition, a spirit of restlessness and nostalgia, and irritable nervous sensibility were features of his personality that helped to shape his passionate, masculine, and deeply romantic art. About 1808, Géricault took his first lessons from Carle Vernet, a fashionable painter of sporting subjects. In 1810–11 he pursued more systematic studies under the rigorous classicist Pierre Guérin, who introduced him to the principles of Davidian history painting. Very soon, Géricault began to work on his own, copying Renaissance and baroque masters at the Louvre. This self-training opened his eyes to the colorism and dynamism of Rubens, Caravaggio, Titian, and Veronese, thus counterbalancing his classicist training. At the Salon of 1812 he exhibited his first independent work, the *Charging Chasseur* (Paris, Louvre), a large equestrian portrait expressive of the war fever of that year, which in its dramatic energy, baroque composition, and Rubens-like colorism seemed a deliberate attack on academic classicism.

In the years that followed, Géricault retreated from this exuberance into a more controlled, compactly sculptural style, closer to classicism. The somber *Wounded Cuirassier* (1814; Louvre), several military portraits (Louvre; and Rouen, Museum of Fine Arts), the three large *Heroic Land-*

Théodore Géricault, *The Raft of the Medusa*. Louvre, Paris. A highly controversial work when first exhibited in the Salon of 1819.

scapes (New York, W. Chrysler and H. Hartford Collections), and a number of classicist projects (*The Death of Paris*; *Gigantomachy*) illustrate his striving for a grand style. A stay in Italy in 1816–17 brought him under the spell of Michelangelo, Raphael, and the baroque masters. From this time date mythological compositions (*Leda*; *Nymph and Centaur*) in a terse graphic style that marks Géricault's closest approach to classicism. At the same time he retained an interest in dramatic modern themes, as is shown by studies of "picturesque" Italian subjects. Two of these, *Cattle Market* (Cambridge, Mass., Fogg Art Museum) and *Riderless Horse Race* (Baltimore, Walters Gallery; Louvre; Lille, Museum of Fine Arts; and Rouen, Museum of Fine Arts), he ultimately translated into monumentally conceived, classical scenes, divested of all modern detail.

On his return to France, in 1817, he sought for a subject that would permit him to combine his interest in grandly monumental stylization with his relish for dramatic modernity. The incident of a shipwreck that was then the subject of violent public debate gave him this opportunity. The *Raft of the Medusa* (1819; Louvre), a very large canvas representing the survivors of the disaster straining toward rescue, was the result of intense year-long labor. It is a composite of realist observation (he made studies after cadavers and hospital patients), dramatic analysis (in a series of compositions he explored every phase of the

disaster), tense formal discipline, and romantic imagination. Synthesizing all that was vital in the art of the period, the painting stirred tremendous controversy. Géricault, disappointed and tired, left for England (1820), where the *Medusa* was being exhibited for a fee.

He was profoundly impressed by what he saw of English art—the landscapes of Constable and the genre and animal scenes of Wilkie, Ward, and Landseer—and his own reaction against classical stylization and heroic subjects was confirmed by it. For some time, he had been experimenting with water-color painting and lithography (military subjects, 1818–19). Stimulated by English art, he renewed his acquaintance with the essentially anticlassical tradition of realist genre to which Carle Vernet had introduced him. His gift for intimate observation and sensuous color came strongly to the fore. In small format and minute execution he drew and painted horsemen, farriers, waggoners, and caged lions, and also produced a fine series of lithographs. The *Epsom Derby* (1821; Louvre), the most important painting of his English stay, presents an interesting contrast to his earlier *Riderless Horse Race*: light, atmosphere, and the effect of speed now are the dominant aspect; landscape prevails over figure composition.

In Géricault's last years he continued in the realist manner of his English genre pieces and cultivated a highly refined colorism in water colors and oils. His *Lime Kiln* (ca. 1822; Louvre), depicting a factory set on muddy slopes, is a remarkably original landscape in its combination of sober realism and romantic sentiment. Akin to it in spirit are the five *Portraits of the Insane* (Louvre; Ghent; Winterthur, Del.; Lyons; Springfield, Mass.), remnants of a series of studies painted in the clinic of Dr. Georget. Observed with scientific accuracy, they also possess great depth of psychological insight and tragic power in their simple dignity. At this time, Géricault also painted several remarkable portraits of Negroes (Rouen, Museum of Fine Arts; Buffalo, Albright-Knox Art Gallery). His last projects were concerned, once again, with monumental compositions of vital, modern subjects: *The Negro Slave Trade* and *The Opening of the Prisons of the Inquisition*; only scattered studies for them remain.

Although he was not the leader of a movement, Géricault strongly influenced the artists of his generation, notably the young Delacroix. His peculiar position midway between classicism and romanticism caused him to be claimed by both movements. Today he appears significant chiefly for having attempted to formulate a modern style that would combine the grandeur of the classical tradition with the freshness and urgency of observed life. His effort became a starting point for such later attempts at monumental realism as are to be found in the work of Delacroix, Courbet, and Cézanne.

Despite the brevity of his career, his range of style is very wide. It includes the fresh, Rubens-like colorism of his early military sketches; the somber, sculptural compactness of his classicist phase, from about 1814 to 1818; the baroque chiaroscuro of the *Raft of the Medusa*; and the color subtlety and refined execution of his late, English-inspired horse genre and Oriental scenes. Thematically, his work extended from classical mythology to modern military anecdote. The drama of physical conflict deeply fascinated him; he returned over and over again to the image of struggle: men fighting, men taming animals, animals attacking one another.

At the time of his death, at the age of thirty-three, Géricault's work was still only fragmentary. In addition to his few finished paintings, he left behind a vast body of studies and sketches, a series of lithographs (1817–23) which are among the earliest masterworks in this technique, and a few sculptural essays (*Nymph and Satyr*; *Negro Attacking a Woman*, Albright-Knox Art Gallery). His paintings are scattered throughout the public and private collections of Europe (chiefly Louvre; museums of Rouen, Bayonne, Lille, Lyons, Montpellier, Besançon, Brussels, Ghent, Munich, and Stockholm; private collections in Paris and Winterthur) and the United States (museums in Buffalo, Springfield, Cambridge, Brooklyn, Chicago, and New York).

BIBLIOGRAPHY. C. Clément, *Géricault*, 3d ed., Paris, 1879; G. Oprescu, *Géricault*, Paris, 1927; K. Berger, *Géricault and His Work*, Lawrence, Kan., 1955; D. Aimé-Azam, *Mazeppa, Géricault et son temps*, Paris, 1956; L. Eitner, *Géricault, An Album of Drawings in the Art Institute of Chicago*, Chicago, 1960.
LORENZ EITNER

GERINES, JACQUES DE (Jacob de Coperslagere). Flemish bronze caster (fl. Brussels, 1392; d. there, 1463). His two destroyed masterpieces are known from sketches and engravings: figures of the tomb of Louis de Male (1455) in St-Pierre de Lille and the tomb of Johanna of Brabant (1458) in the Carmelite church of Brussels. The latter was painted by Rogier van der Weyden. To Gerines are ascribed ten bronze statuettes commissioned by Philip the Good for the Amsterdam City Hall (Amsterdam, Rijksmuseum). Gerines employed a vigorous Gothic manner.

BIBLIOGRAPHY. E. Marchal, *La Sculpture et les chefs-d'oeuvre de l'orfèvrerie belges*, Brussels, 1895.

GERINI, *see* LORENZO DI NICCOLO GERINI; NICCOLO DI PIETRO GERINI.

GERMAIN FAMILY. Silversmiths active in Paris during the 17th and 18th centuries. The first, François, became a freeman in 1643 and was the father of Pierre I. Little is known of his career other than that he was a silversmith, probably from the south of France. Pierre I (b. Paris, 1644/45; d. 1684) was commissioned at the age of seventeen to do the covers of several precious books owned by Louis XIV and thereafter worked often for the king, with the title "orfèvre ordinaire du roi."

Of Pierre's two sons, Charles (fl. 1695) worked in Rome on silver for the Gesù, but Thomas (1673–1748) is the more famous and has been called the ablest silversmith of the 18th century. Trained as an architect and sculptor, he was the finest exponent of the most exuberant rococo design. Pierre II (b. Avignon, 1716; d. Paris, 1783), possibly a nephew of Thomas, called "the Roman" because of his schooling in Rome, worked with J. J. Roëttiers in the Louvre. He is best known for his books of design, *Elements d'orfèvrerie* (1748) and *Livre d'ornements* (1751), which were followed by other craftsmen. Thomas's son, François-Thomas (b. Paris, 1726; d. 1791), took over his father's shop in 1749 and produced large quantities of silver. He was one of the most popular silversmiths of his time and worked extensively for the Portuguese court as well as for the courts of Russia and Poland.

BIBLIOGRAPHY. G. Bapst, *Etudes sur l'orfèvrerie française au XVIIIe siècle*, Paris, 1887; F. Dennis, *Three Centuries of French Domestic Silver...*, New York, 1960.
MARVIN D. SCHWARTZ

GERMAIN OF AUXERRE, ST. Bishop (ca. 378–448). He trained in Rome as an advocate and ruled over part of Gaul. Made bishop of Auxerre in 418, he was sent to Britain by Pope Celestine I in 429 to combat Pelagianism and won British clergy back to orthodoxy. On a second trip, Germain aided the Britons in routing the pagan Picts and Saxons and founded schools for clergy. He may have consecrated Patrick bishop in Auxerre. In 448, he visited Ravenna to plead for Armoricans. He has no attributes. His feast is July 31. *See* GENEVIEVE OF PARIS, ST.

See also SAINTS IN ART.

GERMAN EMBASSY BUILDING, LENINGRAD, *see* BEHRENS, PETER.

GERMANIC ART. The beginning of Germanic art is difficult to establish. Some scholars would trace its origin to the battle-axe–corded-ware cultures of the late Neolithic; others would seek its rise in the coalescence of the diverse elements of the Neolithic which developed into the Scan-

Germanic art. Picture stone from Hablingbo, Gotland, A.D. 400.

dinavian Bronze Age. There is a continuity of cultural and artistic development in the northernmost part of Germany and southern Scandinavia throughout the Bronze Age. These lands shared the same types of tools and weapons, jewelry and ornament, and pottery. This Bronze Age art has a geometric decoration based upon the use of the concentric circle, spiral, and wave motifs. Northern Scandinavia possessed a quite different woodland culture, whose affinities were with similar cultures of the Eurasiatic forest zone.

The unity of the northern Bronze Age lasted until the 8th century B.C., when these Germanic peoples began to expand over the north German plain. This expansion led to the rise of three distinct cultural areas, two of which have interesting forms of art. In the east there was the face-urn culture of Pomerania, characterized by cremation urns with schematized faces, and in the center, between the Elbe and the Oder, the house-urn culture, with cremation urns recalling those of Italy. The third area, in northwestern Germany, is known from the impoverished Wessenstedt and Jastorf cultures, which had nothing of artistic significance. There were obvious Hallstatt influences and even imports from Italy in the 7th and 6th centuries.

It is only in the 5th century B.C., when La Tène influence was penetrating northern Germany and Scandinavia, that one can state with some certainty that the peoples of these lands were Germanic. During this period, when the knowledge of iron reached Scandinavia, there was a tendency for these cultures to differentiate into northern, eastern, and western groups. Some archaeologists would argue that the northwestern German, Rhine-Weser, Elbe, Vistula, and

Oder-Warthe groups were gradually differentiated during the 4th to 1st centuries as the Germanic peoples pushed farther southward. These Germanic groups possessed an impoverished art relieved only by imports from the Celtic La Tène peoples or from the Mediterranean area. During the period of the Roman Empire, Germanic art was strongly affected by Roman provincial influences. In the 3d and 4th centuries of our era new names began to appear for the German tribes beyond the Rhine and Danube, such as Angle, Saxon, Frank, Burgundian, Alamanni, Lombard, Vandal, Visigoth, and Ostrogoth. The Germanic peoples were on the eve of the Migration age.

See also MIGRATION STYLE.

BIBLIOGRAPHY. H. Kühn, *Die vorgeschichtliche Kunst Deutschlands*, Berlin, 1935; C. Schuchhardt, *Vorgeschichte von Deutschland*, 5th ed., Munich, 1943; H. Jankuhn, *Denkmäler der Vorzeit zwischen Nord- und Ostsee*, Schleswig, 1957.

HOMER L. THOMAS

GERMANY, MUSEUMS OF. See under the names of the following cities:

Aachen (Aix-la-Chapelle). Suermondt Museum.

Aschaffenburg. Municipal Museum.

Augsburg. State Gallery and Municipal Art Collections.

Bamberg. New Residence (including State and Municipal Picture Gallery).

Bayreuth. New Residence (State Picture Gallery).

Berlin. West Berlin: Brücke Museum; Charlottenburg Castle; Gallery of the 20th Century; Former State Museums (Egyptian, Greco-Roman, Islamic, Far Eastern, and Sculpture Collections); Former State Museums (Picture Gallery, National Gallery, Print Cabinet, and Museum of Arts and Crafts). East Berlin: Museum Island.

Bielefeld. Municipal Museum.

Bonn. Municipal Art Collections; Rhenish Landesmuseum.

Bremen. Art Gallery (Kunsthalle); Ludwig-Roselius Collection; Paula Becker-Modersohn Collection.

Brunswick (Braunschweig). Guelph Treasury; Herzog-Anton-Ulrich Museum.

Coburg. Veste Coburg Art Collections.

Cologne. Archiepiscopal Diocesan Museum; Schnuetgen Museum; Wallraf-Richartz Museum.

Darmstadt. Hessian Landesmuseum.

Dresden. State Art Collections.

Duisburg. Lehmbruck Museum.

Dusseldorf. Art Museum; Jägerhof Museum.

Essen. Folkwang Museum.

Frankfurt am Main. Municipal Sculpture Collection (Liebieghaus); Städel Art Institute and Municipal Gallery.

Freiburg im Breisgau. Municipal Collections (Augustinermuseum).

Hamburg. Art Gallery; Barlach House.

Hannover. Kestner Museum; Lower Saxony Landesmuseum.

Heidelberg. Palatinate Museum.

Karlsruhe. State Art Gallery.

Kassel. State Picture Collections.

Kiel. Art Gallery.

Konstanz. Rosgarten Museum.

Krefeld. Kaiser-Wilhelm Museum.

Lubeck. Sankt Annen Museum.

Léon Gérôme, *Meeting of the Siamese Ambassador and Napoleon III at Fontainebleau.* Versailles Museum.

Mainz. Museum of Antiquities and Picture Gallery.

Mannheim. Municipal Art Gallery.

Minden. Cathedral Treasury (Domschatzkammer).

Munich. Bavarian National Museum; Bavarian State Picture Galleries (New Pinacothek and New State Gallery, Old Pinacothek, Schack Gallery); Municipal Gallery and Lenbach Gallery; Residence Museum; Residence Treasury (Schatzkammer); State Antiquities Collection (Glyptothek).
See also Schleissheim/Munich.

Nurnberg. Albrecht-Dürer House; Germanic National Museum.

Oldenburg. Landesmuseum for Art and Cultural History.

Recklinghausen. Municipal Art Gallery.

Schleissheim/Munich. Schleissheim Castle and State Picture Gallery.

Stuttgart. Sonnenhalde Artists House; State Gallery: Württemburg Landesmuseum.

Trier. Cathedral Treasury.

Ulm. Municipal Collection of Art and Cultural History.

Wurzburg. Mainfränkisches Museum.

GERMIGNY-DES-PRES, CHURCH OF. French Carolingian oratory near Orléans. It was built for Theodulf of Orléans in 806 and was badly restored in the late 19th century.

This small structure has a Greek-cross plan with nine vaulted compartments. Each of the arms culminates in an apse, with the eastern end having two smaller apsidioles in addition. The central compartment opens into a tall, square, towerlike space, while the corner compartments are vaulted with small domes on squinches. The entire vaulting system is based upon four central piers.

The church was influenced by East Christian and Moorish sources. The former influence derives from such buildings as the Cathedral of Echmiadzin, Armenia, as rebuilt in 628; the latter influence can be seen in the horseshoe arches, in both their plan and elevation.

GERNRODE: ST. CYRIACUS. Ottonian church in Lower Saxony, Germany, dedicated about 961. It is built on a three-aisled basilican plan with both an eastern and a western apse, a transept, and two flanking towers in the west. As such it differs little from other Ottonian buildings of the period, but the articulation of the interior indicates a development in the direction of Romanesque. Despite a flat timber roof, the sophisticated, subtly proportioned relationship of aisle, gallery, and clerestory openings marks a new direction. The aisle arcade rests alternately on pier and on column, creating two arches between each pier. On the gallery level, three arches between the piers are each divided in two, giving a relationship of 6:2 between piers. On the clerestory level a single light is placed over each grouping of gallery arches. This arrangement lends a subtle rhythm to the whole, creating a well-articulated, plastic interior space.

GEROME, LEON. French painter, etcher, and sculptor (b. Vesoul, 1824; d. Paris, 1904). The son of a goldsmith, Jean Léon Gérôme went to Paris and began his studies with Delaroche in 1841. He made his debut in the Salon of 1846 with *Cockfight* (Paris, Luxembourg Museum), which was received with immediate enthusiasm. For the next ten years Gérôme painted subjects drawn from Greek and Roman history, which he painstakingly researched for accuracy. His most successful neoclassic painting was *Age of Augustus*, which was very popular at the World Exhibition of 1855.

In 1856 Gérôme traveled to Egypt and spent four months on a Nile boat studying the natives and landscape. Out of this Egyptian experience came several paintings of Oriental subjects; the most famous is *The Captive* (1857;

Nantes Museum). In the remaining years of his active career, he also painted contemporary subjects (*Meeting of the Siamese Ambassador and Napoleon III at Fontainebleau*, Versailles Museum). As a sculptor, Gérôme is best known for his equestrian statue of Napoleon (formerly Paris, Luxembourg Museum). His style combined the clear linearism of his neoclassic training with a sense of sentimentality and, at times, eroticism in the literary interpretation of subject matter.

BIBLIOGRAPHY. C. Moreau-Vauthier, *Gérôme, peintre et sculpteur*, Paris, 1906.

JULIA M. EHRESMANN

GERONA BEATUS COMMENTARY. Mozarabic illuminated manuscript, in the Cathedral Library, Gerona, Spain. *See* BEATUS OF LIEBANA.

GERONA CATHEDRAL. Spanish Romanesque cathedral, consecrated in 1038, whose tower, cloister, marble high altar, and episcopal throne survive. The *chevet* (1312–47) by Master Enrique, with nine radiating chapels, is modeled after Barcelona Cathedral's. In 1416 a council of master masons decided to continue the church with a single span of about 75 feet. The last of the four bays of this width was vaulted in the late 17th century. In 1580 twin towers were begun for the west façade, but only one was finished. The baroque portal (1680–1733) is by Pedro Costa.

The *chevet* retains much 14th-century glass, and the silver-gilt retable of the high altar (1309) with its *repoussé* baldachino are justly famous. The church is rich in sculptured tombs and houses a magnificent collection of tapestries, paintings, and liturgical instruments as well as notable manuscripts.

BIBLIOGRAPHY. L. Font, *Gerona, la Catedral y el Museo Diocesano*, Gerona, 1952; P. de Palol Salellas, *Gerona*, Barcelona, 1953.

GERONIMO DA FORLI, MAESTRO, *see* MASTER OF THE RESURRECTION PANEL.

GERVASE OF CANTERBURY. Benedictine English chronicler (ca. 1141–1210). After 1163 he was a monk at the abbey of Christchurch, in Canterbury. Later, he became a close friend and disciple of Thomas à Becket. In English art he is sometimes represented with Becket.

GERZSO, GUNTHER. Mexican painter (1915–   ). Born in Mexico City, Gerzso is self-taught, with inspiration from Julio Castellaños and Otto Butterlin. He has worked as a stage designer. His paintings were shown in the National Museum of Modern Art, Mexico City, in 1963, and he represented Mexico at the São Paulo Bienal of 1965. Coloristic geometric abstractions are his forte.

BIBLIOGRAPHY. Instituto Nacional de Bellas Artes, *Günther Gerzso*, Mexico City, 1965.

GESELLIUS, HERMAN. Finnish architect (1874–1916). He studied at the Polytechnic Institute, Helsinki, before becoming head of the influential firm of Gesellius, Lindgren, and Saarinen at the turn of the century. *See* SAARINEN, ELIEL.

GESSI, FRANCESCO. Italian painter (b. Bologna, 1588; d. there, 1649). He studied under Calvaert and Cremonini. At first Gessi adopted the dramatic style of Lodovico Car-

racci, and later he became a slavish follower of Guido Reni, finishing a number of his paintings. Many of Gessi's works hang in the churches and museums of Bologna.

GESSNER, JOHANN CONRAD. Swiss painter (1764–1826). The son of Salomon Gessner, Johann Conrad studied at Dresden with Graff and Zingg, and later went to Rome (1787), where he turned to landscape painting. During a stay in England (1796–1803) he painted in water colors and pioneered in lithography. Stylistically, his landscapes derive from the Dutch tradition.

GESSNER, SALOMON. Swiss painter and graphic artist (b. Zurich, 1730; d. there, 1780). Gessner, who was a well-known poet in the circle of Ramler and Hagedom and an art theorist, also merits recognition as an accomplished visual artist. For a long period after 1762 he turned exclusively to art, producing etchings, engravings, water colors, oils, ink and gouache drawings, and paintings on porcelain. His style was in the best rococo tradition and his ideas of subject matter were equally rococo; he peopled his "ideal" landscapes with shepherds, satyrs, and nymphs. In 1772 he brought forth a new edition of his then famous *Idyllen* (1st ed., 1756), this time illustrated with his own vignettes. His art theory is to be found in *Brief über die Landschaftsmahlerey an Herrn Füesslin* (1787).

BIBLIOGRAPHY. R. Hamann, *Die deutsche Malerei vom 18. bis zum Beginn des 20. Jahrhunderts . . .*, Leipzig, 1925.

GESSO. Mixture of plaster and glue applied to wooden panels as a preparatory ground for painting. Other forms of gesso—for example, gesso d'oro—are used to produce ground for gilding, such as the gilding commonly used on imitation carved picture frames. In northern Europe gesso painting was used primarily with oil colors; in Italy, with tempera media. Two layers, one coarse (gesso grosso) and one finer and less absorbent (gesso sottile), were usually applied one after another over the ground.

BIBLIOGRAPHY. D. V. Thompson, *The Practice of Tempera Painting*, New Haven, 1936.

GESTALT. German word meaning "form" or "shape," but suggesting the totality of the way something is put together. As a concept of psychology, gestalt was first broadly developed by Christian von Ehrenfels (1890), who opposed the mechanistic approach of the 19th century and sought to reemphasize experience as the immediate perception of whole entities with particular qualities relating to their wholeness. As elaborated in the 20th century by Max Wertheimer, Wolfgang Köhler, and Kurt Koffka, the theory has had immense influence in psychology and other disciplines. In aesthetics, gestalt theory and the notion that visual expression and perception are based on laws of organization have been used by Rudolph Arnheim and others in the exploration of the creation and effect of works of art.

GESTEL, LEO. Dutch painter and lithographer (b. Woerden, 1881; d. 1941). He studied with his father, William Gestel, with his uncle, Dimmen Gestel, and at the Amsterdam Academy. Leo's early work recapitulated the styles of the late 19th century, for example, the postimpressionist *Still Life* (1911; Otterlo, Kröller-Müller Museum). By 1913

Il Gesù, Rome, façade, designed by Giacomo della Porta.

he was painting simplified cubistic landscapes and figures. In the 1920s his subjects, showing the influence of Belgian expressionism, were strongly stylized and tightly composed with strong, dull color. Much of his later work consisted of similarly treated figures, often nudes.

BIBLIOGRAPHY. J. Slagter, *Leo Gestel*, The Hague, 1948.

GESU, IL, ROME. Church begun by Vignola in 1568 for Cardinal Alessandro Farnese and consecrated in 1584. Basilican in plan, it has a nave flanked by side chapels, a short transept, and an apse directly behind the domed crossing. Il Gesù was the mother church of the Jesuit order. Its plan, ideally suited for preaching to large numbers of people, established a type followed in countless congregational churches throughout the Roman Catholic world. The façade, with large scrolls connecting the lower chapel roofs and the high front of the nave, was also a prototype for baroque church architecture. It was the work of Giacomo della Porta, who changed Vignola's original scheme. In the interior, architecture, sculpture, and painting, by means of dramatic lighting, are merged to produce exciting and theatrical effects.

BIBLIOGRAPHY. A. E. Brinckmann, *Die Baukunst des 17. und 18. Jahrhunderts in den romanischen Ländern*, Berlin-Neubabelsberg, 1919.

GEYSER, CHRISTIAN GOTTLIEB. German engraver and miniature painter (b. Görlitz, 1742; d. Leipzig, 1803). He was the father of the engraver Friedrich Christian Gottlieb Geyser (b. 1772). Christian is known mainly for his book illustrations, the best of which appear in Heyne's edition of Vergil, after Johann Fiorello, and in Hinchfield's *Theory of Gardening*.

GHANA, see AFRICA, PRIMITIVE ART OF (WEST AFRICA).

GHAT. Hindu landing place with ranges of steps lining the shores of lakes and the banks of rivers, as on the Ganges at Benares.

GHAZNAVID PAINTING, *see* ISLAMIC PAINTING (UMAYYAD AND EARLY ABBASID PERIODS: GHAZNAVID SCHOOL).

GHEERAERTS, MARCUS I. Flemish portrait and history painter (ca. 1525–before 1599). Born in Bruges, he studied with his father, Egbert Gheeraerts. Marcus I was a master in the Bruges guild in 1558. He executed paintings for Bruges churches, notably for the Church of Our Lady, where he finished Bernard van Orley's altarpiece of the Passion. In 1567 Marcus illustrated Aesop's *Fables*, in which his skill in drawing animals is displayed. The next year he went to England; there he is supposed to have painted portraits, but none are known today. He was the father of Marcus II Gheeraerts.

BIBLIOGRAPHY. R. L. Pool, "Marcus Gheeraerts, Father and Son, Painters," *Walpole Society Annual*, III, 1913–14.

GHEERAERTS, MARCUS II. Flemish-English portrait painter (b. Bruges, 1561; d. London, 1635/36). The son of Marcus I Gheeraerts, Marcus II was the most important of the Elizabethan and Jacobean portrait painters. He went to England in 1568; studied with Lucas de Heere, who was also in London; and made at least one trip back to the Continent, in 1577, when he was received in the Antwerp guild. Marcus II spent most of the rest of his life in England. A court painter from 1611 on, he was "his Majestie's paynter" in 1617 and "picture drawer" to James I in 1618. In his numerous life-size, full-length portraits of aristocrats, the emphasis is on the costumes, the rich brocades and laces, and the jewelry rather than on the faces, which are somewhat stereotyped and expressionless. He painted a few group portraits and a number of representations of the royal family. The portrait of Queen Elizabeth preserved at Welbeck Abbey is signed. Marcus II must have had a huge workshop, and countless repetitions of his works exist.

BIBLIOGRAPHY. R. L. Pool, "Marcus Gheeraerts, Father and Son, Painters," *Walpole Society Annual*, III, 1913–14.

GHENT (Gand). City in northern Belgium that has retained an extraordinary ensemble of private houses and public buildings, both ecclesiastical and secular, dating from the 12th to the 16th century. The Abbey of St. Bavon, around which the town began to develop in the 7th century, is the oldest monument. The Castle of the Counts of Flanders (Gravensteen Castle), with its picturesque ramparts along the Lys River, was founded in the 9th century, reconstructed in 1180, and radically restored in the 19th century. The Cathedral of St. Bavon (11th–17th cent.) houses the world-famous *Adoration of the Lamb* by the Van Eycks. The cloth trade, which brought the city great prosperity beginning in the 12th century, is commemorated by the monumental Cloth Hall, begun in 1425 by Simon van Assche. It adjoins the belfry, with its famous carillon, which was constructed in the 13th and 14th centuries. The only remaining example of Burgundian Gothic architecture in Ghent is the old Dominican convent. *See* GRAVENSTEEN CASTLE; ST. BAVON.

Early Flemish paintings and Brussels tapestries are the outstanding exhibits of the Fine Arts Museum. The Cistercian Abbey of La Byloke, built from the 13th to the 17th century, has interesting brick construction, vaulting, and 14th-century frescoes; it now houses an archaeological museum.

See GHENT: FINE ARTS MUSEUM; GHENT SCHOOL.

MADLYN KAHR

GHENT: FINE ARTS MUSEUM. Belgian painting of the 19th and 20th centuries accounts for a large proportion of this general collection of European painting and sculpture. The Belgian sculptor Georges Minne is represented by several works. Outstanding works of earlier periods are Bosch's *Christ Carrying the Cross* and *St. Jerome in Penitence*, Huguet's *Crucifixion of St. Peter*, Rubens's *St. Francis Receiving the Stigmata* and his oil studies for the *Flagellation* and the *Hunt of Atalanta*, and several paintings by Jordaens. The museum also has Dutch 17th-century painting and French 19th-century landscape painting (Corot, Millet, Daubigny, Boudin, Théodore Rousseau, Courbet, Harpignies, and Guillamin), as well as a collection of Brussels tapestries.

BIBLIOGRAPHY. G. Chabot, *La Musée des beaux-arts de Gand*, Brussels, 1951.

GHENT ALTARPIECE (Adoration of the Lamb). Tempera and oil panels by Hubert and Jan Van Eyck, in the Cathedral of St. Bavon, Ghent. *See* VAN EYCK, HUBERT; VAN EYCK, JAN.

GHENT SCHOOL. The Flemish city of Ghent became, for a brief time, the center of a school of painting during the second half of the 15th century. At least two painters of great importance worked there: Justus of Ghent and the Netherlandish Hugo van der Goes. Justus, however, spent only his early career in Ghent; in 1468 he went to Italy, where he worked for the court of Urbino. It was Van der Goes, with an individualistic style characterized by a heightened sense of expression, who gave the Ghent school its revolutionary character, in contrast to the more conventional centers at Bruges and Brussels. *See* GOES, HUGO VAN DER; JUSTUS OF GHENT.

BIBLIOGRAPHY. E. Panofsky, *Early Netherlandish Painting*, 2 vols., Cambridge, Mass., 1953.

GHERARDINI, ALESSANDRO. Italian painter (b. Florence, 1655; d. Livorno, 1726). Gherardini studied with Alessandro Rosi and was influenced by the Neapolitan Luca Giordano and the Venetian Sebastiano Ricci in breaking with the academicized Cortonesque style that dominated Florentine art. Many of Gherardini's frescoes in Tuscan churches emphasize celestial space and dramatically foreshortened *repoussoir* figures done in a brisk manner.

GHERARDO DI GIOVANNI DI MINIATO. Florentine miniaturist (1446–97). He was the son of Giovanni di Miniato del Favilla, the architect for the triumphal arch in Naples. Gherardo's style is indistinguishable from that of his brother, Monte; however, D'Ancona has attributed a choir book in S. Lorenzo, Florence, to Gherardo alone. Known works executed with Monte include the Missal of S. Egidio (1474–76; Florence, National Museum) and the

Bible executed for Matthias Corvinus (1492; Florence, Laurentian Library). Gherardo was also a musician and records show that he was organist at S. Maria Nuova and S. Egidio from 1470 to 1494.

BIBLIOGRAPHY. M. L. D'Ancona, *Miniatura e miniatori a Firenze dal XIV al XVI secolo*, Florence, 1962.

GHERARDO DI JACOPO, *see* STARNINA, GHERARDO.

GHEYN, JACOB DE, II. Netherlandish engraver, etcher, and print publisher (b. Antwerp, 1565; d. The Hague, 1629). He was a pupil of Hendrik Goltzius in Haarlem (1585–87). Unlike many of his contemporary printmakers, De Gheyn worked mainly after his own designs. More than 300 of his prints are his own inventions; more than 100 were made after the designs of others. What he lacked in engraving technique—the skill to achieve a wide range of effects—he more than compensated for in compositional flair and pictorial wit. His allegories and saints, soldiers and masqueraders, are in the high northern mannerist style. Several etched landscapes, however, are in the realistic vein, characteristic in this period of the transition of Dutch art from mannerism to realism.

BIBLIOGRAPHY. F. W. H. Hollstein, *Dutch and Flemish Etchings, Engravings, and Woodcuts, ca. 1450–1700*, vol. 7, Amsterdam, 1952.

GHIBERTI, LORENZO (Lorenzo di Bartolo, di Bartoluccio, or di Bartolo Michele). Italian sculptor, goldsmith, architect, painter, and writer (b. Florence, 1378; d. there, 1455). Trained as a goldsmith, he became a member of the goldsmiths' guild in 1409, the painters' guild in 1423, and the stonemasons' guild in 1426. He belonged to the circle of Florentine humanists, collected antiquities, and wrote a treatise called *Commentarii*, which contains an autobiography and a history and theory of art and is one of the main source books of the early Renaissance.

In 1400 Ghiberti left Florence to avoid the plague and was employed as a painter at the court of Carlo Malatesta, lord of Pesaro. He returned to Florence in 1401 to participate in the competition staged by the merchants' guild for the commission of the second pair of bronze doors for the Baptistery, which he won. His competition relief, representing the sacrifice of Isaac, is preserved with that of another competitor, Filippo Brunelleschi, in the National Museum (Bargello), Florence. Ghiberti's efforts during the next fifty years were dominated by designing and executing this and the third pair of bronze doors for the baptistery, known as the "Gates of Paradise."

Work on the earlier doors began in January, 1404. Containing twenty quatrefoil panels of scenes from the life of Christ and eight panels of figures of the four Evangelists and four Church Fathers, with, at the angles, forty-seven heads of prophets and prophetesses and a self-portrait, the doors were completed in 1424 and installed on the east side of the baptistery. Within a year Ghiberti signed the contract for the third pair of doors, the Gates of Paradise. These are divided into ten nearly square panels containing some thirty-seven scenes from the Old Testament, with twenty-four full-length figures of Old Testament personages and twenty-two heads of prophets and portraits of himself and his son Vittorio in the frames. Work on these doors appears to have begun by 1428; by 1447 all the reliefs were completed; and in 1452 the east doors were moved to the north side and the Gates of Paradise installed in their place on the east side.

Other projects executed by Ghiberti in Florence are the bronze life-size statues of *St. John the Baptist* (1412–16), *St. Matthew* (1419–22), and *St. Stephen* (1425–28), commissioned respectively by the merchants' guild, the bankers' guild, and the wool guild for Or San Michele; a bronze tomb slab of Fra Leonardo Dati (d. 1423) in S. Maria Novella; marble tomb slabs of Lodovico degli Obizzi (d. 1424) and Bartolommeo Valori (d. 1427) in Sta Croce; a bronze shrine of SS. Protus, Hyacinth, and Nemesius for S. Maria degli Angeli (1428), dismantled during the French occupation, later reassembled, and now in the Bargello; a marble tabernacle for Fra Angelico's *Linaiuoli Altarpiece* (1432), in the Museum of San Marco; a bronze shrine of St. Zenobius for the Cathedral, completed in 1442; and a bronze door for a tabernacle by Bernardo Rossellino in S. Egidio (1450). Ghiberti also made two pictorial reliefs for the baptismal font in the Siena Baptistery: *St. John the Baptist before Herod* (1417) and *The Baptism of Christ* (1417–27).

From 1404 on Ghiberti also designed stained-glass windows for the Cathedral of Florence, and from 1417 until 1436 he was involved with Brunelleschi in the building of the dome of the Cathedral. In 1419 he was engaged to design a staircase for a papal apartment in S. Maria Novella. In 1420 he supervised with one Cola di Niccola (Spinelli) work on the choir stalls and other furnishings of the sacristy and the Strozzi Chapel in Sta Trinità. In 1435 he submitted, in competition with Brunelleschi and Angelo di Lazzaro d'Arezzo, a project for the choir of the Cathedral. He made gold and jeweled miters and clasps for Popes Martin V (1419) and Eugene IV (1438), and set an antique carnelian for Cosimo de' Medici (ca. 1430).

For half a century Ghiberti played a leading role in the artistic life of Florence. His workshop, which was continued after his death by his son Vittorio, became the principal training ground for the younger generation of Florentine painters and sculptors. He himself remained throughout his life a transitional master, neither purely Gothic nor purely Renaissance. His humanist instincts and his interest in theory did not quell his Gothic taste for melodious line and lyrical storytelling. Though he borrowed and adapted from Roman sarcophagi and other antique sources, he was almost equally enthusiastic about 14th-century Italian painting and French goldsmiths' work. Indeed, he discovered in the latter that exquisite working of detail and warm feeling for the soft, tactile qualities of the nude that remained ever foremost in his own art.

His development follows an unpredictable course, and is particularly difficult to chart in his work up to about 1425. Now it draws abreast of the *avant-garde* of Florence, and again it asserts the virtues of the waning past. The thread that makes the course intelligible is the artist's passion for pictorial relief, already announced in the competition panel of 1401. This leads in the 1420s to the introduction of the graduated relief, with its spatial implications. And it is this, together with an increased preference for and more subtle employment of antique motifs, that establishes the superiority of the Gates of Paradise. The reliefs of these doors are characterized by the rhythmical unification of a multitude of figures in a rational

space and the harmonious relation of the figures to realistically detailed landscape and architectural settings, some of which are of pure antique design. In such reliefs as the *Story of Isaac*, the *Story of Joseph*, and *Solomon and the Queen of Sheba* Ghiberti succeeds in mating the balance and monumentality of Renaissance design with the delicate refinement of the goldsmith's art.

BIBLIOGRAPHY. J. von Schlosser, *Lorenzo Ghibertis Denkwürdigkeiten*, Berlin, 1912; L. Planiscig, *Lorenzo Ghiberti*, Florence, 1949; J. Pope-Hennessy, *Italian Gothic Sculpture*, London, 1955; R. Krautheimer and T. Krautheimer-Hess, *Lorenzo Ghiberti*, Princeton, 1956; C. Seymour, *Sculpture in Italy, 1400–1500*, Baltimore, 1966.

DARIO A. COVI

GHIBERTI, VITTORIO (Vettorio). Italian goldsmith, bronze caster, and sculptor (1416–96). He was born in Florence and was a pupil of his father, Lorenzo. Vittorio assisted Lorenzo on the third pair of bronze doors of the baptistery, the Gates of Paradise, and after his father's death was engaged in completing the frieze of that door and the frames of all three baptistery doors.

GHIRLANDAJO, BENEDETTO DI TOMMASO. Florentine painter (1458–97). He was one of many assistants associated with his brother Domenico Ghirlandajo, a few of whose works he completed in conjunction with his brother Davide after Domenico's death. Benedetto's individual style, submerged as it is within the all-encompassing Ghirlandajo framework, has never been satisfactorily analyzed; in general, it can only be said at present that his art seems the least refined of all the Ghirlandajo workshop.

Documentary evidence indicates that Benedetto was employed as a miniature painter until the age of about twenty-two, when he gave up this craft because of failing eyesight. At that point he entered the Ghirlandajo workshop. It is known that he accompanied his brothers and Cosimo Roselli, with whom he may have been studying, to Rome to work on the frescoes commissioned for the lower walls of the Sistine Chapel in 1481–82.

The first definite appearance of Benedetto's style occurs in scattered areas of Domenico's great fresco cycle in S. Maria Novella, Florence (completed by 1490). The lateral figures in the *Dormition of the Virgin*, about two-thirds of the *Banquet of Herod*, and *S. Lucy and a Donor* seem to represent the early phase of Benedetto's style. In these works the fundamental Ghirlandajesque formula appears in an earnest attempt to depict narrative content with psychological insight; but the forms are simplified, reduced to broadly conceived planes, with hard facial contours and a rather coarse delineation of features, all rendered in the pale shadowless coloring of Cosimo Roselli.

Benedetto's only authenticated work, a small *Nativity* panel (ca. 1492; Aigueperse, Notre-Dame), was executed during the artist's trip to France late in his life. As in the work in S. Maria Novella attributed to Benedetto, much of the Aigueperse *Nativity* depends on a standard compositional scheme evolved in Domenico's workshop; the figures are arranged in a series of receding planes parallel to that of the picture, balancing each other with the geometric simplicity characteristic of all Ghirlandajo works. However, Benedetto had by this time clearly appended to his brother's style a number of Flemish elements, which were only imperfectly absorbed. These appear in the elon-

Lorenzo Ghiberti, panel of the Gates of Paradise on the east side of the Baptistery, Florence, with scenes from the Creation of Adam and Eve.

gated figure of the Virgin, with her smooth egg-shaped head artificially posed on a thin curving neck, the crumpled papery folds of drapery, and the detailed over-refinement of costume and ornament.

BIBLIOGRAPHY. G. de' Francovich, "Benedetto Ghirlandaio," *Dedalo*, VI, 1925–26; G. Marchini, "The Frescoes in the Choir of Santa Maria Novella," *The Burlington Magazine*, XCV, 1953.

PENELOPE C. MAYO

GHIRLANDAJO, DAVIDE. Italian painter of the Florentine school (1452–1525). He was the principal assistant and partner of his brother Domenico Ghirlandaio until the latter's death in 1494. In 1475 the two brothers collaborated on the decoration of the library of Sixtus IV in Rome. Most of Davide's own works, which are difficult to isolate, were done on the indication of Domenico; moreover, it is not always possible to be sure about the extent of the intervention of his brother Benedetto, who was also an assistant to Domenico. Davide is credited with two mosaics: the *Madonna and Child with Angels* (1496; Paris, Cluny Museum) and the *Annunciation* (1510) in SS. Annunziata in Florence, which was completed by Ridolfo Ghirlandaio. A detached fresco of the *Crucifixion with Two Camaldolese Monks* (Florence, S. Apollonia) shows Davide working in a Castagnesque manner. Most of the other works associated with him are in or near Florence.

BIBLIOGRAPHY. G. Poggi, "Il Reliquiario di S. Pietro Martire e un quadro di David del Ghirlandaio in S. Maria Novella," *Miscellanea d'arte*, I, January, 1903; G. Pudelko, "Davide Ghirlandaio," *Old Master Drawings*, XI, September, 1936; C. de Tolnay, "Two Frescoes by Domenico and David Ghirlandaio in Santa Trinità in Florence," *Wallraf-Richartz-Jahrbuch*, XXIII, 1961.

GHIRLANDAJO (Grillandaio), DOMENICO (Domenico Bigordi). Italian painter of the Florentine school (1449–94). He is said to have been a pupil of Alesso Baldovinetti. Domenico was the leading fresco painter of his generation and had a large workshop, which included his brothers Davide and Benedetto, his son Ridolfo, his brother-in-law Sebastiano Mainardi, and Francesco Granacci. With one exception (a Medici commission that has been lost) all Domenico's important works were public ones, either civic or religious.

In 1475 Domenico painted frescoes depicting the life of Christ in the Chapel of S. Fina in the Collegiata in San Gimignano. Two frescoes in the Church of Ognissanti in Florence, the *St. Jerome* in the church (showing influences from Flemish painting) and the *Last Supper* in the refectory, date from 1480. In 1481 and 1482 he worked in the Sistine Chapel at the Vatican, painting the *Calling of the Apostles* and the *Passage of the Red Sea*, both notable for their monumental, stolid rows of portraits. Later in 1482 he was back in Florence to direct the fresco decoration in the Sala dei Gigli of the Palazzo Vecchio (until 1484). In 1485 he completed the altarpiece of the *Adoration of the Shepherds* (also showing strong Flemish influences) in the Sassetti Chapel in Sta Trinità, where he also painted frescoes of the *Life of St. Francis* and *Portraits of Francesco Sassetti and His Wife*. The *Adoration of the Magi* in the Hospital of the Innocents in Florence is dated 1488, and a *Visitation* in the Louvre, Paris (partly executed by assistants), is dated 1491.

From 1486 to 1490 Domenico and his shop (which at this time included Michelangelo) worked on the fresco decoration of the choir of S. Maria Novella, doing *Scenes from the Lives of the Virgin and St. John the Baptist*, the *Legends of SS. Dominic and Peter*, and others. Painted in a broad and sturdy style, they draw on contemporary Florentine fashions and personnages to evoke a gay, idealized image of Florentine life of the time. In his monumental fresco cycles Domenico attempted to revive something of the simplicity, severity, and power of the heroic style of Masaccio at the beginning of the 15th century. However, Domenico was also fascinated by the exact, closely observed realism of Flemish painting, and often adopted it in order to articulate as sharply as possible the specificity and concreteness of his forms—for example, in the *Portrait of Francesco Sassetti and His Grandson* (New York, Metropolitan Museum).

BIBLIOGRAPHY. A. Warburg, *Bildniskunst und florentinisches Bürgertum*, Leipzig, 1902; J. Lauts, *Domenico Ghirlandajo*, Vienna, 1943; P. Bargellini, *Il Ghirlandaio del bel mondo fiorentino*, Florence, 1945; G. Marchini, "The Frescoes in the Choir of Santa Maria Novella," *The Burlington Magazine*, XCV, 1953.

HELLMUT WOHL

GHIRLANDAJO, MICHELE DI RIDOLFO DEL, *see* TOSINI, MICHELE.

GHIRLANDAJO, RIDOLFO. Italian painter (b. Florence, 1483; d. there, 1561). He was the son of Domenico Ghirlandajo, a pupil of Fra Bartolommeo, and an admirer of Piero di Cosimo and Granacci. Ridolfo maintained the literalism of the Ghirlandajo tradition in spite of the com-

Domenico Ghirlandajo, Adoration of the Magi, 1487. Uffizi, Florence.

promise about 1505–15 with High Renaissance formulas seen in his Bartolommesque *Madonna della Cintola* (1514–15; Prato, Cathedral). This compromise perhaps underlay his success with Florentine officialdom, witnessed by his many commissions for frescoes (now mostly lost), decorations for festive occasions, and portraits.

BIBLIOGRAPHY. C. Gamba, "Ridolfo e Michele di Ridolfo del Ghirlandaio," 2 parts, *Dedalo*, IX, 1928–29; S. J. Freedberg, *Painting of the High Renaissance in Rome and Florence*, 2 vols., Cambridge, Mass., 1961.

GHISI, GIORGIO. Italian printmaker (1520–82). Trained under Giulio Romano in Mantua, after whose designs he executed many prints, Ghisi engraved in a structural, volumetric style deriving from Marcantonio Raimondi. During his first visit to Rome, Ghisi engraved Michelangelo's *Last Judgment*, and during a second trip in 1540, his *Prophets* and *Sibyls* of the Sistine Chapel. He went to Antwerp in 1550 at the request of the publisher Hieronymus Cock, and engraved on a grandiose scale Raphael's *School of Athens* and *Disputa*, but exercised only a fugitive influence on northern printmakers. Although Ghisi returned to Mantua, his engraving of the *Philosopher* after Luca Penni, published by Cock in 1561, suggests a second trip to Flanders.

GHISLANDI, GIUSEPPE (Fra Vittore del Galgario). Italian painter (1655–1743). He was a lay brother in the

Giuseppe Ghislandi, Portrait of Isabella Camozzi de' Gherardi. Gallery of the Carrara Academy, Bergamo, Italy.

Order of the Minims attached to the convent in his native Bergamo. He spent much of his early life in Venice, where he studied with the portrait painter Sebastiano Bombelli, and did not return to Bergamo until about 1700. Known as one of the finest portraitists of the 18th century, Ghislandi also executed numerous "portrait-genre" scenes later in his career; this, however, remained a popular sideline in his *oeuvre*, and his most important works are his portraits of nobility and of professional men, dating from the 1730s and 1740s. Among these paintings, the portrait of Isabella Camozzi de' Gherardi (ca. 1730; Bergamo Museum) reveals Ghislandi's particular combination of psychological characterization, deriving from Moroni, and a brilliance of color and a textural variation absorbed during his stay in Venice. In the portrait of the architect G. B. Caniana (ca. 1740; Alzano, Canonica) Ghislandi demonstrates, through the relaxed pose of the sitter and the extremely free brushwork, the modern sense of immediacy in portraiture so different from the stiff austerity of the earlier Lombard portraitist Ceresa.

BIBLIOGRAPHY. A. Locatelli-Milesi, *Fra Galgario*, Bergamo, 1945; F. Mazzini, *Mostra di Fra Galgario e del Settecento in Bergamo* (catalog), Milan, 1955; E. K. Waterhouse, *Italian Baroque Painting*, London, 1962.   PENELOPE C. MAYO

GHISSI (di Cecco), FRANCESCUCCIO. Marchigian painter (fl. chiefly in Fabriano). His signed works range in date from 1359 to 1374 or, if one includes a controversial panel once in the Fornari Collection in Rome, 1395. The surname "Ghissi" has been questioned as a misreading of "Cicchi," that is, "di Cecco." All of Francescuccio's works represent the Madonna of Humility, and the best example is the undated one in the Vatican Museums. All are modeled after a Madonna by Allegretto Nuzi (1366; Sanseverino Gallery). Francescuccio is considered an important though unoriginal follower of Nuzi.

BIBLIOGRAPHY. A. Colasanti, "Note sull'antica pittura fabrianese: Allegretto Nuzi e Francescuccio di Cecco Ghissi," *L'arte*, IX, 1906.

GHIYAS-UD-DIN (Ghiyath ad-Din; Giyasuddin) TUGHLAK, TOMB OF, DELHI. Indian tomb adjacent to the fortress named Tughlakabad, 12 miles southeast of Delhi. Erected by Ghiyas-ud-Din Tughlak and completed about 1326 after his death, it is set in an artificial lake and is massive and fortresslike in character.

BIBLIOGRAPHY. R. C. Arora, *Delhi: The Imperial City*, New Delhi, 1953.

GIACOMETTI, ALBERTO. Swiss sculptor, painter, draftsman, and poet (b. Stampa, 1901; d. Chur, 1966). His first sculpture was done in 1914, and by 1916 he had begun his series of busts of Diego, his brother. In 1919 Giacometti attended the Geneva School of Arts and Crafts, working under Estoppey. He studied Italian painting, notably Tintoretto and Giotto, while in Italy (1920–22). It was then that he became interested in the immobility of archaic art. In 1922 he took up residence in Paris and for the next three years was a student of Bourdelle, whom he disliked. Giacometti continually drew in the museums from Chaldean and Egyptian sculpture and copied a Fayoum portrait.

About 1926 he left his academic style of sculpture for flat figural forms in idol-like and cubist formations. In

Alberto Giacometti, *Head of Diego*. Brady Collection, Los Angeles.

1926 he began his *Woman-Spoon* series. Toward the end of the decade he came to look upon the figure not as a closed mass but as a transparent construction. In 1929 he joined the surrealists and became their leading sculptor. He did his *Reclining Woman* in 1929, *Study for a Surrealist Cage* in 1930, *Palace at Four A.M.* in 1932–33 (New York, Museum of Modern Art), *Project for a Square* in 1930–31, *The Phallic Embryo* in 1931–32, *Object Difficult to Throw* in 1931, and *Hands Holding the Void* in 1934 (New York, W. Rubin Collection).

About 1935 he broke with the surrealists, feeling the need to return to study from the human model, and did both a cubist *Head* (1935; later destroyed) and a series of portrait busts of Diego. He destroyed many of his figure studies and exhibited none. He found that he kept reducing the scale, detail, and volume of his forms so that they became thin, attenuated, and increasingly fugitive in profile. He was motivated by the truth of vision, rendering in sculpture closer approximations of the way the human is seen from a distance, or, as he put it, "trimming the fat off of space." With these ideas was mingled his conviction of an essential human isolation.

Following an accident in 1938, Giacometti was a patient in a Geneva hospital and was thus permitted valuable time for reflection on his art. During World War II he was again in Geneva (1940–45), working from memory rather than from the model and developing his signature style of hermetic figures and busts. He continued to rework this style in Paris after the war, both in sculpture and in painting: *City Square* (1948), *Man Pointing* (both New York, Museum of Modern Art), and *Head of Diego* (Los Angeles, Brady Collection). Among the few themes of his art is the disembodied gesture, for example, *The Hand* (1947).

Giacometti was the strongest European sculptor working after World War II; his importance lies in the visual and philosophic richness of his work, the intensity of his drive to capture that which he felt constantly escaped his vision of the outer world, and the need to render the human in its entirety.

BIBLIOGRAPHY. P.-M. Grand, "Giacometti," *Portfolio & Art News Annual*, III, 1960; J.-P. Sartre, *Essays in Aesthetics*, London, 1963.

ALBERT ELSEN

GIACOMETTI AS PAINTER

Although Giacometti began to paint and draw at an early age, most of his paintings date after 1947. Like his sculpture, they feature human beings who are perilously slender. They are shown standing erect, or beckoning, or striding. Often they appear to move, and then as if with a sense of purpose. He shows them singly and in groups. His portrait busts have decidedly recognizable gestures. His still-life paintings consist largely of clusters of dusty bottles, sculpture tools, and tin cans on a tabletop. The range of his subjects is thus limited. He shows figures in his paintings in a large, empty, cavernous room with a high ceiling. His palette is severely limited to warm grays, blacks, browns, and creamy whites. His paintings are essentially brush drawings. Giacometti has also made lithographs, which are close to his paintings and drawings in theme and conception.

BIBLIOGRAPHY. A. Giacometti, *Schriften, Fotos, Zeichnungen*, ed. E. Scheidegger, Zurich, 1958.

ROBERT REIFF

GIAMBERTI, GIULIANO, ANTONIO THE ELDER, ANTONIO THE YOUNGER, FRANCESCO, see SAN-GALLO FAMILY.

GIAMBOLOGNA, see BOLOGNA, GIOVANNI.

GIAMBONO, MICHELE. Venetian painter of the last phase of International Gothic (fl. 1420–62). He is often connected with Jacobello del Fiore. In 1447 Giambono agreed to copy a work by Antonio Vivarini, but his major inspiration is Gentile da Fabriano. Typical of his late phase is the flat ornament of twining line, relatively broad and open rather than taut.

His signed works are a small Madonna (Rome, Venezia Palace), a *St. James Altarpiece* (Venice, Academy), and the important but much restored mosaics of the *Life of Mary* in the Mascoli Chapel, S. Marco, Venice (begun 1444). His masterpieces are *Michael Enthroned* (Florence, I Tatti, Berenson Collection) and *St. Crisogonus on Horseback* (Venice, S. Trovaso).

BIBLIOGRAPHY. B. Berenson, *The Venetian Painters of the Renaissance*, 3d ed., New York, 1897; L. Testi, *La storia della pittura veneziana*, vol. 2: *Il divenire*, Bergamo, 1915.

GIAMPIETRINO (Gian Pietro Rizzi). Italian painter (fl. ca. 1520). A group of pictures clearly by one artist has been labeled with this name since the 18th century. They are close imitations of Leonardo in his Milanese phase. Leonardo's notebooks mention a pupil "Gian Pietro," but there are no documents; one painting attributed to Giampietrino is dated 1521.

His paintings are nearly all women and nearly all half-lengths. One group of Madonnas, sometimes with saints,

closely recalls Boltraffio. Another group, recalling Luini, is of single saints (*Magdalene*, Milan, Brera; *St. Catherine*, Florence, Uffizi). His most nearly independent works are nudes of mythological and historical figures (*Cleopatra*, Paris, Louvre; *Egeria*, Milan, Brivio Collection; *Lucretia*, Sarasota, Ringling Museum). These derive from Leonardo's *Leda*. The artist's tone is dry and the typical black backgrounds are flat.

BIBLIOGRAPHY. W. Suida, *Leonardo und sein Kreis*, Munich, 1929.

GIAN GIACOMO D'ALLADIO, see MACRINO D'ALBA.

GIANNICOLA, see GRASSI, NICOLA.

GIANTS. Mythological beings, of tremendous size and strength, born from the blood of the mutilated god Uranus as it fell upon Gaea, the earth. They battled against the Olympian gods but were defeated and imprisoned under mountainous islands, where their occasional movements were thought by the ancient Greeks to be the cause of local upheavals and volcanic eruptions. Fifth-century sculpture depicts them with human bodies, but later works show them with serpent legs. *See* GIGANTOMACHIA.

GIANTS, TEMPLE OF THE, AKRAGAS, see OLYMPIEION, AKRAGAS.

GIBBERD, FREDERICK. English architect (1908–   ). He realizes the quintessential in English planning: the site and the *genius loci*. His two most considerable recent achievements are the Passenger and Terminal Building, London Airport (1955) and Harlow New Town, for which he has been a planner since 1947. He is architect-planner for the future Nuneaton.

BIBLIOGRAPHY. "Men of the Year," *The Architects' Journal*, CXXIII, 1955.

GIBBONS, GRINLING. English sculptor and carver (b. Rotterdam, 1648; d. London, 1721). By 1677–80 he had executed carving at Cassiobury and was appointed Master Carver to the Crown in 1693. He is best documented by official commissions, particularly at Hampton Court (1691–96) and St. Paul's Cathedral (first carvings in stone, 1694–95). There is little documentary evidence for his decorative carving in country houses. He worked at Burghley and Petworth in the 1680s, and carvings at Holme Lacy and Belton are possibly by him. He had a large workshop for stone carving at Blenheim Palace (1700–12), but his monuments are uneven in quality. The best, now rearranged, is the marble tomb of Lord Coventry (1687) at the church in Croome d'Abitot.

BIBLIOGRAPHY. D. Green, *Grinling Gibbons...*, London, 1964.

GIBBS, JAMES. English architect (1682–1754). He was born in Scotland, and toured the Continent as a young man. In Rome (ca. 1707–09), where he studied with Carlo Fontana, he decided to become an architect. His first major English commission, St. Mary-le-Strand, in London (1714–17), reflects his Roman studies and shows mannerist rather than baroque inspiration, particularly in his individual handling of wall surfaces. Because of the Neo-Palladian ascendancy that occurred soon after his return to England, Gibbs altered his style, but he never capitulated to the Palladian

James Gibbs, St. Martin-in-the-Fields, London, 1721–26.

group. Instead he allied himself with the style of Wren. His designs consisted not of running together isolated units, but in handling broad masses often related by uniform fenestration. His St. Martin-in-the-Fields (1721–26), London, is perhaps the most influential of all English churches. Its combination of steeple tower and temple front was widely imitated, particularly in America. *See* ST. MARTIN-IN-THE-FIELDS, LONDON; ST. MARY-LE-STRAND, LONDON.

A Tory rather than a Whig, Gibbs did not receive as many public commissions as he might have when the Tories came to power, but he did have a large private practice. Generally conservative in plan, these private buildings reflect a Palladian line of thinking in that the main house is often connected to flanking buildings by quadrant colonnades. Yet the overall decorative schemes and proportions are his own. Many of these houses were published in his *Book of Architecture* (1728), which also contains designs of Continental origin; this book has been called "the most widely used architectural book of the century." It was geared to the use of amateurs in search of professional advice. Gibbs also wrote other books, including *Rules for Drawing and the Several Parts of Architecture* (1732).

A late monument, the Radcliffe Library, Oxford (1739–49), illustrates Gibbs's persistent individuality in the face of popular styles. Circular, with strong mannerist and baroque gestures, the library is almost a unique excursion on the part of any English architect into these modes of design. Gibbs's influence was extensive, and even profound, in outlying areas of the English-speaking world, primarily because of his books. His style was personal, though derived from a variety of sources, and marked by a sense of technical accomplishment rather than by brilliance in performance.

BIBLIOGRAPHY. J. N. Summerson, *Architecture in Britain, 1530–1830*, 4th rev. ed., Baltimore, 1963.   MATTHEW E. BAIGELL

GIBBS LIMNER, *see* FREAKE MASTER.

GIBEON (El Jib). Important fortified city north of Jerusalem, on a rocky hill in the Jordanian plain. The influence of its many conquerors is still visible in its ruins. Built and destroyed six times, Gibeon was famous for its wine industry; the oldest known winery was unearthed there, capable of producing 25,000 gallons of wine annually.

Ruins of massive city walls have been discovered, as well as tunnels, pools, Roman baths, a large massive building with vaulted rooms, and an ancient cemetery with connecting shaft tombs, cut into the rock, filled with human and animal skeletons and artifacts.

Pottery of various periods has been unearthed, including Mycenaean and Cypriote ware and Bronze and Iron Age vessels, as well as weapons, woven materials, cylinder and stamp seals, engraved scarabs, and a hoard of coins from 103–76 B.C. The famous Biblical Pool of Gibeon has also been excavated.

BIBLIOGRAPHY. J. B. Pritchard, *Gibeon, Where the Sun Stood Still*, Princeton, 1962; J. B. Pritchard, *The Bronze Age Cemetery at Gibeon*, Philadelphia, 1963.

GIBSON, JOHN. English architect (1819–92). A pupil of Charles Barry, Gibson became the most prolific bank architect of his time. His fashionable neo-Renaissance style of the mid-19th century may be seen in more than forty buildings for the National Provincial Bank and in the Imperial Assurance Office (completed 1848).

BIBLIOGRAPHY. H. R. Hitchcock, *Early Victorian Architecture in Britain*, 2 vols., New Haven, 1954.

GIBSON, JOHN. English sculptor (1790–1866). He spent most of his life in Rome, where he studied under Canova, and died there. He is noted for his use of color, which imitated the Greeks, particularly in his *Queen Victoria* and his celebrated *Tinted Venus*.

Gigaku mask. Gokō (Prince of Wu), 7th century. National Museum, Tokyo.

GIGAKU MASK

GIGAKU MASK. Japanese mask used for Gigaku, a farcical pantomime performed to the accompaniment of three musical instruments. Gigaku, which originated in China, is said to have been introduced to Japan in 612 by a Korean immigrant. It was performed frequently at court and temple ceremonies from the Asuka to the early Heian period. Although Gigaku itself was discontinued and forgotten early, no fewer than 223 Gigaku masks of the 7th and 8th centuries have been collected and preserved in the Hōryūji (now transferred to the Tokyo National Museum), the Shōsō-in, and the Tōdaiji. These masks are not only the first masks used in Japan but are among the oldest extant masks in the entire world. They are mostly made of wood, but some are done in the dry-lacquer technique. Gigaku masks are large and heavy, covering the entire head of a dancer. Their facial expressions often tend to be outrageously comical so that they stand out vividly in outdoor performances. Gigaku masks were made most often by Buddhist sculptors, and they reflect the style and technique of the contemporary Buddhist sculpture. *See also* BUGAKU MASK; NOH MASK.

BIBLIOGRAPHY. T. Nogami, *Masks of Japan: The Gigaku, Bugaku and Noh Masks*, Tokyo, 1935; S. Noma, *Masks* (Arts & Crafts of Japan, no. 1), Rutland, Vt., 1957.

MIYEKO MURASE

GIGANTOMACHIA (Gigantomachy). In Greek mythology, the struggle at Phlegra between the gods and the giants. The giants hurled rocks and burning tree trunks against heaven, but the gods, assisted by Heracles, were victorious. The battle is depicted in the famous frieze on the Pergamene Altar of Zeus (ca. 180 B.C.; Berlin, former State Museums, Department of Antiquities).

GIL, EL MULATO, *see* GIL DE CASTRO, JOSE.

GILBERT, SIR ALFRED. English sculptor (1854–1934). His professional reputation was founded upon his early Italian works, such as *Icarus*, which exhibit his ability to combine the delicate and monumental. He is best known for his Shaftesbury Memorial Fountain (1893), the *Eros* in Piccadilly Circus.

GILBERT, CASS. American architect (b. Ohio, 1858; d. 1934). Trained in St. Paul, Minn., and at the Massachusetts Institute of Technology, Gilbert worked briefly for McKim, Mead and White before returning to the Middle West, where he designed the classically styled Minnesota State Capitol (1896–1903). After moving to New York, he became a major architect of commercial, civic, and utilitarian buildings. In the West Street Building (1905) and the Woolworth Tower (1911–13), both in New York City, he pioneered in accommodating Gothic motifs to the skyscraper building.

A stylistic adapter rather than an innovator, and thoroughly competent in the use of eclectic detail, Gilbert was known for his sure sense of design. This is illustrated in the massive, block-square United States Customs House in New York (1901–07) with its Beaux-Arts mixture of Roman and Renaissance forms. He built the state capitols at Arkansas (1912) and West Virginia (1928–32), the United

Cass Gilbert, Woolworth Tower, New York City, 1911–13.

Gilgamesh. Relief of the legendary Sumerian hero, from the Palace of Sargon II, Dur Sharrukin, Khorsabad. Louvre, Paris.

States Treasury Annex (1918), and the Supreme Court Building (1933–35), completed after his death. *See* WOOL-WORTH BUILDING, NEW YORK.

MATTHEW E. BAIGELL

GILBERT, EMILE JACQUES. French architect (b. Paris, 1793; d. there, 1874). A pupil of J. N. L. Durand and Barthélemy Vignon, Gilbert built the Prison de la Nouvelle Force (1842–49; destroyed) in the prevailing radial cellular pattern and the Charenton Lunatic Asylum (1838–45) in a style typical of the regimentation of 19th-century community planning.

GILBERT, SIR JOHN. English historical painter and wood engraver (b. Blackheath, 1817; d. London, 1897). A painter of historical genre scenes (*Sir Lancelot du Lake*, 1878) and water colors, Gilbert was most noted as a designer of woodcut illustrations to editions of Shakespeare, Scott, Milton, Cervantes, and others. He is represented in a number of British museums.

BIBLIOGRAPHY. C. H. G. Baker, "Sir John Gilbert," *The Art Journal*, 1908.

GIL DE CASTRO, JOSE (El Mulato Gil). Peruvian portrait painter (d. ca. 1841). Little is known of the life of José Gil de Castro, the portraitist of South American independence. Born in Lima, Peru, he was active in Chile from 1814 to 1822. Portraits of San Martín (1818; Buenos Aires, National Museum of Fine Arts), Bolívar (1823; Caracas, Alfredo Boulton Collection), and the Peruvian hero Olaya (1823; Lima, Museum of the Republic) show his severe and powerful style.

BIBLIOGRAPHY. A. R. Romera, *Historia de la pintura chilena*, Santiago, 1960.

GIL DE HONTANON, JUAN AND RODRIGO. Spanish architects of the 16th century. The father, Juan (d. 1526), was apparently *maestro mayor* of Segovia Cathedral. His son Rodrigo (ca. 1500–77) later assumed that position, completing the choir according to Juan's plans. Rodrigo, who also worked on Salamanca Cathedral after 1538, is best known as the author of a treatise on construction, written about 1538. It is concerned with proportions and construction and shows that even in the 16th century there was no standard method for computing vault thrusts and buttress requirements. After giving his own complicated system, Rodrigo Gil de Hontañón admits he asked architects for advice and never received the same answer twice.

BIBLIOGRAPHY. G. Kubler, "A Late Gothic Computation of Rib Vault Thrusts," *Gazette des Beaux-Arts*, XXVI, 1944.

GILES, ST. French abbot, one of the Fourteen Holy Helpers (b. Athens; d. ca. 750). He became a hermit near Nîmes, France, where he was accidentally wounded by a huntsman of King Wamba (or Flavius?) of the Visigoths, who was hunting doe. Wamba built a monastery, of which St. Giles became abbot, on the site of the present city of St-Gilles. A Frankish king Charles, possibly Charlemagne, supposedly sought and received intercession from St. Giles for forgiveness of a sin he dared not confess. The tomb of St. Giles became a pilgrimage shrine. St. Giles (Latin name Aegidius) usually appears as a Benedictine; his attributes are the doe and the lily, a pun on his name in Italian. His feast is September 1. *See also* SAINTS IN ART.

GILGAMESH. Hero of Sumerian legend. His life and exploits form the basis of an epic that includes an early version of the Biblical flood story. Gilgamesh is often shown fighting or stabbing monsters, a motif that passed eventually into the medieval repertoire as Daniel flanked by lions. His closest friend was the wild man Enkidu, who accompanied him on his travels in search of immortality.

BIBLIOGRAPHY. S. Moscati, *Ancient Semitic Civilizations*, London, 1957.

GILIOLI, EMILE. French sculptor (1911–   ). Born in Paris, he studied at the Ecole des Beaux-Arts in Nice and then in Boucher's studio at the Ecole des Beaux-Arts in Paris. Gilioli came under the influence of the cubists and works today in an abstract style. He uses many media, and the shifting planes in his pieces produce an interplay of light and shade. He is represented in the Museum of Modern Art, New York, by *Sky and Sea* (1956).

GILL, ERIC. English stone carver, engraver, typographer, and author (1884–1940). Typography and lettering were the major themes of Gill's versatile career. In addition to carving letters and painting signs, he designed ten new printing types, among them the well-known Perpetua; wrote an essay on typography; engraved much for the Golden Cockerel Press; and masterfully illustrated the Gospels and other works. As a sculptor, he worked mainly in low relief but also executed figures in the round. The Stations of the Cross, Westminster Cathedral (1918), the wooden altarpiece at Rossal School Chapel, the figures on Broadcasting House, and the giant torso *Mankind*, now in the Tate Gallery, London, are among his finest achievements.

BIBLIOGRAPHY. E. Gill, *Autobiography*, London, 1940.

GILL, IRVING. American architect (1870–1936). Gill was born in Syracuse, N.Y. After working under Louis Sullivan in Chicago from 1890 to 1892, Gill settled in San Diego, Calif., where he developed a style that approached the clean surfaces of the European modernists, as in his Dodge House in Los Angeles (1916). He helped establish modern architecture in California.

GILLEMANS, JAN PAUWEL, THE ELDER. Flemish painter of still life and flower pieces (b. Antwerp, 1618; d. there, shortly after 1675). He became a member of the Guild of St. Luke in 1648, and was also, after an appeal to the magistrate, accepted as a master goldsmith in 1662. His compositions, mostly done against a dark background, are in the manner of Jan Davidsz. de Heem. Gillemans comes especially close to the master in the rich and sometimes overladen breakfast pieces. *Oysters and Fruit* (1662; Brussels, Fine Arts Museum) can be considered a typical signed and dated example of his art. Other works can be found in the galleries of Lille, Liechtenstein, and elsewhere.

BIBLIOGRAPHY. F. J. van den Branden, *Geschiedenis der Antwerpsche Schilderschool*, Antwerp, 1883.

GILLEMANS, JAN PAUWEL, THE YOUNGER. Flemish painter of still life, occasional portraits, and mythological compositions (b. Antwerp, 1651; d. there, ca. 1704). The artist is mentioned in 1666 as a pupil of Joris van Son, and was inscribed as a member of the Guild of St. Luke in 1674. He is not the same as a painter of similar

Claude Gillot, *Scène de Carosses*. Louvre, Paris.

name who is cited as a member of the Guild of Middelburg. As far as we can judge, the artist's production comes very close to that of his father, Gillemans the Elder, except that the latter showed a marked preference for larger-size compositions. Among numerous attributions lacking certitude, two still-life paintings, one in the Valenciennes Museum and the other in the Schönborn-Buchheim Gallery in Vienna, seem to be by Gillemans the Younger.

BIBLIOGRAPHY. F. J. van den Branden, *Geschiedenis der Antwerpsche Schilderschool*, Antwerp, 1883.

GILLES, WERNER. German painter and lithographer (1894–1961). Born in Rheydt, he studied at the Kassel Academy and with Walter Klemm and Lyonel Feininger at the Weimar Bauhaus. His works of the 1920s are strongly brushed, sometimes thickly painted landscapes, still lifes, and figures. In the 1930s realistic elements became more simple and formalized and his line stronger. At the same time an increasing strain of fantasy and symbolism appeared. In the paintings done after the war Gilles's symbolic interpretation of nature became more lyrical and profound, and his personal touch remained evident despite occasional borrowings from Picasso.

GILLES. Oil painting by Watteau, in the Louvre Museum, Paris. *See* WATTEAU, JEAN-ANTOINE.

GILLIG, JACOB. Dutch still-life and fish painter (b. Utrecht, ca. 1636; d. there, 1701). He was a pupil of Wilem Ormea in Utrecht. In 1661 Gillig married the daughter of the painter Adam Willaerts. Gillig seems to have been only a part-time painter, for he is not mentioned in the records of the Utrecht Guild of St. Luke. He held several municipal posts in Utrecht. He was the father of the portrait painter Michiel Gillig.

BIBLIOGRAPHY. A. P. A. Vorenkamp, *Bijdrage tot de geschiedenis van het Hollandsch stilleven in de zeventiende eeuw*, Leyden, 1934.

GILLOT, CLAUDE. French genre painter and etcher (b. Langres, 1673; d. Paris, 1722). He was the pupil of his father, Jean Gillot, a painter-decorator and embroiderer, and, in Paris, of J. B. Corneille, a painter and engraver of historical and religious subjects. Gillot became an associate of the Royal Academy in 1710. Little is known of his career before his appointment by the Regent in 1715 as Director of Costumes and Decoration at the Opera. Concurrently, he was admitted to membership in the Royal Academy as a painter of *sujets modernes*, though his reception piece was a traditional history painting, *Christ on Calvary* (Corrèze, France, Eglise de Noailles), referred to in the Academy records as the *Mise en Croix*.

His subjects were usually taken from the Dutch genre painters, especially Teniers, and from the Italian *commedia dell'arte*. Gillot's best-known painting from the latter, *Scène de Carosses* (Paris, Louvre), shows a dry, artificial manner untypical of the 18th century, literally but animatedly representing the stage performance. Through such works he revived the dormant spirit of Jacques Callot and initiated theatrical subject matter most typical of the future. His ornamental designs were an important contribution to the formation of the Regency style in the delicacy and tenuousness of their motifs. They are more fanciful than those of J. Berain. Gillot left a few tapestry cartoons; some unfinished paintings; a number of drawings for illustrations, religious subjects, and figure studies; and ornament designs, some of which are thought to exist under an attribution to Claude Audran III, the engraver of Gillot's *Passions* series.

A number of his suites, engraved by G. Huquier, P. Chéreau, and others, were published after his death. He shows himself to be particularly facile with the burin. His best-known etchings are *Diana and Bacchus* and the *Triumphs of Pan and Faunus*. His compositions are always full of movement and are populated with small figures. His drawings possess a brilliance and lightness of touch that is most successful when translated into engraving. His influence on Watteau, whose master he was prior to 1718, is most noticeable in his work concerning the Italian theater. Gillot's portrait was engraved by J. Aubert.

BIBLIOGRAPHY. L. Dimier, *Les Peintres français du XVIIIe siècle...*, vol. 1, Paris, 1928; B. Populus, *Claude Gillot*, Paris, 1930.
GEORGE V. GALLENKAMP

GILLRAY, JAMES.

English caricaturist (b. Chelsea, 1757; d. London, 1815). Gillray's work is often based on Hogarth, but the expressionistic possibilities are considerably enlarged. After the wishes of his patron, the Younger Pitt, Gillray concentrated on politics, sometimes going against his own sentiments. His caricatures, unlike those of Hogarth, do not grow out of a close observation of life but seem to stem from some inner vision. Gillray's borrowing from Hogarth may be seen, for example, in the *Union Club* (1801), which combines elements of Hogarth's *Midnight Modern Conversation* and *Election Entertainment*. But Gillray's drinking scene shows caricatured expressions rather than real persons in actual surroundings. Many other borrowings from Hogarth may be cited; for example, Gillray's engraving *Dilettanti Theatricals* (1803) incorporates the pose of Hogarth's girl undressing in the *Rake's Orgy* but has a swirling baroque quality foreign to Hogarth.

Gillray, unlike Hogarth, was specific in his satire, and often portrayed the leading personalities of the day. Even King George III was subjected to his barbs. In *A New Way to Pay the National Debt* (1786) George and his queen are seen coming out of the Treasury loaded with

money, which is overflowing their pockets. On the right is the Prince of Wales in a very shabby condition gratefully receiving money from the Duc d'Orléans. *Frying Sprats: Toasting Muffins* (1791) is a comment on the parsimonious habits of George III and his queen: the Queen is represented frying her own sprats, and the King is shown toasting his own muffins. In *Market Day* (1788) Lord Thurlow as a grazier is attending Smithfield Market, where he is examining the beasts, whose heads represent the leading political characters of the day. Yet Gillray was also capable of patriotically satirizing Napoleon's aggrandizement. About 1802 he issued a set of four plates entitled *The Consequences of a Successful French Invasion*, in which he depicted the horrors to be expected. These plates helped inspire the people to a more determined resistance.

Gillray is best known as a political and social caricaturist, but not all his work is in this vein. For example, in 1784 he engraved two subjects from Goldsmith's *Deserted Village*, and he engraved a few plates after Lady Spencer's drawings. In 1792 he reproduced a large plate after Northcote representing the delivery of the prisoners from the Bastille and inscribed "Le Triomphe de la Liberté, ou, L'Elargissement de la Bastille." Gillray's closest spiritual descendant was probably Max Beerbohm, who was, however, less vitriolic.

BIBLIOGRAPHY. T. Wright and R. H. Evans, *Historical and Descriptive Account of the Caricatures of James Gillray*, London, 1851; T. S. R. Boase, *English Art, 1800–1870*, Oxford, 1959; F. Antal, *Hogarth and His Place in European Art*, London, 1962.
ABRAHAM A. DAVIDSON

GILLY, FRIEDRICH.

German architect (1772–1800). He worked in Berlin. Although he died young, this gifted architect deeply influenced German architecture through such projects as his 1797 monument to Frederick the Great and his 1800 Prussian National Theater, which carry forward the work of the earlier French architects Boullée and Ledoux.

BIBLIOGRAPHY. A. Oncken, *Friedrich Gilly, 1772–1800*, Berlin, 1935.

James Gillray, *George IV Wedding Mrs. Fitzherbert.*

GILMAN, ARTHUR, *see* Bryant and Gilman.

GILMAN, HAROLD. English painter (1875–1919). Gilman studied at the Hastings Art School and the Slade School in London. In 1904 he went to Spain, where he spent a year copying Velázquez and Goya. His early dark portraits and interiors derive from these masters and from the influence of Whistler and Sickert, but the turning point in his development was the impact of the historic postimpressionist exhibition organized in London by Roger Fry in 1910. Gilman became fiercely involved in the movement among young painters to break through the provincialism of British painting. He helped found the influential Camden Town Group and was the first president of the London Group, its successor. Commissioned by the Canadian government to paint Halifax Harbor for the War Memorial in Ottawa, he went to Canada. His disciplined personal style combined the flaming color and expression of Van Gogh with a controlled observation of English scenes and figures. Examples of his work are in the Tate Gallery, London, and in many English private collections.

BIBLIOGRAPHY. Arts Council of Great Britain, *Harold Gilman: Oil Paintings and Drawings*, London, 1954.

GIMSON, ERNEST. English architect and designer (1864–1919). He ranks among the greatest of English artist-craftsmen. Few were more aware of the virtues of traditional English design. He evolved forms of the utmost simplicity. His buildings, especially the Markfield cottages, are in the best vernacular tradition.

BIBLIOGRAPHY. W. R. Lethaby et al., *Ernest Gimson: His Life and Work*, Stratford-upon-Avon, 1924.

GINES, JOSE. Spanish sculptor (1768–1823). Born in Valencia, and apparently trained in academic circles in Madrid, José Ginés nevertheless preferred the traditional naturalism of polychromed wood sculpture to the neoclassicism then in vogue. In 1794 he was granted the honorary title "Sculptor of the Chamber" by Charles IV. He is best remembered for his contributions to a multiple commission for the grandiose *Birth of the Prince*, ordered by Charles IV, then prince of Asturias, and completed in 1790. A detail from the dismantled ensemble, *The Massacre of the Innocents* (Madrid, San Fernando Academy), reveals Ginés to have been an able craftsman.

BIBLIOGRAPHY. M. Ossorio y Bernard, *Galería biográfica de artistas españoles del siglo XIX*, Madrid, 1883–84; M. E. Gómez-Moreno, *Breve historia de la escultura española*, 2d ed., Madrid, 1951.

GINGERBREAD STYLE. Architectural and, by extension, general artistic style of the late Victorian period. It was characterized by an overornate, almost encrusted, decoration of buildings, furniture, and porcelain.

BIBLIOGRAPHY. J. Maass, *The Gingerbread Age: A View of Victorian America*, New York, 1957.

GINKAKUJI. Japanese Buddhist temple in Kyoto. It was originally built as the mountain retreat of the Ashikaga shogun Yoshimasa, sometime between 1469 and 1486. After Yoshimasa's death the villa was converted into a Buddhist temple named the Jishōji, but it is more popularly known as the Ginkakuji (Temple of the Silver Pavilion). The Silver Pavilion (Ginkaku), facing a pond, was intended to be covered with silver leaf, following the example of the Kinkakuji. Another small building, the Tōgudō standing at the opposite side of the pond, was built as Yoshimasa's study. It is one of the earliest examples of the true shōin type of architecture. These two buildings are the only remains from the original villa, and they represent good examples of residential architecture of the Muromachi period. The temple is also renowned for its garden, modeled after that of the Saihōji. *See* Kinkakuji; Saihoji Garden, Kyoto; Shoin-Zukuri.

BIBLIOGRAPHY. Tokyo National Museum, *Pageant of Japanese Art*, vol. 6: *Architecture and Gardens*, Tokyo, 1952; R. T. Paine and A. Soper, *The Art and Architecture of Japan*, Baltimore, 1955; Kokusai Bunka Shinkōkai, *Tradition of Japanese Garden*, Tokyo, 1962.

GINNER, CHARLES. English painter (b. Cannes, 1878; d. London, 1952). He began as an architecture student in Paris, then studied painting at the Ecole des Beaux-Arts from 1904 to 1908. He settled in London in 1910 and was a founder-member of the Camden Town Group in 1911 and of the London Group in 1913. He was one of the signers of the neorealist statement in 1914. Ginner painted street scenes and landscapes in a detailed, carefully worked style that emphasized texture and a feeling for pattern and decoration. He was made an associate of the Royal Academy in 1942 and was an official war artist during World War II.

GIO, *see* Africa, Primitive Art of (West Africa: Sierra Leone).

GIOCONDA, LA, *see* Mona Lisa.

GIOCONDO, FRA GIOVANNI. Italian architect and humanist (b. Verona, ca. 1433; d. Rome, 1515). Although he was one of the most celebrated architects of his time and one of the leading Vitruvius scholars, little is known about the life and training of Fra Giocondo. His first work, the Loggia del Consiglio (1478–88) in Verona, at

Ginkakuji. Japanese Buddhist temple, Muromachi period, Kyoto.

once conforms to the traditional architectural modes of northern Italy at the end of the 15th century and suggests some of the decorative forms that were to become popular in the 16th century. From 1489 to 1493 he was in Naples at the court of Alfonso, duke of Calabria, engaged in unknown architectural commissions. His acquaintance with Francesco di Giorgio at this time is documented by a payment through Francesco to Fra Giocondo for 126 illustrations to accompany a book on architecture and another on artillery.

In 1495 he was called to Amboise by Charles VIII of France. There Fra Giocondo surrounded himself with a group of Italian artists, although the precise nature of the work executed is still quite vague. His name is associated with the Château at Blois, the Hôtel Alluye at Blois, the lost Chambre Dorée and the Cour des Comptes in the Palais de Justice, Paris, and the Château at Gaillon. In 1506 he was called to Venice, where he designed fortresses for the mainland and helped arrange new canal systems. He published his first edition of Vitruvius in Venice in 1511, and a year later submitted a plan for the new Rialto Bridge. In January, 1514, he was appointed with Raphael *capomastro* of St. Peter's in Rome. Plans for this structure have been attributed to him, but his death in 1515 precluded any participation in the construction of the basilica.

BIBLIOGRAPHY. H. Willich, *Die Baukunst der Renaissance in Italien...*, 2 vols., Berlin, 1914–29.

JOHN R. SPENCER

GIOLFINO, NICCOLO. Italian painter of Verona (1476–1555). He was a member of a large family of sculptors and a pupil of Liberale da Verona. Many documents and works are in Verona. Giolfino exploited the decorative late Gothicism of his master most effectively for secular works, with vivacious narrative and idealized figures, using the old tradition of courtly ornament for the more modern ends of allegorical humanism.

Typical works are *Triumphal Procession, Seven Allegorical Figures*, and *Achilles and Odysseus* (all Verona, Castelvecchio). He also painted standard altarpieces in intense colors, the later ones showing that his vitalism was attracted to Leonardo. Frescoes include both religious cycles for chapels and friezes for the façades of private houses.

BIBLIOGRAPHY. *Capolavori della pittura veronese* (catalog), ed. A. Avena, Verona, 1947.

GIORDANO, LUCA (Luca fa presto). Italian painter (1632–1705). Born in Naples, he first studied with his father, Antonio, a copyist of Ribera's paintings, and then possibly with Falcone and Ribera in Naples. After traveling to Rome to study the Renaissance masters (ca. 1650), Luca is reported to have gone to Parma, Florence, and Venice (in 1653) and to have returned to Naples via Rome. Back in Venice in 1667, in Florence from 1679 to 1682, and in Bergamo in 1685, he was called to Spain by Charles II in 1692, where he remained until 1702, then returned to Naples by way of Genoa, Florence, and Rome.

While Ribera had a profound influence on Luca's style (compare his *Dying Seneca* in the Munich Pinacothek, which once bore a false signature of Ribera, with the Spaniard's *Martyrdom of St. Andrew* in Budapest), his restlessness and eclecticism make it impossible to determine his real master. Surrounded by the works of the *Caravaggisti* and the Carracci school in Naples, he also deliberately exposed himself to the great Romans, and above all to the Venetians, as the strong Venetian influence in his *Marriage at Cana* (ca. 1689; Naples, Capodimonte) indicates. He went so far afield as to imitate the styles of Lucas van Leyden and Dürer in the *Ecce Homo* (Baltimore, Walters Art Gallery). However, in his vast output (which earned him the title "Luca fa presto"), he never copied but rather assimilated from the total tradition, creating his own personal style, which is essentially a combination of Venetian colorism and the grandiose conceptions of Pietro da Cortona. *St. Anne and the Virgin* (1657; Naples, Ascensione a Chiaia), with its Cortonesque composition and Venetian coloring, is an example.

This ability to synthesize is most evident in Luca's large fresco decorations. Even when they are related to 16th-century examples, as is *Christ Driving the Money Changers from the Temple* (1684; Naples, S. Filippo Neri), he adds a high-baroque intensity to the old formulas. However, such frescoes as those in the Grand Gallery of the Medici-Riccardi Palace in Florence (1682) and the *Triumph of Judith* (1704; Naples, S. Martino, Cappella del Tesoro) demonstrate a facility of handling and grandiloquence of statement that had not been present earlier. The combination of lightness and heaviness had a major influence on 18th-century fresco decoration; his style is more closely related to that of the rococo Tiepolo than to baroque artists of his own century.

BIBLIOGRAPHY. W. Valentiner, "An Early Forger," *Art in America*, I, 1913; E. Petraccone, *Luca Giordano*, Naples, 1919; A. Griseri, "I Bozzetti di Luca Giordano per l'Escalera dell'Escorial," *Paragone*, no. 81, 1956.

STEPHEN E. OSTROW

GIORGI, GIORGIO DE. Italian sculptor (1918–   ). He studied in his native Genoa and has traveled throughout Europe and America. Giorgi's work was first exhibited in Bologna (1954) and Paris (1956). After a period of working in a figurative style influenced by Giacometti, he turned to abstraction and more recently to assemblage.

GIORGIO, MAESTRO, see GUBBIO WARE.

GIORGIO, FRANCESCO DI, see FRANCESCO DI GIORGIO (MARTINI).

GIORGIONE. Venetian painter (ca. 1477–1510). Giorgione is one of the greatest and most epoch-making artists, but one of the hardest to pin down. Paucity of records contrasts with richness of citation of him as an inspiration just after his death. His new style dominated Venetian art from Titian on, and indirectly was basic for European painting up to impressionism. His official documented work for the Doge's Palace and the Fondaco dei Tedeschi is lost or badly damaged. Knowledge is based chiefly on a notebook kept by Marcantonio Michiel (ca. 1525–35) on his visits to private collectors. Besides works known through engravings or copies, Michiel lists *The Tempest* (Venice, Academy), *Sleeping Venus* (Dresden, State Art Collections), and *The Three Philosophers* (Vienna, Museum of Art History). A contemporary inscription names Giorgione as the artist of *Laura* (1506; Vienna, Museum of Art History).

Giorgione, *The Tempest*, Academy, Venice. The painting's theme or lack of theme is widely debated.

Among the infinity of paintings suggested as his, only the following are today accepted with near unanimity: the *Castelfranco Altarpiece* (Castelfranco Cathedral), *Judith* (Leningrad, Hermitage), *Portrait of a Youth* (Berlin, former State Museums, Picture Gallery), and *The Concert Champêtre* (Paris, Louvre). The most important debated paintings are *The Adoration of the Shepherds*, also called the *Allendale Nativity* (Washington, D.C., National Gallery) as an early work and the *Portrait of an Old Woman* labeled *col tempo* (Venice, Academy). Others of the highest quality are probably by the young Titian. The certain works are of 1503 and later and are in one mature style; the *Allendale Nativity* might be an early stage toward this, but there are no sure links, and the solidest view holds that it is by a late follower of Giovanni Bellini somewhat affected by Giorgione.

The first technical quality of Giorgione's art to be noticed as unique is the light. Earlier Venetian works made it pervade the entire surface, unlike the tradition of Renaissance Florence, but it is now more positive, determining the visual character of figures and even breaking up forms. The *Castelfranco Altarpiece*, probably the earliest of Giorgione's works, reinforces the dominance of specific light in unusual ways, that is, by un-Venetian restraint of color, using browns and grays, and by leaving the center empty of objects for the action of light (contrary to classic Italian composition) as if it were a theme. The light tends to be soft and hazy and thus suggests mood rather than definition. Also un-Venetian is the motionlessness and isolation of figures, each linked only to the softening light and thus reinforcing the mood by appearing contemplative. All these procedures produce the effect called romantic, lyrical, or Giorgionesque. Though reminiscent of music and poetry, the mood in the altarpiece is conveyed by purely pictorial means; one of the strongest contributions is the balance between hues and values without loss in the function of either.

The implication that the figures are sensitive brings complexity to understanding the themes, especially in *The Tempest*, one of the most debated problems and at the heart of the so-called mystery of Giorgione. Many proposals to identify the story, usually in classical literature, have failed to convince other observers; but since Giorgione certainly transformed his source, one may be right. Other writers hold that there is no subject at all, that it is the earliest European painting in which this is the case. This has been denied as antihistorical, that is, that it would not have occurred to the artist; but it is supported by Michiel's description of it simply as "the tempest, with gypsy and soldier." Even if Michiel was ignorant of an intended theme (unlikely, since he talked with the original owner), his description proves that a painting could be so conceived at the time, denial of which is the main basis for rejecting the no-subject view. It seems supported by the drastic changes made while it was being painted (another nude was replaced by the soldier, impossible in an illustration of a story) and by the composition, where the empty center fills with light in its most positive form of the tempest.

As a "character," the tempest would be present as it is personified in pastoral poetry of the time, something different from modern natural landscape, which indeed is un-historical. (Some who have insisted on a story have assumed this as the only alternative possible or offered.) In any case, it is agreed that the lyrical feeling is the heart of the painting.

The gypsy's facial type, unidealized but romantic, with large intense eyes, recurs in *Laura* but not in the many attributed Madonnas, which are more conventional. It may be typical of the Giorgione problem that *Laura* had never been suggested as a work by Giorgione before its inscription was found, though hundreds of other works had been.

The most literally musical work is *The Concert Champêtre*. The mingling of nudes, landscape, light, and music evokes the pastoral, moody vein. Figures are more active and interrelated than elsewhere, and relatively larger, as they are in *The Three Philosophers*. Here, an original composition places all the figures on one side, while the rock and its rich dusky light dominate the other. Many titles have been given this picture, but today it is generally agreed that it shows the three Magi as astrologers, casting Christ's horoscope as they watch the star. This theme recurs during the period (for example, by Giovanni Francesco Caroto, Florence, Uffizi) and relates to the great interest in astrology. According to Michiel, *The Three Philosophers* was finished by Sebastiano del Piombo, but this may have been a slight touching up since it does not now appear.

Titian did more when he added the Cupid (later painted over) to the *Sleeping Venus*. Lying full length, she is the first of an endless series of the nude in light as a sensuous theme for painters, but differs in being passive and in a landscape. Despite its poor state of preservation, the Berlin *Portrait of a Youth* shows dusky shadow related to intense violets. A sensitive, poetic gaze makes the youth an ideal image of a Giorgione patron.

Recent study still attempts to enlarge the list of Giorgione's works. Of many attributions in a 1955 exhibition, only one won favor, *Sunset* (London, private collection), but it is drastically restored. Another group of recent attributions is based on the hypothesis that in a late phase Giorgione painted monumental active figures, foretelling Titian. But since *The Three Philosophers* and *Sleeping Venus* were left unfinished, it is likely that they were his last word.

BIBLIOGRAPHY. L. Venturi, *Giorgione e il giorgionismo*, Milan, 1913; G. M. Richter, *Giorgio da Castelfranco, Called Giorgione*, Chicago, 1937; G. B. Giorgione, *All the Paintings of Giorgione*, text by L. Coletti, New York, 1962.

CREIGHTON GILBERT

GIOTTESCHI. Group of 14th-century Italian painters who continued the style of Giotto after the master's death. Chief among them were Taddeo Gaddi, Bernardo Daddi, Giottino, and Maso di Banco. *See* DADDI, BERNARDO; GADDI, TADDEO; GIOTTINO; MASO DI BANCO.

GIOTTINO (Giotto di Maestro Stefano; Tommaso di Stefano). Italian painter of the Florentine school (fl. ca. 1325–75). Giottino is still one of the most shadowy figures of early Italian painting. A painter called Giotto di Maestro Stefano was a member of the Florentine Company of St. Luke in 1368 and was working in the Vatican in 1369 with Giovanni da Milano and Agnolo Gaddi. A 15th-century compilation about Florentine artists mentions the name Giottino and attributes to him several lost works.

Vasari, finally, writes of a painter called Tommaso di Stefano or Giottino, but the works that he attributes to him have been proved to be by Maso di Banco.

It is by no means certain that these three names, or even any two of them, refer to the same painter. One of them, at least, must be the author of the large, brilliant *Deposition* from S. Remigio(?) now in the Uffizi Gallery in Florence, which is generally attributed to Giottino. Vasari ascribed it to Tommaso di Stefano detto Giottino, but its style is so individual and distinct that it cannot be by the same hand as the other works, that is, by Maso di Banco.

The identity of Giottino depends, therefore, on the Uffizi *Deposition*. Its high-keyed color and decorative refinements may reflect influences from north Italian painting. But the firm architectural composition of its figures is in the Florentine monumental tradition of Giotto. Clearly, it was painted during the second half of the 14th century, though there are differences of opinion on whether closer to the middle or the end of that century.

BIBLIOGRAPHY. O. Sirén, *Giottino*, Leipzig, 1908; O. Sirén, *Giotto and Some of His Followers*, 2 vols., Cambridge, Mass., 1917; O. Sirén, "Il problema Maso-Giottino," *Dedalo*, VIII, December, 1927; G. Sinibaldi and G. Brunetti, *Pittura italiana del duecento e trecento, catalogó della mostra Giottesca di Firenze del 1937*, Florence, 1943.

HELLMUT WOHL

GIOTTO DI BONDONE. Italian painter and architect (b. probably Colle di Vespignano, near Florence, 1267; d. Florence, 1337). Although his fame is attested in a wide variety of literary sources, nothing is known with certainty about his artistic origins or youthful activity. Nevertheless, a period of apprenticeship, or at least of independent work, in Rome and Assisi before 1304 may be safely postulated. At some time between 1304 and 1310 he was working in Padua, and at various times between 1311 and 1322 he is recorded in Florence. By 1313 he had probably worked in Rimini. In 1327 he was inscribed in the Arte dei Medici e Speziali in Florence, and at the beginning of 1330 he entered the service of King Robert of Anjou in Naples. In 1334 he was nominated chief architect of the Cathedral of Florence, and in that year he laid the cornerstone of the Campanile. In 1336 he was invited by Azzone Visconti to work for him in Milan.

The earliest known preserved work indisputably by Giotto is the series of frescoes of the *Life of the Virgin and Christ* and the *Last Judgment* in the nave of the Arena (Scrovegni) Chapel, Padua. It was consecrated in 1305, but it is not known whether the decoration was completed at the time of the consecration. Written sources permit as late a date as 1313 for the frescoes, although other considerations suggest a terminal date of no later than 1310. After the completion of the Arena Chapel frescoes, Giotto's most important work was done in Florence, where he was responsible among other things for frescoes and altarpieces in four chapels in Sta Croce.

The frescoes in two of the chapels, the Bardi and the Peruzzi, survive, and although those in the former are largely the work of assistants and have suffered extensive losses, these paintings constitute the principal evidence of Giotto's late development. The frescoes in the Bardi Chapel consist mainly of six scenes from the *Legend of St. Francis*, and they were probably executed after 1317, as they include a representation of St. Louis of Toulouse, who was canonized in that year. The frescoes in the Peruzzi Chapel depict events from the lives of SS. John the Baptist and John the Evangelist, and are certainly later. Stylistically they are the most developed of Giotto's pictorial work.

In addition to the murals in the Arena Chapel and Sta Croce, a number of panels belong securely to the *oeuvre* of Giotto. The *Dormition of the Virgin* in the former State Museums, Berlin, is generally regarded as one of the altarpieces that, according to the sources, Giotto executed for the Church of Ognissanti in Florence. Also from Ognissanti is the magnificent panel, *Madonna and Child Enthroned with Angels and Saints*, now in the Uffizi Gallery, Florence. These altarpieces probably date from about 1311 or shortly after. The painted cross in the Arena Chapel may have been executed by Giotto about 1315, when he appears to have returned to Padua.

Three signed altarpieces—the *Coronation of the Virgin* in the Baroncelli Chapel in Sta Croce, Florence; the *Madonna and Saints* from S. Maria degli Angeli, Bologna, now in the National Picture Gallery in that city; and the *St. Francis Receiving the Stigmata* from S. Francesco, Pisa, in the Louvre, Paris—are from the workshop of the master. A reconstructed polyptych, *Christ with the Virgin and Other Saints*, in the National Gallery of Art, Washington, D.C., has been identified as the altarpiece executed by Giotto and assistants for the Peruzzi Chapel in Sta Croce. Other paintings, such as the panels of St. Stephen in the Fondazione Horne, Florence, and a Franciscan monk in the Berenson Collection, Settignano; the painted cross in S. Maria Novella, Florence, perhaps identical with one mentioned as Giotto's in a document of 1312; and a painted cross in the Tempio Malatestiano (S. Francesco), Rimini, are probably by pupils or close followers of Giotto.

The sources mention frescoes by Giotto in the Badia and the Palazzo del Podestà (Bargello), Florence; S. Antonio and the Palazzo della Ragione, Padua; the Tempio Malatestiano, Rimini; the Castel Nuovo, S. Barbara, and S. Chiara, Naples; and elsewhere. Traces of the murals in the Badia have recently been brought to light, and some

Giottino, *The Deposition*. Uffizi, Florence.

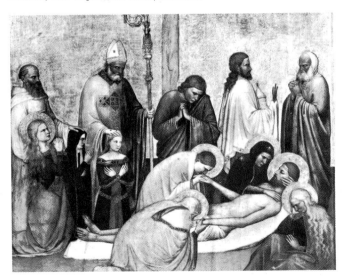

of the frescoes in the Bargello, restored beyond recognition of their original character, have survived. Of the work in Rome, the most important extant example is the celebrated mosaic of the *Navicella* in the narthex of St. Peter's; but it has been so completely altered that it can no longer be considered Giotto's. Two fragments of the original, showing heads of angels, are in S. Pietro Ispano at Boville Ernica and the Petrine Museum in the Vatican. The *Navicella*, as well as an altarpiece identified with a polyptych of *Christ Enthroned* on one side and *St. Peter Enthroned* on the other, by pupils of Giotto in the Vatican Picture Gallery; frescoes, no longer preserved, for the choir of the old Basilica of St. Peter's; and a fresco, *Pope Boniface VIII Proclaiming the Jubilee*, inadmissible in its present state as a work by Giotto, in St. John Lateran—all were ordered from Giotto by Cardinal Jacopo Stefaneschi either in 1300 or, more likely, after 1304.

The identification and dating of Giotto's work in Rome raise problems in the study of the master. Another, and more crucial, problem is the work that he is believed to have left in Assisi. The main source of controversy is the cycle of twenty-eight scenes of the *Legend of St. Francis* in the Upper Church of S. Francesco. Scenes XXVI–XXVIII and possibly I are quite unanimously regarded as the work of the St. Cecilia Master; but II–XXV have been attributed by the majority of writers to Giotto and his assistants, and have been dated either in the last decade of the 13th century or the second quarter of the 14th. Recent studies show rather conclusively that the latter murals belong to approximately the same period as the Arena Chapel frescoes, thus virtually ruling out Giotto's participation. Technical analysis now seems to confirm this. Very probably, as has been proposed, Giotto is the so-called Isaac Master, who is generally held to have painted, in the 1290s, several scenes from the Old and New Testaments above the *Legend of St. Francis* in the Upper Church. Three of these, *The Lamentation, Jacob and Rebecca before Isaac*, and *Esau Seeking Isaac's Blessing*, are particularly impressive and seem worthy of Giotto. *See* ISAAC MASTER.

With Giotto's work in Assisi thus defined, the artistic origins of the master would receive some clarification. In one critical view, he would have served an apprenticeship under Cimabue, who worked in Rome and Assisi during the last quarter of the 13th century; and in Rome he would have come under the influence of Pietro Cavallini. At some time, too, he must have been influenced by the sculpture of Nicola, and especially by Giovanni Pisano. From these masters he could have acquired the appreciation of form that was to be decisive for the subsequent development of western European painting. His mature work at Padua reveals him as an artist possessed of an unfailing sense of composition resolved along classical lines, with each scene rendered poignantly expressive and at the same time linked rhythmically with the others to carry the narrative forward. Giotto's forms are simplified, stressing universal rather than individual traits. They are rounded but remain related to the picture plane; the space is sufficient for their disposition in depth, though never

very deep, and the figures are invested with a human sentiment that is restrained yet dramatic in its concentration. In his latest work, as in the Peruzzi Chapel frescoes, the compositions become more complicated, the actions more varied, and the narrative more complex.

BIBLIOGRAPHY. F. Rintelen, *Giotto und die Giotto-Apokryphen*, Munich, 1912; R. van Marle, *The Development of the Italian Schools of Painting*, vol. 3, The Hague, 1924; R. Salvini, *Giotto: Bibliografia*, Rome, 1938; R. Offner, "Giotto, Non-Giotto," *Burlington Magazine*, LXXIV–LXXV, 1939; P. Murray, "Notes on Some Early Giotto Sources," *Journal of the Warburg and Courtauld Institutes*, XVI, 1953; C. Gnudi, *Giotto*, Milan, 1958; M. Meiss, *Giotto and Assisi*, New York, 1960; L. Tintori and M. Meiss, *The Painting of The Life of St. Francis in Assisi*, New York, 1962; L. Tintori and E. Borsook, *Giotto: The Peruzzi Chapel*, New York, 1965.

DARIO A. COVI

GIOTTO DI MAESTRO STEFANO, *see* GIOTTINO.

GIOVANNI, JEAN, *see* RICHTER, JOHAN.

GIOVANNI, PAOLO DI, *see* PAOLO DI GIOVANNI.

GIOVANNI, STEFANO DI, *see* SASSETTA.

GIOVANNI, TEDESCO (Piero di, or Pietro di). Italian sculptor (fl. Florence, 14th cent.). He worked at the Cathedral from 1386 to 1400, executing statues of SS. Jerome and Ambrose and the decoration of the easternmost pilasters of the southern doors. His inclusion of mythological creatures on the pilasters shows a usage of classical sources for carvings that would become more common in the Renaissance.

BIBLIOGRAPHY. W. G. Waters, *Italian Sculptors*, 2d ed., London, 1926.

GIOVANNI ANGELO DI ANTONIO DA CAMERINO, *see* MASTER OF THE BARBERINI PANELS.

GIOVANNI ANTONIO DE' SACCHI, *see* PORDENONE.

GIOVANNI BATTISTA DI JACOPO DI GASPARE, *see* ROSSO FIORENTINO.

GIOVANNI BOLOGNA, *see* BOLOGNA, GIOVANNI.

GIOVANNI BONSI, *see* BONSI, GIOVANNI.

GIOVANNI DA CAMPIONE. Italian sculptor (b. Lugano, early 14th cent.; fl. Milan, until ca. 1397). The reliefs and figures of the Virtues from his decoration of the doors and exterior angles of S. Maria Maggiore, Bergamo, are especially notable. The Scaliger tombs in Verona were done primarily from his designs.

GIOVANNI DA FAENZA, *see* GIOVANNI DA ORIOLO.

GIOVANNI DA FIESOLE (Da Firenze), *see* ANGELICO, FRA.

GIOVANNI D'ALEMAGNA (Giovanni da Murano). Venetian painter (d. 1450). He is known only through collaboration with Antonio Vivarini, his wife's brother. Since Giovanni is usually named first and died much sooner, he was probably older and the dominant partner. The one early work that Antonio painted alone is somewhat different, but after 1450 he retains the collaborative style.

Giotto, *The Visitation*, from the fresco series *Life of the Virgin*, Scrovegni Chapel, Padua. The earliest known surviving work by the artist.

It is debated whether Giovanni d'Alemagna, or John of Germany, brought the northern Gothic to Venice, where it bore much fruit. The earlier documents call him "of Murano" (the native town of the Vivarini), and he may have been German only by ancestry. In any case, the Venetian Gothic filtered to him through Masolino and Gentile da Fabriano.

BIBLIOGRAPHY. L. Testi, *La storia della pittura veneziana*, vol. 2: *Il divenire*, Bergamo, 1915; B. Berenson, *Italian Pictures of the Renaissance, Venetian School*, rev. ed., 2 vols., London, 1957.

GIOVANNI DA MAIANO, *see* MAIANO, GIOVANNI DA.

GIOVANNI DA MILANO (Giovanni di Jacopo di Guido da Caversaccio; Giovanni di Como). Italian painter of the Florentine school (fl. ca. 1350–75). Giovanni is first mentioned in 1350 in Florence. In 1363 he was registered in the painters' guild there, and in 1365 he was commissioned to paint frescoes in the Rinuccini Chapel in Sta Croce; those are his most important surviving works and his only fully authenticated frescoes. Giovanni's decorations in the Vatican, where he is documented in 1369, have been destroyed, together with all the other commissions of Urban V. Among Giovanni's paintings on panel are the polyptych of the *Madonna and Child with Four Saints*, executed in 1354(?), in the Municipal Museum of Prato; an *Annunciation* in the National Museum of St. Matthew in Pisa; the lovely *Pietà* in the Florentine Academy (signed IO. GOVANI DA MELANO DEPIN-

Giovanni d'Alemagna, *Madonna and Child*. Academy, Venice.

SI QUESTA TAVOLA 1365); panels of *Five Pairs of Saints* (from the high altar of the Ognissanti in Florence) in the Uffizi; and a lunette with the *Madonna and Child* in the Metropolitan Museum of Art in New York. Giovanni's art participates in the hieratic and flat style of his generation in Florence; it stands apart from it, however, through its lyrical and poetic suggestiveness.

BIBLIOGRAPHY. P. Toesca, *La pittura e la miniatura nella Lombardia*, Milan, 1912; A. Marabottini, *Giovanni da Milano*, Florence, 1950.
HELLMUT WOHL

GIOVANNI DA ORIOLO (Giovanni di Giuliano Savoretti? Giovanni Marcio; Giovanni da Faenza?). Italian portrait painter (fl. Faenza, 1443; d. 1473/74). He is known only by a signed portrait (ca. 1447) of Lionello d'Este of Ferrara, which seems to be a free copy of a medal by Pisanello, who may have been his teacher. The portrait, now in the National Gallery, London, is crisply executed in warm colors and with precise detail.

GIOVANNI DA PISTOIA, *see* GIOVANNI DI BARTOLOMMEO CRISTIANI.

GIOVANNI DA SAN GIOVANNI, *see* MANNOZZI, GIOVANNI.

GIOVANNI DA TRAU, *see* DALMATA, GIOVANNI.

GIOVANNI DA UDINE (Giovanni Nanni; Giovanni Recamador). Italian painter, stucco worker, and architect (b. Udine, 1487; d. Rome, 1564). First a pupil of Giovanni Martino da Udine, he later studied with Giorgione (1510/11?). He is known to have been collaborating with Raphael at least by 1516, when he painted the musical instruments in Raphael's *St. Cecilia* (Bologna, National Picture Gallery). Between 1517 and 1519 he assisted Raphael in the *Psyche* loggia of the Villa Farnesina (Rome) and in the Vatican *loggie*. The rich decoration of the second floor of the latter remains the most influential scheme of its kind ever devised. Giovanni was responsible also for the stucco decoration at the Villa Madama (Rome, 1525), and with Perino del Vaga he decorated the ceiling of the Sala dei Pontefici in the Vatican (1523–27). From 1532 to 1534 he worked on the cupola ornamentation of Michelangelo's New Sacristy (Florence, S. Lorenzo), but this work was painted over at a later date. In 1534 he returned to Udine and was active mainly as an architect. According to Vasari, he made a final trip to Rome in 1560 to paint the third floor of the Vatican *loggie*. Inspired by ancient Roman grotesques, he emerged as the foremost decorator of the Renaissance.

NORMAN W. CANEDY

GIOVANNI DA VERONA, FRA. Italian sculptor and architect (b. Verona, ca. 1457; d. there, 1525). Giovanni da Verona was an Olivetan monk, and all knowledge of his career is based on the *Tabulae familiarum* of that order. Until 1506 he was at Monte Oliveto Maggiore, where he executed the Easter candlestick for the cloister of S. Maria in Organo, Verona. From 1506 to 1525 he was in Naples, in Rome, and again in northern Italy. He executed intarsia decorated panels and benches for the Camera della Segnatura in the Vatican (1511–12). His major

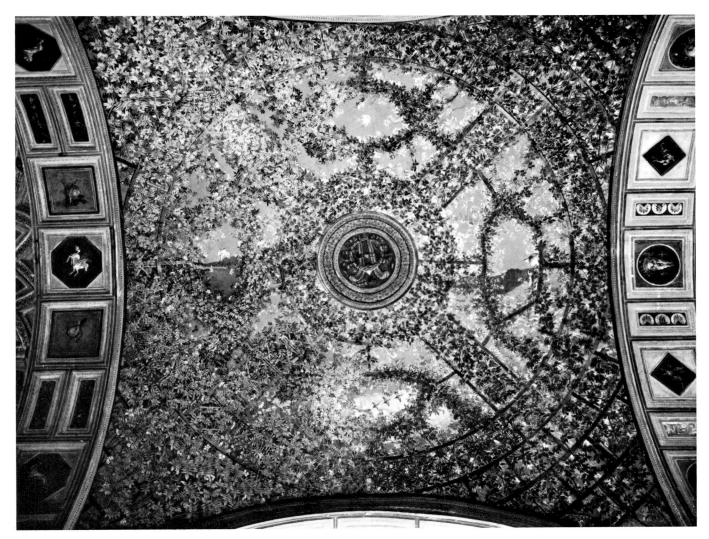

Giovanni da Udine, vault decoration on the first floor of the Vatican loggie, Rome.

work is considered to be the choir stalls of S. Maria in Organo in Verona (begun 1491).

BIBLIOGRAPHY. C. Scherer, *Technik und Geschichte der Intarsia*, Leipzig, 1891; P. Lugano, "Di Fra Giovanni da Verona, maestro d'intaglio e di Tarsia e della sua scuola," *Bollettino Senese di Storia Patria*, XII, 1905.

GIOVANNI DEL BIONDO DAL CASENTINO. Italian painter of the Florentine school (fl. ca. 1350–1400). Giovanni is first recorded in 1356, when he became a Florentine citizen. His earliest work is a panel, *S. Verdiana*, in the sacristy of S. Verdiana at Castelfiorentino (from an altarpiece painted for S. Sofia there in 1360). Among his many signed and dated pictures are the *Madonna and Child* polyptych (1372) in the Bardi di Vernio Chapel in Sta Croce, Florence; the *Coronation of the Virgin* polyptych (1373) in the Bardini Museum at Fiesole; a *Madonna and Child* (1377) in the Picture Gallery of Siena; the polyptych (1379) in the Rinuccini Chapel in Sta Croce, Florence; an *Annunciation with Two Saints* (1385) in the Ospedale degli Innocenti, Florence; and the *Madonna and Child* (1392) in S. Francesco, Figline. Other important works are the *St. Zenobius* in the Florence Cathedral and the *St. John the Evangelist* in the Uffizi Gallery at Florence. Giovanni's style is a product of the Orcagna brothers' workshop. It has little flexibility or variety, though it excels in its frontal severity of form, luminosity of color, and richness of pattern.

BIBLIOGRAPHY. C. Gamba, "Giovanni del Biondo," *Rivista d'arte*, V, 1907; R. van Marle, *The Development of the Italian Schools of Painting*, vol. 3, The Hague, 1924; R. Offner, *Italian Primitives at Yale University*, New Haven, 1927.

HELLMUT WOHL

GIOVANNI DELL'OPERA, *see* BANDINI, GIOVANNI.

GIOVANNI DEL POGGIO, *see* GIOVANNI DI PAOLO.

GIOVANNI DEL PONTE (Giovanni di Marco; Giovanni di Marco dal Ponte). Italian painter of the Florentine school (1385–1437). Giovanni di Marco acquired the name Giovanni del Ponte because he had a studio near S. Stefano a Ponte in Florence. He is believed to have been a pupil of Spinello Aretino. He was one of the few painters brought up in the 14th-century tradition who absorbed the influence of Masaccio's innovations. In 1408 Giovanni was a member of the Company of St. Luke. He worked in Sta Trinità in 1429–30 and 1434, but only the remains of his frescoes of the later date in the Scali Chapel have survived in a tolerable state. Giovanni evolved a somewhat harsh, broad style, imbuing his essentially Gothic forms with a sculptural sense of mass. A triptych of the *Annunciation* in the Vatican is dated 1435; another triptych, the *Ascension of St. John the Evangelist with Saints* in London, is somewhat earlier. Other works by Giovanni are in the Uffizi Gallery in Florence, the Gallery of the Academy in Florence, the Fogg Art Museum in Cambridge, Mass., and the Condé Museum in Chantilly.

BIBLIOGRAPHY. P. Toesca, "Umili pittori fiorentini del principio del Quattrocento," *L'Arte*, 1904; H. Horne, "Giovanni dal Ponte," *The Burlington Magazine*, IX, 1906; R. van Marle, *The Development of the Italian Schools of Painting*, vol. 9, The Hague, 1927.

HELLMUT WOHL

GIOVANNI DI BARTOLOMMEO CRISTIANI (Giovanni da Pistoia). Italian painter of the school of Pistoia (fl. 2d half of 14th cent.). According to Vasari, Giovanni da Pistoia was a follower of Pietro Cavallini; the style of the works associated with him, however, shows no signs of contact with the tradition of the Roman master. Cristiani is recorded in Pistoia in 1366 and 1374; in 1381 and 1382 he was active at the Camposanto in Pisa. Of his works in Pistoia, the only surviving ones are an altarpiece of *St. John the Evangelist* (signed and dated 1370) flanked by eight scenes from the legend of St. John, in the sacristy of S. Giovanni Fuorcivitas; and fragments of the ceiling frescoes with figures of the Virtues in the entrance hall of the Cathedral (1377–78). There are panel paintings by Cristiani in the Metropolitan Museum of Art in New York and at the Yale University Art Gallery in New Haven, Conn. His style shows connections with the hard, tight, and flatly modeled manner of the Pisan school, though it is more monotonous in design and color.

BIBLIOGRAPHY. B. Khvoshinsky and M. Salmi, *I pittori toscani, dal XII al XVI secolo*, vol. 2: *I Fiorentini del Trecento*, Florence, 1914; V. Lasareff, "Some Florentine Pictures of the Trecento in Russia," *Art in America*, XVI, Dec., 1927.

GIOVANNI DI BENEDETTO DA COMO. Italian miniaturist (fl. ca. 1350–75). He illuminated a Book of Hours for Bianca of Savoy (1350/78; Munich, State Library) in a charming, graceful style deriving from the French Gothic, with emphasis on details of setting and costume.

GIOVANNI DI COMO, *see* GIOVANNI DA MILANO.

GIOVANNI DI FRANCESCO DEL CERVELLIERA. Italian painter of the Florentine school (ca. 1428–59). Giovanni di Francesco del Cervelliera was registered in the Florentine painters' guild in 1446. In his tax declaration of 1451 he stated that he was born in Rovezzano, that his age was twenty-three, and that he had been living in Florence for sixteen years. Giovanni's only documented work is the lunette of *God the Father Surrounded by Innocents* over the north door of the Ospedale degli Innocenti, for which he received payments in 1459. The most important works securely attributed to him are the triptych of the *Madonna and Child with Four Saints* in the

Carrand Collection of the National Museum (Bargello), Florence; its predella of *Three Episodes from the Legend of St. Nicholas* in the Casa Buonarroti; a *Crucifix* in S. Andrea, Brozzi; a predella with the *Nativity and the Adoration of the Magi* in the Montpellier Museum; and the altar frontal with *St. Blaise* (dated 1453) in S. Biagio, Petriolo, near Florence. Giovanni's eclectic, linear, and precise manner shows the influence of Fra Filippo Lippi, Castagno, Domenico Veneziano, and, most strongly, Baldovinetti.

BIBLIOGRAPHY. R. Longhi, "Ricerche su Giovanni de Francesco," *Pinacoteca*, I, July–August, 1928; V. Giovanozzi, "Note su Giovanni di Francesco," *Rivista d'arte*, VI, Oct., 1934; R. W. Kennedy, *Alesso Baldovinetti*, New Haven, 1938.

HELLMUT WOHL

GIOVANNI DI GIULIANO SAVORETTI, *see* GIOVANNI DA ORIOLO.

GIOVANNI DI JACOPO DI GUIDO DA CAVERSACCIO, *see* GIOVANNI DA MILANO.

GIOVANNI DI MARCO (Dal Ponte), *see* GIOVANNI DEL PONTE.

GIOVANNI DI MICHELE SCHEGGINI DA LARCIANO, *see* GRAFFIONE.

GIOVANNI DI NICOLA. Italian painter (fl. 1326–60). He is probably the painter mentioned as a student of Lippo Memmi in Siena (1326). He worked in Pisa, where he is recorded as a member of the city council in 1358. The only other date connected with him (1360) appeared on a painting that is now lost. His one signed work is a polyptych with the Madonna flanked by SS. Bona, John the Baptist, Mary Magdalen, and Bartholemew (Pisa, National Museum of St. Matthew). Many works have been attributed to him, including two Madonnas and an Annunciation in the National Museum of St. Matthew. These show the influence of Traini, the linearism of Simone Martini, and the bland faces of Lippo Memmi.

BIBLIOGRAPHY. G. Vigni, *Pittura del due e trecento nel museo di Pisa*, Palermo, 1950.

GIOVANNI DI PAOLO (Giovanni del Poggio). Italian painter of the Sienese school (1403–83). This remarkable artist was most probably a pupil of Taddeo di Bartolo, the leading Sienese painter of the previous generation. He was influenced by Gentile da Fabriano, who worked in Siena in 1424–25, and to a certain extent, though somewhat later, by Florentine painting. The most important factor in the evolution of his style was the art of Sassetta.

Giovanni's earliest documented works are the *Madonna and Child with Angels* (1426) in the Propositura of Castelnuovo Berardenga, near Siena, and the *Madonna and Child* (1427) in the Hirsch Collection in Basel, both related to the late-14th-century Sienese style, though modified by Gentile da Fabriano. The *Madonna and Child* (1428) in the Saracini Collection in Siena is, however, closely aligned with the art of Sassetta. Later signed and dated works are the *Crucifixion* (1440) in the Sienese Academy; the *Coronation of the Virgin* (1445) in S. Andrea in Siena; the *Presentation in the Temple* (1447/48), based on Ambrogio Lorenzetti's formulation of this sub-

Giovanni di Paolo, *The Last Judgment.* **Pinacoteca, Siena. Typical of the poetic Sienese narrative painting.**

ject of 1342, in the Academy in Siena; the *Mystic Marriage of St. Catherine* (1457) in Castiglion Fiorentino; and a *Madonna and Child* (1463) in Pienza. The last two show a decline in Giovanni's artistic powers, with rather stereotyped, mawkish figures and monotonous colors, a tendency which continues until his last documented work, the *Assumption of the Virgin* (1475) in the Academy in Siena.

Giovanni's genius was at its height in his small narrative pictures. The most beautiful are six scenes from the *Life of St. John the Baptist* (ca. 1450) in the Ryerson Collection of the Art Institute of Chicago. Painted in the most felicitous period in the artist's career, they fuse in a most original and moving way the poetic fantasy of medieval Siena with early Renaissance achievements in composition and perspective. Among Giovanni's other narrative pictures are four predella panels (1426) in the Walters Art Gallery in Baltimore and two works from an altarpiece of 1445, the panel representing *Paradise* in the Metropolitan Museum of Art in New York and the equally magical *Creation of the World* in the Lehman Collection.

While Giovanni di Paolo's art is the product of his own unique imagination, it would be inconceivable in its time outside the context of Sienese mysticism and religious fervor. Only within this framework did the visionary and the naturalistic come together as they do in the art of Giovanni di Paolo, with its delicate, often archaic, expressionistic—occasionally grotesque—formal inventions.

BIBLIOGRAPHY. J. Pope-Hennessy, *Giovanni di Paolo*, London, 1937; C. Brandi, *Giovanni di Paolo*, Florence, 1947.

HELLMUT WOHL

GIOVANNI DI PIETRO DA NAPOLI. Italian religious painter (b. Naples; fl. Pisa, 1402–05). In 1402 he worked with Martino di Bartolommeo da Siena on an altarpiece for the Hospital Church of S. Chiara in Pisa. Extant works (1403–05) show linear figures, similar to those of Luca di Tommè, and somber coloring.

GIOVANNI FRANCESCO DA RIMINI. Italian painter (d. before Dec., 1470). He is documented in Padua and Bologna. Knowledge of his work is based on two signed and dated panel paintings: a *Madonna and Child Enthroned* in S. Domenico, Bologna (1459), and a half-length *Madonna and Child with Two Angels* in the National Gallery, London (1461). These and other works attributed to him—for example, the panel of the *Virgin Adoring the Christ Child*, in the National Picture Gallery, Bologna; a predella panel of *The Legend of St. Nicholas*, in the Louvre, Paris; a triptych of the *Madonna and Child with Two Saints*, in the National Gallery of Umbria, Perugia; and a *Scene from the Legend of St. Dominic*, in the Gallery of Pesaro—show the influence of Umbrian and Marchigian masters, such as Fiorenzo di Lorenzo and Matteo da Gualdo. Although the forms are somewhat hard, the pictures have a certain charm because of their melancholy mood and naïveté of narrative expression.

BIBLIOGRAPHY. R. van Marle, *The Development of the Italian Schools of Painting*, vol. 15, The Hague, 1934.

GIOVANNI MARCIO, see GIOVANNI DA ORIOLO.

GIOVANNI MARIA. Italian ceramic artist of Castel Durante (fl. early 16th cent.). He is known for his majolica plates. The one extant signed example of his work is a dish decorated with the arms of Pope Julius II and the arms of the Manzoli family. There is often an element of the grotesque in his inventive and cohesive style.

GIOVANNI MARIA DA PADOVA, see MOSCA, GIOVANNI MARIA.

GIOVANNINO DE' GRASSI. Italian architect, sculptor, painter, and miniaturist of the Lombard School (ca. 1340–98). Giovannino, one of the major personalities in the art of Milan at the beginning of the Renaissance, is most fully documented as architect, sculptor, decorator, and painter in the Cathedral of Milan. His name occurs there from 1389 until his death, and after 1391 with the designation "architect-in-charge." His architectural contribution is, however, difficult to estimate. Among the works he executed for the Cathedral, only a relief of *Christ and the Samaritan Woman* (1396) over the font in the south sacristy has survived. As a miniaturist Giovannino is thought to have painted the illuminations in the Codex Berolo (Bibl. Trivulziana Cod. 2262) and in the prayerbook of Gian Galeazzo Visconti in the Visconti di Modrone Library in Milan. A notable sketchbook containing remarkably detailed, naturalistic studies of animals and designs for vari-

ous figural types is in the library in Bergamo. Giovannino was the leading International Style artist of his time and had considerable influence on northern Italian art; his style shows relationships to the art of the Burgundian court.

BIBLIOGRAPHY. A. van Schendel, *Le Dessin en Lombardie, jusqu'à la fin du XVe siècle*, Brussels, 1938; O. Pächt, "Early Italian Nature Studies and the Early Calendar Landscape," *Journal of the Warburg and Courtauld Institutes*, XIII, Jan., 1950.

HELLMUT WOHL

GIOVANNI PISANO. Italian sculptor (b. prob. Pisa, ca. 1250; d. after 1314). His earliest known work, a *Madonna and Child* (1265; Pisa, Camposanto), was done when he accompanied his father, Nicola, to Pisa. It follows Nicola's style in the beauty of line in the Madonna's torso, while a liveliness of movement is created by the slight backward turn of her head toward the child. Giovanni went with Nicola to Perugia for the decoration of the fountain at the Palazzo Maggiore, completed in 1278. A number of reliefs around the lower basins and the slender Etruscan nymphs forming the jet may be ascribed to Giovanni's hand.

Returning to Pisa, Nicola having died probably in the previous year, Giovanni continued his father's work on the Pisa Baptistery. His predilection for Gothic splendor, rather than Nicola's Romanesque restraint, appears in the elaborate cusping and marble tracery decorating the gallery. This tendency is again apparent in the graceful arcading of the marble loggia in the Camposanto.

Retained as Cathedral architect at Siena in 1284, Giovanni designed a Gothic façade that, although basically northern, retained certain Romanesque elements, as in the proportion of the central dome. Architecturally concise, despite small side turrets and pediment pinnacles, the façade gives a pictorial effect similar to the marble polychromed Orvieto façade, because of the extensive statuary, now largely restored. A powerful, schematic effect is created by the paired figures—David opposite Solomon, Plato opposite Habakkuk—which lean forward from the façade plane to gaze or gesture at each other. This scheme of external plastic decoration, although differing from such great French cathedrals as Amiens by its confinement of statuary to the area above the entrance level and clear identification by isolation of each statue, nonetheless liberated Italian sculpture to the same degree as its French counterpart from its architectural setting.

While the polygonal St. Andrew pulpit in Pistoia (1299) structurally resembles the earlier Siena pulpit, the sharply pointed ogival arches and the delicacy of the capital ornamentation indicate Giovanni's essentially Gothic character. A freedom from architecture is evident in the animated statues, which seem almost to detach themselves from the parapet corners, in harmony with the crowded panel reliefs which they separate rather than with their setting. Such panels as the *Massacre of the Innocents* show increasing compositional awareness. Here, the gesticulating, angular figures mass in oblique lines, one group surging toward Herod's throne, the other being driven back. A new softness of flesh and vividness of hair underline Giovanni's sophisticated handling of marble throughout the pulpit.

The polychromed Scrovegni Chapel *Madonna and Child*

Giovanni Pisano, relief of the Adoration of the Magi on the octagonal pulpit in Sant'Andrea, Pistoia.

flanked by two candle-bearing angels, in Padua, is somewhat later than the Pistoia pulpit. The Mother and Child form an intimate group, as in the Camposanto *Madonna*, with the Child turning to meet the Mother's eyes. However, the strong linear rising curve of the Madonna, with her arched brows above deep-set eyes, contributes to a new sense of grandeur and brooding.

The last of the great Pisan pulpits, in the Cathedral, was commissioned from Giovanni in 1302 (completed in 1400). Architecturally inferior to the Pistoia pulpit, the sculptural execution is also often inferior, as in the confused composition of the Passion scenes of the sixth relief or the coarser figures of the reliefs of the Liberal Arts decorating the polygonal base. Most noteworthy is Giovanni's novel introduction of large-scale figures of saints and virtues, replacing several of the columns. While not wholly classical, the figures indicate a moderation of Gothic turbulence.

This quieter mood is again apparent in comparing a final *Madonna and Child* (Prato Cathedral) with the Scrovegni *Madonna*. Although the later group echoes the pose of the earlier, the delicate smiling profile of the Madonna and the wistful Child stretching one hand forward toward her crown establish a lighter mood in the turbulent list of Giovanni's *oeuvre*.

As a Gothic sculptor, Giovanni, rather than his father, had far-reaching effects on the continuity of Italian 14th-century artists, although perhaps his most direct descendant, after more than a century, was Jacopo della Quer-

cia. Giovanni as an innovator was a liberator of Italian sculpture from its former ancillary position; as a sculptor, he was a dynamic and intellectual artist.

BIBLIOGRAPHY. A. Venturi, *Giovanni Pisano*, Paris, 1928; G. H. and E. R. Crichton, *Nicola Pisano and the Revival of Sculpture in Italy*, Cambridge, 1938; H. Keller, *Giovanni Pisano*, Vienna, 1942; J. Pope-Hennessy, *Italian Gothic Sculpture*, London, 1955.
LYNNE S. MAYO

GIOVENONE, GIROLAMO. Italian painter, active in Vercelli, Piedmont (ca. 1486–1555). His early work is well known, deriving from Spanzotti and showing a formal, Italianized echo of Flemish traditions of the late 15th century, Gothic but bourgeois (altarpiece, 1513, Vercelli Museum; altarpiece, 1514, Turin, Sabauda Gallery; and so on). A later phase, affected in its nervous monumentality by Gaudenzio Ferrari, appears in his *St. Ambrose* (1527; Vercelli, S. Francesco). His last years are unknown.

BIBLIOGRAPHY. Turin, Mostra d'arte a Palazzo Carignano, 2d ed., 1939, *Gotico e Rinascimento in Piemonte, Catalogo*, Turin, 1939.

GIRALDA TOWER, SEVILLE, *see* SEVILLE.

GIRALDI, GUGLIELMO (Del Magro). Italian illuminator of Ferrara (fl. 1445–76). His principal work is a four-volume Bible in the Certosa of S. Cristoforo. He painted miniatures illustrating the works of Tibullus, Appian, and Petrarch. Gradually making use of perspective, he developed a Renaissance style, and his later work is similar to Cosimo Tura's.

BIBLIOGRAPHY. M. Salmi, *Italian Miniatures*, New York, 1954.

François Girardon, *The Rape of Proserpina*, 1699, in the colonnade at Versailles.

GIRALTE, FRANCISCO. Spanish sculptor (fl. 1st half of 16th cent.). Fully trained when he associated with a group under the influence of the style of Alonso Berruguete, Giralte is credited with a major part of the execution of Berruguete's choir stalls on the Epistle side of Toledo Cathedral (1531-40); Felipe Bigarny did those on the Gospel side. Technically skilled, he served the nervous genius of Berruguete. The effective fusion of emotion and technique seen in Berruguete's works was carried into Giralte's own commissions, the altarpiece and sepulchers of the Chapel of the Bishop in S. Andrés, Madrid.

BIBLIOGRAPHY. G. Weise, *Spanische Plastik aus sieben Jahrhunderten*, vol. 2, Reutlingen, 1927; M. E. Gómez-Moreno, *Breve historia de la escultura española*, 2d ed., Madrid, 1951.

GIRANDOLE, BERNARDO DELLE, *see* BUONTALENTI, BERNARDO.

GIRARD D'ORLEANS. French painter (d. Paris, 1361). It is known from documents that he was active in Paris as Court Painter to King Jean II, known as "Jean le Bon," who reigned from 1350 to 1364. Girard is said to have accompanied the King during his captivity in England, which lasted from 1356 to 1360. For these reasons Bouchot attributed to Girard the portrait inscribed JEHAN ROY DE FRANCE (Paris, Louvre), which is generally considered to be the earliest royal portrait painted in Europe. It was probably painted about 1360, judging from the apparent age of the King, who was born in 1319.

BIBLIOGRAPHY. H. Bouchot, *Les Primitifs français, 1292-1500*, 2d ed., Paris, 1904; G. Ring, *A Century of French Painting, 1400-1500*, London, 1949.

GIRARDON, FRANCOIS. French sculptor (b. Troyes, 1628; d. Paris, 1715). Girardon was a pupil of the wood sculptor Baudesson at the Castle of Saint-Liebault in Estissac. He aroused the interest of Chancellor Séguier, who sent him to Rome under the protection of Mignard. By 1650 he was again in Paris, the pupil of Laurent Magnier and François Anguier. He often worked from designs by Charles Le Brun or Claude Perrault. In 1657 Girardon became a member of the Royal Academy; he was professor there in 1659, rector in 1675, and chancellor in 1695.

From 1664 to 1671, Girardon worked under Le Brun in the Gallery of Apollo at the Louvre, also doing stucco works for the Tuileries in 1666-67. From 1666 to 1675, he collaborated with T. Regnaudin on the *Apollo and the Nymphs* group for the Grotto of Thetis (Versailles Gardens). In 1684 he recut Bernini's marble statue of Louis XIV into a work that showed Marcus Curtius plunging into the flames (Versailles Gardens). At Troyes he did a medallion of Louis XIV (1687), a *Christ* (1690) for St-Rémi, and a high altar (1692) for St-Jean. The year 1699 saw his *Rape of Proserpina* for the colonnade at Versailles, inspired by Giovanni da Bologna's *Rape of the Sabines*. From 1690 on, Girardon was Inspector General of Sculpture, creating models to be executed by his pupils. His acknowledged masterpiece is the tomb of Cardinal Richelieu (1694) in the Chapel of the Sorbonne, Paris.

Girardon's most grandiose project came from Bernini via Le Brun: a rock 100 feet high with the colossal statue of Louis XIV crushing Discord and Heresy, with enchained rivers and subjected nations. This project, begun in 1679, came to an end in 1683 with the death of Colbert, but is the probable inspiration for Falconet's statue of Peter the Great.

Girardon also did many private commissions from 1670 to 1675, including the tombs of the Président de Lamoignon (destroyed except bas-relief; Troyes Museum) and the Princesse de Conti (destroyed except relief figure; Paris, private collection). He executed an equestrian statue of Louis XIV (1683-99; destroyed in 1792) for the Place Vendôme, Paris, which was cast by Balthazar Keller in 1692. It was the first time horse and rider were cast together rather than composed from assembled pieces. Upon Girardon's retirement in 1700, Coysevox succeeded him at the works of the Invalides in Paris.

Girardon died on the same day as the monarch he had devoted his life to glorifying. His work is the embodiment of 17th-century French classic sculpture, and although his debt to Bernini is great, he seems to have rejected the pathetic quality of the baroque and to have been drawn to the art of Duquesnoy and Giovanni da Bologna, Italianized northerners.

BIBLIOGRAPHY. J. Guiffrey, "Le Tombeau du cardinal de Richelieu," *Nouvelles Archives de l'Art Français*, V, 1889; A. Michel, *Histoire de l'art*, vol. 6, pt. 2, Paris, 1922; P. Francastel, *Girardon*, Paris, 1928; M. Oudinot, "François Girardon, son rôle dans les travaux de sculpture à Versailles et aux Invalides," *Bulletin de la Société de l'Histoire de l'Art français*, 1937.

W. MC ALLISTER JOHNSON

GIRAUD, JEAN-BAPTISTE. French sculptor (b. Aix-en-Provence, 1752; d. Bouleaux, 1830). The pupil of an anonymous goldsmith, Giraud was a self-taught sculptor. He exhibited only once, in the Salon of 1789, where his *Dying Achilles* won him membership in the Royal Academy. He then went to Italy for eight years, assembling a museum of casts of antique statuary which was later displayed in the Place Vendôme, Paris. His pupils included Pierre-François-Grégoire Giraud, and he helped in the creation of Eméric David's book on statuary in ancient and modern times.

GIRAUD, PIERRE-FRANCOIS-GREGOIRE. French sculptor (b. Le Luc, 1783; d. Paris, 1836). He studied with Jean-Baptiste Giraud and Ramey and won the Prix de Rome in 1806. His relatively few works, animal groups and classical figures, depend more on observation than on neoclassic artistic theory.

GIRGENTI CATACOMBS, AGRIGENTO. Early Christian catacombs in the modern city of Agrigento (Akragas), in southern Sicily, possibly originating in the 2d century but more probably not until the 4th. They are located in the area of the Greek temples of Concord and Heracles (Hercules). One catacomb is composed of a circular room with vaulted tombs.

BIBLIOGRAPHY. C. Mercurelli, "Scavi e scoperte nelle catacombe siciliane (1941)," *Rivista di Archeologia Cristiana*, XXI, 1944-45.

GIRL BEFORE A MIRROR. Oil painting by Picasso, in the Museum of Modern Art, New York. *See* PICASSO, PABLO.

GIRODET-TRIOSON (Girodet de Roussy), ANNE-LOUIS. French painter, printmaker, and poet (b. Montargis, 1767; d. Paris, 1824). Anne-Louis Girodet added the name Trioson to his surname in homage to his benefactor Dr. Trioson. In 1785 he entered David's studio; he won the Prix de Rome in 1789 and painted in Rome during the difficult days of the French Revolution. In 1792 he painted the hard, Davidian *Hippocrates Refusing the Presents of Artaxerxes* (Paris, Faculty of Medicine) and the next year the soft and misty *Endymion's Sleep* (Paris, Louvre). Back in Paris, he was awarded commissions along with other Davidians, his being *Ossian Welcoming the French Heroes* (1801; Rueil, Malmaison, and an excellent oil sketch in the Louvre). His *Deluge* (1806; Louvre) was judged one of the great paintings in the Salon of 1808, the year of his *Funeral of Atala* (Louvre), inspired by Chateaubriand's famous novel.

For the great military series commissioned by Napoleon he painted, in 1808, *Napoleon Receiving the Keys of Vien-*

Anne-Louis Girodet-Trioson, *Funeral of Atala*. Louvre, Paris. This painting was inspired by Chateaubriand's famous novel.

na and, in 1810, *The Revolt of Cairo*, both in the Versailles Museum. Filled with dramatic action, the latter work, an energetic and colorful romantic conception of a historical event, won for him a foremost place as a military painter. For the Château de Compiègne he did a series of seasons and mythological figures on which he worked during the last decade of his life. In 1818 he painted *Pygmalion and Galatea* (Château de Dampierre). Several fine portraits are found in museums: *Deputy Belley* (1797; Versailles, Museum); *Dr. Larrey* (1804; Louvre); and *Chateaubriand* (1811; Versailles, Museum). Numerous fine drawings exist for Girodet's illustrations of the works of Racine, Ossian, Vergil, and Anacreon.

Although one of the outstanding painters of his epoch, Girodet preferred composing long, meandering poems. His painting style was often nebulous and hazy—an effect he sought, but one which David criticized harshly. Girodet was inspired by Poussin, David, and Italian painters, but he added a *sfumato* quality to heighten the poetic effect of lucent figures moving in a strange atmosphere. He was an innovator and an influential theoretician for his contemporaries.

BIBLIOGRAPHY. P.-A. Coupin, ed., *Oeuvres posthumes de Girodet-Trioson...*, 2 vols., Paris, 1829; H. Lemonnier, *Girodet et les héros d' "Ossian"* (Institut de France), Paris, 1913; G. Levitine, "L'Ossian de Girodet et l'actualité politique sous le Consulat," *Gazette des Beaux-Arts*, XLVIII, 1956 (Eng. summary); N. Schlenoff, *Ingres, ses sources littéraires*, Paris, 1956.

NORMAN SCHLENOFF

GIROLAMO, GIOVANNI, see GRANDI, VICENZO.

GIROLAMO DA CARPI. Italian painter of Ferrara (1501–56). He was the favorite painter of Cardinal Ippolito d'Este. He followed Giulio Romano in massive, shadowy, mobile classicism; among his altarpieces and allegories, *Opportunity and Patience* (1541; Dresden, State Art Collections, Picture Gallery) is notable.

GIROLAMO DA COTIGNOLA, see MARCHESI, GIROLAMO.

GIROLAMO DA CREMONA. Italian miniaturist and painter (fl. 1467–75). He is known from sixty-one miniatures in eleven antiphonals in the Piccolomini Library, Siena. One other signed miniature is in the Victoria and Albert Museum, London. He certainly painted one large altarpiece, *The Risen Christ* (1472; Viterbo Cathedral).

If he painted the final part of the *Missal of Marchioness Barbara of Brandenburg* at Mantua, it would indicate his beginnings; the work was started in 1461 with Mantegna as supervisor. The missal (Mantua, Ducal Palace) is inspired by Antonio Vivarini, but Mantegna, whom he varies in mannered swirling forms with cutting line, is Girolamo's main source. He exchanged ideas with Liberale da Verona.

BIBLIOGRAPHY. M. Salmi, "Gerolamo da Cremona, miniatore e pittore," 2 pts., *Bollettino d'Arte*, XVI, Mar., Apr., 1923.

GIROLAMO (Jerome) DA FIESOLE. Italian-French sculptor (fl. 15th–16th cent.). About 1499 he was called to France to collaborate on the tomb of François II (1502–07; Nantes Cathedral), which is often ascribed to Jean Perreal and Michel Colombe. He may have done the tomb of the children of Charles VIII (1506; Tours Cathedral), which is traditionally ascribed to the Giusti. His specialty was ornamental sculpture, and there is much controversy over his works which, however, are in the proto-Renaissance tradition of Colombe.

BIBLIOGRAPHY. P. Vitry, *Michel Colombe...*, Paris, 1901.

GIROLAMO DA TREVISO THE ELDER (Girolamo Pennacchi). Italian painter (1455–97). He was the brother of Pier Maria Pennacchi. The work from his early career in Padua is a provincial reflection of Mantegna, which he soon overlays with imitations of the compositional designs of Giovanni Bellini.

GIROLAMO DA TREVISO THE YOUNGER. Venetian painter (1497–1544). He was influenced by Raphael (*Sleeping Venus*, Rome, Borghese Gallery) even before he went to Bologna, where Parmigianino's influence was added (frescoes in Bologna, S. Petronio, and Faenza, Chiesa della Commenda). After 1538 he worked as an engineer in England.

GIROLAMO DEL SANTO (Tessaro). Italian painter of Padua (b. ca. 1497; d. after 1561). There, under the influence of Romanino, he painted striking frescoes in S. Francesco, in the Scuola del Carmine, and elsewhere. He was incorrectly supposed to have worked simultaneously with Titian in 1511 at the Scuola del Santo.

BIBLIOGRAPHY. L. Pietrogrande, "Nuovi documenti su Girolamo dal Santo," *Rivista d'arte*, XXI, 1939.

GIROLAMO DI BENVENUTO. Italian painter (b. Siena, 1470; d. there, 1524). Girolamo first worked with his father, Benvenuto di Giovanni, from whose paintings he borrowed motifs and compositions throughout his career. His religious paintings and frescoes show the same tendency to verticalism and meticulous realism, although the figure and drapery style is fuller but less consistent.

GIROLAMO DI GIOVANNI DA CAMERINO. Italian religious painter (fl. last half 15th cent.). He was a member of the painters' guild in Padua in 1450. His various works show the influences of Matteo da Gualdo and Giovanni Boccati, as well as those of Piero della Francesca and the Venetian school in his later works. It was formerly believed that only a signed polyptych in Monte San Martino had survived, but in the early 20th century Bernard Berenson identified and grouped several of his paintings by style.

GIROLAMO PENNACCHI, see GIROLAMO DA TREVISO THE ELDER.

GIRTIN, THOMAS. English landscape painter in water color (b. Southwark, London, 1775; d. London, 1802). His first teacher was a Mr. Fisher, but in 1789 he was apprenticed to Edward Dayes, the topographical water-colorist. Probably about 1791–92, there was a serious quarrel, and henceforth Girtin worked more or less independently. Like Dayes, he did much work during the early 1790s for James Moore, an antiquary, contributing drawings to be engraved for Moore's topographical publications. From about 1794 to 1797 he was employed with Turner

Thomas Girtin, *Kirkstall Abbey*. Victoria and Albert Museum, London.

by the connoisseur Dr. Thomas Monro in copying drawings by J. R. Cozens. In 1796 he went on a sketching trip to the north of England and southern Scotland, the first of many such tours of various parts of Great Britain, including Wales. In 1799 he became the leading spirit of a group of young artists who called themselves "The Brothers" and met for the purpose of drawing landscape compositions based on verses of poetry.

Girtin had exhibited water colors at the Royal Academy of Arts since 1794, and his work was beginning to attract the patronage of wealthy collectors such as Sir George Beaumont, Edward Lascelles, and the Earl of Mulgrave. He nevertheless failed in his ambition to be elected a member of the Royal Academy. With this object in mind he had exhibited in 1801 his only recorded oil painting, *Bolton Bridge*, which is now lost.

He went to Paris in November, 1801, stayed there about six months, and drew a series of views of the city from which he later made soft-ground etchings. These were aquatinted and published posthumously in 1803 under the title *A Selection of Twenty of the Most Picturesque Views in Paris and Its Environs*. In November, 1802, six months after his return to London, Girtin died at the age of twenty-seven.

Although his scope was limited to water color and his career so drastically abbreviated, Girtin as much as any artist liberated landscape from the conventions of the 18th century and created the romantic naturalism of the 19th. It was Girtin who swept away the classical formulas of landscape composition and first saw the winding hills and

dales of the English countryside as the romantic goal of the city-dweller's personal quest for freedom.

His early works (ca. 1792–95) are in the 18th-century topographical manner, greatly influenced by Dayes, whom he gradually surpassed in breadth of execution.

In the following years (ca. 1796–99), he began to use stronger and deeper local colors. The paint is more heavily applied, the touch broader, and the drawing looser. At the same time he became more variable in style and more uneven in quality. Exposure to the art of J. R. Cozens had revealed to him a depth of personal feeling unparalleled in topographical art. He was also receptive to other, very different influences—the picturesque domesticity of his friend George Morland and the autographic handling of Monro, among others. He even copied Marco Ricci and other outright classicists, no doubt in an effort to capture the warmth of the Italianate tradition.

Not until 1800 was Girtin able to assimilate these influences and fuse them into an entirely personal idiom, as he did in such masterpieces as *Kirkstall Abbey* (Victoria and Albert Museum) and *The White House at Chelsea* (London, Tate Gallery). In these, the topographical focus —that is, the building or landscape feature from which the painting derives its name—recedes into the distance, where it is swallowed up in a vast expanse of countryside, extending seemingly far beyond the limits of the picture. Solitude prevails, yet never without hints of human presence and warm, nostalgic notes of remembrance. Girtin, like his fellow cockney Turner, could envisage such intimacy only as something distant in space and time, to be recaptured by lyrical striving. Unlike Turner, Girtin reached his goal by simply leaving the foreground entirely empty and blurred in focus, and at times by eliminating it completely. The effect is to make the distant landscape all the more majestic.

BIBLIOGRAPHY. L. Binyon, *Thomas Girtin*, London, 1900; R. Davies, *Thomas Girtin's Water-Colours*, London, 1924; J. Mayne, *Thomas Girtin*, Leigh-on-Sea, 1949; T. Girtin and D. Loshak, *The Art of Thomas Girtin*, London, 1954.

DAVID M. LOSHAK

GISCHIA, LEON. French painter (1904–   ). Gischia was born in Dax. After advanced studies in the history of art and archaeology, he studied art under Friesz and Léger, and in 1926 he visited Spain, Italy, and the United States. In collaboration with Léger and Le Corbusier he decorated the Pavillon des Temps Nouveaux for the 1937 Universal Exposition.

Gischia excels in theater décor and has worked extensively for Jean Vilar and his Théâtre National Populaire. He participated in the foundation of the Salon de Mai (1944) and is a regular exhibitor. His color is decorative and flat with overlapping perspective, as in *The Canvases* (1944). Gischia has written two essays: *La Sculpture en France depuis Rodin* and *Arts primitifs*. A lucid creator of impeccable still lifes, he skillfully combines the lesson of Matisse and that of Léger.

BIBLIOGRAPHY. B. Dorival, *Twentieth-Century French Painters*, 2 vols., New York, 1958; H. Read, *A Concise History of Modern Painting*, London, 1959.

GISLEBERTUS. French sculptor of the 12th century (b. Autun). He first worked at Cluny and by about 1115 was probably one of the chief assistants of the Master of Cluny, working on the great western doorway, of which only a few fragments have been preserved. After his apprenticeship at Cluny, Gislebertus probably went to Vézelay, where there are several fragments from a tympanum that was replaced by the great Vézelay tympanum of about 1140. It has been postulated that Gislebertus carved the earlier tympanum for the main doorway at Vézelay, but left for Autun before the building had actually reached this point. Later on, it seems, a new sculptor carved the present tympanum at Vézelay, and the Gislebertus design was used in another place.

Gislebertus probably stayed at Vézelay for only five years, arriving at Autun about 1125, already a mature artist. Very likely he started work in the eastern part of the church, which was presumably completed at the time of the dedication, in 1130. Soon after this dedication, Gislebertus probably began the west tympanum, which took some four to five years to complete. When this work was near completion, he began about fifty nave capitals that could have been done in roughly one year. Thus his entire work at Autun can possibly be dated between 1125 and 1135.

Gislebertus produced the tympanum sculptures for the main portal of the Cathedral of Autun, of which the *Christ* is exemplary. He also executed the *Last Judgment* and the *Resurrection* for the Cathedral. His figures, especially those of the *Last Judgment*, are abstractly designed to fill architectural space. The demon forms are treated fantastically and prefigure the surrealism of the 20th century. The entire composition has a vitality that is charac-

Gislebertus, detail of *The Last Judgment*. Cathedral of St-Lazare, Autun.

teristic of much of the Burgundian ecclesiastical sculpture executed during the 12th century. *See* AUTUN: CATHEDRAL OF SAINT-LAZARE.

BIBLIOGRAPHY. D. Grivot and G. Zarnecki, *Gislebertus, Sculptor of Autun*, Paris, 1961.

GISORS FAMILY. French architects: Jacques-Pierre (1755–1828), Alexandre-Jean-Baptiste (1762–1835), and Henri-Alphonse (1796–1866). They worked in Paris and were connected with state architecture and with public monuments. Jacques-Pierre is less well known than his brother Alexandre-Jean-Baptiste, who worked on the Arc de Triomphe de l'Etoile, or Henri-Alphonse, nephew of Francis Guy and a pupil of Percier, who was civil architect from 1834.

GIUDINI (Giudici), FRANCESCO, *see* FRANCIABIGIO.

GIULIA, VILLA, ROME, *see* ROME: MUSEUMS (NATIONAL ETRUSCAN MUSEUM OF THE VILLA GIULIA).

GIULIANI, GIOVANNI. Italian sculptor (b. Venice, 1663; d. Heiligenkreuz, Austria, 1744). Perhaps a pupil of A. Faistenberger, although with strong stylistic relations to G. M. Mazza, Giuliani went to Vienna in 1690. There he executed sandstone sculptures (1705–09) for the Rossau Palace. His greatest works were done for St. Maria in Heiligenkreuz, including the pulpit (1719), the organ (1720), the *Column of the Trinity* (1730), and the *Stations of the Cross* (1732). Giuliani was assuredly a decorative sculptor, yet he merged Italian and Alpine style into a high baroque mode which spread to Vienna and became characteristic of the 18th century.

GIULIANO, CARLO. Italian-English goldsmith and jeweler (b. Naples; fl. London ca. 1866–1910; d. London, 1912). Strongly influenced by Castellani's "archaeological jewelry" based on Greek and Etruscan originals, Giuliano later worked in a more elaborate and colorful Neo-Renaissance style. During the 1860s and 1870s his workmanship was considered the finest in England.

BIBLIOGRAPHY. M. Flower, *Victorian Jewelry*, New York, 1951; "Some Pieces by Carlo Giuliano," *The Antique Dealer and Collector's Guide*, VII, Sept., 1952.

GIULIANO DA MAIANO, *see* MAIANO, GIULIANO DA.

GIULIANO DI ARRIGO, *see* PESELLO, GIULIANO.

GIULIO ROMANO, *see* ROMANO, GIULIO.

GIUSTI (Di Giusto Betti; Juste), ANTONIO AND GIOVANNI, I. Italian sculptors of the early 16th century. Antonio Giusti (b. San Martino a Mensola, 1479; d. Tours, 1519) did twelve apostles for the chapel of Cardinal d'Amboise at Gaillon. After 1504 he worked with his brother Giovanni Giusti (b. San Martino a Mensola, 1485; d. Tours, 1549). Their masterpiece is the tomb of Louis XII and Anne de Bretagne (1516–31; St-Denis). Their style is akin to that of Michel Colombe; and with Guido Mazzoni and Girolamo da Fiesole, they are the most important representatives of the Italianate proto-Renaissance mode in France.

BIBLIOGRAPHY. A. de Montaiglon and G. Milanesi, *La Famille des Juste en Italie et en France*, Paris, 1877.

GIUSTO DI GIOVANNI DE' MENABUOI (Giusto Fiorentino; Giusto Padovano). Italian painter of the Florentine school (b. ca. 1340; d. before April, 1393). This artist was active chiefly in Padua. His style shows the influence of Taddeo Gaddi and Giovanni da Milano, in whose shop he may have worked. Giusto's first known work is a *Madonna and Child* (1363) painted for a certain Isotta da Terzago. A polyptych of the *Coronation of the Virgin* in the National Gallery in London is signed and dated 1367. His most important Paduan works are the frescoes commissioned by Fina Buzzaccarina, wife of Francesco Carrara, in the Baptistery in Padua, which were completed in 1376. Fragments have been discovered of Giusto's important frescoes of the Liberal Arts, the Virtues and Vices, and Famous Men (1370) in the Cortellieri Chapel of the Eremitani church in Padua. In 1382 he painted frescoes in the Belludi Chapel of S. Antonio, Padua. Giusto's vivid, monumental style played a key role in the development of art in Padua between Giotto and Altichiero.

BIBLIOGRAPHY. S. Bettini, *Giusto de' Menabuoi e l'arte del trecento a Padova*, Padua, 1944.

HELLMUT WOHL

GIYAN (Tepe Giyan). Archaeological site in western Iran. Tepe Giyan was excavated by the French before World War II. It was first occupied in the chalcolithic period (Giyan V), when it was a village contemporary with the Halaf-Ubaid-Uruk period in Mesopotamia. After a short gap in occupation it was reoccupied during the 3d and 2d millenniums (Giyan IV–I).

GIYASUDDIN TUGHLAK, TOMB OF, DELHI, *see* GHIYAS-UD-DIN TUGHLAK, TOMB OF, DELHI.

GIZA (Gizeh). Plateau on the western bank of the Nile opposite Cairo, renowned for its necropolis (4th–6th dynasties), which contains the pyramids of the Pharaohs Cheops, Chephren, and Mycerinus, and the mastaba tombs of the nobles. *See* CHEOPS, PYRAMID OF; CHEPHREN, PYRAMID OF; MYCERINUS, PYRAMID OF.

The general layout is governed by the location of the three pyramids and their orientation to the cardinal points of the compass. The stone mastaba tombs of the nobles of the 4th dynasty are arranged so that the chapels on their main façades front on north–south streets crossing secondary (east–west) streets to the west of Cheops' pyramid. This follows an orthogonal system of planning which probably imitated that of the preplanned quarters in the contemporary city of Memphis. A wall enclosed the cemetery on the south. Later mastabas of the 5th dynasty were crammed in between the earlier ones, and tombs containing statuary were hewn in the cliff. To the north of Chephren's pyramid stretches an area of leveled bedrock with traces

Giza. The pyramids of the Pharaohs Cheops, Chephren, and Mycerinus, on the west bank of the Nile.

William Glackens, *Promenade*, 1926. Detroit Institute of Arts.

of channeling (ca. 2 ft. wide) that forms a quadrangular mesh and the remains of a quarry of local limestone for the pyramid.

Extensive series of contiguous deep-vaulted rooms along three sides of a long courtyard (north–south) to the west of Chephren's pyramid have been interpreted as barracks for the workmen or perhaps workshops and storehouses. To the south or southeast of each pyramid are one or more smaller pyramids (one in the case of Chephren's, three each for the other two), which were designed for the queens or to house canopic jars containing the Pharaoh's internal organs. Each pyramid had its funerary temple complex abutting its east side and connected to the valley temple by a causeway.

The three valley temples and the Great Sphinx with its temple stood on a waterway along which the boats of the funerary procession and the mourning visitors could sail. On the southern outskirts of the plateau, the so-called pyramid town, or settlement of funerary priests, was built. The area that has been uncovered contains two parallel streets running east and west along the north and south façades of a series of contiguous houses. Beneath the east end of the south street an underpassage, which crossed it at right angles at a lower level, had to be built. *See* SPHINX GREAT; SPHINX, TEMPLE OF THE.

The architectural style of the 4th dynasty is conspicuous for its stark simplicity of design, deriving the utmost effect from the horizontal and vertical lines of its trabeated (flat-beamed) construction, even to the exclusive use of pillars as supports. The layouts of the plans as well as the façades conform closely to a simple harmonic system resulting in successful proportions. This purity of style is aided by the use of variegated hard stones, red or black granite, alabaster, and basalt, all highly polished and practically without relief or decoration. To this architecture is allied, in a most harmonious way, a sculptural style, the so-called Giza Style, which is characterized both by its stylization of the figure and by its idealized portraiture, which has a faraway gaze enhanced by lifelike colors and inlaid eyes of various materials. Pharaoh, as represented in his polished diorite statues, is truly the divine son of Re'.

See also EGYPT.

BIBLIOGRAPHY. W. F. Petrie, *The Pyramids and Temples of Gizeh*, London, 1883; H. Junker, *Giza*, 12 vols., Vienna 1929–55; G. A. Reisner and W. S. Smith, *A History of the Giza Necropolis*, 2 vols., Cambridge, Mass., 1942–55; I. E. S. Edwards, *The Pyramids of Egypt*, Harmondsworth, 1947.   ALEXANDER M. BADAWY

GLACKENS, WILLIAM JAMES. American painter and illustrator (b. Philadelphia, Pa., 1870; d. Westport, Conn., 1938). He studied at the Pennsylvania Academy of Fine Arts while he worked as an illustrator for the *Record*, the *Press*, and the *Public Ledger* in Philadephia. As a newspaper artist, he met Henri, Sloan, Shinn, and Luks, the most important realist members of the future group, The Eight, which exhibited in New York in 1908. In 1895 Glackens went to Paris, where he remained for over a year. On his return he worked as an illustrator and cartoonist for magazines and New York newspapers. In 1898 he was sent to cover the fighting in Cuba by *McClure's Magazine*, and in 1906 he traveled in France and Spain.

Glackens was only briefly involved with Ashcan-school subjects, which he painted with a humorous approach. He soon left the slums as subject matter for more fashionable scenes of holiday activities, although the depiction of the lower classes had a somewhat longer life in his skillfully observed drawings, such as *Washington Square* (*A Holiday in the Park*, 1914; New York, Museum of Modern Art), where he effectively caught movement and gesture.

Glackens's early works were richly painted and relatively dark in tonality, under the influence of Henri and Manet (for example, *Luxembourg Gardens*, 1904; Washington, D.C., Corcoran Gallery). In subject and in the treatment of the figures and still life, the debt to Manet is obvious in *Chez Mouquin* (1905; Art Institute of Chicago). But Glackens's travel in France had introduced him to impressionism and especially to the light and palette of Renoir. *Nude with an Apple* (1910; Brooklyn Museum) immediately recalls Manet's *Olympia* in pose, but the technical sources are Renoir's brushwork and color. The influence of Renoir was to grow until at times it almost overwhelmed Glackens's individuality, although his colors were seldom quite as hot or his forms quite as full as those of his master. Occasionally, in his later paintings, he more successfully fused his own artistic personality with Renoir's technique, in figures, such as the painting of the girl on a donkey called *Promenade* (1926; Detroit Institute of Arts), or in landscapes, such as *Vence* (1930; New York, Whitney Museum).

BIBLIOGRAPHY. F. Watson, ... *William Glackens* ..., New York, 1923; G. P. Du Bois, *William J. Glackens*, New York, 1931; I. Glackens, *William Glackens and the Ashcan Group* ..., New York, 1957.   JEROME VIOLA

GLAIR. Type of size made of the white of eggs and used in bookbinding to bind gold leaf to the leather cover. The area to be stamped is first given a light coating of glair; then the gold leaf is transferred by pressing it on the glairy surface with a moderately heated iron tool.

BIBLIOGRAPHY. E. Diehl, *Bookbinding: Its Background and Technique*, vol. 2, New York, 1946.

GLAMIS CASTLE. Scottish castle comprising an L-shaped 15th-century core to which were added a southwest wing about 1620 and a northwest wing about 1671. Both wings were Gothicized in 1790. The great hall has fine plasterwork dated 1620. Dutch craftsmen were employed in the 1680s.

BIBLIOGRAPHY. O. Hill, *Scottish Castles of the 16th and 17th Centuries*, London, 1953.

GLARNER, FRITZ. American abstract painter (1899–   ). He was born in Zurich, Switzerland, lived as a child in France and Italy, and now lives in New York City. From 1914 to 1920 he studied at the Royal Institute of Fine Arts in Naples, and, from 1924 to 1926, at the Colarossi Academy in Paris. He had his first one-man exhibition in Paris in 1928. By 1933 he had turned from representational painting that showed the influence of impressionism to abstraction, and he became a member of the Abstraction-Création group.

Glarner calls his own work "relational." It is a late development of neoplasticism. Like Mondrian (whom he met in 1943), Glarner limits himself to primary colors, black, white, and gray. He also works for an equivalence of the flat area. He develops planar relationships by introducing the slant or oblique, thus making areas trapezoidal, and frequently composes within a circular format, or *tondo*.

BIBLIOGRAPHY. D. C. Miller, "Fritz Glarner," in J. I. H. Baur, ed., *New Art in America*, New York, 1957.

GLASCO, JOSEPH. American abstract and figure painter (1925–   ). He was born in Pauls Valley, Okla., and now lives in Taos, N. Mex. He studied briefly with Rico Lebrun, in Mexico City, and in New York, and has traveled in Europe. He was included in the Whitney Museum's 1955 show "The New Decade." He frequently composes figures of, or places them before, textured areas resembling richly grained wood or coarse tweed.

GLASGOW: ART GALLERIES AND MUSEUM. Scottish collection established in 1856. Outstanding in this museum are Rembrandt's *Man in Armor*, Whistler's *Arrangement in Grey and Black, No. 2: Thomas Carlyle*, and notable paintings by Rubens, the Master of Moulins, and Delacroix. Scottish, English, and modern French painters are also well represented.

GLASGOW: CATHEDRAL. Scottish church, mainly of the 12th century, although the nave was not finished until the late 13th century. The chapter house is 15th century, and the Blacader aisle and pulpitum are late 15th century. The crypt, or lower church, is one of the high-water marks of Scottish early Gothic.

GLASS. Amorphous substance created by melting together silica with smaller proportions of alkali. Either lime or lead oxide must be added to act as a hardening agent and to lower the temperature required to bring about fusion of the mixture. Glass chemicals melt gradually, the softening point varying from about 500 to 1510°C. When completely melted, they form a viscous, heavy liquid which can be manipulated as it begins to cool and harden. Since glass can be worked only while it remains in a warm, plastic stage, frequent reheating is required for glass to retain its ductility. Annealing and cooling of finished glass must be very gradual in order to prevent glass failures resulting from the formation of internal stresses.

Objects of glass appeared in Egypt by 2500 B.C., deriving from the use of glaze as a coating for beads of stone or clay. By the 18th dynasty (ca. 1500 B.C.), Egyptian artisans were making a type of soda glass, colored by metallic oxides. Most of their glass was opaque in quality, a condition caused by the presence of bubbles in the mixture through the Egyptians' inability to produce high enough temperatures to dispel them. The glass was used to make small, narrow-necked cosmetic containers by means of the mud-core technique, which built up each vessel on a cloth bag filled with mud and tied at the neck with a string. A long rod was inserted as a means of dipping the bag repeatedly into a pot of melted glass. Fine glass threads in contrasting colors were pressed into the surface and combed into patterns. Finally, the rod was withdrawn, the core scraped out, and the vessel polished. Mold pressing was used for making goblets and for the flat figures employed as furniture and wall decorations. Occasionally, glass was treated as a gem material and the lapidary or cold-cutting technique employed.

Vessels and molded figurines were also made in Syria, Palestine, and Mesopotamia. Assyria appears to have had a flourishing glass industry during the 8th and 7th centuries B.C. Little is known of ancient Greek glass, but evidence exists of its manufacture in Cyprus, Crete, Asia Minor, and Olympia. In Hellenistic Egypt, glass containers often imitated the forms used in Greek pottery, with Alexandria becoming famous for luxury wares. Ascribed to it are the richly decorated millefiori, or "mosaic," bowls made by mold pressing. *See* MILLEFIORI. *See also* GLASS, CAMEO.

The invention of the blowing pipe revolutionized glassmaking. Originating perhaps in Syria in the 1st century A.D., the use of the blowpipe made possible a variety of processes still in use today. All of them are based on the gather of hot glass picked up on the end of the pipe and blown by the craftsman into the shape, size, and thinness required. The industry which arose through use of this method, in conjunction with the continued use of both mold pressing and mold blowing, spread quickly throughout the Roman Empire. Inexpensive tableware and costly *objets d'art* were turned out in quantity in Syria, Italy, Spain, Gaul, the Rhineland, and England.

Despite the slow disintegration of the Empire, manufacture of glass continued into the 5th century with soda and lime persisting as the basic glass ingredients. Highly decorated unguentaria are characteristic of the Syrian output of this period, while gilt-glass portraits and religious symbols became popular in Early Christian Rome. In time, elaborate wares ceased to be made in Europe, but in Constantinople, capital of the Byzantine empire, a glass industry was maintained. For hundreds of years it served as a production and design center for mosaic tesserae which were used to decorate palaces, churches, and even mosques throughout the Mediterranean region.

By the 7th century, Islamic conquerors had occupied a large part of western Asia. Building upon the remnants of the Syro-Roman glass industry, they turned out small bottles ornamented with honeycomb facet cutting through the use of the wheel in a manner similar to that employed on rock crystal. Mold-blown pieces were also made, many with applied and tooled ornament. Egypto-Arabic glassworkers began to paint on glass with metallic lusters, and Syrian chemists developed formulas for glassy enamels containing lead. These enamels resulted in the unequaled series of mosque lamps, cups, and bottles made from the 12th through 14th century in both Egypt and Syria. *See* ISLAMIC GLASS AND CRYSTAL.

In the Far East, glass has usually been treated as an artificial gemstone. As a result, its use in China was largely confined to jewelry and to small objects such as snuff bottles. Original tints of glass were created, often in layered form so that cameo cutting might be applied. In Japan, glass was produced as early as the 1st century A.D., and in the year 701 a casting bureau was established at Nara in order to deal with both metalwork and glass. This glass was either fashioned into beads and gems or poured into cloisonné-type compartments as ornaments for precious objects in metal. Glass methods may have come to Japan by way of Korea, where goldsmiths used melted glass for cloisonné decorations and bangles before 668 A.D. In Persia, glass artistry had declined considerably by the 17th century, when it was revived by Venetian workers imported during the reign of Shah Abbas the Great (1587–1628).

The 13th century had seen the rise of Venice as both an important Mediterranean power and a center of glassmaking. Its glass factories had become large enough to be considered a fire hazard and were moved, in 1291, to the nearby island of Murano. In this way, the city hoped to retain for itself a glass monopoly based on the retention of highly skilled workmen and glassmaking secrets. The earliest goblets were heavy in form, deep in color, and decorated with enamels. By the middle of the 15th century, Venice was making *cristallo*, a glass often likened to rock crystal but actually grayish in tone and filled with minute bubbles. This soda glass appeared completely clear only when very thinly blown, despite the use of decolorizers. Venetian artisans brought to perfection their method of blowing the light, brittle material in making a host of delicate wine glasses, some ornamented with swirled serpentine trailings and dragon wings in a clear greenish blue containing gold or other colored threads. Also popular were footed compotes and trays (*tazzas*). Opaque white glass was used to make latticinio rods, drawn out to incredible thinness and incorporated in clear glass to form "ribbon" or intricate "net" glass. Although Venetian glass was too thin for wheel cutting, the technique of diamond-point scratching was used to engrave elaborate designs on luxurious pieces.

Eventually, many Venetian and other Italian glassworkers made their way north and west. In Antwerp, Liège, Amsterdam, Nürnberg, and Hall-in-the-Tirol, glass in the *façon de Venise* was blown and tooled with such skill that it is often indistinguishable from Venetian pieces.

Some examples are larger and heavier in form and ornament than the glasses imported from Venice but were nonetheless able to offer them serious competition. Through the efforts of Verzelini and other Italians brought in from Antwerp, these methods were introduced to England about 1677.

Despite the popularity of the delicate Italian glass, there existed also a continued preference for sturdy dark-green drinking vessels in Holland and in the Rhineland and other parts of Germany. This type was based on an earlier forest-glass tradition when transient glasshouses used the ashes of bracken and fern (potash) as a source of alkali. Few examples appear earlier than the 16th century, when glassworkers began to make roemers and humpen, large drinking vessels whose green color was emphasized by the addition of copper and iron scale to the glass mixture. Prunts, or applied blobs in the form of berries or thorns, were used to decorate them.

In Silesia and Bohemia, increasing knowledge of glassmaking brought about a new crystal glass, made from pounded quartz pebbles, potash, and table salt. Its clarity and strength made it suitable for engraving by means of a copper wheel and abrasives. This technique was practiced by Kaspar Lehmann at the court of Rudolf II in Prague from about 1580 to 1610. His pieces and those of the artists who succeeded him are masterpieces of intaglio engraving. In time, this technique was carried to Scandinavia and Russia, with glassworks firmly established in these areas by the middle of the 18th century. Enameling was another method of decorating German-Bohemian crystal, the colors being heavily applied and fused to the glass by heating. Styles of painting varied from folk-art simplicity to baroque sophistication, but under the influence of neoclassicism in design, enamels were lightened to a thin wash of color by an Austrian glass painter, Samuel Mohn.

In England, a new development was made possible by the research of George Ravenscroft, who produced, by 1677, a softer glass of deep, rich brilliance. This lead glass, mistakenly termed "flint glass," was the result of adding large amounts of lead oxide to produce a slow-cooling, heavy glass. It appeared to best advantage in elegantly simple pieces, with decoration restricted to the stems of drinking vessels, frequently baluster-shaped. Their knops often enclose air bubbles, or "teardrops," which, extended vertically, could be further manipulated to make "air-twist" stems, or if carried out with latticinio rods, "cotton-twist" stems.

By 1750, a prohibitive tax on the weight of glass ingredients caused the more massive types to be succeeded by a lighter variety trimmed with shallow cutting. Some British manufacturers reestablished themselves in Ireland. Opaque white glass became popular in England and was painted to imitate porcelain, but deep colors were also used, often trimmed with loops of opaque white in Nailsea glass. Repeal of the tax in 1845 resulted in an unlimited output of thick glass completely covered with prismatic cutting. The cut-glass craze spread to the United States, and factories in both countries resorted to mechanically produced blanks which were later individually cut.

With the invention of machinery for mass production of glass, hand methods were abandoned for all but luxury wares such as those made by Baccarat in France. Utility

Stiegel glass. Stiegel-type enamel decoration, probably from Pennsylvania, ca. 1765–75. Corning Museum of Glass, Corning, N. Y.

and decorative glass became the products of pressing, molding, and blowing machines. During the era of Crystal Palace influence, designers of factory-made glass employed garish color effects and a bewildering array of eclectic ornament as a means of drawing attention in a highly competitive market. The growth of the Arts and Crafts movement in England at mid-century and the Art Nouveau designers of the 1880s brought about a revolt against both the domination of the machine and the lack of originality in design. Lalique, Gallé, Navarre, and Tiffany introduced a new and poetic version of glass forms and color effects based on experiment and influenced by nature and the art forms of the Orient. *See* LALIQUE; TIFFANY, LOUIS COMFORT.

The 20th century has seen the vigorous combination of function with sound design. With Scandinavia in the vanguard, factory designers in Europe and the United States have raised table glass to high levels. In the United States, an amazing number of industrial and architectural uses for glass have been perfected. Paralleling this large-scale manufacture, there has also been continuous interest by designer-craftsmen in glass as an art medium for studio use. *See also* GLASS, GOLD; GLASS, STIEGEL; GLASS, WISTAR; GLASS PICTURES; STAINED GLASS.

BIBLIOGRAPHY. C. J. Phillips, *Glass: The Miracle Maker*, New York, 1941; W. B. Honey, *English Glass*, London, 1946; D. Daniel, *Cut and Engraved Glass, 1771–1905*, New York, 1950; E. M. Elville, *English Tableglass*, London, 1951; J. R. Vávra, *5000 Years of Glass-Making*, Prague, 1954; D. B. Harden, "Glass and Glazes," in C. Singer, ed., *A History of Technology*, vol. 2, Oxford, 1956; L. M. Angus-Butterworth, "Glass Sections 6–9," in C. Singer, ed., *A History of Technology*, vol. 3, Oxford, 1957; Corning Museum of Glass, *Glass from the Ancient World: The Ray Winfield Smith Collection*, catalog of a special exhibition, Corning, N.Y., 1957; Corning Museum of Glass, *Glass 1959: A Special Exhibition of International Contemporary Glass*, Corning, N.Y., 1959; E. B. Haynes, *Glass through the Ages*, rev. ed., Baltimore, 1959.   EMMA N. PAPERT

GLASS, CAMEO. Translucent colored glass with designs cut in relief. Layers of glass in varying colors are built up to the desired shape, and the designs are then carved into the layers, producing a polychrome decoration. The most famous example of cameo glass is the ancient Roman Portland Vase (London, British Museum). During the 18th and 19th centuries in England there was much interest in this technique; a similar form of glass, influenced by Chinese glass carving, was produced in France at Nancy. *See* PORTLAND VASE.

GLASS, GOLD. Type of decorative glass made by laminating a sheet of gold foil between transparent layers of glass. Designs were frequently cut into the gold. Although the technique seems to have originated in Alexandria, it reached its high point in the Roman glass of the Early Christian period. The technique was revived during the 18th century and applied to some Bohemian glass.

BIBLIOGRAPHY. H. Vopel, *Die altchristlichen Goldgläser*, Freiburg im Breisgau, 1899.

GLASS, STIEGEL. Glass manufactured by the colorful "Baron" Henry William Stiegel, a German immigrant who, in 1763, established glassworks in Lancaster County, Pa. His workmen produced not only bottles and window glass but also fine tableware, frequently decorated by copper-wheel engraving or by bright enameling in the European folk-art tradition. Dip molds were used for making pattern-molded and expanded scent bottles and salts, often in sapphire-blue or amethyst-purple glass. Although his ambitious project ended in bankruptcy in 1774, Stiegel's advertisements mention a large number of standard items. Since none were signed, it is best to apply the term "Stiegel-type" to those that survive.

BIBLIOGRAPHY. R. M. Knittel, *Early American Glass*, New York, 1927; G. Heigs, *Henry William Stiegel*, Manheim, Pa., 1937; G. S. and H. McKearin, *American Glass*, New York, 1941.

GLASS, WISTAR. Graceful objects of household utility ware made in conjunction with bottles and window glass in the factory of Caspar Wistar in Salem County, N.J., from 1739 to 1779. Wistar's workers, trained in European methods, founded the South Jersey glass tradition and later spread it to other New Jersey factories and eventually carried it north to New York State and New England and west to Ohio. Their work was largely of the free-blown variety, using ordinary aquamarine, green, and amber bottle glass to produce pitchers, sugar bowls, and so on, usually ornamented with additional glass, threaded, crimped, or often tooled into distinctive wavelike swirls.

BIBLIOGRAPHY. R. M. Knittel, *Early American Glass*, New York, 1927; G. S. and H. McKearin, *American Glass*, New York, 1941.

GLASS PICTURES. Paintings carried out on small panes of glass so that the glass acts as both foundation and protective cover for the paint. They were extremely popular in the 18th and 19th centuries, when Continental folk painters used either tempera or enamels to make them. In addition, copperplate engravings (mezzotints) were applied to glass in the manner of decalcomanias in order to supply designs which were colored in with oils and varnish.

BIBLIOGRAPHY. H. G. Clarke, *The Story of Old English Glass Pictures, 1690–1810*, London, 1928; J. Vydra, *Folk Painting on Glass*, Prague, 1957 (or 1958); G. Mariacher, *Italian Blown Glass from Ancient Rome to Venice*, New York, 1961.

GLASTONBURY. English town, the legendary site of the establishment of Christianity in England. The great abbey church is now destroyed, but the Lady Chapel (1184–86) is partly preserved and is a key example of the "first" purely English Gothic architectural style.

BIBLIOGRAPHY. G. F. Webb, *Architecture in Britain: The Middle Ages*, Baltimore, 1956.

GLAUBER, JOHANNES. Dutch landscape painter and etcher (b. Utrecht, 1646; d. Schoonhoven, ca. 1726). He was a pupil of Claes Berchem and also worked with Adriaen van der Cabel in Lyons. He was in France (1671–75) and also spent two years in Rome and Venice as well as a year in Padua. He copied Italian paintings for the Amsterdam art dealer Vilenburgh. Glauber was also active in Copenhagen. In Amsterdam he lived in the house of Gerard de Lairesse, who collaborated with him. His Italianate landscapes are influenced by Gaspard Dughet.

BIBLIOGRAPHY. W. Stechow, *Dutch Landscape Painting of the Seventeenth Century*, London, 1966.

GLAZE, *see* CERAMICS.

GLAZING. Technique for toning down the intensity of colors in a painting by the application of a thin coat of raw or burnt sienna. Glazing produces the mellow brown appearance characteristic of old masters. The technique is also used in wall painting when the intensity of the fresco pigment produces an undesirably harsh effect.

GLEANERS, THE. Oil painting by Millet, in the Louvre Museum, Paris. *See* MILLET, JEAN-FRANCOIS.

GLEIZES, ALBERT. French painter (b. Paris, 1881; d. Avignon, 1953). Gleizes was both a painter and a writer, and he was inextricably linked with the evolution of cubism as a leading theoretician and exponent. His early work (1901) was influenced by impressionism, but beginning in 1906 he sought a simplification of color which reflected his ardent desire to simplify form. He naturally turned to cubism, for it responded to his needs, and in 1910 exhibited at the Salon des Indépendants (*L'Arbre*). In 1911 he was one of the exhibitors in the celebrated Cubist Room in the Salon des Indépendants. At the Salon d'Automne of the same year his *Portrait de Nayral* had a *succès de scandale*. Gleizes belonged to the Section d'Or group headed by Jacques Villon, which often met at his studio or in Puteaux, where Villon lived. In 1912 Gleizes (together with Metzinger) published *Du cubisme*, the most important book at that time on the cubist movement and one which constituted a veritable manifesto.

Gleizes traveled extensively; he went to the United States, where he experienced a religious revelation. Henceforth his artistic researches, while still faithful to cubist principles, were influenced by his profound religious interests. He had exhibited in Moscow and Barcelona and at the famous New York Armory Show of 1913. After his visit to

Albert Gleizes, *Support of Contemplation*. Municipal Museum, Menton.

the United States he continued his experiments and in 1923 outlined them in *La Peinture et ses lois*. He proclaimed the impending return of the Christian era and endeavored to develop an objective technique easily transmissible as a means of praising God. In 1932 he published *Homocentricisme ou retour à l'homme chrétien* and *Forme et histoire*, a vast work showing the superiority of an art based on religious thought and expressed by symbolic rhythms. From 1939 on Gleizes lived in retirement at Saint-Rémy-de-Provence, exerting in his writings and lectures as well as in his paintings a marked influence on those young artists of the Rhone Valley separated from Paris.

Gleizes' marriage of traditional Catholic themes with cubist ideas is perhaps best exemplified in his illustrations of Pascal's *Pensées*, fifty-seven original etchings which constituted his last important work. His paintings are in Paris (National Museum of Modern Art), New York (Museum of Modern Art), and numerous private collections. Gleizes was one of the foremost flat-pattern cubists who achieved his goal of sublime precision through a capacity for individual abstractions, as in *The Kitchen* (1911; London, Marlborough Fine Arts, Ltd.). He exercised considerable influence not only on Lhote, Le Corbusier, and Marcoussis but also on all those inspired by cubist theories.

BIBLIOGRAPHY. A. H. Barr, Jr., *Cubism and Abstract Art*, New York, 1936; J. Chevalier, *Le Dénouement traditionnel du cubisme*, *Confluences*, Paris, 1942; D. A. Surchamp, *Destinée du Cubisme*, Lyons, 1947; M. Reynal et al., *Histoire de la peinture moderne*, vol. 3: *De Picasso au Surréalisme*, Geneva, 1950; J. Cassou, ed., *The Sources of the Twentieth Century: The Arts in Europe from 1884 to 1914*, exhibition catalog, Paris, 1960; B. Dorival, *The School of Paris in the Musée d'Art Moderne*, London, 1960.

ARNOLD ROSIN

GLICENSTEIN, ENRICO. Polish sculptor (b. Turek, 1870; d. New York City, 1942). After traveling through Europe Glicenstein, at nineteen, entered the academy in Munich. He was awarded the Prix de Rome for his statue *Aryon* and settled in Rome until 1928, when he moved to the United States. Early recognition was accorded Glicenstein by Rodin, who invited him to exhibit in the Salon of 1906 and requested that their works be shown together in the central rotunda of the Grand Palais. Important one-man shows were given him at the Venice Biennale (1926), the Chicago Art Institute (1929), the Palais des Beaux-Arts, Brussels (1932), and the Petit Palais, Paris (1948).

Although Glicenstein was aloof from the movements of modern art, his work exhibits the vitality of engagement. He worked primarily in wood and stone, and his figures from the beginning retain the form of the block. There is a profound identification, as in primitive sculpture, between the forms that the material will yield and the emotional tensions and content of the work. While early works, such as *Solitude* (1900) and *Caryatid* (1913), are somewhat open and lyrical, the later works strike a balance between the interior energy of forms freed from the block and the exterior restraint caused by the limitations of the block. The interior dynamics may be expressed as a complex interplay (*Motherhood*, 1938), a simple gesture of outcry (*De profundis*, 1942), or a stoically rigid configuration (*The Wounded*, 1940), but the strong tension always exists. In his late works, such as the latter two, Glicenstein turned his uncompromising understanding of the identification of sculptural and human form to the tragic predicament of mankind before and during World War II.

BIBLIOGRAPHY. H. Glicenstein, *Glicenstein*, New York, 1958.

DONALD GODDARD

GLINSKY, VINCENT. American sculptor (1895–). Born near Leningrad, Glinsky received his education in New York City at Columbia University, the City College of New York, and the Beaux-Arts Institute of Design. His first one-man show took place in Paris in 1929. He has since had a number of exhibitions and shows yearly as a member in the Sculptors Guild Exhibition in New York City. He has received awards from the Guggenheim Foundation (1935), the Pennsylvania Academy of Fine Arts (1948), and the Architectural League of New York (1956), among others. His studies of nude figures are conceived in icy sensuality, emphasizing large forms and sweeping, elegant lines.

GLOCKENDON (Glockenton) FAMILY. German artists (15th–16th cent.). The Glockendons were a large artistic family whose members lived and worked in Nürnberg. Among them were glass painters, miniature painters, engravers, and die cutters. The most famous members are brothers, Albrecht Glockendon (d. 1545) and Nikolaus Glockendon (d. 1534). Albrecht painted miniatures for the so-called Glockendon Missal (now in Nürnberg). Nikolaus decorated the Missal of Albrecht of Mainz (now in Aschaffenburg) in 1524 with miniatures done in the style of Dürer and the school of Cranach.

BIBLIOGRAPHY. E. W. Bredt, "Zur Geschichte der Nürnberger Miniatoren und Kleinmeister," *Zeitschrift für Bücherfreunde*, VI, 1903.

"GLORIA DEI," PHILADELPHIA. This steep-roofed edifice, erected by a Swedish congregation between 1698 and 1700, is the oldest surviving church in Philadelphia. It was originally rectangular with a projecting entrance tower, but a porch and vestry were added in 1703 to buttress the walls when they began to spread under the vaulted ceiling. The roof, diminutive steeple, and polygonal ceiling over the east end are probably Swedish in origin, although the character of the cornice and window trim is English. The interior, with its gallery supported by slender posts, is very plain. Two carved cherubim are placed over the altar. Possibly John Smart and John Brett designed the church.

BIBLIOGRAPHY. H. S. Morrison, *Early American Architecture*, New York, 1952.

GLORY. General term for the display of rays of light in various forms around the head or body of a godly or saintly personage. The effect is sometimes used also with allegorical subjects concerning the Divinity. Glory is found in ancient Near Eastern art, as well as in the art of antiquity and in Indian art. It was adopted by Christian art in the 4th century.

The main types of glory are the nimbus (circular disk or ring-shaped), used for all saints and, with a cross, for Christ; the aureole (circular), which surrounds the entire figure of the resurrected Christ; and the mandorla (almond or figure-eight-shaped), which surrounds the figure of Christ in the Last Judgment. *See* AUREOLE; MANDORLA; NIMBUS.

BIBLIOGRAPHY. A. Krücke, *Der Nimbus und verwandte Attribute in der frühchristlichen Kunst*, Strasbourg, 1905.

GLOSENKAMP, HERMAN. Flemish sculptor (fl. 1st half 15th cent.). With Roger de Smet and other sculptors he worked on the famous *Cheminée du Franc* (1528–31), which had been designed by Lancelot Blondeel for the Palace of Justice in Bruges. He was responsible for the five Hapsburg figures in the scene of the coronation of Charles V.

GLOUCESTER CATHEDRAL. The nave, gallery, and clerestory of this English cathedral are powerful examples of the Romanesque style built between 1089 and 1160. The south transept is notable for the early exposition of the court Perpendicular style, following closely St. Stephen's Chapel, Westminster.

BIBLIOGRAPHY. J. Harvey, *The English Cathedrals*, London, 1950.

Enrico Glicenstein, *S. Francis*. Exhibited at the Venice Biennale in 1926.

GLOVER, JOHN. English water-colorist (b. Houghton-on-the-Water, near Leicester, 1767; d. 1849). At nineteen he became a writing master and, during occasional visits to London, began to take lessons in drawing from William Payne and John "Warwick" Smith. He then established himself as a drawing master in Lichfield in 1794, and over the next eleven years had a number of notable pupils. In 1805 he settled in London after some success at the first exhibition of the Old Water-Colour Society, where he continued to exhibit regularly until 1832. During this period he toured extensively in the British Isles, France, Switzerland, and Italy before immigrating in 1831 to Tasmania. His water-color style is lively both in handling and in its silhouette effects. He also painted in monochrome.

BIBLIOGRAPHY. I. Williams, *Early English Watercolours*, London, 1952.

GLUCKSBERG CASTLE, FLENSBURG, see KARIES, NIKOLAUS.

GLUE. Any of a variety of adhesive liquids used for joining purposes or as a binding medium for paintings. Most glues are derived from animal substances, such as bones or skins.

GLYCON. Greek sculptor from Athens (probably fl. 1st cent. B.C.). His signature appears on the *Farnese Heracles* in Naples, which, as the inscription on another copy in Florence attests, is a copy of an original Heracles by Lysippus. No other work by Glycon is known, and he may have been exclusively a copyist.

BIBLIOGRAPHY. G. Lippold, *Kopien und Umbildungen griechischer Statuen*, Munich, 1923.

GLYPH. Groove; more specifically, a carved vertical channel. *See also* TRIGLYPH.

GLYPTOLOGY (Glyptography). Art or study of engraving on precious or semiprecious stones. Since antiquity, engraved gems have been used as seals, and their study, like that of coins, is important for the history of antique art.

GLYPTOTHECA. In Greek antiquity, a building containing sculpture. The 18th-century Glyptothek in Munich was inspired by classical precedents.

GLYPTOTHEK, MUNICH, see KLENZE, LEO VON; MUNICH: MUSEUMS (STATE ANTIQUITIES COLLECTION).

GMUND: HOLY CROSS CHURCH. The Heiligenkreuzkirche is the most important Gothic structure in Lower Swabia, Germany. It was begun in the early 14th century and was completed in the 16th (the vaulting of the nave was in place in 1521) on the foundations of an earlier Romanesque building. It is a Gothic hall church with nave, two aisles, choir, ambulatory, and radiating chapels. The design has been attributed to Heinrich Parler, although the name of his more famous son, Peter Parler (of Prague), has also been associated with it. The northern and southern portals of the choir contain tympanums representing the Last Judgment, executed in the late Gothic style and influenced by French sculpture of the period. The most notable monument in the church is the choir screen surmounted by a series of back-to-back figures of the Apostles (1550).

BIBLIOGRAPHY. A. Naegele, *Die Heilig-Kreuzkirche in Schwäbisch-Gmünd*, Gmünd, 1925; O. Schmitt, *Das Heiligkreuzmünster in Schwäbisch-Gmünd*, Stuttgart, 1951.

GNESEN (Gniezno) CATHEDRAL. Basilican cathedral in western Poland. The present Gothic structure of 1342–1415, which has been altered several times, replaced an earlier building of 1040–64 (rebuilt 1097 and 12th cent.). All that remains of the Romanesque cathedral is the magnificent pair of bronze doors of the main façade.

The doors were in all probability executed in the years 1135 to 1138, in the reign of Boleslaw III. In eighteen scenes, they depict the life of St. Wojciech (St. Adalbert, apostle to the Slavs). They are cast in low relief on horizontally placed rectangular panels. Each door with its nine panels is framed by an inhabited vine rinceau border. The iconography is based upon contemporary texts of the life of the saint and also upon unwritten local legend. This latter point argues a Polish origin for the iconography.

Stylistically, the doors have been related to a Saxon (Hildesheim) workshop or to a Mosan (Liège) source. The latter supposition appears more tenable in view of the relationship between the Gnesen doors and the *Retable of St. Remaclius* in Stavelot, a Liège work.

BIBLIOGRAPHY. A. Goldschmidt, *Die Bronzetüren von Nowgorod und Gnesen*, Marburg an der Lahn, 1932.

GOBBO, IL, see LOMBARDO, CRISTOFORO; SOLARI, CRISTOFORO.

GOBELINS, see TAPESTRY.

GOCH, JOHANN VON. German sculptor (fl. 1470–88). He worked in St. Viktor, Xanten, for which he made pillar figures as well as figures of the Church fathers and saints for the lecterns.

GODDESS OF MERCY, see AVALOKITESVARA.

GODECHARLE, GILLIS LAMBERT. Flemish sculptor (b. Brussels, 1750; d. there, 1835). Godecharle was a pupil of Delvaux before studying in Paris. He later became a professor at the Academy of Brussels. He is known for his rococo reliefs on the palace at Laken, near Brussels, and for bust portraits in the Museum of Fine Arts, Brussels.

BIBLIOGRAPHY. H. Gerson and E. H. ter Kuile, *Art and Architecture in Belgium, 1600–1800*, Baltimore, 1960.

GODEFROY DE CLAIRE. A goldsmith from Huy on the Meuse, Godefroy (fl. 1130–50) was in all probability a product of the workshop of the metalwork master, Renier de Huy. One of the important known Romanesque artists, he was most active in the service of Wibald of Stavelot. Among the works credited to him are a bronze aquamanile head of Bacchus in Brussels (ca. 1130–40) and the impressive engraved silver-gilt reliquary *Triptych of the Holy Cross* in the Metropolitan Museum, New York (ca. 1150). *See also* MOSAN ART.

GODERIS, HANS. Dutch marine painter (fl. from 1625; d. before 1643). Goderis was active in Haarlem, where he was first documented in 1625, until 1638. His best-known work, a marine scene (Rotterdam, Boymans–Van Beuningen Museum) is dated 1625. This painting recalls the style of Jan Porcellis, who was active in Haarlem from 1622.

BIBLIOGRAPHY. F. C. Willis, *Die niederländische Marinemalerei*, Leipzig, 1911.

GODESCALC GOSPELS. Carolingian illuminated manuscript (ca. 781) in the National Library, Paris.

GOD FROM THE SEA, *see* ARTEMISIUM ZEUS.

GODS AND GODDESSES, *see* names of individual deities.

GODS AND GODDESSES, ANCIENT PRECLASSICAL. Primitive man, who was inclined to attribute supernatural powers to anything he did not understand or could not control, wove many myths around those powers. Preoccupied with the mystery of creation, he tried to explain it in his own way; yet in ancient mythologies the stories of the creation of the world present noteworthy similarities, as do the stories of the flood. Thus, according to the general concept, at the very beginning there was "chaos," out of which a powerful spirit established order. Many forces, however, took part in this achievement, and differing names and symbols were given to them. Natural physical phenomena and, eventually, man's ancestors, kings, and heroes were deified. Polytheistic religion thus evolved, and as religion developed so did various forms of art to serve it. Man believed that all things were possessed of spirits. Some were friendly, and these he invoked in times of need or danger; others were hostile, and these he tried to propitiate or win over to his side. In each instance he used prayers, promises, incantations, gifts, offerings, and sacrifices.

In time, gods acquired distinct personalities, with distinct likes and dislikes and with their own particular attributes, often represented by animals. They were considered to have power over certain places or certain phenomena, and statues and temples were dedicated to them. Some gods were considered greater or more powerful than others, and in many ancient religions the sun, the moon, and other heavenly bodies held a very high place in their particular pantheons. The cult of the mother goddess, symbol of fertility and procreation, was also prevalent among ancient peoples, and she was represented in many forms—very early as a mature squatting woman with a fat body, sagging breasts, and an amorphous mass of clay for a head. Much later a face was added.

In a number of ancient religions there was a triad of supreme gods. In Sumer, the supreme triad was composed of Anu, ruler of heaven; Enlil, ruler of earth; and Ea, ruler of the waters.

Later, in Babylonia, a second triad appeared, with Sin, the moon god, whose emblem was the winged bull; his son Shamash, the sun god, considered supreme among the gods; and Adad, the weather god, or storm god, of the Amorites, who was worshiped under different names throughout Asia Minor, Mesopotamia, Syria, and Palestine. Adad was identified with Teshub, the great Hittite god of the elements. His emblem was the thunderbolt, the winged bull his animal attribute. On a limestone slab from Assur, Adad is shown standing on his sacred bull. Shamash was also worshiped as the sun god by the Akkadians and the Sumerians and then by the Assyrians, who attributed to him their victories over their enemies. It was from Shamash that the great Hammurabi, who united Babylonia and Assyria under one rule, received the famous "Code of Hammurabi." *See* HAMMURABI, STELE OF.

The three supreme gods worshiped by the Mitannians were Varuna, the sky god; his twin brother, Mithras, god of the eternal light; and Indra, god of thunder. In Persia, Ahura Mazda was the supreme god of the Achaemenians, creator of heaven and earth; his emblem was the sun disk. Sraosha, the high-ranking god of justice whose animal attribute was the cock, waged war against the enemies of Ahura Mazda and, together with Mithras and Rashnu, judged the souls of the dead. In the Greek pantheon, Zeus, the supreme god, was often portrayed with the combined attributes of other lesser gods.

Of the female divinities, the most important and best known was the great Ishtar, goddess of fertility and love, who was closely associated with the second triad. The planet Venus was considered her domain, and the lion was her animal attribute. Known under various names and forms, she was earlier considered the consort of the great Sumerian god Anu. In Persia, the mother goddess of fecundity was known as Ashi and was the sister of Sraosha. Her emblems were fish and pomegranates, and her animal attributes, the lion and the ibex.

When their rule was threatened by Apsu, god of the waters, and by Tiamat, goddess of the underworld, the great gods chose one of the younger gods, Marduk, the son of Ea, to defend them. In the ensuing combat Marduk won and brought order to the universe. The gods then divided the earth among themselves, and each god chose his own city. Thus, Sin chose Ur, and Ea the city of Eridu.

In Assyria, the role of Marduk was played by Assur, the supreme Assyrian god and patron of the city of Assur, whose consort was Ishtar, there considered the goddess of war. In Syria, Baal became the supreme god of the Syrian pantheon, replacing Anu and Enlil.

The ancient gods behaved like mortals. They ate, drank, loved, quarreled, and fought each other and the mortals. Their temples were their private residences on earth. The more important a god, the more numerous and splendid were the temples built in his honor. In Assur there were many temples of Ishtar, built like palaces. In Babylon, where Marduk held a unique position, his temple Esagila was the largest and most splendid of all Babylonian temples, and the great statue of the seated god, his throne, table, and footstool were of solid gold. Marduk's position and cult were so strong that he reigned supreme for 2,000 years. Even Cyrus the Great, who conquered Babylon in 539 B.C., 1,500 years after the reign of Hammurabi, paid homage to Marduk and gave him credit for his victory, as stated on a cuneiform inscription on a clay cylinder, now in the British Museum, in London.

Many were the gods worshiped by the ancients: gods of mountains, vegetation, forests, winds, water, thunder, rain, rivers, storms, fire, justice, sleep, the underworld, and innumerable others. Some were local gods; others were worshiped far and wide. Each had his own residence or temple, where his statue was enshrined. Each city had its own deity. Migrating or invading people brought their own gods with them, and often both local and foreign gods were worshiped together or became one god. Often, conquerors and vanquished adopted one anothers' gods.

Sometimes the gods of the invaders took precedence over the local gods, and at other times the gods of the vanquished were dethroned or became lesser gods, underworld gods, or even evil spirits. When the lesser gods or the newcomers' gods had no temple of their own, they were given space in a temple of a greater god. In the great temple of Marduk in Babylon there were fifty-five side chapels dedicated to other gods and goddesses. Among these were Zarpanit, the consort of Marduk; Nebo (Nabu) and his son, Ea; Nusku, the fire god; and many others.

Dagan was a fish god whose cult originated in Sumer and spread later in Assyria and Babylonia. In a small temple unearthed in Nimrud, a relief was found portraying Dagan with his attributes.

In the beginning of the 1st millennium, when interest in astrology became widespread, gods and goddesses were depicted in astral splendor. Cylinder seals of the period portray Ishtar surrounded by heavenly bodies. In one hand she holds a star-tipped scepter and in the other a ring. Nebo, the god of writing, holding a double wedge, accompanies her. Both wear miters adorned with stars, and they stand on their animal attributes. On the same cylinders other gods of the heavens are depicted, surrounded by stars, among which the constellation of the Pleiades is represented by seven small circles.

See also CLASSICAL (GREEK AND ROMAN) GODS, under individual names.

BIBLIOGRAPHY. E. Porada, *Mesopotamian Art in Cylinder Seals of the Pierpont Morgan Library*, New York, 1947; A. Godard, *Iran*, Paris, 1948; C. S. Braden, *The World's Religions*, Nashville, Tenn., 1954; O. James, *The Ancient Gods*, New York, 1960; J. Maringer, *The Gods of Prehistoric Man*, New York, 1960; A. Parrot, *Sumer: The Dawn of Art*, New York, 1961; A. Parrot, *Nineveh and Babylon*, London, 1961; L. Woolley, *Mesopotamia and the Middle East*, London, 1961; S. Lloyd, *The Art of the Ancient Near East*, London, 1961; R. Ghirshman, *Persian Art, the Parthian and Sassanian Dynasties*, New York, 1962; S. H. Hooke, *Babylonian and Assyrian Religion*, Norman, Okla., 1963; R. Ghirshman, *The Arts of Ancient Iran: From Its Origins to the Time of Alexander the Great*, New York, 1964.

LUCILLE VASSARDAKI

GODWIN, EDWARD. English architect and designer (1833–86). His Northampton Town Hall (1861), in Italian Gothic, betrays the influence of Ruskin. For Whistler he designed the White House (1878), one of several houses for artists. He participated in the aesthetic and Arts and Crafts movements, of which Liberty's costume studio represents a phase.

BIBLIOGRAPHY. D. Harbron, "Edward Godwin," *Architectural Review*, XCVIII, 1945.

GOELDI, OSWALDO. Brazilian printmaker and draftsman (b. Belém, 1895; d. Rio de Janeiro, 1961). The son of a Swiss naturalist, Goeldi was trained in Switzerland. In 1919 he settled in Brazil. His work consists of large expressionistic woodcuts (e.g., *Cavaleiro*, Rio de Janeiro, National Library) and drawings. He illustrated Poe and Dostoyevsky and did many *danse macabre* themes.

BIBLIOGRAPHY. A. M. Machado, *Goeldi*, Rio de Janeiro, 1955.

GOERG, EDOUARD. French painter (1893–   ). Born in Sydney, Australia, Goerg went to France at the age of seven. In 1912 he enrolled at the Académie Ranson, where Maurice Denis was teaching; he had his first exhibition in 1924. His art has always been inspired by realism. Goerg greatly admires Goya, Daumier, and Rouault, but unlike them he has accentuated the sentimental, condemning genuine plastic emotions in favor of the anecdotal.

His work soon fell into à kind of soft realism, characterized by the representation of nude, barely adolescent young girls, often accompanied by men in evening clothes, all enveloped in a shadowy atmosphere relieved only by conventional gleams of light. Goerg takes his subject matter from the life around him with no attempt at social realism or at a portrayal of the tragic element as seen in Goya and Rouault, being content to represent people, mostly women and girls, as he sees them (*Les Modèles*, 1954; Mme Goerg Collection; *Le Gourmet*, Art Institute of Chicago; *La jolie fille du bar*, Charles Jacquemart Collection).

Goerg is professor of engraving at the Ecole des Beaux-Arts in Paris. He excels in black and white, in which his understanding of contrasts has enabled him to emphasize the dramatic element very skillfully, yet with a certain stress on the macabre. This is seen clearly in two of his best works, the illustrations for *The Tales of Hoffmann*, and for Baudelaire's *Les Fleurs du mal*. Like Van Dongen, Goerg has created a feminine type, often entirely imaginary (*Imaginary Portrait*, 1929; Paris, private collection), yet never lacking in charm. His teaching has had an important influence on young French realistic painters.

BIBLIOGRAPHY. B. Dorival, *The School of Paris in the Musée d'Art Moderne*, London, 1960; R. Nacenta, *School of Paris*, London, 1960; W. George, *Edouard Goerg*, Geneva, 1965.

ARNOLD ROSIN

GOERITZ, MATHIAS. German sculptor (1915–   ). He was born in Danzig, and after studying in Berlin and re-

Edouard Goerg, *La jolie bouquetière*. Museum of Modern Art, Paris.

ceiving his Ph.D., he joined the School of Arts and Crafts in Charlottenburg. He was friendly with the Brücke painters. He traveled through Europe and settled in Paris to work (1936–38). During World War II he lived in Tetuan; in 1945 he moved to Spain, where he founded the school of Altamira (1948). In 1949 he settled in Mexico City, where he worked as both sculptor and architect. He has created such monumental works as Echo Museum (1952–53) and a five-pylon entrance to Satellite City (1957–58). His wood carving is expressionistic.

GOES, HUGO VAN DER. Flemish painter (ca. 1435/40–82). One of the greatest masters of the late 15th century, Hugo brought to his work an emotional intensity new to Flemish art.

The earliest record of Hugo is his admittance to the painters' guild of Ghent in 1467. In 1468 he went to Bruges, as "referee" of the guild, to aid in decorating the city for the marriage of Margaret of York and Charles the Bold. He continued to be patronized by the citizens of Bruges and by Charles and Margaret. In 1469 and 1472 he was active in the decoration of Ghent for their sumptuous entry into that city. In 1473 he was called upon to decorate St. Pharahildis for the funeral services of Philip the Good and Isabella of Portugal. His fame and success increased, and he was named dean of the painters' guild of Ghent in 1474.

At this point in his career, prior to 1475, Hugo forsook Ghent to enter the Red Cloister (Roode Kloster) near Brussels as a lay brother. He remained at the cloister, with considerable privileges, until his death. He continued to paint and receive visitors, and even left the cloister for brief periods. In 1479/80 he went to Louvain to estimate the value of Dirk Bouts's unfinished *Justice Panels*. However, Hugo was subject to increasing fits of depression during which he despaired of salvation and of completing his work, and in 1481 he attempted suicide.

The most firmly dated of Hugo's works is the *Portinari Altarpiece* (ca. 1474–76; Florence, Uffizi). Authorities disagree on the dating inasmuch as the evidence is internal,

Hugo van der Goes, *Adoration of the Shepherds*, from the Portinari Altarpiece, ca. 1474–76. Uffizi, Florence.

deriving from the number of the children of the donor, Tommaso Portinari, and their apparent ages. The work is enormous (over 8 ft. by 19 ft.) by Flemish standards. Despite a debt to Dirk Bouts in the full employment of space, the painting possesses an emotional concentration and intensity hitherto foreign to northern painting. The colors are clear and brilliant, from the deep shadows surrounding the ox and ass to the broadest light on the distant hillside. But all light seems to be concentrated in, or to emanate from, the Christ Child. The entire composition is grouped around the Child, with the dynamic action of the shepherds "bursting" into the scene and the gazes of Mary and the angels all joined to create a psychological tension that pulls the parts together. The wings of the altarpiece are visually joined to the whole by use of a continuous landscape that carries through the three panels (a device used as early as the *Ghent Altarpiece*) and by the intensity with which the donors and their children concentrate on the central Nativity panel. This work, rich and profound iconographically, and emotionally moving, was done at a high point in Hugo's career—just before or at the time of his entry into the Roode Kloster. His other works are therefore considered in relation to the *Portinari Altarpiece*.

The earliest work of his career is probably the diptych with *The Fall of Man* and *The Lamentation* (Vienna, Museum of Art History), which might be dated as early as 1467/68. The figures of Adam and Eve in the former are certainly successors to their counterparts in the *Ghent Altarpiece*. The richly profuse foliate landscape also bespeaks Ghent and the Eyckian tradition. For the newly admitted free master, this seems to have been the major, but not the sole, influence. The companion panel of *The Lamentation* shows the influence of Bouts and Rogier van der Weyden, perhaps deriving from Hugo's unknown, pre-Ghent period. Hence, these traditionalist panels may justifiably be considered at the beginning of Hugo's career. A small triptych of the *Virgin and Child and Donors* (Frankfurt am Main, Städel Institute) seems also to date from this time.

The years between 1467/68 and 1475 are devoid of known works, with the exception of the debatable *Montforte Altarpiece* (Berlin, former State Museums). Of this work, only a monumental *Adoration of the Kings* survives. The dating poses a problem inasmuch as the panel shows the work of a mature, developed artist, which is related to the *Portinari Altarpiece* rather than to the works of 1467/68. Authorities disagree on whether it precedes or follows the Portinari work. This confusion is due to its Italianate quality, which has led some students to hypothesize an Italian journey for Hugo. But our knowledge of his life precludes such a journey, unless it was made prior to 1467. The *Montforte Altarpiece* would then have to be placed early in Hugo's career, a solution that creates greater problems than it solves. The open space in the foreground, around which the composition revolves, and the very restrained movement of the Magi toward the Child seem to foreshadow the Portinari triptych, but the monumental dignity of the figures places it very close to the later work.

A pair of organ shutters done for Sir Edward Bonkil (Edinburgh, Holyrood Palace) can be dated 1478/79 on historical and stylistic grounds. The work was not completed by Hugo; some parts are credited to assistants and others are from an entirely different period.

Hugo's career reached its climax in two panels of intense emotional power. The abandon and psychological release of these works are undoubtedly related to the growth of Hugo's mental torments. The earlier of them, another *Adoration of the Shepherds* (Berlin, former State Museums) is a long, low panel resembling a predella. Within this horizontal framework, Hugo has placed a startling, diffuse composition. In the foreground, at either side, two half-figure prophets draw back curtains to reveal the scene. The tranquillity of the Nativity is shattered by the shepherds "tumbling" into the manger in their anxiety to do homage to the Child. They carry with them a flood of brilliant, pale morning light into a somber darkness lit only by the delicate radiance from the Child and Mary. The sharp contrasts of light and shade, warm darks and cool light, break the surface and space into a dynamically composed, highly fragmented complex, where rational spatial construction or light sources are meaningless.

Hugo's *Death of the Virgin* (Bruges Museum) at first seems unrelated to the Berlin *Adoration*. The Berlin work is a narrow, horizontal panel; the Bruges painting is almost square. The former has a diffuse, fragmented composition; the latter appears to be tightly and compactly composed. The disciples, emotionally distraught, are arranged around the Virgin's bed in attitudes of tragic despair. Their grief seems almost too great to be encompassed by the windowless room. But the compactness is shattered by the blazing aureole of Christ and the angels descending to take the soul of His mother. The colors—off-tones of blues, pinks, greens, reds—seem washed away by the blaze of light, as do the walls of the room. The aureole hovers in an intangible space, made less tangible and more irrational by the disregard of perspective and physical space that is evident in the placement of the Apostles. The total result is a fragmented, irrational spatial composition, psychologically close to the Berlin *Adoration*, which is held together only by the emotional intensity of the participants in the scene.

These last two works clearly show the emotional state that Hugo had already reached. They can therefore be dated about 1481, the time of his attempted suicide.

BIBLIOGRAPHY. M. J. Friedländer, *Die altniederländische Malerei*, vol. 4, Berlin, 1926; E. Panofsky, *Early Netherlandish Painting*, 2 vols., Cambridge, Mass., 1953.

STANLEY FERBER

GOIJEN (Goyen), JAN JOSEPHSZ. VAN. Dutch landscape painter (b. Leyden, 1596; d. The Hague, 1656). Van Goijen studied with a number of different masters from the age of ten. He was first a pupil of Coenraet van Schilperoort, then of Isaak van Swanenburgh, Jan de Man, and the glass painter Hendrick Clock, all at Leyden. He then spent two years with the Hoorn painter Willem Gerritsz. At the age of about nineteen Van Goijen spent a year traveling in France. After his return he studied for a year with the Haarlem landscape painter Esaias van de Velde, whose artistic influence is most apparent in Van Goijen's early development.

In 1631 he moved to The Hague, where he became a citizen in 1634. However, in 1634 he was also active in Haarlem, living in the house of Isaak van Ruisdael. He was an official (*hoofdman*) of the painters' organization in The Hague in 1638 and 1640. His daughter married Jan Steen in 1649. Van Goijen's earliest works are completely dependent upon the style of his last teacher, Esaias van de Velde. His earliest dated work, *Landscape with an Old Tree* (1620; Haarlem, Collection of Th. Hoog), is completely dependent upon Van de Velde, as is his 1623 *Village Street with a River and a Windmill* (Lisbon, Collection of A. de Medeiros e Almeida). In the later 1620s Van Goijen's style deviates from the compositional pattern established by Van de Velde, and in his *Country Road* (1628; Frankfurt am Main, Städel Art Institute) he moves toward a more tonal use of color. However, there are still traces of Van de Velde's influence in the use of detail. The link with his last teacher is broken completely in the 1631 *Wooden Fence* (Brunswick, Herzog Anton Ulrich Museum) with its tonal use of color and unification of detail and compositional sweep.

During the 1630s Van Goijen was the leading painter of the tonal development of Dutch landscape painting, and during this period the use of water as a dominant motif in his landscapes becomes increasingly more apparent, as can be seen, for example, in his *River Scene* (1636; Cambridge, Mass., Fogg Art Museum; on loan from the Collection of James P. Warburg).

In the 1640s Van Goijen turned his considerable talents toward panoramic views of the Dutch countryside, in works such as *View of Rhenen* (1646; Washington, D.C., Corcoran Gallery of Art, W. A. Clark Collection) and *View of Leyden* (1647; Northampton, Mass., Smith College Museum of Art). During this period he also painted a num-

ber of winter landscapes that often combined the panoramic point of view and the magnificent rendering of figural detail (*On the Ice*, 1643; St. Louis, City Art Museum).

As the varied locations of his landscape subjects indicate, Van Goijen traveled frequently throughout the Netherlands. In addition to his painting he was also an art dealer and often arranged auction sales.

BIBLIOGRAPHY. H. van de Waal, *Jan van Goyen*, Amsterdam, 1941; N. Maclaren, *National Gallery Catalogues: The Dutch School*, London, 1960; W. Stechow, *Dutch Landscape Painting of the Seventeenth Century*, London, 1966.
LEONARD J. SLATKES

GOITIA, FRANCISCO. Mexican painter (1882–   ). Born in Patillos, Zacatecas, Goitia went to Mexico City in 1898 and for five years attended the Bellas Artes School. He traveled to Europe in 1904, and studied in Barcelona for four years with Francisco Gali. He also spent four years in Italy. On his return to Mexico in 1912, he lived in Zacatecas for six years and came to Mexico City again in 1918. At that time he began working with Gamio on the archaeology of the Teotihuacán Valley and Oaxaca. From a variety of conservative, technically sophisticated early works, Goitia moved into social painting of high aesthetic interest. Distilling a rich Indian and mestizo background, he painted a number of masterful works in thick oil impasto, including the famous *Tata Jesucristo* of 1927, an archetype of human bereavement. Goitia has been a teacher for many years and now lives in utmost simplicity near Xochimilco. An important retrospective exhibition of his works was held at the Palacio de Bellas Artes in Mexico City (1961).

BIBLIOGRAPHY. M. Helm, *Modern Mexican Painters*, New York, 1941; B. S. Myers, *Mexican Painting in Our Time*, New York, 1956.

Jan Josephsz. van Goijen, *River Scene*. Fogg Art Museum, Cambridge, Mass.

GOLD, ANCIENT USES OF. Gold was used frequently in ancient jewelry and art objects because of its relative abundance in usable form. It was first employed in its unrefined form, alloyed with such other metals as silver, copper, or iron (the silver-gold alloy was sometimes known as "white gold" or "electrum"). Refining was apparently utilized in the gold objects excavated in Troy II (ca. 2600–2300 B.C.) but did not become general until the classical era. *See* JEWELRY, HISTORY OF.

The chief gold mines in ancient times were those in Nubia in the Bronze Age, in Thrace and Macedonia during classical and Hellenistic times (especially because of the efforts of Philip II of Macedonia), and in Spain, Noricum, northern Italy, and the Balkan Peninsula in the Roman era. The chief uses for gold in antiquity were for coinage, jewelry, metal art works, and, less commonly, death masks and entire monumental statues. One particularly Greek practice was the erection of chryselephantine statues—sculptured in ivory and gold—of which the most famous was Phidias's statue of Zeus at Olympia.

See also GOLDSMITH'S WORK; SILVER AND GOLD.

BIBLIOGRAPHY. British Museum, Dept. of Greek and Roman Antiquities, *Catalogue of the Jewellery, Greek, Etruscan and Roman, in the Department of Antiquities, British Museum* by F. H. Marshall, London, 1911; R. A. Higgins, *Greek and Roman Jewellery,* London, 1962.

EVANTHIA SAPORITI

GOLDEN HOUSE OF NERO (Domus Aurea), ROME. Ancient Roman palace complex, built by Nero after the fire A.D. 64. It covered an area of about 125 acres, extending from the Palatine to the Esquiline hill. The palace was destroyed by the Flavian emperors, who returned part of the grounds to the Roman people. The palace area consisted of a conglomeration of buildings, baths, fountains, gardens, and so on. It was approached through a monumental colonnade starting at the Temple of Vesta and leading up to the Velia, where the vestibule was situated. At the center of the vestibule stood a colossal bronze statue of Nero. The buildings were decorated with stucco, marble, and wall paintings. Fine examples of the paintings were found in the cryptoporticus. The rooms were roofed with quadripartite cross vaulting.

BIBLIOGRAPHY. G. T. Rivoira, *Architettura romana*, Milan, 1921; W. J. Anderson, R. P. Spiers, and T. Ashby, *The Architecture of Greece and Rome*, vol. 2: *The Architecture of Ancient Rome*, London, 1927.

GOLDEN LEGEND, *see* LEGENDA AUREA.

GOLDEN MADONNA. German work sometimes known as the Essen Madonna and dated about 1000, now in the Essen Cathedral treasury. This gold-covered, enameled, and jeweled wooden figure has occasionally been considered the forerunner of monumental Romanesque sculpture, although it is not quite 29 inches high. It was probably produced in Essen or Mainz, and its full volume and broad planes aid in its achievement of a monumental feeling.

GOLDEN PAVILION IN ROKUONJI, KYOTO, *see* KINKAKUJI.

GOLDEN SECTION. System of aesthetically pleasing proportions based on the division of a line or figure into parts which correspond to the proportion 3:5—that is, the smaller part is to the size of the greater part approx-

imately as the greater is to the whole. This principle, used in antiquity, was revived during the Italian Renaissance, when it was used primarily in architecture.

GOLD GROUND. Use of a neutral gold background, or *fondo d'oro*, in Christian paintings and mosaics for the purpose of conveying a transcendental and eternal setting. In medieval and Renaissance paintings, the ground was achieved by covering a smooth gesso board with gold leaf, which was burnished and tooled or stamped in patterns. The result was a feeling of great richness in altarpieces and religious panel paintings.

BIBLIOGRAPHY. D. V. Thompson, *The Materials of Medieval Painting*, London, 1936.

GOLD POINT DRAWING. One of the metal point techniques of drawing, like silverpoint and lead point. Of the three, all of which are forerunners of pencil drawing, gold point is the least used. The artist uses a sharpened gold wand on a specially treated paper to produce a thin, delicate, and fragile line.

GOLDSMITH'S WORK. The artistic production of objects of precious metals—gold, silver, and platinum—in the form of vessels, utensils, and jewelry. Repoussé is the technique employed most frequently, although casting and carving are also used to achieve the general forms. Surface decoration is executed by a variety of techniques, including enamel, filigree, niello, and intarsia. *See* CAST AND CASTING; ENAMEL; FILIGREE; INTARSIA; NIELLO; REPOUSSAGE.

GOLE, JACOB. Dutch engraver (b. Amsterdam, 1660; d. there, 1737). Gole worked in both mezzotint and line engraving, but is generally considered more successful in the latter medium. His *oeuvre* consists mainly of portraits, such as *Charles XI of Sweden* (1685); it also includes some genre scenes after Dutch masters.

BIBLIOGRAPHY. P. Kristeller, *Kupferstich und Holzschnitt in vier Jahrhunderten*, Berlin, 1905.

GOL GOMBAZ, BIJAPUR, *see* MUHAMMAD ADIL SHAH, TOMB OF, BIJAPUR.

GOLTZIUS, HENDRICK (Hendrik). Dutch engraver (b. Mulbracht, 1558; d. Haarlem, 1617). His father, Jan Goltz, was a glass painter who moved to Duisburg when Goltzius was three years old. Instructed in drawing and glass painting by his father, Goltzius was also taught engraving by Dirk Volckertz Coornhert and Philipp Galle before going to Haarlem in about 1577. There, two years later, he married the widow of Adriaen Matham. His work can be divided into two phases: the period from 1577 to 1590, when he brought his technique to a high degree of perfection, and the period after his visit to Italy in 1590–91. Technically, Goltzius is justly famous for his skill in the swelled-line method of engraving, which involves the artful control of parallel lines tapering, widening, and tapering again in each stroke. Stylistically, he became the leader of the mannerist school of Dutch engravers. Since both technique and style are contrived, it required masterful engraving to avoid banal consequences. Goltzius's stature as a great engraver derives from his brilliance in both areas.

His earliest work was reproductive. Most of his work

after other artists shows foreign influences, particularly of Bartholomeus Spranger, Dürer, and the Italian painters. Before his trip to Italy in 1590, Goltzius had already produced a number of notable original works. The series *Story of Ruth and Boaz* and *Story of Lucretia* show the emergence of his personal style. In the latter series, the use of 16th-century costume, the emphasis on intricate detail, and the chiaroscuro light effects are particularly interesting. Goltzius then began to develop a broader manner in his series of *Roman Heroes* (1586) and in the astonishing circular perspective studies of the four "Disgracers" (e.g., Tantalus, Icarus) of 1588. Another remarkable engraving of the period is the great *Hercules*, whose mottled body displays an exuberance of muscular anatomy. At this time also there appeared a dated chiaroscuro woodcut of *Hercules and Cacus*. Goltzius's other woodcuts in this technique, of landscapes and mythological figures, have a surprisingly restrained mood. During his trip to Italy in 1590–91, Goltzius drew from the antique, and his style became even more restrained.

During the 1590s he produced a series of large plates on the life of Christ in which he superbly imitated with bravura the styles of six artists: Raphael, Parmigianino, Jacopo Bassano, Dürer, Lucas van Leyden, and Baroccio. A large *St. Jerome* and his *Farnesian Hercules* are other high points of his later work. Among his 500 or so prints are a group of fine, small portraits including those of Henry IV, Mercator, and Christopher Plantin.

BIBLIOGRAPHY. O. Hirschmann, *Hendrik Goltzius*, Leipzig, 1919.
KNEELAND MC NULTY

GOLTZIUS, HUBERT. Flemish engraver, painter, printer, and numismatist (b. Würzburg or Venloo, 1526; d. Bruges, 1583). A pupil of his father and of Lambert Lombard in Liège, he spent a number of years (1558–67) in travel, studying European collections of coins and antiquities. He is known almost exclusively for his work as an engraver of coins and portraits.

GOLUB, LEON. American painter (1922–   ). Golub studied with Paul Wieghardt at the Art Institute School in his native Chicago. He has lived in Italy (1956–57) and Paris (1959–64) and now lives in New York City. The colossal figures in his paintings, sometimes drawn from ancient Greek statuary, often have the brutalized power of late Roman art.

GOMATESVARA, SRAVANA BELGOLA. Statue in Hāssan District, Mysore State, India. Sravana Belgola was for centuries the chief center for the Jain religion in southern India. Here, on the Dodda-betta hill, a colossal image 57 feet high was carved from a boulder; it is one of the largest freestanding statues in the world. Made between 947 and 984, the figure represents the saint Gomateśvara, son of the first Tīrthaṅkara (Jain hero), who gave up his kingdom to become an ascetic. He is shown in benevolent ecstasy, ignoring the plant which has grown up to his shoulder and the serpents around his feet.

BIBLIOGRAPHY. R. Mukerjee, *Culture and Art of India*, New York, 1959.

GONCALVES, NUNO. Portuguese painter (fl. 1450–72). Documentary evidence suggests that Nuno Gonçalves was appointed court painter to Alfonso V, king of Portugal, in 1450. Official account books and archives reveal the progress of his artistic recognition but little else.

His fame rests on two large altarpieces, both with St. Vincent, the patron saint of Lisbon and of the royal house of Portugal, as the principal figure. The one executed for the Cathedral of Lisbon was destroyed in the earthquake of 1755 and is now known only from literary sources. The other, intended for the Convent of St. Vincent-beyond-the-Walls, was discovered in 1882; it can be seen in the National Museum in Lisbon. On the basis of documentary evidence, it has been attributed to Nuno.

The polyptych for St. Vincent's Convent consists of six panels, two large ones and four narrower ones. The large panels, both dominated by the youthful figure of St. Vincent clad in a deacon's dalmatic, may have appeared in the middle with two wings on each side. It is conjectured that a statue of the saint originally stood between the symmetrical halves. The large left-central *Panel of the Infante* shows the saint worshiped by a congregation of personages, among whom Alfonso V, Prince John, Henry the Navigator, and the artist himself have been identified. The two narrow panels represent groups of adoring fishermen and monks. The large central panel to the right, *Panel of the Archbishop*, shows the saint surrounded by clergy and knights, both groups continuing on the adjacent

Hendrick Goltzius, an engraving from the series of the *Roman Heroes* (1586).

Nuno Gonçalves, *Panel of the Infante*. National Museum, Lisbon.

narrow panel. The chief figure in the panel at the extreme right is kneeling and holds a portion of the saint's skull. In the background, the saint's coffin can be seen. These were the two relics of St. Vincent possessed by the convent. It is thought that the work was a votive offering of Alfonso V to his patron saint after the successful capture of Alcácer in 1458. The hair styles and costumes suggest a date between 1460 and 1470 for its execution.

Nuno permits neither landscape nor architectural detail to distract the viewer's attention from the solemn assemblage before him. Though a debt to Flemish art is apparent in the brushwork and in the three-quarter view of some of the heads, the sculpturesque treatment of the portraits owes nothing either to the Flemish painters or to the Italians. Indeed, Nuno was unprecedented in the art of his own country, and he should be considered the founder of the Portuguese school which was to flourish in the next century.

BIBLIOGRAPHY. R. dos Santos, *Nuno Gonçalves*, New York, 1955; A. B. da Fonseca, *O mistério dos painéis*, Lisbon, 1957.

FRANKLIN R. DIDLAKE

GONDI PALACE, *see* SANGALLO FAMILY.

GONDOIN, JACQUES. French architect (1737–1818). Gondoin worked in Paris and was a pupil of Jacques François Blondel. His forward-looking lecture theater of the Ecole de Médecine (1769–76) carried classical ideals beyond Soufflot's Panthéon and was related to advanced contemporary thinking.

GONTARD, KARL VON. German architect (1731–91). He worked in Bayreuth, Potsdam, and Berlin. At first connected with the theater, he turned to architecture through the influence of Carlo Bibiena. After studying with Jacques François Blondel and making an Italian trip, he assumed the title of chief engineer of Bayreuth, taught architecture and perspective at the local academy, and was connected with the court of Fredrick the Great of Prussia. He was the most accomplished and important architect of Bayreuth's prime. A masterly manipulator of form with a strong sense of painterly effects, Gontard founded his art on the baroque style, although later in life he inclined strongly toward classicism.

BIBLIOGRAPHY. P. Wallé, *Leben und Wirken Karl von Gontards*, Berlin, 1891.

GONTCHAROVA, NATALIE. Russian-French scenic designer, painter, and sculptor (b. near Moscow, 1881; d. Paris, 1962). Well known as a Russian artist before her association with the ballet, Gontcharova studied sculpture at the Academy of Fine Arts, Moscow, and later gave up sculpture for painting. In 1905, she created the scenery for *The Wedding of Zobeide* by Hofmannsthal, ignoring the then-accepted rules of perspective. Her costumes for the Moscow Kamerny Theater's production of Goldoni's *The Fan* (1913) did not indicate time or place but pleased the eye with their gay colors. In 1914, she came to Paris and designed the scenery for the Russian Ballet's *Coq d'Or*. Famous for her use of hot, bright colors and rich motifs based on Byzantine mosaics and icons, Gontcharova later rejected bright color for undistracting black, white, and gray costumes and scenery (*Les Noces*, Paris, 1923).

BIBLIOGRAPHY. W. George, "Gontcharova [and] Larionow." *Prisme des Arts*, no. 3, May, 1956.

GONZALEZ, BARTOLOME. Spanish painter (1564–1627). Born in Valladolid, he was named court painter in 1617 and was required to paint almost assembly-line por-

Julio González, *Seated Woman*. Bronze. Collection Roberta González, Paris.

traits of the royal family. He continued the style made popular by Sánchez Coello with a miniaturist detailing of the costumes, but what had produced admirable and original results for Sánchez Coello became onerous and stultifying for González's talents. Bowing to court taste, he took shortcuts in generalizing even the physiognomy of his sitters, as seen, for example, in *Princess Margarita* (1616; Nürnberg, Germanic Museum) and *Prince Ferdinand* (New York, French and Co.).

Something of his ennui can be comprehended from the fact that by 1621 he had been paid for ninety-one portraits of twenty-nine members of the royal house, even down to *Princess Margarita in Her Coffin* (1617; Madrid, Descalzas Reales).

For evidence that he was indeed an artist of stature, one must look at his conceptions of religious themes in such works as *St. John the Baptist* (1621, Budapest Museum). It is an early baroque statement of forceful realism and Caravaggesque *tenebroso*.

BIBLIOGRAPHY. E. Lafuente Ferrari, *Breve historia de la pintura española*, 4th ed., Madrid, 1953; G. Kubler and M. Soria, *Art and Architecture in Spain and Portugal and Their American Dominions, 1500–1800*, Baltimore, 1959.   EILEEN A. LORD

GONZALEZ, JOSE VICTORIANO, *see* GRIS, JUAN.

GONZALEZ, JUAN FRANCISCO. Chilean painter (b. Santiago, 1853; d. there, 1933). González was trained in Santiago. He traveled in Peru and Bolivia, in Europe, and in North Africa. His art is a personal impressionism, as in *Roses* (Santiago, National Museum of Fine Arts).

BIBLIOGRAPHY. A. R. Romera, *Historia de la pintura chilena*, Santiago, 1960.

GONZALEZ, JULIO. Spanish sculptor (b. Barcelona, 1876; d. Arceuil, near Paris, 1942). He learned metalwork from his father and first exhibited in 1893. He studied painting at the Barcelona Art Academy from 1892 to 1898. In 1900 he went to Paris and met Picasso. Except for sculpture made between 1910 and 1912, he worked as a painter until 1926, when he decided to devote himself to sculpture. Between 1930 and 1931 he instructed Picasso in metalwork and joined the constructivist Circle and Square group. His most imaginative constructs in iron date from the 1930s and strongly influenced metal sculptors such as the American David Smith. He worked more naturalistically in iron and plaster from the late 1930s until his death. The Museum of Modern Art, New York, owns *Standing Figure* (1932), *Head* (1934), and *Woman Combing Her Hair* (1936). González developed the idea of metal sculpture as drawing in space and of forming by free association. He gave an unprecedented range and power to sculpture in iron. (See illustration.)

BIBLIOGRAPHY. New York, Museum of Modern Art, *Julio González*, introd. by A. C. Ritchie, New York, 1956.

GONZALEZ CAMARENA, JORGE. Mexican painter (1908–   ). González Camarena was born in Guadalajara and was trained by Rivera and Dr. Atl. He represents the middle generation of the Mexican renaissance. An eclectic, he displays the influence of Rivera and Siqueiros on the one hand, and of pre-Columbian, colonial, and surrealist art on the other. Unlike the major frescoists, he owes as much to private as to public commissions. Since the late thirties his patrons have included manufacturers, bankers, brewers, and churchmen. Among his chief works, which sometimes combine sculptural with pictorial elements, are murals done in varying techniques, such as oil, lacquer, and mosaic. Representative works are those in the Guardiola (1941), Social Security (1950), and the Senate (1957) buildings of Mexico City.

BIBLIOGRAPHY. B. S. Myers, *Mexican Painting in Our Time*, New York, 1956.

GOODEN, STEPHEN. English engraver (1892–1944). He engraved on copper twelve full-page plates and numerous picture initials for Sir Robert L'Estrange's translation of *Aesop's Fables*. On the title page is a medallion portrait of the dwarfed Aesop, with a book and pen, surrounded by a border of interlocked beasts.

BIBLIOGRAPHY. H. F. G., "Aesop's Fables" [Book Review], *The Connoisseur*, XCIX, Apr., 1937.

GOOD GOVERNMENT. Fresco painting by Lorenzetti, in the Palazzo Pubblico, Siena. *See* LORENZETTI, AMBROGIO.

GOODHUE, BERTRAM GROSVENOR. American architect (b. Pomfret, Conn., 1869; d. 1924). Trained under James Renwick between 1884 and 1890, he joined the Boston firm of Cram and Wentworth, becoming a partner in 1899 under Cram, Goodhue, and Ferguson. While a partner, he was responsible for the interior of St. Thomas's Church in New York (1906), considered his finest ecclesiastical interior. Though an ardent Gothicist, after he left the firm in 1914 he helped initiate the Spanish colonial revival in California, particularly with his ornate designs for the San Diego Exposition of 1915. In his skyscraper Nebraska State Capitol (1922), he sought an American style, but in the buildings of this period an eclectic semi-modernism obtained, in which smoother wall surfaces appeared and Gothic detail was shaved clean. *See* CRAM, GOODHUE AND FERGUSON.

BIBLIOGRAPHY. C. H. Whitaker, ed., *Bertram Grosvenor Goodhue, Architect and Master of Many Arts*, New York, 1925.

GOODMAN, PERCIVAL. American architect (1904–   ). He was born in New York City. Noteworthy as a synagogue architect, Goodman designed Temple Beth El in Springfield, Mass. (1953), Temple Beth El in Providence, R.I. (1954), and Temple Beth Shalom in Miami Beach, Fla. (1955). Works by Motherwell, Lassaw, and Lipton decorate Goodman's structures.

BIBLIOGRAPHY. "Vigorous Art in the Temple," *Architectural Forum*, CX, May, 1959.

GOOD SHEPHERD, THE. Early Christian marble sculpture, in the Lateran Museums, Rome.

GOODWIN, FRANCIS. English architect (b. King's Lynn, Norfolk, 1784; d. 1835). Goodwin had a large practice in the industrial cities of the Midlands and northern England during the 1820s. Notable among his Greek revival works was the Manchester Town Hall (1822–25).

GOODWIN, PHILIP LIPPINCOTT. American architect (1885–1957). Born in New York City, he was educated at Yale University and the Columbia School of Architecture (1909–12). Goodwin also studied architecture in Paris (1912–14). After working for Delano and Aldrich (1914–16) and becoming a partner with Bullard and Woolsey, he formed his own office in 1921. He collaborated with Edward Durrell Stone on the design of the Museum of Modern Art in 1939, traveled to Brazil in 1942, and wrote *Brazil Builds* in 1943.

BIBLIOGRAPHY. New York, Museum of Modern Art, *Built in USA, 1932–1944*, ed. by E. Mock, New York, 1944.

GOOVAERTS, *see* GOVAERTS.

GOPURA. South Indian Hindu temple gateway, such as that at Madura. It is a pyramidal type of structure built up of richly sculptured tiers.

GORDION. Site in central western Turkey, approximately 70 miles southwest of Ankara. Gordion was excavated by the University Museum of the University of Pennsylvania, Philadelphia, under the leadership of Rodney S. Young. It is strategically located on one of the main ancient roads across Asia Minor and is on the Sangarios River. Gordion was inhabited continuously from the Early Bronze Age (3d millennium B.C.) to the 2d century B.C.

Shallow cist graves at Gordion are lined with stone and contain pottery offerings of the Early Bronze Age. Remains of the Hittite period (1750–1100 B.C.) include graves, in which the dead are buried in large pottery storage jars, and a few buildings. Evidently Gordion was a provincial town during this period.

The Phrygian empire is first heard of in Asia Minor late in the 2d millennium B.C. Gordion was the Phrygian capital. The extensive city of the early 1st millennium B.C. consisted of a citadel surrounded by a massive 14-foot-thick wall with rubble filling and with a gate approached by a ramp. An open paved area was ringed with brick, stone, and timber buildings with plastered walls. In one house there is a mosaic floor made of blue, white, and red pebbles arranged in a geometrical design. Acroteria (pedimental sculptures) suggest that the houses had gabled roofs.

The grave tumuli of the wealthy Phrygian royalty surround the site. They were wooden structures, for the most part set in pits in the ground and covered with stones. Mounds of earth and clay were heaped over the structures. In the largest, 170 feet high and almost 1,000 feet in diameter, a single male was buried, probably a Phrygian king. Entombed with him were vast quantities of wooden screens and tables, bronze caldrons with siren and bull-head attachments for handles, bowls, pitchers, and a large number of fibulae. A smaller tumulus, possibly that of a young prince, was also excavated, and produced more wooden furniture and bronzes as well as animal-shaped pottery vessels painted with geometrical designs.

After the sack of Gordion about 700 B.C. by the nomadic Cimmerians, the mound to the east was used for a brief time as a fortified garrison by the Lydians. Finally it in turn was destroyed by the Persians, who established themselves on the main site. Their city gate overlay the Phrygian gate, and houses with painted relief tiles occupied the area within the walls. A particularly notable building was filled with fragments of painted plaster with designs of human figures clearly in an Eastern Greek style.

Gordion. Excavations on the site of the ancient Phrygian capital, dating from the 1st millennium B.C.

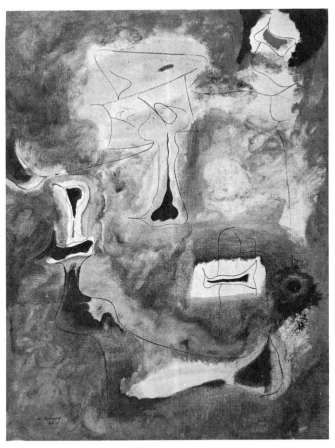

Arshile Gorky, *Charred Beloved II*, 1946. Museum of Modern Art, New York.

After the coming of Alexander the Great in 333 B.C., the site became a small village. In 250 B.C. the Gauls settled there, but by 189 B.C. the greater part of the site was abandoned.

BIBLIOGRAPHY. R. S. Young, "Gordion: Preliminary Report, 1953," *American Journal of Archaeology*, LIX, Jan., 1955; R. S. Young, "The Campaign of 1955 at Gordion: Preliminary Report," *American Journal of Archaeology*, LX, July, 1956; R. S. Young, "Gordion 1956: Preliminary Report," *American Journal of Archaeology*, LXI, Oct., 1957; R. S. Young, "The Gordion Campaign of 1957: Preliminary Report," *American Journal of Archaeology*, LXII, Apr., 1958; G. R. Edwards, "The Gordion Campaign of 1958: Preliminary Report," *American Journal of Archaeology*, LXIII, July, 1959; R. S. Young, "The Gordion Campaign of 1959: Preliminary Report," *American Journal of Archaeology*, LXIV, July, 1960; R. S. Young, "The 1961 Campaign at Gordion," *American Journal of Archaeology*, LXVI, Apr., 1962; R. S. Young, "The 1963 Campaign at Gordion," *American Journal of Archaeology*, LXVIII, July, 1964; R. S. Young, "The Gordion Campaign of 1965," *American Journal of Archaeology*, LXX, July, 1966.

PRUDENCE O. HARPER

GORE, SPENCER FREDERICK. English painter (b. Epsom, 1878; d. Richmond, 1914). He studied at the Slade School from 1896 to 1899. From 1904 to 1906 he was in Dieppe and Paris and met Sickert. He was a founder-member and first president of the Camden Town Group in 1911. Gore was influenced by impressionism through Lucien Pissarro, whom he met in London. Fundamentally, he was a restrained, sensitive painter of English landscape. After 1912 he attempted to assimilate Gauguin and Cézanne by simplifying his subject and arranging his color masses in a formalized way using broad drawing and sharper-edged shapes. The maturation of these experiments was prevented by his early death.

GORGO. In Greek mythology, female monster with wings, snaky locks, and a hideous face. Homer mentions only one Gorgo, but Hesiod names three Gorgones, Stheno, Euryale, and Medusa. They are frequently represented in art; one of the famous early examples is on the pediment of the Temple of Artemis at Corcyra, dating from about 600 B.C. *See* MEDUSA.

BIBLIOGRAPHY. C. Kerenyi, *The Gods of the Greeks*, New York, 1951.

GORIBAR, NICOLAS JAVIER DE. Spanish colonial painter in Ecuador (fl. ca. 1688–1736). A pupil of Miguel de Santiago, Nicolás Javier de Goríbar is best represented by an undated *Prophets* series in the Church of La Compañía and a *Kings of Judah* series in S. Domingo, both in his native city of Quito. *The Assumption*, in the Sanctuary of the Virgin of Guápulo near Quito, is a rare signed work.

BIBLIOGRAPHY. E. Marco Dorta, in D. Angulo Iñiguez, *Historia del arte hispanoamericano*, vol. 2, Barcelona, 1950.

GORIN, JEAN. French sculptor and painter (1899–   ). He studied at the Académie de la Grande Chaumière in Paris and at the Nantes School of Fine Arts. He was first a painter; his earliest sculptures date from the mid-1920s, when he was influenced by de Stijl. He has exhibited with the Cercle et Carré and the Salon des Réalités Nouvelles as well as at the Galerie Colette Allendy. He works especially with rod-formed, rectilinear cage sculptures interspersed and amplified by rectangular metal or plastic shapes. Gorin lives near Paris.

GORKY, ARSHILE. American painter (b. Tiflis, Russia, 1904; d. Sherman, Conn., 1948). A major American abstract artist, Gorky went to the United States in 1920, following two years' study at the Polytechnic Institute in Tiflis, and enrolled as an engineering student at Brown University, Providence, R.I. In 1925 he settled in New York, where he studied briefly at the National Academy of Design and taught at the Grand Central School (1926–32).

Influenced by neoclassicism in the late 1920s, Gorky found inspiration in Picasso's contemporary style during the 1930s, producing cubist still lifes with strong definition and bright colors. His first one-man show was at the Guild Art Gallery, New York, in 1932. During the late 1930s Gorky continued to work under the inspiration of cubism but added the formal devices of Miró. He shared a studio with Willem de Kooning in the early 1940s and the two men interchanged ideas; De Kooning has expressed a debt to Gorky, but the influence was certainly mutual. Another meaningful relationship was that with Stuart Davis, ten years Gorky's senior and an early practitioner of abstraction by way of cubism. It is also probable that Gorky was stimulated to a certain degree by Kandinsky's 1910–13 "biomorphic" abstractions.

These various sources were resolved in Gorky's style shortly after 1940, and by 1943 he was a major figure in

American abstract expressionist painting. His *Waterfall* (1943), with its fluid, organic shapes and rapid linear accents, is typical of his mature style. The highly personal fantasy of Gorky's imagery led André Breton to classify him as a surrealist, and his last works suggest the indirect influence of Matta's surrealist abstractions.

Among Gorky's finest, most inventive canvases of the 1943–47 phase are *The Liver Is the Cock's Comb, Diary of a Seducer, Making the Calendar*, and *Agony*. These paintings are remarkably tense and eloquent because of their whipping, cursive line and free spottings of delicate, fluidly handled color. Gorky was represented by one-man shows after 1945 at the Julien Levy Gallery, the Kootz Gallery (1950), the Whitney Museum of American Art (1951), the Martha Jackson Gallery (1954), and the Sidney Janis Gallery (1955). He can be classified as an abstract surrealist; however, because his work has elements of action painting and because of his influence on the abstract expressionist school, he can just as readily be considered an abstract expressionist.

BIBLIOGRAPHY. New York, Museum of Modern Art, *14 Americans*, ed. D. C. Miller, New York, 1946; E. DeKooning, "Gorky, Painter of His Own Legend," *Art News*, XLIX, 1951; M. Schapiro, "Gorky: The Creative Influence," *Art News*, LVI, 1957; E. Schwabacher, *Arshile Gorky*, New York, 1957; Sidney Janis Gallery, *Thirty-three Paintings by Arshile Gorky*, catalog, New York, 1957.

JOHN C. GALLOWAY

GOSHUN (Matsumura Gekkei). Japanese painter (1752–1811). Goshun studied *haiku* and painting with Buson, but later followed the realistic style of Okyo. His intimate portrayals of animals, fruit, and the landscape around Kyoto are extremely lyrical. His brushwork is less detailed than that of Okyo. He founded the Shijo school of painting. *See* OKYO; SHIJO SCHOOL.

BIBLIOGRAPHY. T. Akiyama, *Japanese Painting* [Geneva?], 1961.

GOSLAR. Historic center in southeastern Lower Saxony, West Germany. It was an imperial city (until 1802) and a member of the Hanseatic League. Founded in the 10th century to protect the rich silver mines in the neighborhood, Goslar attained its greatest prosperity during the Romanesque period. The Kaiserpfalz (imperial palace) was begun about 1050; it was the residence of eleven emperors and the seat of twenty-three imperial diets. Because of the restoration of 1867–70 the original aspect of the palace survives only in part. The Chapel of St. Ulrich has two stories, the lower of Greek-cross plan, the upper an octagon. The Reichssaal displays historical frescoes (1879–99) by Hans Wislicenus. The Kaiserpfalz is one of the rarest extant examples of a Romanesque palace complex.

The Neuwerkkirche is a Romanesque basilica of the 12th century; the interior has contemporaneous wall paintings and an episcopal throne of the 13th century. The Jacobikirche represents a 12th-century basilica "modernized" in the late Gothic manner in the 15th century. Of the once important Collegiate Church of SS. Simon and Jude there survives only the columned hall of the 12th century. The Frankenberg Church is another Romanesque basilica (dating from 1108) with Gothic additions.

Secular monuments include the 13th-century fountain in the marketplace, the Kaiserworth (seat of the tailors' guild, 1494), the Brusttuch (a house of 1526), the Rathaus (town hall; 15th–17th cent.), and remains of the old fortifications.

BIBLIOGRAPHY. P. J. Meier, *Die Stadt Goslar*, Stuttgart, 1926; K. Frölich, *Das Stadtbild von Goslar im Mittelalter*, Giessen, 1949; U. Hölscher, *Die Kaiserpfalz*, Göttingen, 1955; H. G. Griep, *Das Bürgerhaus in Goslar*, Tübingen, 1959.

WAYNE DYNES

GOSPELS, PURPLE. Manuscripts whose vellum leaves were dyed purple to signify the royal or imperial use for which they were intended. The custom, of Byzantine origin, was taken up by the West in the early Middle Ages; an example is the Godescalc Gospels (781; Paris, National Library).

GOSPELS, THE. The four books of the New Testament supposed to have been written by the evangelists Matthew, Mark, Luke, and John. The Gospels, which embody four parallel, yet slightly varying, accounts of the life of Christ, are the primary source for the essential doctrines of Christianity. Illuminated manuscripts of the Gospels have been done since the 5th century of our era in the following styles: Early Christian, East Christian, Byzantine, Ottonian, Carolingian, Hiberno-Saxon, Romanesque, Gothic, and Renaissance. To the extent that the Gospel book was regarded as a holy object in itself, it was often graced with precious covers made of ivory, gold, and gold studded with gems (for example, the Lindau Gospels, ca. 870; New York, Morgan Library).

GOSPELS OF ABBESS UTA. Romanesque illuminated manuscript, in the State Library, Munich.

Goslar. The Neuwerkkirche, 12th century.

Jan Gossaert, *Malvagna Triptych*. National Gallery of Sicily, Palermo.

GOSPELS OF CHARLEMAGNE (Schatzkammer Gospels). Carolingian illuminated manuscript, in the Treasury, Vienna.

GOSPELS OF HENRY II. Ottonian illuminated manuscript, in the State Library, Munich.

GOSPELS OF MOUNT ATHOS. Byzantine illuminated manuscript, in the Monastery of Mt. Athos (Stavroniketa 43).

GOSPELS OF OTTO III. Ottonian illuminated manuscript, in the State Library, Munich.

GOSPELS OF ST. CHAD. Hiberno-Saxon illuminated manuscript, in the Cathedral library, Lichfield, England.

GOSSAERT (Mabuse), JAN. Flemish painter (ca. 1478–1533). Born in Hainaut, Gossaert early attached himself to the court of Philip of Burgundy and accompanied that prince to Rome in 1508. Returning to the north in 1509, Gossaert does not seem to have settled in one place. He had been listed as a member of the Painters' Guild of St. Luke in Antwerp in 1507, but did not settle there after his return from Rome. Moving from one noble house to another, he appears to have set up shop in whichever city his patrons were located, including Utrecht, Bruges, Mechlin, Brussels, and Middelburg, all known residences of the Hapsburg-Burgundian rulers of the Lowlands.

His continuous traveling, and the great impression made on him by Italian art, makes it difficult to recognize specific, local characteristics in Gossaert's work. However, a number of signed, dated works eases the problem of following his development. The earliest dated work is a *Neptune and Amphitrite* (1516; Berlin, former State Museums), painted for Philip of Burgundy. The work is based on Dürer's engraving *Adam and Eve*, but it is replete with reminiscences of antique sculpture. Friedländer has suggested an earlier pen drawing, *Hermaphrodite* (Venice, Academy), dating from the Roman trip of 1508.

On the basis of undated works, it is possible to say that Gossaert achieved a mature style by 1516–17. Dated 1517 is a diptych depicting one of his patrons, *Jean Carondelet Adoring the Virgin and Child* (Paris, Louvre). Of the same date is *Hercules* (Birmingham, Barber Institute). These works show the technical facility for which Gossaert was famed. Among the remaining dated works are an engraving of 1522, another *Hercules* (1523; known through a copy), and the *Danae* (1527; Munich, Pinacothek).

Within this corpus of dated works it is possible, on stylistic grounds, to place other works. The earliest date, about 1512, can be assigned to the *Adoration of the Kings* (London, National Gallery) and to the *Malvagna Triptych* (Palermo Museum). Of the same time, or perhaps a little earlier, is the striking, moonlit *Agony in the Garden* (Berlin, former State Museums). Grouped with these major panels, or possibly as early as 1510, are a number of male portraits. Between these presumably early works and the *Neptune and Amphitrite* of 1516 is a *St. Luke Painting the Virgin* (ca. 1515; Prague, National Museum). Another version of the same subject (Vienna, Museum of Art History) should be about 1520, while an *Ecce Homo*, known through many copies, would be about 1527.

Gossaert's development shows an attempt to achieve a fully Italianate style. His works are filled with classical motifs and fully plastic, sculpturesque figures (preferably nude). However, he frequently shows limitations of imagination by working in the Renaissance mode second-hand —through copies of Dürer engravings. His style moves from the grandiose richness of Gothic baroque to relatively simple, forthright statements of the Renaissance, but always within the meticulous, jewel-like technical tradition of the Netherlands.

BIBLIOGRAPHY. M. J. Friedländer, *Die altniederländische Malerei*, vol. 8, Berlin, 1930.

STANLEY FERBER

GOTEBORG: ART GALLERY. Swedish collection. The principal attractions of this gallery are the *Man with a Falcon* by Rembrandt, *The Acrobat Family* (1905) by Picasso, and paintings by Cranach, Tintoretto, Zurbarán, Rubens, Matisse, and Munch. Of importance, too, are a large group of paintings by Swedish artists, including Ernst Josephson and Anders Zorn, and works by several modern French sculptors as well as by the Swedish neoclassic sculptor Johan Sergel.

GOTHIC ART. Gothic art arose during the middle of the 12th century in north-central France. The first Gothic buildings were cathedrals, and Gothic art for long remained primarily an ecclesiastical style. The Gothic style was created to solve certain technical demands arising from Romanesque building practice, but the discoveries prompted by these problems were so fruitful that they soon spread to the other visual arts. Sculpture and stained glass, which were closely associated with architecture in the Middle Ages, were the first to be affected. In the late 12th and the 13th century the Gothic style was successfully exported from France to England, Spain, Germany, and Italy and even as far afield as Sweden and the Holy Land. Gothic art then underwent a gradual transformation, which led to the emergence of the elegant International Style and an opposing trend toward realism. In the 16th century Gothic art finally yielded before the advancing Renaissance style.

ARCHITECTURE

It is generally agreed that the first appearance of Gothic architecture occurred in Abbot Suger's rebuilding of the abbey church of St-Denis near Paris (1137–43). Inspired by the glorification of light in the mystical writings of Dionysius the Areopagite, Suger created broad windows that he filled with rich stained glass. The introduction of larger glazed areas was facilitated by a recently invented technical device, the rib vault. In the following fifty years north-central France became a kind of laboratory for experimentation with the new way of building. The most important stages of this process are represented by the Cathedrals of Sens (begun ca. 1140), Noyon (begun ca. 1150), Laon (begun ca. 1160), and Paris (begun 1163). *See* LAON CATHEDRAL; NOTRE-DAME CATHEDRAL, PARIS; NOYON CATHEDRAL; SAINT-DENIS, ABBEY OF; SENS, SAINT-ETIENNE.

The end product of this development, the High Gothic cathedral, first appears at Chartres, where the Cathedral was rebuilt after the fire of 1194. The use of the rib vault, the pointed arch, and the flying buttress permitted reduction of solid wall to a mere skeleton or cage, the gaps being filled with stained glass. As a result the interior acquired an ethereal, otherworldly quality unparalleled in the history of art. Chartres Cathedral was followed by the Cathedrals of Bourges (begun before 1200), Reims (begun 1211), and Amiens (begun 1220). These are the classic cathedrals of France. *See* AMIENS: CATHEDRAL; BOURGES; CHARTRES CATHEDRAL; REIMS: CATHEDRAL.

The succeeding Rayonnant phase, which represents a thinning out of High Gothic structural achievements, made its appearance in the new nave of St-Denis (begun 1231). Here the walls were cut through by enormous clerestory windows with radiating tracery patterns. The Rayonnant Gothic reached its greatest refinement in the buildings erected for King Louis IX, notably his Parisian royal chapel (the Ste-Chapelle; early 1240s). The remainder of the 13th century saw a continuation of this process of purification. With such buildings as the abbey church of Ste-Trinité at Vendôme an extreme was reached that seems to signal a definite decline in the artistic powers of French architects. In any case the outbreak of the Hundred Years' War in 1339 prevented a resurgence of French Gothic architecture. It is ironic that while the Gothic was ebbing in the country of its birth it was triumphing in the rest of Europe. *See* RAYONNANT STYLE; SAINTE-CHAPELLE, PARIS.

As early as the middle of the 12th century the austere Cistercian order had produced a kind of stripped-down Gothic architecture, which found a ready reception in other countries, notably Italy and Germany. But English architects proved the aptest pupils of the French; with the rebuilding of Canterbury Cathedral (begun 1175) they were able to participate in the experimental stage of Gothic building, and in the following century they proved capable both of creating a distinctive variant of the High Gothic cathedral (Salisbury and Lincoln) and of competing with the latest French trends (Westminster Abbey). Then the short but brilliant efflorescence of the Decorated style (ca. 1290–1350) made English architecture the most creative in Europe. This style is characterized by the double curve and the ogee arch, star vaults, and profuse enrichments. Although these are the very qualities that were to be distinctive of the later German *Sondergotik* and the French Flamboyant style, the precise relationships have not yet been worked out by scholars. *See* CANTERBURY CATHEDRAL; DECORATED STYLE; FLAMBOYANT STYLE; LINCOLN CATHEDRAL; SALISBURY CATHEDRAL; WESTMINSTER ABBEY, LONDON.

Standing apart from these trends, the late Gothic architects of Languedoc and Spain specialized in broad interior spaces and contrasts between smooth and heavily decorated surfaces. The Cathedral of Albi (1282–1390) and the Cathedral of Barcelona (begun 1298) are examples of this approach. Under the patronage of the mendicant orders Italy developed an austerely beautiful late Gothic style (for example, Sta Croce in Florence and the Cathe-

Gothic Revival. Horace Walpole (with J. Chute), Villa at Strawberry Hill, Twickenham, interior (ca. 1755).

dral of Orvieto, both begun at the end of the 13th century), which in its simplicity and clarity was to prepare the way for Renaissance architecture. See ALBI, ST. CECILIA; SANTA CROCE, FLORENCE.

The Gothic style is also represented in secular building. Although fortifications and castles, because of their essentially defensive nature, proved recalcitrant to the verticality and attenuation of the Gothic style, it could be freely adopted in town halls such as those of Brunswick and Siena and in the residences of the wealthy, for example, the house of Jacques Coeur in Bourges. But Gothic architecture always remained primarily associated with the great cathedrals, which were usually the outstanding feature in a medieval town. See COEUR, JACQUES, HOUSE OF, BOURGES.

SCULPTURE

The evolution of early Gothic sculpture was closely tied to that of architecture. In this phase monumental sculpture was confined to the exterior portals of buildings, and a limited number of problems (most of them inherited from Romanesque art) were worked out in accordance with the structural principles affirmed in architecture. Although the original sculpture of the west front of Suger's St-Denis has largely disappeared, the elaborate iconographical program of the Royal Portal of Chartres Cathedral (mid-12th century) constitutes the true overture and at the same time perhaps the greatest masterpiece of early Gothic sculpture. The main elements appear in three areas, the jambs, tympanums, and voussoirs. The standing figures of the jambs, which are perhaps the most original feature, have a columnar repose that gives them a unique majesty. In the second half of the 12th century early Gothic sculp-

ture developed in various churches of northern France—Senlis, Lisieux, Rouen, Sens, Laon, and Mantes—but for the point of arrival of this early Gothic phase we must turn to the new work at Chartres. The carvings of the north and south transept façades (executed after 1194) show a more humanistic approach, but formally they represent something of a falling off from the clarity and authority of the earlier Royal Portal sculptures. See MANTES: COLLEGIAL OF NOTRE-DAME; ROUEN; SENLIS CATHEDRAL.

The High Gothic phase in sculpture begins with the new work on the west façade of Notre-Dame in Paris (begun ca. 1210). Although the main features are endowed with an almost forbidding severity and monumentality, such subordinate episodes as the hell scenes and the Labors of the Months show a remarkable freshness and sharpness of observation. Toward 1220 the main Parisian current shifted westward to Amiens. The west façade of Amiens Cathedral represented the most ambitious scheme yet attempted by Gothic sculptors, and its comprehensiveness has earned it the sobriquet "Bible of Amiens." The last of the great High Gothic cathedrals, Reims, displays the most freedom and variety. Here, in the famous *Annunciation* group, the Gothic sculptor made his closest approach to the classic art of Greece and Rome.

Although the great cycles of the Spanish Cathedrals of Burgos and León represent the most faithful adherence outside France to the High Gothic program of portal sculpture, French Gothic art never took root in the length and breadth of Spain, which remained attached to Romanesque traditions. More assiduous were the rank and file of German sculptors, but their reception of French prototypes was often only partial. The reliefs of the Naumburg Cathedral choir screen (2d half of 13th cent.) show an astonishing realism that foretells 15th-century trends. Italy followed its own path, which was more attuned to the example of antique sculpture. Occasionally, however, there was a closer approach, as in the impassioned expressiveness of Giovanni Pisano or in the courtly grace of Andrea Pisano, but this is largely a matter of parallel evolution rather than of borrowing. See ANDREA PISANO; GIOVANNI PISANO; NAUMBURG CATHEDRAL.

Late Gothic sculpture is dominated by the imposing creations of Claus Sluter, a Dutchman working in the service of the Burgundian court. His works are imbued with a powerful realism that found a ready reception in central Europe. This appears first in the expressiveness of Nikolaus Gerhard from Leyden and Bernt Notke, then in the sculptural altarpieces of Michael Pacher, Tilman Riemenschneider, and Veit Stoss. See GERHARD, NIKOLAUS, FROM LEYDEN; NOTKE, BERNT; PACHER, MICHAEL; RIEMENSCHNEIDER, TILMAN; SLUTER, CLAUS; STOSS, VEIT.

STAINED GLASS, PAINTING, AND MINOR ARTS

Of all the Gothic arts stained glass has suffered more than any other from vandalism and the passing of time. Stained glass was the Gothic art of color par excellence and formed the ideal complement to the architectural shaping of the interiors of Gothic buildings. Early Gothic windows surviving at St-Denis and Chartres already show the rich color gamut—deep blues, reds, and greens—that was to prevail in the later 13th-century work. The masterpiece of this 13th-century glass is the sixteen windows of Ste-

Chapelle in Paris, a building that seems to have been designed for just this triumph of the glass painter's art. In the 14th century a new fashion for monochrome grisaille windows ousted the richly colored style. Later techniques were more varied; the artists developed a new type of silver-stain work, and damascening and plating were introduced. The realistic perspectical windows of the late Middle Ages announce the decadence of the art. *See* STAINED GLASS.

As the great windows took up more and more of the wall surface in Gothic buildings, wall painting dwindled in significance. Important wall paintings are found mainly in Italy, but the painters there followed the lead of Giotto in minimizing the influence of Gothic art. In fact, the only field where Gothic painting in opaque colors can be followed from beginning to end is book illumination. Early masterpieces such as the Psalter of Queen Ingeburga were succeeded in the reign of Louis IX by a highly sophisticated style of International Gothic painting, which ultimately reached its culmination in the second quarter of the 14th century in manuscripts illuminated by Jean Pucelle and his school. At the end of the 14th century illumination became one of the principal means of spreading the International Style. The fantastic pages painted by the Limbourg brothers for their patron, Jean, duc de Berry, are the high point of this phase. In the middle of the 15th century Gothic illumination had a last blaze of glory in the work of Jean Fouquet, who had traveled in Italy and was able to integrate some features of the early Renaissance into his style. *See* FOUQUET, JEAN; INTERNATIONAL GOTHIC PAINTING; LIMBOURG BROTHERS; PUCELLE, JEAN.

Illuminations formed the essential background for the emergence of panel painting as a great art in 15th-century Flanders. The greatest realizations of this school were the many-leaved altarpieces, such as the *Ghent Altarpiece* by Hubert and Jan van Eyck. Rogier van der Weyden evolved a severe devotional mode in the middle of the 15th century; he was followed by Memling and Hugo van der Goes, whose work marks the end of Flemish Gothic painting. *See* GOES, HUGO VAN DER; MEMLING, HANS; VAN EYCK, HUBERT; VAN EYCK, JAN; WEYDEN, ROGIER VAN DER.

Gothic artists excelled in the minor arts, of which perhaps the most typical branches are enamel work and ivories. The development of such subtle techniques as the use of translucent enamel attests the virtuosity of Gothic metalworkers. The religious ivory carvings, conceived as an intimate substitute for large-scale sculpture, were supplemented by secular ivories illustrating the *chansons de geste. See also* FURNITURE (MIDDLE AGES: ROMANESQUE AND GOTHIC); IVORY.

BIBLIOGRAPHY. J. H. Harvey, *The Gothic World, 1100–1600*, London, 1950; E. Panofsky, *Early Netherlandish Painting*, 2 vols., Cambridge, Mass., 1953; O. G. von Simson, *The Gothic Cathedral*, New York, 1956; P. Frankl, *The Gothic, Literary Sources and Interpretations through Eight Centuries*, Princeton, N.J., 1960; J. Porcher, *French Miniatures from Illuminated Manuscripts*, London, 1960; P. Frankl, *Gothic Architecture*, Baltimore, 1962; H. Jantzen, *High Gothic*, New York, 1962; H. Focillon, *The Art of the West*, vol. 2: *Gothic Art*, London, 1963; W. Sauerländer, *Die Skulptur des Mittelalters*, Frankfurt am Main, 1963.

WAYNE DYNES

GOTHIC REVIVAL. Term referring to the revival of interest in Gothic decoration and architectural forms as part of a deliberate romanticism. It was begun by Horace Walpole in his pseudo-Gothic villa, Strawberry Hill (ca. 1755), and was repeated by many landowners in artificial Gothic "ruins" placed in their parks. Whereas these 18th-century Gothic revivals were mainly domestic buildings, those of the 19th century were primarily churches, built between 1830 and 1875, and also public buildings (town halls, hospitals, prisons, and railroad stations) as well as residences. Among the leading exponents of this style were Pugin in England, Viollet-le-Duc in France, and Cram and Goodhue in the United States. *See* CRAM, RALPH ADAMS; GOODHUE, BERTRAM GROSVENOR; PUGIN, AUGUSTUS WELBY NORTHMORE; STRAWBERRY HILL; VIOLLET-LE-DUC, EUGENE-EMANUEL.

GOTHIC SCRIPT. General term for a variety of lettered hands used from the end of the 12th century until the invention of printing. It is characterized by an extreme angularity that evolved into a script that was very regular in appearance, with few strokes ascending or descending beyond the mean level. The thickness of its letters contrasts with the lighter, more differentiated strokes of antique script. Gothic script was never used in documents.

BIBLIOGRAPHY. E. M. Thompson, *An Introduction to Greek and Latin Palaeography*, Oxford, 1912.

GOTHO-SARMATIAN STYLE, *see* VISIGOTHIC ART.

GOTTLIEB, ADOLPH. American painter (1903–   ). Born in New York, he studied at the Art Students League from 1919 to 1921 with Robert Henri and John Sloan and at the Parsons School of Design in 1923. Gottlieb's first one-man show was at the Dudensing Galleries, New York, in 1930. In 1947 and in the 1950s he had one-man shows at the Kootz Gallery. He has also been represented in many important annuals and international exhibitions, including the Whitney Museum of American Art's "The New Decade," 1955, and the Tokyo International of that year; the 1958 and the 1961 Carnegie International, in which he took a prize; the 1961 Whitney Museum Annual; and the 1963 São Paulo Bienal, at which he won a grand prize.

Gottlieb at first worked in an essentially naturalistic style. In the early 1940s he developed his pictographic semiabstract method with compartmented silhouettes and

Adolph Gottlieb, *The Frozen Sounds.* **Whitney Museum of American Art, New York.**

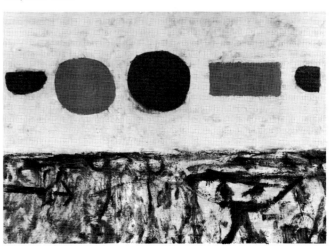

arcane symbols, combining flatly painted shapes and linear enclosures. His 1946 *Voyager's Return* (New York, Museum of Modern Art) is characteristic. Gottlieb changed in the early 1950s to a fully abstract-expressionist idiom (*The Frozen Sounds 1*, 1951; New York, Whitney Museum) and has recently become a leading action stylist (*Ascent*, 1958, and *Counterpoise*, 1959; both East Hampton, N.Y., Mrs. Adolph Gottlieb Collection).

BIBLIOGRAPHY. J. Fitzsimmons, "Adolph Gottlieb," *Everyday Art Quarterly*, no. 25, 1953; Whitney Museum of American Art, *The New Decade*..., New York, 1955; Walker Art Center, *Adolph Gottlieb* (catalog), text by M. Friedman, Minneapolis, 1963; R. Doty and D. Waldman, *Adolph Gottlieb*, New York, 1968.

JOHN C. GALLOWAY

GOUACHE. Method of painting with opaque water color. The pigments are mixed with white and a binding medium, such as gum arabic. When applied, the layers of colors are relatively thick. The colors become lighter when they dry, producing an opaque effect similar to that of pastels.

GOUBAU, ANTOON. Flemish painter of genre scenes and landscapes (b. Antwerp, 1616; d. 1698). From a stay of five years in Italy (1644–49) he returned with a wealth of Roman souvenirs, which he exploited throughout his life. His canvases recall the manner of Pieter van Laer, Johannes Lingelbach, and Karel Dujardin, with occasional reminiscences of David Teniers the Younger and Jacob Duck.

BIBLIOGRAPHY. W. Bernt, *Die niederländischen Maler des 17. Jahrhunderts*..., vol. 1, Munich, 1948.

GOUDA: MUNICIPAL MUSEUM. Dutch collection housed in the Catharina Gasthuis. The building was erected in 1665 and contains furniture, documents, the Chamber of Surgeon's Guild, and other exhibits related to the history of Gouda, as well as paintings by Rubens, Pourbus, Salomon van Ruysdael, Hobbema, and Bol, among others.

GOUDT, HENDRICK. Dutch draftsman and graphic artist (b. Utrecht, 1585; d. there, 1648). Count Hendrick Goudt was a gifted amateur artist. He probably studied with an unknown Utrecht artist. He spent some time in Rome and was an acquaintance of the German painter Adam Elsheimer. Goudt was back in Utrecht by 1611, the year after Elsheimer's death in Italy, and entered the Guild of St. Luke.

Goudt is responsible for the widespread knowledge of the works of Elsheimer in the Netherlands. He seems to have owned works by Elsheimer and made seven engravings, for example, *Tobias and the Angel* (1608), after Elsheimer. Through Goudt's engravings Elsheimer's use of landscape and nocturnes was taken up by such Dutch painters as Hercules Seghers, Willem Buijtenwegh, and Jan van de Velde. As a draftsman Goudt developed a drawing style that was completely dependent upon Elsheimer, and his drawings are often confused with those of Elsheimer.

BIBLIOGRAPHY. H. S. Reitlinger, "Hendrik, Count Goudt," *Print-Collectors Quarterly*, VIII, 1921; H. Weizsäcker, "Hendrick Goudt," *Oud-Holland*, XLV, 1928; J. Rosenberg, S. Slive, and E. H. ter Kuile, *Dutch Art and Architecture, 1600–1800*, Baltimore, 1966.

GOUJON, JEAN. French sculptor (b. near Rouen, ca. 1510; d. Bologna, 1564/68). In 1541 he built the Corinthian columns supporting the organ loft at the Church of St-Maclou in Rouen. He has also been credited with the

Jean Goujon, Nymphs of the Fontaine des Innocents. Louvre, Paris.

tomb of Louis de Brézé, husband of Diane de Poitiers, which was executed between 1531 and 1540 for the Cathedral of Rouen. His profound understanding of the classical orders has led to the assumption that his early training was in architecture rather than sculpture. Documents relating to the Château of Ecouen that refer to him as architect have been recovered by Du Colombier, although the château is usually credited to Bullant. A Victory in relief over the mantelpiece at Ecouen has traditionally been ascribed to Goujon.

In collaboration with the architect Pierre Lescot, in 1544 Goujon executed the rood screen in low relief for the Church of St-Germain-l'Auxerrois (Paris, Louvre), depicting a Pietà, with Evangelists on the side panels. Here are to be seen reminiscences of Parmigianino and Rosso, adapted to the sculptor's classicizing tendency and his feeling for surface pattern and texture.

In 1547 Goujon illustrated with woodcuts the French translation of Vitruvius by Martin. The same year, at the latest, he entered the service of the king. His sculptures for the exterior and the interior of the Louvre Pavilion of Henry II, which Lescot designed, were so completely restored in the 19th century that they no longer serve as reliable examples of his style; this includes the famous Gallery of the Caryatids. From 1547 to 1549 he also worked on the reliefs for the Fontaine des Innocents, most of which are now in the Louvre. The nymphs and sea gods, ingeniously designed to fill the long, narrow spaces assigned to them, display the hallmark of Goujon's style: elongated, elegant figures derived from Primaticcio's canon of proportions, incorporated into well-assimilated reminiscences of the late antique, executed with consummate personal authority. These works represent with distinction the classical moment at which French art arrived in the middle of the 16th century.

BIBLIOGRAPHY. P. Du Colombier, *Jean Goujon*, Paris, 1949.

MADLYN KAHR

GOVAERTS (Goovaerts), ABRAHAM. Flemish landscape painter (1589–1626). He was active in Antwerp. He was a pupil of Jan Breughel I, whose style he followed closely, sometimes imitating it to the point of causing confusion as to authorship. Govaerts also drew upon compositions by Gillis van Coninxloo for his woodland views. The artist excels by dint of his feeling for light and movement.

BIBLIOGRAPHY. Y. Thiery, *Le Paysage flamand au XVIIᵉ siècle*, Brussels, 1953.

GOVAERTS (Goovaerts), HENDRIK. Flemish painter of genre and historical scenes (b. Mechlin, 1669; d. Antwerp, 1720). He traveled extensively in Germany, Hungary, and Austria. His interiors, executed in a delicate color gamut and appealing to bourgeois taste, have been called northern parallels to those of Pietro Longhi.

BIBLIOGRAPHY. R. Oldenbourg, *Die flämische Malerei des 17. Jahrhunderts*, 2d ed., Berlin, 1922.

GOVARDHAN, *see* MUGHAL PAINTING OF INDIA (JAHANGIR PERIOD).

GOWING, LAWRENCE. English painter and writer (1918–). He was born in Store Newington. He has painted portraits but is best known for his volumetric still lifes derived from Cézanne. Gowing has also written perceptively on Vermeer, Turner, Cézanne, Renoir, and Constable, and is now Keeper of the British School of Painting at the Tate Gallery, London.

BIBLIOGRAPHY. L. Gowing, "Painter and Apple," *The Arts* (London), no. 1, 1946.

GOYA Y LUCIENTES, FRANCISCO JOSE. Spanish painter (b. Fuentetodos, 1746; d. Bordeaux, 1828). One of Spain's greatest painters, Goya rose out of the moribund traditions of the rococo in Spain to herald the 19th century. Little is known of his early training besides possible instruction by his father, a master gilder, and an apprenticeship with José Luzán. Most significant were his friendship with Francisco Bayeu, whose sister he married in 1773, his awareness of French artists in Spain (Louis-Michel van Loo), and, especially, his knowledge of Mengs and Tiepolo, both active in Madrid. Goya went to Italy (1770–71), where he may have studied fresco techniques and where he won a prize at Parma. Back in Spain (1771), in his first works he followed imported rococo and baroque formulas; the frescoes for the Pilar Cathedral in Saragossa and for the

Charterhouse of Aula Dei, his first commissions, hark back to Luca Giordano.

In 1774 Mengs commissioned him to execute tapestry cartoons for the Royal Factory of Santa Barbara (whose assistant director he was to become in 1785). Finished in 1791, these masterpieces of rococo decoration rank with his greatest achievements. The earliest, mostly hunting scenes, are still academic and close to Bayeu. But the series on *madrileño* daily activity (Madrid, Prado) established Goya's talent. With bright Tiepolo colors, they broke with the current Teniers-Wouwermans tradition to show completely indigenous subjects. As exemplified in one of these, *The Crockery Vendor*, the mixture of gaiety and gravity, realism of detail, and strong human characterization personalize these basically 18th-century works.

By 1778 Goya was famous. A member of the Academy of San Fernando (1780) and court painter (1789), he became the darling of Madrid society, which he immortalized in portraiture throughout his career. The 1780s marked the initiation of this gallery of portraits, with the depiction of the Count of Floridablanca (1783; Madrid, Urquijo Bank). It is still academic, as is the altarpiece in S. Francisco el Grande, Madrid, of 1784 (influenced by Houasse). Then Goya's art began to show the influence of Velázquez, whose canvases in the Royal Collection he had been commissioned to etch in 1778. The brilliant *Duke of Osuna* (1785; New York, Frick Collection), with its luminous silvery atmosphere, its harmonies in gray touched with pure bright color, typifies the period. Goya proved himself almost unparalleled in rendering drapery. His depth of observation and fluid brushstroke gave a presence and dashing quality to his portraits.

The famous *Fiesta of S. Isidro* (1787; Prado) has been

Francisco José Goya y Lucientes, *What will He Die of?*, aquatint. Number 40 of the *Caprichos*, 1793–1799. British Museum, London.

called a masterpiece of 18th-century *peinture claire*. However, a dramatic change ensued with the darker works that followed Goya's illness in 1792. Left stone-deaf, Goya became extremely analytical and critical; he developed an urgent style marked by a bold, nervous brush and a palette of grays, blacks, and browns, sharply accented by reds, yellows, and blues. His unleashed imagination produced new personal themes. Described by Goya himself as "fancy and invention," the 1793 series of panels, among which are *Madhouse* and *Inquisition* (Madrid, San Fernando Academy), introduced the romantic character of Goya. This expressiveness was continued in the decoration of S. Antonio de la Florida, commissioned in 1798 through court contacts, which Goya was never to dissolve despite his independent character and his political leanings. The painting is boldly executed, as if dashed off in a day. Reinforcing this spontaneous quality is a thorough study of perspective and trompe l'oeil, which creates a wholly pictorial work in the grand manner of Veronese and Tiepolo but one devoid of academic rhetoric. Representing episodes in the life of St. Anthony of Padua, with figures in contemporary dress, this work remains one of his best.

In the same year Goya published *Los caprichos*, a series of etchings that turned his heretofore gay genre scenes into social mockeries. Banned in Spain because of their anticlerical sentiment, they did more to establish Goya's fame outside Spain than did his paintings and influenced such artists as Daumier (see Goya as Graphic Artist below).

The same incisive character can be found in *The Family of Charles IV* (1800; Prado). Its colorful, shimmering virtuosity may have kept the royal family from noticing Goya's keen penetration of their hollow and vain natures. Although inspired by Velázquez's *Las Meninas*, it has an analytical and satirical quality that separates it from the world of Velázquez. In *The Countess of Chinchón* (1800; Madrid, Duchesses of Sueca Collection) Goya laid aside satirical comment to present one of his most sensitive portraits. A symphony of grays and whites, it too recalls Velázquez, especially in its background. Other important portraits painted at this time are the two standing depictions of the *Duchess of Alba* (1797; Madrid, Alba Collection; New York, Hispanic Society) and the two famous *Majas*, done before 1808 (Prado), celebrated as much for the liaison of the artist with this *grande dame* of Spanish society as for their sensuous pictorial qualities. The portrait of Goya's son Xavier, *The Man in Gray* (1805; Paris, Noailles Collection), is an elegant work in the English tradition.

The period from 1792 to 1808 was the pinnacle of Goya's popularity and success. He was elected president of the Royal Academy in 1795 and was named First Painter to the King in 1799. His work was diversified but remained fixed primarily on the observable world, and while its tone was analytical, it was never bitter. After 1808, with the disillusionment of the Napoleonic domination, Goya's art grew steadily introspective and introverted, despite continuing official patronage. As a liberal, he had welcomed Joseph Bonaparte, but the ensuing savagery and corruption repelled him, as did the situation that followed the French withdrawal. With Spanish royalty again ruling in 1814, repression against the liberals became steadily graver, and Goya went into voluntary exile in France in 1824. He has left one of the most vivid chronicles of the horrors of war, both physical and mental, in a series of etchings, *Los desastres de la guerra* (*The Disasters of War*; 1808–14), and in *Los proverbios* (1813–18). Lashing out against hypocrisy and man's inhumanity, they employ eyewitness accounts in the earlier etchings and subjective outbursts, or "dream proverbs," in the later works, made more potent and universal by cryptic captions such as *La vida es sueño* (*Life is a dream*).

These depictions find their counterparts in the historical canvases *The Charge of the Mamelukes* and *Executions on May Third* (1814; Prado), which preface future protests by Géricault, Delacroix, Manet, and Picasso; and in the 1820 "black frescoes" of La Quinta del Sordo, Goya's country retreat. Once more involved with nightmarish monsters, these frescoes translated the dark mood of the *Proverbs* into a painted chiaroscuro slashed out in rapid expressionistic strokes, most modern in feeling, as in *Saturn Devouring His Son* (Prado). The technique of building up from an almost completely dark ground produced a satanic quality distinguishable in other works, namely, the dynamic portrait of Tiburcio Pérez (1820; New York, Metropolitan Museum). The brooding atmosphere in the portrayal of the actor Maiquez (1807; Prado) is echoed in many paintings by Delacroix. In the equestrian portrait of Ferdinand VII (1808) and of the Duke of Wellington (1812) Goya's style remained within the more rigid confines of official portraiture, though enhanced by his freer brushstroke. At the same time came a growth in his religiosity. *The Last Communion of St. Joseph of Calasanz* (1819; Madrid, Escuela Pias) shares in the intense spirituality of this final period.

After 1824 Goya settled in Bordeaux, making occasional brief trips to Madrid to execute portraits. His work in France softened a bit in its treatment of contemporary genre. *The Milkmaid of Bordeaux* (1827; Prado) is surprising for its light, tender tones and has been called a presentiment of impressionism. The five lithographs of *The Bulls of Bordeaux* (1825) nostalgically continue the theme of the 1815 *Tauromachia* etchings, and these works were influential in technique and composition during the 19th century (Daumier and Manet). Goya's last portrait was that of Don José Pio de Molina (1827; Winterthur, Reinhart Foundation).

Goya's importance and genius lie in the transition to a modern idiom. At the beginning of his career he soon enriched the usual French and Italian 18th-century subjects with a luminous style based on Velázquez. Then personal and political crises joined to release an outpouring of poignant and impassioned subjects conceived in a loosened neobaroque style that prefigured Delacroix and envisioned Manet. Goya's previous light genre and conventional portraiture became acutely observed drama and penetrating character analysis. Though he was trained solely in courtly art, his eye turned ever inward to record haunting fantasies and personal reflections, making him one of the truly "subjective" painters. The artist exposed his period and the depths of his soul equally well. Strong and Spanish and complex, Goya could be at once poet and terrorist, visionary, satirist, and unflinching chronicler. Excelling in deco-

Francisco José Goya y Lucientes, *Funeral of the Sardine*. Academy of S. Fernando, Madrid.

ration, portraiture, and graphics, his art, along with that of Velázquez, made Spain one of the dominant influences on 19th-century France, especially in the Romantic sentiment and the expressionistic paint and graphic technique of his later works.

BIBLIOGRAPHY. X. D. Fitz-Gerald, *L'Oeuvre peint de Goya*, 4 vols., Paris, 1928–50; P. Gassier, *Goya, a Biographical and Critical Study*, New York, 1955; A. Malraux, *Saturn, an Essay on Goya*, New York, 1957; F. J. Sánchez Cantón, *Goya*, New York, 1964.

PHILIPPE DE MONTEBELLO

GOYA AS GRAPHIC ARTIST

Goya's highly original and technically refined etchings, aquatints, and lithographs span his entire creative career and always seem to reflect his most deeply felt passions and sensibilities. Some of these works were so private and politically dangerous that they were published only posthumously.

Goya's first experiments with etching are traditionally dated 1770, four years before his earliest-dated oil portrait. Only a few of these first plates escaped Goya's own destruction. One of them, *Flight into Egypt*, shows the influence of the 17th-century Spanish engraver J. G. Hidalgo. From 1770 until just before his death Goya experimented with etching and lithography and produced single pages, in addition to his great series, which reveal his progressive mastery of the techniques. His various series constitute landmarks both of Goya's artistic and intellectual development and of graphics as a fine-arts medium.

His first great series, *Los caprichos*, was done between 1796 and 1798. All but one of the eighty etchings used an aquatint background. Most are based on drawings from Goya's *Madrid Sketchbook* or *Large Sanlúcar Sketchbook* (1795–96) and show a side of his perception seen only in a few paintings that date after his illness of 1792. The range of subject matter is the widest of any of his series: scenes of bullfighting, of a madhouse, and of dreams and pictures of pure caprice. Almost all are reflections of the influences at work on Goya's intellectually attuned awareness. The earlier plates are rococo creations. The later ones are far more serious both in questioning and in style. Themes from Molière and Juvellanos are side by side with plates that show a knowledge of 18th-century occultism and the works of Blake and Fuseli.

After 1805, with military upheavals and the subsequent Napoleonic invasions, Goya used drawings and other graphic media almost exclusively for his most urgent expressions. Between 1808 and 1823 Spain was an arena of suppression and chaos. Goya protested fiercely but privately in the etching series *Los desastres de la guerra* (*The Disasters of War*), made in 1808–09 and 1814 and published long after his death in 1863. In eighty-two plates Goya shows the effects of war with unprecedented realism and ferocity and in an increasingly perfected etching technique.

In the years before his departure for Bordeaux he made two other great series. In 1815–16 he etched the forty-four plates of scenes of bullfighting, the *Tauromachia*, eleven of which appeared after the original thirty-three. His last etching series, *Los proverbios* (or "Follies," as Goya called them), was done in stages between 1813–1815 and 1817–1818. There are twenty-two known plates, although only eighteen were in the original publication of 1864. *Los proverbios*, which are aquatints, are technically Goya's best and at the same time uniformly monstrous in subject matter and mood.

At Bordeaux he worked consistently on single plates and continued the experiments with lithography he had begun in Madrid in 1819. His last series, five lithographs called *The Bulls of Bordeaux* (1825), prefigured the French Romantics. Goya's graphic output, which formed one of the most interesting parts of his total *oeuvre*, was either unpublished or little known until it was "discovered" by French Romantic artists like Delacroix. To them he appeared as a bold and uncompromising patron of their artistic ambitions. Even among today's artists this enthusiasm has hardly diminished.

BIBLIOGRAPHY. L. Delteil, *Le Peintre-graveur illustré*, vols. 14–15, Paris, 1922; P. Vindel, *Los Caprichos . . .*, Madrid, 1928.

JULIA M. EHRESMANN

GOYEN, JAN JOSEPHSZ. VAN, see GOIJEN, JAN JOSEPHSZ. VAN.

GOZLUKULE, see TARSUS.

GOZZOLI, BENOZZO. Italian painter (b. Florence, ca. 1420; d. Pistoia, 1497). Gozzoli is known primarily as a student of Fra Angelico and as the artist responsible for the frescoes decorating the chapel in the Medici-Riccardi Palace, Florence.

The early training of Benozzo di Lese di Sandro, as he is named in the documents, is not known, although he was listed as a painter in a contract of 1444 with Lorenzo and Vittorio Ghiberti. When Gozzoli accompanied Fra Angelico to Rome and Orvieto in 1447, he had probably been a member of the shop for some time. After the death of Fra Angelico, Gozzoli went to Montefalco, where he had begun a series of frescoes in 1450, one depicting scenes from the life of St. Jerome and another illustrating twelve scenes from the life of St. Francis. Between 1453 and 1456 he executed a series of frescoes in S. Rosa, Viterbo, now lost, and a signed and dated (1454) altarpiece now in Perugia. In 1459 he was engaged on the decoration of the Medici-Riccardi Palace in Florence. At San Gimignano he executed a series of frescoes depicting the life of St. Augustine (1463) for S. Agostino and a *St. Sebastian* (1465–66) for the Collegiata. In August, 1467, he was documented in Pisa, where he undertook a series of frescoes in the Camposanto depicting scenes from the Old Testament. These frescoes (destroyed in 1944) were completed in 1484. Gozzoli spent the remaining years of his life in and around Pisa, painting banners, panels, and church furniture.

His earliest dated work is an *Assumption of the Virgin* (1450; Rome, Vatican Museums). The altarpiece and its predella show clearly the influence of Fra Angelico as do the frescoes in Montefalco. It is only with Gozzoli's arrival in Florence that there is evidence of a personal style. His fresco of the *Procession of the Magi* (1459–61) in the private chapel of the Medici family in the Medici-Riccardi Palace recalls Gentile da Fabriano's painting of the same subject created more than thirty years earlier, and it possesses the decorative character of contemporary tapestries; but it is nonetheless quite personal and unique in its expression. The primary intention of the work was to depict an animated and courtly procession of the kings and

Benozzo Gozzoli, *Procession of the Magi*, fresco. Medici-Riccardi Palace, Florence.

their retinue moving toward the *Madonna Adoring the Child* by Fra Filippo Lippi, which had originally stood on the altar.

The *Madonna and Saints* (1461; London, National Gallery) clearly shows the association between Fra Angelico and Gozzoli; the contract stipulated that Gozzoli's model was to be Fra Angelico's altarpiece for S. Marco.

Of the later works only the St. Augustine frescoes in San Gimignano present any clear relationship to Florentine art, although they represent a style that had fallen behind the main stream. The variety of life represented and the fantastic architecture in the Pisa frescoes recall the International Style, and yet there is the same interest in genre detail that prevails throughout Gozzoli's career.

BIBLIOGRAPHY. R. van Marle, *The Development of the Italian School of Painting*, vol. 11, The Hague, 1929.

JOHN R. SPENCER

GRAAT, BARENT. Dutch landscape, history, and portrait painter and draftsman (b. Amsterdam, 1628; d. there, 1709). He was the pupil of his uncle Hans Bodt, a little-known animal painter. Graat's earliest works are land-scapes with animals. Later he painted historical subjects, somewhat under the influence of Guido Reni. In Amsterdam Graat founded an academy of drawing that was attended by many important artists.

BIBLIOGRAPHY. W. Bernt, *Die niederländischen Maler des 17. Jahrhunderts...*, vol. 1, Munich, 1948.

GRACANICA, MONASTERY OF. Medieval monastery in Yugoslavia. Founded by King Milutin in 1321, Gra-čanica is a representative monument of Serbian medieval art. The interior of the church displays noteworthy 14th-century religious frescoes in a style derived from Byzantium. Other frescoes depict members of the Serbian royal house. *See* SERBIAN PAINTING.

BIBLIOGRAPHY. R. H. L. Hamann-Maclean and H. Hallensleben, *Die Monumentalmalerei in Serbien und Makedonien vom 11. bis zum frühen 14. Jahrhundert*, text and plates, Giessen, 1963.

GRACES, THE. Three young and lovely goddesses, named Euphrosyne, Aglaia, and Thalia. They personify everything graceful and enjoyable, such as the pleasures of the banquet. In Greek myths they act as attendants upon Aphrodite, whom they help to robe; Apollo, when he sings with the Muses; and Dionysus, when they dance with the nymphs. In art they are portrayed as maidens who stand in a circle with their arms entwined. They are also known as Charites.

GRADO CATHEDRAL. Italian basilica in the Byzantine-Ravennate style. Its foundation goes back to the 5th century. Several times rebuilt and restored, the Cathedral contains fragments of ancient Roman structures, of 6th-century mosaics, and of later medieval works.

BIBLIOGRAPHY. G. Brusin, *Aquileia e Grado*, 4th ed., Padua, 1956.

GRADUAL. Music sung between the Epistle and the Gospel during the Mass. Gradual is also the book from which this music is sung, varying in accordance with the time in the church year, as well as all other Gregorian chants for the Mass. It contains both the choir's parts (*Concentus*) and the priest's parts (*Accentus*). Graduals were lavishly illuminated in the medieval period.

GRAF, OSKAR. Germain painter and graphic artist (b. Freiburg im Breisgau, 1873; d. Bad Boll, 1957). He studied painting with Knirr, Schmid-Reutte, and Hölzel in Munich and with Cormon in Paris, but was self-taught as an etcher. His weightily realistic works in both media make use of the large forms and sweeping lines of landscape and architectural settings.

GRAF, URS. Swiss woodcut designer, etcher, engraver, goldsmith, and glass painter (b. Solothurn, ca. 1485; d. Basel? 1527/28). He learned goldsmithing under his father, but received his broad artistic training in Basel. In 1503 he was in Strasbourg where he made his earliest book illustrations, twenty-five designs for woodcuts for *Passio domini nostri Jesu Christi*... (1st ed., 1506) published by Johann Knoblouch. Thereafter he made numerous woodcut designs for book illustrations and title borders for books, issued mostly in Basel but also in Paris, including *Decretales diu pape Gregorii* (1511) published by Thielmann Kerver and Johannes Cabiller and *Decretum Gratiani*... (1510) published by François Fradin. In the period from 1505 to 1515 Graf was influenced by Dürer's woodcut illustrations of the early 1490s for the *Ritter vom Turn*... and *Das Narrenshyff*. These had particular bearing on Graf's *Passio*. In 1509 Graf was working in Basel as a goldsmith; in 1510 he drew the title page for the register of the Solothurn guild of goldsmiths. In 1511 he began to learn glass painting. He joined the Basel guild of goldsmiths in 1512.

His style of drawing is crisp and energetic. Numerous drawings by him are extant, nearly all signed and dated, and are in Basel for the most part. Until 1511 he added to his monogram a goldsmith's borax box. In 1512 Graf's draftsmanship reached its full maturity, and the goldsmith's emblem disappeared. In some drawings of 1513–16, he (like many other German and Italian artists) assumed Dürer's monogram tablet. From 1518 he added a Swiss dagger to his initials.

Graf made three etchings, two of them dated 1513. These are the earliest dated etchings extant. Among his most notable achievements are a set of sixteen white-line woodcuts representing the banner carriers of the Swiss cantons. (Lines are cut into a plank of wood much as an

Urs Graf, drawing of a young woman. Public Art Collections, Basel.

engraver with a burin cuts into the surface of a metal plate. The surface of the wood is inked, care being taken that no ink gets into the lines.)

Graf's engravings are ornamental, destined as inspiration to jewelers and armorers. Several of these are said to be in the niello style; that is, they have a preponderance of black areas. Graf was an intense and vivid artist. His work can be cheerful and hearty or fraught with death and demons.

BIBLIOGRAPHY. W. Lüthi, *Urs Graf und die Kunst der alten Schweizer*, Zurich, 1928; E. Major and E. Gradmann, *Urs Graf*, London, 1947.

CAROLINE KARPINSKI

GRAFF, ANTON. Swiss-German painter (b. Winterthur, 1736; d. Dresden, 1813). After studies in Zurich, Augsburg, and Ansbach, Graff moved to Dresden, where he was made court painter (1765) and a professor at the Academy (1766). He became the foremost portrait painter of central and northern Germany and was influenced at first by the elegant English style, particularly that of Gainsborough. A more commanding sense of physical and psychological presence emerges in later portraits of intellectuals and members of the rising middle class, which break with the rococo style.

GRAFFIONE (Giovanni di Michele Scheggini da Larciano). Italian religious painter (b. Florence, 1455; d. there, 1527). He studied in the workshop of Zuccherini and

Francesco Granacci, *Madonna in Glory with Saints*. Academy, Florence.

later became a co-worker and possibly a student of Baldovinetti. His works routinely follow the styles of Filippino Lippi and Pesellino.

GRAFFITO, *see* SGRAFFITO.

GRAFLY, CHARLES. American sculptor (b. Philadelphia, 1862; d. 1929). He began work as a stone carver at the age of seventeen and during the following five years produced numerous marble figures. He attended night classes in art at the Spring Garden Institute and in 1884 entered the Pennsylvania Academy, where he studied with Thomas Eakins. In 1888 Grafly went to Paris, studying first at the Académie Julian and later at the Ecole des Beaux-Arts. He began teaching sculpture at the Drexel Institute and at the Pennsylvania Academy in 1891.

Grafly's sculpture is largely derivative of 19th-century romantic classicism and tends toward naturalistic effects. A thorough understanding of anatomy and the craft of sculpture sometimes enabled him to achieve a forceful and meaningful plastic expression. Typical of his work is the Meade Memorial, Washington, D.C.

BIBLIOGRAPHY. L. Taft, *The History of American Sculpture*, rev. ed., New York, 1930.

GRAMMATICA, ANTIVEDUTO. Italian painter (b. Siena, 1571; d. Rome, 1626). He was a minor but fairly prominent follower of Giandomenico Angelini in Rome,

where he created altarpieces for several churches; his mature style is Caravaggesque. He later became *principe* of the Academy of St. Luke and is known principally for the incident that led to his dismissal from that post—his attempt to replace a Raphael painting of St. Luke, hanging at the Academy, with a copy of his own making.

GRANACCI, FRANCESCO. Italian painter (b. Florence, 1477; d. there, 1543). He was trained in Domenico Ghirlandajo's workshop and studied in Lorenzo de' Medici's Giardino di S. Marco. Departing from the late-15th-century tradition, Granacci gradually adopted more compact and energetic contours, perhaps under the influence of Michelangelo, who was his friend. In 1508 he was sent to Rome to assist Michelangelo in painting the Sistine ceiling, but was dismissed with the other helpers. In Florence once more, Granacci leaned toward Fra Bartolommeo's version of Leonardo's style, while retaining under his Bartolommesque shadows the higher tonalities characteristic of the 15th century (*Madonna della Cintola*, 1508; Florence, Academy); and, though not quite grasping the full High Renaissance style, he moved toward a broader silhouette and more easily unfolding forms, no longer using an ornamental line or observing details for their own sake (*Madonna in Glory with Four Saints* and *Madonna with SS. Zenobius and Francis*, both 1514–16; Florence, Academy).

Granacci's art of about 1517–18 seems to reflect the work of the young mannerists, with whom he was employed in doing scenes from the life of Joseph (now Florence, Uffizi) for a room for Pier Francesco Borgherini. These, and also his predella panels done for the high altar in the Convent of S. Apollonia (1516–17; six panels now in the Academy, two in the Berenson Collection), show elongated figures without structural solidity moving in isolated rhythms across the dreamlike space of the panels. Granacci here reflects the current Florentine tendency to a more emotive, personal art in small works, returning to a more monumental style for large altars.

Like Bugiardini, Franciabigio, and Ridolfo Ghirlandajo, Granacci was a transitional master. His work, spanning the years of the great High Renaissance masters, prolongs the late-15th-century stylistic mannerisms and the observation of details under an adequate adaptation of High Renaissance forms. His late altarpieces repeat this solution with less and less conviction; Granacci claims a considerable place, however, owing to the agreeable dignity and sobriety of his work.

BIBLIOGRAPHY. G. Vasari, *Le Vite...*, ed. G. Milanesi, vol. 5, Florence, 1880; A. Venturi, *Storia dell'arte italiana*, vol. 9, pt. 1, Milan, 1925; S. J. Freedberg, *Painting of the High Renaissance in Rome and Florence*, 2 vols., Cambridge, Mass., 1961.

ALTHEA BRADBURY

GRANADA. Spanish city on the Darro River at the foot of the Sierra Nevada in Andalusia; capital of the province of Granada and the seat of an archbishop. The history of the town goes back to the 5th century B.C., when it was known as Elibyrge. Under the Romans it became Iliberis. The present name derives from Garnata, the name of a village on one of the hills within the town.

Granada began to prosper in the 11th century, after the fall of Cordova and the founding of the Zirite dynasty by Zari Ben Ziri, viceroy of Granada. After the liberation of

Cordova in 1236 Granada became the capital of the last Muslim kingdom on Iberian soil. During the following 250 years it resisted all attempts at capture and enjoyed a matchless cultural flowering, culminating in the building and decoration of the Alhambra Palace in the 14th century. *See* ALHAMBRA.

Liberated by the Catholic kings in 1492, Granada became a center of Renaissance culture and royal patronage. Its most impressive Christian monument is Diego de Siloe's Cathedral (1528–43), the most majestic Plateresque building in Spain. It retains the Gothic emphasis on verticality and the emotive use of light from stained-glass windows with the upper reaches of the vaults lost in obscurity. The ornamental ribbing of the vaults and the inventive attitude toward classical vocabulary are Mudejar. These classical elements are Italianate Renaissance, as are the robust masses and the employment of pure geometric shapes, notably in the rotunda. *See* SILOE, DIEGO DE.

The burial church of the Catholic kings (Royal Chapel), built in 1506–07 in the first Plateresque style by Enriques Egas, is annexed to the south aisle of the Cathedral. Two other Renaissance churches—S. Ana (1537–63) and S. Jeronimo (1496–1547)—are associated with Diego de Siloe. The Hospital of S. Juan de Dios (begun 1552; portal 1609) is a vast Renaissance block containing a basilican church with a rich baroque façade decorated with statues and reliefs (1738–59). The most brilliant baroque work in Granada is the sacristy of the Charterhouse (Cartuja) by Luis de Arevalo and Fray J. M. Vázquez (1727–64) from the design of Francisco Hurtado of Cordova. *See* GRANADA: MUSEUM OF THE ROYAL CHAPEL.

On the site of the ancient Iliberis and within the remains of an Arab wall is the Alcazaba Cadima quarter with several churches of the early 16th century. The Albaicín quarter outside the town and enclosed by another Arab wall contains narrow streets and white-washed houses typical of many old sections of Andalusian towns.

BIBLIOGRAPHY. K. E. Schmidt, *Cordoba und Granada*, Leipzig, 1902.

HELLMUT WOHL

GRANADA: MUSEUM OF THE ROYAL CHAPEL.
Spanish collection. The Royal Chapel was built by Charles V as a mausoleum and is dominated by Domenico Fancelli's marble tomb of Ferdinand and Isabella. Among the objects exhibited in the sacristy is a remarkable group of early Netherlandish paintings, by Memling, Bouts, and Rogier van der Weyden.

BIBLIOGRAPHY. A. Gallego y Burín, *La Capilla Real de Granada*, Madrid, 1952; R. van Schoute, *La Chapelle Royale de Granade*, Brussels, 1963.

GRANATA, ANGELO JOHN. American sculptor (1922–   ). He studied at Iowa State University and taught at the University of Alabama after 1949. Granata has exhibited widely in the Southeast and his work was seen in the 1959 show, "Recent Sculpture U.S.A.," of the Museum of Modern Art in New York. *Arch Form* (1959), an abstract work in cast iron, is characteristic of his more recent works.

BIBLIOGRAPHY. New York, Museum of Modern Art, *Recent Sculpture U.S.A.*, New York, 1959.

GRANDE CHARTREUSE, LA. Parent house of the Carthusian monastic order, founded near Grenoble in 1084

La Grande Chartreuse. Panoramic view.

by St. Bruno. By the end of the 15th century the hermit-like order included 206 monasteries, whose names—Certosa, Charterhouse—derived from the Chartreuse region of France, where the original house was located. This monastery, covering 12 acres, is famed for its extensive size. The Great Cloister, which preserves some fragmentary portions of 13th-century architectural ornament (1145–1235) in its upper parts, is crossed by two transverse galleries (1326), which enclose the cemetery between them. Individual dwelling units for thirty-six monks border the cloister, each providing facilities for prayer, study, and manual labor, as well as a small garden. The monks meet for services in a 15th-century church.

The monastery has burned and been reconstructed eight times, so that very little remains of its older buildings, with the exception of the Chapel of St. John the Baptist (founded 1132), the Refectory (14th–15th cent.), and the Clock Tower (1371). The Chapel of St. Louis has ornate polychrome marbles ordered for its interior by Louis XVIII. The main building (1688) is constructed on three sides of a courtyard and includes a central block flanked by side pavilions. All have steeply pitched slate roofs in strong rhythmical contrast to the stringcourses dividing the three stories. The ensemble presents a typically French design of great austerity and in harmony with its mountainous setting.

BIBLIOGRAPHY. Y. Christ, *Abbayes de France*, Paris, 1955.

EMMA N. PAPERT

GRANDES BAIGNEUSES, LES (The Bathers). Oil painting by Cézanne; versions in the Museum of Art, Philadelphia, and the National Gallery, London. *See* CEZANNE, PAUL.

GRANDES MISERES DE LA GUERRE. Etching series by Callot. *See* CALLOT, JACQUES.

GRANDE-THEATRE, BORDEAUX, *see* LOUIS, VICTOR.

GRANDI, ERCOLE, *see* ROBERTI, ERCOLE DE'.

GRANDI, VINCENZO (Giovanni Girolamo; Il Vicentino). Italian sculptor (d. Padua, 1562). Grandi's sole extant work is the tomb monument of Fra Gonfalionieri, in the small church of S. Maria Maddalena in Padua, which features a finely expressive bust of the deceased.
BIBLIOGRAPHY. N. Pietrucci, *Biografia degli artisti padovani,* Padua, 1858.

GRANDJEAN DE MONTIGNY, AUGUSTE-HENRI-VICTOR. Brazilian architect (1776–1850). Born in Germany and trained in Paris, he was court architect of Westphalia in 1808 and to Maximilian I of Munich in 1814. He published his influential *Architecture toscane* in Munich. After moving to Brazil in 1816 he trained Brazilian architects in the Empire style.

GRANDVILLE, SEAN (Ignace-Isidore Gerard). French graphic artist (b. Nancy, 1803; d. Vanves, near Paris, 1847). Grandville was highly celebrated in his day for his perceptive caricatures of what he called the "comedy of life." In his satires people usually took the guise of animals, although his works include some charming nonanthropomorphic illustrations. He was on the staff of *La Caricature* and *Le Charivari* with another famous contemporary, Daumier. Grandville taught himself lithography and produced his first lithograph series in 1827. He was most expressive in his satirical series, including *Métamorphoses du jour* (1829), *Animaux parlants* (1840–42), *Les Animaux peints par eux-mêmes* (1842), and *Petites misères de la vie humaine* (1843). All are anthropomorphic satires and the last two show him at his best. His illustrations, though somewhat more dry than his satire, were highly expressive, for example, those for *Gulliver's Travels* (1838).
BIBLIOGRAPHY. H. Béraldi, *Les Graveurs du XIXe siècle...,* vol. 7, Paris, 1900; E. Bayard, *La Caricature et les caricaturistes,* Paris, 1901.

GRANET, FRANCOIS MARIUS. French painter (b. Aix-en-Provence, 1775; d. there, 1849). In 1799, after a short apprenticeship with J. A. Constantin in Aix, Granet entered the studio of J. L. David in Paris. He studied further between 1802 and 1819 in Rome, where he was a member of the Salon after 1806. In 1826 he was appointed conservator of the Louvre in Paris and, in 1830, director of the painting collections at Versailles. In his will he left a large bequest for the Granet Museum in his native Aix. As a painter, Granet specialized in depicting interiors, particularly Italian church and cloister interiors, for example, the Choir of the Capuchin Church of St. Mary of the Conception, Rome (1815; New York, Metropolitan Museum). *See* AIX-EN-PROVENCE: GRANET MUSEUM.
BIBLIOGRAPHY. H. Marcel, *La Peinture française au XIXe siècle,* Paris, 1905; L. Bénédite, *La Peinture au XIXe siècle...,* Paris, 1909.

GRANPRE-MOLIERE, M. J. Dutch architect (1883–   ). Professor of architecture at the Technische Hogeschool,

Delft, until 1953, Granpré-Molière has been the leader of the Delft school since the 1930s. This group has reacted against the new architecture in favor of a more traditional and nationalistic form. One of his best works is the rustic suburban design Vreewijk, in Rotterdam (1916).
BIBLIOGRAPHY. J. J. Vriend, *Reflexen, Nederlands bouwen na 1945,* Amsterdam, 1959.

GRANT, DUNCAN. Scottish painter and designer (1885–   ). Born in Rothiemurchus, he visited Italy and in 1906 studied with Jacques-Emile Blanche in Paris. Grant was greatly affected by Roger Fry's 1910 London exhibition of postimpressionists, and for several years his paintings reflected their immediate influence as well as that of Matisse and Picasso. In 1913 he designed pottery, furniture, and fabrics for Fry's Omega Workshops, and he was active as a room decorator in the early 1920s. Even in his later decorative panels Grant always retains some of the feeling for volume and mass evidenced in the *Still Life* (ca. 1912) in the Courtauld Institute of Art, London.
BIBLIOGRAPHY. R. Mortimer, *Duncan Grant,* Harmondsworth, 1948.

GRANULATION. Technique whereby the Greeks and, especially, the Etruscans decorated gold-leaf jewelry surfaces with almost microscopic gold bosses. These fine balls of gold are sometimes no larger than two-hundredths of a millimeter in diameter but are, nevertheless, very regular in shape. The exact means by which the bosses or granules were made and the way in which they were soldered are still unknown.
BIBLIOGRAPHY. R. Bloch, *The Etruscans,* New York, 1958.

GRAPHIC ART. In general, a term describing all two-dimensional media within the field of the fine arts, including photography. Specifically, it includes only those media that make use of the printing press to produce original, fine prints. Sometimes, especially in Europe, it is used to describe the various types of drawing as well.

GRAPINELLI, FLAMINIO. Italian painter (b. Pieve d'Alpago, late 17th cent.; d. ca. 1750). In the six powerful figures of apostles he painted for the Belluno Cathedral, the vigorous brushwork and dramatic contrasts of light and shade are more typical of the 17th than the 18th century.

GRASSER, ERASMUS. German sculptor and architect (b. Schmidmühlen, ca. 1450; d. Munich, 1518). Grasser's early artistic training is unknown. He appeared on the artistic scene about 1480, when he produced the red marble relief for the grave monument of Kaiser Ludwig the Bavarian in the Frauenkirche in Munich. This work showed the artist to be a member of the Upper Rhenish school, which in the previous generation was strongly influenced by the German sculptor Nikolaus Gerhard from Leyden. In the same period he created the famous *Moriskentänzer* for the festival hall of the Munich Rathaus. His religious works include a *Pietà* (1490–92; Freising Cathedral). Grasser's style is more dramatic than monumental; he was intensely interested in spatial movement, and this aspect of his work has led to his being grouped with other artists of the late Gothic baroque.
BIBLIOGRAPHY. P. Halm, *Erasmus Grasser,* Augsburg, 1928; A. Feulner and T. Müller, *Geschichte der deutschen Plastik,* Munich, 1953.

GRASSET, EUGENE. Swiss-French architect, illustrator, and designer (b. Lausanne, 1841; d. Scéaux, 1917). Influenced by Japanese art and important in the evolution of the Parisian Art Nouveau, Eugene Grasset developed a style of typography which bears his name (ca. 1898). He also produced posters, designs for textiles and wall hangings, glass paintings, and mosaics.

BIBLIOGRAHPY. P. Selz, ed., *Art Nouveau...*, New York, 1959.

GRASSHOUSE. Dome-shaped dwelling of the American Wichita Indian. Built of poles set in earth and thatched with grass, it had a smoke hole near the top.

GRASSI, ANTON. Austrian sculptor and ceramist (b. Vienna, 1775; d. there, 1807). He studied with Christian Friedrich Wilhelm Beyer at the Vienna Academy and became chief modeler at the Vienna porcelain manufacture in 1784. Traveling to Rome, Florence, and Naples in 1792, he made numerous studies from ancient statuary, reliefs, and vases. The drawings are now to be found in the National Library, Vienna. After this sojourn the style of his biscuit sculptures moved from rococo to academic neoclassicism.

GRASSI, NICOLA (Giannicola). Italian portrait and religious painter (b. before 1682; d. ca. 1750). Grassi was born in Formeaso in Carnia. Little is known about him, but he was regarded as a good portraitist. He was possibly a pupil of G. A. Cassana. Although there are etchings after his portraits and several paintings are attributed to him, none of his works can be identified with certainty. He is often confused with Giovanni Grassi.

GRASSMAN, MARCELO. Brazilian draftsman and printmaker (1925–   ). Born in São Paulo, Grassman is self-taught. He has won many prizes, including the travel prize from the Modern Art Salon in Rio de Janeiro (1954–55); first prize for graphics at the São Paulo Bienal (1955); and a prize for sacred art at the Venice Biennale (1958). His drawings follow Renaissance models and show monstrous human-animal fusions (for example, *Taming of the Beast*, 1958; artist's collection).

BIBLIOGRAPHY. L. de Almeida Cunha, *Brasil* (Art in Latin America Today, vol. 1), Washington, D.C., 1960.

GRAU, ENRIQUE. Colombian painter (1920–   ). Born in Cartagena, Grau studied at the Art Students League in New York from 1940 to 1943. He has exhibited widely (for example, at the Venice Biennale of 1950 and 1958). His subjects are mainly figures, such as *La calletana* (1963; Bogotá, Museum of Modern Art), and still lifes. He uses a semiabstract representational style.

BIBLIOGRAPHY. M. Traba and H. Díaz, *Seis artistas contemporáneos colombianos*, Bogotá, 1963.

GRAVELOT, HUBERT FRANCOIS (Le Bourguignon). French draftsman and engraver (b. Paris, 1699; d. there, 1773). He attended the Collège des Quatres Nations, but soon dropped out in order to devote more of his time to drawing. However, he spent so much money on books and became so involved in the theater that his father sent him to the island of Santo Domingo. While there Gravelot became interested in trade, but his commercial venture ended in shipwreck. Returning to Paris and to art, he be-

Hubert François Gravelot, illustration for Tasso's *Gerusalemme Liberata*, published in Paris, 1792.

came the pupil of Restout and Boucher. At the urging of the engraver Dubosc, Gravelot went to England in 1732; he remained there for fifteen years. He made the acquaintance of British artists, connoisseurs, and particularly the actor Garrick. Of his work in England, his engraved illustrations after drawings by Hayman for Shakespeare are considered the best, although he also published a series of draped male and female figures in the style of Boucher and illustrated British novels.

Again returning to Paris, Gravelot undertook a variety of decorating assignments, in accordance with the fashionable demands of 18th-century French life, such as painting spinets, embellishing the lids of little boxes, designing irons for bookbinding, and the like. However, it is as a book illustrator that he is famous. He was a favorite of Boucher and his work influenced the younger artist. He had an acute sensitivity to the life and manners of his time, and portrayed with a delicate line the luxurious settings and dress of his stylish subjects. Though primarily a draftsman, he engraved some of his own work and executed a few engravings after the work of other artists. Often he would draw a figure study in the nude and drape it when the pose was correct.

Among the books he illustrated were *Il decamerone di M. Giovanni Boccaccio* (1757, 5 vols.), which also contained designs by Boucher, Cochin, and Eisen, engraved by Aliamet, Flipart, Saint-Aubin, Tardieu, and others; the *Théâtre de Pierre Corneille* (1764, 12 vols.), with commentary by Voltaire and some of Gravelot's best work; Marmontel's *Contes Moraux* (1765, 3 vols.); an annual series called *Almanach Iconologique*; and Ovid's *Les Métamorphoses* (1767-71, 4 vols.), a most sumptuous set. His work became so popular that publishers tried to include at least one Gravelot design in every book. Of his few satirical plates, that of the author and critic E. C. Fréron, made for Voltaire, is perhaps the best known.

BIBLIOGRAPHY. E. and J. de Goncourt, *L'art du XVIIIe siècle*, 4th ed., vol. 2, Paris, 1881-84; V. Salomons, *Gravelot*, London, 1911.

KNEELAND MC NULTY

GRAVENSTEEN CASTLE, GHENT. Belgian castle founded in the 9th cent. The stronghold was rebuilt in 1180 by Count Philip of Alsace on his return from the Holy Land. From 1407 until 1778 the palace was the seat of the Counts of Flanders. Restored to its former appearance, the ensemble affords an almost unique picture of an early medieval fortress. The central portion of the inner castle is the donjon, a massive structure of four stories, the foundations of which date from the 11th century. This is adjoined on the northwest side by the palace, or residence of the owner. Below the palace is a reception hall with groined vaulting and a dungeon 18 feet deep.

BIBLIOGRAPHY. A. Heyse, ed., *Gand, guide illustré*, Ghent, 1928.

GRAVER, *see* BURIN.

GRAVES, MORRIS. American painter (1910–   ). Born in Fox Valley, Ore., he now lives in Seattle. From 1928 to 1930 Graves traveled in Japan and China. Mainly self-taught as a painter, he was influenced by Mark Tobey early in his career. He worked with the Federal Art Project in the 1930s and won first prize at the Northwest Annual Exhibition of the Seattle Art Museum in 1933. His first one-man show, at the Seattle Art Museum, was in 1936. In 1938-39 Graves traveled in Europe, and from 1942 to 1945 he served in the Armed Forces. He received a Guggenheim fellowship in 1946, and won first prize at the Art Institute of Chicago in 1948 and a University of Illinois purchase prize in 1955. Graves has had one-man shows in Oslo (1955) and at the Whitney Museum of

American Art, New York (1956). He again traveled to the Orient in 1956, when he also visited Ireland.

A serious student of Oriental religion, Graves has long been deeply influenced in his iconography and to some extent in his style by Eastern philosophy. His 1938–40 gouaches, such as *Bird Singing in the Moonlight* and *Blind Bird* (both New York, Museum of Modern Art), are characteristic of his earlier style. The *Flight of Plover* (1955; Whitney Museum) is more nearly abstract; and his pictures of the 1960s, which show an almost completely nonfigurative aesthetic, are less manifestly Oriental in quality.

BIBLIOGRAPHY. New York, Museum of Modern Art, *Americans 1942 . . .*, New York, 1942; K. Rexroth, "The Visionary Painting of Morris Graves," *Perspectives USA*, no. 10, 1955; F. S. Wight et al., *Morris Graves*, Berkeley, 1956.

JOHN C. GALLOWAY

GRAY, HENRY PETERS. American portrait and figure painter (b. New York, 1819; d. there, 1877). He studied painting with Daniel Huntington, traveled in Italy, and was a president of the National Academy of Design (1869–71). His cabinet-size portraits and academic figure pieces reveal an imaginative sweetness and emulate the golden tonalities of Correggio and Titian.

BIBLIOGRAPHY. E. P. Richardson, *Painting in America*, New York, 1956.

GRAY, MILNER C. British industrial designer (1899–   ). First known as an illustrator, he developed an interest in designing for industry and commerce in sympathy with the Bauhaus spirit. He has been a longtime partner in the Design Research Unit, and his articles, lectures, and designs have made him a leading figure in the industrial art movement in England.

BIBLIOGRAPHY. G. Butler, "Designer: Milner Gray, R.D.I., F.S.I.A.," *Art and Industry*, XLIX, November, 1950.

GRAZ: LANDESMUSEUM JOANNEUM. Austrian museum, founded in 1811. The collection encompasses natural history, prehistoric, and historical exhibits as well as a group of art works deriving primarily from the area of Styria. Prehistoric objects include finds from Klein-Glein and Flavia Solva. Austrian painting, sculpture, and applied arts range from the 15th century to the present. Outstanding early works are Hans von Tübingen's *Altarpiece of St. Lambert* and Pacher's two scenes from the life of Thomas à Becket. Austrian baroque painting is well

Gravensteen Castle, Ghent. **A restored but typical early medieval fortress.**

Morris Graves, *Flight of Plover*, 1955. **Whitney Museum of American Art, New York.**

represented in works by Altomonte, Maulbertsch, Rottmayr, M. J. Schmidt, Troger, Willman, and others. The New Gallery is devoted to paintings, sculpture, and prints of the 19th and 20th centuries.

BIBLIOGRAPHY. *Meisterwerke der österreichischen und deutschen Barockmalerei in der alten Galerie am Landesmuseum Joanneum in Graz*, Vienna, 1961.

GREAT BRITAIN, MUSEUMS OF.
See under the names of the following cities:

Birmingham. Barber Institute of Fine Arts; City Museum and Art Gallery.

Bristol. City Art Gallery; City Museum.

Cambridge. Fitzwilliam Museum.

Edinburgh. Corporation Museums; National Gallery of Scotland; Royal Scottish Museum.

Glasgow. Art Galleries and Museum.

Leeds. City Art Gallery.

Liverpool. Walker Art Gallery.

London. British Museum; Courtauld Institute of Art; Dulwich College Picture Gallery; London Museum; National Gallery; National Portrait Gallery; Queen's Gallery; Sir John Soane's Museum; Tate Gallery; Victoria and Albert Museum; Wallace Collection.

Manchester. Whitworth Art Gallery.

Oxford. Ashmolean Museum.

GREAT DEPARTURE.
Subject of Buddhist art. It shows Siddhārtha's leave-taking from his father's palace in order to go out into the world seeking enlightenment. He is riding his faithful horse, Kaṇṭhaka, and the Lokapālas hold up its hoofs lest their sound awaken the sleeping guard. Siddhārtha is accompanied by Channa, his faithful charioteer.

GREAT PALACE OF CONSTANTINOPLE, see SACRED PALACE, ISTANBUL.

GREAT SERPENT MOUND, OHIO, see MOUND BUILDERS; NORTH AMERICAN INDIAN ART (EASTERN UNITED STATES AND CANADA).

GREAT WALL OF CHINA.
Chinese fortification, called in Chinese the Wan-li ch'ang-ch'eng (long wall of 10,000 li). It is one of the focal points of Chinese history and folklore. Conceived and engineered by Shih-huang-t'i (r. 221–210 B.C.), China's first emperor, the Great Wall was actually a joining and extension of several smaller walls built during the late Chou period by the northern states as a defense against barbarian invasions. Innumerable alterations and repairs have since taken place; the last great rebuilding of the wall occurred in the 15th and 16th centuries under the Ming emperors.

The total length of the wall, including the great loops and contours, measures nearly 2,500 miles, extending from Shan-hai-kuan on the coast in Hopei Province to Chia-yü-kuan in westernmost Kansu Province. The original wall was of rammed earth, and in several locations in the western sections rammed earth is still to be seen. The Ming rebuilding included refacing with stone and brick. The actual structure varied, as did the building materials, depending on local techniques and supplies. The height of the wall also varies, as does the thickness. On the top a paved road was built, measuring on the average 16 feet in width, and towers were placed at irregular intervals, rising some 13 feet above the wall. At the crossing points of the major trade routes main gates were established.

BIBLIOGRAPHY. L. N. Hayes, *The Great Wall of China*, Shanghai, 1929; J. Needham, *Science and Civilization in China*, 4 vols. in 5, Cambridge, Eng., 1954–65; A. C. H. Boyd, *Chinese Architecture and Town Planning, 1500 B.C.-A.D. 1911*, Chicago, 1962.

MARTIE W. YOUNG

GREAVES, WALTER.
English painter and etcher (b. London, 1841; d. there, 1930). Greaves was a friend and pupil of Whistler. He and his brother Henry were boatmen who rowed Whistler about the Thames, and in 1863 Whistler accepted both as pupils. Walter's work, in obvious imitation of the master's, gained some recognition. The Art Institute of Chicago owns an oil portrait of Whistler that Greaves painted in 1869.

GREBBER, PIETER FRANSZ. DE.
Dutch history and portrait painter (b. Haarlem, ca. 1600; d. there? 1652/53). De Grebber was a pupil of his father, Frans Pietersz. de Grebber, and of Hendrick Goltzius. He was active in Haarlem and, from 1638, in Delft. His large compositions show the influence of Peter Paul Rubens and Jacob Jordaens. He was also influenced by the Caravaggesque movement.

BIBLIOGRAPHY. V. Bloch, "Haarlemer Klassizisten," *Oud-Holland*, LVII, 1940.

GRECHETTO, IL, see CASTIGLIONE, GIOVANNI BENEDETTO.

GRECO, EL (Domenikos Theotokopoulos; Domenico Theotocopuli, Greco, or Griego).
Greek-Spanish painter, architect, and sculptor (b. in or near Candia, Crete, ca. 1541; d. Toledo, 1614); known by his Spanish nickname, El Greco ("the Greek"). His Byzantine background and early training in icon painting gave him a natural disregard for optical truth in favor of the expression of unseen, inner values. It has been surmised that he arrived in Venice from Crete as early as 1558. There he studied under Titian and absorbed a variety of influences: Titian's architectonic compositions and sumptuous color, Jacopo Bassano's realism and genre interest, and, most notably, Tintoretto's dematerialized mass and frenetic vitality confined within a geometric format.

In 1570 he went to Rome with a letter of introduction describing him as "a follower of Titian." Apparently he remained in the papal city about two years. There the spiritual force infused into mannerism by Michelangelo in his late sculptural works had a potent effect upon the mystically inclined Cretan who, when discovered in his darkened Roman studio, explained that "the light of the day impaired his inner light."

Nothing of El Greco's Venetian or Roman periods is documented with absolute certainty, but there is some agreement among authorities about a number of works that he appears to have executed; other works, known to be his, fall into these periods, depending on the dates assigned to them. *The Marriage at Cana* (ca. 1568–70; Stras-

El Greco, *Pentecost*, detail. Pendant to the *Resurrection*. Prado, Madrid.

bourg, Museum of Fine Arts) embodies Titian's spatial clarity, Tintoretto's use of precipitous recession, and Veronese's revelation of material opulence. *The Healing of the Blind Man* (ca. 1571–73; Dresden, State Art Collections) has a Mantegna-like construction of space that recedes from the picture plane in a series of stepped stages, and it has a suggestion of Raphael in the classicistic idealized forms. It is believed that El Greco was acknowledging his artistic debts when he inserted in his *Purification of the Temple* (ca. 1574–75; Minneapolis Institute of Fine Arts) the portrait busts of Titian, Michelangelo, Raphael, and Giulio Clovio (the last a mannerist miniaturist and the benefactor and teacher of El Greco in Rome).

He returned to Venice in 1572 after arrogantly informing Pope Pius V that if the Sistine frescoes were removed he would replace them with better ones. Possibly in 1575, he settled in Toledo, Spain, the recognized center of the Church's Counter Reformation activities. Here he developed a style uniquely his own. To him the nobility's proud asceticism, the inquisitors' zealous conviction of their own rectitude, and the peasants' unquestioning acceptance of the human state in a Christian perspective provided an ideal social climate. Together these attributes ignited El Greco's imagination and gave a directional certainty to the evolution of his art. In addition, he became acquainted with the sculpture of Alonso Berruguete, whose intense mysticism and fervid concept of spiritual drama caused his works to be more true to the abstract idea than to the substance.

Attempts have been made to subdivide El Greco's chronological development (for example, Italian period, ca. 1558–75; early period in Spain, ca. 1575–86; middle period, 1586–1604; late period, 1604–14). Although this classification system has a general validity, it cannot be rigidly applied to the corpus of his works, for he reverted to earlier ways of "seeing" whenever he felt the subject of his art would be injured by his more personalized manner. Notable among these exceptions are several portraits. *The Burial of Count Orgaz* (1586; Toledo, S. Tomé) serves as an apt proof that El Greco's style involved deliberate choice. In the lower, earthly scene, all except for the indefinitely compressed space is naturalistically represented; in the heavenly group above, the heads of those attending the burial, a physical surrealistic situation is rendered. The artist's full genius was called upon to harmonize the halves into a single, unified expression.

His style, at its most typical, is characterized by sinuous forms simultaneously sculptural and impalpable, figures distorted by their attenuation and their markedly reduced heads, and an irrationally dispersed chiaroscuro organized in a broken but urgent vertical movement. From focal areas established in intricate, geometric schemas, attention is distracted by rapidly changing values and regained by the illusion of spatial compression. A work that may be cited as an archetype is the *Adoration of the Shepherds* (New York, Metropolitan Museum).

El Greco's fame in Spain was immediately established by his 1577 paintings for S. Domingo el Antiguo, Toledo, and for the sacristy of the Cathedral there. He then sought the favor of the king by presenting him with two small paintings: the *Espolio* (*Disrobing of Christ on Calvary*), now in Upton House, Oxfordshire, and the *Adoration of*

the Holy Name of Jesus in the National Gallery, London. In the latter he represented Philip II kneeling in the company of St. Paul, the Pope, and the doge of Venice. The delighted monarch ordered a large version of this for the Escorial and later commissioned the *Martyrdom of St. Maurice and the Theban Legion* (1580–82; El Escorial) from El Greco. In previous works El Greco had strongly evidenced his Italianate training, but his conception of the martyrdom as a revelation of the intangible spirituality of the saint and his fellow victims led him into a more abstract, expressionistic interpretation. Philip II was puzzled and repelled by the result, and El Greco never again enjoyed royal favor.

Self-trained in architecture and sculpture, he demonstrated his ability in both arts in the handsome architectural settings and statuary that he designed for the two altarpieces of 1577. Hundreds of figures that he executed in wax, clay, and plaster as preliminary studies for his paintings have been lost, but his *Savior* (1595–98; Toledo, Duchess of Lerma Collection) is one of two works in polychromed wood that survive. Surprisingly, it reveals that, despite the pronounced abstraction in his painting, he retained an admiration for the ideals of the Greek golden age: Christ is portrayed as a canonically beautiful Apollo.

If his art was unpleasing to Philip II, El Greco had many ardent Spanish admirers with the wealth and inclination to keep him busy with commissions. In fact, he employed assistants to execute copies of popular works. His son Jorge Manuel Theotocopuli was also a painter, architect, and sculptor. *See* TOLEDO, SPAIN: MUSEUMS (EL GRECO MUSEUM).

BIBLIOGRAPHY. M. B. Cossio, *El Greco*, 2 vols., Madrid, 1908; A. L. Mayer, *El Greco*, Berlin, 1931; L. Goldscheider, *El Greco*, New York, 1938; J. Camón Aznar, *Doménico Greco*, 2 vols., Madrid, 1950. EILEEN A. LORD

GRECO, EMILIO. Italian sculptor (1913–   ). Born in Catania, he began exhibiting in Rome in 1933. His early work consists mainly of portraits, but he has since turned to the female nude as his primary mode of expression. His work manifests a lyrical classicism verging, at times, on mannerism, but embodying a sense of fantasy and removal in the elongated linear movements of his figures.

BIBLIOGRAPHY. F. Sapori, *Modern Italian Sculpture*, Rome, 1949; R. Salvini, *Modern Italian Sculpture*, New York, 1962.

GRECO-BUDDHIST ART, *see* AFGHANISTAN; ASIA, CENTRAL; GANDHARA.

GRECO-ROMAN STYLE. Term used in reference to the art of classical antiquity during the period of Roman domination over Greece (2d cent. B.C.–A.D. 2d cent.); sculpture and painting produced by Greek artists for Roman patrons, in Italy and Greece. Most prominent were the works of the neo-Attic school, which revived and maintained the style of Greek classicism. The term is also employed in analyzing the style of a nonancient work to indicate certain characteristics that cannot be traced back to a specific source in Greek or Roman art but are nonetheless recognizably antique. *See* NEO-ATTIC STYLE.

Greco-Roman Style. Salpion, Crater with Hermes entrusting the infant Dionysos to a nymph, mid-1st century B.C. National Archaeological Museum, Naples.

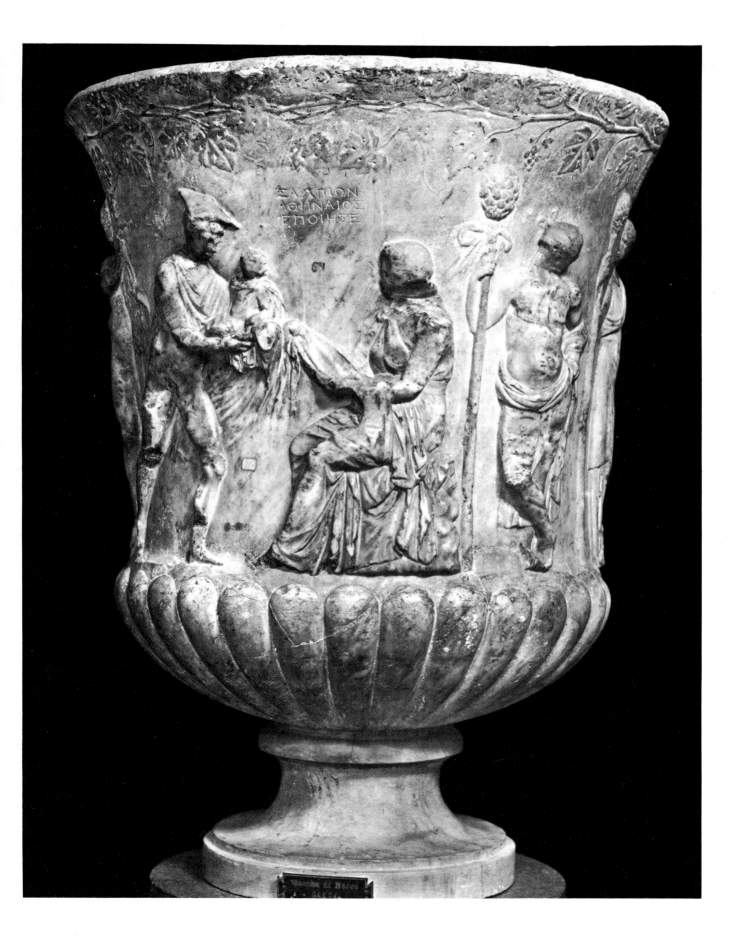